New Perspectives on

HTML, XHTML, and XML

3rd Edition

Comprehensive

Patrick Carey

COURSE TECHNOLOGY
CENGAGE Learning™

Australia • Brazil • Japan • Korea • Mexico • Singapore • Spain • United Kingdom • United States

COURSE TECHNOLOGY
CENGAGE Learning™

**New Perspectives on HTML, XHTML, and XML,
3rd Edition—Comprehensive**

Vice President, Publisher: Nicole Jones Pinard

Executive Editor: Marie L. Lee

Associate Acquisitions Editor: Brandi Shailer

Senior Product Manager: Kathy Finnegan

Associate Product Manager: Leigh Robbins

Editorial Assistant: Julia Leroux-Lindsey

Director of Marketing: Cheryl Costantini

Marketing Manager: Ryan DeGrote

Marketing Coordinator: Kristen Panciocco

Developmental Editors: Mary Kemper, Robin M. Romer

Senior Content Project Manager: Jennifer Goguen McGrail

Composition: GEX Publishing Services

Text Designer: Steve Deschene

Art Director: Marissa Falco

Cover Designer: Elizabeth Paquin

Cover Art: Bill Brown

Copyeditor: Suzanne Huizenga

Proofreader: Kathy Orrino

Indexer: Alexandra Nickerson

For product information and technology assistance, contact us at
Cengage Learning Customer & Sales Support, 1-800-354-9706

For permission to use material from this text or product, submit all requests online at **cengage.com/permissions**
Further permissions questions can be emailed to
permissionrequest@cengage.com

Some of the product names and company names used in this book have been used for identification purposes only and may be trademarks or registered trademarks of their respective manufacturers and sellers.

Microsoft and the Office logo are either registered trademarks or trademarks of Microsoft Corporation in the United States and/or other countries. Course Technology, Cengage Learning is an independent entity from the Microsoft Corporation, and not affiliated with Microsoft in any manner.

Disclaimer: Any fictional data related to persons or companies or URLs used throughout this book is intended for instructional purposes only. At the time this book was printed, any such data was fictional and not belonging to any real persons or companies.

ISBN-13: 978-0-495-80640-0

ISBN-10: 0-495-80640-4

Course Technology
20 Channel Center Street
Boston, Massachusetts 02210
USA

Cengage Learning is a leading provider of customized learning solutions with office locations around the globe, including Singapore, the United Kingdom, Australia, Mexico, Brazil, and Japan. Locate your local office at:
international.cengage.com/region

Cengage Learning products are represented in Canada by Nelson Education, Ltd.

To learn more about Course Technology, visit **www.cengage.com/coursetechnology**
To learn more about Cengage Learning, visit **www.cengage.com**

Purchase any of our products at your local college store or at our preferred online store **www.ichapters.com**

Printed in the United States of America
1 2 3 4 5 6 7 8 9 13 12 11 10 09

Preface

The New Perspectives Series' critical-thinking, problem-solving approach is the ideal way to prepare students to transcend point-and-click skills and take advantage of all that the World Wide Web has to offer.

Our goal in developing the New Perspectives Series was to create books that give students the software concepts and practical skills they need to succeed beyond the classroom. With this new edition, we've updated our proven case-based pedagogy with more practical content to make learning skills more meaningful to students.

With the New Perspectives Series, students understand *why* they are learning *what* they are learning, and are fully prepared to apply their skills to real-life situations.

"This text is filled with excellent explanations and activities. My students vary in their abilities, and this text covers exactly what they need in a logical, incremental fashion. It's a great reference book that students will find useful for years."
—Kenneth Wade
Champlain College

About This Book

This book provides complete coverage of HTML, XHTML, and XML, including:

- Up-to-date coverage of using HTML and XHTML to create and design Web sites
- Instruction on using CSS to create styles that enhance Web page design and layout
- Expanded and in-depth coverage of embedding multimedia content; creating Web forms; and combining XHTML and other XML vocabularies
- Reinforcement of code compliance with strict applications of HTML and XHTML and compliance with Section 508 accessibility guidelines
- Coverage of XML validation, including the creation and application of DTDs and schemas
- An Online Companion, which provides supplemental information related to the content of each tutorial as well as access to the student data files
- Updated business case scenarios throughout, which provide a rich and realistic context for students to apply the concepts and skills presented

System Requirements

This book assumes that students have an Internet connection, a text editor, and a current Web browser that supports HTML 4.0 and XHTML 1.1 standards. The following is a list of the most recent versions of the major browsers at the time this text was published: Windows—Firefox 2.0, Internet Explorer 7.0, Opera 9.25, and Safari 3.0; Macintosh—Safari 3.0. All Web browsers interpret HTML and CSS code in slightly different ways. It is highly recommend that students have several different browsers installed on their systems, for comparison purposes. Students might also want to run older versions of these browsers to highlight compatibility issues, but the code in this book is designed to support those browser versions. Students who intend to validate their XML documents in Tutorials 13 and 14 should either have access to Internet Explorer for Windows or to an XML validating parser such as XMLSpy, oXygen, or an online validation service. The screenshots in this book were produced using Internet Explorer 7.0 running on Windows Vista, unless otherwise noted. If students are using a different browser or operating system, their screens will vary slightly from those shown in the book; this does not present any problems for students in completing the tutorials.

www.cengage.com/ct/newperspectives

"The New Perspectives Series approach, which combines definition and real-world application of content, makes it an easy choice for me when selecting textbooks. I am able to teach concepts that students can immediately apply."
—Brian Morgan
Marshall University

The New Perspectives Approach

Context
Each tutorial begins with a problem presented in a "real-world" case that is meaningful to students. The case sets the scene to help students understand what they will do in the tutorial.

Hands-on Approach
Each tutorial is divided into manageable sessions that combine reading and hands-on, step-by-step work. Colorful screenshots help guide students through the steps. **Trouble?** tips anticipate common mistakes or problems to help students stay on track and continue with the tutorial.

InSight

InSight Boxes
New for this edition! InSight boxes offer expert advice and best practices to help students better understand how to work with HTML, XHTML, and XML. With the information provided in the InSight boxes, students achieve a deeper understanding of the concepts behind the features and skills presented.

Tip

Margin Tips
New for this edition! Margin Tips provide helpful hints and shortcuts for more efficient use of HTML, XHTML, and XML. The Tips appear in the margin at key points throughout each tutorial, giving students extra information when and where they need it.

Reality Check

Reality Checks
New for this edition! Comprehensive, open-ended Reality Check exercises give students the opportunity to practice skills by completing practical, real-world tasks, such as creating a personal Web site and creating and posting an online resume.

Review

In New Perspectives, retention is a key component to learning. At the end of each session, a series of Quick Check questions helps students test their understanding of the concepts before moving on. Each tutorial also contains an end-of-tutorial summary and a list of key terms for further reinforcement.

Apply

Assessment
Engaging and challenging Review Assignments and Case Problems have always been a hallmark feature of the New Perspectives Series. Colorful icons and brief descriptions accompany the exercises, making it easy to understand, at a glance, both the goal and level of challenge a particular assignment holds.

Reference Window

Reference
While contextual learning is excellent for retention, there are times when students will want a high-level understanding of how to accomplish a task. Within each tutorial, Reference Windows appear before a set of steps to provide a succinct summary and preview of how to perform a task. In addition, each book includes a combination Glossary/Index to promote easy reference of material.

Our Complete System of Instruction

Coverage To Meet Your Needs

Whether you're looking for just a small amount of coverage or enough to fill a semester-long class, we can provide you with a textbook that meets your needs.

- Brief books typically cover the essential skills in just 2 to 4 tutorials.
- Introductory books build and expand on those skills and contain an average of 5 to 8 tutorials.
- Comprehensive books are great for a full-semester class, and contain 9 to 12+ tutorials.

So if the book you're holding does not provide the right amount of coverage for you, there's probably another offering available. Visit our Web site or contact your Course Technology sales representative to find out what else we offer.

Online Companion

This book has an accompanying Online Companion Web site designed to enhance learning. This Web site, www.cengage.com/webdesign/np/xml3, includes the following:

- Supplemental information tied directly to the content of each tutorial, for further student exploration and reference
- Student Data Files needed to complete the tutorials and end-of-tutorial exercises

CourseCasts – Learning on the Go. Always available…always relevant.

Want to keep up with the latest technology trends relevant to you? Visit our site to find a library of podcasts, CourseCasts, featuring a "CourseCast of the Week," and download them to your mp3 player at http://coursecasts.course.com.

Ken Baldauf, host of CourseCasts, is a faculty member of the Florida State University Computer Science Department where he is responsible for teaching technology classes to thousands of FSU students each year. Ken is an expert in the latest technology trends; he gathers and sorts through the most pertinent news and information for CourseCasts so your students can spend their time enjoying technology, rather than trying to figure it out. Open or close your lecture with a discussion based on the latest CourseCast.

Visit us at http://coursecasts.course.com to learn on the go!

Instructor Resources

We offer more than just a book. We have all the tools you need to enhance your lectures, check students' work, and generate exams in a new, easier-to-use and completely revised package. This book's Instructor's Manual, ExamView testbank, PowerPoint presentations, data files, solution files, figure files, and a sample syllabus are all available on a single CD-ROM or for downloading at http://www.cengage.com/coursetechnology.

Blackboard

Skills Assessment and Training

SAM 2007 helps bridge the gap between the classroom and the real world by allowing students to train and test on important computer skills in an active, hands-on environment. SAM 2007's easy-to-use system includes powerful interactive exams, training or projects on critical applications such as Word, Excel, Access, PowerPoint, Outlook, Windows, the Internet, and much more. SAM simulates the application environment, allowing students to demonstrate their knowledge and think through the skills by performing real-world tasks. Powerful administrative options allow instructors to schedule exams and assignments, secure tests, and run reports with almost limitless flexibility.

Online Content

Blackboard is the leading distance learning solution provider and class-management platform today. Course Technology has partnered with Blackboard to bring you premium online content. Content for use with *New Perspectives on HTML, XHTML, and XML, 3rd Edition, Comprehensive* is available in a Blackboard Course Cartridge and may include topic reviews, case projects, review questions, test banks, practice tests, custom syllabi, and more. Course Technology also has solutions for several other learning management systems. Please visit http://www.cengage.com/coursetechnology today to see what's available for this title.

Acknowledgments

No one writes a book alone, and I want to thank all of the following people who collaborated on this venture. Special thanks to my developmental editors, Mary Kemper and Robin Romer, for their hard work and valuable insights, and to my Product Manager, Kathy Finnegan, who has worked tirelessly in overseeing this project and made my task so much easier with her enthusiasm and good humor. Other people at Course Technology who deserve credit are Marie Lee, Executive Editor; Brandi Shailer, Associate Acquisitions Editor; Leigh Robbins, Associate Product Manager; Julia Leroux-Lindsey, Editorial Assistant; Jennifer Goguen McGrail, Senior Content Project Manager; Christian Kunciw, Manuscript Quality Assurance (MQA) Supervisor; and John Freitas, Serge Palladino, Danielle Shaw, Teresa Storch, and Susan Whalen, MQA testers.

Feedback is an important part of writing any book, and thanks go to the following reviewers for their helpful ideas and comments: William Frankhouser, Everett Community College; Janos Fustos, Metropolitan State College of Denver; Heith Hennel, Valencia Community College; Jean Insinga, Middlesex Community College; Chang-Yang Lin, Eastern Kentucky University; Angela McFarland, B.T. Washington High School, Escambia; Brian Morgan, Marshall University; and Sylvia Unwin, Bellevue Community College. My thanks as well to the members of the New Perspectives HTML Advisory Board for their insights and suggestions for this new edition: Lisa Macon, Valencia Community College; Don Mangione, Baker College of Muskegon; Chuck Riden, Arizona State University; and Kenneth Wade, Champlain College.

I want to thank my wife Joan for her love and encouragement and my children for taking me away from my desk every now and then. I especially want to thank all of the people at Course Technology who have provided me the opportunity to write these books over the past 15 years, and the instructors who have given me such valuable feedback during that time.

– Patrick Carey

Brief Contents

Table of Contents

HTML and XHTML—Level II Tutorials

Tutorial 3 Working with Cascading Style Sheets

Designing a Web Site . . . .*HTML 121*

Tutorial 4 Creating Special Effects with CSS

Adding Advanced Styles to a Web Site . . .*HTML 199*

HTML, XHTML, and XML— Level IV Tutorials

Tutorial 11 Creating an XML Document

Developing a Document for a Cooking Web Site . . . . .HTML 617

Tutorial 12 Working with Namespaces

Combining XML Vocabularies in a Compound Document . . . . .HTML 663

Tutorial 13 Validating Documents with DTDs

Working with Document Type Definitions .HTML 707

Tutorial 14 Validating Documents with Schemas

Exploring the XML Schema Vocabulary ...HTML 765

Objectives

Session 1.1
- Learn the history of the Web and HTML
- Describe HTML standards and specifications
- Understand HTML elements and markup tags
- Create the basic structure of an HTML file
- Insert an HTML comment

Session 1.2
- Work with block-level elements
- Create ordered, unordered, and definition lists
- Work with inline elements
- Understand the div and span elements

Session 1.3
- Add attributes to HTML elements
- Format page content using the style attribute
- Mark empty elements with one-sided tags
- Add an inline image to a Web page
- Work with character sets and codes

Developing a Web Page

Creating a Product Page for a Startup Company

Case | Dave's Devil Sticks

Dave Vinet is a machinist in Auburn, Maine. In his spare time, Dave builds and juggles devil sticks—juggling props used in circuses and by street performers. In recent years, he has made customized sticks for his friends and colleagues. Encouraged by their enthusiasm for his work, Dave has decided to start a business called Dave's Devil Sticks. So far his customers have come through word of mouth; now Dave wants to advertise his business on the Web. To do that, Dave needs to create a Web page that describes his company and its products. He has the text describing his company in a flyer that he hands out at juggling conventions. He has also contacted a graphic artist to design a logo. He wants to use this material in his Web page.

He has come to you for help in designing a Web page and writing the code. He wants the Web page to contain the same information and graphics contained in his flyer. To create Dave's Web page, you'll have to learn how to work with HTML, the markup language used to create documents on the World Wide Web.

Starting Data Files

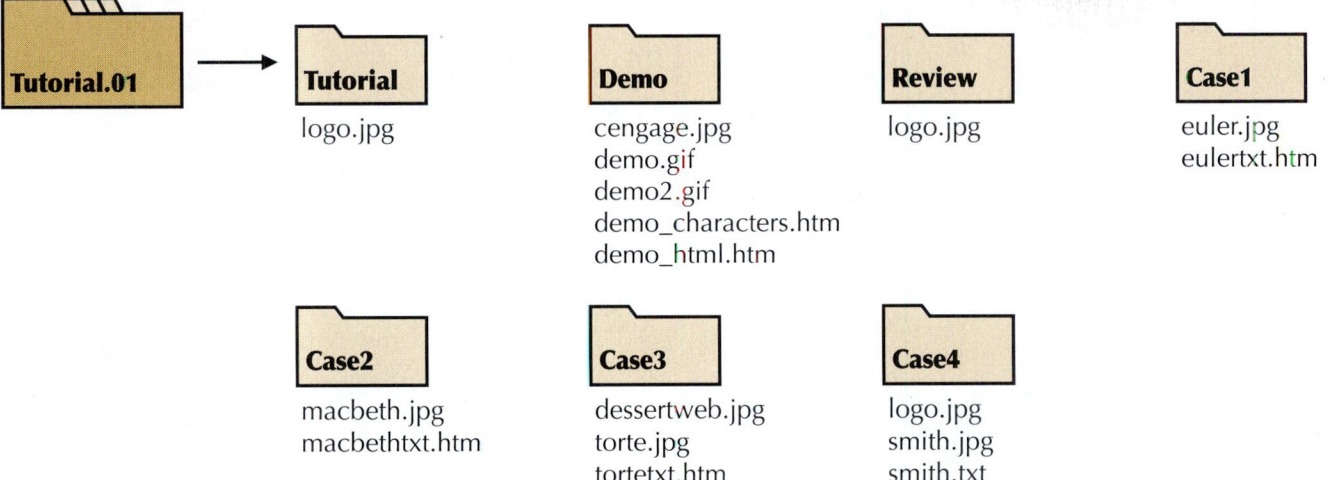

Tutorial.01 → Tutorial
logo.jpg

Demo
cengage.jpg
demo.gif
demo2.gif
demo_characters.htm
demo_html.htm

Review
logo.jpg

Case1
euler.jpg
eulertxt.htm

Case2
macbeth.jpg
macbethtxt.htm

Case3
dessertweb.jpg
torte.jpg
tortetxt.htm

Case4
logo.jpg
smith.jpg
smith.txt

Session 1.1

Exploring the History of the World Wide Web

Before you start creating a Web page for Dave, it's helpful to first look at the history of the Web and how HTML was developed. You'll start by reviewing networks.

Networks

A **network** is a structure that links several points called **nodes** allowing for the sharing of information and services. For computer networks, each node is a device such as a computer or a printer or a scanner, capable of sending and receiving data electronically over the network. A computer node is also called a **host** to distinguish it from other node devices.

As the network operates, nodes are either providing data to other nodes on the network or requesting data. A node that provides information or a service is called a **server**. For example, a **print server** is a network node that provides printing services to the network; a **file server** is a node that provides storage space for saving and retrieving files. A computer or other device that requests services from a server is called a **client**. Networks can follow several different designs. One of the most commonly used designs is the **client-server network** in which several clients access information provided by one or more servers. You might be using such a network to access your data files for this tutorial.

Networks can also be classified based on the range they cover. A network confined to a small geographic area, such as within a building or department, is referred to as a **local area network** or **LAN**. A network that covers a wider area, such as several buildings or cities, is called a **wide area network** or **WAN**. Wide area networks typically consist of two or more local area networks connected together.

The largest WAN is the Internet. The origins of the Internet can be traced backed to a WAN called the **ARPANET**, which started with two network nodes located at UCLA and Stanford connected by a single phone line. Today, the **Internet** has grown to an uncountable number of nodes involving computers, cell phones, PDAs, MP3 players, gaming systems, and television stations. The physical structure of the Internet uses fiber-optic cables, satellites, phone lines, wireless access points, and other telecommunications media, enabling a worldwide community to communicate and share information. See Figure 1-1. It is within this expansive network that Dave wants to advertise his devil sticks business.

Figure 1-1 | **Structure of the Internet**

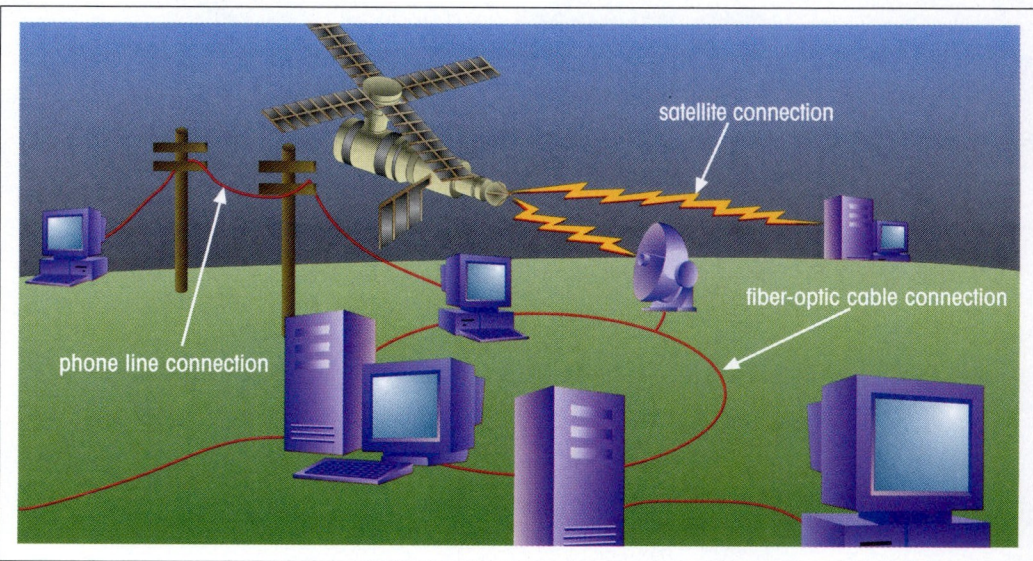

Locating Information on a Network

One of the biggest obstacles to effectively using a network is not mechanical—it's the human element. Users must be able to easily navigate the network and locate the information and services they need. Most of the early Internet tools required users to master a bewildering array of terms, acronyms, and commands. Because network users had to be well versed in computers and network technology, Internet use was limited to universities and departments of the government. To make the Internet accessible to the general public, it needed a simpler interface. This interface proved to be the World Wide Web.

The foundations for the **World Wide Web**, or the **Web** for short, were laid in 1989 by Timothy Berners-Lee and other researchers at the CERN nuclear research facility near Geneva, Switzerland. They needed an information system that would make it easy for their researchers to locate and share data with minimal training and support. To meet this need, they developed a system of hypertext documents that enabled users to easily navigate from one topic to another. **Hypertext** is a method of organization in which information is not presented linearly, but in whatever order is requested by the user. For example, if you read the operating manual for your car starting with page 1 and proceeding to the end, you are processing the information linearly and in the order determined by the manual's author. A hypertext approach would place the same information in a series of smaller documents, with each document dedicated to a single topic, allowing you—and not the author—to choose the order and selection of topics you'll view.

The key to hypertext is the use of **links**, which are the elements in a hypertext document that allow you to jump from one topic or document to another, usually by clicking a mouse button. Hypertext is ideally suited to use with networks because the end user does not need to know where a particular document, information source, or service is located—he or she only needs to know how to activate the link. In the case of an expansive network like the Internet, documents can be located anywhere in the world; but that is largely unseen by the user because of the hypertext structure. The fact that the Internet and the World Wide Web are synonymous in many users' minds is a testament to the success of the hypertext approach.

The original Web supported only textual documents, but the use of hypertext links has expanded through the years to encompass information in any form, including video, sound, interactive programs, conferencing, and online gaming. While the Web has greatly expanded to include these services, the basic foundation is still the same: a collection of interconnected documents linked through the use of hypertext.

Web Pages and Web Servers

Each document on the World Wide Web is referred to as a **Web page**. Web pages are stored on **Web servers**, which are computers that make Web pages available to any device connected to the Internet. To view a Web page, the end user's device needs a software program called a **Web browser**, which retrieves the page from the Web server and renders it on the user's computer or other device. See Figure 1-2.

Figure 1-2   **Using a browser to view a Web document from a Web server**

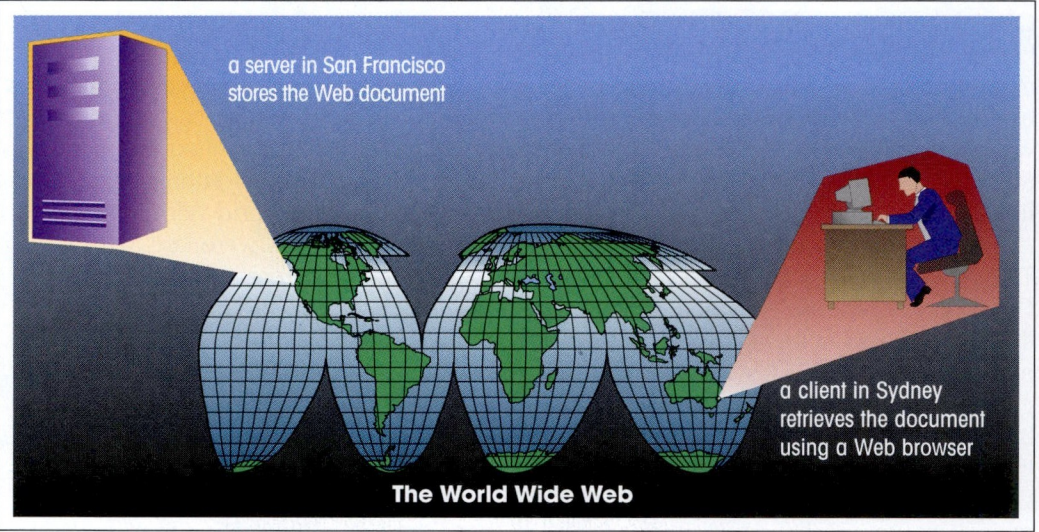

The earliest browsers, known as **text-based browsers**, were limited to displaying only text. Today's browsers are capable of displaying text, images, video, sound, and animations. In the early days of the Internet, Web browsing was limited to computers. Now browsers are installed on cell phones, PDAs (personal digital assistants), MP3 players, and gaming systems. How does a Web page work with so many combinations of browsers and clients and devices? To understand, you need to look at how Web pages are created.

Introducing HTML

A Web page is actually a text file written in **Hypertext Markup Language** or **HTML**. We've already discussed hypertext, but what is a markup language? A **markup language** is a language that describes the content and structure of a document. If this tutorial were written using a markup language, the language would identify the parts of the document, indicating which sections correspond to paragraphs, figure captions, tables, page headings, and so forth.

There are several things that HTML is not. While Web pages often contain interactive programs, HTML is not a programming language. In addition, while HTML can describe the content of a document, it is not a formatting language because it does not necessarily describe how content should be rendered. This is a necessary facet of HTML: the Web page author has no control over what device is used to view the Web page, so the browser—not the HTML—determines how the Web page will look. The end user might be using a large-screen television monitor, a cell phone, or even a device that renders Web pages in Braille or in aural speech.

If you want to format your document, the preferred method is to use styles. **Styles** are formatting rules written in a separate language from HTML telling the browser how to render each element for particular devices. A Web page author can write a style that displays page headings one way for computer monitors and another way for printed output. You'll explore some basic styles as you create your first Web pages.

The History of HTML

HTML evolved as the Web itself evolved. Thus in order to fully appreciate the nuances of HTML, it's a good idea to review the language's history. The first popular markup language was the **Standard Generalized Markup Language** (**SGML**). Introduced in the 1980s, SGML is device- and system-independent, meaning that it can be applied to almost any type of document stored in almost any format. While powerful, SGML is also quite complex; and for this reason SGML is limited to those organizations that can afford the cost and overhead of maintaining complex SGML environments. However, SGML can also be used to create other markup languages that are tailored to specific tasks and are simpler to use and maintain. HTML is one of the languages created with SGML.

In the early years after HTML was created, no single organization was responsible for the language. Web developers were free to define and modify HTML in whatever ways they thought best. Eventually, competing browsers, seeking to dominate the market, added new features called **extensions** to the language. The two major browsers during the 1990s, Netscape Navigator and Microsoft Internet Explorer, added the most extensions to HTML. Netscape provided an extension to add background sounds to documents, while Internet Explorer added an extension to provide marquee-style text that would scroll automatically across the page. These extensions and others provided Web page authors with more options, but at the expense of complicating Web page development. A Web page that took advantage of extensions might work in one browser but not in another.

Thus Web page authors faced the challenge of determining which browser or browser version supported a particular extension, and they had to create a workaround for browsers that did not. By adding this layer of complexity to Web design, extensions, while often useful, diminished the promise of simplicity that made HTML so attractive in the first place.

Ultimately, a group of Web developers, programmers, and authors called the **World Wide Web Consortium**, or the **W3C**, created a set of standards or specifications that all browser manufacturers were to follow. The W3C has no enforcement power; but because a uniform language is in everyone's best interest, the W3C's recommendations are usually followed, though not always right away. The W3C also provides online tutorials, documentation, and quizzes that you can use to test your knowledge of HTML and other languages. For more information on the W3C and the services it offers, see its Web site at *www.w3c.org*.

Figure 1-3 summarizes the various versions of HTML that the W3C has released over the past decade. While you may not grasp all of the details of these versions yet, it's important to understand that HTML doesn't come in only one version.

Figure 1-3 **History of HTML and XHTML**

Version	Date of Release	Description
HTML 1.0	1989	The first public version of HTML which included browser support for inline images and text controls.
HTML 2.0	1995	The first version supported by all graphical browsers. It introduced interactive form elements such as option buttons and text boxes. A document written to the HTML 2.0 specification is compatible with almost all browsers on the World Wide Web.
HTML 3.0	1996	A proposed replacement for HTML 2.0 that was never widely adopted.
HTML 3.2	1997	This version included additional support for creating and formatting tables and expanded the options for interactive form elements. It also supported limited programming using scripts.
HTML 4.01	1999	This version added support for style sheets to give Web designers greater control over page layout. It added new features to tables and forms and provided support for international features. This version also expanded HTML's scripting capability and added increased support for multimedia elements.
HTML 5.0	not yet released	This version supports elements that reflect current Web usage, including elements for Web site navigation and indexing for use with search engines. This version also removes support for purely presentational elements because those effects can be better handled with styles.
XHTML 1.0	2001	This version is a reformulation of HTML 4.01 in XML and combines the strength of HTML 4.0 with the power of XML. XHTML brings the rigor of XML to Web pages and provides standards for more robust Web content on a wide range of browser platforms.
XHTML 1.1	2002	A minor update to XHTML 1.0 that allows for modularity and simplifies writing extensions to the language.
XHTML 2.0	not yet released	The latest version, designed to remove most of the presentational features left in HTML. XHTML 2.0 is not backward compatible with XHTML 1.1.
XHTML 5.0	not yet released	A version of HTML 5.0 written under the specifications of XML, unlike XHTML 2.0, XHTML 5.0 will be backward-compatible with XHTML 1.1.

Tip

You can learn more about deprecated features by examining the documentation available at the W3C Web site and by viewing the source code of various pages on the Web.

When you work with HTML, you should keep in mind not only what the W3C has recommended, but also what HTML features the browser market actually supports. This might mean dealing with a collection of approaches: some browsers are new and meet the latest W3C specifications, while some are older but still widely supported. Older features of HTML are often **deprecated**, or phased out, by the W3C. While deprecated features might not be supported in current or future browsers, that doesn't mean that you won't encounter them—indeed, if you are supporting older browsers that recognize only early versions of HTML, you might need to use them. Because it's hard to predict how quickly deprecated features will disappear from common usage, it's crucial to be familiar with them.

Current Web developers are increasingly using **XML (Extensible Markup Language)**, a language for creating markup languages, like SGML, but without SGML's complexity and overhead. Using XML, developers can create documents that obey specific rules for their content and structure. This is in contrast with a language like HTML, which supported a wide variety of rules but did not include a mechanism for enforcing those rules.

Indeed, one of the markup languages created with XML is **XHTML (Extensible Hypertext Markup Language)**, a stricter version of HTML. XHTML is designed to confront some of the problems associated with the various competing versions of HTML and to better integrate HTML with other markup languages like XML. The current version of XHTML is XHTML 1.1, which is mostly (but still not completely) supported by all browsers. Because XHTML is an XML version of HTML, most of what you learn about HTML can be applied to XHTML.

Another version of XHTML, **XHTML 2.0**, is still in the draft stage and has proved to be controversial because it is not backward-compatible with earlier versions of HTML and XHTML. In response to this controversy, another working draft of HTML called **HTML 5.0** is being developed. It provides greater support for emerging online technology while still providing support for older browsers. HTML 5 is also being developed under the XML specifications as **XHTML 5.0**. At the time of this writing, none of these versions has moved beyond the development stage nor has been adopted by the major browsers. This book discusses the syntax of HTML 4.01 and XHTML 1.1, but also brings in deprecated features and browser-supported extensions where appropriate.

Writing HTML Code | InSight

Part of writing good HTML code is being aware of the requirements of various browsers and devices as well as understanding the different versions of the language. Here are a few guidelines for writing good HTML code:

- Become well versed in the history of HTML and the various versions of HTML and XHTML. Unlike other languages, HTML's history does impact how you write your code.
- Know your market. Do you have to support older browsers, or have your clients standardized on one particular browser or browser version? Will your Web pages be viewed on a single device like a computer, or do you have to support a variety of devices?
- Test your code on several different browsers and browser versions. Don't assume that if your page works in one browser it will work on other browsers or even on earlier versions of the same browser. Also check on the speed of the connection. A large file that performs well under a high-speed connection might be unusable under a dial-up connection.
- Read the documentation on the different versions of HTML and XHTML at the W3C Web site and review the latest developments in new versions of the languages.

In general, any HTML code that you write should be compatible with the current versions of the following browsers: Internet Explorer (Windows), Firefox (Windows and Macintosh), Netscape Navigator (Windows), Opera (Windows), and Safari (Macintosh).

Tools for Creating HTML Documents

Because HTML documents are simple text files, you can create them with nothing more than a basic text editor such as Windows Notepad. Specialized HTML authoring programs, known as HTML converters and HTML editors, are also available to perform some of the rote work of document creation. An **HTML converter** is a program that translates text written in another language into HTML code. You can create the source document with a word processor such as Microsoft Word, and then use the converter to save the document as an HTML file. Converters free you from the laborious task of typing HTML code; and because the conversion is automated, you usually do not have to worry about introducing coding errors into your document. However, converters tend to create large and complicated HTML files resulting in "bloated" code, which is more difficult to edit if you need to make changes. So while a converter can speed up Web page development, you will probably still have to invest time in cleaning up the code.

An **HTML editor** is a program that helps you create an HTML file by inserting HTML codes for you as you work. HTML editors can save you a lot of time and can help you work more efficiently. Their advantages and limitations are similar to those of HTML converters. Like converters, HTML editors allow you to set up a Web page quickly, but you will still have to work directly with the underlying HTML code to create a finished product.

Creating an HTML Document

Now that you've had a chance to explore some of the history of the Web and HTML's role in its development, you are ready to work on the Web page for Dave's Devil Sticks. It's always a good idea to plan your Web page before you start coding it. You can do this by drawing a sketch or by creating a sample document using a word processor. The preparatory work can weed out errors or point to potential problems. In this case, Dave has already drawn up a flyer he's passed out at juggling and circus conventions. The handout provides information about Dave's company and his products. Figure 1-4 shows Dave's current flyer.

Figure 1-4   Elements of the Dave's Devil Sticks flyer

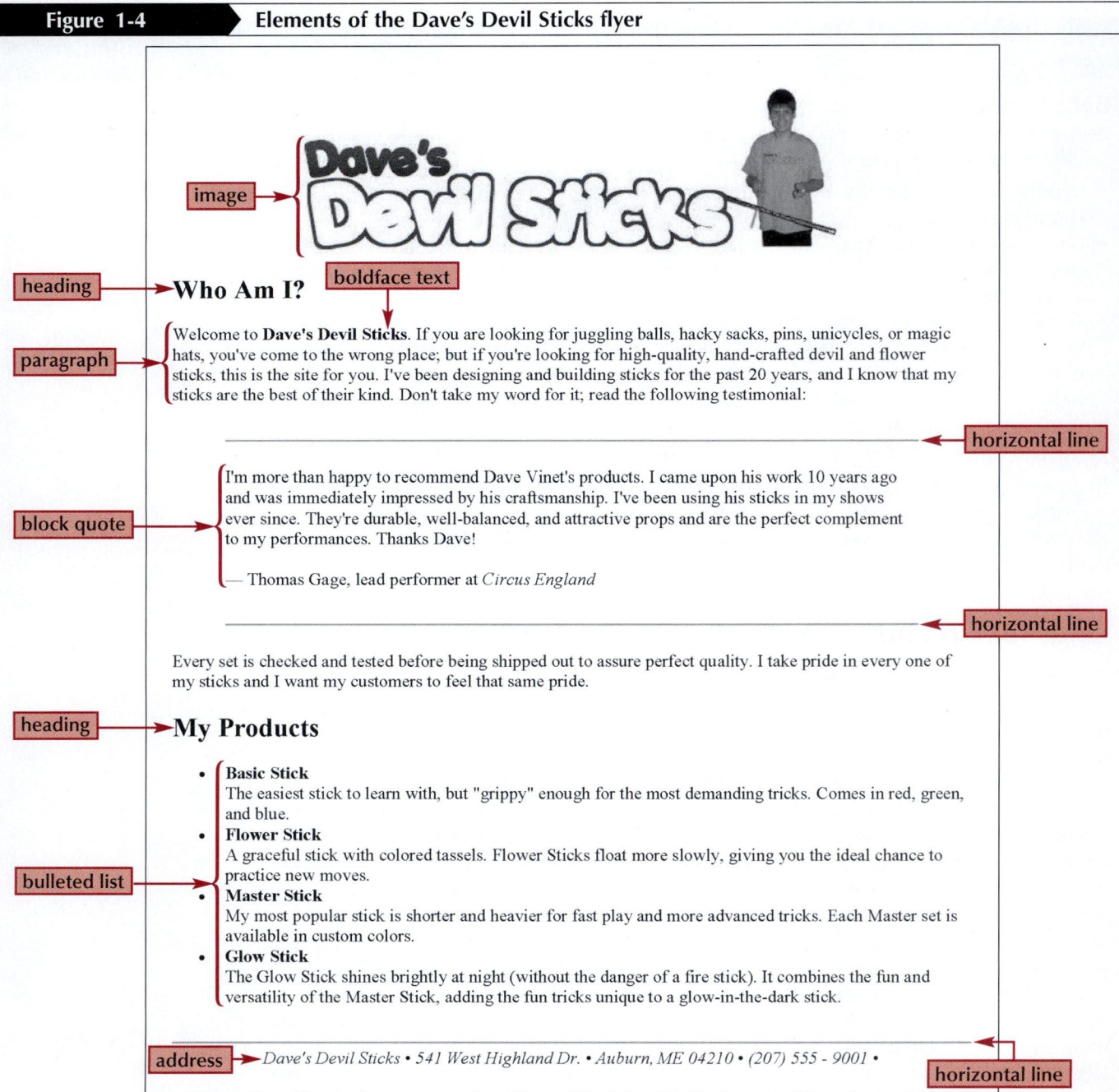

When you sketch a sample document, it is a good idea to identify the document's various elements. An **element** is a distinct object in the document, like a paragraph, a heading, or the page's title. Even the whole document is considered an element. Dave's flyer includes several elements: an image displays his company's logo, several headings break his flyer into sections, the text in his flyer is laid out in paragraphs, a bulleted list describes his products, and the address of his company is at the bottom of the flyer. Note that some elements are marked by their appearance in the text. For example, the name of his company is displayed in boldface text at the top of the flyer to set it off from other text in the opening paragraph. Italics are also used in several locations on the page. As you recreate this flyer as a Web page, you should periodically refer to Figure 1-4.

Marking Elements with Tags

The core building block of HTML is the **tag**, which marks the presence of an element. If the element contains content such as text or another element, it is marked using a **two-sided tag** in which an **opening tag** indicates the beginning of the content and a **closing tag** indicates the content's end. The syntax of a two-sided tag is:

```
<element>content</element>
```

where *element* is the name of the element and *content* is any content contained within the element. For example, the following code is used to mark a paragraph element within a document:

```
<p>Welcome to Dave's Devil Sticks.</p>
```

In this example, the <p> tag marks the beginning of the paragraph, the text "Welcome to Dave's Devil Sticks." constitutes the content of the paragraph element and the </p> tag marks the end of the paragraph.

Note that an "element" is an object in the Web document, and a "tag" is the part of the HTML code that marks the element. So you would mark a paragraph element in a document by enclosing the paragraph content within opening and closing paragraph tags.

Elements can also contain other elements. For example, the paragraph tags in the following code

```
<p>Welcome to <b>Dave's Devil Sticks</b>.</p>
```

enclose both the text of the paragraph as well as another set of tags <b> ... </b> that are used to mark content that should be treated by the browser as boldface text. Note that the <b> tags have to be completely enclosed or nested within the <p> tags. It's improper syntax to have tags overlap as in the following code sample:

```
<p>Welcome to <b>Dave's Devil Sticks.</p></b>
```

In this example, the closing </b> tag is placed *after* the closing </p> tag, which is improper because the boldface text marked with these tags must be completely enclosed *within* the paragraph.

The Structure of an HTML Document

All documents written in a markup language need to have a **root element** that contains all of the elements used in the document. For HTML documents, the root element is marked using the <html> tag as follows

```
<html>
  document content
</html>
```

where *document content* is the content of the entire document, including all other elements. The presence of the opening <html> tag in the first line of the file tells any device reading the document that this file is written in HTML. The closing </html> tag signals the end of the document and should not be followed by any other content or markup tags.

Web pages are divided into two main sections: a head and a body. The **head element** contains information about the document—for example, the document's title or a list of key-words that would aid a search engine on the Web identifying this document for other users. The **body element** contains all of the content that will appear on the Web page. Taken together, the syntax of the entire HTML file including the head and body elements is

```
<html>
    <head>
        head content
    </head>
    <body>
        body content
    </body>
</html>
```

where *head content* and *body content* are the content you want to place within the document's head and body. Note that the body element is always placed after the head element and that no other elements can be placed between the html, head, and body elements.

Tip

Enter your tags using all lowercase letters. For example, use <html> rather than <HTML>. While many browsers accept uppercase tag names, XHTML code requires tag names to be lowercase.

Reference Window | Creating the Basic Structure of an HTML Document

- Enter the following HTML tags
  ```
  <html>
      <head>
          head content
      </head>
      <body>
          body content
      </body>
  </html>
  ```
  where *head content* and *body content* are the content you want to place within the document's head and body.
- To specify the page title, enter the following tag within the head section
  ```
  <title>content</title>
  ```
  where *content* is the text of the Web page title.

Now that you've learned about the basic structure of an HTML file, you can start writing the HTML code for Dave's Web page.

To create the basic structure of an HTML document:

► **1.** Start your text editor, opening it to a blank document.

Trouble? If you don't know how to start or use your text editor, ask your instructor or technical support person for help.

► **2.** Type the following lines of code in your document. Press the **Enter** key after each line. Press the **Enter** key twice for a blank line between lines of code. See Figure 1-5.

```
<html>

<head>
</head>

<body>
</body>

</html>
```

Basic structure of an HTML document   Figure 1-5

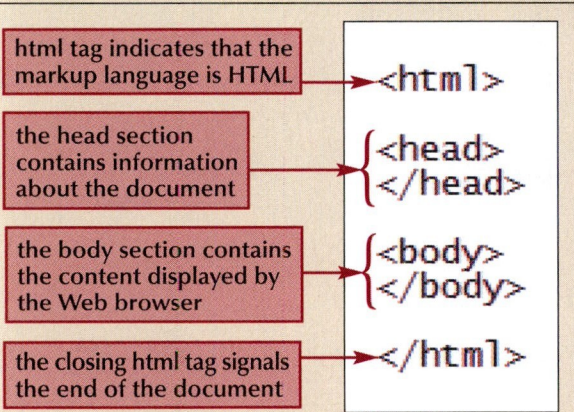

html tag indicates that the markup language is HTML → `<html>`

the head section contains information about the document → `<head>` `</head>`

the body section contains the content displayed by the Web browser → `<body>` `</body>`

the closing html tag signals the end of the document → `</html>`

► **3.** Save the file as **dave.htm** in the tutorial.01\tutorial folder included with your Data Files.

Trouble? If you are using the Windows Notepad text editor to create your HTML file, make sure you don't save the file with the extension .txt, which is the default file extension for Notepad. Instead, make sure you save the file with the file extension .htm or .html. Using the incorrect file extension might make the file unreadable to Web browsers, which require file extensions of .htm or .html.

Tip

To make it easier to link to your Web pages, follow the Internet convention in which HTML filenames and folder names use only lowercase letters with no spaces.

InSight | **Converting an HTML Document into XHTML**

There is considerable overlap between HTML and XHTML. You can quickly change an HTML document into an XHTML document just by altering the first three lines of code. To convert an HTML file into an XHTML file, replace the opening <html> tag with the following three lines of code:

```
<?xml version="1.0" encoding="UTF-8" standalone="no" ?>
<!DOCTYPE html PUBLIC "-//W3C//DTD XHTML 1.0 Strict//EN"
    "http://www.w3.org/TR/xhtml1/DTD/xhtml1-strict.dtd">
<html xmlns="http://www.w3.org/1999/xhtml">
```

Each line has an important role in converting the HTML document into XHTML. XHTML documents are written in XML, so the first line notifies the browser that the document is an XML file. The version number—1.0—tells the browser that the file is written in XML 1.0.

XHTML files differ from HTML files in that XHTML files have to be tested against a set of rules that define exactly which markup tags are allowed and how they can be used. To reference the set of rules, you have to include a DOCTYPE declaration in the second line of the file, indicating the collection of rules to be used. XHTML documents can be tested against several different rules. The code sample above assumes a strict interpretation of the rules is being enforced.

The third line of the file contains the opening <html> tag. In XHTML, the <html> tag must include what is known as a namespace declaration indicating that any markup tags in the document should, by default, be considered part of the XHTML language. This is necessary because XML documents can contain a mixture of several different markup languages and there must be a way of defining the default language of the document.

With these three lines in place, browsers recognize the file as an XHTML rather than an HTML document. After these three lines, there is little difference between the code in an HTML file and in an XHTML file.

Defining the Page Title

One of the elements you can add to the document head is the document title. The syntax of the document title is

```
<title>document title</title>
```

where *document title* is the text of the document title. The document title is not displayed within the page, but is usually displayed in the browser's title bar. The document title is also used by search engines like Google or Yahoo! to report on the contents of the file.

To add a title to a Web page:

▶ 1. Click at the end of the <head> tag, and then press the **Enter** key to insert a new line in your text editor.

▶ 2. Press the **Spacebar** three times to indent the new line of code, and then type **<title>Dave's Devil Sticks</title>** as shown in Figure 1-6.

Tip

Indent your markup tags and insert extra blank spaces as shown in this book to make your code easier to read. It does not affect how the page is rendered by the browser.

Defining the page title ◀ Figure 1-6

```
<html>

<head>
Web page title ─────▶ <title>Dave's Devil Sticks</title>
</head>

<body>
</body>

</html>
```

Adding Comments

As you create a Web page, you might want to add notes or comments about your code. These comments might include the name of the document's author and the date the document was created. Such notes are not intended to be displayed by the browser, but are instead used to help explain your code to yourself and others. To add notes or comments, insert a **comment tag** with the syntax

```
<!-- comment -->
```

where *comment* is the text of the comment or note. For example, the following code inserts a comment describing the page you'll create for Dave's business:

```
<!-- Page created for Dave Vinet's devil stick business -->
```

A comment can also be spread out over several lines as follows:

```
<!-- Dave's Devil Sticks
     A Web page created for Dave Vinet -->
```

Because they are ignored by the browser, comments can be added anywhere within the HTML document.

<table>
<tr><td style="background:#9b1c2e;color:white">Adding an HTML Comment</td><td style="background:#9b1c2e;color:white" align="right">| Reference Window</td></tr>
</table>

- To insert an HTML comment anywhere within your document, enter
    ```
    <!-- comment -->
    ```
  where *comment* is the text of the HTML comment.

You'll add a comment to the head of Dave's file indicating its purpose, author, and date created.

To add a comment to Dave's file:

▶ **1.** Click at the end of the <head> tag, and then press the **Enter** key to insert a new line directly above the title element you've just entered.

▶ **2.** Type the following lines of code, as shown in Figure 1-7

```
<!-- Dave's Devil Sticks
     Author: your name
     Date:   the date
-->
```

where *your name* is your name and *the date* is the current date.

Figure 1-7 | Adding a comment tag

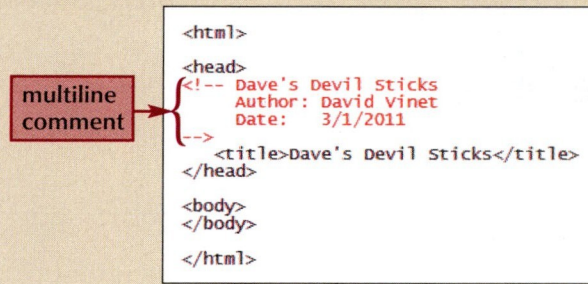

Displaying an HTML File

As you continue modifying the HTML code, you should occasionally view the page with your Web browser to verify that you have not introduced any errors. You might even want to view the results using different browsers to check for compatibility. In this book Web pages are displayed using the Windows Internet Explorer 7.0 browser. Be aware that if you are using a different browser or a different operating system, you might see slight differences in the layout and appearance of the page.

To view Dave's Web page:

1. Save your changes to the **dave.htm** file.

2. Start your Web browser. You do not need to be connected to the Internet to view local files stored on your computer.

   Trouble? If you start your browser and are not connected to the Internet, you might get a warning message. Click the OK button to ignore the message and continue.

3. After your browser loads its home page, open the **dave.htm** file from the tutorial.01\tutorial folder.

   Trouble? If you're not sure how to open a local file with your browser, check for an Open or Open File command under the browser's File menu. If you are still having problems accessing the dave.htm file, talk to your instructor or technical resource person.

   Your browser displays the Web page shown in Figure 1-8. Note that the page title appears in the browser's title bar; and if your browser supports tabs, it also appears in the tab title. The page itself is empty because you have not yet added any content to the body element.

Viewing a page title in the browser window   Figure 1-8

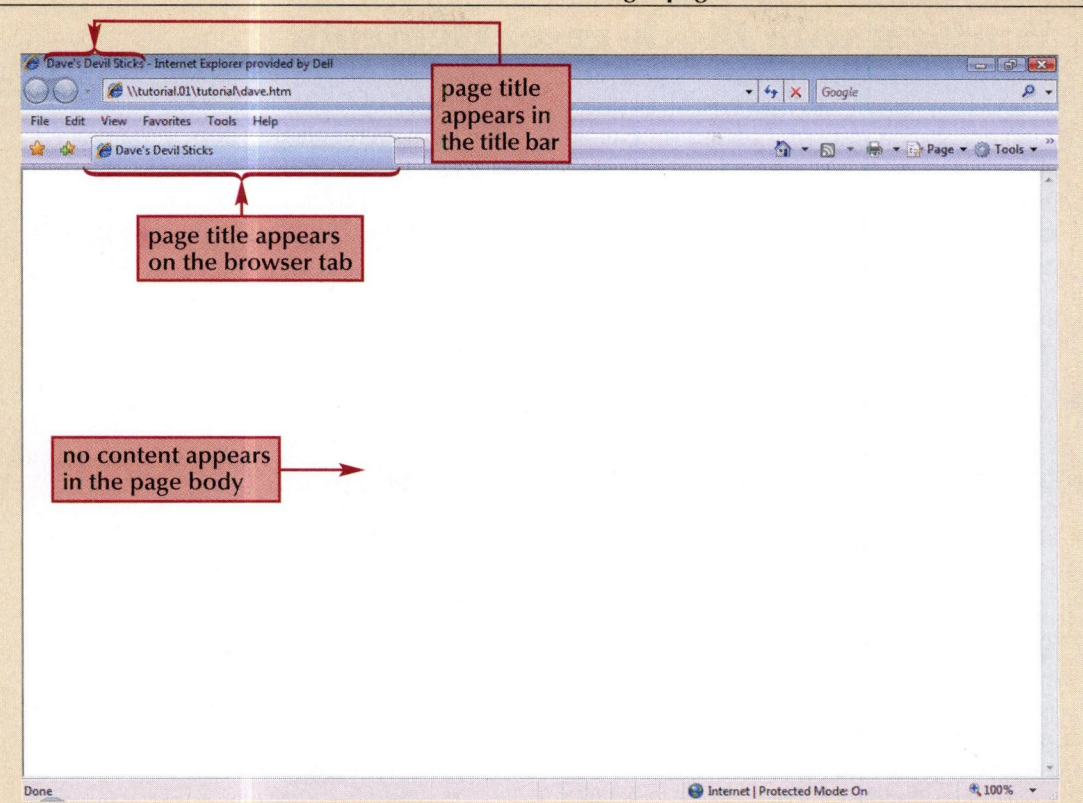

You've completed the head section of the HTML document. In the next session, you'll define the elements that are displayed in the body section. For now, you can close your files and Web browser if you want to take a break before starting the next session.

Session 1.1 Quick Check | Review

1. What is a hypertext document?
2. What is a Web server? What is a Web browser? Describe how they work together.
3. How do HTML documents differ from documents created with a word processor such as Word or WordPerfect?
4. What is a deprecated feature?
5. What element do you use to mark the beginning and end of an HTML document?
6. What code would you enter in your document to set the page title to "Technical Support"? Where would you enter this code?
7. Specify the code needed to add the comment "Page Updated on 4/15/2011" to an HTML file.
8. What error was made in the following HTML code?:

```
<head>
   <title>Customer Comments Form
   </head>
</title>
```

Session 1.2

Working with Block-Level Elements

You're now ready to begin entering content into the body of Dave's Web page. The first elements you'll add are **block-level elements**, which are elements that contain content that is viewed as a distinct block within the Web page. When rendered visually, block-level elements start on a new line in the document. Paragraphs are one example of a block-level element. To explore block-level and other HTML elements, a demo page has been prepared for you.

To open the HTML Tags demo page:

▶ **1.** Use your browser to open the **demo_html.htm** file from the tutorial.01\demo folder.

▶ **2.** If your browser prompts you to allow code on the Web page to be run, click the **OK** button.

Working with Headings

The first block-level elements you'll explore are heading elements. **Heading elements** are elements that contain the text of main headings on the Web page. They are often used for introducing new topics or dividing the page into topical sections. The syntax to mark a heading element is

```
<hn>content</hn>
```

where *n* is an integer from 1 to 6. Content marked with the <h1> tag is considered a major heading and is usually displayed in large bold text. Content marked with <h2> down to <h6> tags is used for subheadings and is usually displayed in progressively smaller bold text. To see how these headings appear on your computer, use the demo page.

Reference Window | Marking Block-Level Elements

- To mark a heading, enter
   ```
   <hn>content</hn>
   ```
   where *n* is an integer from 1 to 6 and *content* is the text of heading.
- To mark a paragraph, enter
   ```
   <p>content</p>
   ```
- To mark a block quote, enter
   ```
   <blockquote>content</blockquote>
   ```
- To mark a generic block-level element, enter
   ```
   <div>content</div>
   ```

To view heading elements:

▶ **1.** Click in the blue box on the bottom left of the demo page, type **<h1>Dave's Devil Sticks</h1>** and then press the **Enter** key to go to a new line.

▶ **2.** Type **<h2>Auburn, ME 04210</h2>**.

3. Click the **Preview Code** button located below the blue code window. Your browser displays a preview of how this code would appear in your Web browser (see Figure 1-9).

Marking an h1 and h2 element | **Figure 1-9**

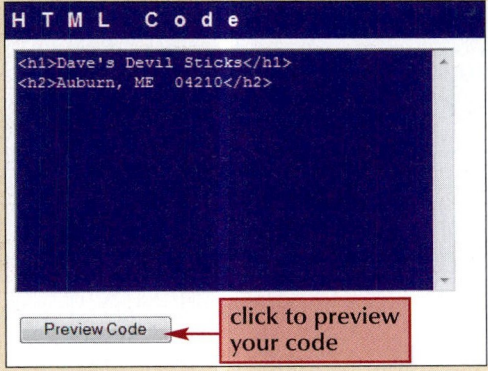
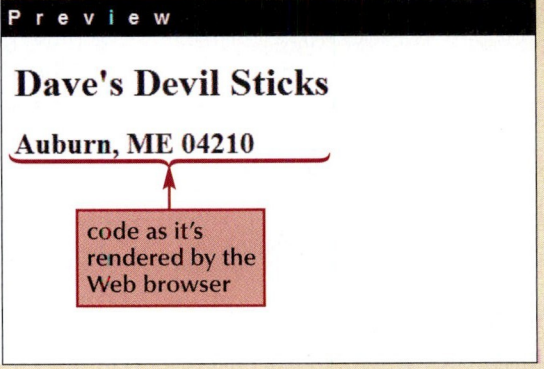

Trouble? If you are using a browser other than Internet Explorer 7.0 running on Windows Vista, your screen might look slightly different from that shown in Figure 1-9.

4. To see how an h3 heading would look, change the opening and closing tags for the store's city and state information from <h2> and </h2> to **<h3>** and **</h3>**. Click the **Preview Code** button again.

Your browser renders the code again, this time with the city and state information displayed in a smaller font. If you continued to change the heading element from h2 down to h6, you would see the text in the Preview box get progressively smaller.

It's important not to treat markup tags as simply a way of formatting the Web page. The h1 through h6 elements are used to identify headings, but the exact appearance of these headings depends on the browser and the device being used. Remember that the headings might not even be displayed visually. A browser that renders content aurally might convey an h1 heading using increased volume preceded by an extended pause.

Now that you've seen how to mark page headings, you can add some to Dave's Web page. Dave has three headings he wants to add to his document. The first is an h1 heading that will contain the company's name. The other two are h2 headings that preface two different sections of the document: one titled "Who Am I?" and the other titled "My Products."

To add headings to Dave's document:

1. Return to the **dave.htm** file in your text editor.

2. Between the opening and closing <body> tags, insert the following code:

```
<h1>Dave's Devil Sticks</h1>
<h2>Who Am I?</h2>
<h2>My Products</h2>
```

Indent your code to make it easy to read, as shown in Figure 1-10.

| Figure 1-10 | Adding <h1> and <h2> markup tags |

```
<body>
    <h1>Dave's Devil Sticks</h1>
    <h2>Who Am I?</h2>
    <h2>My Products</h2>
</body>
```

▶ **3.** Save your changes to the file, and then reload or refresh the **dave.htm** file in your Web browser. Figure 1-11 shows the revised Web page.

| Figure 1-11 | Headings on the Web page |

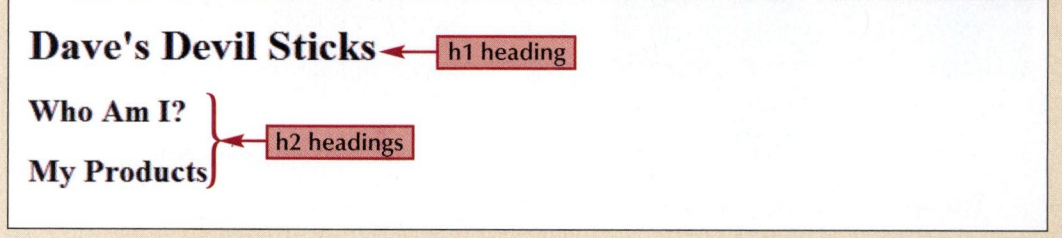

The next block-level elements you'll add are paragraphs about Dave's company and its wares.

Marking Paragraph Elements

As you saw earlier, you can mark a paragraph element using the <p> tag

```
<p>content</p>
```

where *content* is the content of the paragraph. When rendered in a browser, paragraphs are started on a new line. In older HTML code, you might occasionally see paragraphs marked with only the opening <p> tag but without a closing tag. In those situations, the <p> tag marks the start of each new paragraph. While this convention is still accepted by many browsers, it does violate HTML's syntax rules; if you want XHTML-compliant code, you must include the closing tags.

To add two paragraphs to Dave's Web page:

▶ **1.** Return to the **dave.htm** file in your text editor.

▶ **2.** Directly below the Who Am I? h2 heading, insert a new line, and then type the following code, as shown in Figure 1-12:

```
<p>Welcome to Dave's Devil Sticks. If you are looking for juggling
balls, hacky sacks, pins, unicycles, or magic hats, you've come
to the wrong place; but if you're looking for high-quality,
hand-crafted devil and flower sticks, this is the site for you.
I've been designing and building sticks for the past 20 years,
and I know that my sticks are the best of their kind.</p>

<p>Every set is checked and tested before being shipped out to
  assure perfect quality. I take pride in every one of my sticks
  and I want my customers to feel that same pride.</p>
```

Marking paragraph elements | **Figure 1-12**

```
<body>
    <h1>Dave's Devil Sticks</h1>
    <h2>Who Am I?</h2>
    <p>Welcome to Dave's Devil Sticks. If you are looking for juggling balls,
        hacky sacks, pins, unicycles, or magic hats, you've come to the wrong
        place; but if you're looking for high-quality, hand-crafted devil and
        flower sticks, this is the site for you. I've been designing and building
        sticks for the past 20 years, and I know that my sticks are the best of
        their kind.</p>

    <p>Every set is checked and tested before being shipped out to assure perfect
        quality. I take pride in every one of my sticks and I want my customers to
        feel that same pride.</p>

    <h2>My Products</h2>
</body>
```

paragraphs

Trouble? Don't worry if your lines do not wrap at the same locations shown in Figure 1-12. As you'll see shortly, line wrap in the HTML code does not affect how the page is rendered by the browser.

3. Save your changes to the file and then refresh the **dave.htm** file in your Web browser. Figure 1-13 shows the new paragraphs added to the Web page.

Paragraphs added to Dave's Web page | **Figure 1-13**

Dave's Devil Sticks

Who Am I?

Welcome to Dave's Devil Sticks. If you are looking for juggling balls, hacky sacks, pins, unicycles, or magic hats, you've come to the wrong place; but if you're looking for high-quality, hand-crafted devil and flower sticks, this is the site for you. I've been designing and building sticks for the past 20 years, and I know that my sticks are the best of their kind.

Every set is checked and tested before being shipped out to assure perfect quality. I take pride in every one of my sticks and I want my customers to feel that same pride.

My Products

paragraphs

White Space and HTML

If you compare the paragraph text from the HTML code in Figure 1-12 to the way it's rendered on the Web page in Figure 1-13, you'll notice that the line returns in the code are not reflected in the Web page. When the browser renders HTML code, it ignores the presence of white space within the HTML text file. **White space** consists of blank spaces, tabs, and line breaks. As far as the browser is concerned, there is no difference between a blank space, a tab, or a line break. To explore this issue further, you'll experiment with the HTML demo page.

To explore how white space is treated by the Web browser:

1. Return to the **demo_html.htm** file in your Web browser.

2. Delete the HTML code in the left box and replace it with the following:

```
<p>Dave's Devil Sticks</p>

<p>Dave's                Devil                    Sticks</p>

<p>Dave's
   Devil
   Sticks</p>
```

3. Click the **Preview Code** button. Figure 1-14 shows how the browser renders the three paragraphs of code.

| Figure 1-14 | Viewing the effects of white space on HTML code |

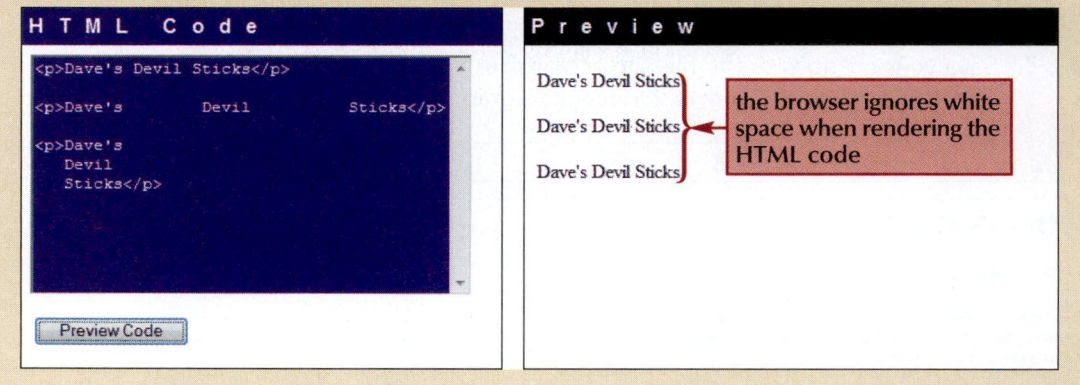

Each paragraph is rendered exactly the same by the browser. Notice that even adding blank spaces within the paragraph does not change the appearance of the text. This is because the browser ignores extra blank spaces. Consequently, you are free to use white space however you wish as you lay out the HTML code to make it easier for you to read—without impacting the appearance of the Web page.

Tip

To force the browser to retain the extra blank spaces, tabs, and line breaks from your HTML code, enclose the white space within a set of opening and closing <pre> tags.

Marking a Block Quote

The next element that Dave wants you to enter into his document is a quote from a satisfied customer. Dave wants the quote, shown earlier in Figure 1-4, to be indented from the surrounding paragraphs to make it stand out more. However, as you just saw, any indenting you do in the HTML file will be ignored by the browser. So how do you achieve this effect? Remember that HTML is used to mark up document content, and so you need a markup tag that identifies quoted material. The syntax for marking an extended quote is

```
<blockquote>content</blockquote>
```

where *content* is the text of the quote. Most browsers will by default indent block quotes on the Web page, so you'll still achieve the visual effect that Dave wants. Note that some browsers might display block quotes differently, and the only way to ensure that block quotes are always indented is by using styles. You'll explore how to apply styles shortly.

To create a block quote:

▶ **1.** Return to the **dave.htm** file in your text editor.

▶ **2.** At the end of the first paragraph, directly *before* the closing </p> tag, insert a space and then type the following text:

```
Don't take my word for it; read the following testimonial:
```

▶ **3.** Between the closing </p> tag from the first paragraph and the opening <p> tag of the second paragraph, insert the following code, as shown in Figure 1-15:

```
<blockquote>

    <p>I'm more than happy to recommend Dave Vinet's products. I came
    upon his work 10 years ago and was immediately impressed by his
    craftsmanship. I've been using his sticks in my shows ever since.
    They're durable, well-balanced, and attractive props and are
    the perfect complement to my performances. Thanks Dave!</p>

    <p>Thomas Gage, lead performer at Circus England</p>

</blockquote>
```

Marking a block quote ◀ **Figure 1-15**

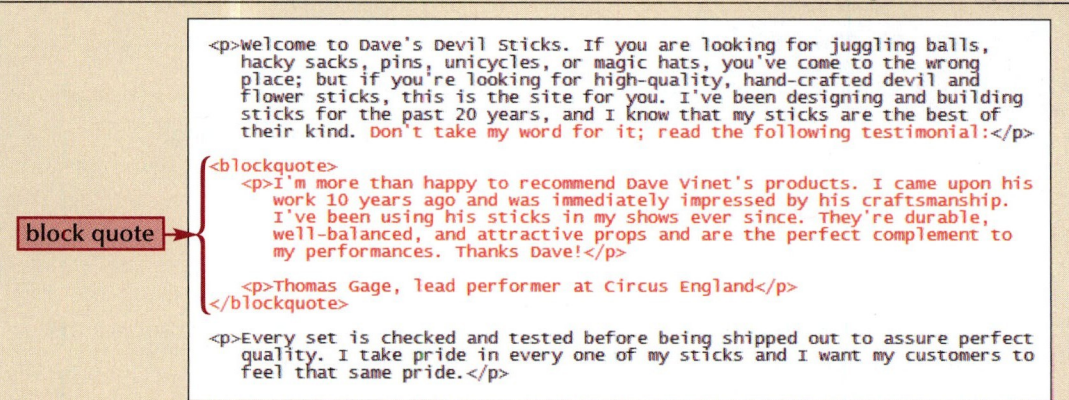

▶ **4.** Save your changes to the file, and then reload **dave.htm** in your Web browser. Figure 1-16 shows the revised page with the quoted material.

Dave's Web page with customer comment ◀ **Figure 1-16**

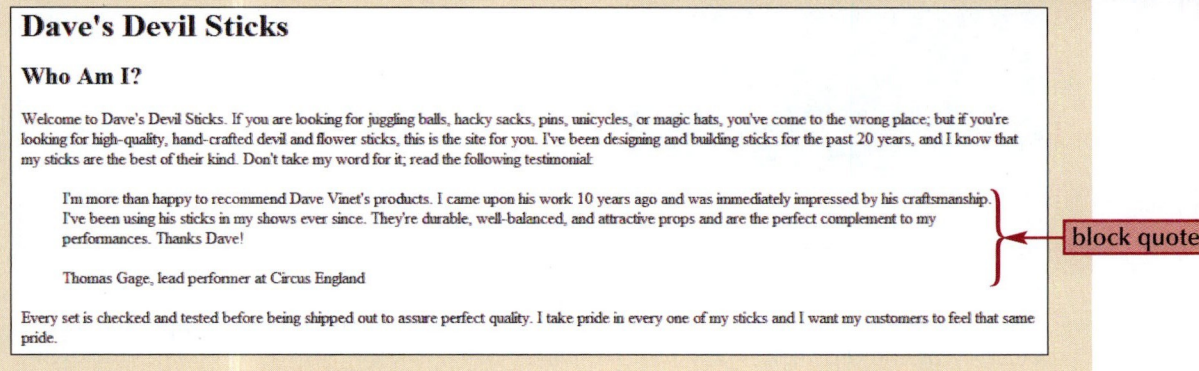

Note that the customer quote also included two paragraph elements nested within the blockquote element. The indentation applied by the browser to the block quote was also applied to any content within that element, so those paragraphs were indented even though browsers do not indent paragraphs by default.

Marking a List

Dave has a list of products that he wants to display on his Web page. This information is presented on his flyer as a bulleted list. He wants something similar on the Web site. HTML supports three kinds of lists: ordered, unordered, and definition.

Ordered Lists

Use an **ordered list** for items that must appear in a numeric order. The beginning of an ordered list is marked by the <ol> (ordered list) tag. Each item within that ordered list is subsequently marked using the <li> (list item) tag. The syntax of an ordered list is therefore

```
<ol>
    <li>item1</li>
    <li>item2</li>
...
</ol>
```

where *item1*, *item2*, and so forth are the items in the list. To explore creating an ordered list, return to the HTML demo page.

To create an ordered list:

1. Return to the **demo_html.htm** file in your Web browser.

2. Delete the HTML code in the left box and replace it with the following:

```
<ol>
    <li>First Item</li>
    <li>Second Item</li>
    <li>Third Item</li>
</ol>
```

3. Click the **Preview Code** button. Figure 1-17 shows how the browser renders the ordered list contents.

Figure 1-17 **Viewing an ordered list**

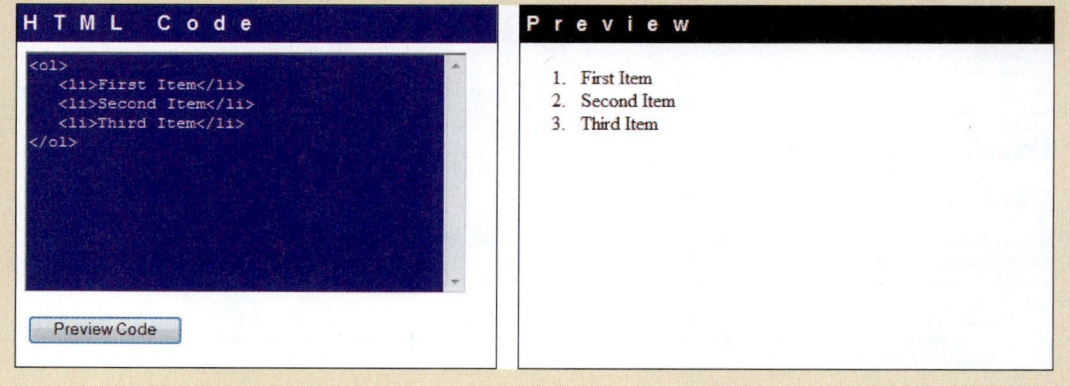

By default, entries in an ordered list are numbered, with the numbers supplied automatically by the browser.

Unordered Lists

To mark a list in which the items do not need to occur in any special order, create an **unordered list**. The structure of ordered and unordered lists is the same, except that the list contents are contained with a set of <ul> (unordered list) tags:

```
<ul>
    <li>item1</li>
    <li>item2</li>
...
</ul>
```

Try creating an unordered list with the demo page.

To create an unordered list:

▶ **1.** Delete the HTML code in the left box and replace it with the following:

```
<ul>
    <li>Basic Stick</li>
    <li>Flower Stick</li>
    <li>Master Stick</li>
    <li>Glow Stick</li>
</ul>
```

▶ **2.** Click the **Preview Code** button. Figure 1-18 shows how the browser renders the unordered list.

Viewing an unordered list | Figure 1-18

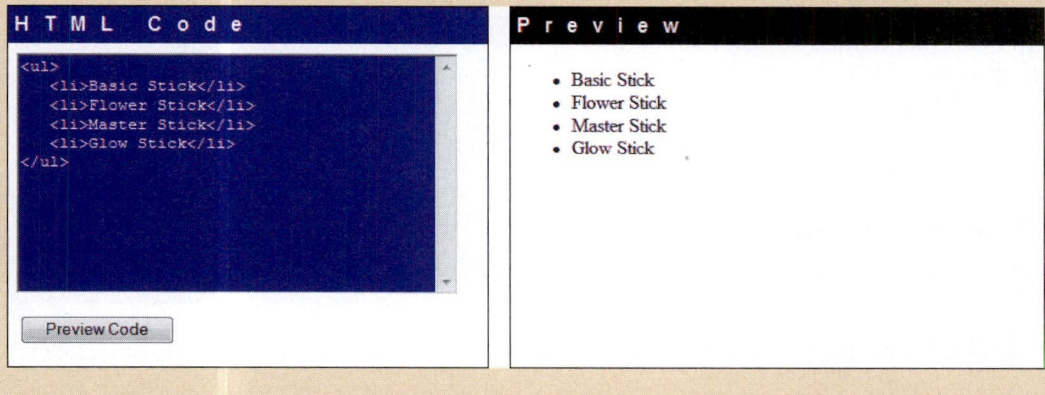

Trouble? On some browsers, the list appears with diamond shapes rather than circular bullets.

By default, unordered lists appear as bulleted lists. The exact bullet marker depends on the browser. Most browsers use a filled-in circle.

Reference Window | **Marking Lists**

- To mark an ordered list, enter

```
<ol>
    <li>item1</li>
    <li>item2</li>
. . .
</ol>
```

  where *item1*, *item2*, and so forth are the items in the list.
- To mark an unordered list, use

```
<ul>
    <li>item1</li>
    <li>item2</li>
. . .
</ul>
```

- To mark a definition list, use

```
<dl>
    <dt>term1</dt>
    <dd>description1</dd>
    <dt>term2</dt>
    <dd>description2a</dd>
    <dd>description2b</dd>
. . .
</dl>
```

  where *term1*, *term2*, etc. are the terms in the list and *description1*, *description2a*, *description2b*, etc. are the descriptions associated with each term.

Nesting Lists

You can place one list inside of another to create several levels of list items. The top level of the nested list contains the major items, with each sublevel containing items of lesser importance. Most browsers differentiate the various levels by using a different list symbol. Use the demo page to see how this works with unordered lists.

To create an unordered list:

▶ 1. Click at the end of the <li>Basic Stick</li> line, and then press the **Enter** key to insert a new blank line.

▶ 2. Insert the following code between the <li>Basic Stick</li> and <li>Flower Stick</li> lines:

```
<ul>
    <li>Red</li>
    <li>Blue</li>
    <li>Green</li>
</ul>
```

▶ 3. Click the **Preview Code** button. Figure 1-19 shows the result of creating a nested list.

Viewing a nested list   Figure 1-19

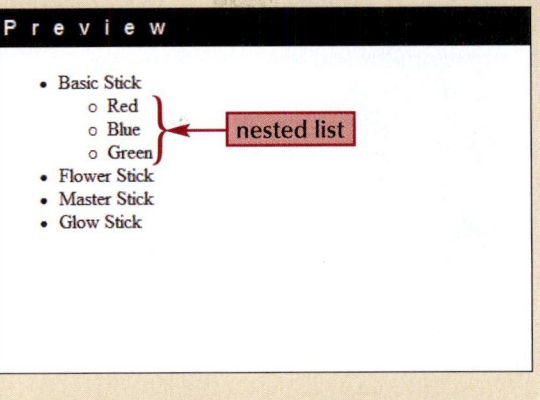

Trouble? Depending on your browser, the sublist of basic stick colors might appear with solid bullets rather than open circles.

The lower level of items is displayed using an open circle as the list bullet and indented on the page. Once again, the exact choice of formatting a nested list is left to the browser at this point. As you continue your study of HTML you'll learn how to specify the appearance of nested lists using styles.

Definition Lists

A third type of list is the **definition list**, which contains a list of terms, each followed by the term's description. The syntax for creating a definition list is

```
<dl>
    <dt>term1</dt>
    <dd>description1</dd>
    <dt>term2</dt>
    <dd>description2a</dd>
    <dd>description2b</dd>
...
</dl>
```

where *term1*, *term2*, etc. are the terms in the list and *description1*, *description2a*, *description2b*, etc. are the descriptions associated with each term. Note that definition lists must follow a specified order, with each dt (definition term) element followed by one or more dd (definition description) elements.

To create a definition list:

1. Replace the code in the left box of the HTML demo page with:

   ```
   <dl>
       <dt>Basic Stick</dt>
       <dd>Easiest stick to learn</dd>
       <dt>Flower Stick</dt>
       <dd>A graceful stick with tassels</dd>
       <dt>Master Stick</dt>
       <dd>Our most popular stick</dd>
   </dl>
   ```

2. Click the **Preview Code** button. Figure 1-20 shows the appearance of the definition list in the browser.

Figure 1-20 **Viewing a definition list**

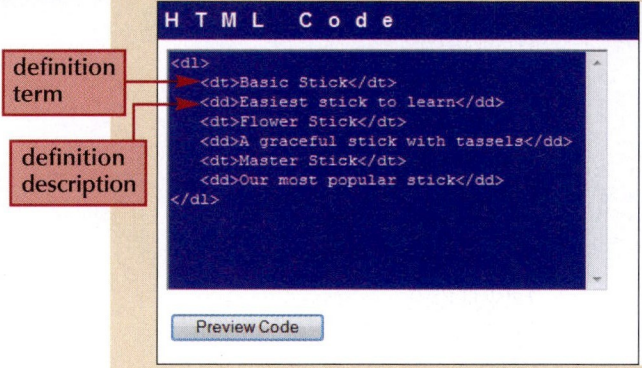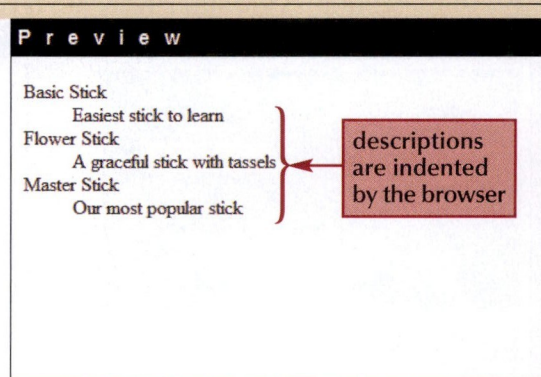

> **Tip**
>
> Definition lists can also mark dialogs, with each dt element naming a speaker, and each dd element containing the speaker's words. For long speeches, use multiple dd elements per speaker to break the speaker's words into separate blocks.

The demo page shows each term followed by a description that is placed in a new block below the term and indented on the page. If you had included multiple dd elements, each description would have been contained within its own block and indented.

Now that you've experimented with the three types of HTML lists, you'll add an unordered list of products to Dave's Web page. By default, the product names will appear as a bulleted list.

To add an unordered list to Dave's Web page:

1. Return to the **dave.htm** file in your text editor.

2. Directly below the <h2>My Products</h2> heading, insert the following code, as shown in Figure 1-21:

```
<ul>
   <li>Basic Stick</li>
   <li>Flower Stick</li>
   <li>Master Stick</li>
   <li>Glow Stick</li>
</ul>
```

Figure 1-21 **Adding an unordered list**

```
<h2>My Products</h2>
<ul>
   <li>Basic Stick</li>
   <li>Flower Stick</li>
   <li>Master Stick</li>
   <li>Glow Stick</li>
</ul>
</body>
```

3. Save your changes to the file, and then refresh the **dave.htm** file in your Web browser. As shown in Figure 1-22, the list of products appears as a bulleted list at the bottom of the page.

Product list on Dave's Web page **Figure 1-22**

Dave's Devil Sticks

Who Am I?

Welcome to Dave's Devil Sticks. If you are looking for juggling balls, hacky sacks, pins, unicycles, or magic hats, you've come to the wrong place; but if you're looking for high-quality, hand-crafted devil and flower sticks, this is the site for you. I've been designing and building sticks for the past 20 years, and I know that my sticks are the best of their kind. Don't take my word for it; read the following testimonial:

I'm more than happy to recommend Dave Vinet's products. I came upon his work 10 years ago and was immediately impressed by his craftsmanship. I've been using his sticks in my shows ever since. They're durable, well-balanced, and attractive props and are the perfect complement to my performances. Thanks Dave!

Thomas Gage, lead performer at Circus England

Every set is checked and tested before being shipped out to assure perfect quality. I take pride in every one of my sticks and I want my customers to feel that same pride.

My Products

- Basic Stick
- Flower Stick   bulleted list
- Master Stick   of products
- Glow Stick

Exploring Other Block-Level Elements

HTML supports several other block-level elements you'll find useful. Dave wants to display the company's address at the bottom of the body of his page. Contact information like addresses can be marked using the <address> tag

```
<address>content</address>
```

where *content* is the contact information. Most browsers render addresses in italics, and some also indent or right-justify addresses. You'll use the address element to display the address of Dave's company.

To add an address to the bottom of Dave's Web page:

► 1. Return to the **dave.htm** file in your text editor.

► 2. Directly above the </body> tag, insert the following code, as shown in Figure 1-23:

```
<address>Dave's Devil Sticks
        541 West Highland Dr.
        Auburn, ME 04210
        (207) 555 - 9001
</address>
```

Adding an address element **Figure 1-23**

```
<address>Dave's Devil Sticks
        541 West Highland Dr.
        Auburn, ME 04210
        (207) 555 - 9001
</address>
</body>

</html>
```

► 3. Save your changes to the file, and then refresh **dave.htm** in your Web browser. Figure 1-24 shows the revised page with the address text.

Figure 1-24 **Address text on Dave's Web page**

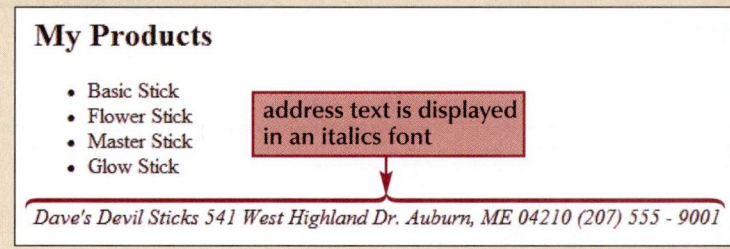

The address text appears in italics at the bottom of the page. Note that the company name, street address, city, state, and phone number all appear to run together. Remember that the browser ignores the occurrence of line breaks, tabs, and other white space in your text document. In the next session, you'll learn how to make this text more readable. For now, you'll leave the address text as it is.

At this point, you're done adding block-level elements to Dave's Web page. Figure 1-25 summarizes the properties and uses of HTML's block-level elements, including information on some block-level elements you did not add to Dave's document.

Figure 1-25 **Block-level elements**

Block-Level Element	Marks	Usual Visual Appearance
`<address> ... </address>`	Contact information	*Italicized text*
`<blockquote> ... </blockquote>`	An extended quotation	Plain text indented from the left and right
`<center> ... </center>`	Text horizontally centered with the block (**deprecated**)	Plain text, centered
`<dd> ... </dd>`	A definition description	Plain text
`<dir> ... </dir>`	A multicolumn directory list (**deprecated**)	Plain text
`<div> ... </div>`	A generic block-level element	Plain text
`<dl> ... </dl>`	A definition list	Plain text
`<dt> ... </dt>`	A definition term from a definition list	Plain text
`<hn> ... </hn>`	A heading where n is a value from 1 to 6 with h1 as the most prominent heading and h6 the least prominent	**Boldfaced text of various font sizes**
`<li> ... </li>`	A list item from an ordered or unordered list	Bulleted or numbered text
`<menu> ... </menu>`	A single column menu list (**deprecated**)	Plain text
`<ol> ... </ol>`	An ordered list	Plain text
`<p> ... </p>`	A paragraph	Plain text
`<pre> ... </pre>`	Preformatted text, retaining all white space and special characters	`Fixed width text`
`<ul> ... </ul>`	An unordered list	Plain text

Working with Inline Elements

Block-level elements place their content starting on a new line within the page. Another type of element is an **inline element**, which marks a section of text within a block-level element. If you think of a block-level element as a paragraph, an inline element is like a phrase or a collection of characters within that paragraph. Inline elements do not start out on a new line or block, but instead flow "in-line" with the rest of the characters in the block.

Character Formatting Elements

Inline elements are often used to format characters and words. For example, you can use an inline element to make a name or title appear in **boldface** letters or *italics*. Inline elements used in this fashion are referred to as **character formatting elements**. Figure 1-26 describes some of the inline elements supported by HTML.

Inline elements Figure 1-26

Inline Element	Marks	Usual Visual Appearance
`<abbr> ... </abbr>`	An abbreviation	Plain text
`<acronym> .. </acronym>`	An acronym	Plain text
`<b> ... </b>`	Boldfaced text	**Boldfaced text**
`<big> ... </big>`	Big text	Larger text
`<cite> ... </cite>`	A citation	*Italicized text*
`<code> ... </code>`	Program code	Fixed width text
`<del> ... </del>`	Deleted text	~~Strikethrough text~~
`<dfn> ... </dfn>`	A definition term	*Italicized text*
`<em> ... </em>`	Emphasized content	*Italicized text*
`<i> ... </i>`	Italicized text	*Italicized text*
`<ins> ... </ins>`	Inserted text	Underlined text
`<kbd> ... </kbd>`	Keyboard-style text	Fixed width text
`<q> ... </q>`	Quoted text	"Quoted text"
`<s> ... </s>`	Strikethrough text (**Deprecated**)	~~Strikethrough text~~
`<samp> ... </samp>`	Sample computer code	Fixed width text
`<small> ... </small>`	Small text	Smaller text
`<span> ... </span>`	A generic inline element	Plain text
`<strike> ... </strike>`	Strikethrough text (**Deprecated**)	~~Strikethrough text~~
`<strong> ... </strong>`	Strongly emphasized content	**Boldfaced text**
`<sub> ... </sub>`	Subscripted text	Subscripted text
`<sup> ... </sup>`	Superscripted text	Superscripted text
`<tt> ... </tt>`	Teletype text	Fixed width text
`<u> ... </u>`	Underlined text (**Deprecated**)	Underlined text
`<var> ... </var>`	Programming variables	*Italicized text*

To see how to use inline elements in conjunction with block-level elements, you'll return to the HTML demo page.

To explore the use of inline elements:

1. Return to the **demo_html.htm** file in your Web browser.

2. In the left box, enter the HTML code:

   ```
   <p>Welcome to Dave's Devil Sticks, owned and operated by David
   Vinet.</p>
   ```

3. Click the **Preview Code** button to display this paragraph in the Preview box.

   To mark "Dave's Devil Sticks" as boldface text, you can enclose that phrase within a set of <b> tags.

4. Insert a **<b>** tag directly before the word "Dave's" in the box on the left. Insert the closing **</b>** tag directly after the word "Sticks." Click the **Preview Code** button to confirm that "Dave's Devil Sticks" is now displayed in bold.

   You can use the <i> tag to mark italicized text. Try this now by enclosing "David Vinet" within a set of <i> tags.

5. Insert an **<i>** tag directly before the word "David" and insert the closing **</i>** tag directly after "Vinet". Click the **Preview Code** button to view the revised code. Figure 1-27 shows the result of applying the <b> and <i> tags to the paragraph text.

Figure 1-27	Using the <b> and <i> tags

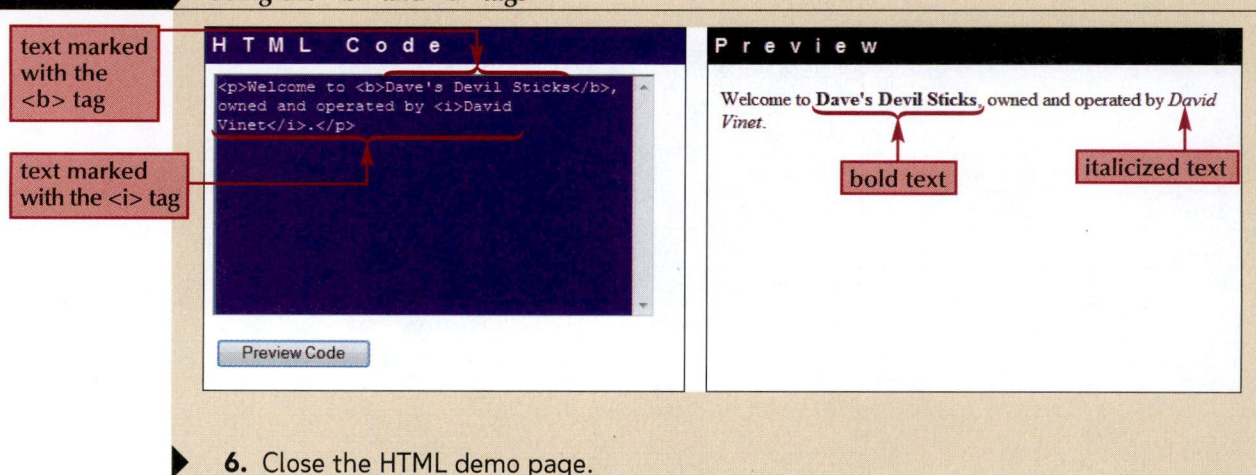

6. Close the HTML demo page.

You can nest inline elements to mark text with more than one character-formatting element. The code

```
<p>Welcome to <b><i>Dave's Devil Sticks</i></b>.</p>
```

displays "Dave's Devil Sticks" in a ***bold italic*** font.

Dave wants to use the <b> and <i> tags in several locations in his document. He wants to display the name of his company and the names of all of his devil stick products in bold. He would also like to display the name of the juggling troupe, *Circus England*, in italics. Make these changes to his document now.

Marking Inline Elements	Reference Window

- To mark boldface text, enter
  ```
  <b>content</b>
  ```
  where *content* is the text to be displayed in boldface.
- To mark italicized text, use
  ```
  <i>content</i>
  ```
- To mark text with a generic inline element, use
  ```
  <span>content</span>
  ```

To mark boldface and italicized text:

1. Return to the **dave.htm** file in your text editor.

2. Go to the first paragraph of the body section and enclose the text "Dave's Devil Sticks" within a set of opening and closing <b> tags.

3. Go to the second paragraph within the blockquote element and enclose the text "Circus England" within a set of opening and closing <i> tags.

4. Go to the unordered list and enclose each product item within a set of opening and closing <b> tags. Nest the <b> tags within the <li> tags. Figure 1-28 highlights the revised code of Dave's document.

Marking bold and italicized text | Figure 1-28

```
<body>
    <h1>Dave's Devil Sticks</h1>
    <h2>Who Am I?</h2>
    <p>Welcome to <b>Dave's Devil Sticks</b>. If you are looking for juggling balls,
       hacky sacks, pins, unicycles, or magic hats, you've come to the wrong
       place; but if you're looking for high-quality, hand-crafted devil and
       flower sticks, this is the site for you. I've been designing and building
       sticks for the past 20 years, and I know that my sticks are the best of
       their kind. Don't take my word for it; read the following testimonial:</p>

    <blockquote>
        <p>I'm more than happy to recommend Dave Vinet's products. I came upon his
           work 10 years ago and was immediately impressed by his craftsmanship.
           I've been using his sticks in my shows ever since. They're durable,
           well-balanced, and attractive props and are the perfect complement to
           my performances. Thanks Dave!</p>

        <p>Thomas Gage, lead performer at <i>Circus England</i></p>
    </blockquote>

    <p>Every set is checked and tested before being shipped out to assure perfect
       quality. I take pride in every one of my sticks and I want my customers to
       feel that same pride.</p>

    <h2>My Products</h2>
    <ul>
        <li><b>Basic Stick</b></li>
        <li><b>Flower Stick</b></li>
        <li><b>Master Stick</b></li>
        <li><b>Glow Stick</b></li>
    </ul>

    <address>Dave's Devil Sticks
             541 West Highland Dr.
             Auburn, ME 04210
             (207) 555 - 9001
    </address>
</body>
```

5. Save your changes to the file.

6. Refresh the **dave.htm** file in your Web browser. Figure 1-29 shows the revised appearance of the Web page.

Figure 1-29   Dave's revised Web page

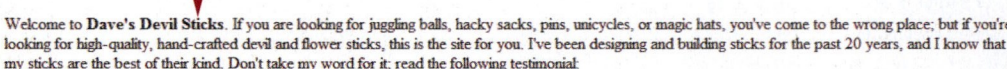

Dave's Devil Sticks

Who Am I?   bold text

Welcome to **Dave's Devil Sticks**. If you are looking for juggling balls, hacky sacks, pins, unicycles, or magic hats, you've come to the wrong place; but if you're looking for high-quality, hand-crafted devil and flower sticks, this is the site for you. I've been designing and building sticks for the past 20 years, and I know that my sticks are the best of their kind. Don't take my word for it; read the following testimonial:

> I'm more than happy to recommend Dave Vinet's products. I came upon his work 10 years ago and was immediately impressed by his craftsmanship. I've been using his sticks in my shows ever since. They're durable, well-balanced, and attractive props and are the perfect complement to my performances. Thanks Dave!

> Thomas Gage, lead performer at *Circus England*   italicized text

Every set is checked and tested before being shipped out to assure perfect quality. I take pride in every one of my sticks and I want my customers to feel that same pride.

My Products

- **Basic Stick**
- **Flower Stick**
- **Master Stick**
- **Glow Stick**

bold text

Dave's Devil Sticks 541 West Highland Dr. Auburn, ME 04210 (207) 555 - 9001

▶ **7.** If you want to take a break before starting the next session, you can close your browser and any open files now.

Using the Generic Elements: div and span

Most of the block-level and inline elements you've examined have a specific meaning or purpose in your document. Sometimes you will want an element that represents a text block or a string of inline text without it having any other meaning. HTML supports two types of generic elements: div and span. The div element is used to mark general block-level content and has the syntax

```
<div>content</div>
```

The span element, used to mark general inline content, has the syntax

```
<span>content</span>
```

Browsers recognize both elements but do not assign any default format to content marked with those elements. Web authors like using the div and span elements because they know they can completely control the appearance of the content through the use of styles. This is not the case with elements such as addresses or headings, which have default formats assigned to them by the Web browser.

Logical Elements vs. Physical Elements | InSight

As you learn more HTML, you'll notice some overlap in how certain elements are displayed by the browser. To display italicized text, you could use the <dfn>, <em>, <i>, or <var> tags, or if you want to italicize an entire block of text, you could use the <address> tag. It's important to distinguish between how a browser displays an element and the element's purpose in the document. Page elements can be organized into two types: logical elements and physical elements. A logical element, marked with tags like <cite> or <code>, describes the nature of the enclosed content but not necessarily how that content should appear. A physical element, on the other hand, marked with tags like <b> or <i>, describes how content should appear but doesn't indicate the content's nature.

While it can be tempting to use logical and physical elements interchangeably, your HTML code benefits in several ways when you respect the distinction. For one, different browsers can and do display logical elements differently. For example, both Netscape's browser and Internet Explorer display text marked with the <cite> tag in italics, but the text-based browser Lynx displays the citation text using a fixed width font. An aural browser that doesn't render pages visually might increase the volume when it encounters cited text. In addition, Web programmers can also use logical elements to extract information from a page. For example, a program could automatically generate a bibliography from all of the citations listed within a Web site.

In general, you should use a logical element that accurately describes the enclosed content whenever possible, letting the browser determine the appearance based on its function, and use physical elements only for general content.

You're finished working with block-level elements and inline elements. In the next session you'll learn how to add images to the document as well as how to use styles to control the appearance of your Web pages.

Session 1.2 Quick Check | Review

1. What is the difference between a block-level element and an inline element?
2. If you want to add an extra blank line between paragraphs on your Web page, why can't you simply add an extra blank line to the HTML file?
3. Specify the code to mark the main heading on your Web page.
4. Specify the tag to mark an extended quotation. How would that quotation be rendered in most visual browsers?
5. Specify the code you would use to display the seasons of the year (Winter, Spring, Summer, and Fall) as an unordered list.
6. The following is a dialog from Shakespeare's *Hamlet*. Indicate how you would use a definition list to mark up this text, distinguishing between the speaker and the lines spoken.

   HAMLET
   There's ne'er a villain dwelling in all Denmark; but he's an arrant knave.
   HORATIO
   There needs no ghost, my lord, come from the grave to tell us this.
7. What code would you enter to display the following text as a paragraph in your Web page? Include both the block-level and inline element tags.

   Hamlet, a play by William Shakespeare.
8. What are the two generic page elements?

Session 1.3

Using Element Attributes

So far you've used markup tags only to create Dave's Web page. However, many markup tags contain **attributes** that control the use, behavior, and in some cases the appearance of elements in the document. You apply an attribute to an element by adding it to the element's markup tag using the syntax

```
<element attribute1="value1" attribute2="value2" ...>content</element>
```

where *attribute1*, *attribute2*, etc. are the names of attributes associated with the element and *value1*, *value2*, etc. are the values of those attributes. You can list attributes in any order, but you must separate them from one another with white space.

One attribute that is associated with most elements is the id attribute, which uniquely identifies the element in the Web page. The following code assigns the id value of "mainhead" to the h1 heading "Dave's Devil Sticks," distinguishing it from other h1 headings that might exist in the document:

```
<h1 id="mainhead">Dave's Devil Sticks</h1>
```

You'll learn more about the id attribute in the next tutorial. For a list of attributes associated with each element, you can also refer to the appendices.

> **Tip**
>
> Attribute names should be entered in lowercase letters to be completely compliant with the syntax rules of XHTML. Attribute values must be enclosed within single or double quotation marks.

Reference Window | **Adding an Attribute to an Element**

- To add an element attribute, enter
  ```
  <element attribute1="value1" attribute2="value2" ...>content
  </element>
  ```
  where *attribute1*, *attribute2*, etc. are the names of attributes associated with the element and *value1*, *value2*, etc. are the values of those attributes.

The Style Attribute

Another important attribute is the style attribute. As you've seen, an element's appearance on the Web page is determined by the browser. If you want to change how the browser displays an element, you can use the style attribute. The syntax of the style attribute is

```
<element style="rules" ...>content</element>
```

where *rules* is a set of style rules. Style rules are entered by specifying a style name followed by a colon and then a style value. You can have multiple style rules with each style name/value pair, separated from each other by a semicolon. The general form of the style attribute is therefore

```
style="name1:value1; name2:value2; ..."
```

where *name1*, *name2*, etc. are style names and *value1*, *value2* and so forth are the values of those styles.

As you proceed in your study of HTML you'll learn more about styles and how to apply them. For now you'll focus only on a few basic ones. The first is a style to align text. As you may have noticed, Web page text is usually aligned with the page's left margin. To choose a different alignment, you can apply the following text-align style to the element

```
style="text-align: alignment"
```

where *alignment* is left, right, center, or justify. For example, to center an h1 heading, you would enter the following markup tag:

```
<h1 style="text-align: center"> ... </h1>
```

A second style you'll explore defines the text color used in an element. Most browsers display text in a black font. To apply a different text color, use

```
style="color: color"
```

where *color* is a color name such as red, blue, green, and so forth. Applying the following attribute to an h1 heading causes the browser to render the heading text in a red font:

```
<h1 style="color: red"> ... </h1>
```

You can both center the text and change its font color to red by combining the two styles in one style attribute:

```
<h1 style="text-align: center; color: red"> ... </h1>
```

Applying the Style Attribute | Reference Window

- To add the style attribute, in the opening tag enter
  ```
  style="name1:value1; name2:value2; ..."
  ```
  where *name1*, *name2*, etc. are style names and *value1*, *value2* and so forth are the values of those styles.
- To center text horizontally, use
  ```
  style="text-align: alignment"
  ```
  where *alignment* is left, right, center, or justify.
- To set the font color, use
  ```
  style="color: color"
  ```
  where *color* is a color name.

To explore how to apply these two styles to a page element, you'll return to the HTML demo page.

To explore the style attribute:

1. Return to the **demo_html.htm** file in your Web browser.

2. Enter the following code in the left box, and then click the **Preview Code** button:

   ```
   <h1>Dave's Devil Sticks</h1>
   ```

   The demo page displays Dave's Devil Sticks as an h1 heading in the Preview box. Now you'll change the font color to red and center this heading in the box.

▶ **3.** Within the opening <h1> tag, insert a space after "h1," and then type the attribute

```
style="text-align: center; color: red"
```

▶ **4.** Click the **Preview Code** button. As shown in Figure 1-30, the h1 heading is now centered and displayed in a red font.

Figure 1-30 Applying styles to an element

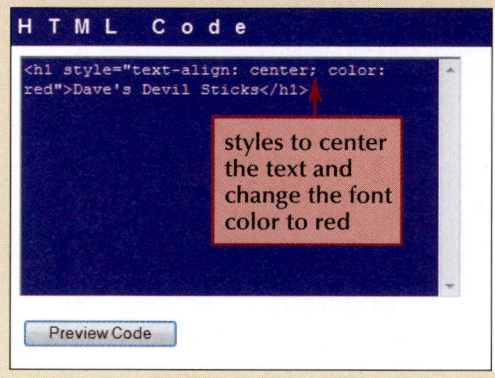
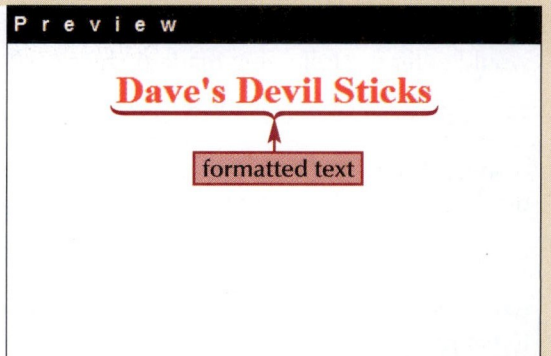

▶ **5.** Continue exploring the text-align and color styles by creating headings right-aligned or centered in a blue, green, and gray-colored text.

▶ **6.** Close the HTML demo page when you are finished exploring these two styles.

Dave has had a chance to examine your progress on his Web page and suggests that you center the address text at the bottom of the page. Now that you've explored the uses of the style attribute, you can make this change to his document.

To apply a style to the address element:

▶ **1.** Return to the **dave.htm** file in your text editor.

▶ **2.** Locate the address element at the bottom of the file and insert the following style attribute, as shown in Figure 1-31:

```
style="text-align: center"
```

Figure 1-31 Apply the text-align style to an address

```
<address style="text-align: center">Dave's Devil Sticks
          541 West Highland Dr.
          Auburn, ME 04210
          (207) 555 - 9001
</address>
</body>

</html>
```

▶ **3.** Save your changes to the file and refresh the **dave.htm** file in your Web browser. Verify that the address text is centered horizontally at the bottom of the page.

Presentational Attributes

You learned in the first session that early versions of HTML were used mostly by scientists and researchers. HTML was intended to be a language that described the structure but not necessarily the appearance of documents. Scientists and researchers didn't need flashy graphics, various fonts, or even much color on a page. The earliest Web pages weren't fancy and did not require much from the browsers that displayed them. This changed as the Web became more popular and attracted the attention of graphic designers and artists.

One way that HTML changed to accommodate this new class of users was to introduce **presentational attributes**, which are attributes that specifically describe how any element should be rendered. Rather than using styles, early versions of HTML would align text using the align attribute

```
<element align="alignment">content</element>
```

where *alignment* is either left, right, center, or justify. Thus to center an h1 heading you could use either of the following:

```
<h1 style="text-align: center">Dave's Devil Sticks</h1>
```

or

```
<h1 align="center">Dave's Devil Sticks</h1>
```

Almost all presentational attributes are now deprecated in favor of styles, but you will still see them used. Many HTML editors and converters use presentational attributes in place of styles. Even though using a deprecated attribute like align will probably not cause your Web page to fail, you should still use styles because that will ensure compatibility with future browser versions and with XHTML.

Working with Empty Elements

As he examines your work on the Web page, Dave notices that the product list you created in the last session lacks descriptions of the items. Dave wants you to take the information from his original flyer and add it to the Web page.

To add a description of each item in the product list:

1. Return to the **dave.htm** file in your text editor.

2. Locate the first closing </b> tag in the unordered list directly after the text "Basic Stick." Press the **Enter** key and type the following text, indenting it to make the code easier to read:

   ```
   The easiest stick to learn with, but "grippy" enough for the most
   demanding tricks. Comes in red, green, and blue.
   ```

3. Insert the following description for the Flower Stick, directly after the closing </b> tag for that product name:

   ```
   A graceful stick with colored tassels. Flower Sticks float more
   slowly, giving you the ideal chance to practice new moves.
   ```

4. Add the following description for the Master Stick after the closing </b> tag:

   ```
   My most popular stick is shorter and heavier for fast play and more
   advanced tricks. Each Master set is available in custom colors.
   ```

5. Finally, add the following description for the Glow Stick:

```
The Glow Stick shines brightly at night (without the danger of a fire
stick). It combines the fun and versatility of the Master Stick,
adding the fun tricks unique to a glow-in-the-dark stick.
```

Figure 1-32 highlights the newly added product descriptions.

Figure 1-32 **Adding product descriptions**

```
<h2>My Products</h2>
<ul>
    <li><b>Basic Stick</b>
        The easiest stick to learn with, but "grippy" enough for the most demanding
        tricks. Comes in red, green, and blue.</li>
    <li><b>Flower Stick</b>
        A graceful stick with colored tassels. Flower Sticks float more slowly, giving
        you the ideal chance to practice new moves.</li>
    <li><b>Master Stick</b>
        My most popular stick is shorter and heavier for fast play and more advanced
        tricks. Each Master set is available in custom colors.</li>
    <li><b>Glow Stick</b>
        The Glow Stick shines brightly at night (without the danger of a fire stick).
        It combines the fun and versatility of the Master Stick, adding the fun tricks
        unique to a glow-in-the-dark stick.</li>
</ul>
```

6. Save your changes to the file and then refresh the **dave.htm** file in your Web browser. Figure 1-33 shows the new product descriptions as they appear in the browser.

Figure 1-33 **Product descriptions on the Web page**

My Products

- **Basic Stick** The easiest stick to learn with, but "grippy" enough for the most demanding tricks. Comes in red, green, and blue.
- **Flower Stick** A graceful stick with colored tassels. Flower Sticks float more slowly, giving you the ideal chance to practice new moves.
- **Master Stick** My most popular stick is shorter and heavier for fast play and more advanced tricks. Each Master set is available in custom colors.
- **Glow Stick** The Glow Stick shines brightly at night (without the danger of a fire stick). It combines the fun and versatility of the Master Stick, adding the fun tricks unique to a glow-in-the-dark stick.

Dave thinks the revised product list is difficult to read and suggests that you place the descriptions on a new line directly below the product name. To do that you'll have to insert a line break into the Web page. The line break element is an example of an **empty element** because it contains no content. Empty elements appear in code as **one-sided tags** using

```
<element />
```

where *element* is the name of the empty element. As with other markup tags, one-sided tags can also contain attributes that define how the element is used in the document. The one-sided tag to mark a line break is

```
<br />
```

Line breaks need to be placed within block-level elements such as paragraphs or headings. Some browsers accept line breaks placed anywhere within the body of the Web page, but this is not good coding technique. XHTML in particular will reject code in which an inline element like the br element is not placed within a block-level element.

Use the br element now to mark a line break between the names and descriptions in Dave's product list.

To create line breaks between the product names and descriptions:

1. Return to the **dave.htm** file in your text editor.

2. Insert a **
** tag directly after the closing </b> tag for the Basic Stick product description.

3. Add a **
** tag after the closing </b> tag for each of the remaining three product names. Figure 1-34 shows the revised HTML code.

Adding line breaks to the Web page   Figure 1-34

```
<h2>My Products</h2>
<ul>
    <li><b>Basic Stick</b><br />
        The easiest stick to learn with, but "grippy" enough for the most demanding
        tricks. Comes in red, green, and blue.</li>
    <li><b>Flower Stick</b><br />
        A graceful stick with colored tassels. Flower Sticks float more slowly, giving
        you the ideal chance to practice new moves.</li>
    <li><b>Master Stick</b><br />
        My most popular stick is shorter and heavier for fast play and more advanced
        tricks. Each Master set is available in custom colors.</li>
    <li><b>Glow Stick</b><br />
        The Glow Stick shines brightly at night (without the danger of a fire stick).
        It combines the fun and versatility of the Master Stick, adding the fun tricks
        unique to a glow-in-the-dark stick.</li>
</ul>
```

forces the browser to insert a line break before rendering the next line of text

4. Save your changes to the file and then refresh the Web page in your browser. Verify that each of the four product descriptions is displayed on a new line directly below the product name.

Marking a Horizontal Rule

Another useful empty element is the hr or horizontal rule element, which places a horizontal line across the Web page. The syntax of the hr element is

`<hr />`

The exact appearance of the horizontal rule is left to the browser. Most browsers display a gray-shaded line a few pixels in height. Horizontal rules are considered block-level elements because they are displayed starting on a new line in the Web page. The hr element can be nested either within the <body> tag, in which case the horizontal rule will extend across the width of the Web page, or within a blockquote element, in which case the horizontal rule will be indented like other contents of the block quote.

Horizontal rules are useful in breaking up a long Web page into topical sections. Dave suggests that you place a horizontal rule above and one below the customer quotation and a third at the bottom of the page directly above the company address.

To create three horizontal rules:

1. Return to the **dave.htm** file in your text editor.

2. Directly below the opening <blockquote> tag, press the **Enter** key to insert a blank line, and then insert an **<hr />** tag.

3. Insert one **<hr />** tag directly above the closing </blockquote> tag and another above the opening <address> tag. Figure 1-35 highlights the revised code.

Figure 1-35 | **Marking horizontal rules with the <hr /> tag**

```
<blockquote>
    <hr />
    <p>I'm more than happy to recommend Dave Vinet's products. I came upon his
        work 10 years ago and was immediately impressed by his craftsmanship.
        I've been using his sticks in my shows ever since. They're durable,
        well-balanced, and attractive props and are the perfect complement to
        my performances. Thanks Dave!</p>

    <p>Thomas Gage, lead performer at <i>Circus England</i></p>
    <hr />
</blockquote>

<p>Every set is checked and tested before being shipped out to assure perfect
    quality. I take pride in every one of my sticks and I want my customers to
    feel that same pride.</p>

<h2>My Products</h2>
<ul>
    <li><b>Basic Stick</b><br />
        The easiest stick to learn with, but "grippy" enough for the most demanding
        tricks. Comes in red, green, and blue.</li>
    <li><b>Flower Stick</b><br />
        A graceful stick with colored tassels. Flower Sticks float more slowly, giving
        you the ideal chance to practice new moves.</li>
    <li><b>Master Stick</b><br />
        My most popular stick is shorter and heavier for fast play and more advanced
        tricks. Each Master set is available in custom colors.</li>
    <li><b>Glow Stick</b><br />
        The Glow Stick shines brightly at night (without the danger of a fire stick).
        It combines the fun and versatility of the Master Stick, adding the fun tricks
        unique to a glow-in-the-dark stick.</li>
</ul>

<hr />

<address style="text-align: center">Dave's Devil Sticks
        541 West Highland Dr.
        Auburn, ME 04210
        (207) 555 - 9001
</address>
</body>
```

4. Save your changes to the file and then refresh the Web page in your browser. As shown in Figure 1-36, three horizontal rules have been added to the document, visually breaking the Web page into sections.

Figure 1-36 | **Adding horizontal rules to the Web page**

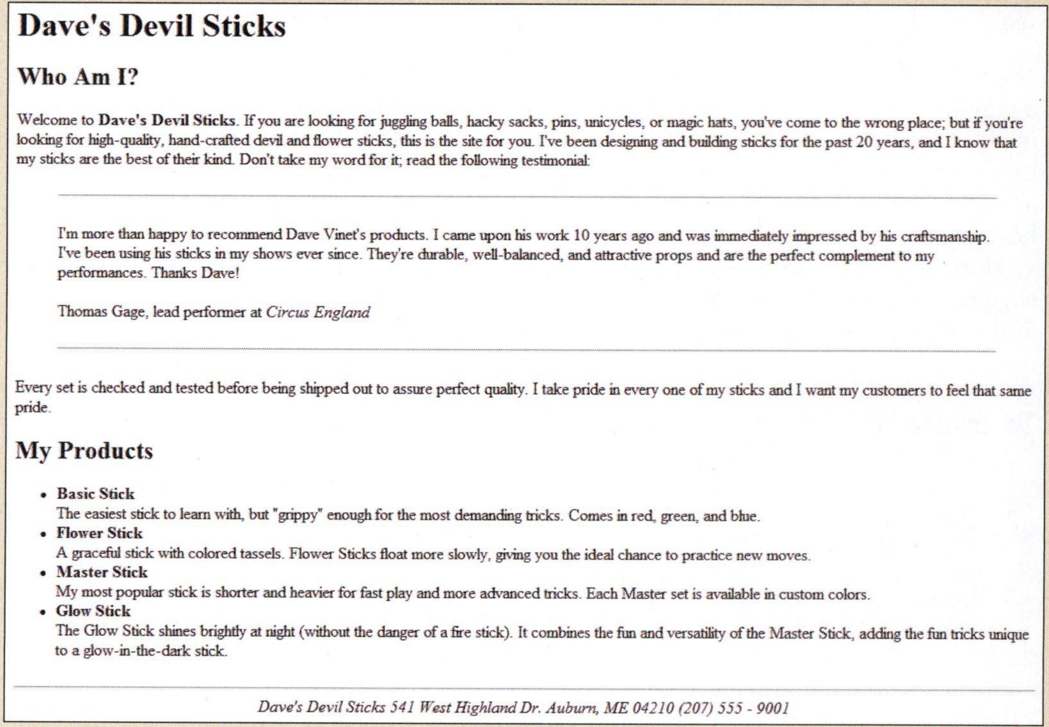

Dave's Devil Sticks

Who Am I?

Welcome to **Dave's Devil Sticks**. If you are looking for juggling balls, hacky sacks, pins, unicycles, or magic hats, you've come to the wrong place; but if you're looking for high-quality, hand-crafted devil and flower sticks, this is the site for you. I've been designing and building sticks for the past 20 years, and I know that my sticks are the best of their kind. Don't take my word for it; read the following testimonial:

I'm more than happy to recommend Dave Vinet's products. I came upon his work 10 years ago and was immediately impressed by his craftsmanship. I've been using his sticks in my shows ever since. They're durable, well-balanced, and attractive props and are the perfect complement to my performances. Thanks Dave!

Thomas Gage, lead performer at *Circus England*

Every set is checked and tested before being shipped out to assure perfect quality. I take pride in every one of my sticks and I want my customers to feel that same pride.

My Products

- **Basic Stick**
  The easiest stick to learn with, but "grippy" enough for the most demanding tricks. Comes in red, green, and blue.
- **Flower Stick**
  A graceful stick with colored tassels. Flower Sticks float more slowly, giving you the ideal chance to practice new moves.
- **Master Stick**
  My most popular stick is shorter and heavier for fast play and more advanced tricks. Each Master set is available in custom colors.
- **Glow Stick**
  The Glow Stick shines brightly at night (without the danger of a fire stick). It combines the fun and versatility of the Master Stick, adding the fun tricks unique to a glow-in-the-dark stick.

Dave's Devil Sticks 541 West Highland Dr. Auburn, ME 04210 (207) 555 - 9001

You show the revised page to Dave and he's pleased with the addition of the horizontal rules. They have made the text easier to read and have nicely highlighted Thomas Gage's tribute.

Inserting an Inline Image

Dave wants you to replace the name of the company with the company logo centered at the top of the page. Because HTML files are simple text files, nontextual content like graphics must be stored in separate files, which are then loaded by the browser as it renders the page. The location of the graphic is marked as an **inline image** using the one-sided tag

```
<img src="file" alt="text" />
```

where *file* is the name of the graphic image file and *text* is text displayed by the browser in place of the graphic image. In this tutorial, you'll assume that the graphic image file is located in the same folder as the Web page, so you don't have to specify the location of the file. In the next tutorial, you'll learn how to reference files placed in other folders or locations on the Web.

As the name implies, inline images are another example of an inline element and thus must be placed within a block-level element such as a heading or a paragraph. Inline images are most widely stored in one of two formats: GIF (Graphics Interchange Format) or JPEG (Joint Photographic Experts Group). You can use an image editing application such as Adobe Photoshop to convert images to either of these two formats. Dave has already created such a graphic and stored it with the filename **logo.jpg**, located in the tutorial.01\tutorial folder included with your Data Files.

Marking Empty Elements | Reference Window

- To mark a line break, use
  ```
  <br />
  ```
- To mark a horizontal rule, use
  ```
  <hr />
  ```
- To mark an inline image, use
  ```
  <img src="file" alt="text" />
  ```
  where *file* is the name of the graphic image file and *text* is text displayed by the browser in place of the graphic image.

To insert Dave's logo centered at the top of the page:

1. Return to the **dave.htm** file in your text editor.

2. Go to the h1 heading element at the top of the body section and insert the following attribute into the opening <h1> tag:

   ```
   style="text-align: center"
   ```

3. Delete the text **Dave's Devil Sticks** from between the opening and closing <h1> tags and replace it with

   ```
   <img src="logo.jpg" alt="Dave's Devil Sticks" />
   ```

   Figure 1-37 shows the revised code in the **dave.htm** file.

Figure 1-37 ▸ **Adding an inline image to a Web page**

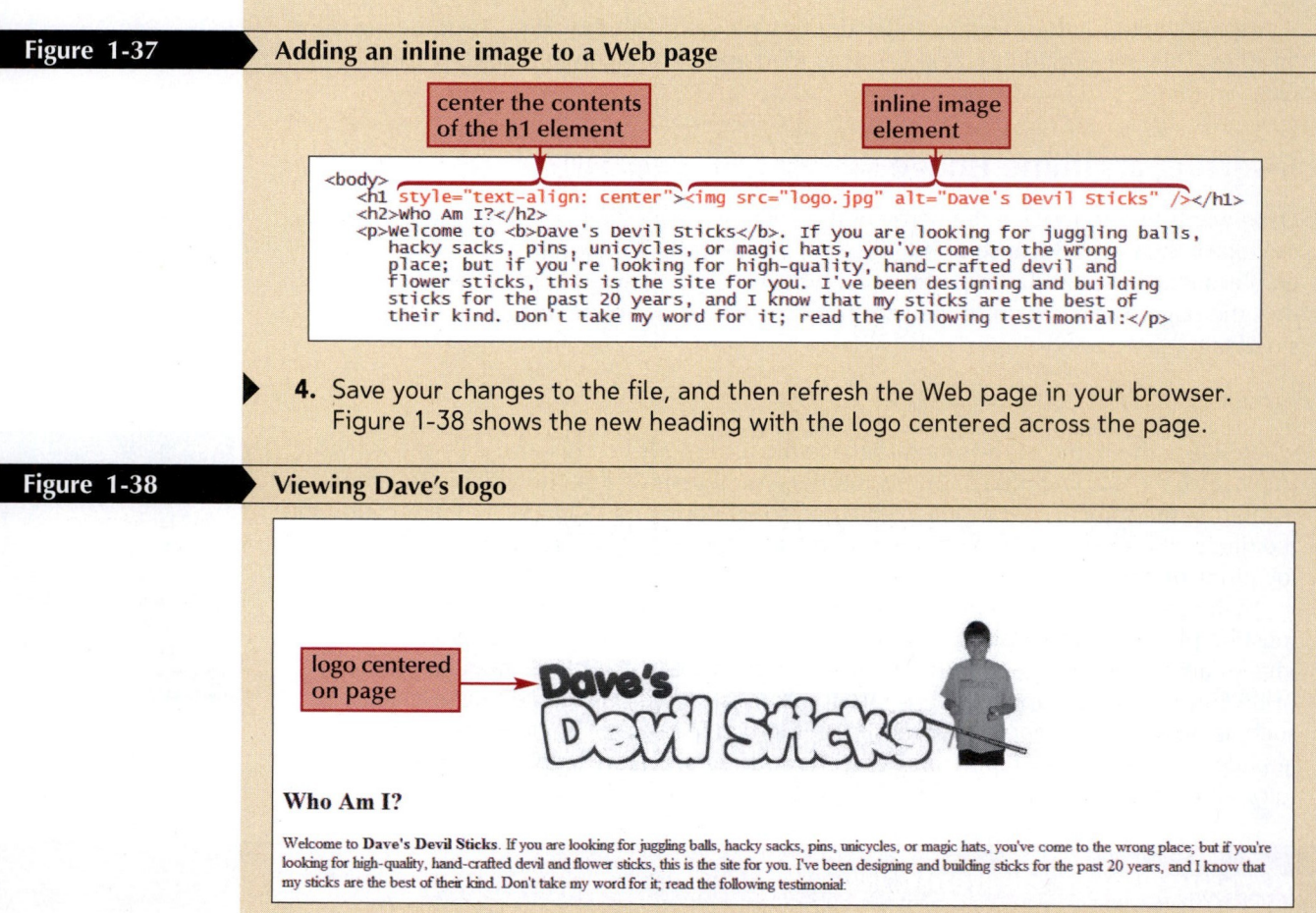

4. Save your changes to the file, and then refresh the Web page in your browser. Figure 1-38 shows the new heading with the logo centered across the page.

Figure 1-38 ▸ **Viewing Dave's logo**

Working with Character Sets and Special Characters

Dave likes the work you've done so far on the Web page. He has only one remaining concern: he feels that the address information at the bottom of the page is difficult to read and would like you to add a solid circular marker separating the different sections of the address. However, this marker is not represented by any keys on your keyboard. How then do you insert this symbol into the Web page?

Character Sets

To add dots to Dave's address, you must reference a symbol that your browser will be able to display but is not found on your keyboard. This is done by using a collection of characters and symbols called a **character set**. Character sets come in a wide variety of sizes, based on the number of symbols required for communication in the chosen language. For English, no more than about 127 characters are needed to represent all of the upper- and lowercase letters, numbers, punctuation marks, spaces, and special typing symbols in the English language. Other languages, such as Japanese or Chinese, require character sets containing thousands of symbols.

Each character set has a name. The character set representing the alphabet of English characters is called **ASCII** (**American Standard Code for Information Interchange**). A more extended character set called **Latin-1** or the **ISO 8859-1** character set supports 255 characters and can be used by most languages that employ the Latin alphabet, including English, French, Spanish, and Italian. The most extended character set is **Unicode**, which can be used for any of the world's languages, supporting up to 65,536 symbols. The most commonly used character set on the Web is **UTF-8**, which is a compressed version of Unicode and is probably the default character set assumed by your browser. You can learn more about character sets by visiting the W3C Web site and the Web site for the Internet Assigned Numbers Authority at *www.iana.org*.

Numeric Character References

To store a character set, browsers need to associate each symbol with a number in a process called **character encoding**. The number is called the **numeric character reference**. For example, the copyright symbol © from the UTF-8 character set has the number 169. If you know the numeric reference, you can insert the number directly into your code to display the symbol. The syntax to insert a numeric character reference is

```
&#code;
```

where *code* is the reference number. Thus to display the © symbol in your Web page, you would enter

```
&#169;
```

into your HTML file. To render a numeric character reference correctly, the browser needs to know the character set and encoding being used in the Web page. This information is typically sent by the Web server as it transfers the HTML page to the browser; and unless you are working with specialized international documents, you usually do not have to worry about specifying the character set for the browser.

Character Entity References

Another way to insert a special symbol is to use a **character entity reference**, in which a short memorable name is used in place of the numeric character reference. The syntax to insert a character entity reference is

```
&char;
```

where *char* is the character's name. The character entity reference for the copyright symbol is "copy," so to display the © symbol in your Web page you could also insert

```
&copy;
```

into your HTML code. One of the advantages of character entity references is that browsers can use them without knowing the character set or encoding. A disadvantage is that older browsers might not recognize the character entity reference and will thus display the reference name but not the symbol it represents.

Reference Window | Inserting Character Codes

- To insert a character based on a numeric character reference, use
  `&#code;`
  where *code* is the character code number.
- To insert a character based on the character entity reference, use
  `&char;`
  where *char* is the name assigned to the character.
- To insert a nonbreaking space, use
  ` `
- To insert the < symbol, use
  `&lt;`
- To insert the > symbol, use
  `&gt;`

To explore various numeric character references and character entity references, you can view a demo page supplied with your Data Files.

To view the demo page:

▶ 1. Use your Web browser to open the **demo_characters.htm** file from the tutorial.01\demo data folder.

▶ 2. Type **£** in the input box at the top of the page, and then click the **Show** button. The Web browser displays the £ symbol in the ivory-colored box below. As you can see, to display the British pound symbol (£), you can use the &#163 numeric character reference.

▶ 3. Now try to display a special symbol using a character entity reference. Replace the value in the input box with **®** and then click the **Show** button. The browser now displays the ® symbol, which is the symbol for registered trademarks.

You can view a collection of numeric character references and character entity references by selecting a table from the list box on the page.

▶ 4. Verify that General Symbols is displayed in the selection list box, and then click the **Show Table** button. As shown in Figure 1-39, the browser displays a list of 35 symbols with the character entity reference and numeric references displayed beneath each symbol.

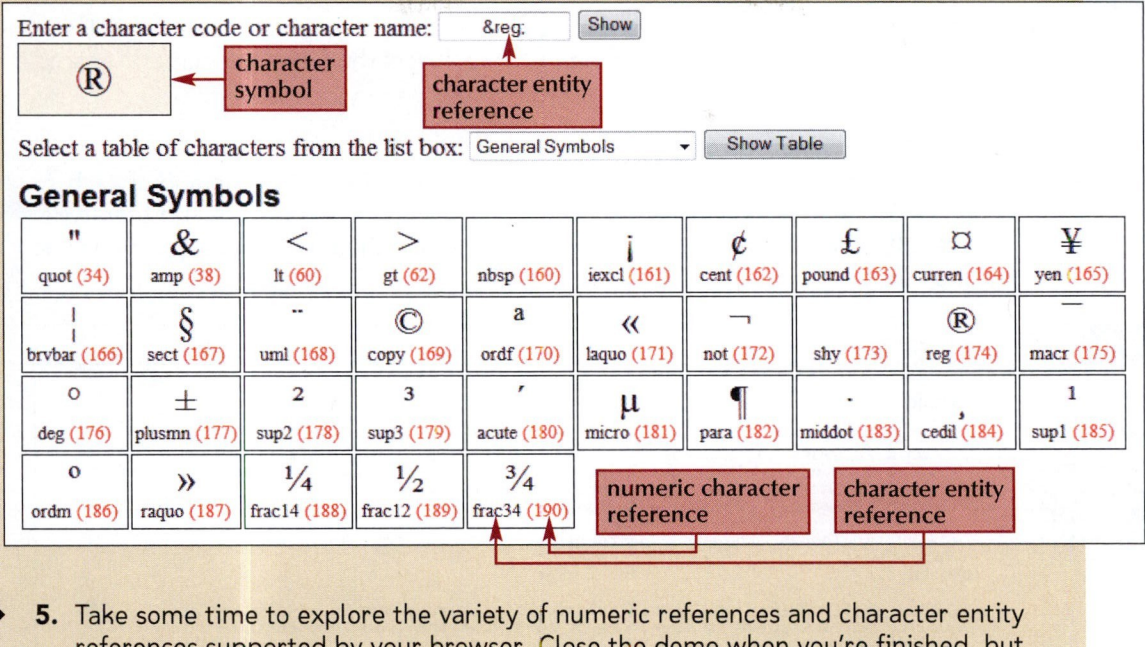

HTML characters demo page ◄ **Figure 1-39**

5. Take some time to explore the variety of numeric references and character entity references supported by your browser. Close the demo when you're finished, but leave your browser open.

Special Characters

One use of character codes is to insert text about HTML itself. For example, if you want your Web page to describe the use of the <h1> tag, you cannot simply type

```
The <h1> tag is used to mark h1 headings.
```

because the browser will interpret the <h1> text as marking the beginning of an h1 heading! Instead, you have to use the < and > entity references to insert the < and > symbols. The text would then be

```
The &lt;h1&gt; tag is used to mark h1 headings.
```

Another use of character codes is to add extra spaces to your Web page. Remember that browsers ignore extra blank spaces in the HTML file. To insert additional spaces, use the   entity reference ("nbsp" stands for nonbreaking space), which forces the browser to insert extra spaces.

On Dave's Web page, you decide to use the bullet symbol to break up the address text into sections. The symbol has the numeric character code value of 8226 and the entity character reference name "bull." Dave suggests you also add a long horizontal line called an em-dash to mark Thomas Gage's name as the author of the recommendation for Dave's business. The character code and entity reference for an em-dash are 8212 and "mdash," respectively.

To add bullets and an em-dash to Dave's Web page:

▶ **1.** Return to the **dave.htm** file in your text editor.

▶ **2.** Locate the paragraph within the blockquote element containing the name of Thomas Gage. Directly after the opening <p> tag, insert the following numeric character code, followed by a space:

—

▶ **3.** Scroll down to the address element at the bottom of the file. At the end of each line within the address element (except the last line), insert a space and then type the **•** character entity reference. Figure 1-40 highlights the newly added code in the file.

Figure 1-40	Adding character references to the HTML file

```
<blockquote>
    <hr />
    <p>I'm more than happy to recommend Dave Vinet's products. I came upon his
       work 10 years ago and was immediately impressed by his craftsmanship.
       I've been using his sticks in my shows ever since. They're durable,
       well-balanced, and attractive props and are the perfect complement to
       my performances. Thanks Dave!</p>

    <p>&#8212; Thomas Gage, lead performer at <i>Circus England</i></p>
    <hr />
</blockquote>

<p>Every set is checked and tested before being shipped out to assure perfect
   quality. I take pride in every one of my sticks and I want my customers to
   feel that same pride.</p>

<h2>My Products</h2>
<ul>
    <li><b>Basic Stick</b><br />
        The easiest stick to learn with, but "grippy" enough for the most demanding
        tricks. Comes in red, green, and blue.</li>
    <li><b>Flower Stick</b><br />
        A graceful stick with colored tassels. Flower Sticks float more slowly, giving
        you the ideal chance to practice new moves.</li>
    <li><b>Master Stick</b><br />
        My most popular stick is shorter and heavier for fast play and more advanced
        tricks. Each Master set is available in custom colors.</li>
    <li><b>Glow Stick</b><br />
        The Glow Stick shines brightly at night (without the danger of a fire stick).
        It combines the fun and versatility of the Master Stick, adding the fun tricks
        unique to a glow-in-the-dark stick.</li>
</ul>

<hr />

<address style="text-align: center">Dave's Devil Sticks &bull;
        541 West Highland Dr. &bull;
        Auburn, ME 04210 &bull;
        (207) 555 - 9001 &bull;
</address>
</body>
```

numeric character reference

character entity reference

▶ **4.** Close the file, saving your changes.

▶ **5.** Refresh the **dave.htm** file in your Web browser. Figure 1-41 shows the final version of Dave's Web page.

Who Am I?

Welcome to **Dave's Devil Sticks**. If you are looking for juggling balls, hacky sacks, pins, unicycles, or magic hats, you've come to the wrong place; but if you're looking for high-quality, hand-crafted devil and flower sticks, this is the site for you. I've been designing and building sticks for the past 20 years, and I know that my sticks are the best of their kind. Don't take my word for it; read the following testimonial:

I'm more than happy to recommend Dave Vinet's products. I came upon his work 10 years ago and was immediately impressed by his craftsmanship. I've been using his sticks in my shows ever since. They're durable, well-balanced, and attractive props and are the perfect complement to my performances. Thanks Dave!

— Thomas Gage, lead performer at *Circus England*

Every set is checked and tested before being shipped out to assure perfect quality. I take pride in every one of my sticks and I want my customers to feel that same pride.

My Products

- **Basic Stick**
  The easiest stick to learn with, but "grippy" enough for the most demanding tricks. Comes in red, green, and blue.
- **Flower Stick**
  A graceful stick with colored tassels. Flower Sticks float more slowly, giving you the ideal chance to practice new moves.
- **Master Stick**
  My most popular stick is shorter and heavier for fast play and more advanced tricks. Each Master set is available in custom colors.
- **Glow Stick**
  The Glow Stick shines brightly at night (without the danger of a fire stick). It combines the fun and versatility of the Master Stick, adding the fun tricks unique to a glow-in-the-dark stick.

Dave's Devil Sticks • 541 West Highland Dr. • Auburn, ME 04210 • (207) 555 - 9001 •

▶ **6.** If you plan on taking a break before working on the end of tutorial problems, you can close your Web browser and any other open files or programs.

You show the completed Web page to Dave. He's pleased that you were able to duplicate much of what was on his original flyer. As you and Dave grow in your understanding of HTML and the Web, you'll add more pages to his site; but for now, this is a good start on giving him a presence on the Internet.

| InSight | **Publishing Your Page on the Web** |

Once you've completed your Web page, your next step is to research ways of getting it on the Web. You first need to find a Web server to host the page. Some of the issues you'll need to consider are how much you want to pay, how much space you need, and how important it is for you to have a highly trafficked Web site. You might first look toward the company that provides your Internet access. Most **ISPs** (**Internet Service Providers**) offer space on their Web server as part of their regular service or for a small fee. However, they usually limit the amount of space available to you, unless you pay an extra fee to host a larger site. There are also free Web hosts, which provide space on servers for personal or noncommercial use. Once again, the amount of space you get is limited. Free Web hosting services make their money from selling advertising space on your site, so you should be prepared to act as a billboard in return for space on their server.

Web sites are identified by their domain names. If you're planning to create a commercial site to advertise a product or service, you want the domain name to reflect your business. Free Web hosts usually include their names in your Web address. Thus instead of having a Web address like

> davesdevilsticks.com

you might have something like

> freewebhosting.net/members/~davesdevilsticks.html

If you're running a site for personal use, this might not be a problem—but it would look unprofessional on a commercial site. If you are planning a commercial site and simply want to advertise your product by publishing an online brochure, you can usually find an inexpensive host and pay a nominal yearly fee to reserve a Web address that reflects your company's name. On the other hand, if you intend to run an e-commerce site where users can purchase products online, you will need to invest in software and storage space to manage customer orders and inventory. You will also need to invest in getting your Web site noticed in the increasingly crowded Internet market. Commercial pages require careful planning and good design so that the investment in publishing the site is not wasted.

| Review | **Session 1.3 Quick Check** |

1. Specify the code you would enter to display the text "Product List" as an h2 heading, centered horizontally on the page.
2. What is a presentational attribute? What is a reason for using presentational attributes? What is a reason for avoiding them?
3. Specify the code you would enter to mark the text "Hamlet by William Shakespeare" as a centered h1 heading with a line break after the word "Hamlet."
4. You want to add the graphic file portrait.gif to your Web page as an inline image. For nonvisual browsers, your page should display the text "David Vinet" in place of the image. Specify the code to do this.
5. What is ISO-8859-1?
6. The trademark symbol ™ has the Unicode number 8482. How would you enter this symbol into your Web page?
7. The Greek letter b has the character entity name of "beta." How would you enter this symbol into your Web page?
8. Specify the code you would enter to add three consecutive blank spaces to your Web page.
9. Specify the code you would enter to display the text "<h2>Hamlet</h2>" on your Web page.

Tutorial Summary | Review

In this tutorial you learned how to create a basic Web page using HTML. The tutorial began by examining concepts and history surrounding networks and the development of the World Wide Web. It then explored the history of HTML, explaining how the development of HTML was a key component in the development of the Web. The first session concluded with the creation of a simple Web page consisting only of the page head. Work on designing the page body began in the second session by first exploring how to mark block-level elements. The discussion of block-level elements included work with headings, paragraphs, block quotes, and lists. The second session concluded with coverage of inline elements and discussed the issue of physical elements versus logical elements. The third session began by exploring element attributes, showing how to use the style attribute to center the contents of a block-level element. Because Web pages often need to display nontextual content, the third session then examined how to use empty elements such as line breaks, horizontal rules, and inline images. The session and the tutorial concluded by discussing character sets and explored how to insert special character symbols into a Web page.

Key Terms

ARPANET
ASCII
attribute
block-level element
body element
character encoding
character entity reference
character formatting
    element
character set
client
client-server network
closing tag
comment tag
definition list
deprecated
element
empty element
Extensible Hypertext
    Markup Language
Extensible Markup
    Language
extensions
file server
head element
heading element
host
HTML

HTML 5.0
HTML converter
HTML editor
hypertext
Hypertext Markup
    Language
inline element
inline image
Internet Service Provider
ISO-8859-1
ISP
LAN
Latin-1
link
local area network
logical element
markup language
network
node
numeric character
    reference
one-sided tag
opening tag
ordered list
physical element
presentational attribute
print server

root element
server
SGML
Standard Generalized
    Markup Language
style
tag
text-based browser
two-sided tag
Unicode
unordered list
UTF-8
W3C
WAN
Web
Web browser
Web page
Web server
white space
wide area network
World Wide Web
World Wide Web
    Consortium
XHTML
XHTML 2.0
XHTML 5.0
XML

| Practice | Review Assignments |

Practice the skills you learned in the tutorial using the same case scenario.

Data File needed for the Review Assignments: logo.jpg

Dave has found a host for his Web page and has published the document you helped him create on the Internet. He wants to start adding more pages to his Web site. He's come to you for help in creating a page describing his basic stick. He's already written the text for the Web page; he needs you to translate that text into HTML code. Figure 1-42 shows a preview of the page you'll create for Dave.

Figure 1-42

The Basic Stick

The Basic Stick is the perfect stick for beginners. The stick rotates slowly to provide extra time for performing stick tricks, but is flashy enough to impress your friends.

Patented Dura-Coat® finish ensures sticks can withstand all weather conditions. More durable than other sticks, these props will keep looking like new for as long as you own them.

Enhanced stick flexibility provides more bounce, allowing for better tricks. A soft rubber core adds a whole new element to the sticking experience that you have to feel to believe!

Full customization will give you the chance to own a pair of sticks unlike any others out there. I make exactly what you want, with your colors and your designs.

A personal touch through both my customization options and hand-crafted designs.

Specifications

- Main Stick
  - Weight: 7 oz.
  - Length: 24 inches
  - Tape: Dura-Coat® finish with laser-style color choices
- Handle Sticks (one pair)
  - Weight: 2 oz.
  - Length: 18 inches
  - Tape: Soft ivory tape with rubber core

Dave's Devil Sticks ◆ 541 West Highland Dr. ◆ Auburn, ME 04210 ◆ (207) 555 - 9001

Complete the following:

1. Use your text editor to create a new file named **basic.htm**, and save it in the tutorial.01\review folder included with your Data Files.

2. Within the basic.htm file, insert the structure of the HTML file, including the head and body sections.

3. Within the head section, insert a comment containing
   Dave's Devil Sticks
   Basic Stick
   Author: *your name*
   Date: *the date*
   where *your name* is your name and *the date* is the current date.

4. Add the page title **Basic Sticks** to the head section.

5. Within the body section, insert an h1 heading centered horizontally on the page and containing the inline image file **logo.jpg**, located in the tutorial.01\review folder included with your Data Files. Specify the following alternate text for the image: **Dave's Devil Sticks: The Basic Stick**.

6. Add two h2 headings containing the text **The Basic Stick** and **Specifications**. Set the font color of the heading 2 text to red.

7. Directly below the first h2 heading, insert a paragraph containing the text: **The Basic Stick is the perfect stick for beginners. The stick rotates slowly to provide extra time for performing stick tricks, but is flashy enough to impress your friends.**

8. Directly below the paragraph but above the second h2 heading, insert a block quote that contains the following:

    a. Place a horizontal rule at the top and the bottom of the block quote.

    b. Between the two horizontal rules, insert the following four paragraphs:

    Patented Dura-Coat finish ensures sticks can withstand all weather conditions. More durable than other sticks, these props will keep looking like new for as long as you own them.

    Enhanced stick flexibility provides more bounce, allowing for better tricks. A soft rubber core adds a whole new element to the sticking experience that you have to feel to believe!

    Full customization will give you the chance to own a pair of sticks unlike any others out there. I make exactly what you want, with your colors and your designs.

    A personal touch through both my customization options and hand-crafted designs.

    c. Change the first few words of each of the four paragraphs to a bold font, as indicated in Figure 1-42.

9. Directly below the second h2 heading, insert an unordered list. The list should contain two items: **Main Stick** and **Handle Sticks (one pair)**.

10. Directly below the Main Stick list item, insert an unordered list containing the following items:
    Weight: 7 oz.
    Length: 24 inches
    Tape: Dura-Coat finish with laser-style color choices

11. Directly below the Handle Sticks (one pair) list item, insert an unordered list containing:
    Weight: 2 oz.
    Length: 18 inches
    Tape: Soft ivory tape with rubber core

12. Locate the two occurrences of "Dura-Coat" in the document. Directly after the word "Dura-Coat," insert the registered trademark symbol ®. The character entity name of the ® symbol is "reg." Display the ® symbol as a superscript by placing the character within the sup inline element.

13. At the bottom of the body section, insert the company's address:
    Dave's Devil Sticks
    541 West Highland Dr.
    Auburn, ME 04210
    (207) 555 - 9001

14. Center the address on the page.

15. Separate the different sections of the address using a solid diamond ◆ (character code 9830).

16. Add a horizontal rule directly above the address element.

17. Save your changes to the file, and then open it in your Web browser to verify that the content and layout are correct.

18. Submit your completed files to your instructor.

Apply | **Case Problem 1**

Apply your knowledge of HTML to create a Web page for a mathematics department at a university.

Data Files needed for this Case Problem: euler.jpg and eulertxt.htm

Mathematics Department, Coastal University Professor Lauren Coe of the Mathematics Department of Coastal University in Anderson, South Carolina, is preparing material for a course on the history of mathematics. As part of the course, she has written biographies of famous mathematicians. Lauren would like you to use content she's already written to create Web pages that students can access on Coastal University's Web server. You'll create the first one in this exercise. Figure 1-43 shows a preview of this page, which profiles the mathematician Leonhard Euler.

Figure 1-43

Leonhard Euler (1707-1783)

The greatest mathematician of the eighteenth century, **Leonhard Euler** was born in Basel, Switzerland. There, he studied under another giant of mathematics, **Jean Bernoulli**. In 1731 Euler became a professor of physics and mathematics at St. Petersburg Academy of Sciences. Euler was the most prolific mathematician of all time, publishing over *800 different books and papers*. His influence was felt in physics and astronomy as well. Euler's work on mathematical analysis, *Introductio in analysin infinitorum* (1748) remained a standard textbook for well over a century. For the princess of Anhalt-Dessau he wrote *Lettres à une princesse d'Allemagne* (1768-1772), giving a clear non-technical outline of the main physical theories of the time.

One can hardly do math without copying Euler. Notations still in use today, such as e and π, were introduced in Euler's writings. He is perhaps best known for his research into mathematical analysis. Euler's formula

$$\cos(x) + i\sin(x) = e^{(ix)}$$

demonstrates the relationship between algebra, complex analysis, and trigonometry. From this equation, it's easy to derive the equation

$$e^{(\pi i)} + 1 = 0$$

which relates the fundamental constants: 0, 1, π, e, and i in a single beautiful and elegant statement.

Leonhard Euler died in 1783, leaving behind a legacy perhaps unmatched, and certainly unsurpassed, in the annals of mathematics.

Math 895: The History of Mathematics

Complete the following:

1. Open the **eulertxt.htm** file from the tutorial.01\case1 folder included with your Data Files. Save the file as **euler.htm** in the same folder.

2. Add opening and closing <html> tags to the file. Insert a head section and enclose Lauren's text on Euler within a body element.

3. Within the head section, insert a comment containing

   History of Math 895: Leonhard Euler

   Author: *your name*

   Date: *the date*

   where *your name* is your name and *the date* is the current date.

4. Add the page title **History of Math 895: Leonhard Euler** to the head section.

5. Directly below the opening <body> tag, insert a paragraph containing the inline image file **euler.jpg**, located in the tutorial.01\case1 folder included with your Data Files. Specify "Portrait of Leonhard Euler" as the alternative text.

6. Mark the next line containing "Leonhard Euler (1707 - 1783)" as an h1 heading.

7. Mark the five blocks of text describing Euler's life as paragraphs.

8. Mark the two equations as block quotes. Change the font color of the two block quotes to red.

9. Mark the name of the course title at the bottom of the file as an address.

10. Insert horizontal rules directly above the h1 heading and the address element.

⊕ EXPLORE 11. Within the first paragraph, display the names "Leonhard Euler" and "Jean Bernoulli" in boldface. Mark the phrase "800 different books and papers" as emphasized text using the em element. Mark the phrase "Introduction in analysin infinitorum" as a citation.

12. In the phrase, "Lettres a une princesse d'Allemagne" replace the one-letter word a with à (the character entity name is "agrave"). Mark the entire publication as a citation.

13. In the second paragraph, italicize the notation for e and replace "pi" with the character π (the character name is "pi").

14. In the first equation, italicize the letters e, x, and i (but do not italicize the "i" in "sin"). Display the term (ix) as a superscript.

15. In the second equation, replace "pi" with the character π. Italicize the letter e and i. Display (πi) as a superscript.

16. In the last paragraph, italicize the notations for e and i and replace "pi" with π.

17. Save your changes to the file, and then verify that the page appears correctly in your Web browser.

18. Submit your completed files to your instructor.

| Apply | **| Case Problem 2** |

Apply your knowledge of HTML to create a page showing text from a scene of a Shakespeare play.

Data Files needed for this Case Problem: macbeth.jpg and macbethtxt.htm

Mansfield Classical Theatre Steve Karls is the director of Mansfield Classical Theatre, a theatre company for young people located in Mansfield, Ohio. This summer the company is planning to perform the Shakespeare play *Macbeth*. Steve wants to put the text of the play on the company's Web site and has asked for your help in designing and completing the Web page. Steve wants to have a separate page for each scene from the play. A preview of the page you'll create for Act I, Scene 1 is shown in Figure 1-44. Steve has already typed the text of the scene. He needs you to supply the HTML code.

Figure 1-44

Macbeth

ACT I

SCENE 1.

Summary A thunderstorm approaches and three witches convene. They agree to confront the great Scot general Macbeth upon his victorious return from a war between Scotland and Norway. Soon, heroic Macbeth will receive the title of Thane of Cawdor from King Duncan. However, Macbeth learns from the witches that he is fated for greater things and he will be led down to the path of destruction by his unquenchable ambition.

A desert place.

Thunder and lightning. Enter three Witches.

First Witch
    When shall we three meet again
    In thunder, lightning, or in rain?
Second Witch
    When the hurlyburly's done,
    When the battle's lost and won.
Third Witch
    That will be ere the set of sun.
First Witch
    Where the place?
Second Witch
    Upon the heath.
Third Witch
    There to meet with Macbeth.
First Witch
    I come, Graymalkin!
Second Witch
    Paddock calls.
Third Witch
    Anon.
ALL
    Fair is foul, and foul is fair:
    Hover through the fog and filthy air.

Exeunt

Go to Scene 2 ⇒

Text provided by Online Shakespeare

Complete the following:

1. Open the **macbethtxt.htm** file from the tutorial.01\case2 folder included with your Data Files. Save the file as **macbeth.htm** in the same folder.

2. Enclose the entire Macbeth text within the structure of an HTML document.

3. Within the head section, insert a comment containing the following text:
   Macbeth: Act I, Scene 1
   Author: *your name*
   Date: *the date*

4. Add the page title **Macbeth: Act I, Scene 1** to the head section.

5. Directly below the opening <body> tag, insert an h1 heading containing the inline image file **macbeth.jpg** (located in the tutorial.01\case2 folder included with your Data Files) with **Macbeth** as the alternate text for nonvisual browsers. Add a horizontal rule directly below the h1 heading.

6. Mark the text "ACT I" as an h2 heading. Mark "SCENE 1." as an h3 heading.

7. Mark the summary of the scene as a paragraph. Display the word "Summary" in bold.

8. In the text of the play, mark the descriptions of setting, scene, and exits as separate paragraphs, and italicize the text, as shown in Figure 1-44.

EXPLORE
9. Mark the dialog as a definition list, with each character's name marked as a definition term and each speech marked as a definition description. Where the speech goes over one line, use a line break to keep the speech on separate lines, as shown in the figure.

10. Directly below the Exeunt paragraph, insert the line **Go to Scene 2**. Mark this line as a div element and align it with the right page margin. (Steve will mark this as a link later.) At the end of the line, insert a right arrow character using the 8658 character number. Add horizontal rules directly above and below this statement.

EXPLORE
11. Mark the line "Text provided by Online Shakespeare" as a paragraph, with the text itself marked with the cite element. Align the text with the right page margin.

12. Save your changes to the file, and then confirm the layout and content of the page in your Web browser.

13. Submit the completed files to your instructor.

Challenge | **Case Problem 3**

Explore how to use HTML to create a recipe page.

Data Files needed for this Case Problem: dessertweb.jpg, torte.jpg, and tortetxt.htm

dessertWEB   Amy Wu wants to take her love of cooking and sharing recipes to the World Wide Web. She's interested in creating a new Web site called *dessertWEB* where other cooks can submit and review dessert recipes. Each page within her site will have a photo and description of the dessert, the ingredients, the cooking directions, and a list of reviews. Each recipe will be rated on a 5-star scale. She already has information on one recipe: Apple Bavarian Torte. She's asked for your help in creating a Web page from the data she's collected. A preview of the completed page is shown in Figure 1-45.

Figure 1-45

dessertWEB

Apple Bavarian Torte (★★★★)

A classic European torte baked in a springform pan. Cream cheese, sliced almonds, and apples make this the perfect holiday treat (12 servings).

INGREDIENTS

1/2 cup butter
1/3 cup white sugar
1/4 teaspoon vanilla extract
1 cup all-purpose flour
1 (8 ounce) package cream cheese
1/4 cup white sugar
1 egg
1/2 teaspoon vanilla extract
6 apples - peeled, cored, and sliced
1/3 cup white sugar
1/2 teaspoon ground cinnamon
1/4 cup sliced almonds

DIRECTIONS

1. Preheat oven to 450° F (230° C).
2. Cream together butter, sugar, vanilla, and flour.
3. Press crust mixture into the flat bottom of a 9-inch springform pan. Set aside.
4. In a medium bowl, blend cream cheese and sugar. Beat in egg and vanilla. Pour cheese mixture over crust.
5. Toss apples with sugar and cinnamon. Spread apple mixture over all.
6. Bake for 10 minutes. Reduce heat to 400° F (200° C) and continue baking for 25 minutes.
7. Sprinkle almonds over top of torte. Continue baking until lightly browned. Cool before removing from pan.

REVIEWS

★★★★ ★
I loved the buttery taste of the crust which complements the apples very nicely.
— Reviewed on Sep. 22, 2010 by MMASON.
★★ ★★★
Nothing special. I like the crust, but there was a little too much of it for my taste, and I liked the filling but there was too little of it. I thought the crunchy apples combined with the sliced almonds detracted from the overall flavor.
— Reviewed on Sep. 1, 2010 by GLENDACHEF.
★★★★★
Delicious!! I recommend microwaving the apples for 3 minutes before baking, to soften them. Great dessert - I'll be making it again for the holidays.
— Reviewed on August 28, 2010 by BBABS.

Complete the following:

1. Open the **tortetxt.htm** file from the tutorial.01\case3 folder included with your Data Files. Save the file as **torte.htm** in the same folder.

2. Add the structure of an HTML document around the recipe text. Within the head section, insert a comment containing the following text:
   Apple Bavarian Torte
   Author: *your name*
   Date: *the date*

3. Add the page title **Apple Bavarian Torte Recipe** to the head section.

4. Directly below the opening <body> tag, insert a div element containing the inline image **dessertweb.jpg** located in the tutorial.01\case3 folder included with your Data Files. Specify the alternative text **dessertWEB**. Insert a horizontal rule directly below the div element.

EXPLORE

5. Mark the text "Apple Bavarian Torte" as an h2 heading.

6. Change the text "(4 stars)" to a set of 4 star symbols (character number 9733). Enclose the star symbols in a span element, setting the font color to teal.

7. Directly below the h2 heading, insert another div element containing the inline image **torte.jpg**, located in the tutorial.01\case3 folder included with your Data Files. Specify the alternative text **Torte image**.

8. Mark the description of the dessert as a paragraph.

9. Mark "INGREDIENTS," "DIRECTIONS," and "REVIEWS" as h3 headings.

10. Enclose the list of ingredients in a block quote. Add line breaks after each item in the list.

EXPLORE

11. Mark the list of directions as an ordered list, with each direction a separate item in the list. Replace the word "degrees" with the degree symbol (character name deg).

12. Enclose the list of reviews in a block quote. Turn the list into a definition list. Mark up the definition list as follows:

EXPLORE

   a. The definition term is the number of stars assigned by each reviewer. Change the number of stars in the text file to star symbols (character number 9733). Amy wants you to display 5 stars for each review with the number of stars displayed in a teal font matching the stars given by the reviewer and the remaining stars displayed in a gray font. Use the span element to enclose the two different groups of stars.

   b. There are two definition descriptions for each review. The first encloses the text of the review. The second encloses the date of the review and the name of the reviewer.

   c. Insert an em-dash (character name "mdash") before the word "Reviewed" in each of the reviews.

13. Save your changes to the file, and then verify the layout and content of the page in your Web browser.

14. Submit the completed files to your instructor.

| Create | | **Case Problem 4** |

Test your knowledge of HTML and use your creativity to design a Web page for an exercise equipment company.

Data Files needed for this Case Problem: logo.jpg, smith.jpg, and smith.txt

Body Systems   Body Systems is a leading manufacturer of home gyms. The company recently hired you to assist in developing its Web site. Your first task is to create a Web page for the LSM400, a popular weight machine sold by the company. You've been given a text file describing the features of the LSM400. You've also received two image files: one of the company's logo and one of the LSM400. You are free to supplement these files with any other resources available to you. You are responsible for the page's content and appearance.

Complete the following:

1. Create a new HTML file named **smith.htm** and save it in the tutorial.01\case4 folder included with your Data Files.

2. Add a comment to the head section of the document describing the document's content and containing your name and the date.

3. Add an appropriate page title to the document.

4. Use the contents of the **smith.txt** document (located in the tutorial.01\case4 folder) as the basis of the text in the Web page. Include at least one example of each of the following:
   - a heading
   - a paragraph
   - an ordered or unordered list
   - an inline element
   - an inline image
   - a horizontal rule
   - a special character
   - an element attribute
5. Structure your HTML code so that it will be easy for others to read and understand.
6. Save your changes to the file, and then open it in your Web browser to verify that it is readable and attractive.
7. Submit your completed files to your instructor.

| Review | **| Quick Check Answers** |

Session 1.1

1. A hypertext document is an electronic file containing elements that users can select, usually by clicking a mouse, to open other documents.
2. A Web server is a computer on a network that stores a Web site and makes it available to clients. Users access the Web site by running a program called a Web browser on their computers.
3. HTML documents do not exactly specify the appearance of a document; rather they describe the purpose of various elements in the document and leave it to the Web browser to determine the final appearance. A word processor like Microsoft Word exactly specifies the appearance of each document element.
4. Deprecated features are those features that are being phased out by the W3C and might not be supported by future browsers.
5. The html element.
6. In the head section of the document you would enter the code
   `<title>Technical Support</title>`
7. `<!-- Page Updated on 4/15/2011 -->`
8. The title element was not properly nested within the head element.

Session 1.2

1. Block-level elements contain content that is displayed in a separate section within the page, such as a paragraph or a heading. An inline element is part of the same block as its surrounding content—for example, individual words or phrases within a paragraph.
2. Web browsers will strip out extra occurrences of white space and thus will ignore the extra blank line.
3. `<h1>content</h1>`
4. Use the blockquote element. Most browsers indent blockquote text.

5.
```
<ul>
    <li>Winter</li>
    <li>Spring</li>
    <li>Summer</li>
    <li>Fall</li>
</ul>
```

6.
```
<dl>
    <dt>HAMLET</dt>
    <dd> There's ne'er a villain dwelling in all Denmark; but he's
an arrant knave.</dd>
    <dt>HORATIO</dt>
    <dd> There needs no ghost, my lord, come from the grave to tell
us this.</dd>
</dl>
```

7. `<p><i>Hamlet</i>, a play by William Shakespeare</p>`

8. div and span

Session 1.3

1. `<h2 style="text-align: center">Product List</h2>`

2. Presentational attributes are HTML attributes that exactly specify how the browser should render an HTML element. Most presentational attributes have been deprecated, replaced by styles. You should use presentational attributes when you need to support older browsers.

3. `<h1 style="text-align: center">Hamlet<br /> by William Shakespeare</h1>`

4. `<img src="portrait.gif" alt="David Vinet" />`

5. ISO-8859-1 is a character set that supports 255 characters and can be used by most languages that use the Latin alphabet.

6. `&#8482;`

7. `&beta;`

8. `   `

9. `&lt;h2&gt;Hamlet&lt;/h2&gt;`

Ending Data Files

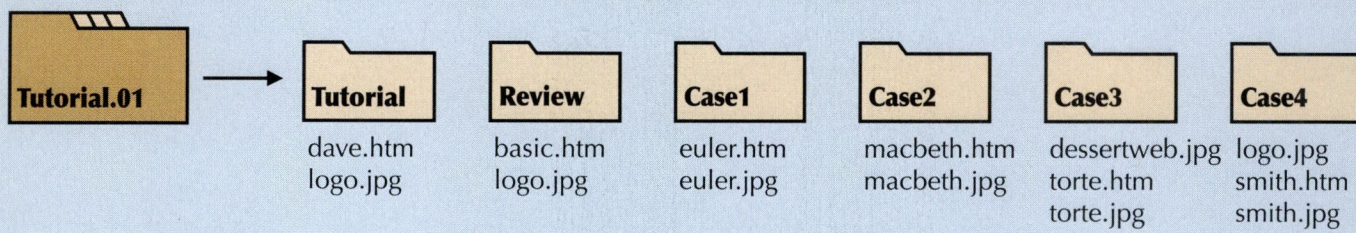

Tutorial.01 → **Tutorial**
dave.htm
logo.jpg

Review
basic.htm
logo.jpg

Case1
euler.htm
euler.jpg

Case2
macbeth.htm
macbeth.jpg

Case3
dessertweb.jpg
torte.htm
torte.jpg

Case4
logo.jpg
smith.htm
smith.jpg

Developing a Web Site

Creating a Web Site for Digital Photography Enthusiasts

Case | CAMshots

Gerry Hayward is an amateur photographer and digital camera enthusiast. He's decided to create a Web site named CAMshots, where he can offer advice and information to people who are just getting started with digital photography or who are long-time hobbyists like himself and are looking to share tips and ideas. Gerry's Web site will contain several pages, with each page dedicated to a particular topic. He has created a few pages for the Web site, but he hasn't linked them together. He has asked your help in designing his site. You'll start with only a few pages and then Gerry can build on your work as he adds more information to the site.

Starting Data Files

Tutorial.02 →

Tutorial
glosstxt.htm
hometxt.htm
tipstxt.htm
+ 3 graphic files

Demo
demo_mailto.htm
+ 3 graphic files

Review
childtxt.htm
contesttxt.htm
flowertxt.htm
scenictxt.htm
+ 22 graphic files

Case1
colleges.txt
uwlisttxt.htm
+ 1 graphic file

Case2
hometxt.htm
slide1txt.htm
slide2txt.htm
slide3txt.htm
slide4txt.htm
slide5txt.htm
slide6txt.htm
+ 18 graphic files

Case3
classtxt.htm
hometxt.htm
indextxt.htm
memtxt.htm
+ 1 graphic file

Case4
characters.txt
notes.txt
tempest.txt
+ 1 graphic file

Session 2.1

Exploring Web Site Structures

You meet with Gerry to discuss his plans for the CAMshots Web site. Gerry has already created a prototype for the Web site. He's created three Web pages: one page is the site's home page and contains general information about CAMshots; the second page contains tips about digital photography; and the third page contains a partial glossary of photographic terms. The pages are not complete, nor are they linked to one another. You'll begin your work for Gerry by viewing these files in your text editor and browser.

To view Gerry's Web pages:

▶ 1. Start your text editor, and then one at a time, open the **hometxt.htm**, **tipstxt.htm**, and **glosstxt.htm** files, located in the tutorial.02\tutorial folder included with your Data Files.

▶ 2. Within each file, go to the comment section at top of the file and add *your name* and *the date* in the space provided.

▶ 3. Save the files as **home.htm**, **tips.htm**, and **glossary.htm**, respectively, in the tutorial.02\tutorial folder.

▶ 4. Take some time reviewing the HTML code within each document so that you understand the structure and content of the files.

▶ 5. Start your Web browser, and then one at a time, open the **home.htm**, **tips.htm**, and **glossary.htm** files. Figure 2-1 shows the current layout and appearance of Gerry's three Web pages.

Figure 2-1	Pages in the CAMshots Web site

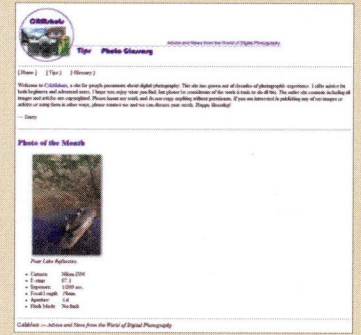

home.htm
the CAMshots home page

tips.htm
the CAMshots tip of the day

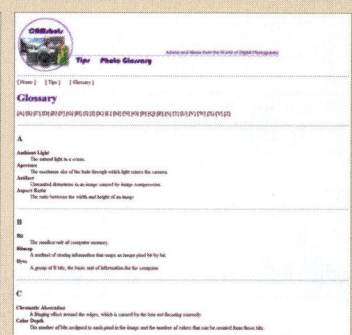

glossary.htm
a partial glossary of
photography terminology

Gerry wants to create links among the three pages so that users can easily navigate from one page to another. Before you write code for the links, it's worthwhile to map out exactly how you want the pages to relate to each other, using a technique known as storyboarding. A **storyboard** is a diagram of a Web site's structure, showing all the pages in the site and indicating how they are linked together. Because Web sites use a variety of structures, it's important to storyboard your Web site before you start creating your pages. This helps you determine which structure works best for the type of information your site contains. A well-designed structure ensures that users will able to navigate the site without getting lost or missing important information.

Every Web site starts with a single **home page** that acts as a focal point for the Web site. It is usually the first page that users see. Starting from the home page, you add the links to other pages in the site, creating the site's overall structure. The Web sites you commonly encounter as you navigate the Web use one of several different Web structures. Examine some of these structures to help you decide how to design your own sites.

Linear Structures

If you wanted to create an online version of a famous play, like Shakespeare's *Hamlet*, one method would be to link the individual scenes of the play in a long chain. Figure 2-2 shows the storyboard for this type of **linear structure**, in which each page is linked with the pages that follow and precede it. Readers navigate this structure by moving forward and backward through the pages, much as they might move forward and backward through the pages of a book.

A linear structure ◀ **Figure 2-2**

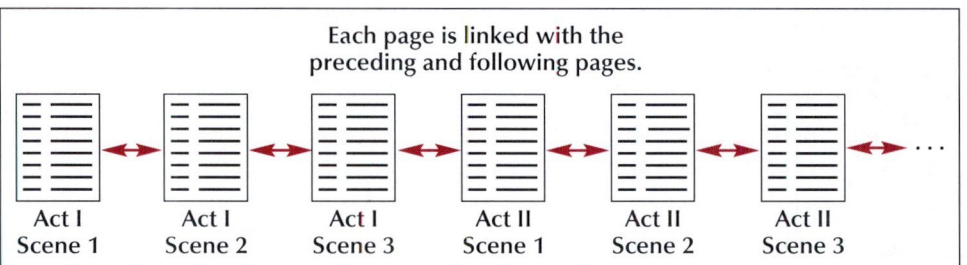

Linear structures work for Web sites with a clearly defined order of pages that are small in size. However, they can be difficult to work with as the chain of pages increases in length. An additional problem is that in a linear structure you move farther and farther away from the home page as you progress through the site. Because home pages often contain important general information about the site and its author, this is usually not the best design technique.

You can modify this structure to make it easier for users to return immediately to the home page or other main pages. Figure 2-3 shows this online play with an **augmented linear structure**, in which each page contains an additional link back to the opening page of each act.

An augmented linear structure ◀ **Figure 2-3**

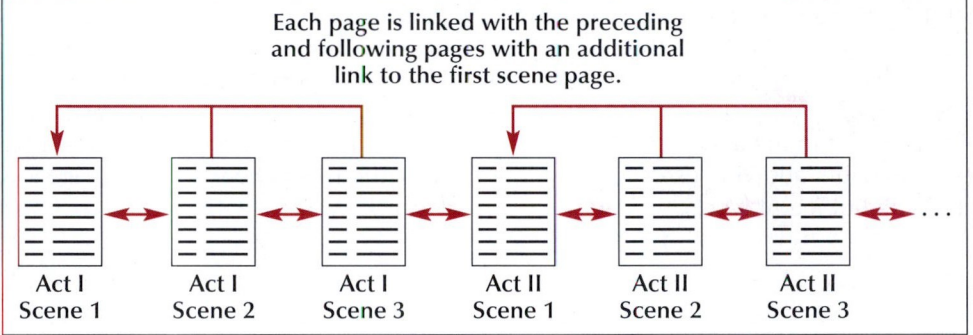

Hierarchical Structures

Another popular structure is the **hierarchical structure**, in which the pages are linked going from the home page down to pages dedicated to specific topics. Those pages, in turn, can be linked to even more specific topics. So, a hierarchical structure allows users to easily move from general to specific and back again. In the case of the online play, you can link an introductory page containing general information about the play to pages that describe each of the play's acts, and within each act you can include links to individual scenes. See Figure 2-4. With this structure, a user can move quickly to a specific scene within the page, bypassing the need to move through each scene in the play.

Figure 2-4	A hierarchical structure

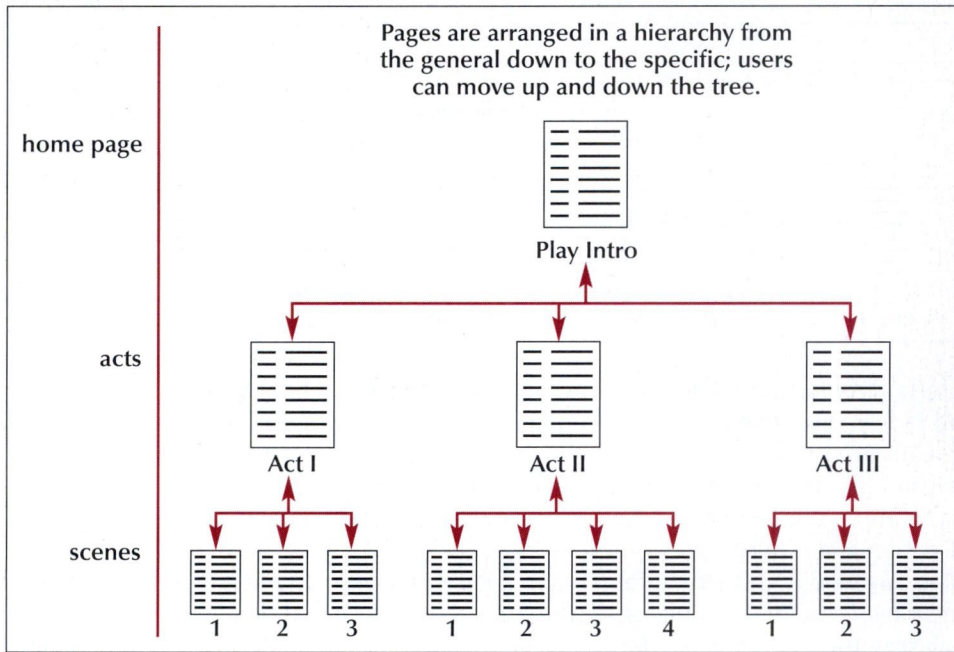

Mixed Structures

With larger and more complex Web sites, you often need to use a combination of structures. Figure 2-5 shows the online play using a mixture of the three main structures. The overall form is hierarchical, as users can move from a general introduction down to individual scenes; however, users can also move through the site in a linear fashion, going from act to act and scene to scene. Finally, each individual scene contains a link to the home page, allowing users to jump to the top of the hierarchy without moving through the different levels.

A mixed structure   Figure 2-5

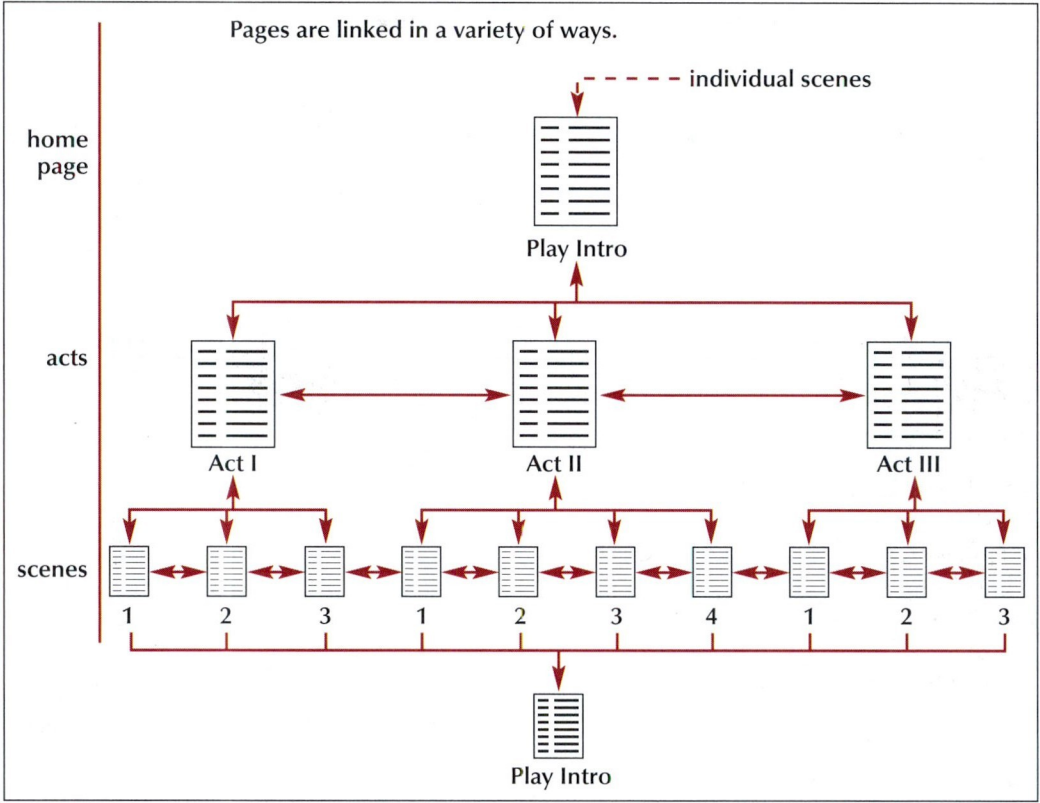

As these examples show, a little foresight can go a long way toward making your Web site easier to use. Also keep in mind that search results from a Web search engine such as Google or Yahoo! can point users to any page in your Web site—not just your home page—so they will need to quickly understand what your site contains and how to navigate it. At a minimum, each page should contain a link to the site's home page or to the relevant main topic page. In some cases, you might want to supply your users with a **site index**, which is a page containing an outline of the entire site and its contents. Unstructured Web sites can be difficult and frustrating to use. Consider the storyboard of the site displayed in Figure 2-6.

Figure 2-6 ▶ Web site with no coherent structure

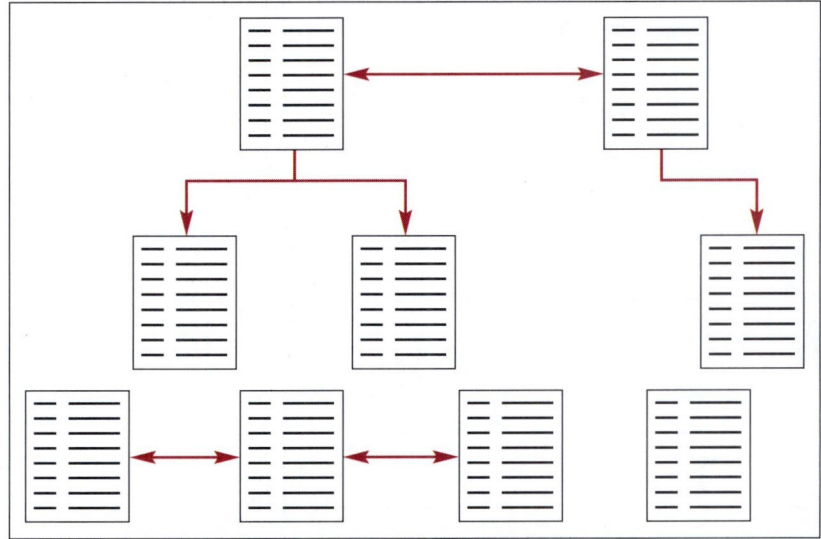

This confusing structure makes it difficult for users to grasp the site's contents and scope. The user might not even be aware of the presence of some pages because there are no connecting links, and some of the links only point in one direction. The Web is a competitive place; studies have shown that users who don't see how to get what they want within the first few seconds often leave a Web site. How long would a user spend on a site like the one shown in Figure 2-6?

Protected Structures

Sections of most commercial Web sites are off-limits except to subscribers and registered customers. As shown in Figure 2-7, these sites have a password-protected Web page that users must go through to get to the off-limits areas. The same Web site design principles apply to the protected section as the regular, open section of the site.

Figure 2-7 ▶ A protected structure

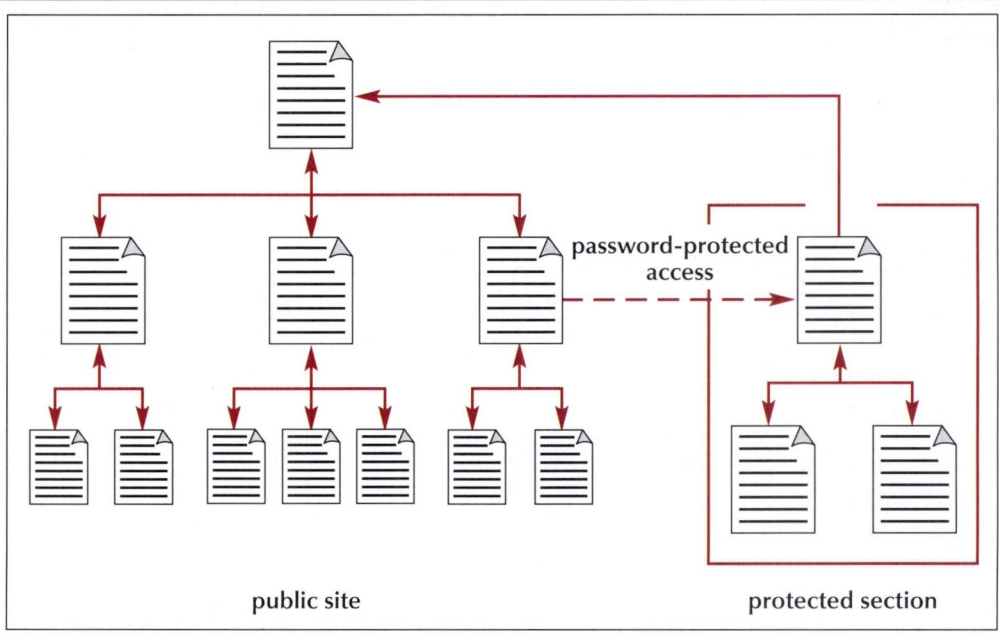

public site   protected section

Storyboarding a protected structure is particularly important to ensure that no unmonitored "back doors" to the protected area are allowed in the site design.

Creating a Hypertext Link

Gerry wants his site visitors to be able to move effortlessly among the three documents he's created. To do that, you'll link each page to the other two pages. Figure 2-8 provides the storyboard for the simple structure you have in mind.

Storyboard for the CAMshots Web site — Figure 2-8

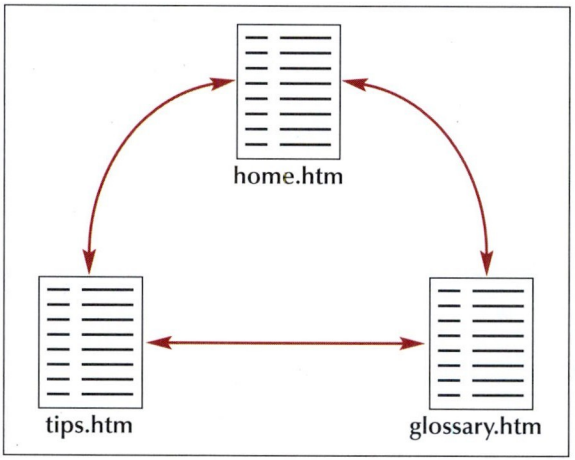

To create these links, you have to add hypertext links to each of the three documents. Hypertext links are created by enclosing some document content with a set of opening and closing <a> tags. The general syntax to create a hypertext link is

```
<a href="reference">content</a>
```

where *reference* is the location being linked to and *content* is the document content that is being marked as a link. The *reference* value can be a page on the World Wide Web, a local file, an e-mail address, or a network server. For example, to create a hypertext link to the tips.htm file, you could enter the following code:

```
<a href="tips.htm">Photography Tips</a>
```

This code marks the text "Photography Tips" as a hypertext link. When rendered by the browser, the words "Photography Tips" will be underlined, providing a visual clue to the user that the text is linked to another document. If the user clicks the text with a mouse, the browser will load the linked document (tips.htm).

Filenames are case sensitive on some operating systems, including the UNIX and Macintosh operating systems. Web servers running on those systems differentiate between a file named tips.htm and Tips.htm. For this reason, you might find that links you create on your computer do not work when you transfer your files to a Web server. To avoid this problem, the current standard is to always use lowercase filenames for all Web site files and to avoid using special characters such as blanks and slashes (/).

At the top of the home.htm, tips.htm, and glossary.htm files, Gerry has already entered the names of each of his three documents. Your first task is to mark these names as hypertext links to each of Gerry's three files. You'll start with the names in the home.htm file.

> **Tip**
>
> Keep your filenames short so that users are less apt to make a typing error when accessing your Web site.

To create a hypertext link to a document:

► 1. Return to the **home.htm** file in your text editor and locate the second div element at the top of the file.

► 2. Mark the text "Home" as a hypertext link using a set of <a> tags as follows:

   `<a href="home.htm">Home</a>`

► 3. Mark the text "Tips" as a hypertext link using the following code:

   `<a href="tips.htm">Tips</a>`

► 4. Mark the text "Glossary" as a hypertext link as follows:

   `<a href="glossary.htm">Glossary</a>`

   Figure 2-9 highlights the revised text in the home.htm file.

Figure 2-9 | **Marking hypertext links in the home.htm file**

```
<body>
    <div>
        <img src="camshots.jpg" alt="CAMshots" />
    </div>
    <hr />

    <div>
        [ <a href="home.htm">Home</a> ]
             
        [ <a href="tips.htm">Tips</a>  ]
             
        [ <a href="glossary.htm">Glossary</a>  ]
    </div>
```

► 5. Save your changes to the file.

► 6. The two other files have the same headings at the top of the document. Go to the **tips.htm** file in your text editor and repeat Steps 2 through 5 for the Home, Tips, and Glossary titles at the top of that file.

► 7. Go to the **glossary.htm** file in your text editor and repeat Steps 2 through 5 to mark the titles in that document as hypertext links as well.

   Now that you've added hypertext links to each of the three documents, test those links in your browser.

► 8. Reload or refresh the **home.htm** file in your Web browser. As indicated in Figure 2-10, the titles at the top of the page should now be underlined, providing visual evidence that these words are treated as hypertext links.

Hypertext links in the home page ◄ Figure 2-10

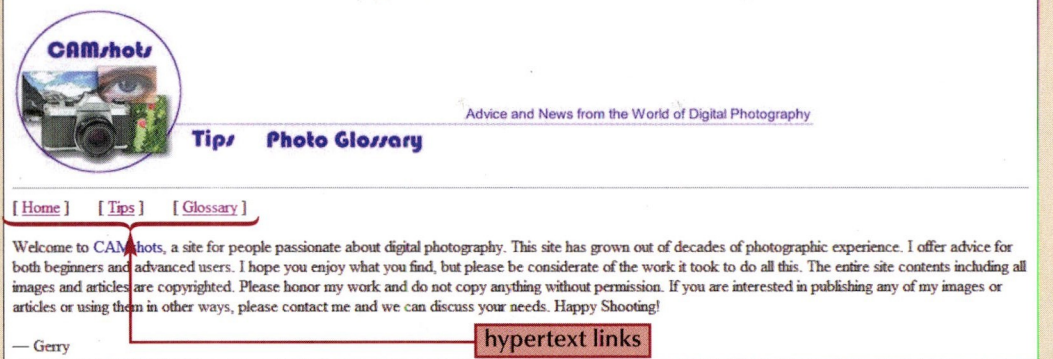

> **9.** Click the **Tips** link from the list of page names. Verify that the browser loads and displays the Tips page.
>
> **10.** Click the **Glossary** link. Verify that the Glossary page is opened by the browser.
>
> **11.** Continue to click the hypertext links from the list, confirming that you can jump from any of the three pages to each of the other two pages.
>
>   **Trouble?** If the links do not work, check the spelling of the filenames in the href attributes of the <a> tags. Because some Web servers require you to match capitalization in a filename, you should verify this in your attributes as well.

Specifying a Folder Path

In the links you've just created, you specified only the filename and not the location of the file. When you specify only the filename, the browser searches for the file in the same folder as the document containing the hypertext link; however, large Web sites containing hundreds of documents often place those documents in separate folders to make them easier to manage.

As Gerry adds more files to his Web site, he will probably want to use folders to organize the files. Figure 2-11 shows a preview of how Gerry might employ those folders. In this case, the topmost folder is named camshots. Gerry has placed some of his HTML files within the pages folder, which he has then divided into three subfolders named tips, glossary, and articles. He has also created separate folders for the images and video clips used on his Web site. Figure 2-11 displays the location of four HTML files named index.htm, tips1.htm, tips2.htm, and glossary.htm.

Figure 2-11 ▸ **A sample folder structure**

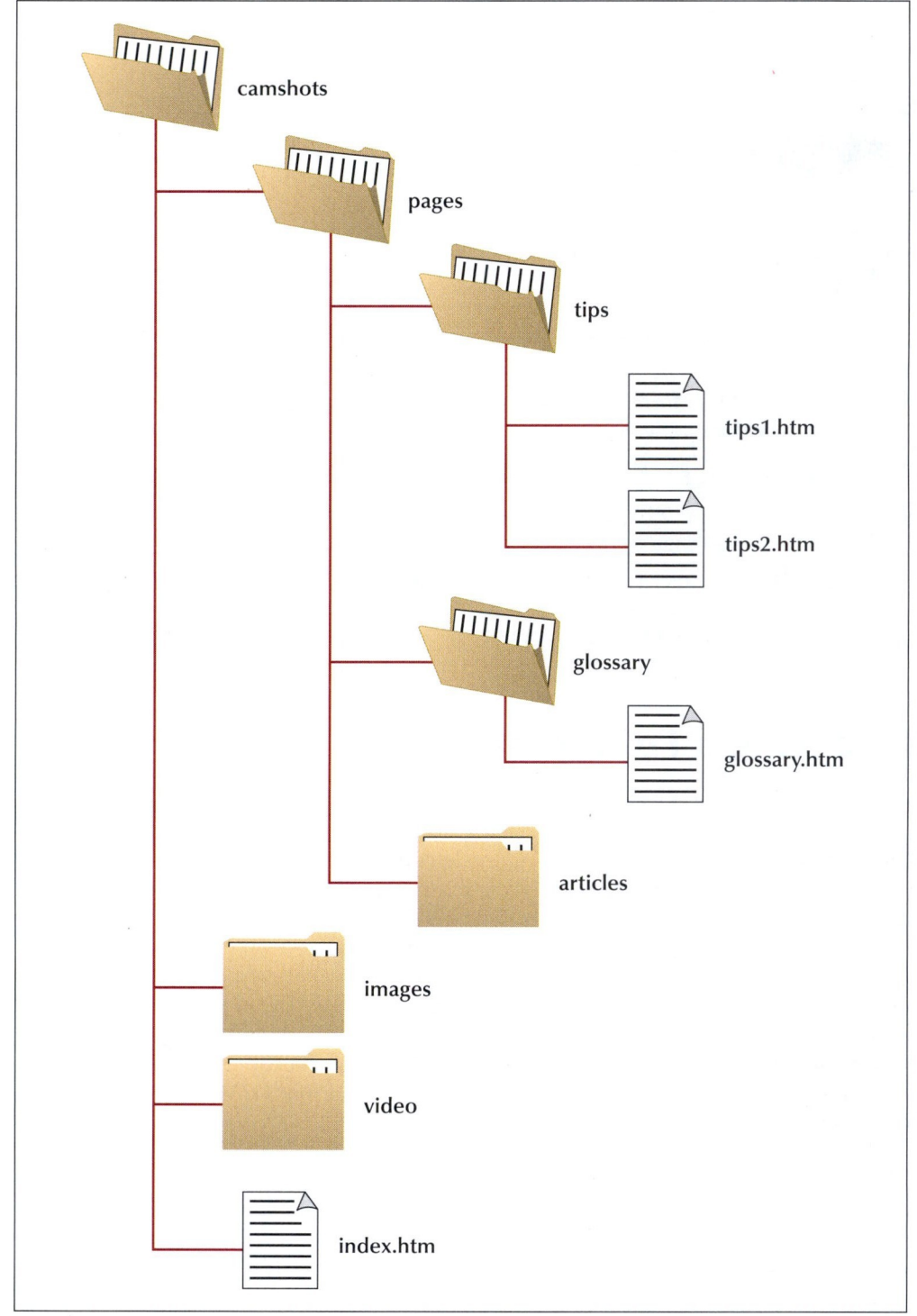

To create a link to a file located in a different folder than the current document, you must specify the file's location, or **path**, so that browsers can find it. HTML supports two kinds of paths: absolute and relative.

Absolute Paths

An **absolute path** specifies a file's precise location within a computer's entire folder structure. Absolute pathnames employ the syntax

/folder1/folder2/folder3/file

where *folder1* is the topmost folder in the computer's folder tree, followed by *folder2*, *folder3*, and so forth, down to the file you want to link to. Figure 2-12 shows how you would express absolute paths to the four files listed in Figure 2-11.

Tip

To make your Web site easier to maintain, organize your folders to match the organization of the pages on the Web site and group images and other media files within folders separate from your HTML files.

Absolute paths — Figure 2-12

Absolute Path	Interpretation
/camshots/pages/tips/tips1.htm	The tips1.htm file located in the pages/tips subfolder
/camshots/pages/tips/tips2.htm	The tips2.htm file located in the pages/tips subfolder
/camshots/pages/glossary/glossary.htm	The glossary.htm file located in the pages/glossary subfolder
/camshots/index.htm	The index.htm file located in the camshots folder

If files are located on different drives as well as in different folders, you must include the drive letter in the form

/drive | /folder1/folder2/folder3/file

where *drive* is the letter assigned to the drive. For example, the tips1.htm file located on drive C in the /camshots/pages/tips folder would have the absolute path:

```
/C|/camshots/pages/tips/tips1.htm
```

Remember that you don't have to include a drive letter if the destination document is located on the same drive as the document containing the link.

Relative Paths

When many folders and subfolders are involved, absolute pathnames can be cumbersome and confusing. For that reason, most Web designers prefer to use relative paths. A **relative path** specifies a file's location in relation to the location of the current document. If the file is in the same location as the current document, the relative path is simply the filename. If the file is in a subfolder of the current document, include the name of the subfolder without the forward slash in the form

folder/file

where *folder* is the name of the subfolder. To go farther down the folder tree to other subfolders, include those in the relative path separated by forward slashes, i.e.

folder1/folder2/folder3/file

where *folder1*, *folder2*, *folder3*, and so forth are subfolders of the current folder. Finally, a relative path can go up the folder tree by starting the pathname with a double period (..) followed by a forward slash and the name of the file. The path

../file

references the *file* document located in the parent folder of the current document. To reference a different folder on the same level of the folder tree, known as a **sibling folder**, you move up the folder tree using the double period (..) and then down using the name of the sibling folder. The general syntax is

../folder/file

where *folder* is the name of the sibling folder. Figure 2-13 shows the relative paths to the six files in the tree from Figure 2-11, starting from the camshots/pages/tips subfolder.

Figure 2-13	Relative paths

Relative Path from the /camshots/pages/tips Subfolder	Interpretation
tips1.htm	The tips1.htm file located in the current folder
tips2.htm	The tips2.htm file located in the current folder
../glossary/glossary.htm	The glossary.htm file located in the sibling glossary folder
../../index.htm	The index.htm file located in the parent camshots folder

Tip

You can reference the current folder using a single period (.) character.

You should almost always use relative paths in your links. If you have to move your files to a different computer or server, you can move the entire folder structure without having to change the relative pathnames you created. If you use absolute pathnames, you will probably have to revise each link to reflect the new location of the folder tree on the computer.

Changing the Base

As you've just seen, a browser resolves relative pathnames based on the location of the current document. You can change this behavior by specifying a different base or starting location for all relative paths. The code to specify a different base is

```
<base href="path" />
```

where *path* is the folder location that you want the browser to use when resolving relative paths in the current document. The base element has to be added to the head section of the HTML file and will be applied to all hypertext links found within the document.

Reference Window	**Using the Base Element to Set the Default Location of Relative Paths**

- To set the default location for a relative path, add the element
  ```
  <base href="path" />
  ```
  to the document head, where *path* is the folder location that you want the browser to use when resolving relative paths in the current document.

The base element is useful when a single document is moved to a new folder. Rather than rewriting all of the relative paths to reflect the document's new location, the base element redirects browsers to the document's old location, allowing any relative paths to be resolved as they were before.

Managing Your Web Site | InSight

Web sites can quickly grow from a couple of pages to dozens or hundreds of pages. As the size of the site increases, it becomes more difficult to get a clear picture of the site's structure and content. Imagine deleting or moving a file in a Web site that contains dozens of folders and hundreds of files. Can you easily project the effect of this change? Will all of your hypertext links still work after you move or delete the file?

To effectively manage a Web site, you should follow a few important rules. The first is to be consistent in how you structure the site. If you decide to collect all image files in one folder, you should follow that rule as you add more pages and images. Web sites are more likely to break down if files and folders are scattered throughout the server without a consistent rule or pattern. Decide on a structure early on and stick with it.

The second rule is to create a folder structure that matches the structure of the Web site itself. If the pages can be easily categorized into different groups, that grouping should also be reflected in the grouping of the subfolders. The names you assign to your files and folder should also reflect their use on the Web site. This makes it easier for you to predict how modifying a file or folder will impact other pages on the site.

Finally, you should document your work by adding comments to each new Web page. Comments are useful not only for colleagues who may be working on the site, but also for the author who has to revisit those files months or even years after creating them. The comments should include:

- The page's filename and location
- The page's author and the date the page was initially created
- A list of any supporting files used in the document, such as image and audio files
- A list of the files and their locations that link to the page
- A list of the files and their locations that the page links to

By following these rules, you can reduce a lot of the headaches associated with maintaining a large and complicated Web site.

You've completed your initial work linking the three files in Gerry's Web site. In the next session, you'll learn how to work with hypertext links that point to locations within files. If you want to take a break before starting the next session, you can close your files and your Web browser now.

Session 2.1 Quick Check | Review

1. What is storyboarding? Why is it important in creating a Web page system?
2. What is a linear structure? What is a hierarchical structure?
3. What code would you enter to link the text "Sports Info" to the sports.htm file? Assume that the current document and sports.htm are in the same folder.
4. What's the difference between an absolute path and a relative path?
5. Refer to Figure 2-11. If the current file is in the camshots/pages/glossary folder, what are the relative paths for the four files listed in the folder tree?
6. What is the purpose of the base element?

Session 2.2

Tip

In general, Web pages should not span more than one or two screen heights. Studies show that long Web pages are often skipped by busy users.

Linking to Locations within Documents

Gerry likes the links you've created in the last session and would like you to add some more links to the Glossary page. Recall that the Glossary page contains a list of digital photography terms. The page is very long, requiring users to scroll through the document to find a term of interest. At the top of the page Gerry has listed the letters A through Z. Gerry wants to give users the ability to jump to a specific section of the document by clicking a letter from the list. See Figure 2-14.

Figure 2-14	Jumping to a location within a Web page

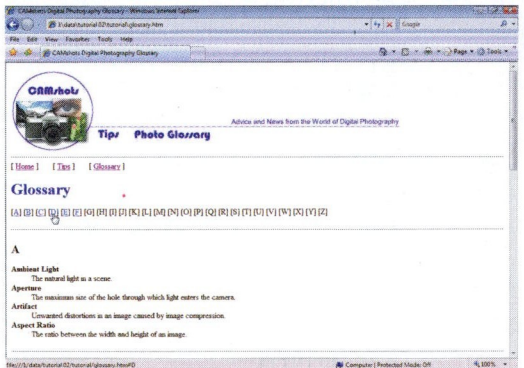 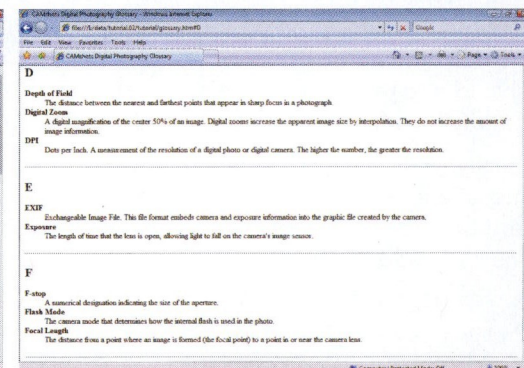

clicking the letter D from the alphabetical list …

…jumps the user to the D section of the glossary

Using the id Attribute

To jump to a specific location within a document, you first need to mark that location. One way of doing this is to add an id attribute to an element at that location in the document. The syntax of the id attribute is

```
id="id"
```

where *id* is the value of the element id. For example, the following code marks the h2 element with an id value of H:

```
<h2 id="H">H</h2>
```

Note that id names must be unique. If you assign the same id name to more than one element on your Web page, the browser uses the first occurrence of the id name. XHTML documents will be rejected if they contain elements with duplicate ids. Id names are not case sensitive, so browsers do not differentiate between ids named top and TOP.

Reference Window	**Defining an Element id**

- To define the id of a specific element in a Web document, use the attribute
  ```
  id="id"
  ```
  where *id* is the value of the element id.

The Glossary page has only a partial list of the photography terms that Gerry will eventually add to his Web site. For now, you'll only mark sections in the glossary corresponding to the letters A through F.

To add the id attribute to h2 headings:

1. Return to the **glossary.htm** file in your text editor.

2. Scroll down the file and locate the h2 heading for the letter A. Within the opening <h2> tag, insert the following attribute:

   `id="A"`

3. Locate the h2 heading for the letter B and insert the following attribute in the opening <h2> tag:

   `id="B"`

   Figure 2-15 highlights the revised code.

Adding the id attribute to h2 headings   Figure 2-15

```
<hr />
<h2 id="A">A</h2>
<dl>
    <dt><b>Ambient Light</b></dt>
    <dd>The natural light in a scene.</dd>
    <dt><b>Aperture</b></dt>
    <dd>The maximum size of the hole through which light enters the camera.</dd>
    <dt><b>Artifact</b></dt>
    <dd>Unwanted distortions in an image caused by image compression.</dd>
    <dt><b>Aspect Ratio</b></dt>
    <dd>The ratio between the width and height of an image.</dd>
</dl>

<hr />
<h2 id="B">B</h2>
<dl>
    <dt><b>Bit</b></dt>
    <dd>The smallest unit of computer memory.</dd>
    <dt><b>Bitmap</b></dt>
    <dd>A method of storing information that maps an image pixel bit by bit.</dd>
    <dt><b>Byte</b></dt>
    <dd>A group of 8 bits, the basic unit of information for the computer.</dd>
</dl>
```

4. Continue going down the file, adding id attributes to the opening <h2> heading tags for C, D, E, and F corresponding to the letters of those headings.

For longer documents like the Glossary page, it's also helpful to the reader to be able to jump directly from the bottom of a long page to the top of the page rather than having to scroll back up. With that in mind, you'll also add an id attribute marking the element at the top of the page.

To mark the top of the page:

1. Scroll up the **glossary.htm** file in your text editor and locate the div element directly below the opening <body> tag.

2. Insert the following attribute within the opening <div> tag, as shown in Figure 2-16:

   `id="top"`

Adding an id attribute to the div element   Figure 2-16

```
<body>
    <div id="top">
        <img src="camshots.jpg" alt="CAMshots" />
    </div>
    <hr />
```

Linking to an id

Once you've marked an element using the id attribute, you can create a hypertext link to that element using the hypertext link

```
<a href="#id">content</a>
```

where *id* is the value of the id attribute of the element. For example, to create a link to the h2 heading for the letter A in the glossary document, you would enter the following code:

```
<a href="#A">A</a>
```

Use this code to change the entries on the Glossary page to hypertext links pointing to the section of the glossary corresponding to the selected letter.

To change the list of letters to hypertext links:

1. Locate the letter A in the list of letters at the top of the **glossary.htm** file.

2. After the [character, insert the following opening tag:

   ```
   <a href="#A">
   ```

3. Between the letter A and the] character, insert closing **</a>** tag. Figure 2-17 shows the revised code.

Figure 2-17 | Creating a hypertext link for "A"

```
<h1 style="color: teal">Glossary</h1>
<p>
    [<a href="#A">A</a>] [B] [C]
    [D] [E] [F]
    [G] [H] [I]
    [J] [K] [L]
    [M] [N] [O]
    [P] [Q] [R]
    [S] [T] [U]
    [V] [W] [X]
    [Y] [Z]
</p>
```

4. Mark the letters B through F in the list as hypertext links pointing to the appropriate h2 headings in the document. Figure 2-18 shows the revised code for the list of letters.

Figure 2-18 | Hypertext links for the list of letters

```
<h1 style="color: teal">Glossary</h1>
<p>
    [<a href="#A">A</a>] [<a href="#B">B</a>] [<a href="#C">C</a>]
    [<a href="#D">D</a>] [<a href="#E">E</a>] [<a href="#F">F</a>]
    [G] [H] [I]
    [J] [K] [L]
    [M] [N] [O]
    [P] [Q] [R]
    [S] [T] [U]
    [V] [W] [X]
    [Y] [Z]
</p>
```

Gerry also wants you to create a hypertext link at the bottom of the file that points to the top (using the id attribute you created in the last set of steps).

5. Scroll to the bottom of the file and locate the text "Return to Top."

6. Mark the text as hypertext, pointing to the element with an id value of top. See Figure 2-19.

Hypertext link to return to the top of the document ◀ Figure 2-19

```
<hr />
<div><a href="#top">Return to Top</a> &#8657;</div>
<hr />
<address>
    CAMshots &#8250;&#8250;&#8250; Tips and News from the World of Digital Photography
</address>
```

▶ **7.** Save your changes to the file and then reload or refresh the **glossary.htm** file in your Web browser.

▶ **8.** As shown in Figure 2-20, the letters A through F in the alphabetic list are displayed as hypertext links. Click the link for **F** and verify that you jump down to the end of the document, where the photographic terms starting with the letter F are listed.

Hypertext links in the glossary page ◀ Figure 2-20

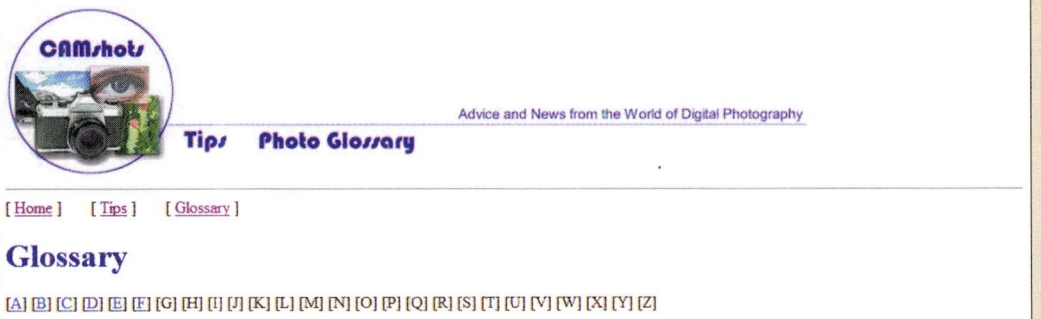

▶ **9.** Click the **Return to Top** hypertext link and verify that you jump back to the top of the document.

▶ **10.** Click the other links within the document and verify that you jump to the correct sections of the glossary.

Trouble? The browser cannot scroll farther than the end of the page. So, you might not see any difference between jumping to the E section of the glossary and jumping to the F section.

InSight | **Working with Anchors**

Early browser versions might not support the use of the id attribute as a way of marking document elements. These early browser versions instead used anchors or bookmarks to mark document locations. The syntax of the anchor element is

```
<a name="anchor">content</a>
```

where *anchor* is the name of the anchor that marks the location of the document *content*. For example, to mark the h2 heading with an anchor of "A," you would enter the following code:

```
<h2><a name="A">A</a></h2>
```

Marking a location with an anchor does not change your document's appearance in any way; it merely creates a destination within your document.

You use the same syntax to link to locations marked with an anchor as you would with locations marked with id attributes. To link to the above anchor, you could use the following code:

```
<a href="#A">A</a>
```

The use of anchors is a deprecated feature of HTML and is not supported in strict applications of XHTML, but you will still see anchors used in older code and in code generated by HTML editors and converters.

Creating Links between Documents

Gerry knows that the glossary will be one of the most useful parts of his Web site, especially for novice photographers. However, he's also aware that most people do not read through glossaries. He would like to create links from the words he uses in his articles to glossary entries so that readers of his articles can quickly access definitions for terms they don't understand. His articles are not on the same page as his Glossary page, so he will have to create a link between those pages and specific glossary entries.

To create a link to a specific location in another file, enter the code

```
<a href="reference#id">content</a>
```

where *reference* is a reference to an HTML or XHTML file and *id* is the id of an element marked within that file. For example, the code

```
<a href="glossary.htm#D">"D" terms in the Glossary</a>
```

creates a hypertext link to the D section in the glossary.htm file. This assumes that the glossary.htm file is located in the same folder as the document containing the hypertext link. If not, you have to include either the absolute or relative path information along with the filename, as described in the last session.

Reference Window | **Linking to an id**

- To link to a specific location within the current file, use
  ```
  <a href="#id">content</a>
  ```
  where *id* is the id value of an element within the document.
- To link to a specific location in another file, use
  ```
  <a href="reference#id">content</a>
  ```
  where *reference* is a reference to an external file and *id* is the id value of an element in that file.

On Gerry's home page, he wants to showcase a Photo of the Month, displaying a photo that his readers might find interesting or useful in their own work. Along with the photo, he has included the digital camera settings used in taking the photo. Many of the camera settings are described on the Glossary page. Gerry suggests that you create a link between the setting name and the glossary entry. The five entries he wants to link to are: F-stop, Exposure, Focal Length, Aperture, and Flash Mode. Your first step is to mark these entries in the glossary using the id attribute.

To mark the glossary entries:

1. Return to the **glossary.htm** file in your text editor.

2. Scroll down the file and locate the Aperture definition term.

3. As shown in Figure 2-21, within the opening <dt> tag, insert the attribute

   `id="aperture"`

Inserting an id attribute   Figure 2-21

```
<hr />
<h2 id="A">A</h2>
<dl>
    <dt><b>Ambient Light</b></dt>
    <dd>The natural light in a scene.</dd>
    <dt id="aperture"><b>Aperture</b></dt>
    <dd>The maximum size of the hole through which light enters the camera.</dd>
    <dt><b>Artifact</b></dt>
    <dd>Unwanted distortions in an image caused by image compression.</dd>
    <dt><b>Aspect Ratio</b></dt>
    <dd>The ratio between the width and height of an image.</dd>
</dl>
```

4. Scroll down the file and locate the Exposure definition term.

5. Within the opening <dt> tag, insert the following attribute:

   `id="exposure"`

6. Go to the F section of the glossary and mark the terms with the following ids:

   F-stop with the id f-stop

   Flash Mode with the id flash_mode

   Focal Length with the id focal_length

7. Save your changes to the **glossary.htm** file.

Next you'll go to the Home page and create links from these terms in the Photo of the Month description to their entries on the Glossary page.

To create links to the glossary entries:

1. Open the **home.htm** file in your text editor.

2. Scroll down the file and locate the F-stop term from the unordered list.

3. Mark "F-stop" as a hypertext link using the following code:

   `<a href="glossary.htm#f-stop">F-stop</a>`

4. Mark "Exposure" as a hypertext link with:

   `<a href="glossary.htm#exposure">Exposure</a>`

5. Mark the remaining three entries in the unordered list as hypertext pointing to their corresponding entries on the Glossary page. Figure 2-22 highlights the revised code in the file.

Figure 2-22 | **Linking to a location within another document**

```
                                  <i>Pear Lake Reflection</i></blockquote>
<ul>
    <li>Camera:
                
        Nikon D50</li>
    <li><a href="glossary.htm#f-stop">F-stop</a>:
                  
        f/7.1</li>
    <li><a href="glossary.htm#exposure">Exposure</a>:
                                 document file
        1/200 sec.</li>
    <li><a href="glossary.htm#focal_length">Focal Length</a>:
         
        18mm</li>
    <li><a href="glossary.htm#aperture">Aperture</a>:
                         element id
        3.6</li>
    <li><a href="glossary.htm#flash_mode">Flash Mode</a>:
           No Flash</li>
</ul>
```

▶ **6.** Save your changes to the file.

▶ **7.** Refresh the **home.htm** file in your Web browser. As shown in Figure 2-23, the settings from the Photo of the Month description are now displayed as hypertext links.

Figure 2-23 | **Linked photography terms**

Photo of the Month

Pear Lake Reflection

- Camera: Nikon D50
- F-stop: f/7.1
- Exposure: 1/200 sec.
- Focal Length: 18mm
- Aperture: 3.6
- Flash Mode: No flash

▶ **8.** Click the **F-stop** hypertext link and verify that you jump to the Glossary page with the F-stop entry displayed in the browser window.

▶ **9.** Return to the **CAMshots home page** and click the hypertext links for the other terms in the list of photo settings, verifying that you jump to the section of the glossary that displays that term's definition.

Working with Linked Images and Image Maps

A standard practice on the Web is to turn the Web site's logo into a hypertext link pointing to the home page. This gives users a quick reference point to the home page rather than searching for a link to the home page. To mark an inline image as a hypertext link, you enclose the <img> tag within a set of <a> tags as follows:

```
<a href="reference"><img src="file" alt="text" /></a>
```

Once the image has been linked, clicking anywhere within the image jumps the user to the linked file.

Introducing Image Maps

When you mark an inline image as a hypertext link, the entire image is linked to the same destination file; however, HTML also allows you to divide an image into different zones, or **hotspots,** each linked to a different destination. Therefore, a single inline image can be linked to several locations. Gerry is interested in doing this with the CAMshots logo. He would like you to create hotspots for the logo so that if the user clicks anywhere within the CAMshots circle on the left side of the logo, the user jumps to the Home page, while clicking either Tips or Photo Glossary in the logo takes the user to the Tips page or the Glossary page. See Figure 2-24.

Tip

Always include alternative text for your linked images to allow nongraphical browsers to display a text link in place of the linked image.

Hotspots within the CAMshots logo   **Figure 2-24**

| home.htm | tips.htm | glossary.htm |

To define these hotspots, you create an **image map** that matches a specified region of the inline image to a specific destination. HTML supports two kinds of image maps: client-side image maps and server-side image maps. You'll first study how to create a client-side image map.

Client-Side Image Maps

A **client-side image map** is an image map that is handled entirely by the Web browser running on the user's computer. Client-side image maps are defined with the map element

```
<map id="map" name="map">
   hotspots
</map>
```

where *map* is the name of the image map and *hotspots* are the locations of the hotspots within the image. Each image map has to be given an id and a name. You have to include both attributes, setting them to the same value, because HTML code requires the name attribute and XHTML requires the id attribute. As long as you include both, your code will work under all browsers. For example, the following code creates a map element named logomap:

```
<map id="logomap" name="logomap">
...
</map>
```

Map elements can be placed anywhere within the body of the Web page because they are not actually displayed by the browser, but used as references for mapping hotspots to inline images. The common practice is to place the map element below the inline image.

Defining Hotspots

The individual hotspots are defined using the area element

```
<area shape="shape" coords="coordinates" href="reference" alt="text" />
```

where *shape* is the shape of the hotspot region, *coordinates* are the list of points that define the boundaries of the region, *reference* is the file or location that the hotspot is linked to, and *text* is alternate text displayed for nongraphical browsers. Hotspots can be created in the shape of rectangles, circles, or polygons (multisided figures). So, the shape attribute can have the value rect for a rectangular hotspot, "circle" for a circular hotspot, and "poly" for a polygonal or multisided hotspot. A fourth shape option is "default," representing the remaining area of the inline image not covered by hotspots. There is no limit to the number of area elements you can add to an image map. Hotspots can also overlap. If they do and the user clicks an overlapping area, the browser opens the link of the first hotspot defined in the map.

Hotspot coordinates are measured in **pixels**, which are the smallest unit or dot in a digital image or display. Your computer monitor might have a size of 1024 x 768 pixels, which means that the display is 1024 dots wide by 768 dots tall. The CAMshots logo that Gerry uses in his Web site has a dimension of 778 pixels wide by 164 pixels tall. When used with the coords attribute of the area element, the pixel values exactly define the location and size of the hotspot region.

Each hotspot shape has a different set of coordinates that define it. To define a rectangular hotspot, enter

```
<area shape="rect" coords="x1, y1, x2, y2" ... />
```

where *x1, y1* are the coordinates of the upper-left corner of the rectangle and *x2, y2* are the coordinates of the rectangle's lower-right corner. Figure 2-25 shows the coordinates of the rectangular region surrounding the Photo Glossary hotspot.

Rectangular hotspot and area element ◀ **Figure 2-25**

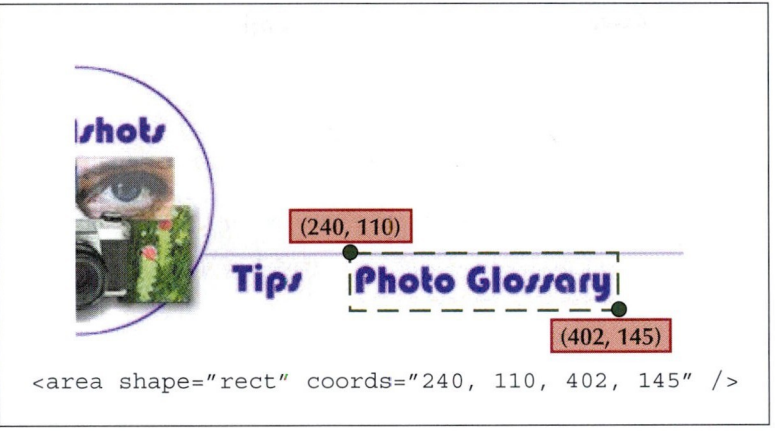

```
<area shape="rect" coords="240, 110, 402, 145" />
```

The upper-left corner of the rectangle has the coordinates (240, 110). The lower-right corner is found at the coordinates (402, 145). Coordinates are always expressed relative to the image's top-left corner. A coordinate of (240, 110) refers to a point that is 240 pixels to the right and 110 pixels down from the image's top-left corner.

Circular hotspots are defined using the area element

```
<area shape="circle" coords="x, y, r" ... />
```

where *x* and *y* are the coordinates of the center of the circle and *r* is the circle's radius. Figure 2-26 shows the coordinates for a circular hotspot around the CAMshots image from the Web site logo. The center of the circle is located at the coordinates (82, 78) and the circle has a radius of 80 pixels.

Circular hotspot and area element ◀ **Figure 2-26**

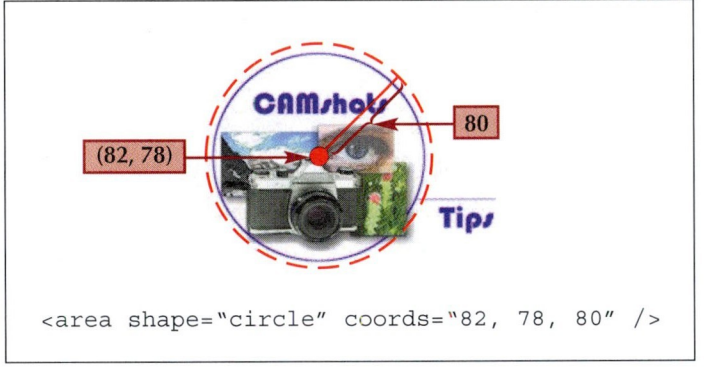

```
<area shape="circle" coords="82, 78, 80" />
```

Polygonal hotspots are defined with

```
<area shape="poly" coords="x1, y1, x2, y2, x3, y3, ..." ... />
```

where (*x1, y1*), (*x2, y2*), (*x3, y3*) and so forth define the coordinates of each corner in the multisided shape. Figure 2-27 shows the coordinates for a triangular-shaped hotspot with corners at (30, 142), (76, 80), and (110, 142). With polygonal hotspots, you can create a wide variety of shapes as long you know the coordinates of each corner.

Figure 2-27 ▶ **Polygonal hotspot and area element**

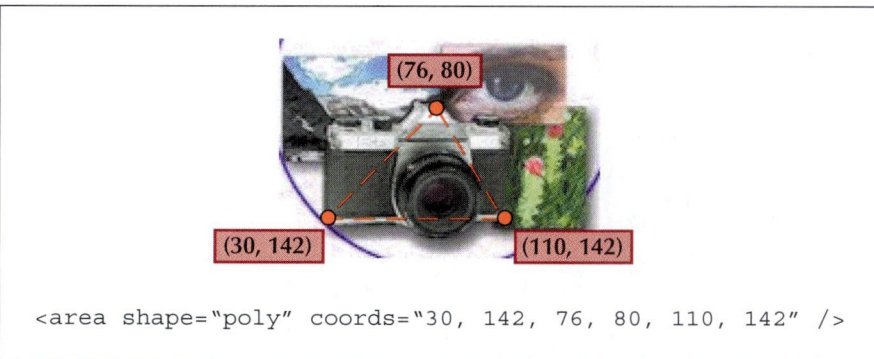

```
<area shape="poly" coords="30, 142, 76, 80, 110, 142" />
```

Finally, to define the default hotspot for the image use

```
<area shape="default" coords="0, 0, x, y" ... />
```

where *x* is the width of the inline image in pixels and *y* is the image's height. Any spot in the inline image that is not covered by another hotspot will activate the default hotspot link.

To determine the coordinates of a hotspot, you can use either a graphics program such as Adobe Photoshop or image map software that automatically generates the HTML code for the hotspots you define.

In this case, assume that Gerry has already determined the coordinates for the hotspots in his image map and provided them for you. He has three hotspots that he wants you to create, shown earlier in Figure 2-24. The first is a circular hotspot linked to the home.htm file, centered at the point (82, 78) and having a radius of 80 pixels. The second is a rectangular hotspot, linked to the tips.htm file with corners at (168, 110) and (225, 145). The third is also rectangular, linked to the glossary.htm file with corners at (240, 110) and (402, 145). You do not have to create a polygonal hotspot.

You'll name the image map containing these hotspots logomap.

To create an image map:

1. Return to **home.htm** file in your text editor.

2. Directly below the <img> tag for the CAMshots inline image, insert the following map element:

   ```
   <map id="logomap" name="logomap">
   </map>
   ```

3. Within the map element, insert a circular hotspot that points to the home.htm file using the following area element:

   ```
   <area shape="circle" coords="82, 78, 80"
       href="home.htm" alt="Home" />
   ```

4. Directly below the <area> tag for the circular hotspot, insert the following two rectangular hotspots pointing to the tips.htm and glossary.htm files:

   ```
   <area shape="rect" coords="168, 110, 225, 145"
       href="tips.htm" alt="Tips" />
   <area shape="rect" coords="240, 110, 402, 145"
       href="glossary.htm" alt="Glossary" />
   ```

   Figure 2-28 highlights the new code in the file.

Creating an image map ◀ Figure 2-28

```
<body>
    <div>
        <img src="camshots.jpg" alt="CAMshots" />
        <map id="logomap" name="logomap">
            <area shape="circle" coords="82, 78, 80"
                  href="home.htm" alt="Home" />
            <area shape="rect" coords="168, 110, 225, 145"
                  href="tips.htm" alt="Tips" />
            <area shape="rect" coords="240, 110, 402, 145"
                  href="glossary.htm" alt="Glossary" />
        </map>
    </div>
    <hr />
```

hotspots

▶ **5.** Save your changes to the file.

Creating a Client-Side Image Map | Reference Window

- To create a client-side image map, insert the map element
  ```
  <map name="map" id="map">
     hotspots
  </map>
  ```
  anywhere within the Web page body, where *map* is the name and id of the image map
  and *hotspots* is a list of hotspot areas defined within the image map.
- To add a hotspot to the image map, place the element
  ```
  <area shape="shape" coords="coordinates" href="reference"
  alt="text" />
  ```
  within the map element, where *shape* is the shape of the hotspot region, *coordinates*
  are the list of points that define the boundaries of the region, *reference* is the file or
  location that the hotspot is linked to, and *text* is alternate text displayed for nongraphical
  browsers.
- To define a rectangular-shaped hotspot, use the area element
  ```
  <area shape="rect" coords="x1, y1, x2, y2" ... />
  ```
  where x1, y1 are the coordinates of the upper-left corner of the rectangle and x2, y2 are
  the coordinates of the rectangle's lower-right corner.
- To define a circular hotspot, use
  ```
  <area shape="circle" coords="x, y, r" ... />
  ```
  where *x* and *y* are the coordinates of the center of the circle and *r* is the circle's radius.
- To define a polygonal hotspot, use
  ```
  <area shape="poly" coords="x1, y1, x2, y2, x3, y3, ..." ... />
  ```
  where (x1, y1), (x2, y2), (x3, y3), and so forth define the coordinates of each corner in the
  multisided shape.
- To define the default hotspot, use
  ```
  <area shape="default" coords="0, 0, x, y" ... />
  ```
  where *x* is the width of the inline image in pixels and *y* is the height in pixels.
- To apply an image map to an inline image, add the usemap attribute
  ```
  <img src="file" alt="text" usemap="#map" />
  ```
  to the img element, where *map* is the name or id of the map element.

Now that you've defined the image map, your next task is to apply the map to the
CAMshots logo.

Applying an Image Map

To apply an image map to an image, add the usemap attribute to the inline image's <img> tag. The syntax is

```
<img src="file" alt="text" usemap="#map" />
```

where *map* is the id or name of the map element. If you place the map element in a separate file, you can reference it using the code

```
<img src="file" alt="text" usemap="reference#map" />
```

where *reference* is a reference to an HTML or XHTML file containing the map element. Unfortunately, most browsers do not support this option, so you should always place the image map in the same file as the inline image. You'll apply the logomap to the CAMshots logo and then test it on your Web browser.

To apply the logomap image map:

▶ 1. Add the following attribute to the <img> tag for the CAMshots logo, as shown in Figure 2-29.

```
usemap="#logomap"
```

Figure 2-29 ▶ **Applying an image map**

▶ 2. Save your changes to the file and reload or refresh the **home.htm** file in your Web browser.

Trouble? Depending on your browser, you might see a border around the CAMshots logo, which you can ignore for now. You'll remove it shortly.

▶ 3. Click anywhere within the word **Tips** in the logo image and verify that the browser opens the Tips page.

▶ 4. Return to the home page and click anywhere within the word **Photo Glossary** to verify that the browser opens the Glossary page.

Tip

If you need to be compatible with older browsers, use the attribute border="0" in place of the border-width style. Note that the border attribute has been deprecated and is not supported in strict applications of XHTML.

After changing the logo to a hypertext link, you may have noticed that you have added a border around the image. Hypertext links are usually underlined in the Web page; but with inline images, the image is displayed with a lined border. Gerry would prefer not to have a border because he feels that it detracts from the logo's appearance. He asks if you can remove the border but still keep the logo functioning as a hypertext link.

To remove the border, you can apply a border-width style to the inline image. By setting the width of the border to zero, you will effectively remove it from the logo. The style attribute to change the width of a border is

```
style="border-width: 0"
```

Removing the Border from an Inline Image

- To remove a border from an inline image, add the following attribute to the `<img>` tag:
  `style="border-width: 0"`

Use the border-width style to remove the border from the CAMshots logo on the three pages of Gerry's Web site.

To set the border width of the CAMshots logo to 0:

1. Return to the **home.htm** file in your text editor.

2. Add the following style attribute to the `<img>` tag for the logo inline image, as shown in Figure 2-30.

   `style="border-width: 0"`

Removing an inline image border   Figure 2-30

```
<body>
   <div>
      <img src="camshots.jpg" alt="CAMshots" usemap="#logomap" style="border-width: 0" />
      <map id="logomap" name="logomap">
         <area shape="circle" coords="82, 78, 80"
               href="home.htm" alt="Home" />
         <area shape="rect" coords="168, 110, 225, 145"
               href="tips.htm" alt="Tips" />
         <area shape="rect" coords="240, 110, 402, 145"
               href="glossary.htm" alt="Glossary" />
      </map>
   </div>
   <hr />
```

set the width of the image border to 0

3. Save your changes to the file.

4. Reload the **home.htm** file in your browser and verify that the border has been removed from the image.

Now that you've created an image map for the logo on the home page, you can create similar image maps for the logos on the Tips and Glossary pages.

To add image maps to the other Web pages:

1. Return to the **tips.htm** file in your text editor.

2. Replace the code within the div element for the logo image with the code shown earlier in Figure 2-30. (Hint: You can use the copy and paste feature of your text editor to copy the code from the home.htm file into the tips.htm file.)

3. Save your changes to the file.

4. Go to the **glossary.htm** file in your text editor.

5. As you did for the tips.htm file, replace the code within the div element for the logo image with the code from the home.htm file. Save your changes to the file.

6. Return to the **home.htm** file in your Web browser and verify that you can switch among the three Web pages by clicking the hotspots in the CAMshots logo.

7. If you want to take a break before starting the next session, close your files and programs now.

Server-Side Image Maps

The other type of image map you might encounter on the Web is a **server-side image map**, which is stored on the Web server rather than entered into the HTML code of the Web page. When you click a hotspot on a server-side image map, the coordinates of the mouse click are sent to the server, which activates the corresponding link, downloading the page to your Web browser.

The server-side image map was the original HTML standard and is still supported on the Web. However, this map has some limitations compared to client-side image maps. Because the map is located on the server, you cannot test your Web page without server access. Also, server-side image maps might be slower because information must be sent to the server with each mouse click. Finally, unlike client-side image maps, server-side image maps require the use of a mouse. This makes them unsuitable for users with disabilities or users running nongraphical browsers.

To create a server-side image map, enclose the inline image with a hypertext link such as

```
<a href="map">
   <img src="file" alt="text" ismap="ismap" />
</a>
```

where *map* is the name of a program or file running on the Web server that will handle the image map. The ismap attribute tells the Web browser to treat the inline image as an image map.

At this time, you do not foresee a need to use a server-side image map in the CAMshots Web site. In any future projects, you'll continue to work with client-side maps.

| InSight | **Writing Effective Hypertext Links** |

To make it easier for users to navigate your Web site, you should follow a few key design tips. Write the text of your hypertext links so that they tell the reader exactly what type of document the link points to. For example, the link text

Click here for more information.

doesn't tell the user what type of document will appear when "here" is clicked. In the place of phrases like "click here," use descriptive link text such as:

For more information, view a list of frequently asked questions.

If the link points to a non-HTML file, such as a PDF document, include that information in the link text. If the linked document is extremely large and will take a while to download to the user's computer, include that information in your link text so that users can decide whether or not to initiate the transfer. The following link text informs users of the size of the video clip before they initiate the link:

Download the video clip (16 MB).

Make your link text easy to locate. Because most browsers underline hypertext links, don't use underlining for other text elements; use italic or boldface fonts instead. Users should never be confused about what is a link and what is not. Also, if you apply a color to your text, do not choose colors that will make the linked text harder to pick out against the Web page background.

Gerry is pleased with the progress you've made on his Web site. Adding the links to the glossary and within the CAMshots logo has made his site easier to navigate. However, there are many other sources of information about digital photography and digital cameras that Gerry wants to make available to his readers. In the next session you'll examine how to create links between his Web site and other sites on the World Wide Web.

1. Specify the code for marking the text "CAMshots FAQ" as an h2 heading with the id "faq."
2. Specify the code for marking the text "Read our FAQ" as hypertext linked to an element in the current document with the id "faq."
3. Specify the code for marking the text "Read our FAQ" as a hypertext link, pointing to an element with the id "faq" in the help.htm file. Assume that help.htm lies in the same folder as the current document.
4. Specify the code for placing an anchor with the name "faq" within the h2 heading "CAMshots FAQ."
5. For marking locations within a Web page, what is one advantage of using anchors rather than the id attribute? What is one disadvantage?
6. The CAMmap image map has a circular hotspot centered at the point (50, 75) with a radius of 40 pixels pointing to the faq.htm file. Specify the code to create this map element with that circular hotspot.
7. An inline image based on the logo.jpg file with the alternative text "CAMshots" needs to use the CAMmap image map. Specify the code to apply the image map to the image.
8. What attribute do you add to the inline image from the previous question to remove its border?

Session 2.3

Linking to Resources on the Internet

Gerry has a final set of tasks for you. In the tips.htm file, he has listed some of the Web sites he finds useful in his study of photography. He would like to change the entries in this list to hypertext links that his readers can click to quickly access the sites.

Introducing URLs

To create a link to a resource on the Internet, you need to know its URL. A **URL**, or **Uniform Resource Locator**, specifies the precise location of a resource on the Internet. Examples of URLs include *www.whitehouse.gov*, the home page of the President of the United States, and *www.w3.org*, the home page of the World Wide Web consortium. All URLs share the common form

```
scheme:location
```

where *scheme* indicates the type of resource referenced by the URL and *location* is the location of that resource. For Web pages, the location refers to the location of the HTML file; but for other resources, the location might simply be the name of the resource. For example, a link to an e-mail account has the e-mail address as the resource.

The name of the scheme is taken from the protocol used to access the resource. A **protocol** is a set of rules defining how information is passed between two devices. Your Web browser communicates with Web servers using the **Hypertext Transfer Protocol** or **HTTP**. Therefore, the URLs for all Web pages must start with the http scheme. This tells the browser to use http when it tries to access the Web page. Other Internet resources, described in Figure 2-31, use different communication protocols and have different scheme names.

> **Tip**
>
> Because URLs cannot contain blank spaces, avoid blank spaces in Web site file and folder names.

Figure 2-31 | **Internet protocols**

Protocol	Used To
file	access documents stored locally on a user's computer
ftp	access documents stored on an FTP server
gopher	access documents stored on a gopher server
http	access Web pages stored on the World Wide Web
https	access Web pages over a secure encrypted connection
mailto	open a user's e-mail client and address a new message
news	connect to a Usenet newsgroup
telnet	open a telnet connection to a specific server
wais	connect to a Wide Area Information Server database

Linking to a Web Site

The URL for a Web page has the general form

```
http://server/path/filename#id
```

where *server* is the name of the Web server, *path* is the path to the file on that server, *filename* is the name of the file, and if necessary, *id* is the name of an id or anchor within the file. A Web page URL can also contain specific programming instructions for a browser to send to the Web server (a topic beyond the scope of this tutorial). Figure 2-32 shows the URL for a sample Web page with all of the parts identified.

Figure 2-32 | **Parts of a URL**

You might have noticed that a URL like *http://www.camshots.com* doesn't include any pathname or filename. If a URL doesn't specify a path, then it indicates the topmost folder in the server's directory tree. If a URL doesn't specify a filename, the server will return to the default home page. Many servers use index.html as the filename for the default home page, so a URL like *http://www.camshots.com/index.html* would be equivalent to *http://www.camshots.com*.

Understanding Domain Names | InSight

The server name portion of the URL is also called the **domain name**. By studying the domain name you learn about the server hosting the Web site. Each domain name contains a hierarchy of names separated by periods (.), with the topmost level appearing at the end. The top level, called an **extension**, indicates the general audience supported by the Web server. For example, .edu is the extension reserved for educational institutions, .gov is used for agencies of the United States government, and .com is used for commercial sites or general-use sites.

The next lower level appearing before the extension displays the name of the individual or organization hosting the site. A domain name like camshots.com indicates a commercial or general use site owned by CAMshots. To avoid duplicating domain names, the two top-most levels of the domain have to be registered with the IANA (Internet Assigned Numbers Authority) before they can be used. You can usually register your domain name through your Internet Service Provider. Be aware that you will have to pay an annual fee to keep the domain name.

The lowest levels of the domain, which appear farthest to the left in the domain name, are assigned by the individual or company hosting the site. Large Web sites involving hundreds of pages typically divide their domain names into several levels. For example, a large company like Microsoft might have one domain name for file downloads—*downloads. microsoft.com*—and another for customer service—*service.microsoft.com*. Finally, the lowest level of the domain, the first part of the domain name, displays the name of the hard drive or resource storing the Web site files. Many companies have standardized on using "www" as the name of the lowest level in their domain.

Gerry has listed four Web pages that he wants his readers to be able to access. He's provided you with the URLs for these pages, which are shown in Figure 2-33.

Web site URLs ◀ **Figure 2-33**

Web Site	URL
Apogee Photo	http://www.apogeephoto.com
Outdoor Photographer	http://www.outdoorphotographer.com
PCPhoto	http://www.pcphotomag.com
Popular Photography and Imaging	http://www.popphoto.com

To create a link to these Web sites from your document, you need to mark some text as a hypertext link, using the URL of the Web site as the value of the href attribute. So to link the text "Apogee Photo" to the Apogee Photo Web site, you would enter the following code:

```
<a href="http://www.apogeephoto.com">Apogee Photo</a>
```

Use the information that Gerry has given you to create links to all four of the Web sites listed on his tips page.

To create links to sites on the Web:

▶ 1. Return to the **tips.htm** file in your text editor.

▶ 2. Scroll to the bottom of the file and locate the definition list containing the list of Web sites.

3. Mark the entry for Apogee Photo as a hypertext link using the following code:

```
<a href="http://www.apogeephoto.com">Apogee Photo</a>
```

4. Mark the remaining three entries in the list as hypertext links pointing to each company's Web site. Figure 2-34 highlights the revised code in the file.

Figure 2-34 ▶ **Linking to sites on the Web**

```
<h2 style="color: blue">Photography Sites on the Web</h2>
<p>The Web is an excellent resource for articles on photography and digital cameras.
   Here are a few of my favorites.</p>
<dl>
   <dt>&#9758; <a href="http://www.apogeephoto.com">Apogee Photo</a></dt>
   <dd>An established online photography magazine with articles by top pros,
       discussion forums, workshops, and more.</dd>
   <dt>&#9758; <a href="http://www.outdoorphotographer.com">Outdoor Photographer</a></dt>
   <dd>The premier magazine for outdoor photography. The site includes extensive tips
       on photographing wildlife, action sports,
       scenic vistas, and travel sites.</dd>
   <dt>&#9758; <a href="http://www.pcphotomag.com">PCPhoto</a></dt>
   <dd>An excellent site for novices and professionals with informative reviews and
       buying guides for the latest equipment and software.</dd>
   <dt>&#9758; <a href="http://www.popphoto.com">Popular Photography and Imaging</a></dt>
   <dd>A useful and informative site with articles from the long-established
       magazine of professional and amateur photographers.</dd>
</dl>
```

5. Save your changes to the file.

6. Reload or refresh the **tips.htm** file in your Web browser. Figure 2-35 shows the revised list with each entry appearing as a hypertext link.

Figure 2-35 ▶ **Links on the tips page**

Photography Sites on the Web

The Web is an excellent resource for articles on photography and digital cameras. Here are a few of my favorites.

☞ Apogee Photo
    An established online photography magazine with articles by top pros, discussion forums, workshops, and more.
☞ Outdoor Photographer
    The premier magazine for outdoor photography. The site includes extensive tips on photographing wildlife, action sports, scenic vistas, and travel sites.
☞ PCPhoto
    An excellent site for novices and professionals with informative reviews and buying guides for the latest equipment and software.
☞ Popular Photography and Imaging
    A useful and informative site with articles from the long-established magazine of professional and amateur photographers.

7. Click each of the links on the page and verify that the appropriate Web site opens.

Trouble? To open these sites, you must be connected to the Internet. If you are still having problems, compare your code to the URLs listed in Figure 2-34 to confirm that you have not made a typing error. Also keep in mind that because the Web is constantly changing, the Web sites for some of these links might have changed, or a site might have been removed since this book was published.

Web pages are only one type of resource that you can link to. Before continuing work on the CAMshots Web site, you should explore how to access some of these other resources.

Linking to FTP Servers

Another method of storing and sharing files on the Internet is through FTP servers. **FTP servers** are file servers that act like file cabinets in which users can store and retrieve data files, much as they store and retrieve files from their own computer. FTP servers transfer information using a communications protocol called **File Transfer Protocol**, or **FTP** for short. The URL to access an FTP server follows the general format

```
ftp://server/path/
```

where *server* is the name of the FTP server and *path* is the folder path on the server that contains the files you want to access. When you access the FTP site, you can navigate through its folder tree as you would navigate the folders on your own hard disk. Figure 2-36 shows how someone can use Internet Explorer to view the FTP site and how the site appears as a collection of folders that can be opened and viewed.

FTP site appearing in the browser and in Windows Explorer   Figure 2-36

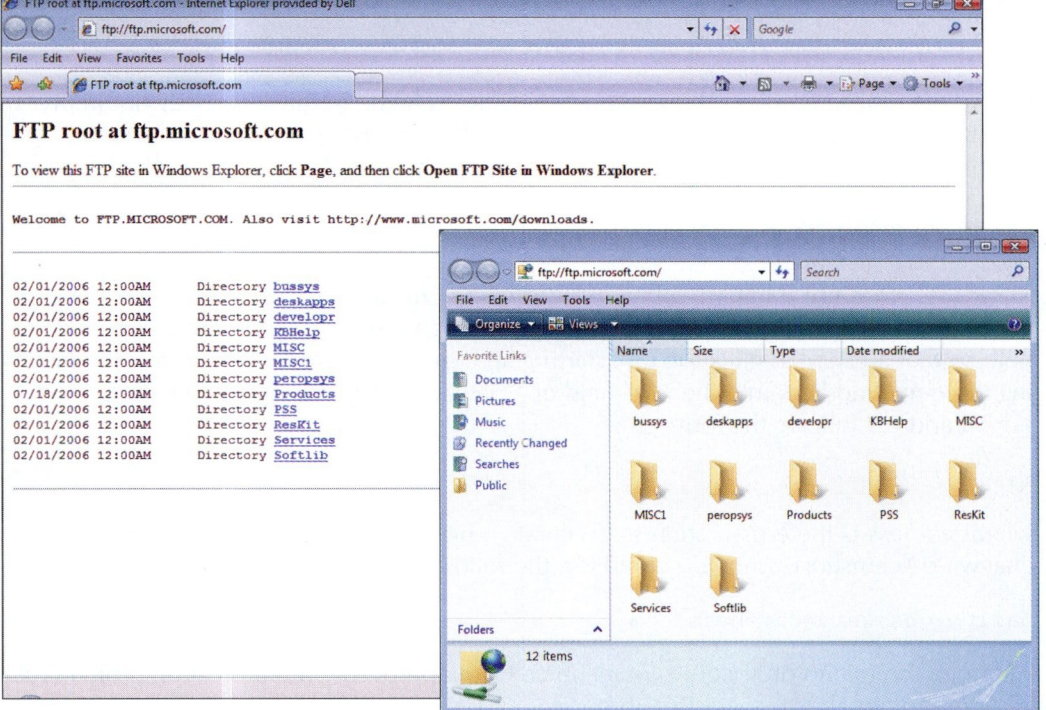

FTP servers require each user to enter a password and a username to gain access to the server's files. The standard username is anonymous and requires no password. Your browser supplies this information automatically, so in most situations you don't have to worry about passwords and usernames. However, some FTP servers do not allow anonymous access. In these cases, either your browser prompts you for the username and the password, or you can supply a username and password within the URL using the format

```
ftp://username:password@server/path
```

where *username* and *password* are a username and password that the FTP server recognizes. It is generally *not* a good idea, however, to include usernames and passwords in URLs, as it can allow others to view your sensitive login information. It's better to let the browser send this information or to use a special program called an **FTP client**, which can encrypt or hide this information during transmission.

Linking to a Local File

HTML is a very useful language for creating collections of linked documents. Many software developers have chosen to distribute their online help in the form of HTML files. The Web site for their help files then exist locally on the user's computer or network. If the Web site needs to reference local files (as opposed to files on the Internet or another wide area network), the URL needs to reflect this fact. The URL for a local file has the general form

```
file://server/path/filename
```

where *server* is the name of the local network server, *path* is the path on that server to the file, and *filename* is the name of the file. If you're accessing a file from your own computer, the server name can be omitted and replaced by an extra slash (/). So, a file from the documents/articles folder might have the URL:

```
file:///documents/articles/tips.htm
```

If the file is on a different disk within your computer, the hard drive letter would be included in the URL as follows:

```
file://D:/documents/articles/tips.htm
```

Unlike the other URLs you've examined, the "file" scheme in this URL does not imply any particular communication protocol; instead, the browser retrieves the document using whatever method is the local standard for the type of file specified in the URL.

Linking to an E-Mail Address

Many Web sites use e-mail to allow users to communicate with a site's owner, sales representative, or technical support staff. You can turn an e-mail address into a hypertext link, so that a user can click the link starting an e-mail program and automatically inserting the e-mail address into the "To" field of a new outgoing message. The URL for an e-mail address follows the form

```
mailto:address
```

where *address* is the e-mail address. To create a hypertext link to the e-mail address ghayward@camshots.com, you could use the following URL:

```
mailto:ghayward@camshots.com
```

Tip

To link to more than one e-mail address, add the addresses to the mailto link in a comma-separated list.

Although the mailto protocol is not technically an approved communication protocol, it is supported by almost every Web browser.

The mailto protocol also allows you to add information to the e-mail, including the subject line and the text of the message body. To add this information to the link, you use the form

```
mailto:address?header1=value1&header2=value2& ...
```

where *header1*, *header2*, etc. are different e-mail headers and *value1*, *value2*, and so on are the values of the headers. So to create the e-mail message

```
TO: ghayward@camshots.com
SUBJECT: Test
BODY: This is a test message
```

you would use the following URL:

```
mailto:ghayward@camshots.com?Subject=Test&Body=This%20is%20a%20test%20message
```

Notice that the spaces in the message body "This is a test message" have been replaced with %20 characters. This is necessary because URLs cannot contain blank spaces. To preserve information about blank spaces, URLs use **escape characters**, which are symbols that represent characters including nonprintable characters such as spaces, tabs, and line feeds. Escape characters use many of the same values as HTML character codes, though the syntax of escape characters is different. So, when the browser receives the following character string in a URL such as

```
This%20is%20a%20test%20message
```

it interprets the %20 escape character as a blank space and resolves the string as

```
This is a test message
```

Figure 2-37 lists some of the escape characters that can be used in any URL in place of printable or nonprintable characters.

Escape character codes | Figure 2-37

Escape Character Code	Character	Escape Character Code	Character
%20	space	%5B	[
%0D%0A	new line	%5D	]
%3C	<	%60	`
%3E	>	%3B	;
%23	#	%2F	/
%25	%	%3F	?
%7B	{	%3A	:
%7D	}	%40	@
%7C			%3D	=
%5C	\	%26	&
%5E	^	%24	$
%7E	~		

To further explore how to convert an e-mail message into a URL, you can experiment with a demo page.

To view the e-mail demo:

1. Use your Web browser to open the **demo_mailto.htm** file from the tutorial.02\demo folder included with your Data Files.

2. Scroll down the page, and in the TO: input box, enter the e-mail address **ghayward@camshots.com**.

3. Type **CAMshots Message** in the SUBJECT input box.

4. Type the following in the BODY input box:

   ```
   This is a message generated by the CAMshots Web site for
   Gerry Hayward.
   ```

5. Click the **Generate URL** button to create the URL for this e-mail message.

   As shown in Figure 2-38, the demo page generates the URL for the e-mail message. All of the blank spaces in the mail message have been replaced with the %20 escape character.

Figure 2-38 ▶ **Converting an e-mail message to a URL**

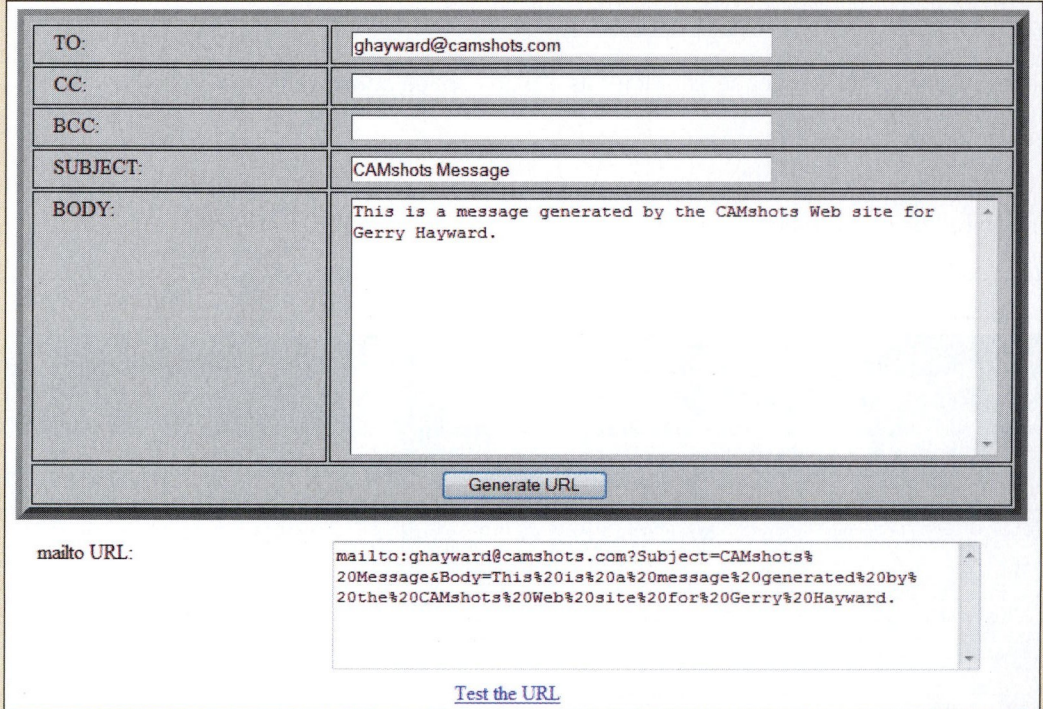

6. Click the **Test the URL** button at the bottom of the page. As shown in Figure 2-39, the browser opens the user's e-mail program, with the e-mail fields already filled in, based on the text of the URL.

Figure 2-39 ▶ **E-mail message generated by the hypertext link**

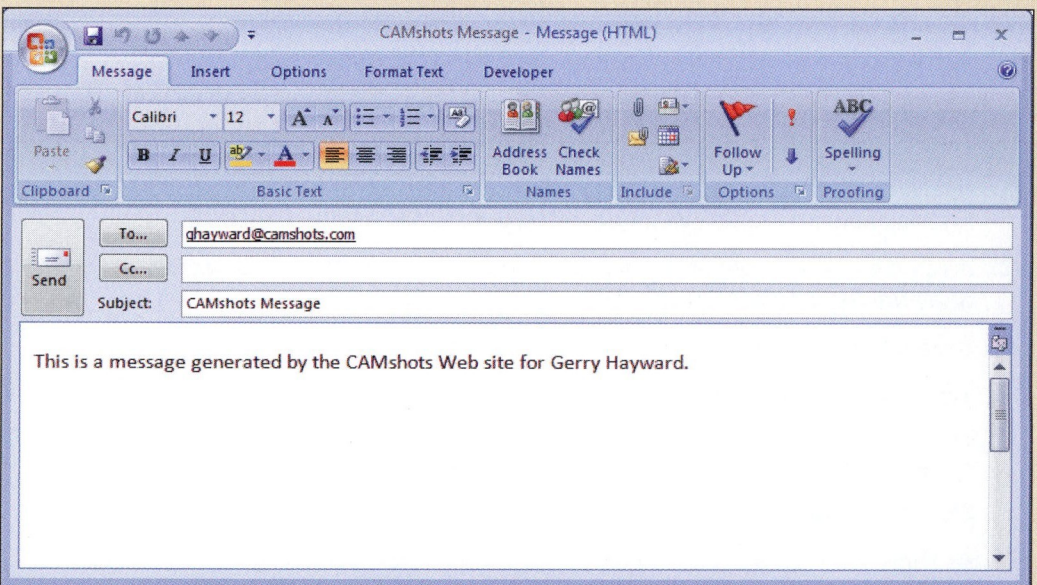

Trouble? Your e-mail window might look different depending on the e-mail program installed on your computer. If you do not have access to an e-mail program, you might not see any result or you might receive an error message after clicking the Test the URL button.

7. Close the message window without saving the message.

8. Continue experimenting with the demo page, exploring the effects of different e-mail messages on the URL text. Close the demo page when you are finished.

Gerry wants you to add to a link to his e-mail address on the CAMshots home page. This gives people who read his site the ability to contact him with additional questions or ideas.

To link to an e-mail address on Gerry's home page:

1. Return to the **home.htm** file in your text editor.

2. Go to the first paragraph and locate the text "contact me."

3. Mark "contact me" as a hypertext link using the following code, as shown in Figure 2-40:

```
<a href="mailto:ghayward@camshots.com?subject=CAMshots%20Message">
   contact me
</a>
```

Adding an e-mail link to the CAMshots home page ◄ Figure 2-40

```
<p>Welcome to <span style="color: blue">CAMshots</span>, a site for people passionate about
   digital photography. This site has grown out of decades of photographic experience.
   I offer advice for both beginners and advanced users. I hope you enjoy what you find,
   but please be considerate of the work it took to do all this.
   The entire site contents including all images and articles are copyrighted.
   Please honor my work and do not copy anything without permission. If you are
   interested in publishing any of my images or articles or using them in other ways,
   please <a href="mailto:ghayward@camshots.com?subject=CAMshots%20Message">contact me</a>
   and we can discuss your needs. Happy Shooting!</p>
<p>&mdash; Gerry</p>
```

4. Save your changes to the file.

5. Refresh the **home.htm** file in your browser. Verify that the text "contact me" in the opening paragraph now appears as a hypertext link.

6. Click **contact me** and verify that your e-mail program displays a message with ghayward@camshots.com as the recipient and CAMshots Message as the subject.

7. Close your message window without saving the message.

InSight | **E-Mail Links and Spam**

Use caution when adding e-mail links to your Web site. While it may make it more convenient for users to contact you, it also might make you more vulnerable to spam. **Spam** is unsolicited e-mail sent to large numbers of people, promoting products, services, and in some cases inappropriate Web sites. Spammers create their e-mail lists by scanning discussion groups, stealing Internet mailing lists, and using programs called **e-mail harvesters** to scan HTML code for the e-mail addresses contained in mailto URLs. Many Web developers have removed e-mail links from their Web sites in order to foil these harvesters, replacing the links with Web forms that submit e-mail requests to a secure server. If you need to include an e-mail address on your Web page, you can take a few steps to reduce your exposure to spammers:

- Replace the text of the e-mail addresses with inline images that are more difficult for e-mail harvesters to read.
- Write a program to scramble any e-mail addresses in the HTML code, unscrambling the e-mail address only when it is clicked by the user.
- Replace the characters of the e-mail address with escape characters. For example, you can replace the "@" symbol with the escape sequence %40.

There is no quick and easy solution to this problem. Fighting spammers is an ongoing battle, and they have proved very resourceful in overcoming some of the defenses people have created. As you develop your Web site, you should carefully consider how to handle e-mail addresses and review the most current methods for safeguarding that information.

Reference Window | **Linking to Various Interent Resources**

- The URL for a Web page has the form
  `http://server/path/filename#id`
  where *server* is the name of the Web server, *path* is the path to a file on that server, *filename* is the name of the file, and if necessary *id* is the name of an id or anchor within the file.
- The URL for an FTP site has the form
  `ftp://server/path/filename`
  where *server* is the name of the FTP server, *path* is the folder path, and *filename* is the name of the file.
- The URL for an e-mail address has the form
  `mailto:address?header1=value1&header2=value2& ...`
  where *address* is the e-mail address; *header1*, *header2*, etc. are different e-mail headers; and *value1*, *value2*, and so on are the values of the headers.
- The URL to reference a local file has the form
  `file://server/path/filename`
  where *server* is the name of the local server or computer, *path* is the path to the file on that server, and *filename* is the name of the file. If you are accessing a file on your own computer, the server name is replaced by a third slash (/).

Tip

All of the hypertext attributes applied to the <a> tag can also be applied to the <area> tags within your image maps.

Working with Hypertext Attributes

HTML provides several attributes to control the behavior and appearance of your links. Gerry suggests that you study a few of these to see whether they would be effective in his Web site.

Opening a Secondary Window or Tab

By default, each page you open replaces the contents of the current page in the browser window. This means that when Gerry's readers click on one of the four external links listed on the tips page, they leave the CAMshots Web site. To return to the Web site, users would have to click their browser's Back button.

Gerry wants his Web site to stay open when a user clicks one of the links to the external Web sites. Most browsers allow users to open multiple browser windows or multiple tabs within the same browser window. Gerry suggests that links to external sites be opened in a second browser window or tab. He wants these external sites to be displayed in a second browser window or tab. This arrangement allows continual access to his Web site, even as users are browsing other sites.

To force a document to appear in a new window or tab, add the target attribute to the <a> tag. The general syntax is

```
<a href="url" target="window">content</a>
```

where *window* is a name assigned to the new browser window or browser tab. The value you use for the target attribute doesn't affect the appearance or content of the page being opened; the target simply identifies the different windows or tabs that are currently open. You can choose any name you wish for the target. If several links have the same target name, they all open in the same location, replacing the previous content. HTML also supports several special target names, described in Figure 2-41.

Target names for browser windows and tabs ◄ Figure 2-41

Target Name	Description
target	Opens the link in a new window or tab named *target*
_blank	Opens the link in a new, unnamed window or tab
_self	Opens the link in the current browser window or tab

Whether the new page is opened in a tab or in a browser window is determined by the browser settings. It cannot be set by the HTML code.

Opening a Link in a New Window or Tab | Reference Window

- To open a link in a new browser window or browser tab, add the attribute
    ```
    target="window"
    ```
    to the <a> tag, where *window* is a name assigned to the new browser window or tab.

Gerry suggests that all of the external links from his page be opened in a browser window or tab identified with the target name "new."

To specify a link target:

1. Return to the **tips.htm** file in your text editor.

2. Scroll to the bottom of the file and locate the four links to the external Web sites.

3. Within each of the opening <a> tags, insert the following attribute, as shown in Figure 2-42.

    ```
    target="new"
    ```

Figure 2-42 | **Setting a target for a hyperlink**

```
<h2 style="color: blue">Photography Sites on the Web</h2>
<p>The Web is an excellent resource for articles on photography and digital cameras.
    Here are a few of my favorites.</p>
<dl>
    <dt>&#9758; <a href="http://www.apogeephoto.com" target="new">Apogee Photo</a></dt>
    <dd>An established online photography magazine with articles by top pros,
        discussion forums, workshops, and more.</dd>
    <dt>&#9758; <a href="http://www.outdoorphotographer.com" target="new">Outdoor Photographer</a></dt>
    <dd>The premier magazine for outdoor photography. The site includes extensive tips
        on photographing wildlife, action sports,
        scenic vistas, and travel sites.</dd>
    <dt>&#9758; <a href="http://www.pcphotomag.com" target="new">PCPhoto</a></dt>
    <dd>An excellent site for novices and professionals with informative reviews and
        buying guides for the latest equipment and software.</dd>
    <dt>&#9758; <a href="http://www.popphoto.com" target="new">Popular Photography and Imaging</a></dt>
    <dd>A useful and informative site with articles from the long-established
        magazine of professional and amateur photographers.</dd>
</dl>
```

4. Save your changes to the file.

5. Refresh the **tips.htm** file in your browser. Click each of the four links to external Web sites and verify that each opens in the same new browser window or tab.

6. Close the secondary browser window or tab.

Tip

To force all hypertext links in your page to open in the same target, add the target attribute to a base element located in the document's header.

You should use the target attribute sparingly in your Web site. Creating secondary windows can clutter up the user's desktop. Also, because the page is placed in a new window, users cannot use the Back button to return to the previous page in that window; they must click the browser's program button or the tab for the original Web site. This confuses some users and annoys others. Many Web designers now advocate not using the target attribute at all, leaving the choice of opening a link in a new tab or window to the user. Note that the target attribute is not supported in strict XHTML-compliant code.

Creating a Tooltip

If you want to provide additional information about a link on your Web page, you can add a tooltip to the link. A **tooltip** is descriptive text that appears when a user positions the mouse pointer over a link. Figure 2-43 shows an example of a tooltip applied to one of Gerry's links.

Figure 2-43 | **Viewing a tooltip**

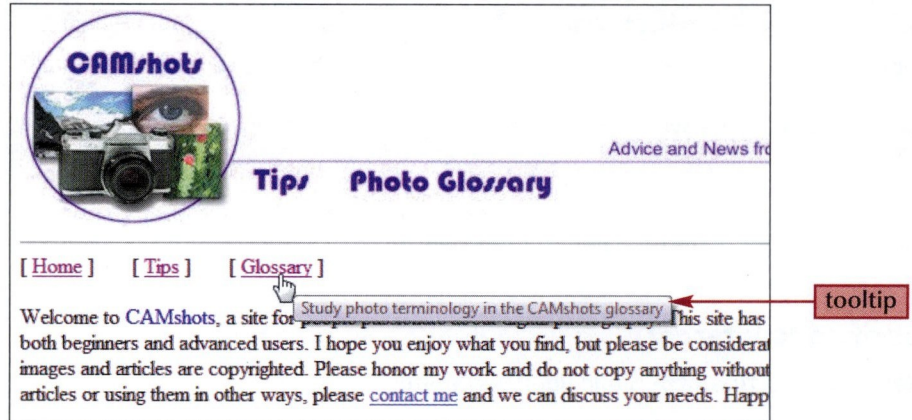

To create the tooltip, add the title attribute to the opening <a> tag in the form

```
<a href="url" title="text">content</a>
```

where *text* is the text that appears in the tooltip. To create the tooltip shown in Figure 2-43, you would enter the following HTML code:

```
<a href="glossary.htm"
   title="Study photo terminology in the CAMshots glossary">
   Glossary
</a>
```

Note that because some browsers do not support this feature, you should not place crucial information in a tooltip.

Creating a Semantic Link

The text of a hypertext link should always describe the type of document that will be called up by the link. You can also use the rel and rev attributes to add information about the link. The rel attribute describes the relation of the current document to the linked document. For example, in the link to the Glossary page, Gerry could insert the following rel attribute:

```
<a href="glossary.htm" rel="glossary">Glossary</a>
```

The rev attribute describes the reverse relationship: how the linked document views the current document. For example, if you're linking to the Glossary page from the home page, the reverse relation is "home" (because that is how the Glossary page views the home page). The HTML code would be:

```
<a href="glossary.htm" rel="glossary" rev="home">Glossary</a>
```

Links containing the rel and rev attributes are called **semantic links** because the tag contains information about the relationship between the link and its destination. This information is not designed for the user, but for the browser. A browser could display all hypertext links marked having a rel value of glossary with a special icon. The browser could also collect all of the hypertext links within the Web page and place them within a customized toolbar. Few browsers currently take advantage of these attributes, but future browsers may do so.

Although rel and rev are not limited to a fixed set of attribute values, the specifications for HTML and XHTML include a proposed list of rel and rev names. Figure 2-44 shows some of these proposed relationship values.

Figure 2-44 Link relations for the rel and rev attributes

Link Relation	Description
alternate	A substitute version of the current document, perhaps in a different language or in a different medium
appendix	An appendix
bookmark	A bookmark in a collection of documents
chapter	A document serving as a chapter in a collection of documents
contents	A table of contents
copyright	A copyright statement
glossary	A glossary
help	A help document
index	An index
next	The next document in a linear sequence of documents
prev	The previous document in a linear sequence of documents
section	A document serving as a section in a collection of documents
start	The first document in a collection of documents
top	The Web site's home page
stylesheet	An external style sheet
subsection	A document serving as a subsection in a collection of documents

At this point, Gerry decides against using the rel and rev attributes on his Web site. However, he'll keep them in mind as an option as his Web site expands in size and complexity.

Using the Link Element

Another way to add a hypertext link to your document is to add a link element to the document's head. Link elements are created using the one-sided tag

```
<link href="url" rel="text" rev="text" target="window" />
```

where the *href*, *rel*, *rev*, and *target* attributes serve the same purpose as in the <a> tag. For example, to use the link element to create semantic links to the three pages of Gerry's Web site, you could add the following link elements to the heading of each document:

```
<link rel="top" href="home.htm" />
<link rel="help" href="tips.htm" />
<link rel="glossary" href="glossary.htm" />
```

Because they are placed within a document's head, link elements do not appear as part of the Web page. Instead, if the browser supports them, link elements are displayed in a browser toolbar. Figure 2-45 shows how the three link elements described above would appear in the Opera's Navigation toolbar. If you click an entry on the toolbar, the browser loads the referenced page.

Navigation toolbar in Opera — Figure 2-45

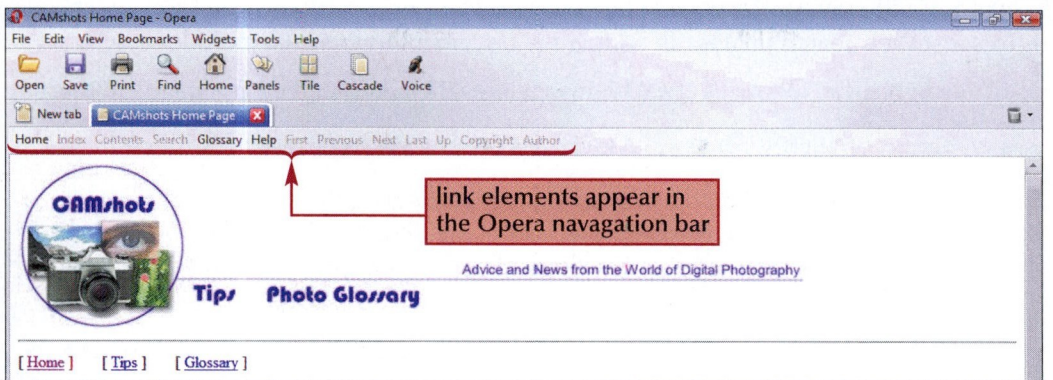

The advantage of the link element is that it places the list of links outside of the Web page, freeing up page space for other content. Also, because the links appear in a browser toolbar, they are always easily accessible to users. Currently, Opera is one of the few browsers with built-in support for the link element. Third party software exists to provide this support for Internet Explorer and Firefox. Because no single list of relationship names is widely accepted, you must check with each browser's documentation to find out what relationship names it supports. Until link elements are embraced by more browsers, you should use them only if you duplicate that information elsewhere on the page.

Working with Metadata

Gerry is happy with the work you've done on the design for his CAMshots Web site. Now he wants to start working on getting the site noticed. When someone searches for "digital photography tips" or "camera buying guide," will they find Gerry's Web site? There are thousands of photography sites on the Web. Gerry knows he needs to add a few extra touches to his home page to make it more likely that the site will be picked up by major search engines such as Yahoo! and Google.

Optimizing a Web site for search engines can be a long and involved process. For the best results, Web authors often turn to companies that specialize in making sites appear more prominently in search engines. CAMshots is a hobby site and Gerry does not want to invest any money in improving the site's visibility, but he would like to do a few simple things that would help.

Using the Meta Element

To be noticed on the Web, a site needs to include information about itself so the search engines can read it and add the site to their search indices. Information about the site is called **metadata**. You can add metadata to your Web pages by adding a meta element to the head section of the document. The syntax of the meta element is

```
<meta name="text" content="text" scheme="text" http-equiv="text" />
```

where the name attribute specifies the type of metadata, the content attribute stores the metadata value, the scheme attribute defines the metadata format, and the http-equiv attribute is used to attach metadata or commands to the communication stream between the Web server and the browser. There are three uses of the meta element:

- To store information about the document that can be read by the author, other users, or the Web server.

- To control how the browser handles the document, including forcing the browser to automatically refresh the page at timed intervals.
- To assist Web search engines in adding the document to their search index.

For example, the following meta element stores the name of the Web page's author:

```
<meta name="author" content="Gerry Hayward" />
```

For search engines, you should include metadata describing the site and the topics it covers. This is done by adding a meta element containing the site description and another meta element with a list of keywords. The following two elements would summarize the CAMshots Web site for any search engines running on the Web:

```
<meta name="description" content="CAMshots provides advice on digital
cameras and photography" />
<meta name="keywords" content="photography, cameras, digital imaging" />
```

Figure 2-46 lists some other examples of metadata that you can use to describe your document.

Figure 2-46 | Metadata

Meta Name	Example	Description
author	`<meta name="author" content="Gerry Hayward" />`	Supplies the name of the document author
classification	`<meta name="classification" content="photography" />`	Classifies the document
copyright	`<meta name="copyright" content="&copy; 2011 CAMshots" />`	Provides a copyright statement
description	`<meta name="description" content="Digital photography and advice" />`	Provides a description of the document
generator	`<meta name="generator" content="Dreamweaver" />`	Indicates the name of the program that created the HTML code for the document
keywords	`<meta name="keywords" content="photography,cameras, digital" />`	Provides a list of keywords describing the document
owner	`<meta name="owner" content="CAMshots" />`	Indicates the owner of the document
rating	`<meta name="rating" content="general" />`	Provides a rating of the document in terms of its suitability for minors
reply-to	`<meta name="reply-to" content="ghayward@camshots.com (G. Hayward)" />`	Supplies a contact e-mail address and name for the document

In recent years, search engines have become more sophisticated in evaluating Web sites. In the process, the meta element has decreased in importance. However, it is still used by search engines when adding a site to their indexes. Because adding metadata requires very little effort, you should still include meta elements in your Web documents.

Working with Metadata | Reference Window

- To document the contents of your Web page, use the meta element

   `<meta name="text" content="text" />`

   where the name attribute specifies the type of metadata and the content attribute stores the metadata value.
- To add metadata or a command to the communication stream between the Web server and Web browser, use

   `<meta http-equiv="text" content="text" />`

   where the http-equiv attribute specifies the type of data or command attached to the communication stream and the content attribute specifies the data value or command.

Having discussed metadata issues with Gerry, he asks that you include a few meta elements to describe his new site.

To add metadata to Gerry's document:

▶ 1. Return to the **home.htm** file in your text editor.

▶ 2. Directly below the opening <head> tag, insert the following meta elements, as shown in Figure 2-47:

```
<meta name="author" content="your name" />
<meta name="description" content="A site for sharing information on
         digital photography and cameras" />
<meta name="keywords" content="photography, cameras, digital
imaging" />
```

Adding meta elements to the CAMshots home page ◀ Figure 2-47

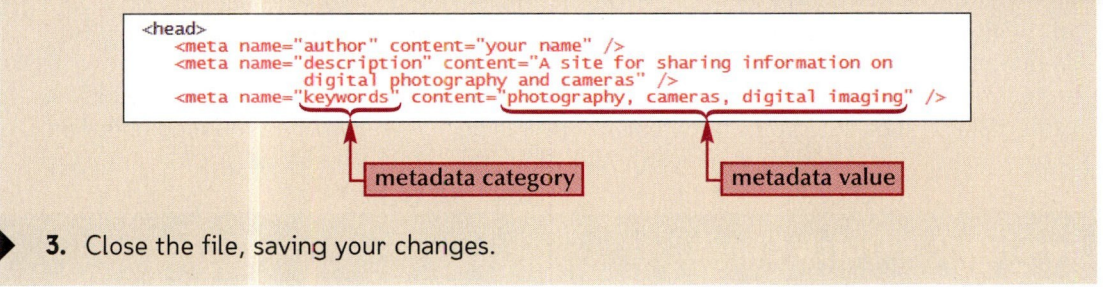

```
<head>
    <meta name="author" content="your name" />
    <meta name="description" content="A site for sharing information on
         digital photography and cameras" />
    <meta name="keywords" content="photography, cameras, digital imaging" />
```

metadata category   metadata value

▶ 3. Close the file, saving your changes.

Applying Metadata to the Communication Stream

Describing your document is not the only use of the meta element. As you learned earlier, servers transmit Web pages using a communication protocol called HTTP. You can add information and commands to this communication stream with the meta element's http-equiv attribute. One common use of the http-equiv attribute is to force the browser to refresh the Web page at timed intervals, which is useful for Web sites that publish scoreboards or stock tickers. For example, to automatically refresh the Web page every 60 seconds, you would apply the following meta element:

`<meta http-equiv="refresh" content="60" />`

Another use of the meta element is to redirect the browser from the current document to a new document. This might prove useful to Gerry someday if he changes the URL of his site's home page. As his readers get accustomed to the new Web address, he can keep the old address online, automatically redirecting readers to the new site. The meta element to perform an automatic redirect has the general form

```
<meta http-equiv="refresh" content="sec;url=url" />
```

where *sec* is the time in seconds before the browser redirects the user and *url* is the URL of the new site. To redirect users after five seconds to the Web page at *http://www. camshots.com*, you could enter the following meta element:

```
<meta http-equiv="refresh" content="5;url=www.camshots.com" />
```

Tip

When redirecting a Web site to a new URL, always include text notifying the user that the page is being redirected. This avoids confusion and provides users several seconds to read the text.

Another use of the http-equiv attribute is to specify the character set used by the document. (For a discussion of character sets, see Tutorial 1.) This is particularly useful for international documents in which the browser might need to know the character set being used to correctly interpret the document. The syntax to specify the character set for an HTML document is

```
<meta http-equiv="Content-Type" content="text/html;charset=char-set" />
```

where *char-set* is the character set used by the document. So to indicate that the browser uses the ISO-8859-1 character set, you would include the following meta element in the document's header:

```
<meta http-equiv="Content-Type" content="text/html;charset=ISO-
8859-1" />
```

With the Web expanding its international presence, many Web developers advocate always including metadata about the character set so there is no ambiguity in the interpretation of the character encoding used in the document.

At this point, Gerry does not need to use the meta element to send data or commands through the HTTP communication protocol. However, he will keep this option in mind if moves the site to a new address.

Gerry is happy with the Web site you've started. He'll continue to work on the site and will come back to you for more assistance as he adds new pages and elements. For now you can close any open files or applications used to create the site.

Review | **Session 2.3 Quick Check**

1. What are the five parts of a URL?
2. Specify the code to link the text "White House" to the URL *http://www.whitehouse. gov*, with the destination document displayed in a new unnamed browser window.
3. Specify the code to link the text "Washington" to the FTP server at *ftp.uwash.edu*.
4. Specify the code to link the text "President" to the e-mail address *president@whitehouse.gov*.
5. What attribute would you add to a hypertext link to display the popup title "Tour the White House"?
6. What attribute would you add to a link specifying that the destination is the next page in a linear sequence of documents?
7. Specify the code to add the description "United States Office of the President" as metadata to a document.
8. Specify the code to automatically refresh the document every 5 minutes.

In this tutorial you explored some of the issues involved in creating a Web site with several linked pages. The first session began with an overview of storyboarding as a tool for designing and maintaining complex Web site structures. The session then turned to creating a simple Web site involving three Web pages linked together with the <a> tag element. The second session focused on creating links to locations within documents, first examining how to mark a location by using the id attribute and the anchor element. It then covered how to create links to these locations from within the same document and from within another document. The second session concluded by examining how to use inline images and image maps to create links to several documents. The third session expanded the discussion of hypertext by showing how to create links to sites on the World Wide Web and non-Web locations, including FTP sites and e-mail addresses. The third session then examined how to set different hypertext attributes to control how the browser displays and reacts to hypertext links. The session and the tutorial concluded by discussing the uses of the meta element for conveying information to Web search engines.

Key Terms

absolute path
augmented linear structure
client-side image map
domain name
e-mail harvester
escape characters
extension
File Transfer Protocol
FTP
FTP server
hierarchical structure

home page
hotspot
HTTP
Hypertext Transfer
    Protocol
image map
linear structure
metadata
mixed structure
protected structure
protocol

relative path
semantic link
server-side image map
sibling folder
site index
spam
storyboard
tooltip
Uniform Resource Locator
URL

Practice	**Review Assignments**

Practice the skills you learned in the tutorial using the same case scenario.

Data Files needed for the Review Assignments: child1.jpg - child3.jpg, childtxt.htm, contest0.jpg - contest3.jpg, contesttxt.htm, flower1.jpg - flower3.jpg, flowertxt.htm, scenic1.jpg - scenic3.jpg, scenictxt.htm, and thumb1.jpg - thumb9.jpg

Gerry has been working on the CAMshots Web site for a while. During that time, the site has grown in popularity with amateur photographers. Gerry wants to host a monthly photo contest to highlight the work of his colleagues. Each month Gerry will pick the three best photos from different photo categories. He's asked for your help in creating the collection of Web pages highlighting the winning entries. Gerry has already created four pages. The first page contains information about the photo contest; the next three pages contain the winning entries for child photos, scenic photos, and flower photos. Although Gerry has already entered much of the page content, he needs you to work on creating the links between and within each page. Figure 2-48 shows a preview of the photo contest's home page.

Figure 2-48

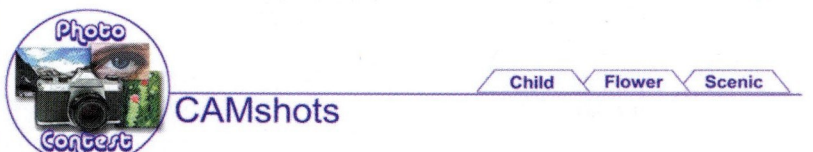

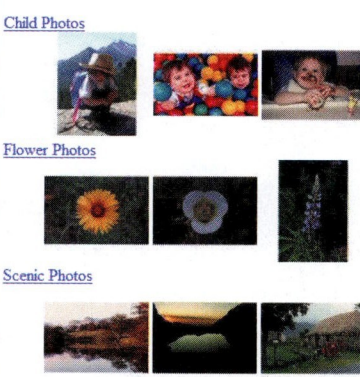

Complete the following:

1. Use your text editor to open the **contesttxt.htm**, **childtxt.htm**, **scenictxt.htm**, and **flowertxt.htm** files from the tutorial.02\review folder included with your Data Files. Enter *your name* and *the date* within each file, and then save them as **contest.htm**, **child.htm**, **scenic.htm**, and **flower.htm**, respectively, in the same folder.

2. Go to the **child.htm** file in your text editor. Locate the inline image within the first div element at the top of the file. Directly below the inline image insert an image map with the following properties:
   - Set the id and name of the image map to contestmap.
   - Add a polygonal hotspot pointing to the child.htm file containing the points (457, 84), (474, 63), (549, 63), and (566, 84). Specify "Child Photos" as the alternate text for the hotspot.
   - Add a polygonal hotspot pointing to the flower.htm file containing the points (554, 84), (571, 63), (646, 63), and (663, 84). Specify "Flower Photos" as the alternate text for the hotspot.
   - Add a polygonal hotspot pointing to the scenic.htm file containing the points (651, 84), (668, 63), (743, 63), and (760, 84). Specify "Scenic Photos" as the alternate text for the hotspot.
   - Add a circular hotspot pointing to the contest.htm file centered at the point (82, 82) and having a radius of 78 pixels. Specify "Contest Results" as the alternate text for the hotspot.

3. Apply the contestmap image map to the logo image at the top of the page. Set the width of the border to 0.

4. Locate the three h2 elements naming the three child photo winners. Assign the h2 elements the ids child1, child2, and child3, respectively.

5. Save your changes to the **child.htm** file.

6. Go to the **scenic.htm** file in your text editor. Repeat Steps 2 and 3 for the logo image at the top of the page.

7. Assign the ids scenic1, scenic2, and scenic3 to the three h2 elements located farther down in the file. Save your changes to the document.

8. Go to the **flower.htm** file in your text editor and repeat the same edits you applied to the child.htm and scenic.htm files. Assign the ids flower1 through flower3 to the three h2 headings located at the bottom of the document. Save your changes.

9. Go to the **contest.htm** file in your text editor. Repeat Steps 2 and 3 for the logo image at the top of the page.

10. Scroll to the definition list at the bottom of the file. Mark the definition term "Child Photos" as a hypertext link pointing to the child.htm file. Mark the definition term "Flower Photos" as a link to the flower.htm file. Mark the term "Scenic Photos" as a link to the scenic.htm file.

11. Following each definition term is a definition description containing three thumbnail images of the winning photos. Mark the nine thumbnail images as hypertext links pointing to the larger images (contained in the child.htm, flower.htm, and scenic.htm files). For example, mark the first child photo (thumb1.jpg) as a hypertext link pointing to the h2 element with the id child1 in the child.htm file. Set the border width of each of the nine thumbnail images to 0.

12. Scroll up and locate the fourth paragraph. Mark the text "Gerry Hayward" as a hypertext link to an e-mail message sent to *ghayward@camshots.com* with the subject line "Photo Contest."

13. Go to the sixth paragraph and mark the text "BetterPhoto.com" as a hypertext link pointing to the URL *http://www.betterphoto.com*. Set the attribute of the link so that it opens in a new browser window or tab.

14. Save your changes to the **contest.htm** file.

15. Open **contest.htm** in your Web browser. Verify that the e-mail link opens a new mail message window with the subject line "Photo Contest." Verify that the link to BetterPhoto.com opens that Web site in a new browser window or tab. Verify that the three links to the photo pages are connected to the child.htm, scenic.htm, and flower.htm files. Finally, click each of the nine thumbnail images at the bottom of the page and verify that they connect to the larger image of the photo.

16. Open **child.htm** in your Web browser. Verify that the Scenic Photos link at the top of the page is connected to the scenic.htm file. Navigate forward and backward through the three photo pages by clicking the links at the top of each page. Verify that on each page you can return to the contest page by clicking the contest logo.

17. Submit your completed files to your instructor.

| Apply | **Case Problem 1** |

Apply your knowledge of hypertext links to create a directory of universities and colleges.

Data Files needed for this Case Problem: colleges.txt, highered.jpg, and uwlisttxt.htm

HigherEd   Adella Coronel is a guidance counselor for Eagle High School in Waunakee, Wisconsin. She wants to take her interest in helping students choose colleges to the Web by starting a Web site called *HigherEd*. She's come to you for help in creating the site. The first page she wants to create is a simple directory of Wisconsin colleges and universities. She's created the list of schools, but has not yet marked the entries in the list as hypertext links. Also, the list is very long, so she has broken it down into three categories: private colleges and universities, technical colleges, and public universities. Because of the length of the page, she wants to include hypertext links that allow students to jump down to a specific college category. Figure 2-49 shows a preview of the page you'll create for Adella.

Figure 2-49

Higher ◆ Ed

The Directory of Higher Education Opportunities

Wisconsin Colleges and Universities

[Private Colleges and Universities]   [Technical College System]   [University of Wisconsin System]

Private Colleges and Universities

Alverno College
Beloit College
Cardinal Stritch University
Carroll College
Concordia University Wisconsin
Edgewood College
Lakeland College
Lawrence University
Marian College
Medical College of Wisconsin
Milwaukee Institute of Art and Design
Milwaukee School of Engineering

Complete the following:

1. In your text editor, open the **uwlisttxt.htm** file from the tutorial.02\case1 folder included with your Data Files. Enter *your name* and *the date* in the comment section of the file. Save the file as **uwlist.htm** in the same folder.

2. Mark each of the school entries on the page as a hypertext link. Use the URLs provided in the colleges.txt file. (Hint: Use the copy and paste feature of your text editor to efficiently copy and paste the URL text.)

⊕ EXPLORE

3. Adella wants the links to the school Web sites to appear in a new tab or window. Because there are so many links on the page, add a base element to the document header specifying that all links will open by default in a new browser window or tab named "collegeWin."

4. Add the id names "private," "technical," and "public" to the three h2 headings that categorize the list of schools.

5. Create hyperlinks from the entries in the category list at the top of the page to the three headings.

⊕ EXPLORE

6. For each of the hypertext links you marked in Step 5, set the link to open in the current browser window and not in a new browser window or tab.

7. Save your changes to the file.

8. Open **uwlist.htm** in your Web browser and verify that the school links all open in the same browser window or tab and that the links within the document to the different school categories bring the user to those locations on the page but not in a new window tab.

9. Submit your completed files to your instructor.

Apply	**| Case Problem 2**

Apply your knowledge of HTML to create a slide show Web site.

Data Files needed for this Case Problem: back.jpg, end.jpg, fiddler.jpg, forward.jpg, home.jpg, hometxt.htm, slide1.jpg - slide6.jpg, slide1txt.htm - slide6txt.htm, start.jpg, and thumb1.jpg - thumb6.jpg

Lakewood School Tasha Juroszek is a forensics teacher at Lakewood School, a small private school in Moultrie, Georgia. Tasha has just finished directing her students in *Fiddler on the Roof Jr.* and wants to place a slide show of the performances on the Web. She has already designed the layout and content of the pages, but needs help to finish the slide show. She has asked you to add hypertext links between the slide pages and the site's home page. Figure 2-50 shows a preview of one of the slide pages on the Web site.

Figure 2-50

Matchmaker (L:R) Karen Unger, Rachel Paulson, Lucy Davis, Judy French, Catherine Lewis

Complete the following:

1. Use your text editor to open the **hometxt.htm**, and **slide1txt.htm** through **slide6txt.htm** files from the tutorial.02\case2 folder included with your Data Files. Enter *your name* and *the date* in the comment section of each file. Save the files as **home.htm** and **slide1.htm** through **slide6.htm,** respectively.

2. Return to the **slide1.htm** file in your text editor. At the top of the page are five buttons used to navigate through the slide show. Locate the inline image for the home button (home.jpg) and mark it as a hypertext link pointing to the home.htm file.

3. There are six slides in Tasha's slide show. Mark the start button as a hypertext link pointing to the slide1.htm file. Mark the end button as a link to the slide6.htm file. Link the back button to slide1.htm, the first slide in the show. Link the forward button to the slide2.htm file.

4. Directly below the slide show buttons are thumbnail images of the six slides. Link each thumbnail image to its slide page.

5. Set the border width of each linked image to 0, *except* the thumbnail image for slide1. Set the border width of that thumbnail to 5.

6. Save your changes to the file.

EXPLORE

7. Repeat Steps 2 through 6 for the five remaining slide pages. Within each page, set the navigation buttons to go back and forth through the slide show. For the slide6.htm file, the forward button should point to the slide6.htm file since it is the last slide in the show. The border width of each linked image should be set to 0 *except* the border width of the current slide, which should be set to 5.

8. Go to the **home.htm** file in your text editor. Go to the second paragraph and mark the text "slide show" as a hypertext link pointing to the slide1.htm file.

EXPLORE

9. Go to the end of the second paragraph and mark the phrase "contact me" as a hypertext link pointing to the following e-mail message:
   TO: tashajur@lakewood.edu
   SUBJECT: Photo CD
   BODY: Please send me a copy of the photos.

10. Save your changes to the file.

11. Load the **home.htm** file in your Web browser. Test the links in the Web site and verify that they work correctly.

12. Submit your completed files to your instructor.

Challenge	**Case Problem 3**

Broaden your knowledge of HTML by exploring how to use anchors and pop-up titles in a Web site for a health club.

Data Files needed for this Case Problem: classtxt.htm, diamond.jpg, hometxt.htm, indextxt.htm, and memtxt.htm

Diamond Health Club, Inc. You work for Diamond Health Club, a health club in Boise, Idaho that has been serving active families for 25 years. The director, Karen Padilla, has asked you to help work on their Web site. The site contains three pages: the home page describing the club, a page listing classes offered, and a page describing the various membership options. You need to add links within the main page and add other links connecting the pages. Because this Web site will need to support older browsers, you will have to use the anchor tag to mark specific locations in the three documents. Karen would also like you to create pop-up titles for some of the links in the site to supply additional information about the links to the users.

Finally, this new site will replace the old company Web site. Karen wants to keep the old Web site address and redirect users automatically to the new home page. She wants you to insert the code required to do this.

Figure 2-51 shows a preview of the completed home page.

Figure 2-51

Complete the following:

1. Use your text editor to open the **hometxt.htm**, **indextxt.htm**, **classtxt.htm**, and **memtxt.htm** files from the tutorial.02\case3 folder included with your Data Files. Enter *your name* and *the date* in the comment section of each file. Save the files as **home.htm**, **index.htm**, **classes.htm**, and **members.htm** respectively.

⊕EXPLORE

2. Go to the **index.htm** file. Use the <a> tag to add the anchor names fac, hours, and staff to the h3 headings "Facilities," "Hours," and "For More Information, E-mail our Staff."

⊕EXPLORE

3. Scroll up to the top of the file. Below the logo image at the top of the page, add an image map with the following properties:
   - Give the image map a name and id of diamondmap.
   - Create a rectangular hotspot with the coordinates (225, 7) and (333, 40). Point the hotspot to the classes.htm file with the alternate text "Classes." Add the tooltip "View our classes."

- Create a rectangular hotspot with the coordinates (258, 44) and (437, 82). Point the hotspot to the members.htm file with the alternate text "Memberships." Add the tooltip "View our membership options."
- Create a default hotspot for the inline image. (*Hint:* the image is 548 pixels wide and 150 pixels tall.) Point the default hotspot to the index.htm file with the alternate text "Home Page." Add the tooltip "Return to the Home Page."

4. Apply the diamondmap hotspot to the logo image. Remove the border around the inline image.

5. In the list at the top of the page, mark "Facilities" as a link pointing to the fac anchor within the index.htm document. Mark "Staff" as a link pointing to the staff anchor within the index.htm file. Mark "Hours" as a link pointing to the hours anchor within the index.htm file.

⊕ EXPLORE

6. Add the tooltip "Learn more about our facilities" to the Facilities link. Add the tooltip "Meet the DHC staff" to the Staff link. Add the tooltip "View the DHC hours of operation" to the Hours link.

7. Go to the staff list at the bottom of the page. Format each name as a link that points to the individual's e-mail address. The e-mail addresses are:

Ty Stoven: tstoven@dmond-health.com

Yosef Dolen: ydolen@dmond-health.com

Sue Myafin: smyafin@dmond-health.com

James Michel: jmichel@dmond-health.com

Ron Chi: rchi@dmond-health.com

Marcia Lopez: mlopez@dmond-health.com

8. Save your changes to the file.

9. Go to the **members.htm** file in your text editor and repeat Steps 3 through 6.

10. Use the <a> tag to add anchors named "ind" to the "Individual memberships" h3 heading, "fam" to the "Family memberships" h3 heading, and "temp" to the "Temporary memberships" h3 heading.

11. Format the phrase "e-mail Ron Chi" in the first paragraph as a link pointing to Ron Chi's e-mail address. Save your changes to the file.

12. Go to the **classes.htm** file in your text editor and repeat Steps 3 through 6 for the entries at the top of that page.

13. Use the <a> tag to add the following anchors to h3 headings in the file: "senior" for "Senior Classes," "adult" for "Adult Classes," "teen" for "Teen Classes," and "child" for "Children's Classes."

14. Format the phrase "e-mail Marcia Lopez" in the first paragraph as a link pointing to Marcia Lopez's e-mail address. Save your changes to the file.

15. Return to the **index.htm** file in your text editor. Within the first paragraph, link the word "children" to the child anchor in the classes.htm file. Link the word "teens" to the teen anchor in the classes.htm file. Link the word "adults" to the adult anchor in classes.htm. Finally, link "seniors" to the senior anchor in classes.htm.

16. Within the second paragraph of index.htm, link the word "individual" to the ind anchor in the members.htm file. Link the word "family" to the fam anchor in members.htm. Finally, link the first occurrence of the word "temporary" to the temp anchor in members.htm.

17. Go to the head section of the document and add the following metadata directly below the opening <head> tag:
    - The description: "The Diamond Health Club is your year-round source for fun family health."
    - The keywords: health club, exercise, family, seattle
18. Save your changes to the file.

EXPLORE

19. Go to the **home.htm** file in your text editor. Within the head section, insert a meta element to redirect the browser to the index.htm file after a 5 second delay.
20. Mark the phrase "this link to our new Web site" as a hypertext link pointing to the index.htm file. Save your changes to the file.
21. Open the **home.htm** file in your Web browser. Verify that the browser loads the index.htm file after a 5 second delay.
22. Once the index.htm file is loaded, verify that all of your links work correctly, including the links that point to sections within documents and the links within the image map. Verify that tooltips appear as you move your mouse pointer over the links at the top of each page. (Note: Internet Explorer does not currently support tooltips found within image map hotspots.)
23. Submit your completed files to your instructor.

| Create | **Case Problem 4** |

Test your knowledge of HTML and use your creativity to design a Web site documenting a Shakespeare play.

Data Files needed for this Case Problem: characters.txt, notes.txt, tempest.jpg, and tempest.txt

Mansfield Classical Theatre   Steve Karls continues to work as the director of Mansfield Classical Theatre in Mansfield, Ohio. The next production he plans to direct is *The Tempest*. Steve wants to put the text of this play on the Web, but he also wants to augment the dialog of the play with notes and commentary. However, he doesn't want his commentary to get in the way of a straight-through reading of the text, so he has hit on the idea of linking his commentary to key phrases in the dialog. Steve has created text files containing an excerpt from *The Tempest* as well as his commentary and other supporting documents. He would like you to take his raw material and create a collection of linked pages.

Complete the following:

1. Create HTML files named **tempest.htm**, **commentary.htm**, and **cast.htm** and save them in the tutorial.02\case4 folder included with your Data Files. Add comment tags to the head section of each document containing *your name* and *the date*. Add an appropriate page title to each document.
2. Using the contents of the tempest.txt, notes.txt, and characters.txt text files, create the body of the three Web pages in Steve's Web site. The design of these pages is left to your imagination and skill. Make the pages easy to read and visually interesting. You can supplement the material on the page with appropriate material you find on your own.
3. Use the **tempest.jpg** file as a logo for the page. Create an image map from the logo pointing to the tempest.htm, commentary.htm, and cast.htm files. The three rectangular boxes on the logo have the following coordinates for their upper-left and lower-right corners:
   - The Play: (228, 139) (345, 173)
   - Commentary: (359, 139) (508, 173)
   - The Cast: (520, 139) (638, 173)
   Use this image map in all three of the Web pages from this Web site.

4. Create links between the dialog on the play page and the notes on the commentary page. The notes contain line numbers to aid you in linking each line of dialog to the appropriate note.

5. Create a link between the first appearances of each character's name from the tempest.htm page with the character's description on the cast.htm page.

6. Include a link to Steve Karl's e-mail address on the tempest.htm page. Steve's e-mail address is *stevekarls@mansfieldct.com*. E-mail sent to Steve's account from this Web page should have the subject line "Comments on the Tempest."

7. Add appropriate meta elements to each of the three pages documenting the page's contents and purpose.

8. Search the Web for sites that would provide additional material about the play. Add links to these pages on the tempest.htm page. The links should open in a new browser window or tab.

9. Submit your completed files to your instructor.

Review | **Quick Check Answers**

Session 2.1

1. Storyboarding is the process of diagramming a series of related Web pages, taking care to identify all links among the various pages. Storyboarding is an important tool in creating Web sites that are easy to navigate and understand.

2. A linear structure is one in which Web pages are linked from one to another in a direct chain. Users can go to the previous page or the next page in the chain, but not to a page in a different section of the chain. A hierarchical structure is one in which Web pages are linked from general to specific topics. Users can move up and down the hierarchy tree.

3. `<a href="sports.htm">Sports Info</a>`

4. An absolute path indicates the location of the file based on its placement in the computer. A relative path indicates the location of the file relative to the location of the current document.

5. glossary.htm
   ../tips/tips1.htm
   ../tips/tips2.htm
   ../../index.htm

6. The base element specifies the default location that the browser should use to resolve all relative paths.

Session 2.2

1. `<h2 id="faq">CAMshots FAQ</h2>`

2. `<a href="#faq">Read our FAQ</a>`

3. `<a href="help.htm#faq">Read our FAQ</a>`

4. `<h2><a name="faq">CAMshots FAQ</a></h2>`

5. Anchors are supported by older browsers. Some older browsers do not support using the id attribute to mark a location in a document. However, use of anchor tags has been deprecated, so it is not supported in strict applications of XHTML. Also, because it is deprecated, use of the anchor tag may be phased out in future browser releases.

6. ```
<map name="CAMmap" id="CAMmap">
    <area shape="circle" coords="50, 75, 40" href="faq.htm" />
</map>
```

7. `<img src="logo.jpg" alt="CAMshots" usemap="#CAMmap"/>`

8. `style="border-width: 0"`

## Session 2.3

1. The protocol, the hostname, the folder name, the filename, and the anchor name or id.

2. `<a href="http://www.whitehouse.gov target="_blank">White House</a>`

3. `<a href="ftp://ftp.uwash.edu">Washington</a>`

4. `<a href="mailto:president@whitehouse.gov">President</a>`

5. `title="Tour the White House"`

6. `rel="next"`

7. `<meta name="description" content=" United States Office of the President" />`

8. `<meta http-equiv="refresh" content="300" />`

## Ending Data Files

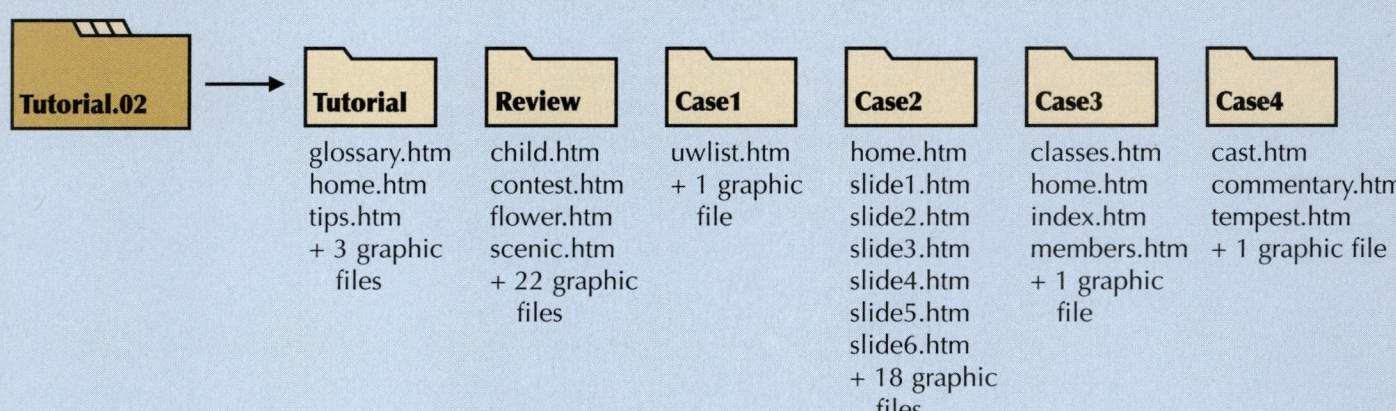

**Tutorial.02** →

**Tutorial**
glossary.htm
home.htm
tips.htm
+ 3 graphic
files

**Review**
child.htm
contest.htm
flower.htm
scenic.htm
+ 22 graphic
files

**Case1**
uwlist.htm
+ 1 graphic
file

**Case2**
home.htm
slide1.htm
slide2.htm
slide3.htm
slide4.htm
slide5.htm
slide6.htm
+ 18 graphic
files

**Case3**
classes.htm
home.htm
index.htm
members.htm
+ 1 graphic
file

**Case4**
cast.htm
commentary.htm
tempest.htm
+ 1 graphic file
```

Reality Check

The Web has become an important medium for advertising products and one's self. By making your resume available online, you can quickly get prospective employers information they need to make a hiring decision. There are many sites that will assist you in writing and posting your resume. They will also, for a fee, present your online resume to employers in your chosen field. Assuming you don't want to pay to use such a site, you can also create your own Web site containing your employment history and talents. In this exercise, you'll use the skills and tasks you learned in Tutorials 1 and 2 to design your own Web site and create an online resume.

1. Collect material on yourself that would be useful in an online resume. You should include material for a page on your employment history, talents and special interests, a general biography, and a summary of the main points of your resume.

2. Create a storyboard outlining the pages on your Web site. Clearly indicate the links between the pages. Make sure that your site is easy to navigate no matter which page the user starts on.

3. Collect or create graphical image files to make your site interesting to the viewer. If you obtain graphics from the Web, be sure to follow all copyright restrictions on the material.

4. Start designing your site's home page. It should include an interesting and helpful logo. The home page should be brief and to the point, summarizing the main features of your resume. Its height should not be greater than two screens.

5. Add other pages containing more detailed information. Each page should have a basic theme and topic. The pages should follow a unified theme and design.

6. Use boldface fonts and italics to highlight important ideas. Do not overuse these page elements; doing so can distract from your page's readability rather than enhancing it.

7. Use numbered and bulleted lists to list the main points in your resume.

8. Use block quotes to highlight recommendations from colleagues and former employers.

9. Use horizontal rules to divide longer pages into topical sections.

10. If there are sites on the Web that would be relevant to your online resume (such as the Web sites of former or current employers), include links to those sites.

11. Include a link to your e-mail address. Write the e-mail address link so that it automatically adds an appropriate subject line to the e-mail message.

12. Save your completed Web site and present it to your instructor.

Working with Cascading Style Sheets

Designing a Web Site

Case | Sunny Acres

Tammy Nielsen and her husband Brent live and work at Sunny Acres, a 200-acre farm near Council Bluffs, Iowa. Over the past 25 years, the Nielsen family has expanded the farm's operations to include a farm shop, which sells fresh produce, baked goods, jams and jellies, and gifts; a pick-your-own garden, which operates from May through October and offers great produce at discounted prices; a petting barn, with over 100 animals and the opportunity to bottle-feed the baby animals; a corn maze, with over 4 miles of twisting trails through harvested corn fields; and a Halloween Festival featuring the corn maze haunted with dozens of spooks and tricks. The farm also hosts special holiday events during the winter.

Tammy created a Web site for Sunny Acres several years ago to make information about the farm easily accessible to her current customers. The Web site has become outdated, so Tammy would like to enliven it with a new design. She also wants to catch the attention of new customers via the Web. She has several pictures she wants to use on the Web site and has ideas for the look and feel of each Web page. Tammy's knowledge of HTML and Web styles is limited, so she's come to you for help in creating a new look for the Sunny Acres Web site.

Starting Data Files

Tutorial.03 →

Tutorial
farmtxt.css
haunttxt.htm
hometxt.htm
indextxt.htm
mazetxt.htm
pettingtxt.htm
producetxt.htm
+ 9 graphic files

Demo
demo_color_names.htm
demo_css.htm
demo_safety_palette.htm
+ 3 graphic files

Review
holidaytxt.htm
sunnytxt.css
+ 3 graphic files

Case1
algo.htm
crypttxt.htm
enigma.htm
history.htm
public.htm
single.htm
+ 5 graphic files

Case2
bmtourtxt.htm
wheelstxt.css
+ 4 graphic files

Case3
centertxt.css
kingtxt.htm
+ 7 graphic files

Case4
casttxt.htm
hebtxt.htm
hightxt.htm
lakestxt.htm
+ 6 graphic files

Session 3.1

Introducing CSS

You and Tammy have recently discussed the work she wants done on the new Web site. She's already entered the content for six pages of the Web site. The six pages are:

- index.htm—the page that users see when first accessing the site, currently blank
- home.htm—the home page, describing the operations and events sponsored by the farm
- maze.htm—a page describing the farm's corn maze
- haunted.htm—a page describing the farm's annual Halloween Festival and haunted maze
- petting.htm—a page describing the farm's petting barn
- produce.htm—a page describing the Sunny Acres farm shop and the pick-your-own produce garden

  Figure 3-1 shows the links among these sites in the Sunny Acres storyboard. Open these files now in your text editor and browser.

Figure 3-1 ▶ **Storyboard of the Sunny Acres Web site**

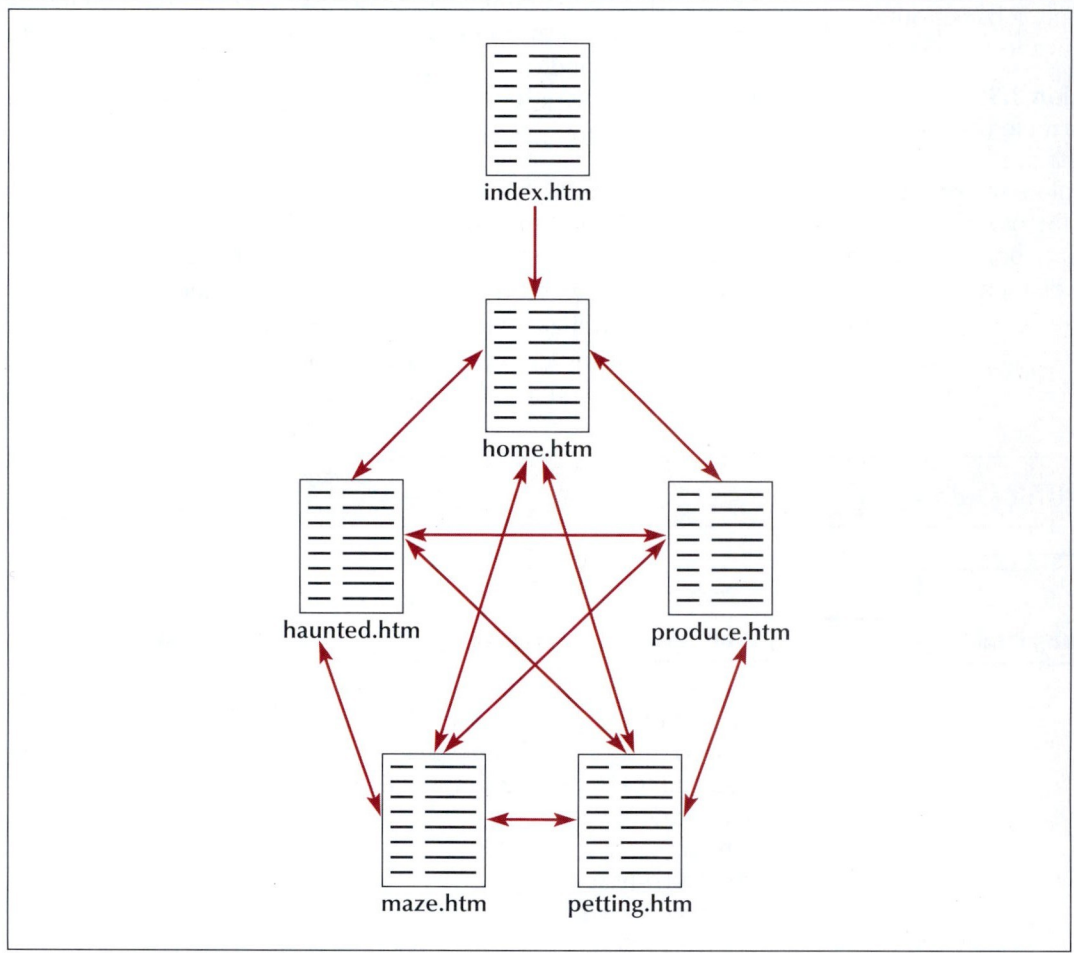

To view the Sunny Acres Web pages:

1. Use your text editor to open the **haunttxt.htm**, **hometxt.htm**, **indextxt.htm**, **mazetxt.htm**, **pettingtxt.htm**, and **producetxt.htm** files, located in the tutorial.03\tutorial folder included with your Data Files. Within each file, go to the comment section at top of the file and add *your name* and *the date* in the space provided. Save the files as **haunted.htm**, **home.htm**, **index.htm**, **maze.htm**, **petting.htm**, and **produce.htm**, respectively, in the same folder.

2. Take some time to review the HTML code within each document so that you understand the structure and content of the files.

3. Open the **home.htm** file in your Web browser, and then click the links at the top of the page to view the current appearance of the haunted.htm, maze.htm, petting.htm, and produce.htm files. Figure 3-2 shows the current layout and appearance of the Sunny Acres home page. Note that currently the index.htm file does not have any page content. You'll add that later in this tutorial.

Initial Sunny Acres home page ◄ **Figure 3-2**

Sunny Acres

Tammy and Brent Nielsen
1973 Hwy G
Council Bluffs, IA 51503

Home The Corn Maze The Haunted Maze Petting Barn Produce

Welcome

Welcome to the home page of our family farm, Sunny Acres, where there's always something happening. With the coming of fall, we're gearing up for our big AutumnFest and Farm Show. If you haven't visited our famous Corn Maze, be sure to do so before it gets torn down on November 5. This year's maze is bigger and better than ever.

Farms can be educational and Sunny Acres is no exception. Schools and home-schooling parents, take an afternoon with us at our Petting Barn. We have over 100 friendly farm animals in a clean environment. Kids can bottle feed the baby goats, lambs, and calves while they learn about nature and the farming life. Please call ahead for large school groups.

When the sun goes down this time of year, we're all looking for a good fright. Sunny Acres provides that too with another year of the Haunted Maze. Please plan on joining us during weekends in October or on Halloween for our big Halloween Festival.

Of course, Sunny Acres is above all, a *farm*. Our Farm Shop is always open with reasonable prices and great produce. Save even more money by picking your own fruits and vegetables from our orchards and gardens.

We all hope to see you soon, down on the farm.

— Tammy & Brent Nielsen

Hours

- Farm Shop: 9 am - 5 pm Mon - Fri; 9 am - 3 pm Sat
- The Corn Maze: 11 am - 9 pm Sat; 11 am - 5 pm Sun
- The Haunted Maze: 5 pm - 9 pm Fri & Sat
- Petting Barn: 9 am - 4 pm (Mon - Fri); 11 am - 3pm (Sat & Sun)

Directions

- From Council Bluffs, proceed east on I-80
- Take Exit 38 North to the Drake Frontage Road
- Turn right on Highway G
- Proceed east for 2.5 miles
- Sunny Acres is on your left&watch for the green sign

Sunny Acres ☀ *Tammy & Brent Nielsen* ☀ *1977 Highway G* ☀ *Council Bluffs, IA 51503*

The home page has all of the content that Tammy needs, but its design needs work. In Figure 3-3 she sketches how she would like the home page to appear.

Figure 3-3 ▶ **Proposed design for the Sunny Acres home page**

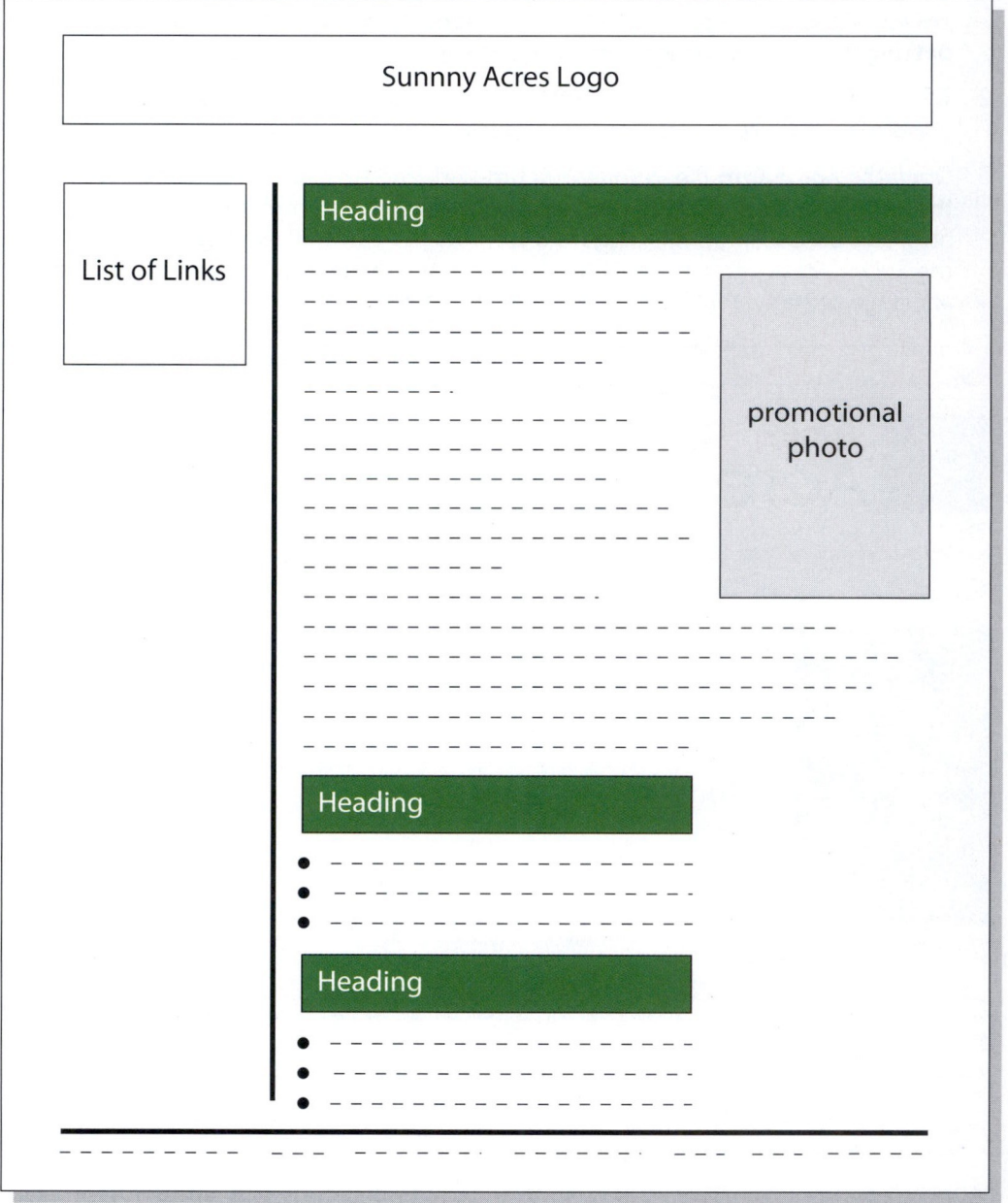

To apply this design not just to the Sunny Acres home page but also to the other pages on the Sunny Acres Web site, you'll create a page design using style sheets.

The History of CSS

A **style sheet** is a set of declarations describing the layout and appearance of a document. As you learned in Tutorial 1, HTML specifies a document's content and structure but not necessarily its appearance. To create a document design, you have to work in a different language. Several style sheet languages exist, but the most commonly used on the Web by far is the **Cascading Style Sheets** language, also known as **CSS**. You've actually been using CSS since Tutorial 1, when you used the style attribute. While the style attribute is part of the specifications for HTML and XHTML, the text of the attribute value is written in the CSS language.

Like HTML and XHTML, the specifications for CSS are maintained by the World Wide Web Consortium (W3C); and like those languages, several versions of CSS exist with varying levels of browser support. The first version of CSS, called **CSS1**, was introduced in 1996, but it was not fully implemented by any browser for another three years. CSS1 introduced styles for the following document features:

- *Fonts*: Setting font size, type, and other properties
- *Text*: Controlling text alignment and applying decorative elements such as underlining, italics, and capitalization
- *Color*: Specifying background and foreground colors of various page elements
- *Backgrounds*: Setting the background image for an element
- *Block-level elements*: Setting the margins, internal space, and borders of block-level elements

The second version of CSS, **CSS2**, was introduced in 1998. It expanded the language to support styles for:

- *Positioning*: Placing elements at specific locations on the page
- *Visual formatting*: Clipping and hiding element content
- *Media types*: Creating styles for various output devices, including printed media and aural devices
- *Interfaces*: Controlling the appearance and behavior of browser features such as scroll bars and mouse cursors

An update to CSS2, **CSS 2.1,** was introduced by the W3C in April 2002. Although the update did not add any new features to the language, it cleaned up minor errors that were introduced in the original specification. Even as browsers are implementing all of the features of CSS2, the W3C has pressed forward to the next version, **CSS3**. Still in development as of this writing, CSS3 will add styles for:

- *User interfaces*: Adding dynamic and interactive features
- *Accessibility*: Supporting users with disabilities and other special needs
- *Columnar layout*: Giving Web authors more page layout options
- *International features*: Providing support for a wide variety of languages and typefaces
- *Mobile devices*: Supporting the device requirements of PDAs and cell phones
- *Scalable vector graphics*: Making it easier for Web authors to add graphic elements to their Web pages

CSS3 will break up all of the style sheet specifications into individual modules. This approach should make it easier for developers of Web browsers to create products that support only those parts of CSS that are relevant to their products. For example, an aural browser might not need to support the CSS styles associated with printed media, so the browser's developers would need to concentrate only on the CSS3 modules that deal with aural properties. This CSS revision promises to make browser development easier; and the resulting browser products will therefore be more efficient and compact.

As with HTML, the usefulness of style sheets depends on the support of the browser community. Currently, CSS 2.1 enjoys good browser support—though there are some important differences between the major browsers that you'll explore later in this tutorial. As always, a Web page designer needs to be aware of compatibility issues that arise not just among different versions of CSS, but also among different versions of the same browser.

Applying a Style Sheet

You can apply styles to a Web site in three ways: with inline styles, with an embedded style sheet, and with an external style sheet. Each approach has its own advantages and disadvantages; you'll probably use some combination of all three in developing your Web sites. Tammy suggests that you explore each approach.

Using Inline Styles

An **inline style** is a style that is applied directly to an element through the use of the following style attribute

```
style = "style1: value1; style2: value2; style3: value3; ..."
```

where *style1*, *style2*, *style3*, and so forth are the names of the style properties, and *value1*, *value2*, *value3*, and so on are the values associated with each style property. So to center an h1 heading and display it in a red font, add the following inline style to the opening <h1> tag:

```
<h1 style="text-align: center; color: red">Sunny Acres</h1>
```

Inline styles are easy to interpret because they are applied directly to the elements they affect. However, this also makes them cumbersome. For example, if you wanted to use inline styles to make all of your headings the same font color, you would have to locate all of the h1 through h6 elements on the Web site and apply the same color style to them. This would be no small task on a large Web site containing hundreds of headings spread out among dozens of Web pages.

In addition, some developers point out that inline styles aren't consistent with the goal of separating content from style. After all, there is arguably little difference between using the inline style

```
<h1 style="text-align: center"> ... </h1>
```

and the deprecated align attribute

```
<h1 align="right"> ... </h1>
```

One goal of style sheets is to separate the development of a document's style from the development of its content. Ideally, the HTML code and CSS styles should be separate so that one person could work on content using HTML and another on design using CSS. This isn't possible with inline styles.

Using an Embedded Style Sheet

The power of style sheets becomes evident when you move style definitions away from document content. One way of doing this is to collect all of the styles used in the document in an **embedded style sheet** that is placed in the head section of the document. Embedded style sheets are created using the style element

```
<style type="text/css">
   style declarations
</style>
```

where *style declarations* are the declarations of the various styles to be applied to elements in the current document. Each style declaration has the syntax

```
selector {style1: value1; style2: value2; style3: value3; ...}
```

where *selector* identifies an element or elements within the document and the *style*: *value* pairs follow the same syntax that you've been using with inline styles. So to display all of the h1 headings in the documents in centered red text, add the following embedded style to the document head:

```
<style type="text/css">
   h1 {text-align: center; color: red}
</style>
```

You can apply the same style to several elements by entering the elements in a comma-separated list before the list of style properties. The following embedded style applies the centered-red font style to all of the h1 and h2 headings in the current document:

```
<style type="text/css">
   h1, h2 {text-align: center; color: red}
</style>
```

To see how to create and apply an embedded style, add one now to the home.htm file, setting the font color of all h2 and h3 headings in the document to green.

To apply an embedded style to Tammy's home page:

▶ **1.** Return to the **home.htm** file in your text editor.

▶ **2.** Directly above the closing </head> tag, insert the following embedded style, as shown in Figure 3-4:

```
<style type="text/css">
   h2, h3 {color: green}
</style>
```

Creating an embedded style sheet ◀ Figure 3-4

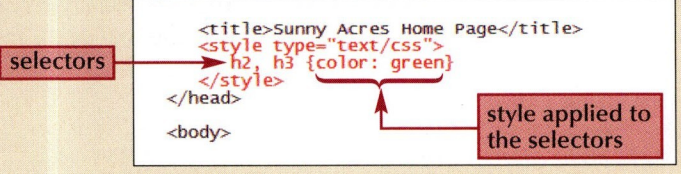

```
<title>Sunny Acres Home Page</title>
<style type="text/css">
h2, h3 {color: green}
</style>
</head>

<body>
```

selectors

style applied to the selectors

▶ **3.** Save your changes to the file and refresh the **home.htm** file in your Web browser. The Welcome heading (an h2 element) and the Hours and Directions headings (both h3 elements) should now be displayed in a green font.

Styles from an embedded style sheet are applied to each of the elements listed in the style declaration—unless one of those elements has an inline style. In the case of conflicts, an inline style takes precedence over an embedded style sheet.

Using an External Style Sheet

Note that an embedded style sheet is limited to the page elements of the current document. If you wanted to use embedded styles to apply a style to an entire Web site, you would have to repeat the styles in the head section of each document. For a large Web site with many documents, this would be a cumbersome and error-prone process. Instead, you can place the style declarations in an external style sheet. An **external style sheet** is a text file that contains style declarations. The file can then be linked to any or all pages on the Web site, allowing the same styles to be applied to the entire site. The file-name extension indicates the language of the style sheet. The extension for CSS style sheets is .css. An external style sheet looks like a list of embedded styles, except that the style declarations are not enclosed within opening and closing <style> tags. The following style declaration in an external style sheet

```
h1 {text-align: center; color: red}
```

would cause all Web pages linked to that style sheet to have their h1 headings displayed in centered red text. The great advantage of external style sheets is that you can create and change the style for an entire Web site by modifying one style sheet rather than editing the code of dozens of Web pages.

Adding Style Comments

Tip

Style comments can also be added to embedded style sheets as long as they are placed between the opening and closing <style> tags.

Style sheets can be as long and complicated as HTML files. To help others interpret your style sheet code, you should document the content and purpose of the style sheet using style sheet comments. The syntax to add a style sheet comment is

```
/* comment */
```

where *comment* is the text of the comment. CSS ignores the presence of whitespace, so as with HTML code, you can place style comments and style text on several lines to make your document easier to read. For example, the following style comment extends over four lines in the style sheet:

```
/*
    Sunny Acres
    Style Sheet
*/
```

Tammy would like you to use an external style sheet for the design of her Sunny Acres Web site. She has provided a text file with the main structure of a style sheet already entered. She'd like you to start by adding a style to center the text of all the address elements.

To create an external style sheet:

1. Use your text editor to open the **farmtxt.css** file from the tutorial.03\tutorial folder included with your Data Files. Enter **your name** and **the date** in the comment section at the top of the file.

2. Below the comment section, insert the following style declaration. Figure 3-5 shows the completed style sheet.

   ```
   address {text-align: center}
   ```

Creating an external style sheet ◀ Figure 3-5

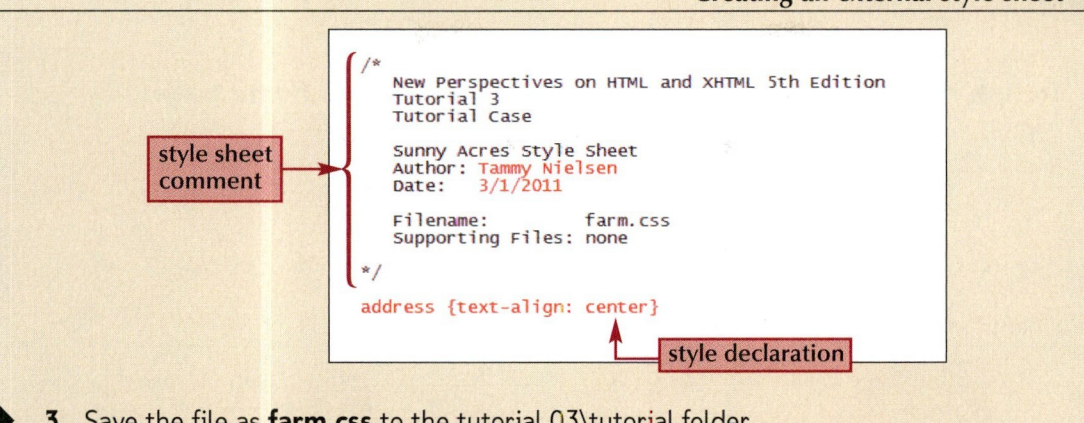

style sheet comment →

```
/*
   New Perspectives on HTML and XHTML 5th Edition
   Tutorial 3
   Tutorial Case

   Sunny Acres Style Sheet
   Author: Tammy Nielsen
   Date:   3/1/2011

   Filename:        farm.css
   Supporting Files: none

*/

address {text-align: center}
```

style declaration

▶ **3.** Save the file as **farm.css** to the tutorial.03\tutorial folder.

To apply this style to Tammy's document, you have to create a link between the home.htm file and the farm.css style sheet.

Linking to an External Style Sheet

You create a link between Web pages and external style sheets using the same link element discussed in Tutorial 2. The code to create a style sheet link is

```
<link href="url" rel="stylesheet" type="text/css" />
```

where *url* is the URL of the external style sheet. As with the link elements discussed in Tutorial 2, link elements used for style sheets must be placed in the head section of the Web page document. For example, to create a link to a styles.css style sheet, you would insert the following element into the head section of the HTML file:

```
<link href="styles.css" rel="stylesheet" type="text/css" />
```

The URL in the href attribute is interpreted in the same way as URLs for linked Web pages. In this case, you assume that the styles.css file is located in the same folder as the current document because no additional path information has been provided.

Applying a Style | Reference Window

- To apply an inline style to a page element, insert the HTML attribute
    ```
    style="style1: value1; style2: value2; style3: value3; ..."
    ```
  where *style1*, *style2*, *style3*, and so on are the names of the style properties, and *value1*, *value2*, *value3*, and so on are the values associated with each style property.
- To apply an embedded style sheet to a Web page, add to the document's head
    ```
    <style type="text/css">
       style declarations
    </style>
    ```
  where *style declarations* are lists of styles in the form
    ```
    selector {style1: value1; style2: value2; style3: value3; ...}
    ```
  with *selector* identifying the element or elements within that document receiving the style.
- To apply an external style sheet, use your text editor to create a text file containing style declarations. Use the .css filename extension. To link to the external style sheet, add
    ```
    <link href="url" rel="stylesheet" type="text/css" />
    ```
  to the document head, where *url* is the URL of the external style sheet.

You'll use the link element to create a link between Tammy's home.htm file and the farm.css style sheet.

To link the farm.css external style sheet to Tammy's home page:

▶ **1.** Return to the **home.htm** file in your text editor.

▶ **2.** Between the closing </style> tag and the closing </head> tag, insert the following link element, as shown in Figure 3-6:

```
<link href="farm.css" rel="stylesheet" type="text/css" />
```

Figure 3-6	Linking to an external style sheet

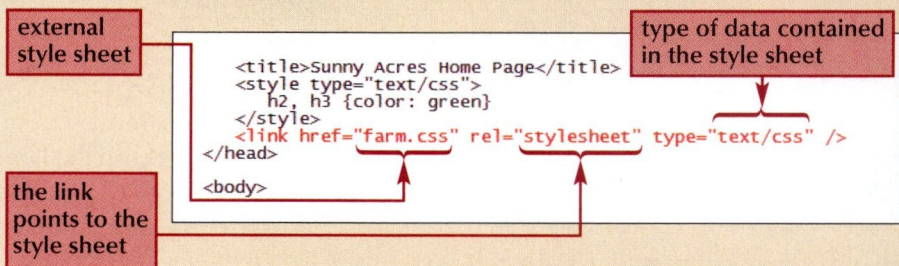

▶ **3.** Save your changes to the file and then reload or refresh the **home.htm** file in your Web browser.

▶ **4.** Scroll to the bottom of the page and confirm that the address text for the Sunny Acres farm is now centered horizontally on the page.

InSight	**Importing Style Sheets**

On large Web sites that involve hundreds of pages, you might decide to use different styles for different groups of pages to give a visual cue to users about where they are on the site. One way of organizing these different styles is to break them into smaller, more manageable units. The different style sheets can then be imported into a single sheet. To import a style sheet, add the following statement to either an embedded style sheet or an external style sheet file

```
@import url(url)
```

where (*url*) is the URL of an external style sheet file. For example, a company might have one style sheet named company.css that contains basic styles used in all Web pages and another style sheet named support.css that only applies to Web pages containing technical support information. The following embedded style sheet imports both files:

```
<style type="text/css">
    @import url(company.css)
    @import url(support.css)
</style>
```

The @import statement must always come before any other style declarations in the embedded or external style sheet. When the browser encounters the @import statement, it imports the content of the style sheet file directly into current style sheet, much as if you had typed the style declarations yourself.

Setting up Alternate Style Sheets

Many browsers allow Web pages to support alternative style sheets. This is particularly useful in situations with users who have special needs (such as a need for large text with highly contrasting colors). To support these users, you can create an alternate style sheet with the link element

```
<link href="url1" rel="alternate stylesheet"
      type="text/css" title="title1" />
<link href="url2" rel="alternate stylesheet"
      type="text/css" title="title2" />
```

where *url1*, *url2*, and so forth are the URLs of the style sheet files, and *title1*, *title2*, etc. are the titles of the alternate style sheets. For example, the following HTML code creates links to two style sheets named Large Text and Regular Text:

```
<link href="large.css" rel="alternate stylesheet" type="text/css"
      title="Large Text" />
<link href="regular.css" rel="alternate stylesheet" type="text/css"
      title="Regular Text" />
```

Browsers that support alternate style sheets provide a menu option for the user to select which style sheet to apply. Figure 3-7 shows how users could choose between the Large Text and the Regular Text style sheets under the Firefox browser.

Choosing between alternate style sheets in Firefox   Figure 3-7

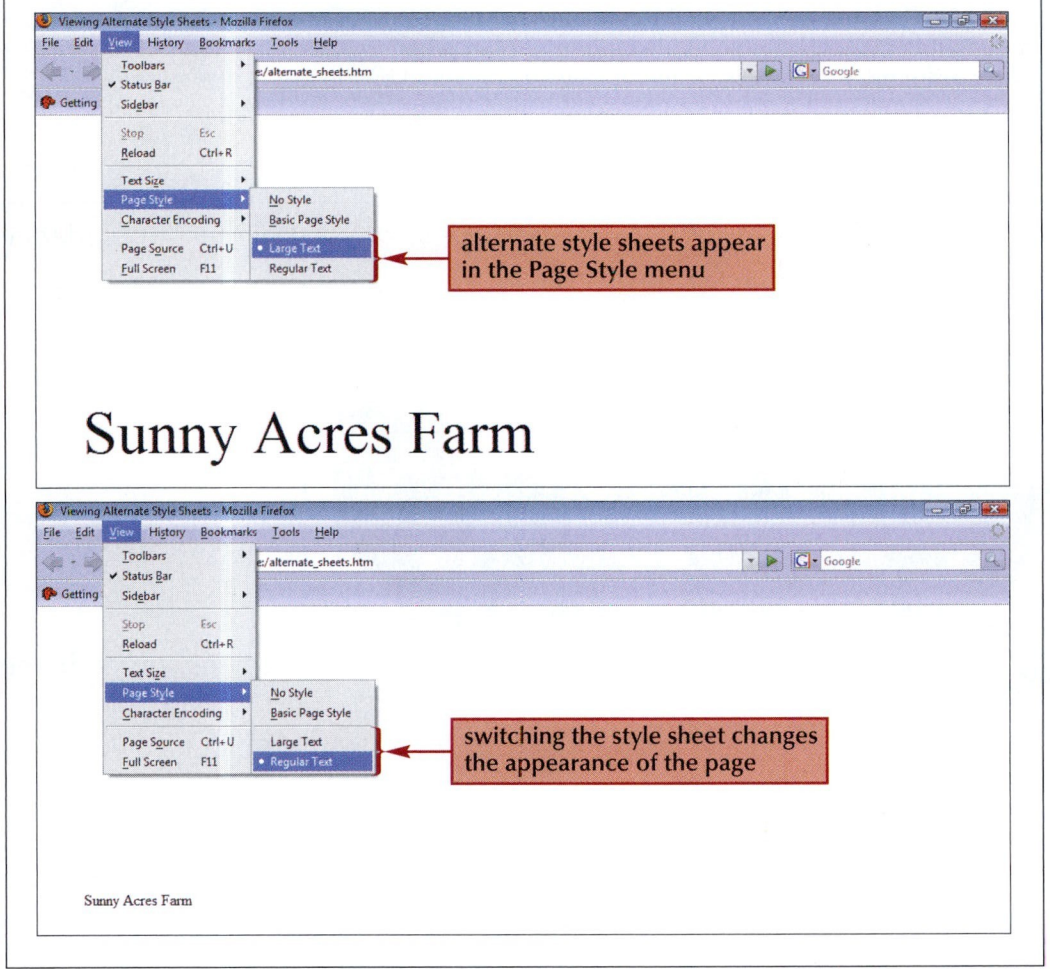

Among the major browsers, currently Netscape, Firefox, Opera, and Safari support alternate style sheets. At the time of this writing, Internet Explorer supports them only if a specialized add-in program is installed on the user's computer. Tammy wants you to be aware of alternate style sheets for the future; but for now, you will not be specifying alternate style sheets for the Sunny Acres Web site.

Understanding Cascading Order

With so many ways of applying styles to a Web site, you might wonder which style is ultimately used by the browser when the page is rendered. For example, consider a Web page that is linked to an external style sheet that sets all h1 elements in bold, red font. But the author also has an inline style for one of the h1 elements specifying centered blue font. Furthermore, the browser specifies that all h1 elements are rendered in a regular black font that is not centered on the page. Which style rule is ultimately applied to the page? To answer that question, you have to examine the principals of style precedence and style inheritance.

Style Precedence

Style precedence is the rule that determines which style is applied when one or more styles conflict. The general rule is that in the case of conflict, the more specific style has precedence over the more general style.

As shown in Figure 3-8, the most general style is the one that is built into the Web browser. Each browser has an internal style sheet that it uses for rendering page elements. The reason that most browsers indent block quotes or display h1 headings in a large font is that they are applying an internal style sheet that governs how those elements are rendered. Unless a different style is specified by the Web page author or the user viewing the page, these browser styles are used.

Figure 3-8 | **Levels of style precedence**

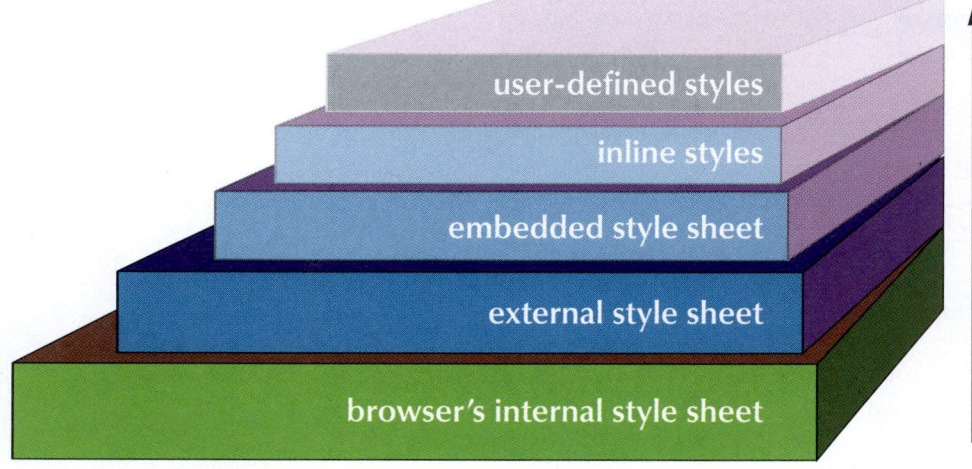

The next three levels of styles are those defined by the Web site author. The first are styles defined in an external style sheet. When linked to a Web page, those styles will have precedence over the browser's built-in styles. In the same way, an embedded style sheet applied to a specific Web page has precedence over external style sheets. Finally, inline styles applied to specific elements within a Web page have precedence over the styles defined in the embedded style sheet.

The highest level of style rules includes those defined by the user of the Web page. Most browsers allow users to modify the style sheets used by the browser and the Web page. For example, the Accessibility dialog box in Internet Explorer shown in Figure 3-9 is often used by people with disabilities to set up style sheets that meet specific needs. These user-defined styles take precedence over the browser's internal styles and any styles specified by the Web page author.

Accessibility dialog box in Internet Explorer | Figure 3-9

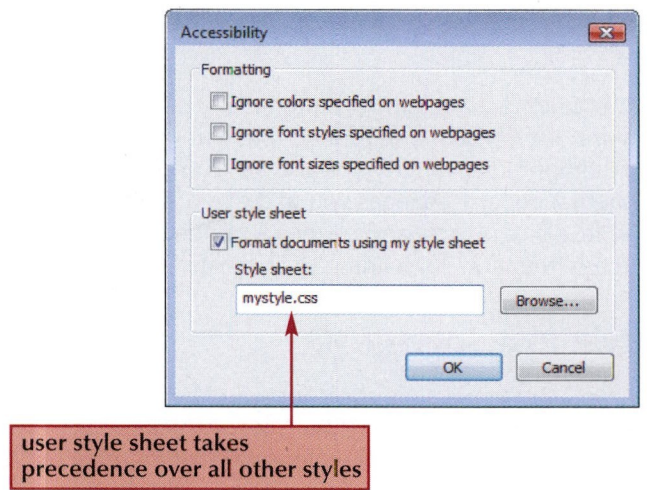

user style sheet takes precedence over all other styles

When conflicting styles are on the same level, the one declared last has precedence. For example, the following embedded style sheet

```
<style type="text/css">
   h1 {color: orange; text-align: center}
   h1 {color: blue}
</style>
```

results in h1 headings displayed in centered blue text. The text is blue because the second style declaration has precedence over the first. However, the text is still centered because the second style declaration did not alter the text-align style, so the text-align setting from the first style declaration is still in force.

You can override the precedence rules by adding the !important property to a style declaration. The style sheet

```
<style type="text/css">
 h1 {color: orange !important }
 h1 {color: blue; text-align: center }
</style>
```

results in h1 headings rendered in centered orange text because the orange style is given a higher weight than the blue style even though the blue style is declared last. The !important property is useful in situations where you want to ensure that a particular style is always enforced regardless of its location in the order of precedence.

Note that even with the !important property, any styles you specify can still be overridden by users who set up their own style sheets with their browsers.

Style Inheritance

Where there is no conflict, styles are passed down from the more general levels to the more specific in what is known as **style inheritance**. When you use an external style sheet to set the font color of h1 headings to blue, that color is assumed in all other h1 heading styles unless a different color is specified. This is also true for page elements that are nested within other page elements. For example, to set the font color of every element on the page to blue, you could enter the following style declaration:

```
body {color: blue}
```

Every element nested within the body element (that is, every element on the page) would inherit this style. This means that every h1 heading, every paragraph, every numbered list, and so forth would be displayed in blue text. To override style inheritance, you specify an alternate style for one of the descendant elements of the parent. The styles

```
body {color: blue}
p    {color: red}
```

set the text color to blue for every element on the page; paragraphs and elements contained within them are displayed in a red font. Note that you can override style inheritance using the same !important property you use for overriding style precedence.

Through style inheritance, any changes you make to a style sheet will automatically be passed down the levels of objects and elements on the Web site. This cascade of style changes is the source of the term "cascading style sheets."

Applying a Style to a Specific ID

Sometimes you'll have an external style sheet for your Web site, but will still want to apply a style to a specific element. If that is the case, you can mark the element with the id attribute, as discussed in Tutorial 2. To create a style for that marked element, apply the style declaration

```
#id {style rule}
```

where *id* is the value of the element's id attribute and *style rule* stands for the styles applied to that specific element. For example, if you have the h2 element

```
<h2 id="subtitle">A Fun Family Farm</h2>
```

in your code, you can set the font color to red using the following style:

```
#subtitle {color: red}
```

You do the same with an inline style, but using the id attribute has the advantage of moving the style declaration out of the HTML file, where it can be more easily maintained and revised.

Reference Window | **Applying a Style to an ID**

- To apply a style to an element marked with a specific id value, use the declaration
  `#id {style rule}`
  where *id* is the value of the element's id attribute and *style rule* stands for the styles applied to that specific element.

You'll create styles for specific element ids later in this tutorial.

Working with Color in HTML and CSS

Now that you've seen how embedded and external style sheets work, you'll begin exploring various aspects of the CSS language. You'll start by examining how to work with color. If you've worked with graphics software, you've probably made your color choices without much difficulty due to the graphical interfaces that those applications employ. Graphical interfaces, known as WYSIWYG (what you see is what you get), allow you to select colors visually. Specifying a color with CSS is somewhat less intuitive because CSSis a text-based language and requires you to define your colors in textual terms. This can be done by specifying either a color value or a color name.

Color Values

A **color value** is a numerical expression that precisely describes a color. To better understand how numbers can represent colors, it helps to review some of the basic principles of color theory and how they relate to the colors that your monitor displays.

White light is made up of three primary colors (red, green, and blue) mixed at equal intensities. By adding two of the three primary colors you can generate a trio of complementary colors: yellow, magenta, and cyan, as shown Figure 3-10.

Primary color model for light ◄ **Figure 3-10**

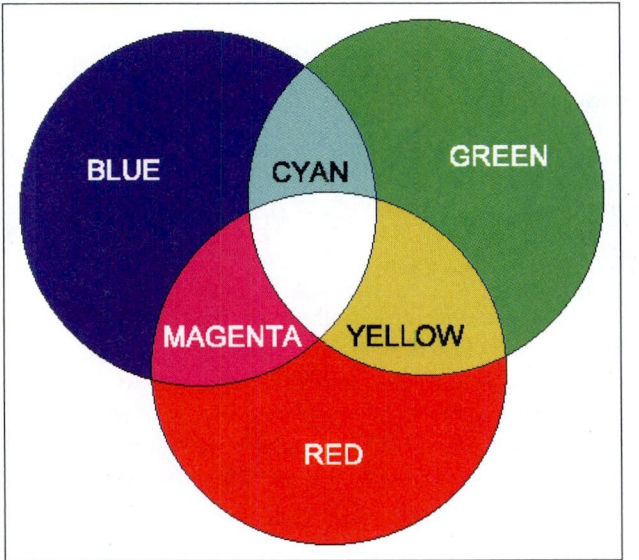

To generate a wider range of colors, you simply vary the intensity of the red, green, and blue light. For example, orange is created from a high intensity of red light, a moderate intensity of green light, and an absence of blue light. Your computer monitor generates colors by emitting red, green, and blue light at different intensities. CSS represents these intensities mathematically. Each color is represented by a triplet of numbers called an **RGB triplet**, whose values are based on the strength of its red, green, and blue components. This triplet has the form

```
rgb(red, green, blue)
```

where *red*, *green*, and *blue* are the intensity values of the red, green, and blue components. The intensity values range from 0 (absence of color) to 255 (highest intensity). For example, the RGB triplet for white is (255, 255, 255), indicating that red, green, and blue are equally mixed at the highest intensity. Orange has the triplet (255, 165, 0) which means it results from a mixture of high-intensity red, moderate-intensity green, and no blue. You can also enter each component value as a percentage, with 100% representing the highest intensity. In this form, you specify the color orange with

```
rgb(100%, 65%, 0%)
```

The percentage form is less commonly used than RGB values. RGB triplets can specify 256^3 (16.7 million) possible colors, which is more colors than the human eye can distinguish.

Originally, HTML required that color values be entered using the hexadecimal system. A **hexadecimal** is a number expressed in the base 16 numbering system rather than in the base 10 form you use every day. In base 10 counting, you use combinations of 10 characters (0 through 9) to represent numerical values. The hexadecimal system includes six extra characters: A (for 10), B (for 11), C (for 12), D (for 13), E (for 14), and F (for 15). For values above 15, you use a combination of those 16 characters. Therefore, to represent a number in hexadecimal terms, you convert the value to multiples of 16, plus a remainder. For example, 16 is equal to (16 × 1) + 0, so its hexadecimal representation is 10. A value of 21 is equal to (16 × 1) + 5, for a hexadecimal representation of 15. The number 255 is equal to (16 × 15) + 15, or FF in hexadecimal format (remember that F = 15 in hexadecimal). In the case of the number 255, the first F represents the number of times 16 goes into 255 (which is 15), and the second F represents the remainder of 15. A color value represented as a hexadecimal number has the form

```
#redgreenblue
```

where *red*, *green*, and *blue* are the hexadecimal values of the red, green, and blue components. Therefore, the color yellow could be represented either by the RGB triplet

```
rgb(255,255,0)
```

or in the hexadecimal form

```
#FFFF00
```

At this point, you might be wondering whether you have to become a math major before you can start adding color to your Web pages! Fortunately, this is not the case. You can specify most colors on your Web pages with styles that use RGB triplets rather than the hexadecimal form. However, you might see HTML or CSS code that sets a color value to something like #FFA500, and now you know where such a representation comes from—even if you can't tell at a glance that it specifies the color orange.

Using Color Names

If you don't want to use color values, you can also specify colors by name. HTML and XHTML support 16 basic color names. These color names are also supported by CSS 2.1, with the addition of orange to make 17 color names. The 17 color names and their RGB and hexadecimal color values are shown in Figure 3-11.

The 17 basic color names from CSS 2.1 ◄ Figure 3-11

Color Name	RGB Triplet	Hexadecimal	Color Name	RGB Triplet	Hexadecimal
Aqua	(0, 255, 255)	00FFFF	Olive	(128, 128, 0)	808000
Black	(0, 0, 0)	000000	Orange	(255, 165, 0)	FFA500
Blue	(0, 0, 255)	0000FF	Purple	(128, 0, 128)	800080
Fuchsia	(255, 0, 255)	FF00FF	Red	(255, 0, 0)	FF0000
Gray	(128, 128, 128)	808080	Silver	(192, 192, 192)	C0C0C0
Green	(0, 128, 0)	008000	Teal	(0, 128, 128)	008080
Lime	(0, 255, 0)	00FF00	White	(255, 255, 255)	FFFFFF
Maroon	(128, 0, 0)	800000	Yellow	(255, 255, 0)	FFFF00
Navy	(0, 0, 128)	000080			

Seventeen colors are not a lot, so most browsers support an extended list of 140 color names, including such colors as crimson, khaki, and peachpuff. Although this extended color list is not part of the specifications for either HTML or CSS, most browsers support it. You can view these color names in a demo page.

To view the extended list of color names:

▶ 1. Use your browser to open the **demo_color_names.htm** file from the tutorial.03\demo folder included with your Data Files.

▶ 2. As shown in Figure 3-12, the demo page displays the list of 140 color names along with their color values expressed both as RGB triplets and in hexadecimal form. The 17 color names supported by CSS 2.1 are highlighted in the table.

A partial list of extended color names ◄ Figure 3-12

Sample	Name	RGB	Hexadecimal
	aliceblue	(240,248,255)	#F0F8FF
	antiquewhite	(250,235,215)	#FAEBD7
	aqua	(0,255,255)	#00FFFF
	aquamarine	(127,255,212)	#7FFFD4
	azure	(240,255,255)	#F0FFFF
	beige	(245,245,220)	#F5F5DC
	bisque	(255,228,196)	#FFE4C4
	black	(0,0,0)	#000000
	blanchedalmond	(255,235,205)	#FFEBCD
	blue	(0,0,255)	#0000FF
	blueviolet	(138,43,226)	#8A2BE2
	brown	(165,42,42)	#A52A2A
	burlywood	(222,184,135)	#DEB887

▶ 3. Close the page when you are finished reviewing the extended color names list.

Depending on the design requirements of your site, you might sometimes need to use color values to get exactly the right color. However, if you know the general color that you need, you can usually enter the color name without having to look up its RGB value.

Defining Text and Background Colors

Now that you've studied how to specify a color in HTML and CSS, you can start applying it to the elements of Tammy's Web pages. CSS supports styles to define the text and background color for each element on your page. You've already worked with the color style to define text color. The style to define the background color is

```
background-color: color
```

where *color* is either a color value or a color name. If you do not define an element's color, it takes the color of the element that contains it. For example, if you specify red text on a gray background for the Web page body, all elements within the page inherit that color combination unless you specify different styles for specific elements.

Reference Window | **Setting the Background Color**

- To set the background color of an element, use
  ```
  background-color: color
  ```
  where *color* is a color name or a color value.

Tammy wants each of her pages to have a slightly different color theme. For the home page, she wants a white page background, and she wants the heading text to appear in white text on a dark green background. Although most browsers assume a white background by default, it's a good idea to make this explicit in case a browser has a differentsetting. You'll add to this style to the farm.css external style sheet because you'll eventually apply this to the entire Sunny Acres Web site. For the background color of the heading, you'll use the value

```
rgb(0, 154, 0)
```

You'll add this to an embedded style sheet in the home.htm file because Tammy doesn't intend to use the same heading background on her other pages.

To set the text and background colors on Tammy's home page:

1. Return to the **home.htm** file in your text editor.

2. As shown in Figure 3-13, change the style for h2 and h3 headings to:
   ```
   h2, h3 {color: white; background-color: rgb(0, 154, 0)}
   ```

Figure 3-13 | **Specifying text color and background colors**

```
<title>Sunny Acres Home Page</title>
<style type="text/css">
   h2, h3 {color: white; background-color: rgb(0, 154, 0)}
</style>
<link href="farm.css" rel="stylesheet" type="text/css" />
</head>
```

3. Save your changes to the file.

4. Return to the **farm.css** file in your text editor.

5. As shown in Figure 3-14, above the style declaration for the address element, insert the following style:
   ```
   body {background-color: white}
   ```

◀ Figure 3-14

```
body    {background-color: white}
address {text-align: center}
```

▶ **6.** Save your changes to the file.

▶ **7.** Reload the **home.htm** file in your Web browser. As shown in Figure 3-15, the h2 and h3 heading text should now appear as white text on a dark green background.

Formatted heading ◀ Figure 3-15

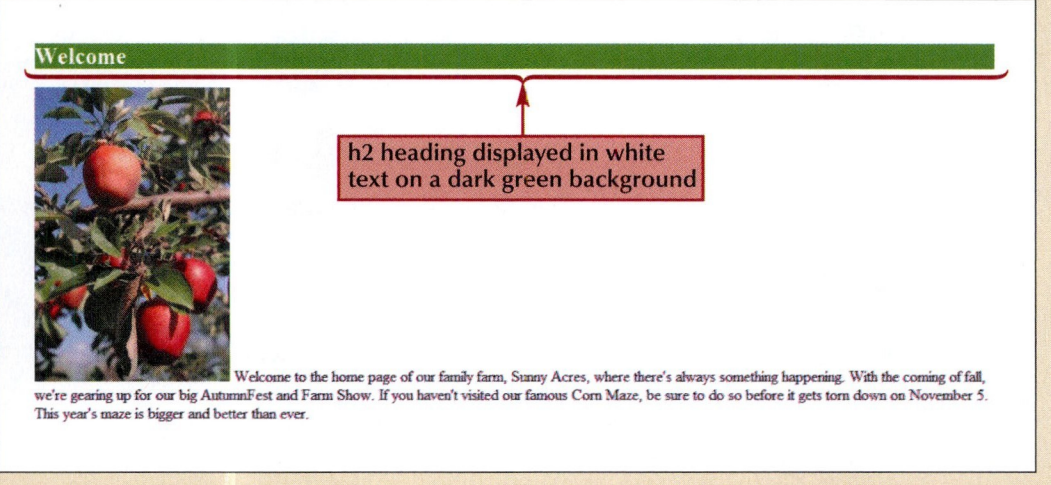

Welcome

h2 heading displayed in white text on a dark green background

Welcome to the home page of our family farm, Sunny Acres, where there's always something happening. With the coming of fall, we're gearing up for our big AutumnFest and Farm Show. If you haven't visited our famous Corn Maze, be sure to do so before it gets torn down on November 5. This year's maze is bigger and better than ever.

▶ **8.** If you want to take a break before starting the next session, you can close your files and applications now.

CSS was not part of the original HTML specifications. If you need to work with older HTML code or need to support older browser versions, you might need to use several deprecated attributes such as bgcolor and text. Both attributes require you to enter either the hexadecimal color value or a recognized color name. You use the bgcolor attribute in the <body> tag to define the background color for an entire page. To define the text color for the entire page, use the text attribute. For example, the following code changes the page background to yellow and the page's text color to sky blue with the hexadecimal value 99CCFF:

```
<body bgcolor="yellow" text="#99CCFF">
```

If you need to color a section of text on your page, enclose the text within the two-sided <font> tag. The <font> tag is a deprecated element that supports several design attributes. Among those supported is the color attribute, which you can use to specify a color name or a hexadecimal color value. For example, the following HTML code sets the text color of an h1 heading to green:

```
<h1><font color="green">Sunny Acres</font></h1>
```

Note that the bgcolor and text attributes and the font element are not part of XHTML and will be rejected by documents that require a strict application of XHTML standards.

You show Tammy the work you've done on colors. She's pleased with the ease of CSS to modify the design and appearance of elements on the Sunny Acres home page. In the next session, you'll continue to explore CSS styles, focusing on text and image styles.

Review | Session 3.1 Quick Check

1. What are inline styles, embedded styles, and external style sheets? Which would you use to create a design for an entire Web site?
2. Specify the code to enter the following comment into a CSS file:

   ```
   Sunny Acres Style Sheet
   ```

3. Specify the code to set the text color of every paragraph element within the Web page to red.
4. If a style sheet has the following declarations, how will address text be rendered by the browser?:

   ```
   address {color: red; text-align: left}
   address {color: blue}
   ```

5. If a style sheet has the following declarations, how will paragraph text be rendered by the browser?:

   ```
   body {background-color: ivory}
   p    {color: red}
   ```

6. What property do you add to a style to override style precedence and style inheritance?
7. Specify the style to display block quote text in a color with a red intensity of 221, a green intensity of 128, and a blue intensity of 0.

Session 3.2

Working with Fonts and Text Styles

Tammy has noticed that all of the text on her pages is displayed in the same typeface. She'd like to see more variety in the page fonts. To modify the text, you'll work with the CSS text and font styles.

Choosing a Font

By default, browsers display Web page text in a single font—usually Times New Roman. You can specify a different font for any page element using the style

```
font-family: fonts
```

where *fonts* is a comma-separated list of fonts that the browser can use in any element. Font names can be either specific or generic. A **specific font** is a font that is actually installed on a user's computer; examples are Times New Roman, Arial, and Garamond. A **generic font** is a name for a grouping of fonts that share a similar appearance. Browsers recognize five generic font groups: serif, sans-serif, monospace, cursive, and fantasy. Figure 3-16 shows examples of each.

Note that within a font family, the actual appearance of the text might vary widely and you cannot be sure which font a given user's browser will use. For this reason, CSS allows you to specify a list of specific fonts along with a generic font. You list the specific fonts first, in order of preference, and then end the list with the generic font. If the browser cannot find any of the specific fonts listed, it uses the generic font. For example, to specify a sans-serif font, you could enter the following style:

```
font-family: Arial, Helvetica, 'Trebuchet MS', sans-serif
```

This style tells the browser to first look for the Arial font; if Arial is not available, the browser looks for Helvetica, and then Trebuchet MS. If none of those fonts is available, the browser uses a generic sans-serif font. Note that font names containing one or more blank spaces (such as Trebuchet MS) must be enclosed within single or double quotes.

To see how the generic fonts appear on your browser, you can use a demo page on text styles.

To use the demo to view your browser's generic fonts:

▶ 1. Use your Web browser to open the **demo_css.htm** file from the tutorial.03\demo folder included with your Data Files.

The demo page contains a collection of text styles you'll explore in this session. You can select a text style value from the drop-down lists on the left side of the demo. You can specify the text to apply the style to in the top-right box. The style as applied to the sample text appears in the middle box. The CSS code for the style appears in the bottom-right box. You press the Tab key to apply the style.

▶ 2. Click the top-right corner box, select and delete the text "Enter sample text here" and type **Sunny Acres**, press the **Enter** key, and then type **Corn Maze**. Press the **Tab** key to display this text in the Preview box.

▶ 3. In the three color input boxes, enter the RGB value

```
rgb(255, 255, 255)
```

and in the three background-color input boxes, enter

```
rgb(153, 102, 102)
```

and then press the **Tab** key.

> **4.** Select **sans-serif** from the font-family list box. As shown in Figure 3-17, the demo page shows the effect of the styles applied to the sample text. The CSS code for these styles is shown in the Style box.

Figure 3-17 ▶ **Viewing the sans-serif font**

> If you think users will want to print your Web pages, be aware that the general rule is to use sans-serif fonts for headlines and serif fonts for body text. For computer monitors, which have lower resolutions than printed material, the general rule is to use sans-serif fonts for headlines and body text, leaving serif fonts for special effects and large text. Tammy expects that her Web page will only be viewed on computer monitors, so you'll use a sans-serif font for all of the body text. You'll do this in the farm.css external style sheet so it can be applied to all pages on the site.

To apply a sans-serif font to the body text in Tammy's external style sheet:

> **1.** Return to the **farm.css** file in your text editor.

> **2.** Add the style
>
> ```
> font-family: Arial, Helvetica, sans-serif
> ```
>
> to the style declaration for the body element. Be sure to use a semicolon to separate this new style from the background-color style. Figure 3-18 shows the revised code.

Figure 3-18 ▶ **Setting the font-family style for the body text**

```
body    {background-color: white; font-family: Arial, Helvetica, sans-serif}
address {text-align: center}
```

> **3.** Save your changes to the file and then reload the **home.htm** file in your Web browser. As shown in Figure 3-19, all of the body text in the Web page should now be displayed in a sans-serif font.

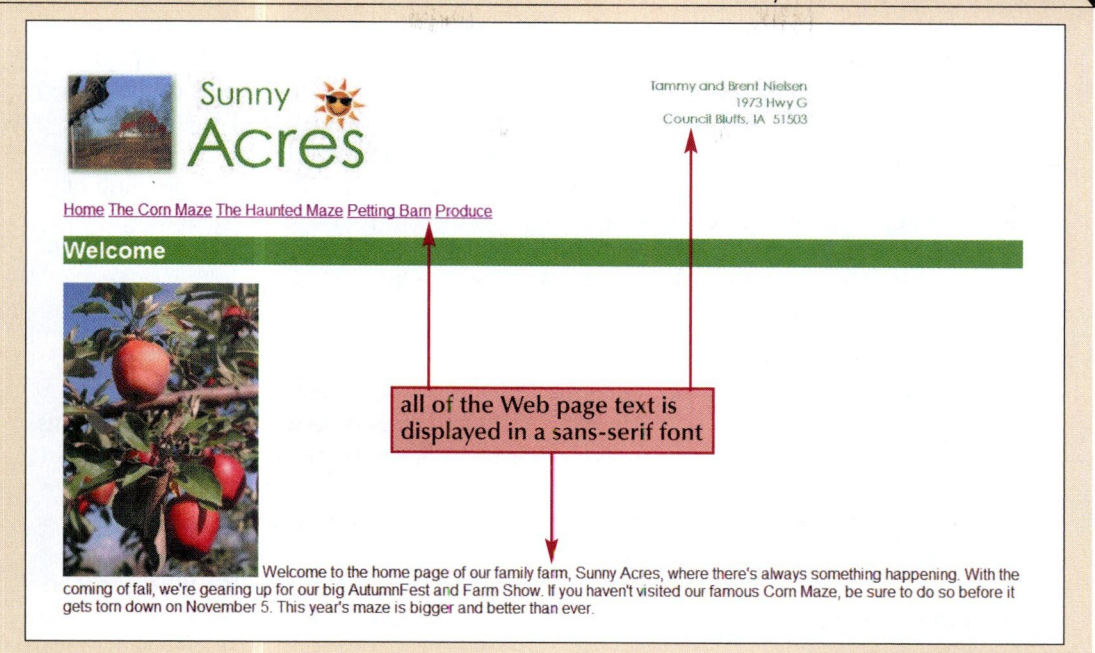

Note that the sans-serif font is applied to all page elements on the Sunny Acres home page. This is because you applied the style to the body element, and so it cascades through all the elements on the page.

Setting the Font Size

Tammy would like the Welcome heading on her home page to be displayed in slightly larger text than the rest of her site. The style to change the font size of the text within an element is

```
font-size: length
```

where *length* is a length measurement. Lengths can be specified in four different ways:

- with a unit of measurement
- with a keyword description
- as a percentage of the size of the containing element
- with a keyword expressing the size relative to the size of the containing element

If you choose to specify lengths using measurement units, you can use absolute units or relative units. Because absolute and relative units appear in several styles, it's worthwhile to spend some time understanding them. **Absolute units** are units that are fixed in size regardless of the device rendering the Web page and are specified in one of five standard units of measurement: mm (millimeters), cm (centimeters), in (inches), pt (points), and pc (picas). The points and picas measurements might not be as familiar to you as inches, millimeters, and centimeters. For comparison, there are 72 points in an inch, 12 points in a pica, and 6 picas in an inch. Size values for any of these measurements can be whole numbers (0, 1, 2 ...) or decimals (0.5, 1.6, 3.9 ...). For example, ifyou want your text to be 1/2 inch in size, you can use any of the following styles (note that you should not insert a space between the size value and the unit abbreviation):

```
font-size: 0.5in
font-size: 36pt
font-size: 3pc
```

Absolute measurements are appropriate when you know the physical properties of the output device and want to fix the size to a specific value. Of course this is not often the case with Web pages because they can be displayed on a variety of devices, monitor sizes, and resolutions. This is one of the fundamental differences between Web page design and print design (in which you usually know the size and properties of the paper).

To cope with a wide variety of output devices and sizes, many Web page designers opt to use **relative units**, which are expressed relative to the size of other objects within the Web page. One commonly used relative unit is the **em unit**. The exact meaning of the em unit depends on its use in the style sheet. If the em unit is used for setting font size, it expresses the size relative to the font size of the parent element. For an h1 heading, the parent element is the Web page body. So the style

```
h1 {font-size: 2em}
```

sets the font size of h1 headings to twice the font size of body text. If the browser has been configured to display body text in a 12-point font, this style will cause h1 headings to be displayed in a 24-point font. On the other hand, if the h1 heading is nested within another element such as a blockquote element or div element, then the size of the h1 heading will be twice the size of text in that containing element. Context is important when interpreting the effect of the em unit.

When used for sizing objects other than fonts, the em unit is equal to a little over the width of the capital letter "M" in the font size of the current element. The style

```
h1 {width: 20em}
```

sets the width of the h1 heading to a little over the width of 20 capital Ms. Of course, the actual size of the Ms depends on the font used in the h1 heading. Because capital Ms take up the most width of any character, another way to think of the em unit is as about the length of two characters. The above style would fit about 40 characters of text in the h1 heading.

One of the great advantages of relative units like the em unit is that they can make your page **scalable**, allowing the page to be rendered the same way no matter what font size is used by the browser. For example, one user with a large monitor might have body text set to 18 points, while another user with a smaller monitor might have body text setto 10 points. Regardless of the size of the monitor, your heading text should be about 50% larger than the body text. Setting the font size of h1 headings to 1.5 em ensures that they are sized appropriately.

Another relative unit is the percentage. Like the em unit, percentages have one meaning when used for font sizes and another meaning when used to size other objects. When used for font sizes, the percentages are based on the font size of the parent element. The style

```
h1 {font-size: 200%}
```

sets the font size of h1 headings to be 200% or twice that of body text. When used to set the size of other objects, the percentage refers to the width of the parent element. So the style

```
h1 {width: 50%}
```

sets the width of the h1 heading to be 50% or half that of the body text. You'll learn more about the width style later in this tutorial.

The final unit of measurement used in Web pages is the pixel, which represents a single dot on the output device.

Be aware that the exact size of a pixel depends on the output device. Different devices have different resolutions, which are typically expressed in terms of dots per inch or dpi. For example, a 600 dpi printer has six times more pixels per inch than a typical computer monitor.

Finally, you can express font sizes using seven descriptive keywords: xx-small, x-small, small, medium, large, x-large, or xx-large. Each browser is configured to display text at a particular size for each of these keywords, but the exact size is determined by the browser's internal style sheet. You can also use the relative keywords larger and smaller to make a font one size larger or smaller than the surrounding text. For example, the following set of styles causes the body text to be displayed in a small font, while h2 text is displayed in a font one size larger (medium in this case):

```
body {font-size: small}
h2 {font-size: larger}
```

Tammy suggests that you make the h2 headings twice the size of body text. You'll add this style to the external style sheet because you want to eventually apply it to her entire Web site.

To set the font size of h2 headings in Tammy's external style sheet:

▶ **1.** Return to the **farm.css** file in your text editor.

▶ **2.** Directly below the style for the body element, insert the following style, as shown in Figure 3-20:

```
h2 {font-size: 2em}
```

Setting the font size of h2 headings   Figure 3-20

```
body    {background-color: white; font-family: Arial, Helvetica, sans-serif}
h2      {font-size: 2em}  ◀──
address {text-align: center}          h2 headings will be twice
                                      the size of body text
```

▶ **3.** Save your changes to the file and then reload the **home.htm** file in your Web browser. Verify that the font size used for the h2 heading at the top of the page is larger than before.

Web designers often have to work in both the em and pixel units of measure. Trying to translate between the two measuring units can be a challenge. One popular approach to defining sizes on a Web page is the so-called 62.5% hack. The idea, introduced by Richard Rutter in his Web design blog called Clagnut, is to define the default font size of the body text in a Web page as 62.5% of the width of the Web page using the following style:

```
body {font-size: 62.5%}
```

The reasoning behind the 62.5% hack is that most Web browsers display body text in a medium font, with the text at a height of 16 pixels. Taking 62.5% of this value assigns the value of 1 em to 10 pixels for body text. With these numbers, you can easily translate between the em unit and the pixel unit. The width of an element can be set to either 100 pixels or its equivalent of 10 em.

You have to be careful when using the 62.5% hack because the value of the em unit depends on its context in the document. As you nest one element within another, the em unit is expressed relative to the font size of the parent element. Several sites on the Web provide em calculators, making it easier for you to track the changing values of the em unit as you drill down through a series of nested elements.

Despite the complication with nesting, the 62.5% hack has become so popular with Web designers that it is considered a standard tool for designing challenging and visually interesting Web pages.

Controlling Spacing and Indentation

Tammy thinks that the text for the Welcome heading looks too crowded. She's wondering if you can spread it out more across the width of the page. She also would like to see more space between the first letter, "W," and the left edge of the green background.

CSS supports styles that allow you to perform some basic typographic tasks, such as kerning and tracking. **Kerning** refers to the amount of space between characters, while **tracking** refers to the amount of space between words. The styles to control an element's kerning and tracking are

```
letter-spacing: value
word-spacing: value
```

where *value* is the size of space between individual letters or words. You specify these sizes with the same units that you use for font sizing. As with font sizes, the default unit of length for kerning and tracking is the pixel (px). The default value for both kerning and tracking is 0 pixels. A positive value increases the letter and word spacing. A negative value reduces the space between letters and words. If you choose to make your pages scalable for a variety of devices and resolutions, you will want to express kerning and tracking values as percentages or in em units.

To see how modifying these values can affect the appearance of your text, return to the CSS styles demo page.

To use the demo to explore kerning and tracking styles:

▶ **1.** Return to the **css_demo.htm** file in your Web browser.

▶ **2.** Enter **2** in the font-size input box, and then select **em** from the corresponding unit drop-down list.

▶ **3.** Select **center** from the text-align list box.

4. Enter **0.3** in the letter-spacing input box and **em** from the corresponding drop-down list. Press the **Tab** key.

5. Enter **0.8** in the word-spacing input box and **em** from the corresponding drop-down list. Press the **Tab** key. Figure 3-21 shows the revised appearance of the text after applying the letter-spacing and word-spacing styles.

Setting kerning and tracking styles | Figure 3-21

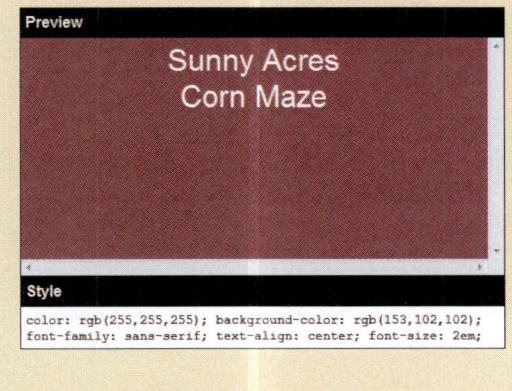

default kerning and tracking

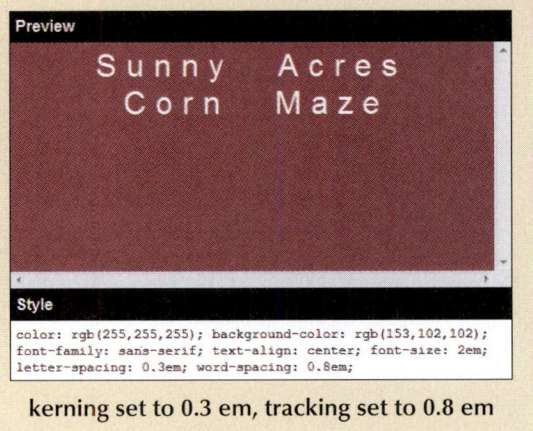

kerning set to 0.3 em, tracking set to 0.8 em

Another typographic feature that you can set is **leading**, which is the space between lines of text. The style to set the leading for the text within an element is

```
line-height: length
```

where *length* is a specific length or a percentage of the font size of the text on those lines. If no unit is specified, most browsers interpret the number to represent the ratio of the line height to the font size. The standard ratio is 1.2:1, which means that the line height is usually 1.2 times the font size. On the other hand, the style

```
p {line-height: 2}
```

makes all paragraphs double-spaced. A common technique is to create multiline titles with large fonts and small line heights in order to give title text more impact. Use the demo page to see how this works.

To use the demo to explore leading styles:

1. Enter **0.75** in the line-height input box, and then select **em** from the corresponding unit drop-down list.

2. Press the **Tab** key to apply the line-height style. Figure 3-22 shows the revised appearance of the text.

Figure 3-22	Setting the line-height style

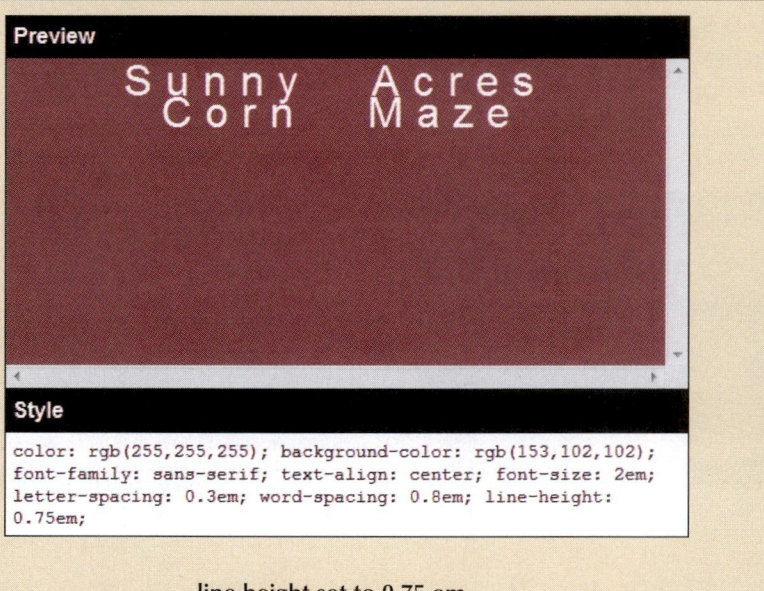

line height set to 0.75 em

An additional way to control text spacing is to set the indentation for the first line of a block of text. The style is

```
text-indent: value
```

where *value* is a length expressed in absolute or relative units or as a percentage of the width of the text block. For example, an indentation value of 5% indents the first line by 5% of the width of the block. The indentation value can also be negative, extending the first line to the left of the text block to create a **hanging indent**.

Reference Window | **Setting the Font Face and Sizes**

- To define the font face, use the style property
    ```
    font-family: fonts
    ```
  where *fonts* is a comma-separated list of fonts that the browser can use with the element. List specific fonts first and complete the list with a generic font.
- To set the font size, use
    ```
    font-size: length
    ```
  where *length* is a CSS unit of length in either relative or absolute units.
- To set the kerning (the space between letters), use
    ```
    letter-spacing: length
    ```
- To set the tracking (the space between words), use
    ```
    word-spacing: length
    ```

Now you can use what you've learned about spacing to make the changes that Tammy has suggested. To make her heading text more spread out, you'll set the kerning of the h2 elements to 0.4 em. You'll also set the indentation to 1 em, moving the text of all h2 headings to the left.

To change the spacing of the h2 headings in Tammy's external style sheet:

▶ 1. Return to the **farm.css** style sheet in your text editor.

▶ 2. Add the following attributes to the h2 style as shown in Figure 3-23. Be sure to separate each attribute with a semicolon.

```
letter-spacing: 0.4em; text-indent: 1em
```

Applying the letter-spacing and text-indent styles to h2 headings	Figure 3-23

```
body     {background-color: white; font-family: Arial, Helvetica, sans-serif}
h2       {font-size: 2em; letter-spacing: 0.4em; text-indent: 1em }
address  {text-align: center}
```

▶ 3. Save your changes to the file and then refresh the Sunny Acres home page in your Web browser. Figure 3-24 shows the revised appearance of the h2 heading on that page.

Formatted h2 heading	Figure 3-24

W e l c o m e

Welcome to the home page of our family farm, Sunny Acres, where there's always something happening. With the coming of fall, we're gearing up for our big AutumnFest and Farm Show. If you haven't visited our famous Corn Maze, be sure to do so before it gets torn down on November 5. This year's maze is bigger and better than ever.

By increasing the kerning in the h2 heading, you've made the text appear less crowded, making it easier to read.

Applying Font Features

As you saw in the first tutorial, browsers often apply default font styles to particular types of elements. Text marked with an <address> tag, for example, usually appears in italics. This is handy when you don't have a specific design in mind for your text. However, you can also choose a specific font style, such as italics, bold, underline, and so forth. You can specify font styles using the style

```
font-style: type
```

where *type* is normal, italic, or oblique. The italic and oblique styles are similar in appearance, but might differ subtly depending on the font in use.

You have also seen that browsers render certain elements in heavier fonts. For example, most browsers render headings in a boldfaced font. You can specify the font weight for any page element using the style

```
font-weight: weight
```

where *weight* is the level of bold formatting applied to the text. You express weights as values ranging from 100 to 900, in increments of 100. In practice, however, most browsers cannot render nine different font weights. For practical purposes, you can assume that 400 represents normal (unbolded) text, 700 is bold text, and 900 represents heavy bold text. You can also use the keywords normal or bold in place of a weight value, or you can express the font weight relative to the containing element, using the keywords bolder or lighter.

Another style you can use to change the appearance of your text is

```
text-decoration: type
```

where *type* is none (for no decoration), underline, overline, line-through, or blink (to create blinking text). You can apply several decorative features to the same element by listing them as part of the text-decoration style. For example, the style

```
text-decoration: underline overline
```

places a line under and over the text in the element. Note that the text-decoration style cannot be applied to nontextual elements, such as inline images.

To control the case of the text within an element, use the style

```
text-transform: type
```

where *type* is capitalize, uppercase, lowercase, or none (to make no changes to the text case). For example, if you want to capitalize the first letter of each word in the element, you could use the style

```
text-transform: capitalize
```

Finally, you can display text in uppercase letters and a small font using the style

```
font-variant: type
```

where *type* is normal (the default) or small caps (small capital letters). Small caps are often used in legal documents, such as software agreements, in which the capital letters indicate the importance of a phrase or point, but the text is made small so as to not detract from other elements in the document.

Setting Font and Text Appearance | Reference Window

- To specify the font style, use
    `font-style: type`
    where *type* is normal, italic, or oblique.
- To specify the font weight, use
    `font-weight: type`
    where *type* is normal, bold, bolder, light, lighter, or a font weight value.
- To specify a text decoration, use
    `text-decoration: type`
    where *type* is none, underline, overline, line-through, or blink.
- To transform the text, use
    `text-transform: type`
    where *type* is capitalize, uppercase, lowercase, or none.
- To display a font variant of the text, use
    `font-variant: type`
    where *type* is normal or small-caps.

To see the impact of these styles, return to the demo page.

To use the demo to view the various font styles:

▶ **1.** Return to the **CSS demo page** in your Web browser.

▶ **2.** Select **bold** from the font-weight list box.

▶ **3.** Select **small-caps** from the font-variant list box. Figure 3-25 shows the impact of applying the font-weight and font-variant styles.

Applying the font-weight and font-variant styles ◀ **Figure 3-25**

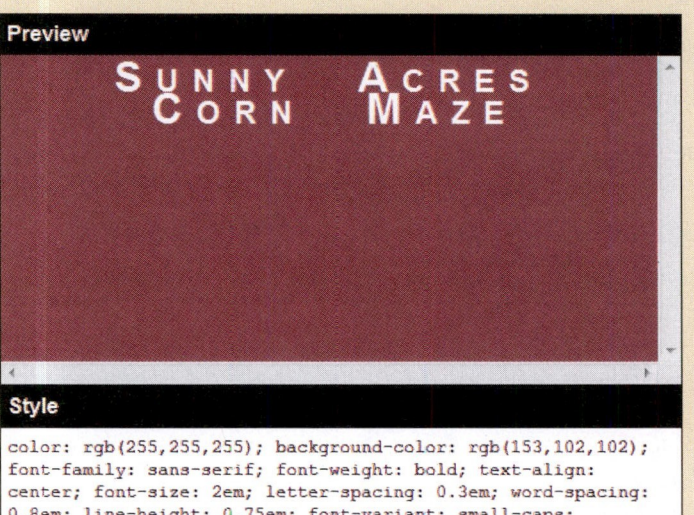

```
Style
color: rgb(255,255,255); background-color: rgb(153,102,102);
font-family: sans-serif; font-weight: bold; text-align:
center; font-size: 2em; letter-spacing: 0.3em; word-spacing:
0.8em; line-height: 0.75em; font-variant: small-caps;
```

▶ **4.** You've completed your work with the CSS demo page. You can continue to explore different CSS font and text styles or close the demo Web page now.

Aligning Text Vertically

In Tutorial 1, you learned how to align text horizontally using the text-align style. You can also vertically align inline elements within the content of the surrounding block. The style for setting vertical alignment is

```
vertical-align: type
```

where *type* is one of the keywords described in Figure 3-26.

Figure 3-26   **Values of the vertical-align style**

Value	Description
baseline	Aligns the element with the bottom of lowercase letters in surrounding text (the default)
bottom	Aligns the bottom of the element with the bottom of the lowest element in surrounding content
middle	Aligns the middle of the element with the middle of the surrounding content
sub	Subscripts the element
super	Superscripts the element
text-bottom	Aligns the bottom of the element with the bottom of the font of the surrounding content
text-top	Aligns the top of the element with the top of the font of the surrounding content
top	Aligns the top of the element with the top of the tallest object in the surrounding content

Instead of using keywords, you can specify a length or a percentage for the element to be aligned relative to the surrounding content. A positive value moves the element up and a negative value lowers the element. For example, the style

```
vertical-align: 50%
```

raises the element by half of the line height of the surrounding content, while the style

```
vertical-align: -100%
```

drops the element an entire line height below the baseline of the current line.

Combining All Text Formatting in a Single Style

You've learned a lot of different text and font styles. You can combine most of them into a single declaration, using the style

```
font: font-style font-variant font-weight font-size/line-height
font-family
```

where *font-style* is the font's style, *font-variant* is the font variant, *font-weight* is the weight of the font, *font-size* is the size of the font, *line-height* is the height of each line, and *font-family* is the font face. For example, the style

```
font: italic small-caps bold 16pt/24pt Arial, sans-serif
```

displays the text of the element in italics, bold, and small capital letters in Arial or another sans-serif font, with a font size of 16pt and spacing between the lines of 24pt. You do not have to include all of the properties of the font style; the only required properties are size and font-family. A browser assumes the default value for any omitted property. However, you must place any properties that you do include in the order indicated above.

Tammy thinks that the size of the address text at the bottom of the page is too large, and would like it in a smaller, non-italics, small caps, sans-serif font. You should modify the style for the address element in the farm.css style sheet so that Tammy can apply the style to any page on her Web site.

To change the style of the address element in Tammy's external style sheet:

▶ 1. Return to the **farm.css** file in your text editor.

▶ 2. Within the style declaration for the address element, add the following style attributes. See Figure 3-27.

```
font: normal small-caps 0.8em sans-serif
```

Applying the font style to the address element ◀ **Figure 3-27**

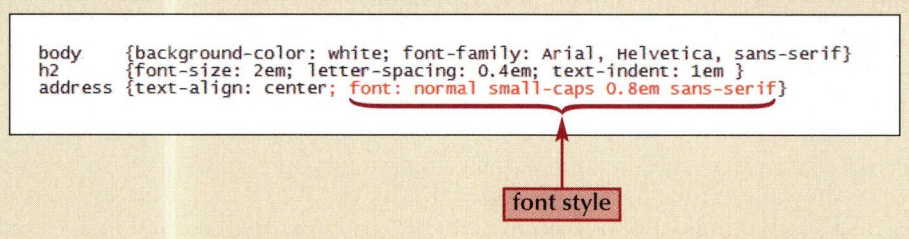

```
body     {background-color: white; font-family: Arial, Helvetica, sans-serif}
h2       {font-size: 2em; letter-spacing: 0.4em; text-indent: 1em }
address  {text-align: center; font: normal small-caps 0.8em sans-serif}
```

font style

▶ 3. Save your changes to the file.

▶ 4. Refresh the **home.htm** file in your Web browser. Scroll to the bottom of the page and verify that the style of the address element has been changed as shown in Figure 3-28.

Formatted address text ◀ **Figure 3-28**

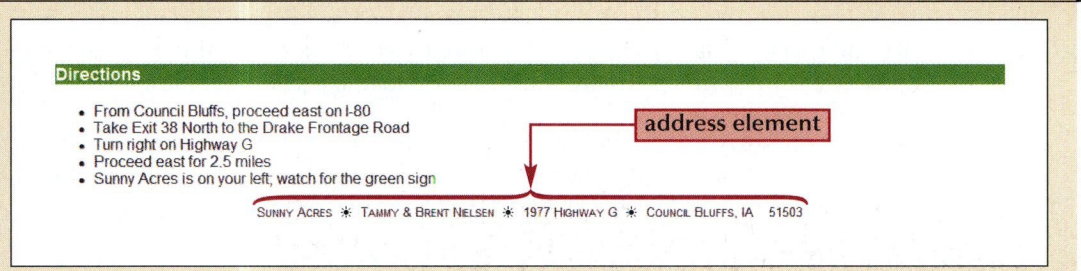

Directions

- From Council Bluffs, proceed east on I-80
- Take Exit 38 North to the Drake Frontage Road
- Turn right on Highway G
- Proceed east for 2.5 miles
- Sunny Acres is on your left; watch for the green sign

address element

SUNNY ACRES �֎ TAMMY & BRENT NIELSEN �֎ 1977 HIGHWAY G ✦ COUNCIL BLUFFS, IA 51503

Tammy likes the way the fonts appear on her Web site. She especially likes the fact that because these changes were made in a CSS style sheet, she can apply the styles to any Web page she adds to the site in the future.

Working with Images

Tammy wants you to turn your attention to her Web site's graphic images. Graphic images can greatly increase the size of the Web page so you must balance the goal of creating an interesting and attractive page against the need to keep the size of your page and its supporting files small. Many users will turn away from Web pages that take a long time to load.

Web browsers support three graphic formats: GIF, JPEG, and PNG. Each file format has its advantages and disadvantages, and you will probably use a combination of all three formats in your Web page designs. First, you'll look at the advantages and disadvantages of using GIF image files.

Working with GIF Images

GIF (**Graphics Interchange Format**) is a common image format first developed for the CompuServe online information service. GIF files are limited to 256 colors, so they are most often used for graphics requiring fewer colors, such as clip art images, line art, logos, and icons. Images that require more color depth, such as photographs, can appear grainy when saved as GIF files. GIF image files can be large. One way to reduce the size of a GIF is to reduce the number of colors in its color palette. For example, if an image contains only 32 different colors, you can use an image editing program to reduce the palette to those 32 colors, resulting in a smaller image file that loads faster.

Another feature of GIFs is their ability to use transparent colors. A **transparent color** is a color that is not displayed when the image is viewed in an application. In place of the transparent color, a browser displays whatever is on the page background. The process by which you create a transparent color depends on the graphics software you are using. Many applications include the option to designate a transparent color when saving an image, while other packages include a transparent color tool, which you use to select the color that you want to treat as transparent.

GIFs also support animation. An **animated GIF** is composed of several images that are displayed one after the other, creating the illusion of motion. There are many online collections of animated GIFs on the Web. You can also create your own with animated GIF software, which allows you to control the rate at which an animation plays (as measured by frames per second) and to determine the number of times the animation repeats before stopping (or to set it to repeat without stopping).

Animated GIFs are a mixed blessing. They make a Web page appear more dynamic, but they are larger than static GIF files, using them can slow down the loading of a Web page. Also, as with all formatting features, you should be careful not to overuse animated images. Animated GIFs can quickly irritate users once the novelty wears off, especially because there is no way for users to turn them off! Finally, keep in mind that like static GIF files, animated GIFs are limited to 256 colors.

One of the pages Tammy is planning for the Sunny Acres Web site is the index.htm file, which acts as a splash screen. A **splash screen** is a Web page containing interesting animation or graphics that introduces a Web site. Tammy suggests that you use an animated GIF for her splash screen. You've located a fun animated GIF of a scarecrow and another GIF that contains the Sunny Acres logo. You'll add both of these graphics as inline images to the index.htm file.

To insert GIF files into the splash screen page:

1. Open the **index.htm** file in your text editor.

2. Within the div element, insert the following inline image for the Sunny Acres logo:

   ```
   <img src="salogo.gif" alt="Sunny Acres" /><br />
   ```

3. Tammy wants the animated GIF to also function as a hypertext link, pointing to the home.htm file. As shown in Figure 3-29, insert the following linked graphic directly below the Sunny Acres logo:

   ```
   <a href="home.htm">
    <img src="scarecrow.gif" alt="animated GIF"
         style="border-width: 0" />
   </a>
   ```

Inserting GIF images Figure 3-29

```
<body>
   <div style="text-align: center">
      <img src="salogo.gif" alt="Sunny Acres" /><br />
      <a href="home.htm"><img src="scarecrow.gif" alt="animated GIF" style="border-width: 0" /></a>
   </div>
</body>
```

4. Save your changes to the file and then open the **index.htm** file in your Web browser. As shown in Figure 3-30, an animated scarecrow appears on the Web page directly below the Sunny Acres logo.

Sunny Acres splash screen Figure 3-30

JPEG Images

The other main image file format for Web pages is JPEG. **JPEG** stands for **Joint Photographic Experts Group**. JPEGs differ from GIFs in several ways. In the JPEG format, you can create images that use all 16.7 million colors available in the color palette. Because of this, JPEG files are most often used for photographs and other images that cover a wide spectrum of color. In addition, despite the fact that JPEGs use the full color palette, the image compression algorithm used by JPEG files yields image files that are usually (though not always) smaller than their GIF counterparts. (Note that in some situations, though, the GIF format creates a smaller and better-looking image—for example, when an image contains large sections covered with a single color.) You can set the amount of compression applied to JPEGs in your imaging editing software, allowing you to balance the desire for a high-quality image versus the need to keep images compact.

As a general rule, you should use JPEGs for photos and use GIFs for illustrations that involve only a few colors. All of the photos on the Sunny Acres Web site are in JPEG format. Note that JPEGs do not support animation or transparent colors.

PNG Images

A third graphic format gaining wider acceptance is the **Portable Network Graphics** or **PNG** format. PNG files include most of the same features as GIFs (including animation and transparency) but also provide file compression and the full 16.7 million colors available with JPEGs. You can also designate several transparent colors in a PNG file, rather than the single color that GIFs support. The only problem with the PNG format is that older browsers do not support it. This is becoming less of a problem as time goes by. Figure 3-31 summarizes the features of the three major graphics formats on the Web.

| Figure 3-31 | Comparison of Web graphic formats |

Feature	GIF	JPEG	PNG
Color resolution	256	16.7 million	16.7 million
Useful for line art	Yes	No	Yes
Useful for photographs	No	Yes	Yes
Interlacing/progressive encoding	Yes	Yes	Yes
Compressible	Yes	Yes	Yes
Transparent colors	Yes (1)	No	Yes (multiple)
Supported by older browsers	Yes	Yes	No

| InSight | **Other Image Formats** |

The GIF, JPEG, and PNG formats are not the only ways to add graphic images and animation to your Web site. The World Wide Web Consortium (W3C) promotes the **Scalable Vector Graphics (SVG)** specification, which is a graphic format written with XML that you can use to create line art composed of straight lines and curves. SVG also supports animation, and it can be used with programmable scripts that control the behavior and appearance of the animation. Because SVG files are written in XML, they are transferred as simple text files, allowing the application to interpret the SVG commands and render the graphic. Most browsers do not support SVG without the addition of specialized add-in programs.

Another popular approach is to use the Flash software program from Macromedia. You can use Flash to create interactive animations, scalable graphics, animated logos, and navigation controls for a Web site. To view a Flash animation, users must have the Flash player installed on their computers. Users can download and install the player for free, and are generally prompted to do this the first time they open a Web page that uses Flash. Flash players are available for all browsers and operating systems, so Flash is a safe and well supported method of creating animated effects and specialized graphics.

Setting the Image Size

By default, browsers display an image at its saved size. You can specify a different size by adding the HTML attributes

```
width="value" height="value"
```

to the <img /> tag, where the width and height values represent the dimensions of the image in pixels.

Changing an image's dimensions within the browser does not affect the file size. If you want to decrease the file size of an image, you should do so using an image editing application so that the image's file size is reduced in addition to its dimensions. Because of the way that browsers work with inline images, it is a good idea to specify the height and width of an image even if you're not trying to change its dimensions. When a browser encounters an inline image, it calculates the image size and then uses this information to lay out the page. If you include the dimensions of the image, the browser does not have to perform that calculation, reducing the time required to render the page. You can obtain the height and width of an image as measured in pixels using an image editing application such as Adobe Photoshop, or by viewing the properties of the graphic file in your computer's operating system.

The salogo.gif image is 599 pixels wide by 223 pixels high. The animated scarecrow graphic is 500 pixels wide by 300 pixels high. You decide to specify these dimensions in the HTML code of the index.htm file so that browsers won't have to calculate the images' dimensions when loading the page.

Tip

You can also set the image dimensions using the CSS width and height styles.

To set the dimensions for Tammy's splash screen images:

▶ 1. Return to the **index.htm** file in your text editor.

▶ 2. Within the <img> tag for the Sunny Acres logo, add the following attributes:

```
width="599" height="223"
```

▶ 3. Within the <img> tag for the animated scarecrow graphic, add the following attributes:

```
width="500" height="300"
```

Place the attributes on a new line to make your HTML code easier to read. Figure 3-32 shows the revised code for the index.htm file.

Specifying image width and height ◀ **Figure 3-32**

```
<body>
   <div style="text-align: center">
      <img src="salogo.gif" alt="Sunny Acres" width="599" height="223" /><br />
      <a href="home.htm"><img src="scarecrow.gif" alt="animated GIF"
                        width="500" height="300" style="border-width: 0" /></a>
   </div>
</body>
```

Formatting Backgrounds

Tammy has one more suggestion for the splash screen page. She would like you to change the background from its plain white color to the image shown in Figure 3-33.

Figure 3-33 **Tammy's proposed background image**

You can add a background image to any element. The style to apply a background image to an element is

```
background-image: url(url)
```

where (*url*) defines the name and location of the image file. When a browser loads the background image, it repeats the image in both the vertical and the horizontal directions until the background of the entire element is filled. This process is known as **tiling** because of its similarity to the process of filling up a floor or other surface with tiles. Let's see how Tammy's image looks in the splash screen page by adding it as a background for the entire page body. The image is saved as background.jpg.

To add a background image to the body element of Tammy's splash screen:

▶ **1.** Within the opening <body> tag, insert the following style attribute, as shown in Figure 3-34:

```
style="background-image: url(background.jpg)"
```

Figure 3-34 **Setting the background image for the page body**

```
<body style="background-image: url(background.jpg)">
    <div style="text-align: center">
        <img src="salogo.gif" alt="Sunny Acres" width="599" height="223" /><br />
        <a href="home.htm"><img src="scarecrow.gif" alt="animated GIF"
                        width="500" height="300" style="border-width: 0" /></a>
    </div>
</body>
```

▶ **2.** Close the file, saving your changes.

3. Reload the **index.htm** file in your Web browser. Verify that the Web page has the tiled background image shown in Figure 3-35.

Final splash screen page ◄ **Figure 3-35**

Tip

When using splash screens, include a meta element that automatically redirects the user to the site's home page after a few seconds have passed.

Note that both of the GIF images on this page employ a transparent color. This allows you to see the tiled background image behind the logo and the animated scarecrow graphic.

4. If you want to take a break before starting the next session, close any open files or applications now.

Background Image Options

By default, background images are tiled both horizontally and vertically until the entire background of the element is filled up. You can specify the direction of the tiling using the style

```
background-repeat: type
```

where *type* is repeat (the default), repeat-x, repeat-y, or no-repeat. Figure 3-36 describes each of the repeat types and Figure 3-37 shows examples of the style values.

Values of the background-repeat style ◄ **Figure 3-36**

Value	Description
repeat	The image is tiled both horizontally and vertically until the entire background of the element is covered
repeat-x	The image is tiled only horizontally across the width of the element
repeat-y	The image is tiled only vertically across the height of the element
no-repeat	The image is not repeated at all

Figure 3-37 **Tiling the background image**

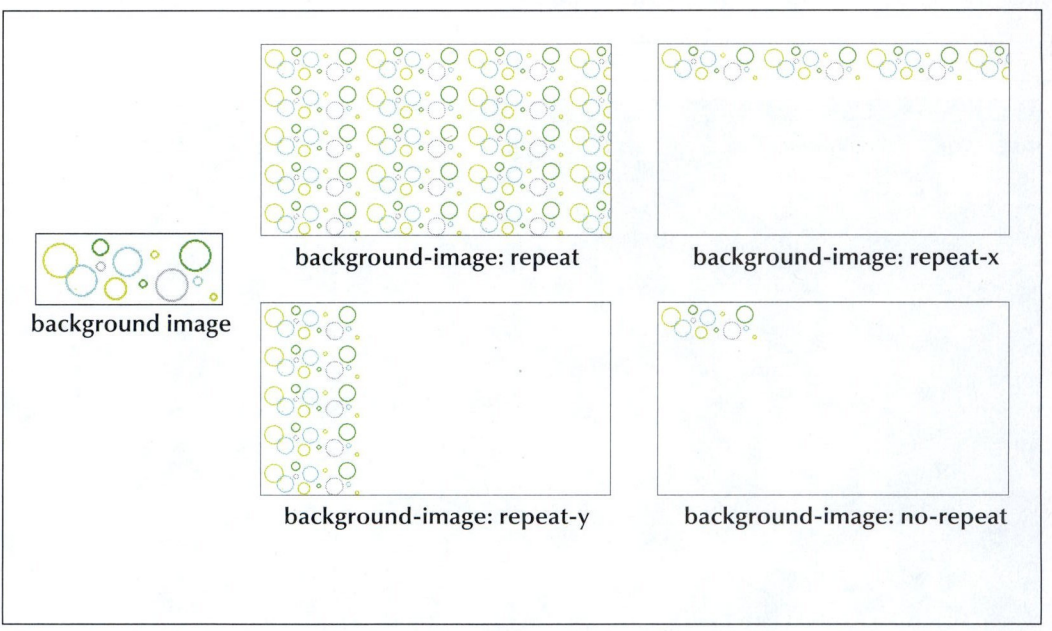

Browsers initially place a background image in an element's upper-left corner; and then if the code specifies tiling, the image is repeated from there. You can change the initial position of a background image using the style

```
background-position: horizontal vertical
```

where *horizontal* is the horizontal position of the image and *vertical* is its vertical position. You can specify a position as the distance from the top-left corner of the element, as a percentage of the element's width or height, or with a keyword. Keyword options are top, center, or bottom for vertical position, and left, center, or right for horizontal placement. For example, the style

```
background-position: 10% 20%
```

specifies an initial position for the background image 10% to the right and 20% down from the upper-left corner of the element. The style

```
background-position: right bottom
```

places the background image at the lower-right corner of the element. If you include only one position value, the browser applies that value to the horizontal position and vertically centers the image. So the style

```
background-position: 30px
```

places the background image 30 pixels to the right of the element's left border and centers it vertically.

By default, a background image moves along with its element as a user scrolls through a page. You can change this using the style

```
background-attachment: type
```

where *type* is either scroll or fixed. Scroll (the default) scrolls the image along with the element, while fixed places the image in a fixed place in the browser's display window, preventing it from moving even if the user scrolls down through the Web page. Fixed background images are often used to create the effect of a watermark, which is a translucent graphic impressed into the very fabric of paper, often found on specialized stationery.

The Background Style

Like the font style discussed in earlier in this session, you can combine the various background styles into the following single style

```
background: color url(url) repeat attachment horizontal vertical
```

where *color*, *(url)*, *repeat*, *attachment*, *horizontal*, and *vertical* are the values for the background style attributes that set the background color and control the placement and tiling of a background image. For example, the style

```
background: yellow url(logo.gif) no-repeat fixed center center
```

creates a yellow background on which the image file logo.gif is displayed. The image file is not tiled across the background, but is instead fixed in the horizontal and vertical center. You do not have to enter all of the values of the background style. However, those values that you do specify should follow the order indicated by the syntax to avoid unpredictable results.

Setting the Background Style | Reference Window

- To set the background style of an element, use
  ```
  background color url(url) repeat attachment horizontal vertical
  ```
  where *color* is a color name or a color value, *(url)* is the URL of the background image file, *repeat* specifies how the background image is tiled across the background (repeat, repeat-x, repeat-y, or no-repeat), *attachment* specifies whether the image scrolls with the Web page (scroll or fixed), and *horizontal* and *vertical* specify the initial position of the tiled background image.

You've completed your work with styles for the text and graphic images on the Sunny Acres Web site. You still have work to do to make the page layout interesting and attractive. In the next session you'll work with styles for block-level elements and lists.

Session 3.2 Quick Check | Review

1. Specify the style declaration to display all code elements in the Courier New font; and if that font is unavailable, use a monospace font.
2. If the font size of blockquote element text is set to 12 points, what will be the size of h2 headings nested within a blockquote if the following style declaration is applied to the Web page?

```
h2 {font-size: 1.5em}
```

3. Specify the style declaration to display all h3 headings with both an overline and an underline.

4. Specify the style declaration to set the kerning of address text to 0.5 em and tracking to 0.9 em.

5. Specify the style declaration to display the text of all definition term elements in uppercase letters.

6. Which graphic image format should you use for photographic images—GIF or JPEG—and why?

7. What attributes do you add to the <img /> tag to set the size of the image to 200 pixels wide by 100 pixels high?

8. Specify the style to use the image file mark.jpg as the background image for all blockquote elements. Fix the image at the top left of the block quote with no tiling.

Session 3.3

Floating an Element

Tammy wants you to return to work on her home page. She notices that the inline image below the Welcome heading forces a large space between the heading and the following paragraph (see Figure 3-24 from the last session). She would like the image placed alongside the right margin and the paragraph text to wrap around it. You can do this by floating the inline image.

Floating an element like an inline image causes the element to move out of the normal document flow on the page, moving to a position along the left or right margins of the parent element. The other elements on the Web page that are not floated are then moved up to occupy the position previously occupied by the floating element. Figure 3-38 shows a diagram of an element that is floated along the right margin of the page body.

Figure 3-38 ▶ **Floating an element**

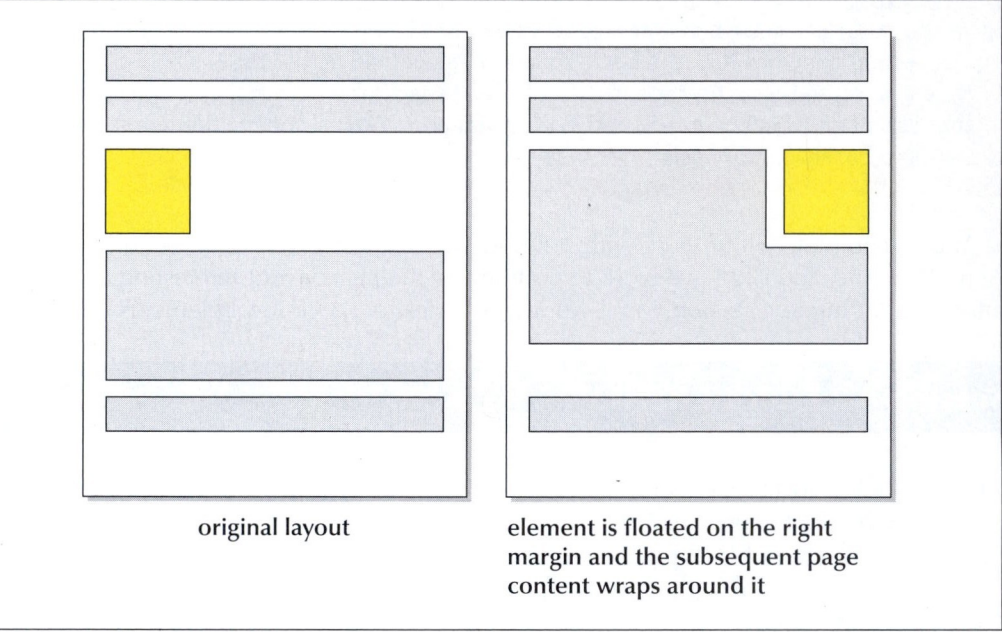

original layout

element is floated on the right margin and the subsequent page content wraps around it

To float an element, apply the style

```
float: position
```

where *position* is none (the default to turn off floating), left, or right. Most page elements can be floated. You can also stack floating elements to create a column effect in your page layout, as in Figure 3-39.

Floating multiple elements to create columns | **Figure 3-39**

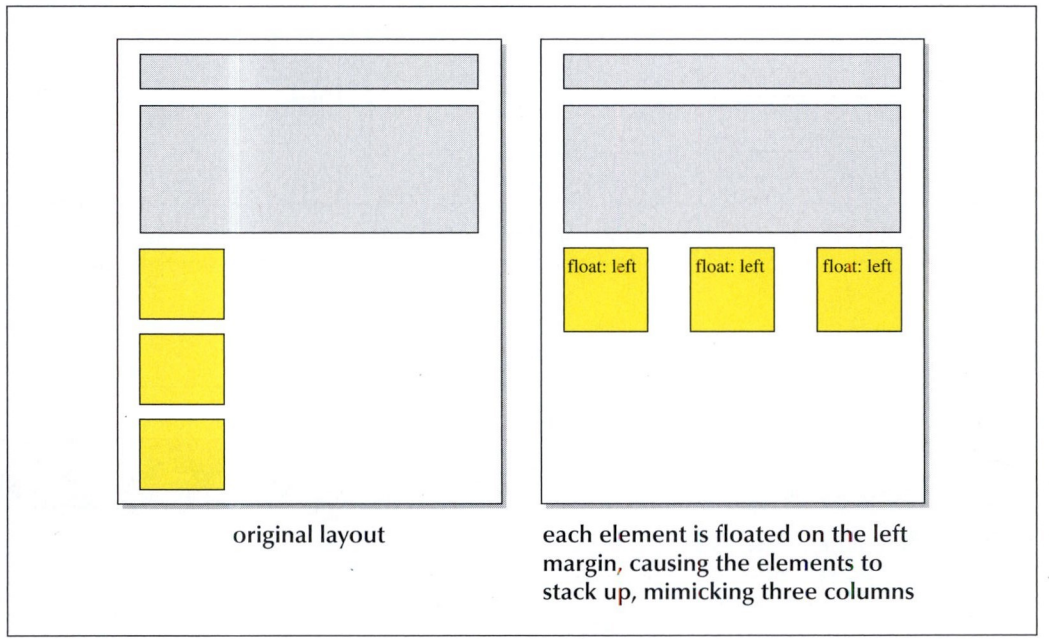

original layout

each element is floated on the left margin, causing the elements to stack up, mimicking three columns

Sometimes you will want to prevent an object from wrapping around a floating element. For example, you might not want headings to wrap around inline images. To prevent an element from wrapping, apply the clear style

```
clear: position
```

where *position* is none (the default), left, right, or both. For example, the style declaration

```
clear: right
```

causes the element not to be displayed until the right margin of the parent element is clear of floating objects. See Figure 3-40.

Figure 3-40 | **Using the clear style**

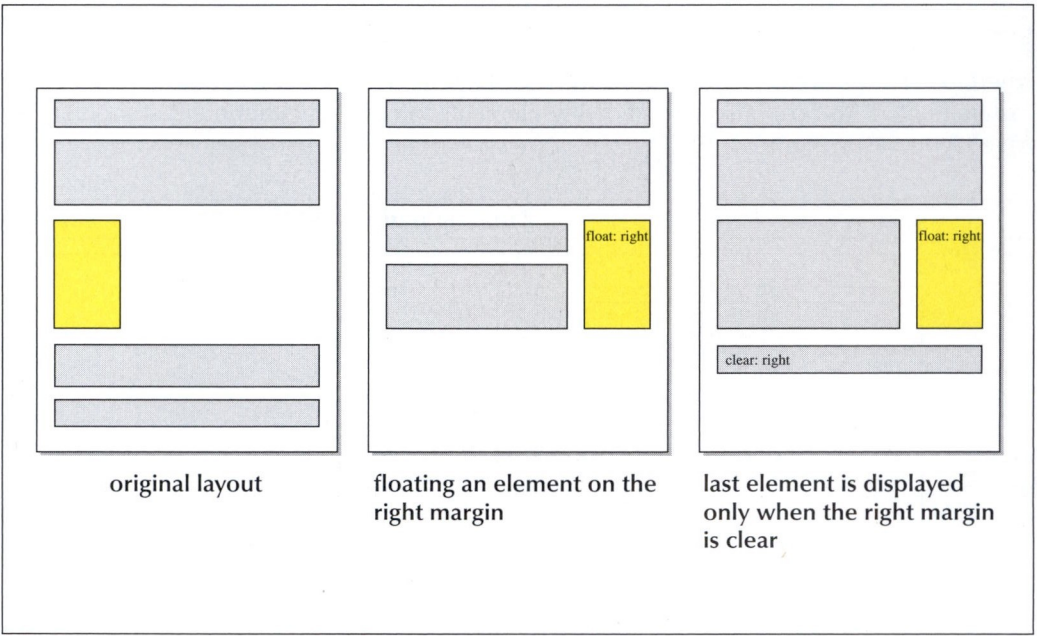

original layout

floating an element on the right margin

last element is displayed only when the right margin is clear

---

Reference Window | **Floating an Element**

- To float an element, use the style
    ```
    float: position
    ```
  where *position* is none (to turn off floating), left or right.
- To display an element clear of a floating element, use the style
    ```
    clear: position
    ```
  where *position* is none, left, right, or both.

Tammy wants you to use what you've learned about the floating style to float the inline image from the home page on the right margin of the paragraph that contains it. You could add the float style as an inline style directly to the <img> tag for the image, but Tammy has similar promotional photos on several of the pages from her Web site. She has given each promotional photo the id promoimage. Recall from the first session that you can create style declarations for elements based on their id values. This means you can use the farm.css style sheet to float all of these images with the following style declaration:

```
#promoimage {float: right}
```

Tammy wants you to add this style to the farm.css style sheet.

To float the promotional images on the Sunny Acres Web site:

► **1.** Return to the **farm.css** style sheet in your text editor.

► **2.** At the bottom of the file, add the following style as shown in Figure 3-41:

```
#promoimage {float: right}
```

```
body     {background-color: white; font-family: Arial, Helvetica, sans-serif}
h2       {font-size: 2em; letter-spacing: 0.4em; text-indent: 1em }
address  {text-align: center; font: normal small-caps 0.8em sans-serif}

#promoimage {float: right}
```

id of promotional images (points to `#promoimage`)

float the image on the right margin (points to `{float: right}`)

> **Tip**
> The float style floats the object on the margin of the parent element, not necessarily the margin of the Web page.

▶ **3.** Save your changes to the file.

▶ **4.** Refresh the **home.htm** file in your Web browser. As shown in Figure 3-42, the promotional inline image is now floated on the right margin of the first paragraph. The subsequent page content flows around the image.

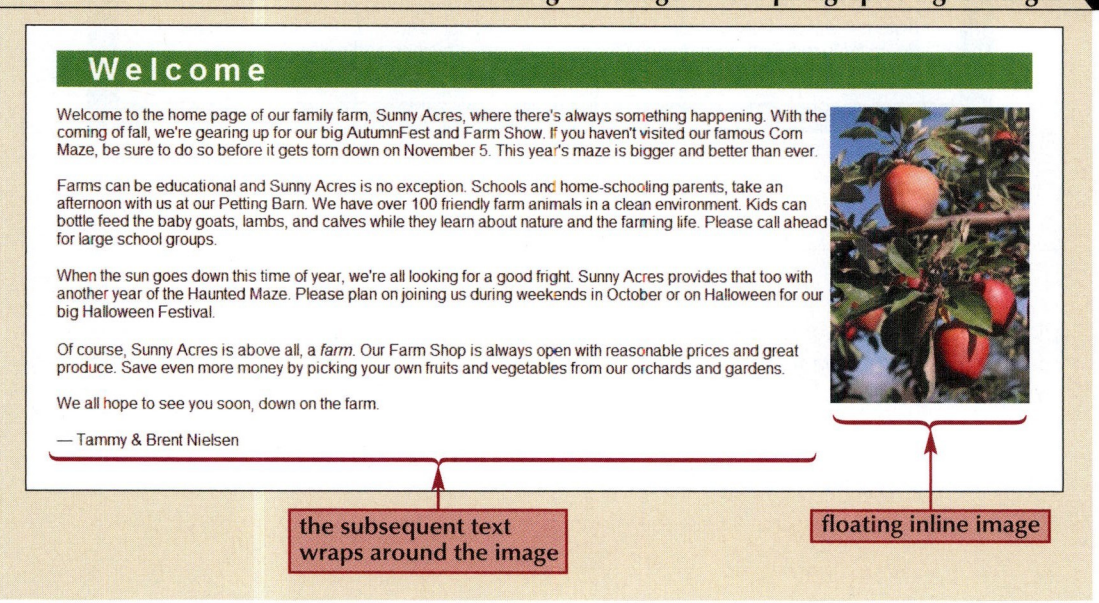

Welcome

Welcome to the home page of our family farm, Sunny Acres, where there's always something happening. With the coming of fall, we're gearing up for our big AutumnFest and Farm Show. If you haven't visited our famous Corn Maze, be sure to do so before it gets torn down on November 5. This year's maze is bigger and better than ever.

Farms can be educational and Sunny Acres is no exception. Schools and home-schooling parents, take an afternoon with us at our Petting Barn. We have over 100 friendly farm animals in a clean environment. Kids can bottle feed the baby goats, lambs, and calves while they learn about nature and the farming life. Please call ahead for large school groups.

When the sun goes down this time of year, we're all looking for a good fright. Sunny Acres provides that too with another year of the Haunted Maze. Please plan on joining us during weekends in October or on Halloween for our big Halloween Festival.

Of course, Sunny Acres is above all, a *farm*. Our Farm Shop is always open with reasonable prices and great produce. Save even more money by picking your own fruits and vegetables from our orchards and gardens.

We all hope to see you soon, down on the farm.

— Tammy & Brent Nielsen

the subsequent text wraps around the image

floating inline image

In older HTML code, you might see inline images floated using the align attribute. The general syntax of the align attribute is

```
<img align="position" ... />
```

where *position* is left or right. Note that the align attribute has been deprecated and is not supported in strict applications of XHTML.

Working with the Box Model

Floating the promotional image improved the appearance of the page. Tammy wants you to work with the size and placement of other elements on the page such as the heading and address elements. She wants a page layout that is easy to read and attractive to the eye.

A study of the technique of Web page layout starts with an appreciation of the CSS box model. The **box model** describes the structure of page elements as they are laid out on the Web page. In the box model, each element is composed of the four sections shown in Figure 3-43:

- the **margin** between the element and other page content
- the **border** of the box containing the element content
- the **padding** between the element's content and the box border
- the **content** of the element itself

Figure 3-43   **The box model**

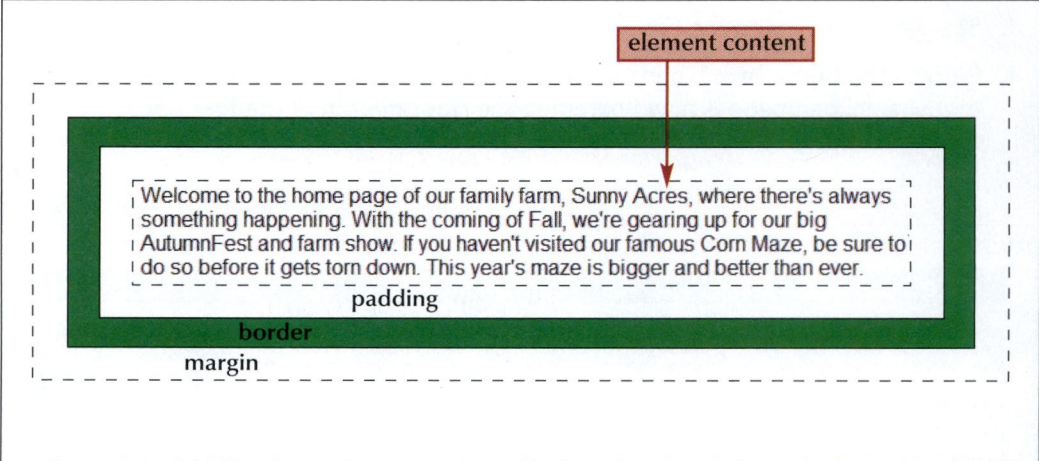

The size and appearance of these four sections determine how the element is displayed by the browser and play an important role in determining the layout of the elements on the Web page. Start exploring the box model by examining how to set the margins around an element.

Margin Styles

CSS supports several styles to set the element margin. The following four styles

```
margin-top: length
margin-right: length
margin-bottom: length
margin-left: length
```

set the sizes of the top, right, bottom, and left margins. Here *length* is a length expressed in one of the CSS units of measure discussed in the last session. You can also use the keyword auto, which leaves it to the browser to determine the margin size. The style declaration

```
h1 {margin-top: 10px; margin-right: 20px; margin-bottom: 10px;
    margin-left: 20px}
```

creates margins of 10 pixels above and below the h1 heading and margins of 20 pixels to the left and right of the heading.

These four margin styles can be combined into the single style

```
margin: top right bottom left
```

where *top*, *right*, *bottom*, and *left* are the sizes of the top, right, bottom, and left margins. (To help remember this order, think of moving clockwise around the element, starting with the top margin.) The style

```
h1 {margin: 10px 20px 10px 20px}
```

applies an identical set of margins to the longer style described above.

You don't have to supply values for all of the margins. If you specify only three values, they are applied to the top, right, and bottom margins. If you specify only two values, they're applied to the top and bottom margins. If you specify only a single value, a browser applies that value to all four margins. So the style

```
h1 {margin: 10px 20px}
```

applies a 10-pixel margin above and below the h1 heading and a 20-pixel margin to the left and right. The style

```
h1 {margin: 10px}
```

creates a 10-pixel margin around the entire heading.

One of the changes that Tammy suggested is to add more space between the promotional image and the surrounding text. She thinks that the text is too tight around the image and suggests that you set a 1-em margin below and to the left of the image. The top margin and the right margin can be set to 0 em units. Remember that you are making these changes to the CSS style sheet so that Tammy can apply them to any image she marks with the promotional id.

To set the margins around the promotional image in Tammy's external style sheet:

▶ **1.** Return to the **farm.css** style sheet in your text editor.

▶ **2.** Add the following margin style to the style declaration for the promotional image, as shown in Figure 3-44:

```
margin: 0em 0em 1em 1em
```

Setting margins around the promotional images ◀ **Figure 3-44**

```
body     {background-color: white; font-family: Arial, Helvetica, sans-serif}
h2       {font-size: 2em; letter-spacing: 0.4em; text-indent: 1em }
address  {text-align: center; font: normal small-caps 0.8em sans-serif}

#promoimage {float: right; margin: 0em 0em 1em 1em}
```

▶ **3.** Save your changes to the file.

▶ **4.** Reload the **home.htm** file in your Web browser. Verify that the margin to the left and below the promotional image has been increased slightly.

The margin styles can also be applied to the body element. By setting the margin around the page body to 0, you can remove the extra space many browsers insert by default between the page content and the edge of the browser window.

Padding Styles

The styles for the size of the padding in the box model are similar to the margin styles. The following four styles set the size of the padding above, to the right, below, and to the left of the element content:

```
padding-top: length
padding-right: length
padding-bottom: length
padding-left: length
```

You can also combine these four styles in a single padding style

```
padding: top right bottom left
```

where *top*, *right*, *bottom*, and *left* are the padding sizes around the element content. As with the margin style, you can specify any or all of the four padding values. When you specify a single value, it is applied to all four padding values. The style

```
h1 {padding: 5px}
```

sets the padding space around the h1 heading content to 5 pixels in each direction. By default, elements have no padding. The space between elements such as between adjacent paragraphs is set by the margins alone.

Reference Window | **Setting Margin and Padding Space in the Box Model**

- To set the margin space around an element, use
  ```
  margin: length
  ```
  where *length* is the size of the margin using one of the CSS units of measure.
- To set the padding space within an element, use
  ```
  padding: length
  ```
- To set a margin or padding for one side of the box model only, specify the direction (top, right, bottom, or left). For example, use
  ```
  margin-right: length
  ```
  to set the length of the right margin.

Border Styles

CSS supports three types of styles for the box model border. You can set the border width, the border color, or the border style. As with the margin and padding styles, there are styles that affect the top, right, bottom, and left borders or all borders at once. To define the width of the border, use

```
border-top-width: length
border-right-width: length
border-bottom-width: length
border-left-width: length
```

or the following single border-width style for setting the width for any or all of the borders:

```
border-width: top right bottom left
```

You've already worked with the border-width style in Tutorial 2, where you used it to remove the border around a linked image. The style

```
img {border-width: 0px}
```

could be used to remove the borders around all of the inline images on the Web page or Web site. Border widths can also be expressed using the keywords thin, medium, or thick. The exact meaning of these sizes depends on the browser.

The next set of styles set the color of the border (if one exists) around an element. These styles are

```
border-top-color: color
border-right-color: color
border-bottom-color: color
border-left-color: color
border-color: top right bottom left
```

where *color* is a color name, color value, or the keyword transparent to create an invisible border. For example, the following style adds a 4-pixel red border directly above the address element:

```
address {border-top-width: 4px; border-top-color: red}
```

If you don't specify a color, the browser uses the text color of the element within the box.

The final border style defines the border design. The five border styles are

```
border-top-style: type
border-right-style: type
border-bottom-style: type
border-left-style: type
border-style: top right bottom left
```

where *type* is one of the nine border style displayed in Figure 3-45.

Tip

You can create the illusion of a drop shadow by adding borders of different thicknesses around the element. Try border styles such as
```
border-width: 1px
4px 4px 1px
```
to create this effect.

Border style designs ◄ **Figure 3-45**

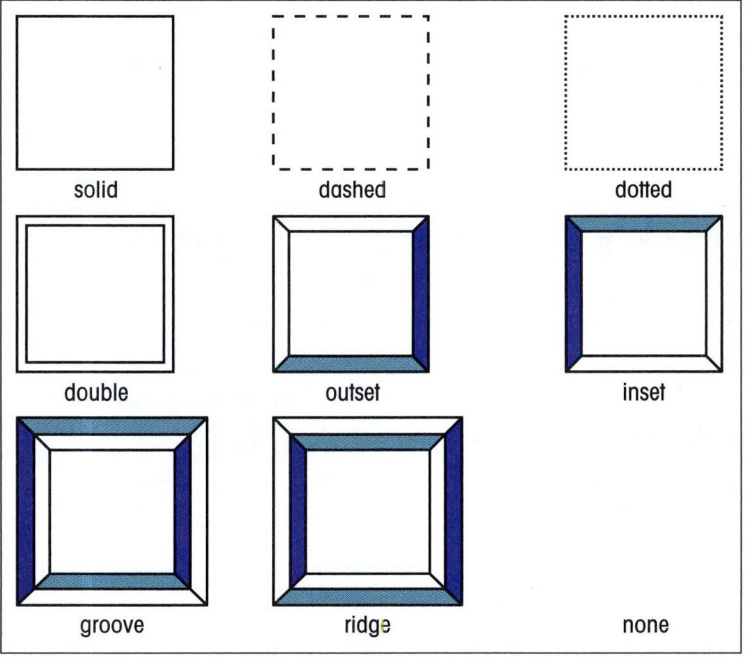

For example, to place a double border below an element, use the style:

```
border-style-bottom: double.
```

All of the border styles discussed above can be combined into a single style that defines each or all of the borders around the element. The syntax of these border styles is

```
border-top: width style color
border-right: width style color
border-bottom: width style color
border-left: width style color
border: width style color
```

where *width* is the width of the border, *style* is the style of the border, and *color* is the border color. The three properties must be entered in that order. For example, the style

```
h1 {border: 2px solid blue}
```

adds a 2-pixel wide solid blue border around every h1 heading.

Reference Window | **Setting Border Styles in the Box Model**

- To set the border width, use
     ```
     border-width: length
     ```
  where *length* is the width of the border using one of the CSS units of measure.
- To set the border color, use
     ```
     border-color: color
     ```
  where *color* is a color name or value.
- To set the border design, use
     ```
     border-style: type
     ```
  where *type* is none, solid, dashed, dotted, double, outset, inset, groove, or ridge.
- To set all of the border options in one style, use
     ```
     border: length color type
     ```
  in that order.

Having discussed the wide varieties of border styles with Tammy, she suggests you add a top border to the address element on the Sunny Acres home page. She thinks a double green border 0.5 em in height would look good. To keep the border from crowding the address text, you'll increase the padding between the text and the border to 1 em.

To create a border for the address element in Tammy's external style sheet:

1. Return to the **farm.css** style sheet in your text editor.

2. Add the following styles to the address element as shown in Figure 3-46. Place the styles on a new line to make your code easier to read. Be sure to separate all styles with a semicolon.

   ```
   border-top: 0.5em double green; padding-top: 1em
   ```

Using the border-top and padding-top styles ◀ Figure 3-46

```
body     {background-color: white; font-family: Arial, Helvetica, sans-serif}
h2       {font-size: 2em; letter-spacing: 0.4em; text-indent: 1em }
address  {text-align: center; font: normal small-caps 0.8em sans-serif;
          border-top: 0.5em double green; padding-top: 1em}

#promoimage {float: right; margin: 0em 0em 1em 1em}
```

▶ **3.** Save your changes to the file.

▶ **4.** Reload the **home.htm** file in your Web browser. Scroll to the bottom of the page and verify that a double green border has been added to the top of the address element, as shown in Figure 3-47.

Adding a double top border to the address element ◀ Figure 3-47

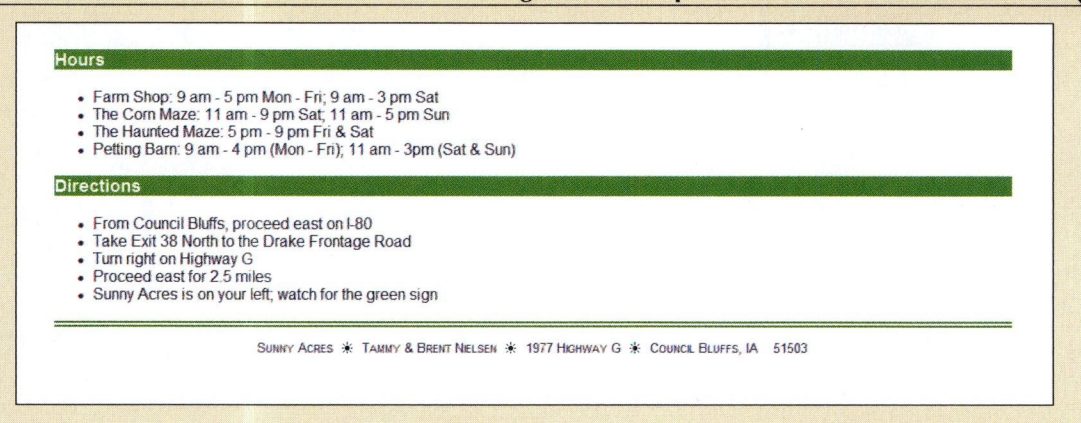

Because of their flexibility, border styles are usually applied in place of the hr (horizontal rule) element discussed in Tutorial 1 as a way of creating section breaks on Web pages.

Width and Height Styles

The final aspect of the box model that can be controlled with CSS styles is the box's width and height. The default width and height are determined by the browser. For inline elements, the width is the width of the element content and the height is the height of a single line. Block-level elements extend across the width of their parent element with a height that expands to meet the content enclosed within the block. So a heading element will have a width than spans the width of the Web page. If the heading is nested within a blockquote element, its width will span the width of the blockquote, and so on. You can set a different width using the style

```
width: value
```

where *value* is the width of the content expressed in one of the CSS units of measure discussed in the last session. According to the CSS specifications, the width value does not take into account the size of the margins, padding space, or borders. It applies only to the actual content of the element. Most browsers follow the CSS specifications, except Internet Explorer. With Internet Explorer, the width style value is applied to element content, padding, and borders. This means that if you are using the box model for page layout, you can end up with different layouts under different browsers. For example, the style declaration

```
p {width: 500px; padding: padding: 30px; border: 10px solid green}
```

results in a paragraph that is 500 pixels wide under Internet Explorer with 420 pixels reserved for the width of the element content. Under other browsers that follow the CSS specifications (such as Firefox, Opera, and Safari), the element content is 500 pixels wide and the width of the entire box (including the padding and borders) is 580 pixels. See Figure 3-48.

Figure 3-48 Interpretations of the box model width style

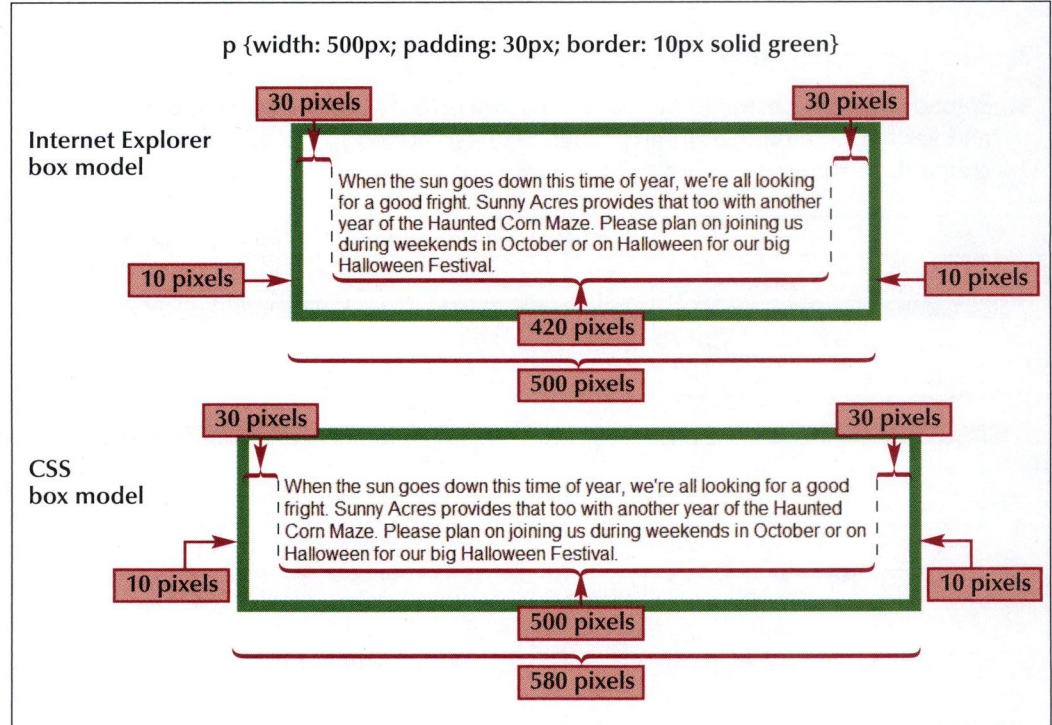

There are several ways of reconciling these interpretations of the box model that we'll discuss later. For now, you should simply be aware that this is an ongoing concern for designers trying to do precise Web page layout.

Quirks Mode and Standards Mode | InSight

Internet Explorer has two modes it can work in. One is **quirks mode**, in which the browser applies the Internet Explorer interpretation of the box model and other features of CSS. However, starting with Internet Explorer 6, you can force the IE browser to adopt the CSS interpretation of the box model styles by putting it into **standards mode**. This is done by changing the code of your Web page from HTML to XHTML by replacing the opening <html> tag with the following three lines:

```
<?xml version="1.0" encoding="UTF-8" standalone="no" ?>

<!DOCTYPE html PUBLIC "-//W3C//DTD XHTML 1.0 Strict//EN"
   "http://www.w3.org/TR/xhtml1/DTD/xhtml11-strict.dtd">

<html xmlns="http://www.w3.org/1999/xhtml">
```

When the IE browser encounters these lines, it interprets all CSS styles in accord with a strict interpretation of the CSS guidelines. Standards mode also enforces other aspects of the CSS specifications; so to be more compliant with CSS, you should use the three lines of code above to put the IE browser in standards mode. By default, Internet Explorer works in quirks mode, which is often necessary to support older HTML and CSS code written before the CSS 2.1 standards were introduced.

As long as you are not doing exact Web page design in which the difference of a few pixels can render your page unreadable, you can work in either standards or quirks mode. However, as you gain confidence in Web design and attempt more intricate layouts, you might find a need to work in standards mode. Note that all browsers, not just Internet Explorer, support a standards mode and quirks mode. You can learn more by reading the browser's technical documentation or by doing a Web search on the differences between quirks and standards models.

To set the height of the element content, use the height style

```
height: value
```

where *value* is the height of the content expressed in CSS units of measure. If you set a height value that is insufficient to display all of the element content, the browser will ignore the height value and still expand the height of the box. There are styles to override this behavior that you explore in Tutorial 4.

Setting the Width and Height in the Box Model | Reference Window

- To set the box model width, use
  ```
  width: length
  ```
  where *length* is the width of the box content in one of the CSS units of measure. (Note that Internet Explorer applies the width value to the box model content, padding space, and border.)
- To set the box model height, use
  ```
  height: length
  ```
  where *length* is the height of the box content in one of the CSS units of measure.

Tammy doesn't like the appearance of h3 headings on the home page shown earlier in Figure 3-47. The headings identify two subsections of the document: one for the hours the farm is open and the other for directions to the farm. Currently the two headings extend across the width of the Web page. Tammy suggests that the headings would look better if they were about the same width as the text of the bulleted lists they introduce. You'll also increase the size of the left padding to offset the text a few spaces from the box's left border. You'll apply this style to other h3 headings on the Sunny Acres Web site, so you'll add the style to the farm.css external style sheet.

To set the style of the h3 headings in Tammy's external style sheet:

▶ 1. Return to the **farm.css** style sheet in your text editor.

▶ 2. Insert the following style directly below the style for the h2 heading, as shown in Figure 3-49:

```
h3 {width: 20em; padding-left: 1em}
```

Figure 3-49	Setting the width and left padding of the h3 element

```
body     {background-color: white; font-family: Arial, Helvetica, sans-serif}
h2       {font-size: 2em; letter-spacing: 0.4em; text-indent: 1em }
h3       {width: 20em; padding-left: 1em}
address {text-align: center; font: normal small-caps 0.8em sans-serif;
         border-top: 0.5em double green; padding-top: 1em}

#promoimage {float: right; margin: 0em 0em 1em 1em}
```

▶ 3. Save your changes to the file.

▶ 4. Reload the **home.htm** file in your Web browser. Figure 3-50 shows the revised appearance of the two h3 headings.

Figure 3-50	Reformatted h3 headings

Hours

- Farm Shop: 9 am - 5 pm Mon - Fri; 9 am - 3 pm Sat
- The Corn Maze: 11 am - 9 pm Sat; 11 am - 5 pm Sun
- The Haunted Maze: 5 pm - 9 pm Fri & Sat
- Petting Barn: 9 am - 4 pm (Mon - Fri); 11 am - 3pm (Sat & Sun)

Directions

- From Council Bluffs, proceed east on I-80
- Take Exit 38 North to the Drake Frontage Road
- Turn right on Highway G
- Proceed east for 2.5 miles
- Sunny Acres is on your left; watch for the green sign

Controlling Page Layout with div Containers

Tammy is pleased with the layout of the Sunny Acres home page. But when she displayed it on her laptop's wide-screen monitor, she expressed concern about the text that extends across the screen. Studies show that text gets more difficult to read as the length of the line extends beyond about 30 to 50 characters per line. A page layout like that shown in Figure 3-51 is difficult enough to read that many people will skip over it.

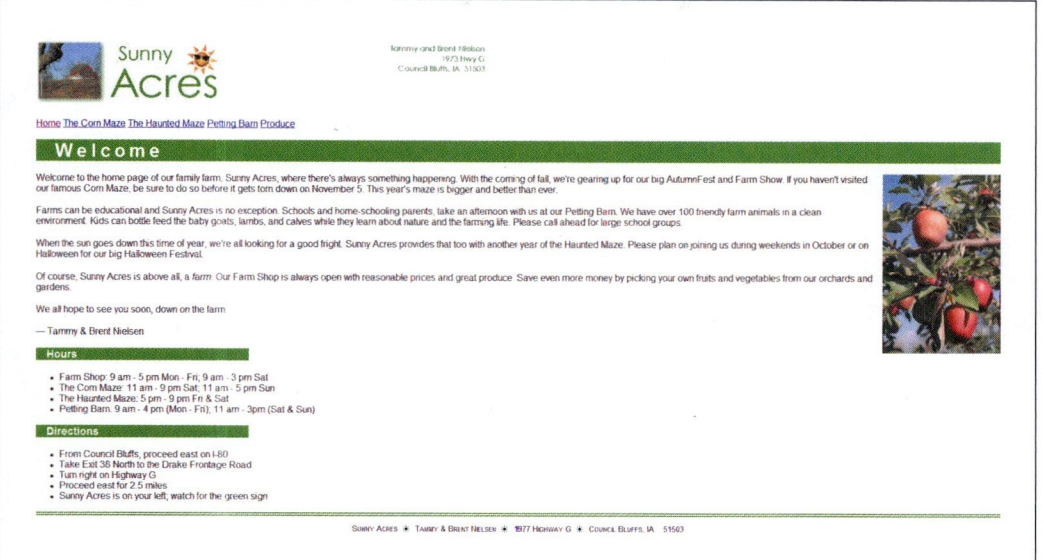

Tammy wants you to modify the page layout so that the length of the line is always kept within an acceptable limit under any monitor resolution. To do that, you'll use the style associated with the box model to set the width and margins of the different sections of the page. The technique involves placing different sections of the page within div elements called **div containers**, which you can then resize and float to create different page layouts. Recall that the div element is a generic block-level element. Browsers do not have default styles for the element's padding, border, margins, or width, so you can set all of these with your style sheet without worrying about conflicts with the browser's default settings.

The first div container that you'll add to the Sunny Acres home page will enclose the entire page content. You'll give this div container the id, outer.

To create the outer div container on Tammy's home page:

1. Open the **home.htm** file with your text editor.

2. Directly below the opening <body> tag, insert the following:

   ```
   <div id="outer">
   ```

3. Scroll down to the bottom of the file. Directly above the closing </body> tag, insert the following:

   ```
   </div>
   ```

   Figure 3-52 highlights the newly added code.

Figure 3-52 ▸ Adding the outer div container

```
<body>
<div id="outer">
    <h1><img src="salogo.jpg" alt="Sunny Acres" /></h1>
    <div id="links">
        <a href="home.htm">Home</a>
        <a href="maze.htm">The Corn Maze</a>
        <a href="haunted.htm">The Haunted Maze</a>
        <a href="petting.htm">Petting Barn</a>
        <a href="produce.htm">Produce</a>
    </div>

    <h2>Welcome</h2>



    <address>
        Sunny Acres  &#9728; 
        Tammy &amp; Brent Nielsen  &#9728; 
        1977 Highway G  &#9728; 
        Council Bluffs, IA    51503
    </address>

</div>
</body>
```

▸ **4.** Save your changes to the file.

Now that you've enclosed the page content within a div container, you can specify the width of the content. Rather than letting the content extend across the width of the browser window, you'll set the width to 50 em.

To set the width of the outer div container:

▸ **1.** Return to the **farm.css** style sheet in your text editor.

▸ **2.** Add the following style to the bottom of the file, as shown in Figure 3-53:

    #outer {width: 50em}

Figure 3-53 ▸ Setting the width of the outer div container

```
body     {background-color: white; font-family: Arial, Helvetica, sans-serif}
h2       {font-size: 2em; letter-spacing: 0.4em; text-indent: 1em }
h3       {width: 20em; padding-left: 1em}
address  {text-align: center; font: normal small-caps 0.8em sans-serif;
          border-top: 0.5em double green; padding-top: 1em}

#promoimage {float: right; margin: 0em 0em 1em 1em}
#outer      {width: 50em}
```

▸ **3.** Save your changes to the file, and then reload **home.htm** in your Web browser. Verify that the width of the page content has been changed.

Note that by setting the width of the outer div container to 50 em, you've set the width to a defined size. Most monitors can fit this size; but if the user is using a smaller monitor, it's possible that the page width will extend beyond the browser window. If that is the case, the user will have to scroll horizontally through the browser window to view the entire page text. This is considered bad design, so you should test your Web pages on a variety of devices and resolutions to ensure this doesn't happen. Setting a page width is often a balancing act between competing needs.

Tammy has included a list of links at the top of the home page. She would like to display these links to the left of the Sunny Acres introduction. The links have been placed in a div container of their own with the id named links, so you can apply the following styles to the links div container:

Tip

You can set the page width by applying the width style to the body element.

- float it on the left margin of the outer div container
- set the width to 10 em
- set the background color to white
- add an outset border 0.5 em in width

You'll add this style declaration to the farm.css external style sheet so that Tammy can use it throughout her Web site.

To set the style for the list of links:

1. Return to the **farm.css** style sheet in your text editor.

2. As shown in Figure 3-54, add the following style:

```
#links {float: left; width: 10em; background-color: white;
        border-style: outset; border-width: 0.5em}
```

Setting the style of the links div container | Figure 3-54

```
#promoimage {float: right; margin: 0em 0em 1em 1em}
#outer      {width: 50em}
#links      {float: left; width: 10em; background-color: white;
             border-style: outset; border-width: 0.5em}
```

3. Save your changes to the file, and then reload **home.htm** in your Web browser. Figure 3-55 shows the revised appearance of the Sunny Acres home page.

List of links floated on the left margin | Figure 3-55

Sunny Acres

Tammy and Brent Nielsen
1973 Hwy G
Council Bluffs, IA 51503

links floated
on the left

Home The Corn
Maze The Haunted
Maze Petting Barn
Produce

Welcome

Welcome to the home page of our family farm, Sunny Acres, where there's always something happening. With the coming of fall, we're gearing up for our big AutumnFest and Farm Show. If you haven't visited our famous Corn Maze, be sure to do so before it gets torn down on November 5. This year's maze is bigger and better than ever.

Floating the list of links on the left page margin has saved some vertical space, but the layout is not attractive. Tammy thinks it would look much better if the welcoming text did not wrap around the links box, but instead was placed in a separate column. You can do this by enclosing the welcoming text within a div container of its own and then setting the left margin large enough to clear the links box.

To create the div container:

▶ 1. Return to the **home.htm** file in your text editor.

▶ 2. Directly above the opening <h2> tag for the Welcome title, insert:

   `<div id="inner">`

▶ 3. Scroll down the file and directly above the opening <address> tag, insert:

   `</div>`

   Figure 3-56 highlights the revised text.

Figure 3-56 ▶ **Adding the inner div container**

```
<div id="inner">
<h2>welcome</h2>
<p>
    <img src="photo1.jpg" alt="home page photo" id="promoimage" />
    welcome to the home page of our family farm,
    sunny Acres, where there's always something
    happening. with the coming of fall, we're gearing up for our big AutumnFest
    and Farm show. If you haven't visited our famous corn Maze, be sure to do
    so before it gets torn down on November 5. This year's maze is bigger and
    better than ever.
</p>




    <h3>Directions</h3>
    <ul>
        <li>From council Bluffs, proceed east on I-80</li>
        <li>Take Exit 38 North to the Drake Frontage Road</li>
        <li>Turn right on Highway G</li>
        <li>Proceed east for 2.5 miles</li>
        <li>sunny Acres is on your left; watch for the green sign</li>
    </ul>
</div>
```

▶ 4. Save your changes to the file.

Now you can set the styles for the inner div container. To separate the text in the inner div container from the links box, you'll apply styles to:

- set the left margin to 12 em
- display a solid green border 0.1 em wide on the left side of the container
- set the left padding to 1 em

You want to add this style to the farm.css style sheet so that Tammy can use it in any of her pages.

To create a style for the inner div container:

▶ 1. Return to the **farm.css** style sheet in your text editor.

▶ 2. Add the following style, as shown in Figure 3-57:

```
#inner {margin-left: 12em; padding-left: 1em;
     border-left: 0.1em solid green}
```

Setting the style of the inner div container ◀ **Figure 3-57**

```
#promoimage {float: right;  margin: 0em 0em 1em 1em}
#outer      {width: 50em}
#links      {float: left;  width: 10em;  background-color: white;
             border-style: outset;  border-width: 0.5em}
#inner      {margin-left: 12em;  padding-left: 1em;
             border-left: 0.1em solid green}
```

▶ 3. Save your changes to the file and then reload or refresh **home.htm** in your Web browser. Figure 3-58 shows the revised layout of the Sunny Acres home page.

Layout of the inner div container ◀ **Figure 3-58**

Sunny **Acres**

Tammy and Brent Nielsen
1973 Hwy G
Council Bluffs, IA 51503

Home The Corn
Maze The Haunted
Maze Petting Barn
Produce

Welcome

Welcome to the home page of our family farm, Sunny Acres, where there's always something happening. With the coming of fall, we're gearing up for our big AutumnFest and Farm Show. If you haven't visited our famous Corn Maze, be sure to do so before it gets torn down on November 5. This year's maze is bigger and better than ever.

Farms can be educational and Sunny Acres is no exception. Schools and home-schooling parents, take an afternoon with us at our Petting Barn. We have over 100 friendly farm animals in a clean environment. Kids can bottle feed the baby goats, lambs, and calves while they learn about nature and the farming life. Please call ahead for large school groups.

When the sun goes down this time of year, we're all looking for a good fright. Sunny Acres provides that too with another year of the Haunted Maze. Please plan on joining us during weekends in October or on Halloween for our big Halloween Festival.

left margin is
set to 12 em

The page looks much better with the two div containers separating the content on the home page.

InSight

The Box Model and Nested div Containers

One source of page layout conflicts come from the different ways browsers apply the padding space. One way to avoid this problem is to set the padding space to 0 and only use the margin style with nested div containers. For example, if you need to set the padding space around your paragraphs to 10 pixels, but you worry that this will adversely affect the layout for IE users, place the paragraph in a div container and set the margin around the paragraph to 10 pixels. Because margins are interpreted the same way by all browsers, you will find that the paragraph's width will be the same under the IE box model and the CSS box model.

Setting the Display Style

Tammy likes the revised page layout but still finds the list of links difficult to read. She thinks it would be better if each link were on a separate line. You could fix this by enclosing each link within its own paragraph or by inserting a line break between each link. However, Tammy wants to move as much of the formatting into style sheets as she can, rather than making these changes to document content. She also might want to explore different layouts in the future—for example, laying out the links horizontally at the top of the page—and doesn't want to have to remove paragraph tags or line breaks if she does that.

As you've seen, most page elements are classified as either inline elements or block-level elements. Browsers treat links as inline elements, which is why all of the entries in the links list run together on a single line. You can use CSS to change the display style applied to any element, allowing you to make inline elements appear as block-level elements and vice versa. The syntax of the display style is

```
display: type
```

where *type* is one of the CSS display types described in Figure 3-59.

| Figure 3-59 | Values of the display style |

Display	Description
block	Display as a block-level element
inline	Display as an inline element
inline-block	Display as an inline element with some of the properties of a block (much like an inline image or frame)
inherit	Inherit the display property of the element's parent
list-item	Display as a list item
none	Do not display the element
run-in	Display as either an inline or block-level element depending on the context (CSS2)
table	Display as a block-level table
inline-table	Display as an inline table
table-caption	Treat as a table caption
table-cell	Treat as a table cell
table-column	Treat as a table column
table-column-group	Treat as a group of table columns
table-footer-group	Treat as a group of table footer rows
table-header-group	Treat as a group of table header rows
table-row	Treat as a table row
table-row-group	Treat as a group of table rows

To display all hypertext links as block-level elements rather than inline elements, apply the following style

```
a {display: block}
```

which has the same effect on page layout as turning the hypertext link into a generic div element.

Setting the Display Style | Reference Window

- To set the display style of an element, use
  display: *type*
  where *type* is the type of display. Use inline for inline elements and block for block-level elements.

You'll add this style to the farm.css style sheet. You'll also set the margin around each of the hypertext links to 0.1 em to provide more space between the links and the links box.

To set the display style for the links container:

▶ 1. Return to the **farm.css** file in your text editor.

▶ 2. As shown in Figure 3-60, add the following style:

```
a {display: block; margin: 0.3em}
```

The final farm.css style sheet ◀ **Figure 3-60**

```
body    {background-color: white; font-family: Arial, Helvetica, sans-serif}
h2      {font-size: 2em; letter-spacing: 0.4em; text-indent: 1em }
h3      {width: 20em; padding-left: 1em}
address {text-align: center; font: normal small-caps 0.8em sans-serif;
         border-top: 0.5em double green; padding-top: 1em}
a       {display: block; margin: 0.3em}

#promoimage {float: right; margin: 0em 0em 1em 1em}
#outer      {width: 50em}
#links      {float: left; width: 10em; background-color: white;
             border-style: outset; border-width: 0.5em}
#inner      {margin-left: 12em; padding-left: 1em;
             border-left: 0.1em solid green}
```

▶ 3. Save your changes to the file and then refresh **home.htm** in your Web browser. Figure 3-61 shows the final layout of the entire Sunny Acres home page.

Figure 3-61 | **The final layout of the Sunny Acres home page**

Sunny **Acres**

Tammy and Brent Nielsen
1973 Hwy G
Council Bluffs, IA 51503

Home
The Corn Maze
The Haunted Maze
Petting Barn
Produce

Welcome

Welcome to the home page of our family farm, Sunny Acres, where there's always something happening. With the coming of fall, we're gearing up for our big AutumnFest and Farm Show. If you haven't visited our famous Corn Maze, be sure to do so before it gets torn down on November 5. This year's maze is bigger and better than ever.

Farms can be educational and Sunny Acres is no exception. Schools and home-schooling parents, take an afternoon with us at our Petting Barn. We have over 100 friendly farm animals in a clean environment. Kids can bottle feed the baby goats, lambs, and calves while they learn about nature and the farming life. Please call ahead for large school groups.

When the sun goes down this time of year, we're all looking for a good fright. Sunny Acres provides that too with another year of the Haunted Maze. Please plan on joining us during weekends in October or on Halloween for our big Halloween Festival.

Of course, Sunny Acres is above all, a *farm*. Our Farm Shop is always open with reasonable prices and great produce. Save even more money by picking your own fruits and vegetables from our orchards and gardens.

We all hope to see you soon, down on the farm.

— Tammy & Brent Nielsen

Hours

- Farm Shop: 9 am - 5 pm Mon - Fri; 9 am - 3 pm Sat
- The Corn Maze: 11 am - 9 pm Sat; 11 am - 5 pm Sun
- The Haunted Maze: 5 pm - 9 pm Fri & Sat
- Petting Barn: 9 am - 4 pm (Mon - Fri); 11 am - 3pm (Sat & Sun)

Directions

- From Council Bluffs, proceed east on I-80
- Take Exit 38 North to the Drake Frontage Road
- Turn right on Highway G
- Proceed east for 2.5 miles
- Sunny Acres is on your left; watch for the green sign

SUNNY ACRES ☀ TAMMY & BRENT NIELSEN ☀ 1977 HIGHWAY G ☀ COUNCIL BLUFFS, IA 51503

Compared to the initial design of this page shown earlier in Figure 3-2, you've improved the appearance of the page and made it easier to read. There are four other pages on the Sunny Acres Web site that you haven't yet formatted. However, they share a common document structure with the home page, so you can apply the same style rules you've created for the home.htm file to those files. This is why external style sheets are so powerful: You can apply the same styles to many pages without having to duplicate your work.

Tammy wants those other pages to have slightly different color schemes, so you'll have to apply some embedded styles to each of them. They already have the outer and inner div containers, so you will not have to add those elements to the files.

To apply Tammy's external style sheet to the rest of the pages on her Web site:

1. Open the **haunted.htm** file from the tutorial.03\tutorial folder included with your Data Files.

2. Directly above the closing </head> tag, insert the following code, as shown in Figure 3-62:

```
<style type="text/css">
   h2, h3 {color: white; background-color: black}
</style>
<link href="farm.css" rel="stylesheet" type="text/css" />
```

Applying the style sheet to the haunted.htm file ▶ **Figure 3-62**

```
<title>Sunny Acres Haunted Maze</title>
<style type="text/css">
   h2, h3 {color: white; background-color: black}
</style>
<link href="farm.css" rel="stylesheet" type="text/css" />
</head>
```

3. Close the file, saving your changes.

4. Open the **maze.htm** file and repeat Steps 2 and 3, using a background color value of (200, 105, 0).

5. Open the **petting.htm** file and repeat Steps 2 and 3, using a background color of blue.

6. Open the **produce.htm** file and repeat Steps 2 and 3, using a background color of red.

7. Return to the Sunny Acres home page in your Web browser, and then click the links in the links box to view the appearance of the other four Web pages to verify that you've applied a uniform design to the Web site. Figure 3-63 shows the appearance of each of the four other pages.

Revised design of the Sunny Acres Web site ▶ **Figure 3-63**

haunted.htm   maze.htm   petting.htm   produce.htm

8. Close any remaining open files or applications.

You've completed your work on the Sunny Acres Web site. Through the use of style sheets, you've managed to create a common look and feel for all of Tammy's Web pages. Style sheets also speeded up the development time as you were able to apply previously created style sheets to other pages on the site. Finally, if you or Tammy decide to make a change to the site's design style, you can make your modifications to the farm.css style sheet and have your revisions instantly applied to all of the Web site pages. Tammy will continue to work with the Web site, adding new material and making other design decisions.

Review	**Session 3.3 Quick Check**

1. An inline image has the id photoImage. Specify the style declaration you would enter to float this inline image on the left margin.

2. Specify the style declaration to set the right and bottom margins of the photoImage inline image to 5 pixels each.

3. You want your paragraphs to have a padding space above and below the paragraph equal to 10 pixels. Specify the style declaration to do this.

4. You want your block quotes to have a 20-pixel left margin and to have a solid gray 4-pixel-wide left border. Specify the style declaration to do this.

5. You want the h1 heading with the mainHeading id to be displayed in a green font with a double green border 8 pixels wide. Specify the style declaration to do this.

6. Describe the difference between how Internet Explorer and CSS calculate element widths under the box model.

7. By default, images are displayed as inline elements. Specify the style declaration you would enter to display all inline images as block-level elements.

In this tutorial, you learned how to use the CSS language to create and apply style sheets. In the first session, you learned how to apply inline styles, embedded styles, and external style sheets. You also explored the parts of style declarations and saw how they relate to elements within Web page documents. The first session concluded by examining how both foreground and background color can be described and rendered under CSS and HTML. In the second session, you began by working with the different CSS styles associated with text and fonts. You also learned about several different measuring units that can be applied to font sizes and letter, word, and line spacing. The second session also provided an overview of different image types supported by most browsers and showed how to use these images to create animated graphics and wallpaper-style backgrounds. The final session began by looking at how to float elements within a Web page layout. You then explored the box model, showing how to define an element's internal and external space. The session also showed how to add borders to any page element. The session concluded by looking at div containers, showing how they can be used as tools to create dynamic and interesting page layouts.

Key Terms

absolute unit
animated GIF
box model
Cascading Style Sheets
color value
CSS
CSS2
CSS 2.1
CSS3
div container
em unit
embedded style sheet
external style sheet
Flash
floating
generic font
GIF

Graphics Interchange
   Format
hanging indent
hexadecimal
inline style
Joint Photographic
   Experts Group
JPEG
kerning
leading
margin
padding
PNG
Portable Network
   Graphics
quirks mode
relative unit

RGB triplet
scalable
Scalable Vector Graphics
specific font
splash screen
standards mode
style inheritance
style precedence
style sheet
SVG
tiling
tracking
transparent color

Practice | **Review Assignments**

Practice the skills you learned in the tutorial using the same case scenario.

Data Files needed for the Review Assignments: greenbar.jpg, holiday.jpg, holidaytxt. htm, salogo.jpg, and sunnytxt.css

Tammy has been working with the Web site you designed. She's returned to you for help with another Web page. The Sunny Acres farm is planning a festival called *Holiday on the Farm* to bring people to Sunny Acres during the months of November and December. They're planning to offer sleigh rides, sledding (weather permitting), and a visit with Santa Claus. Tammy has already created the content for this page and located a few graphics she wants you to use. One is the Sunny Acres logo that she's placed at the top of the page. Another is a promotional photo that she wants placed in a box floated on the right margin of the Web page. The third graphic displays a green bar that Tammy wants to tile as a background. A preview of the page you'll create for Tammy is shown in Figure 3-64.

Figure 3-64

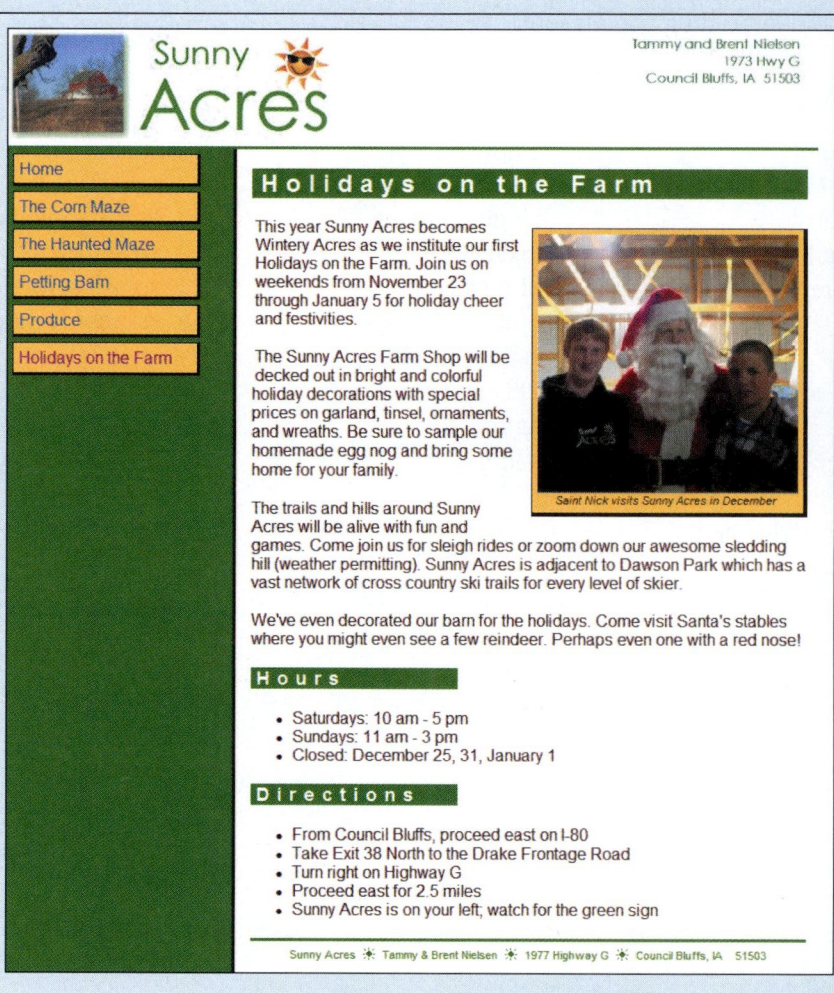

Complete the following:

1. Use your text editor to open the **holidaytxt.htm** and **sunnytxt.css** files from the tutorial.03\review folder included with your Data Files. Enter *your name* and *the date* in the comment section within each file and save them as **holiday.htm** and **sunny.css**, respectively, in the same folder. Take some time to review the content and appearance of the holiday.htm file in your text editor and Web browser.

2. Go to the holiday.htm file in your text editor. Add a div container named outer that encloses the entire page content within the opening and closing <body> tags.

3. Add a second div container named inner that encloses the page content from the h2 heading down to the address element.

4. Locate the photo inline image. Set the width and height of this image to 250 pixels.

5. Link the **holiday.htm** file to the **sunny.css** style sheet. Close the file, saving your changes.

6. Return to the **sunny.css** file in your text editor. Add the following style for the page body:
   - Set the margin to 0 pixels.
   - Set the default font face to Arial, Helvetica, or the generic sans-serif font.
   - Change the background color to white and display the background image file **greenbar.jpg** tiled in the vertical direction only starting from the top left corner of the page.

7. Display the h1 headings with a 3-pixel-wide solid green bottom border and a margin of 0 pixels.

8. Display the h2 and h3 headings in white text on a green background. Set the left padding to 5 pixels and the kerning to 7 pixels. Set the width of the h3 headings to 200 pixels.

9. Display the address text in an 8-point normal green font. Center the address text with a top padding of 5 pixels. Add a 3-pixel solid green border to the top of the address text.

10. Set the width of the outer div container to 770 pixels.

11. Set the left margin of the inner div container to 225 pixels. Set the left padding of the inner div container to 10 pixels.

12. The holiday.htm file contains the photobox paragraph, which displays the photo inline image followed by a caption for the image. Apply the following styles to the photobox paragraph:
    - Float the paragraph on the right margin.
    - Center the text horizontally within the box.
    - Display the text in an 8-point italic font.
    - Change the background color to the value (255, 215, 71).
    - Add a 10-pixel margin to the top of, below, and to the left of the box, and set the right margin to 0 pixels.
    - Add a solid black border that is 1 pixel wide on the box's top and left, and 4 pixels wide on the right and bottom.

13. Display the photo image within the photobox paragraph as a block-level element.

14. Tammy has placed a list of links within the links div container. Float this container on the left margin.

15. Display all hypertext links using the following styles:
    - Remove any underlining from the hypertext links by setting the text decoration to none.

- Display each link as a block-level element 180 pixels wide with a 5-pixel margin and 5 pixels of internal padding.
- Set the background to the color value (255, 215, 71).
- Add a solid black border that is 1 pixel wide on the top and left, and 3 pixels wide on the right and bottom.

16. Save your changes to the file and then open the **holiday.htm** file in your Web browser. Verify that the page layout appears similar to that shown in Figure 3-64. Note that Figure 3-64 displays the page as rendered by the Internet Explorer browser; you will see some slight differences under other Web browsers.

17. Submit your completed files to your instructor.

| Apply | **Case Problem 1** |

Apply your knowledge of hypertext links to create a Web page for the International Cryptographic Institute.

Data Files needed for this Case Problem: algo.htm, back1.gif, back2.gif, crypttxt.htm, enigma.htm, history.htm, locks.jpg, logo.gif, public.htm, scytale.gif, and single.htm

International Cryptographic Institute Sela Dawes is the media representative for the ICI, the International Cryptographic Institute. The ICI is an organization of cryptographers who study the science and mathematics of secret codes, encrypted messages, and code breaking. Part of the ICI's mission is to inform the public about cryptography and data security. Sela has asked you to work on a Web site containing information about cryptography for use by high school science and math teachers. She wants the design to be visually interesting in order to help draw students into the material. Figure 3-65 shows a preview of your design.

Figure 3-65

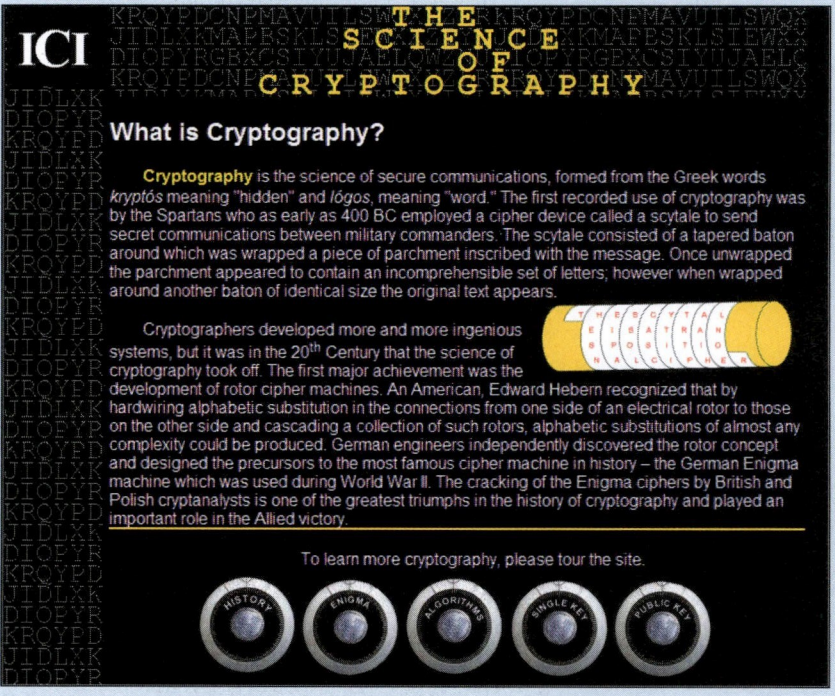

Complete the following:

1. In your text editor, open **crypttxt.htm** from the tutorial.03\case1 folder included with your Data Files. Enter *your name* and *the date* in the comment section of the file. Save the file as **crypt.htm** in the same folder.

2. Add a div container covering the page content from the h1 heading through the end of the third paragraph. Give the div element the id pageContent.

3. Add an embedded style sheet to the head section of the document. With the style sheet, create the following style for the page body:
   - Set the background color to black and the text color to white.
   - Use the file **back1.gif** as a background image tiled in the vertical direction only.
   - Sets the margin to 0 pixels.

4. Apply the following styles to the pageContent div container:
   - Set the width to 670 pixels and the left margin to 100 pixels.
   - Set the default font to Arial, Helvetica, or sans-serif.

5. Apply the following styles to the h1 element:
   - Set the font family to Courier New or monospace.
   - Set the font size to 24 points, the kerning to 10 points, and the leading to 0.7 points.
   - Center the text of the h1 heading horizontally.
   - Change the font color to yellow.
   - Use **back2.gif** as the background image.
   - Set the margin to 0 pixels.

6. Create a style to display bold text in a yellow font.

7. Create a style to indent paragraphs by 2 em units.

8. Locate the inline image for the **logo.gif** file. Set the width and height for the image to 95 pixels wide by 78 pixels high. Float the image on the left page margin.

9. Locate the **scytale.gif** image. Set the dimensions to 250 pixels wide by 69 pixels high. Float the image on the right margin.

10. Use an inline style to add a 2-pixel solid yellow border to the bottom of the second paragraph. Change the bottom padding of the paragraph to 10 pixels.

11. Use an inline style to center the contents of the third paragraph.

12. Locate the **locks.jpg** inline image and set the dimensions of the image to 510 pixels wide by 110 pixels high.

13. Directly below the locks.jpg inline image, create an image map with the name and id, locks. Add the following hotspots to the image map:
    - A circular hotspot linked to history.htm centered at the coordinate (52, 52) with a radius of 43 pixels; the alternate text should be "History"
    - A circular hotspot with a radius of 43 pixels located at the coordinate (155, 52); link the hotspot to enigma.htm and set the alternate text to "Enigma"
    - A circular hotspot with a radius of 43 pixels located at the coordinate (255, 52); link the hotspot to algo.htm and set the alternate text to "Algorithms"
    - A circular hotspot with a radius of 43 pixels located at the coordinate (355, 52); link the hotspot to single.htm and set the alternate text to "Single Key"
    - A circular hotspot with a radius of 43 pixels located at the coordinate (455, 52); link the hotspot to public.htm and set the alternate text to "Public Key"

14. Apply the locks image map to the **locks.jpg** inline image. Use an inline style to remove the border around the inline image.

15. Save your changes to the file. Load **crypt.htm** in your Web browser. Verify that the layout appears similar to that shown in Figure 3-65 and that the image map hotspots open the appropriate pages on your Web site.

16. Submit your completed files to your instructor.

Apply	**Case Problem 2**

Apply your knowledge of CSS to create a three-column layout for a bike touring company.

Data Files needed for this Case Problem: block.jpg, bmtourtxt.htm, body.jpg, h1back. jpg, h1title.gif, and wheelstxt.css

Mountain Wheels   Adriana and Ivan Turchenko are the co-owners of Mountain Wheels, a bike shop and touring agency in Littleton, Colorado. One of their most popular tours is the Bike the Mountains Tour, a six-day excursion over some of the highest roads in Colorado. Adriana wants to update the company's Web site, providing more information about the Bike the Mountains Tour. She envisions a three-column layout with a list of links in the first column and descriptive text in the second and third columns. She has asked for your help in working up a design. As a first step, you'll design the page containing the tour's itinerary. Adriana has already created all of the page content and provided all of the graphics needed for page backgrounds. She needs your help in working with the CSS. Figure 3-66 shows a preview of the Web page you'll create.

Figure 3-66

Bike the Mountains Tour

Home
Learn More
Testimonials
Route Maps
Register
Lodging
Meals
Training
Equipment
Forums
FAQs
Contact Us

INTRODUCTION

The Bike the Mountains Tour rises from the town of Littleton, Colorado and explores the Colorado Front Range. Our tour crosses the Continental Divide twice, giving you the opportunity to bike the highest paved roads in the United States. This tour is a classic showcase of Colorado's Rocky Mountain scenery.

Not designed for the weekend cyclist, this tour is offered only for those fit enough to ride high mountain passes. We provide sag wagons and support. Your lodging and meals are also part of the registration fee. We guarantee tough climbs, amazing sights, sweaty jerseys, and lots of fun.

"The Bike the Mountains Tour is *amazing*. I highly recommend it and would gladly return."

This is the seventh year we've offered the Bike the Mountains Tour. It is our most popular tour and riders are returning again and again. Our experienced tour leaders will be there to guide, help, encourage, draft, and lead you every stroke of the way. Come join us!

ITINERARY

Day 1

We start from the foothills above Littleton, Colorado, promptly at 9am. Be sure to fuel up at Kate's House of Pancakes before starting your ride. The first day is a chance to get your legs in shape, test your gearing, and prepare for what's to come. Be aware that there are several steep grades as we climb out of the valley into the Front Range. Optional side tours and shortcuts will be provided.

Day 2

Day 2 starts with a climb up Bear Creek Canyon to Lookout Mountain, followed by a swift and winding descent into the town of Golden. Refresh yourself at the famous Coors Brewery. You'll need the break to get yourself ready for a great climb through Golden Gate Canyon to the Peak to Peak Highway, ending in the gambling town of Blackhawk. Try your hand at poker and blackjack, but watch your wallet.

Day 3

Day 3 takes you along the Peak to Peak Highway. Established in 1918 this is Colorado's oldest scenic byway. This 55-mile route showcases the mountains of the Front Range, providing amazing vistas from Golden Gate Canyon State Park to Rocky Mountain National Park. We'll stop at Estes Park for fun and refreshment. Get a good night's sleep; you'll need it the next day.

Day 4

Now for the supreme challenge: Day 4 brings some real high-altitude cycling through Rocky Mountain National Park and up Trail Ridge Road. It's an amazing ride, high above timberline, topping out at over 11,000 feet. Stop and rest at the Alpine Visitor's Center before all of that hard work is rewarded with a fast and joyous descent into the town of Grand Lake.

Day 5

We start Day 5 on the west side of the Continental Divide. From Grand Lake, you'll bike to Winter Park, a great ski town summer resort. From Winter Park it's a steady and scenic climb over Berthoud Pass, and back to the eastern side of the Continental Divide. We'll stay at Idaho Springs, where you can enjoy the natural hot springs at the hotel.

Day 6

On Day 6 choose your pleasure or your poison. You can ride back to Littleton over Squaw Pass and Bear Creek. The ride is beautiful and enjoyable in its own right. However, if you're "up" to it, this is your opportunity to tackle Mount Evans. The 7-mile side trip to the top of Mt Evans, at over 14,000 feet, is something that can't be found anywhere else in the country. We'll provide the sag wagon, you provide the legs and lungs.

Once you're back to Littleton, please join us for a celebratory dinner as we share memories of an amazing 6 days of riding the Colorado mountains.

Bike the Mountains Tour • Littleton, CO 80123 • (303) 555 - 5499

Complete the following:

1. In your text editor, open **bmtourtxt.htm** and **wheelstxt.css** from the tutorial.03\case2 folder included with your Data Files. Enter *your name* and *the date* in the comment section of each file. Save the files as **bmtour.htm** and **wheels.css** in the same folder.

2. Review the contents and current layout of the **bmtour.htm** file in your text editor and browser. Create three div containers for the three columns that Adriana wants to use in her proposed page layout. To create the three div containers:
   - Locate the div container for the list of links at the top of the file. Give this div element the id, column1.
   - Enclose the page content starting with the h2 Introduction heading through the paragraph describing the Day 2 activities of the tour in another div container. Give this div element the id, column2.
   - Enclose the page content starting with the Day 3 heading through the last paragraph describing the Day 6 activities in a div element with the id, column3.

3. Within the head section, create a link to the external style sheet, **wheels.css**. Save your changes to the **bmtour.htm** file.

4. Go to the **wheels.css** style sheet in your text editor. Create a style for the page body containing the following style rules:
   - Set the font family to Verdana, Helvetica, or sans-serif.
   - Set the margin size to 0 pixels.
   - Set the background color to white and add a background image using the body.jpg file tiled in the vertical direction.

5. Create the following style for the first column in the layout of the **bmtour.htm** file:
   - Set the width to 140 pixels. Set the left padding to 10 pixels and the top padding to 20 pixels.
   - Float the column on the left page margin.

6. Create the following style for the second column of the **bmtour.htm** file:
   - Set the width to 40% of the width of the page body.
   - Float the column on the left margin.
   - Add a 1-pixel-wide solid black border to the left and right of the column.

7. Set the width of the third column to 40% of the width of the page body and also float this column on the left.

8. Create the following style for the h1 heading:
   - Center the contents of the heading, setting the height to 100 pixels and the margin to 0 pixels.
   - Set the background color to white with the file h1back.jpg as the background image, tiled in the horizontal direction.
   - Add a 1-pixel-wide solid black bottom border.

9. Create the following style for the h2 headings:
   - Indent the text 30 pixels.
   - Set the font color to white and the background to the color value (108, 87, 12).
   - Set the kerning to 8 points and the margin to 0 pixels.
   - Display the text in small caps.

10. Set the left margin of h3 headings to 10 pixels.

11. Set the margins of all paragraphs to 10 pixels on the top and left and 20 pixels on the right and bottom.

12. Apply the following styles to blockquote elements on the page:
    - Set the width of every blockquote element to 200 pixels with 10 pixels of padding.
    - Display the text in a 16-point white font.
    - Add a 3-pixel-wide solid black border.

- Change the background color to the value (255, 204, 0) with the image file **block.jpg** as the background, tiled in the horizontal direction.
- Set the margins around the blockquote to 5 pixels, except for the right margin, which should be set to 10 pixels.
- Float the blockquote on the right margin.

13. Apply the following styles to hypertext elements:
    - Display hypertext elements as block-level elements with 2 pixels of padding.
    - Set the top, right, and bottom margins to 5 pixels. Set the left margin to 0 pixels.
    - Set the font size to 10 points.
    - Remove underlining from the hypertext links by setting the text decoration to none.
    - Add a 1-pixel-wide solid black border.
    - Change the background color to the value (255, 255, 192).

14. Apply the following styles to the address element:
    - Center the address text.
    - Display the text in a 10-point normal font (no italics).
    - Set the background color to white.
    - Set the padding size to 10 pixels and add a 1-pixel-wide solid black top border.
    - ⊕ EXPLORE Display the address only when both margins are clear of floating elements.

15. Save your changes to the file.
16. Open the **bmtour.htm** file in your Web browser. Verify that the layout resembles that shown in Figure 3-66.
17. ⊕ EXPLORE Try to locate a wide screen monitor and view the Web page under that monitor's resolution. What aspect of your style sheet allowed the columns to be resized to fit the increased width of the monitor? This type of page layout is called a fluid or liquid layout. Explain why.
18. Submit your completed files to your instructor.

| Challenge | **Case Problem 3** |

Broaden your knowledge of CSS and HTML by creating an image with an irregular text wrap.

Data Files needed for this Case Problem: banner.jpg, king1.gif – king6.gif, kingtxt.htm, and centertxt.css

Center for Diversity Stewart Tompkins is the project coordinator for the Midwest University Center for Diversity. He is currently working on a Web site titled The Voices of Civil Rights, containing Web pages with extended quotes from civil rights leaders of the past and present. He has asked you to help develop a design for the pages in the series. He has given you the text for one of the pages, which is about Dr. Martin Luther King, Jr.

Stewart has supplied a photo of Dr. King that he would like you to include on the page. He has seen how text can be made to wrap irregularly around a photo in graphic design software, and he wonders if you can do the same thing on a Web page. Although you cannot use this same technique with page elements, which are always rectangular, you can break a single image into a series of rectangles of different sizes. When the text wraps around these stacked rectangles, they provide the appearance of a single image with an irregular line wrap. Stewart asks you to try this with his Dr. King photo. Figure 3-67 shows a preview of the page you'll create. Note how the right margin of the text seems to wrap around Dr. King's image along a diagonal line, rather than a vertical one.

Figure 3-67

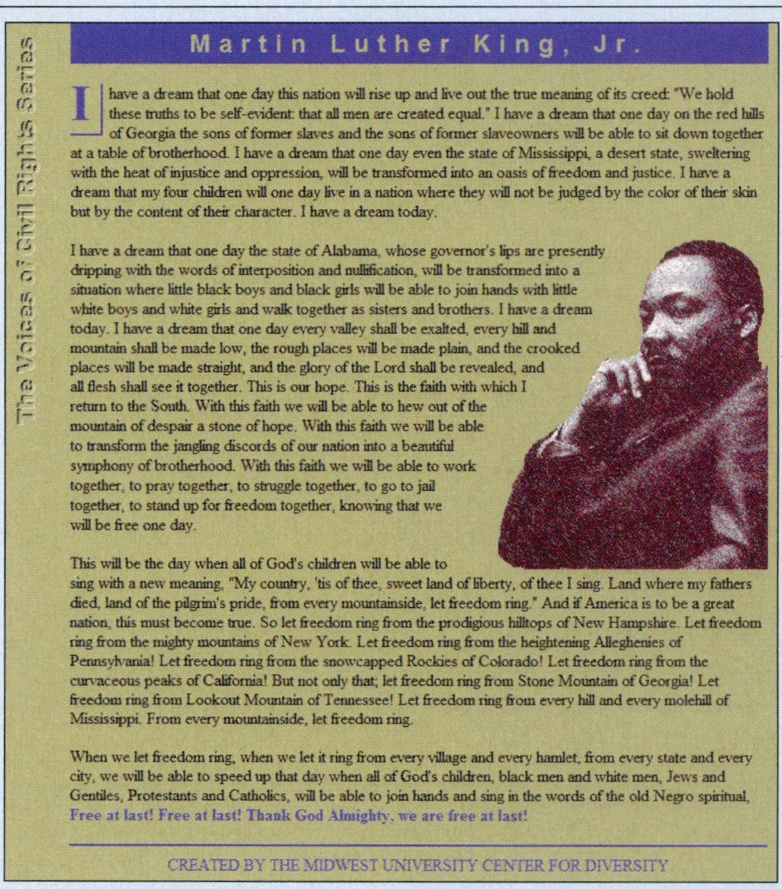

Complete the following:

1. In your text editor, open the **kingtxt.htm** and **centertxt.css** files from the tutorial.03\case3 folder included with your Data Files. Enter *your name* and *the date* in the comment section of each file. Save the files as **king.htm** and **center.css** in the same folder. Take some time to study the content and layout of the king.htm file as it appears in your text editor and Web browser.

2. Return to the **king.htm** file in your text editor. Directly below the opening <body> tag, insert a div element with the id banner. Within the div element, insert an inline image for the **banner.jpg** graphic file. Give the inline image the id, bannerImage, and specify the alternate text "The Voices of Civil Rights Series."

3. Enclose the rest of the page content, starting with the h1 heading at the top of the page through the address at the bottom of the file, in a div element with the id, pageContent.

4. Save your changes to the file.

5. In your text editor, go to the **center.css** file. Create a style for the body element that sets the font color to black, the background color to the value (204, 204, 153), and the margin to 0 em.

6. Float the banner div container on the left page margin.

7. Set the width of the pageContent div container to 42 em and the left margin to 4 em.

8. Apply the following styles to h1 headings:
   - Set the font face to Arial, Helvetica, or sans-serif.

- Set the font size to 1.5 em and the kerning to 0.5 em. Center the h1 heading text.
- Set the padding to 0.2 em.
- Set the font color to the value (204, 204, 153) and the background color to the value (102, 102, 204).

9. Display text marked as an em element in a normal bold font. Set the font color to the value (102, 102, 204).

10. Apply the following styles to the address element:
    - Set the font style to normal to remove the default italics style.
    - Display the text in uppercase letters. Set the font color to (102, 102, 204).
    - Center the address text.
    - Set the padding to 0.5 em.
    - Add a solid top border 0.1 em wide in the color value (102, 102, 204).

11. Save your changes to the **center.css** style sheet.

12. Return to the **king.htm** file in your text editor. Add a link to the center.css to the head of the document.

EXPLORE 13. Stewart wants the opening word from Dr. King's speech to appear as a drop cap. To create this effect, enclose the word in a span element and apply the following inline styles:
    - Float the span element on the left paragraph margin.
    - Set the font weight to bold and the font size to 3 em.
    - Set the font color to the value (102, 102, 240).
    - Set the line height to 0.8 em.
    - Add a solid border 0.05 em wide with the color value (102, 102, 204) to the right and bottom edge of the span element.
    - Set the bottom and right padding to 0.2 em.
    - Set the right margin to 0.2 em.

EXPLORE 14. To create an irregular line wrap around the image, you have to break the image into several files and then stack them on the left or right margin, displaying an image only when the margin is clear of the previous image. To remove the seams between the images, you have to set the top and bottom margins to 0. The Dr. Martin Luther King, Jr. graphic has been broken into six files for you. To stack them:
    - Directly below the first paragraph, insert a div element containing six inline images for the graphic files **king1.gif** through **king6.gif**. For each image, set the alternate text to an empty text string.
    - Use inline styles to set the width of the six inline images to the following values: king1.gif = 6.7 em, king2.gif = 7.85 em, king3.gif = 11.45 em, king4.gif = 14.25 em, king5.gif = 15.5 em, king6.gif = 16.6 em.

15. Scroll to the top of the file and add an embedded style sheet to the head section of the document.

16. Within the embedded style sheet, create the following styles for inline images in the document:
    - Float the images on the right margin.
    - Set the clear style so that the image is only displayed when the right margin is clear of other floating images.
    - Set the left margin to 2 em and the other margins to 0 em.

17. Directly below the style you just created, add the following styles for the inline image with the bannerImage id:
    - Set the width to 3.5 em.

- Set the value of the float style to none (to prevent this inline image from floating on the page).
- Set the margin to 0 em.

18. Save your changes to the file. Open the **king.htm** file in your Web browser and verify that it resembles the layout shown in Figure 3-67. Verify that the first letter in the speech appears as a drop cap and that the image of Dr. King is surrounded by an irregular line wrap with no seams appearing between the six stacked images.

⊕ **EXPLORE**

19. Using Firefox or another browser that allows the user to increase and decrease the browser's default font size, increase and decrease the font size on the Dr. King Web page. What happens to the size of the images and the general appearance of the page layout? This type of design is called an elastic layout. Can you see why? How did choosing the em unit to size the page elements and the graphic images create this effect?

20. Submit your completed files to your instructor.

| Create | | **Case Problem 4** |

Test your knowledge of CSS and HTML by creating a design for a Scottish touring company's Web site.

Data Files needed for this Case Problem: castles.jpg, casttxt.htm, Hebrides.jpg, hebtxt. htm, highland.jpg, hightxt.htm, lake.jpg, lakestxt.htm, parch.jpg, and tslogo.gif

Travel Scotland!   Fiona Henderson is the owner of *Travel Scotland!*, a touring company specializing in guided tours of Scotland. She's come to you for help in creating a design for the *Travel Scotland!* Web site. Fiona has four Web pages describing four of the company's tours. She's already inserted the content and gathered some graphic images to supplement her text. She wants you to take her unformatted Web pages and create an interesting design and layout.

Complete the following:

1. In your text editor, open the **casttxt.htm**, **hebtxt.htm**, **hightxt.htm**, and **lakestxt.htm** from the tutorial.03\case4 folder included with your Data Files. Enter **your name** and **the date** in the comment section of each file. Save the files as **castles.htm**, **hebrides.htm**, **highland.htm**, and **lakes.htm** in the same folder. Take some time to study the content of these four files. You are free to supplement the content of these Web pages with additional material you find on your own. You may also edit the HTML tags and attributes within these pages if they help you achieve your final design.

2. Use your text editor to create an external style sheet named **ts.css**, placed in the tutorial.03\case4 folder. Add a comment section to the style sheet containing **your name**, **the date**, a description of the style sheet, and its purpose in the Web site.

3. Add styles to the ts.css style sheet that you'll apply to the four pages on the *Travel Scotland!* Web site. The design of the Web site is up to you, but it should include at least one example of each of the following:

   - A style that modifies the text and background colors of page elements
   - A style that modifies the font size, face, and appearance of element text
   - A style that defines an element's padding and margins, distinctly different in at least two directions
   - A style to define the border appearance of an element
   - A style that floats an inline image or element
   - A style that adds a background image to an element
   - A style applied to a div container identified by an id value

4. Each of the four Web pages should have a slightly different appearance. Add an embedded style sheet to each file that provides a slightly different color scheme for each Web page.

5. Link your Web pages to your style sheet, and then test your Web page under a variety of browsers and monitor resolutions. Correct any problems that arise from those differing environments.

6. Submit your completed files to your instructor.

Review	**| Quick Check Answers**

Session 3.1

1. Inline styles are styles applied directly to an element through the use of the style attribute in the element's tag. Embedded styles are styles placed in the head section of a document and apply to elements within that document. External style sheets are files separate from the document and can be applied to any document on a Web site. External style sheets are best for setting the styles of an entire Web site.

2. `/* Sunny Acres Style Sheet */`

3. `p {color: red}`

4. As left-aligned blue text

5. In red text with an ivory-color background

6. `!important`

7. `blockquote {color: rgb(221, 128, 0)}`

Session 3.2

1. `code {font-family: Courier New, monospace}`

2. 18 points

3. `h3 {text-decoration: overline underline}`

4. `address {letter-spacing: 0.5em; word-spacing: 0.9em}`

5. `dt {text-transform: uppercase}`

6. JPEG because the JPEG format supports a much larger color palette, while GIFs are limited to 256 colors and so will not display photographic images without dithering the colors.

7. `width = "200" height = "100"`

8. `blockquote {background-image: url(mark.jpg);`
   `            background-repeat: no-repeat;`
   `            background-position: left top;`
   `            background-attachment: fixed}`

Session 3.3

1. `#photoImage {float: left}`

2. `#photoImage {margin-right: 5px; margin-bottom: 5px}`

3. `p {padding-top: 10px; padding-bottom: 10px}`

4. `blockquote {margin-left: 20px; border-left: 4px solid gray}`

5. `#mainHeading {color: green; border: 8px double green}`

6. Internet Explorer applies the width property to the entire box, including the padding and border spaces. The CSS box model applies the width property to the content of the box, but not to the padding and margins.

7. `img {display: block}`

Ending Data Files

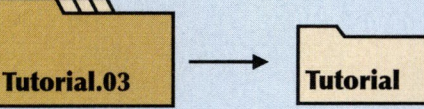

Tutorial
farm.css
haunted.htm
home.htm
index.htm
maze.htm
petting.htm
produce.htm
+ 9 graphic files

Review
holiday.htm
sunny.css
+ 3 graphic files

Case1
algo.htm
crypt.htm
enigma.htm
history.htm
public.htm
single.htm
+ 5 graphic files

Case2
bmtour.htm
wheels.css
+ 4 graphic files

Case3
center.css
king.htm
+ 7 graphic files

Case4
castles.htm
hebrides.htm
highland.htm
lakes.htm
ts.css
+ 6 graphic files

Creating Special Effects with CSS

Adding Advanced Styles to a Web Site

Case | Online Scrapbooks

Scrapbooking is the popular hobby of creating albums containing photos, memorabilia, writing, and other embellishments. This hobby has become a multimillion-dollar industry with companies that specialize in scrapbooking supplies and support. One of these companies is Online Scrapbooks.

Kathy Pridham, who leads the Web development team at Online Scrapbooks, has hired you to work on the style for the new company's Web site. The Web site's home page will have information on how to get started in scrapbooking and links to other pages that contain a wide variety of information. Because the Web site will have so many pages, Kathy is using Cascading Style Sheets to manage the layout, design, and function of the pages. She has a style sheet providing the site's basic layout and design. She would like you to add features such as graphical bullets, rollover effects, and drop caps. To make those enhancements, you'll need to use some of the special features supported by CSS.

Kathy knows that many users want to access the Web site from mobile devices, while others want to be able to print some of the site's contents. She wants the site to work with any kind of output, including mobile devices and printed output.

Starting Data Files

Tutorial.04 →

Tutorial
printtxt.css
samptxt.htm
scrapstxt.css
starttxt.htm
+ 4 graphic files

Demo
demo_positioning.htm
+ 5 graphic files

Review
gallerytxt.htm
printertxt.css
screentxt.css
+ 7 graphics files

Case1
h01txt.htm-h18txt.htm
printtxt.css
willettxt.css
+ 21 graphic files

Case2
cwpagetxt.htm
cwtxt.css
+ 2 graphic files

Case3
longstxt.htm
+ 11 graphic files

Case4
bizetbio.txt
bizetlist.txt
mozartbio.txt
mozartlist.txt
puccinibio.txt
puccinilist.txt

verdibio.txt
verdilist.txt
wagnerbio.txt
wagnerlist.txt
+ 5 graphic files

Session 4.1

Working with Selector Patterns

Kathy has already created a basic Web page describing how to get started in scrapbooking. She's written an article and created the basic Web page layout using an external style sheet. She's provided you with her HTML document, her graphic files, and her style sheet to study. Kathy suggests that this Web page would be a good place to start in your task of enhancing her basic design.

To view Kathy's data files:

▶ **1.** In your text editor, open the **starttxt.htm** and **scrapstxt.css** files, located in the tutorial.04\tutorial folder included with your Data Files. Within the comment section at the top of each file, add *your name* and *the date* in the space provided. Save the files as **start.htm** and **scraps.css**, respectively, in the same folder.

▶ **2.** Take some time to review the code in both the external style sheet file and the HTML document. Note how the CSS styles are applied to specific elements in the start.htm file to create an interesting layout and design.

▶ **3.** Open **start.htm** in your Web browser. Figure 4-1 shows the current appearance of the start.htm file.

Figure 4-1 | **Initial design for the Getting Started page**

SCRAPBOOKS ONLINE

- Home
- Getting Started
- Scrapbooking Tips
- Supply List
- Glossary
- Online Classes
- Sample Pages
- Online Store
- Shopping Cart
- Checkout
- Your Account
- Order Status
- Wish List
- Customer Service
- About Us
- Newsletter
- FAQ
- Contact Us

Getting Started

Scrapbooking is the practice of combining photos, memorabilia, and stories in an album, preserving memories for future generations. In recent years, scrapbooking has become a $300 million dollar industry as the public has discovered the joys of creating albums for families and friends. Online Scrapbooks is here to help you with all of your scrapbooking needs.

Preserving Your Memories

Scrapbook albums have existed since the beginning of photography. However, the sad fact is that photographs and most printed material are not permanent: they will fade and yellow with age. Scrapbookers of today are aware of these problems, and the industry is providing remedies to minimize deterioration. For the best results, avoid using materials with high acid content which can cause photos and paper to deteriorate. Another thing to avoid is lignin, a material that is the bonding element in wood fibers. Over time, paper with lignin will become yellow and brittle, so you should only use lignin-free products.

Your albums should contain page protectors to shield the pages from smudges, oil, and dirt that can be transferred from your hands. You should never use albums with sticky "magnetic" pages. The sticky substance will be transferred to the photo and backing paper causing deterioration. Never crop Polaroid® photos: they will curl and fall apart. Mount all memorabilia on acid-free cardstock paper, and photocopy all newspaper clippings on acid-free paper.

Basic Materials

- Acid-free paper, card stock, and stickers
- Acid-free pen, markers, and adhesive
- Acid-free memory book album
- Straight and pattern edge scissors
- Photos and photo corners
- Paper punches
- Journalling templates
- Decorative embellishments

ONLINE SCRAPBOOKS · 212 SUNSET DRIVE · RICHMOND, KY 40475 · (859) 555-8100

As you can see from Figure 4-1, Kathy has applied a layout in which the list of links floats on the left page margin and a box describing basic scrapbooking materials floats on the right margin. There is one main heading marked as an h1 element displayed at the top of page, providing a logo with the company name.

The three other headings—Getting Started, Preserving Your Memories, and Basic Materials—are marked as h2 elements. Kathy wants to apply a slightly different format to the Basic Materials h2 heading than the one applied to the Getting Started and Preserving Your Memories h2 headings. One way of applying a specific format to this heading is through the use of an id attribute. However, Kathy doesn't want to maintain a list of id values for all the various elements on her Web page. Instead, she would like to create styles for elements based on their location or their use in the document. She asks if this can be done with CSS.

Contextual Selectors

So far, the only styles you've worked with are ones in which the style selector references either an element (or a group of elements) or an element identified by an id. For example, the style

```
b {color: blue}
```

displays all boldface text in a blue font. What would you do, however, if you didn't want every example of boldface text to be displayed in a blue font? What if you wanted this style applied only to boldface text located within an ordered or unordered list?

Recall that on a Web page, elements are nested within other elements, forming a hierarchical tree structure. The top element on the Web page is the body element because it contains all of the content appearing in the page. From this top element, other elements descend. Figure 4-2 shows an example of such a tree structure for a Web page consisting of a few headings, a couple of paragraphs, some boldface elements, and a span element nested within a paragraph.

A sample tree hierarchy of page elements ◀ Figure 4-2

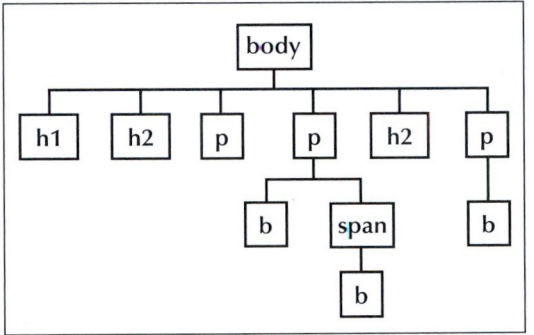

To take advantage of this tree structure, CSS allows you to create **contextual selectors** that express the location of an element within the hierarchy of elements. The general syntax of a contextual selector has the form

```
parent descendant {styles}
```

where *parent* is the parent element, *descendant* is a descendant of the parent, and *styles* are the styles to be applied to the descendant element. To apply a blue color only to boldface text found in lists, you would use the style:

```
li b {color: blue}
```

In this case, li is the parent element and b is the descendant element (because it is contained within the list item). Any bold element not nested within a list element is not affected by this style. Note that the descendant element does not have to be a direct child of the parent element; it can appear several levels below the parent element in hierarchy. For example in the code

```
<li>
    <span><b>Special</b>Orders</span> this month!
</li>
```

the bold element is a descendant of the list item, but it is a direct child only of the span element. So the word "Special" would appear in a bold font if the above style is applied to the document. Contextual selectors can be grouped with other selectors. The following style applies a blue font to h2 headings and to boldface list items, but nowhere else:

```
li b, h2 {color: blue}
```

Contextual selectors can also be applied with elements marked with a specific id. The style

```
#notes b {color: blue}
```

displays bold text in a blue font if it is nested within an element with an id of notes.

The parent/descendant form is only one example of a contextual selector. Figure 4-3 describes some of the other contextual forms supported by CSS.

Figure 4-3   **Contextual selectors**

Selector	Description
*	Matches any element in the hierarchy
e	Matches any element, e, in the hierarchy
e1, e2, e3, ...	Matches the group of elements: e1, e2, e3, ...
e f	Matches any element, f, that is a descendant of an element, e
e > f	Matches any element, f, that is a direct child of an element, e
e + f	Matches any element, f, that is immediately preceded by a sibling element, e

For example, the style

```
* {color: blue}
```

causes *all* of the elements in the document to appear in a blue font. On the other hand, the style

```
p > b {color: blue}
```

applies the blue font only to boldface text that is contained within a paragraph element as a child of that element and not any descendent. Figure 4-4 provides additional examples of how to select different elements of the Web page document based on the expression in the contextual selector. Selected elements are highlighted in red for each pattern. Remember that because of style inheritance, any style applied to an element is passed down the document tree. So a style applied to a paragraph element is automatically passed down to elements contained within that paragraph unless it conflicts with a more specific style.

Simple and contextual selectors ◄ Figure 4-4

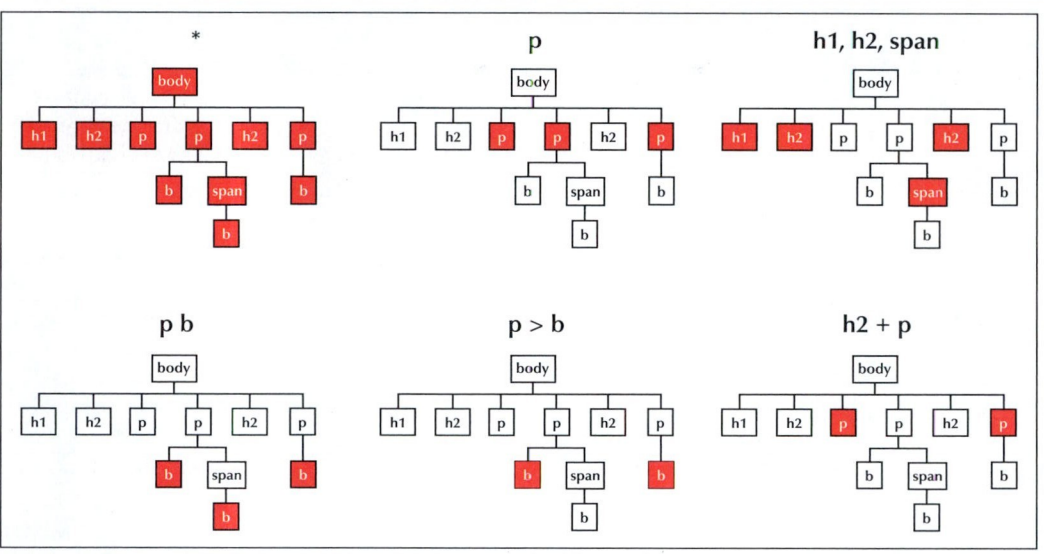

Although the contextual selectors listed in Figure 4-3 are part of the specifications for CSS2, they are not well supported by earlier versions of the Internet Explorer browser. In particular, the *e* > *f* and *e* + *f* contextual selectors should be used with caution if you need to support Internet Explorer. Other browsers, including Firefox, Opera, and Safari, do support all of the contextual selectors described in Figure 4-3.

Attribute Selectors

On occasion you might also need to select elements based on their attribute values. For example, if you want to display link text in a blue font, you might use the following declaration:

```
a {color: blue}
```

However, this declaration makes no distinction between <a> tags used to mark links and <a> tags used to mark document anchors (for a discussion of anchors, see Tutorial 2). HTML makes this distinction based on the presence or absence of the href attribute. To select an element based on the element's attributes, you can create an **attribute selector** that has the form

```
element[att] {styles}
```

where *element* is a page element, *att* is the name of an attribute associated with the element, and *styles* are the styles applied to the element. The declaration

```
a[href] {color: blue}
```

applies the blue font color style only to link elements that contain an href attribute. Any <a> tag used to mark anchors would not contain the href attribute, and therefore would not be affected by this style. Figure 4-5 describes some of the other attribute selectors supported by CSS.

Figure 4-5 ▸ **Attribute selectors**

Selector	Description	Example	Interpretation
elem[att]	The element contains the *att* attribute	a[href]	Matches hypertext elements containing the href attribute
elem[att="val"]	The element's *att* attribute equals *val*	a[href="gloss.htm"]	Matches hypertext elements whose href attribute equals "gloss.htm"
elem[att~="val"]	The element's *att* attribute value is a space-separated list of words, one of which is exactly *val*	a[rel~="glossary"]	Matches hypertext elements whose rel attribute contains the word "glossary"
elem[att|="val"]	The element's *att* attribute value is a hyphen-separated list of words beginning with *val*	p[id|="first"]	Matches paragraphs whose id attribute starts with the word "first" in a hyphen-separated list of words
elem[att^="val"]	The element's *att* attribute begins with *val* (CSS3)	a[rel^="prev"]	Matches hypertext elements whose rel attribute begins with "prev"
elem[att$="val"]	The element's *att* attribute ends with *val* (CSS3)	a[href$="org"]	Matches hypertext elements whose href attribute ends with "org"
elem[att*="val"]	The element's *att* attribute contains the value *val* (CSS3)	a[href*="faq"]	Matches hypertext elements whose href attribute contains the text string "faq"

Browser support for attribute selectors is mixed. For this reason, you should use attribute selectors with caution. Note that some of the attribute selectors listed in Figure 4-5 are part of the proposed specifications for CSS3 and have scattered browser support at the present time. As with contextual selectors, attribute selectors enjoy good support from Firefox, Opera, and Safari, but poor support from Internet Explorer. IE does support attribute and contextual selectors if you write your HTML code to put Internet Explorer into standards mode (for a discussion of standards mode, see Tutorial 3).

Using Selector Patterns | Reference Window

- To apply a style to all elements in the document, use the * selector.
- To apply a style to a single element, use the *e* selector, where *e* is the name of the element.
- To apply a selector to a descendant element, *f*, use the *e f* selector, where *e* is the name of the parent element and *f* is an element nested within the parent.
- To apply a selector to a child element, *f*, use the *e > f* selector, where *e* is the name of a parent element and *f* is an element that is a direct child of the parent.
- To apply a selector to a sibling element, use the *e + f* selector, where *e* and *f* are siblings and *f* immediately follows *e* in the document tree.

Applying a Selector Pattern

After discussing how to use selector patterns, you and Kathy decide to apply them to her Getting Started document. You decide to create a style for the h2 heading in the Basic Materials box so that you can use the style in similar boxes on other pages in the Online Scrapbooking site. You'll center this heading, change the background color to white, reduce the top margin to 0 pixels, and add a solid orange border to the bottom of the element. Because this heading appears within a div element that is identified with an id value of pullout, you'll add the following style to the style sheet:

```
#pullout h2 {text-align: center; background-color: white; margin-top:
  0px;
          border-bottom: 2px solid orange}
```

Add this style declaration to the scraps.css file.

To add a contextual selector to the style sheet:

▶ 1. Go to the **scraps.css** file in your text editor.

▶ 2. Directly below the style for the #pullout selector, insert the following style, as shown in Figure 4-6:

```
#pullout h2 {text-align: center; background-color: white;
            margin-top: 0px; border-bottom: 2px solid orange}
```

Using a contextual selector ◀   Figure 4-6

```
#pullout           {float: right; width: 250px; margin: 0px 0px 10px 10px;
                    border: 5px outset orange; background-color: ivory;
                    font-size: 10pt; font-family: Arial, Helvetica, sans-serif}
#pullout h2         {text-align: center; background-color: white; margin-top: 0px;
                    border-bottom: 2px solid orange}
```

selector references only those h2 elements within an element with the pullout id

▶ 3. Save your changes to the file and then reload **start.htm** in your Web browser. Figure 4-7 shows the revised appearance of the document.

Figure 4-7 ▶ Applying a style to a nested h2 element

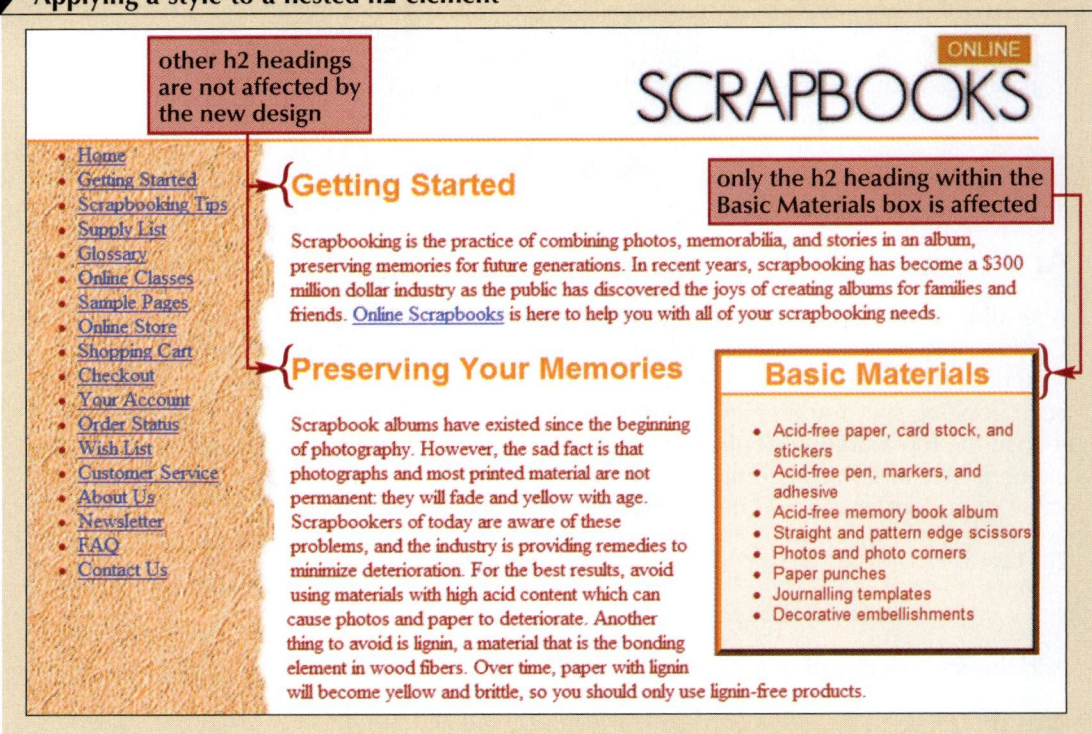

As shown in Figure 4-7, the appearance of the h2 element nested within the Basic Materials box has been modified under the new style, but h2 elements located elsewhere in the document retain their original appearance.

Conditional Comments and Internet Explorer | InSight

Several versions of the Internet Explorer browser don't follow all of the CSS specifications for selectors and styles. You can correct many of the incompatibilities by converting your HTML code to XHTML and putting IE into standards mode rather than quirks mode. However, this might not work for older versions of Internet Explorer, such as IE5 and even IE6. For those browser versions, you can use **conditional comments** that allow you to apply different HTML code for different versions of Internet Explorer. The general syntax of a conditional comment is

```
<!--[if condition IE version]><!-->
    HTML code
<!--<![endif]-->
```

where *condition* is a condition that is either true or false, *version* is the version number of an IE browser, and *HTML code* is code that will be run if *condition* is true. For example, the code

```
<!--[if lt IE 6]><!-->
    <link rel="stylesheet" type="text/css" href="old.css" />
<!--<![endif]-->
```

links the Web page to the old.css style sheet file, but only if the browser version in use is older than Internet Explorer 6. In this case, the *condition* value is lt for "less than." Other *condition* values include lte (less than or equal to), gt (greater than), gte (greater than or equal to), and ! (not equal to). If you specify no *condition* value, the *HTML code* will be run only for the specified version of Internet Explorer. You can also leave off the version number to apply the HTML code to Internet Explorer but not to other browsers. So the code

```
<!--[if IE]><!-->
    <link rel="stylesheet" type="text/css" href="ie_styles.css" />
<!--<![endif]-->
```

links the file to the ie_styles.css style sheet file, but only if Internet Explorer is being used.

Conditional comments are one of the best ways you can tailor your HTML code to match the capabilities of different versions of Internet Explorer and other browsers.

Applying Styles to Lists

Kathy has her Web page links in an unordered list that is displayed in a box floated on the left page margin. Like all unordered lists, the browser displays the items in this list with bullet markers. Kathy would like to remove the bullet markers from this list. To remove the markers you can apply one of the many CSS list styles.

Choosing a List Style Type

To specify the list marker displayed by the browser, you can apply the style

```
list-style-type: type
```

where *type* is one of the markers shown in Figure 4-8.

Figure 4-8 **List style types**

list-style-type	Marker (s)
disc	●
circle	○
square	□
decimal	1, 2, 3, 4, ...
decimal-leading-zero	01, 02, 03, 04, ...
lower-roman	i, ii, iii, iv, ...
upper-roman	I, II, III, IV, ...
lower-alpha	a, b, c, d, ...
upper-alpha	A, B, C, D, ...
none	no marker displayed

For example, to create a list with alphabetical markers such as

A. Home
B. Getting Started
C. Scrapbooking Tips
D. Supply List

you would apply the following list style to the ol list element:

```
ol {list-style-type: upper-alpha}
```

List style types can be used with contextual selectors to create an outline style for several levels of nested lists. Figure 4-9 shows an example in which several levels of list style markers are used in formatting an outline. Note that each marker style is determined by the location of each ordered list within the levels of the outline. The top level is displayed with uppercase Roman numerals; the bottom level, nested within three other ordered lists, uses lowercase letters for markers.

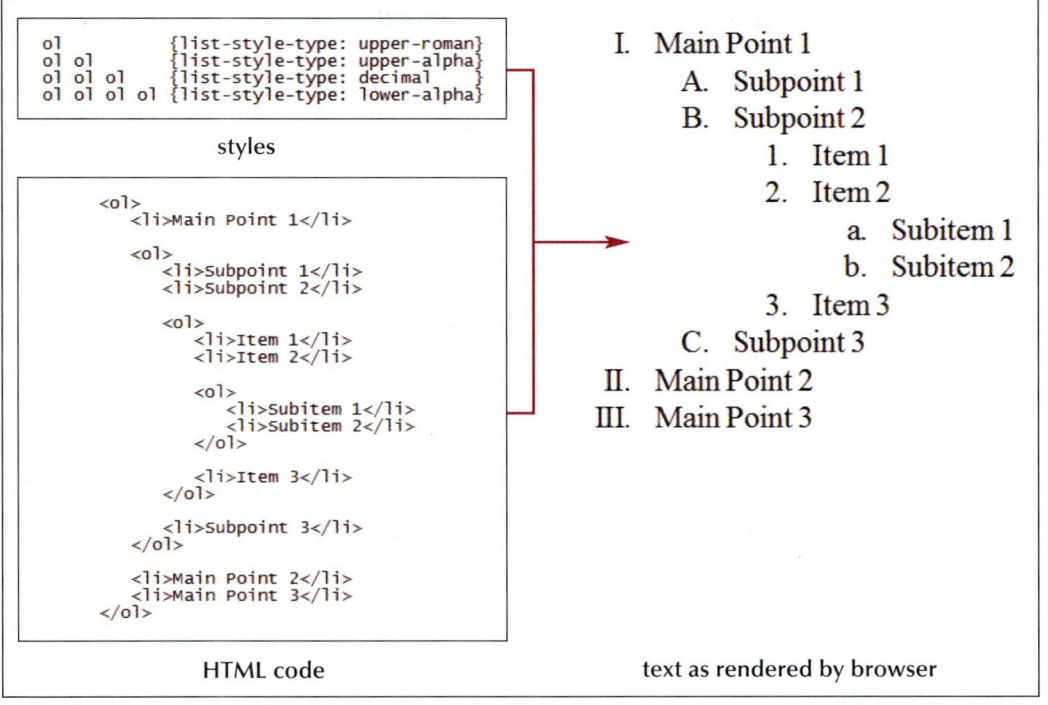

```
ol            {list-style-type: upper-roman}
ol ol         {list-style-type: upper-alpha}
ol ol ol      {list-style-type: decimal    }
ol ol ol ol   {list-style-type: lower-alpha}
```

styles

```
<ol>
    <li>Main Point 1</li>

    <ol>
        <li>Subpoint 1</li>
        <li>Subpoint 2</li>

        <ol>
            <li>Item 1</li>
            <li>Item 2</li>

            <ol>
                <li>Subitem 1</li>
                <li>Subitem 2</li>
            </ol>

            <li>Item 3</li>
        </ol>

        <li>Subpoint 3</li>
    </ol>

    <li>Main Point 2</li>
    <li>Main Point 3</li>
</ol>
```

HTML code

I.   Main Point 1
   A.   Subpoint 1
   B.   Subpoint 2
      1.   Item 1
      2.   Item 2
         a.   Subitem 1
         b.   Subitem 2
      3.   Item 3
   C.   Subpoint 3
II. Main Point 2
III. Main Point 3

text as rendered by browser

If you don't find the marker you want from the list-style-type style, you can supply your own in a graphic image file. To use a graphic image for the list marker, use the style

```
list-style-image: url(url)
```

where (*url*) is the URL of the graphic image file. The style

```
ul {list-style-image: url(redball.gif) }
```

displays items in an unordered list marked with the graphic image in the redball.gif file.

Kathy wants her list of links to appear without any bullet marker, but she wants the list of basic materials to appear with a bullet marker based on one of her graphic image files. She suggests that you use both the list-style-type and list-style-image attributes to modify the appearance of the two lists. To differentiate between the two lists, you'll use contextual selectors. The list of links is an unordered list nested within a div container with the id named links, while the list of basic materials is nested within the pullout div box.

To apply a list style to Kathy's list of links:

▶ 1. Return to the **scraps.css** file in your text editor.

▶ 2. Directly below the style for the #links selector, enter:

```
#links ul    {list-style-type: none}
```

▶ 3. Directly below the style for the #pullout h2 selector, enter:

```
#pullout ul {list-style-image: url(bullet.jpg)}
```

Figure 4-10 shows the revised code in the style sheet.

Figure 4-10 ▶ **Setting the style of the list marker**

```
body        {margin: 0px; color: brown;
             background: white url(back.jpg) repeat-y}
h1, h2, h3 {font-family: Arial, Helvetica, sans-serif; color: orange}
h1          {border-bottom: 2px solid orange; background-color: white; margin: 0px; padding: 0px}
ul          {margin-top:0px}

#outer_container  {width: 780px}
#head             {text-align: right}

#links            {float: left; width: 200px}
#links ul         {list-style-type: none}

#article          {margin-left: 200px}

#pullout          {float: right; width: 250px; margin: 0px 0px 10px 10px;
                   border: 5px outset orange; background-color: ivory;
                   font-size: 10pt; font-family: Arial, Helvetica, sans-serif}
#pullout h2       {text-align: center; background-color: white; margin-top: 0px;
                   border-bottom: 2px solid orange}
#pullout ul       {list-style-image: url(bullet.jpg)}

address           {text-align: center; font-style: normal; font-variant: small-caps;
                   border-top: 2px solid orange; color: orange}
```

no marker is used with the list

the graphic file bullet.jpg is used for the list marker

▶ 4. Save your changes to the file, and then refresh **start.htm** in your Web browser. Figure 4-11 shows the revised appearance of the two lists in the document.

Figure 4-11 ▶ **Formatted lists**

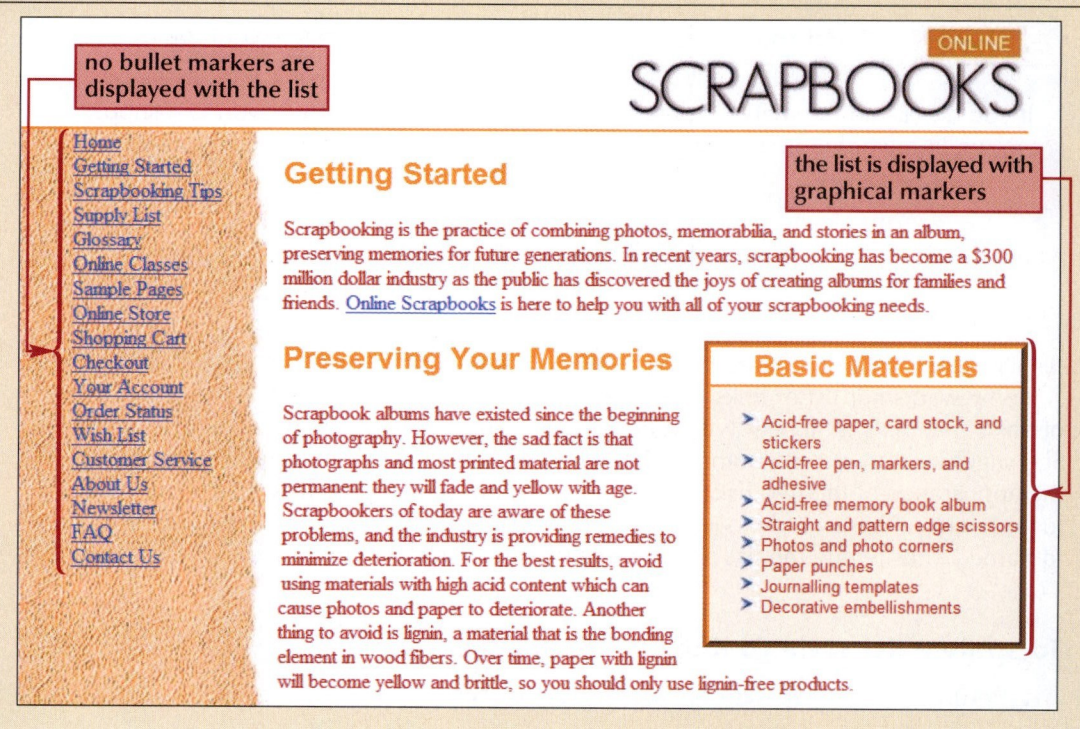

no bullet markers are displayed with the list

the list is displayed with graphical markers

The bullet markers have been removed from the list of links and have been replaced by blue arrows in the Basic Materials list.

Tip

Web browsers always place bullets to the left of the list text. To create a right-side bullet marker, add a background image containing the marker symbol to each list item, placing the image on the right border of the list element.

Defining the List Position and Layout

Kathy likes the revised markers, but she thinks there's too much empty space to the left of the lists. She would like you to modify the layout to remove the extra space. As you learned in Tutorial 1, each list is treated as a block-level element. By default, most browsers place the list marker to the left of this block, lining up the markers with each list item. You can change this default behavior by using the style

```
list-style-position: position
```

where *position* is either "outside" (the default) or "inside." Placing the marker inside of the block causes the list text to flow around the marker. Figure 4-12 shows how the list-style-position affects the appearance of a bulleted list.

Formatted lists Figure 4-12

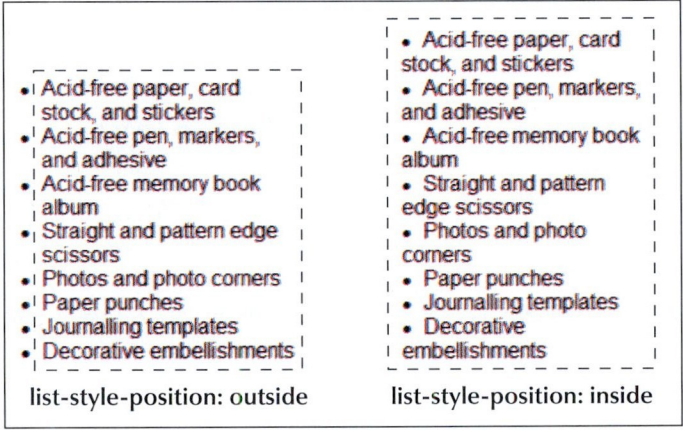

list-style-position: outside   list-style-position: inside

By specifying "inside" for the list-style-position value, you force both the list text and the list marker to be displayed inside of the block. With the addition of the list marker, you will have less space available for the list text.

When a browser renders a list, it offsets the list text a certain distance from the bullet marker. At this time there is no style for specifying the space between the list marker and the list text. The browser also indents the entire list a certain distance from other elements on the page. There is no commonly accepted value for the length that the entire list is indented. Browsers indent lists by setting a value for either the list's left margin or left padding. Firefox indents the list by setting the left padding value, while Opera and Internet Explorer set the size of the left margin. So to have a consistent layout across all browsers, you need to set a value for both the left padding and the left margin.

The internal style sheets for Explorer and Opera set the left margin size to 40 pixels or about 2.5 em and set the left padding space to 0 pixels. Firefox's internal style sheet does the opposite, setting the size of the left margin to 0 pixels and the left padding space to 40 pixels or 2.5 em. So if you want to reduce the indent applied by the browser, you should choose a style that reduces the sum of the left margin and left padding spaces to less than 40 pixels or 2.5 em. Finding the right combination of left padding and left margin values is often a matter of trial and error; you'll have to test your choices under different browsers and different resolutions.

Reference Window | **Applying List Styles**

- To define appearance of the list marker, use the style
  ```
  list-style-type: type
  ```
  where *type* is disc, circle, square, decimal, decimal-leading-zero, lower-roman, upper-roman, lower-alpha, upper-alpha, or none.
- To insert a graphic image as a list marker, use the style
  ```
  list-style-image: url(url)
  ```
  where (*url*) is the URL of the graphic image file.
- To set the position of the list marker, use the style
  ```
  list-style-position: position
  ```
  where *position* is inside or outside.
- To define all of the list style properties in a single style, use
  ```
  list-style: type url(url) position
  ```

After some work, you decide to indent Kathy's list of links by 15 pixels and the Basic Materials list by 25 pixels. You'll add these styles to the scraps.css external style sheet.

To change the margins and padding for the two lists:

▶ 1. Return to the **scraps.css** file in your text editor.

▶ 2. Add the following style to the style declaration for the #links ul selector:

   margin-left: 15px; padding-left: 0px

▶ 3. Add the following to the style declaration for the #pullout ul selector:

   margin-left: 25px; padding-left: 0px

   Figure 4-13 shows the revised style code.

Figure 4-13 ▶ **Setting the spacing within the lists**

```
#outer_container    {width: 780px}
#head               {text-align: right}

#links              {float: left; width: 200px}
#links ul           {list-style-type: none; margin-left: 15px; padding-left: 0px}

#article            {margin-left: 200px}

#pullout            {float: right; width: 250px; margin: 0px 0px 10px 10px;
                     border: 5px outset orange; background-color: ivory;
                     font-size: 10pt; font-family: Arial, Helvetica, sans-serif}
#pullout h2         {text-align: center; background-color: white; margin-top: 0px;
                     border-bottom: 2px solid orange}
#pullout ul         {list-style-image: url(bullet.jpg); margin-left: 25px; padding-left: 0px}

address             {text-align: center; font-style: normal; font-variant: small-caps;
                     border-top: 2px solid orange; color: orange}
```

▶ 4. Save your changes to the file, and then reload or refresh **start.htm** in your Web browser. Verify that both lists moved slightly to the left as a result of the reduced left margin and left padding values in the scraps.css style sheet.

You can combine all of the CSS styles for lists into a single style attribute. The syntax of this combined style is

```
list-style: type url(url) position
```

where *type* is one of the CSS marker types, (*url*) is the location of a graphic file containing a marker image, and *position* is the position of the list markers relative to the containing box.

Nongraphical browsers use the marker defined by the *type* value, while graphical browsers use the image from the graphic file. For example, the style

```
ul {list-style: circle url(dot.gif) inside}
```

displays unordered lists using the marker stored in the dot.gif file; unless a nongraphical browser is displaying the page, in which case the circle marker is applied. In both cases, the marker will be displayed on the inside of the box surrounding the list.

Working with Classes

The list of links on the Getting Started page covers three main areas: pages that teach scrapbooking, pages that sell products, and pages that provide information about the company. Although Kathy has ordered the links by area, the sections are not separated visually on the rendered page. Kathy suggests that you increase the space between the three groups so it's clear where one group ends and another starts. One method for doing this is to mark the first link in each group, and then to increase the size of the margin above those links. You can mark those links using the class attribute. The class attribute is used when you want to identify elements that share a common characteristic. It has the syntax

```
<elem class="class"> ... </elem>
```

where *elem* is an element in the body of the Web page and *class* is a name that identifies the class of objects to which the element belongs. The HTML code

```
<h2 class="subtitle">Getting Started</h2>
<h2 class="subtitle">Preserving Your Memories</h2>
```

marks both of the h2 headings—Getting Started and Preserving Your Memories—as belonging to the subtitle class. Note that unlike the id attribute, several elements can share the same class value. The class values need not be assigned to the same type of element. You can, for example, also mark h3 headings and address elements as belonging to the subtitle class if it suits your purpose. Also, unlike the id attribute, you can place several class values in a space-separated list in the class attribute. The h2 element

```
<h2 class="subtitle mainpage">Preserving Your Memories</h2>
```

belongs to both the subtitle and the mainpage classes.

The advantage of the class attribute is that you can use it to assign the same style to multiple elements sharing the same class value. The selector for the class attribute is

```
.class {styles}
```

where *class* is the name of the class and *styles* are the styles applied to that class of element. So to display all elements belonging to the subtitle class in a blue font, you could apply the following style:

```
.subtitle {color: blue}
```

Because the same class name can be used with elements of different types, you might need to specify exactly which elements of a particular class receive a defined style. This is done using the selector

```
elem.class {styles}
```

where *elem* is the element and *class* is the class. The style

```
h2.subtitle {color: blue}
```

applies a blue font to elements of the subtitle class, but only if they are h2 headings. You can also use class selectors with other selectors in more complicated expressions. The style

```
blockquote h2.subtitle {color: blue}
```

applies the blue font color only to h2 headings of the subtitle class nested within a blockquote element.

Reference Window | **Applying a Style to an Element Class**

- To assign an element to a class, add the attribute
  `class="class"`
  to the element's markup tag, where *class* is the name of the class.
- To apply a style to a class of elements, use the selector
  `.class`
  where *class* is the name of the class.
- To apply a style to an element of a particular class, use the selector
  `elem.class`
  where *elem* is the name of the element and *class* is the name of the class.

Now that you've seen how to create and apply a style to an element class, you can create a style for the list of links on the Getting Started page. The three links that indicate the start of a new link group are named Home, Online Store, and About Us. You need to mark these as belonging to the newGroup class and then apply a style that increases the top margin of these elements.

To create a style for a class of elements:

▶ **1.** Go to the **start.htm** file in your text editor.

▶ **2.** Locate the div element containing the list of links, and then insert the attribute

`class="newGroup"`

in the opening <li> tag for the Home, Online Store, and About Us links. See Figure 4-14.

Figure 4-14 ▶ **Inserting the class attribute**

```
<div id="links">
    <ul>
        <li class="newGroup"><a href="#">Home</a></li>
        <li><a href="#">Getting Started</a></li>
        <li><a href="#">Scrapbooking Tips</a></li>
        <li><a href="#">Supply List</a></li>
        <li><a href="#">Glossary</a></li>
        <li><a href="#">Online Classes</a></li>
        <li><a href="#">Sample Pages</a></li>
        <li class="newGroup"><a href="#">Online Store</a></li>
        <li><a href="#">Shopping Cart</a></li>
        <li><a href="#">Checkout</a></li>
        <li><a href="#">Your Account</a></li>
        <li><a href="#">Order Status</a></li>
        <li><a href="#">Wish List</a></li>
        <li><a href="#">Customer Service</a></li>
        <li class="newGroup"><a href="#">About Us</a></li>
        <li><a href="#">Newsletter</a></li>
        <li><a href="#">FAQ</a></li>
        <li><a href="#">Contact Us</a></li>
    </ul>
</div>
```

▶ **3.** Save your changes to the file.

Next you'll go to the style sheet and create a style for the class of newGroup elements.

4. Return to the **scraps.css** file in your text editor. Directly below the style for the #links ul selector, insert the following style:

```
#links li.newGroup {margin-top: 15px}
```

Note that the selector includes both the element name and the class name to make it clear that elements receive the margin-top style. Figure 4-15 shows the revised style code.

Defining a style for the newGroup class ◄ **Figure 4-15**

```
#links            {float: left; width: 200px}
#links ul         {list-style-type: none; margin-left: 15px; padding-left: 0px}
#links li.newGroup {margin-top: 15px}
```

5. Save your changes to the file and then refresh **start.htm** in your Web browser. As shown in Figure 4-16, the list of links is now divided into three topical areas.

Links list separated into groups ◄ **Figure 4-16**

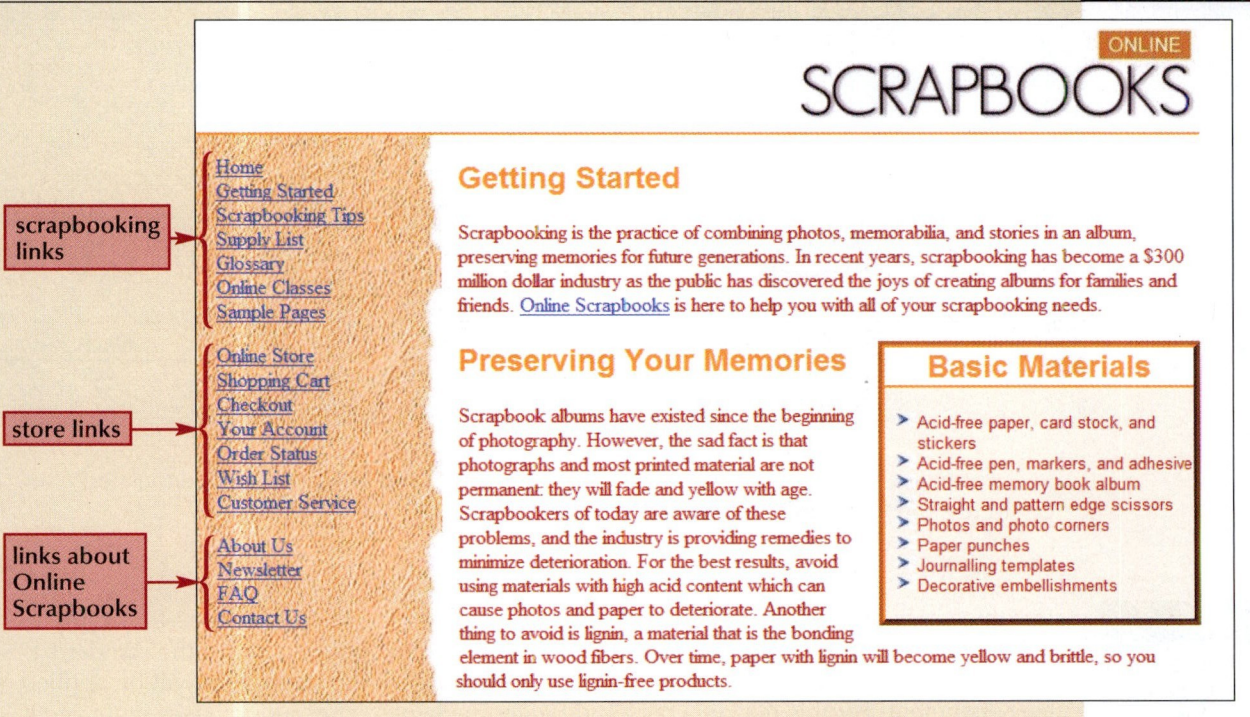

Kathy likes the layout of the list of links. Now she wants to focus on some design elements to enhance the user's interaction with those links.

Using Pseudo-Classes and Pseudo-Elements

Although she realizes that most browsers underline linked text by default, Kathy thinks that a large block of underlined text is difficult to read. She's seen sites in which links are underlined only when the mouse pointer hovers over the linked text. This type of effect is called a **rollover effect** because it is applied only when a user "rolls" the mouse pointer over an element. She would like you to make underlining a rollover effect for the list of links.

Creating a Link Rollover

Rollover effects for links can be created using pseudo-classes. A **pseudo-class** is a classification of an element based on its current status, position, or use in the document. For example, one pseudo-class indicates whether a link has been previously visited by the user. Another pseudo-class indicates whether a link is currently being activated or clicked. To create a style for a pseudo-class, use the style

```
selector:pseudo-class {styles}
```

where *selector* is an element or group of elements within a document, *pseudo-class* is the name of a pseudo-class, and *styles* are the styles you want to apply. Figure 4-17 lists some of the pseudo-classes supported by CSS.

Figure 4-17	**Pseudo-classes**

Pseudo-class	Description	Example
link	The link has not yet been visited by the user	`a:link {color: red}`
visited	The link has been visited by the user	`a:visited {color: green}`
active	The link is in the process of being activated by the user	`a:active {color: yellow}`
hover	The mouse pointer is hovering over the link	`a:hover {color: blue}`
focus	The element has received the focus of the keyboard or mouse pointer	`input.focus {background-color: yellow}`
first-child	The element is the first child of its parent	`p:first-child {text-indent: 0}`
lang	Specifies the language to be used with the element	`q:lang(FR) {quotes: '<<' '>>'}`

If you want the font color of your links to change to red after they've been visited, you could use the following style declaration:

```
a:visited {color: red}
```

Tip

You can achieve interesting rollover effects by having the browser change the background image or background color of the hypertext link.

In some cases, two or more pseudo-classes can apply to the same element—for example, a link can be both previously visited and hovered over. In such situations, the standard cascading rules apply: the pseudo-class that is listed last in the style sheet will be applied to the element. For this reason, you should enter the hypertext pseudo-classes in an order that reflects how users interact with hypertext links. The link pseudo-class should come first, followed by the visited class, the hover class, and finally the active class. The link pseudo-class comes first because it represents a hypertext link that has not yet been visited or even clicked by the user. The visited pseudo-class comes next, for the link that has been previously visited or clicked. The hover pseudo-class comes next, for the situation in which the user has once again moved the mouse pointer over the hypertext link before clicking the link. The active pseudo-class is last, representing the exact instant in which the link is clicked by the user.

Creating a Hypertext Rollover | Reference Window

- To create a rollover for a hypertext link, apply these styles to the link element

  ```
  a:link      {styles}
  a:visited   {styles}
  a:hover     {styles}
  a:active    {styles}
  ```
  where *styles* are the CSS styles applied to hypertext links that have not been visited (link), already visited (visited), have the mouse pointer over them (hover), or are actively being clicked (active).

Kathy wants to remove the underlining from all of the links on her Getting Started page. If the mouse pointer is hovering over a link, however, she wants the link text to appear in a black font and underlined. The style declarations to remove the underlining and to create this rollover effect are:

```
#links a:link {text-decoration: none}
#links a:visited {text-decoration: none}
#links a:hover {color: black; text-decoration: underline}
#links a:active {text-decoration: none}
```

Add these styles now to the scraps.css style sheet.

To create a rollover effect for hypertext links:

▶ 1. Return to the **scraps.css** file in your text editor.

▶ 2. Directly below the style for the #links li.newGroup selector, insert the following style declarations, as shown in Figure 4-18:

```
#links a:link {text-decoration: none}
#links a:visited {text-decoration: none}
#links a:hover {color: black; text-decoration: underline}
#links a:active {text-decoration: none}
```

Using pseudo-classes in a selector ◄ Figure 4-18

```
#links              {float: left; width: 200px}
#links ul           {list-style-type: none; margin-left: 15px; padding-left: 0px}
#links li.newGroup  {margin-top: 15px}
#links a:link       {text-decoration: none}
#links a:visited    {text-decoration: none}
#links a:hover      {color: black; text-decoration: underline}
#links a:active     {text-decoration: none}
```

▶ 3. Save your changes to the file, and then refresh the **start.htm** file in your Web browser.

▶ 4. Verify that the links in the list of links are no longer underlined (because you have set the text-decoration style to have a value of none).

▶ 5. Hover your mouse pointer over a link in the list and verify that when the mouse pointer hovers over the link, it appears in a black font and is underlined. See Figure 4-19.

Figure 4-19 | **Viewing a rollover effect**

SCRAPBOOKS ONLINE

Home
Getting Started
Scrapbooking Tips
Supply List
Glossary
Online Classes
Sample Pages

Online Store
Shopping Cart
Checkout
Your Account
Order Status
Wish List
Customer Service

About Us
Newsletter
FAQ
Contact Us

Getting Started

Scrapbooking is the practice of combining photos, memorabilia, and stories in an album, preserving memories for future generations. In recent years, scrapbooking has become a $300 million dollar industry as the public has discovered the joys of creating albums for families and friends. Online Scrapbooks is here to help you with all of your scrapbooking needs.

Preserving Your Memories

Scrapbook albums have existed since the beginning of photography. However, the sad fact is that photographs and most printed material are not permanent: they will fade and yellow with age. Scrapbookers of today are aware of these problems, and the industry is providing remedies to minimize deterioration. For the best results, avoid using materials with high acid content which can cause photos and paper to deteriorate. Another thing to avoid is lignin, a material that is the bonding element in wood fibers. Over time, paper with lignin will become yellow and brittle, so you should only use lignin-free products.

Basic Materials

➤ Acid-free paper, card stock, and stickers
➤ Acid-free pen, markers, and adhesive
➤ Acid-free memory book album
➤ Straight and pattern edge scissors
➤ Photos and photo corners
➤ Paper punches
➤ Journalling templates
➤ Decorative embellishments

InSight | **Presentational Attributes for Hypertext Links**

Earlier versions of HTML did not include support for the link, visited, and active pseudo-classes. If a Web page author wanted to change the color of a hypertext link, he or she would have to add to the page's <body> tag the attributes

```
<body link="color" vlink="color" alink="color">
```

where the link attribute specifies the color of unvisited links, the vlink attribute specifies the color of visited links, and the alink attribute specifies the color of active links. Colors had to be entered either as a supported color name or as a hexadecimal color value. There is no HTML attribute for creating a rollover effect, so for older browsers you would have to use CSS (if it was supported) or a programming language such as JavaScript to display rollovers.

The link, vlink, and alink attributes have been deprecated and are not supported by strictly compliant XHTML code, but you might still see them used in the code of older Web pages.

Creating a Drop Cap

Kathy has a few more formatting changes she would like you to make to the Getting Started page. She wants you to add the following effects to the first paragraph on the page:

• The first line should be displayed in a small caps style.
• The first letter should be increased in size and displayed as a drop cap.

So far all of our selectors have been based on elements that exist somewhere in the document hierarchy. We can also define selectors based on **pseudo-elements** that are not part of the document tree, but instead are abstracted from what we know of an element's content, use, or position in the document. For example, a paragraph element is part of the document tree and is marked with the <p> tag, but the first line of that paragraph is not—there is no "first line" element even though people intuitively know what page content corresponds to the paragraph's first line. CSS's support for pseudo-elements enables you to create styles for objects such as a paragraph's first line.

The selector for a pseudo-element is similar to what we use for a pseudo-class. The syntax of the pseudo-element selector is

```
selector:pseudo-element {styles}
```

where *selector* is an element or group of elements within the document, *pseudo-element* is an abstract element based on the selector, and *styles* are the styles that you want to apply to the pseudo-element. Figure 4-20 lists some of the pseudo-elements supported by CSS.

Pseudo-elements   Figure 4-20

Pseudo-element	Description	Example
first-letter	The first letter of the element text	`p:first-letter {font-size:14pt}`
first-line	The first line of the element text	`p:first-line {text-transform: uppercase}`
before	Content inserted directly before the element	`p:before {content:"Special!"}`
after	Content appended to the element	`p:after {content:"eof"}`

For example, to display the first letter of every paragraph in a gold fantasy font, you could apply the following style:

```
p:first-letter {font-family: fantasy; color: gold}
```

The advantage of this pseudo-element is that you don't have to mark the first letter in the HTML document; its position is inferred by the browser when it applies the style.

A pseudo-element is also useful for a design element such as a drop cap. To create a drop cap, you increase the font size of an element's first letter and float it on the left margin. Drop caps also generally look better if you decrease the line height of the first letter, enabling the surrounding content to better wrap around the letter. Finding the best combination of font size and line height is a matter of trial and error; and unfortunately what looks best in one browser might not look as good in another. After trying out several combinations for the Getting Started page, you settle on a drop cap that is 400% the size of the surrounding text, with a line height of 0.8. The following style will create this effect:

```
p:first-letter {float: left; font-size: 400%; line-height: 0.8}
```

However, Kathy only wants to apply this style to the first paragraph on each page. The first paragraph on the Getting Started page has already been given the id value firstp, so the style declaration becomes

Tip

Older browsers might not support the first-letter pseudo-element. If you still want to create a drop cap for those browsers, mark the first letter with a span element and apply your style to that element.

```
#firstp:first-letter {float: left; font-size: 400%; line-height: 0.8}
```

Because Kathy also wants the first line of that paragraph to be displayed in small caps, you will also use the first-line pseudo-element in the following style:

```
#firstp:first-line {font-variant: small-caps}
```

Add both of these styles to the scraps.css style sheet.

To create the drop cap effect:

1. Return to the **scraps.css** file in your text editor.

2. Directly above the style for the #article selector, insert the following two styles involving the first-letter and first-line pseudo-elements. See Figure 4-21:

   ```
   #firstp:first-line {font-variant: small-caps}
   #firstp:first-letter {float: left; font-size: 400%; line-height: 0.8}
   ```

| Figure 4-21 | Specifying a style for the first-line and first-letter pseudo-elements |

```
#firstp:first-line   {font-variant: small-caps}
#firstp:first-letter {float: left; font-size: 400%; line-height: 0.8}

#article             {margin-left: 200px}
```

3. Close the **scraps.css** file, saving your changes, and then refresh the **start.htm** file in your Web browser. Figure 4-22 shows the final layout of the Getting Started page.

| Figure 4-22 | Final appearance of the Getting Started page |

4. If you want to take a break before starting the next session, close any open files or programs now.

Working with Pseudo-Elements | Reference Window

- To apply a style to the first line of an element, use the pseudo-element selector
    ```
    selector:first-line
    ```
  where *selector* is the name of the element or elements in the document.
- To apply a style to the first letter of an element, use the pseudo-element selector
    ```
    selector:first-letter
    ```
- To insert a text string before an element, use the style
    ```
    selector:before {content: "text"}
    ```
  where *text* is the content of the text string.
- To insert a text string after an element, use the style
    ```
    selector:after {content: "text"}
    ```

Generating Text with Pseudo-Elements

You can use CSS to insert text into your Web page using the before and after pseudo-elements. The before pseudo-element places text directly before the element, while the after pseudo-element placed the text directly after the element. The syntax of both pseudo-elements is

```
selector:before {content: "text"}
selector:after {content: "text"}
```

where *selector* is an element to which you want to add the *text* string. For example, the style

```
em:after {content: " !"}
```

appends an exclamation point to the end of every element marked with a <em> tag. You can use the before and after pseudo-elements in conjunction with other pseudo-elements and pseudo-classes. The code

```
a:hover:before {content: "<"}
a:hover:after {content: ">"}
```

creates a rollover effect in which the < and > characters are placed around a hypertext link when a mouse pointer hovers over the link.

The content value must be entered as a text string, and you cannot use the content property to insert HTML code. The browser displays the HTML code rather than the element the code represents. For example, if you apply the style

```
em:after {content: "<b>!</b>"}
```

the browser displays the text of opening and closing <b> tags in addition to the exclamation point. Although you cannot insert an HTML element, you can insert an HTML attribute. This is useful because attribute values are usually not displayed on the Web page, but you can automatically insert an attribute value using the attr property

```
content: attr(attribute)
```

where *attribute* is an attribute of the element. For example, the following style appends every hypertext link with the link's URL (as stored in the href attribute):

```
a:after {content attr(" [" attr(href) "] ")}
```

Note that in this example, the href attribute will be enclosed within a set of opening and closing square brackets [.]. This makes your text easy to read by using spaces or brackets to offset the generated content from its surrounding text.

Using the before and after pseudo-elements, you can create truly dynamic Web pages whose content can change based on the styles stored in different style sheets. Internet Explorer does not support the before and after pseudo-elements unless your code puts the IE browser in standards mode. You will not need to use the before and after pseudo-elements in Kathy's Web site.

Kathy is pleased with the work you've done adding special effects to the Getting Started page. She feels that the use of the first-letter and first-line pseudo-elements to create the drop cap effect added a great deal to the appearance of the page. She's also pleased with your work on the rollover effect in the list of links and the graphic image used in the Basic Materials list. In the next session, you'll expand your understanding of CSS by using the styles to directly position elements on the rendered Web page.

Review | Session 4.1 Quick Check

1. Specify the style to italicize the content of all span elements nested within paragraphs.
2. Specify the style to italicize the content of all span elements that are direct children of paragraph elements.
3. Specify the style to italicize all h2 headings that directly follow h1 headings.
4. Specify a style to display all elements that belong to the newsAlert class in boldface text.
5. Specify a style to display only span elements belonging to the newsAlert class in boldface text.
6. Specify a style in which every hypertext link is displayed with a yellow background when the mouse pointer hovers over the link.
7. Specify a style in which hovering over a hypertext link causes the Web browser to change the link's background image to the graphic file hover.jpg.
8. Specify a style that displays the first letter of every block quote in a red font.
9. Specify a style that displays the first line of every block quote in a red font.

Session 4.2

Positioning Objects with CSS

One purpose of the Online Scrapbooks Web site is to teach new scrapbookers how to create beautiful and interesting pages. Every month Kathy wants to highlight a scrapbook page that displays some noteworthy features. Figure 4-23 shows the current Samples page. (Note that because of the scraps.css style sheet, this page uses the same layout as the other pages in the Web site.) The scrapbooking sample is displayed in the main section of the document.

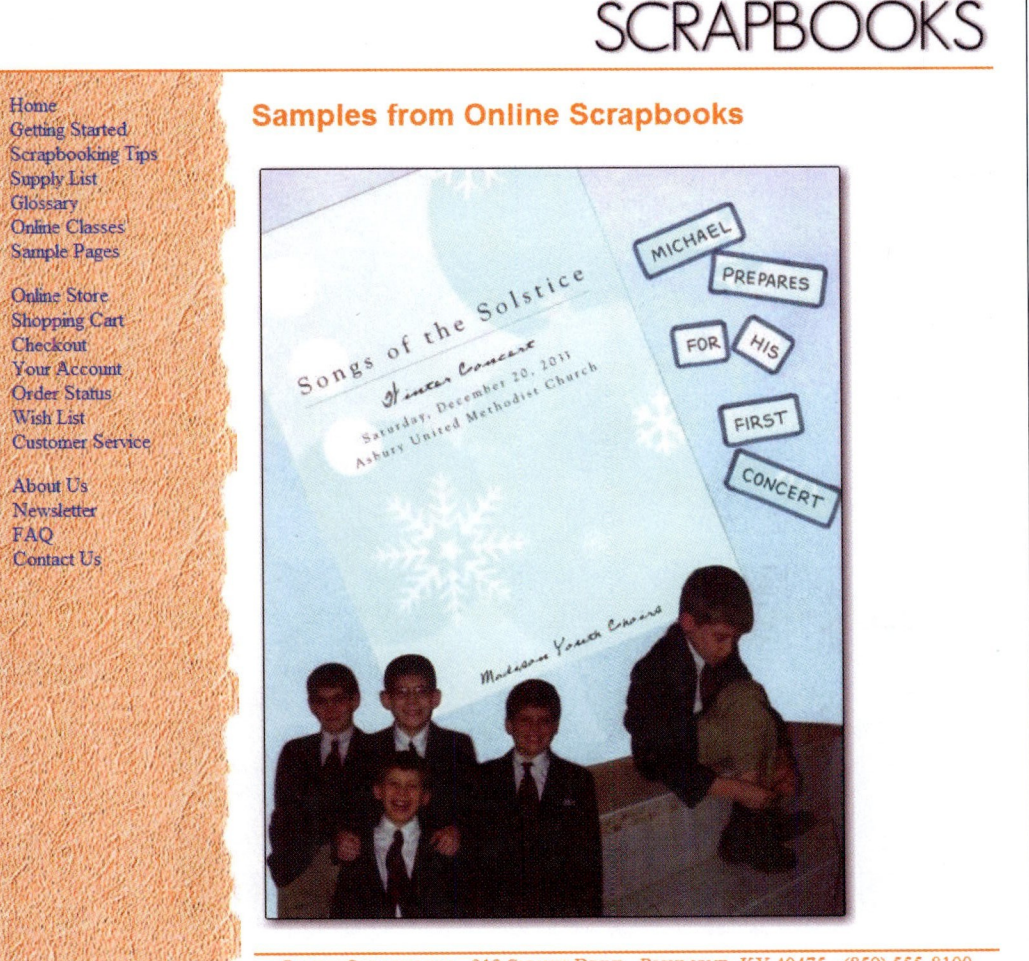

Kathy wants to augment the page by inserting callouts that highlight certain portions of the scrapbooking sample for the reader. She wants each callout to be placed close to the feature that it highlights. Kathy has drawn in the locations of the three callouts that she wants to add in the sketch shown in Figure 4-24.

Figure 4-24   **Sketch of the Samples page**

Figure 4-25 shows the text of the three callout notes.

Figure 4-25   **Text of the three callout notes**

Note	Text
note 1	Paste cut-out letters and words in your scrapbook to create a 3D effect. Online Scrapbooks sells professionally designed cut-out letters, words, and phrases for all occasions.
note 2	Clippings, flyers, programs, and other memorabilia are valuable sources of information that can enhance your scrapbook pages. Make sure that any material is copied to acid-free paper. Newspaper clippings are especially susceptible to deterioration.
note 3	Photographic cut-outs and textured backgrounds can add visual interest to your pages. See the online store for our wide variety of textured and embossed papers.

You'll insert each of these notes in div containers placed within the main section of the page. You'll set the id values of the three elements to note1, note2, and note3, respectively, and you'll add the class value notes to each element so that you can apply a common set of styles to all of the notes.

To insert the three notes:

▶ 1. Use your text editor to open the **samptxt.htm** from the tutorial.04\tutorial folder included with your Data Files. Enter **your name** and **the date** in the comment section of the file and save it as **samples.htm** in the same folder.

▶ 2. Directly below the h2 heading, Samples from Online Scrapbooks, insert the following div container elements, as shown in Figure 4-26:

```
<div id="note1" class="notes">
    <p>Paste cut-out letters and words in your scrapbook to create
    a 3D effect. Online Scrapbooks sells professionally  designed
    cut-out letters, words, and phrases for all occasions.</p>
</div>
<div id="note2" class="notes">
    <p>Clippings, flyers, programs, and other memorabilia are valuable
    sources of information that can enhance your scrapbook pages.
    Make sure that any material is copied to acid-free paper.
    Newspaper clippings are especially susceptible to deterioration.
    </p>
</div>
<div id="note3" class="notes">
    <p>Photographic cut-outs and textured backgrounds can add
    visual interest to your pages. See the online store for our
    wide variety of textured and embossed papers.</p>
</div>
```

Inserting text for the three notes ◀ **Figure 4-26**

```
<div id="article">
    <h2>Samples from Online Scrapbooks</h2>

    <div id="note1" class="notes">
        <p>Paste cut-out letters and words in your scrapbook to create
        a 3D effect. Online Scrapbooks sells professionally
        designed cut-out letters, words, and phrases for all occasions.</p>
    </div>
    <div id="note2" class="notes">
        <p>Clippings, flyers, programs, and other memorabilia are valuable
        sources of information that can enhance your scrapbook pages.
        Make sure that any material is copied to acid-free paper.
        Newspaper clippings are especially susceptible to deterioration.</p>
    </div>
    <div id="note3" class="notes">
        <p>Photographic cut-outs and textured backgrounds can add visual
        interest to your pages. See the online store for our wide
        variety of textured and embossed papers.</p>
    </div>

    <div id="sample_image">
        <img src="sample.jpg" alt="sample page" width="474" height="616" />
    </div>
```

Because the styles in this task will apply only to this page and no others in Kathy's Web site, you'll add an embedded style sheet to the samples.htm file to format the appearance of the three notes. Kathy wants the text to appear in a brown 8-point sans-serif font on an ivory background. She wants the note boxes to be displayed with a 3-pixel light gray inset border. The notes should be 130 pixels wide with a margin space of 5 pixels around the paragraphs.

To define a style for the three notes:

▶ **1.** Scroll to the top of the samples.htm file.

▶ **2.** Directly below the link element, insert the following embedded style sheet as shown in Figure 4-27:

```
<style type="text/css">
 .notes  {font-family: sans-serif; font-size: 8pt; color: brown;
          background-color: ivory;
          border: 3px inset rgb(212, 212, 212); width: 130px}
.notes p {margin: 5px}
</style>
```

Figure 4-27	Setting the styles for the notes text

```
<title>Samples from Online Scrapbooks</title>
<link href="scraps.css" rel="stylesheet" type="text/css" />
<style type="text/css">
    .notes   {font-family: sans-serif; font-size: 8pt; color: brown;
             background-color: ivory; border: 3px inset rgb(212, 212, 212);
             width: 130px}
    .notes p {margin: 5px}
  </style>
</head>
```

▶ **3.** Save your changes to the file.

▶ **4.** Open the **samples.htm** file in your Web browser. Figure 4-28 shows the formatted appearance of the three note boxes. Note that although the boxes are placed side-by-side in this figure to make them easier to read, they should be stacked one on top of the other at the top of your Web page.

Figure 4-28	Formatted note boxes

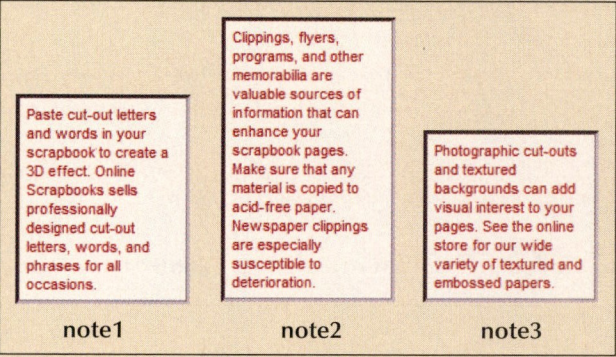

note1   note2   note3

Trouble? Depending on your browser, your note boxes may look slightly different than those shown in Figure 4-28.

Now that you've entered the text and the formatting styles for the three callout notes, your next task is to position them at appropriate locations on the Samples page.

The Position Style

Positioning was one of the first enhancements to the original CSS1 specifications. Collectively, the various positioning styles were known as **CSS-Positioning**, or more commonly, **CSS-P**. CSS-P became part of the specification for CSS2, and positioning styles were some of the first CSS2 styles to be adopted by browsers.

To place an element at a specific position on the page, use the styles

```
position: type; top: value; right: value; bottom: value; left: value;
```

where *type* indicates the type of positioning applied to the element, and the top, right, bottom, and left styles indicate the coordinates of the top, right, bottom, and left edges of the element. In practice, usually only the left and top coordinates are used because the right and bottom coordinates can be inferred given the element's height and width. Coordinates can be expressed in any of the CSS measuring units.

The position style has five possible values: static, absolute, relative, fixed, and inherit. The default position is static, which enables browsers to place an element based on where it flows in the document. This is essentially the same as not using any CSS positioning at all. Any values specified for the left or top styles with a static position are ignored by the browser. You'll explore each of the other values (absolute, relative, fixed, and inherit) so that you can use them to position the notes on Kathy's Sample Pages page.

Absolute Positioning

Absolute positioning enables you to place an element at specific coordinates either on a page or within a containing element. For example, the declaration

```
position: absolute; left: 100px; top: 50px
```

places an element at the coordinates (100, 50), or 100 pixels to the right and 50 pixels down from upper-left corner of the page or the containing element. Once an element has been placed using absolute positioning, it affects the placement of other objects on the Web page. To explore how absolute positioning affects page layout, you'll use a demo containing objects that can be positioned on the Web page.

To explore absolute positioning:

1. Use your Web browser to open the **demo_positioning.htm** file from the tutorial.04\demo folder included with your Data Files.

   The demo page contains two colored boxes that you can move by changing the values in the Positioning Styles box. The boxes are initially set to their default position, which is within the flow of the other elements on the demo page. To make it easier to place the boxes at specific positions, a grid marked in pixels has been added to the page background.

2. Select **absolute** from the list box for the outer box, and then press the **Tab** key.

3. Enter **275** in the left box, and then press the **Tab** key. Enter **350** in the top box, and then press the **Tab** key again. As shown in Figure 4-29, the red outer box is placed at the page coordinates (275, 350).

Figure 4-29 ▸ **Viewing absolute positioning**

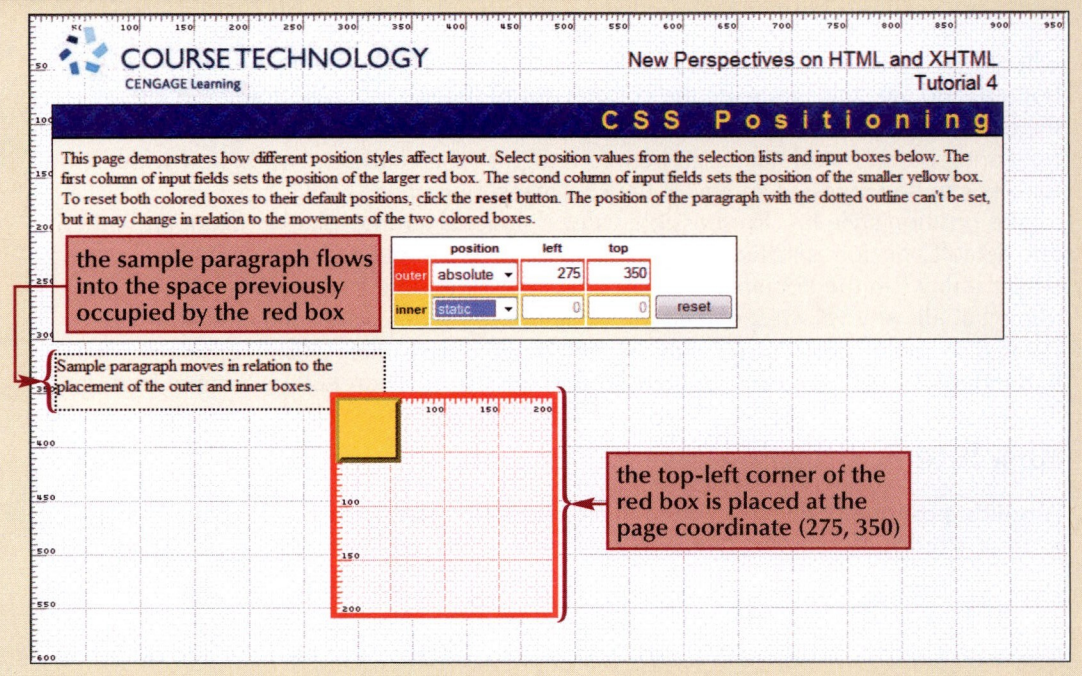

Absolute positioning takes an element out of the normal flow of a document, so that any subsequent content flows into the space previously occupied by the element. Note that on the demo page, the sample paragraph moves up into the space that was previously occupied by the red outer box.

When elements are nested within one another, the position of the element is based on the coordinates within the parent object if that object is itself placed on the page using a CSS positioning style. If the parent object is not positioned using a CSS style, then the position of the nested object is set within the next object higher up in the hierarchy of elements positioned on the page. If no other objects are positioned on the page, the top and left coordinates are based on the browser window. To see this effect, return to the demo page.

To view absolute positioning with a nested object:

▸ **1.** Within the demo page, select **absolute** from the list box for the inner element.

▸ **2.** Enter **90** in the left box for the inner object and **75** for the top box. As shown in Figure 4-30, the inner yellow box is placed at the (90, 75) coordinate within the outer box, not within the Web page.

Positioning a nested object ◄ **Figure 4-30**

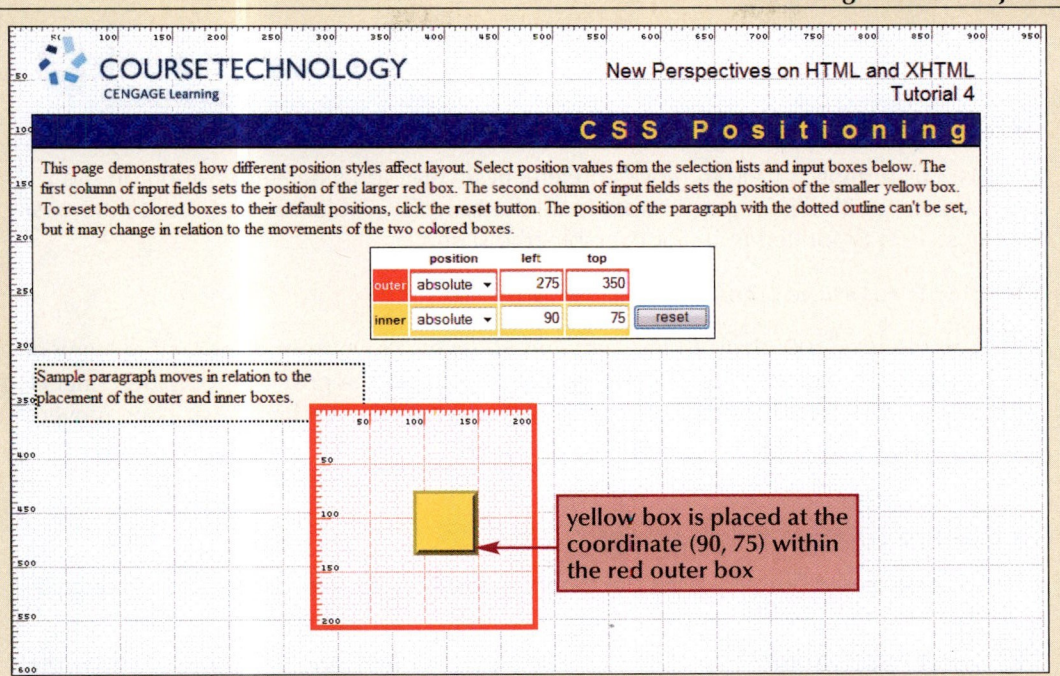

Now examine what occurs when the outer box is no longer placed on the Web page using a positioning style.

▶ **3.** Select **static** from the list box for the outer element.

As shown in Figure 4-31, the red outer box is returned to its default position on the Web page. The yellow inner box is now placed at the coordinate (90, 75), but within the Web page.

Absolute positioning within a nonpositioned element ◄ **Figure 4-31**

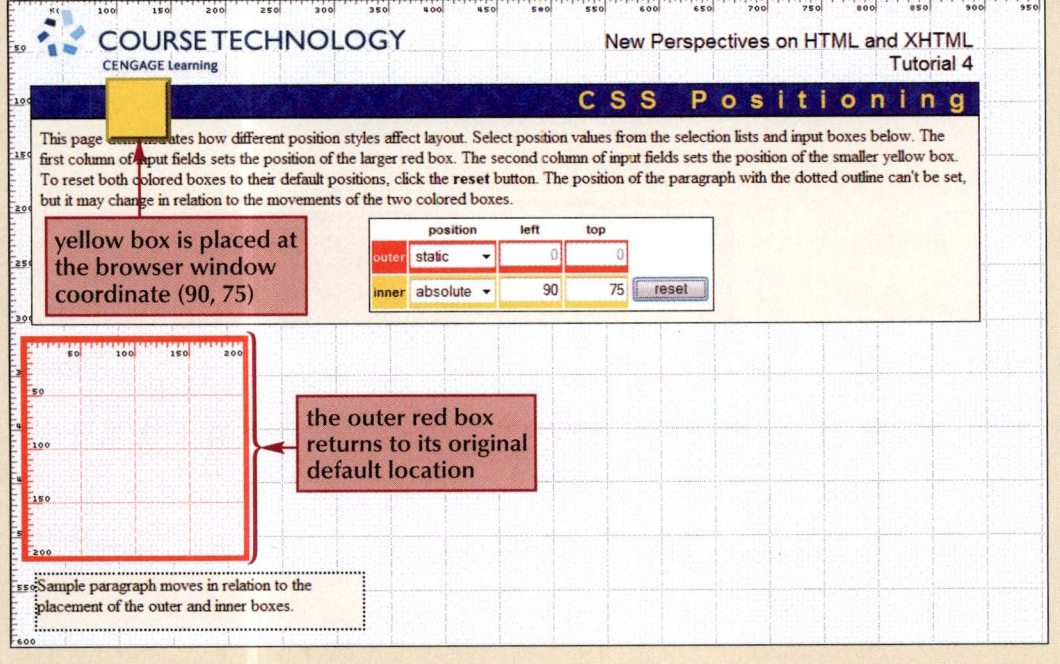

Tip

You can enter negative values for the top and left styles to move page elements up and to the left from their default locations.

> **4.** Continue experimenting with the demo page by entering values for the top and left coordinates and observing the effect on the placement of the boxes.

Relative Positioning

Relative positioning is used to move an element relative to its default position on the page. An element's default position is where the browser would have placed it if no positioning style was applied to it. For example, the style

```
position: relative; left: 100px; top: 50px
```

places an element 100 pixels to the right and 50 pixels down from its normal placement in a browser window. Relative positioning does not affect the position of other elements on a page, which retain their original positions as if the element had never been moved. You'll use the demo page to experiment with this.

To explore relative positioning:

> **1.** Click the **reset** button within the demo page to return both boxes to their default locations on the Web page.

> **2.** Select **relative** from the list box for the outer element, and then enter **275** for the left value and **50** for the top value. As shown in Figure 4-32, the outer box moves 275 pixels to the right and 50 pixels down from its default location.

Figure 4-32 | **Relative positioning**

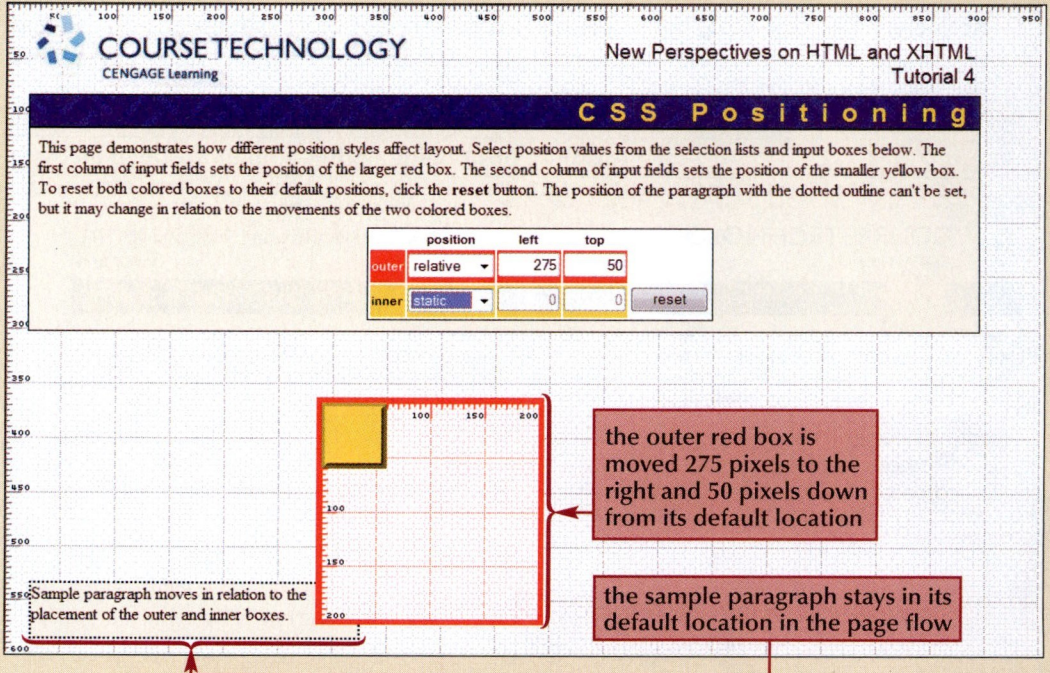

Also note that the sample paragraph does not flow into the space previously occupied by the colored boxes. The layout of the rest of the page is unaffected when relative positioning is applied.

> **3.** Explore other combinations of absolute and relative positioning to see their effect on the layout of the demo page.

In many Web page layouts, you might want to position any object nested within a div container, but you don't need to move the container itself. In those cases, use relative positioning to place the div container with the top and left values set to 0 pixels. The position you apply to the nested object will then be based on coordinates within the div container object.

Fixed and Inherited Positioning

An element placed with absolute or relative positioning scrolls with the rest of the document. Alternately, you can fix an element at a specific spot in the document window while the rest of the page scrolls by setting the value of the position style to fixed. Note that not all browsers support the fixed position, so you should use it with some caution if it is a crucial part of your Web page layout.

You can also assign the inherit position style to an element so that it inherits the position value of its parent element. You'll explore both positioning styles on the demo page.

To explore fixed and inherited positioning:

> **1.** Click the **reset** button within the demo page to return both boxes to their default locations on the Web page.

> **2.** Select **fixed** from the list box for the outer element, and then enter **300** for the left and top values.

  The red box is placed at the window coordinates (300, 300). The sample paragraph moves up into the space previously occupied by the red box.

  Trouble? If you are running an older browser, you might not see any change in the position of the red box.

> **3.** Select **inherit** from the list box for the inner element, and then enter **600** for the left value and **300** for the top value.

  The yellow box inherits the position style of its parent. In this case it uses fixed positioning and is placed to the right of the outer red box. See Figure 4-33.

Figure 4-33   **Fixed and inherited positioning**

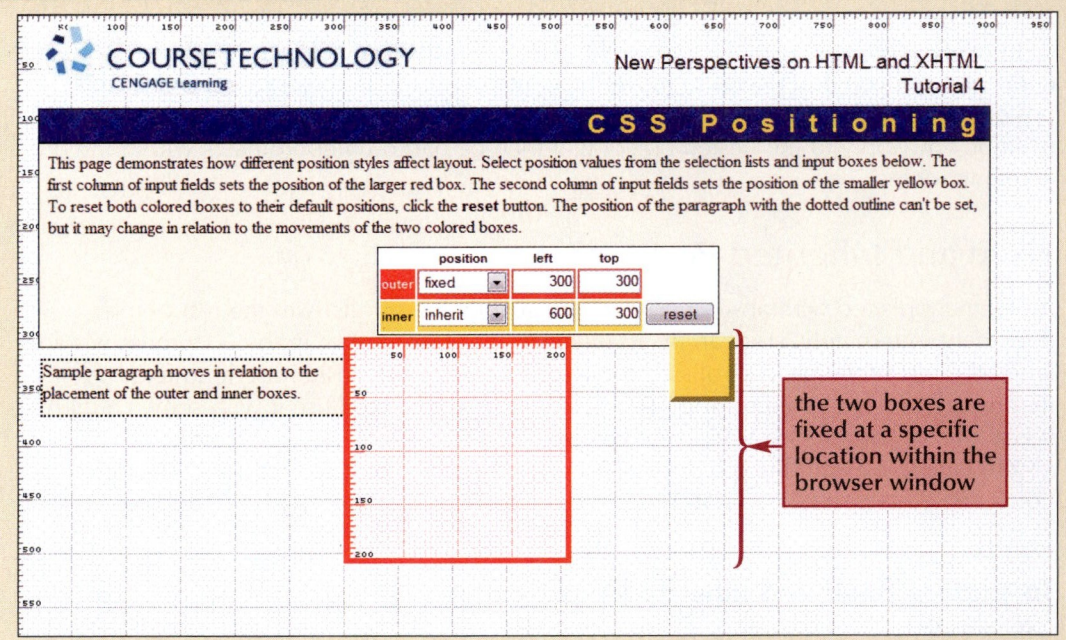

Trouble? Internet Explorer does not support the inherit position style at the time of this writing. To fix the position of the inner box, you have to choose fixed drop in the list box.

▶ 4. Resize the browser window so it's small enough to force the browser to display the vertical and horizontal scroll bars. Scroll through the document and verify that the two color boxes remain fixed at the same location within the window.

▶ 5. Continue to experiment with different positioning combinations. Close the demo page when you're finished.

Reference Window | **Positioning an Object with CSS**

- To position an object at a specific coordinate, use the style
  ```
  position: type; top: value; right: value; bottom: value;
              left: value;
  ```
  where *type* indicates the type of positioning applied to the object (absolute, relative, static, fixed, or inherit) and the top, right, bottom, and left styles indicate the coordinates of the object.

Now that you've seen how to work with the different positioning styles of CSS, you can apply your knowledge to position the three callout notes. After trying different values, you and Kathy settle on the following coordinates using absolute positioning:

```
note1: (600, 120)
note2: (170, 400)
note3: (570, 550)
```

You'll add styles for these positions to the embedded style sheet in the samples.htm file.

To position the three notes for the Samples page:

▶ **1.** Return to the **samples.htm** file in your text editor.

▶ **2.** Add the following styles to the embedded style sheet, as shown in Figure 4-34:

```
#note1 {position: absolute; left: 600px; top: 120px}
#note2 {position: absolute; left: 170px; top: 400px}
#note3 {position: absolute; left: 570px; top: 550px}
```

Setting the position of the three note boxes ◀ **Figure 4-34**

```
<style type="text/css">
    .notes    {font-family: sans-serif; font-size: 8pt; color: brown;
               background-color: ivory; border: 3px inset rgb(212, 212, 212);
               width: 130px}
    .notes p {margin: 5px}
    #note1    {position: absolute; left: 600px; top: 120px}
    #note2    {position: absolute; left: 170px; top: 400px}
    #note3    {position: absolute; left: 570px; top: 550px}
</style>
```

▶ **3.** Save your changes, and then reload the **samples.htm** file in your Web browser. Figure 4-35 shows the placement of the three sample notes.

Notes placed with absolute positioning ◀ **Figure 4-35**

You show Kathy the revised page. She likes the position of the notes, but she points out that they are pretty big and they hide too much of the scrapbooking sample. Kathy would like you to investigate ways of making the notes less intrusive.

Working with Overflow and Clipping

Reducing the height of each note by lowering the value of its height attribute might seem like an easy solution to Kathy's first request. Unfortunately, though, this would not meet her needs because the height of each note expands to accommodate its content. If you want to force an element into a specified height and width, you have to define how the browser should handle a situation where content overflows the space allotted to the object. The syntax of the overflow style is

```
overflow: type
```

where *type* is visible (the default), hidden, scroll, or auto. A value of visible instructs browsers to increase the height of an element to fit the overflow content. The hidden value keeps an element at the specified height and width, but cuts off excess text. The scroll value keeps an element at the specified dimensions, but adds horizontal and vertical scroll bars to allow users to scroll through the overflow. Finally, the auto value keeps an element at the specified size, adding scroll bars only as they are needed. Figure 4-36 shows examples of the effect of each overflow value.

Figure 4-36 **Values of the overflow style**

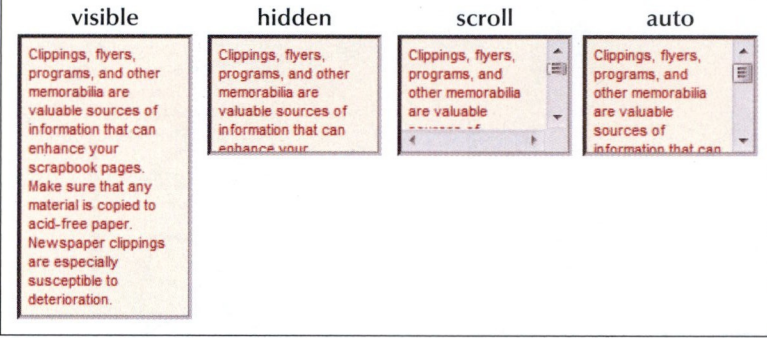

You decide to limit the height of each callout note to 90 pixels and have the browser display scroll bars as needed by setting the value of the overflow style to auto.

To define the overflow style for the callout notes:

1. Return to the **samples.htm** file in your text editor.

2. Add the following styles to the .notes selector, as shown in Figure 4-37:

```
height: 90px; overflow: auto
```

Figure 4-37 **Setting the overflow style for the notes**

```
<style type="text/css">
    .notes    {font-family: sans-serif; font-size: 8pt; color: brown;
               background-color: ivory; border: 3px inset rgb(212, 212, 212);
               width: 130px; height: 90px; overflow: auto}
    .notes p {margin: 5px}
    #note1    {position: absolute; left: 600px; top: 120px}
    #note2    {position: absolute; left: 170px; top: 400px}
    #note3    {position: absolute; left: 570px; top: 550px}
</style>
```

3. Save your changes, and then refresh the **samples.htm** file in your Web browser. Figure 4-38 shows the appearance of the three callout notes with heights limited to 90 pixels and scroll bars added.

Notes with scroll bars   Figure 4-38

4. Use the scroll bars to verify that the entire content of each note is still available to the user.

   Trouble? Depending on your browser, you might not see scrollbars around each note box.

5. If you want to take a break before starting the next session, you can close any open files or programs now.

Clipping an Element

Closely related to the overflow style is the clip style. The clip style allows you to define a rectangular region through which the element's content can be viewed. Anything that lies outside the boundary of the rectangle is hidden. The syntax of the clip style is

```
clip: rect(top, right, bottom, left)
```

where *top*, *right*, *bottom*, and *left* define the coordinates of the clipping rectangle. For example, a clip value of rect(10, 175, 125, 75) defines a clip region whose top and bottom edges are 10 and 125 pixels from the top of the element, and whose right and left edges are 175 and 75 pixels from the left side of the element. See Figure 4-39.

Figure 4-39 ▶ **Clipping an element**

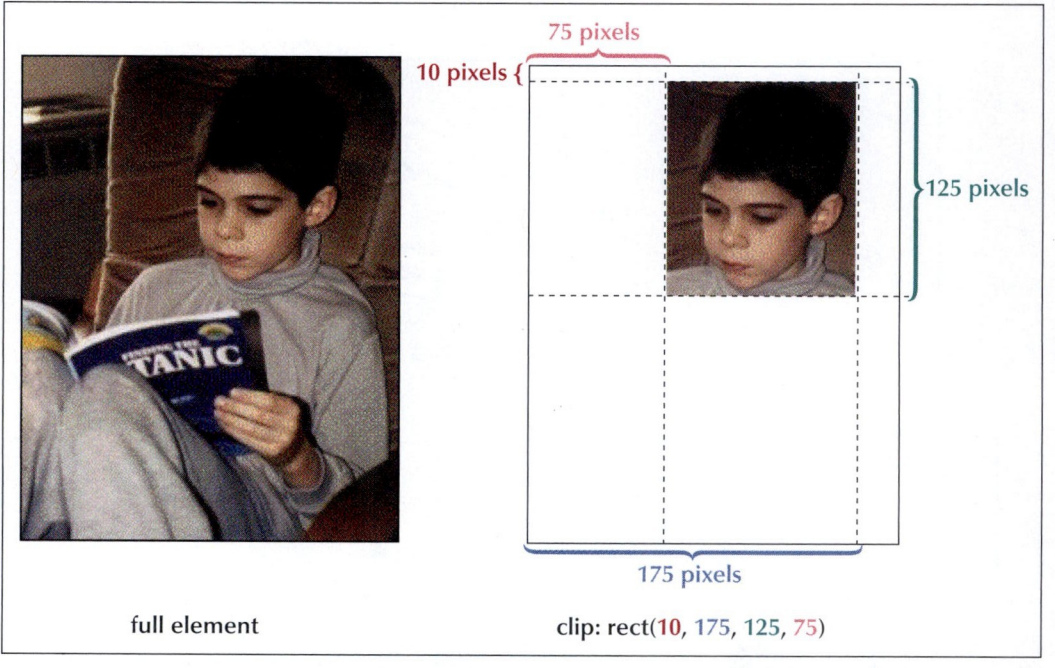

| full element | clip: **rect(10, 175, 125, 75)** |

The *top*, *right*, *bottom*, and *left* values can also be set to auto, which matches the specified edge of the clipping region to the edge of the parent element. For example, a clip value of rect(10, auto, 125, 75) creates a clipping rectangle whose right edge matches the right edge of the parent element.

Reference Window | **Working with Content Overflow and Clipping**

- To specify how the browser should handle content that overflows an element's boundary, use the style
    ```
    overflow: type
    ```
 where *type* is visible (to expand the element height to match the content), hidden (to hide the excess content), scroll (to always display horizontal and vertical scroll bars), or auto (to display scroll bars if needed).
- To clip an element's content, use the style
    ```
    clip: rect(top, right, bottom, left)
    ```
 where *top*, *right*, *bottom*, and *left* define the boundaries of the clipping rectangle.

Limiting Width and Height

In some page layouts, you might want to limit an element's height or width. This is often desirable when you've specified the element's size using relative units that can expand or contract depending on the size of the browser window. If the browser window is very wide, the element might become too wide to be easily readable. If the browser window is too narrow, the element might be reduced to a size that is also difficult to view. Rather than allowing these problems to occur, you can specify an element's minimum or maximum height or width using the styles

```
min-width: value
min-height: value
max-width: value
max-height: value
```

where *value* is the width or height value in one of the CSS units of measure. The min and max values are usually used alongside the height and width styles to set a possible range of values for an element. For example, the style declaration

```
div {width: 80%; min-width: 200px; max-width: 700px}
```

sets the width of the div element to 80% of the Web browser window. If the browser window is 800 pixels wide, the div element will be 640 pixels wide. However, browser windows can vary in size and many users will resize their browser windows to free up desktop space. In that case, the size of the div element will vary accordingly, but it will never be allowed to get smaller than 200 pixels or larger than 700 pixels. Using the min and max styles enables the Web page designer to have some control over the page layout and avoid problems caused by either very large or very small windows.

Max-Width and Internet Explorer | InSight

As mentioned in Tutorial 3, usability studies have shown that most users are comfortable reading text that extends no more than 60 to 70 characters per line or about 30 em. Beyond this length, reading comprehension goes down rapidly and eye fatigue increases. To deal with this problem, Web page designers often use the max-width style to ensure that their Web pages are not too wide on large monitors or screens set to high resolutions.

Internet Explorer did not fully support maximum widths until IE 7. For browser versions earlier than IE7, Web page authors have had to adopt workarounds to approximate the effect of the max-width style. One popular approach, offered by Svend Tofte, is to use a CSS command introduced and supported by Internet Explorer to automatically size the width of an element based on the width of the browser window. For example, the following set of styles defines a maximum width of 800 pixels for an object:

```
max-width:800px;
width:expression(document.body.clientWidth > 800? "800px":
"auto" );
```

In this code, browsers that support maximum widths use the max-width style in the first line to set the maximum width of the object to 800 pixels. Those browsers then ignore the next line and continue on to the rest of the style sheet. Internet Explorer on the other hand, ignores the max-width style in the first line and goes directly to the second line. The second line contains a command that tests whether the browser window is wider than 800 pixels. If it is, it sets the width of the object to 800 pixels. If the browser window is not wider than 800 pixels, the object will be automatically sized by the browser to fit into whatever space is available. The result is that the object will have a maximum width under both IE and browsers that support the max-width style.

This particular workaround can be adapted for different widths and different units of measure. For more information, you can view Svend Tofte's work at *www.svendtofte.com/ code/max_width_in_ie/* or do a Web search for IE workarounds to the max-width problem. As always, you should test any code to ensure that it works with a variety of browsers and operating systems.

Stacking Elements

Positioning elements can sometimes lead to objects that overlap each other. By default, elements that are formatted later in an HTML or XHTML document are stacked on top of earlier elements. In addition, elements placed using CSS positioning are stacked on top of elements that are not. To specify a different stacking order, use the style

```
z-index: value
```

where *value* is a positive or negative integer or the keyword "auto." As shown in Figure 4-40, objects are stacked based on their z-index values, with the highest z-index values placed on top. A value of auto allows the browser to determine stacking order using the default rules.

| Figure 4-40 | Using the z-index style to stack elements |

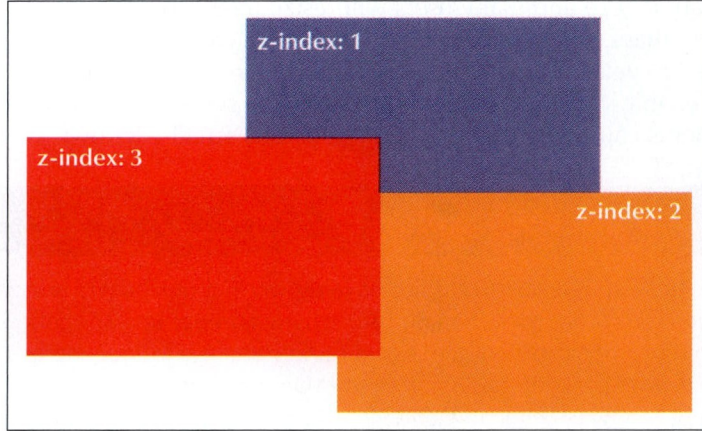

The z-index style only works for elements that are placed with absolute positioning. Also, an element's z-index value determines its position relative only to other elements that share a common parent; the style has no impact when applied to elements with different parents. Figure 4-41 shows a diagram in which the object with a high z-index value of 4 is still covered because it is nested within another object that has a low z-index value of 1.

| Figure 4-41 | Nesting z-index values |

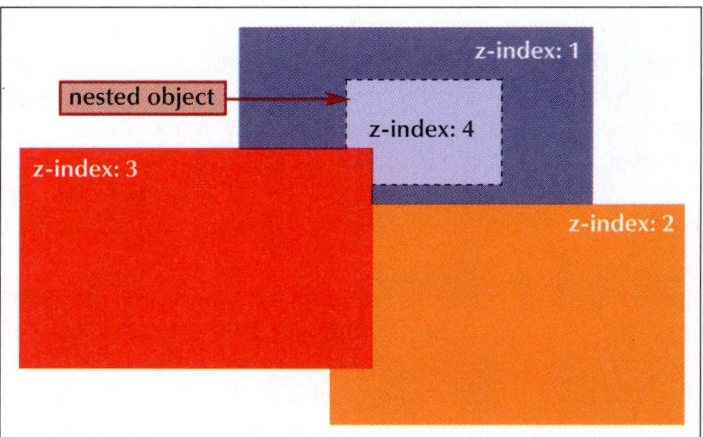

Kathy is pleased with how the notes are positioned over the scrapbooking sample, so you don't need to use the clip or z-index styles. The page looks good on computer monitors. In the next session, you'll explore styles to make your Web pages ready for print media and portable devices.

Session 4.2 Quick Check | Review

1. Specify the style to place an element with the id named logo at the coordinates (150, 75) using absolute positioning.
2. Specify a style to place the logo element 25% down from the top of the page and 10% to the right.
3. What is the style to move span elements belonging to the class highlight up 10 pixels?
4. Specify a style that moves all link elements 5 pixels down when the mouse pointer hovers over them.
5. What is the style to fix an element with the links id at the browser window coordinates (10, 50)?
6. Specify a style to set the width of all block quotes to 70% of the browser window width with a minimum width of 250 pixels and a maximum width of 650 pixels.
7. Specify a style to set the height of all block quotes to 25% of the browser window height. If the content of the block quote cannot fit within this space, include a style to add scroll bars to the block quote as needed.
8. The #title element has a z-index of 1. The #subtitle has a z-index of 5. Will the #subtitle element always be displayed on top of the #title element? Explain why or why not.

Session 4.3

Working with Different Media

Many users of the Online Scrapbooks Web site have reported to Kathy that they enjoy the monthly Samples page so much that they print the samples and store them for future reference. However, these users often find that the pages don't print well. Most users would prefer to print only the scrapbook sample, without the Online Scrapbooks header, links list, and footer. Also, they enjoy the notes that Kathy adds to the sample page, but they would like those notes to be printed on a separate page from the scrapbook sample. In Figure 4-42, Kathy has sketched the design she envisions for the printed version of the Samples page.

Figure 4-42 ▶ **Kathy's proposed printed output**

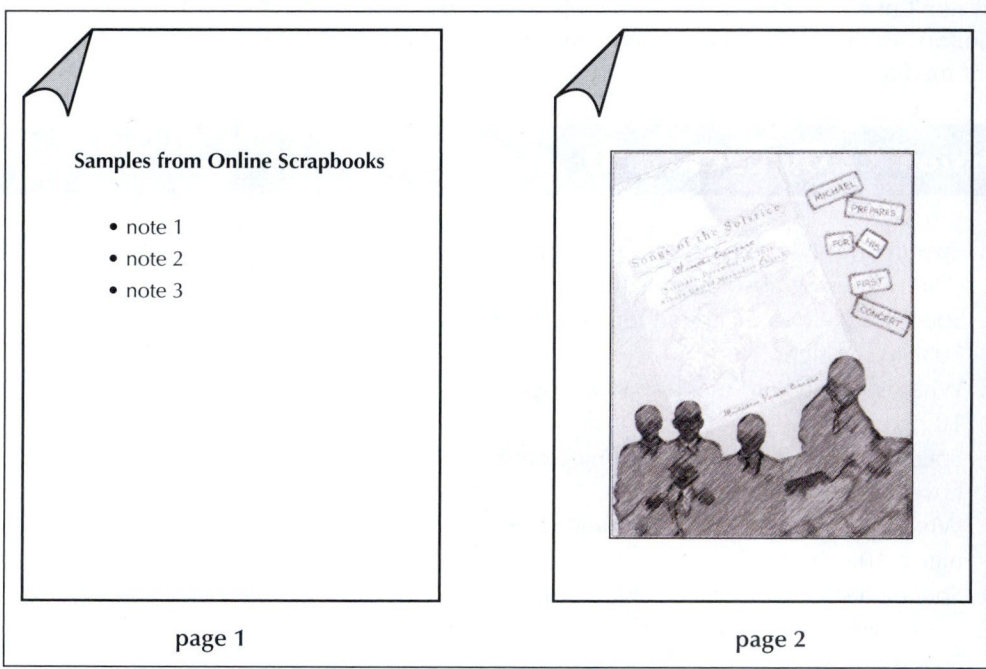

One solution to Kathy's problem would be to create two versions of the Samples page: one for computer screens and the other for printouts. However, Kathy would like to avoid having multiple versions of the same file on her Web site. She would much prefer having a separate style sheet: one that is designed for printed output. She would like you to examine how to create style sheets that are designed for specific devices such as a printer.

Media Types

By default, a style sheet is applied to all devices, and each device must determine how best to match the styles to its own requirements. For example, when you print a Web page, the Web browser and its built-in styles prepare the document for the printer. The user also has some control over that process—for example, determining the size of the page margins or the content of the printout's header or footer. However, beyond that, the user cannot control how the page is printed.

CSS2 and subsequent versions have given more control to Web page authors to specify output styles for particular devices. To do that, you use the media attribute to specify an output device in either the style element (for embedded style sheets) or in the link element (for external style sheets). The syntax of the media attribute is

```
<style type="text/css" media="type">
   ...
</style>
```

or

```
<link href="url" type="text/css" media="type" ... />
```

where *type* is the type of media used by the style sheet. Figure 4-43 lists the different values of the media attribute.

Value	Used for
all	All output devices (the default)
aural	Speech and sound synthesizers
braille	Braille tactile feedback devices
embossed	Paged Braille printers
handheld	Small or handheld devices with small screens, monochrome graphics, and limited bandwidth
print	Printers
projection	Projectors
screen	Computer screens
tty	Fixed-width devices like teletype machines and terminals
tv	Television-type devices with low resolution, color, and limited scrollability

For example, to specify that aural browsers should render your Web page using the sounds.css style sheet, you would enter the following link element in the HTML file:

```
<link href="sounds.css" type="text/css" media="aural" />
```

In the same way, you would use the following media attribute in an embedded style sheet to indicate that its styles are intended for aural devices:

```
<style type="text/css" media="aural">
   . . .
</style>
```

The media attribute can also contain a comma-separated list of media types. The following link element points to a style sheet designed for both print and screen media:

```
<link href="output.css" type="text/css" media="print, screen" />
```

Style sheets cascade through the media types in the same way they cascade through a document tree. A style sheet in which the output device is not specified is applied to all devices, unless it is superseded by a style designed for a particular device. In the following set of embedded style sheets, h1 headings are displayed in a sans-serif font for all devices; however, the text color is red for computer screens and black for printed pages:

```
<style type="text/css">
   h1 {font-family: sans-serif}
</style>
<style type="text/css" media="screen">
   h1 {color: red}
</style>
<style type="text/css" media="print">
   h1 {color: black}
</style>
```

When no value is given to the media attribute, any style defined in the embedded or external style sheet is used for all media, where applicable.

The @media Rule

It's not always convenient to maintain several different style sheets for the same document. In place of several style sheets, you can use a single style sheet broken down into different sections for each media type. This is done using the rule

```
@media type {
    styles declarations
}
```

where *type* is one of the supported media types and *style declarations* are style declarations associated with that media type. For example, the following style sheet is broken into four sections with a different collection of styles for screen, print, handheld, and television media:

```
@media screen    { body {font-size: 1em}  h1 {font-size: 2em}  }
@media print     { body {font-size: 12pt} h1 {font-size: 16pt} }
@media handheld  { body {font-size: 8pt}  h1 {font-size: 12pt} }
@media tv        { body {font-size: 16pt} h1 {font-size: 24pt} }
```

In this style sheet, the font size is smallest for a handheld device (which presumably has a limited screen area), and largest for a television (which is usually viewed from a greater distance). Similar to the media attribute, the @media rule also allows you to place media types in a comma-separated list, as in the following declaration:

```
@media screen, print, handheld, tv {
    h1 {font-family: sans-serif}
}
```

Both the media attribute and the @media rule come with their own benefits and disadvantages. The @media rule enables you to consolidate all of your styles within a single style sheet; however, this consolidation can result in larger and complicated files. The alternative—placing media styles in different sheets—can make those sheets easier to maintain; however, if you change the design of your site, you might have to duplicate your changes across several style sheets.

Media Groups

The distinction among the different media types is not always immediately clear. For example, how is projection media different from screen media? The difference lies in what kind of output can be sent to the media. All output media can be described based on some common properties. CSS uses **media groups** to describe how different media devices render content. There are four media groups based on the following characteristics:

- continuous or paged
- visual, aural, or tactile
- grid (for character grid devices) or bitmap
- interactive (for devices that allow user interaction) or static (for devices that allow no interaction)

Figure 4-44 shows how all output media are categorized based on the four media groups. For example, a printout is paged (because the output comes in discrete units or pages), visual, bitmap, and static (you can't interact with it). A computer screen, on the other hand, is continuous, visual, bitmap, and can be either static or interactive.

Media groups ◄ Figure 4-44

Media type	continuous/ paged	visual/aural/ tactile	grid/bitmap	interactive/ static
aural	continuous	aural	N/A	both
braille	continuous	tactile	grid	both
embossed	paged	tactile	grid	both
handheld	both	visual	both	both
print	paged	visual	bitmap	static
projection	paged	visual	bitmap	static
screen	continuous	visual	bitmap	both
tty	continuous	visual	grid	both
tv	both	visual, aural	bitmap	both

Media groups are important because the CSS2 specifications indicate which media *group* a particular style belongs to, rather than the specific media *device*. For example, the font-size style belongs to the visual media group because it describes the visual appearance of the document content; and as indicated in Figure 4-44, this means you can use the font-size style with handheld, print, projection, screen, tty, and tv media. However, it would have no meaning to—and will in fact be ignored by—devices whose output consists of Braille or aural communication. On the other hand, the pitch style, used to define the pitch or frequency of a speaking voice, belongs to the aural media group and is supported by aural and tv devices. By studying the media groups, you can choose the styles that apply to a given output device.

Creating Styles for Different Media | Reference Window

- To create a style sheet for specific media, add the attribute
    media = "*type*"
  to either the link element or the style element, where *type* is one or more of the following: aural, braille, embossed, handheld, print, projection, screen, tty, tv, or all. If you don't specify a media type, the style sheet applies to all media. Multiple media types should be entered in a comma-separated list.
- To create a style for specific media from within a style sheet, add to the sheet the rule
    @media *type* {*style declarations*}
  where *type* is the media type and *style declarations* are the styles that are applied to the different page elements within that media.

Now that you've seen how to define the style sheet for a particular media device, you decide to create one for printers.

To create a style sheet for print media:

▶ 1. Use your text editor to open the **printtxt.css** style sheet from the tutorial.04\tutorial folder included with your Data Files. Enter **your name** and **the date** in the comment section of the file.

▶ 2. Save the file as **print.css** in the same folder.

Kathy wants you to use the print.css style sheet for any paged visual media, which includes both printed media and projected media. You'll use the scraps.css style sheet for continuous visual media, which includes computer screens, television monitors, and ttys. In the samples.htm file, add a link to the print.css style sheet and insert the media attribute to indicate which style sheets to use for which output devices.

To link Kathy's Samples page to the print.css style sheet:

▶ 1. Return to the **samples.htm** file in your text editor.

▶ 2. Directly above the link element in the document head, insert the following link element for the print.css style sheet:

```
<link href="print.css" rel="stylesheet" type="text/css"
    media="print, projection" />
```

▶ 3. Add the following media attribute to the link element for the scraps.css file to indicate that it should be used for screen, tv, and tty media:

```
media="screen, tv, tty"
```

Figure 4-45 highlights the new code in the samples.htm file.

Figure 4-45 | **Linking to external style sheets for different media**

```
<title>Samples from Online Scrapbooks</title>
<link href="print.css" rel="stylesheet" type="text/css" media="print, projection" />
<link href="scraps.css" rel="stylesheet" type="text/css" media="screen, tv, tty" />
```

The samples.htm file also includes an embedded style sheet. Like the external style sheet, you need to create two embedded sheets: one for printers and projection devices, and the other for screens, tvs, and ttys.

To create an embedded style sheet for print media:

▶ 1. Within the samples.htm file, directly above the embedded style sheet, insert the following HTML code:

```
<style type="text/css" media="print, projection">
</style>
```

▶ 2. Add the following media attribute to the opening <style> tag for the first embedded style sheet. See Figure 4-46.

```
media="screen, tv, tty"
```

Figure 4-46 | **Embedded style sheets for different media**

```
<style type="text/css" media="print, projection">
</style>

<style type="text/css" media="screen, tv, tty">
    .notes    {font-family: sans-serif; font-size: 8pt; color: brown;
              background-color: ivory; border: 3px inset rgb(212, 212, 212);
              width: 130px; height: 90px; overflow: auto}
    .notes p {margin: 5px}
    #note1    {position: absolute; left: 600px; top: 120px}
    #note2    {position: absolute; left: 170px; top: 400px}
    #note3    {position: absolute; left: 570px; top: 550px}
</style>
```

> **3.** Save your changes to the file, and then reload the **samples.htm** file in your Web browser. Confirm that the appearance of the page has not changed. (It should not change because your Web browser is treated as screen media and you haven't changed the style sheet for that media type.)

With two sets of style sheets for the different media types, you are ready to start defining the styles for printed output.

Hiding Elements

The first thing you notice when examining Kathy's sketch of the printed version of the Samples page is that many elements from the Web page—such as the list of links on the left and the address at the bottom—are missing. CSS has two styles that you can use to keep an element from being displayed in the output: the display style and the visibility style. As you've already seen in Tutorial 3, the display style supports the value "none," which causes the element to not be rendered by the output device. Alternately, you can use the visibility style, which has the syntax

```
visibility: type
```

where *type* is visible, hidden, collapse, or inherit (the default). A value of "visible" makes an element visible; the "hidden" value hides the element; a value of "collapse" is used with the tables to prevent a row or column from being displayed; and the "inherit" value causes an element to inherit the visibility style from its parent. Unlike the display style, the visibility style hides an element, but does not remove it from the flow of elements on the page. As shown in Figure 4-47, setting the display style to none not only hides an element, but also removes it from the page flow.

Comparing the visibility and display styles Figure 4-47

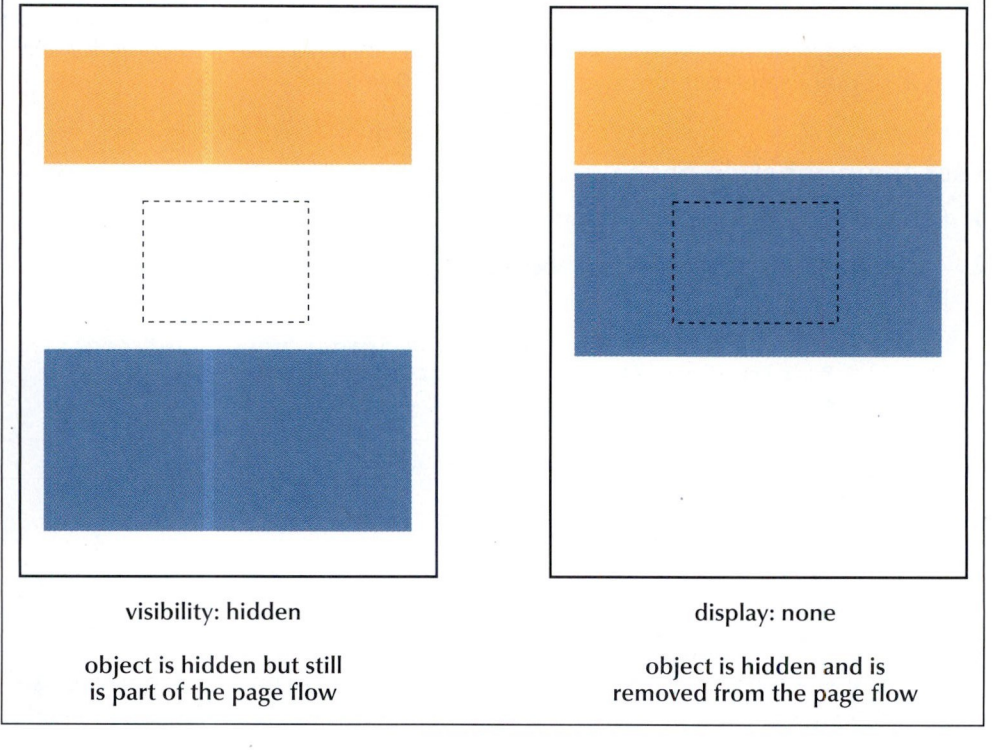

visibility: hidden

object is hidden but still
is part of the page flow

display: none

object is hidden and is
removed from the page flow

The display: none style is more appropriate for hiding elements in most cases. Use of the visibility: hidden style is usually reserved for scripts in which an element is alternatively hidden and made visible to create an animated effect. You'll use the display: none style to hide the #head, #links, and address selectors in the printed output.

To apply the display: none style:

1. Return to the **print.css** file in your text editor.

2. Add the following style declaration below the comment section:

   `#head, #links, address {display: none}`

3. Kathy still wants all headings to appear in a sans-serif font in the printed version of the page. Add the following style to the sheet:

   `h1, h2, h3, h4, h5, h6 {font-family: sans-serif}`

   Figure 4-48 shows the code from the print.css style sheet.

> **Tip**
>
> You can also hide an element by stacking other elements on top of it using CSS positioning and the z-index style.

Figure 4-48 | Using the display:none style

```
#head, #links, address {display: none}
h1, h2, h3, h4, h5, h6 {font-family: sans-serif}
```

4. Save your changes to the file.

Next, you need to modify the style for the callout notes. Kathy wants the notes to be displayed as items in a bulleted list. You can change the style of the notes to list items by applying the following display style:

`display: list-item`

Once the display style has been set to list-item, you can apply the same list styles you would use with elements marked with HTML's <li> tag. You decide to display each note with the bullet.jpg graphic image you used earlier in Session 1. You'll also set the text style to a 12-point sans-serif font with a margin of 20 pixels.

To set the print style of the callout notes:

1. Return to the **samples.htm** file in your text editor.

2. Add the following style to the embedded style sheet for printed output. See Figure 4-49.

   ```
   .notes {display: list-item; list-style-image: url(bullet.jpg);
           font-family: sans-serif; font-size: 12pt;
           margin: 20px}
   ```

Figure 4-49 | Setting the print styles for the callout notes

```
<style type="text/css" media="print, projection">
    .notes {display: list-item; list-style-image: url(bullet.jpg);
            font-family: sans-serif; font-size: 12pt; margin: 20px}
</style>
```

3. Save your changes to the file.

   Now test whether the styles you've defined have been applied to the printed version of the page.

4. Reload the **samples.htm** file in your Web browser. Verify that the appearance of the page within the browser window has *not* changed.

5. Either print the Web page from within your browser or use your browser's Print Preview command to preview the printed version of the page. Figure 4-50 shows how the page appears when printed.

Preview of the Samples page | Figure 4-50

Samples from Online Scrapbooks   Page 1 of 1

notes printed as a bulleted list

Samples from Online Scrapbooks

> Paste cut-out letters and words in your scrapbook to create a 3D effect. Online Scrapbooks sells professionally designed cut-out letters, words, and phrases for all occasions.

> Clippings, flyers, programs, and other memorabilia are valuable sources of information that can enhance your scrapbook pages. Make sure that any material is copied to acid-free paper. Newspaper clippings are especially susceptible to deterioration.

> Photographic cut-outs and textured backgrounds can add visual interest to your pages. See the online store for our wide variety of textured and embossed papers.

Kathy likes the printout you created; however, she still wants the notes to appear on a separate sheet. To do this, you'll have to place a page break in the middle of the document. Although page breaks are not supported by media types such as computer screens, they are supported in printed output and for projection devices.

Using Print Styles

CSS defines printed pages by extending the box model described in Tutorial 3 to incorporate the entire page in a **page box**. As shown in Figure 4-51, the page box is composed of two areas: the **page area**, containing the content of the document, and the **margin area**, containing the space between the printed content and the edges of the page.

Figure 4-51   ▶   **The page box**

As with the box model, you can specify the size of a page box, the page margins, the internal padding, and other features. The general rule to create and define a page box is

```
@page {styles}
```

where *styles* are the styles you want applied to the page. For example, the following @page rule sets the page margin for the printed output to 5 inches:

```
@page {margin: 5in}
```

A page box does not support all of the measurement units you've used with the other elements. For example, pages do not support the em or ex measurement units. In general, you should use measurement units that are appropriate to the dimensions of your page, such as inches or centimeters.

Page Pseudo-Classes and Named Pages

If your Web pages will require several pages when printed, you might want to define different styles for different pages. You can do this with pseudo-classes that reference specific pages. The syntax to apply a pseudo-class to a page uses the following rule

```
@page:pseudo-class {styles}
```

where *pseudo-class* is first (for the first page of the printout), left (for the pages that appear on the left in double-sided printouts), and right (for pages that appear on the right in double-sided printouts).

For example, if you are doing two-sided printing, you might want to mirror the margins of the left and right pages of the printout. The following styles result in pages in which the inner margin is set to 5 centimeters and outer margin is set to 2 centimeters:

```
@page:left {margin: 3cm 5cm 3cm 2cm}
@page:right {margin: 3cm 2cm 3cm 5cm}
```

To format specific pages other than the first, left, or right pages, you first must create a page name that contains a set of styles for the page. The syntax to create a page name is

```
@page name {styles}
```

where *name* is the label assigned to the page style. The following code creates the large_margins page name that defines a page box with 10-centimeter margins:

```
@page large_margins {margin: 10cm}
```

Once you define a page name, you can apply it to any block-level element in your document. The content of the block-level element will appear on its own page, with the browser automatically inserting page breaks before and after the element if required. To assign a page name to a block-level element, use the style

```
selector {page: name}
```

where *selector* is a CSS selector that points to a block-level element and *name* is the name of a defined page. For example, the style

```
blockquote {page: large_margins}
```

causes all block quotes to be displayed on their own separate pages using the styles defined for the large_margins page.

Setting the Page Size

Because printed media can vary in size and orientation, one of the styles supported by the page box is the size style that allows the Web author to define the default dimensions of the printed page as well as whether the pages should be printed in portrait or landscape orientation. The syntax of the size style is

```
size: width height orientation
```

where *width* and *height* are the width and height of the page, and *orientation* is the orientation of the page (portrait or landscape). If you don't specify the orientation, browsers assume a portrait orientation. To format a page as a standard-size page in landscape orientation with a 1-inch margin, you would apply the following style:

```
@page {size: 8.5in 11in landscape; margin: 1in}
```

If you remove the orientation value, as in the style

```
@page {size: 8.5in 11in; margin: 1in}
```

browsers print the output in portrait by default. Note that the page sizes and orientations chosen by the Web page author can still be overridden by the user, who may choose different settings when actually printing the page.

You can also replace the width, height, and orientation values with the keyword "auto" (to let the browser determine the page dimensions) or "inherit" (to inherit the page size from the parent element). If a page does not fit into the dimensions specified by the style, browsers will either rotate the page box 90 degrees or scale the page box to fit the sheet size.

Use the @page rule to define the print layout of the Samples page. Kathy suggests that you set the page size to 8.5 × 11 inches, in portrait orientation, with 0.5-inch margins.

To set the style of the printed page:

► **1.** Return to the **print.css** file in your text editor.

► **2.** As shown in Figure 4-52, add the following rule to the top of the list of style declarations:

```
@page {size: 8.5in 11in portrait; margin: 0.5in}
```

Figure 4-52 ▶ Setting the print style with the @print rule

```
@page {size: 8.5in 11in portrait; margin: 0.5in}
#head, #links, address {display: none}
h1, h2, h3, h4, h5, h6 {font-family: sans-serif}
```

► **3.** Save your changes to the file.

Working with Page Breaks

When a document is sent to the printer, the printer decides the location of the page breaks unless that information is included as part of the print style. To specify a page break that occurs either before or after a page element, you apply the following styles:

```
page-break-before: type
page-break-after: type
```

The *type* style attribute has the following values:

- **always**, to always place a page break before or after the element
- **avoid**, to never place a page break
- **left**, to place a page break where the next page will be a left page
- **right**, to place a page break where the next page will be a right page
- **auto**, to allow the printer to determine whether or not to insert a page break
- **inherit**, to insert the page break style from the parent element

For example, if you want h1 headings to always be placed at the start of a new page, you would apply the following style in your style sheet:

```
h1 {page-break-before: always}
```

Or, if you want block quotes to always appear on their own page, you could place a page break before and after the block quote using the style:

```
blockquote {page-break-before: always; page-break-after: always}
```

Preventing a Page Break

Sometimes you want to keep the printer from inserting a page break inside of an element. This usually occurs when you have a long string of text that you don't want broken into two pages. You can prevent the printer from inserting a page break by using the style

```
page-break-inside: type
```

where *type* is auto, inherit, or avoid. To prevent a block quote from appearing on two separate pages, you could apply the following style:

```
blockquote {page-break-inside: avoid}
```

Note that the avoid type does not guarantee that there will not be a page break within the element. If the content of an element exceeds the dimensions of the sheet, the browser will be forced to insert a page break.

Working with Widows and Orphans

Even with the three page break styles, there will be situations where a printer will have to divide the contents of an element across two pages. Although this situation is largely unavoidable, designers can control the occurrence of widows and orphans in their printed output. A **widow** occurs when only a few ending lines of an element appear at the top of a page. An **orphan** is just the opposite: it occurs when only a few beginning lines of an element appear at the bottom of a page. Leaving one or two lines "stranded" on a page either as a widow or an orphan makes the material more difficult to read and is considered poor page design. The styles to control the appearance of widows and orphans in the printout are

```
widow: value
orphan: value
```

where *value* is the number of lines that must appear within the element before a page break can be inserted by the printer. The default value is 2, which means the widow or orphan must contain at least two lines of text. If you want to increase the size of widows and orphans to three lines for the paragraphs of your document, you could use the style declaration

```
p {widow: 3; orphan: 3}
```

and the printer will not insert a page break if less than three lines of a paragraph will be stranded at either the top or the bottom of a page. It's important to note that the widow and orphan values might not always be followed. Browsers attempt to use page breaks that obey the following guidelines:

- Insert all of the manual page breaks as indicated by the page-break-before, page-break-after styles, and page-break-inside styles.
- Avoid inserting page breaks where indicated in the style sheet.
- Break the pages as few times as possible.
- Make all pages that don't have a forced page break appear to have the same height.
- Avoid page breaking inside a block-level element that has a border.
- Avoid breaking inside a table.
- Avoid breaking inside of a floating element.

Only after attempting to satisfy these constraints are the Web page designer's recommendations for the widow and orphan styles applied.

You can combine all of the various page styles described above to provide the greatest control over the appearance of your printed document. The following set of styles shows how to create a style for the blockquote element that places each block quote on a separate 8.5 × 11 sheet of paper in landscape orientation:

```
@page quote_page {8.5in 11in landscape}
blockquote     {page: quote_page; page-break-before: always;
                                   page-break-inside: avoid;
                                   page-break-after: always}
```

Browser support for the various CSS print styles is very uneven, so you should always test your print styles on a wide variety of browsers and operating systems.

Reference Window | **Working with Print Styles**

- To define a page box for a printout that indicates the page size, margins, and orientation, use the declaration
    ```
    @page {styles}
    ```
  where *styles* are the styles that define the page.
- To set the page size and orientation, use the style
    ```
    size: width height orientation
    ```
  where *width* and *height* are the width and height of the page, and *orientation* is the orientation of the page (portrait or landscape).
- To insert a page break before an element, use the style
    ```
    page-break-before: type
    ```
  where *type* is always (to always place a page break), avoid (to never place a page break), left (to force a page break where the succeeding page will be a left page), right (to force a page break where the succeeding page will be a right page), auto (to allow the browser to determine whether or not to insert a page break), or inherit (to inherit the page break style of the parent element).
- To insert a page break after an element, use the style
    ```
    page-break-after: type
    ```
  where *type* has the same values as the page-break-before style.
- To apply a page break inside an element, use the style
    ```
    page-break-inside: type
    ```
  where *type* is auto, inherit, or avoid.

Now that you've seen how to insert page breaks into printed output, you are ready to insert a break into the printed version of the Samples page. Recall that Kathy wants the list of notes to appear on one page and the scrapbooking sample to appear on another. To do this, you can either place a page break after the third callout note or place a page break before the inline image of the scrapbooking sample. You decide to place a page break before the image. This will enable you to insert additional callout notes later without having to revise the page break structure. The sample image has been placed within a div container element with the id sample_image. To ensure that this container will start on a new page, you'll add the style below to the print.css style sheet. Kathy also wants the image centered horizontally on the page. The complete style for the #sample_image selector is:

```
#sample_image {page-break-before: always;
               text-align: center}
```

Kathy also wants the sample image itself resized to better fit the size of the page. She suggests you increase the size of the printed image to 7 inches wide by 9.1 inches tall. Because the img element for the sample image is nested within the #sample_image div container, you can set the size using the following style:

```
#sample_image img {width: 7in; height: 9.1in}
```

Add both of these styles to the print.css style sheet.

To complete the print.css style sheet:

▶ **1.** As shown in Figure 4-53, add the following styles to the bottom of the **print.css** style sheet:

```
#sample_image        {page-break-before: always;
                       text-align: center}
#sample_image img {width: 7in; height: 9.1in}
```

Final print.css style sheet ◀ **Figure 4-53**

```
@page {size: 8.5in 11in portrait; margin: 0.5in}
#head, #links, address {display: none}
h1, h2, h3, h4, h5, h6 {font-family: sans-serif}

#sample_image        {page-break-before: always;
                       text-align: center}

#sample_image img {width: 7in; height: 9.1in}
```

▶ **2.** Close the file, saving your changes.

▶ **3.** Reload the **samples.htm** file in your Web browser.

▶ **4.** Either print the Web page or use the Print Preview feature of your Web browser to view the layout and design of the printed version of the document. As shown in Figure 4-54, the printed version covers 2 pages, with the list of notes on one page and the sample image resized and centered on the second page.

Figure 4-54   Two-page printout of the samples.htm file

Samples from Online Scrapbooks

> Paste cut-out letters and words in your scrapbook to create a 3D effect. Online Scrapbooks sells professionally designed cut-out letters, words, and phrases for all occasions.

> Clippings, flyers, programs, and other memorabilia are valuable sources of information that can enhance your scrapbook pages. Make sure that any material is copied to acid-free paper. Newspaper clippings are especially susceptible to deterioration.

> Photographic cut-outs and textured backgrounds can add visual interest to your pages. See the online store for our wide variety of textured and embossed papers.

5. Close your Web browser and any other programs and files.

Styles for Handheld Devices | InSight

Although CSS allows you to create styles for handheld devices such as cell phones, PDAs, and MP3 players, effectively translating a large Web page into a smaller space is not easy. Some handheld devices support screens only up to 120 pixels wide; so you might quickly find your graphics-intensive Web page does not translate well into a portable world.

In general, if you want your Web page to be accessible to handheld devices, you should avoid using decorative images, and you should always specify alternative text for your graphic images. Also avoid floating elements. In the small, confined space of a handheld device, a floating element can behave unpredictably and ruin your page layout. Instead try to limit your page layout to a single column.

Use relative units such as the em unit and percent values to set the size of your fonts and block-level elements. If you must use pixels to specify a margin or padding size, try to keep your sizes within 5 pixels. Using larger pixel values such as 15 or 20 pixel widths can have an unpredictable effect on your page.

Finally, you have to pick and choose the features that are the most crucial to your Web page. A long list of links, while useful on a computer screen, can be distracting and difficult to navigate in a portable browser. Use the display:none style to control which elements will be sent to handheld devices.

Support for handheld browsing is still in its infancy, so don't be surprised to find a great deal of variation in the support for your HTML and CSS code among the various portable devices.

You've completed your work on the Samples page for the Online Scrapbooks Web site, and you'll be able to apply what you've learned about print styles to the other pages in the site. At the moment, most browsers support few of the page styles other than page breaking. This is sure to change in the future, however, as Web pages expand beyond the limitations of the computer screen into new media. Kathy finds this an exciting prospect, providing the opportunity to advertise the company to a whole new set of potential customers.

Session 4.3 Quick Check | Review

1. What attribute would you add to an embedded or external style sheet link to apply a style sheet to a mobile phone?
2. Which media types belong to the continuous/visual group?
3. Which media types would be most appropriate for Web browsers designed for the visually impaired?
4. What is the difference between the display:none and visibility:hidden styles?
5. Specify a style to set the page size of the printed document to 11 inches wide by 14 inches high in landscape orientation with a 1.5-inch margin.
6. Specify the style to insert a page break before every h1 heading in your document.
7. In page design, what is a widow? What is an orphan?

In this tutorial, you learned how to use Cascading Style Sheets to create interesting and flexible layouts and designs. The first session examined different types of CSS selectors, providing the Web author flexibility in creating and applying specific design styles. The first session also explored how to apply styles to unordered lists. It concluded by examining how to use CSS to create rollover effects and drop caps. The second session focused on CSS positioning styles and explored how to use CSS positioning to place elements in absolute and relative coordinates. The final session looked at applying styles to media other than computer screens, focusing on creating styles for printed output. In the session you learned how to work with page flow within printed materials by controlling the placement of page breaks before, after, and within page elements.

Key Terms

absolute positioning	media group	pseudo-element
attribute selector	orphan	relative positioning
conditional comment	page box	rollover effect
contextual selector	pseudo-class	widow

| Practice | **Review Assignments** |

Practice the skills you learned in the tutorial using the same case scenario.

Data Files needed for the Review Assignments: back.jpg, gallerytxt.htm, marker.gif, printertxt.css, sample1.jpg – sample4.jpg, scraps.jpg, and screentxt.css

Kathy stopped by to ask for your help in designing a new Web page to display scrapbooking samples sent in by different visitors to the Web site. The screen version of the Web page will show four new sample scrapbook pages each month, laid out on the page in a 2 × 2 grid. The print version of the same page will display enlarged versions of the four samples, printed on separate pages. Kathy also has some changes she wants you to make to the size navigation links. A preview of the design you'll apply to the Scrapbook Gallery page is shown in Figure 4-55.

Figure 4-55

Scrapbook Gallery

Every month Online Scrapbooks presents the best scrapbooking samples from our customers. Scroll through the list of images to view this month's submissions. Click the image to view a full-size version of the sample page.

Interested in showcasing your work? Contact kathy_pridham@onlinescraps.com to receive a copy of our submission guidlines. Please one submission per person.

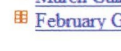 April Gallery
 March Gallery
 February Gallery

Paint Ball Fun

Longs Peak Memories

Trick or Treat!

Michael's First Concert

Home
  Getting Started
  Scrapbooking Tips
  Supply List
  Glossary
  Online Classes
  Sample Pages

Online Store
  Shopping Cart
  Checkout
  Your Account
  Order Status
  Wish List
  Customer Service

About Us
  Newsletter
  FAQ
  Contact Us

ONLINE SCRAPBOOKS · 212 SUNSET DRIVE · RICHMOND, KY 40475 · (859) 555-8100

Complete the following:

1. Use your text editor to open the **gallerytxt.htm**, **printertxt.css**, and **screentxt.css** files from the tutorial.04\review folder included with your Data Files. Enter *your name* and *the date* in the comment section of each file. Save the files as **gallery.htm**, **printer.css**, and **screen.css**, respectively, in the same folder. Take some time to study the content and layout of the Gallery Web page and observe how the styles in the screen.css style sheet file affects the layout and appearance of the page as it appears in your Web browser.

2. Return to the **gallery.htm** file in your text editor. Kathy wants you to format the appearance of the list of links by indenting links belonging to a particular group or class. To define the class of links, do the following:
   - Add a class attribute to the li elements in the list of links, placing the Home, Online Store, and About Us links in the newgroup class.
   - Place the other li elements in the list of links in the subgroup class.

3. The Gallery page contains four images of scrapbook page samples chosen for the May gallery. Scroll down to the four div container elements (marked with ids sample1 through sample4) and place each of the div containers in the samples class.

4. Save your changes to the **gallery.htm** file and then go to the **screen.css** style sheet file in your text editor. This style sheet will be used to design the layout of the Gallery page as it appears on computer screens.

5. Kathy wants to remove the bullet markers from the list of links. She also wants to change the layout of the links, moving them farther to the left and indenting links belonging to the subgroup class. To apply these styles, do the following:
   - For ul elements nested within the #links selector, change the marker style to none.
   - To move the list of links to the left on the Web page, set the size of the left margin to 15 pixels and the size of the left padding to 0 pixels.
   - Set the top margin of elements belonging to the newgroup class to 20 pixels.
   - Set the left margin of elements belonging to the subgroup class to 20 pixels.

6. The Gallery page also includes links to galleries from the months of February, March, and April. These links also appear in a list nested within the content div container. Kathy would like you to replace the bullet marker on this list with a graphical marker. To apply this style, set all the ul elements nested within the #content selector to use the **marker.gif** file as their bullet marker.

7. Kathy would like you to create a rollover effect for the list of links displayed on the left margin of the Web page. To create the rollover effect, add the following styles to the style sheet:
   - For links within the #links selector, remove any underlining by setting the text-decoration style to none. Do this for the link, visited, and active pseudo-classes.
   - When the mouse pointer is hovering over those links, change the font color to black and change the background color to white, and use the text-decoration style to add an underline and an overline to the link text.

8. Kathy wants the four scrapbook samples to be reduced in size and placed in a 2 x 2 grid on the Web page. To create this effect, add the following styles to the style sheet:
   - Apply absolute positioning to all elements belonging to the samples class.
   - For all img elements nested within the samples class, set the width of the image to 150 pixels, the height to 193 pixels, and the border width to 0 pixels.

- All four scrapbook samples are nested within a div container with the id samples_container. Place this div container on the Web page using relative positioning. Set the top and left coordinates of the element to 0 pixels. Set the height of samples_container to 450 pixels.
- Place the #sample1 selector at the page coordinates (0, 0). Place the #sample2 selector at the coordinates (170, 0). Place the #sample3 selector at the coordinates (0, 220). Place the #sample4 selector at the coordinates (170, 220).

9. Save your changes to the **screen.css** file. Load the **gallery.htm** file in your Web browser and verify that its layout resembles that shown in Figure 4-55. Confirm that the Web browser displays the correct rollover effect when you hover your mouse pointer over any of the links in the list on the left page margin.

10. Kathy also wants you to create a style sheet for printed versions of the Gallery page in which only the four scrapbook samples and their headings are shown, each on its own page. To create this style, return to the **printer.css** file in your text editor.

11. Add the following styles to the style sheet:
- Set the page size to 8.5 × 11 inches, in portrait orientation, with a margin of 0.5 inches.
- Prevent the display of the #head and #links selectors as well as the address, ul, and h2 elements and paragraphs nested within the #content selector.
- Horizontally center all elements belonging to the samples class, and add a page break after every occurrence of this class of element.
- Set the font size of h3 headings nested within the samples class to 18 points and the font family to sans-serif.
- Set the size of img elements nested within the samples class to 6.5 inches wide by 8.35 inches tall. Set the border width to 0 pixels.

12. Save your changes to the **printer.css** file and return to the **gallery.htm** file.

13. Edit the link element pointing to the screen.css style sheet, adding an attribute that indicates that this style sheet should only be used for screen output.

14. Add a link pointing to the printer.css style sheet with an attribute indicating that this style sheet is used for printed output.

15. Save your changes to the **gallery.htm** file and refresh the page in your Web browser. Confirm that the appearance of the page within the browser window is unchanged. Print the Web page or use your browser's Print Preview command to confirm that the printed version of the page displays only the four scrapbook samples and their headings.

16. Submit your completed files to your instructor.

Apply | **Case Problem 1**

Apply your knowledge of Web site design to create a Web site for a golf course.

Data Files needed for this Case Problem: h01txt.htm – h18txt.htm, hole01.jpg – hole18.jpg, next.jpg, prev.jpg, printtxt.css, willet.jpg, and willettxt.css

Willet Creek Golf Course   Willet Creek is a popular public golf course in central Idaho. You've been asked to work on the design of the course's Web site by Michael Carpenter, the head of promotion for the course. Part of the Web site contains a preview of each of the course's 18 holes, complete with yardages and shot recommendations. Each hole has been given its own Web page with a set of links to navigate from one page to another. Figure 4-56 shows a preview of the design you'll use to show one of the pages on the golf course Web site.

Figure 4-56

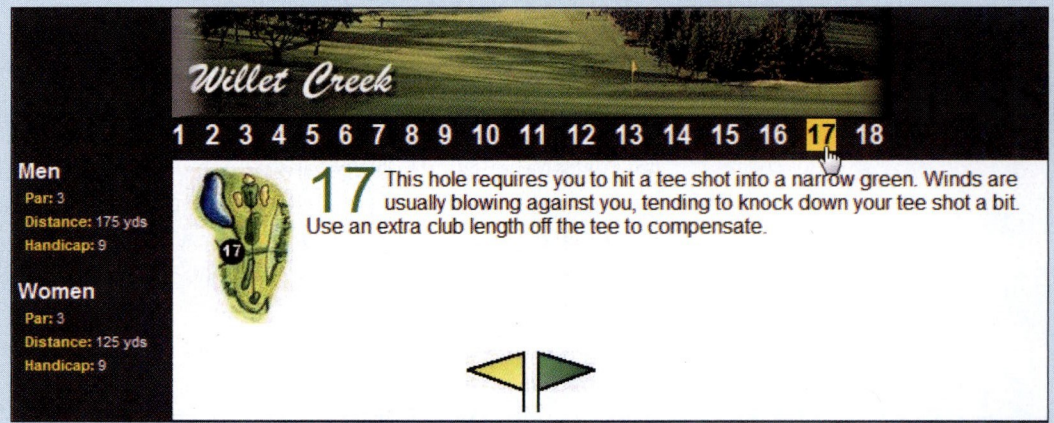

Michael also wants another style sheet designed for printed output. Figure 4-57 shows a preview of the print style used with the golf course pages.

Figure 4-57

Willet Creek Golf Course: 17th Hole

Men

- **Par:** 3
- **Distance:** 175 yds
- **Handicap:** 9

Women

- **Par:** 3
- **Distance:** 125 yds
- **Handicap:** 9

Hole 17

This hole requires you to hit a tee shot into a narrow green. Winds are usually blowing against you, tending to knock down your tee shot a bit. Use an extra club length off the tee to compensate.

1 of 1

Michael has already done a lot of work in setting up the page content and has even applied a few CSS styles to the page elements. He needs you to complete the task, getting the Web pages ready for the next round of golfers.

Complete the following:

1. In your text editor, open the files **h01txt.htm** through **h18txt.htm** from the tutorial.04\case1 folder included with your Data Files. Enter *your name* and *the date* in the comment section of each file and save the files as **h01.htm** through **h18.htm** in the same folder.

2. Use your text editor to open the **printtxt.css** and **willettxt.css** files, also from the tutorial.04\case1 folder included with your Data Files. Enter *your name* and *the date* in each file and save them as **print.css** and **willet.css**, respectively, in the same folder. Take some time to review the contents and layout of the Web pages, paying particular attention to the use of div container tags and id attributes to mark off different sections of the document. Also take some time to review the contents of the **willet.css** style sheet to examine what styles Michael has already created for the Web site.

3. Return to the **willet.css** file in your text editor. The list of links to each page in the Web site is contained within a div container with the id hole_list. Apply the following styles to the list and the links it contains:
   - Display each link in a bold, white font, with a font size of 1.25 em.
   - When a mouse pointer hovers over a link, change the background color to yellow and the font color to black.
   - Display each li element within the #hole_list selector as an inline element with a margin of 0 pixels, a padding space of 0 pixels above and below the element, and padding space of 5 pixels to the left and right.

4. The hole_stats div container stores statistical information about each hole, providing the par score, distance, and handicap value for men and women. Apply the following styles to this element:
   - Use absolute positioning to place the div container at the page coordinates (0, 115).
   - For h2 elements nested within the container, set the font size to 1 em and the left margin to 5 pixels. Set the size of the other margins to 0 pixels.
   - Remove the list markers from the unordered list within the container. Also, set the left margin of the list to 10 pixels, the left padding to 0 pixels, and the top margin to 0 pixels. Display the unordered list in a 0.7 em size font.
   - Display the contents of the strong element within the container in a yellow font.

5. The hole_summary div container contains a text summary of the hole and how to play it. Add a style to place the container at the coordinates (120, 115). Use absolute positioning.

6. The hole_image div container stores an image of the hole. Use absolute positioning to place this element at the coordinates (10, 5).

7. The hole_description div container contains a text description of the hole. Use absolute positioning to place this element at the coordinates (100, 5).

8. Within the hole_description container is a span element that contains the hole number. Michael would like this number to appear as a drop cap. Create this effect by floating the span element on the left margin with a line height of 0.75 with 2 pixels of padding on the right. Set the font color to green and the font size to 300%.

9. At the bottom of each page are a pair of flag images that can be clicked to move to the next hole on the course. The images are nested within a div container with the id flags. Apply the following styles to the div container and the images it contains:
   - Set the border width of img elements within the flags container to 0 pixels.

- Use absolute positioning to place the #prevFlag selector at the coordinates (220, 145).
- Use absolute positioning to place the #nextFlag selector at the coordinates (270, 145).

10. Save your changes to the **willet.css** file. Go to the **h01.htm** through **h18.htm** files in your text editor and link each file to the willet.css style sheet, specifying that the sheet is to be used with screen and tv media. Save your changes to each file, and then view the Web site in your browser. Verify that the layout resembles that shown in Figure 4-57 and that the list of links at the top of the page has a rollover effect.

11. Return to the **print.css** file in your text editor. Add the following styles to the style sheet:
    - Set the page size to 8.5 × 11 inches in portrait orientation.
    - Set the font family of the h1, h2, and h3 headings to sans-serif.
    - Horizontally align the contents of the #head selector.
    - Prevent the display of the #hole_list and #flags selectors.
    - Float the #hole_stats selector on the left margin with a 0.2-inch right margin and 0.1 inches of padding. Add a 0.1-inch double black border to the right and bottom of the element.
    - Set the font size of h2 elements nested within the #hole_stats selector to 12 points.
    - Use absolute positioning to place the #hole_image selector 3 inches from the top of the page and 3 inches from the page's left margin.
    - Set the width of img elements within the #hole_image selector to 3.54 inches wide by 5 inches tall.
    - Display the span element nested within the #hole_description selector as a block-level element. Display the text in a 20-point bold sans-serif font.

EXPLORE
    - Use the before pseudo-element to place the text "Hole" directly before the content of the span element.

12. Save your changes to the **print.css** file. Return to the **h01.htm** through **h18.htm** files in your text editor. Link each file to the print.css style sheet, indicating that this style sheet is used for print media.

13. Print **h01.htm** (or use the Print Preview feature on your Web browser) to verify that the layout of the printed Web page resembles that shown in Figure 4-57. (Note: Internet Explorer does not support the before pseudo-element, so in this browser you will not see the word "Hole" next to the hole number in the printed version of the page.)

14. Submit your completed files to your instructor.

| Challenge | **Case Problem 2** |

Test your knowledge of Web site design by completing a Civil War history page.

Data Files needed for this Case Problem: cwlogo.gif, cwpagetxt.htm, cwtxt.css, and tan.jpg

Civil War Studies Adanya Lynne is a professor of military history at Ridgeview State College in Bartlett, Tennessee. She has been working on a Web site for a course she is preparing in Civil War studies. Professor Lynne has already created some sample pages and done work on the design and layout, but she needs your help in completing the project. She would like to create a list of links in an outline format by nesting one ordered list inside of another. She's also interested in using CSS to create a drop-shadow effect on the main topic headings on her pages. To test your design, you'll create a style for a page containing the text of Lincoln's second inaugural address. A preview of the page you'll create for Professor Lynne is shown in Figure 4-58.

Figure 4-58

Complete the following:

1. Use your text editor to open the **cwpagetxt.htm** and **cwtxt.css** files from the tutorial.04\case2 folder included with your Data Files. Enter *your name* and *the date* in the comment section of each file. Save the files as **cwpage.htm** and **cw.css**, respectively, in the same folder. Take some time to examine the contents and structure of the HTML file and the external style sheet.

2. Return to the **cwpage.htm** file in your text editor. Create a link to the cw.css style sheet. You do not have to specify a media attribute.

3. Scroll down the file and locate the h2 heading "Lincoln's Second Inaugural." Directly below this heading, insert another h2 heading containing exactly the same text but with the class name shadow.

4. Go to the paragraphs within the article div container. Give the first paragraph the class name first_para and give the remaining paragraphs the class name following_para.

5. Save your changes to the **cwpage.htm** file and then return to the **cw.css** file in your text editor.

6. The page_content div container contains the entire contents of the Web page. Add the following styles for the container:
   - Use relative positioning to place the container with top and left coordinates of 0 pixels.
   - Set the width of the container to 95% of the width of the document window.
   - Insert styles to set the minimum width of the container to 800 pixels and the maximum width to 1000 pixels.

 **EXPLORE**

7. The linkList div container contains the list of links in Adanya's Web site. Use absolute positioning to place this element at the coordinates (5, 140). Set the width to 280 pixels. Add a 1-pixel-wide solid black border to the right edge of the element.

8. Remove the underlining from the links nested within the linkList container, and change the font color to black. If a mouse pointer hovers over any of the links, have the browser underline the link text.

9. The links appear in a set of nested ordered lists. Adanya wants these links to appear in an outline format. To create the outline, do the following:
   - Display the ol element using uppercase Roman numerals as the bullet marker. Set the font size to 0.9 em.
   - Display ol elements nested within another ordered list using uppercase letters as bullet markers.
   - Display ol elements nested within *two* levels of ordered lists using decimal numbers as bullet markers.

10. Use absolute positioning to place the article div container at the coordinates (320, 190).

11. You can create a drop-shadow around a heading by duplicating the heading and then offsetting one heading from another. You've already duplicated the heading in the cwpage.htm file; complete the drop-shadow by applying the following styles:
   - Use absolute positioning to place the h2 element at the coordinates (320, 125). Set the font color of the heading to the RGB value (237, 227, 178) and the z-index value to 2.
   - Directly below the h2 style, insert a style to place the element belonging to the shadow class at the coordinates (321, 126), once again using absolute positioning. Set the font color to black and the z-index value to 1.

12. Adanya wants you to create drop caps and a special first line style for the paragraphs that contain the text of Lincoln's second inaugural address. Add the following styles to the style sheet:
   - Display the first line of the paragraph belonging to the first_para class in small capital letters.
   - Float the first letter of the "first_para" paragraph on the left margin of the paragraph with top and left margin values of 0 pixels and right bottom margins of 5 pixels. Set the font size to 300% and the line height to 0.75.
   - Use the text-indent style to indent the paragraphs belonging to the following_para class by 10 pixels each.

13. Save your changes to the style sheet.

14. Load the **cwpage.htm** file in your Web browser and verify that the layout matches that shown in Figure 4-58. Confirm that the Lincoln's Second Inaugural heading appears with a drop-shadow. Verify that the list of links appears in outline form and that links within the outline display a rollover effect.

15. If you have a large screen monitor and access to Firefox, Opera, or another Web browser that supports minimum and maximum widths, resize your browser window and verify that the width of the page content does not exceed 1000 pixels or fall below 800 pixels even as you resize the browser window. (Note: Internet Explorer does not support minimum and maximum width styles.)

16. Submit your completed files to your instructor.

Challenge		Case Problem 3

Broaden your knowledge of CSS styles by creating an interactive map for a national park Web site.

Data Files needed for this Case Problem: image0.jpg – image9.jpg, longstxt.htm, and lpmap.jpg

Longs Peak Interactive Map Longs Peak is one of the most popular attractions of Rocky Mountain National Park (RMNP). Each year during the months of July, August, and September, thousands of people climb Longs Peak by the Keyhole Route to reach the 14,255-foot summit. Ron Bartlett, the head of the RMNP Web site team, has asked for your help in creating an interactive map of the Keyhole Route. The map will be installed at electronic kiosks in the park's visitor center. Ron envisions a map with 10 numbered waypoints along the Keyhole Route, displaying photos and text descriptions of each waypoint when a mouse pointer hovers over its corresponding numbered point. Figure 4-59 shows a preview of the online map with the first waypoint highlighted by the user.

Figure 4-59

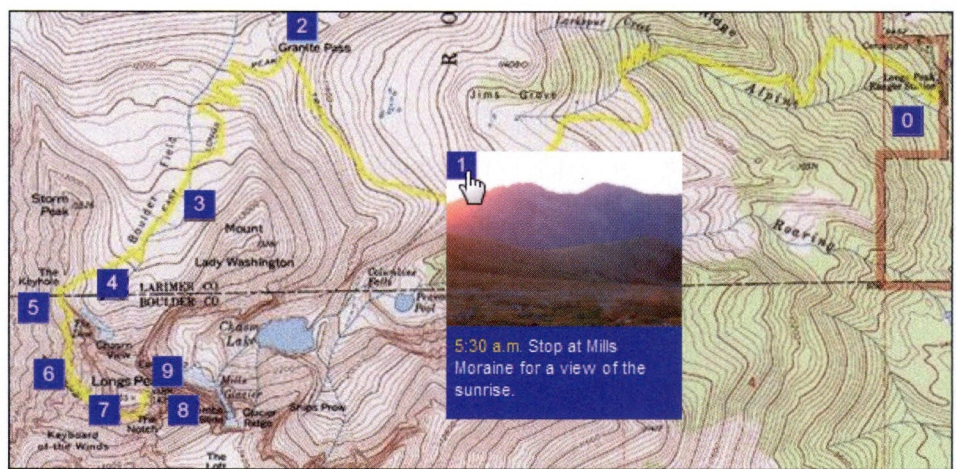

Longs Peak Online Trail Map

At 14,255 feet, Longs Peak towers above all other summits in Rocky Mountain National Park. The summer is the only season in which the peak can be climbed by a non-technical route. Early mornings break calm, clouds build in the afternoon sky, often exploding in storms of brief, heavy rain, thunder and dangerous lightning. Begin your hike early, way before dawn, to be back below timberline before the weather turns for the worse.

The Keyhole Route, Longs Peak's only non-technical hiking pathway, is a 16 mile round trip with an elevation gain of 4,850 feet. Though non-technical, the Keyhole Route is still challenging and is not recommended for those who are afraid of heights or exposed ledges. Hikers should be properly outfitted with clothing, food and water. Use caution when ascending or descending steep areas. Don't be afraid to back down when bad weather threatens.

Move your mouse pointer over the numbered landmarks in the map to preview the hike.

Ron also wants to create a print version of the waypoint descriptions. Users can print the map elsewhere on the park's Web site, so he wants the print style sheet to display just the list of waypoints in a bulleted list.

Complete the following:

1. Use your text editor to open the **longstxt.htm** file from the tutorial.04\case3 folder included with your Data Files. Enter *your name* and *the date* in the comment section at the top of the file. Save the file as **longs.htm** in the same folder. Take some time to study the contents of the file. Notice that the waypoint descriptions are nested within the online_map div container. Each waypoint description has been placed in a separate div container with the class name notes and id names ranging from point0 to point9.

2. To create a rollover effect for the nine waypoints, you need to mark the waypoint contents as hyperlinks. Within each of the nine div containers, enclose the img element and paragraph element within a single <a> tag. Point each link to the **longs.htm** file so that if a user clicks the link, it will simply refresh the current Web page.

3. Add a style to the embedded style sheet at the top of the file to remove underlining from all hypertext links.

4. Currently the online_map div container does not display the Longs Peak map. Add the following style to the embedded style sheet to display the map:
   - Set the width of the container to 600 pixels wide by 294 pixels high.
   - Add a 1-pixel-wide solid black border to the container.
   - Apply the **lpmap.jpg** graphic file as the background image.
   - Use relative positioning to place the container on the page. Set the top and left coordinates to 0 pixels.

5. In the embedded style sheet, add the following styles for all of the div containers belonging to the notes class:
   - For paragraphs nested within each note, set the font size to 8 points and the margin to 5 pixels.
   - Set the font color to yellow for each span element nested within a note.

EXPLORE 6. For each link nested within a notes class element, apply the following styles:
   - Set the width and height of the link to 20 pixels.
   - Hide any content that overflows the boundary of the link.
   - Set the background color to blue and the font color to white.
   - Set the z-index value to 1.

EXPLORE 7. When the mouse hovers over a link within a notes class element, have the browser apply the following style:
   - Change the width to 150 pixels and the height to 170 pixels.
   - Change the overflow property to visible.
   - Set the z-index value to 2.

8. Use absolute positioning to place the link nested within the #point0 selector at the coordinates (560, 60).

9. Repeat Step 8 for the nine remaining waypoints:
   - #point1 at (277, 90)
   - #point2 at (175, 0)
   - #point3 at (110, 115)
   - #point4 at (55, 165)
   - #point5 at (5, 180)

- #point6 at (15, 222)
- #point7 at (50, 245)
- #point8 at (100, 245)
- #point9 at (90, 220)

10. Go to the top of the file and add a media attribute to the embedded style sheet indicating that the sheet is designed for screen and tv media.

11. Save your changes to the file and then open **longs.htm** in your Web browser. Verify that the placement of the waypoints follows the locations shown in Figure 4-59. Confirm that when you hover your mouse over each of the nine waypoints, a description of the waypoint appears on the top of the trail map.

12. Return to the **longs.htm** file in your text editor. Create a new embedded style sheet designed for print media.

13. Scroll down to the "Longs Peak Online Trail Map" h2 heading and enclose the text "Online Trail Map" within a span element.

14. Add the following styles to the embedded print style sheet:
    - Set the font family for the page body to sans-serif.
    - Remove underlining from all hypertext links.
    - Do not display the #instructions selector, the span element nested within the h2 element, or the img element nested within elements belonging to the notes class.
    - Display the notes class of elements as list items with a disc marker. Set the margin to 20 pixels.
    - Change the display property of paragraphs nested within the notes class of elements to inline.
    - Display span elements nested within the notes class of elements in a bold font.

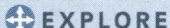 **EXPLORE**   15. Add a style that inserts the text string "Trail Itinerary" after the h2 heading.

16. Save your changes to the file.

17. Refresh the **longs.htm** file in your Web browser. By either printing the page or viewing the page within the Print Preview window, confirm that the printed page only shows a bulleted list of the waypoint descriptions. If you are running Firefox, Opera, or Safari, confirm that the heading at the top of the page reads "Longs Peak Trail Itinerary." (If you are using Internet Explorer, the title will simply read "Longs Peak.")

18. Submit your completed files to your instructor.

| Create | **Case Problem 4** |

Test your knowledge of CSS and HTML by creating a Web page design for a children's choir.

Data Files needed for this Case Problem: bizet.jpg, bizetbio.txt, bizetlist.txt, mozart.jpg, mozartbio.txt, mozartlist.txt, puccini.jpg, puccinibio.txt, puccinilist.txt, verdi.jpg, verdibio.txt, verdilist.txt, wagner.jpg, wagnerbio.txt, and wagnerlist.txt

Gresham Children's Choir   Faye Dawson is an instructor for Gresham Children's Choir in Gresham, Oregon. The choir is a chance for talented youth to perform and to learn about music history. Faye is working on a Web site describing the history of opera. She's asked for your help in creating a design. Faye has provided you with information on five different composers: Bizet, Mozart, Puccini, Verdi, and Wagner. For each composer, she's given you an image file containing the composer's picture, a text file listing the composer's works, and a text file containing a biographical sketch. Use this information to design your Web site. You may supplement these files with any other material you think will enhance your site's design.

Complete the following:

1. Use your text editor to create four HTML files named **bizet.htm**, **mozart.htm**, **puccini.htm**, **verdi.htm**, and **wagner.htm**, placing them in the tutorial.04\case4 folder included with your Data Files. Enter *your name* and *the date* in a comment section of each file. Include any other comments you think will aptly document the page's purpose and history.

2. Use the provided text files and image files to create a Web page describing each composer's life and accomplishments. Include hypertext links between the five composer Web pages.

3. Create an external style sheet named **gresham.css** for your Web site. Insert a comment section in the style sheet file that includes *your name* and *the date* as well as other comments that describe the style sheet.

4. The content of the gresham.css style sheet is up to you, but it must include the following features:
   - Styles that use contextual selectors
   - A style that uses a pseudo-element and a pseudo-class
   - Styles that use positioning styles (either absolute or relative)
   - A style that creates or modifies an ordered or unordered list
   - A style to create a rollover effect

5. Create another style sheet named **printer.css** containing styles for a printed version of the pages in your Web site. Add appropriate comments to the different parts of your style sheet.

6. Test your Web site on a variety of browsers to ensure your design works under different conditions.

7. Submit your completed files to your instructor.

| Review | **| Quick Check Answers** |

Session 4.1

1. `p span {font-style: italic}`
2. `p > span {font-style: italic}`
3. `h1 + h2 {font-style: italic}`
4. `.newsAlert {font-weight: bold}`
5. `span.newsAlert {font-weight: bold}`
6. `a:hover {background-color: yellow}`
7. `a:hover {background-image:url(hover.jpg)}`
8. `blockquote:first-letter {color: red}`
9. `blockquote:first-line {color: red}`

Session 4.2

1. `#logo {position: absolute; top: 75px; left: 150px}`
2. `#logo {position: relative; top: 25%; left: 10%}`
3. `span.highlight {position: relative; top: -10px}`
4. `a:hover {position: relative; top: 5px}`
5. `#links {position: fixed; top: 50px; left: 10px}`
6. `blockquote {width: 70%; min-width: 250px; max-width: 650px}`
7. `blockquote {height: 25%; overflow: auto}`
8. No. It will only be on top of other elements for which it shares a common parent.

Session 4.3

1. `media = "handheld"`
2. screen, tv, tty
3. aural, Braille, embossed
4. The display:none style hides the element and removes it from the document flow. The visibility:hidden style hides the element, but does not remove it from the document flow.
5. `@page {11in 14in landscape ; margin 1.5 in}`
6. `h1 {page-break-before: always}`
7. A widow occurs when a page break divides a block of text, leaving only one or two lines of text on the succeeding page. An orphan occurs when the page break occurs near the start of the block of text, leaving only one or two lines of text on the first page.

Ending Data Files

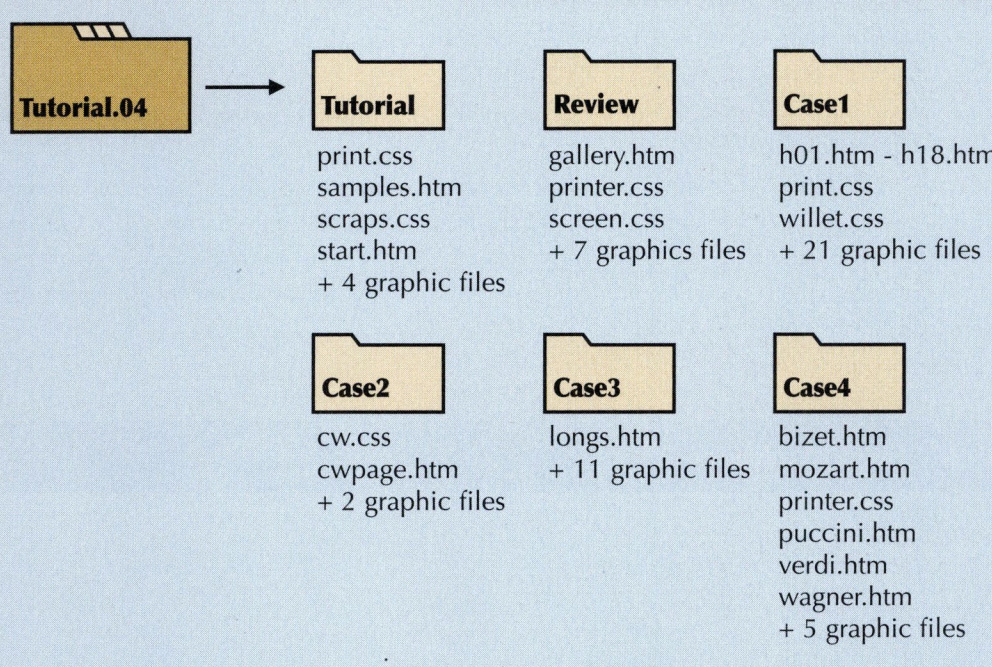

Tutorial.04 →

Tutorial
print.css
samples.htm
scraps.css
start.htm
+ 4 graphic files

Review
gallery.htm
printer.css
screen.css
+ 7 graphics files

Case1
h01.htm - h18.htm
print.css
willet.css
+ 21 graphic files

Case2
cw.css
cwpage.htm
+ 2 graphic files

Case3
longs.htm
+ 11 graphic files

Case4
bizet.htm
mozart.htm
printer.css
puccini.htm
verdi.htm
wagner.htm
+ 5 graphic files

Objectives

Session 5.1
- Explore the structure of a Web table
- Create headings and cells in a table
- Create cells that span multiple rows and columns
- Create row and column groups
- Add a caption and a summary to a table

Session 5.2
- Format a table using HTML attributes
- Format a table using CSS styles
- Collapse table borders
- Display page elements in tabular form

Session 5.3
- Create a jigsaw layout
- Explore the use of tables for page layout
- Create rounded borders

Working with Web Tables

Creating a Radio Program Schedule

Case | KPAF Radio

Kyle Mitchell is the program director at KPAF, a public radio station broadcasting out of Bismarck, North Dakota. To remain viable, it's important for the station to have a presence on the Internet. With this in mind, Kyle has begun upgrading the KPAF Web site. He envisions a site in which listeners have quick and easy access to information about the station and its programs.

The Web site needs to include pages listing the KPAF morning, afternoon, and evening schedules. Kyle decides that this information is best conveyed to the listener in a table, with each column of the table displaying one day's program schedule and each row displaying the broadcast times for the various KPAF programs. Kyle has never created a Web table, so he's come to you for help in designing a Web page describing the KPAF evening schedule. Kyle wants the table you create to be easy to read and informative. He also wants you to add table styles that will enhance the appearance of the Web page.

Starting Data Files

Tutorial.05 →

Tutorial
kpaftxt.css
newshows.css
newshows.txt
roundedtxt.css
schedtxt.htm
tablestxt.css
+ 9 graphic files

Review
kpaf.css
morningtxt.htm
programstxt.css
+ 5 graphic files

Case1
jpftxt.css
stabletxt.css
sudokutxt.htm
+ 6 graphic files

Case2
caltxt.css
ccctxt.css
febtxt.htm
+10 graphic files

Case3
dhometxt.htm
dometxt.css
dtabletxt.css
+ 14 graphic files

Case4
rooms.txt
+ 9 graphic files

Session 5.1

Introducing Web Tables

You meet with Kyle in his office at KPAF to discuss the design of the new Web site. Kyle has already created a basic Web page displaying the KPAF logo and a list of links to other pages. Open this file now.

To view Kyle's data files:

▶ 1. In your text editor, open the **schedtxt.htm** and **kpaftxt.css** files, located in the tutorial.05\tutorial folder included with your Data Files. Enter *your name* and *the date* in the comment section of each file. Save the files as **schedule.htm** and **kpaf.css** in the same folder.

▶ 2. Review the **schedule.htm** file in your text editor to become familiar with its content and structure. Insert the following link element below the opening <title> tag to link the schedule.htm file to the kpaf.css style sheet:

```
<link href="kpaf.css" rel="stylesheet" type="text/css" />
```

▶ 3. Save your changes to the file and then open the **schedule.htm** file in your Web browser. Figure 5-1 shows the current appearance of the Web page.

| Figure 5-1 | Initial schedule page |

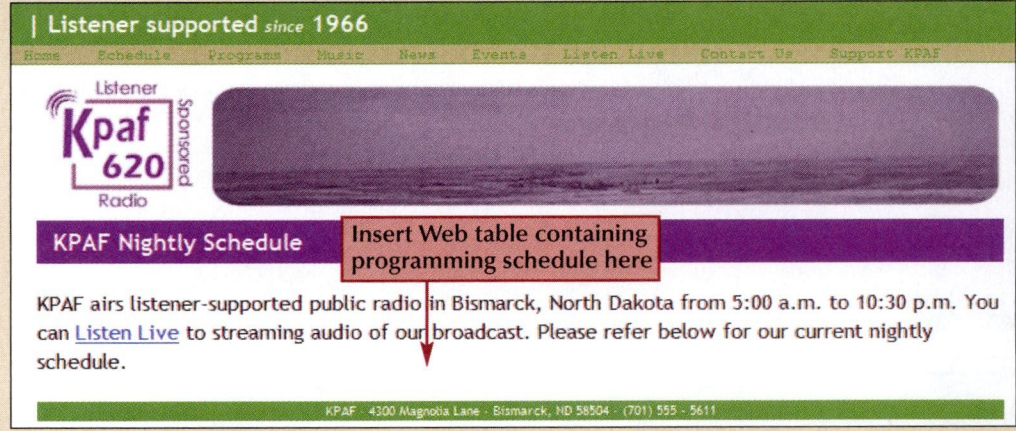

▶ 4. Go to the **kpaf.css** style sheet in your text editor. Review the styles and compare them to the elements contained within the schedule.htm file to fully understand Kyle's design for the schedule page.

▶ 5. Close the style sheet file when you're finished reviewing it.

The first thing that Kyle needs you to add to the schedule page is KPAF's nightly schedule, which covers from 6:00 p.m. to 10:30 p.m. Kyle hands you a printout of the KPAF schedule shown in Figure 5-2. At 10:30 p.m. the station goes dark and does not broadcast again until 5:00 a.m. the following day. Kyle wants you to use HTML to recreate this table.

Time	Monday	Tuesday	Wednesday	Thursday	Friday	Saturday	Sunday
6:00	National News	National News	National News	National News	National News	National News	National News
6:30	Local News	Local News	Local News	Local News	Local News	Local News	Local News
7:00	Opera Fest	Radio U	Science Week	The Living World	Word Play	Agri-Week	Folk Fest
7:30					Brain Stew	Bismarck Forum	
8:00	The Classical Music Connection				Old Time Radio	Saturday Nite Jazz	The Indie Connection
8:30					The Inner Mind		
9:00					Open Mike Nite		
9:30							
10:00	World News Feed	World News Feed	World News Feed	World News Feed	World News Feed	World News Feed	World News Feed

To create this program listing in HTML, you have to first understand the HTML table structure.

Marking Tables and Table Rows

Each table in a Web page follows a basic structure consisting of the table element and a collection of table rows nested in the table element. The general HTML code for a Web table is

```
<table>
   <tr>
   table cells
   </tr>
   <tr>
   table cells
   </tr>
...
</table>
```

where <table> marks the table element, <tr> marks each row, and *table cells* are the cells within each row. Note that the dimension of a Web table is defined by the number of rows and the number of cells within the rows. There is no HTML element to mark a table column. You'll explore how to create table cells shortly. Tables are considered block-level elements, so when rendered by a browser, they'll appear on a new line on the Web page. Like other block-level elements, you can float tables and resize them using the same styles you've already studied.

Kyle's proposed Web table has 10 rows, with the first row containing the days of the week, followed by nine rows listing the KPAF shows from 6:00 p.m. to 10:30 p.m. in half-hour intervals. For now, you'll insert tr elements for just the first three rows of the table. You'll also include a class attribute, placing the table in the schedule class of elements to distinguish it from other tables on the KPAF Web site.

To insert the table and tr elements:

▶ 1. Return to the **schedule.htm** file in your text editor.

▶ 2. Directly above the address element, insert the following code, as shown in Figure 5-3:

```
<table class="schedule">
    <tr>
    </tr>
    <tr>
    </tr>
    <tr>
    </tr>
</table>
```

Figure 5-3 ▶ Marking a table and table rows

At this point you have a table with three rows but nothing within those rows. The next part of the table structure is the cells within each row.

Marking Table Headings and Table Data

There are two types of table cells: those that contain headings and those that contain data. The two tags are different so that the headings in a table are formatted differently than the rest of the cells. **Table headings**, the cells that identify the contents of a row or column, are marked using a <th> tag. You can place a <th> tag anywhere in a table, but you'll most often place one at the top of a column or at the beginning of a row. Most browsers display table headings in a bold font, centered within the table cell.

Kyle wants you to mark the cells in the first row of the radio schedule as headings because the text identifies the contents of each column. He also wants the first cells in the remaining rows displaying the time to be marked as headings. Add these cells to the first three columns of the schedule table.

To insert the table headings:

▶ 1. Return to the **schedule.htm** file in your text editor.

▶ 2. In the first table row, insert the following th elements:

```
<th>Time</th>
<th>Monday</th>
<th>Tuesday</th>
<th>Wednesday</th>
<th>Thursday</th>
<th>Friday</th>
<th>Saturday</th>
<th>Sunday</th>
```

3. Insert the heading

   ```
   <th>6:00</th>
   ```

   in the second table row.

4. In the third table row insert the following heading:

   ```
   <th>6:30</th>
   ```

5. Figure 5-4 shows the revised code in the schedule table.

Inserting table heading cells ◀ Figure 5-4

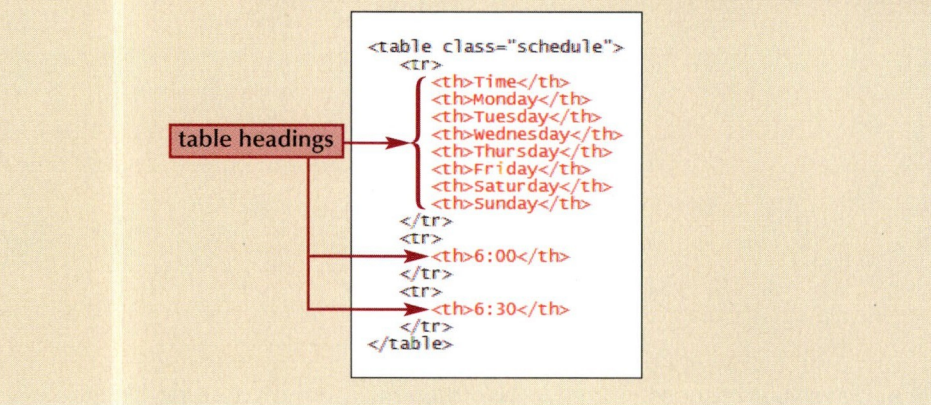

The other type of table cells is **data cells**, which are marked with the <td> tag and are used for any content that is not considered a heading. Most browsers display table data using unformatted text, left-aligned within the cell. You'll use table data cells to insert the names of the KPAF programs. KPAF airs the national and local news at 6:00 and 6:30, respectively, every night of the week. Add these broadcasts to the schedule table.

To insert table data for the next two rows of the table:

1. Return to the **schedule.htm** file in your text editor.

2. In the second table row, insert the following td elements:

   ```
   <td>National News</td>
   <td>National News</td>
   <td>National News</td>
   <td>National News</td>
   <td>National News</td>
   <td>National News</td>
   <td>National News</td>
   ```

3. In the third table row, insert the following elements:

   ```
   <td>Local News</td>
   <td>Local News</td>
   <td>Local News</td>
   <td>Local News</td>
   <td>Local News</td>
   <td>Local News</td>
   <td>Local News</td>
   ```

   Figure 5-5 shows the newly inserted HTML code.

Figure 5-5 | **Inserting table data cells**

```
<table class="schedule">
    <tr>
        <th>Time</th>
        <th>Monday</th>
        <th>Tuesday</th>
        <th>Wednesday</th>
        <th>Thursday</th>
        <th>Friday</th>
        <th>Saturday</th>
        <th>Sunday</th>
    </tr>
    <tr>
        <th>6:00</th>
        <td>National News</td>
        <td>National News</td>
        <td>National News</td>
        <td>National News</td>
        <td>National News</td>
        <td>National News</td>
        <td>National News</td>
    </tr>
    <tr>
        <th>6:30</th>
        <td>Local News</td>
        <td>Local News</td>
        <td>Local News</td>
        <td>Local News</td>
        <td>Local News</td>
        <td>Local News</td>
        <td>Local News</td>
    </tr>
</table>
```

table data cells

4. Save your changes to the file, and then refresh the **schedule.htm** file in your Web browser. Figure 5-6 shows the current appearance of the programming schedule. The headings are in bold and centered, and the table data is in a normal font and left-aligned.

Figure 5-6 | **Viewing the Web table**

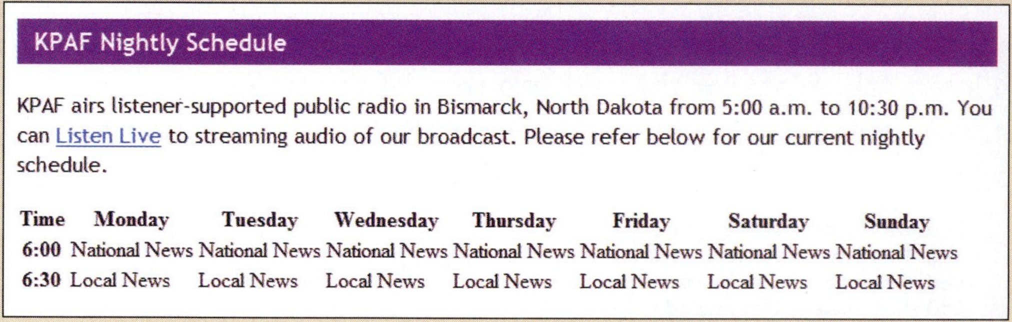

KPAF Nightly Schedule

KPAF airs listener-supported public radio in Bismarck, North Dakota from 5:00 a.m. to 10:30 p.m. You can <u>Listen Live</u> to streaming audio of our broadcast. Please refer below for our current nightly schedule.

Time	Monday	Tuesday	Wednesday	Thursday	Friday	Saturday	Sunday
6:00	National News	National News	National News	National News	National News	National News	National News
6:30	Local News	Local News	Local News	Local News	Local News	Local News	Local News

Trouble? If your table looks different than Figure 5-6, you might have inserted an incorrect number of table cells. Check your code and verify that you've inserted one table header and seven table data cells in each row.

| Reference Window

Defining a Table Structure

- To mark a Web table, use the element
    ```
    <table>rows</table>
    ```
    where *rows* are the rows of the table.
- To mark a table row, use the element
    ```
    <tr>cells</tr>
    ```
    where *cells* are the table cells contained within the row.
- To mark a cell containing a row or column heading, use the element
    ```
    <th>content</th>
    ```
    where *content* is the content of the heading.
- To mark a cell containing table data, use the element
    ```
    <td>content</td>
    ```
    where *content* is the content of the table data.

Tip

To place an empty table cell anywhere within a row, insert the <td> </td> tag into the row.

The table you created for Kyle has three rows and eight columns. Remember that the number of columns is determined by the maximum number of cells within each row. If one row has four cells and another row has five, the table will have five columns. The row with only four cells will have an empty space at the end, where the fifth cell should be.

Adding a Table Border

By default, there are no gridlines displayed in a Web table, making it difficult to see the table structure. You decide the table would be easier to read with gridlines marking each cell in the table. To add gridlines, insert the attribute

```
<table border="value">
    ...
</table>
```

in the table element, where *value* is the width of the table border in pixels. Figure 5-7 shows how different border values affect the appearance of a sample table.

Tables with different border sizes ◄ **Figure 5-7**

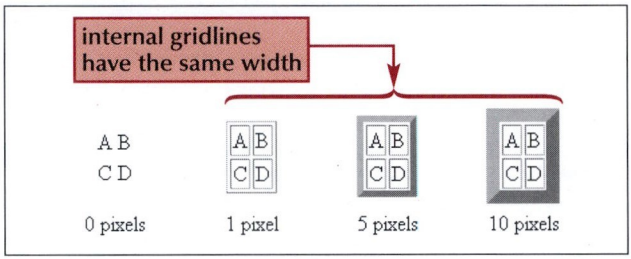

Note that the border attribute does not control the width of internal gridlines; however, to display internal gridlines you must add a border to the table. You can change the width of the internal gridlines by changing the space between the table cells, an issue you'll examine in the next session.

<table>
<tr><td>Reference Window |</td><td>**Adding a Table Border Using HTML**</td></tr>
</table>

- To add a border to a Web table using HTML, use the border attribute
  `<table border="value"> ... </table>`
  where *value* is the size of the border in pixels.

You decide to add a 1-pixel border to the schedule table. Because of the border, your browser will also insert gridlines around each of the table cells.

To add a border to the schedule:

▶ 1. Return to the **schedule.htm** file in your text editor and add the attribute

   `border="1"`

   to the opening <table> tag, as shown in Figure 5-8.

Figure 5-8	Adding a table border

```
<table class="schedule" border="1">
    <tr>
        <th>Time</th>
        <th>Monday</th>
        <th>Tuesday</th>
        <th>Wednesday</th>
        <th>Thursday</th>
        <th>Friday</th>
        <th>Saturday</th>
        <th>Sunday</th>
    </tr>
```

table cells will be surrounded by a 1-pixel-wide border

▶ 2. Save your changes to the file, and then reload the schedule page in your Web browser. Figure 5-9 shows the revised table with the border and the internal gridlines added.

Figure 5-9	Web table with cell borders

KPAF Nightly Schedule

KPAF airs listener-supported public radio in Bismarck, North Dakota from 5:00 a.m. to 10:30 p.m. You can Listen Live to streaming audio of our broadcast. Please refer below for our current nightly schedule.

Time	Monday	Tuesday	Wednesday	Thursday	Friday	Saturday	Sunday
6:00	National News	National News	National News	National News	National News	National News	National News
6:30	Local News	Local News	Local News	Local News	Local News	Local News	Local News

Table Border Colors | InSight

Most browsers display the table border in gray in a raised style that gives the border a 3D effect. There is no HTML attribute to change the border style, but many browsers allow you to change the color by adding the bordercolor attribute

```
<table border="value" bordercolor="color"> ... </table>
```

to the table element, where *color* is either a recognized color name or a hexadecimal color value. For example, the following HTML code adds a 10-pixel blue border to a table:

```
<table border="10" bordercolor="blue"> ... </table>
```

The exact appearance of the table border differs among browsers. Internet Explorer and Safari display the border in a solid blue color, Firefox displays the border in a raised style using two shades of blue, and Opera does not support the bordercolor attribute at all. So you should not rely on getting a consistent border color across all browsers with this attribute.

The bordercolor attribute has been deprecated by the World Wide Web Consortium (W3C) and is being gradually phased out. The recommended method is to use one of the CSS border styles discussed in Tutorial 3, but you will still see this attribute used in many Web pages.

Spanning Rows and Columns

Reviewing the schedule from Figure 5-2, you notice that several programs are longer than a half hour, and some are repeated across several days. For example, every day of the week there is national and local news at 6:00 and 6:30, respectively. Likewise, from Monday through Thursday, the hour from 7:00 to 8:00 is needed for the shows Opera Fest, Radio U, Science Week, and The Living World. And finally, the Classical Music Connection airs Monday through Thursday for two hours from 8:00 to 10:00. Rather than repeat the names of programs in all of the half-hour slots, Kyle would prefer that the table cells stretch across those hours and days.

To do this, create a **spanning cell** in which a single cell occupies more than one row or one column in the table. Spanning cells are created by inserting a rowspan or colspan attribute into a <th> or <td> tag. The syntax is

```
<th rowspan="value" colspan="value"> ... </th>
```

or

```
<td rowspan="value" colspan="value"> ... </td>
```

where *value* is the number of rows or columns that you want the table cell to cover. The spanning starts in the cell where you put the rowspan and colspan attributes and goes downward and to the right from that cell. For example, to create a data cell that spans two columns and three rows, enter the <td> tag as:

```
<td colspan="2" rowspan="3"> ... </td>
```

It's important to remember that when a cell spans multiple rows or columns, you must adjust the number of cells used elsewhere in the table. For column-spanning cells, you have to reduce the number of cells in the current row. For example, if a row contains five columns but one of the cells in the row spans three columns, you need only three cell elements in the row: two cells that occupy a single column each and one cell that spans the remaining three columns.

To see how column-spanning cells works, you'll replace the cells for the National News and Local News programs that currently occupy seven cells a piece with two cells that each span seven columns in each row.

Tip

For every extra column that a cell spans, you must delete one cell from the table row. So for a cell spanning four columns, you must delete three cells to keep from having extra cells in the row.

To create cells that span several columns:

1. Return to the **schedule.htm** file in your text editor and add the attribute

   `colspan="7"`

   to the second table cell in the second and third rows of the table.

2. Delete the remaining six table cells in both the second and the third table rows. Figure 5-10 shows the revised code for the schedule table.

Figure 5-10 ▶ **Creating cells to span several columns**

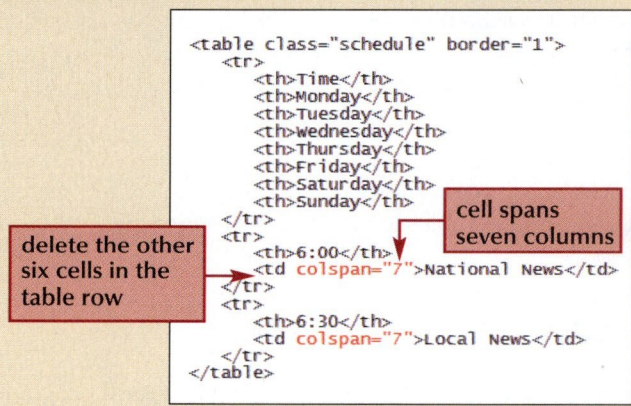

```
<table class="schedule" border="1">
    <tr>
        <th>Time</th>
        <th>Monday</th>
        <th>Tuesday</th>
        <th>wednesday</th>
        <th>Thursday</th>
        <th>Friday</th>
        <th>Saturday</th>
        <th>Sunday</th>
    </tr>
    <tr>
        <th>6:00</th>
        <td colspan="7">National News</td>
    </tr>
    <tr>
        <th>6:30</th>
        <td colspan="7">Local News</td>
    </tr>
</table>
```

cell spans seven columns

delete the other six cells in the table row

3. Save your changes to the file, and then refresh the **schedule.htm** file in your Web browser. Figure 5-11 shows the revised appearance of the Web table.

Figure 5-11 ▶ **Column-spanning cell**

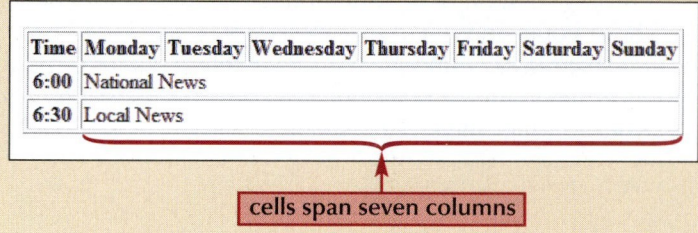

Time	Monday	Tuesday	Wednesday	Thursday	Friday	Saturday	Sunday
6:00	National News						
6:30	Local News						

cells span seven columns

To make the cell for the hour-long shows on Monday through Thursday, you'll need to span two rows, which lengthens the height of the cell. For row-spanning cells, you need to remove extra cells from the rows below the spanning cell. Consider the table shown in Figure 5-12, which contains three rows and four columns. The first cell spans three rows. You need four table cells in the first row, but only three in the second and third rows. This is because the spanning cell from row one occupies a position reserved for a cell that would normally appear in those rows.

Cells spanning several rows ◄ **Figure 5-12**

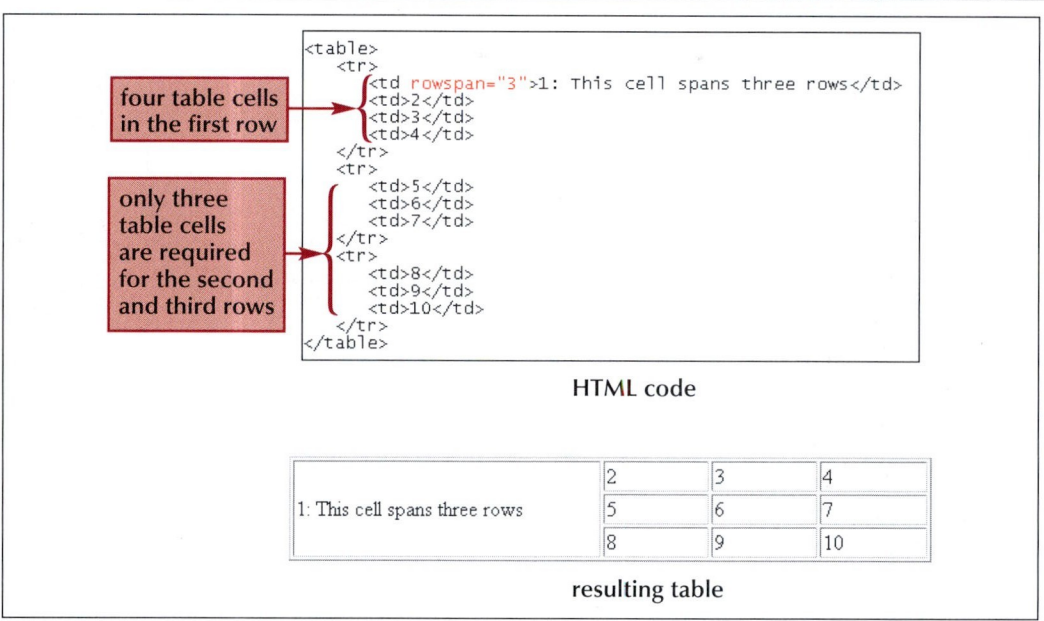

four table cells
in the first row

only three
table cells
are required
for the second
and third rows

```
<table>
  <tr>
    <td rowspan="3">1: This cell spans three rows</td>
    <td>2</td>
    <td>3</td>
    <td>4</td>
  </tr>
  <tr>
    <td>5</td>
    <td>6</td>
    <td>7</td>
  </tr>
  <tr>
    <td>8</td>
    <td>9</td>
    <td>10</td>
  </tr>
</table>
```

HTML code

1: This cell spans three rows	2	3	4
	5	6	7
	8	9	10

resulting table

Creating a Spanning Cell | Reference Window

- To create a table cell that spans several columns, add the attribute
    `colspan="value"`
  to the cell, where *value* is the number of columns covered by the cell.
- To create a table cell that spans several rows, add the attribute
    `rowspan="value"`
  to the cell, where *value* is the number of rows covered by the cell.

The 7:00 to 8:00 section of the KPAF schedule contains several programs that run for
an hour. To insert these programs, you'll create row-spanning cells that span two rows in
the schedule table. To keep the columns lined up, you must reduce the number of cells
entered in the subsequent row.

To span several table rows:

▶ **1.** Return to the **schedule.htm** file in your text editor and add the following row to
the bottom of the schedule table:

```
<tr>
    <th>7:00</th>
    <td rowspan="2">Opera Fest</td>
    <td rowspan="2">Radio U</td>
    <td rowspan="2">Science Week</td>
    <td rowspan="2">The Living World</td>
    <td>Word Play</td>
    <td>Agri-Week</td>
    <td rowspan="2">Folk Fest</td>
</tr>
```

2. The next row should display table cells only for the two programs that start at 7:30. The HTML code for this table row is:

```
<tr>
    <th>7:30</th>
    <td>Brain Stew</td>
    <td>Bismarck Forum</td>
</tr>
```

Figure 5-13 shows the code for the two new table rows.

Figure 5-13   **Inserting cells that span two rows**

```
<tr>
    <th>6:30</th>
    <td colspan="7">Local News</td>
</tr>
<tr>
    <th>7:00</th>
    <td rowspan="2">Opera Fest</td>
    <td rowspan="2">Radio U</td>
    <td rowspan="2">Science Week</td>
    <td rowspan="2">The Living World</td>
    <td>Word Play</td>
    <td>Agri-Week</td>
    <td rowspan="2">Folk Fest</td>
</tr>
<tr>
    <th>7:30</th>
    <td>Brain Stew</td>
    <td>Bismarck Forum</td>
</tr>
</table>
```

3. Save your changes to the file, and then refresh the **schedule.htm** file in your Web browser. As shown in Figure 5-14, the Sunday through Thursday 7:00 p.m. programs each last an hour, spanning two table rows.

Figure 5-14   **Schedule table with several one-hour programs spanning two table rows**

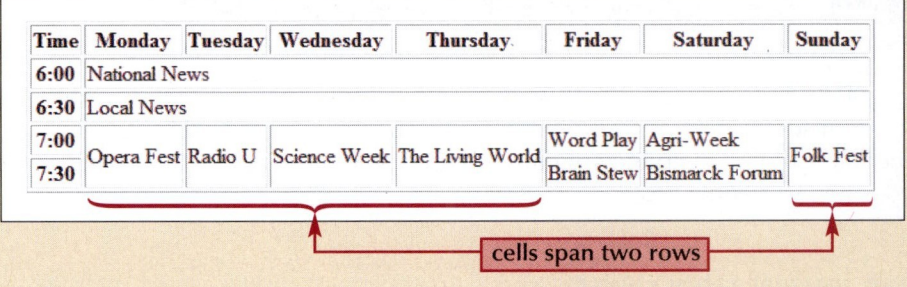

Time	Monday	Tuesday	Wednesday	Thursday	Friday	Saturday	Sunday
6:00	National News						
6:30	Local News						
7:00	Opera Fest	Radio U	Science Week	The Living World	Word Play	Agri-Week	Folk Fest
7:30					Brain Stew	Bismarck Forum	

cells span two rows

The final part of the evening schedule includes the program Classical Musical Connection, which spans two hours on Monday through Thursday. Like the news programs, you don't want to repeat the name of the show each day; and like the four hour-long programs you just entered, you don't want to repeat the name of the show in each half-hour cell. Kyle suggests that you use both the colspan and rowspan attributes to enter a table cell that spans four rows and four columns.

Other programs in the 8:00 to 10:00 time slots, such as Saturday Nite Jazz and The Indie Connection, also span four rows, but only one column. The last program aired before KPAF signs off is the World News Feed, which is played every night from 10:00 to 10:30. You'll add these and the other late evening programs to the schedule table now.

To add the remaining KPAF evening programs:

▶ **1.** Return to the **schedule.htm** file in your text editor and enter the following table row for programs airing starting at 8:00:

```
<tr>
    <th>8:00</th>
    <td rowspan="4" colspan="4">The Classical Music Connection</td>
    <td>Old Time Radio</td>
    <td rowspan="4">Saturday Nite Jazz</td>
    <td rowspan="4">The Indie Connection</td>
</tr>
```

▶ **2.** The Inner Mind is the only program that starts at 8:30 during the week. Add the 8:30 starting time to the table using the following row:

```
<tr>
    <th>8:30</th>
    <td>The Inner Mind</td>
</tr>
```

▶ **3.** The only program that starts at 9:00 is Open Mike Nite. Add the following row to the table to display this program in the schedule:

```
<tr>
    <th>9:00</th>
    <td rowspan="2">Open Mike Nite</td>
</tr>
```

▶ **4.** There are no programs that start at 9:30, so you'll add the table row but without any programs listed. Add the following row:

```
<tr>
    <th>9:30</th>
</tr>
```

▶ **5.** Complete the schedule table by adding the last table row for the World News Feed occurring every night from 10:00 to 10:30. This single program occupies a single row and spans seven columns. Add the following row:

```
<tr>
    <th>10:00</th>
    <td colspan="7">World News Feed</td>
</tr>
```

Figure 5-15 shows the code completing the structure of the schedule table.

Adding the remaining KPAF evening programs | Figure 5-15

```
<tr>
    <th>7:30</th>
    <td>Brain Stew</td>
    <td>Bismarck Forum</td>
</tr>
<tr>
    <th>8:00</th>
    <td rowspan="4" colspan="4">The Classical Music Connection</td>
    <td>Old Time Radio</td>
    <td rowspan="4">Saturday Nite Jazz</td>
    <td rowspan="4">The Indie Connection</td>
</tr>
<tr>
    <th>8:30</th>
    <td>The Inner Mind</td>
</tr>
<tr>
    <th>9:00</th>
    <td rowspan="2">Open Mike Nite</td>
</tr>
<tr>
    <th>9:30</th>
</tr>
<tr>
    <th>10:00</th>
    <td colspan="7">World News Feed</td>
</tr>
</table>
```

> **6.** Save your changes to the file, and refresh the **schedule.htm** file in your Web browser. Figure 5-16 shows the complete evening schedule of programs offered by KPAF.

Figure 5-16 **The complete KPAF evening schedule**

Time	Monday	Tuesday	Wednesday	Thursday	Friday	Saturday	Sunday
6:00	National News						
6:30	Local News						
7:00	Opera Fest	Radio U	Science Week	The Living World	Word Play	Agri-Week	Folk Fest
7:30					Brain Stew	Bismarck Forum	
8:00	The Classical Music Connection				Old Time Radio	Saturday Nite Jazz	The Indie Connection
8:30					The Inner Mind		
9:00					Open Mike Nite		
9:30							
10:00	World News Feed						

The Web table you created matches the printout of KPAF's evening schedule. Kyle likes the clear structure of the table. He notes that many KPAF listeners tune into the station over the Internet, listening to KPAF's streaming audio feed. Since those listeners might be located in different time zones, Kyle suggests that you add a caption to the table indicating that all times in the schedule are based on the Central time zone.

Creating a Table Caption

Table captions are another part of the basic table structure and are marked using the caption element

```
<table>
   <caption>content</caption>
   ...
</table>
```

where *content* is the content contained within the caption. You can nest inline elements within a caption element. For example, the following code marks the text *Program Schedule* using the em element:

```
<table>
   <caption><em>Program Schedule</em></caption>
   ...
</table>
```

Only one caption is allowed per Web table and the <caption> tag must be listed directly after the opening <table> tag. The caption is treated as a block-level element, placed directly above the table, but you can change the placement of the caption using the following align attribute:

```
<caption align="position">content</caption>
```

In this code, *position* equals top, bottom, left, or right, to place the caption either above, below, or to the left or right sides of the table.

The interpretation of the left and right align value is not consistent among the major browsers. Netscape and Firefox follow the W3C specifications and place the captions to the left or right of the Web table. Internet Explorer and Opera still place the caption above the table, but horizontally align the caption text to the left or right. The align attribute is another example of a presentational attribute that has been deprecated in favor of style sheets, though you'll still often find it used on Web sites, both old and new.

Tip

You can also use the CSS caption-side style to align caption text.

Creating a Table Caption | Reference Window

- To create a table caption, add the caption element directly below the opening <table> tag with the syntax
  ```
  <caption>content</caption>
  ```
  where *content* is the content of the table caption.

Add Kyle's suggested caption to the program schedule. You do not have to specify an align value because you want the caption to be above the table.

To create a caption for the program schedule:

1. Return to the **schedule.htm** file in your text editor and insert the following caption element directly below the opening tag, as shown in Figure 5-17.

   ```
   <caption>All times listed in central time</caption>
   ```

Inserting a table caption | Figure 5-17

```
<table class="schedule" border="1">
    <caption>All times listed in central time</caption>
    <tr>
        <th>Time</th>
        <th>Monday</th>
        <th>Tuesday</th>
        <th>Wednesday</th>
        <th>Thursday</th>
        <th>Friday</th>
        <th>Saturday</th>
        <th>Sunday</th>
    </tr>
```

2. Save your changes to the file and refresh the **schedule.htm** file in your Web browser. As shown in Figure 5-18, Kyle's suggested caption appears centered above the Web table.

Table caption for the KPAF programming schedule | Figure 5-18

All times listed in central time

Time	Monday	Tuesday	Wednesday	Thursday	Friday	Saturday	Sunday
6:00	National News						
6:30	Local News						
7:00	Opera Fest	Radio U	Science Week	The Living World	Word Play	Agri-Week	Folk Fest
7:30					Brain Stew	Bismarck Forum	
8:00	The Classical Music Connection				Old Time Radio	Saturday Nite Jazz	The Indie Connection
8:30					The Inner Mind		
9:00					Open Mike Nite		
9:30							
10:00	World News Feed						

Although table captions might lie outside of the borders of the Web table, they are still part of the Web table's structure. This means that they'll inherit any styles associated with the table. For example, if you create a style for the table that sets the font color to red, the caption text will also be in a red font. You'll explore how to apply styles to table captions in the next session.

Marking Row Groups

You can divide a table's rows into **row groups**, in which each group element contains different types of content and can be formatted differently. HTML supports three row groups: one to mark the header rows, another for the body rows, and a third for the footer rows. The syntax to create these three row groups is:

```
<table>
   <thead>
      table rows
   </thead>
   <tfoot>
      table rows
   </tfoot>
   <tbody>
      table rows
   </tbody>
</table>
```

where *table rows* are rows from the Web table. For example, the following code marks two rows as belonging to the table header row group:

```
<thead>
   <tr>
      <th colspan="2">KPAF Programs</th>
   </tr>
   <tr>
      <th>Time</th>
      <th>Program</th>
   </tr>
</thead>
```

Tip

The table header, table body, and table footer must all contain the same number of columns.

Order is important. The thead element must appear first, and then the tfoot element, and finally the tbody element. A table can contain only one set of thead and tfoot elements, but it can have any number of tbody elements. The reason the body group appears last and not the footer group is to allow the browser to render the footer before receiving what might be numerous groups of table body rows.

One purpose of row groups is to allow you to create different styles for groups of rows in your table. Any style that you apply to the thead, tbody, or tfoot elements is inherited by the rows those elements contain. Row groups are also used for tables that import their data from external data sources such as databases or XML documents. In those situations, a single table can span several Web pages, and it's helpful to have the rows within the thead and tfoot elements repeated on every page.

Creating Row Groups | Reference Window

- Row groups must be entered in the following order: table header rows, table footer rows, and then table body rows.
- To create a row group consisting of header rows, add the element
  ```
  <thead>
      rows
  </thead>
  ```
  within the table, where *rows* are the row elements within the table header.
- To create a row group consisting of footer rows, add the following element:
  ```
  <tfoot>
      rows
  </tfoot>
  ```
- To create a row group consisting of rows used in the body of the table, add the following element:
  ```
  <tbody>
      rows
  </tbody>
  ```
  A table can have multiple table body row groups.

To indicate the structure of the schedule table, you decide to the use the thead element to mark the header row in the program schedule and the tbody element to mark the rows that include the broadcast times of each program. You do not need to specify a footer for this table.

To mark the row groups:

▶ 1. Return to the **schedule.htm** file in your text editor and enclose the first row of the table within an opening and closing set of **<thead>** tags.

▶ 2. Enclose the remaining rows of the table within an opening and closing set of **<tbody>** tags. Figure 5-19 shows the markup tags for the two new row groups.

Figure 5-19   **Marking the table header and table body row groups**

```
<table class="schedule" border="1">
    <caption>All times listed in central time</caption>

    <thead>
    <tr>
        <th>Time</th>
        <th>Monday</th>
        <th>Tuesday</th>
        <th>Wednesday</th>
        <th>Thursday</th>
        <th>Friday</th>
        <th>Saturday</th>
        <th>Sunday</th>
    </tr>
    </thead>

    <tbody>
    <tr>
        <th>6:00</th>
        <td colspan="7">National News</td>
    </tr>


    <tr>
        <th>9:30</th>
    </tr>
    <tr>
        <th>10:00</th>
        <td colspan="7">World News Feed</td>
    </tr>
    </tbody>

</table>
```

Marking Column Groups

As you've seen, there is no HTML tag to mark table columns—the columns are created implicitly from the number of cells within each row. However, once the columns have been determined by the browser, you can reference them through the use of **column groups**. Column groups give you the ability to assign a common format to all of the cells within a given column. Column groups are defined using the colgroup element

```
<colgroup>
    columns
</colgroup>
```

where *columns* are the individual columns with the group. The columns themselves are referenced using the following empty element:

```
<col />
```

The number of col elements must match the number of columns in the Web table. Once you create a column group, you can add id or class attributes to identify or classify individual columns. For example, the following code creates a column group consisting of three columns, each with a different class name:

```
<colgroup>
    <col class="column1" />
    <col class="column2" />
    <col class="column3" />
</colgroup>
```

The browser takes any style specified for the col element and applies it to cells within the column. So to create columns with different background colors, you could apply the inline styles

```
col.column1 {background-color: red}
col.column2 {background-color: blue}
col.column3 {background-color: yellow}
```

and the browser will display the first table column with a background color of red, the second with blue, and the third with yellow. Note that not all CSS styles can be applied to table columns. You'll explore column styles in more detail in the next session.

The col element also supports the span attribute, allowing a column reference to cover several table columns. The syntax of the span attribute is

```
<col span="value" />
```

where *value* is the number of columns referenced by the col element. The column structure

```
<colgroup>
   <col class="column1" />
   <col class="nextColumns" span="2" />
</colgroup>
```

references a group of three columns; the first column belongs to the column1 class and the next two columns belong to the nextColumns class. Note that you can also apply the span attribute to a column group itself. The following code uses two column groups to also reference three columns, the first belonging to the column1 class and the last two belonging to the nextColumns class:

```
<colgroup class="column1"></colgroup>
<colgroup class="nextColumns span="2"></colgroup>
```

Notice that in this case there are no col elements within the column group. The browser will assume the number of columns indicated by the span attribute; if no span attribute is present, the column group is assumed to have only one column.

Creating Column Groups | Reference Window

- To create a column group, add the element
  ```
  <colgroup>
      columns
  </colgroup>
  ```
  to the Web table, where *columns* are individual columns within the group.
- To define a column or columns within a column group, use the element
  ```
  <col span="value" />
  ```
  where *value* is the number of defined columns. The span attribute is not required if only one column is defined.

Now that you've seen how columns can be referenced through the use of column groups, you'll create a column group for the programming table. You'll place the first column containing the broadcast times for the different KPAF programs in one column with the class name firstCol and the remaining seven columns containing the daily program listings in a column group with the class name dayCols. These groupings will allow you to format the two sets of columns in different ways later on.

To mark the column groups:

▶ **1.** Return to the **schedule.htm** file in your text editor.

▶ **2.** Directly below the table caption, insert the following code, as shown in Figure 5-20:

```
<colgroup>
   <col class="firstCol" />
   <col class="dayCols" span="7" />
</colgroup>
```

Figure 5-20 ▶ **Inserting a column group**

```
<table class="schedule" border="1">
   <caption>All times listed in central time</caption>

   <colgroup>
      <col class="firstCol" />
      <col class="dayCols" span="7" />        col element spans
   </colgroup>                                  seven columns
```

▶ **3.** Save your changes to the file.

▶ **4.** Creating row groups and column groups adds to the structure and flexibility of the table, but should not alter its appearance. To confirm that the row and column groups have not modified the table's appearance, refresh the **schedule.htm** file in your browser. Verify that the table layout is the same as that shown earlier in Figure 5-18.

Adding a Table Summary

Nonvisual browsers (such as aural browsers that are often used by visually impaired people) can't display tables, and it's cumbersome to listen to each cell being read. For these situations, it is useful to include a summary of a table's contents. While a caption and the surrounding page text usually provide clues about the table and its contents, the summary attribute allows you to include a more detailed description. The syntax of the summary attribute is

```
<table summary="description"> ... </table>
```

where *description* is a text string that describes the table's content and structure. The summary attribute fills the same role that the alt attribute fills for inline image: providing a textual (aural) alternative to what could be a long and complicated table. A user running a screen reader or other type of aural browser will first hear the summary of the table's contents, which can then aid in interpreting the subsequent reading of the table's content.

Kyle definitely wants the KPAF Web page to be accessible to users with all types of disabilities and asks that you include a summary description of the program schedule.

To add a summary to the table:

▶ **1.** Return to the **schedule.htm** file in your text editor.

▶ **2.** Within the opening <table> tag insert the following attribute as shown in Figure 5-21.

```
summary="This table contains the nightly KPAF program schedule aired
from Bismarck, North Dakota. Program times are laid out in
thirty-minute increments from 6:00 p.m. to 10:00 p.m., Monday through
Sunday night."
```

```
<table class="schedule" border="1"
       summary="This table contains the nightly KPAF program schedule aired
                from Bismarck, North Dakota. Program times are laid out in
                thirty-minute increments from 6:00 p.m. to 10:00 p.m., Monday
                through Sunday night.">

   <caption>All times listed in central time</caption>
```

▶ **3.** Save your changes to the file, and then reload the **schedule.htm** file in your Web browser. Verify that the summary description does *not* appear in the browser window.

▶ **4.** If you plan on taking a break before starting the next session, close your open files and programs now.

Tip

In some browsers, you can view the summary description by right-clicking the table and selecting Properties from the shortcut menu.

Creating Tables with Preformatted Text   InSight

As you learned in Tutorial 1, browsers strip out white space from the HTML code when they render Web pages. You can force the browser the keep certain white space by marking your document text as **preformatted text**, in which the browser displays the spacing and line breaks exactly as you enter it. Preformatted text is created using the tag

```
<pre>content</pre>
```

where *content* is the text that will appear preformatted in the browser. One use of preformatted text is to quickly create tables, neatly laid out in rows and columns. For example, the code

```
<pre>
Time     Friday      Saturday
====     ==========  ==============
7:30     Brain Stew  Bismarck Forum
</pre>
```

is displayed by the browser exactly as typed, with the spaces as shown:

```
Time     Friday      Saturday
====     ==========  ==============
7:30     Brain Stew  Bismarck Forum
```

Preformatted text is displayed by the browser in a **monospace font** in which each letter takes up the same amount of space. One of the advantages of monospace fonts that make them useful for entering tabular data is that the relative space between characters is unchanged as the font size increases or decreases. This means that if the font size of the above table were increased or decreased, the columns would still line up.

Although you should probably use Web tables to display most of your data, you might want to consider using preformatted text for simple and quick text tables.

You've completed your work in laying out the basic structure of the KPAF program schedule. The next thing Kyle wants you to focus on is formatting the table to be attractive and professional. In the next session you'll explore how to apply design styles to make an interesting and attractive Web table.

| Review | | Session 5.1 Quick Check |

1. There is no HTML tag that marks a column; how is the number of columns in a Web table determined?
2. How does a browser usually render text marked with the <th> tag?
3. Specify the code to add a 10-pixel-wide border to a Web table.
4. A cell contains the text "Monday" and should stretch across 2 rows and 3 columns. Specify the HTML for the cell.
5. What adjustment do you have to make when a cell spans multiple columns?
6. Captions usually appear above or below their Web tables. Explain why a caption is still part of a table's structure.
7. What are the three table row groups, and in what order should they be specified in the code?
8. Specify the code to create a column group in which the first two columns belong to the introCol class and the next three columns belong to the col1, col2, and col3 classes, respectively.
9. What is the purpose of the table summary attribute?

Session 5.2

Formatting Tables with HTML Attributes

After specifying the content and structure of the program schedule, you and Kyle are ready to format the table's appearance. There are two approaches to formatting Web tables. One is to use HTML attributes, and the other is to use CSS styles. Because you'll see both approaches used on the Internet, you'll examine both techniques, starting with the HTML attribute approach.

Setting Cell Spacing with HTML

Web tables are one of the older HTML page elements, predating the introduction of cascading style sheets. Because of this, HTML has long supported several attributes controlling a table's layout and appearance. In the last session you used one of those attributes, the border attribute, to create a table border and display internal table gridlines. The next attribute you'll consider controls the amount of space between table cells, which is known as the **cell spacing**. By default, browsers set the cell spacing to 2 pixels. To set a different cell spacing value, add the cellspacing attribute

```
<table cellspacing="value"> ... </table>
```

to the table element, where *value* is the size of the cell spacing in pixels. If you have applied a border to your table, changing the cell spacing value also impacts the size of the internal gridlines. Figure 5-22 shows how different cell spacing values affect the appearance of the table border and internal gridlines. Note that if the cell spacing is set to 0 pixels, the browser will still display an internal gridline that comes from the drop shadow that browsers apply to cell and table borders.

Cell spacing values ◄ Figure 5-22

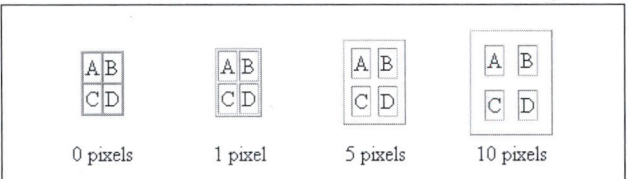

Cell spacing essentially sets the outside margins of the table cells. Unlike the CSS margin style, you can specify cell spacing values only in pixels and not other measuring units, nor can you set different cell spacing values for the different sides of the cell. Also, the effect of setting the cell spacing value is limited by the width allotted to the entire table. The browser ignores cell spacing values that would push the table beyond its defined width.

Setting Cell Padding with HTML

Related to cell spacing is **cell padding**, which is the space between the cell contents and the cell border. You set the padding using the attribute

```
<table cellpadding="value"> ... </table>
```

where *value* is the size of the cell padding. Like the cellspacing attribute, the cellpadding attribute applies to every cell in the table. Figure 5-23 shows the impact of various cell padding values on the table's appearance. Cell padding is similar to the CSS padding style, though there is no option to define padding values for different sides of the cell; and like the cellspacing attribute, cell padding values can only be expressed in pixels and not other units of measure.

Cell padding values ◄ Figure 5-23

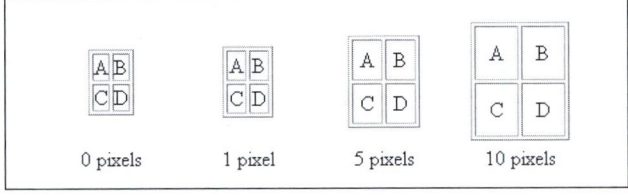

Setting Cell Padding and Cell Spacing with HTML | Reference Window

- To define the padding within table cells, add the attribute
    ```
    <table cellpadding="value"> ... </table>
    ```
  to the table element, where *value* is the size of the padding space in pixels.
- To define the space between table cells, add the attribute
    ```
    <table cellspacing="value"> ... </table>
    ```
  to the table element, where *value* is the space between table cells in pixels.

Kyle would like you to experiment with how the cellpadding and cellspacing attributes might affect the appearance of the program schedule, so you'll add these two attributes to the table element, setting the cell spacing to 3 pixels and the cell padding to 5 pixels.

To set the cell padding and cell spacing:

▶ **1.** Return to the **schedule.htm** file in your text editor.

▶ **2.** Within the opening <table> tag, insert the following attribute, as shown in Figure 5-24.

```
cellspacing="3" cellpadding="5"
```

Figure 5-24	Setting the cell spacing and padding values

```
<table class="schedule" border="1" cellspacing="3" cellpadding="5"
       summary="This table contains the nightly KPAF program schedule aired
                from Bismarck, North Dakota. Program times are laid out in
                thirty-minute increments from 6:00 p.m. to 10:00 p.m., Monday
                through Sunday night.">
```

▶ **3.** Save your changes to the file, and then open **schedule.htm** in your Web browser. As shown in Figure 5-25, the space between and within the table cells has been increased from their default values.

Figure 5-25	Table with increased cell spacing and padding

Time	Monday	Tuesday	Wednesday	Thursday	Friday	Saturday	Sunday
6:00	National News						
6:30	Local News						
7:00	Opera Fest	Radio U	Science Week	The Living World	Word Play	Agri-Week	Folk Fest
7:30					Brain Stew	Bismarck Forum	
8:00	The Classical Music Connection				Old Time Radio	Saturday Nite Jazz	The Indie Connection
8:30					The Inner Mind		
9:00					Open Mike Nite		
9:30							
10:00	World News Feed						

Setting Table Widths and Heights in HTML

You can use HTML to set the overall width and height of the table, and of the individual cells within the table. By default, the width of tables will range from the minimum necessary to display all the cell contents without the line wrapping up to the width of the container element. To set the width of the table to a specific value, add the width attribute

```
<table width="value"> ... </table>
```

to the table element, where *value* is the width either in pixels or as a percentage of the width of the containing element. If the containing element is the page itself, you can set the table to fill the entire page width by specifying a width value of 100%. You can still never reduce a table to a width smaller than is required to display the content or larger than the width of its container. For example, if the table content requires a width of 450 pixels, then the browser will ignore any width attribute that attempts to set a smaller table size.

Many browsers also support the height attribute, which has the syntax

```
<table height="value"> ... </table>
```

where *value* is the height of the table either in pixels or as a percentage of the height of the containing element. Even though the height attribute is widely supported, it is not part of the HTML specifications nor is it supported by XHTML. Like the width attribute, the height attribute indicates only the minimum height of the table. If the table content cannot fit into the specified height, the table height increases to match the content.

You can also set the width of individual columns by applying the width attribute to either an individual column or a column group. For example, the HTML code

```
<colgroup width="100" span="7">
</colgroup>
```

sets the width of each of seven columns from the table to 100 pixels. To specify different column widths, apply the width attribute to individual col elements as in the code

```
<colgroup>
   <col width="50" />
   <col width="100" span="5" />
   <col width="50" />
</colgroup>
```

which sets the widths of the five middle columns to 100 pixels, but sets the width of the first and seventh columns to 50 pixels each. Column widths can also be expressed as a percentage of the total width of the table. A column width of 50% causes a column to occupy half of the table width. Column widths are always limited by the total width of the table and the content that each cell contains. For example, if you try to set the width of each column in a five-column table to 200 pixels but only 800 pixels of space is available, the browser will adjust the column widths down to fit the content.

In the code for many Web tables, you might see the width attribute applied to individual table cells. This is another way to set the width of an entire column because the remaining cells in the column will adopt that width to keep the column cells aligned. Even so, the width value for a single cell might be overridden by the browser if other cells in the column require a larger width to display their content. With the introduction of column groups, there is little need to apply the width attribute to individual table cells. Also, the W3C has deprecated the use of the width attribute with the td and th elements. As you might expect, however, you will still see it supported by many of the current browsers.

> **Tip**
>
> Width and height values should always be thought of as minimum widths and heights because they will be overridden whenever the content of the table requires it.

Setting Row Heights with HTML

You can use HTML to set the row heights by applying the height attribute

```
<tr height="value"> ... </tr>
```

to the tr element, where *value* is the height of the row in pixels. Internet Explorer also allows you to specify height values as a percentage of the height of the table. The height attribute is not part of the W3C specifications, but most browsers support it. As with setting the column width by setting the width of an individual cell, you can also set the row height by applying the height attribute to an individual cell within the row. This approach is also supported by most browsers even though it has been deprecated by the W3C.

Formatting Table Borders with HTML

In the last session you used the border attribute to add a border around the table and each of the table cells. You can modify the placement of the table borders using table frames and table rules. A **table frame** specifies which sides of the table (or which sides of the table cells) will have borders. To apply a frame to a table, apply the frame attribute

```
<table border="value" frame="type"> ... </table>
```

to the table element, where *value* is the width of the table border and *type* is box (the default), above, border, below, hsides, vsides, lhs, rhs, or void. Figure 5-26 describes each of these frame options.

Figure 5-26 | **Values of the frame attribute**

Frame Value	Border Appearance
above	only above the table
below	only below the table
border	around all four sides of the table
box	around all four sides of the table
hsides	on the top and bottom sides of the table (the horizontal sides)
lhs	only on the left side
rhs	only on the right side
void	no border is drawn around the table
vsides	on the left and right sides of the table (the vertical sides)

Figure 5-27 shows the impact of these frame attribute values on a sample table grid.

Figure 5-27 | **Frame examples**

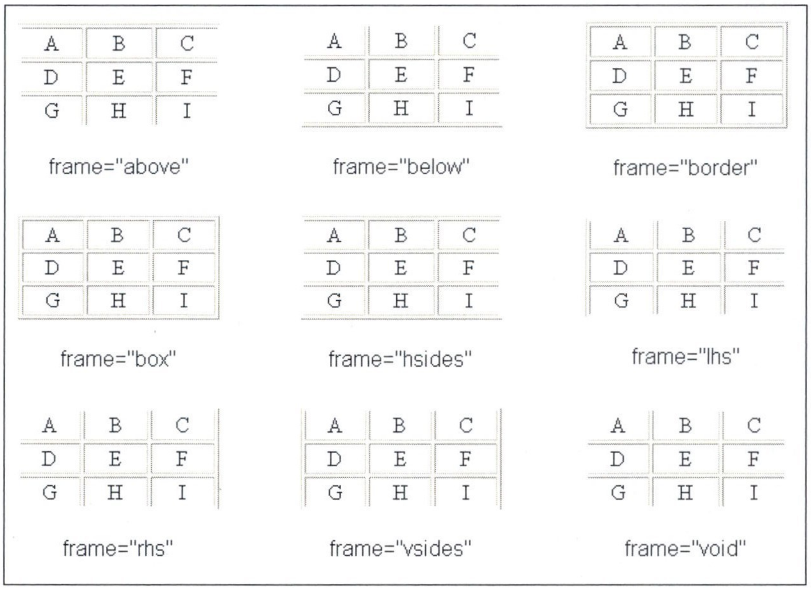

A **table rule** specifies how the internal gridlines are drawn within the table. To apply a table rule, add the rules attribute

```
<table border="value" rules="type"> ... </table>
```

to the table element, where *type* is all (the default), cols, groups, none, or rows. Figure 5-28 describes the impact of each of these rules attribute values on the placement of the internal table gridlines.

Values of the rules attribute | Figure 5-28

Rules Value	Description of Rules
all	places gridlines around all table cells
cols	places gridlines around columns
groups	places gridlines around row groups
none	displays no gridlines
rows	places gridlines around rows

Figure 5-29 shows how these rules values would appear in a sample table.

Rules examples | Figure 5-29

By combining frame and rules values, you can duplicate many of the same effects you could achieve using the CSS border-style property, which you'll explore shortly. Some Web page authors prefer to work with these HTML attributes because they enable them to set the appearance of the table borders from within the <table> tag rather than through an external style sheet.

Aligning Cell Contents with HTML

The final set of HTML table attributes you'll examine before looking at CSS table styles are those attributes that control how content is aligned within each table cell. By default, browsers horizontally center the contents of table header cells and left-align the contents of table data cells. You can specify a different horizontal alignment using the align attribute

```
align="position"
```

where *position* is left, center, right, justify or char. The align attribute can be applied to table rows, row groups, columns, column groups, or individual table cells. For example, the code

```
<colgroup>
    <col align="left" />
    <col span="6" align="right" />
</colgroup>
```

left-aligns the first column of the Web table and right-aligns the remaining six columns. When you apply the align attribute to the table element, it aligns the entire table with the surrounding page content but does not affect the alignment of the cells within the table. The align attribute has been deprecated for use with the table element, but not for the row, column, and cell elements within the table.

InSight | **Character Alignment**

Another alignment option included with the align attribute is the char value, which tells the browser to align the values in a cell based on the position of a particular character. The default character is a decimal point, which is represented by a period in the English language and by commas in some European languages (such as French). To line up all of the data values within a column by their decimal points, enter the following code:

```
<col align="char" />
```

You can specify a different character by adding the char attribute to the tag. You can also specify how much the alignment character is offset from the cell borders using the charoff attribute. The syntax of these attributes is

```
align="char" char="character" charoff="position"
```

where *character* is the alignment character and *position* is the position of the character within the table cell either in pixels or as a percentage of the cell's width. So the HTML code

```
<col align="char" char="," charoff="50%" />
```

aligns all of the column values by the position of the comma character. The comma character itself will be placed in the center of each cell in the column.

While useful for displaying financial or scientific data, the character alignment attributes have not received much support in the browser market, so their potential is still mostly unfulfilled.

Vertical Alignment in HTML

You can also use HTML to vertically align the contents of each table cell. The default is to place the text in the middle of the cell. To choose a different placement, apply the valign attribute

```
valign="position"
```

where *position* is top, middle, bottom, or baseline. The top, middle, and bottom options align the content with the top, middle, and bottom borders of the cell. The baseline option places the text near the bottom of the cell but aligns the bases of each letter. The valign attribute can be applied to table rows, row groups, columns, and column groups to set the vertical alignment of several cells at once.

Kyle feels that having the program names placed in the middle of each cell makes the program schedule more difficult to read. He prefers having all of the program names lined up with the top of the cells. To change the cell alignment for all of the cells in the table body, you'll apply the valign attribute to the tbody row group.

To vertically align the text in the table:

▶ 1. Return to the **schedule.htm** file in your text editor.

▶ 2. Within the opening <tbody> tag, insert the following attribute, as shown in Figure 5-30:

```
valign="top"
```

```
<tbody valign="top">
    <tr>
        <th>6:00</th>
        <td colspan="7">National News</td>
    </tr>
```

3. Save your changes to the file, and then reload or refresh the **schedule.htm** file in your Web browser. As shown in Figure 5-31, the text is aligned at the top of the cells.

Cell content aligned with the top of each table cell | Figure 5-31

Time	Monday	Tuesday	Wednesday	Thursday	Friday	Saturday	Sunday
6:00	National News						
6:30	Local News						
7:00	Opera Fest	Radio U	Science Week	The Living World	Word Play	Agri-Week	Folk Fest
7:30					Brain Stew	Bismarck Forum	
8:00	The Classical Music Connection				Old Time Radio	Saturday Nite Jazz	The Indie Connection
8:30					The Inner Mind		
9:00					Open Mike Nite		
9:30							
10:00	World News Feed						

Kyle likes the appearance of the program table. But he notes that this is only the evening schedule; he plans to create other Web pages for the morning and afternoon schedules. To have the tables match each other, you'll have to insert the various HTML attributes into each table's markup tags. Kyle would rather use CSS so he can easily apply the formatting he likes to all of the schedules at once. He suggests that you explore the CSS table styles before continuing your design of the evening schedule.

Formatting Tables with CSS

Starting with CSS2, Cascading Style Sheets included support for Web tables. With more browser support for these styles, CSS has gradually replaced the HTML attributes you've just reviewed (though you will still see those HTML attributes frequently used on the Web). Kyle suggests that you replace the HTML table attributes with an external style sheet that he can apply to all of the program schedule tables on the KPAF Web site.

To create the style sheet:

1. Open the **tablestxt.css** file from the tutorial.05\tutorial folder included with your Data Files. Enter *your name* and *the date* in the comment section of the file. Save the file as **tables.css** in the same folder.

2. Return to the **schedule.htm** file in your text editor and insert the following link element directly above the closing </head> tag:

   ```
   <link href="tables.css" rel="stylesheet" type="text/css" />
   ```

3. Because you'll be replacing the HTML attributes with CSS styles, delete the border, cellpadding, and cellspacing attributes from the opening <table> tag.

4. Delete the valign attribute from the opening <tbody> tag.

5. Save your changes to the file.

Tip

Don't combine HTML table attributes and CSS table styles in your Web table design. Choose one or the other to avoid conflicts in the two approaches.

Now that you've linked the schedule.htm file to the tables.css style sheet and you've removed the old HTML table attributes, you are ready to begin creating the style sheet. You'll start with styles for the table border.

Table Border Styles

The first styles you'll apply to the program schedule are the border styles. Web tables use the same border styles you've already used with other page elements in previous tutorials. Unlike the HTML border attribute, you can apply one set of borders to the Web table itself and another set of borders to the individual cells within the table. You decide to add a 10-pixel purple border around the entire schedule table in the outset style. You'll also add a 1-pixel solid gray border around each cell within the table.

To add the table border styles:

1. Return to the **tables.css** file in your text editor. Add the following style to apply a border to the entire Web table:

   ```
   table.schedule {border: 10px outset rgb(153, 0, 153)}
   ```

2. Add the following style to apply borders to each table cell. See Figure 5-32.

   ```
   table.schedule th, table.schedule td
                    {border: 1px solid gray}
   ```

Figure 5-32	Setting the table border styles

```
table.schedule          {border: 10px outset rgb(153,0,153)}
table.schedule th, table.schedule td
                        {border: 1px solid gray}
```

Notice that the style sheet uses contextual selectors to apply these styles only to the schedule table and not other tables that might exist on the KPAF Web site.

3. Save your changes to the style sheet and then reload the **schedule.htm** file in your Web browser. As shown in Figure 5-33, borders have now been added to the entire table and to each table cell.

Table and cell borders   Figure 5-33

All times listed in central time							
Time	**Monday**	**Tuesday**	**Wednesday**	**Thursday**	**Friday**	**Saturday**	**Sunday**
6:00	National News						
6:30	Local News						
7:00	Opera Fest	Radio U	Science Week	The Living World	Word Play	Agri-Week	Folk Fest
7:30					Brain Stew	Bismarck Forum	
8:00	The Classical Music Connection				Old Time Radio		
8:30					The Inner Mind	Saturday Nite Jazz	The Indie Connection
9:00					Open Mike Nite		
9:30							
10:00	World News Feed						

CSS provides for two ways of drawing the table borders. The default, shown in Figure 5-33, is to draw separate borders around the table cells and the entire table. The other approach is to collapse the borders in upon each other as shown in Figure 5-34, removing any space between the borders.

Separate and collapsed borders   Figure 5-34

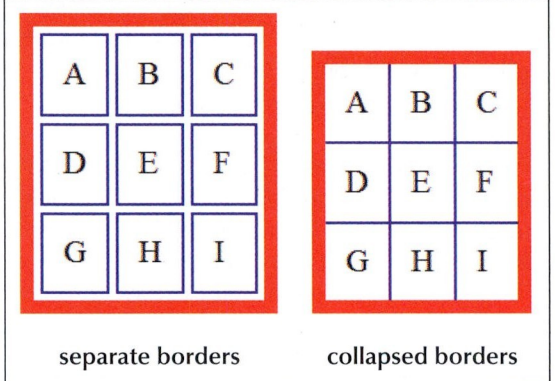

separate borders   collapsed borders

To determine whether to use the separate or collapsed border model, you apply the style

```
border-collapse: type
```

to the table element, where *type* is either separate (the default) or collapse. One of the key differences between the separate and collapse border models is that under the separate border model you can only apply borders to the table itself or to table cells. Under the collapse border model, any table object can have a border, including table rows, row groups, columns, and column groups. If the separate borders model is used, you can specify the distance between the borders by applying the style

```
border-spacing: value
```

to the table, where *value* is the space between the borders in one of the CSS units of measure. For example, the following style specifies that all borders within the table should be separated by a distance of 10 pixels:

```
table {border-collapse: separate; border-spacing: 10px}
```

The separate borders model, therefore, has the same effect as the HTML cellspacing attribute in providing additional space between table cells.

In the collapsed border model, there is no space between borders; in fact, the adjacent borders are merged together to form a single line. It's important to understand that the borders are not simply moved together, but rather they are combined into a single border. For example, if two adjacent 1-pixel-wide borders are collapsed together, the resulting border is not 2 pixels wide, but only 1 pixel wide. The situation is more complicated when the adjacent borders have different widths, styles, or colors. How would you merge a double red border and a solid blue border into a single border of only one color and style? Those kinds of differences must be reconciled before the two borders can be merged. CSS employs five rules to determine the style of the collapsed border. Listed in decreasing order of importance, the rules are:

1. If either border has a border style of hidden, the collapsed border is hidden.
2. A border style of none is overridden by any other border style.
3. If neither border is hidden, the style of the wider border takes priority over the narrower.
4. If the two borders have the same width but different styles, the border style with the highest priority is used. Double borders have the highest priority, followed by solid, dashed, dotted, ridge, outset, groove, and finally inset borders.
5. If the borders differ only in the color, the color from the table object with the highest priority is used. The highest priority color belongs to the border surrounding individual table cells, followed by the borders for table rows, row groups, columns, column groups, and finally the border around the entire table.

Any situation not covered by these rules is left to the browser to determine which border dominates when collapsing the two borders. Figure 5-35 provides an example of the first rule in action. In this example, the border around the entire table is hidden but a 1-pixel blue border is assigned to the cells within the table. When collapsed, any cell borders that are adjacent to the table border adopt the hidden border property.

Figure 5-35 ▸ **Reconciling hidden borders**

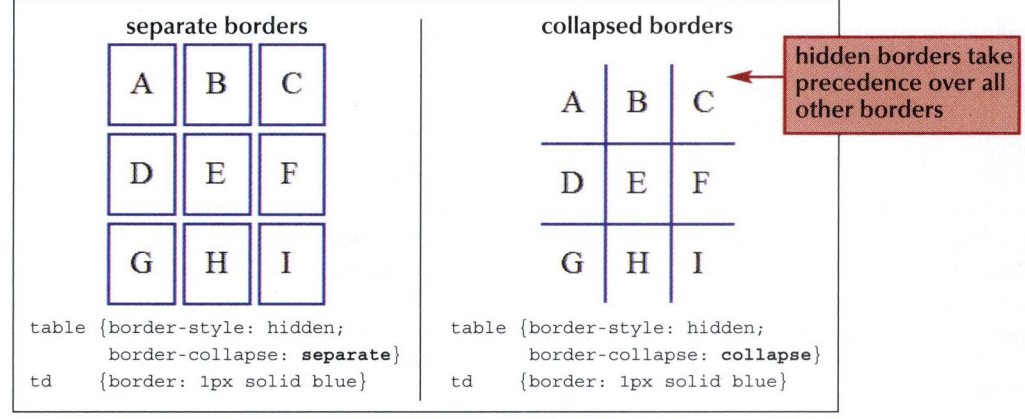

Figure 5-36 shows what happens when two borders of the same width but different styles meet. In this case, because of Rule 4, the table cell borders with the double blue lines have precedence over the solid red lines of the table border.

Reconciling different border styles ◄ **Figure 5-36**

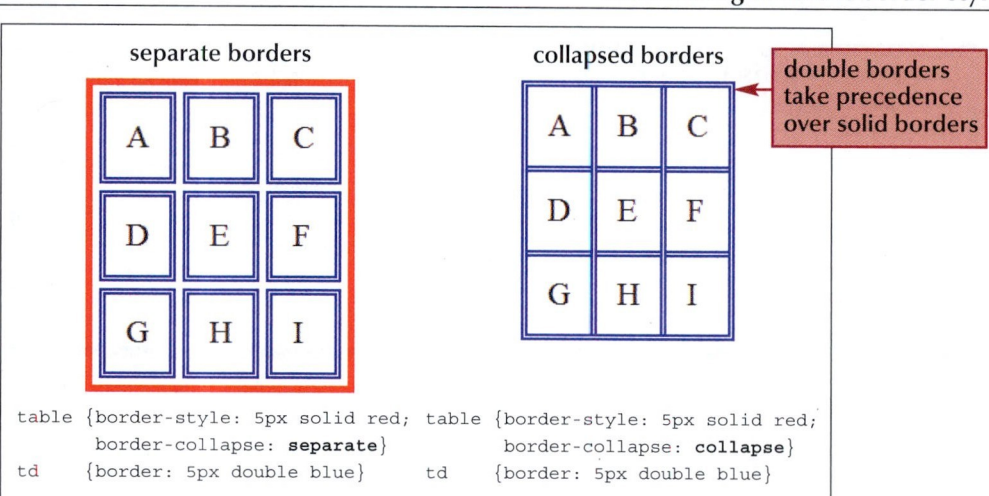

separate borders

collapsed borders

double borders take precedence over solid borders

```
table {border-style: 5px solid red;    table {border-style: 5px solid red;
       border-collapse: separate}             border-collapse: collapse}
td    {border: 5px double blue}         td    {border: 5px double blue}
```

Although the collapse model appears more complicated at first, the rules are reasonable and allow for a wide variety of border designs.

Setting Table Borders with CSS | Reference Window

- To define the border model used by the table, apply the table style
    ```
    border-collapse: type
    ```
  where *type* is separate (the default) to keep all borders around cells and the table itself, separate, or collapse to merge all adjacent borders.
- To set the space between separated borders, apply the table style
    ```
    border-spacing: value
    ```
  where *value* is the space between the borders in any of the CSS units of measure.

For the KPAF program schedule, Kyle thinks the table would look better if there were no space between the table cells. He asks you to collapse the borders.

To collapse the cell borders:

▶ 1. Return to the **tables.css** file in your text editor. Add the following style to the table element, as shown in Figure 5-37.

```
border-collapse: collapse
```

Adding the border-collapse style ◄ **Figure 5-37**

```
table.schedule          {border: 10px outset rgb(153,0,153); border-collapse: collapse}
table.schedule th, table.schedule td
                        {border: 1px solid gray}
```

▶ **2.** Save your changes to the style sheet, and then reload **schedule.htm** in your Web browser. Figure 5-38 shows the revised table design with the collapsed border layout.

Figure 5-38 ▶ **Table with collapsed borders**

All times listed in central time						

Time	Monday	Tuesday	Wednesday	Thursday	Friday	Saturday	Sunday
6:00	National News						
6:30	Local News						
7:00	Opera Fest	Radio U	Science Week	The Living World	Word Play	Agri-Week	Folk Fest
7:30					Brain Stew	Bismarck Forum	
8:00	The Classical Music Connection				Old Time Radio	Saturday Nite Jazz	The Indie Connection
8:30					The Inner Mind		
9:00					Open Mike Nite		
9:30							
10:00	World News Feed						

Notice that the browser still uses the purple outset style for the border around the entire table. This is due to Rule 3 above. Because the border around the entire table is 10 pixels wide, it takes priority over the 1-pixel-wide borders around the individual table cells under the collapsed border model.

Applying Styles to Rows and Columns

Kyle doesn't like the appearance of the table text. He suggests changing the table text to a sans-serif font that is 0.7 em units in size. He also suggests that the text in the header row appear in a white font on a purple background and that the first column of the schedule, containing the program times, appear on a light yellow background.

You can apply these styles to the row groups and column groups you created in the last session. Recall that the header row is part of the thead row group (see Figure 5-19), and the first column of the table belongs to the firstCol class of columns (see Figure 5-20). So to apply Kyle's suggested styles, you could add the following declarations to the tables.css style sheet:

```
table.schedule              {font-family: Arial, Helvetica, sans-
                            serif; font-size: 0.7em}
table.schedule thead        {color: white; background-color:
                            rgb(203,50,203)}
table.schedule col.firstCol {background-color: rgb(255,255,192)}
```

However, you notice a small problem. The first cell in the table belongs to both the header row and the first column. Will this cell have a purple background or a yellow background? Which style has precedence? Table objects, like other parts of CSS, have levels of precedence in which the more specific object has priority over the more general. Figure 5-39 shows a diagram of the different levels of precedence in the Web table structure.

Levels of precedence in Web table styles ◀ **Figure 5-39**

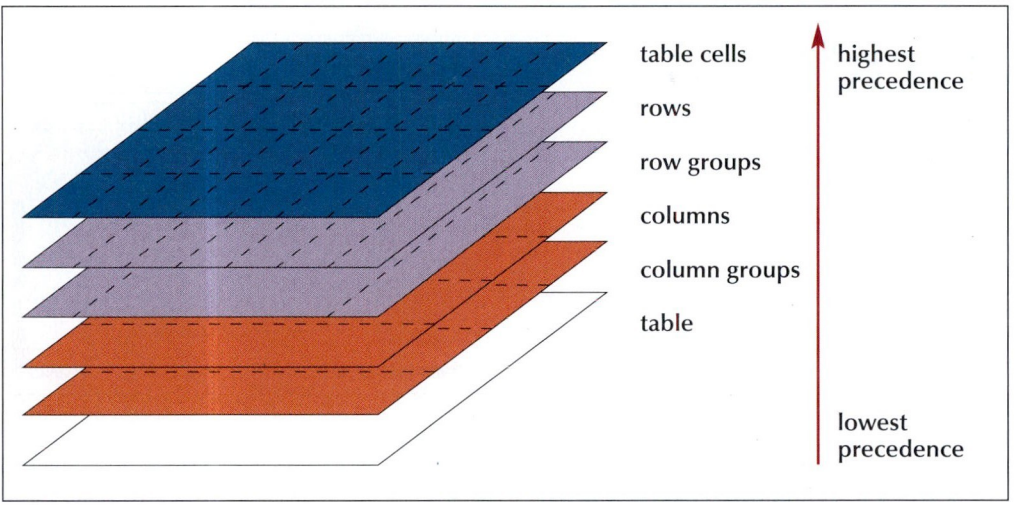

The most general styles are those applied to the entire table. Those styles are overruled by styles that are applied to column groups and then to columns. The next level up in precedence contains those styles applied to row groups and then rows. The highest level of precedence is given to those styles applied to table cells. Be aware that not all styles are supported by different layers of the table structure. In particular, columns and column groups accept only four styles: border, background, width, and visibility.

With Kyle's proposed design, the first cell should have a purple background because row groups take priority over columns or column groups. To see that this is the case, add Kyle's proposed styles to the tables.css style sheet.

To set the text and background styles in the schedule table:

▶ **1.** Return to the **tables.css** file in your text editor. Add the following styles to the style declaration for the schedule table:

```
font-family: Arial, Helvetica, sans-serif; font-size: 0.7em
```

▶ **2.** Go to the bottom of the style sheet and insert the following lines to create styles for the table's header row and first column as shown in Figure 5-40:

```
table.schedule thead        {color: white; background-color:
                             rgb(203,50,203)}
table.schedule col.firstCol {background-color: rgb(255,255,192)}
```

Adding font and color styles to the schedule table ◀ **Figure 5-40**

```
table.schedule        {border: 10px outset rgb(153,0,153); border-collapse: collapse;
                        font-family: Arial, Helvetica, sans-serif; font-size: 0.7em}     ◀ table font styles
table.schedule th, table.schedule td
                       {border: 1px solid gray; font-family: Arial}
table.schedule thead   {color: white; background-color: rgb(203,50,203)} ◀ style applied to
                                                                            thead row group
table.schedule col.firstCol
                       {background-color: rgb(255,255,192)} ◀ style applied to
                                                               first table column
```

3. Save your changes to the style sheet, and then reload **schedule.htm** in your Web browser. The revised table design is shown in Figure 5-41.

| Figure 5-41 | Applying styles to the header row and first column |

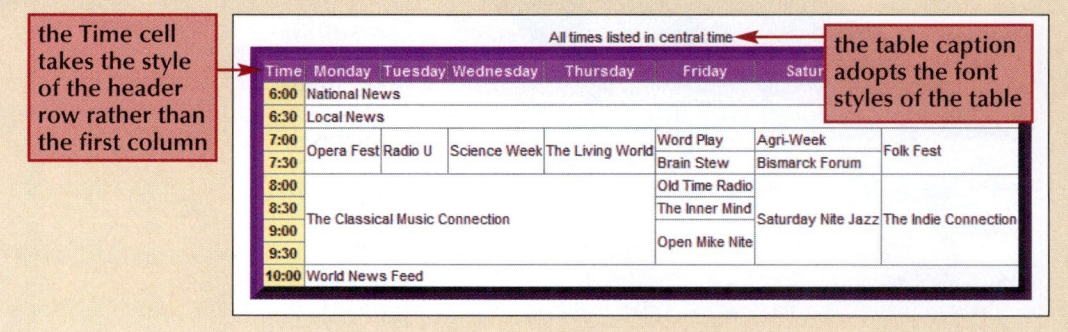

the Time cell takes the style of the header row rather than the first column

the table caption adopts the font styles of the table

As you expected, the cell in the first column of the header row does indeed have a purple, and not a light yellow, background. Also note that all of the cells in the table and the table caption have adopted the smaller sans-serif font. This is because the font style you entered for the schedule table is inherited by all table objects unless a different font style is specified.

Using the Width and Height Styles

Reducing the font size and changing the font family has resulted in a more compact table, but Kyle thinks it could be difficult to read and wonders if you could enlarge the table. Recall that browsers will set the table width to efficiently use the page space, never making tables wider than necessary to display the content. You can use the CSS width style to specify a different table size. Widths are expressed in one of the CSS units of measure or as a percentage of the containing element. Kyle suggests that you set the width of the table to 100% so that it covers the entire width of its div container.

To set the width of the table:

1. Return to the **tables.css** file in your text editor. Add the following style to the table element, as shown in Figure 5-42.

```
width: 100%
```

| Figure 5-42 | Setting the width of the schedule table |

```
table.schedule          {border: 10px outset rgb(153,0,153); border-collapse: collapse;
                         font-family: Arial, Helvetica, sans-serif; font-size: 0.7em;
                         width: 100%}
```

2. Save your changes to the file, and then reload **schedule.htm** in your Web browser. Figure 5-43 shows the layout of the enlarged table.

Table width set to 100% ◀ **Figure 5-43**

You notice that the column widths are inconsistent, with very little width given to the Time column and different widths given to different days of the week. This is because the space allotted to each column is a function of the column's content. The Web browser will attempt to fit the most content possible within each column without having the text wrap to a new line. This means that columns with more text are wider than those with less text. When the width of the entire table is increased, the added space is divided evenly among the table columns.

You can set column widths using the same width style you applied to the table itself. The column width is expressed either in a CSS unit of measure or as a percentage of the entire width of the table. You decide to set the width of the first column to 7% of the entire table width, while setting each of the seven remaining columns to 13% of the table width. Added together, 98% of the table width will be allotted to the eight table columns. The remaining table width is reserved for table and cell borders.

You can set the column widths by applying the width style to the two column groups. The width values are applied to the individual columns within those groups. The styles are:

```
table.schedule col.firstCol  {width: 7%}
table.schedule col.dayCols   {width: 13%}
```

Add these styles to the tables.css style sheet.

> **Tip**
>
> Always set the total width of the table columns to be less than 100% of the table width to allow space for table borders and padding.

To set the width of the table columns:

▶ 1. Return to the **tables.css** file in your text editor. Add the following style to the first-Col selector:

```
width: 7%
```

2. Insert the following style declaration to set the widths of the columns in the day-Cols class to 13% as shown in Figure 5-44:

```
table.schedule col.dayCols {width: 13%}
```

Figure 5-44 | **Setting the width of the schedule table columns**

```
table.schedule col.firstCol
                           {background-color: rgb(255,255,192); width: 7%}

table.schedule col.dayCols
                           {width: 13%}
```

3. Save your changes to the file, and then reload **schedule.htm** in your Web browser. Figure 5-45 shows the revised layout of the table.

Figure 5-45 | **Revised table column widths**

widths for the day columns are equal

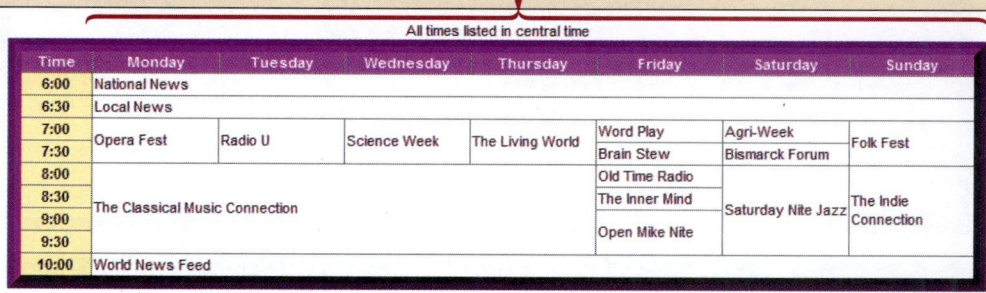

				All times listed in central time			
Time	**Monday**	**Tuesday**	**Wednesday**	**Thursday**	**Friday**	**Saturday**	**Sunday**
6:00	National News						
6:30	Local News						
7:00	Opera Fest	Radio U	Science Week	The Living World	Word Play	Agri-Week	Folk Fest
7:30					Brain Stew	Bismarck Forum	
8:00					Old Time Radio		
8:30	The Classical Music Connection				The Inner Mind	Saturday Nite Jazz	The Indie Connection
9:00							
9:30					Open Mike Nite		
10:00	World News Feed						

Kyle also wants you to increase the height of the table rows to provide more visual space for the table contents. Heights are set using the CSS height style. You can apply heights to entire table rows or individual table cells. You can also use the height style to set the height of the entire table. As with the width style, the height style should be interpreted as the minimum height for these table objects since the browser will enlarge the table, table row, or table cell if the content requires it.

You decide to set the height of the rows in the table header to 20 pixels and the height of the rows in the table body to 30 pixels. The styles to do this are:

```
table.schedule thead tr {height: 20px}
table.schedule tbody tr {height: 30px}
```

Note that you don't apply the height style to the row groups themselves because that would set the width of the entire group and not the individual rows within the group.

To set the height of the table rows:

1. Return to the **tables.css** file in your text editor and add the following styles to the bottom of the style sheet, as shown in Figure 5-46.

```
table.schedule thead tr {height: 20px}
table.schedule tbody tr {height: 30px}
```

Figure 5-46 | **Setting the height of the table rows**

```
table.schedule col.dayCols
                           {width: 13%}

table.schedule thead tr {height: 20px}
table.schedule tbody tr {height: 30px}
```

▶ **2.** Save your changes to the file, and then reload **schedule.htm** in your Web browser. Verify that the heights in the table header and table body have changed.

 With the increased row height, Kyle would like all of the program names in the schedule to be vertically aligned with the top of the cell borders as you did earlier with the valign HTML attribute. The equivalent CSS style is the vertical-align property introduced in Tutorial 3. Kyle also wants to increase the padding within each cell to add more space between the program names and the cell border. You'll add the following style to the style sheet:

```
table.schedule tbody td {vertical-align: top; padding: 5px}
```

To place the program names at the top of each table cell:

▶ **1.** Return to the **tables.css** file in your text editor and add the following style as shown in Figure 5-47.

```
table.schedule tbody td {vertical-align: top; padding: 5px}
```

Aligning the data cells within the table body   Figure 5-47

```
table.schedule thead tr {height: 20px}
table.schedule tbody tr {height: 30px}

table.schedule tbody td {vertical-align: top; padding: 5px}
```

▶ **2.** Save your changes to the file, and then reload **schedule.htm** in your Web browser. As shown in Figure 5-48, the program names are now placed at the top of each cell and the padding space between the program names and the cell borders has been increased.

Revised table layout   Figure 5-48

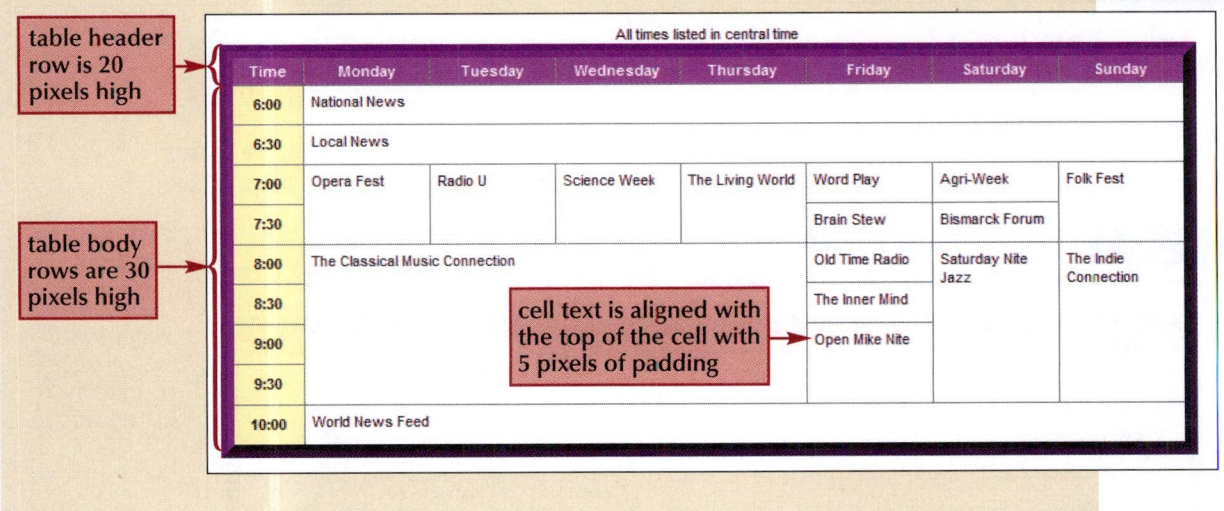

Notice that only the data cells within the tbody rows are placed at the top of the cell. The header cells are still centered vertically because they were not included in the contextual selector you specified in the style sheet.

Caption Styles

Kyle likes the new table design. His only remaining suggestion is that you align the table caption with the top-right corner of the table. Browsers usually place captions above the table, but you can specify the caption location using the caption-side style with the syntax

```
caption-side: position
```

where *position* is either top (the default) or bottom to place the caption below the Web table. To horizontally align the caption text you use the CSS text-align style. So to place the schedule caption at the top-right corner of the table, you would enter the following CSS style:

```
caption {caption-side: top; text-align: right}
```

Reference Window | **Formatting a Table Caption with CSS**

- To position a table caption, apply the style
  ```
  caption-side: position
  ```
  where *position* is top or bottom.

Add this style to the tables.css style sheet.

To apply a style to the table caption:

1. Return to the **tables.css** file in your text editor and add the following style, as shown in Figure 5-49:

   ```
   table.schedule caption {caption-side: top; text-align: right}
   ```

Figure 5-49 | **Setting the caption position**

```
table.schedule tbody td {vertical-align: top; padding: 5px}
table.schedule caption  {caption-side: top; text-align: right}
```

2. Close the file, saving your changes, and then reload the **schedule.htm** file in your Web browser. Figure 5-50 shows the final appearance of the Web table.

Figure 5-50 | **Final design of the schedule table**

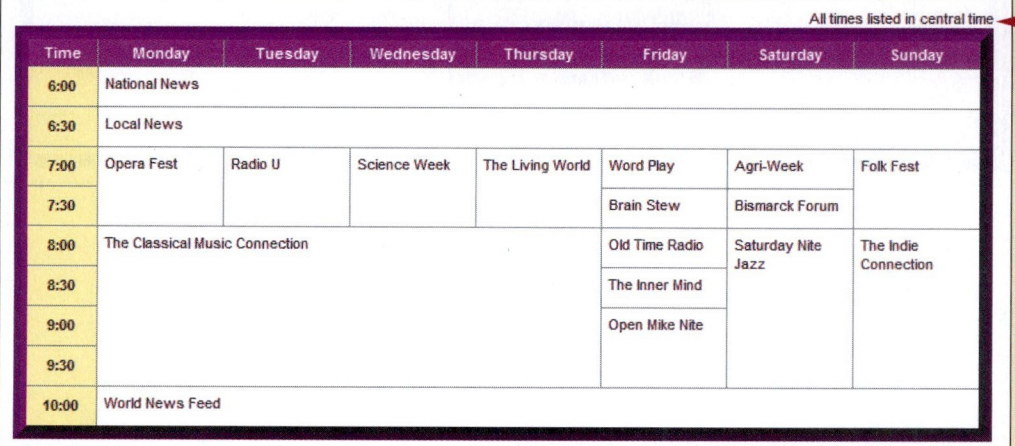

All times listed in central time ← caption is aligned with the top-right corner of the table

Time	Monday	Tuesday	Wednesday	Thursday	Friday	Saturday	Sunday
6:00	National News						
6:30	Local News						
7:00	Opera Fest	Radio U	Science Week	The Living World	Word Play	Agri-Week	Folk Fest
7:30					Brain Stew	Bismarck Forum	
8:00	The Classical Music Connection				Old Time Radio	Saturday Nite Jazz	The Indie Connection
8:30					The Inner Mind		
9:00					Open Mike Nite		
9:30							
10:00	World News Feed						

▶ **3.** If you want to take a break before starting the next session, close all of your files and programs now.

Applying Table Styles to Other Page Elements

As you can see, tables are useful for displaying information in an organized structure of rows and columns. Tables are so useful, in fact, that there's no reason to limit the table structure to Web tables. Using the CSS display style, you can apply the table layout to other HTML elements, such as paragraphs, block quotes, or lists. Figure 5-51 describes the various CSS table display styles and their HTML equivalents.

Table display styles — Figure 5-51

Display Style	Equivalent HTML Element
display: table	table (treated as a block-level element)
display: table-inline	table (treated as an inline element)
display: table-row	tr
display: table-row-group	tbody
display: table-header-group	thead
display: table-footer-group	tfoot
display: table-column	col
display: table-column-group	colgroup
display: table-cell	td or th
display: table-caption	caption

For example, the following definition list contains definitions of several networking terms:

```
<dl>
   <dt>bandwidth</dt>
   <dd>A measure of data transfer speed over a network</dd>
   <dt>HTTP</dt>
   <dd>The protocol used to communicate with Web servers</dd>
</dl>
```

Rather than accepting the default browser layout for this list, it might be useful to display the text in a table. But you don't want to lose the meaning of the markup tags. After all, HTML is designed to mark content, but not indicate how that content should be rendered by the browser. To display this definition list as a table, you first enclose each set of terms and definitions within a div container tag, as follows:

```
<dl>
   <div>
      <dt>bandwidth</dt>
      <dd>A measure of data transfer speed over a network</dd>
   </div>
   <div>
      <dt>HTTP</dt>
      <dd>The protocol used to communicate with Web servers</dd>
   </div>
</dl>
```

You then apply the following style sheet to the list, which treats the entire definition list as a table, the div elements as table rows, and the definition terms and descriptions as table cells within those rows:

```
dl      {display: table; border-collapse: collapse; width: 300px}
dl div {display: table-row}
dt, dd {display: table-cell; border: 1px solid black;
        vertical-align: top; padding: 5px}
```

When viewed in a Web browser, the definition list looks exactly as if it were created using the HTML table tags as shown in Figure 5-52.

Figure 5-52 ▶ **Applying table styles to a definition list**

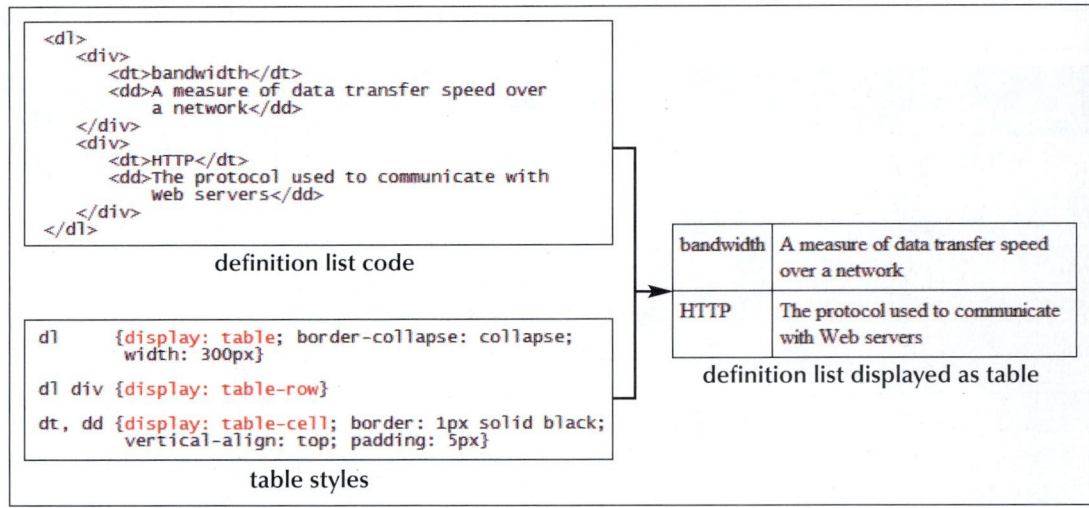

```
<dl>
    <div>
        <dt>bandwidth</dt>
        <dd>A measure of data transfer speed over
            a network</dd>
    </div>
    <div>
        <dt>HTTP</dt>
        <dd>The protocol used to communicate with
            web servers</dd>
    </div>
</dl>
```
definition list code

```
dl      {display: table; border-collapse: collapse;
        width: 300px}

dl div {display: table-row}

dt, dd {display: table-cell; border: 1px solid black;
        vertical-align: top; padding: 5px}
```
table styles

| bandwidth | A measure of data transfer speed over a network |
| HTTP | The protocol used to communicate with Web servers |

definition list displayed as table

In the same way, you can display other page elements in tabular form. As long as the markup tags are nested in a way that mimics the table structure, it doesn't matter if they're table tags or not. You can display them as tables using CSS.

Kyle is pleased with the work you've done on the programming schedule page. In the next session you'll explore how to use tables for page layout and you'll study various CSS layout designs.

Review | **Session 5.2 Quick Check**

1. What HTML attribute do you add to the table element to set the space between cells to 10 pixels?
2. What HTML attribute would you add to the table element to display a 1-pixel border around the table but no gridlines within the table?
3. What HTML attribute would you add to the table element to add borders around the table columns?
4. What CSS style would you enter to collapse all adjacent borders in the table into single borders?
5. Two table cells have adjacent borders. One cell has a 5-pixel-wide double border and the other cell has a 6-pixel-wide solid border. If the table borders are collapsed, what type of border will the two cells share?
6. In the case of conflicting styles, which has highest precedence: the style of the row group or the style of the column group?

7. What style should you enter to align the content of all table header cells with the bottom of the cell?

8. What style would you enter to display the table caption below the table?

9. Specify the style to display ordered lists as table elements and list items as table cells.

Session 5.3

Using Tables for Page Layout

Kyle is very pleased with the work you've done on the KPAF evening schedule. He thinks the page would look even better if it included summaries of upcoming broadcasts. Figure 5-53 shows a sketch of Kyle's proposed addition. He suggests placing the program summaries in a new column to the right of the schedule table.

Kyle's proposed addition to the evening schedule page ◄ **Figure 5-53**

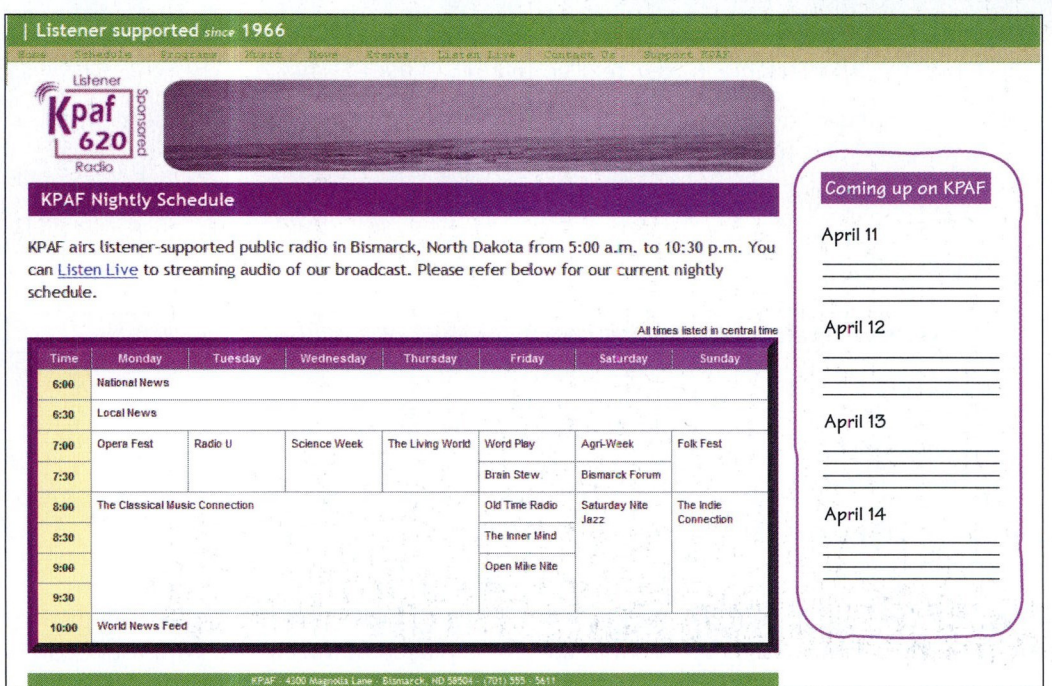

To create this new column, you'll add a new div container named right_col to the schedule.htm file.

To create the new column:

▶ **1.** Return to the **schedule.htm** file in your text editor.

▶ **2.** Scroll to the bottom of the file, and directly above the closing </body> tag, insert the following div container as shown in Figure 5-54.

```
<div id="right_col">
</div>
```

Figure 5-54 | **Inserting the right_col div element**

```
<address>
    KPAF &#183;
    4300 Magnolia Lane &#183;
    Bismarck, ND 58504 &#183;
    (701) 555 - 5611
</address>

</div>

<div id="right_col">
</div>

</body>
```

▶ **3.** Save your changes to the file.

Now you'll add styles to the kpaf.css style sheet to set the width of this new column to 200 pixels. You'll use absolute positioning to place it alongside the nightly program schedule, creating a two-column layout.

To create styles for a two-column layout:

▶ **1.** Open the **kpaf.css** file in your text editor.

▶ **2.** Directly below the style declaration for the #page_content selector, insert the following style for the #right_col selector:

```
#right_col {width: 200px; position: absolute; top: 55px; left:
770px}
```

Figure 5-55 highlights the new style sheet code.

Figure 5-55 | **Adding styles to create a two-column layout**

```
body                    {margin: 0px}
#heading                {color: white; background-color: rgb(215, 205, 151);
                         border-bottom: 1px solid rgb(105, 177, 60)}
#page_content           {width: 730px; position: absolute; top: 55px; left: 20px}
#right_col              {width: 200px; position: absolute; top: 55px; left: 770px}
```

▶ **3.** Close the style sheet file, saving your changes.

Next you'll start creating the bar that lists upcoming programs. To avoid having this look too "boxy," Kyle has proposed that the list be placed in a rectangle with rounded corners. There is no HTML element or CSS style for rounded corners, but you can simulate the effect using background images and a Web table.

Introducing the Jigsaw Layout

So far in this tutorial you've only placed text into your Web tables; however, tables can contain any page content, including inline images, headings, paragraphs, lists, and other tables. Because of this, Web designers began using tables for page layout, allowing them to have more control over the placement of different page elements. For example, a three-column layout could be simulated by enclosing the entire page within a table containing a single row with three columns. The table borders would be hidden from the user, leaving only the table content visible.

Tables support a wide variety of possible page layouts. The one that you'll explore in this session is known as a **jigsaw layout**, so called because it involves breaking up the page content into separate table cells that are then joined together like pieces in a jigsaw puzzle. Figure 5-56 shows an example of a jigsaw layout in which the page content is broken into fourteen table cells, including an image file that has been sliced into nine distinct pieces and placed on the page as a background image. When the cells are reassembled in the complete table after removing the table borders, it appears that the page content flows naturally alongside and within the graphic images or other features of the page.

A jigsaw layout   **Figure 5-56**

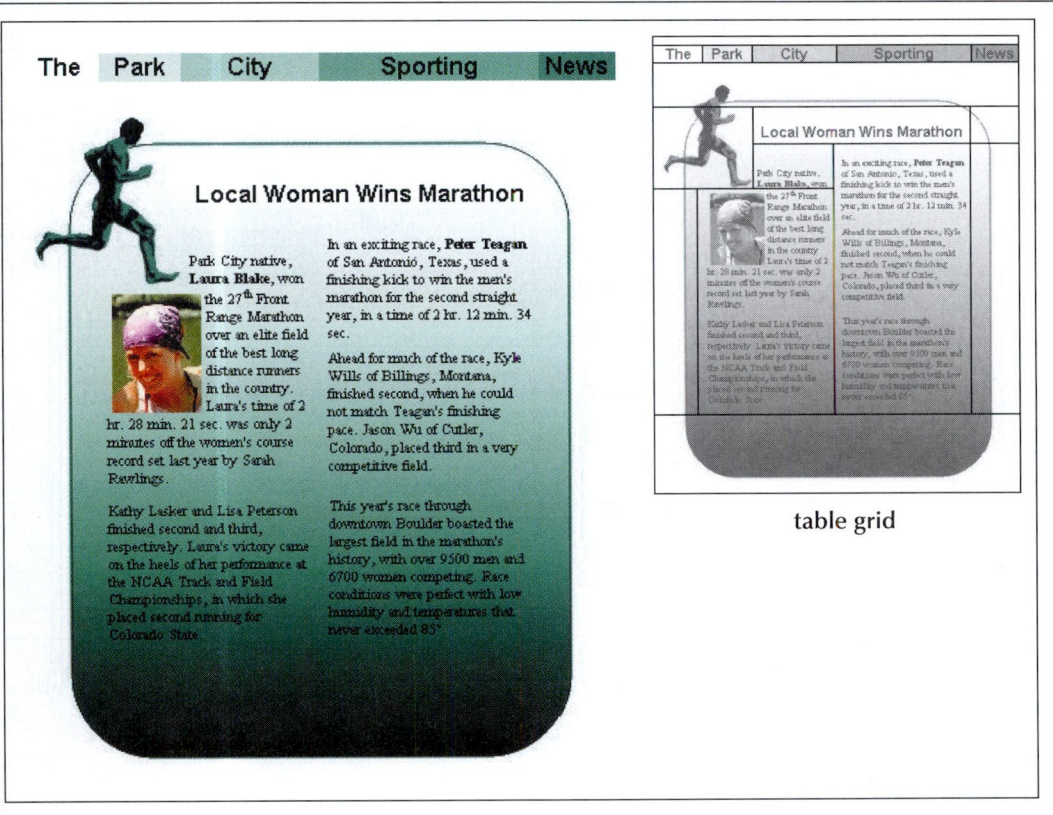

table grid

Defining the Structure of a Jigsaw Table

Figure 5-57 shows a similar jigsaw layout for Kyle's list of upcoming programs. The cell borders have been added to make the table structure clear, but they are removed in the final version of the object. The table contains three rows and three columns with eight background images. Only the middle cell contains any actual content; the remaining cells are used to display the graphic images that constitute the rounded border. When rendered by the browser without the table gridlines, it appears like a rectangle with rounded borders.

Figure 5-57 ▶ **Creating a box with rounded corners**

jigsaw layout   the box as it appears to user

Kyle is interested in this technique and asks you to add the structure for this 3x3 table to the schedule.htm file.

To create the table:

1. Return to the **schedule.htm** file in your Web browser.

2. Within the right_col container, insert the following table. See Figure 5-58.

```
<table class="roundedBox">
   <tr>
      <td></td>
      <td></td>
      <td></td>
   </tr>
   <tr>
      <td></td>
      <td></td>
      <td></td>
   </tr>
   <tr>
      <td></td>
      <td></td>
      <td></td>
   </tr>
</table>
```

Basic table structure for the roundedBox layout | Figure 5-58

```
<div id="right_col">
    <table class="roundedBox">
        <tr>
            <td></td>
            <td></td>
            <td></td>
        </tr>
        <tr>
            <td></td>
            <td></td>
            <td></td>
        </tr>
        <tr>
            <td></td>
            <td></td>
            <td></td>
        </tr>
    </table>
</div>
```

Next you have to assign class names to the nine cells contained within the table. Remember that only the center cell will contain any content. The remaining cells will be used to display the outside borders of the rounded box. You'll assign the outside cells the class names topLeft, top, topRight, left, right, bottomLeft, bottom, and bottomRight. You'll give the inside cell the class name boxContent.

To add class values to the table cells:

1. Return to the **schedule.htm** file and add the class values **topLeft**, **top**, **topRight**, **left**, **right**, **bottomLeft**, **bottom**, and **bottomRight** to the eight outside table cells.

2. Add the class value **boxContent** to the center table cell. Figure 5-59 shows the class values in the roundedBox table.

Inserting the class attributes | Figure 5-59

```
<div id="right_col">
    <table class="roundedBox">
        <tr>
            <td class="topLeft"></td>
            <td class="top"></td>
            <td class="topRight"></td>
        </tr>
        <tr>
            <td class="left"></td>
            <td class="boxContent"></td>
            <td class="right"></td>
        </tr>
        <tr>
            <td class="bottomLeft"></td>
            <td class="bottom"></td>
            <td class="bottomRight"></td>
        </tr>
    </table>
</div>
```

3. Save your changes to the file.

Now that you've created the basic structure of the roundedBox table, you can start working on the design. Rounded boxes are useful elements of page design that Kyle will probably want to repeat throughout the KPAF Web site. So you'll insert the styles for the roundedBox table in an external style sheet named rounded.css.

To open the style sheet file and link it to the schedule file:

▶ 1. Use your text editor to open the **roundedtxt.css** file from the tutorial.05\tutorial folder included with your Data Files. Enter *your name* and *the date* in the comment section of the file. Save the file as **rounded.css**.

▶ 2. Return to the **schedule.htm** file in your text editor.

▶ 3. Directly above the closing </head> tag, insert the following link element:

```
<link href="rounded.css" rel="stylesheet" type="text/css" />
```

▶ 4. Save your changes to the file.

In a jigsaw layout, you don't want any seams to appear between the cells, so you have to collapse the table borders and set the cell padding to 0 pixels. For the KPAF Web site you also want to add space between the table and any surrounding page content, so you'll set the margin space around the table to 5 pixels.

To set the table styles:

▶ 1. Return to the **rounded.css** file in your text editor.

▶ 2. Add the following styles to the sheet, as shown in Figure 5-60:

```
table.roundedBox    {margin: 5px; border-collapse: collapse}
table.roundedBox td {padding: 0px}
```

Figure 5-60 ▶ **Setting the table styles to control the spaces within the table**

```
table.roundedBox    {margin: 5px; border-collapse: collapse}
table.roundedBox td {padding: 0px}
```

▶ 3. Save your changes to the file.

Next you must define the sizes of the eight cells that constitute the outer edges of the table. Because the box will vary in width and height depending on its content, the different cells need to be free to move in different directions. The left and right sides should expand in the vertical direction to accommodate the table content, while the top and bottom sides should expand horizontally. The four corner cells are fixed in size and should not expand or contract based on the table content. See Figure 5-61.

The outside table cells ◄ Figure 5-61

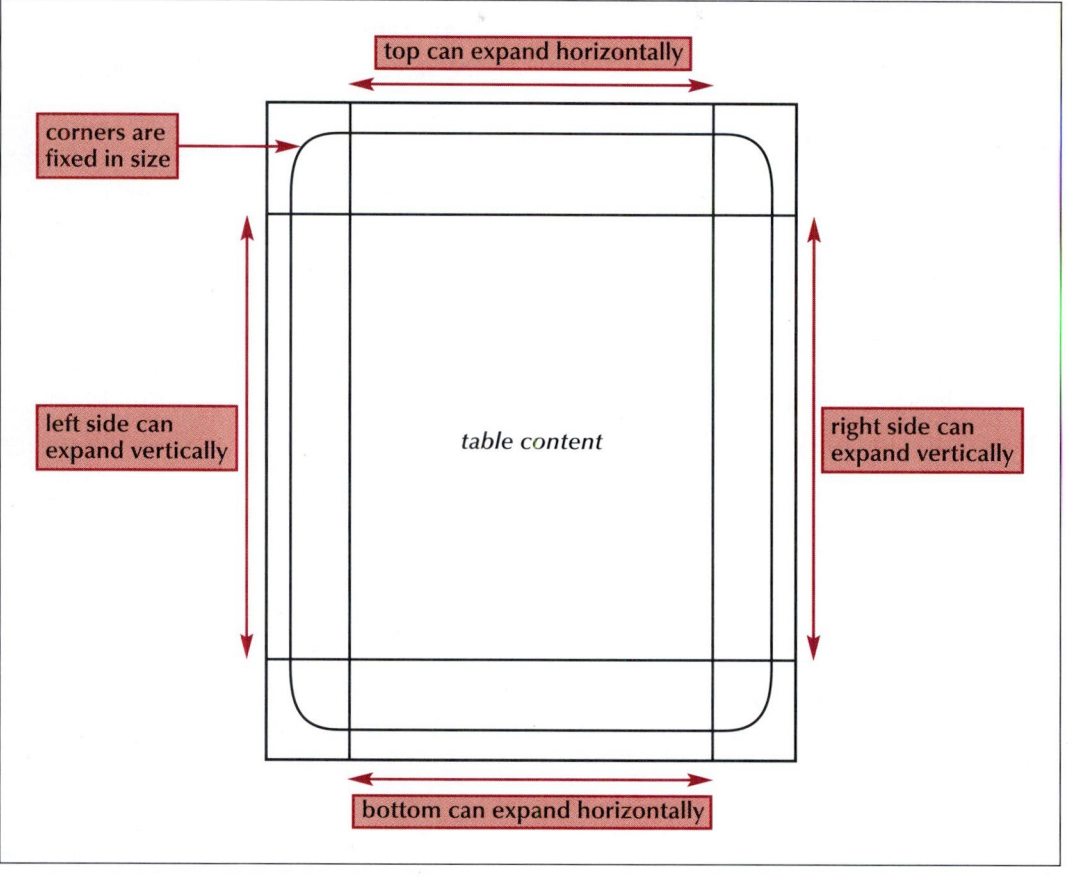

Each cell still must be large enough to display the border image files, which you'll add shortly. For example, the corner cells must be 16 pixels wide by 16 pixels high. The style for the top-left corner cell would therefore be:

```
table.roundedBox td.topLeft {width: 16px; height: 16px}
```

On the other hand, the top border is free to expand horizontally, but it must be tall enough to display the top border image. Its style would be:

```
table.roundedBox td.top {width: auto; height: 16px}
```

Remember that a width or height value of auto allows the browser to change the element to match the content. The other six border cells have similar width and height values. Add these styles to the rounded.css style sheet.

To set the dimensions of the outside cells:

► **1.** To set the dimensions of the four corner cells, add the following styles to the bottom of the **rounded.css** style sheet:

```
table.roundedBox td.topLeft      {width: 16px; height: 16px}
table.roundedBox td.topRight     {width: 16px; height: 16px}
table.roundedBox td.bottomLeft   {width: 16px; height: 16px}
table.roundedBox td.bottomRight  {width: 16px; height: 16px}
```

► **2.** For the top and bottom cells, add the styles:

```
table.roundedBox td.top      {width: auto; height: 16px}
table.roundedBox td.bottom   {width: auto; height: 16px}
```

3. Finally, for the left and right cells, add the styles:

```
table.roundedBox td.left          {width: 16px; height: auto}
table.roundedBox td.right         {width: 16px; height: auto}
```

Figure 5-62 highlights the styles of the eight cells on the outside edge of the table.

Figure 5-62 | **Setting cell widths and heights**

```
table.roundedBox     {margin: 5px; border-collapse: collapse}
table.roundedBox td {padding: 0px}
```

corner cells →
```
table.roundedBox td.topLeft      {width: 16px; height: 16px}
table.roundedBox td.topRight     {width: 16px; height: 16px}
table.roundedBox td.bottomLeft   {width: 16px; height: 16px}
table.roundedBox td.bottomRight  {width: 16px; height: 16px}
```

top and bottom cells →
```
table.roundedBox td.top          {width: auto; height: 16px}
table.roundedBox td.bottom       {width: auto; height: 16px}
```

left and right cells →
```
table.roundedBox td.left         {width: 16px; height: auto}
table.roundedBox td.right        {width: 16px; height: auto}
```

You won't set a width or height for the boxContent cell because that should expand to match whatever content you place inside.

Adding the Rounded Border

The last part of the jigsaw table is to put background images in the eight outside cells. Kyle has created eight separate files that cover the four corners and four sides of the box. The files—named topleft.png, top.png, topright.png, left.png, right.png, bottomleft.png, bottom.png, and bottomright.png—are shown in Figure 5-63.

Figure 5-63 | **The layout of the eight border images**

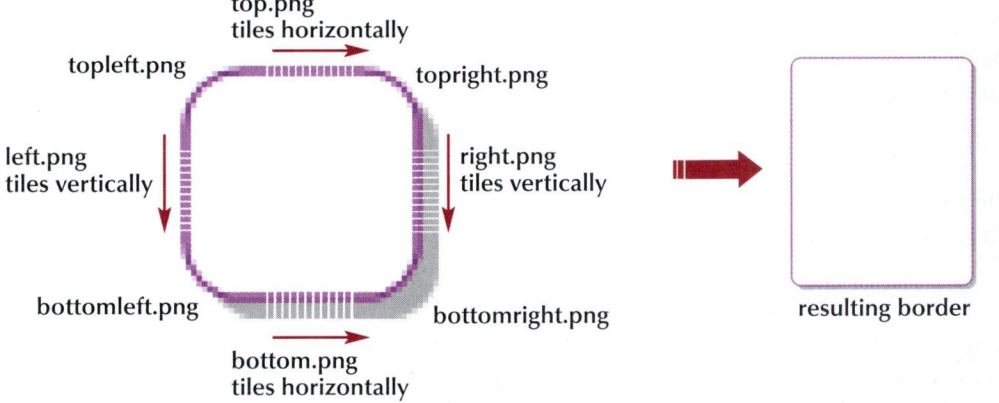

Each background image is tiled in a different way. The left and right images are tiled only in the vertical direction, filling up the entire background of the left and right cells. The top and bottom images are tiled horizontally, filling up the backgrounds of the top and bottom cells. Finally, the corner cells do no tiling, remaining fixed.

So to set the background of the top-left corner cell, you would use the following background style:

```
.topLeft {background: url(topleft.png) no-repeat top left}
```

Note that this style places the topleft.png image without tiling and fixes it in the top-left corner of the cell (if you're unclear about the background style, review the material on background styles from Tutorial 3). The style for the top border would appear as:

```
.top {background: url(top.png) repeat-x top}
```

Here the background image starts at the top of the cell and tiles in the x or horizontal direction only. The style for the left border would appear as

```
.left {background: url(left.png) repeat-y left}
```

with the tiling done only in the y or vertical direction.

Notice this style is applied to any element belonging to the topLeft, top, or left classes. This is not an accident. Later in this session, you'll reuse these background image styles, applying them to page elements other than table cells.

Add these styles to the rounded.css style sheet to insert and tile the eight background images for the roundedBox table.

Tip

If you have an object with a fixed width and height, you can create a rounded border with a single background image. If the object can vary in size, break the border graphic into separate pieces in a jigsaw layout.

To add the table background images to the style sheet:

▶ 1. Go to the bottom of the **rounded.css** style sheet and add the following styles to set the background images for the four corner cells:

```
.topLeft {background: url(topleft.png) no-repeat top left}
.topRight {background: url(topright.png) no-repeat top right}
.bottomLeft {background: url(bottomleft.png) no-repeat bottom left}
.bottomRight {background url(bottomright.png) no-repeat bottom right}
```

▶ 2. Add the styles for the top and bottom cell backgrounds:

```
.top {background: url(top.png) repeat-x top}
.bottom {background: url(bottom.png) repeat-x bottom}
```

▶ 3. Finally add the background images for the left and right cells:

```
.left {background: url(left.png) repeat-y left}
.right {background: url(right.png) repeat-y right}
```

Figure 5-64 shows the newly inserted style code.

Setting the background images for the eight corners ◀ **Figure 5-64**

```
table.roundedBox      {margin: 5px; border-collapse: collapse}
table.roundedBox td {padding: 0px}

table.roundedBox td.topLeft      {width: 16px; height: 16px}
table.roundedBox td.topRight     {width: 16px; height: 16px}
table.roundedBox td.bottomLeft   {width: 16px; height: 16px}
table.roundedBox td.bottomRight  {width: 16px; height: 16px}

table.roundedBox td.top          {width: auto; height: 16px}
table.roundedBox td.bottom       {width: auto; height: 16px}

table.roundedBox td.left         {width: 16px; height: auto}
table.roundedBox td.right        {width: 16px; height: auto}
```

corners →
```
.topLeft     {background: url(topleft.png) no-repeat top left}
.topRight    {background: url(topright.png) no-repeat top right}
.bottomLeft  {background: url(bottomleft.png) no-repeat bottom left}
.bottomRight {background: url(bottomright.png) no-repeat bottom right}
```

top and bottom sides →
```
.top         {background: url(top.png) repeat-x top}
.bottom      {background: url(bottom.png) repeat-x bottom}
```

left and right sides →
```
.left        {background: url(left.png) repeat-y left}
.right       {background: url(right.png) repeat-y right}
```

▶ 4. Save your changes to the file.

Adding the Box Content

Now that you've created the styles that define the size and backgrounds of the eight outside cells, you can enter sample text into the roundedBox table. You'll test your styles by first inserting some simple text to verify that you have not made any errors in entering the table tags or CSS styles.

To enter sample text into the box:

1. Return to the **schedule.htm** file in your text editor.

2. Locate the center cell in the roundedBox table and insert the following text, as shown in Figure 5-65.

   `Coming Up on KPAF`

Figure 5-65 | Inserting the sample text

```
            <address>
               KPAF &#183;
               4300 Magnolia Lane &#183;
               Bismarck, ND 58504 &#183;
               (701) 555 - 5611
            </address>

         </div>

         <div id="right_col">
            <table class="roundedBox">
               <tr>
                  <td class="topLeft"></td>
                  <td class="top"></td>
                  <td class="topRight"></td>
               </tr>
               <tr>
                  <td class="left"></td>
                  <td class="boxContent">Coming Up on KPAF</td>
                  <td class="right"></td>
               </tr>
               <tr>
                  <td class="bottomLeft"></td>
                  <td class="bottom"></td>
                  <td class="bottomRight"></td>
               </tr>
            </table>
         </div>

   </body>
```

3. Save your changes to the file, and then reload **schedule.htm** in your Web browser. As shown in Figure 5-66, the sample text is displayed within a rounded box that is tightly fit to the text.

Figure 5-66 | Sample text placed in a rounded box

> Coming Up on KPAF

Trouble? If your box does not resemble the box shown in Figure 5-66, check your style sheet code against the code shown in Figure 5-64. Make sure you have separated all of the style values with semicolons, that you have entered all of the background image file names correctly, and that you have the images correctly tiled.

The advantage of the table design you've created is that it's flexible and will expand to match the content you place in the center cell.

You've tested your code against the sample text; now you can replace that text with the complete list of upcoming KPAF programs. Kyle has already written HTML code listing upcoming KPAF programs and has created a style sheet for that list. You can copy and paste that code directly into the rounded box table and then link the page to Kyle's style sheet.

To insert the descriptions of upcoming programs at KPAF:

1. In your text editor, open the **newshows.txt** file from the tutorial.05\tutorial folder included with your Data Files.

2. Copy all of the HTML code describing upcoming KPAF programs.

3. Return to the **schedule.htm** file in your text editor and scroll down to the bottom of the file.

4. Paste the copied HTML code into the center table cell, replacing the sample text you just entered (you might want to insert a line break into your text file to make the new code easier to read). Figure 5-67 shows the newly inserted code.

Inserting the text of the upcoming KPAF programs ◀ **Figure 5-67**

```
<td class="boxContent">
<h1 class="newshows">Coming Up on KPAF</h1>

<ul class="newshows">
    <li>
        <h2 class="newshows">April 11 - 14</h2>
        <h3 class="newshows">The Classical Music Connection</h3>
        <p>Peter Thiesen shares his eclectic
            selections from the world of classical
            music.</p>
    </li>
    <li>
        <h2 class="newshows">April 11</h2>
        <h3 class="newshows">Opera Fest</h3>
        <p>Excerpts from <i>Turandot</i> by Giacomo Puccini.</p>
    </li>
    <li>
        <h2 class="newshows">April 12</h2>
        <h3 class="newshows">Radio U</h3>
        <p>Novelist Karen Graves reads from her latest
            work, <i>Hellion of Troy</i>.</p>
    </li>
    <li>
        <h2 class="newshows">April 13</h2>
        <h3 class="newshows">Science Week</h3>
        <p>Prof. Thomas Glass from UND discusses
            <i>String Theory and Spooky Action at a Distance</i>.</p>
    </li>
    <li>
        <h2 class="newshows">April 14</h2>
        <h3 class="newshows">The Living World</h3>
        <p>A panel discussion on
            the <i>Return of the Electric Car</i> and the latest
            in eco-news.</p>
    </li>
</ul>
</td>
```

Styles for the list of upcoming shows are contained in the newshows.css style sheet that Kyle created. You need to add a link to this style sheet to the schedule.htm file.

5. Scroll to the top of the file. Directly above the closing </head> tag, insert the following link element:

```
<link href="newshows.css" rel="stylesheet" type="text/css" />
```

6. Save your changes to the file, and then reload **schedule.htm** in your Web browser. As shown in Figure 5-68, the list of upcoming KPAF programs is presented in a box with rounded corners.

Figure 5-68 **The upcoming programs sidebar**

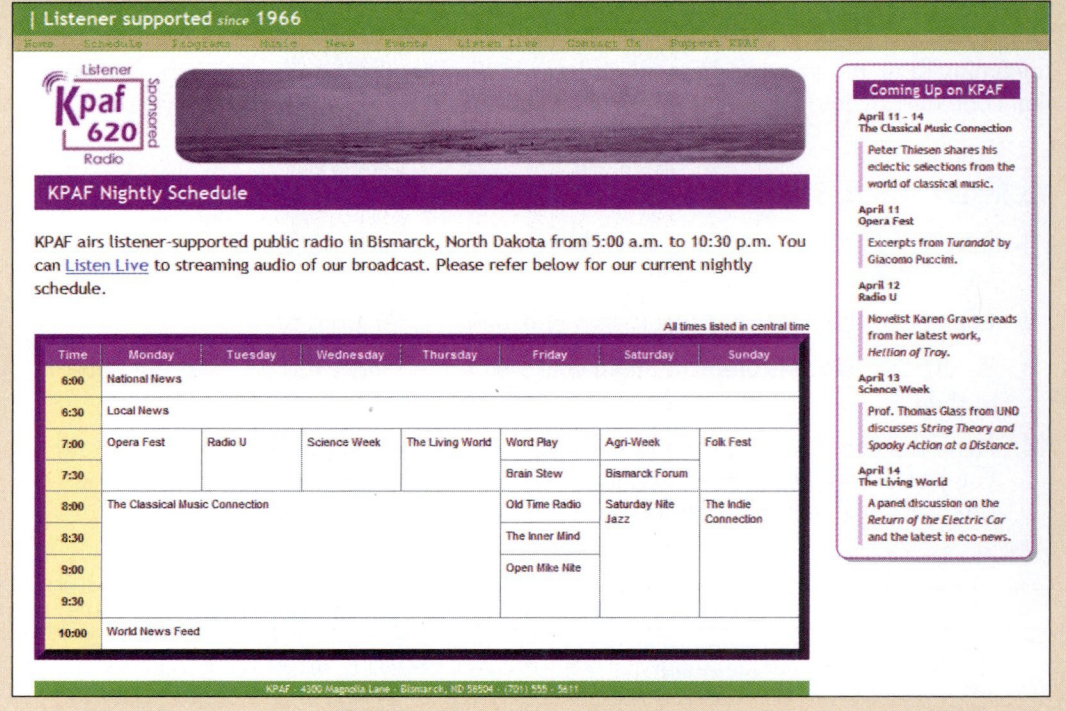

As you expected, the box expanded to fit the contents of the program list without showing any seams in the rounded border. Kyle is happy to know that this design can be easily adapted to any page content and complements you on your work.

Kyle wonders whether you should use Web tables to design other parts of his Web site. He asks you which is better for doing page layout: div containers or Web tables? You'll explore this question next.

Exploring the Controversy over Table Layouts

Using Web tables for page layout predates the introduction of CSS, and for many years the technique was one of the essential tools of the Web page designer. However, this changed with the introduction of CSS, which held the promise of simplifying the process of Web page design. But browser support for CSS was scattered and inconsistent at first, so many designers were reluctant to give up their Web table layouts. Then as more browsers began to support CSS and in particular the CSS positioning styles, Web designers began to advise against using Web tables for page layout—arguing that tables should be reserved for strictly tabular data, such as the KPAF program schedule. There are several good reasons for this:

- **Table layouts are not in the spirit of HTML**. A basic philosophy of Web page design is that the HTML code should indicate the structure of the document, but not how it should be rendered by the browser. Tables take control of layout from style sheets, putting page design back into the HTML file.

- **Table layouts are difficult to revise**. Imagine a complex table layout consisting of two columns with several levels of additional tables nested within each column. Now imagine having to revise that table structure, changing it into a three-column layout. This would not be an easy task because the page content is intertwined with the page layout. Now further imagine the difficulty of having to repeat that design change for dozens of pages across a large Web site. On the other hand, a layout created with a properly designed style sheet is much easier to maintain and revise because it is separate from the page content.
- **Tables take longer to render**. Unless the size of every element in the table is specified, the browser needs to first load the table content and then run an algorithm to determine how to size each element of the table. This can be time-consuming for a large, complex table that involves many cells and nested elements.
- **Tables can be code-heavy**. Creating a visually striking table layout often requires several table cells, rows, and columns, and some nested tables. This is particularly true if you create a jigsaw layout. Therefore, the ratio of HTML code to actual page content becomes more heavily weighted toward the HTML code, resulting in a longer file that takes longer to load and that can be difficult to interpret by people who need to edit the underlying code.
- **Tables can be inaccessible to users with disabilities**. People who use an aural or Braille browser to access a Web page formatted with a table layout can find it difficult to interpret the page content. The problem is that screen readers and speech output browsers read the HTML source code line-by-line in a linear direction, but tables sometimes convey information in several different directions. Figure 5-69 shows how a table whose content is quite clear visually becomes jumbled when presented aurally. This example shows the problems associated with a simple 3x3 table; comprehending a truly complex table layout with several levels of nested tables might be insurmountable to the visually impaired. On the other hand, an aural style sheet could be written that would more easily convey this information.

Aural browsers and tables Figure 5-69

```
<table>
   <tr>
      <th>Time</th>
      <th>Thursday</th>
      <th>Friday</th>
   </tr>
   <tr>
      <th>7:00</th>
      <th colspan="2">The Living World</th>
      <th>World Play</th>
   </tr>
   <tr>
      <th>7:30</th>
      <th>Brain Stew</th>
   </tr>
</table>
```

HTML table code

With the current strong browser support for CSS, there is less reason to use tables for page layout. In fact, the jigsaw layout shown earlier in Figure 5-56 could also be done using div containers positioned on the Web page with CSS. However, Web table layouts will not disappear immediately, so Web page designers must be conversant with both approaches, especially if they are called upon to support older browser versions or have the task of maintaining the code of an older Web site.

Creating a Rounded Box Using div Containers

You tell Kyle what you've learned about the controversy over Web table layouts and he agrees that the KPAF Web site should limit the use of tables to strictly tabular information. Kyle wants to add another rounded box to the schedule page, one that displays the name and description of the program currently running on KPAF. He understands your concern about using table layouts and asks whether you can create the same rounded box design using only div containers and CSS styles. As with your work on the table layout, whatever you create must be flexible enough to accommodate content of any size.

After researching the issue on the Internet, you discover there are actually hundreds of techniques that Web designers have developed over the years to create rounded borders without using tables. You decide to use one that was introduced by the Web designer Tedd Sperling (*www.sperling.com*).

Nesting div Containers

The basic idea of Tedd Sperling's approach is to nest several levels of div elements within one another. Since the div elements have no padding and no margin spaces, they will be completely superimposed upon one another—creating a stack of div elements that all occupy the same space on the Web page. Because they're stacked on top of each other, when these div elements are displayed by the browser, any background image from an element lower in the stack will be visible as long as it is not obstructed by another background image higher in the stack. Figure 5-70 shows how eight different background images from eight nested div elements would appear as a single curved border when rendered by the browser.

| Figure 5-70 | Creating a rounded border using nested div elements |

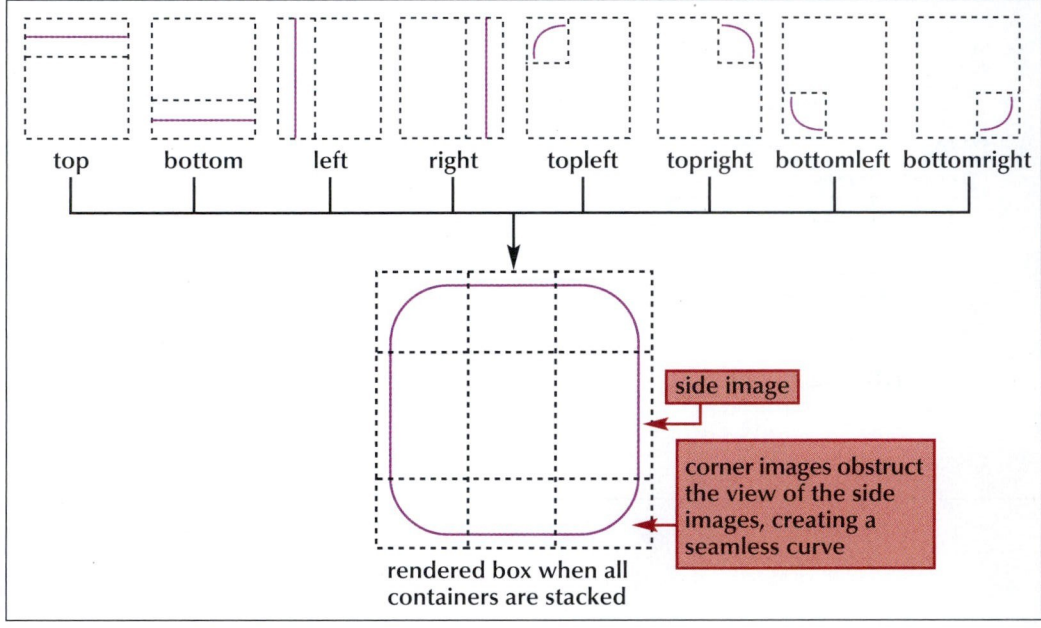

top   bottom   left   right   topleft   topright   bottomleft   bottomright

side image

corner images obstruct the view of the side images, creating a seamless curve

rendered box when all containers are stacked

Notice that the corner images obstruct the view of the side images, so that it appears as one seamless curve around the content. To create this effect in HTML, you can nest these eight div elements

```
<div class="top"><div class="bottom">
<div class="left"><div class="right">
<div class="topLeft"><div class="topRight">
<div class="bottomLeft"><div class="bottomRight">
   <div class="boxContent">
      content
   </div>
</div></div></div></div>
</div></div></div></div>
```

where *content* is the page content you would surrounded by the rounded border. The order of the div elements is important. The corner borders must be on top of the stack because they connect the side borders, and so you list the top, bottom, left, and right sides first. The div elements for the corners (topleft, topright, bottomleft, and bottomright) are nested within them. When the browser renders these elements, it starts from the outside and moves in. The corners are therefore displayed last, appearing on top of the side borders.

Add this basic structure of nested div elements to the schedule.htm page.

To insert the div containers:

1. Return to the **schedule.htm** file in your text editor.

2. Scroll down to the bottom of the file and directly after the opening tag

   ```
   <div id="right_col">
   ```

   insert the following code as shown in Figure 5-71:

   ```
   <div class="roundedBox">
      <div class="top"><div class="bottom">
      <div class="left"><div class="right">
      <div class="topLeft"><div class="topRight">
      <div class="bottomLeft"><div class="bottomRight">

         <div class="boxContent">
         </div>

      </div></div></div></div>
      </div></div></div></div>
   </div>
   ```

Creating a set of nested div elements | **Figure 5-71**

```
<div id="right_col">

   <div class="roundedBox">
      <div class="top"><div class="bottom">
      <div class="left"><div class="right">
      <div class="topLeft"><div class="topRight">
      <div class="bottomLeft"><div class="bottomRight">

         <div class="boxContent">
         </div>

      </div></div></div></div>
      </div></div></div></div>
   </div>

   <table class="roundedBox">
      <tr>
         <td class="topLeft"></td>
         <td class="top"></td>
         <td class="topRight"></td>
      </tr>
```

3. Save your changes to the file.

You might have noticed that you repeated the same class names used earlier in Figure 5-58. That's no accident—the eight div elements fulfill the same role of creating the rounded border as the eight table cells did in the table layout. Also, because you assigned background images to any element belonging to the topLeft, topRight, and so forth classes, these div elements will have the same background images as the table cells did in the roundedBox table. The only thing you must add to this set of div elements is a style to place a 5-pixel margin around the roundedBox and 16 pixels of padding space to the boxContent element. Finally, because of how Internet Explorer treats nested div elements, you'll place the box using relative positioning to ensure that all of the nested div elements line up properly in that browser. Add these styles to the rounded.css file.

To define the style for the box and its contents:

1. Return to the **rounded.css** file and insert the following style to define the appearance of the containing box:

   ```
   div.roundedBox {margin: 5px; position: relative}
   ```

2. Add the following style to set the display properties of the box's content:

   ```
   div.boxContent {padding: 16px}
   ```

   Figure 5-72 shows the final style definitions for the rounded box style sheet.

Figure 5-72 | Defining the styles for the box contents

```
.topLeft      {background: url(topleft.png) no-repeat top left}
.topRight     {background: url(topright.png) no-repeat top right}
.bottomLeft   {background: url(bottomleft.png) no-repeat bottom left}
.bottomRight  {background: url(bottomright.png) no-repeat bottom right}

.top          {background: url(top.png) repeat-x top}
.bottom       {background: url(bottom.png) repeat-x bottom}

.left         {background: url(left.png) repeat-y left}
.right        {background: url(right.png) repeat-y right}

div.roundedBox {margin: 5px; position: relative}
div.boxContent {padding: 16px}
```

3. Close the **rounded.css** file, saving your changes.

4. Reload the **schedule.htm** file in your Web browser. The page should now show an empty rounded box directly above the list of upcoming programs.

   Kyle asks that you add text to this box describing the program currently airing on KPAF.

5. Return to the **schedule.htm** file in your text editor and insert the following code within the boxContent div element as shown in Figure 5-73:

   ```
   <h1 class="newshows">On the Air Now</h1>
   <h2 class="newshows">Folk Fest</h2>
   <p class="newshows">Featuring the best of traditional and
           contemporary folk music</p>
   ```

Adding text for the current program ◄ **Figure 5-73**

```
<div class="roundedBox">
   <div class="top"><div class="bottom">
   <div class="left"><div class="right">
   <div class="topLeft"><div class="topRight">
   <div class="bottomLeft"><div class="bottomRight">

   <div class="boxContent">
      <h1 class="newshows">On the Air Now</h1>
      <h2 class="newshows">Folk Fest</h2>
      <p  class="newshows">Featuring the best of traditional
         and contemporary folk music</p>
   </div>

   </div></div></div></div>
   </div></div></div></div>
</div>
```

6. Save your changes to the file, and then reload **schedule.htm** in your Web browser. As shown in Figure 5-74, the name of the program currently airing on KPAF is shown in a rounded box at the top of the page.

The final KPAF nightly schedule page ◄ **Figure 5-74**

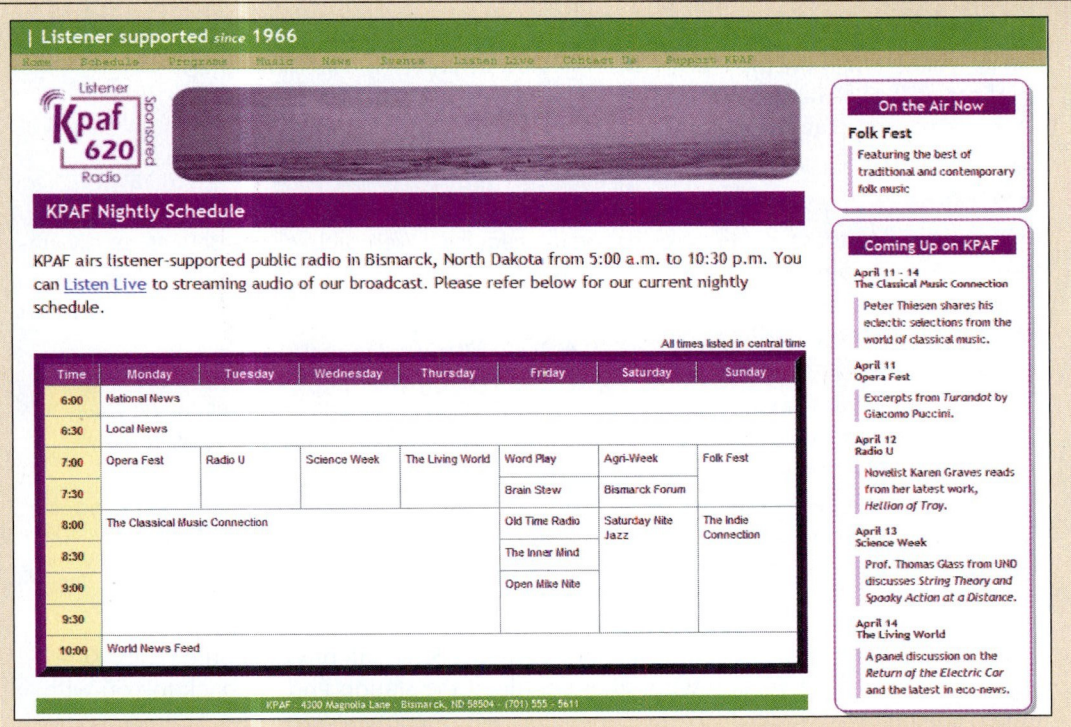

Trouble? If your rounded box does not resemble that shown in Figure 5-74, check your style code against that shown in Figure 5-72 and Figure 5-73. Common errors include misspelling class names, forgetting to separate style properties with semi-colons, neglecting to close style declarations with right curly braces, and misspelling the names of style properties.

7. You can close any open files or programs now.

Kyle will talk to the KPAF programmers to write code that will automatically insert the name of the currently airing program into the rounded box you created, but for now this gives him a good idea of how the page will look to KPAF listeners.

InSight | **Rounded Boxes and CSS3**

The Web is a competitive environment in which designers are always looking for ways to make their pages stand out. One way is with specialized design elements like the rounded box you created in this session. Such designs can be challenging the first few times. One reason is that CSS 2.1 allows only one background image per element, so you have to "trick" browsers into displaying several images at once. How much easier the task would be if you could place multiple background images that automatically resized with the element!

This is starting to change with the introduction and adoption of CSS3 styles. In CSS3, you can define multiple backgrounds by entering them in a comma-separated list for the background-image style. The syntax is

```
background image: url(image1), url(image2), ...
```

where *image1*, *image2*, and so forth are the image files you want displayed as a background for the element. To position the images, you once again enter a comma-separated list of position values matching the background image. For example, the style

```
background-position: top left, center left
```

places the first background image in the top-left corner of the element and the second image on the center-left edge. As you increase the number of background images, you add more background-position values, one for each image.

Finally, you specify how the images are repeated by entering each repeat property in another list. The style

```
background-repeat: no-repeat, repeat-y
```

fixes the first background image in place and tiles the second image in the vertical direction.

You can see from these styles that what would require a Web table or several nested div elements can be accomplished in CSS3 with one element and a style sheet. CSS3 will also introduce styles to allow for more decorative borders, including rounded borders. To create a rounded border, you will be able to apply the style

```
border-radius: value
```

where *value* defines the curvature of the rounded corners of the border. This style has scattered browser support at the moment, though Firefox does support the following equivalent style:

```
-moz-border-radius: value
```

CSS3 is still in the development stage, so you cannot rely on it yet for designing Web sites. However, as these and other CSS3 styles are finalized and adopted by the browser market, designers will explore new possibilities for their Web sites.

You've completed your work on the design of the KPAF nightly schedule page. Kyle will discuss your final version with other people at the station and get back to you with future projects.

Review | **Session 5.3 Quick Check**

1. What is a jigsaw layout?
2. You are creating a table structure for a table that will be used to develop a jigsaw layout. One of the cells in the table with the id midCell needs to have a height of 20 pixels, but the width can be calculated by the browser. Specify a style to apply to the midCell table cell.
3. Why are tables especially challenging for the visually impaired?
4. You want to use the image tlcorner.jpg as the top-left background corner image for a div element with the id mainLogo. What style would you enter?

5. A div element with the id name subLogo needs to use a background image for the left side border. The div element could be any height, so the image will need to tile vertically down the element. The image comes from the file lborder.jpg. Specify a style to apply this image to the element's background.

6. You want to use an image file named bborder.jpg as the bottom border for the div element mainContent. The width of the mainContent element can vary freely, so the image file will need to tile horizontally across the element. Specify the style you would use.

7. An old Web page uses a table with one row and two columns to create a two-column layout. The Web site manager wants to move away from using table layouts. Suggest two ways of creating a two-column layout without tables.

Tutorial Summary | Review

In this tutorial you learned how to create and design Web tables, and you explored the issues surrounding using tables for page layout. The first session introduced the basic structure of the Web table. You learned how to define table rows, table cells, row groups, column groups, and captions. The session also explored how to create cells that span multiple rows and columns. The session concluded by introducing the summary attribute as a way of making table content accessible in nonvisual browsers. The second session explored how to format a table's appearance. The first half of the session looked at various HTML attributes that have long been used to format tables. The second half of the session concentrated on the CSS styles that can be applied to tables. The session ended by showing how to use CSS to make almost any page element appear as a table. The third session looked at the special topic of creating page boxes with rounded borders. The first method examined was the use of a Web table to lay out the graphical borders of the box. The second method explored how to do the same thing with nested div elements. The third session discussed the advantages and disadvantages of using tables for page layout and examined the prevalence of table-based designs on the Web today.

Key Terms

cell padding	monospace font	table data cell
cell spacing	preformatted text	table frame
column group	row group	table heading
jigsaw layout	spanning cell	table rule

| Practice | **| Review Assignments** |

Practice the skills you learned in the tutorial using the same case scenario.

Data Files needed for the Review Assignments: kpaf.css, kpaf.jpg, left.jpg, morningtxt.htm, programstxt.css, right.jpg, topleft.jpg, and topright.jpg

Kyle has had a chance to work with the KPAF nightly schedule page. He wants you to make a few changes to the layout and apply the new design to a page that displays the KPAF morning schedule. Kyle has already entered much of the Web page content and style. He wants you to complete his work by creating the Web table with the morning schedule. He wants you to add some rounded and shaped corners to the table to make it stand out more on the page. Figure 5-75 shows a preview of the table you'll create for Kyle.

Figure 5-75

Complete the following:

1. Use your text editor to open the **morningtxt.htm** and **programstxt.css** files from the tutorial.05\review folder included with your Data Files. Enter *your name* and *the date* in the comment section of each file. Save the files as **morning.htm** and **programs.css**, respectively, in the same folder.
2. Go to the **morning.htm** file in your text editor. Insert a link to the **programs.css** style sheet.

3. Scroll down the file and directly below the paragraph element, insert a Web table with the class name programs.

4. Add a caption containing the text "All times central".

5. Below the caption, create a column group containing three columns. The first column element should have the class name timeColumn. The second column element should have the class name daysColumn and span six columns in the table. The last column element should have the class name lastColumn.

6. Insert the following summary for the table: "Lists the morning programs aired by KPAF from 5:00 a.m. to 12:00 p.m. (central time)".

7. Add the table header row group containing the headings shown in Figure 5-75.

8. Enter the tbody row group containing the times and names of the different KPAF programs from 5:00 a.m. to 12:00 p.m., Monday through Sunday, in half-hour intervals. Create row- and column-spanning cells to match the layout of the days and times shown in Figure 5-75.

9. Assign the cell in the top-left corner of the table the id name topLeft. Assign the cell in the top-right corner the id name topRight.

10. Close the **morning.htm** file, saving your changes.

11. Go to the **programs.css** file in your text editor. Create the following styles for the programs table:
    - Set the width of the table to 100%.
    - Display the table text according to the following list of fonts: Trebuchet MS, Arial, Verdana, and sans-serif.
    - Set the table borders to collapse.

12. Align the table caption with the bottom-right border of the table. Set the caption font size to 0.8 em.

13. Add the following styles for the table cells:
    - Set all table cells to a font size of 0.7 em.
    - Vertically align the text of all table data cells with the top of the cell.
    - Add a 1-pixel solid gray border to the left and bottom of every table data cell.
    - Add a 1-pixel solid gray border to the bottom of every table header cell.

14. Set the height of all table rows to 25 pixels.

15. Display the header row group in white font with a background color of (105, 177, 60).

16. Add the following styles for the three column types in the table:
    - Set the width of the timeColumn to 7%. Change the background color to the value (215, 205, 151). Add the background image file **left.jpg** to the column, repeated vertically and set against the left border of the column.
    - Set the width of the columns in the dayColumns group to 13%.
    - Set the width of the lastColumn column to 13%. Set the background color to white and add the background image file **right.jpg**, tiled vertically and set against the right border of the column.

17. For the table cell with the id topLeft, set the background color to the value (105, 177, 60) and add the background image file **topleft.jpg** set against the top-left corner of the cell. Do not tile the background image.

18. For the table cell with id topRight, set the background color also to the value (105, 177, 60) and add the background image file **topright.jpg**. Set the background image against the top-right border of the cell and do not tile the image.

19. Save your changes to the **programs.css** file.

20. Open the **morning.htm** file in your Web browser and verify that the table layout and design resembles that shown in Figure 5-75. (Note: If you are using Internet Explorer, you might see the caption aligned with the top-right corner of the table rather than the bottom-right.)

21. Submit your completed files to your instructor.

Apply	**Case Problem 1**

Apply your knowledge of Web tables and table styles to create a puzzle page.

Data Files needed for this Case Problem: gold.jpg, green.jpg, jpf.jpg, jpftxt.css, left.jpg, stabletxt.css, sudokutxt.htm, topleft.jpg, and topright.jpg

The Japanese Puzzle Factory Rebecca Peretz has a passion for riddles and puzzles. Her favorites are the Japanese logic puzzles that have become very popular in recent years. Rebecca and a few of her friends have begun work on a new Web site called The Japanese Puzzle Factory (JPF), where they plan to create and distribute Japanese-style puzzles. Eventually the JPF Web site will include interactive programs to enable users to solve the puzzles online, but for now Rebecca is interested only in the design and layout of the pages. You've been asked to help by creating a draft version of the Web page describing the Sudoku puzzle. Figure 5-76 shows a preview of the design and layout you'll create for Rebecca.

Figure 5-76

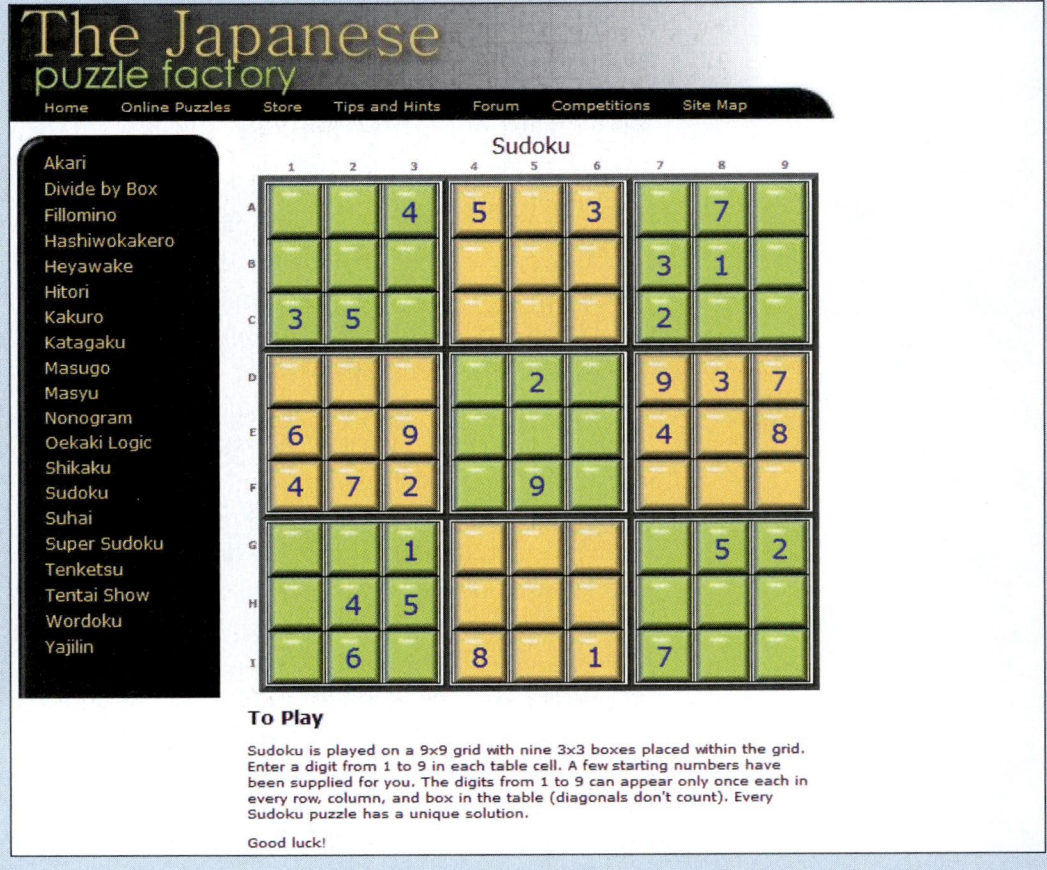

Rebecca has created some of the content and designs for this page. Your task is to complete the page by entering the code and styles for the Sudoku table as well as adding some background images to other sections of the page layout.

Complete the following:

1. Use your text editor to open the **jpftxt.css**, **stabletxt.css**, and **sudokutxt.htm** from the tutorial.05\case1 folder included with your Data Files. Enter *your name* and *the date* in the comment section of each file. Save the files as **jpf.css**, **stable.css**, and **sudoku.htm**, respectively, in the same folder.

2. Return to the **sudoku.htm** file in your text editor. Add a link to the **jpf.css** and **stable.css** style sheets.

3. Scroll down to the links div element. Rebecca wants the list of links to have rounded top corners and a shaded left corner. Mark the corner and sides by nesting the ul element within three div elements with class names of left, topLeft, and topRight.

4. Save your changes to the file, and then go to the **jpf.css** style sheet in your text editor. At the bottom of the style sheet, add the following styles:
   - For the div element belonging to the topLeft class, display the background image file **topleft.jpg** in the top-left corner of the element. Do not tile the image.
   - For the div element from the topRight class, display the background image file **topright.jpg** in the top-right corner without tiling.
   - For the div element from the left class, display the **left.jpg** background image file placed on the left border of the element and tiled in the vertical direction only.

5. Save your changes to the file, and then display the **sudoku.htm** file in your Web browser. Verify that the list of Japanese puzzles on the left margin of the page is displayed with rounded top corners and a shaded left border.

6. Return to the **sudoku.htm** file in your text editor. Scroll down to the rightColumn div element. Directly below the opening <div> tag, insert a table element that will be used to display the Sudoku puzzle. Give the table element the class name spuzzle.

7. Add a caption to the spuzzle table containing the text Sudoku.

8. Create a table head row group containing a single row. The row should display 10 heading cells. The first heading cell should be blank and the remaining nine cells should display the digits from 1 to 9.

9. Create the table body row group. The tbody should contain the following structure:
   - There are nine rows in the tbody.
   - The first cell in each row should contain a table heading cell displaying the letters A through I.
   - Starting with the first row, every third row should contain three table data cells with each cell spanning three rows and three columns. All together, these table cells will store the nine 3x3 boxes that are part of the Sudoku puzzle.
   - In the first row, put the three table data cells in the greenBox, goldBox, and greenBox classes, respectively. In the fourth row, the three data cells belong to the goldBox, greenBox, and goldBox classes. In the seventh row, the three data cells belong to the greenBox, goldBox, and greenBox classes.

⊕ EXPLORE

10. Go to each of the nine table data cells you created in the last step. Within each data cell, insert a nested table belonging to the subTable class. Within each nested table, insert three rows and three columns of data cells. Enter the digits from Figure 5-76 in the appropriate table cells. Where there is no digit, leave the table cell empty.

11. Save your changes to the file, and then go to the **stable.css** file in your text editor.

12. Collapse the borders of the spuzzle and subTable tables.

13. Add a 5-pixel outset gray border to the data cells within the spuzzle table. Set the font size of header cells within the spuzzle table to 8 pixels and the font color to gray. Set the height of header cells within the body row group of the spuzzle table to 40 pixels.

14. For data cells within the subTable table, add the following styles:
    - Set the font size to 20 pixels and the font color to blue.
    - Set the width and height to 40 pixels and center the cell text both horizontally and vertically.
    - Add a 1-pixel solid black border around the cell.

15. For table cells nested within the goldBox class of table cells, apply the background image file gold.jpg centered within the cell and not tiled (*Hint*: Use background position values of 50% for both the horizontal and vertical directions.) For cells nested within the greenBox class of table cells, set the background image to the green.jpg file, once again centered within the cell without tiling.

16. Save your changes to the file and then reload **sudoku.htm** in your Web browser. Verify that the layout and design of the Sudoku table resembles that shown in Figure 5-76.

17. Submit your completed files to your instructor.

Apply	**Case Problem 2**

Create a calendar table for a community civic center.

Data Files needed for this Case Problem: bottom.jpg, bottomleft.jpg, bottomright.jpg, caltxt.css, ccc.jpg, ccctxt.css, febtxt.htm, left.jpg, right.jpg, tab.jpg, top.jpg, topleft.jpg, and topright.jpg

The Chamberlain Civic Center   Lewis Kern is an events manager at the Chamberlain Civic Center in Chamberlain, South Dakota. The center is in the process of updating its Web site and Lewis has asked you to work on the pages detailing events in the upcoming year. He's asked you to create a calendar page for the month of February. Lewis wants the page design to catch the reader's eye and so he suggests that you create a Web table with a background showing a spiral binding. The spiral binding graphic must be flexible to accommodate calendars of different sizes, so you'll build the borders for this image by nesting the February calendar table within eight div elements. The February calendar must list the following events:

- Every Sunday, the Carson Quartet plays at 1:00 p.m. ($8)
- February 1, 8:00 p.m.: Taiwan Acrobats ($16/$24/$36)
- February 5, 8:00 p.m.: Joey Gallway ($16/$24/$36)
- February 7-8, 7:00 p.m.: West Side Story ($24/$36/$64)
- February 10, 8:00 p.m.: Jazz Masters ($18/$24/$32)
- February 13, 8:00 p.m.: Harlem Choir ($18/$24/$32)
- February 14, 8:00 p.m.: Chamberlain Symphony ($18/$24/$32)
- February 15, 8:00 p.m.: Edwin Drood ($24/$36/$44)
- February 19, 8:00 p.m.: The Yearling ($8/$14/$18)
- February 21, 8:00 p.m.: An Ellington Tribute ($24/$32/$48)
- February 22, 8:00 p.m.: Othello ($18/$28/$42)
- February 25, 8:00 p.m.: Madtown Jugglers ($12/$16/$20)
- February 28, 8:00 p.m.: Ralph Williams ($32/$48/$64)

Lewis wants the weekend events (Friday and Saturday night) to be displayed with a light red background. A preview of the page you'll create is shown in Figure 5-77.

Figure 5-77

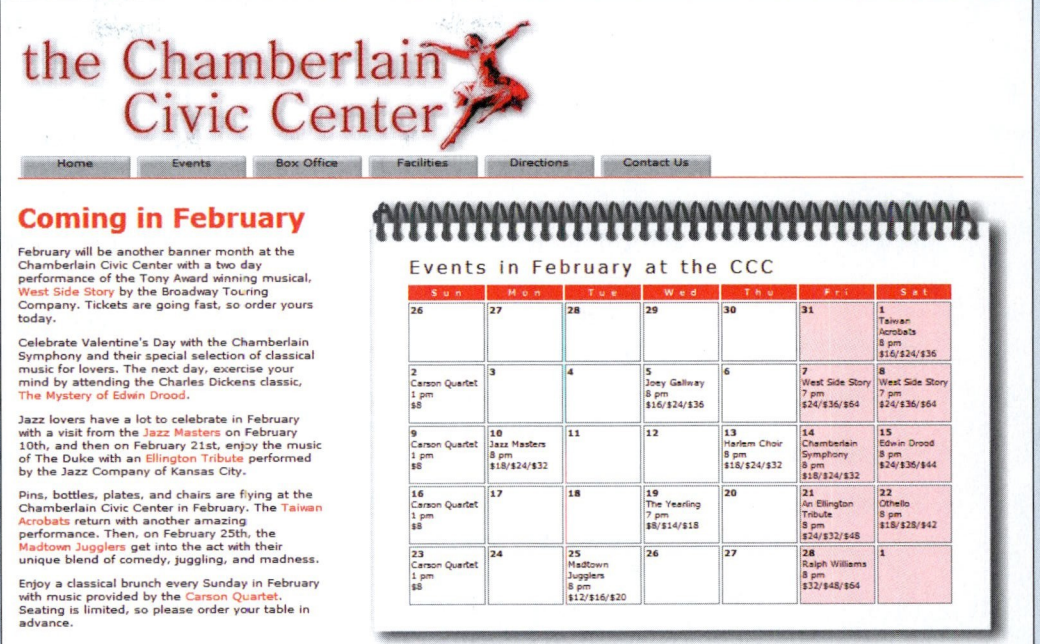

Complete the following:

1. Use your text editor to open the **caltxt.css**, **ccctxt.css**, and **febtxt.htm** from the tutorial.05\case2 folder included with your Data Files. Enter *your name* and *the date* in the comment section of each file. Save the files as **calendar.css**, **ccc.css**, and **feb.htm**, respectively, in the same folder.

2. Go to the **feb.htm** file in your text editor. Create links to the **calendar.css** and **ccc.css** style sheets.

3. Scroll down to the rightColumn div element. Within the div element, insert a table with the class name calendar. Add the caption "Events in February at the CCC" to the calendar.

4. Create a column group for the calendar consisting of two col elements. The first col element should belong to the weekdays class and span five columns. The second col element should belong to the weekends class and span two columns.

5. Create a table header row group consisting of one row of table headings displaying the three-letter abbreviations of the days of the week, starting with Sun and ending with Sat.

6. Create a table body row group containing the days in the month of February. The row group should contain five rows and seven columns of table data cells. There are no spanning cells in any of the rows or columns.

7. Each table data cell should have the following content:
   - The day of the month marked as an h3 heading (refer to Figure 5-77 for the starting and ending days in the calendar).
   - On the days in which there is a CCC event, enter the event information as a definition list with the name of the event marked as a dt element, and the time and price of the event each marked with dd elements.

8. Enclose the entire table within a set of nine nested div elements. The four outermost elements should have the ids tBorder, lBorder, rBorder, and bBorder. The next four innermost elements should have the ids tlCorner, trCorner, blCorner, and brCorner. The innermost div element should have the id boxContent.

9. Save your changes to the file, and then go to the **ccc.css** file in your text editor.

10. Apply the following background image styles to the eight div container elements:

   - For the tlCorner element, display the **topleft.jpg** image in the top-left corner of the element without tiling.
   - For the trCorner element, display the **topright.jpg** image in the top-right corner without tiling.
   - For the blCorner element, display the **bottomleft.jpg** image in the bottom-left corner without tiling.
   - For the brCorner element, display the **bottomright.jpg** image in the bottom-right corner without tiling.

EXPLORE
   - For the tBorder element, display the **top.jpg** image 39 pixels from the left edge aligned at the top border, tiling the image horizontally.
   - For the lBorder element, display the **left.jpg** image on the left border and tiled vertically.
   - For the rBorder element, display the **right.jpg** image on the right border and tiled vertically.
   - For the bBorder element, display the **bottom.jpg** image on the bottom border and tiled horizontally.

11. Set the padding space of the boxContent div element to 50 pixels.

12. Save your changes to the file, and then go to the **calendar.css** file in your text editor. Add the table styles described in the next steps to the style sheet.

EXPLORE
13. Display the borders of the table as separate borders with the space between the borders set to 5 pixels. Set the font size of the table text to 8 pixels.

14. Align the table caption with the top left of the calendar table. Set the font size of the caption to 16 pixels and the letter spacing to 3 pixels.

15. Set the width of the table columns to 14% of the width of the table. For columns belonging to the weekend class, change the background color to the value (255, 232, 232).

16. For table headings in the table header row group of the calendar table, set the background color to red, the font color to white, and the letter spacing to 5 pixels.

17. Set the height of the table row within the table header row group of the calendar table to 5%. Set the height of the table rows within the table body row group to 19% each.

18. Add a 1-pixel solid gray border to every table data cell within the calendar table. Set the vertical alignment of the cell content to the top of the cell.

19. Set the font size of h3 headings with the data table cells of the calendar table to 8 pixels and set the margin and padding spaces of the h3 headings to 0 pixels.

20. Set the margin and padding spaces of the definition list, definition descriptions, and definition terms within the tables to 0 pixels.

21. Save your changes to the file, and then open **feb.htm** in your Web browser. Verify that the layout and design of the page resemble that shown in Figure 5-77.

22. Submit your completed files to your instructor.

| Challenge | **Case Problem 3** |

Explore additional CSS table styles and image techniques by designing the home page for a manufacturer of geodesic domes.

Data Files needed for this Case Problem: blank.gif, bottom.jpg, bottomleft.jpg, bottomright.jpg, dhometxt.htm, dlogo.jpg, domepaper.css, dometxt.css, dtabletxt.css, left.jpg, leftbox.jpg, right.jpg, rightbox.jpg, tableback.jpg, top.jpg, topleft.jpg, and topright.jpg

dHome, Inc. Olivia Moore is the director of advertising for dHome, one of the nation's newest manufacturers of geodesic dome houses. She's hired you to work on the company's Web site. Olivia has provided you with all of the text you need for the Web page, and your job is to design the page's layout. You'll start by designing a draft of the company's home page. Olivia wants the page to include information about dHome's pricing structure for various dome models. The page should also contain links to other pages on the Web site. A preview of the design you'll create for Olivia is shown in Figure 5-78.

Figure 5-78

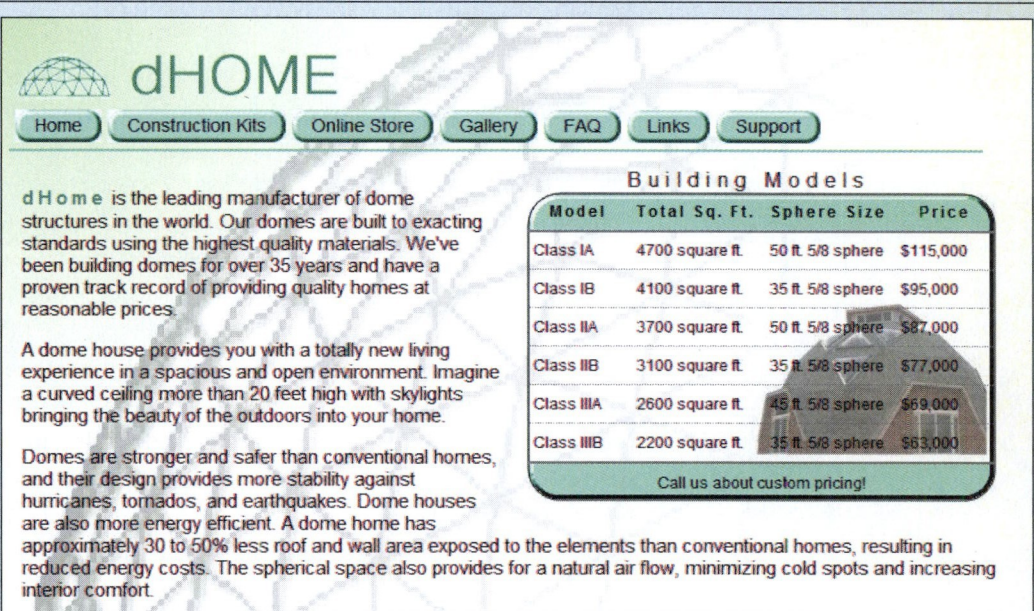

Complete the following:

1. Use your text editor to open **dhometxt.htm**, **dometxt.css**, and **dtabletxt.css** from the tutorial.05\case3 folder included with your Data Files. Enter *your name* and *the date* in the comment section of each file. Save the files as **dhome.htm**, **dome.css**, and **dtable.css**, respectively, in the same folder.

2. Go to the **dhome.htm** file in your text editor. Create links to the **dome.css** and **dtable.css** style sheets.

3. Scroll down to the pageContent div element, and above the paragraphs within that element, insert a table with the class name domeSpecs. Add the table summary, "A table describing six dome models sold by dHome, Inc." and add the caption, "Building Models".

4. Create a column group containing three col elements with class names of firstColumn, middleColumns, and lastColumn. The middleColumns element should span two columns in the table.

5. Create a table header row group containing a single table row with four table heading cells. The cells should contain the headings Model, Total Sq. Ft., Sphere Size, and Price. Mark the first cell with the id value topLeft and the last cell with the id value topRight.

EXPLORE

6. Insert a table footer row group containing a single row and three data cells. The first and third cells should be left blank. The middle cell should contain the text, "Call us about custom pricing!" and should span two columns. Mark the first cell with the id bottomleft and the last cell with the id bottomright.

7. Create the table body row group consisting of six table rows with four cells each. Insert the model, square feet, sphere size, and price values from Figure 5-78.

8. Save your changes to the **dhome.htm** file, and then go to the **dome.css** file in your text editor.

9. Many of the styles for the dHome Web page have been entered for you. Your job is to insert styles for the list of links. Make the following style changes to the unordered list within the links div element:
   - Remove the bullet marker.
   - Set the padding space to 0 pixels.
   - Set the top and left margins to 5 pixels and the right and bottom margins to 0 pixels.

10. Make the following style changes to the list elements:
    - Change the list items to inline objects, floating on the left margin.
    - Set the font size to 14 pixels and the right margin to 5 pixels.
    - Display the background image file **rightbox.jpg**, placed on the center of the right margin. Do not tile the image.

11. Make the following changes to hypertext links within list elements:
    - Display the hypertext links as block-level elements.
    - Set the font color to black and remove underlining from the links.
    - Set the top and bottom padding space to 10 pixels and the left and right padding spaces to 15 pixels.
    - Display the background image file **leftbox.jpg**, placed on the center of the left margin. Do not tile the image.

12. Change the font color of the hyperlinks within the list element to blue whenever the mouse pointer hovers over the link.

13. Save your changes to the file, and then load **dhome.htm** in your Web browser. Verify that the list of links is displayed in a single line below the dHome logo and that each link is enclosed within a rounded box of varying lengths.

EXPLORE

14. The technique used to create the rounded box behind the links is known as the *sliding door* technique. Open the **rightbox.jpg** and **leftbox.jpg** files in a graphics program and notice that the rightbox.jpg image file is extremely long compared to the text it lies behind. Why is the entire image not displayed? (Hint: Think about how the hypertext links are nested within list elements.) Look up the sliding door technique on the Web to learn more about this approach.

15. Go to **dtable.css** in your text editor. Create a style for the domeSpecs table that floats the table on the right border, sets the font size to 12 pixels, and sets the top and right margins to 0 pixels, the bottom margin to 10 pixels, and the left margin to 20 pixels. Collapse all the borders in the table.

16. Create a style for the caption, setting the font size to 16 pixels and the kerning to 5 pixels. Center the caption horizontally above the table.

17. Set the width of the first and last columns to 22% of the width of the table. Set the width of the middle columns to 28% of the table width.
18. Make the following style changes to the table row groups:

EXPLORE

   - Add a 2-pixel-wide solid gray border to the bottom of the table head row group.
   - Add a 2-pixel-wide solid gray border to the top of the table footer row group and center the text of the table footer.
   - Add a 1-pixel dotted gray border to the table rows within the table body row group.
19. Make the following style changes to individual table cells and rows:
   - Set the padding of all table cells to 0 pixels above and 5 pixels on the sides.
   - Set the kerning of the table heading cells to 2 pixels.
   - Set the height of all table rows to 30 pixels.

EXPLORE 20. Add the following background images to the table:
   - Apply the **left.jpg** image as a background for the first table column, placed on the left border of the column and tiled vertically.
   - Apply the **blank.gif** image as a background for the middle table columns tiled in all directions.
   - Apply the **right.jpg** image as a background for the last column, placed on the right border and tiled vertically.
   - Apply the **top.jpg** image to the table header row group, placed on the top border of the object and tiled horizontally.
   - Add the **tableback.jpg** image to the background of the entire table, placed at the 98%, 70% position with no tiling.
   - Add the **topleft.jpg**, **topright.jpg**, **bottomleft.jpg**, and **bottomright.jpg** image files to the background corners of the topLeft, topRight, bottomLeft, and bottomRight table cells. Do not tile the images.
21. Save your changes to the **dtable.css** file, and then open the **dhome.htm** file in the Firefox, Opera, or Safari browsers. Verify that the design of the table resembles that shown in Figure 5-78. (Note: Internet Explorer is unable to display the borders within the three row groups.)
22. Submit your completed files to your instructor.

| Create | **Case Problem 4** |

Create a Web page describing room reservations at a popular conference center.

Data Files needed for this Case Problem: bottom.png, bottomleft.png, bottomright.png, hcclogo.jpg, left.png, right.png, rooms.txt, top.png, topleft.png, and topright.png

Hamilton Conference Center   Yancy Inwe is the facilities manager at the Hamilton Conference Center in Hamilton, Ohio. The conference center, a general-use facility for the community, hosts several organizations and clubs as well as special events and shows by local vendors. The center has recently upgraded its intranet capabilities and Yancy would like to create a Web site where employees and guests can easily track which conference rooms are available and which are being used. She would like this information displayed in a table that lays out the room use from 8:00 a.m. to 5:00 p.m. for seven rooms and halls. Eventually this process will be automated by the conference's Web server, but for now she has come to you for help in setting up a sample Web page layout and design.

Complete the following:

1. Use your text editor to create an HTML file named **conference.htm** and two style sheets named **hcc.css** and **schedule.css**. Enter *your name* and *the date* in a comment section of each file. Include any other comments you think aptly document the purpose and content of the files. Save the files in the tutorial.05\case4 folder included with your Data Files.

2. Use the text files provided to create a Web page containing the reservation information. The design of the Web page is up to you and you may supplement your Web page with any material you feel is appropriate. Place any CSS styles you design for the page in the **hcc.css** style sheet.

3. Create a table containing the room reservation information. The table structure should contain the following elements:
   - A table caption and summary
   - Table row and column groups
   - Examples of row- and/or column-spanning cells
   - Examples of both table heading and table data cells

4. Create a style for your table in the **schedule.css** style sheet. The layout and appearance of the table is up to you, but it should include the following:
   - A border style applied to one or more table objects
   - Multiple background colors
   - Use of horizontal and vertical alignment of the table cell contents
   - Different widths applied to different table columns
   - Styles applied to the table caption

5. Add a rounded-box object to your final Web page. You may use nested div elements, a Web table, or another approach to create the rounded border effect. You may use the border style graphics included in the tutorial.05\case4 folder included with your Data Files, or you may find or create your own.

6. Test your Web site on a variety of browsers to ensure your design works under different conditions.

7. Submit your completed files to your instructor.

Review | Quick Check Answers

Session 5.1

1. The number of columns is determined by the maximum number of cells within the table rows.

2. Horizontally centered and in a bold font

3. `<table border="10"> ... </table>`

4. `<td colspan="3" rowspan="2">Monday</td>`

5. You have to reduce the number of cells in the row to accommodate the spanning cell.

6. Because styles that are applied to the table element will be inherited by the caption.

7. thead, tfoot, and tbody (they should be specified in that order).

8.
```
<colgroup>
<col span="2" class="introCol" />
<col class="col1" />
<col class="col2" />
<col class="col3" />
</colgroup>
```

9. To provide more information to visually impaired users whose browsers have difficulty interpreting text in a tabular form.

Session 5.2

1. `<table cellspacing="10"> ... </table>`
2. `<table border="1" rules="none"> ... </table>`
3. `rules="cols"`
4. `border-collapse: collapse`
5. 6-pixel solid border because it is the border with the larger width
6. the row group
7. `th {vertical-align: bottom}`
8. `caption {caption-side: bottom}`
9. `ul {display: table}`

   `ul li {display: table-cell}`

Session 5.3

1. A layout in which the page content is broken down into smaller pieces which are then reassembled like pieces from a jigsaw puzzle
2. `#midCell {height: 20px; width: auto}`
3. Table text is read as it appears in the browser code, which can be confusing to users who cannot see the relationship between the rows and columns of the table.
4. `#mainLogo {background: url(tlcorner.jpg) no-repeat 0% 0%}`
5. `#subLogo {background: url(lborder.jpg) repeat-y 0% 0%}`
6. `#mainContent {background: url(bborder.jpg) repeat-x 0% 100%}`
7. You could float two div elements on the page's left page or you could place the div elements using absolute positioning.

Ending Data Files

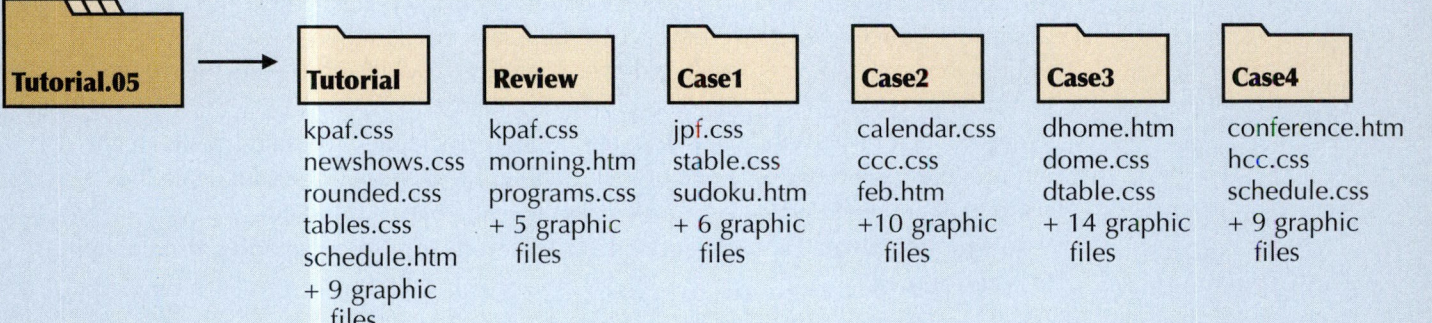

Tutorial.05 →	**Tutorial**	**Review**	**Case1**	**Case2**	**Case3**	**Case4**
	kpaf.css	kpaf.css	jpf.css	calendar.css	dhome.htm	conference.htm
	newshows.css	morning.htm	stable.css	ccc.css	dome.css	hcc.css
	rounded.css	programs.css	sudoku.htm	feb.htm	dtable.css	schedule.css
	tables.css	+ 5 graphic	+ 6 graphic	+10 graphic	+ 14 graphic	+ 9 graphic
	schedule.htm	files	files	files	files	files
	+ 9 graphic					
	files					

Reality Check

The Web is a valuable source of information and it is particularly valuable for those who want to learn how to write Web pages. Each Web site presents an opportunity to study how other Web page designers solved problems involving layout and design. And most Web designers are eager to share the methods, techniques, and sometimes tricks they've used to get the most out of HTML, CSS, and an occasional uncooperative browser. In this exercise, you'll use the skills and tasks you learned in Tutorials 3 through 5 to create a Web site on a hobby or personal interest of yours. First you'll research and evaluate the techniques of published Web page designers.

Please be sure *not* to include any personal information of a sensitive nature in the files you create to be submitted to your instructor for this exercise. Later on, you can update the files with such information for your personal use.

1. Web designers have come up with a variety of approaches to creating two-, three-, and four-column layouts. Search the Web for designer pages and report on the different techniques designers have used to create these classic layouts.

2. In the course of your research, you'll come across information on fixed and liquid layouts. Summarize the two approaches and compare each one's advantages and disadvantages.

3. The W3C specifications for HTML and CSS represent a "gold standard" by which all browsers are rated. Do a Web search to determine the browsers that provide the best support for the W3C specifications. Which browsers provide the poorest level of support?

4. Designers must come up with work-arounds or "hacks" to deal with the incompatibilities between browsers in implementing HTML and CSS. Search the Web and come up with three different hacks that designers use in their Web sites. Describe each hack and the problem it solves.

5. Locate a Web page whose content and layout you enjoy. Take some time to download the underlying HTML and CSS code and reconstruct exactly how the Web designer created the page. A few caveats: be respectful about your use of copyrighted material and avoid large and over-complicated Web sites. A site for a large company or organization would be difficult to interpret.

6. When you're finished studying the page's code, recreate the layout and design techniques on a page describing one of your hobbies or interests. Try to duplicate the same look and feel (as much as possible) of the site that you studied.

7. Save your completed Web site and the answers from your research and present them to your instructor.

Objectives

Session 6.1
- Explore how Web forms interact with Web servers
- Create form elements
- Create field sets and legends
- Create input boxes and form labels

Session 6.2
- Creation option buttons
- Create selection lists
- Create check boxes
- Create text area boxes
- Apply styles to Web forms

Session 6.3
- Work with form buttons
- Explore image elements and hidden fields
- Work with form actions and methods

Working with Web Forms

Creating a Donation Form

Case | The Lighthouse

Terry Ives is the director of The Lighthouse, a community center in St. Peters, Missouri. The Lighthouse provides social services, focusing on drug addiction counseling, job placement, child care, and tutoring disadvantaged youths. The Lighthouse's mission is broad and challenging, and as a nonprofit organization, money is always tight.

You've been volunteering at the center for several months, helping to upgrade the Web site's design and adding new features that will make the site more useful for clients, volunteers, and donors. Terry would like your help with one important feature: creating a page for online donations. She knows that many social service organizations receive a good percentage of their donations online; therefore, she's been working with an Internet service provider (ISP) to find out how to facilitate secure online donations. She has learned that the donations page needs a Web form that can be used to transfer payment data to the ISP's Web server for processing. Terry has asked you to create a Web form that will supply the server with the needed financial data.

Starting Data Files

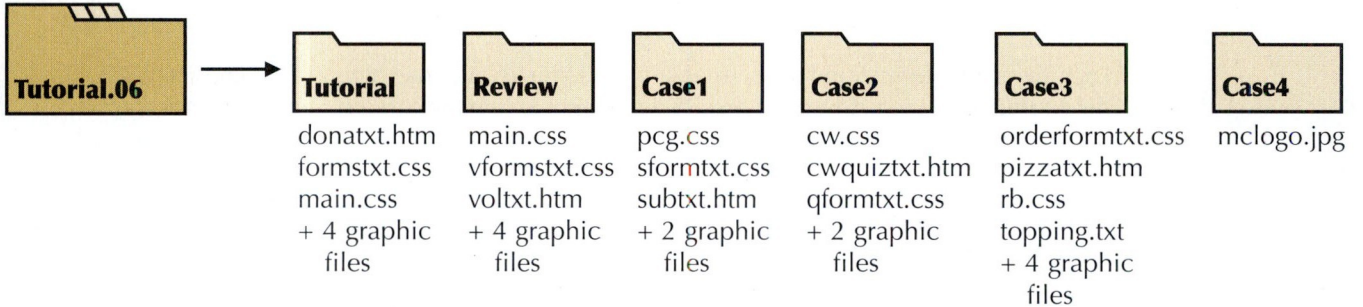

Tutorial.06 →	Tutorial	Review	Case1	Case2	Case3	Case4
	donatxt.htm	main.css	pcg.css	cw.css	orderformtxt.css	mclogo.jpg
	formstxt.css	vformstxt.css	sformtxt.css	cwquiztxt.htm	pizzatxt.htm	
	main.css	voltxt.htm	subtxt.htm	qformtxt.css	rb.css	
	+ 4 graphic files	+ 4 graphic files	+ 2 graphic files	+ 2 graphic files	topping.txt	
					+ 4 graphic files	

Session 6.1

Introducing Web Forms

You meet with Terry to discuss the new donations page for The Lighthouse's Web site. She sketches out the appearance of a form shown in Figure 6-1 that she would like to display on the center's Web site.

Figure 6-1   **Terry's proposed donations form**

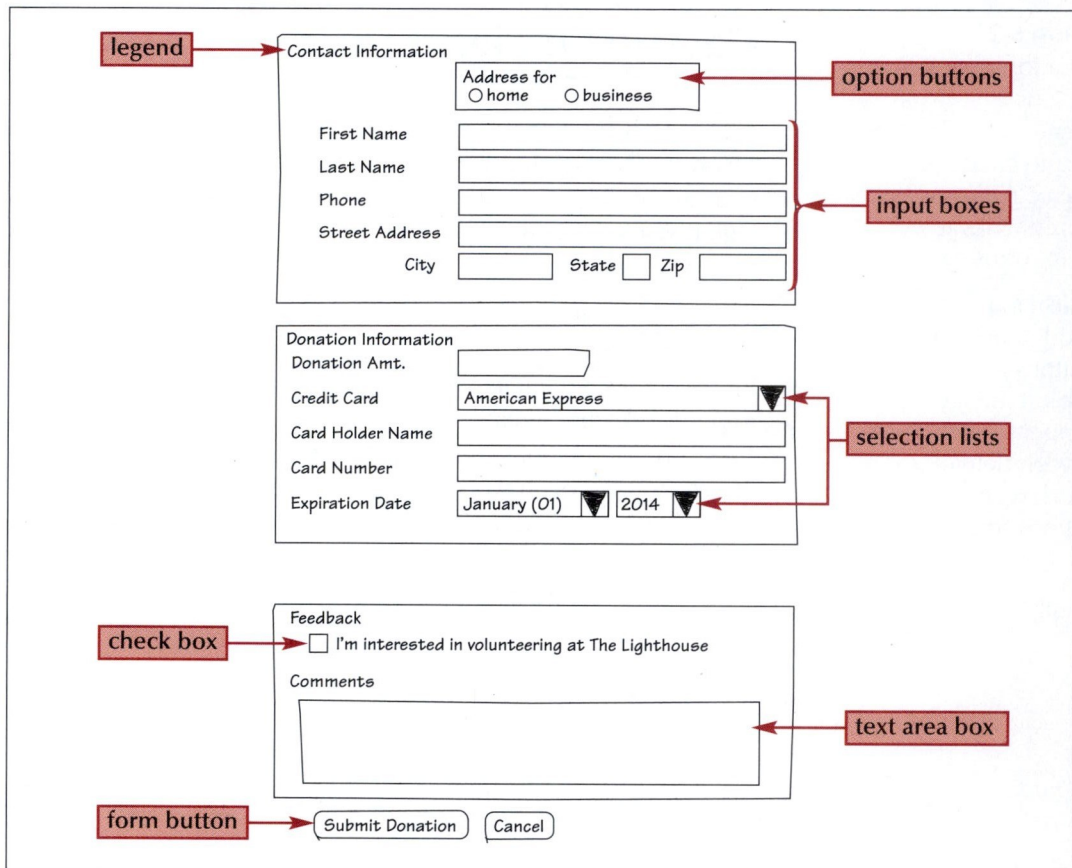

The form is divided into three topical areas. The first requests contact information from the donor, including the donor's name, phone number, and mailing address. In the second part of the form, the donor specifies the amount of the donation and provides credit card information. The final part of the form is reserved for any comments the donor has and offers a check box where donors can indicate an interest in volunteering at the center.

Parts of a Web Form

Each piece of information for a form is stored in a **field**, and the value itself is known as the **field value**. In some fields, users are free to enter anything they choose, while other fields are limited to a set of possible values. Users enter or select a field value using **control elements**, which are buttons, boxes, lists, and so on, that provide a way of associating a field value with a particular field. HTML supports the following control elements:

• **input boxes** for text and numerical entries

- **option buttons**, also called **radio buttons**, for selecting a single option from a predefined list
- **selection lists** for long lists of options, usually appearing in a **drop-down list box**
- **check boxes** for specifying yes or no
- **text areas** for extended entries that can include several lines of text

Terry's donation form includes several examples of these different control elements, each one associated with a particular field. As you'll see later, users will enter their first and last names in the firstName and lastName fields through the use of an input box control element. They'll indicate their credit card through the use of a selection list.

Forms and Server-Based Programs

Before you start work on Terry's Web form, you should understand how forms are processed on the Web. As shown in Figure 6-2, the Web form is used to collect information, but the data itself is stored and analyzed using a program running on a Web server.

The interaction between the Web form and the Web server ◄ Figure 6-2

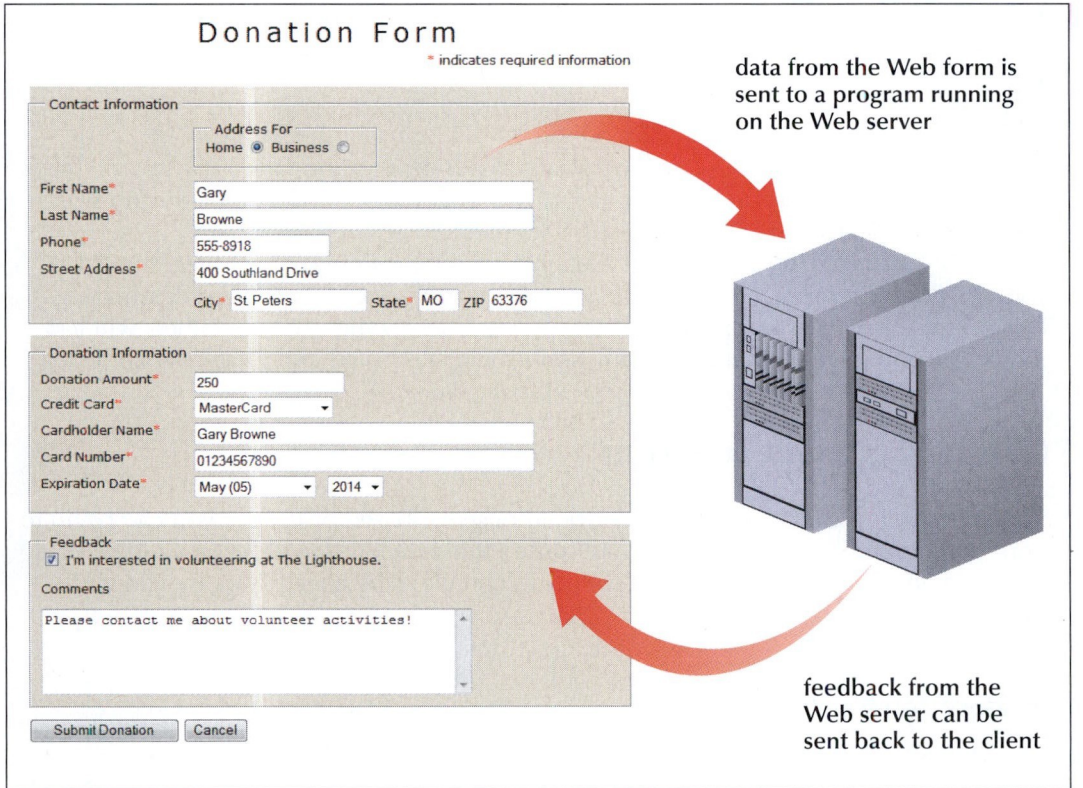

data from the Web form is sent to a program running on the Web server

feedback from the Web server can be sent back to the client

The pairing of server-based programs and Web forms early in the development of HTML represented a dramatic shift in how the Web was perceived and used. By giving users access to programs that react to user input, the Web became a more dynamic environment where companies and users could interact. Server-based programs have made many things possible, including:

- online databases containing customer information
- online catalogs for ordering and purchasing merchandise
- dynamic Web sites with content that is constantly modified and updated
- message boards for hosting online discussion forums

Because these programs run on Web servers, rather than locally, you might not have permission to create or edit them. Instead, you'll receive information about how to interact with the programs on the Web server. This usually includes a list of fields that are required by the program and a description of the type of values expected in those fields. The Web form code needs to work in conjunction with the requirements of the server-based program.

There are several reasons to restrict direct access to these programs. The primary reason is that when you run a server-based program, you are interacting directly with the server environment. Mindful of the security risks that computer hackers present and the drain on system resources caused by large numbers of programs running simultaneously, system administrators are understandably careful to maintain strict control over their servers and systems. Otherwise, people could use malicious code to inject programming into the server and possibly change the prices of items or degrade the performance of the server.

Server-based programs are written in a variety of languages. The earliest and most common of these languages are called **Common Gateway Interface (CGI) scripts**, written in a language called **Perl**. Other popular languages widely used today for writing server-based programs include:

- ASP
- ColdFusion
- C/C++
- PHP
- VBScript

Which language your Web form will interact with depends on your Web server. Check with your ISP or system administrator to find out what programs are available and what rights and privileges you have in working with them.

The ISP that hosts The Lighthouse's Web site has scripts in place to receive the data from the donation form and process it. You will not have access to these programs, so Terry just wants you to work with the Web form portion of this process. Others will test your Web form to verify that the information is being collected and processed correctly.

Creating a Web Form

Now that you're familiar with the background of server-based programs, you can begin to work on Terry's donation form. Terry has created the design of the page, leaving the right column empty for the form. Your job will be to complete the page by adding the Web form. Open Terry's document now.

To view Terry's document:

► 1. Start your text editor, and then open the **donatxt.htm** file located in the tutorial.06\tutorial folder included with your Data Files. Enter *your name* and *the date* in the comment section of the file. Save the file as **donations.htm** in the same folder.

► 2. Review the file to become familiar with its contents and structure, and then open the file in your Web browser. Figure 6-3 shows the current appearance of the page.

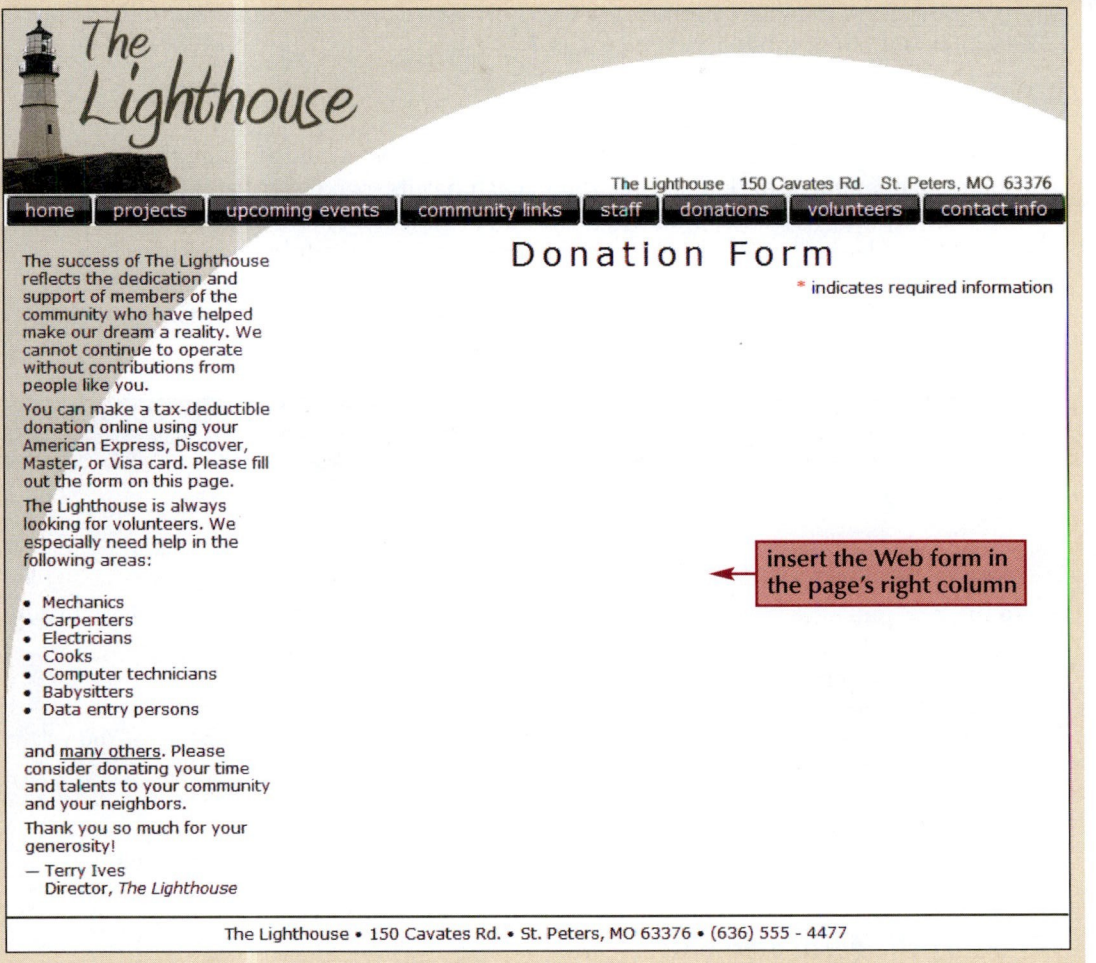

The initial donations page — Figure 6-3

Terry suggests that you insert the Web form in the page's right column. She has already inserted a heading above where she wants the form to appear. Forms are created using the form element

```
<form attributes>
    elements
</form>
```

where *attributes* are the attributes that name the form and control how it is processed, and *elements* are the elements placed within the form. Forms typically contain many of the control elements that were discussed earlier, but can also contain page elements such as tables, paragraphs, inline images, and headings. The form element can be placed anywhere within the HTML file and a single page can contain multiple forms.

Form attributes tell the browser the location of the server-based program to be used on the form's data, how that data is to be transferred to the script, and so forth. These attributes are not needed when first designing the form, and it's actually useful to omit them at first. This prevents you from accidentally running the program on an unfinished form, causing the Web server to process incomplete information. After you've finalized the form's appearance, you can add the attributes required by the server program. You'll have a chance to do this in the last session of this tutorial.

Two attributes identify the form: the id attribute and the name attribute. Naming a form is useful for pages that contain multiple forms so you can differentiate one form from another, and it might be required for server-based programs that accept form values. The syntax of both of these attributes is

```
<form name="name" id="id"> . . . </form>
```

where *name* is the name of the form, and *id* is the id of the form. Although these two attributes might appear to do the same thing, each has its own history and role. The name attribute represents the older standard for form identification, and so is often required for older browsers and older server programs. The id attribute, on the other hand, represents the current standard under HTML and XHTML for identifying a form. For maximum compatibility with older and newer browsers and CGI scripts, you should include both attributes, setting them to the same value.

Reference Window | **Inserting a Web Form**

- To insert a Web form, add the elements
  ```
  <form attributes>
      elements
  </form>
  ```
  to the Web page, where *attributes* are the attributes that name the form and control how it is processed, and *elements* are the elements placed within the form.
- To identify the form, add the attributes
  ```
  id="id" name="name"
  ```
  to the opening <form> tag, where *id* is the form id and *name* is the form name. You will often set these attributes to the same value.

You are ready to add a form element named donationForm to Terry's Web page.

To insert the form element:

1. Return to the **donations.htm** file in your text editor and scroll down the file to the rightColumn div container.

2. Insert the following form element within the rightColumn div container, as shown in Figure 6-4.

   ```
   <form name="donationForm" id="donationForm">
   </form>
   ```

Figure 6-4 | **Inserting a form element**

```
<div id="rightColumn">
    <h1>Donation Form</h1>
    <p><span>*</span> indicates required information</p>

    <form name="donationForm" id="donationForm">
    </form>

</div>
```

With the form element added to the donations page, you can start populating it with control elements and other form features. You'll start by adding field sets.

Creating a Field Set

A Web form like the donation form can have dozens of different fields. One way of organizing a form is to group similar fields into **field sets**. When rendered by the browser, a field set usually appears as a box surrounding the fields, separating those fields from other field sets. Field sets are created using the fieldset element, which has the syntax

```
<fieldset id="id">
   controls
</fieldset>
```

Tip

Field sets make it easier for users with aural browsers and screen readers to navigate your Web form.

where *id* identifies the field set and *controls* are the control elements associated with fields within the field set. The *id* value is not required, but it is useful in distinguishing one field set from another. Terry wants to organize the donation form into three field sets named contact, donation, and feedback. Add these field sets to her donation form.

Creating a Field Set | Reference Window

- To create a field set, add the element
  ```
  <fieldset id="id">
     controls
  </fieldset>
  ```
  to the form, where *id* identifies the field set and *controls* are the control elements associated with fields within the field set.

To insert a field set:

▶ **1.** Return to the **donations.htm** file.

▶ **2.** Within the form element, insert the following three field sets, as shown in Figure 6-5:

```
<fieldset id="contact">
</fieldset>

<fieldset id="donation">
</fieldset>

<fieldset id="feedback">
</fieldset>
```

Inserting field sets ◀ **Figure 6-5**

```
<form name="donationForm" id="donationForm">
    <fieldset id="contact">
    </fieldset>

    <fieldset id="donation">
    </fieldset>

    <fieldset id="feedback">
    </fieldset>
</form>
```

▶ **3.** Save your changes to the file.

Every field set can contain a legend describing its contents. The syntax of the legend element is

```
<legend>text</legend>
```

where *text* is the text of the legend. The legend element can only contain text and not other page elements. Based on Terry's sketch from Figure 6-1, you'll add the legends Contact Information, Donation Information, and Feedback to the three field sets you created.

To insert legends for the field sets:

1. Return to the **donations.htm** file.

2. Within the first field set, insert the following legend element:

   ```
   <legend>Contact Information</legend>
   ```

3. In the second field set, insert the following legend element:

   ```
   <legend>Donation Information</legend>
   ```

4. In the last field set, insert the following legend element:

   ```
   <legend>Feedback</legend>
   ```

   Figure 6-6 highlights the revised text of the HTML file.

Figure 6-6 | Creating field set legends

```
<form name="donationForm" id="donationForm">
    <fieldset id="contact">
        <legend>Contact Information</legend>
    </fieldset>

    <fieldset id="donation">
        <legend>Donation Information</legend>
    </fieldset>

    <fieldset id="feedback">
        <legend>Feedback</legend>
    </fieldset>
</form>
```

5. Now you can view the three field sets in your Web browser. Save your changes to the file, and reload the **donations.htm** file in your Web browser. Figure 6-7 shows the current appearance of the form.

Figure 6-7 | Appearance of the field set and legend elements

Field sets are block-level elements that expand to accommodate their content. Currently, there are no control or other page elements within the three field sets, so the field set boxes are small and narrow. By default, browsers display the legend text in the upper-left corner of the field set box. However, you can use the CSS positioning styles to move the legend position. Terry does not need you to modify the legend, so you'll leave it in its default position. Now that you've created the three field sets, you can begin to populate them with form control elements.

Creating Input Boxes

Most of the control elements in which users either type or select a data value are marked as input elements. The general syntax of this element is

```
<input type="type" name="name" id="id" />
```

where *type* specifies the type of input control, and the name and id attributes provide the field's name and id, respectively. As with the form element, you should provide both the name and the id attributes, setting them to the same value to ensure compatibility with older browsers. HTML supports 10 different input types, which are described in Figure 6-8. If no type attribute value is specified, the browser will assume a type value of text.

Appearance of control elements ◀ **Figure 6-8**

Type Value	Description	General Appearance
button	Displays a button that can be clicked to perform an action from a script	Run Program
checkbox	Displays a check box	☑ ☐
file	Displays a Browse button to locate and select a file	donations.htm Browse...
hidden	Creates a hidden field, not viewable on the form	
image	Displays an inline image that can be clicked to perform an action from a script	
password	Displays an input box that hides text entered by the user	•••••••••
radio	Displays an option button	◉ ○
reset	Displays a button that resets the form when clicked	Cancel Donation
submit	Displays a button that submits the form when clicked	Submit Donation
text	Displays an input box that displays text entered by the user	Terry Ives

The exact appearance of each control element varies among browsers and operating systems. Figure 6-9 highlights the differences among four major browsers in how they render a control button. Because of this variation, you should not rely on the exact appearance of any particular control element when designing your Web form.

Figure 6-9 Control elements under different browsers

When a form is submitted to the server, the server program receives the data in **name/value pairs** in which the name or id of each field is paired with whatever field value is entered into the corresponding control element. The program then processes the data according to each name/value pair. Some server-based programs require a particular field or group of fields. For example, a CGI script whose purpose is to register users might require e-mail addresses entered into a field named e_mail. This means that before specifying a name or id value for a control, you have to learn what the server program expects that data to be named and write your HTML code accordingly. Be aware that case is usually important in specifying field names. A program might not interpret a field named e_mail in the same way as a field named E_MAIL.

The first controls you'll add to the donation form will be input boxes in which donors can enter their first and last names. The syntax to create an input box is:

```
<input type="text" name="name" id="id" />
```

You ask Terry for the ids of the first and last name fields in her donation form. She checks with the ISP hosting The Lighthouse's Web site and tells you that fields containing the donor's first and last name should be given name and id values of firstName and lastName, respectively. You can add these two input boxes to the Contact Information field set. To describe these input boxes for the user, you'll insert the text First Name and Last Name before the input boxes.

Reference Window | **Inserting a Text Input Box**

- To create a text input box control, use the element
  ```
  <input type="text" name="name" id="id" />
  ```
  where the name and id attributes identify the field associated with the input box.

To insert the input boxes:

▶ 1. Return to the **donations.htm** file in your text editor and scroll down to the Contact Information field set element.

▶ 2. Within the field set element, add the following text strings and input elements, as shown in Figure 6-10.
```
First Name
   <input type="text" id="firstName" name="firstName" />
Last Name
   <input type="text" id="lastName" name="lastName" />
```

Adding input box controls | Figure 6-10

```
<form name="donationForm" id="donationForm">
    <fieldset id="contact">
        <legend>Contact Information</legend>
        First Name
        <input type="text" id="firstName" name="firstName" />
        Last Name
        <input type="text" id="lastName" name="lastName" />
    </fieldset>
```

text type indicates an input text box

3. Save your changes to the file, and then reload **donations.htm** in your Web browser. Your browser should show two input boxes within the Contact Information field set box. Terry suggests that you test the input boxes.

4. Type *your first name* in the First Name box, press the **Tab** key, and then type *your last name* in the Last Name box. Figure 6-11 shows the input boxes with the sample text.

Input controls with sample data | Figure 6-11

Contact Information
First Name Terry   Last Name Ives
Donation Information
Feedback

HTML treats all form control elements as inline elements, so the input boxes that you created for Terry's form appear within the same line rather than in separate blocks. You can change this by applying the CSS display style to the input box.

Adding Field Labels

In the last set of steps, you entered descriptive text alongside the input boxes to indicate the purpose of the input box to the user. However, nothing in the HTML code explicitly associates that text with the input box. To associate text with a control element, you can use the label element

```
<label for="id">label text</label>
```

where *id* is the value of the id attribute for the field's control element, and *label text* is the text of the label. The for attribute associates the text of the label with the control element id. For example, the following code associates the label text First Name with the first-Name control element:

```
<label for="firstName">First Name</label>
<input type="text" id="firstName" />
```

Using the for attribute explicitly associates the label with the control element. You can also make this association implicitly by nesting the control element within the label as in the following code:

```
<label>
    First Name
    <input type="text" id="firstName" />
</label>
```

Notice that you do not need to include a for attribute when you nest the control element within the label element.

Which approach you take depends on how you want to lay out the form's contents. When you use the for attribute, you can place the label text anywhere within the Web page and it will still be associated with the control element. However, by nesting the control element within the label, you can treat both the control element and its label as a single object, which might make it easier to do form layout as you can move both label text and the control element around the page. Depending on the layout of your Web form, you might use both approaches.

Reference Window | **Creating a Field Label**

- To explicitly associate a text label with a control element, use the label element
  ```
  <label for="id">label text</label>
  ```
  where *id* is the id of the control element.
- To implicitly associate a text label with a control element, nest the control element within the label as follows
  ```
  <label>
      label text
      control
  </label>
  ```
  where *control* is the control element. You do not have to include a for attribute.

For the firstName and lastName fields, you'll use the second approach, in which the control elements are nested within their label elements.

To insert the field labels:

1. Return to the **donations.htm** file in your text editor.

2. Enclose the First Name and Last Name text strings within opening and closing **<label>** tags. Indent your code to make it easier to read, as shown in Figure 6-12.

Figure 6-12 Adding field labels

```
<fieldset id="contact">
    <legend>Contact Information</legend>

    <label>
        First Name
        <input type="text" id="firstName" name="firstName" />
    </label>
    <label>
        Last Name
        <input type="text" id="lastName" name="lastName" />
    </label>

</fieldset>
```

3. Save your changes to the file, and reload the page in your Web browser.

4. Test the labels by clicking each label and verifying that the cursor appears within the corresponding control element.

Working with Form Styles and HTML Attributes

Terry stops by to see your progress on the donation form. She would prefer to have the labels placed in one column and the input boxes put in another column, rather than having both strung together in a single line. Placing labels and control elements in separate columns is a common form layout, one that has often been done with Web tables. However, you've learned that the use of Web tables for page layout is frowned upon. So, instead of a Web table, you'll lay out the form using positioning styles placed in an external style sheet. This has the advantage of making it easier to modify the form layout later on because you will not have to modify the markup code in the HTML file.

To create the form style sheet:

1. Use your text editor to open the **formstxt.css** file from the tutorial.06\tutorial folder included with your Data Files. Enter *your name* and *the date* in the comment section of the file, and then save it as **forms.css** in the same folder.

2. Return to the **donations.htm** file in your text editor and add the following link to the forms.css style sheet directly above the closing </head> tag.

```
<link href="forms.css" rel="stylesheet" type="text/css" />
```

You decide to change the display style of the label elements from inline to block so that the labels will appear on a separate line from the input boxes. Because this particular style might not apply to other labels in the donation form or on The Lighthouse's Web site, you'll add a class element named blockLabel to the label elements having this design format.

To create the blockLabel class:

1. Scroll down the **donations.htm** file and insert the class attribute

```
class="blockLabel"
```

in the First Name and Last Name labels, as shown in Figure 6-13.

Adding class names to the field labels   **Figure 6-13**

```
<label class="blockLabel">
    First Name
    <input type="text" id="firstName" name="firstName" />
</label>
<label class="blockLabel">
    Last Name
    <input type="text" id="lastName" name="lastName" />>
</label>
```

2. Save your changes to the file.

Next, you'll create a style for the blockLabel class of labels. The style will set the display property of the label to block, and set the margins to 12 pixels above and below the label and to 0 pixels to the left and right. You'll also place the label using relative positioning, but you will not define any coordinates so that the label stays in its default position in the page flow. The complete style declaration is:

```
label.blockLabel {display: block; position: relative; margin: 12px 0px}
```

The input elements within each label will be placed using absolute positioning 150 pixels from the left margin of the label. The style declaration is:

```
label.blockLabel input {position: absolute; left: 150px}
```

Add these two styles to the forms.css style sheet.

To create styles for the blockLabel class:

1. Return to the **forms.css** file in your text editor and add the following styles to the style sheet, as shown in Figure 6-14.

   ```
   label.blockLabel       {display: block; position: relative;
                           margin: 12px 0px}

   label.blockLabel input {position: absolute; left: 150px}
   ```

Figure 6-14 Styles for the blockLabel labels and input elements

```
label.blockLabel       {display: block; position: relative; margin: 12px 0px}
label.blockLabel input {position: absolute; left: 150px}
```

2. Save your changes to the style sheet, and reload the donations page in your Web browser. Figure 6-15 shows the new layout of the form fields.

Figure 6-15 Revised layout of the form elements

There are some fields in the donation form that the server-based program will require for the donation to be processed. Terry wants you to mark such required fields with a red asterisk. The firstName and lastName fields are both required, so you'll mark their labels with an asterisk, adding the red style to the forms.css style sheet.

To mark the required fields:

1. Return to the **donations.htm** file in your text editor.

2. At the end of the label text for the firstName and lastName fields, insert the code

   ```
   <span>*</span>
   ```

   as shown in Figure 6-16.

Marking a required field | **Figure 6-16**

```
<label class="blockLabel">
    First Name<span>*</span>
    <input type="text" id="firstName" name="firstName" />
</label>

<label class="blockLabel">
    Last Name<span>*</span>
    <input type="text" id="lastName" name="lastName" />
</label>
```

▶ **3.** Save your changes to the file and then return to the **forms.css** style sheet. Add the following style to the bottom of the sheet to display all span elements from the donation form in a red font:

```
#donationForm span {color: red}
```

▶ **4.** Save your changes to the style sheet and then reload **donations.htm** in your Web browser. Verify that the labels for the firstName and lastName variables end with a red asterisk.

Terry wants the same style applied to input boxes for each donor's phone number and street address. Both of these fields are required, so you'll also append an asterisk to the field labels.

To insert additional fields to the donation form:

▶ **1.** Return to the **donations.htm** file in your text editor.

▶ **2.** Directly below the label for the lastName field, insert the following fields and labels as shown in Figure 6-17.

```
<label class="blockLabel">
    Phone<span>*</span>
    <input type="text" id="phone" name="phone" />
</label>
<label class="blockLabel">
    Street Address<span>*</span>
    <input type="text" id="street" name="street" />
</label>
```

Adding the phone and street fields | **Figure 6-17**

```
<fieldset id="contact">
    <legend>Contact Information</legend>

    <label class="blockLabel">
        First Name<span>*</span>
        <input type="text" id="firstName" name="firstName" />
    </label>

    <label class="blockLabel">
        Last Name<span>*</span>
        <input type="text" id="lastName" name="lastName" />
    </label>

    <label class="blockLabel">
        Phone<span>*</span>
        <input type="text" id="phone" name="phone" />
    </label>

    <label class="blockLabel">
        Street Address<span>*</span>
        <input type="text" id="street" name="street" />
    </label>

</fieldset>
```

3. Save your changes to the file and then reload the donations page in your browser. Verify that the two additional input boxes have been added to the page in the same style and layout as the First Name and Last Name boxes, as shown in Figure 6-18.

Figure 6-18 | **Required contact information in the donations form**

Contact Information

First Name*

Last Name*

Phone*

Street Address*

The next fields in the Contact Information field set are the city, state, and zip fields. Terry has indicated that she wants these three fields to be displayed on the same line in the form, just as they usually appear in mailing addresses. You'll add the labels for these control elements without the blockLabel class attribute so that the browser treats them as inline elements; however, you'll indent the first label for the city field by 150 pixels, lining it up with the rest of the columns in the form. You learn from Terry that the city and state fields are required by the CGI script that will process this form, so you'll add red asterisks to those two labels.

To add the city, state, and zip fields:

1. Return to the **donations.htm** file in your text editor.

2. Add the following elements to the form, as shown in Figure 6-19.

```
<label class="indentLabel">
   City<span>*</span>
   <input type="text" id="city" name="city" />
</label>
<label>
   State<span>*</span>
   <input type="text" id="state" name="state" />
</label>
<label>
   ZIP
   <input type="text" id="zip" name="zip" />
</label>
```

Figure 6-19 | **Adding the city, state, and zip fields**

```
<label class="blockLabel">
   Street Address<span>*</span>
   <input type="text" id="street" name="street" />
</label>

<label class="indentLabel">
   City<span>*</span>
   <input type="text" id="city" name="city" />
</label>
<label>
   State<span>*</span>
   <input type="text" id="state" name="state" />
</label>
<label>
   ZIP
   <input type="text" id="zip" name="zip" />
</label>

</fieldset>
```

3. Save your changes to the file and then return to the **forms.css** file in your text editor to create a style for the indentLabel class.

4. Add the following style to the bottom of the style sheet:

   ```
   label.indentLabel {margin-left: 150px}
   ```

5. Save your changes to the style sheet and then reload the **donations.htm** file in your Web browser. Figure 6-20 shows the current layout of the form.

Form layout for the city, state, and zip fields ◀ **Figure 6-20**

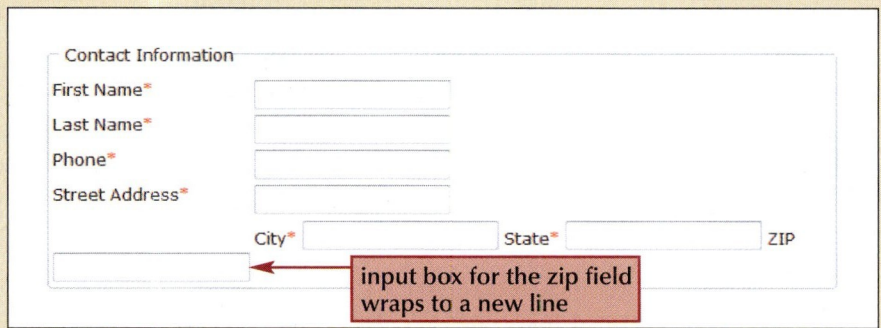

Trouble? Under some browsers such as Safari, the three input boxes will not wrap onto a new line but will instead be displayed on a single line, crossing the boundary of the field set box.

The three input boxes for the city, state, and zip fields do not fit onto a single line, causing the input box for the zip field to wrap onto a second line. By default, most browsers set the width of the input boxes to display about 20 characters of text at any one time. You can change the width of these input boxes using the CSS width style.

Setting the Width of an Input Box

Because Terry wants users to enter only a two-letter abbreviation for the state input box, you can reduce the width of that box to 3 em. The width of the zip code input box can be reduced to 7 em. Finally, she would like the width of the city and phone input boxes set at 10 em. Terry thinks the other input boxes could be wider and suggests that you set the width of the firstName, lastName, and street input boxes to 25 em. Add these styles to the forms.css style sheet.

To set the width of the input boxes:

1. Return to the **forms.css** style sheet and add the following styles to the bottom of the sheet, as shown in Figure 6-21.

   ```
   #firstName, #lastName, #street {width: 25em}
   #phone, #city                  {width: 10em}
   #state                         {width: 3em}
   #zip                           {width: 7em}
   ```

Figure 6-21 ▶ **Setting the widths of the input boxes**

```
#donationForm span        {color: red}

label.indentLabel         {margin-left: 150px}

#firstName, #lastName, #street {width: 25em}
#phone, #city                  {width: 10em}
#state                         {width: 3em}
#zip                           {width: 7em}
```

▶ **2.** Save your changes to the style sheet and reload the **donations.htm** file in your Web browser. Figure 6-22 shows the layout of the form with the new widths for the input boxes.

Figure 6-22 ▶ **Input boxes with modified widths**

Contact Information
First Name*
Last Name*
Phone*
Street Address*
City* State* ZIP

Applying new widths to the different input boxes has removed the line wrap from the form and made the form easier to read. The width style is one way of setting the size of an input box. For older browsers, you can also apply the size attribute to the input element as follows

```
<input type="text" size="chars" />
```

where *chars* is the number of characters displayed in the input box. For example, the tag

```
<input type="text" id="zip" name="zip" size="7" />
```

sets the width of the input box for the zip field to seven characters. This is not an exact measure because the width of individual characters varies (unless you specify a monospace font for the input box text).

Setting the Maximum Width of an Input Box

Setting the width of an input box does not limit the number of characters the box can hold. If a user tries to enter text longer than a box's width, the text scrolls to the left, hiding the extra characters. A user would not be able to see the entire text entered into the input box, but all of it would still be sent to the server for processing.

There are times when you want to limit the number of characters a user can enter in order to reduce the chance of erroneous data entry. For example, if you have a Social Security Number field, you know that only nine characters are required and that any attempt to enter more than nine characters would indicate a mistake. To set the maximum number of characters allowed for an input box, you add the attribute

```
<input type="text" maxlength="chars" />
```

to the input element, where *chars* is the maximum number of characters that can be stored in the field. For the donation form, Terry wants users to enter the two-letter state abbreviation, so she suggests that you limit the size of that input box to two characters. She also wants to limit the width of the zip code field to 10 characters, allowing users to enter a nine-digit zip code that incorporates a hyphen.

To set the maximum width of the state and zip input fields:

▶ **1.** Return to the **donations.htm** file in your text editor and add the attribute

```
maxlength="2"
```

to the input box for the state field.

▶ **2.** Add the attribute

```
maxlength="10"
```

to the input box for the zip field. Figure 6-23 shows the revised code.

Setting the maximum number of characters for an input box ◀ Figure 6-23

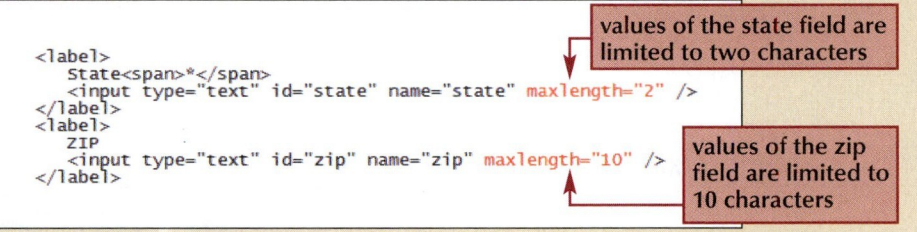

▶ **3.** Save your changes to the file and reload **donations.htm** in your Web browser.

▶ **4.** Click the input boxes for the state and zip fields, and verify that you cannot type more than two characters into the state field and more than 10 characters into the zip field.

Setting a Default Value for a Field

If you expect that most people will enter the same value into a field in your form, it might make sense to define a default value for that field. This makes data entry easier for users who want that default value, and it increases the accuracy of data entered into your Web form. To define a default value, you add the value attribute

```
<input value="value" />
```

to the input control element, where *value* is the default text or number that is displayed in the field. In the case of an input box, the default value appears in the input box when the form is initially opened.

Working with Input Box Attributes

- To set the size of the input box in characters, add the attribute
  `size="chars"`
  to the input element, where *chars* is the number of characters displayed in the input box.
- To set the maximum number of characters in the input box, use the attribute
  `maxlength="chars"`
  where *chars* is the maximum number of characters that can be entered into the input box.
- To set the default value of the field in the input box, use the attribute
  `value="value"`
  where *value* is the default value that will appear in the input box when the form is initially displayed.

About 80% of the online donations to The Lighthouse come from donors in St. Peters, Missouri. Terry suggests that you enter the city and state abbreviation into the form as a default value.

To set the default value for the city and state fields:

1. Return to the **donations.htm** file in your text editor and add the attribute

   `value="St. Peters"`

   to the input box for the city field.

2. Add the attribute

   `value="MO"`

   to the input box for state field, as shown in Figure 6-24.

Figure 6-24 **Defining a default city and state value**

St. Peters is the default value for the city field

MO is the default value for the state field

3. Save your changes to the **donations.htm** file and then reload it in your browser. As shown in Figure 6-25, the default values of St. Peters and MO appear in the city and state fields, respectively.

Web form with default city and state values ◄ **Figure 6-25**

Contact Information
First Name*
Last Name*
Phone*
Street Address*
City* St. Peters   State* MO   ZIP

4. If you want to take a break before starting the next session, you can close your files and programs now.

Note that if donors from places other than St. Peters, Missouri use this Web form, they can remove the default value by selecting the text and pressing the Delete key.

Navigating Forms with Access Keys | InSight

In this session, you've activated control elements either by using your mouse button or by tabbing from one control element to another. As your forms get larger with more elements, you might want to give users the ability to jump to a particular element in the form. This can be done with an access key. An **access key** is a single key on the keyboard that you type in conjunction with the Alt key for Windows users, or the Control key for Macintosh users, to jump to one of the control elements in the form. You can create an access key by adding the accesskey attribute to any of the control elements discussed in this tutorial. For example, to create an access key for the lastName field, enter the following code:

```
<input type="text" name="lastName" id="lastName" accesskey="l" />
```

If a user types Alt+l (or Command+l for Macintosh users), the input box for the lastName field is selected. Note that you must use letters that are not reserved by your browser. For example, Alt+f is used by many browsers including Internet Explorer to access the File menu. If you use an access key, you should provide some visual clues about the key's existence. The accepted method is to underline the character corresponding to the access key. For example, in the previous code, you might display the Last Name label as Last Name.

You've completed the text input boxes for the Contact Information section of the donation form. In the next session, you'll complete the layout of the form by adding new fields to the form, including option buttons, selection lists, and check boxes.

Session 6.1 Quick Check | Review

1. What is a CGI script?
2. Specify the code to create a form with the name registration.
3. Specify the code to create a field set with the id contactInfo and the legend Contact Information.
4. What are two ways of associating a field label with a control element?
5. Specify the code to create a field label with the text Phone that is associated with an input box containing the phone field.

6. What attribute would you add to the Phone input box to allow no more than 10 characters to be entered?
7. Specify the code to create an input box named subscribe with a default value of Yes.
8. What style would you enter to display all text input boxes as block-level elements?

Session 6.2

Creating Option Buttons

Donations to The Lighthouse come from both private individuals and businesses. Terry handles the receipts and thank you notes for private donations differently than those for business donations, so she would like the form to indicate whether the contact information is associated with a business or represents a home address. Terry doesn't want donors to enter this information in an input box; she would prefer that they enter the information with option buttons.

Option buttons, also called **radio buttons**, allow users to select a data value from a limited set of possible values. With option buttons, users can select only one button at a time from a group. The syntax to create a collection of option buttons is

```
<input type="radio" name="name" id="id1" value="value1" />
<input type="radio" name="name" id="id2" value="value2" />
<input type="radio" name="name" id="id3" value="value3" />
...
```

where *name* identifies the field associated with the collection of option buttons; *id1*, *id2*, *id3*, etc. identify the specific options; and *value1*, *value2*, *value3*, etc. are the field values associated with each option. Notice that all options within the group have the same *name* value. In fact, the id attribute is required only if you intend to use a field label with the option button or need some way of distinguishing one option button from another for use with a program or script.

When a group of option buttons share the same name, this puts them in a group—so that selecting one option button automatically deselects all of the others. Figure 6-26 shows an example of a Web form that uses an option button group to indicate political party affiliations.

Figure 6-26	Creating a group of option buttons

```
<fieldset>
    <legend>Party Affiliation</legend>

    <label for="demOption">Democrat</label>
    <input type="radio" name="party" id="demOption" value="dem" />

    <label for="gopOption">Republican</label>
    <input type="radio" name="party" id="gopOption" value="gop" />

    <label for="indOption">Independent</label>
    <input type="radio" name="party" id="indOption" value="ind" />

</fieldset>
```

HTML code

Party Affiliation
Democrat ● Republican ● Independent ●

open buttons

In this sample code, all of the option buttons have the field name party but each has a different value. Because they share the same name, a user can select only one of the option buttons. The field set box provides a visual clue that all of these option buttons are part of the same field, but the field set is only there to aid in the form's appearance—it is not part of the option button syntax.

By default, an option button is unselected; but you can set an option button to be selected by adding the checked attribute to the input element:

```
<input type="radio" checked="checked" />
```

In older Web pages, you might see this code also entered as

```
<input type="radio" checked />
```

with no value provided for the checked attribute. However, this format is not supported in the official specifications for HTML and XHTML and should be avoided in new Web pages.

Creating a Group of Option Buttons | Reference Window

- To create a group of option buttons associated with a single field, add the elements
  ```
  <input type="radio" name="name" id="id1" value="value1" />
  <input type="radio" name="name" id="id2" value="value2" />
  <input type="radio" name="name" id="id3" value="value3" />
  ```
  to the Web form, where *name* identifies the field associated with the collection of option buttons; *id1, id2, id3*, etc. identify the specific options; and *value1, value2, value3*, etc. are the field values associated with each option.
- To specify the default option, add the following attribute to the <input> tag:
  ```
  checked="checked"
  ```

Terry wants you to insert two option buttons at the top of the Contact Information field set with the labels Home and Business. The field name you'll use for this group of option buttons is addressType. To make it clear to donors that the two option buttons are related, you'll enclose them in a field set box.

To create the option buttons for the addressType field:

▶ 1. Reopen the **donations.htm** file in your text editor.

▶ 2. Directly below the Contact Information legend, insert the following field set containing two option buttons with associated field labels:

```
<fieldset id="addressOptions">
    <legend>Address For</legend>

        <label for="homeType">Home</label>
        <input type="radio" id="homeType" name="addressType"
               value="home" />

        <label for="busType">Business</label>
        <input type="radio" id="busType" name="addressType"
               value="business" />

</fieldset>
```

Figure 6-27 shows the revised code.

Figure 6-27 | **Inserting a field set containing an option button group**

```
<form name="donationForm" id="donationForm">

   <fieldset id="contact">
       <legend>Contact Information</legend>

       <fieldset id="addressOptions">
           <legend>Address For</legend>

           <label for="homeType">Home</label>
           <input type="radio" id="homeType" name="addressType" value="home" />
           <label for="busType">Business</label>
           <input type="radio" id="busType" name="addressType" value="business" />

       </fieldset>

       <label class="blockLabel">
           First Name<span>*</span>
           <input type="text" id="firstName" name="firstName" />
       </label>
```

▶ **3.** Save your changes to the **donations.htm** file and then reload it in your browser. Figure 6-28 shows the new field set containing the two option buttons from the addressType field.

Figure 6-28 | **Option buttons in the donations form**

```
┌─ Contact Information ──────────────────────────────┐
│ ┌─ Address For ──┐                                  │
│ Home ⊙  Business ⊙                                  │
│                                                      │
│ First Name*     [                              ]     │
│                                                      │
│ Last Name*      [                              ]     │
│                                                      │
│ Phone*          [              ]                     │
│                                                      │
│ Street Address* [                              ]     │
│                                                      │
│         City* [St Peters      ]  State* [MO]  ZIP [ ]│
└──────────────────────────────────────────────────────┘
```

▶ **4.** Test the option buttons by clicking each one, verifying that you can select only one option at a time. Also verify that you can select an option button by clicking the field label associated with the button.

You decide that the option button group would look better if it weren't as wide and if it were lined up with the other control elements in the form. You'll add this code to the style sheet.

To change the appearance of the option group:

▶ **1.** Reopen the **forms.css** file in your text editor.

▶ **2.** The fieldset element containing the option buttons has the id addressOptions. Add the following style to the bottom of the style sheet, as shown in Figure 6-29.

```
#addressOptions {width: 180px; margin-left: 150px}
```

Setting the format of the addressOptions field set | Figure 6-29

```
#firstName, #lastName, #street {width: 25em}
#phone, #city                  {width: 10em}
#state                         {width: 3em}
#zip                           {width: 7em}

#addressOptions       {width: 180px; margin-left: 150px}
```

▶ **3.** Save your changes to the style sheet and reload the **donations.htm** file in your Web browser. Figure 6-30 shows the new appearance of the control elements in the form.

Revised format of the addressOptions field set | Figure 6-30

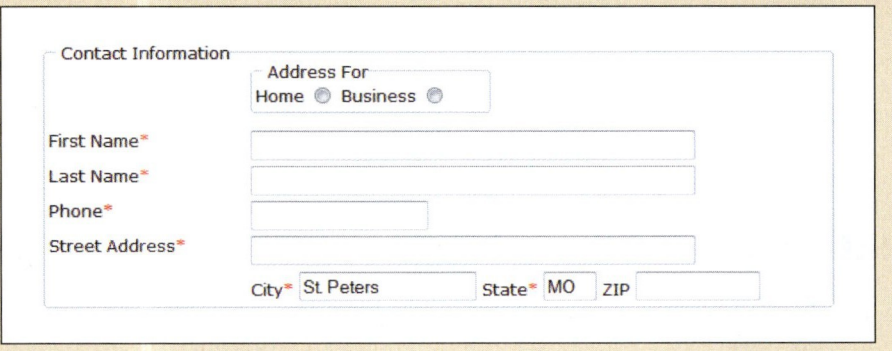

You've now entered all of the control elements for the Contact Information part of the form. Next you'll add fields that store the amount of the donation and the method of payment. You'll start by creating an input box in which donors enter the amount of their donation. You'll name this new field amount. You'll use the same blockLabel class style you used earlier in the form to format the input box and field label.

To insert an input box for the amount of the donation:

▶ **1.** Return to the **donations.htm** file in your text editor.

▶ **2.** Scroll down the file. Within the Donation Information field set, insert the following code, as shown in Figure 6-31.

```
<label class="blockLabel">
   Donation Amount<span>*</span>
   <input type="text" id="amount" name="amount" />
</label>
```

Adding an input box for the donation amount | Figure 6-31

```
<fieldset id="donation">
   <legend>Donation Information</legend>

   <label class="blockLabel">
      Donation Amount<span>*</span>
      <input type="text" id="amount" name="amount" />
   </label>
</fieldset>
```

▶ **3.** Save your changes to the file and then reload **donations.htm** in your Web browser. Figure 6-32 shows the new donation amount input box.

Figure 6-32 ▶ **Donation amount input box**

Contact Information

Address For
Home ○ Business ○

First Name*

Last Name*

Phone*

Street Address*

City* St Peters   State* MO   ZIP

Donation Information

Donation Amount*

In the next field in the donation form, donors are asked to specify the credit card type. To insert this information you'll use a selection list.

Creating a Selection List

A **selection list** is a list box that presents users with a group of possible field values. A selection list fulfills the same role as a group of option buttons and is used in situations where there are too many options to be easily listed on the form with option buttons. As with option buttons, selection lists help prevent spelling mistakes and erroneous data entries that can occur with text input boxes. A selection list is created using the elements

```
<select name="name" id="id">
   <option value="value1">text1</option>
   <option value="value2">text2</option>
   ...
</select>
```

where *name* and *id* identify the field associated with the selection list; *value1*, *value2*, etc. are the possible field values; and *text1*, *text2*, etc. are the entries in the selection list. The text entries are displayed to the user, while CGI scripts retrieving data from a selection list will often work with either the field value or the text entry. Figure 6-33 shows a selection list version of the party affiliation field described earlier with option buttons.

Figure 6-33 ▶ **Creating a selection list**

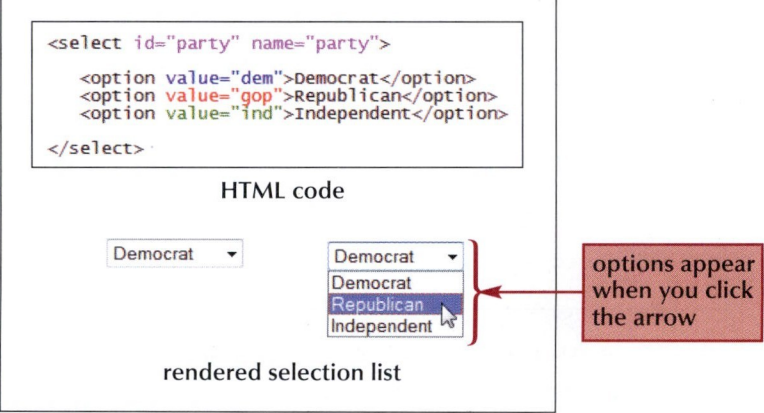

```
<select id="party" name="party">

   <option value="dem">Democrat</option>
   <option value="gop">Republican</option>
   <option value="ind">Independent</option>

</select>
```

HTML code

Democrat ▾

Democrat ▾
Democrat
Republican
Independent

options appear
when you click
the arrow

rendered selection list

Although the first text entry is displayed in a selection list, this is not a default value for the list. To specify which of the options should be selected by default, add the following selected attribute to the option element:

```
<option selected="selected" value="value">text</option>
```

In older code, you might also see the selected attribute entered without an attribute value, appearing as

```
<option selected value="value">text</option>
```

but this is considered poor syntax and is rejected in XHTML documents.

Grouping Selection Options

In a selection list, the options are presented in the same order as they appear in the HTML code. In long selection lists it might be difficult for users to locate a particular option value. You can organize the selection list options by placing them in **option groups** using the optgroup element

```
<select>
    <optgroup label="label1">
        <option>text1</option>
        <option>text2</option>
...
    </optgroup>
    <optgroup label="label2">
        <option>text1</option>
        <option>text2</option>
...
    </optgroup>
</select>
```

where *label1*, *label2*, and so forth are the labels for the different groups of options. The text for the label appears in the selection list above each group of items but is not a selectable item from the list. Figure 6-34 shows an example of a selection list in which the options are divided into two groups.

Figure 6-34 ▶ **Organizing a selection list with option groups**

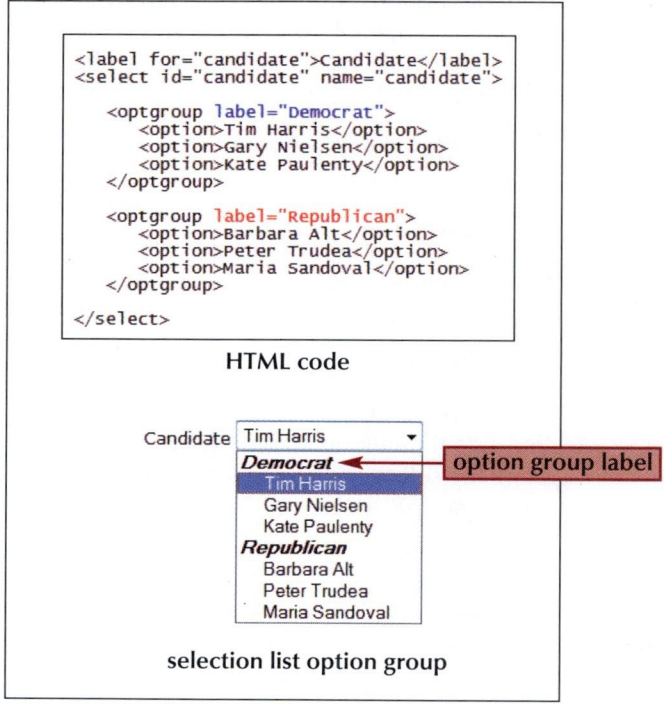

```
<label for="candidate">Candidate</label>
<select id="candidate" name="candidate">

   <optgroup label="Democrat">
      <option>Tim Harris</option>
      <option>Gary Nielsen</option>
      <option>Kate Paulenty</option>
   </optgroup>

   <optgroup label="Republican">
      <option>Barbara Alt</option>
      <option>Peter Trudea</option>
      <option>Maria Sandoval</option>
   </optgroup>

</select>
```

HTML code

option group label

selection list option group

The appearance of the option group label is determined by the browser. You can apply a style to an entire option group including its label, but there is no CSS style to change the appearance of the option group label alone.

Setting the Selection List Size

By default, selection lists display only the currently selected option value. You can change the number of options displayed by applying the size attribute

```
<select size="value"> ... </select>
```

to the select element, where *value* is the number of items that the selection list displays in the form at a time. By specifying a value greater than 1, you change the selection list from a drop-down list box to a list box with a scroll bar that allows a user to scroll through the selection options. If you set the size attribute to be equal to the number of options in the selection list, the scroll bar either is not displayed or is dimmed, as shown in Figure 6-35.

Figure 6-35 ▶ **Setting the size of the selection list**

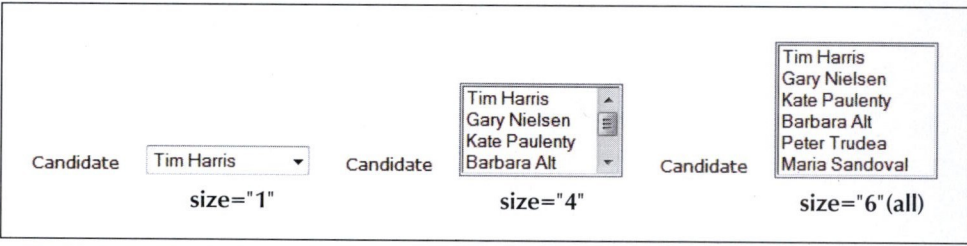

Although the size attribute defines the number of options displayed in the list box, there is no HTML attribute to set the width of the list box. The browser will make the width large enough to display the longest option text. If you want to change the width of a list box, you can use the CSS width style.

Creating a Selection List
Reference Window

- To create a selection list, add the elements
```
<select name="name" id="id">
   <option value="value1">text1</option>
   <option value="value2">text2</option>
   . . .
</select>
```
to the Web form, where *name* and *id* identify the field associated with the selection list; *value1*, *value2*, etc. are the possible field values; and *text1*, *text2*, etc. are the entries in the selection list.
- To specify the default option, add the following attribute to the <option> tag:
```
selected="selected"
```
- To set the number of options displayed at one time in the selection list, add the attribute
```
size="value"
```
to the <select> tag, where *value* is the number of options displayed in the selection list at any one time.

Now that you've learned about selection lists, you can add one to the donation form for entering the credit card brand. The Lighthouse accepts payments from American Express, Discover, MasterCard, and Visa. The field values Terry wants you to use for these three vendors are Amex, Disc, MC, and Visa, respectively. She wants the values to be stored in a field named creditCard. The code for the selection is:

```
<select id="creditCard" name="creditCard">
   <option value="Amex">American Express</option>
   <option value="Disc">Discover</option>
   <option value="MC">MasterCard</option>
   <option value="Visa">Visa</option>
</select>
```

Terry wants the selection list displayed as a block-level element, with the field label placed alongside it.

To create a selection list for the credit card vendors:

1. Return to the **donations.htm** file in your text editor.

2. Below the donation amount input box, insert the following code, as shown in Figure 6-36.

```
<label class="blockLabel">
   Credit Card<span>*</span>
   <select id="creditCard" name="creditCard">
      <option value="Amex">American Express</option>
      <option value="Disc">Discover</option>
      <option value="MC">MasterCard</option>
      <option value="Visa">Visa</option>
   </select>
</label>
```

Figure 6-36 ▷ **Inserting a selection list**

```
<fieldset id="donation">
    <legend>Donation Information</legend>

    <label class="blockLabel">
        Donation Amount<span>*</span>
        <input type="text" id="amount" name="amount" />
    </label>

    <label class="blockLabel">
        Credit Card<span>*</span>
        <select id="creditCard" name="creditCard">
            <option value="Amex">American Express</option>
            <option value="Disc">Discover</option>
            <option value="MC">MasterCard</option>
            <option value="Visa">Visa</option>
        </select>
    </label>

</fieldset>
```

selection list options

3. Save your changes to the file, and then return to the **forms.css** style sheet in your text editor. Like the input boxes you created earlier, you want the selection list positioned 150 pixels from the left margin of the field label. Add the following style to the bottom of the style sheet, as shown in Figure 6-37:

```
#creditCard {position: absolute; left: 150px}
```

Figure 6-37 ▷ **Formatting the selection list**

```
#firstName, #lastName, #street {width: 25em}
#phone, #city                  {width: 10em}
#state                         {width: 3em}
#zip                           {width: 7em}

#addressOptions         {width: 180px; margin-left: 150px}

#creditCard             {position:absolute; left: 150px}
```

4. Save your changes to the style sheet, and then reload **donations.htm** in your Web browser. Figure 6-38 shows the selection list for the creditCard field.

Figure 6-38 ▷ **Credit card selection list in the donations form**

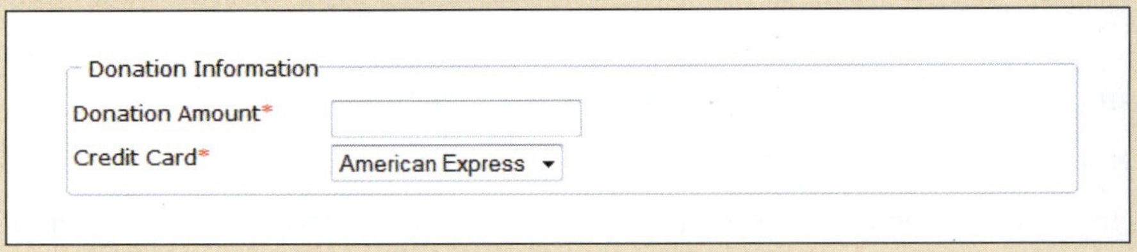

Donation Information
Donation Amount*
Credit Card*   American Express ▾

5. Click the selection list control for the creditCard field and verify that it displays the names of the four credit cards accepted by The Lighthouse.

The next two fields in the donation form are the cardHolder and cardNumber fields, which will be input boxes for users to enter the name on the credit card and the credit card number. You'll format these elements using the blockLabel label class, setting the width of both input boxes to 25 em.

To create input boxes for the card holder name and the credit card number:

▶ **1.** Return to the **donations.htm** file in your text editor.

▶ **2.** Below the selection list, insert the following control elements, as shown in Figure 6-39.

```
<label class="blockLabel">
   Cardholder Name<span>*</span>
   <input type="text" id="cardHolder" name="cardHolder" />
</label>

<label class="blockLabel">
   Card Number<span>*</span>
   <input type="text" id="cardNumber" name="cardNumber" />
</label>
```

Adding input boxes for the cardholder name and credit card number ◄ Figure 6-39

```
<label class="blockLabel">
   Credit Card<span>*</span>
   <select id="creditCard" name="creditCard">
      <option value="Amex">American Express</option>
      <option value="Disc">Discover</option>
      <option value="MC">MasterCard</option>
      <option value="Visa">Visa</option>
   </select>
</label>

<label class="blockLabel">
   Cardholder Name<span>*</span>
   <input type="text" id="cardHolder" name="cardHolder" />
</label>

<label class="blockLabel">
   Card Number<span>*</span>
   <input type="text" id="cardNumber" name="cardNumber" />
</label>

</fieldset>
```

▶ **3.** Save your changes to the file, and then return to the **forms.css** style sheet in your text editor. Add the following styles at the bottom of the file to set the width on the cardHolder and cardNumber input boxes:

```
#cardHolder, #cardNumber {width: 25em}
```

▶ **4.** Save your changes to the style sheet, and then reload **donations.htm** in your Web browser. Figure 6-40 shows the input boxes for the cardHolder and cardNumber fields.

Cardholder Name and Card Number input boxes ◄ Figure 6-40

The final credit card information you need to add to the form is the expiration date. You'll add two selection lists to collect this information. One selection list will contain the month values from January (01) to December (12). The other selection list will contain the year value, ranging from 2011 to 2015.

To create selection lists for the credit card expiration date:

▶ **1.** Return to the **donations.htm** file in your text editor.

▶ **2.** Below the credit card number input box, insert the following code, as shown in Figure 6-41.

```
<label class="blockLabel">
    Expiration Date<span>*</span>
    <select id="expMonth" name="expMonth">
        <option value="01">January (01)</option>
        <option value="02">February (02)</option>
        <option value="03">March (03)</option>
        <option value="04">April (04)</option>
        <option value="05">May (05)</option>
        <option value="06">June (06)</option>
        <option value="07">July (07)</option>
        <option value="08">August (08)</option>
        <option value="09">September (09)</option>
        <option value="10">October (10)</option>
        <option value="11">November (11)</option>
        <option value="12">December (12)</option>
    </select>
    <select id="expYear" name="expYear">
        <option value="2011">2011</option>
        <option value="2012">2012</option>
        <option value="2013">2013</option>
        <option value="2014">2014</option>
        <option value="2015">2015</option>
    </select>
</label>
```

Figure 6-41   **Creating selection lists for the expiration month and year**

```
<label class="blockLabel">
    Card Number<span>*</span>
    <input type="text" id="cardNumber" name="cardNumber" />
</label>

<label class="blockLabel">
    Expiration Date<span>*</span>
    <select id="expMonth" name="expMonth">
        <option value="01">January (01)</option>
        <option value="02">February (02)</option>
        <option value="03">March (03)</option>
        <option value="04">April (04)</option>
        <option value="05">May (05)</option>
        <option value="06">June (06)</option>
        <option value="07">July (07)</option>
        <option value="08">August (08)</option>
        <option value="09">September (09)</option>
        <option value="10">October (10)</option>
        <option value="11">November (11)</option>
        <option value="12">December (12)</option>
    </select>
    <select id="expYear" name="expYear">
        <option value="2011">2011</option>
        <option value="2012">2012</option>
        <option value="2013">2013</option>
        <option value="2014">2014</option>
        <option value="2015">2015</option>
    </select>
</label>

</fieldset>
```

▶ **3.** Save your changes to the file.

You also have to add styles to the forms.css style sheet to line up the expMonth and expYear selection lists with the other entries in the donation form.

4. Go to the **forms.css** file in your text editor and add the following styles to the bottom of the file, as shown in Figure 6-42.

```
#expMonth {position: absolute; left: 150px}
#expYear  {position: absolute; left: 280px}
```

Positioning the expiration month and year selection lists ◄ **Figure 6-42**

```
#creditCard              {position:absolute; left: 150px}

#cardHolder, #cardNumber {width: 25em}

#expMonth                {position: absolute; left: 150px}
#expYear                 {position: absolute; left: 280px}
```

5. Save your changes to the style sheet and reload **donations.htm** in your Web browser. Figure 6-43 shows all of the control elements that collect credit card data.

Control elements collecting credit card data ◄ **Figure 6-43**

6. Test the selection lists by clicking the selection list arrows to verify that all of the year and month options are present.

Allowing for Multiple Selections

In the code you just entered for the donation form, donors were limited to a single option—a certain kind of credit card and a specific month and year for the expiration date. However, selection lists also allow for multiple selections by applying the following multiple attribute to the select element:

```
<select multiple="multiple"> . . . </select>
```

In older code, you might see the minimized version of this attribute, removing the attribute value as follows:

```
<select multiple> . . . </select>
```

However, as with the selected attribute, this is not correct HTML or XHTML syntax and so you should avoid using it.

There are two ways for users to select multiple items from a selection list. For noncontiguous selections, press and hold the Ctrl key (or the Command key on a Macintosh) while making the selections. For a contiguous selection, select the first item, press and hold the Shift key, and then select the last item in the range. This selects the two items as well as all the items between them.

If you decide to use a multiple selection list in a form, be aware that the form sends a name/value pair to the server for each option the user selects from the list. This requires the server-based program to be able to handle a single field with multiple values. Check and verify that your server-based programs are designed to handle this before using a multiple selection list. In most cases, you are better served using check boxes rather than selection lists with multiple values. You'll examine check boxes next because Terry wants donors to be able to indicate if they're interested in volunteering at The Lighthouse.

Working with Check Boxes

You use a **check box** control in situations where you are checking for the presence or absence of something, such as whether or not a donor is interested in volunteering at the center. Check boxes are created using the input element with the type attribute set to checkbox, as follows:

```
<input type="checkbox" name="name" id="id" value="value" />
```

The value attribute contains the value of the field when the check box is checked. If no value is provided, the value On is used by default. For example, the following code creates a check box for determining whether the user is a member of the Democratic party:

```
<label for="dem">Democrat?</label>
<input type="checkbox" name="dem" id="dem" value="yes" />
```

If the check box is selected, the browser will submit the name/value pair of dem/yes to the CGI script running on the Web server. A name/value pair is only sent to the server when the check box is checked by the user. By default, check boxes are not selected. To make a check box selected by default, add the following checked attribute to the input element:

```
<input type="checkbox" checked="checked" />
```

As with other form attributes, you will also see older code with this attribute used as:

```
<input type="checkbox" checked />
```

But once again, you should always provide an attribute value, even if most browsers accept this attribute without a value.

Reference Window | **Creating a Check Box**

- To create a check box, add the element
  ```
  <input type="checkbox" name="name" id="id" value="value" />
  ```
  to the Web form, where *name* and *id* identify the check box field and *value* is the value of the check box field if the check box is selected.
- To specify that the check box is selected by default, add the following attribute to the <input> tag:
  ```
  checked="checked"
  ```

In the next section of the donation form, Terry wants you to add a few fields for recording customer feedback and comments. Terry wants donors to be able to select a check box indicating whether they're interested in doing volunteer work at The Lighthouse in addition to providing financial support. You'll insert this field with a check box control element.

To create a check box for volunteers:

▶ **1.** Return to the **donations.htm** file in your text editor and go to the Feedback field set near the bottom of the file.

▶ **2.** Directly below the legend element, insert the following code, as shown in Figure 6-44.

```
<label>
    <input type="checkbox" id="volunteer" name="volunteer" />
    I'm interested in volunteering at The Lighthouse.
</label>
```

Adding a check box for the volunteer field ◀ **Figure 6-44**

```
<fieldset id="feedback">
    <legend>Feedback</legend>

    <label>
        <input type="checkbox" id="volunteer" name="volunteer" />
        I'm interested in volunteering at The Lighthouse.
    </label>

</fieldset>

</form>
```

▶ **3.** Save your changes to the file, and reload **donations.htm** in your Web browser. Figure 6-45 shows the new check box control added to the Feedback field set box.

The volunteer check box control ◀ **Figure 6-45**

```
┌─ Feedback ──────────────────────────────────────────┐
│ ☐ I'm interested in volunteering at The Lighthouse.  │
│                                                       │
└───────────────────────────────────────────────────────┘
```

▶ **4.** Click the check box, and then click the field label to verify that you can alternately select and deselect the field with both the check box and its label.

Note that you did not specify a value for the volunteer field. When the form is eventually submitted to a CGI script, it will send the name/value pair as volunteer/on when the check box is selected in the form, which means the person would like Terry to contact him or her for volunteering. If the check box is not selected, no name/value pair will be sent, and Terry will not contact the person.

InSight | **Specifying the Tab Order**

Typically, users navigate through a Web form using the Tab key, which moves the cursor from one field to another in the order that the field tags are entered into the HTML file.

You can specify an alternate order by adding the tabindex attribute to any control element in your form. When each element is assigned a tab index number, the cursor moves through the fields from the lowest index number to the highest. For example, to assign the tab index number 1 to the firstName field from the donation form, you would enter the following tab-index attribute to the control element:

```
<input name="firstName" id="firstName" tabindex="1" />
```

This code would ensure that the cursor is in the firstName field when the form is first opened. (Fields with zero or negative tab indexes are omitted from the tab order entirely.)

Web page designers can use tab index numbers in their forms without worrying about older browsers that do not support this new standard. Such browsers simply ignore the tabindex attribute and continue to tab to the fields in the order that they appear in the HTML file.

Working with Text Area Controls

The final part of the Feedback field set includes a place where donors can offer comments about The Lighthouse. Because their comments might contain several lines of text, it would not be appropriate to enter those comments in an input box because input boxes are limited to a single line of text. Instead, you can create a control element that allows for extended text entries using the textarea element

```
<textarea name="name" id="id">
   text
</textarea>
```

where *text* is default text that is placed in the text area box. You do not have to specify default text—this would leave the text area box empty on the form.

The size of the text area box is determined by the browser. Most browsers create a text area box that is about 20 characters long and two or three lines high. To change the dimensions of the text area box, you add the row and cols attributes

```
<textarea rows="value" cols="value"> ... </textarea>
```

where the rows attribute specifies the number of lines in the text area box and the cols attribute specifies the number of characters per line. You can also set the dimensions of the textarea element using the CSS width and height styles.

As you type text into a text area box, the text automatically wraps to a new line as it extends beyond the box's width. If more text is entered into the box than can be displayed, the browser automatically adds horizontal and vertical scroll bars to the box. You can control how the browser handles extra text by using the wrap attribute

```
<textarea wrap="type"> ... </textarea>
```

where *type* is one of the values described in Figure 6-46.

Tip

The rows and cols attributes are required under strict applications of XHTML.

Value	Description
off	All the text is displayed on a single line, scrolling to the left if the text extends past the width of the box. Text goes to the next row in the box only if the Enter key is pressed. The text is sent to the CGI script in a single line.
soft	Text wraps automatically to the next line when it extends beyond the width of the input box. The text is still sent to the CGI script in a single line without any information about how the text was wrapped within the text area box.
hard	Text wraps automatically to the next line when it extends beyond the width of the input box. When the text is sent to the CGI script, the line-wrapping information is included, allowing the CGI script to work with the text exactly as it appears in the text area box.

The wrap attribute is not part of the World Wide Web Consortium (W3C) specifications for HTML or XHTML, but all browsers support it. The default wrap value is soft, which allows the text to wrap automatically to a new line—note that this information is not sent to the CGI script. If you need to include the line wraps as part of the field value, use the following attribute value:

```
wrap="hard"
```

Creating a Text Area Box | Reference Window

- To create a text area box for multiple lines of text, use the element
  ```
  <textarea name="name" id="id">
     text
  </textarea>
  ```
  where *name* and *id* identify the field associated with the text area box and *text* is the default text that appears in the box.
- To specify the dimensions of the box, add the attributes
  ```
  rows="value" cols="value"
  ```
  to the <textarea> tag, where the rows attribute specifies the number of lines in the text area box and the cols attribute specifies the number of characters per line.

You decide to use a text area box for the donor comments, setting the size of the box to 50 characters wide by five lines high.

To create the comments text area box:

▶ 1. Return to the **donations.htm** file in your text editor.

▶ 2. Below the volunteer check box, insert the following elements to create the text area box, as shown in Figure 6-47.

```
<label for="comments" class="blockLabel">Comments</label>
<textarea id="comments" name="comments"
          rows="5" cols="50">
</textarea>
```

Figure 6-47 | Adding a text area box

```
<fieldset id="feedback">
    <legend>Feedback</legend>

    <label>
        <input type="checkbox" id="volunteer" name="volunteer" />
        I'm interested in volunteering at The Lighthouse.
    </label>

    <label for="comments" class="blockLabel">Comments</label>
    <textarea id="comments" name="comments" rows="5" cols="50"></textarea>

</fieldset>
```

the text area box will have five lines of 50 characters each

▶ **3.** Close the file, saving your changes, and then reload **donations.htm** in your Web browser. Figure 6-48 shows the comments text area box.

Figure 6-48 | Text area box in the Feedback section

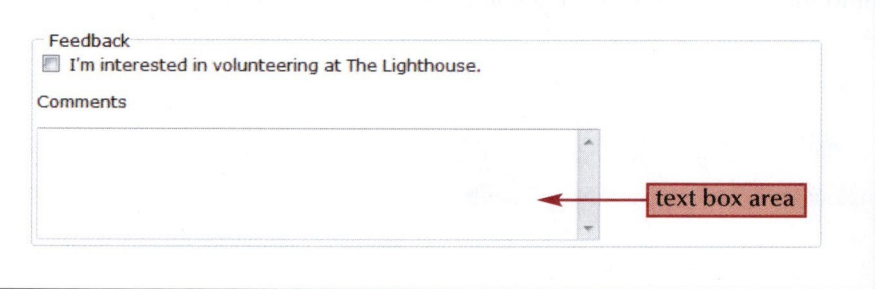

Feedback
☐ I'm interested in volunteering at The Lighthouse.
Comments

← text box area

▶ **4.** Type some sample text into the text area box and verify that the text wraps to a new line as you exceed the width of the box.

Trouble? Line wraps do not occur in the middle of words. If you find your sample text is not wrapping to a new line, make sure you are entering individual words rather than a long character string.

You've added the last field to the donation form. Terry likes the layout of the form, but she thinks the field sets would look better if they had a light brown background similar to the color used in the page's background image. She also wants you to increase the space between and within each of the field set boxes.

To format the field set boxes:

▶ **1.** Go to the **forms.css** style sheet file in your text editor.

▶ **2.** At the top of the style sheet, add the following style, as shown in Figure 6-49.

```
fieldset {margin-bottom: 10px; padding: 10px;
          background-color: rgb(237, 233, 223)}
```

Figure 6-49 | Setting the style of the fieldset elements

```
fieldset               {margin-bottom: 10px; padding: 10px; background-color: rgb(237,233,223)}
label.blockLabel       {display: block; position: relative; margin: 12px 0px}
label.blockLabel input {position: absolute; left: 150px}
```

3. Close the file, saving your changes, and then reload **donations.htm** in your Web browser. Figure 6-50 shows the revised design of the entire donation form.

Layout and design of the donation form — Figure 6-50

Trouble? Depending on your browser, the tan background might not extend beyond the borders of the field set.

4. Take some time to work with all of the control elements you've entered, pressing the **Tab** key to move from one element to another and entering sample data into each field.

5. If you want to take a break before starting the next session, you can close all open files and programs now.

InSight | Web Forms and CSS

When you complete a Web form, you will probably want to ensure that the various form elements appear the same across different browsers and operating systems. The most natural way of doing this would appear to be with CSS. For example, you can apply the following style to display all command buttons with blue text on a yellow background:

```
input[type=button] {color: blue; background-color: yellow}
```

The degree to which these control elements can be formatted varies from browser to browser. Safari, for example, does not apply the above style, nor does it allow any changes to be made to any input element's border or background style. Other browsers are much more lenient. However, an important question for Web designers is whether to make these kinds of style changes even if the browser allows them.

One school of thought holds that any and all parts of a Web form should be open to CSS styles to enhance creativity in the design process. A different point of view holds that control elements such as input boxes and form buttons need to be, above all, usable. The most usable control element is one that has the same design and appearance as the other control elements found elsewhere on the user's computer. When users have come to expect a certain appearance for input boxes, command buttons, check boxes, and radio buttons, they can become confused by a Web format that has a totally different style.

However, the bottom line is that because the appearance of control elements is determined by the operating system and the browser, different browsers will apply CSS styles to control elements in different ways. Research has shown that trying to achieve a uniform look for control elements is a fruitless task. The best approach is to use CSS to lightly style form controls by modifying only properties such as font color, font size, and background colors—and realize that your style changes will not be seen by all of your users. As always, any styles applied to a Web form need to be checked under a variety of browsers and operating systems.

Terry likes the design and layout of the donations form. In the next session you'll add elements to the page to enable the donation form to interact with the CGI script running on The Lighthouse's Web server.

Review | Session 6.2 Quick Check

1. Specify the code to create two option buttons for the Computer field with the values PC and Macintosh.
2. In Question 1, what attribute would you add to the code to make PC the default value for the Computer field?
3. Specify the code to create a selection list for the State field with possible values of California, Nevada, Oregon, and Washington.
4. What attribute would you add to the code in Question 3 to make Oregon the default value for the State field?
5. In Question 3, what attribute would you add to the code to display all of the possible field values in the selection list?
6. How would you modify the code in Question 3 to allow for multiple selections?
7. Specify the code to create a check box and a label for the Computer field. The text of the label should be "I use a PC" and the value of the check box should be Yes.
8. Specify the code to create a text area box for the Memo field that displays 10 lines of text, each of which displays up to 40 characters.

Session 6.3

Working with Form Buttons

Up to now, all of your control elements have involved entering field values. Another type of control element is one that performs an action. In forms, this is usually done with **form buttons**, which perform one of three actions:

- run a command
- submit the form to the CGI script running on the server
- cancel the data entry done in the form

The first type of button you'll examine is the command button.

Creating a Command Button

A **command button** runs a command on the Web page. This command can be a call to a program running on a Web server or to a program installed within the Web browser. Command buttons are created using the input element

```
<input type="button" value="text" />
```

where *text* is the text that appears on the button. By itself, a command button performs no actions on a Web page. To create an action for a command button, you have to write a script or program that runs when the button is clicked. This can be done using a programming language such as JavaScript. Because that is beyond the scope of this tutorial, we won't examine how to use command buttons on the donation page.

Creating Submit and Reset Buttons

The two other kinds of form buttons are submit and reset buttons. A **submit button** submits a form to the server for processing when clicked. Clicking the **reset button** resets a form, changing all field values to their original default values and deleting any values that the user might have entered into the form. The syntax for creating these two buttons is

```
<input type="submit" value="text" />
<input type="reset" value="text" />
```

where the *value* attribute defines the text that appears on the button.

You can also specify name and id attributes for command, submit, and reset buttons, although these attributes are not required. You would use these attributes when a form contains multiple buttons and you're running a program that needs to distinguish one button from another. You won't need to add id and name attributes to the buttons on the donation form.

> **Tip**
>
> Avoid overpopulating your forms with buttons; too many buttons can be confusing. If more than one button is displayed, use CSS styles to give more visual emphasis on the button that will be most often clicked by the user.

Creating Form Buttons

- To create a form button to run a command, use the element

  ```
  <input type="button" value="text" />
  ```
  where *text* is the text that appears on the button.
- To create a form button to submit the form and its fields and values to a CGI script, use the element

  ```
  <input type="submit" value="text" />
  ```
- To create a form button to reset the form to its default values and appearance, use

  ```
  <input type="reset" value="text" />
  ```

Terry wants the donation form to include both a submit button and a reset button. The submit button, which she wants labeled Send Donation, will send the form data to the server for processing when clicked. The reset button, which she wants labeled Cancel, will erase the user's input and reset the fields to their default values.

To add the submit and reset buttons to the donation form:

1. Return to the **donations.htm** file in your text editor.

2. Scroll to the bottom of the file. Directly below the closing </fieldset> tag for the feedback field set, insert the following input elements, as shown in Figure 6-51:

   ```
   <input type="submit" value="Submit Donation" />
   <input type="reset" value="Cancel" />
   ```

Figure 6-51 | Adding submit and reset buttons

```
          </fieldset>

          <input type="submit" value="Submit Donation" />
          <input type="reset" value="Cancel" />

          </form>

     </div>

     <address>
          The Lighthouse &bull;
          150 Cavates Rd. &bull;
          St. Peters, MO  63376 &bull;
          (636) 555 - 4477
     </address>
```

3. Save your changes to the file, and then reload **donations.htm** in your Web browser. Figure 6-52 shows the complete donations page with the Web form.

The Lighthouse

The Lighthouse   150 Cavates Rd.   St. Peters, MO   63376

| home | projects | upcoming events | community links | staff | donations | volunteers | contact info |

Donation Form

* indicates required information

The success of The Lighthouse reflects the dedication and support of members of the community who have helped make our dream a reality. We cannot continue to operate without contributions from people like you.

You can make a tax-deductible donation online using your American Express, Discover, Master, or Visa card. Please fill out the form on this page.

The Lighthouse is always looking for volunteers. We especially need help in the following areas:

- Mechanics
- Carpenters
- Electricians
- Cooks
- Computer technicians
- Babysitters
- Data entry persons

and many others. Please consider donating your time and talents to your community and your neighbors.

Thank you so much for your generosity!

— Terry Ives
  Director, *The Lighthouse*

Contact Information

Address For
Home ○ Business ○

First Name*   [   ]
Last Name*   [   ]
Phone*   [   ]
Street Address*   [   ]
City* [St. Peters]   State* [MO]   ZIP [   ]

Donation Information

Donation Amount*   [   ]
Credit Card*   [American Express ▾]
Cardholder Name*   [   ]
Card Number*   [   ]
Expiration Date*   [January (01) ▾] [2011 ▾]

Feedback

☐ I'm interested in volunteering at The Lighthouse.

Comments
[   ]

[Submit Donation] [Cancel]

The Lighthouse • 150 Cavates Rd. • St. Peters, MO 63376 • (636) 555 - 4477

▶ **4.** Test the Cancel button by entering data into the form and then clicking the **Cancel** button. Verify that the form is reset to its initial state and default values.

Designing a Custom Button

The text of a command, submit, or reset button is determined by the value attribute. You are only allowed to specify the button label text. You can't add other elements such as an inline image to the button value. For more control over a form button's appearance you can use the button element

```
<button name="name" id="id" value="value" type="type">
   content
</button>
```

where the *name* and *value* attributes identify the button and the value sent to a server-based program, respectively; the *id* attribute specifies the button's id; the *type* attribute specifies the button type (submit, reset, or button); and *content* are page elements displayed within the button. The page content can include formatted text, inline images, and other design elements supported by HTML. Figure 6-53 shows an example of a button that contains both formatted text and an inline image.

Figure 6-53	Creating a custom button

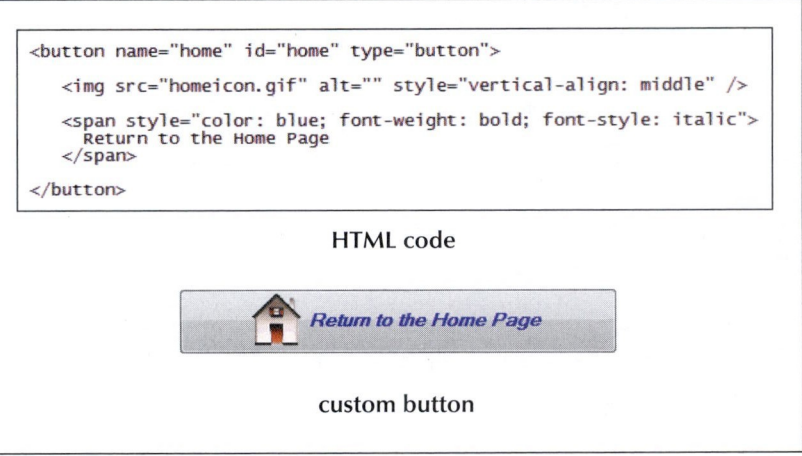

```
<button name="home" id="home" type="button">

   <img src="homeicon.gif" alt="" style="vertical-align: middle" />

   <span style="color: blue; font-weight: bold; font-style: italic">
     Return to the Home Page
   </span>

</button>
```

HTML code

custom button

Creating File Buttons

Another type of button supported by HTML is the **file button**, which is used to select files so that their contents can be submitted for processing to a program. File buttons are created by applying the attribute

```
type="file"
```

to the input element as follows:

```
<input type="file" name="name" id="id" />
```

Most browsers render file buttons as input boxes accompanied by a Browse button. As shown in Figure 6-54, when the user clicks the Browse button, a window opens from which the user can select a file. The file's location and name are then automatically inserted into the input box. When the form is submitted for processing, a script could use the value of the input box to retrieve the file as long as the Web server has access to the folder in which the file is stored.

Using a file button ◀ Figure 6-54

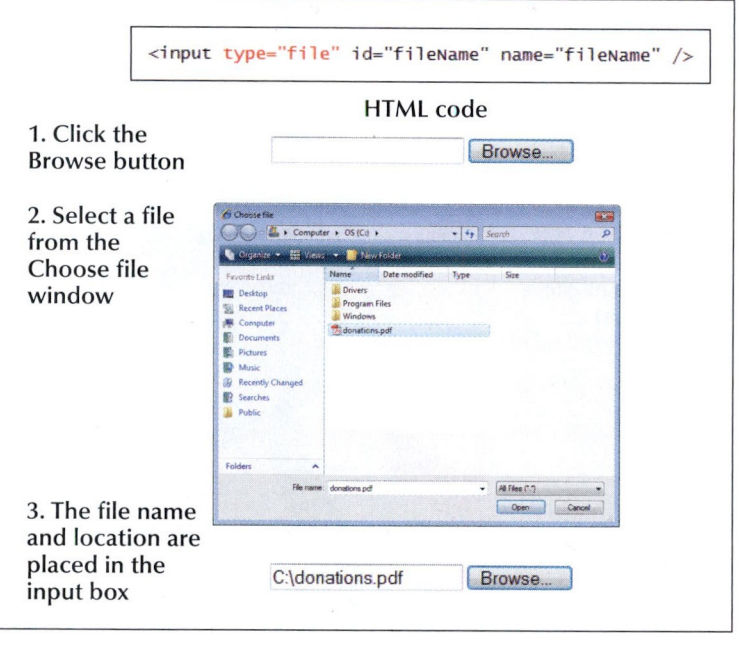

You cannot change the label for the Browse button, but you can increase the size of the input box using either a CSS style or the HTML size attribute.

Creating Image Field Buttons

Another control element you can use in your Web form is an image button. Image buttons act like submit buttons, allowing a user to click an image to submit a form. The syntax for this type of control element is

```
<input type="image" src="url" name="text" id="id" />
```

where *url* is the filename and location of the inline image. The user interacts with this control element by clicking somewhere within the image.

The image field can also act as an image map by recording where within the image the user clicked. When the form is submitted to a server-based program, the coordinates of that mouse click are attached to the image's name in the format

```
name.x=coordinate&name.y=coordinate
```

where *name* is the name of the image field and *coordinate* are the coordinates of the mouse click in the *x* and *y* direction. For example, suppose your Web page contains the following inline image form element:

```
<input type="image" src="usamap.gif" name="usa" id="usa" />
```

If a user clicks the inline image at the coordinates (15, 30), the Web form sends the text string "usa.x=15&usa.y=30" to the server. Once the server-based program receives this data, it performs an action in response to that mouse click, as shown in Figure 6-55.

Figure 6-55 ▶ **Using an image control field with a server-based program**

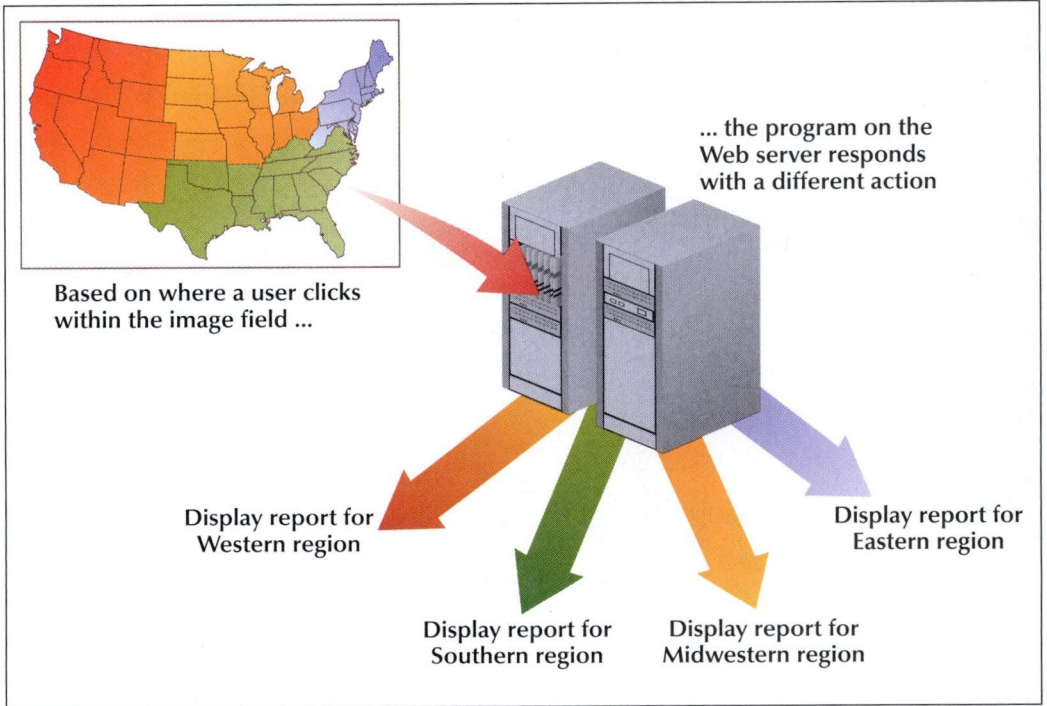

Based on where a user clicks within the image field ...

... the program on the Web server responds with a different action

Display report for Western region

Display report for Southern region

Display report for Midwestern region

Display report for Eastern region

Terry doesn't need any inline image controls or file buttons in the Web form for The Lighthouse.

Working with Hidden Fields

Terry is pleased with the final appearance of the donation form. She shows the code for the form to Warren Kaughman, one of the programmers responsible for the CGI script that will process the donations. Warren notices only one thing missing from the code: the e-mail address that will receive and processes a new donation.

Unlike the other fields you've created so far, this field has a predefined value that users of the Web form should not be able to change. In fact, the e-mail address for donations should not even be displayed on the form. To accomplish this, you can use a **hidden field**, which is added to the form but not displayed on the Web page. The syntax for creating a hidden field is:

```
<input type="hidden" name="name" id="id" value="value" />
```

You've learned from Warren that the name of the e-mail field should be eMail; the e-mail address that will receive the new donations is *donations@thelighthouse.org* (note that this is a fictional address used for the purposes of this tutorial). Now that you know both the field name and the field value, you can add the hidden field to the donation form.

Because the field is hidden, you can place it anywhere within the form element. A common practice is to place all hidden fields in one location, usually at the beginning of the form, to make it easier to read and interpret your HTML code. You should also include a comment describing the purpose of the field.

To add the hidden field to the donation form:

▶ **1.** Return to the **donations.htm** file in your text editor.

▶ **2.** Directly below the opening <form> tag, insert the following element, as shown in Figure 6-56.

```
<input type="hidden" name="eMail" id="eMail"
       value="donations@thelighthouse.org" />
```

Adding a hidden field ◀ Figure 6-56

```
<form name="donationForm" id="donationForm">

    <input type="hidden" name="eMail" id="eMail"
           value="donations@thelighthouse.org" />

    <fieldset id="contact">
        <legend>Contact Information</legend>
```

▶ **3.** Save your changes to the file.

Creating a Hidden Field | Reference Window

• To create a hidden field, add the control element

```
<input type="hidden" name="name" id="id" value="value" />
```

to the form, where *value* is the value of the hidden field, and *name* and *id* identify the hidden field.

With the e-mail field now included in the donation form, you'll return to the first tag you entered into this document, the <form> tag, and insert the attributes needed for it to interact with the CGI script running on the organization's Web server.

Working with Form Attributes

You've added all the elements needed for the form. Your final task is to specify where to send the form data and how to send it. You do this by adding the attributes

```
<form action="url" method="type" enctype="type"> ... </form>
```

to the form element, where *url* specifies the filename and location of the program that processes the form, the *method* attribute specifies how your Web browser sends data to the server, and the *enctype* attribute specifies the format of the data stored in the form's field. Next you'll examine the method and enctype attributes in more detail.

There are two possible values for the method attribute: get or post. The **get method**, the default, appends the form data to the end of the URL specified in the action attribute. The **post method**, on the other hand, sends form data in a separate data stream, allowing the Web server to receive the data through what is called **standard input**. Because it is more flexible, most Web designers prefer the post method for sending data to a server. Also, because browsers limit the size of URLs, the post method is safer—avoiding the possibility of data being truncated (this can happen using the get method if a long string is appended to a URL). The post method is also safer because the content of an extended URL can be viewed by other users and automated programs.

Don't be concerned if you don't completely understand the difference between get and post. Your Internet service provider can supply the necessary information about which of the two methods you should use when accessing the CGI scripts running on its server.

The enctype attribute determines how the form data should be encoded as it is sent to the server. Figure 6-57 describes the three most common encoding types.

Figure 6-57 ▶ **Values of the enctype attribute**

Value	Description
application/x-www-form-urlencoded	The default format. In this format, form data is transferred as a long text string in which spaces are replaced with the + character and nontext characters (such as tabs and line breaks) are replaced with their hexadecimal code values. Field names are separated from their field values with a = symbol.
multipart/form-data	Used when sending files to a server. In this format, spaces and nontext characters are preserved, and data elements are separated using delimiter lines. The action type of the form element must be set to post for this format.
text/plain	Form data is transferred as plain text with no encoding of spaces or nontext characters. This format is most often used when the action type of the form element is set to mailto.

Finally, another attribute you might use with the form element is the target attribute, used to send form data to a different browser window or frame. This is not a concern with the donation form.

Now that you've been introduced to the issues involved in sending form data to a server-based program, you are ready to make some final modifications to the donations. htm file. Warren tells you that a CGI script that processes the form is located at the URL *http://www.thelighthouse.org/cgi-bin/donation* (a fictional address) and uses the post method. You do not have to specify a value for the enctype attribute, so the browser will assume a value of application/x-www-form-urlencoded.

To add attributes to the form element:

▶ 1. Return to the **donations.htm** file and add the following attributes to the opening <form> tag, as shown in Figure 6-58.

```
action="http://www.thelighthouse.org/cgi-bin/donation"
method="post"
```

Figure 6-58 ▶ **Setting the form attributes**

```
<form name="donationForm" id="donationForm"
    action="http://www.thelighthouse.org/cgi-bin/donation"
    method="post">

<input type="hidden" name="eMail" id="eMail"
    value="katherinehayes@thelighthouse.org" />
```

▶ 2. Close the **donations.htm** file, saving your changes.

▶ 3. You can close any other open files or programs.

Using the mailto Action

The data from the donation form must be processed using a CGI script running on the center's Web server. There is, however, a way to send form information from the Web form to an e-mail address. You can do this with the mailto action, which accesses the user's own e-mail program and uses it to mail form information to a specified e-mail address, bypassing the need to use a CGI script. The syntax of the mailto action is

```
<form action="mailto:e-mail" method="post" enctype="text/plain"> ...
</form>
```

where *e-mail* is the e-mail address of the recipient of the form. Because the mailto action does not require a server-based program, you don't have to coordinate your form with a CGI script running on the Web server.

The mailto action is not supported by earlier versions of many browsers. Another concern is that using the mailto action requires the user filling out the form to have an e-mail client program that will be able to accept the output from the Web form and use it to send an e-mail message. This might not always be the case, as different users run different types of e-mail clients or might have no e-mail client at all. Finally, messages sent via the mailto action are not encrypted for privacy and therefore are a security risk. For these reasons, you should carefully consider all of the ramifications of the mailto action before using it in one of your forms. However, if these issues are not obstacles to your project, you can use the mailto action for situations where you need to send form data to an e-mail address and a CGI script is not available.

Tips for Effective Forms | InSight

Web forms are one of the main ways of communicating with your users, so it's important for the forms to be friendly and easy to use. A well-designed form can often be the difference between a new customer and a disgruntled user who leaves your site to go elsewhere. Here are some tips to remember when designing your form:

- Mark fields that are required, but also limit the number of unrequired fields. Don't overwhelm your users with requests for information that is not really essential. Keep your forms short and to the point.
- If you need to collect a lot of information, break the form into manageable sections spread out over several pages. Allow users to easily move backward and forward through the forms without losing data.
- Provide detailed instructions about what users are expected to do. Don't assume that your form is self-explanatory.
- If you ask for personal data and financial information, provide clear assurances that the data will be secure. If possible, provide a link to a Web page describing your security practices.
- Clearly indicate what users will receive once the form is submitted, and provide feedback on the Web site and through e-mail that tells them when their data has been successfully submitted.

Finally, every Web form should undergo usability testing before it is made available to the general public. Weed out any mistakes and difficulties before your users see the form.

You've finished the donation form, and Terry has placed a copy of donation.htm in a folder on the company's Web server. From there it can be fully tested to verify that the CGI script and the form work properly together. Terry is pleased with your work on this project and will come back to you for future Web page development at The Lighthouse.

1. Specify the code to create a submit button with the text Send Form.
2. Specify the code to create a reset button with the text Cancel Form.
3. Specify the code to create an image field named Sites displaying the graphic file sites.gif.
4. Specify the code to create a hidden field named Subject with the field value Form Responses.
5. You need your form to work with a CGI script located at *http://www.j_davis.com/cgi-bin/post-query*. The Web server uses the get method. Specify the code for the form element.
6. You want to use the mailto action to send your form to the e-mail address *walker@j_davis.com*. Assume that the message is sent as plain text. Specify the code for the form element.

Review | **Tutorial Summary**

In this tutorial, you learned how to create and use Web forms. The first session dealt with the fundamentals of Web forms, discussing how Web forms interact with the Web server to submit information to programs running on the server. You learned how to create and format simple input boxes with form labels, and you learned how to create field sets. You also saw how to use CSS styles to format the appearance and layout of a Web form. The second session examined other types of control elements, including option buttons, selection lists, and check boxes. The session concluded by examining how to create text area boxes for extended text input. The last session showed how to create form buttons for resetting a form or submitting it to a program for processing. The session also examined some special input fields that can be used to create server-side image maps and file input boxes. The session and the tutorial concluded by examining various form attributes and discussed how data from the Web form is transferred to a CGI script running on a Web server.

Key Terms

access key	field set	Perl
CGI script	field value	post method
check box	form button	radio button
command button	get method	reset button
Common Gateway Interface script	hidden field	selection list
	input box	standard input
control element	name/value pair	submit button
drop-down list box	option button	text area box
field	option group	

| Practice | **Review Assignments** |

Practice the skills you learned in the tutorial using the same case scenario.

Data Files needed for the Review Assignments: back.jpg, left.jpg, lhouse.jpg, main.css, right.jpg, vformstxt.css, and voltxt.htm

Terry and the staff at The Lighthouse have been working with your form and the CGI script running on the Web server for several weeks now. They're pleased with the work you've done, so they have asked for your help in creating another Web form for the center's Web site. Terry would like a form that Lighthouse volunteers can fill out indicating their talents and interests, and ways they can help the center. A CGI script is already in place to process the information, and much of the work in designing the volunteer page has been done except for the form itself. Terry wants you to complete the page by adding the HTML and CSS code for the volunteer form. A preview of the form you'll create is shown in Figure 6-59.

Figure 6-59

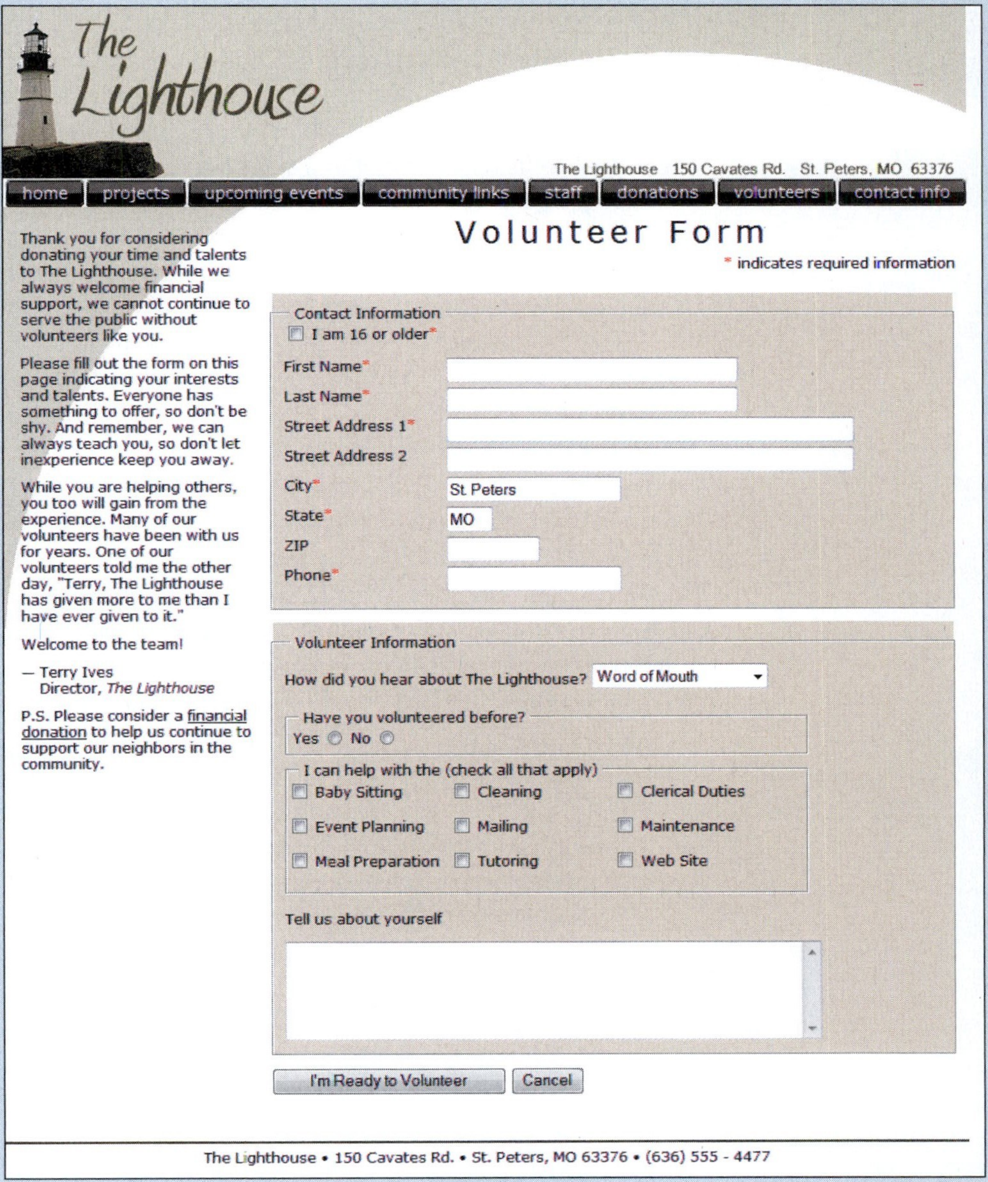

When the form is filled out, it should be sent to a CGI script at *http://www.thelighthouse.org/volunteer*. The CGI script will collect the information and e-mail it to Steve Jones, the volunteer coordinator.

Complete the following:

1. Use your text editor to open the **voltxt.htm** and **vformstxt.css** files from the tutorial.06\review folder included with your Data Files. Enter **your name** and **the date** in the comment section of each file. Save the files as **volunteer.htm** and **vforms.css**, respectively, in the same folder.

2. Go to the **volunteer.htm** file in your text editor. Scroll down to the rightColumn div container and directly below the paragraph element, insert a form element with the name and id volunteerForm. Have the form perform the action of submitting the form data to the CGI script at *http://www.thelighthouse.org/cgi-bin/volunteer* using the post method.

3. Directly below the opening <form> tag, insert a hidden field named eMail with the value *stevejones@thelighthouse.org*.

4. Create a field set with the legend Contact Information. Give the fieldset element the id contactFields.

5. Below the field set legend, insert a label element with the text "I am 16 or older*". Enclose the asterisk symbol in a span element. Directly before the label text, but still nested within the label element, insert a check box with the field name ageOK.

6. Below the label element you just entered, insert the contact information for the volunteer. There are eight contact fields: fName, lName, street1, street2, city, state, zip, and phone. For each field, do the following:
   - Create an input box nested within a label element. The labels for the eight fields are First Name*, Last Name*, Street Address 1*, Street Address 2, City*, State*, ZIP, and Phone*.
   - Enclose the asterisks within a span element.
   - Place each label element within the blockLabel class.

7. Set the maximum number of characters in the state and zip fields to two and 10 characters, respectively.

8. Set the default value of the city and state fields to St. Peters and MO, respectively.

9. Below the contactFields field set, insert another field set with the legend Volunteer Information. Give the field set the id volunteerInfo.

10. Directly below the Volunteer Information legend, insert a selection list for the infoSource field. Add the following code for the selection list:
    - Enclose the selection list within a label element with the class blockLabel.
    - Directly before the selection list within the label element, insert the text "How did you hear about The Lighthouse?"
    - Add the following five options to the selection list: Word of Mouth, TV or Radio Ad, The Internet, The Phonebook, and College/High School. Give the five options the values talk, ads, internet, phonebook, and schools, respectively.

11. After the selection list label, insert a field set with the id experience and the legend "Have you volunteered before?" Within the field set, create two option buttons with the following code:
    - Before each option button, insert a label with the text strings "Yes" and "No". Use the for attribute to assign the labels to the prevYes and prevNo fields, respectively.
    - After each label, insert an option button belonging to the prevExp field. The ids of the option buttons should be prevYes and prevNo, respectively, and the values of the buttons should be yes and no.
12. After the experience field set, insert another field set with the id interestFields and the legend "I can help with the (check all that apply)".
13. Within the interestFields field set, insert nine check boxes. Format the check boxes as follows:
    - Enclose each check box within a label element. Give the label elements ids of interest1 through interest9.
    - Give the check box controls the field names of babysitting, cleaning, clerical, events, mailing, maintenance, food, tutoring, and web.
    - After each check box within the label element, insert the text strings "Baby Sitting", "Cleaning", "Clerical Duties", "Event Planning", "Mailing", "Maintenance", "Meal Preparation", "Tutoring", and "Web Site".
14. Below the interestFields field set, insert a label associated with the comments field. Place the label in the blockLabel class and give it the text "Tell us about yourself".
15. After the label, insert a text area box for the comments field. The text area box should have five lines of 55 characters each.
16. After the text area box, insert submit and reset buttons. The text of the submit button should be "I'm Ready to Volunteer" and the text of the reset button should be "Cancel".
17. Go to the top of the file and link the file to the **vforms.css** style sheet.
18. Close the **volunteer.htm** file, saving your changes.
19. Go to the **vforms.css** file in your text editor and add the following styles to the style sheet:
    - Set the background color of all fieldset elements to the value (237, 233, 223) with 10 pixels of padding and a bottom margin of 10 pixels.
    - Display all span elements within field sets in a red font.
    - Display all labels belonging to the blockLabel class as block-level elements, with relative positioning. Set the width of the labels to 450 pixels. Set the top and bottom margins to 12 pixels and the left and right margins to 0 pixels.
    - Place all input elements nested within blockLabel labels with absolute positioning 140 pixels to the left of the label's left margin.
    - Set the width of the fName and lName input boxes to 250 pixels. Set the width of the street1 and street2 input boxes to 350 pixels. Set the width of the phone and city input boxes to 150 pixels. Set the width of the state input box to 40 pixels and the width of the zip input box to 80 pixels.
    - Set the width of the experience field to 450 pixels with 5 pixels of padding.
20. Terry wants the nine check boxes that constitute different volunteer opportunities to be displayed in a grid of three rows and three columns. To create this layout:
    - Place the interestFields field set with relative positioning. Set the size of the field set box to 450 pixels wide by 120 pixels high. Set the padding to 5 pixels.
    - Place the interest1 through interest9 label elements with absolute positioning.

- Set the top coordinate of the interest1 through interest3 labels to 20 pixels, interest4 through interest6 to 50 pixels and interest7 through interest9 to 80 pixels.
- Set the left coordinate of the interest1, interest4, and interest7 labels to 0 pixels; interest2, interest5, and interest8 to 140 pixels; and interest3, interest6, and interest9 to 280 pixels.

21. Save your edits to **vforms.css**, and then open **volunteer.htm** in your Web browser. Verify that the layout and design of the form resembles that shown in Figure 6-59.

22. Submit your completed files to your instructor.

| Apply | | **Case Problem 1** |

Apply your knowledge of Web forms to create a subscription form for a newspaper.

Data Files needed for this Case Problem: parch.jpg, pcg.css, pcglogo.jpg, sformtxt.css, and subtxt.htm

The Park City Gazette   Kevin Webber, the editor of the Park City Gazette of Estes Park, Colorado, has asked for your help in developing a subscription page for the newspaper's Web site. The page includes a form where customers can enter the length of the subscription they want to purchase, their mailing address, and their credit card information. Kevin has already created much of the layout and text of the Web page. Your job is to add the fields and control elements for the subscription form. A preview of the Web page you'll create for Kevin is shown in Figure 6-60.

Figure 6-60

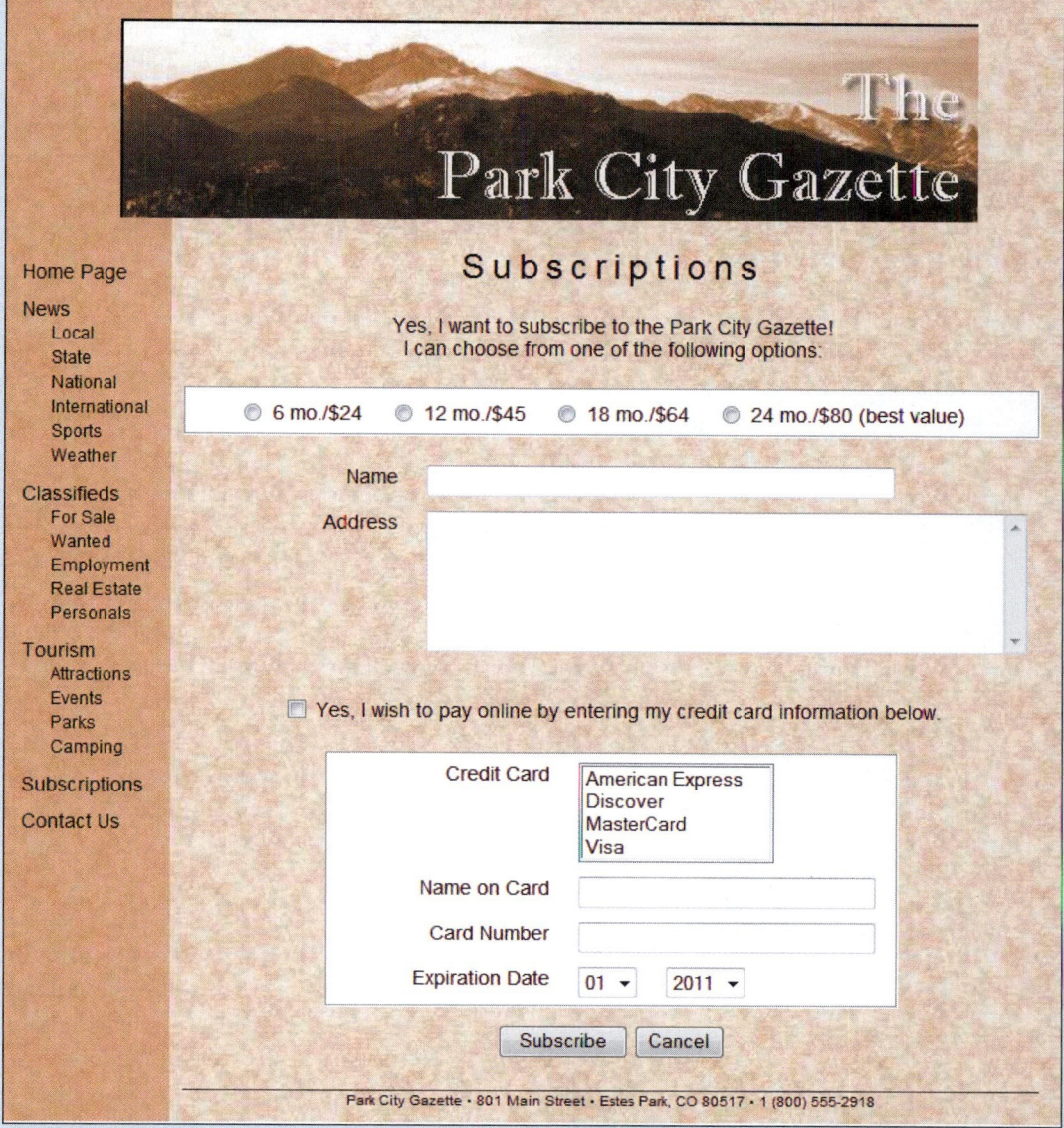

The form contains several labels and control elements placed side-by-side in two columns. To create this two-column layout, you'll float the labels and control elements on the left margin. You'll identify the labels that are floated by putting them into the float-Label class. The floated control elements will belong to the floatCtrl class.

Complete the following:

1. Use your text editor to open the **sformtxt.css** and **subtxt.htm** files from the tutorial.06\case1 folder included with your Data Files. Enter *your name* and *the date* in the comment section of each file. Save the files as **sform.css** and **subscription.htm**, respectively, in the same folder.

2. Go to the **subscription.htm** file in your text editor and insert a link to the **sform.css** style sheet.

3. Scroll down the file and insert a form element with the id subForm, directly below the paragraph in the rightColumn div container.

4. At the top of the form, Kevin wants an option list showing the four different payment plans. Insert a field set with the id subPlans. Within the field set do the following:
   - Insert four option buttons belonging to the subplan field.
   - Give the option buttons the ids plan1 through plan4 and the values 1 through 4.
   - After each option button, insert a label element associated with the preceding option button. The text of the four labels is "6 mo./$24", "12 mo./$45", "18 mo./$64", and "24 mo./$80 (best value)".

5. After the subPlans field set, insert a label containing the text "Name". Associate the label with the cName field and put it in the class floatLabel.

6. After the label, insert an input box for the cName field. Place the input box in the floatCtrl field and set the size of the input box to 50 characters.

7. Insert another label containing the text "Address" associated with the address field and belonging to the floatLabel class. After the label, insert a text area box for the address field. Set the size of the box to six rows by 50 columns and place the text area box in the floatCtrl field.

8. Insert a label with the id agreeLabel associated with the agree field. Place the label in the floatLabel class. Within the label element, insert a check box for the agree field. After the check box, but within the label element, insert the text "Yes, I wish to pay online by entering my credit card information below."

9. Insert a field set with the id payment. At the top of the field set, insert a label belonging to the floatLabel class, containing the text "Credit Card" and associated with the cardType field.

⊕ EXPLORE 10. Insert a selection list for the cardType field. Do the following for the selection list:
   - Place the selection list in the floatCtrl class.
   - Set the selection list to display four items.
   - Add the following options to the selection list: American Express, Discover, MasterCard, and Visa.
   - Set the values of the four options to: Amex, Disc, MC, and Visa.

11. Below the selection list, insert two labels. The first label should contain the text "Name on Card" and should be associated with the cardName field. The second label should contain the text "Card Number" and should be associated with the cardNumber field. Put both labels in the floatLabel class.

12. Directly after each label, insert an input box. The first input box should be for the cardName field; the second input box is for the cardNumber field. For both input boxes, set the width to 30 characters and place the input box into the floatCtrl class.

13. Insert a label belonging to the floatLabel class and containing the text "Expiration Date". After the label, insert two selection lists for the expMonth and expYear field. Do the following for the selection lists:
   - Place both selection lists in the floatCtrl class.
   - Add 12 options to the expMonth selection list containing the text "01" through "12". The values of the options should range from 1 to 12.
   - Add five options to the expYear selection list containing the text "2011" through "2015". Set the values of each option to match the option text.

14. Insert a field set with the id buttons. Within the field set, insert a submit and reset button. Give the submit button the value Subscribe. Give the reset button the value Cancel.

15. Use the CGI script at *http://www.theparkcitygazette.com/subscribe* with the post method.

16. Save your changes to the file.

17. Go to the **sform.css** file in your text editor and add the following styles to the style sheet:
    - Set the background color of the subPlans field set to white. Set the padding to 5 pixels and the bottom margin to 20 pixels. Center the contents of the field set.
    - For label elements within the subPlans fieldset element, set the right margin to 15 pixels.
    - Display objects belonging to the floatLabel class as block-level elements, floated on the left margin but only when the left margin is clear. (*Hint*: Use the clear style.) Set the width to 150 pixels and the bottom margin to 10 pixels. Right-align the label text.
    - Display objects belonging to the floatCtrl class as block-level elements, floated on the left margin. Set the left margin to 20 pixels and the bottom margin to 10 pixels.
    - Set the width of the agreeLabel label to 600 pixels with top/bottom margins of 20 pixels and left/right margins of 0 pixels. Center the label text.
    - Display the payment field set only when the left margin is clear. Set the background color to white. Set the width of the field set to 400 pixels with a left margin of 100 pixels and 5 pixels of padding.
    - Center the contents of the buttons field set with top/bottom margins of 10 pixels and left/right margins of 0 pixels. Set the border style to none.
18. Save your changes to the **sform.css** file and open **subscription.htm** in your Web browser. Verify that the layout and content of the Web form resemble that shown in Figure 6-60.
19. Submit your completed files to your instructor.

| Apply | **Case Problem 2** |

Apply your knowledge of Web forms to create a form for an online quiz.

Data Files needed for this Case Problem: cw.css, cwlogo.gif, cwquiztxt.htm, qformtxt. css, and tan.jpg

Civil War Studies Adanya Lynne, a professor of military history at Ridgeview State College in Bartlett, Tennessee, has been preparing a series of online quizzes for her students. She has created the basic Web page design and layout, but has come to you for help in designing the quiz form. She envisions a series of multiple choice questions displayed in a collection of option buttons. Students will be able to click answers on the form and then submit their answers to a CGI script running on the Web server for their scores. Figure 6-61 shows a preview of the page you'll create for Professor Lynne.

Figure 6-61

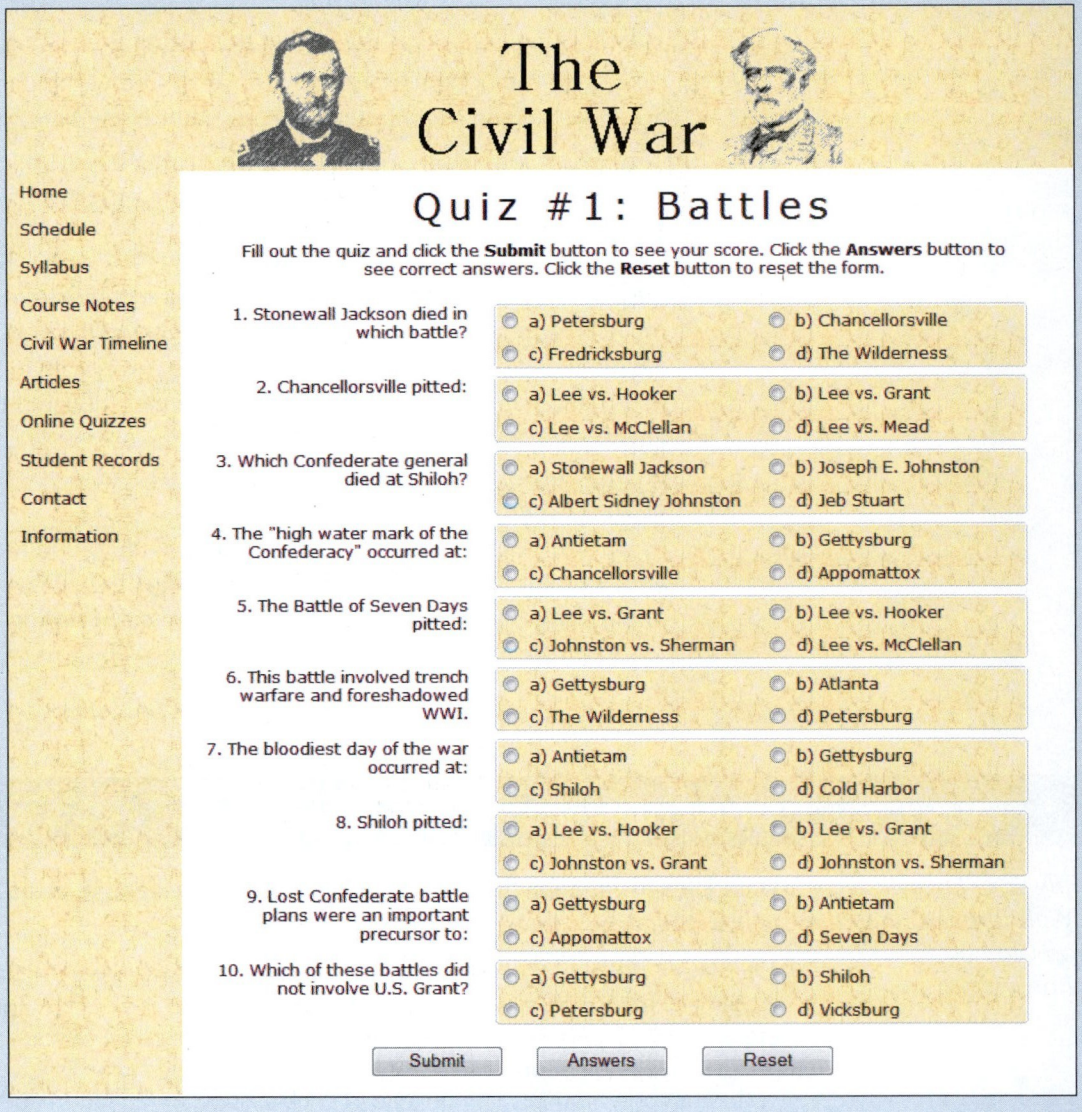

Complete the following:

1. Use your text editor to open the **cwquiztxt.htm** and **qformtxt.css** files from the tutorial.06\case2 folder included with your Data Files. Enter *your name* and *the date* in the comment section of each file. Save the files as **cwquiz.htm** and **qform.css**, respectively.

2. Go to the **cwquiz.htm** file in your text editor and insert a link to the **qform.css** style sheet.

3. Scroll down the file to the rightColumn div element. Professor Lynne has inserted the 10 questions for the online quiz. Enclose the questions in a form element with the id quizForm. Call the CGI script at *http://www.ridgeviewcollmil.edu/quiz* using the post method.

4. Go to the first question and enclose the text of the question in a div element with the class name question.

5. Enclose the set of answers for the first question within a field set.

6. Place a label element around each possible answer for the first question. Put the first answer in the class answerA, the second answer in the class answerB, the third answer in the class answerC, and the fourth answer in the class answerD.

7. Within each of the four labels for the answers to the first question, insert an option button directly before the text of the answer. Assign the ids ans1a, ans1b, ans1c, and ans1d to the four option buttons. Assign the field name question1 to each of the four option buttons. Finally, set the values for the four option buttons to a, b, c, and d.

8. Associate each of the four labels with a different id. Associate the first label with the ans1a field, the second with ans1b, the third with ans1c, and the fourth with ans1d.

9. Repeat Steps 4 through 8 for the remaining nine questions in the quiz, with the following changes:
   - Change the ids for the four option buttons to the question number. For example, the ids for the second question are: ans2a, ans2b, ans2c, and ans2d.
   - Change the field name of the four option buttons to the number of the question. For example, the field name for the second question is question2, for the third question is question3, and so forth.

10. After the last question, insert a div element with the id buttons. Within the element, insert a submit button with the value Submit, a command button with the value Answers, and a reset button with the value Reset.

11. Save your changes to the file.

12. Go to the **qform.css** file in your text editor and add the following styles to the style sheet:
    - Float all elements of the question class on the left margin. Set their widths to 200 pixels and right-align the text. Set the clear style to left so that the element is only displayed when the left margin is clear.
    - Display all field sets as block-level elements floated on the left margin. Set the size of the field sets to 400 pixels wide by 50 pixels high. Add a 20-pixel left margin and a 5-pixel bottom margin. Set the position property to relative. Finally, display the **tan.jpg** file as the background image for the field sets.
    - Use absolute positioning to place all elements of the answerA class at the coordinates (0, 0), place answerB class elements at the coordinates (200, 0), place answerC class elements at (0, 25), and place answerD class elements at (200, 25).
    - Center the contents of the div element with the buttons id. Set the width to 600 pixels and the top/bottom padding to 10 pixels. Set the left/right padding to 0 pixels.
    - For input elements within the buttons div element, set the width to 100 pixels, set the top/bottom margin to 0 pixels, and set the left/right margin to 10 pixels.

13. Save your changes to the file and open **cwquiz.htm** in your Web browser. Verify that the layout and design resemble that shown in Figure 6-61.

14. Submit your completed files to your instructor.

Explore different form controls needed to create an online order form for a pizzeria.

Data Files needed for this Case Problem: buttonball.jpg, leftball.jpg, orderformtxt.css, pizzatxt.htm, rb.css, redball.jpg, rightball.jpg, and topping.txt

Red Ball Pizza Alice Nichols is the owner of Red Ball Pizza, a new pizzeria in Ormond Beach, Florida. You've been working with Alice on creating a Web site for the restaurant. Alice wants to give customers the ability to submit orders online. She has contacted programmers at the restaurant's ISP to process the orders, but she needs a Web form to collect those orders. She's asked you to design a form that would allow customers to select items from the Red Ball Pizza menu. A preview of the Web page you'll create is shown in Figure 6-62.

Figure 6-62

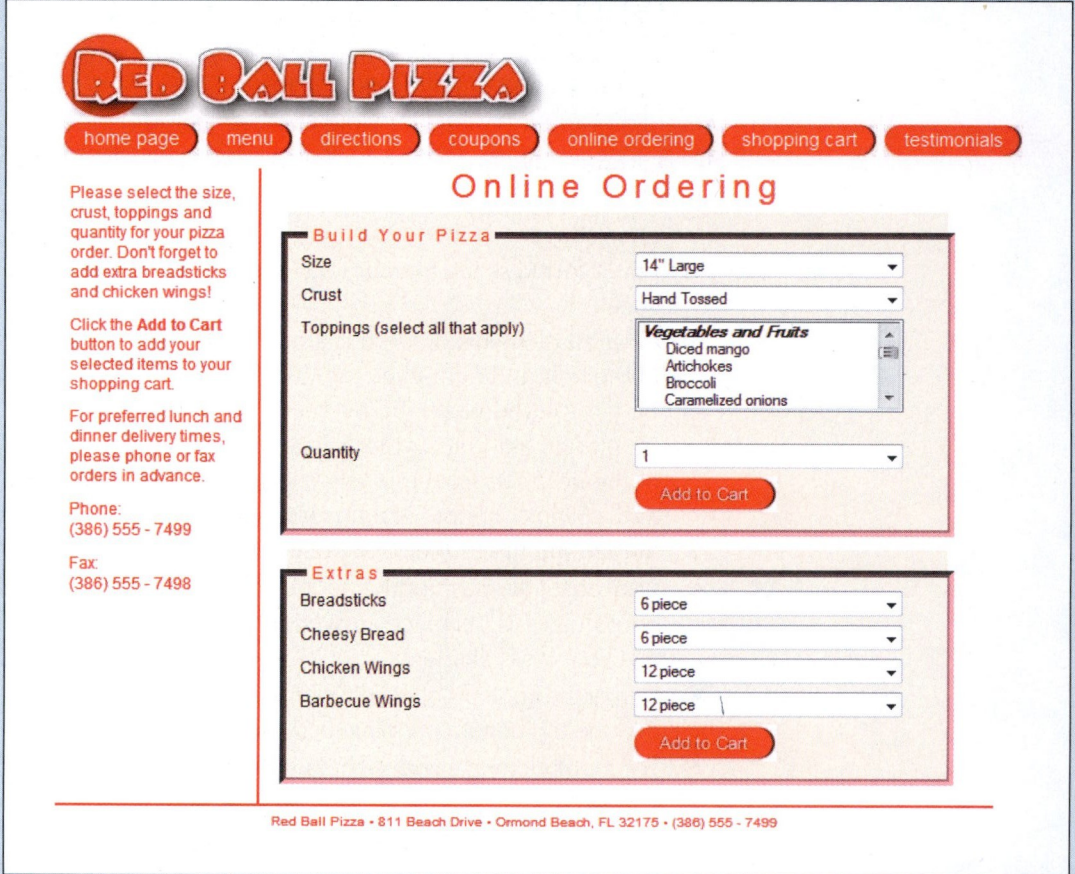

Complete the following:

1. Use your text editor to open the **orderformtxt.css** and **pizzatxt.htm** files from the tutorial.06\case3 folder included with your Data Files. Enter *your name* and *the date* in the comment section of each file. Save the files as **orderform.css** and **pizza.htm**, respectively.

2. Go to the **pizza.htm** file in your text editor and create a link to the **orderform.css** style sheet.

3. Scroll down the file to the rightCol div element and insert a form element directly below the h1 heading.

4. Create a field set with the id pizzaType and the legend Build your Pizza.

EXPLORE
5. Insert a label element with the text Size. Within the label element, insert a selection list for the size field. Add the following options: 12″ Regular, 14″ Large, 16″ Extra Large, and 20″ Family Size. Set the option values to 12, 14, 16, and 20. Make 14″ Large the default selection.

6. Insert a label element with the text "Crust". Within the label element, insert a selection list for the crust field. Add the following options: Thin, Thick, Hand Tossed, and Deep Dish. Make the option values thin, thick, hand, and dish. Make Hand Tossed the default selection.

EXPLORE
7. Insert a label element containing the text "Toppings (select all that apply)". Within the label element, insert the toppings field. Set the size of the selection list to five entries and allow users to make multiple selections.

EXPLORE
8. Within the topping selection list, insert the list of toppings from the **topping.txt** file. Break the options into option groups with labels Vegetables and Fruits, Meats, and Cheeses. You do not have to specify option values.

9. Insert a label element with the text Quantity. Give the label the id qLabel. Within the label element, insert a selection list for the qty field. Insert the numbers 1 through 10 for both the option text and option values.

EXPLORE
10. After the selection list, insert an image control element displaying the image **buttonball.jpg**.

11. Insert a field set with the id extras and the legend Extras.

12. Within the field set, insert a label element containing the text "Breadsticks". Inside the label, insert a selection list for the bread field containing the options 6 piece, 12 piece, and 18 piece. The option values are 6, 12, and 18.

13. Repeat Step 12 for the cheesy bread menu item. The label text is "Cheesy Bread" and the field name is cbread.

14. Insert a label element containing the text "Chicken Wings". Inside the label, insert a selection list for the wings field containing the options 6 piece, 12 piece, 18 piece, and 24 piece with the values 6, 12, 18, and 24. Make 12 the default selection.

15. Repeat Step 14 for the Barbecue Wings menu item. The label text is "Barbecue Wings" and the field name is bwings.

16. After the selection list, insert an image control element displaying the image **buttonball.jpg**.

17. Save your changes to the **pizza.htm** file.

18. Go to the **orderform.css** file in your text editor and add the following styles to the style sheet:
    - Set the margin and padding space of the form element to 0 pixels.
    - Set the bottom margin of the fieldset element to 10 pixels. Set the other margin sizes to 0 pixels. Change the background color to ivory. Add a 5-pixel inset border with the color value (255, 192, 192).
    - Display field set legends in a red font with the kerning set to 3 pixels.
    - Display label elements as blocks with relative positioning. Set the width to 400 pixels, set the top margin to 5 pixels, the bottom margin to 10 pixels, and the left/right margins to 0 pixels.
    - Display select elements using absolute positioning with the top coordinate set to 0 pixels and the left coordinate set to 250 pixels. Set the font size to 12 pixels.
    - For the label with the id qLabel, set the top margin to 80 pixels.
    - Display input elements with a left margin of 250 pixels.

19. Save your changes to the file and then open **pizza.htm** in your Web browser. Verify that the design and layout resemble that shown in Figure 6-62.

20. Submit your completed files to your instructor.

| Create | **Case Problem 4** |

Test your knowledge of Web forms by creating an order form for an online computer store.

Data Files needed for this Case Problem: mclogo.jpg

Millennium Computers You are employed at Millennium Computers, a discount mail-order company specializing in computers and computer components. You've been asked by your supervisor, Sandy Walton, to create an order form Web page so that customers can purchase products online. Your order form is for computer purchases only. There are several options for customers to consider when purchasing computers from Millennium. Customers can choose from the following:

- Processor Speed: 2.4 GHz, 3.2 GHz, 4 GHz
- Memory: 1 GB, 2 GB, 4 GB, 8 GB
- Monitor Size: 15", 17", 19", 21"
- Hard Drive: 240 GB, 500 GB, 750 GB, 1 TB
- DVD burner: yes/no
- LAN card: yes/no
- Media card reader: yes/no

Complete the following:

1. Use your text editor to create an HTML file named **pc.htm** and two style sheets named **mill.css** and **oform.css**. Enter *your name* and *the date* in a comment section of each file. Include any other comments you think will aptly document the purpose and content of the files. Save the files in the tutorial.06\case4 folder included with your Data Files.

2. Design a Web page for the Millennium Computers Web page. Insert any styles you create in the mill.css style sheet. You are free to use the **mclogo.jpg** file and whatever text or images you wish to complete the look and content of the Web page.

3. Within the **pc.htm** file, insert a Web form containing the following elements:
   - Input boxes for the customer's first name, last name, street address, city, state, zip code, and phone number. The field names are fName, lName, street, city, state, zip, and phone.
   - Selection lists for the processor speed, memory, monitor size, and hard drive size. The field names are pSpeed, mem, monitor, and hd. The option values should match the option text.
   - Option buttons for the DVD burner, LAN card, and media card reader options. The field names are dvd, LAN, and mCard.
   - A check box for the warranty field that asks whether customers want the 24-month extended warranty.
   - A text area box requesting additional information or comments on the order.
   - Three form buttons: a submit button with the text "Send Order", a reset button with the text "Cancel Order", and a command button with the text "Contact Me".
   - Name the form cOrder and submit the form using the post method to the CGI script located at *http://www.mill_computers.com/orders/process.cgi*.

4. Create a style for your form in the **oform.css** style sheet. The layout and appearance of the form is up to you.

5. Test your Web site on a variety of browsers to ensure your design works under different conditions.

6. Submit your completed files to your instructor.

Session 6.1

1. A CGI script is a program running on a Web server that receives data from a form and uses it to perform a series of tasks.

2. `<form id="registration" name="registration"> ... </form>`

3. `<fieldset id="contactInfo">`
   `<legend>Contact Information</legend>`
   `</fieldset>`

4. Either with the for attribute (explicitly) or by nesting the control element within the label (implicitly)

5. `<label for="phone">Phone</label>`

6. `maxlength="10"`

7. `<input type="text" id="subscribe" name="subscribe" value="Yes" />`

8. `input[type="text"]{display: block}`

Session 6.2

1. `<input type="radio" name="Computer" value="PC" />`
   `<input type="radio" name="Computer" value="Macintosh" />`

2. `<input type="radio" name="Computer" value="PC`
   `" checked="checked" />`

3. `<select id="State" name="State">`
   `<option>California</option>`
   `<option>Nevada</option>`
   `<option>Oregon</option>`
   `<option>Washington</option>`
   `</select>`

4. `<option selected="selected">Oregon</option>`

5. `<select id="State" name="State" size="4">`

6. `<select id="State" name="State" multiple="multiple">`

7. `<label for="Computer">I use a PC</label>`
   `<input type="checkbox" name="Computer" id="Computer" value="Yes" />`

8. `<textarea rows="10" cols="40" id="Memo" name="Memo">`
   `</textarea>`

Session 6.3

1. `<input type="submit" value="Send Form" />`

2. `<input type="reset" text="Cancel Form" />`

3. `<input type="image" id="Sites" name="Sites" src="sites.gif" />`

4. `<input type="hidden" id="Subject" name="Subject" value="Form Responses" />`

5. `<form action="http:www.j_davis.com/cgi-bin/post-query" method="get"> ...</form>`

6. `<form action="mailto:walker@j_davis.com" method="text/plain" />`

Ending Data Files

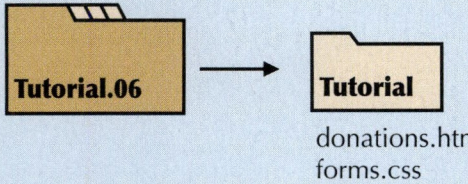

Tutorial.06 →

Tutorial
donations.htm
forms.css
main.css
+ 4 graphic files

Review
main.css
vforms.css
volunteer.htm
+ 4 graphic files

Case1
pcg.css
sform.css
subscription.htm
+ 2 graphic files

Case2
cw.css
cwquiz.htm
qform.css
+ 2 graphic files

Case3
orderform.css
pizza.htm
rb.css
+ 4 graphic files

Case4
mill.css
oform.css
pc.htm
+ 1 graphic file

Working with Multimedia

Enhancing a Web Site with Sound, Video, and Applets

Case | Jumbo Popcorn

Maxine Michaels is a movie buff and has a special fondness for classic movies and musicals. To pursue her interests, she's started a Web site called Jumbo Popcorn containing articles, reviews, and news about movies and cinematic history.

Maxine wants to enhance her Web site by adding sound and video so that users can not only read about movies, but also enjoy audio and video clips of famous movie moments. Maxine is aware that there are several technical issues involved with putting multimedia clips on her Web site. She's asked you to help complete a sample page describing the 1951 classic movie, *Royal Wedding*, starring Fred Astaire and Jane Powell. Note: To complete this tutorial, you should have Adobe Flash and Apple QuickTime on your computer. If you are running Windows, you should also have Windows Media Player.

Starting Data Files

Tutorial.07 →

Tutorial
CreditRoll.class
jp.css
jumbotxt.htm
overture.mp3
rwdance.mov
rwdance.swf
rwdance.wmv
+ 2 text files
+ 15 graphic files

Review
CreditRoll.class
astairetxt.htm
fabio.css
fasong.mp3
hatrack.mov
hatrack.swf
hatrack.wmv
+ 1 text file
+ 16 graphic files

Case1
devotion.mp3
fireice.mp3
poetry.css
PopBtn.class
PopMenu.class
rftxt.htm
+ 6 graphic files

Case2
roadtxt.txt
rw.css
rwlogo.jpg
trailridge.swf

Case3
Cmplx.class
Controls.class
fractaltxt.htm
FracPanel.class
fstyles.css
Mandel.class
mandel.swf
+ 2 graphic files

Case4
beethoven.mp3
CreditRoll.class
+ 2 text files
+ 2 graphic files

Session 7.1

Introducing Multimedia

You and Maxine sit down to discuss her new cinema Web site. She's completed much of the work on the *Royal Wedding* Web page and wants to show you her progress. Open her page now.

To view Maxine's document:

▶ 1. In your text editor, open the **jumbotxt.htm** file located in the tutorial.07\tutorial folder included with your Data Files. Enter *your name* and *the date* in the comment section of the file. Save the file as **jumbo.htm** in the same folder.

▶ 2. Take some time to review the contents of the file. Maxine has already created a style sheet for the document stored in the **jp.css** file. You will not have to make any changes to the style sheet file.

▶ 3. Open **jumbo.htm** in your Web browser. Figure 7-1 shows the current layout of the page.

The initial Royal Wedding Web page | Figure 7-1

A Web site for lovers of classic films

Jumbo Popcorn

| Home | Movies | Actors | Directors | Genres | My Picks | Links |

Royal Wedding (1951) ★★★

Overview
Title Page
User Comments
Reviews
Quotes
Trivia
Awards

Showings
Trailers
TV Schedule
DVD Details
Technical Specs
Soundtrack

Featuring
Fred Astaire
Jane Powell
Peter Lawford
Keenan Wynn
Alan Jay Lerner

You Might Also Enjoy
Finian's Rainbow
Seven Brides for 7 Brothers
Top Hat
Swing Time
Three Little Words
Roberta
Shall We Dance?
The Gay Divorcee
Easter Parade
Funny Face
Daddy Long Legs

Cast

Tom Bowen ... Fred Astaire
Ellen Bowen ... Jane Powell
Lord John Brindale ... Peter Lawford
Anne Ashmond ... Sarah Churchill
Irving Klinger ... Keenan Wynn
Edgar Klinger ... Keenan Wynn
James Ashmond ... Albert Sharpe

Listen Up

The music for *Royal Wedding* was composed by Burton Lane, who is best known for his work in *Finian's Rainbow* (1947) and his Grammy Award-winning *On a Clear Day You Can See Forever* (1965). Lane's greatest musical accomplishment may very well be his discovery of an 11-year-old singing phenom named Frances Gumm, whom the world now knows better as Judy Garland.

insert audio clip of the film overture

Synopsis

Tom Bowen (Fred Astaire) and Ellen Bowen (Jane Powell) are a brother and sister dance team from New York. Their agent (Keenan Wynn) books them in London for performances during the time of the royal wedding. Aboard a cruise ship to London, Ellen becomes involved with aristocrat and playboy, Lord John Brindale (Peter Lawford). In London, Tom meets and falls in love Anne Ashmond (Sarah Churchill), a dancer in his show. Despite a few minor complications, it all ends happily as the two couples find love and marriage on the day of the royal wedding.

Royal Wedding is famous for several dance sequences, including a classic number in which Astaire appears to dance on the ceiling and walls of his hotel room. Jane Powell proves to be an elegant and athletic partner for Astaire; though perhaps his best duet of the movie takes place with a hat rack he discovers on the cruise to England. This is one of Astaire's best and I highly recommend it.

In Focus

The high point of *Royal Wedding* is the "Ceiling Dance" in which Fred Astaire appears to literally dance on the ceiling and walls of his hotel room. The effect was accomplished by putting the whole set inside of a 20-foot diameter rotating cage. As the cage turned, Astaire would seamlessly dance across the four sides of the box, creating the illusion of weightlessness. The same technique would later be used to simulate a zero gravity environment in *2001: A Space Odyssey*.

insert video clip of a dance sequence

| Home | Movies | Actors | Directors | Genres | My Picks | Links |

Royal Wedding is one of a handful of Metro-Goldwyn-Mayer productions from the early 1950s whose original copyrights were never renewed. This means that versions of the movie are now in the public domain and that Maxine can add sound and video clips from the film to this Web page without worrying about the copyright. One of her audio clips contains the first few seconds from the film's overture. She would like to add that clip to the Listen Up box in the upper-right corner of the Web page. She also has a brief excerpt from a Fred Astaire dance number that she wants to add to the In Focus box in the lower-right corner of the page.

Multimedia and Bandwidth

When creating Web pages that include multimedia elements such as sound and video, one of the most important factors that you need to consider is the issue of bandwidth. **Bandwidth** is a measure of the amount of data that can be sent through a communication pipeline each second. Bandwidth values range from slow connections—such as land-lines, which can transfer data at a maximum rate of 56 kilobits per second—to high-speed direct network connections capable of transferring data at several gigabytes per second. In the early days of the Web, efforts to include multimedia elements in Web sites were hampered by low-bandwidth connections, as most users connected to the Internet over slow landlines. Under those conditions, a Web site containing more than one or two multimedia clips would be inaccessible to most users.

This situation led to two developments. One was to make high-speed Internet access more available to the general public through the use of cable modems and DSL. The second development was reducing the size of large multimedia clips through file compression technology that doesn't sacrifice sound or video quality. Paired together, the two developments have made multimedia much more accessible to most Internet users. One of the most popular sites on the Web is YouTube, which is almost solely dedicated to the creation and dissemination of user-created video.

External and Embedded Media

As shown in Figure 7-2, multimedia is made available on the Web in two different ways: as external and embedded media. With **external media**, the media file is accessed through a link that the user clicks to download the media file to his or her computer. An advantage of using an external file is that users don't have to retrieve a multimedia clip; they do so only if they want to. This is useful in situations where a user has a low-bandwidth connection and wants to choose whether to spend time downloading a large multimedia file.

Figure 7-2   **Comparing external and embedded media**

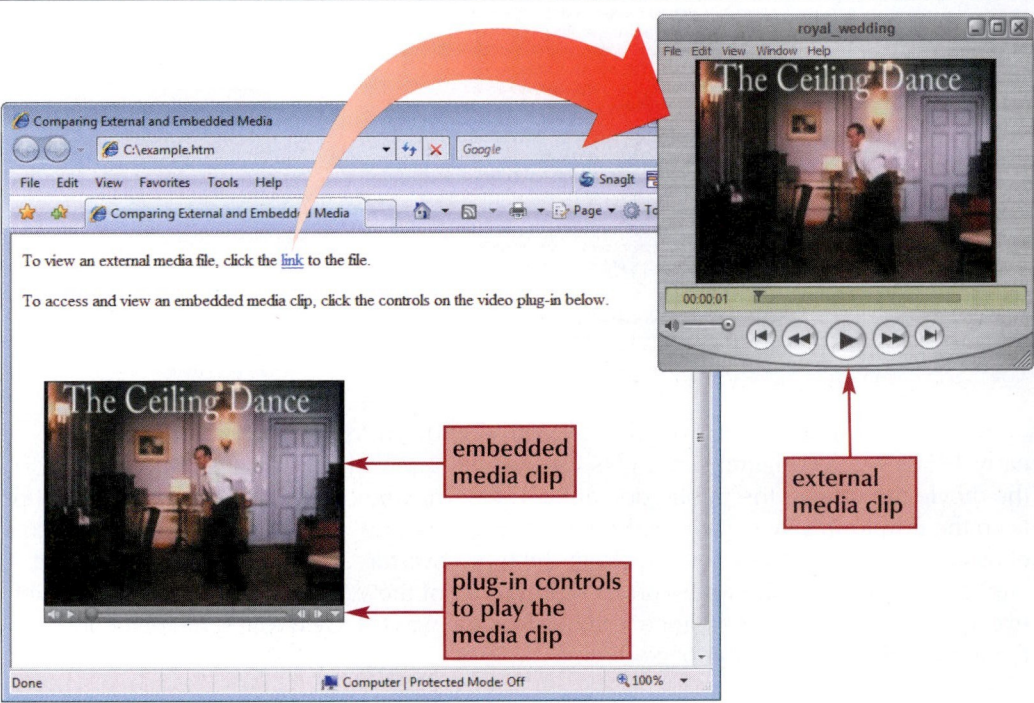

You add external media to a Web page through a hypertext link. For example, to create a link to a sound file named royal.mp3, you could add the following hypertext link to your Web page:

```
<a href="royal.mp3">Music from Royal Wedding</a>
```

When this link is clicked, the royal.mp3 sound file will be downloaded to the user's computer, where it can be played by a media player program such as Apple's QuickTime Player. The sound file will also be stored in one of the user's folders, where it can be played again and again.

Embedded media, on the other hand, is displayed within the Web page in a fashion similar to an inline image. The controls to play the media clip are also displayed as part of the Web page. Users who wish to play the clip do not leave the Web page to do so; instead, they click the player controls. Because embedded media appears within the page, you can supplement it with other material such as text that describes the clip's content and purpose. In essence, embedded media becomes part of the content of the page just as inline images become part of the page content.

To play embedded media, users' browsers often will have access to a **plug-in** or **add-on**—an extra component added to a program (such as a Web browser) to provide a feature or capability not included in the program. In Figure 7-2, a video plug-in has been added to the Web browser to provide the capability of displaying and playing a video clip within the Web page. Most browsers have a collection of plug-ins preinstalled for your use; you can also download and install additional plug-ins from the browser's manufacturer as the need arises.

Maxine has decided that she would like to use embedded media on her Web site to provide users with even more information about classic movies and the actors who appear in them. Your first task will be to embed an audio clip on the *Royal Wedding* Web page. Before doing that, you should learn about the various audio formats available and explore the differences in their sound quality and file size.

Tip

You can view a list of plug-ins installed on Firefox and Opera by entering *about: plugins* in the browser address bar. For Internet Explorer, click Manage Add-ons from the Tools menu and then select Enable or Disable Add-ons to view the list.

Exploring Digital Audio

If you want to add sound to your Web site, it's helpful to understand some of the issues involved in converting sound into a format that can be played on your users' computers and over their Internet connections. Sound is composed of combinations of sound waves; and every sound wave can be described on the basis of two components: amplitude and frequency. Figure 7-3 shows a basic sound wave. The **amplitude** is the height of the sound wave and it relates to the sound's volume—the higher the amplitude, the louder the sound. The **frequency** is the speed at which the sound wave moves and it relates to the sound's pitch—the higher the frequency, the higher the pitch.

A simple sound wave ◀ Figure 7-3

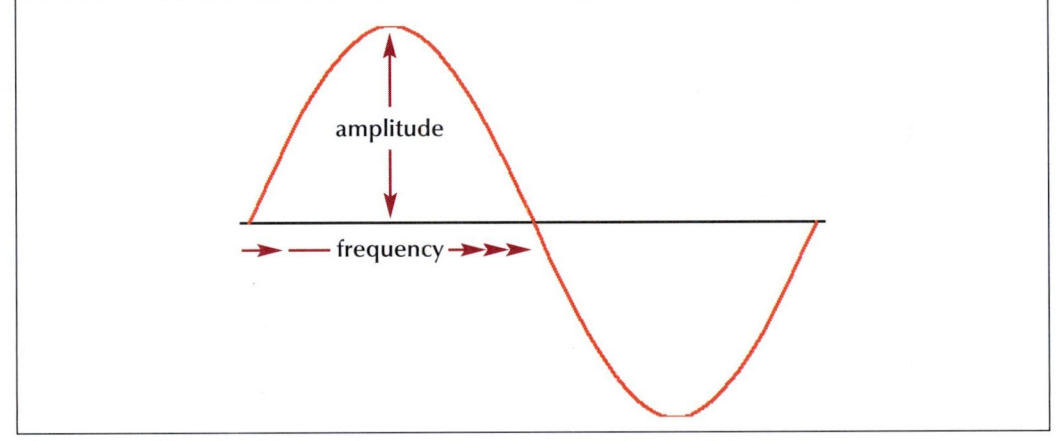

When you hear sound, your ears hear a continuously varying signal created by the vibrations that sound makes on your eardrum; to store that sound in a computer file, it must be converted into discrete pieces or bits of information. A digital recording of that sound takes measurements of the amplitude at different moments in time; each measurement is called a **sample**. The number of samples taken per second is called the **sampling rate**, a value that is measured in kilohertz (kHz). As shown in Figure 7-4, a higher sampling rate means that more samples are taken per second, resulting in a digital recording that more closely matches the original sound. There is a trade-off, however, as increasing the sampling rate also increases the size of a sound file. This might not be a problem with a CD recording, but it can be an issue when transferring sound over an Internet connection—where it's important to keep file sizes compact.

Figure 7-4 ▶ **Different sampling rates**

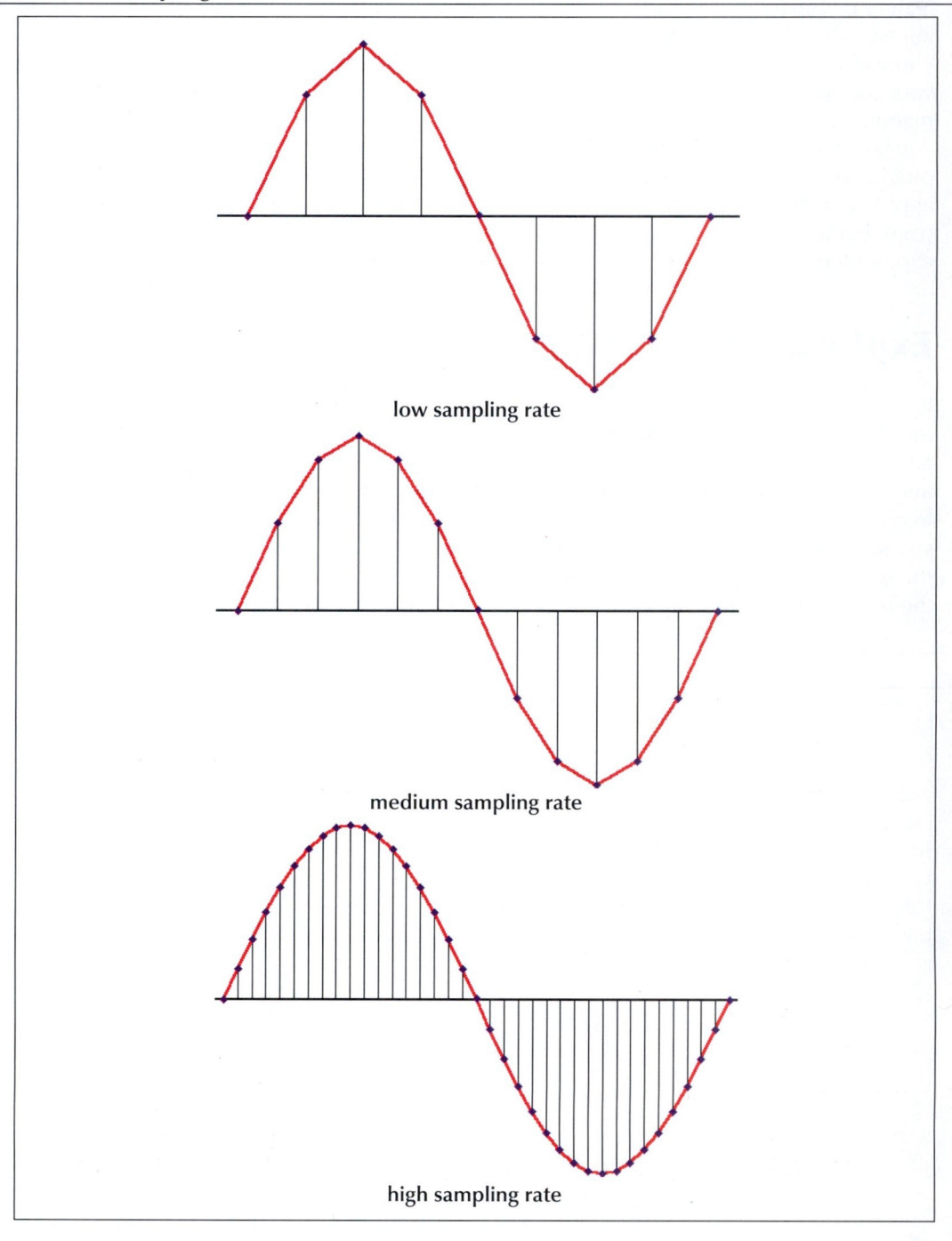

low sampling rate

medium sampling rate

high sampling rate

The second factor in converting sound to digital form is the sample resolution. **Sample resolution** or **bit depth** indicates the precision in measuring the sound within each sample. Three commonly used sample resolution values are 8 bit, 16 bit, and 32 bit. As shown in Figure 7-5, increasing the sample resolution creates a digital sound file that represents the analog signal more accurately, but this results in a larger file. For most applications, saving sound files at the 16-bit resolution provides a good balance between sound quality and file size.

Different sampling resolutions ◄ Figure 7-5

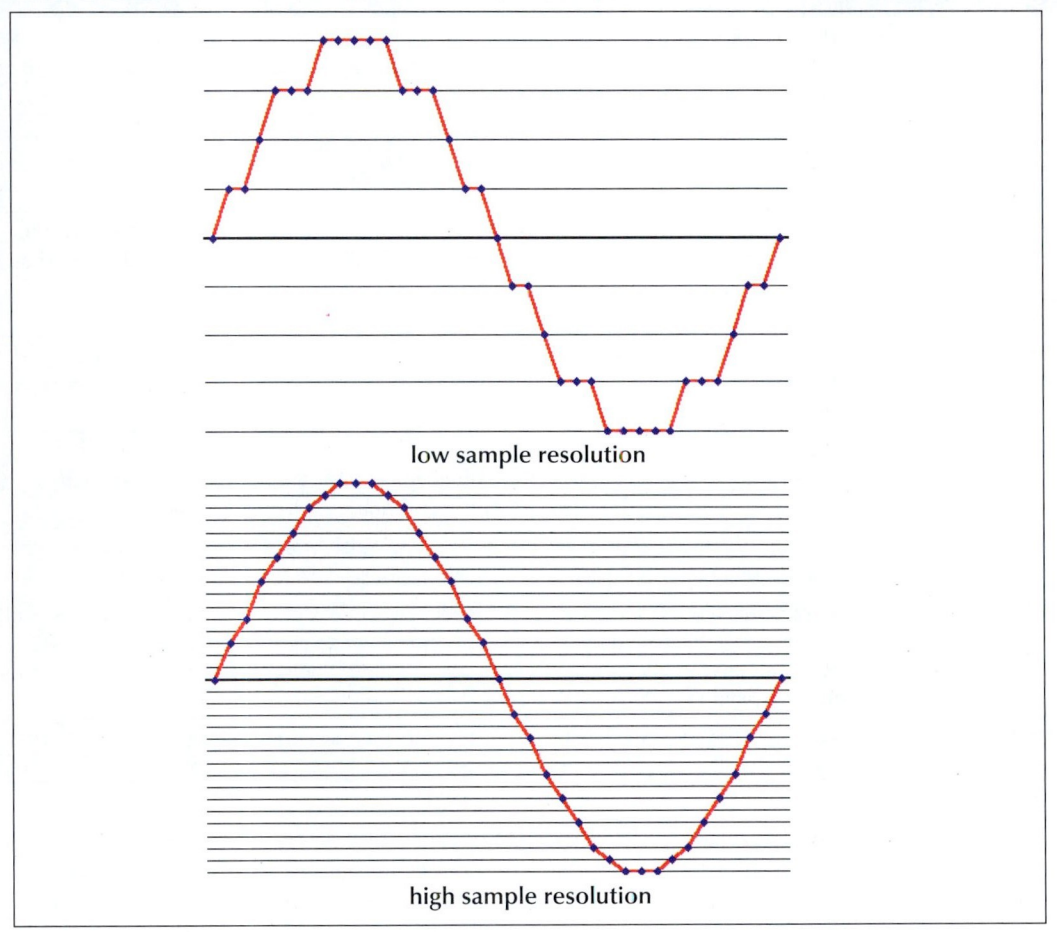

low sample resolution

high sample resolution

Another factor affecting audio quality is the number of sound channels. Typically, the choice is between stereo (two channels) or monaural (a single channel). Stereo provides a richer sound than mono, but with the trade-off of approximately doubling the size of the sound file.

The size of an audio clip is therefore related to the sampling rate, the sample resolution, and the number of channels. The total size can be expressed in terms of the **bitrate**, which is the number of bits of data required for each second of sound. For music stored on compact discs, the bitrate is determined by multiplying the sampling rate by the sample resolution by the number of channels. A typical CD track has a bitrate value of 1411 Kbps, which is too high for practical use on the Web. Therefore, sound files used on the Web must employ **file compression**, a process that reduces the size of the audio file but sometimes at the expense of sound quality. The most common file compression format is the MP3 format used throughout the Web as well as on portable music players and cell phones. MP3s can achieve near-CD quality sound at bitrates of 192 to 320 Kbps. The standard bitrate for MP3s is 192 Kbps, which results in some minor sound degradation but also requires only 13% of the size required for CD-quality sound. If the sound clip involves spoken words and not music, even greater sound compression can be used without affecting the overall quality of the recording. Therefore, MP3 is one of the sound formats ideally suited for use on the Internet. Figure 7-6 lists some of the other common sound file formats that Maxine might consider for her Web site.

Figure 7-6 | **Common sound file formats on the Web**

Format	Description
AIFF/AIFC	Audio Interchange File Format. AIFF was developed by Apple for use on the Macintosh operating system. AIFF sound files can be either 8 bit or 16 bit, can be mono or stereo, and can be recorded at several different sampling rates.
AU	Also called mlaw (mu-law) format. One of the oldest sound formats, it is primarily used on UNIX workstations. AU sound files have 8-bit sample resolutions, use a sampling rate of 8 kHz, and are recorded in mono.
MIDI	Musical Instrument Digital Interface. MIDI files cannot be used for general sound recording, like other sound formats, but are limited to synthesizers and music files. The MIDI format represents sound by recording each note's pitch, length, and volume. MIDI files tend to be much smaller in size than other sound formats.
MP3	The most popular format for downloading and storing music, MP3 compresses sound files to roughly one-tenth the size of uncompressed files while maintaining good audio quality.
RealAudio	A popular sound format on the Web, RealAudio files are designed for real-time playing over low- to high-bandwidth connections. RealAudio files tend to be much smaller than AU or WAV files, but the sound quality is usually not as good.
SND	The SND format is used primarily on the Macintosh operating system for creating system sounds. This format is not widely supported on the Web.
WAV	WAV is the standard audio format for Windows PCs and is commonly used for storing uncompressed CD-quality sound files. In its uncompressed format, a WAV file will require about 10 megabytes per minute of sound; however, compression algorithms are available to reduce the file size.
WMA	Windows Media Audio is a proprietary audio format developed by Microsoft to compete with MP3s, offering near or better levels of compression than MP3s.

Maxine has created a 30-second MP3 sound clip from the overture of *Royal Wedding* and stored it in a sound file named overture.mp3. The file is a monaural recording with sample rate of 44 kHz and a bitrate of 96 Kbps, which she feels is adequate for use on her Web site. You'll next explore how to embed this clip into her Web page.

Another popular sound format for the Web is the MIDI format. **MIDI (Musical Instrument Digital Interface)**, a standard sound format for synthesizers and sound cards, uses mathematical functions to describe the pitch, length, and volume of each note in a musical piece. Because MIDI is a widely supported standard, sounds created on one synthesizer can be played and manipulated on another synthesizer. Sound-editing software can also be used to manipulate the MIDI files, creating new sounds and sound effects. An additional advantage of MIDI files is that they are much smaller compared with most sound formats. A MIDI composition lasting several minutes is less than 20 kilobytes in size, while a similar file in WAV format would be several megabytes in size, and MP3s for similar musical pieces might be several hundred kilobytes in size. However, the major drawback of the MIDI format is that it is limited to instrumental music—it cannot be used for general sounds, such as speech.

Working with Embedded Objects

Most browsers support two elements for embedding objects such as sound clips within a Web page: the embed element and the object element. The embed element is the older approach, initially introduced by the Netscape browser to support multimedia plug-ins; it is supported by most browsers. However, because it is not part of the World Wide Web Consortium (W3C) specifications, it will be rejected by strict applications of XHTML. To be in strict compliance with the W3C specifications, you should use the object element, which is supported by all major browsers. You'll explore both the object element and the embed element in this tutorial, starting with the object element. The syntax of the object element is

```
<object attributes>
   parameters
</object>
```

where *attributes* are the attributes that define the object and *parameters* are values that determine how the embedded object is rendered and played within the browser. The object element can be used with almost any type of content, from sound and video clips to graphic images, PDF files, and even the content of other Web pages. The W3C's original vision was to have the object element used for all nontextual content. For example, the object element could be used in place of the img element for the display of inline images, though this is rarely done. The primary use of the object element is for sound and video clips.

Object Data Sources and MIME Types

To specify the source of the content displayed within the object, you add the data attribute

```
<object data="url"> ... </object>
```

to the opening <object> tag, where *url* is the filename and location of the object file. For example, the following code specifies the overture.mp3 file as the object's data source:

```
<object data="overture.mp3"> ... </object>
```

Because the object element can be used with a wide variety of data types, you indicate the type of object by adding the type attribute

```
type="MIME type"
```

to the <object> tag, where *MIME type* describes the type of data contained in the object. **MIME types** or **Multipurpose Internet Mail Extension types** identify the type of data contained in the file and provide information about how that data should be interpreted. One common MIME type you've used since Tutorial 3 is text/css, which identifies a text file as containing CSS style declarations. The MIME type for mp3 files is audio/mpeg, though audio/x-mpeg is also supported by most browsers. Figure 7-7 lists the MIME types for other sound file formats.

Figure 7-7 | Sound file MIME types

Format	File Extension	MIME Type
AIFC	aifc	audio/x-aiff
AIFF	aif	audio/x-aiff
AIFF	aiff	audio/x-aiff
AU	au	audio/basic
MIDI	mid	audio/mid
MIDI	rmi	audio/mid
MP3	mp3	audio/mpeg
MP3	mp3	audio/x-mpeg
RealAudio	ra	audio/x-pn-realaudio
RealAudio	ram	audio/x-pn-realaudio
SND	snd	audio/basic
WAV	wav	audio/wav
WAV	wav	audio/x-wav

InSight | MIME Types

The MIME type designation was first introduced as a way of attaching nontextual content to e-mail messages. With the growth of the World Wide Web, the use of MIME types expanded to include the flow of information across the Web. Each MIME type contains a header that indicates the type of data content. The header has the general form

   type/subtype

where *type* is the general data type and *subtype* is a special classification of data within that type. The possible values for *type* are: application, audio, image, message, model, multipart, text, and video. Within these types there can be dozens or hundreds of subtypes. The subtype value can often be determined by examining the file extension of the object. For example, a JPEG image is identified as image/jpeg. Note that different file extensions can be associated with the same MIME type. JPEG image files can end in .jpe, .jfif, .jpg, or .jpeg, but all are designated as image/jpeg.

MIME types also include information that tells the computer how to handle and interpret the object data. Most operating systems give the administrator the ability to associate MIME types with specific programs. You can view and change these associations in the Windows or Macintosh Control Panel. For example, you can direct your computer to associate image/jpeg content with a particular graphics program, which tells the operating system to use that graphics program to always open files containing image/jpeg content. Note that any changes you make in the Control Panel might impact how your browser handles and displays multimedia content.

Maxine is ready for you to add an object element for the overture.mp3 file to the jumbo.htm file.

To insert the object element:

▶ **1.** Return to the **jumbo.htm** file in your text editor and scroll down to the section in the middle of the document containing a short bio of Burton Lane, the composer of the music for *Royal Wedding*.

▶ **2.** Directly after the h2 heading, insert the following HTML code, as shown in Figure 7-8:

```
<p style="text-align: center">

   <object data="overture.mp3" type="audio/mpeg">
   </object>

</p>
```

Inserting the object element	Figure 7-8

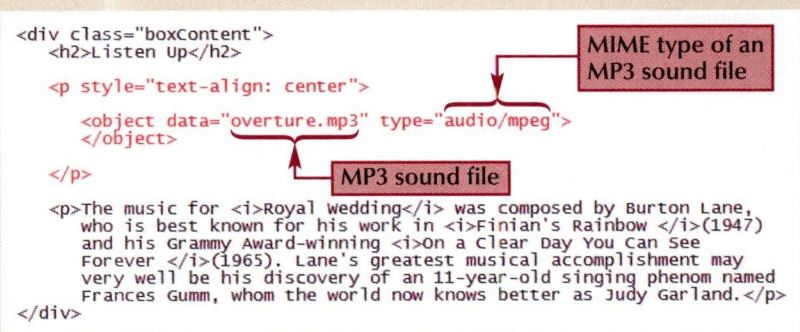

Tip

For large media clips, you can have your browser display a text message as it loads the media file by adding the attribute `standby="text"` where *text* is the text to be displayed temporarily in place of the media clip.

The code you've just entered tells the browser the source and type of object, but it doesn't give any indication of how the sound clip should be rendered and played. Some of that will be determined by the plug-in used by the browser, but you can also add explicit instructions to control how the plug-in will operate and interact with the sound file.

Setting the Object Width and Height

An embedded sound clip is displayed with controls that allow the user to start, pause, rewind, and control the volume of the playback. So part of inserting the sound clip also includes defining how many of these controls appear on the Web page. This is done by setting the size of the sound clip using the attribute

```
width="value" height="value"
```

where the width and height attributes set the size of the control in pixels. The width and height attributes are required for XHTML code.

For sound clips, you should set the height to at least 25 pixels to allow enough space to display the control buttons. The width determines how many control buttons are displayed. In some cases, you might only need to display the play button; while in other cases, you'll want to display all of the buttons available with the plug-in. Figure 7-9 shows the minimum widths needed to display controls for two popular sound plug-ins: QuickTime and Windows Media Player.

Figure 7-9 **Plug-in controls under different width values**

Plug-in	Width	Description	Image
QuickTime Player	17px	Displays only the play button	
	33px	Adds the popup menu button	
	49px	Adds a volume control	
	74px	Adds a progress bar	
	106px	Adds fast-forward and reverse buttons	
	150px	Extends the length of the progress bar	
Windows Media Player	42px	Displays only the play button	
	66px	Adds the stop button	
	164px	Adds fast-forward and reverse buttons	
	279px	Adds a volume control	

You decide to set the height of the sound control for Maxine's Web page to 25 pixels and the width to 280 pixels to ensure all of the sound control buttons appear on the Web page.

To set the width and height of the sound control:

1. Return to the **jumbo.htm** file in your text editor and add the following attributes to the <object> tag, as shown in Figure 7-10:

   ```
   width="280" height="25"
   ```

Figure 7-10 **Setting the object width and height**

```
<p style="text-align: center">
    <object data="overture.mp3" type="audio/mpeg"
     width="280" height="25">
    </object>
</p>
```

2. Save your changes to the file.

The width and height attributes define the space allotted to the controls for the sound clip. But to define how users will interact with those controls, you must specify the control parameters.

Working with Parameters

Every plug-in has a collection of **parameters** that define the appearance and behavior of the embedded object. These parameters are defined by adding the parameter elements

```
<object attributes>
   <param name="name1" value="value1" />
   <param name="name2" value="value2" />
   <param name="name3" value="value3" />
...
</object>
```

within the <object> tag, where *name1*, *name2*, *name3*, and so forth are the parameter names and *value1*, *value2*, *value3*, etc. are the values of each parameter. The parameter names and values are based on the type of object being embedded and on the plug-in used to display the object. One parameter common to most plug-ins for embedded sound is the src parameter, which defines the source of the sound file. So to set the source of your object to the overture.mp3 file, you would enter the following src parameter:

```
<object attributes>
   <param name="src" value="overture.mp3" />
</object>
```

Although the src parameter is similar to the data attribute you've already studied, it's required for some browsers such as Internet Explorer, so you should include it in addition to the data attribute. Figure 7-11 list some other parameters supported by QuickTime and Windows Media Player.

Figure 7-11 **Parameters for QuickTime and Windows Media Player**

Plug-in	Parameter	Description	Value(s)
QuickTime Player	autoplay	Starts playing the clip automatically when the page loads	true | false
	bgcolor	Sets the background color for the space allotted to the object	#rrggbb | color name
	controller	Specifies whether or not to show the object controls	true | false
	endtime	Specifies the time in the clip at which playback ends	hh:mm:ss
	href	Specifies a page to load when the user clicks on the object	url
	loop	Plays the clip in a continuous loop, forward, backward, or both (palindrome)	true | false | palindrome
	src	The source of the clip	url
	starttime	Specifies the time in the clip at which playback begins	hh:mm:ss
	volume	Sets the initial audio volume	0 - 255
Windows Media Player	autostart	Starts playing the clip automatically when the page loads	true | false
	filename	The source of the clip	url
	mute	Specifies whether or not the clip should be initially muted	true | false
	selectionstart	Specifies the time in the clip at which playback begins	seconds
	selectionstop	Specifies the time in the clip at which playback ends	seconds
	playcount	Specifies the number of times the clip will play	integer
	showcontrols	Specifies whether or not to show the object controls	true | false
	volume	Sets the initial audio volume	-10,000 - 0

For example, if you want your sound clip to play automatically when the page is opened, you would enter the following parameter if the browser uses the QuickTime plug-in:

```
<param name="autoplay" value="true" />
```

For Windows Media Player, the parameter to start the clip automatically is:

```
<param name="autostart" value="true" />
```

If a plug-in encounters a parameter it doesn't recognize, it will ignore it. So if you don't know which plug-in the browser will use to play your multimedia clip, you should include both parameter values in your HTML code. Figure 7-11 shows only a small list of the parameters associated with the two popular media players. You can get more information on other parameters and their values from each player's home page on the Web. Remember that users can always set the default options for their plug-ins. So if you are not sure, for example, that the sound controls will be displayed by the plug-in, you can always turn on that feature using either the controller parameter (for QuickTime) or the showcontrols parameter (for Windows Media Player).

Inserting an Object Element

- To insert an object, use the general syntax

```
<object data="url" type="MIME type"
 width="value" height="value">
    parameters
</object>
```
where *url* is the URL of the filename and location of the object file, *MIME type* specifies the data type of the object, *value* specifies the width and height sizes in pixels, and *parameters* are parameters associated with the embedded object.
- To insert a parameter, use the tag

```
<param name="name" value="value" />
```
where *name* is the name of the parameter and *value* is the parameter's value.

Maxine suggests that you add a few parameter elements to the code for the overture.mp3 sound clip. She wants to ensure that the browser always displays the sound clip controls and she doesn't want the clip to start automatically. Because you don't know which plug-in the browser will run, you'll add the following parameter elements to the file:

```
<param name="src" value="overture.mp3" />
<param name="autoplay" value="false" />
<param name="autostart" value="false" />
<param name="controller" value="true" />
<param name="showcontrols" value="true" />
```

Add this code to the jumbo.htm file.

To enter parameter values for the embedded sound clip:

1. Return to the **jumbo.htm** file in your text editor, and within the object tag, insert the following parameter elements as shown in Figure 7-12:

```
<param name="src" value="overture.mp3" />
<param name="autoplay" value="false" />
<param name="autostart" value="false" />
<param name="controller" value="true" />
<param name="showcontrols" value="true" />
```

Adding object parameters — **Figure 7-12**

```
<object data="overture.mp3" type="audio/mpeg"
  width="280" height="25">
    <param name="src" value="overture.mp3" />
    <param name="autoplay" value="false" />
    <param name="autostart" value="false" />
    <param name="controller" value="true" />
    <param name="showcontrols" value="true" />
</object>
```

2. Save your changes to the file and then reload **jumbo.htm** in your Web browser. Depending on your browser, you might see controls for the QuickTime Player or for the Windows Media Player, as shown in Figure 7-13.

Figure 7-13	Plug-ins for the overture.mp3 plug-in

sound clip with Windows Media Player   sound clip with QuickTime Player

Trouble? If you don't see any sound controls on the Web page, your browser might not have the necessary plug-ins installed. If this is the case, you might be prompted by the browser to either activate or download and install the necessary plug-ins. You can also install plug-ins by going to the Web site for your browser; it should have links to all of the popular multimedia plug-ins. Talk to your instructor or technical resource person for permission before installing any programs on a lab computer.

▶ **3.** Click the embedded sound clip and then click the **Play** button on the sound controls to start playing the sound clip.

You show the Web page to Maxine. She appreciates the work you've done but wonders why some users will see the QuickTime plug-in and others will see Windows Media Player. You explain that the choice of plug-in is determined by the settings on users' browsers. Maxine would prefer that QuickTime Player be used because it is a standard that is available for both Windows and Macintosh. She asks whether you can specify a particular plug-in to be used with a media clip.

Working with ActiveX Components

Different browsers support embedded media in different ways. For example, Internet Explorer supports a technology called ActiveX to play embedded media. **ActiveX** is a technology developed by Microsoft involving reusable software components that can be run from within a variety of Windows programs. For example, a programmer could create an ActiveX component to display a drop-down list box to be run within Internet Explorer, and that same component could be run from within Microsoft Word or Microsoft Excel. Another ActiveX component could be created to play video clips or sound files. The media player shown in Figure 7-13 is one example of an ActiveX control for playing such files.

There are literally thousands of ActiveX components available to the programmer and end user. The problem is that ActiveX is a technology designed only for Windows, and thus you cannot rely solely upon it if you're developing a program or Web site that will be used under a variety of operating systems.

The classid Attribute

Each ActiveX control is identified by a unique string of characters called the **class id**. The class id value is determined by the manufacturer of the ActiveX control. Figure 7-14 lists the class id values for several ActiveX controls that Maxine can use in creating her Web site.

Class ids for ActiveX controls ◀ **Figure 7-14**

ActiveX Control	Class ID
Flash Shockwave Player	D27CDB6E-AE6D-11cf-96B8-444553540000
QuickTime Player	02BF25D5-8C17-4B23-BC80-D3488ABDDC6B
RealAudio Player	CFCDAA03-8BE4-11cf-B84B-0020AFBBCCFA
Windows Media Player	6BF52A52-394A-11d3-B153-00C04F79FAA6
Java applet	8AD9C840-044E-11D1-B3E9-00805F499D93

To insert a specific ActiveX control into your Web page, you would add the classid attribute

```
classid="clsid:id"
```

to the <object> tag, where *id* is the class id of the ActiveX control. For example, to insert the ActiveX control for the QuickTime Player, you would add the following classid attribute to the <object> tag:

```
classid="clsid:02BF25D5-8C17-4B23-BC80-D3488ABDDC6B"
```

Class id values are not case sensitive, so you can use upper- or lower-case letters in your HTML code; but you do have to enter the entire class id string with no omissions or errors. Given the length of the class id text string, this makes writing code for ActiveX objects a bit cumbersome. You can find the class id values for each ActiveX control by viewing the manufacturer's documentation.

The codebase Attribute

When browsers encounter plug-ins or ActiveX controls they don't recognize, they usually leave a blank space where the embedded object would normally appear. One way of dealing with this problem is to provide the browser with information about where a working version of the plug-in or control can be downloaded. This is done by adding the codebase attribute

```
codebase="url"
```

to the <object> tag, where *url* is the filename and location of the program. In some cases, these programs are stored in installation files called **cab** or **cabinet files**, which automatically install the necessary software on the user's computer. You can usually find the location of installation programs in the manufacturer's documentation. For the ActiveX QuickTime Player, the URL for the cabinet file is *http://www.apple.com/qtactivex/qtplugin.cab*. So to embed an object using the ActiveX version of the QuickTime Player, you would enter the following code in your Web page:

```
<object classid="clsid:02BF25D5-8C17-4B23-BC80-D3488ABDDC6B"
        codebase="http://www.apple.com/qtactivex/qtplugin.cab">

    parameters

</object>
```

When Internet Explorer encounters this object, it will first attempt to insert the ActiveX QuickTime control into the Web page. If it can't find an ActiveX control on the computer with that class id value, it will then access the cab file at the URL specified in the codebase attribute and prompt the user to install the ActiveX control from that location. This frees the user from having to search for the program file.

Reference Window | **Inserting an ActiveX Control**

- To insert an ActiveX control for Internet Explorer, use the object element

```
<object data="url" type="MIME type"
 width="value" height="value"
 classid="clsid:id" codebase="url">
   parameters
</object>
```

where *id* is the class id of the ActiveX control, and the codebase attribute specifies the location where the ActiveX control can be downloaded and installed.

Maxine wants you to add both the classid and codebase attributes for the QuickTime Player to the <object> tag for the overture.mp3 sound clip. This will cause the browser to either play the clip using the ActiveX control for the QuickTime Player or to prompt the user to download the control from Apple's Web site.

To insert the classid and codebase attributes:

▶ 1. Return to the **jumbo.htm** file in your text editor.

▶ 2. Within the opening <object> tag for the overture.mp3 sound clip, insert the following attributes, as shown in Figure 7-15:

```
classid="clsid:02BF25D5-8C17-4B23-BC80-D3488ABDDC6B"
codebase="http://www.apple.com/qtactivex/qtplugin.cab"
```

| **Figure 7-15** | **Adding the classid and codebase attributes** |

```
<object data="overture.mp3" type="audio/mpeg"
 classid="clsid:02BF25D5-8C17-4B23-BC80-D3488ABDDC6B"
 codebase="http://www.apple.com/qtactivex/qtplugin.cab"
 width="280" height="25">
   <param name="src" value="overture.mp3" />
   <param name="autoplay" value="false" />
   <param name="autostart" value="false" />
   <param name="controller" value="true" />
   <param name="showcontrols" value="true" />
</object>
```

Trouble? The file **activexlist.txt** located in the tutorial.07/tutorial folder contains a list of class ids and codebases for various ActiveX components. You can use the copy and paste feature of your text editor to copy the code values from that file into the jumbo.htm file, rather than typing them.

▶ 3. Save your changes to the file and then reload **jumbo.htm** in the Internet Explorer Web browser. Verify that the browser either displays the QuickTime Player controls to play this audio clip or prompts you to activate or download the QuickTime ActiveX component for the QuickTime Player.

▶ 4. Open **jumbo.htm** in a non-Internet Explorer browser such as Firefox or Opera. Note that the QuickTime Player controls are now missing from the Web page. What happened?

With the classid and codebase attributes, you were able to embed the ActiveX Quick-Time control for the Internet Explorer browser, but at the expense of removing it from other browsers. The problem is that ActiveX controls are designed for the Internet Explorer browser; other browsers do not support them. When those browsers encounter the classid attribute in the code you just entered, they're unable to process the <object> tag and so they ignore the embedded object altogether.

One way to resolve this problem is with Internet Explorer conditional comments.

Internet Explorer Conditional Comments

By now you've realized that Internet Explorer implements HTML and CSS differently than other browsers. Sometimes the easiest way to reconcile the two approaches is to run one set of code for Internet Explorer and another set of code for the other browsers. In Tutorial 4, you were briefly introduced to Internet Explorer's conditional comment, which allows you to run different code for different versions of Internet Explorer as well as for different browsers. The general syntax of an Internet Explorer conditional comment is

```
<!--[if condition IE version]><!-->
   HTML code
<!--<![endif]-->
```

where *condition* is a condition that is either true or false, *version* is the version number of an IE browser, and *HTML code* is code that will be run if the condition is true. If you want to run code only for Internet Explorer (regardless of the version), you would enter the following code:

```
<!--[if IE]><!-->
   HTML code
<!--<![endif]-->
```

If a non-IE browser encounters this code structure, it will interpret the whole structure as one long HTML comment and will not attempt to parse any of the HTML code within the comment tags. So you can insert the entire opening <object> tag within the following structure and it will be run only within Internet Explorer:

```
<!--[if IE]><!-->
   <object data="overture.mp3" type="audio/mpeg"
    classid="02BF25D5-8C17-4B23-BC80-D3488ABDDC6B"
    codebase=http://www.apple.com/qtactivex/qtplugin.cab
    width="280" height="25">
<!--<![endif]-->
```

You can also mark code that will only be run if the browser is *not* Internet Explorer. The general syntax uses conditional comments in the form

```
<!--[if !IE]><!-->
   HTML code
<!--<![endif]-->
```

where *HTML code* is code that will only be parsed if the browser is *not* Internet Explorer. Here, !IE is a conditional statement that means "not Internet Explorer." So to create an opening <object> tag for non-IE browsers that doesn't have the classid and codebase attributes, you would enter the following code:

```
<!--[if !IE]><!-->
   <object data="overture.mp3" type="audio/mpeg"
    width="280" height="25">
<!--<![endif]-->
```

Reference Window | Inserting IE Conditional Comments

- To insert an Internet Explorer conditional comment, use the general syntax
```
<!--[if condition IE version]><!-->
   HTML code
<!--<![endif]-->
```
where *condition* is a condition that is either true or false, *version* is the version number of an IE browser, and *HTML code* is code that will be run if the condition is true.
- To insert a conditional comment that runs code only for Internet Explorer, enter the following:
```
<!--[if IE]><!-->
   HTML code
<!--<![endif]-->
```
- To insert a conditional comment that runs code only for non-IE browsers, enter:
```
<!--[if !IE]><!-->
   HTML code
<!--<![endif]-->
```

Figure 7-16 shows how you can insert a sound clip tailored to both IE and non-IE browsers using both sets of conditional comments. Internet Explorer will insert the sound clip using the ActiveX QuickTime control, while non-IE browsers will insert the sound clip using a plug-in chosen by the browser.

Figure 7-16 **Writing code for IE and non-IE browsers**

Internet Explorer will run the code for the ActiveX QuickTime component

```
<!--[if IE]><!-->
   <object data="overture.mp3" type="audio/mpeg"
    classid="clsid:02BF25D5-8C17-4B23-BC80-D3488ABDDC6B"
    codebase="http://www.apple.com/qtactivex/qtplugin.cab"
    width="280" height="25">
<!--<![endif]-->

<!--[if !IE]><!-->
   <object data="overture.mp3" type="audio/mpeg"
    width="280" height="25">
<!--<![endif]-->

      <param name="src" value="overture.mp3" />
      <param name="autoplay" value="false" />
      <param name="autostart" value="false" />
      <param name="controller" value="true" />
      <param name="showcontrols" value="true" />
   </object>
```

Non-IE browsers will run the standard code for the embedded MP3 sound clip

```
<!--[if IE]><!-->
   <object data="overture.mp3" type="audio/mpeg"
    classid="clsid:02BF25D5-8C17-4B23-BC80-D3488ABDDC6B"
    codebase="http://www.apple.com/qtactivex/qtplugin.cab"
    width="280" height="25">
<!--<![endif]-->

<!--[if !IE]><!-->
   <object data="overture.mp3" type="audio/mpeg"
    width="280" height="25">
<!--<![endif]-->

      <param name="src" value="overture.mp3" />
      <param name="autoplay" value="false" />
      <param name="autostart" value="false" />
      <param name="controller" value="true" />
      <param name="showcontrols" value="true" />
   </object>
```

Add this structure to the jumbo.htm file.

To insert a set of conditional comments:

1. Return to the **jumbo.htm** file in your text editor.

2. Directly above the opening <object> tag for the overture.mp3 sound clip, insert:

   ```
   <!--[if IE]><!-->
   ```

3. Directly below the opening <object> tag, insert:

   ```
   <!--<![endif]-->

   <!--[if !IE]><!-->
      <object data="overture.mp3" type="audio/mpeg"
       width="280" height="25">
   <!--<![endif]-->
   ```

   Figure 7-17 shows the revised code for the overture.mp3 embedded sound clip.

Conditional comments for the overture.mp3 sound file | **Figure 7-17**

```
<!--[if IE]><!-->
   <object data="overture.mp3" type="audio/mpeg"
    classid="clsid:02BF25D5-8C17-4B23-BC80-D3488ABDDC6B"
    codebase="http://www.apple.com/qtactivex/qtplugin.cab"
    width="280" height="25">
<!--<![endif]-->

<!--[if !IE]><!-->
   <object data="overture.mp3" type="audio/mpeg"
    width="280" height="25">
<!--<![endif]-->

      <param name="src" value="overture.mp3" />
      <param name="autoplay" value="false" />
      <param name="autostart" value="false" />
      <param name="controller" value="true" />
      <param name="showcontrols" value="true" />
   </object>
```

4. Save your changes to the file and then verify that the embedded sound clip appears in both Internet Explorer and in non-Internet Explorer browsers such as Firefox and Opera.

5. If you want to take a break before starting the next session, you can close your files and programs now.

You tell Maxine that you've found a workaround for the class id issue and now both Internet Explorer and non-Internet Explorer browsers should be able to display the overture.mp3 file using QuickTime Player (if it is installed). Conditional comments are only one way of writing code that reconciles the differences between how browsers handle embedded objects. You'll explore another technique later in this tutorial that involves nesting one object within another.

Creating Background Sound

The clip you've entered into Maxine's Web page will play only when clicked by the user. You might want to enhance a Web page by adding background music that starts when the page is loaded by the browser and whose controls are hidden on the Web page. The parameters for Windows Media Player to create a hidden clip that starts automatically are

```
<param name="autostart" value="true" />
<param name="showcontrols" value="false" />
```

while for QuickTime Player the parameter values are

```
<param name="autoplay" value="true" />
<param name="hidden" value="true" />
```

If you want the background music to play continuously as long as the page is open, you would add the parameter

```
<param name="playcount" value="0" />
```

for Windows Media Player, and you would use

```
<param name="loop" value="true" />
```

for QuickTime Player. In both cases, once the background music reaches the end of the file, this code will make it loop back to the beginning.

Another way of creating background sound for Internet Explorer is to use the bgsound element

```
<bgsound src="url" balance="value" loop="value" volume="value" />
```

where *url* is the filename and location of the background sound clip, the balance attribute defines how the sound should be balanced between the left and right speakers, the loop attribute defines how many times the sound clip is played, and the volume attribute indicates the volume, ranging from 0 (muted) to 10,000 (the loudest). To have the sound clip play continuously, set the loop value to infinite. The bgsound element is supported only by Internet Explorer and is not part of the specifications for HTML or XHTML.

If you choose to create background music for your Web site, make sure you pick a sound clip that will not irritate your users. Background music can be annoying, especially if the music clip is set to loop indefinitely with no way of shutting it off!

Maxine is pleased with your work on the overture.mp3 sound clip. In the next session you'll use the same techniques to embed a video clip on her Web page.

Tip

Most background music is created from MIDI files because that format allows for longer music clips with a much smaller file size.

Review | Session 7.1 Quick Check

1. Describe two ways of making multimedia content available on your Web site.
2. Define the following terms: bandwidth, sampling rate, sample resolution, and bitrate.
3. Specify the code to create an embedded object containing the sound file royal.wav.
4. What are two possible MIME types that you could use to specify the data type of the royal.wav sound file?
5. Assuming that the royal.wav file will be played using Windows Media Player, what attribute would you add to the <object> tag to display only the play and stop buttons?
6. What parameter would you enter to start playing the royal.wav file when the page is loaded? (Assume that Windows Media Player is used to play the sound clip.)
7. What classid value would you add to the <object> tag to tell the browser to use the Windows Media Player ActiveX control to play the royal.wav file?
8. Specify the code you would enter to run all of the commands from Questions 3 through 7 only for the Internet Explorer browser.

Session 7.2

Exploring Digital Video

Maxine's next task for you is to embed a video clip on her Web page of Fred Astaire dancing in *Royal Wedding*. Displaying video is one of the most popular uses of the Web. With high-speed connections more available to the public, video has transitioned from simply a source of entertainment to an essential source of content and information. For example, sites such as *www.cnn.com* routinely include important information in embedded video clips to supplement their news articles.

Digital video can be recorded using digital camcorders, digital cameras, and cell phones, and with video capture boards installed on computers to record images from television, DVDs, and VCRs. You can also create video clips using computer animation software. When creating a video clip for distribution on the Web, you must determine what size and type of video will work best when played back over the viewer's Internet connection. You also must consider what video format will be most accessible to your users. The goal is to create video that will be easily playable by the most people, with a smooth playback that is easy to watch. Before embedding Maxine's video clip, you'll first examine some of the issues involved in creating digital video files.

Data Rates and Video Quality

A video file is composed of a series of single images or **frames** that are played in rapid succession to create the illusion of motion. Most frames are sized to have width-to-height ratios or **aspect ratios** of 4:3. The two most common frame sizes for the Web are 160 × 120 pixels and 320 × 240 pixels. With high-bandwidth connections becoming increasingly available, frame sizes as high as 640 × 480 pixels are becoming more common.

When a video is played, the frames are rapidly shown in sequence, giving the illusion of motion. The number of frames shown in a given amount of time is called the **frame rate**, commonly expressed in frames per second (fps). Higher frame rates usually, but not always, result in a smoother animation. For comparison, DVDs typically render video at 24 fps, while frame rates of 10 to 15 fps, commonly used on the Web, can still result in videos of good quality.

However, the frame rate is not the only factor that determines the quality of a video. Another more important factor is the **data rate**, which is the amount of data that has to be processed by the video player each second to play the video clip. The size of the frame, the frame rate, and the bit rate of any audio attached to the video also are factored into the calculation of the data rate. When settling on a data rate for video embedded on a Web site, you should take into account the bandwidth of the connection to your Web site. The bandwidth must be large enough to accommodate the amount of information processed each second to smoothly play the video. If the user attempts to play a video with too high of a data rate, the playback will be choppy and uneven as the connection tries in vain to keep up with the pace of the clip. A common mistake is to assume that a high-quality video clip with a fast frame rate will result in the best video for the user. This is not necessarily the case. For slower connections, a lower-quality clip with a slower frame rate might actually look and perform better.

A general rule of thumb is that for a local area network, you should be able to get good quality playback at a data rate of 400 to 600 kilobytes per second (Kbps). For DSL and ISDN, keep the data rate at 350 Kbps or less. If your viewers are connecting at low bandwidth such as through a dial-up line, the data rate should be kept below 100 Kbps. If you are running a video installed on your own computer or on a very fast network connection, you can work with data rates of a megabyte per second or more.

Tip

Use video editing software to create several versions of your video clips, varying the frame rate, frame size, and bit rate to determine which combinations result in the best playback for your target bandwidth.

You can reduce the data rate by reducing the frame size, using monaural rather than stereo sound, and reducing the frame rate. The content of your video clip also has an impact on the data rate. A so-called "talking head" video in which there is a narrator in front of a largely static background can be saved with a low frame rate at little cost in video quality; on the other hand, a clip with a lot of motion (such as the dance sequence that Maxine wants to use for her site) would become choppy and uneven when played at a low frame rate.

Finally, video size can be greatly reduced through the use of file compression. When a compressed video is replayed, each frame is decompressed as it is rendered. The technology that compresses and decompresses a media clip is called a **codec** (short for *compression/decompression*). Many different codecs are available, each with its own advantages and disadvantages. Some codecs create smaller video files but at the expense of choppier playback. Video editing software allows you to choose the codec for your video clip, but you might need to experiment to determine which codec provides the best file compression without sacrificing video quality. Recent developments in video editing have introduced codecs that greatly reduce video size, resulting in high-quality video at data rates that are reasonable even under lower bandwidths.

Video File Formats

As with the sound formats you examined in the last session, there are a variety of video formats in use on the Web. Figure 7-18 lists some of the video file formats that Maxine will consider for her Web site.

Format	Filename Extension	MIME Type	Description
AVI	.avi	video/x-msvideo	Audio/Video Interleaved. AVI is a common video file format developed by Microsoft for use with Windows. It is not always possible to play AVI files on non-Windows computers unless special software has been installed on the computer.
Flash Video	.flv	video/x-flv	FLV is a proprietary file format developed by Adobe to deliver video over the Internet using the popular Adobe Flash Player. It is the preferred file format for online video sites such as YouTube and Google Video.
MPEG	.mpg, .mpeg, .mp3	video/mpeg	Moving Pictures Group. The MPEG format allows for high compression of the video file, resulting in a smaller file size. MPEG files have good support across various browsers and operating systems but tend to be much larger than flash videos.
QuickTime	.mov	video/quicktime	QuickTime is a video format developed by Apple Computer for Windows and Apple computers. Like MPEG, QuickTime employs a compression algorithm that can result in smaller file sizes. QuickTime files require QuickTime Player, available for either Windows or the Macintosh.
RealVideo	.rm, .rv	application/vnd.rn-realmedia	RealVideo is a video format developed by RealNetworks for transmitting live video over the Internet at both low and high bandwidths. It uses a variety of data compression techniques and requires the installation of the RealPlayer media player.
Shockwave Flash	.swf	application/x-shockwave-flash	SWF is a proprietary file format developed by Adobe to deliver multimedia and vector graphics on the Web. An SWF file can contain animations, video, audio, interactive scripts, and control buttons. SWF files can be played using Adobe Flash Player either as a browser plug-in or a stand-alone player.
Windows Media	.wmv	video/x-ms-wmv	Developed by Microsoft, WMV is a popular video format for creating streaming video on the Web. The WMV format offers good compression and video quality, but is primarily designed for Windows users.

The format you should use for your Web page depends a great deal on your target audience. You want a video format that users will be able to play without having to install additional software, and it should be a format that will result in good video quality with reasonable data rates. Currently, the most popular video format by far is Flash video, which is used throughout the Web, including such popular sites as YouTube, MySpace, and Google Video.

Media Players

There are four standard media players for use with video on the Web: Windows Media Player, QuickTime, Flash, and RealPlayer. In the last session, you examined Windows Media Player and QuickTime Player for use with audio clips. You can apply similar techniques to play video clips with those players. Figure 7-19 details the video formats that each player typically supports. Note that these media players support other formats than those listed here, and in some cases the user can install additional codecs to enable the player to support even more formats.

Figure 7-19 ▶ **Video formats, media players and plug-ins**

Video Format	Adobe Flash Player	Windows Media Player	QuickTime Player	RealPlayer
.asf		yes		
.avi		yes		
.mov	yes		yes	
.mp4	yes		yes	yes
.mpg		yes	yes	yes
.rm				yes
.swf	yes			
.wmv		yes		

No matter which video format Maxine chooses for her Web site, her viewers will need to have access to a media player to view the files. Windows Media Player comes preinstalled on Windows computers, QuickTime comes preinstalled on the Macintosh, Flash comes preinstalled on both operating systems, and RealPlayer comes preinstalled on neither. Recent market surveys have indicated that almost 99% of Internet viewers have access to Adobe Flash Player, 83% can run Microsoft Windows Media Player, 68.4% have access to QuickTime Player, and 52.6% have RealPlayer (source: *www.adobe.com/ products/player_census/flashplayer*). Based on these findings, you strongly recommend to Maxine that she develop video for her site to take advantage of the popularity of Adobe Flash Player.

Working with Flash

Now that Maxine has decided on Flash for her video clips, she can either use a free online service such as YouTube (*www.youtube.com*) to host her video or she can host the video on her own Web site. One problem with an online service is that she has no control over the final video quality. Online services tend to apply heavy compression to their video files and limit the choices for both frame rate and frame size. For example, the dimension of a YouTube video is set to 320 × 240 pixels with a data rate of 314 Kbps and frame rates of 25 fps. If these settings do not work well for your video clip, you do not have the option of changing them within YouTube.

Maxine decides that she will create and edit the video clip herself so that she has control over the final appearance of the video and its quality. There are several software packages available for creating a Flash video. The most expensive and extensive is Adobe Flash Professional, which is used by professional video developers. Users who don't want to spend several hundreds of dollars can find decent editing programs for much less. Look for editing software that allows you to convert other video file formats into Flash and gives you control over video quality.

There are two main file formats involved in creating a Flash video. The first is the **flv** or **Flash Video** format that contains the video clip that will be displayed by Adobe Flash Player. An flv file is usually created by converting video from another format such as avi or mpeg. To play Flash video, the video must be stored within a Shockwave Flash file. A **Shockwave Flash** or **swf** file contains the video, audio, animations, interactive scripts, program controls, and other features that provide real-time interactive animation for the viewer. One advantage of an swf file is that programmers can create their own players, containing video controls tailored to the specific needs of their Web site. It's not uncommon to observe Web sites containing players reflecting the Web site's content or design. For example, video played with YouTube's player will display the YouTube logo at the bottom-right corner of each frame. This is different from QuickTime Player and Windows Media Player, whose controls are designed by Apple and Microsoft, respectively, and therefore have a common look and feel on any Web site.

Working with Flash editing software, Maxine has created an swf file containing the video clip of Fred Astaire dancing on the ceiling from *Royal Wedding*. She wants you to insert this file as an embedded object on her Web page.

Embedding a Flash Player

To embed a Flash Player, you use many of the same techniques you used in the last session to embed the overture.mp3 sound clip. Most browsers embed a Flash Player using the object element

```
<object type="application/x-shockwave-flash"
      data="file.swf" width="value" height="value">
   <param name="movie" value="file.swf" />
   parameters
</object>
```

where *file.swf* is the swf file containing the Flash animation. On the other hand, Internet Explorer inserts the Flash Player as an ActiveX control. The object code for Internet Explorer is

```
<object type="application/x-shockwave-flash"
      data="file.swf" width="value" height="value"
      classid="clsid:D27CDB6E-AE6D-11cf-96B8-444553540000"
      codebase="http://download.macromedia.com/pub/shockwave/cabs/
              flash/swflash.cab#version=9,0,115,0">
   <param name="movie" value="file.swf" />
   parameters
</object>
```

You can support both approaches by applying the same conditional comments you used in the last session for the QuickTime plug-in.

Reference Window | **Embedding Shockwave Flash**

- To embed a Shockwave Flash file as an ActiveX control, enter

```
<object type="application/x-shockwave-flash"
        data="file.swf" width="value" height="value"
        classid="clsid:D27CDB6E-AE6D-11cf-96B8-444553540000"
        codebase="http://download.macromedia.com/pub/shockwave/cabs/
                  flash/swflash.cab#version=9,0,115,0">

    <param name="movie" value="file.swf" />
    parameters

</object>
```

where *file.swf* is the Shockwave Flash file and *parameters* are parameters associated with the Flash Player.

- To embed a Shockwave Flash file for non-IE browsers, use the following:

```
<object type="application/x-shockwave-flash"
        data="file.swf" width="value" height="value">

    <param name="movie" value="file.swf" />
    parameters
</object>
```

Maxine has stored her video clip in a Flash Player with the filename rwdance.swf. The clip has a frame size of 280 × 210 pixels and a frame rate of 25 fps. Because she'll be testing this on her local computer only, she set the data rate at 500 Kbps. Later, when she places this clip on her Web server, she might reduce the frame and data rates to something more appropriate for the lower bandwidth.

Add this clip to her Web page now.

To embed the Flash Player:

▶ **1.** Return to the **jumbo.htm** file in your text editor.

▶ **2.** Scroll down the file to the In Focus paragraph. Directly after the paragraph, insert the following code to define the properties of the object element for Internet Explorer users:

```
<p style="text-align: center">

<!--[if IE]><!-->
   <object data="rwdance.swf" type="application/x-shockwave-flash"
   classid="clsid:D27CDB6E-AE6D-11cf-96B8-444553540000"
   codebase=http://download.macromedia.com/pub/shockwave/
cabs/flash/swflash.cab#version=9,0,115,0"
   width="280" height="239">
<!--<![endif]-->
```

Trouble? You can copy and paste the class id and codebase values from the **activexlist.txt** file located in the tutorial.07\tutorial folder included with your Data Files. Despite its length, enter the class id value without inserting blank spaces or pressing the Enter key.

▶ **3.** Next, insert the following code to define the properties of the object element under non-IE browsers.

```
<!--[if !IE]><!-->
   <object data="rwdance.swf" type="application/x-shockwave-flash"
   width="280" height="239">
<!--<![endif]-->
```

4. Finally, complete the code for the Flash video by adding the param element and the closing `</object>` and `</p>` tags. Figure 7-20 shows the complete code for the embedded object.

```
    <param name="movie" value="rwdance.swf" />
  </object>

</p>
```

Embedding a Shockwave Flash file | Figure 7-20

```
<div class="boxContent">
  <h2>In Focus</h2>

  <p>The high point of <i>Royal Wedding</i> is the "Ceiling Dance" in
     which Fred Astaire appears to literally dance on the ceiling and walls
     of his hotel room. The effect was accomplished by putting the whole set
     inside of a 20-foot diameter rotating cage. As the cage turned, Astaire
     would seamlessly dance across the four sides of the box, creating the
     illusion of weightlessness. The same technique would later be used
     to simulate a zero gravity environment in <i>2001: A Space
     Odyssey</i>.</p>

  <p style="text-align: center">

  <!--[if IE]><!-->
    <object data="rwdance.swf" type="application/x-shockwave-flash"
      classid="clsid:D27CDB6E-AE6D-11cf-96B8-444553540000"
      codebase="http://download.macromedia.com/pub/shockwave/cabs/flash/swflash.cab#version=9,0,115,0"
      width="280" height="239">
  <!--<![endif]-->

  <!--[if !IE]><!-->
    <object data="rwdance.swf" type="application/x-shockwave-flash"
      width="280" height="239">
  <!--<![endif]-->

      <param name="movie" value="rwdance.swf" />
    </object>

  </p>
</div>
```

5. Save your changes to the file.

6. Refresh or reload the **jumbo.htm** file in your Web browser.

7. Below the In Focus paragraph, your browser should display an embedded video clip, as shown in Figure 7-21. Click the **play** button to begin playing the clip.

The embedded video clip from *Royal Wedding* | Figure 7-21

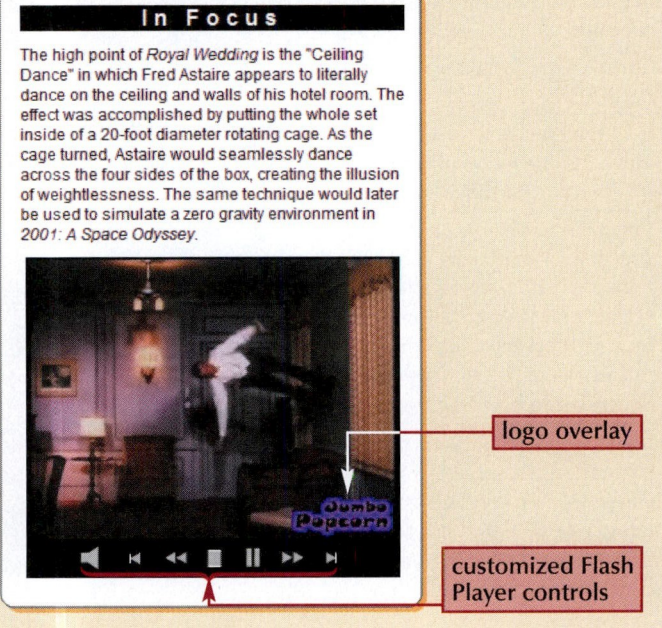

Trouble? If the clip doesn't play or it doesn't appear on the Web page, check your code against that shown in Figure 7-20 and in Steps 2 through 4. It is also possible that you do not have Flash Player installed on your computer. Contact your instructor or technical resource person if you need to install Flash.

Note that the codebase attribute specified above is for version 9 of Flash Player. If a more recent version of the player is available, Internet Explorer checks this Web site using the url from this codebase and prompts the user to install the most recent version. Also note that the URL references the Macromedia.com Web site. Macromedia, the original creator of Flash, was acquired by Adobe Systems in 2005. Adobe choose to keep the Macromedia Web site URL's active to accommodate current HTML code.

The Flash Player that Maxine created for her Web site has a few interesting features. She customized the video control buttons, and she placed the Jumbo Popcorn logo in the lower-right corner of the player. This demonstrates a few of the features of Flash that have made it so popular for designers who want to customize the multimedia on their Web sites.

Tip

You can also use Shockwave Flash Player to embed audio clips on your Web site, customizing the player and appearance of the clip using Flash editing software.

Flash Parameters

The movie you just embedded had a single parameter that identified the swf file. Flash supports other parameters to give more control over the appearance and behavior of the Flash file. Figure 7-22 lists some of the other Flash attributes and parameters.

Figure 7-22 ▶ **Flash Player parameters and values**

Parameter	Description	Value(s)
bgcolor	Sets the background color of the Flash player	*#rrggbb*	*color name*
flashvar	Contains text values that are passed to the Flash player as variables to control the behavior and content of the movie	*text*
id	Identifies the embedded Flash movie so that it can be referenced	*text*
loop	Plays the movie in a continuous loop	true	false
menu	Displays the full Flash pop-up when the user right-clicks the movie	true	false
name	Names the embedded Flash movie so that it can be referenced	*text*
play	Starts playing the movie automatically when the page loads	true	false
quality	Sets the playback quality of the movie; low values favor playback speed over quality; high values favor display quality over playback speed	low	autolow	autohigh	medium	high	best
scale	Defines how the movie clip is scaled within the defined space; a value of showall makes the entire clip visible in the specified area without distortion; a value of noborder scales the movie to fill the specified area, without distortion but possibly with some cropping; a value of exactfit makes the entire movie visible in the specified area without trying to preserve the original aspect ratio	showall	noborder	exactfit
wmode	Sets the appearance of the Flash player against the page background; a value of window causes the movie to play within its own window on the page; a value of opaque hides everything on the page behind the clip; a value of transparent allows the page background to show through transparent colors in the movie	window	opaque	transparent

For example, if you want to set the playback quality of the Flash movie to high, you would add the following parameter to the object element:

```
<param name="quality" value="high" />
```

Note that Flash movies with high display quality may suffer from ragged playback, so you must test your video clips to ensure that the speed of the clip is still sufficient for the viewer.

Maxine suggests that you set the playback quality of the rwdance.swf clip to high. She also asks you to change the menu settings so that viewers will only see the brief version of the pop-up menu rather than the full version. Using a brief Flash pop-up menu is a standard approach on the Web so that viewers cannot change the playback settings chosen by the clip's author.

To add parameters to the Flash Player:

▶ 1. Return to the **jumbo.htm** file in your text editor.

▶ 2. Add the following parameters to the object element for the rwdance.swf file, as shown in Figure 7-23:

```
<param name="quality" value="high" />
<param name="menu" value="false" />
```

Adding the quality and menu parameters ◀ Figure 7-23

```
<!--[if !IE]><!-->
    <object data="rwdance.swf" type="application/x-shockwave-flash"
     width="280" height="239">
<!--<![endif]-->

        <param name="movie" value="rwdance.swf" />
        <param name="quality" value="high" />
        <param name="menu" value="false" />
    </object>
```

▶ 3. Save your changes to the file and then reload **jumbo.htm** in your Web browser.

▶ 4. Click the **play** button to verify that the clip still plays properly within your browser.

▶ 5. Right-click the embedded video and verify that the pop-up menu has only two entries: Settings and About Adobe Flash Player.

You show Maxine the embedded video. She agrees that it adds a lot to the Web page and that the player is easy to use. Although she will continue to use Flash for this site, it's possible that she'll want to use a different video format in the future. She asks you to research how to create embedded video clips with QuickTime Player and Windows Media Player.

Exploring QuickTime Video

QuickTime movies are displayed in the same player you used in the last session for the overture.mp3 file, and therefore much of the code you used for that audio clip can be applied to a QuickTime movie. Once again you need two sets of opening <object> tags: one for Internet Explorer, in which the QuickTime Player is inserted as an ActiveX control, and the other for non-IE browsers, in which the video clip is inserted as a plug-in. You can use the same classid and codebase attribute values for the movie player. The MIME type for QuickTime videos is video/quicktime.

Maxine has created a QuickTime version of the dance clip, saved as rwdance.mov, that she wants you to embed on a sample Web page. Because the code structure will be pretty close to what you used to embed the Flash Player, you can use the jumbo.htm file as a starting point.

To embed the QuickTime movie:

▶ 1. Return to the **jumbo.htm** file in your text editor and save the file as **jumbo_mov.htm** in the tutorial.07\tutorial folder. Scroll down to the section of the file containing the Flash movie.

▶ 2. Change the data attribute in both <object> tags from

```
data="rwdance.swf"
```

to

```
data="rwdance.mov"
```

▶ 3. Change the type attribute in both <object> tags from

```
type="application/x-shockwave-flash"
```

to

```
type="video/quicktime"
```

▶ 4. Change the value of the classid attribute to:

```
classid="clsid:02BF25D5-8C17-4B23-BC80-D3488ABDDC6B"
```

Trouble? You can copy and paste the classid value from the code you entered earlier for the embedded overture.mp3 sound clip.

▶ 5. Change the value of the codebase attribute to:

```
codebase="http://www.apple.com/qtactivex/qtplugin.cab"
```

▶ 6. Delete the three parameters from the embedded object and replace them with the following QuickTime parameters:

```
<param name="src" value="rwdance.mov" />
<param name="autoplay" value="false" />
<param name="controller" value="true" />
```

These are the same parameters you used in the last session for the overture.mp3 sound clip. Figure 7-24 highlights the revised code for the embedded QuickTime movie.

Figure 7-24 ▶ **Embedding a QuickTime movie**

```
<p style="text-align: center">

<!--[if IE]><!-->
   <object data="rwdance.mov" type="video/quicktime"
      classid="clsid:02BF25D5-8C17-4B23-BC80-D3488ABDDC6B"
      codebase="http://www.apple.com/qtactivex/qtplugin.cab"
      width="280" height="239">
<!--<![endif]-->

<!--[if !IE]><!-->
   <object data="rwdance.mov" type="video/quicktime"
      width="280" height="239">
<!--<![endif]-->

      <param name="src" value="rwdance.mov" />
      <param name="autoplay" value="false" />
      <param name="controller" value="true" />
   </object>

</p>
```

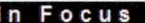

7. Save your changes to the **jumbo_mov.htm** file and then open it in your browser. Your browser should show controls for the QuickTime Movie Player, as shown in Figure 7-25. Click the **play** button to start the movie.

The QuickTime video player   Figure 7-25

All of the parameters discussed earlier in Figure 7-11 for sound also apply to video. The player also supports other parameters specifically related to video. Figure 7-26 lists some of the other QuickTime parameters you can use with embedded video.

Figure 7-26   **Parameters of the QuickTime Player**

Parameter	Description	Value(s)
autohref	Automatically loads the Web page specified in *url*	*url*
goto	Plays a movie from the numbered list specified in the qtnext parameter	*integer*
href	Loads *url* when the viewer clicks the movie	*url*
kioskmode	Does not include the Save option in the movie controller bar	true
movieid	Identifies the movie so that it can be referenced	*text*
moviename	Names the movie so that it can be referenced	*text*
playeveryframe	Does not drop any frames from the video playback	true | false
qtnext	Specifies a numbered list of movies to play in the player	n=<*url*>T<target> | GOTO*n*
qtsrc	Loads a file or stream different from the one specified in the src parameter	*url*
qtsrcchokedspeed	Limits the outgoing bandwidth from the server to a specified data rate	*date rate*
saveembedtags	Preserves the current parameter values when loading a new movie	true
scale	Defines how the movie should be rescaled to fit the defined space; use tofit to change the movie's dimension to fit the space, aspect to fit the movie to the space while retaining the aspect ratio, and *n* to scale the movie by a factor of *n*	tofit | aspect | *n*
showlogo	Shows the QuickTime logo until the movie is ready to play	true | false
target	Places the movie within the QuickTime player or within a named frame, or replaces the current movie with the new movie	quicktimeplayer | *frame* | myself

For example, you can use the QuickTime parameters to format the size of the video clip. The width and height attributes define the space reserved for the QuickTime Player, but within that space you can resize the video clip using the parameter

```
<param name="scale" value="scale" />
```

where *scale* is tofit, aspect, or a numeric value. A value of tofit fits the video clip and the video controls exactly to the available space (even if that distorts the image). The aspect value fits the width of the video clip and player to space while retaining its aspect ratio. If a numeric value is specified, it indicates the factor by which the video is rescaled while retaining its aspect ratio. For example, to reduce the video to 70% of its size, you would enter the following parameter:

```
<param name="scale" value="0.7" />
```

If you reduce the size of the player relative to the space available for it, you can apply a background color using the bgcolor parameter. Background colors are entered using either the color name or a hexadecimal color value (for discussion of hexadecimal color values, see Tutorial 3). Maxine suggests you experiment with these parameters by reducing the size of the player and presenting it on a light brown background.

To format the video's appearance:

▶ **1.** Return to the **jumbo_mov.htm** file in your text editor.

▶ **2.** Add the following parameters to the QuickTime object as shown in Figure 7-27:

```
<param name="scale" value="0.7" />
<param name="bgcolor" value="#F0BC4C" />
```

Setting the movie scale and background color ◀ **Figure 7-27**

```
<!--[if !IE]><!-->
    <object data="rwdance.mov" type="video/quicktime"
    width="280" height="239">
<!--<![endif]-->

        <param name="src" value="rwdance.mov" />
        <param name="autoplay" value="false" />
        <param name="controller" value="true" />
        <param name="scale" value="0.7" />
        <param name="bgcolor" value="#F0BC4C" />
    </object>
```

▶ **3.** Close the file, saving your changes, and then reload **jumbo_mov.htm** in your Web browser. As shown in Figure 7-28, the video is rescaled to 70% of its original size and displayed on a light brown background.

Rescaling the QuickTime Player ◀ **Figure 7-28**

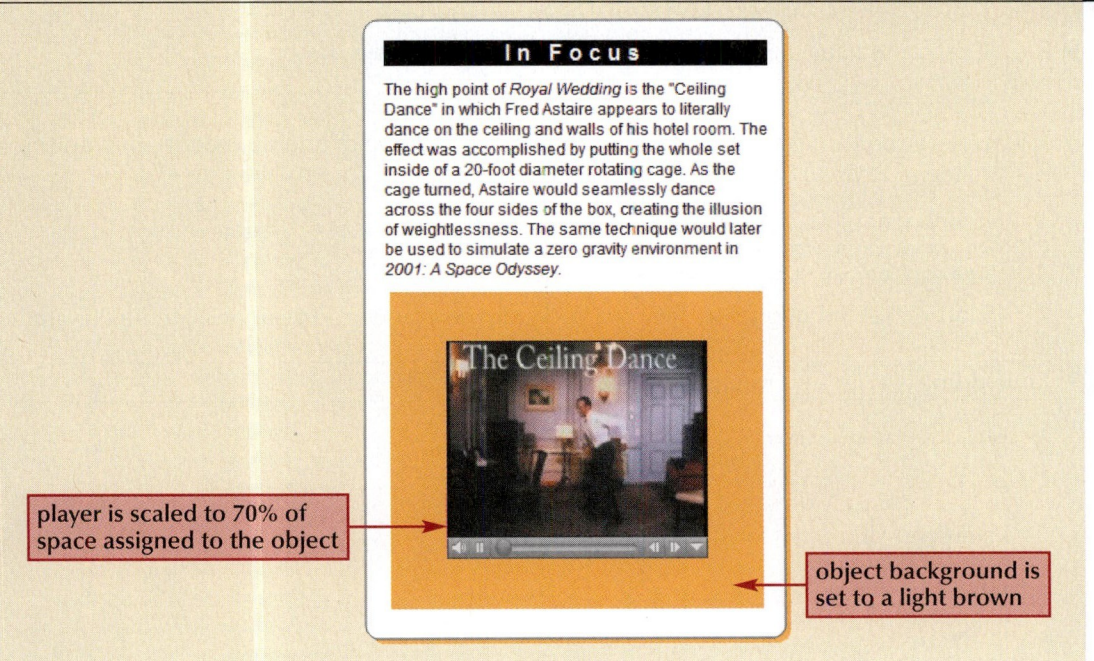

player is scaled to 70% of space assigned to the object

object background is set to a light brown

Rescaling the video does not change the file size or the data rate. It only changes how the browser renders the clip on the page. If you need to resize the clip to reduce its file size or data rate, you must use video editing software.

Exploring Windows Media Player

Maxine has also created a version of the video clip for Windows Media Player that she wants you to test. You can embed this clip as an ActiveX object for IE browsers and as a plug-in for non-IE browsers. Once again, you'll use the same structure for the Windows Media Player as you did for the Flash Player you created earlier.

To embed the Windows Media Player:

1. Reopen the **jumbo.htm** file in your text editor and save the file as **jumbo_wmv.htm** to the tutorial.07\tutorial folder. Scroll down to the code for the embedded Flash Player.

2. Change the data attribute in both <object> tags from

   ```
   data="rwdance.swf"
   ```
   to
   ```
   data="rwdance.wmv"
   ```

3. Change the type attribute in both <object> tags from

   ```
   type="application/x-shockwave-flash"
   ```
   to
   ```
   type="video/x-ms-wmv"
   ```

4. Change the value of the classid attribute to:

   ```
   classid="clsid:6BF52A52-394A-11d3-B153-00C04F79FAA6"
   ```

   Trouble? You can copy and paste the classid value from the **activexlist.txt** file located in the tutorial.07\tutorial folder.

5. Change the value of the codebase attribute to:

   ```
   codebase="http://activex.microsoft.com/activex/controls/
             mplayer/en/nsmp2inf.cab#Version=6,4,5,715"
   ```

6. Change the value of the height attribute in both <object> tags to

   ```
   height="245"
   ```

7. Delete the three parameters from the embedded object and replace them with the following Windows Media Player parameters:

   ```
   <param name="url" value="rwdance.wmv" />
   <param name="autostart" value="false" />
   <param name="showcontrols" value="true" />
   ```

   Figure 7-29 highlights the revised code for the embedded Windows Media Player.

Tip

To display the movie controls, add about 30 pixels to the height of a video played by Windows Media Player. For QuickTime Player, increase the height by about 20 pixels.

Figure 7-29 | **Embedding a Windows Media video**

```
<p style="text-align: center">

<!--[if IE]><!-->
    <object data="rwdance.wmv" type="video/x-ms-wmv"
      classid="clsid:6BF52A52-394A-11d3-B153-00C04F79FAA6"
      codebase="http://activex.microsoft.com/activex/controls/mplayer/en/nsmp2inf.cab#Version=6,4,5,715"
      width="280" height="245" >
<!--<![endif]-->

<!--[if !IE]><!-->
    <object data="rwdance.wmv" type="video/x-ms-wmv"
      width="280" height="245" >
<!--<![endif]-->

      <param name="url" value="rwdance.wmv" />
      <param name="autostart" value="false" />
      <param name="showcontrols" value="true" />
    </object>

</p>
```

8. Close the file, saving your changes to the **jumbo_wmv.htm** file and then open it in your browser. Your browser should show controls for the Windows Media Player, as shown in Figure 7-30. Click the **play** button to start the movie.

The Windows Media Player | **Figure 7-30**

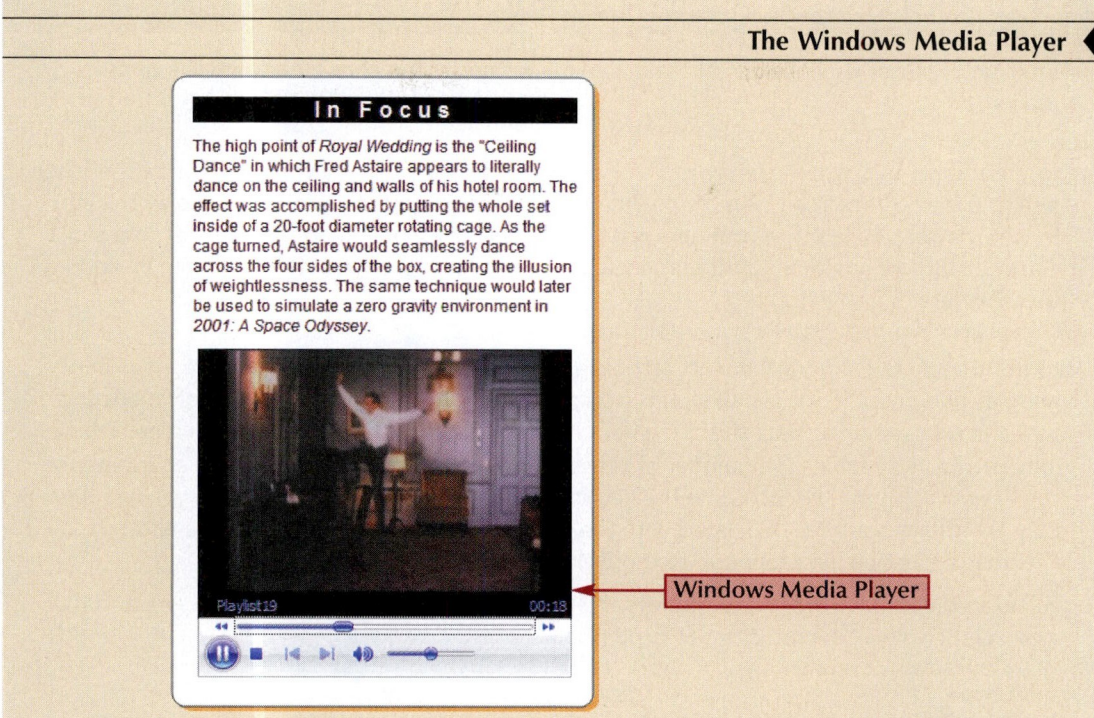

In Focus

The high point of *Royal Wedding* is the "Ceiling Dance" in which Fred Astaire appears to literally dance on the ceiling and walls of his hotel room. The effect was accomplished by putting the whole set inside of a 20-foot diameter rotating cage. As the cage turned, Astaire would seamlessly dance across the four sides of the box, creating the illusion of weightlessness. The same technique would later be used to simulate a zero gravity environment in *2001: A Space Odyssey*.

Windows Media Player

Like the other players, the Windows Media Player includes support for several parameters specifically related to playing videos. Figure 7-31 lists some of the parameters you might consider using in addition to those shown earlier in Figure 7-11.

Video-related parameters of the Windows Media Player | **Figure 7-31**

Parameter	Description	Value(s)
fullscreen	Specifies whether the video content is played back in full-screen mode	true | false
rate	Specifies the playback rate, where a value of 0.5 indicates a playback at half-speed and a value of 2 plays the video back at twice normal speed	*value*
stretchtofit	Specifies whether the video automatically sizes to fit the video window	true | false
url	Specifies the name of the media file to play	*url*
windowlessvideo	Specifies whether the Windows Media player renders the video in windowless mode, in which the video is rendered directly on the page where you can apply special effects or overlay the video with text	true | false

Maxine does not need you to make any other changes to the code for Windows Media Player.

Internet Explorer users can combine inline images and video clips by adding the dynsrc attribute

```
<img src="url" dynsrc="url" />
```

to the <img> tag, where the dynsrc attribute specifies the url of a video version of the inline image. Browsers that can display the video version will automatically load and play the clip for the viewer, while other browsers will display only the inline image. By default, the video clip will start automatically and play once; however, you can control this behavior by adding the attributes

```
start="type" loop="value" controls
```

to the <img> tag, where the start attribute tells the browser when to start the video clip and has two possible values: fileopen to start playing the clip when the browser opens the file, and mouseover to start the clip when the user hovers the mouse over the video. The loop attribute specifies the number of times to play the clip and can be either an integer or the keyword infinite. By including the keyword controls within the <img> tag, you can display any player controls associated with the video clip. Be aware that the space allotted to the image must be large enough for both the clip and the player controls.

For example, the following tag displays the rwdance.jpg inline for non-IE browsers and the video clip rwdance.avi for Internet Explorer:

```
<img src="rwdance.jpg" dynsrc="rwdance.avi" start="mouseover"
loop="1" />
```

The movie will not start until the user hovers the mouse pointer over the video; then the clip will play once and stop. No player controls will be displayed with the image.

Because the dynsrc attribute is supported only by Internet Explorer, you should use it only in situations where you are sure that the IE browsers will be used by viewers, such as for Web pages on a company's intranet.

Introducing the embed Element

The <object> tag represents the W3C standard for inserting multimedia content. Although it is supported by current browsers, it might not be supported by older browser versions. To make your pages backward compatible, you can use the embed element along with the object tag to insert multimedia content. The syntax of the embed element is

```
<embed src="url" attributes></embed>
```

where *url* is the source of the multimedia content and *attributes* are the attributes that define that content and how it is rendered by the browser. Figure 7-32 lists some of the attributes associated with the embed element. Note that many of the attributes match the attributes and parameters associated with the object element. The only required attribute is the src attribute; the other attributes listed in Figure 7-32 are optional.

Attribute	Description	Value(s)
align	Specifies the horizontal alignment of the embedded element	absbottom	absmiddle	baseline	bottom	left	middle	right	texttop	top
alt	Specifies alternate text to be displayed in place of the embedded element	text
classid	Provides the classid for an ActiveX object or Java applet inserted as an embedded element	text
code	The location of class file used with embedded Java applets	url
codebase	The location of a Java applet class file if it differs from the location of the Web page	url
height	The height of the embedded element in pixels	value
id	Provides the id of the embedded element	text
name	Provides the name of the embedded element	text
pluginspage	Provides the location of a document containing instructions for installing the plug-in if it is not already installed	url
pluginurl	Provides the location of an installation file for installing the plug-in specified by the embedded element	url
src	The source of the media file used by the embedded element	url
type	The MIME type of the embedded element	mime-type
width	The width of the embedded element in pixels	value

For example, to insert a Flash Player using the <embed> tag, you would enter the following HTML code:

```
<embed src="file.swf" type="application/x-shockwave-flash"
    pluginspage="http://www.macromedia.com/go/getflashplayer"
    width="value" height="value">
</embed>
```

Note that the pluginspage attribute provides a url for browsers that do not have the Shockwave Flash plug-in. Users running such a browser would be prompted with an option to install the player so they wouldn't have to search for the player on their own.

The <embed> tag to insert the QuickTime Player is:

```
<embed src="file.mov" type="video/quicktime"
    pluginspage="http://www.apple.com/quicktime/download"
    width="value" height="value">
</embed>
```

Finally, the <embed> tag to insert the Windows Media Player has the following form:

```
<embed src="file.wmv" type="video/x-ms-wmv"
    pluginspage="http://www.microscft.com/Windows/MediaPlayer"
    width="value" height="value">
</embed>
```

The embed element does not support the <param> tag, so any features specific to a particular player are added as attributes to the <embed> tag. So the parameter element

```
<param name="name" value="value" />
```

for an object would be entered using the following attribute in the <embed> tag:

```
<embed name="value" ...> </embed>
```

For example, the following code applies the autostart, bgcolor, controller, and scale values as attributes rather than parameters in embedding the rwdance.mov QuickTime video:

```
<embed src="rwdance.mov" type="video/quicktime"
       pluginspage="http://www.apple.com/quicktime/download"
       width="280" height="239"
       autoplay="false" controller="true" scale="0.7"
       bgcolor="#FOBC4C">
</embed>
```

Compare this code to the code you entered earlier, shown in Figure 7-27. Notice that all of the <param> tags in that code have been replaced by attributes within the <embed> tag.

Reference Window | Using the embed Element

- To insert an object using the embed element, enter
  `<embed src="url" attributes></embed>`
  where *url* is the url of the embedded file and *attributes* are attributes associated with the embedded object.

Nesting Embedded Objects

When you add embedded content to your Web pages, you need to provide support for as many browser configurations as possible. Users might access your page using an older browser that supports only the <embed> tag and not the <object> tag. Other users might be running browsers without the capability of displaying embedded content, or they might have turned off those features for their browsers to speed up their Web browsing. To accommodate all of those situations, your code needs to match the capabilities of the variety of browsers and browser settings. You've already studied one way of accommodating different browser capabilities through the use of conditional comments; another important approach is to nest media objects within one another.

As shown in Figure 7-33, the idea behind nesting media clips is to first attempt to display the clip using the <object> tag; if that fails, the browser attempts to display the media clip using the <embed> tag. Finally, if the browser is unable to embed the media clip using either the <object> or the <embed> tag, it will still be able to display a hypertext link to the media clip.

Nesting embedded objects ◀ **Figure 7-33**

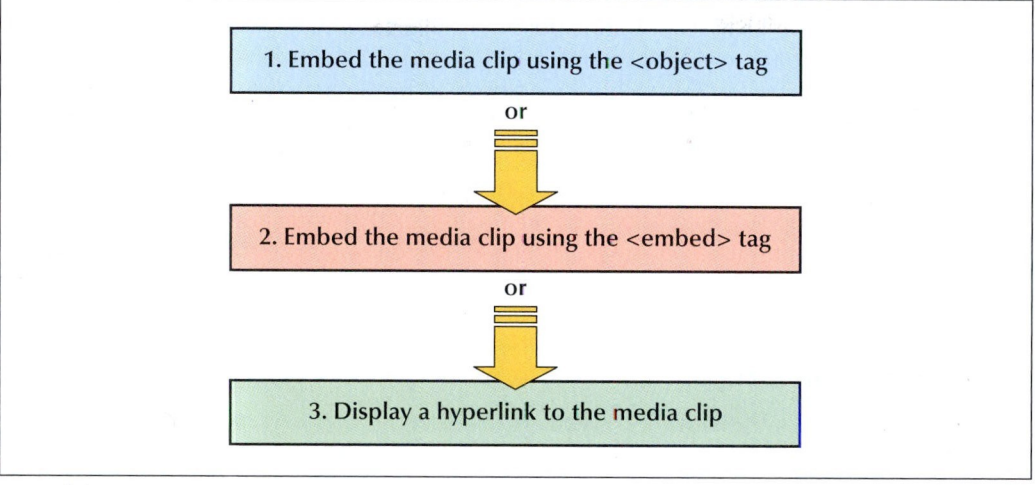

The general syntax of this approach is therefore:

```
<object data="url" attributes>
   <embed src="url" attributes>
      <a href="url">Link to media clip</a>
   </embed>
</object>
```

Browsers that can display the media clip using the <object> tag will ignore any elements nested within the<object> tag other than <param> tags. If a browser cannot work with the <object> tag, it will ignore it and attempt to display the contents of the <embed> tag. Finally, if the browser cannot display the contents of the <embed> tag, it will ignore it as well and display the hypertext link.

Figure 7-34 shows how to use this approach to insert a QuickTime movie clip first as an ActiveX control, then as an embedded object using the <embed> tag, and finally as a hypertext link.

HTML code to nest a QuickTime movie ◀ **Figure 7-34**

display as an ActiveX control

display using the <embed> tag

display as a hypertext link

```
<object data="video.mov" type="video/quicktime"
   classid="clsid:02BF25D5-8C17-4B23-BC80-D3488ABDDC6B"
   codebase="http://www.apple.com/qtactivex/qtplugin.cab"
   width="320" height="260">

      <param name="src" value="video.mov" />
      <param name="autoplay" value="false" />

      <embed src="video.mov" type="video/quicktime"
         pluginspage="http://www.apple.com/quicktime/download"
         width="320" height="260" autoplay="false">

         Click to <a href="video.mov">download</a> the movie clip.

      </embed>
</object>
```

You can also nest <object> tags within one another. The following general code shows three levels of nested objects:

```
<object data="video.mov" type="video/quicktime">
   <object data="video.wmv" type="video/x-ms-wmv">
      Click to <a href="video.avi">download</a> the movie clip.
   </object>
</object>
```

The uppermost level uses the <object> tag to insert a QuickTime movie clip. If that video format is not supported by the browser, the browser will then attempt to display the clip in .wmv format. If the browser supports neither of those objects, it will display a hypertext link to the video file in .avi format.

Nesting <object> tags in this fashion works for all browsers other than Internet Explorer prior to version 7. Earlier versions of Internet Explorer will treat the nested <object> tags as separate objects and will display both of them within the Web page. You can override this behavior by hiding one of the embedded objects using CSS.

You discuss this option with Maxine, and she agrees that you should augment the code for the jumbo.htm file with several levels of nested objects for the sound and video clips from *Royal Wedding*.

To nest the media clips:

1. Return to the **jumbo.htm** file in your text editor.

2. Scroll to the object element for the overture.mp3 audio clip.

3. Directly above the closing </object> tag, insert the following embed element, as shown in Figure 7-35:

```
<embed src="overture.mp3" type="audio/mpeg"
 width="280" height="25"
 autoplay="false" autostart="false"
 controller="true" showcontrols="true">

    Click to <a href="overture.mp3">download</a> the movie overture.

</embed>
```

Figure 7-35	Object nesting for the overture.mp3 file

```
<!--[if IE]><!-->
    <object data="overture.mp3" type="audio/mpeg"
     classid="clsid:02BF25D5-8C17-4B23-BC80-D3488ABDDC6B"
     codebase="http://www.apple.com/qtactivex/qtplugin.cab"
     width="280" height="25">
<!--<![endif]-->

<!--[if !IE]><!-->
    <object data="overture.mp3" type="audio/mpeg"
     width="280" height="25">
<!--<![endif]-->

        <param name="src" value="overture.mp3" />
        <param name="autoplay" value="false" />
        <param name="autostart" value="false" />
        <param name="controller" value="true" />
        <param name="showcontrols" value="true" />

        <embed src="overture.mp3" type="audio/mpeg"
         width="280" height="25"
         autoplay="false" autostart="false"
         controller="true" showcontrols="true">

            Click to <a href="overture.mp3">download</a> the movie overture.

        </embed>

    </object>
```

the <embed> tag will be used by browsers that do not support the <object> tag

browsers that do not support embedded MP3 files will still display a hypertext link to the file

Note that the attributes of the embed element duplicate the parameters and parameter values used for the object element.

4. Scroll down to the object element for the rwdance.swf file. Above the closing
   </object> tag, insert the following code as shown in Figure 7-36:

```
<embed src="rwdance.swf" type="application/x-shockwave-flash"
 width="280" height="239"
 movie="rwdance.swf" quality="high" menu="false">

    To view the movie clip, install Adobe Flash.

</embed>
```

Object nesting for the rwdance.swf file | Figure 7-36

```
<!--[if IE]><!-->
    <object data="rwdance.swf" type="application/x-shockwave-flash"
     classid="clsid:D27CDB6E-AE6D-11cf-96B8-444553540000"
     codebase="http://download.macromedia.com/pub/shockwave/cabs/flash/swflash.cab#version=9,0,115,0"
     width="280" height="239">
<!--<![endif]-->

<!--[if !IE]><!-->
    <object data="rwdance.swf" type="application/x-shockwave-flash"
     width="280" height="239">
<!--<![endif]-->

    <param name="movie" value="rwdance.swf" />
    <param name="quality" value="high" />
    <param name="menu" value="false" />

    <embed src="rwdance.swf" type="application/x-shockwave-flash"
     width="280" height="239"
     movie="rwdance.swf" quality="high" menu="false">

        To view the movie clip, install Adobe Flash.

    </embed>

</object>
```

browsers that do not support Flash will display a message suggesting that Flash be installed

5. Save your changes and then reload the **jumbo.htm** file in your Web browser. Verify
   that both embedded media clips still play correctly within your browser.

As long as you have support for MP3 files and Flash, you should not see any change
within your Web page. The nested objects and hypertext links only appear to users who
do not have the plug-ins or add-ons installed for these objects. You can test object nesting
within your browser by temporarily disabling the multimedia plug-ins. Each browser has
a different method for disabling plug-ins. For example, the Opera browser allows users to
turn off plug-ins from the Preferences window. Firefox requires the user to remove or
rename the plug-in files from the Mozilla Firefox\plugins folder. Under Internet Explorer,
you can disable plug-ins and add-ons by selecting Manage Add-ons from the Tools menu
and clicking Enable or Disable Add-ons to open the Manage Add-Ons dialog box. From
that dialog box, you can select and disable each plug-in associated with Internet
Explorer. Figure 7-37 shows the appearance of the Web page in Internet Explorer with
both QuickTime and Flash disabled.

Figure 7-37 **The Web page with disabled plug-ins**

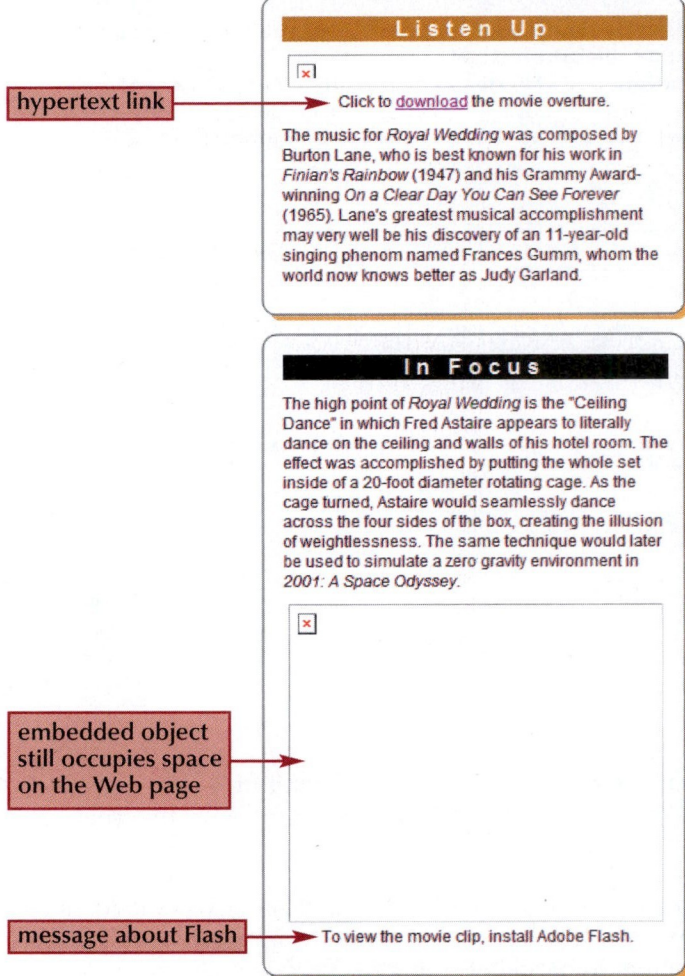

Notice that the embedded objects still occupy space within the Web page even if they're unable to be displayed by the browser.

Embedded Video and YouTube | InSight

One of the largest and most popular online sites for sharing videos is YouTube. Exact numbers are difficult to come by, but the site is estimated to house tens of millions of videos viewed by millions of users each day. YouTube applies a common format to all of its videos, limiting them to a frame size of 320 × 240 pixels with a data rate of 314 Kbps. Although the site accepts videos in wmv, avi, mov, mpeg, and mp4 formats, the files are converted to flv format before being added to the YouTube library. Audio is stored in mp3 format at a bit rate of 65 Kbps.

A video stored on the YouTube server can be viewed either by going to the YouTube Web site or by embedding the YouTube movie player on one's own Web site. The HTML code to embed a YouTube video on your Web site is

```
<object width="425" height="355">
    <param name="movie" value="http://www.youtube.com/v/id"/>
    <param name="wmode" value="transparent" />
    <embed src="http://www.youtube.com/v/id"
            type="application/x-shockwave-flash" wmode="transparent"
            width="425" height="355">
    </embed>
</object>
```

where the url *www.youtube.com/v/id* points to a video file stored on the YouTube server. The id string *youtube_id* is a special id that YouTube assigns to each video in its library. For example, the source for a clip from *Royal Wedding* is (as of this writing) at *www.youtube.com/v/ac6o8PXthzQ&hl=en*.

Maxine is pleased with the work you've done embedding video in several different formats on sample pages for her Web site. In the next session, you'll explore how to work with applets by adding a scrolling marquee to Maxine's sample Web page.

Session 7.2 Quick Check | Review

1. What are four factors that contribute to the calculation of a video's data rate?
2. Why does saving Web video at a high frame rate and data rate not always result in a high-quality video?
3. What is a codec?
4. What is the difference between a Flash flv file and a Flash swf file?
5. What is the MIME type of a Flash animation?
6. What parameter do you add to an embedded Flash animation to set the playback quality to high?
7. What parameter do you add to an embedded QuickTime video to fit the video clip to the object space while retaining its aspect ratio?
8. Specify the code you would enter to insert an embed element containing the QuickTime movie file astaire.mov. Assume the dimensions of the clip are 320 × 160 pixels.

Session 7.3

Introducing Java

Maxine has included a cast list for *Royal Wedding* on her Web site. Currently, the list displays only a few of the actors and actresses from the movie. Maxine would like to expand the list to include more of the cast as well as the director, producers, and writers; however, doing so would result in a list so long that it would ruin her page layout. Instead of a long list, Maxine envisions a scrolling cast list mimicking the credits that appear at the end of a movie. Maxine has seen scrolling text on other Web sites and wonders if you could add a similar feature to her Web page. You can do so with a programming language called Java.

As with many computing innovations, Java came from some unexpected sources. In the early 1990s, programmers at Sun Microsystems envisioned a day when common appliances and devices, such as refrigerators, toasters, and garage door openers, would be networked and controllable using a single operating system. Such an operating system would need to be portable because it would obviously need to be able to work with a wide variety of devices. The programmers began development on such an operating system and based it on a language called **Oak**. The project did not succeed at that point (perhaps the world was not ready for toasters and refrigerators to communicate), but the initial work on Oak was so promising that Sun Microsystems saw its potential for use on the Internet. Oak was modified in 1995 and renamed **Java**.

Each Java program works with a **Java Virtual Machine** (**JVM**), a software program that runs the Java code and returns the results to the user's computer. Java Virtual Machines can be created for different operating systems, so a Java program can be run from any operating system, including UNIX, Windows, DOS, and the Macintosh. Just as Web pages were designed at the beginning to be platform-independent, so was Java, and it became a natural fit for use on the Web. Netscape incorporated a Java Virtual Machine into Netscape Navigator version 2.0. Microsoft wasted little time in including its own JVM with Internet Explorer version 3.0. Because of the popularity of Java, JVMs are usually installed as part of the operating system or along with the user's Web browser. Java is still used throughout the Web today, though many of the uses of Java are now being supplied by Flash, which is easier to program.

A Java program is not a stand-alone application, but instead runs in conjunction with a hosting program such as a Web browser. The program is therefore a "mini" application or **applet**. When the user connects to a Web page containing a Java applet, the applet is downloaded along with the Web page from a Web server, but the applet itself runs within the user's Web browser. This frees up the Web server for other tasks, as shown in Figure 7-38.

Applets and Java Virtual Machines | Figure 7-38

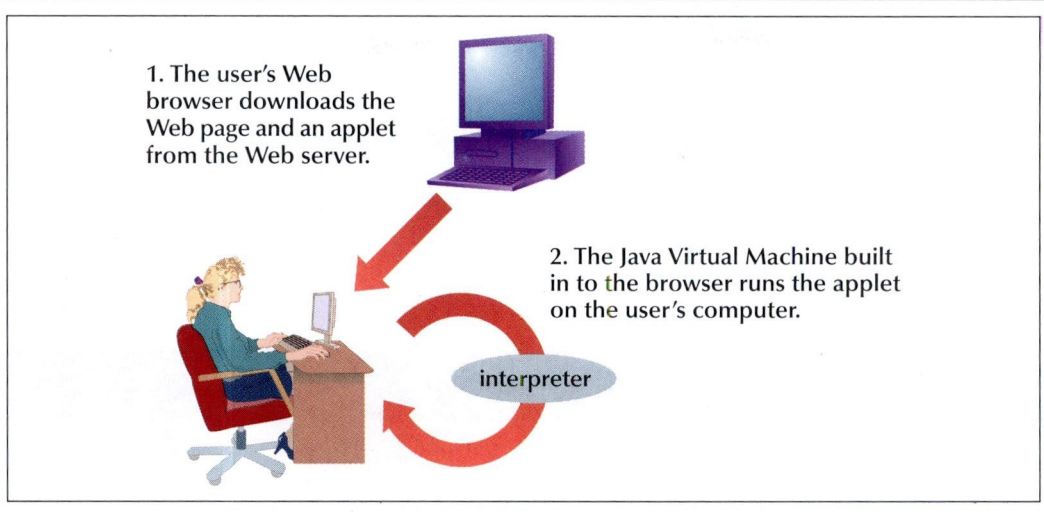

1. The user's Web browser downloads the Web page and an applet from the Web server.

2. The Java Virtual Machine built in to the browser runs the applet on the user's computer.

interpreter

Applets are embedded within Web pages just like the sound and video clips you embedded in the first two sessions of this tutorial. The applet runs within an **applet window**, which can be resized and positioned anywhere within the page.

Several libraries of Java applets are available on the Web. Some applets are free to download and use for non-commercial purposes. In other cases, programmers charge a fee for use of their applets. You can find Java applets for a variety of tasks, including stock market tickers, games, animations, and utilities for your browser or Web page.

A Java program is stored in an executable file called a **class file**, which has the file extension .class. Some Java applets might require several .class files to run properly. Each class file is run within a Java Virtual Machine. This is different from other programs on your computer, such as your Web browser, which are run by your computer's operating system.

Working with Java Applets

Java applets are embedded using the same <object> tag you used for sound and video clips. The general syntax of an embedded Java applet is

```
<object classid="id" type="application/x-java-applet"
        width="value" height="value">
   parameters
</object>
```

where *id* is the class id of the Java applet, the width and height attributes define the dimensions of the applet window, and *parameters* are the parameters associated with the applet. Internet Explorer and non-IE browsers differ in the class id values they use for Java. To embed a Java applet under Internet Explorer, you would use the code

```
<object classid="clsd:clsid:8AD9C840-044E-11D1-B3E9-00805F499D93"
        type="application/x-java-applet"
        width="value" height="value">
   <param name="code" value="file" />
   parameters
</object>
```

where *file* is the name of the file containing the Java applet. For non-IE browsers, Java is installed as a plug-in and the object code is

```
<object classid="java:file" type="application/x-java-applet"
        width="value" height="value">
   parameters
</object>
```

where once again *file* is the name of the file containing the Java applet. Note that for non-IE browsers, you do not need the code parameter. To reconcile the two approaches, you can use IE conditional comments as you did for the embedded sound and video clips in the first two sessions.

Reference Window | **Embedding a Java Applet**

- To embed a Java applet as an ActiveX object for Internet Explorer, enter
  ```
  <object classid="clsd:clsid:8AD9C840-044E-11D1-B3E9-00805F499D93"
          type="application/x-java-applet"
          width="value" height="value">
     <param name="code" value="file" />
     parameters
  </object>
  ```
  where the width and height attributes define the dimensions of the applet window, *file* is the filename of the class file, and *parameters* are the parameters associated with the applet.
- To embed a Java applet for non-IE browsers, use
  ```
  <object classid="java:file" type="application/x-java-applet"
          width="value" height="value">
     parameters
  </object>
  ```

Embedding a Java Applet

Maxine has located a Java applet to display text in a scrolling marquee. The name of the class file is CreditRoll.class. Embed this applet in her Web page both as an ActiveX object for Internet Explorer and a plug-in for non-IE browsers.

To embed the Java applet:

▶ 1. Return to the **jumbo.htm** file in your text editor and scroll up to the paragraph listing the cast members.

▶ 2. Directly above the cast list within the paragraph, insert the following code for IE browsers:

```
<!--[if IE]><!-->
   <object classid="clsid:8AD9C840-044E-11D1-B3E9-00805F499D93"
     type="application/x-java-applet"
     width="260" height="130">
      <param name="code" value="CreditRoll.class" />

<!--<![endif]-->
```

Trouble? You can copy and paste the ActiveX classid from the **activexlist.txt** file located in the tutorial.07\tutorial folder included with your Data Files.

3. Add the following code to insert the <object> tag for non-IE browsers:

```
<!--[if !IE]><!-->
    <object classid="java:CreditRoll.class"
            type="application/x-java-applet"
            width="260" height="130">
<!--<![endif]>
```

4. After the cast list, insert the following closing tag:

```
</object>
```

Figure 7-39 highlights the newly inserted code.

Insert an object element for a Java applet ◀ **Figure 7-39**

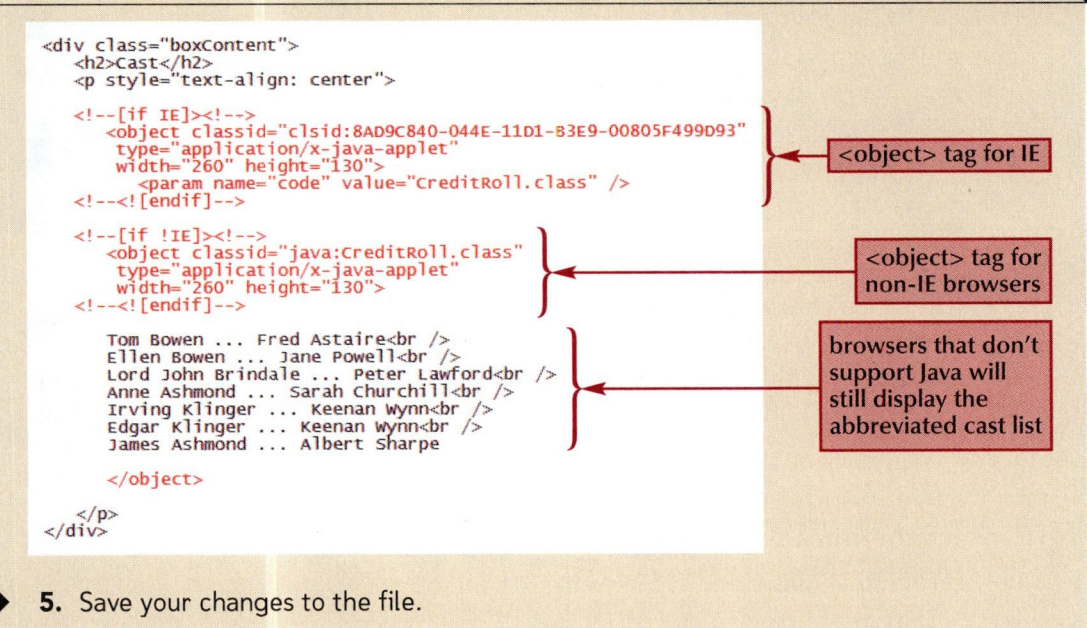

```
<div class="boxContent">
  <h2>Cast</h2>
  <p style="text-align: center">

  <!--[if IE]><!-->
    <object classid="clsid:8AD9C840-044E-11D1-B3E9-00805F499D93"
      type="application/x-java-applet"
      width="260" height="130">
        <param name="code" value="CreditRoll.class" />
  <!--<![endif]-->

  <!--[if !IE]><!-->
    <object classid="java:CreditRoll.class"
      type="application/x-java-applet"
      width="260" height="130">
  <!--<![endif]-->

    Tom Bowen ... Fred Astaire<br />
    Ellen Bowen ... Jane Powell<br />
    Lord John Brindale ... Peter Lawford<br />
    Anne Ashmond ... Sarah Churchill<br />
    Irving Klinger ... Keenan Wynn<br />
    Edgar Klinger ... Keenan Wynn<br />
    James Ashmond ... Albert Sharpe

    </object>

  </p>
</div>
```

<object> tag for IE

<object> tag for non-IE browsers

browsers that don't support Java will still display the abbreviated cast list

5. Save your changes to the file.

Notice that you kept the cast list that Maxine previously entered in this document nested within the <object> tag. If this page is opened by a browser that does not support Java, it will ignore the <object> tags but will still display the abbreviated cast list.

Inserting Java Parameters

The CreditRoll applet contains several parameters that define the text being scrolled, the speed of the scrolling, and the font and background styles. Figure 7-40 describes the parameters used by the CreditRoll applet.

Figure 7-40 ▸ **Parameters of the CreditRoll.class**

Parameter	Description
bgcolor	The background color of the applet window, expressed as a hexadecimal color value
fadezone	The text in the applet window fades in and out as it scrolls; this parameter sets the size of the area in which the text fades (in pixels)
textcolor	The color value of the text in the applet window
font	The font used for the scrolling text in the applet window
text$x$	Each line of text in the applet window requires a separate text$x$ parameter, where x is the line number; for example, the parameter text1 sets the text for the first line in the applet window, text2 sets the text for the second line in the applet window, and so forth
url	Specifies the Web page that is opened if the applet window is clicked
repeat	Specifies whether the text in the applet window is repeated; setting this parameter's value to yes causes the text to scroll continuously
speed	The speed at which the text scrolls, expressed in milliseconds between each movement
vspace	The space between each line of text, in pixels
fontsize	The point size of the text in the applet window

Maxine would like the credit roll to appear in a 14-point white font on a brown background. She suggests setting the speed of the scrolling to 100, which is 100 milliseconds or 1/10 of a second between each movement of the text. She wants 3 pixels of space between each line of text and a fadezone value of 20 pixels. The scrolling should run continuously. Add these parameters and values to the object code for the CreditRoll applet.

To insert the parameters for the CreditRoll applet:

▸ **1.** Return to the **jumbo.htm** file in your text editor.

▸ **2.** Add the following parameters directly above the text for the cast list to set the font style of the scrolling text:

```
<param name="fontsize" value="14" />
<param name="bgcolor" value="CE9314" />
<param name="textcolor" value="FFFFFF" />
```

▸ **3.** Add the following parameters to set the scrolling speed, the space between the lines of text, and the size of the fadezone:

```
<param name="speed" value="100" />
<param name="vspace" value="3" />
<param name="fadezone" value="20" />
```

▸ **4.** Finally, set the CreditRoll applet to repeatedly scroll the text without stopping by adding the following parameter, as shown in Figure 7-41:

```
<param name="repeat" value="yes" />
```

Adding parameters for font style and scrolling speed   Figure 7-41

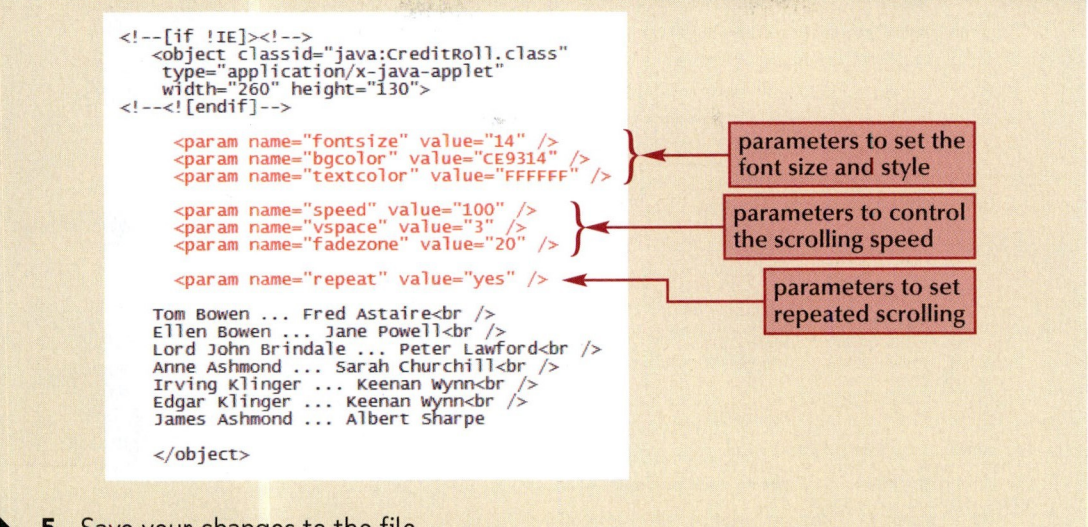

```
<!--[if !IE]><!-->
    <object classid="java:CreditRoll.class"
      type="application/x-java-applet"
      width="260" height="130">
<!--<![endif]-->
        <param name="fontsize" value="14" />
        <param name="bgcolor" value="CE9314" />
        <param name="textcolor" value="FFFFFF" />

        <param name="speed" value="100" />
        <param name="vspace" value="3" />
        <param name="fadezone" value="20" />

        <param name="repeat" value="yes" />

    Tom Bowen ... Fred Astaire<br />
    Ellen Bowen ... Jane Powell<br />
    Lord John Brindale ... Peter Lawford<br />
    Anne Ashmond ... Sarah Churchill<br />
    Irving Klinger ... Keenan Wynn<br />
    Edgar Klinger ... Keenan Wynn<br />
    James Ashmond ... Albert Sharpe

    </object>
```

- parameters to set the font size and style
- parameters to control the scrolling speed
- parameters to set repeated scrolling

5. Save your changes to the file.

Next you must specify the text of the rolling marquee. The credit roll text is entered into parameters named text*x*, where *x* is the number of the line in the credit roll. Because of the length of the cast list, parameters named text1 through text19 have already been created for you and stored in a separate file in the tutorial.07\tutorial folder.

The credit roll applet also supports a parameter named url that adds a link to the credit roll, opening a Web page when a user clicks the applet window. Maxine suggests that you link the credit roll to a Web page from the Internet Movie Database describing *Royal Wedding*. The url of the Web page is *www.imdb.com/title/tt0043983/*.

Add parameters for the credit roll text and the url to the embedded applet.

To add the scrolling text and url:

1. Copy the parameter text from the **creditlist.txt** (in the tutorial.07\tutorial folder included with your Data Files).

2. Return to the **jumbo.htm** file in your text editor and paste the parameter text directly below the <param> tag for the repeat parameter.

3. Add the following parameter to set the url associated with the CreditRoll applet:

```
<param name="url" value="http://www.imdb.com/title/tt0043983" />
```

Figure 7-42 shows the revised code of the file.

Figure 7-42   **Specifying the marquee text**

```
<param name="repeat" value="yes" />

<param name="text1" value="Royal Wedding" />
<param name="text2" value="Produced by: Arthur Freed" />
<param name="text3" value="Directed by: Stanley Donen" />
<param name="text4" value="Written by: Alan Jay Lerner" />
<param name="text5" value="Orignal Music by: Burton Lane" />
<param name="text6" value="---- o ----" />
<param name="text7" value="" />
<param name="text8" value="Fred Astaire ... Tom Bowen" />
<param name="text9" value="Jane Powell ... Ellen Bowen" />
<param name="text10" value="Peter Lawford ... Lord John Brindale" />
<param name="text11" value="Sarah Churchill ... Anne Ashmond" />
<param name="text12" value="Keenan Wynn ... Irving Klinger" />
<param name="text13" value="Keenan Wynn ... Edgar Klinger" />
<param name="text14" value="Albert Sharpe ... James Ashmond" />
<param name="text15" value="Eddie ... Wilson Benge" />
<param name="text16" value="Charles Gordon ... Francis Bethencourt" />
<param name="text17" value="Dick ... William Cabanne" />
<param name="text18" value="Harry ... Jimmy Fairfax" />
<param name="text19" value="Billy ... John Hedloe" />

<param name="url" value="http://www.imdb.com/title/tt0043983" />

Tom Bowen ... Fred Astaire<br />
Ellen Bowen ... Jane Powell<br />
Lord John Brindale ... Peter Lawford<br />
Anne Ashmond ... Sarah Churchill<br />
Irving Klinger ... Keenan Wynn<br />
Edgar Klinger ... Keenan Wynn<br />
James Ashmond ... Albert Sharpe

</object>
```

marquee text

url of the scrolling marquee

▶ **4.** Save your changes to the file and then reload **jumbo.htm** in your Web browser. Verify that the Cast box contains a scrolling marquee of the cast from *Royal Wedding*. Figure 7-43 shows the completed Web page with all of the embedded objects.

Completed Web page | **Figure 7-43**

A Web site for lovers of classic films

Jumbo Popcorn

Home | Movies | Actors | Directors | Genres | My Picks | Links

Royal Wedding (1951) ★★★

Overview
Title Page
User Comments
Reviews
Quotes
Trivia
Awards

Showings
Trailers
TV Schedule
DVD Details
Technical Specs
Soundtrack

scrolling marquee

Featuring
Fred Astaire
Jane Powell
Peter Lawford
Keenan Wynn
Alan Jay Lerner

You Might Also Enjoy
Finian's Rainbow
Seven Brides for 7 Brothers
Top Hat
Swing Time
Three Little Words
Roberta
Shall We Dance?
The Gay Divorcee
Easter Parade
Funny Face
Daddy Long Legs

Cast

Royal Wedding
Produced by: Arthur Freed
Directed by: Stanley Donen
Written by: Alan Jay Lerner

Synopsis

Tom Bowen (Fred Astaire) and Ellen Bowen (Jane Powell) are a brother and sister dance team from New York. Their agent (Keenan Wynn) books them in London for performances during the time of the royal wedding. Aboard a cruise ship to London, Ellen becomes involved with aristocrat and playboy, Lord John Brindale (Peter Lawford). In London, Tom meets and falls in love Anne Ashmond (Sarah Churchill), a dancer in his show. Despite a few minor complications, it all ends happily as the two couples find love and marriage on the day of the royal wedding.

Royal Wedding is famous for several dance sequences, including a classic number in which Astaire appears to dance on the ceiling and walls of his hotel room. Jane Powell proves to be an elegant and athletic partner for Astaire; though perhaps his best duet of the movie takes place with a hat rack he discovers on the cruise to England. This is one of Astaire's best and I highly recommend it.

Listen Up

The music for *Royal Wedding* was composed by Burton Lane, who is best known for his work in *Finian's Rainbow* (1947) and his Grammy Award-winning *On a Clear Day You Can See Forever* (1965). Lane's greatest musical accomplishment may very well be his discovery of an 11-year-old singing phenom named Frances Gumm, whom the world now knows better as Judy Garland.

In Focus

The high point of *Royal Wedding* is the "Ceiling Dance" in which Fred Astaire appears to literally dance on the ceiling and walls of his hotel room. The effect was accomplished by putting the whole set inside of a 20-foot diameter rotating cage. As the cage turned, Astaire would seamlessly dance across the four sides of the box, creating the illusion of weightlessness. The same technique would later be used to simulate a zero gravity environment in *2001: A Space Odyssey*.

Home | Movies | Actors | Directors | Genres | My Picks | Links

5. Click the scrolling marquee box and verify that your Web browser opens a Web page from the Internet Movie Database describing the film.

You show Maxine the scrolling marquee, which she likes very much. She asks how the page will appear for users who don't have Java. You tell her that the page will show the abbreviated cast list used earlier. That text is still present in the Web page, though it won't be displayed if the CreditRoll applet can be run.

Maxine also wants you to include information for users about how to install Java if they don't have it. For Internet Explorer, you can do this by adding the following codebase attribute to the <object> tag:

```
codebase="http://java.sun.com/update/1.6.0/jinstall-6-windows-i586.cab"
```

If Internet Explorer doesn't have Java installed or has a later version installed, this code prompts users to decide whether or not to upgrade their Java support. For other browsers, you can insert a link to a Java download page at *http://www.java.com/en/download*, which users can click to manually install or update their version of Java.

Maxine would like you to add code for both approaches to the jumbo.htm file.

To provide installation support for Java:

▶ **1.** Return to the **jumbo.htm** file in your text editor.

▶ **2.** Add the following codebase attribute to the <object> tag for Internet Explorer users, as shown in Figure 7-44:

```
codebase="http://java.sun.com/update/1.6.0/jinstall-6-windows-
i586.cab"
```

Figure 7-44	Specifying the codebase for Internet Explorer

```
<!--[if IE]><!-->
    <object classid="clsid:8AD9C840-044E-11D1-B3E9-00805F499D93"
        codebase="http://java.sun.com/update/1.6.0./jinstall-6-windows-i586.cab"
        type="application/x-java-applet"
        width="260" height="130">
        <param name="code" value="CreditRoll.class" />
<!--<![endif]-->
```

▶ **3.** Scroll down the file and add the following code after the last cast entry, as shown in Figure 7-45:

```
<br /><br />
To view a scrolling marquee, get the latest
<a href="http://java.sun.com/products/plugin/downloads">
    Java Plug-in.
</a>
```

Figure 7-45	Text displayed when Java is not installed

```
Tom Bowen ... Fred Astaire<br />
Ellen Bowen ... Jane Powell<br />
Lord John Brindale ... Peter Lawford<br />
Anne Ashmond ... Sarah Churchill<br />
Irving Klinger ... Keenan Wynn<br />
Edgar Klinger ... Keenan Wynn<br />
James Ashmond ... Albert Sharpe

<br /><br />
To view a scrolling marquee, get the latest
<a href="http://java.sun.com/products/plugin/downloads">
    Java Plug-in.
</a>

</object>
```

▶ **4.** Close the file, saving your changes.

You can temporarily disable Java in your Web browser to test whether or not the message from Figure 7-45 will be displayed to the user. The commands to disable Java will usually be found in the Options or Preferences window of your browser. For example, to disable Java in the Firefox browser, select Options from the Tools menu to open the Options dialog box, and then click the Content tab. Deselect the Enable Java check box to disable Java. The Enable Java check box for Opera is located under the Advanced tab in the Preferences dialog box. For Safari, it's located under the Security tab of the Preferences dialog box. Finally, for Internet Explorer, you can disable Java by opening the Manage Add-ons dialog box and disabling the Java plug-in. Figure 7-46 shows the appearance of the movie credit box when Java is disabled.

Text for Java-less browsers ◄ Figure 7-46

```
                Cast

        Tom Bowen ... Fred Astaire
        Ellen Bowen ... Jane Powell
   Lord John Brindale ... Peter Lawford
    Anne Ashmond ... Sarah Churchill
      Irving Klinger ... Keenan Wynn
      Edgar Klinger ... Keenan Wynn
    James Ashmond ... Albert Sharpe

  To view a scrolling marquee, get the latest Java
                   Plug-in.
```

Creating a Scrolling Marquee with Internet Explorer | InSight

As an alternative to using a Java applet to create a box with scrolling text, if you know that users accessing your Web page will be using Internet Explorer, you can take advantage of Internet Explorer's marquee element to create a theater-style marquee. The general syntax of the marquee element is

```
<marquee attributes>content</marquee>
```

where *attributes* are the attributes that control the behavior of the marquee and *content* is the text content that appears in the marquee box. To control the scrolling of the text within the marquee, use the attributes

```
behavior="type" direction="type" loop="value"
```

where behavior is either scroll (to scroll the text across the box), slide (to slide the text across the box and stop), or alternate (to bounce the text back and forth across the box); the direction attribute defines the direction of the scrolling (left, right, down, or up); and the loop attribute determines how often the marquee plays (either an integer or infinite).

To control the speed of the text within a marquee, use the attributes

```
scrollamount="value" scrolldelay="value"
```

where the scrollamount attribute determines the amount of space, in pixels, that the text moves each time it advances across the page, and the scrolldelay attribute is the amount of time, in milliseconds, between text advances.

Browsers that do not support the marquee element display the entire marquee text without any scrolling; so if you use this element, be sure to leave room for your text to appear in non-IE browsers.

Exploring the Applet Element

Older browsers might not support the <object> tag for inserting Java applets. If you expect some users to be running older browsers, you can still allow them to view your applet by using the applet element

```
<applet code="file" width="value" height="value" alt="text">
    parameters
</applet>
```

where *file* is the name of the Java class file, the width and height attributes set the dimension of the applet window, the alt attribute defines alternate text to be displayed by the browser if it doesn't support Java, and *parameters* are the parameters associated with the applet. For example, to embed the CreditRoll.class applet using the <applet> tag, you could enter the code

```
<applet code="CreditRoll.class" width="260" height="130">
    parameters
</applet>
```

with *parameters* being the same <param> tags you used with the object element. Like the <embed> tag discussed in the last session, the <applet> tag is not part of the W3C specifications for HTML and XHTML and is gradually being phased out, though you might still encounter it in the code for older Web pages.

Embedding Other Objects

In this tutorial you've used the object element to embed sound clips, video clips, and Java applets. However, you can use the object element for many other purposes. Any type of content can be embedded using <object> tags. In fact, the original vision of the object element was to act as a general container for any content not directly entered into the HTML code of the Web page. Maxine suggests that you explore a few examples.

Inserting Inline Images

You can use the <object> tag to insert all of your inline images. One advantage of entering images as embedded objects is that you can apply markup tags for the alternate text. For example, the inline image

```
<img src="jplogo.jpg" alt="Jumbo Popcorn" width="300" height="200" />
```

can be replaced with the embedded object

```
<object data="jplogo.jpg" type="image/jpeg"
 width="300" height="200">
    <h1>Jumbo Popcorn</h1>
</object>
```

Another advantage of treating images as embedded objects is that you can provide the user with different formats of the same graphic image. For example, the following code allows the browser to first display the Jumbo Popcorn logo in png format:

```
<object data="jplogo.png" type="image/png">
    <object data="jplogo.jpg" type="image/jpg">
        <h1>Jumbo Popcorn</h1>
    </object>
</object>
```

If that format is not supported, the browser displays the logo as a jpeg. Finally, if the browser does not support either format or is a nongraphical browser, it displays the text Jumbo Popcorn marked as an h1 heading.

You can also nest videos and inline images. For example, you can embed a video clip and nest an image object within the video clip, allowing the browser to choose which type of object to display.

Embedding an HTML file

Web pages themselves can be embedded as objects. To embed a Web page you use the <object> tags

```
<object data="url" type="text/html"
        width="value" height="value">
</object>
```

where *url* is the URL of the HTML file to be embedded. When you embed a Web page, that file is displayed within the dimensions specified by the width and height attributes. The browser will automatically add horizontal and vertical scroll bars to allow users to scroll around the document. Figure 7-47 shows an example that Maxine might want to use on the Jumbo Popcorn Web site in which previews of two Web pages are shown embedded within her Web site.

Embedding Web pages as objects **Figure 7-47**

Embedding one Web page within another can also be accomplished using frames, a topic that will be discussed in the next tutorial.

You've completed your work on Maxine's sample page describing the *Royal Wedding* movie. She likes the media clips and Java applet you've inserted in the Web page and looks forward to adding more features.

1. What is a Java Virtual Machine?
2. What are class files?
3. Specify the code you would enter to display the stockmarket.class applet in an applet window that is 500 pixels wide × 400 pixels high. Assume that the code is written for Internet Explorer.
4. What code would you enter for the previous question for non-IE browsers?
5. What Internet Explorer element could you use to create a scrolling marquee?
6. Specify the code to embed the image file logo.jpg as an object. If the browser does not support embedded objects, have it display the text "Millennium Computers" as an h2 heading.
7. Specify the code to display the HTML file glossary.htm as an embedded Web page in a window that is 400 pixels wide × 200 pixels high.

Review | **Tutorial Summary**

In this tutorial, you learned how to work with multimedia on your Web pages. The tutorial explored the use of the object element to embed various types of multimedia. The first session focused on sound, starting with a discussion of the issues surrounding working with digital sound. The session then explored how to embed sound files of different types either as plug-ins or ActiveX objects. The second session explored the use of video, focusing on three video formats: Flash, QuickTime, and Windows Media video. The session also examined some of the issues involved with working with video servers such as YouTube. The final session looked at embedded Java applets within a Web page. The tutorial ended by examining how to embed other objects, such as images and other Web pages, into a Web page.

Key Terms

ActiveX	class id	MIDI
add-on	data rate	MIME type
amplitude	embedded media	MP3
applet	external media	Multipurpose Internet Mail
applet window	file compression	Extension type
aspect ratio	Flash video	Oak
bandwidth	flv	parameter
bit depth	frame (video file)	plug-in
bitrate	frame rate	sample resolution
cab files	frequency	sampling rate
cabinet files	Java	Shockwave Flash
class file	Java Virtual Machine	swf

Practice	**Review Assignments**

Practice the skills you learned in the tutorial using the same case scenario.

Data Files needed for the Review Assignments: astairetxt.htm, bottom.png, bottomleft.png, bottomright.png, button.jpg, CreditRoll.class, fa1.gif - fa5.gif, fabio.css, fasong.mp3, filmlist.txt, hatrack.mov, hatrack.swf, hatrack.wmv, jplogo.jpg, left.png, popcorn.jpg, right.png, top.png, topleft.png, and topright.png

Maxine has been working on the Jumbo Popcorn Web site for several weeks now. She has come back to you for help with completing another page. This page will feature the life of Fred Astaire. She has created a sound clip and a video clip that she wants you to embed on the Web page. She's also interested in creating another scrolling marquee, this one listing some of the many movies that Fred Astaire starred in during his life. A preview of the page you'll create is shown in Figure 7-48.

Figure 7-48

Complete the following:

1. Use your text editor to open the **astairetxt.htm** file from the tutorial.07\review folder included with your Data Files. Enter *your name* and *the date* in the comment section of the file. Save the files as **astaire.htm** in the same folder.

2. Scroll down the file and locate the paragraph below the Career Highlights heading. Within this paragraph, Maxine would like to insert a rolling marquee displaying a list of classic Fred Astaire movies. Insert an embedded object to display the CreditRoll applet both as an ActiveX object (for Internet Explorer) and as a plug-in (for non-IE browsers). Set the dimensions of the applet window to 260 pixels wide × 100 pixels high.

3. Add the following parameters to the CreditRoll applet:
   - Display the marquee text in a 12-point font with a background hexadecimal color value of 996600 and a text color of FFFFFF.
   - Set the scrolling speed to 150, the vspace value to 3 pixels, and the fadezone value to 10 pixels. Have the marquee repeat the scrolling without stopping.
   - When users click the marquee, have the browser display the IMDB Fred Astaire biography located at *www.imdb.com/name/nm0000001*.
   - Copy and paste the parameters from the **filmlist.txt** file (located in the tutorial.07\review folder included with your Data Files) to insert the marquee text.

4. For browsers that do not support Java, display the brief list of Astaire movies found in the original data file, followed by a hypertext link to the page *www.java.com/en/download*.

5. Scroll down the file and locate the second paragraph below the Listen Up heading. Within this heading, insert an embedded object to play the **fasong.mp3** sound clip within the QuickTime Media Player. The clip should be inserted as an ActiveX control for Internet Explorer and as a plug-in for non-IE browsers. Set the dimensions of the player to 280 pixels wide × 16 pixels high.

6. Add QuickTime parameters to the sound clip to set the source to the fasong.mp3 file, to display the QuickTime sound controls, and to not autoplay the sound file.

7. For older browsers that do not support the <object> tag, nest the embed element within the <object> tag to play the fasong.mp3 sound clip.

8. For browsers that do not support embedded sound files, have the Web page display a hypertext link to the fasong.mp3 file.

9. Scroll down to the second paragraph below the In Focus heading. Insert an embedded Flash Player both as an ActiveX control and as a plug-in to play the **hatrack.swf** file. Set the dimensions of the movie clip to 310 pixels wide × 260 pixels high.

10. Set the parameters of the movie clip to play the movie at high quality and to turn off the Flash Player menu.

11. For older browsers that may not support the object element, nest the embed element within the <object> tag to play the hatrack.swf file. For browsers that do not support Java at all, have the browser display a message telling users that they must have Adobe Flash Player installed to play the movie clip.

12. Save your changes to the file and then open **astaire.htm** in your Web browser. Verify that you can play the embedded sound file and movie file, and that the CreditRoll applet starts automatically within the page.

13. Return to the **astaire.htm** file in your text editor. Save the file as **astaire_mov.htm** in the same folder. Change the embedded movie from Flash Player to QuickTime Player, playing the **hatrack.mov** file. Set the autoplay parameter to false and the controller parameter to true. For users who do not have QuickTime installed, have the browser display text suggesting that they install QuickTime Player.

14. Save your changes to the file and then open **astaire_mov.htm** in your Web browser. Verify that you can play the embedded movie clip with QuickTime Player.

15. Return to the **astaire_mov.htm** file in your text editor and save it as **astaire_wmv.htm** in the same folder. Change the embedded movie from QuickTime Player to Windows Media Player, playing the **hatrack.wmv** file. Change the parameter values and the text message accordingly to match the parameters required by Windows Media Player.

16. Save your changes and open **astaire_wmv.htm** in your Web browser. Verify that you can play the embedded movie clip using Windows Media Player.

17. Submit your completed files to your instructor.

| Apply | **Case Problem 1** |

Apply your knowledge of multimedia to create a poetry page with audio samples from an American poet.

Data Files needed for this Case Problem: button0.gif - button3.gif, devotion.mp3, fireice.mp3, poetry.css, PopBtn.class, PopMenu.class, rflogo.gif, rftxt.htm, and tan.jpg

American Poetry 121 Professor Debra Li of the English Department at Carston University in Columbia, Mississippi has asked you to help her create a Web page devoted to the works of the poet Robert Frost for her American Poetry 121 class. With your help, she has created a Web page that contains a short biography of the poet and the complete text of two of his works. Professor Li would like to add sound clips of the two poems to the page so that her students can listen to Frost's poetry as well as read it.

She also wants you to create links to other Frost pages on the Web. She's located a Java applet that creates a set of graphical buttons that act as hypertext links. Professor Li thinks this applet would also make her page more interesting. The Java applet uses the PopMenu.class file with the parameters shown in Figure 7-49.

Figure 7-49

Parameter	Defines
labelpos="type"	The default label position for all of the buttons on the menu, where type is either right or below.
labelposn="type"	The label position for the nth button, starting with labelpos0, labelpos1, etc.
textn="text"	The text for the nth button, starting with text0, text1, etc.
srcn="url"	The URL of the image file to be displayed in the nth button, starting with src0, src1, etc.
hrefn="url"	The URL to be opened when the nth button is clicked, starting with href0, href1, etc.
frame="target"	The target of the links when the applet is used with frames; the default is _top.

A preview of the completed page is shown in Figure 7-50.

Figure 7-50

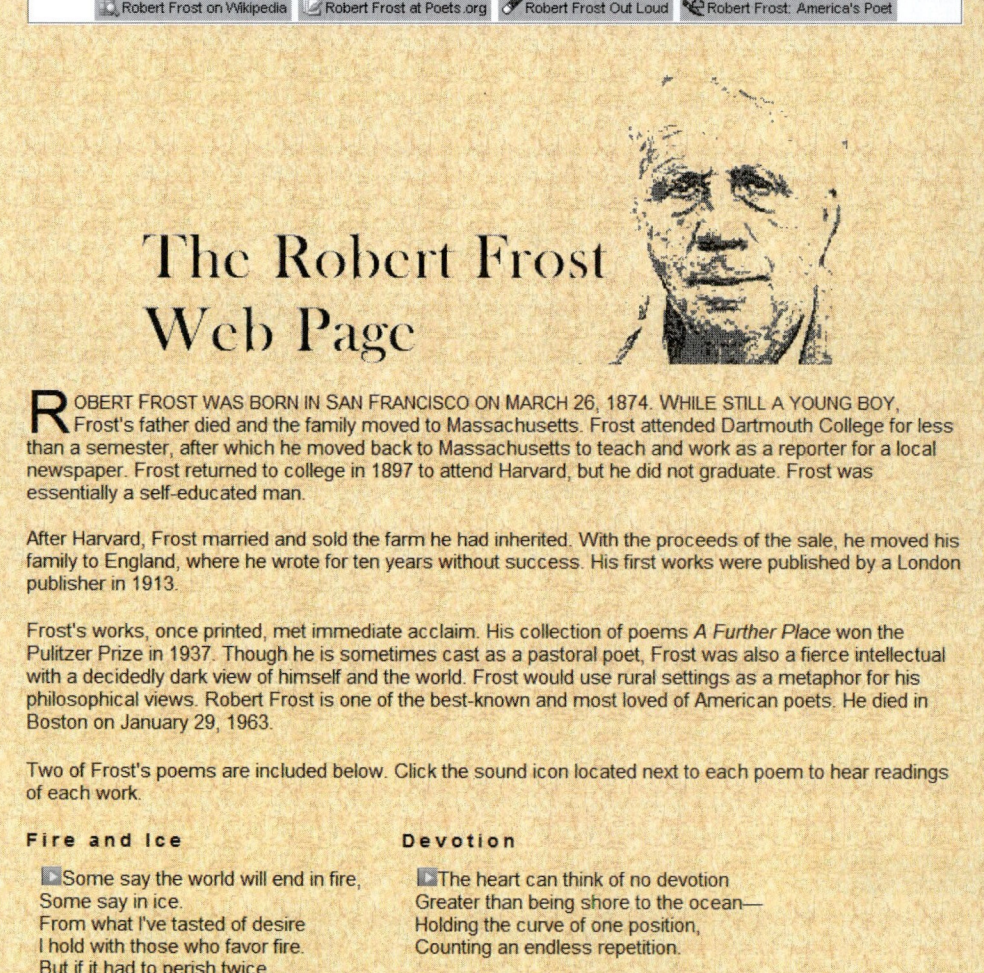

Complete the following:

1. Use your text editor to open the **rftxt.htm** file from the tutorial.07\case1 folder included with your Data Files. Enter *your name* and *the date* in the comment section of the file. Save the file as **rf.htm** in the same folder. Scroll to the links div container. Within the container, Debra has already inserted linked text to four Robert Frost sites on the Web.

2. Insert the **PopMenu.class** Java applet as both an ActiveX object and a plug-in. Set the width of the applet to 700 pixels wide × 30 pixels high.

3. Set the labelpos parameter of the applet to right.

4. Insert parameters src0 through src3, text0 through text3, and href0 through href3 to store the source of the button image, the button text, and the button hypertext link for the four linked buttons. Use the values button0.gif through button3.gif for the button images and the hypertext links to the four Robert Frost sites for the values of the text and href parameters.

5. If the user's browser does not support Java, have it display the hypertext links to the four Robert Frost sites.

6. Scroll down the file to the paragraph for the Fire and Ice poem. Directly above the first line of the poem, insert an embedded QuickTime Player to play the **fireice.mp3** file. Have your code support the QuickTime Player both as an ActiveX object and as a plug-in. Set the height of player to 16 pixels and set the width to only display the QuickTime play button.

7. Add the src, autoplay, and controller parameters to set the source of the QuickTime audio file, to turn off autoplay, and to display the player's sound controls.

8. If the user's browser does not support the QuickTime Player, use the following code instead:

```
<p>Click to <a href="fireice.mp3">download</a> the sound clip</p>
```

9. Repeat Steps 6 through 8 for the Devotion poem, using the sound file **devotion.mp3**.

10. Save your changes to the file and then view it in your Web browser. Verify that the four linked buttons at the top of the page connect the user to the four Robert Frost sites. Also verify that by clicking the player buttons, you can hear a reading of each of the Robert Frost poems.

11. Turn off support for Java and QuickTime within your browser. Verify that your browser displays the hypertext links you specified as alternatives to the embedded media.

12. Submit your completed files to your instructor.

Apply	**Case Problem 2**

Apply your knowledge of embedded video to create a travel guide page with a video tour.

Data Files needed for this Case Problem: roadtxt.htm, rw.css, rwlogo.jpg, and trailridge.swf

Roadways   Karen Upton loves to travel and spends more than half of the year behind the wheel exploring the byways and roadways for her online travel guide, *Roadways*. Karen's Web site is a place where others who share her passion for travel can gather to share stories, advice, and their love for travel. Karen would like to upgrade her site by adding video tours of some of her favorite roadways. She's come to you for help in adding this feature to her site. Karen presents you with a sample page; she has already created the video and descriptive text for Trail Ridge Road, the highest paved continuous highway in the United States. A preview of the page you'll create for Karen is shown in Figure 7-51.

Figure 7-51

Home

Classic Rides

North America
South America
Europe
Asia
Africa
Australia

Tips and Traps

Maintenance
Weather
Law
Enforcement
Local Customs

The Mailbag

Hot Topics
Chat
Archives
FAQs

Contact Me

Travelling the Scenic Byways of the World

Trail Ridge Road

Trail Ridge Road covers the stretch of U.S. Highway 34 from Rocky Mountain National Park near Estes Park, Colorado in the east to Grand Lake, Colorado in the west. The road reaches a maximum elevation of 12,183 feet near Fall River Pass. Trail Ridge Road is the highest paved continuous highway in the United States, spending 10 miles above the tundra line. The road is closed from late fall until early summer due to the snowpack at the higher elevations.

Travellers on Trail Ridge Road climb 4,000 feet in a matter of minutes. The changes that occur en route are dramatic. The drive begins in a forest of aspen and ponderosa pine, but the terrain will soon change to forests of fir and spruce. At 11,000 feet, drivers will encounter treeline and the last stunted trees which soon yield to heavy winds and the alpine tundra.

As you drive, be sure to stop and take in the views at Rainbow Curve, Many Parks Curve, and at Forest Canyon Overlook. On clear days, you can gaze north to Wyoming and east down to the cities along the Front Range. Looking south and west you can gaze further into the heart of the Rocky Mountains. Reserve at least half a day for the drive between Estes Park and Grand Lake.

A simulated drive from Estes Park to the Alpine Visitor Center

Complete the following:

1. Use your text editor to open the **roadtxt.htm** file from the tutorial.07\case2 folder included with your Data Files. Enter *your name* and *the date* in the comment section of the file. Save the file as **roadways.htm** in the same folder.

2. Scroll down to the div element with the id movie. Within the div container, insert an embedded object for the **trailridge.swf** file. The file should be inserted as an ActiveX control for Internet Explorer users and as a plug-in for users of non-IE browsers.

3. Set the dimensions of the video clip to 320 pixels × 280 pixels.

4. Set the value of the movie parameter to trailridge.swf, the quality parameter to high, and the menu parameter to false.

5. For users of older browsers, nest within your video object an embed element to play the trailridge.swf video clip. Set the attributes of the embed element similar to those that you used for the object element.

6. If users do not have Adobe Flash Player installed, display the message "To play this clip you need Adobe Flash Player."

7. Save your changes to file and then view the page in your Web browser. Verify that you can play the embedded video clip.

8. Submit your completed files to your instructor.

| Challenge | **Case Problem 3** |

Explore how to use a Java applet to create a Web page describing the mathematics of fractals.

Data Files needed for this Case Problem: Cmplx.class, Controls.class, fback.jpg, flogo.jpg, FracPanel.class, factaltxt.htm, fstyles.css, Mandel.class, and mandel.swf

Franklin High School   Fractals are geometric objects that closely model the seemingly chaotic world of nature. Doug Hefstadt, a mathematics teacher at Franklin High School in Lake Forest, Illinois, has just begun a unit on fractals for his senior math class. He's used the topic of fractals to construct a Web page to be placed on the school network, and he needs your help to complete the Web page. He has a video clip of a fractal that he wants placed on the Web page, along with a Java applet that allows students to interactively explore the Mandelbrot Set, a type of fractal object. He wants your assistance in putting these two objects on his Web page. A preview of the page you'll create is shown in Figure 7-52.

Figure 7-52

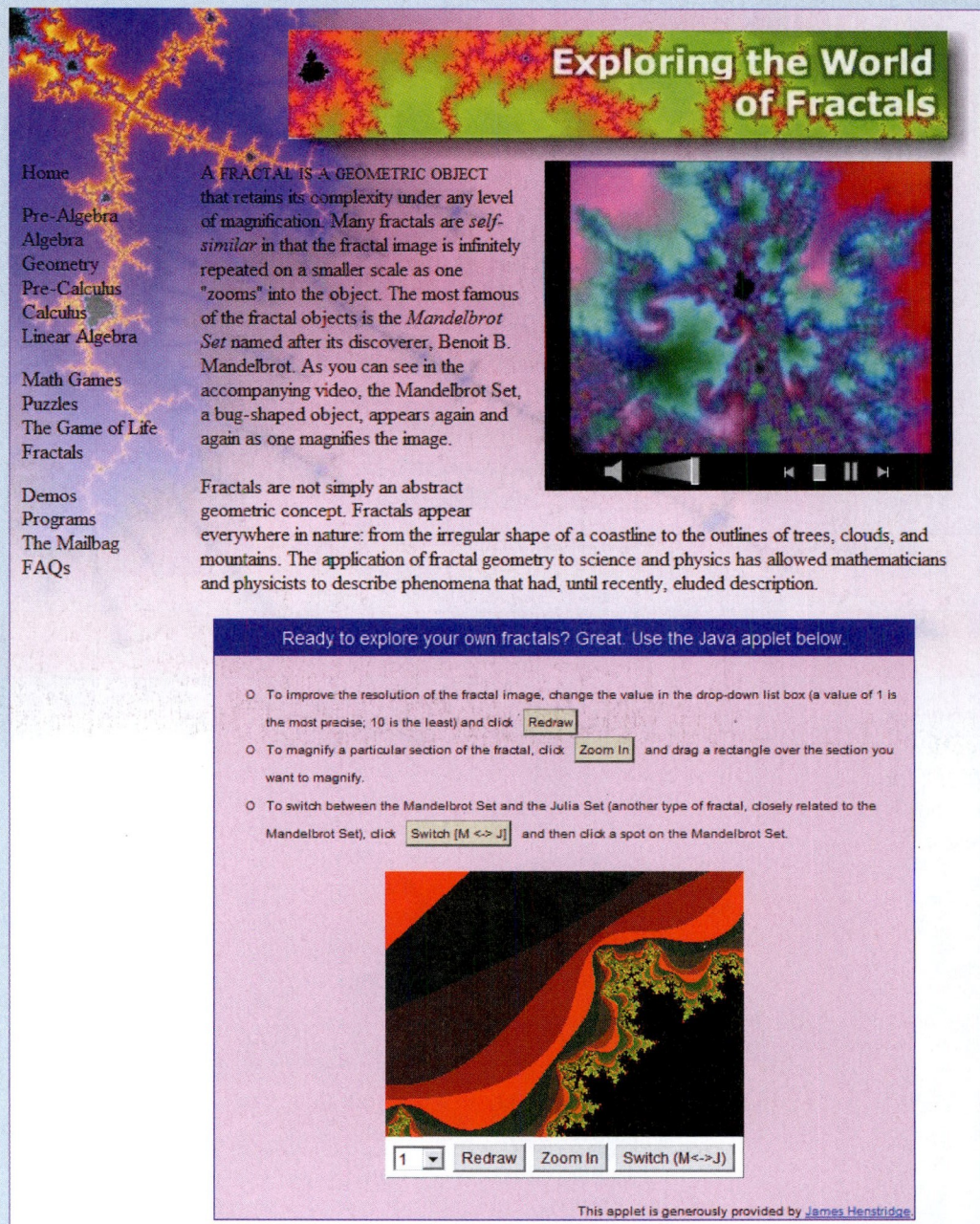

Complete the following:

1. Use your text editor to open the **fractaltxt.htm** file from the tutorial.07\case3 folder included with your Data Files. Enter *your name* and *the date* in the comment section of the file. Save the file as **fractal.htm** in the same folder.

2. Scroll down to the div element with the id movie. Within this div element, insert the **mandel.swf** Flash file both as an ActiveX object and as a plug-in, set the width of the player window to 320 pixels and the height to 260 pixels.

⊕ EXPLORE
3. The fractal movie might take several seconds to load into the Web page. Doug would like the object window to display a message indicating this fact. For both <object> tags, insert the standby attribute to display the text message "Loading movie. Please wait."

4. Set the value of the movie parameter to mandel.swf, the value of the quality parameter to high, and the value of the menu parameter to false.

5. For older browsers, nest an embed element within your <object> tags to insert the **mandel.swf** file. Include all necessary attributes for the embed element.

6. Within the embed element, insert the text string "To play this clip, you need Adobe Flash Player" to have a message for users who do not have Adobe Flash Player installed.

7. Scroll down to the demo div element. Within this element, insert a Java applet for the **Mandel.class** file, both as an ActiveX object and as a plug-in. Set the width of the applet window to 280 pixels and the height to 240 pixels.

⊕ EXPLORE
8. Within the <object> tag, insert the Mandel.class file using the applet object. Set the width of the applet to 280 pixels and the height to 240 pixels.

9. If the browser does not support Java, have it display the text "Your browser does not support Java applets" in place of the Mandel.class applet.

10. Save your changes to the file.

11. Open the Web page in your browser and verify that the video plays correctly.

⊕ EXPLORE
12. Test the fractal applet to verify that you can use it to zoom into the Mandelbrot Set at different levels of magnification.

13. Submit your completed files to your instructor.

Create | **Case Problem 4**

Test your knowledge of embedded media by creating a multimedia Web page for a youth orchestra.

Data Files needed for this Case Problem: beethoven.mp3, byso.jpg, bysoinfo.txt, bysologo.jpg, CreditRoll.class, and schedule.txt

Boise Youth Symphony Orchestra The Boise Youth Symphony Orchestra is one of the premier young people's orchestras in the United States. Denise Young, the BYSO artistic director, has asked you to help create a Web site that contains information about the orchestra. Denise has a short excerpt from the first movement of Beethoven's *Symphony No. 8 in F Major, Op. 93* that the orchestra played in their most recent spring concert. She would like you to embed the clip in the Web page. She also has a schedule of upcoming events and concerts that she would like displayed in a scrolling marquee.

The design of the Web site is up to you, but you can use the following files in creating the Web page:

- **beethoven.mp3**, an MP3 containing an excerpt from the first movement of Beethoven's *Symphony No. 8 in F Major, Op. 93*
- **byso.jpg**, a photo of the orchestra
- **bysoinfo.txt**, general information about the orchestra

- **bysolog.jpg**, the BYSO logo
- **CreditRoll.class**, the scrolling marquee applet
- **schedule.txt**, the orchestra's schedule of upcoming events

Complete the following:

1. Use your text editor to create an HTML file named **byso.htm** and a style sheet named **bstyles.css**. Enter *your name* and *the date* in a comment section of each file. Include any other comments you think will aptly document the purpose and content of the files. Save the files in the tutorial.07\case4 folder included with your Data Files.

2. Go to the **byso.htm** file in your text editor and design the Web page using the files you've been given and any other supplements you have. Place all of your styles in the **bstyles.css** style sheet.

3. The page should contain the **beethoven.mp3** sound file embedded with the Quick-Time Player. Make sure your code works with both as an ActiveX control and a browser plug-in for non-IE browsers.

4. Include code to support browsers that use the embed element rather than the object element to display your media clip.

5. If the users do not have support for embedded media, have your Web page display a link to the **beethoven.mp3** file.

6. Use the schedule information from the **schedule.txt** file to create a scrolling marquee of upcoming BYSO events. The exact parameter values are left up to you. The scrolling marquee should be readable by both IE and non-IE browsers. Set the URL of the CreditRoll applet to *www.cityofboise.org*.

⊕ EXPLORE

7. Within the code for the scrolling marquee, include code for older browsers that might only support the applet element.

8. If the user's browser does not support Java at all, have the Web page display a message indicating this fact and suggesting that Java be installed to view the marquee. Include a hypertext link to a Web site where Java can be downloaded and installed.

9. Save your changes to the file and view the page in your Web browser. Verify that you can play both media clips and view the scrolling marquee.

⊕ EXPLORE

10. If you are working on your own computer or have permission to turn off support within your browser for embedded media and Java, turn off that support temporarily and verify that the page degrades well, showing the hypertext links and the message about installing Java.

11. Submit your completed files to your instructor.

Review | Quick Check Answers

Session 7.1

1. Either as external media in which the user downloads the multimedia file from a hypertext link or as embedded media that is displayed within the Web page.
2. Bandwidth is a measure of the amount of data that can be sent through the communication pipeline each second. Sampling rate is the number of samples taken per second from a sound source. Sample resolution indicates the precision in measuring the sound within each sample. Bitrate is a measure of the amount of data required for each second of sound.
3. `<object data="royal.wav" type="audio/wav"></object>`
4. audiop/wav and audio/x-wav
5. `<param name="showcontrols" value="true" />`
6. `<param name="autostart" value="true" />`
7. `classid ="clsid: 6BF52A52-394A-11d3-B153-00C04F79FAA6"`
8.
```
<!--[if IE]><!-->
    <object data="royal.wav" type="audio/wav"
      classid ="clsid: 6BF52A52-394A-11d3-B153-00C04F79FAA6">
        <param name="showcontrols" value="true" />
        <param name="autostart" value="true" />
    </object>
<!--<![endif]-->
```

Session 7.2

1. The frame size, the frame rate, the bitrate of the audio, the amount of compression.
2. If the bandwidth is not sufficient to keep up with the data rate required by the video, the quality of the video will be greatly degraded.
3. An algorithm that compresses and decompresses a video clip to reduce the overall file size.
4. The Flash flv file is the actual video file. The swf file is a container that contains the video file, other animations, scripts, and special controls to play the video.
5. application/x-shockwave-flash
6. `<param name="quality" value="high" />`
7. `<param name="scale" value="aspect" />`
8. `<embed src="astaire.mov" type="video/quicktime" width="320" height="160"></embed>`

Session 7.3

1. A Java Virtual Machine is a program in which a Java applet is run, thus making Java applets portable across a variety of operating systems.

2. Class files are the executable Java applet files that are run by a Java Virtual Machine.

3.
```
<object classid="clsid: 8AD9C840-044E-11D1-B3E9-00805F499D93"
   type="application/x-java-applet" width="500" height="400">
     <param name="code" value="stockmarket.class" />
</object>
```

4.
```
<object type="application/x-java-applet"
  classid="java:stockmarket.class"
  width="500" height="400">
</object>
```

5. the <marquee> tag

6.
```
<object data="logo.jpg" type="image/jpeg">
     <h2>Millennium Computers</h2>
</object>
```

7.
```
<object data="glossary.htm" type="text/html" width="400"
  height="200">
</object>
```

Ending Data Files

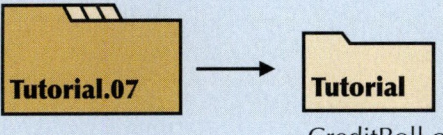

Tutorial.07 →

Tutorial
CreditRoll.class
jp.css
jumbo.htm
jumbo_mov.htm
jumbo_wmv.htm
overture.mp3
rwdance.mov
rwdance.swf
rwdance.wmv
+ 15 graphic files

Review
astaire.htm
astaire_mov.htm
astaire_wmv.htm
CreditRoll.class
fabio.css
fasong.mp3
hatrack.mov
hatrack.swf
hatrack.wmv
+ 16 graphic file

Case1
devotion.mp3
fireice.mp3
poetry.css
PopBtn.class
PopMenu.class
rf.htm
+ 6 graphic files

Case2
roadways.txt
rw.css
rwlogo.jpg
trailridge.swf

Case3
Cmplx.class
Controls.class
FracPanel.class
fractal.htm
fstyles.css
Mandel.class
mandel.swf
+ 2 graphic files

Case4
bstyles.css
beethoven.mp3
byso.htm
CreditRoll.class
+ 2 graphic files

Objectives

Session 8.1
- Explore the uses of frames in a Web site
- Create a frameset consisting of rows and columns of frames
- Display a document within a frame
- Format the appearance of a frame

Session 8.2
- Create links targeted at frames
- Direct a link to a target outside of a frame layout
- Format the color and size of frame borders
- Create an inline frame

Designing a Web Site with Frames

Using Frames to Organize a Web Site

Case | Cliff Hangers

One of the most popular climbing schools and touring agencies in Colorado is Cliff Hangers. Located in Boulder, Cliff Hangers specializes in teaching beginning through advanced climbing techniques. The school also sponsors several climbing tours, leading individuals on some of the most exciting climbs in North America.

Debbie Chen is the owner of the school and is always looking for ways to market her programs and improve the visibility of the school.

She knows that some Web sites use frames to display several Web pages in a single browser window and has asked you to help develop a frame-based Web site for Cliff Hangers.

Starting Data Files

Tutorial.08 →

Tutorial
clifftxt.htm
linkstxt.htm
philosphtxt.htm
tourstxt.htm
+ 17 HTML
  files
+ 3 style sheets
+ 29 graphic
  files

Review
lefttxt.htm
lessonstxt.htm
links1txt.htm
links2txt.htm
links3txt.htm
middletxt.htm
newlayouttxt.htm
righttxt.htm
+ 16 HTML files
+ 4 style sheets
+ 25 graphic files

Case1
maptxt.htm
nhpolytxt.htm
notestxt.htm
+ 13 HTML
  files
poli.css
+ 2 graphic
  files

Case2
browyer.css
listingtxt.htm
+ 17 graphic
  files

Case3
messtxt.htm
mxxtxt.htm
+ 9 HTML files
+ 2 style sheets
+ 22 graphic
  files

Case4
tempa1stxt.htm -
  tempa5s1txt.htm
tempest.jpg

Session 8.1

Introducing Frames

Web authors often dedicate individual Web pages to a particular topic or group of topics. One page might contain a list of links, another page might display contact information for the company or organization, and another page might describe the business philosophy. As more pages are added to the site, the designer often needs a way to display information from several pages at the same time—such as a list of links remaining on the page at the same time as the contact information is displayed.

One common solution is to duplicate that information (such as the list of links) across the Web site, but this strategy presents problems. It requires a great deal of time and effort to repeat (or copy and paste) the same information over and over again. Also, each time a change is required, the edit must be repeated on each page where the information appears—a process that could easily result in errors.

Such considerations contributed to the creation of frames. A **frame** is a section of a browser window capable of displaying the contents of an entire Web page. Figure 8-1 shows an example of a browser window containing two frames. The frame on the left displays the contents of a Web page containing a list of links for the University of Michigan Documents Center. The frame on the right displays the site's home page.

Figure 8-1	A framed Web site

first frame

second frame

This Web site illustrates a common use of frames: displaying a table of contents in one frame, while showing individual pages from the site in another frame. Figure 8-2 illustrates how a list of links can remain on the screen while the user navigates through the contents of the site. Using this layout, a designer can easily change the list of links without having to change every page on the site because the links are stored on only one page.

Activating a link within a frame | Figure 8-2

Drawbacks of Frame-Based Layouts | InSight

As convenient as they look at first, frame-based Web sites do have drawbacks. One drawback is that the browser must load multiple HTML files, increasing the amount of time a user must wait to work with the site. With high-speed connections this is less of a concern than it once was, but it is still something to consider.

Another problem with frames is that they make it difficult for users to bookmark the Web site contents. Browsers will allow the user to bookmark the entire frame or individual pages, but there is no way to create a bookmark that displays a page as it appears within the frame.

Also, some frame-based sites don't work well with Internet search engines such as Yahoo! and Google. The problem is that most search engines base their results on the contents and keywords found within the Web page. However, because frames do not have any content (they only display the content from other pages), the home page from a frame-based site might not score high on the results from a search engine.

For these reasons, many Web designers suggest that if you want to use frames, you should also provide a nonframed version of your Web site, giving users links to both versions so they can choose which version they wish to use.

Planning Your Frames

Before you start creating your frames, you must plan their appearance and determine how you want to use them. There are several issues to consider:

- What information will be displayed in each frame?
- How do you want the frames placed on the Web page? What is the size of each frame?
- Which frames will be static—that is, always showing the same content?
- Which frames will change in response to links being clicked?
- What Web pages will users first see when they access the site?
- Should users be permitted to resize the frames to suit their needs?

As you progress with your design for the Cliff Hangers Web site, you'll consider each of these questions. Debbie has already created the Web pages for the site; your job is to create the frame layout and insert the correct files into the various frames. Figure 8-3 describes the different Web pages you'll work with in this project.

Figure 8-3	Web pages on the Cliff Hangers Web site

Topic	Filename	Content
Biographies	staff.htm	Links to biographical pages of Cliff Hangers staff
Home page	home.htm	The Cliff Hangers home page
Lessons	lessons.htm	Climbing lessons offered by Cliff Hangers
Logo	head.htm	A page containing the company logo
Philosophy	philosph.htm	Business philosophy of Cliff Hangers
Table of contents	links.htm	Links to Cliff Hangers Web pages
Tours	diamond.htm	Description of the Diamond climbing tour
Tours	eldorado.htm	Description of the Eldorado Canyon climbing tour
Tours	grepon.htm	Description of the Petit Grepon climbing tour
Tours	kieners.htm	Description of the Kiener's Route climbing tour
Tours	lumpy.htm	Description of the Lumpy Ridge climbing tour
Tours	nface.htm	Description of the North Face climbing tour

Debbie has organized the pages by topic, such as tour descriptions, climbing lessons, and company philosophy. Two of the files, links.htm and staff.htm, do not focus on a particular topic, but contain links to other Cliff Hangers Web pages.

Debbie has carefully considered how this material should be organized on the Web site and what information the user should see first. She has sketched a layout that illustrates how she would like the frames to be organized, as shown in Figure 8-4.

Debbie's proposed frame layout   Figure 8-4

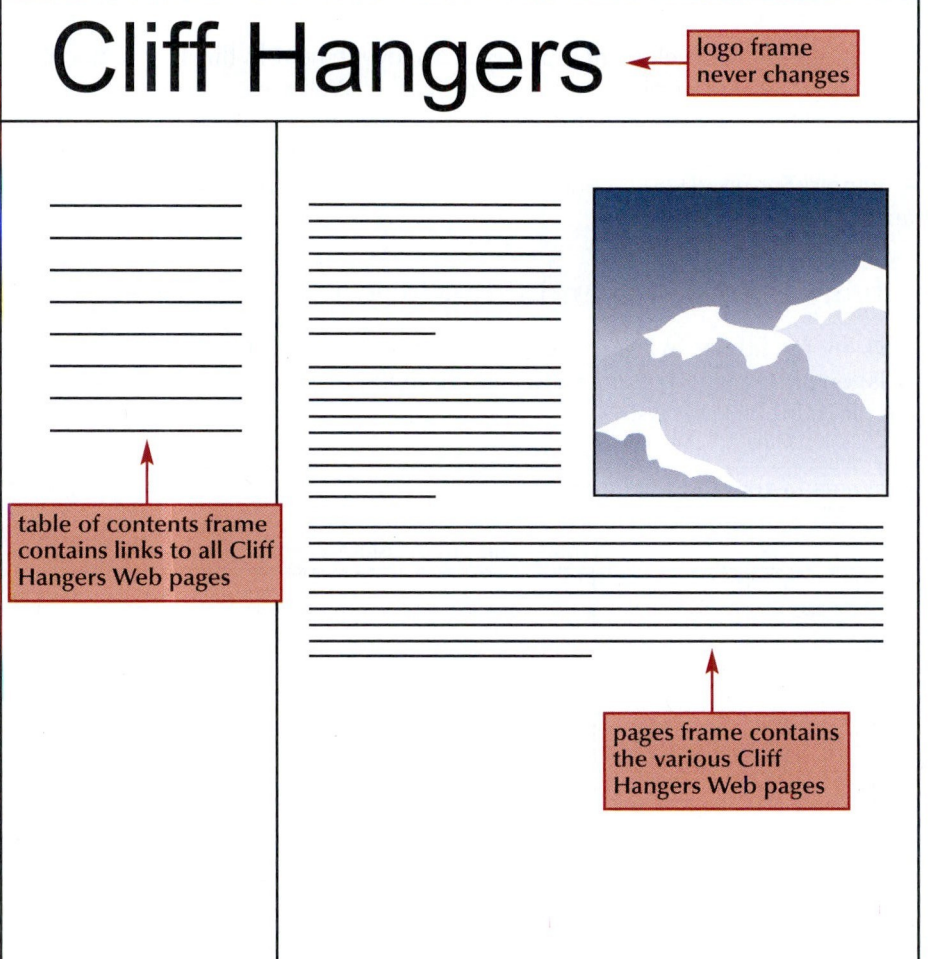

As you can see in Figure 8-4, Debbie would like you to create three frames. She would like the school's logo (which will contain the phone and address information) to appear in the top frame, and she wants that frame to always display that information. She wants the frame on the left to display a list of the Web pages on the Cliff Hangers Web site. Finally, Debbie wants the frame on the lower right to display the contents of the page corresponding to the link that a user clicks from the left frame.

Your first task is to enter the HTML code for the frame layout that Debbie has described.

Creating a Frameset

Frames are organized into a **frameset**, which is HTML code that defines the layout and content of the frames within the browser window. The syntax for creating a frameset is

```
<html>
   <head>
      <title>title</title>
   </head>
   <frameset>
      frames
   </frameset>
</html>
```

where *frames* are the individual frames within the frameset. You'll learn how to create these frames shortly. An HTML file can contain several framesets nested within one another.

Note that the frameset element replaces the body element in this HTML document. Because this HTML file displays the contents of other Web pages, it is not technically a Web page and thus does not include a page body. Later in the tutorial, you'll explore situations in which you would include a body element to support browsers that do not display frames. For now, you'll concentrate on defining the appearance and content of the frames.

Specifying Frame Size and Orientation

Framesets lay out frames in either rows or columns, but not both. Figure 8-5 shows two framesets: one in which the frames are laid out in three columns, and another in which they are placed in three rows.

Figure 8-5 **Frame layouts in rows and columns**

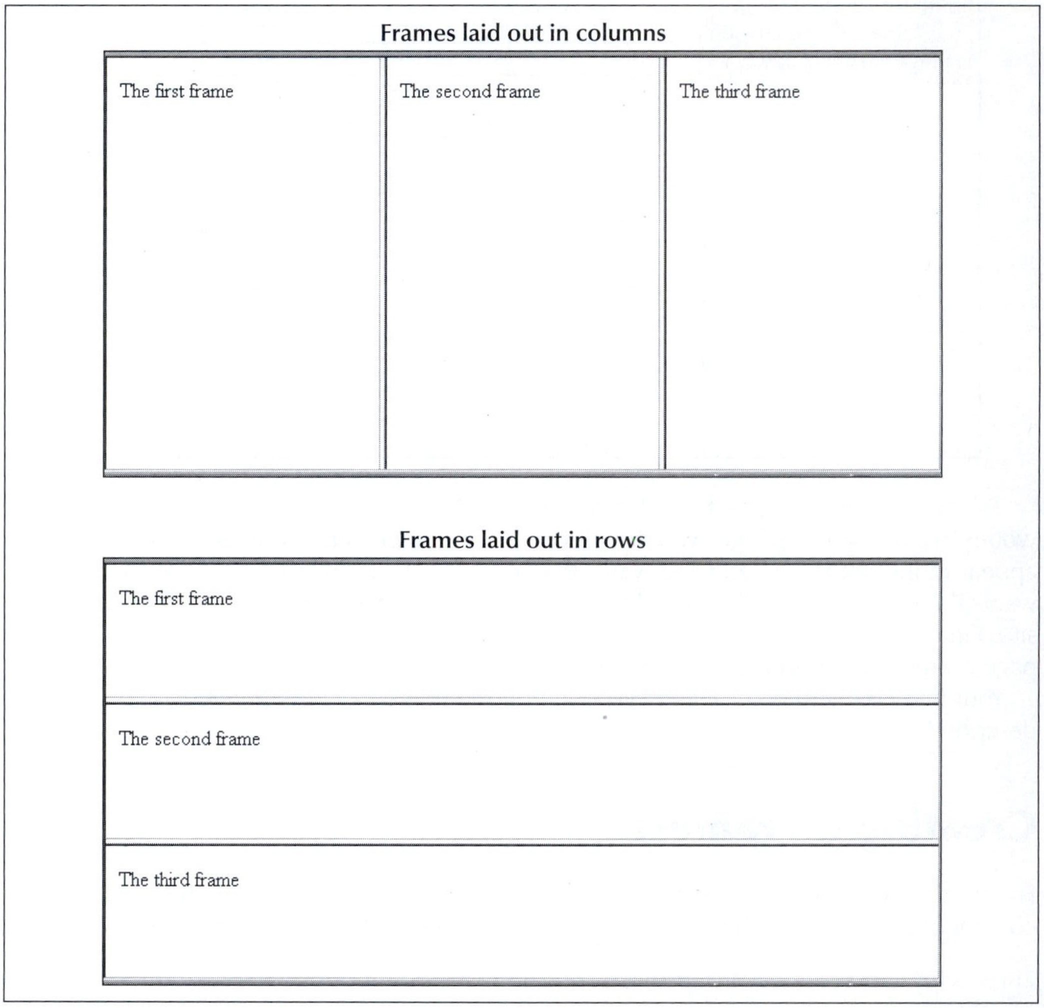

To lay out the frames in rows, you add the rows attribute

```
<frameset rows="row1,row2,row3,..."> ... </frameset>
```

to the <frameset> tag, where *row1*, *row2*, *row3*, etc. is the height of each row in the frameset. To lay out the frames in columns, you use the cols attribute

```
<frameset cols="col1,col2,col3,...">  ...  </frameset>
```

where *col1*, *col2*, *col3*, etc. are the widths of each column. There is no limit to the number of rows or columns you can specify for a frameset; however, you can lay out a frameset only in rows or in columns, but not both. If your site requires frames in both rows and columns, you must nest one frameset within another.

Row and column sizes can be specified in three ways: in pixels, as a percentage of the total size of the frameset, or by an asterisk (*), which instructs the browser to allocate any unclaimed space in the frameset to the given row or column. For example, the attribute

```
rows="160, *"
```

creates two frames set up as rows. The first row has a height of 160 pixels, and the height of the second row is equal to whatever space remains in the browser window area. You can combine all three units of measure to make your framed site look good on different-sized monitors. The attribute

```
cols="160, 25%, *"
```

creates a layout consisting of three columns, with the first column at 160 pixels wide, the second column at 25% of the width of the frameset, and the third column covering whatever space is left, as shown in Figure 8-6.

Sizing frames | **Figure 8-6**

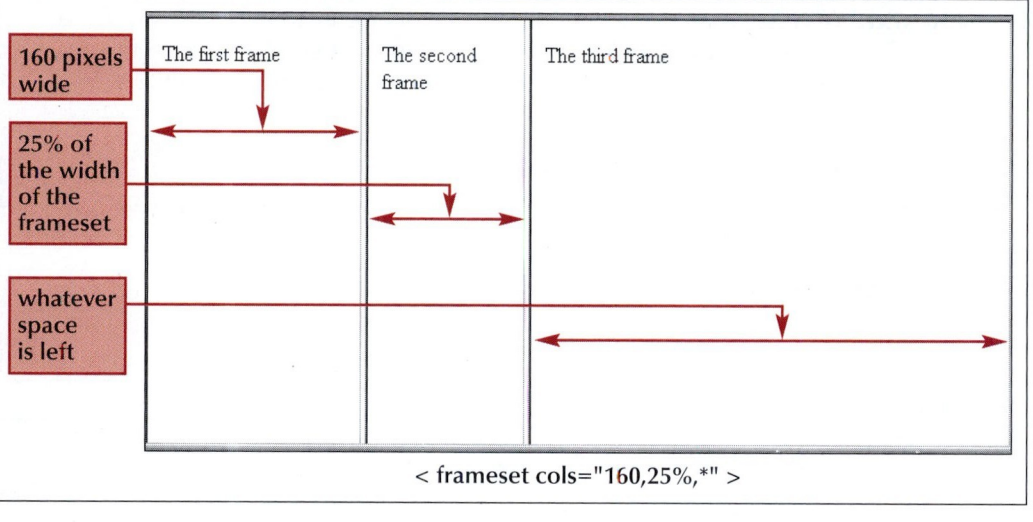

< frameset cols="160,25%,*" >

Tip

Set the size of at least one of the rows or columns to * to ensure that the frames fill up the entire browser window.

You can also use multiple asterisks. In that case, the browser divides the remaining display space equally among the frames designated with asterisks. For example, the attribute

```
rows="*, *, *"
```

creates three rows, each with a height that is one-third of the total height of the frameset.

Creating a Frameset

- To create a frameset, enter the frameset element
  ```
  <frameset>
      frames
  </frameset>
  ```
  where *frames* are the individual frames within the frameset.
- The frames of a frameset must be laid out in rows or columns. To lay out the frames in rows, add the attribute
  ```
  rows="row1, row2, row3, ..."
  ```
  to the opening <frameset> tag, where *row1*, *row2*, *row3*, etc. are the heights of the rows in pixels or percentages. To allow a row to fill the browser window space not specified for other rows, use the value *.
- To lay out the frames in columns, add the attribute
  ```
  cols="col1, col2, col3, ..."
  ```
  to the opening <frameset> tag, where *col1*, *col2*, *col3*, etc. are the widths of the columns in pixels or percentages.

The first frameset you'll create for the Cliff Hangers Web site has two rows. The top row will display the company logo. You'll set the height of the row to 85 pixels. The rest of the Web site will be displayed in the second row, and you'll set that row's height to occupy the rest of the browser window.

To create a frameset:

▶ 1. Use your text editor to open the **clifftxt.htm**, **linkstxt.htm**, **philosphtxt.htm**, and **tourstxt.htm** files from the tutorial.08\tutorial folder included with your Data Files. Enter **your name** and **the date** in the comment section of each file and save them as **cliff.htm**, **links.htm**, **philosph.htm**, and **tours.htm**, respectively, in the same folder.

▶ 2. Return to the **cliff.htm** file in your text editor.

▶ 3. Insert the following frameset directly after the closing </head> tag, as shown in Figure 8-7:

<frameset rows="85,*">

</frameset>

| Figure 8-7 | Inserting a frameset |

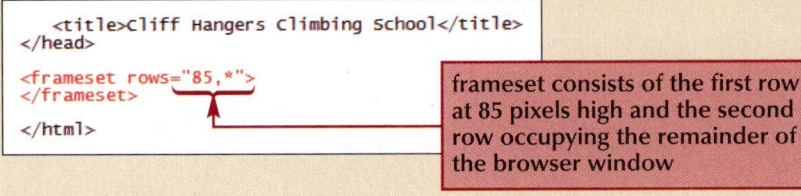

```
    <title>Cliff Hangers Climbing School</title>
</head>

<frameset rows="85,*">
</frameset>

</html>
```

frameset consists of the first row at 85 pixels high and the second row occupying the remainder of the browser window

The initial frameset is now defined. Next you must specify the content of the frameset.

Creating a Frame

The first row of the frameset will contain a frame displaying the company logo. To create a frame, you use the frame element

```
<frame src="url" />
```

where *url* is the URL of the document displayed within the frame.

Debbie saved the page containing the company logo and address as head.htm. You'll place this document in the first frame of the frameset, as shown in Figure 8-8.

Tip

The frame source does not need to be an HTML file. You can insert graphics files within frames as well. However, frames must always be nested within a frameset.

Placing the head.htm file ◀ **Figure 8-8**

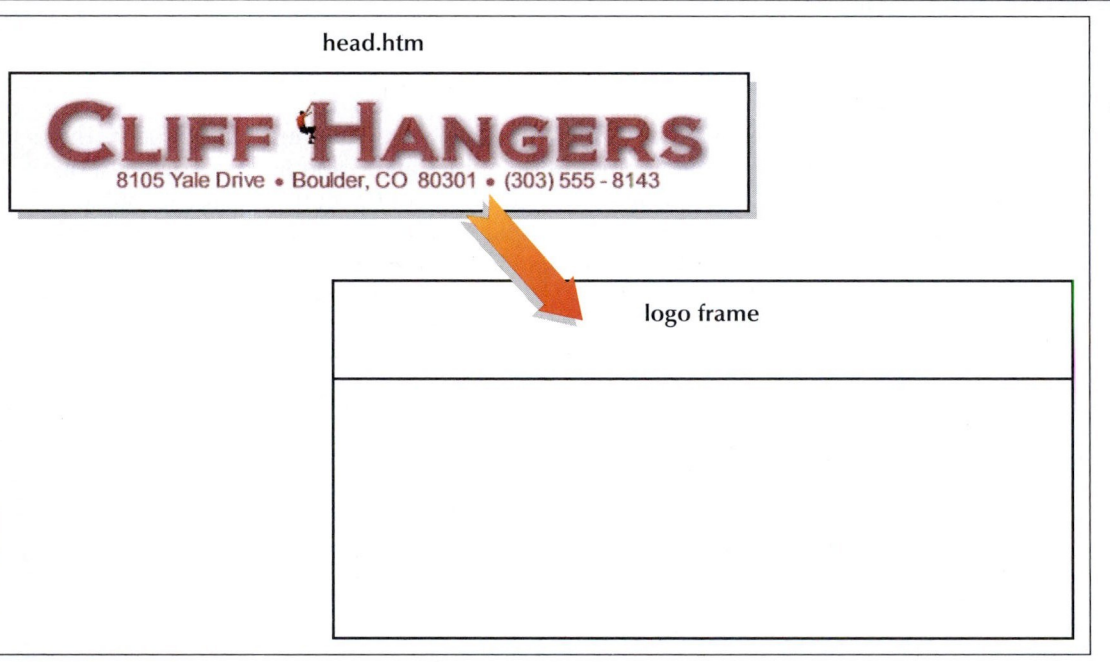

head.htm

logo frame

Create a Frame | Reference Window

- To create a frame, use the element
    ```
    <frame src="url" />
    ```
  where *url* is the URL of the document displayed in the frame.

To set the source of the first frame:

▶ **1.** After the opening <frameset> tag, insert the following frame element, as shown in Figure 8-9.

   <!-- Company Logo -->

   <frame src="head.htm" />

Tip

Add comments to your <frame /> tags so that it's clear what content will be displayed within each frame.

Figure 8-9 ▶ **Inserting the frame element**

```
<frameset rows="85,*">
    <!-- Company Logo -->
    <frame src="head.htm" />
</frameset>

</html>                          file displayed within the frame
```

▶ **2.** Save your changes to the file.

You have successfully specified the source for the first row of the frameset. In the second row you'll insert another frameset.

Nesting Framesets

As noted earlier, a frameset places frames in either rows or columns, but not both. Therefore, to create a layout containing frames in both rows and columns, you must nest one frameset within another. Debbie wants the second row of the current frame layout to contain two columns: the first column will display a table of contents, and the second column will display the Web pages for the various lessons and tours that Cliff Hangers offers. You'll specify a width of 140 pixels for the first column, and whatever remains in the display area will be allotted to the second column.

To nest a frameset:

▶ **1.** Directly below the <frame /> tag you just entered, insert the following lines of code, as shown in Figure 8-10:

<!-- Nested Frameset -->

<frameset cols="140,*">

</frameset>

Figure 8-10 ▶ **Nesting a frameset**

```
<frameset rows="85,*">
    <!-- Company Logo -->
    <frame src="head.htm" />

    <!-- Nested Frameset -->
    <frameset cols="140,*">
    </frameset>

</frameset>
```

▶ **2.** Save your changes to the file.

Next, you'll specify the sources for the two frames in the nested frameset. The frame in the first column should display the links.htm file, which is Debbie's table of contents. The Cliff Hangers home page, home.htm, should be displayed in the second frame. Figure 8-11 shows the contents of these two pages and their locations in the frameset.

Placing the links.htm and home.htm files in the frame layout ◄ **Figure 8-11**

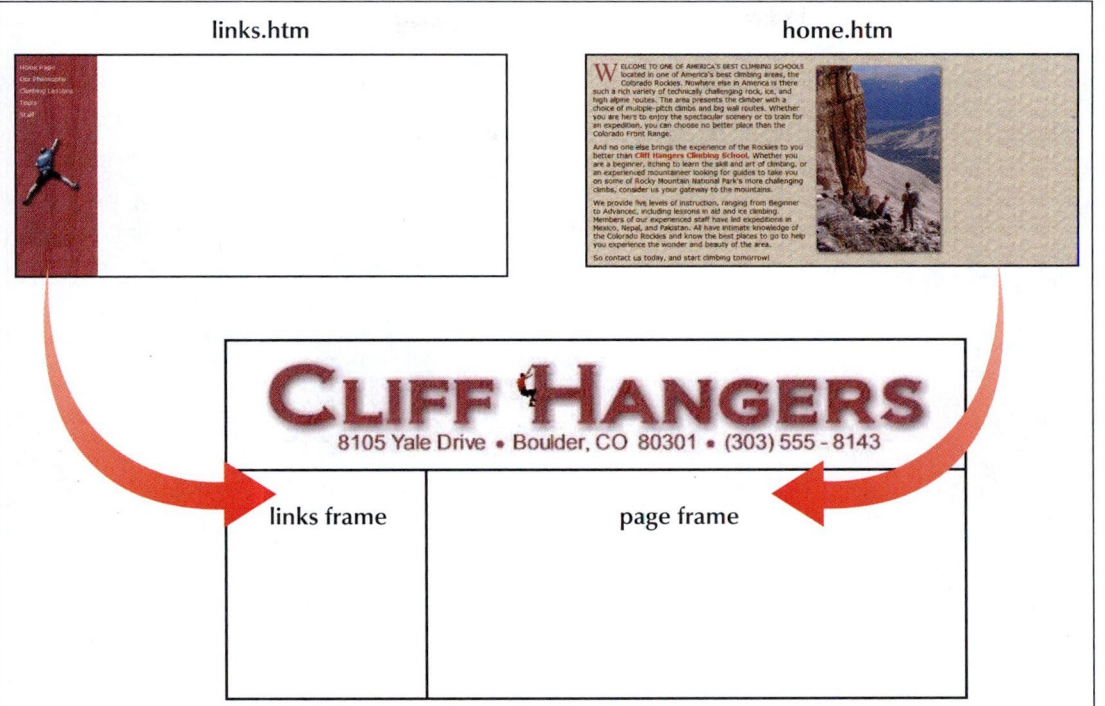

To insert the two frames of the nested frameset:

▶ **1.** Directly below the opening <frameset> tag of the nested frameset, insert the following code, as shown in Figure 8-12.

<!-- List of Links -->

<frame src="links.htm" />

<!-- Cliff Hangers Web Pages -->

<frame src="home.htm" />

Inserting the frame columns ◄ **Figure 8-12**

```
<frameset rows="85,*">
    <!-- Company Logo -->
    <frame src="head.htm" />

    <!-- Nested Frameset -->
    <frameset cols="140,*">
        <!-- List of Links -->
        <frame src="links.htm" />

        <!-- Cliff Hangers Web Pages -->
        <frame src="home.htm" />
    </frameset>

</frameset>
```

▶ **2.** Save your changes to the file.

▶ **3.** Open the **cliff.htm** file in your Web browser. As shown in Figure 8-13, the browser lays out the contents of the three Web pages within frames in the browser window.

Figure 8-13 | **Initial frame layout of the Cliff Hangers Web site**

Although the browser window displays the three Web pages from the Cliff Hangers Web site, the design of the frame layout could use some refinement. Part of the logo has been cut off in the head frame. Whenever page content does not entirely fit within the frame borders, the browser displays horizontal and vertical scroll bars to allow the user to scroll through the rest of the page content within the frame. Scroll bars do not appear in the two other frames because all of the page content from the links.htm and home.htm files fits within their frames. Debbie doesn't want the scroll bars to appear, so you need to format the frame so that it displays all of the company logo.

Formatting a Frame

You can control three attributes of a frame: the appearance of scroll bars, the size of the margin between the source document and the frame border, and whether or not users are allowed to change the frame size. The first attribute you'll work with is the scrolling attribute.

Hiding and Displaying Scroll Bars

By default, a scroll bar is displayed when the content of the source page does not fit within a frame. You can override this setting using the scrolling attribute. The syntax for this attribute is

```
scrolling="type"
```

where *type* can be either yes (to always display a scroll bar) or no (to never display a scroll bar). If you don't specify a setting for the scrolling attribute, the browser displays a scroll bar when the page content doesn't fit in the frame.

Debbie thinks that a scroll bar is inappropriate for the logo frame, and she wants to ensure that a scroll bar is never displayed for that frame. Therefore, you need to add the

```
scrolling="no"
```

attribute to the frame element. However, Debbie does want scroll bars for the other two frames, as needed, so the default value for those frames is sufficient.

To remove the scroll bars from the logo frame:

▶ 1. Return to the **cliff.htm** file in your text editor.

▶ 2. Within the frame element for the logo frame, insert the following attribute, as shown in Figure 8-14:

scrolling="no"

Removing the scroll bars from the logo frame ◀ **Figure 8-14**

```
                                        hide the frame scroll bars
<frameset rows="85,*">
    <!-- Company Logo -->
    <frame src="head.htm" scrolling="no" />

    <!-- Nested Frameset -->
    <frameset cols="140,*">
        <!-- List of Links -->
        <frame src="links.htm" />

        <!-- Cliff Hangers Web Pages -->
        <frame src="home.htm" />
    </frameset>

</frameset>
```

▶ 3. Save your changes to the file and then reload **cliff.htm** in your Web browser. Verify that the scroll bars have been removed from the logo frame.

Although the scroll bar for the logo frame has been removed, depending on your screen size, the logo contained in the head.htm file might still be cut off.

Tip

To view changes in the frame layout or for frame properties in some older browsers, you might have to reload rather than simply refresh the Web site.

When working with frames, keep in mind that you should remove scroll bars from a frame only when you are convinced that the entire Web page will be visible in the frame. To do this, you should view your Web page using several different monitor settings. Few things are more irritating to Web site visitors than to discover that some content is missing from a frame with no scroll bars available to reveal the missing content. To ensure that the head.htm file will fit in the logo frame, you need to modify the frame margins.

Setting Frame Margins

When your browser displays a Web page in a frame, it places a margin between the Web page and the frame borders. If the margin is too large, part of the Web page might not fit within the frame. This is what occurred with the logo frame. Generally, you want the margin to be big enough to keep the source's text or images from running into the frame's borders. However, you do not want the margin to take up too much space, either.

You've already noted that the margin height for the logo frame is too large, and this has shifted some of the text beyond the border of the frame. To fix this problem, you need to specify a smaller margin for the frame so that the logo can move up and allow all of the text to be displayed in the frame.

The attribute for specifying margin sizes for a frame is

```
marginheight="value" marginwidth="value"
```

where the marginheight value specifies the amount of space, in pixels, above and below the frame source, and the marginwidth value specifies the amount of space to the left and right of the frame source. You do not have to specify both the margin height and width. However, if you specify only one, the browser assumes that you want to use the same value for both. Setting margin values is a process of trial and error as you determine what combination of margin sizes looks best.

To correct the problem with the logo frame, you'll decrease its margin size to 0 pixels. This setting will allow the entire logo to be displayed within the frame. You don't need to change the margins of the other frames.

To set the size of the internal frame margins:

1. Return to the **cliff.htm** file in your text editor.

2. Within the frame element for the logo frame, insert the following attribute, as shown in Figure 8-15:

   marginheight="0"

Figure 8-15 | Set the frame margin height

```
<frameset rows="85,*">
   <!-- Company Logo -->
   <frame src="head.htm" scrolling="no" marginheight="0" />

   <!-- Nested Frameset -->
   <frameset cols="140,*">
      <!-- List of Links -->
      <frame src="links.htm" />

      <!-- Cliff Hangers Web Pages -->
      <frame src="home.htm" />
   </frameset>

</frameset>
```

the margin above and below the head.htm file will be 0 pixels

3. Save your changes to the file and then reload **cliff.htm** in your Web browser. As shown in Figure 8-16, the entire logo should now be visible within the frame with no scroll bars showing.

Figure 8-16 | Revised frame layout

the entire Cliff Hangers logo appears within the frame

Formatting a Frame | Reference Window

- To control whether a frame contains a scroll bar, add the attribute
    ```
    scrolling="type"
    ```
  to the frame element, where *type* is either yes (scroll bar) or no (no scroll bar). If you do not specify the scrolling attribute, a scroll bar appears only when the content of the frame source cannot fit within the boundaries of the frame.
- To control the amount of space between the frame source and the frame boundary, add the attribute
    ```
    marginwidth="value" marginheight="value"
    ```
  to the frame element, where the width and height values are expressed in pixels. The margin width is the space to the left and right of the frame source. The margin height is the space above and below the frame source. If you do not specify a margin height or width, the browser assigns dimensions based on the content of the frame source.
- To keep users from resizing frames, add the following attribute to the frame element:
    ```
    noresize="noresize"
    ```

Debbie is satisfied with the changes you've made to the Web page. Your next task is to prevent users from resizing the frames.

Controlling Frame Resizing

By default, users can resize frame borders in the browser by simply clicking and dragging a frame border with their mouse. However, some Web designers prefer to freeze, or lock, frames so that users cannot resize them. This ensures that the Web site appears as the designer intended. Debbie would like you to do this for the Cliff Hangers Web site. The attribute for controlling frame resizing is

```
noresize="noresize"
```

Many browsers also allow you to insert this attribute as simply

```
noresize
```

without an attribute value. However, this form is not supported by XHTML because XHTML requires all attributes to have attribute values. You'll follow this principle in the code we create for Debbie's Web site.

To prevent users from resizing the frames on the Cliff Hangers site:

1. Return to the **cliff.htm** file in your text editor.

2. Within each of the three <frame /> tags in the file, add the attribute

   noresize="noresize"

3. Save your changes to the file and then reload **cliff.htm** in your Web browser.

4. Verify that the frames are now locked in and cannot be resized by the user.

5. If you want to take a break before starting the next session, you can close any open files and programs now.

Debbie is pleased with the progress you've made on the Cliff Hangers site. In the next session you'll modify the properties of the links in the table of contents frame so that all links open with the page frame.

1. What are frames, and why are they useful in displaying and designing a Web site?
2. Why is the <body> tag unnecessary for pages that contain frames?
3. What HTML code do you use to create three rows of frames with the height of the first row set to 200 pixels, the height of the second row set to 50% of the display area, and the height of the third row set to occupy the remaining space?
4. What HTML code do you use to specify home.htm as a source for a frame?
5. What HTML code do you use to remove the scroll bars from the frame for home.htm?
6. What HTML code do you use to set the size of the margin above and below the contents of the home.htm frame to 3 pixels?
7. What is the size of the margins to the right and left of the frame in Question 6?
8. What code would you use to prevent users from moving the frame borders in home.htm?

Session 8.2

Working with Frames and Links

Now that you've created frames for the Cliff Hangers Web site, you're ready to work on formatting the links for the Web page. The links page contains five links, which point to the pages as shown in Figure 8-17:

• The Home Page link points to home.htm.
• The Our Philosophy link points to philosph.htm.
• The Climbing Lessons link points to lessons.htm.
• The Tours link points to tours.htm.
• The Staff link points to a frameset stored in the staff.htm file.

Links within the table of contents frame | Figure 8-17

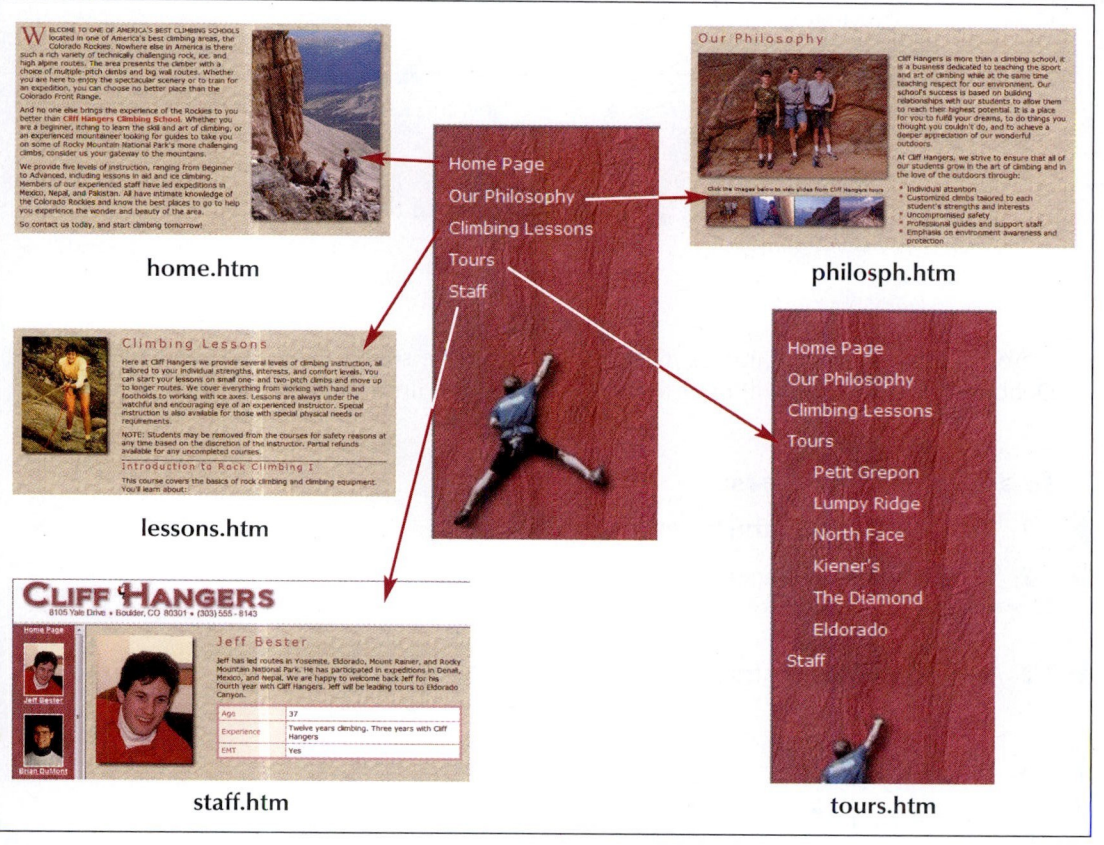

By default, clicking a link within a frame opens the linked file inside the same frame. However, this is not the way Debbie wants each of the links to work. She wants the links to work as follows:

- The Home, Our Philosophy, and Climbing Lessons pages should appear in the lower-right frame.
- The Tours page should appear in the table of contents frame.
- The frameset from the staff.htm file should occupy the entire browser window.

To specify the location in which to open a hypertext link, you must first assign each frame a name. This is done by adding the attribute

```
name="name"
```

to the frame element, where *name* is the name assigned to the frame. Case is important in assigning names. The frame name "information" differs from the frame name "INFORMATION." Also, frame names cannot contain spaces. For the Cliff Hangers frameset, you'll name the three frames logo, links, and pages.

- First, assign a name to a frame by adding the name attribute
  `name="name"`
  to the <frame> tag, where *name* is the name of the frame.
- To point the target of a link to a named frame, add the following attribute to the hypertext link:
  `target="name"`
- To point all links in a document to the same target, add the following element to the head section of the document:
  `<base target="name" />`

You need to name the frames in the Cliff Hanger site so that you can specify where Debbie's various pages will open when users click the links in the left frame.

To assign frame names:

► **1.** Return to the **cliff.htm** file in your text editor.

► **2.** Within the first <frame /> tag, insert the following attribute:

   name="logo"

► **3.** Within the second <frame /> tag, insert the following attribute:

   name="links"

► **4.** Within the last <frame /> tag, insert the following attribute:

   name="pages"

   Figure 8-18 highlights the revised code in the file.

Figure 8-18 ❯ **Setting the frame names**

```
<frameset rows="85,*">
    <!-- Company Logo -->
    <frame src="head.htm" scrolling="no" marginheight="0" noresize="noresize" name="logo"

    <!-- Nested Frameset -->
    <frameset cols="140,*">
        <!-- List of Links -->
        <frame src="links.htm" noresize="noresize" name="links" />

        <!-- Cliff Hangers Web Pages -->
        <frame src="home.htm" noresize="noresize" name="pages" />
    </frameset>

</frameset>
```

► **5.** Save your changes to the file.

Now that you've named the frames, the next task is to specify the pages frame as the target for the Home Page, Our Philosophy, and Climbing Lessons links—so that clicking each of these links opens the corresponding file in the pages frame. In Tutorial 2, you learned how the target attribute can be used to open a hypertext link in a new browser window. You can also use the target attribute to open a linked target in a frame. To point the link to a specific frame, add the attribute

`target="name"`

to the <a> tag for the hypertext link, where *name* is the name you've assigned to a frame on your Web page. For the links to home.htm, philosph.htm, and lesson.htm, the *name* value is pages because all of these links should open within the pages frame of the Cliff Hangers frameset. Add these target names to the hypertext links within the links.htm file.

To specify the target for the hypertext links:

1. Open the **links.htm** file from the tutorial.08\tutorial folder with your text editor.

2. Within the <a> tags for the Home Page, Our Philosophy, and Climbing Lessons links, enter the following attribute, as shown in Figure 8-19:

   target="pages"

Assigning a target to a link | **Figure 8-19**

```
<ul>
    <li><a href="home.htm" target="pages">Home Page</a></li>
    <li><a href="philosph.htm" target="pages">Our Philosophy</a></li>
    <li><a href="lessons.htm" target="pages">Climbing Lessons</a></li>
    <li><a href="tours.htm">Tours</a></li>
    <li><a href="staff.htm">Staff</a></li>
</ul>
```

3. Save your changes to the file.

4. Reload the **cliff.htm** file in your Web browser.

5. Click the **Our Philosophy** link in the links frame. Verify that the Our Philosophy page opens in the pages frame, as shown in Figure 8-20.

Viewing the philosophy page | **Figure 8-20**

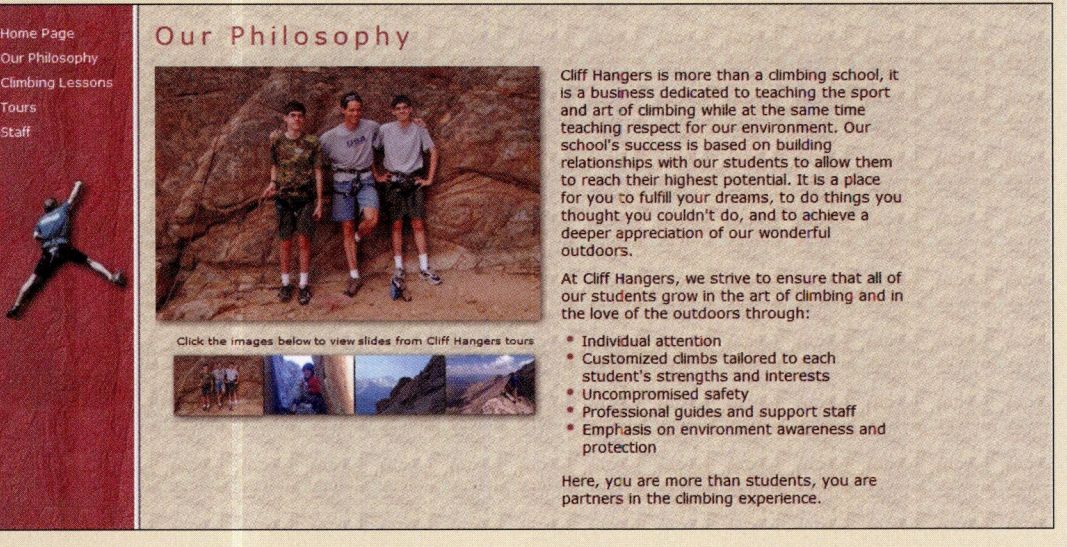

6. Click the links for the **Home Page** and the **Climbing Lessons** links and verify that both pages are also displayed within the pages frame.

   Trouble? If you click one of the other links in the frame, the browser will open the file in the links frame. Reload or refresh the **cliff.htm** file to restore the frameset to its original appearance.

Using Reserved Target Names

The remaining two tags in the list of links point to a list of the tours offered by Cliff Hangers, stored in the tours.htm file, and to a staff information page, stored in the staff.htm file. The tours.htm file does not contain information about individual tours; instead, it is an expanded table of contents of pages on the Cliff Hangers Web site. The purpose of the tours.htm page is to replace the links.htm page when a user clicks the Tours link. The links frame will then display the table of contents shown in Figure 8-21. A user can click on an individual tour name to open a page about that tour.

| Figure 8-21 | Links to the tour pages |

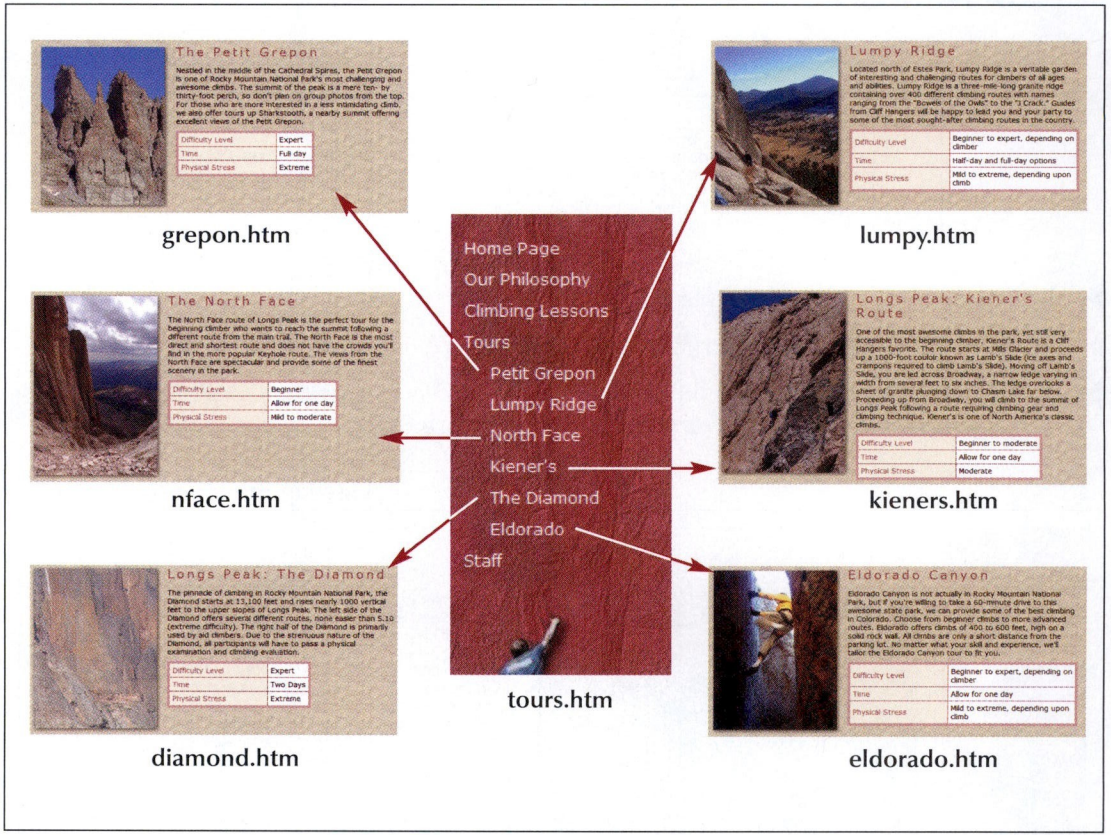

To have tours.htm appear in the links frame when a user clicks the Tours link, you can specify links (the name of the frame) as the target. However, you can also do this using reserved target names. A **reserved target name** is a special name that can be used in place of a frame name as a target. This is useful when the name of the frame is unavailable, when you want the page to appear in a new window, or when you want the page to replace the current browser window. Figure 8-22 describes the reserved target names.

Reserved target names ◄ Figure 8-22

Reserved Target Name	Function in a Frameset
_blank	Loads the target document into a new browser window
_self	Loads the target document into the frame containing the link
_parent	Loads the target document into the parent of the frame containing the link
_top	Loads the document into the full display area, replacing the current frameset

All reserved target names begin with the underscore character (_) to distinguish them from other target names. Note that reserved target names are case-sensitive, so you must enter them in lowercase letters. Debbie wants the contents of the tours.htm file to be displayed in the links frame. You can specify this behavior by adding the target

```
_self
```

to the hypertext link for the tours.htm file.

To add the _self reserved target name to the Tours link:

▶ 1. Return to **links.htm** in your text editor.

▶ 2. Within the hypertext link for the tours.htm file, insert the following attribute, as shown in Figure 8-23:

   target="_self"

Using the _self target ◄ Figure 8-23

```
<ul>
    <li><a href="home.htm" target="pages">Home Page</a></li>
    <li><a href="philosph.htm" target="pages">Our Philosophy</a></li>
    <li><a href="lessons.htm" target="pages">Climbing Lessons</a></li>
    <li><a href="tours.htm" target="_self">Tours</a></li>
    <li><a href="staff.htm">Staff</a></li>
</ul>
```

▶ 3. Save your changes to the file.

▶ 4. Reload **cliff.htm** in your Web browser and verify that when you click the Tours link, the tours.htm file opens in the links frame.

Next you'll work with the links in the tours.htm file. Debbie wants each tour page that is linked to the tours.htm page to appear in the pages frame when a user clicks its respective link. When a Web site contains many links that should all open in the same frame, instead of inserting the same target attributes for each link, you can instead specify the target by inserting the base element

```
<base target="name" />
```

in the head section of the document. This way, hypertext links will by default open in the target specified by *name*. You decide to use the base element in the tours.htm file, setting the default target for all hypertext links to the pages frame. The tours.htm file also contains a link that takes the user back to the links.htm file when the user clicks the Tours link again. So, when a user clicks the Tours link the first time, the browser loads the tours.htm file (the expanded table of contents); and when a user clicks the Tours link again, the browser returns to the links.htm file. You'll specify _self as the target for this particular link.

To modify the targets for the tours.htm file:

1. Use your text editor to open the **tours.htm** file from the tutorial.08\tutorial folder included with your Data Files.

2. Insert the following tag directly above the </head> closing tag:

   <base target="pages" />

3. Add the attribute

   target="_self"

   to the hypertext link in the links.htm file. Figure 8-24 highlights the revised code in the tours.htm file.

Figure 8-24 | **Adding targets to the tours page**

```
<base target="pages" />
</head>

<body style="background: url(wall3.jpg) repeat-y">

    <ul>
        <li><a href="home.htm">Home Page</a></li>
        <li><a href="philosph.htm">Our Philosophy</a></li>
        <li><a href="lessons.htm">Climbing Lessons</a></li>
        <li><a href="links.htm" target="_self">Tours</a></li>
        <ul>
            <li><a href="grepon.htm">Petit Grepon</a></li>
            <li><a href="lumpy.htm">Lumpy Ridge</a></li>
            <li><a href="nface.htm">North Face</a></li>
            <li><a href="kieners.htm">Kiener's</a></li>
            <li><a href="diamond.htm">The Diamond</a></li>
            <li><a href="eldorado.htm">Eldorado</a></li>
        </ul>
        <li><a href="staff.htm">Staff</a></li>
    </ul>
```

by default, all links will open in the page frame

4. Save your changes to the file and then reload **cliff.htm** in your Web browser.

5. Verify that the Tours link works as you intended. When you click the link, the table of contents list should alternately collapse and expand.

6. Click some of the links to the individual tour pages to verify that they appear correctly in the pages frame, as shown in Figure 8-25.

Figure 8-25 | **Viewing the Lumpy Ridge tour page**

As you can see, clicking the Tours link gives the effect that the list is expanding and contracting; but in reality, one table of contents file is simply being replaced by another.

The final link you must create points to a Web page of staff biographies. Debbie asked another employee to produce the contents of this Web page, and the results are shown in Figure 8-26.

The Cliff Hangers staff page **Figure 8-26**

As you can see, this Web page also uses frames. If you specify the pages frame as the target for the staff.htm page, the result is a series of nested framesets, as shown in Figure 8-27.

Nesting one frameset within another **Figure 8-27**

This is not what Debbie wants. She wants the Staff Web page to load into the full display area, replacing the frame layout with its own layout. To target a link to the full display area, you use the _top reserved target name. The _top target is often used when one frameset is accessed from another frameset.

You should also use the _top target when you are linking to pages outside of your Web site. For example, if Debbie wanted to add a link to the Colorado Tourism Board Web site, she wouldn't want that Web site to appear within a frame on the Cliff Hangers Web site. Having the Tourism Board Web site appear within the Cliff Hangers frameset could easily confuse users, making it appear as if the Colorado Tourism Board is a component of the Cliff Hangers Climbing School.

Tip

In a frame layout, always have Web pages that lie outside of your Web site open in a new Window or tab to avoid making external pages appear to be part of your frameset.

To apply the _top target to the staff link:

▶ 1. Return to the **links.htm** file in your text editor.

▶ 2. Enter the attribute

   target="_top"

   to the <a> tag for the Staff link, as shown in Figure 8-28.

Figure 8-28 ▶ **Setting the target of the Staff link**

```
<ul>
    <li><a href="home.htm" target="pages">Home Page</a></li>
    <li><a href="philosph.htm" target="pages">Our Philosophy</a></li>
    <li><a href="lessons.htm" target="pages">Climbing Lessons</a></li>
    <li><a href="tours.htm" target="_self">Tours</a></li>
    <li><a href="staff.htm" target="_top">Staff</a></li>
</ul>
```

the staff.htm page will occupy the complete browser window

▶ 3. Save your changes to the file.

▶ 4. Return to the **tours.htm** file in your text editor, and repeat Step 2 to ensure that the Staff link on that page also opens in the full browser window. Save your changes to the file.

▶ 5. Reload **cliff.htm** in your Web browser. Verify that clicking the **Staff** link displays the full frameset for the Staff pages within the browser window.

▶ 6. Click the **Home Page** link at the top of the links frame to return to the cliff.htm file in your browser.

Debbie has viewed all the links on the Cliff Hangers Web site and is quite satisfied with the results. However, she wonders what would happen if a user accesses her site with a browser that does not display frames. Although most browsers do display frames, she also must consider the needs of people who access the Cliff Hangers Web site with screen readers and other nonvisual browsers. If possible, she wants to accommodate browsers that don't support frames.

Using the noframes Element

You can use the noframes element to make your Web site viewable with browsers that do not support frames (known as frame-blind browsers). The noframes element marks a section of your HTML file as code that browsers incapable of displaying frames can use. The noframes element is nested within the frameset element and uses the syntax

```
<html>
<head>
    <title>title</title>
</head>
<frameset>
    frames
    <noframes>
        <body>
            page content
        </body>
    </noframes>
</frameset>
</html>
```

where *page content* is the content that you want the browser to display in place of the frames. There can be only one noframes element in the document. When a browser that supports frames processes this code, it ignores everything within the noframes element and concentrates solely on the code to create the frames. When a browser that doesn't support frames processes this HTML code, it ignores the frameset and frame elements and renders whatever appears within the <body> tags. This way, both types of browsers are supported within a single HTML file.

Cliff Hangers has been using the nonframed Web site displayed in Figure 8-29 for several years.

Frameless version of the Cliff Hangers home page **Figure 8-29**

8105 Yale Drive • Boulder, CO 80301 • (303) 555 - 8143

Home Page
Our Philosophy
Climbing Lessons
Tours
　Petit Grepon
　Lumpy Ridge
　North Face
　Kiener's
　The Diamond
　Eldorado
Staff

WELCOME TO ONE OF AMERICA'S best climbing schools located in one of America's best climbing areas, the Colorado Rockies. Nowhere else in America is there such a rich variety of technically challenging rock, ice, and high alpine routes. The area presents the climber with a choice of multiple-pitch climbs and big wall routes. Whether you are here to enjoy the spectacular scenery or to train for an expedition, you can choose no better place than the Colorado Front Range.

And no one else brings the experience of the Rockies to you better than **Cliff Hangers Climbing School**. Whether you are a beginner, itching to learn the skill and art of climbing, or an experienced mountaineer looking for guides to take you on some of Rocky Mountain National Park's more challenging climbs, consider us your gateway to the mountains.

We provide five levels of instruction, ranging from Beginner to Advanced, including lessons in aid and ice climbing. Members of our experienced staff have led expeditions in Mexico, Nepal, and Pakistan. All have intimate knowledge of the Colorado Rockies and know the best places to go to help you experience the wonder and beauty of the area.

So contact us today, and start climbing tomorrow!

Reference Window | **Supporting Frame-Blind Browsers**

- To provide content for browsers that do not support frames, add the code
  ```
  <noframes>
  <body>
   page content
  </body>
  </noframes>
  ```
  to the document, where *page content* is the content that will appear on the Web page.

To display this page for frame-blind browsers, while still making your framed version available as the default, you decide to copy the HTML code from the nonframed Web page and place it within a pair of <noframes> tags in the cliff.htm file.

To insert the noframes code:

▶ **1.** Return to the **cliff.htm** file in your text editor.

First you must create a link to the noframes.css style sheet, which contains the style declarations for the elements in the noframes version of the Web page.

▶ **2.** Directly above the closing </head> tag, insert the following link to the noframes. css style sheet:

<link href="noframes.css" rel="stylesheet" type="text/css" />

▶ **3.** Scroll down the file and directly after the closing </frameset> tag near the middle of the file, insert the following:

<!-- Noframes version of this page -->

<noframes>

</noframes>

▶ **4.** Save your changes to the file.

Now copy the body content from the noframes.htm file into the cliff.htm file.

▶ **5.** Open the **noframes.htm** file in the tutorial.08\tutorial.folder included with your Data Files.

▶ **6.** Copy the HTML code for the page content, including both the opening and the closing <body> tags in the selection.

▶ **7.** Return to the **cliff.htm** file in your text editor and paste the copied code within the noframes element you inserted in Step 3. Figure 8-30 shows the revised code in the cliff.htm file.

Inserting the noframes version of the Cliff Hangers home page ◀ Figure 8-30

```
       <title>Cliff Hangers Climbing School</title>
       <link href="noframes.css" rel="stylesheet" type="text/css" />
</head>

<frameset rows="85,*">
    <!-- Company Logo -->
    <frame src="head.htm" scrolling="no" marginheight="0" noresize="noresize" name="logo" />

    <!-- Nested Frameset -->
    <frameset cols="140,*">
        <!-- List of Links -->
        <frame src="links.htm" noresize="noresize" name="links" />

        <!-- Cliff Hangers Web Pages -->
        <frame src="home.htm" noresize="noresize" name="pages" />
    </frameset>

    <!-- Noframes version of this page -->
    <noframes>
        <body>
            <div id="head"><img src="chlogo.jpg" alt="Cliff Hangers" /></div>

            <div id="pageContent">
                <div id="leftCol">
```

```
                <p>We provide five levels of instruction, ranging from Beginner to Advanced,
                   including lessons in aid and ice climbing. Members of our experienced staff
                   have led expeditions in Mexico, Nepal, and Pakistan. All have intimate
                   knowledge of the Colorado Rockies and know the best places to go
                   to help you experience the wonder and beauty of the area.</p>
                <p>So contact us today, and start climbing tomorrow!</p>
            </div>

        </div>
        </body>

    </noframes>

</frameset>
```

▶ **8.** Save your changes to the file and then reload **cliff.htm** in your Web browser. Browsers that support frames should not look any different because the noframes version will be rendered only by frame-blind browsers.

Of the major browsers, only Opera allows the user to disable frames to test the noframes element. To disable frames in Opera, click Preferences from the Tools menu to open the Preferences dialog box, click Content from the Advanced tab, and then click the Style options button. Deselect the Enable frames check box to turn off support for frames.

Tip

You can also support frame-blind browsers by creating two versions of your Web site: one using frames and the other without frames. Provide your users with an opening splash screen to let them pick which version to load.

InSight | **Making Frames Work with Search Engines**

By their nature, frames are not friendly to search engines because they don't have any page content for the search engines to index. However, there are a few things you can do to make your frames more accessible. One is to add <meta /> tags to the head section of the document with keywords that the search engines can use in creating their search indices. However, <meta /> tags are only a partial solution because not all search engines use them.

For a more complete solution, always include page content within a <noframes> element. The page content should be extensive enough to describe your site's purpose and contents, providing enough information for search engines to create a proper index for your site. Search engines also take into account that most Web sites cover multiple pages. Therefore, part of the indexing process undertaken by a search engine is to navigate through all of the links within a Web site, creating a list of important keywords as it goes. This means that you should also include any navigation links within the <noframes> section of your file so that the search engines will be able to see those links and act upon them.

By using <meta /> tags and enclosing important page content within the <noframes> tag, you can make your site much more accessible to search engines, removing one of the drawbacks often associated with frames.

Working with Frame Borders

Some browsers support additional attributes that you can use to change border size and appearance. For example, you can remove borders from your frames to free up more space for text and images, or you can change the color of the frame borders so that they match or complement the color scheme for your Web site.

Setting the Frame Border Color

To change the color of a frame's border, many browsers support the bordercolor attribute. The syntax for this attribute is

```
bordercolor="color"
```

where *color* is either a color name or a hexadecimal color value. The attribute can be applied either to an entire set of frames, by applying it to the frameset element, or to individual frame elements within the frameset. The bordercolor attribute is not part of the official specifications for HTML and XHTML, so you should not rely on it for your frame design.

Debbie wonders how the Cliff Hangers Web site would look with brown frame borders. You'll use the bordercolor attribute to experiment with this.

To set the frame border color:

▶ **1.** Return to the **cliff.htm** file.

▶ **2.** In the opening <frameset> tag, enter the following attribute:

    bordercolor="brown"

▶ **3.** Save your changes to the file and then reload **cliff.htm** in your Web browser. If your Web browser supports the bordercolor attribute for frames and framesets, your Web site should look like Figure 8-31.

Setting the Frame Border Width

You can also remove the frame borders entirely by applying the frameborder attribute

```
<frame frameborder="value" />
```

to the frame element, where a frameborder value of 0 removes the frame border and a value of 1 displays the border. Different browsers respond in different ways to this attribute, and some browsers do not support the attribute at all. Other browsers require you to apply the border attribute

```
<frameset border="value"> ... </frame>
```

to the frameset element to remove frame borders, where value is the size of the border in pixels. Note that the border attribute is applied to the frameset element, while the frameborder attribute is applied only to the frame element. Like bordercolor, the border attribute is not part of the specifications for HTML and is not supported by XHTML.

Hiding a Frame Border | Reference Window

- To specify whether a frame border is displayed, add the attribute
  frameborder="value"
  to the <frame> tag, where value is 0 to hide the border and 1 to display it.

Debbie decides that although the brown borders look fine, the page might look cleaner without any borders at all. To ensure compatibility with the greatest number of browsers, you'll use both the frameborder and the border attributes in your HTML code.

To remove the frame borders:

▶ **1.** Return to the **cliff.htm** file in your Web browser.

▶ **2.** Delete the bordercolor attribute that you added to the opening <frameset> tag in the previous set of steps. You don't need this attribute because you're going to remove the frame borders entirely.

▶ **3.** Insert the attribute

border="0"

within the opening <frameset> tag.

▶ **4.** Insert the attribute

frameborder="0"

within each of the three <frame> tags. Figure 8-32 highlights the revised code.

Figure 8-32 ▶ **Removing frame borders**

```
<frameset rows="85,*" border="0">
    <!-- Company Logo -->
    <frame src="head.htm" scrolling="no" marginheight="0" noresize="noresize" name="logo" frameborder="0" />

    <!-- Nested Frameset -->
    <frameset cols="140,*">
        <!-- List of Links -->
        <frame src="links.htm" noresize="noresize" name="links" frameborder="0" />

        <!-- Cliff Hangers Web Pages -->
        <frame src="home.htm" noresize="noresize" name="pages" frameborder="0" />
    </frameset>
```

▶ **5.** You've finished your edits on this file. Close the **cliff.htm** file, saving your changes.

▶ **6.** Reload **cliff.htm** in your Web browser. As shown in Figure 8-33, the borders are removed from the frames in the frame layout.

Figure 8-33 ▶ **Final frame layout**

CLIFF HANGERS
8105 Yale Drive • Boulder, CO 80301 • (303) 555 - 8143

Home Page
Our Philosophy
Climbing Lessons
Tours
Staff

WELCOME TO ONE OF AMERICA'S BEST CLIMBING SCHOOLS located in one of America's best climbing areas, the Colorado Rockies. Nowhere else in America is there such a rich variety of technically challenging rock, ice, and high alpine routes. The area presents the climber with a choice of multiple-pitch climbs and big wall routes. Whether you are here to enjoy the spectacular scenery or to train for an expedition, you can choose no better place than the Colorado Front Range.

And no one else brings the experience of the Rockies to you better than **Cliff Hangers Climbing School**. Whether you are a beginner, itching to learn the skill and art of climbing, or an experienced mountaineer looking for guides to take you on some of Rocky Mountain National Park's more challenging climbs, consider us your gateway to the mountains.

We provide five levels of instruction, ranging from Beginner to Advanced, including lessons in aid and ice climbing. Members of our experienced staff have led expeditions in Mexico, Nepal, and Pakistan. All have intimate knowledge of the Colorado Rockies and know the best places to go to help you experience the wonder and beauty of the area.

So contact us today, and start climbing tomorrow!

By removing the borders, you've created more space for the text and images on each Web page. You've also created the impression of a seamless Web page, which some Web designers prefer in order to give the illusion of a single Web page rather than three separate ones. However, other Web designers believe that hiding frame borders can confuse users as they navigate the Web site.

Creating Inline Frames

Another type of frame used on Web sites is an **inline frame** in which the frame appears not within a frameset but within the body of a Web page. Much like an inline image displays the contents of graphics file or an embedded object displays a video clip, an inline frame displays the contents of a Web page. Inline frames are created using the iframe element

```
<iframe src="url" width="value" height="value">
   alternate content
</iframe>
```

where *url* is the URL of the document you want displayed in the inline frame and *alternate content* is content displayed by browsers that don't support inline frames. The width and height attributes are required, and they set the size of the inline frame in pixels. For example, the following code displays the contents of the jobs.htm file within an inline frame that is 500 pixels wide × 200 pixels high; browsers that don't support inline frames will display a paragraph containing a link to the jobs.htm file:

```
<iframe src="jobs.htm" width="500" height="200">
   <p>
      View the online <a href="jobs.htm">jobs listings</a>.
   </p>
</iframe>
```

If the contents of the jobs.htm file cannot fit within the specified dimensions, the Web browser will automatically add the necessary horizontal and vertical scroll bars to enable the user to scroll through the contents of the file.

Inline frames support many of the same features as inline images. You can resize them, float them on the page margins, and specify the size of the margin around the frame. You can also use many of the attributes associated with frame elements. Figure 8-34 summarizes some of the attributes associated with inline frames. Note that some of the listed attributes have been deprecated by the World Wide Web Consortium (W3C). You can replace many of these attributes using CSS style sheets.

> **Tip**
>
> You can also use the <object> tag discussed in Tutorial 7 to display the contents of one Web page within another.

Figure 8-34 ▶ **Attributes of inline frames**

Attribute	Description
align="*position*"	Aligns the inline frame with the surrounding content (deprecated)
border="*value*"	Sets the size of the border around the frame in pixels (deprecated)
frameborder="1 | 0"	Specifies whether to display the inline frame border (1 = display; 0 = no frame border)
height="*value*"	Sets the height of the frame in pixels
hspace="*value*"	Sets the horizontal margin around the frame in pixels (deprecated)
marginheight="*value*"	Sets the vertical margin within the frame in pixels
marginwidth="*value*"	Sets the horizontal margin within the frame in pixels
name="*text*"	Specifies the name of the frame
scrolling="yes | no"	Specifies whether or not to display scroll bars around the frame
src="*url*"	Sets the source of the document within the inline frame
style="*styles*"	Provides inline styles to be applied to the frame
vspace="*value*"	Sets the vertical margin around the frame in pixels (deprecated)
width="*value*"	Sets the width of the frame in pixels

Debbie would like to use inline frames on the Cliff Hangers Philosophy page to create a slide show for users to view high-resolution images from Cliff Hangers tours and classes. As shown in Figure 8-35, Debbie wants to give users the option to click on thumbnail versions of the photo images that would then load the larger images onto the Web page.

Figure 8-35 ▶ **Creating a slide show with inline frames**

clicking the thumbnail image loads a new image into the inline frame

Like frames within framesets, inline frames support the name attribute. This attribute provides a way of targeting the inline frame for hypertext links. For example, if you set the name of an inline frame to docs, the hypertext link

```
View the online <a href="jobs.htm" target="docs">job listings</a>
```

will open the jobs.htm file within the docs inline frame.

Creating an Inline Frame | Reference Window

- To create an inline frame within a Web page, add the code

```
<iframe src="url" width="value" height="value">
   alternate content
</iframe>
```

where *url* is the URL of the document you want displayed in the inline frame and *alternate content* is content displayed by browsers that don't support inline frames. The width and height attributes define the size of the inline frame in pixels.

- To create a link to an inline frame, first add the name attribute

```
<iframe src="url" width="value" height="value" name="name">
   alternate content
</iframe>
```

to the <iframe>, where *name* is the name of the inline frame. Then, add the name of the frame to the hypertext link as follows:

```
<a href="url" target="name"> text </a>
```

The linked document will then appear within the *name* inline frame.

To create the inline frame:

1. Open the **philosph.htm** file in your text editor.

2. Scroll down to the leftCol div container and locate the inline image for the philosph1.jpg file.

3. Directly after the opening <div id="leftCol"> tag, insert the following opening <iframe> tag:

   <iframe src="philosph1.jpg" name="slide" width="380" height="260"

       scrolling="no" marginwidth="0" marginheight="0"

       frameborder="0">

4. Directly below the inline image for the philosph1.jpg file, insert the closing **</iframe>** tag, as shown in Figure 8-36.

Tip

To replace an inline image with an inline frame, match the size of the frame to the size of the image and remove any internal margins and frame borders.

Creating an inline frame | Figure 8-36

```
<div id="leftCol">
    <iframe src="philosph1.jpg" name="slide" width="380" height="260"
            scrolling="no" marginwidth="0" marginheight="0" frameborder="0">

        <img src="philosph1.jpg" alt="" width="380" height="260" />

    </iframe>
    <p>Click the images below to view slides from Cliff Hangers tours<br />
        <img src="slides.jpg" alt="" width="380" height="73" />
    </p>
```

frame-blind browsers will still display the inline image

the size and the source of the inline frame match the size and source of the inline image

5. Save your changes to the file and then reload the **cliff.htm** file in your Web browser. Click the **Our Philosophy** link from the links frame and verify that the Our Philosophy page still displays the philosph1.jpg image.

Because you sized the inline frame to match the size of the inline image and removed the frame border and internal margins, you should not see any difference between the appearance of the inline frame and the appearance of the inline image. Note that you've given the inline image the name slide. Like the other frames in this tutorial, you must assign the inline frame name so that it can be a target for hypertext links in other documents.

Next you'll create an image map for the image containing the thumbnail versions of the high-resolution images. Recall from Tutorial 2 that image maps are created using the map and area elements. For the thumbnail images, each image map hot spot can be defined using a rectangular shape. Figure 8-37 shows the coordinates of the four rectangular hot spots.

Figure 8-37   **Rectangular hot spots in the thumbnail images**

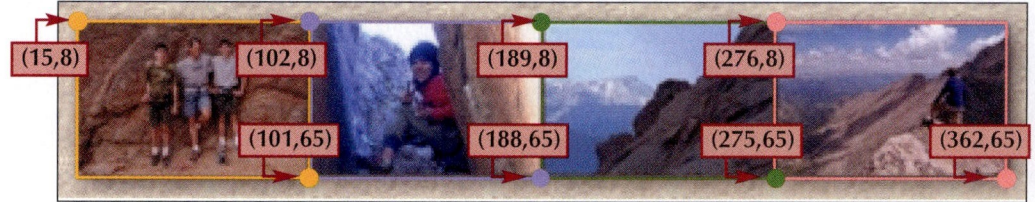

The area elements corresponding to these four hot spots are:

```
<area shape="rect" coords="15,8,101,65" href="philosph1.jpg" />
<area shape="rect" coords="102,8,188,65" href="philosph2.jpg" />
<area shape="rect" coords="189,8,275,65" href="philosph3.jpg" />
<area shape="rect" coords="276,8,362,65" href="philosph4.jpg" />
```

To have each hot spot open the high-resolution jpeg image within the inline frame, you also must add the attribute

```
target="slide"
```

to the <area> tag because you named the inline frame with the slide target name. Debbie wants you to add the image map to the philosph.htm file using the hot spots listed above.

To create an image map for the thumbnail images:

▶ 1. Within the **philosph.htm** file, scroll down to the slides.jpg inline image and insert the following attributes:

   usemap="#thumbmap" style="border-width: 0px"

▶ 2. Directly below the inline image, insert the following thumbmap image map:

   <map name="thumbmap" id="thumbmap">

       <area shape="rect" coords="15,8,101,65" href="philosph1.jpg"

           target="slide" />

       <area shape="rect" coords="102,8,188,65" href="philosph2.jpg"

           target="slide" />

       <area shape="rect" coords="189,8,275,65" href="philosph3.jpg"

           target="slide" />

       <area shape="rect" coords="276,8,362,65" href="philosph4.jpg"

           target="slide" />

   </map>

   Figure 8-38 highlights the revised code for the file.

Adding the image map for the inline frame ◀ Figure 8-38

```
<div id="leftCol">
   <iframe src="philosph1.jpg" name="slide" width="380" height="260"
           scrolling="no" marginwidth="0" marginheight="0" frameborder="0">

      <img src="philosph1.jpg" alt="" width="380" height="260" />

   </iframe>

   <p>Click the images below to view slides from Cliff Hangers tours<br />
      <img src="slides.jpg" alt="" width="380" height="73"
           usemap="#thumbmap" style="border-width: 0px" />

      <map name="thumbmap" id="thumbmap">
         <area shape="rect" coords="15,8,101,65" href="philosph1.jpg" target="slide" />
         <area shape="rect" coords="102,8,188,65" href="philosph2.jpg" target="slide" />
         <area shape="rect" coords="189,8,275,65" href="philosph3.jpg" target="slide" />
         <area shape="rect" coords="276,8,362,65" href="philosph4.jpg" target="slide" />
      </map>
   </p>
```

▶ **3.** Close the **philosph.htm** file, saving your changes.

▶ **4.** Reload the **cliff.htm** file in your Web browser and click the **Our Philosophy** link.

▶ **5.** Click each of the four thumbnail images and verify that the Web page displays the corresponding image in the inline frame above the row of thumbnails.

▶ **6.** You can close any open files or programs now.

Keeping Pages Within Their Frames | InSight

In a frame-based layout, ideally you want all of your Web pages to be accessed only within the context of the frameset. However, with Web search engines such as Google and Yahoo!, this might not always be the case. For example, a user might enter your Web site not from the home page containing the frameset but from another page, thereby bypassing the frame layout you created for all the pages in your Web site. Accessing the Web page outside of its frame context can make it difficult for the user to navigate through the rest of your Web site, especially if you've placed all of your hypertext links on another page.

One way to avoid this problem is to force browsers to always access your Web site through the frameset. You can do this by running a short JavaScript program. JavaScript is a programming language developed for use with HTML and Web browsers. Use the code

```
<script type="text/javascript">
   if (top.location == self.location) top.location = "frame.htm";
</script>
```

in the head section of any document within the site, where *frame.htm* is the file containing the frameset. When the browser attempts to open the page outside of the frameset, this code will force the browser to open the frame.htm file instead. This code can also be used with documents that should only appear within an inline frame. In that case, frame.htm is the Web page containing the inline frame and the code prevents documents from appearing outside of the inline frame.

You've completed your work for Debbie and the Cliff Hangers Climbing School. Using frames, you've created an interesting presentation that is both attractive and easy to navigate. Debbie is pleased and will get back to you if she needs any additional work done.

Review | Session 8.2 Quick Check

1. When you click a link inside a frame, in what frame does the target Web page appear by default?
2. What attribute would you use to assign the name Address to a frame?
3. What attribute would you add to a link to direct it to a frame named News?
4. What attribute would you use to point a link to the document sales.htm, with the result that the sales.htm file is displayed in the entire browser window?
5. What tag would you use to direct all links in a document to the News target?
6. Describe what you would do to make your Web page readable both by browsers that support frames and by those that do not.
7. How would you set the frame border width to 5 pixels?
8. Specify the code to create an inline frame that is 300 pixels wide × 200 pixels high and contains the Web page glossary.htm.

Review | Tutorial Summary

In this tutorial, you learned how to create and use frames. In the first session, you learned how to create a frameset and arrange the frames in rows or columns within a set. You also learned how to specify which document appears within each frame. The first session concluded with a discussion of some of the frame attributes used to control the frame's appearance. The second session explored how to direct a link's target to a specific frame. In addition, you learned some of the other attributes that can be used to format a frame's appearance. The session also showed how to support browsers that don't recognize frames. The tutorial concluded by demonstrating how to create inline frames.

Key Terms

frame (Web design)
frameset
inline frame
reserved target name

Practice		**Review Assignments**

Practice the skills you learned in the tutorial using the same case scenario.

Data Files needed for the Review Assignments: lefttxt.htm, lessonstxt.htm, links1txt.htm, links2txt.htm, links3txt.htm, middletxt.htm, newlayouttxt.htm, righttxt.htm, 16 HTML files, 4 external style sheets, and 25 graphic files

Debbie has asked you to revise the layout for the Cliff Hangers Web site. She would like the links to appear in separate frames so that users can always click a link for a specific page or collection of pages no matter where they are on the Web site. Figure 8-39 shows a preview of the new frame layout you'll create for her Web site.

Figure 8-39

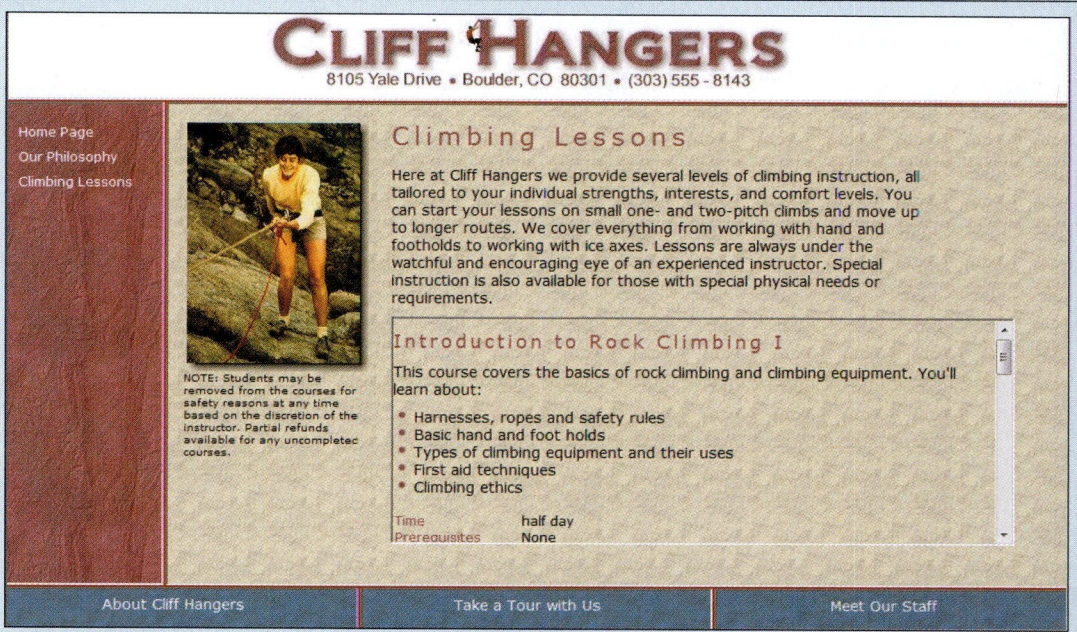

This is a large Web site containing 53 files; however, you'll only have to create the following files in order to complete the frame layout for the site:

- left.htm   a file containing a link to a list of Web pages describing Cliff Hangers
- lessons.htm   a file describing the lessons offered by Cliff Hangers
- links1.htm   a file containing the list of Web pages describing Cliff Hangers
- links2.htm   a file containing the list of tours offered by Cliff Hangers
- links3.htm   a file containing the list of Cliff Hangers staff members
- middle.htm   a file containing a link to the list of tours offered by Cliff Hangers
- newlayout.htm   a frame layout for the Cliff Hangers Web site
- right.htm   a file containing a link to the list of Cliff Hangers staff members

Complete the following:

1. Use your text editor to open the **lefttxt.htm**, **lessonstxt.htm**, **links1txt.htm**, **links2txt.htm**, **links3txt.htm**, **middletxt.htm**, **newlayouttxt.htm**, and **righttxt.htm** from the tutorial.08\review folder included with your Data Files. Enter *your name* and *the date* in the comment section of each file and save them as **left.htm**, **lessons. htm**, **links1.htm**, **links2.htm**, **links3.htm**, **middle.htm**, **newlayout.htm**, and **right.htm**, respectively, in the same folder.

2. Go to the **newlayout.htm** file in your text editor. This file will contain the frame layout for the Cliff Hangers Web site. Create a frameset consisting of three rows. Set the height of the first row to 85 pixels, set the height of the third row to 40 pixels, and let the second row occupy the remaining space between the first and third rows. Set the border color of the frameset to brown.

3. Within the frameset, insert a frame and nest two more framesets. Name the frame top and display the head.htm file within it. Set the margin height of the frame to 0 pixels. Set the first frameset to display two columns, with the first column 150 pixels wide and the second column occupying the remaining space. Set the second frameset to display three columns of equal width.

4. Within the first nested frameset, insert two frames named links and docs. Set the margin width of both frames to 0 pixels. Display the links1.htm file in the first frame and the home.htm file in the second frame.

5. Within the second nested frameset, insert three frames containing the files left.htm, middle.htm, and right.htm. Name the frames left, middle, and right. Set the margin width of all frames to 0 pixels.

6. Within the head section of the file, insert a link to the **noframes.css** style sheet.

7. For browsers incapable of displaying frames, have the file display page contents copied from the **noframes.htm** file. Remember to include the opening and closing <body> tags.

8. Close the file, saving your changes to the file.

9. Go to the **links1.htm** file in your text editor. Set the default target for all links in the file to the docs frame. Close the file, saving your changes.

10. Repeat Step 9 for the **links2.htm** and **links3.htm** files.

11. Go to the **left.htm** file in your text editor. Set the target of the hypertext link in the file to the links frame. Close the file, saving your changes.

12. Repeat Step 11 for the **middle.htm** and **right.htm** files.

13. Go to the **lessons.htm** file in your text editor. Deb wants to insert an inline frame within this file, displaying a list of lessons offered by Cliff Hangers. At the bottom of the page, insert an inline frame in which to display the **lessonlist.htm** file. Set the width of the inline frame to 600 pixels wide × 220 pixels high.

14. For browsers that do not support inline frames, have the browsers display a hypertext link pointing to the **lessonslist.htm** file.

15. Close the **lessons.htm** file, saving your changes.

16. Open the **newlayout.htm** file in your Web browser. Verify that you can view all of the Web pages from the Cliff Hangers site within the appropriate frames.

17. Go to the **Climbing Lessons** page on the Web site and verify that the list of climbing lessons appears within an inline frame with a vertical scroll bar.

18. Submit your completed files to your instructor.

| Apply | Case Problem 1 |

Apply your knowledge of frames to create a politics Web site.

Data Files needed for this Case Problem: belknap.htm, carroll.htm, cheshire.htm, coos.htm, elections.htm, grafton.htm, hillsborough.htm, maptxt.htm, merrimack.htm, nhmap.jpg, nhplogo.jpg, nhpolytxt.htm, notestxt.htm, poli.css, rockingham.htm, statewide.htm, strafford.htm, sullivan.htm, and title.htm

NH PoliWeb Kevin Unger runs a Web site in New Hampshire called NH PoliWeb, which provides articles and news on New Hampshire politics. On part of his Web site, Kevin wants to post recent election results for statewide offices broken down by county. He's decided to use a frame layout with an image map of the New Hampshire counties in one frame and the election results in another. He's asked for your help in creating the frame design. Figure 8-40 shows a preview of the Web site you'll create for Kevin.

Figure 8-40

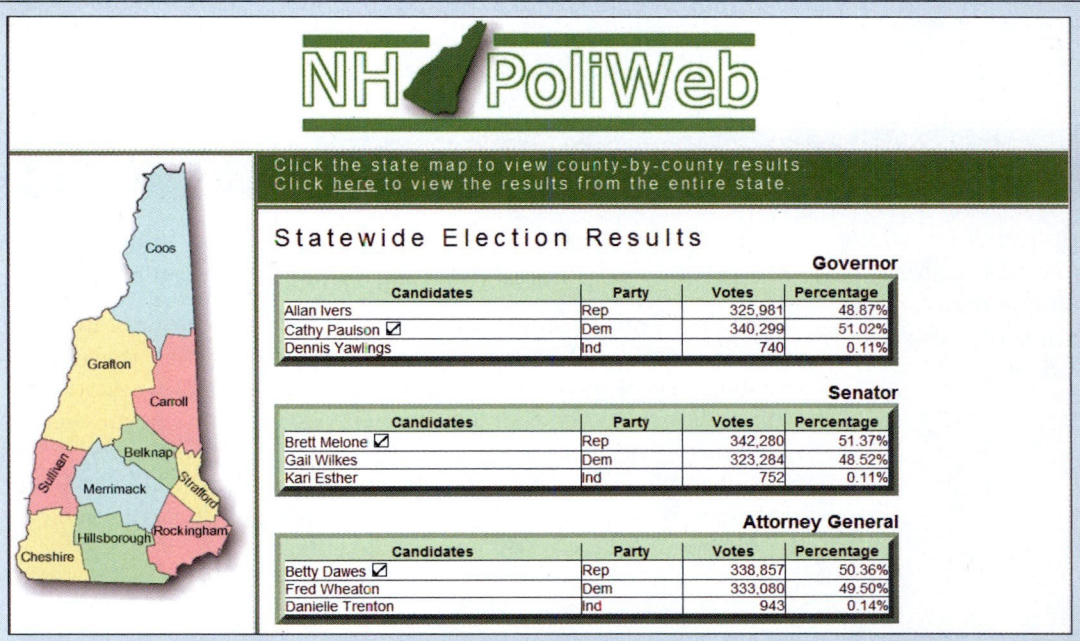

Complete the following:

1. Use your text editor to open **maptxt.htm**, **nhpolytxt.htm**, and **notestxt.htm** from the tutorial.08\case1 folder included with your Data Files. Enter *your name* and *the date* in the comment section of each file. Save the files as **map.htm**, **nhpoly.htm**, and **notes.htm**, respectively, in the same folder.

2. Go to the **nhpoly.htm** file in your text editor. Create a frameset that consists of two rows, with the top row set at 130 pixels and the bottom row occupying the remaining space in the browser window. Set the frame border color to green.

3. Display the title.htm file in the first frame of the frameset. Set the margin width of the frame to 0 pixels and name the frame top.

4. Nest a second frameset within the first frameset consisting of two columns, with the left column set at 235 pixels wide and the right column occupying the remaining space in the browser window.

5. Display the map.htm file in the first frame of the nested frameset. Name the frame links and set the margin width to 0 pixels.

6. Nest a third frameset within the main frameset, consisting of two rows. Set the width of the first row to 50 pixels and the second row to whatever space is left in the browser window.

7. Display the notes.htm file in the first frame. Name the frame notes and set the margin width to 0 pixels. Name the second frame documents and display the statewide. htm file in it. Set the margin width to 0.

8. For browsers that don't support frames, display the page content copied from the elections.htm file.

9. Save your changes to the **nhpoly.htm** file.

10. Return to the **map.htm** file in your text editor. Set the default target of all hypertext links in the file to the documents frame. Save your changes to the file.

11. Return to the **notes.htm** file in your text editor. Set the target of the hypertext link in the file to the documents frame. Save your changes to the file.

12. Open **nhpoly.htm** in your Web browser. Verify that the frame layout resembles that shown in Figure 8-40. Also verify that all the links open in the documents frame.

13. Submit your completed files to your instructor.

| Apply | **Case Problem 2** |

Apply your knowledge of frames to create inline frames for photos on a realty Web site.

Data Files needed for this Case Problem: back.jpg, brlogo.jpg, browyer.css, img01.jpg - img13.jpg, l20481.jpg, listingtxt.htm, and pback.jpg

Browyer Realty   Linda Browyer is the owner of Browyer Realty, a real estate company in Owatonna, Minnesota. She's asked you to help her design a Web page for her current listings. Linda envisions a Web page that displays basic information about a listing, including the owner's description. She would like to have several photos of the listing on the page; but rather than cluttering up the layout with several images, she would like users to be able to view different images by clicking a link on the page. Linda wants the images to open within the listing page, not on a separate Web page. Figure 8-41 shows a preview of the page you'll create for Linda.

Figure 8-41

Complete the following:

1. Use your text editor to open **listingtxt.htm** from the tutorial.08\case2 folder included with your Data Files. Enter *your name* and *the date* in the comment section of the file and save it as **listing.htm**.
2. Locate the inline image for the img01.jpg file (it's floated off the left side of the second paragraph). Use this image as the alternate content for an inline frame, enclosing the image within an inline frame with the following attributes:
   * The source of the frame is the img01.jpg file.
   * The name of the frame is slide.
   * The frame is 300 pixels wide and 225 pixels high.
   * The frame's internal margin width and height are 0 pixels.
   * Do not display scroll bars around the frame.
3. Insert a comment above the floating frame indicating its purpose on the Web page.
4. Change each of the 13 entries in the list of photos to a link. Direct the first entry to img01.jpg, the second entry to img02.jpg, and so forth.
5. Direct the 13 links you created in the previous step to the inline frame (named slide in Step 2).
6. Save your changes to the file.
7. Using your Web browser, open **listing.htm**. Verify that each link displays a different photo on the Web page and that the rest of the page remains unchanged.
8. Submit your completed files to your instructor.

Challenge | **Case Problem 3**

Explore how to nest inline frames to create an interactive slide show for an astronomy Web site.

Data Files needed for this Case Problem: messtxt.htm, mxxtxt.htm, 9 HTML files, 2 external style sheets, and 22 graphic files

SkyWeb Astronomy Dr. Andrew Weiss of Central Ohio University maintains an astronomy page called SkyWeb for his students. On his Web site, he discusses many aspects of astronomy and observing. One of the pages he wants your help with involves the Messier catalog, which is a list of deep sky objects of particular interest to astronomers and amateur observers.

Dr. Weiss wants his page to contain a slide show of various Messier objects, displaying both a photo of the object and a text box describing the object's history and features. He wants his users to be able to click a forward or backward button to move through the slide show, and he wants the rest of the Web page to remain unchanged as users view the presentation. Figure 8-42 shows a preview of the page that Dr. Weiss wants to create.

Figure 8-42

| Home Page | The Night Sky | The Moon | The Planets | Messier Objects | Stars |

The Messier Objects

 **Messier objects** are stellar objects, classified by astronomer **Charles Messier** in the 18th century, ranging from distant galaxies to star clusters to stellar nebula. The catalog was a major milestone in the history of astronomy, as it was the first comprehensive list of deep sky objects. Ironically, Charles Messier wasn't all that interested in the objects in his list. He made the catalog in order to *avoid* mistaking those objects for comets, which were his true passion.

Messier objects are identified by **Messier Numbers**. The first object in Messier's catalog, the Crab Nebula, is labelled **M1**. The last object, **M110** is a satellite galaxy located in the constellation Andromeda. There is no systematic ordering in the Messier Catalog. Messier entered objects into the list as he found them. Sometimes he made mistakes and once he entered the same stellar object twice. The catalog has undergone some slight revisions since Messier's time, correcting the mistakes in the original.

One of the great pursuits for amateur astronomers is to do a **Messier Marathon**, trying to view all of the objects in Messier's catalog in one night. Unfortunately, if you want to see all of them, you have to start looking right after sunset and continue until just before sunrise - hence the term, "marathon." March is the only month in the year in which an astronomer can run the complete marathon.

Use the buttons to view some of the more popular objects in Messier's catalog.

M31: The Andromeda Galaxy

The Andromeda Galaxy, M31, is our nearest large galaxy. At a distance of 2.9 million lightyears, the galaxy is one of the chief items in the "Local Group" of galaxys, of which our own is part.

Andromeda can be easily

To create a presentation like this, you can nest one inline frame inside of another. Dr. Weiss has created the text you need for the Web site. Your job is to create the frames needed to complete the Web page.

Complete the following:

1. Using your text editor, open **mxxtxt.htm** from the tutorial.08\case3 folder included with your Data Files. This file will act as a model for pages that display descriptions and images of the Messier objects. You'll start by using this file to create the page for Messier object M01. Enter *your name* and *the date* in the comment section of this file and save the file as **m01.htm** in the same folder.

2. Replace the text of the page title and the h1 heading with M01: The Crab Nebula.

3. Replace the inline image mxx.jpg with the image file **m01.jpg**.

4. Replace the inline image mxxdesc.jpg with an inline frame with the same id name and dimensions. Set the source of the inline frame to the **m01desc.htm** file.

5. Copy the page content (excluding the opening and closing <body> tags) from the **m01desc.htm** file and paste that content within the inline frame to provide alternate text for browsers that don't support inline frames.

6. Point the hypertext link for the Previous button to the file **m57.htm**. (You'll create this file shortly.)

7. Point the hypertext link for the Next button to the file **m13.htm**. (This is another file you'll create shortly.)

8. Close the file, saving your changes.

 EXPLORE

9. Using your work on the m01.htm file as a guide, use your text editor with the **mxxtxt.htm** file to create similar Web pages for the other eight Messier objects. Save the files as **m13.htm**, **m16.htm**, **m20.htm**, **m27.htm**, **m31.htm**, **m42.htm**, **m51.htm**, and **m57.htm**. Be sure to enter *your name* and *the date* in the comment section of each file. The titles for these pages are:

   - M13: Hercules Globular Cluster
   - M16: The Eagle Nebula
   - M20: The Trifid Nebula
   - M27: The Dumbbell Nebula
   - M31: The Andromeda Galaxy
   - M42: The Orion Nebula
   - M51: The Whirlpool Galaxy
   - M57: The Ring Nebula

   The inline frame for each page should point to the file containing descriptive text on the Messier object. For example, the floating frame for the m13.htm file should display the m13desc.htm file, and so forth.

   The Previous and Next buttons on each page should point to the previous and next Messier object files. For example, the buttons in m27.htm should point to m20.htm and m31.htm. The Next button for m57.htm should point to m01.htm. Save your changes to all the files, and then close them.

10. Use your text editor to open the **messtxt.htm** file. Enter *your name* and *the date* in the comment section of the file. Save the file as **messier.htm**.

11. Scroll down to the div container with the slide show id. Within the id, insert an inline frame with the following properties:

    - Set the source of the frame to the **m01.htm** file.
    - Set the frame dimensions to 460 pixels wide × 240 pixels high.
    - Set the internal margins to 0 pixels.
    - Set the width of the frame border to 0 pixels.
    - For browsers that don't display inline frames, display a text message indicating that they need inline frames to view the slide show and include a hypertext link to the **m01.htm** file.

⊕ **EXPLORE**　12.　Save your changes to the file, and then open **messier.htm** in your Web browser. Click the Previous and Next buttons and verify that you can navigate through the list of Messier objects without disturbing the rest of the Web page. Verify that you can use the scroll bars around the description box to view descriptions of each object.

⊕ **EXPLORE**　13.　Return to the **m01.htm** file in your text editor. Add code to the head section of the document to force the file to always appear within the inline frame of the messier. htm file.

14.　Repeat Step 13 for **m13.htm**, **m16.htm**, **m20.htm**, **m27.htm**, **m31.htm**, **m42.htm**, **m51.htm**, and **m57.htm**.

⊕ **EXPLORE**　15.　Attempt to the open the **m01.htm** file in your Web browser. Verify that when you attempt to load the file, the browser automatically opens the **messier.htm** file (with the m01.htm file showing) instead, preventing users from seeing the m01.htm file outside the contents of the rest of the Web site.

16.　Submit your completed files to your instructor.

Create　| **Case Problem 4**

Test your knowledge of frames by creating a frame layout for a Shakespeare play.

Data Files needed for this Case Problem: tempa1s1txt.htm, tempa1s2txt.htm, tempa2s1txt.htm, tempa2s2txt.htm, tempa3s1txt.htm, tempa3s2txt.htm, tempa3s3txt.htm, tempa4s1txt.htm, tempa5s1txt.htm, and tempest.jpg

Mansfield Classic Theatre　Steve Karls, the director of Mansfield Classic Theatre in Mansfield, Ohio, has come back to you for help on his Web site listing the great plays of classic theatre. He has decided to place the entire text of Shakespeare's *The Tempest* on his Web site. He would like to use a frame layout, with the dialog from the scenes displayed in one frame and a list of links to each scene in the play displayed in another frame. He wants a third frame that displays the logo for the company's production of *The Tempest* and a fourth frame that contains links to sites on the Web containing commentary on William Shakespeare and *The Tempest*. He has already created the HTML files for nine scenes from the play and has created a graphics file containing the logo. He needs your help in creating the frame layout.

Complete the following:

1.　Open the **tempa1s1txt.htm** through **tempa5s1txt.htm** files from the tutorial.08\case4 folder in your text editor. Within each file, insert a comment section containing *your name* and *the date*. Save the files as **tempa1s1.htm** through **tempa5s1.htm**, respectively, in the same folder.

2.　You are free to design the pages with any styles or content you think will enhance the site. Save any styles in an external style sheet named **ws.css** in the tutorial.08\case4 folder.

3.　Use your text editor to create an HTML file named **tempest.htm** that will contain the frame layout for the Web site. Save the file in the tutorial.08\case4 folder included with your Data Files. Enter *your name* and *the date* in a comment section of the file. Include any other comments you think will aptly document the purpose and content of the file.

4.　Use your text editor to create an HTML file named **scenelist.htm** that will contain a list of links to the nine scenes from the five acts of *The Tempest*. Save the file in the tutorial. 08\case4 folder. Enter *your name* and *the date* in a comment section of the file.

5. Use your text editor to create an HTML file named **weblinks.htm** that will contain a list of links to five sites you locate on the Web containing commentary or articles on *The Tempest* or Shakespeare. Save the file in the tutorial.08\case4 folder. Enter *your name* and *the date* in a comment section of the file.

6. In the **tempest.htm** file, create a frameset layout containing the following four frames:
   - A frame displaying the dialog from a scene in the play
   - A frame displaying the **scenelist.htm** file
   - A frame displaying the logo for the production of *The Tempest* (use the file tempest.jpg)
   - A frame containing the **weblinks.htm** file

7. The layout of the frameset is up to you, but it should be designed so that links to each scene from the play open in the frame displaying the scene dialogue, and links to external Web sites open in the entire browser window, replacing the frameset.

8. For sites that do not support frames, have them display a Web page with the name of the play in an h1 heading and the text "Read an online version of Shakespeare's *The Tempest* from the Mansfield Classic Theatre."

⊕ EXPLORE 9. Add JavaScript code to the head section of each page on the Web site so that if a user attempts to open the file in a browser, the browser will load the entire frameset from tempest.htm.

10. Open **tempest.htm** in your Web browser and verify that all of the pages are readable within the frame layout and all of the hypertext links open in the correct frame or browser window.

⊕ EXPLORE 11. Open the individual files in your Web browser and verify that the frameset contained within the **tempest.htm** file opens instead.

12. Submit your completed files to your instructor.

Review | Quick Check Answers

Session 8.1

1. A frame is a section of a browser window capable of displaying the contents of an entire Web page. Frames do not require the same information (such as a list of links) to be repeated on multiple pages of a Web site. They also enable a Web designer to update content in one place in order to affect an entire Web site.

2. Because there is no page body in a frame document. The frame document displays the content of other pages.

3. `<frameset rows="200,50%,*"> ... </frameset>`

4. `<frame src="home.htm" />`

5. `<frame src="home.htm" scrolling="no" />`

6. `<frame src="home.htm" marginheight="3" />`

7. 3 pixels

8. `<frame src="home.htm" noresize="noresize" />`

Session 8.2

1. The frame containing the link

2. `name="Address"`

3. `target="News"`

4. `target="_top"`

5. Place the tag `<base target="News" />` in the head element of the document.
6. Create a section starting with the `<noframes>` tag. After the `<noframes>` tag, enter a `<body>` tag to identify the text and images you want frame-blind browsers to display. Complete this section with a `</body>` tag followed by a `</noframes>` tag.
7. `<frameset border="5">`
8. `<iframe src="glossary.htm" width="300" height="200"></iframe>`

Ending Data Files

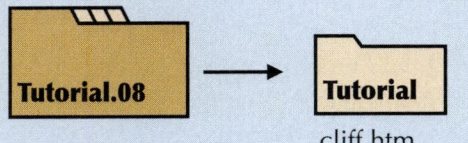

Tutorial

cliff.htm
links.htm
philosph.htm
tours.htm
+ 17 HTML files
+ 3 style sheets
+ 29 graphic files

Review

left.htm
lessons.htm
links1.htm
links2.htm
links3.htm
middle.htm
newlayout.htm
right.htm
+ 16 HTML files
+ 4 style sheets
+ 25 graphic files

Case1

map.htm
nhpoly.htm
notes.htm
poli.css
+ 13 HTML files
+ 2 graphic files

Case2

browyer.css
listing.htm
+ 17 graphic files

Case3

messier.htm
+ 9 HTML files
+ 2 style sheets
+ 21 graphic files

Case4

scenelist.htm
tempa1s1.htm - tempa5s1.htm
tempest.htm
tempest.jpg
weblinks.htm
ws.css

Working with XHTML

Creating a Well-Formed, Valid Document

Case | Wizard Works Fireworks

Wizard Works is one of the largest sellers of brand-name and customized fireworks in the central states. Its Web site produces the bulk of the company's sales. Tom Blaska, the head of advertising for Wizard Works, helps develop the content and design of the company's Web site. Because the Web site has been around for many years, some of the code dates back to the earliest versions of HTML. Tom would like the Web site code to be updated to reflect current standards and practices. Specifically, he wants you to look into rewriting the Web site code in XHTML rather than HTML. He also would like you to find ways to verify that the code used by Wizard Works meets XHTML standards.

Starting Data Files

Tutorial.09 →

Tutorial	Review	Case1	Case2	Case3	Case4
dtd_list.txt	dtd_list.txt	breaktxt.htm	dtd_list.txt	casttxt.htm	address.txt
workstxt.htm	founttxt.htm	dinnrtxt.htm	gargtxt.htm	dtd_list.txt	astro.txt
wwtxt.css	+ 2 graphic	dtd_list.txt	+ 5 graphic	+ 6 graphic	chem.txt
+ 4 graphic	files	lunchtxt.htm	files	files	dtd_list.txt
files		+ 4 graphic		hebdtxt.htm	+ 1 graphic
		files		hightxt.htm	file
				laketxt.htm	elect.txt
				scottxt.htm	eng.txt
				+ 4 HTML	physics.txt
				files	

Session 9.1

Introducing XHTML

You meet with Tom to discuss upgrading the Wizard Works site to conform to the current standards for XHTML. He has brought files for the site's home page to the meeting and he suggests that you upgrade the home page file to XHTML standards before continuing to the rest of the Web site.

To open the Wizard Works home page:

▶ 1. Use your text editor to open the **workstxt.htm** and **wwtxt.css** files from the tutorial.09\tutorial folder included with your Data Files. Enter *your name* and *the date* in the comment section of each file and save them as **works.htm** and **ww.css**, respectively, in the same folder.

▶ 2. Open **works.htm** in your Web browser. Figure 9-1 shows the current layout and design of the page.

Figure 9-1	Wizard Works home page

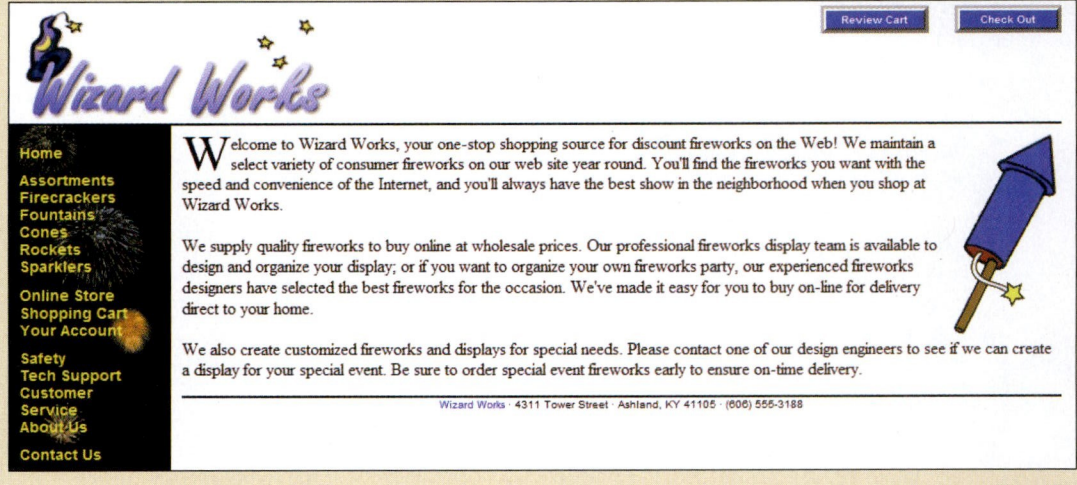

Before you can create your first XHTML document, you should review some of the history of the language. The beginnings of XHTML go back to SGML.

SGML

Standard Generalized Markup Language or **SGML** is a language introduced in 1980 that describes the structure and content of documents or any type of information that is readable by machines. SGML is **device-independent** and **system-independent**, meaning that documents written in SGML can be used, in theory, on almost any type of device under almost any type of operating system. SGML has been and remains the chosen vehicle for creating structured documents in businesses and government organizations of all sizes. Think of the daunting task involved in documenting all of the parts used in a jet airplane while at the same time organizing those documents so that engineers, mechanics, and developers can use them to quickly retrieve and edit information they need. SGML provides tools to manage documentation projects of this magnitude.

However, because of its power, scope, and flexibility, SGML is a difficult language to learn and apply. The official specification for SGML is over 150 pages long and covers some scenarios and cases that are rarely encountered by even the most experienced programmer. This means that the use of SGML is limited to organizations that can afford the cost and overhead of maintaining complex SGML environments. For example, SGML is not intended for the World Wide Web, where Web page authors need a language that is easy to use.

HTML as an SGML Application

SGML is more often used in creating **SGML applications**, which are markup languages that are based on the SGML architecture and that can be applied to specific, not general, types of information. One such SGML application is HTML. Because HTML is an SGML application, it shares several of the properties of SGML, such as device-independence, which is why the same Web page can be rendered by PCs, cell phones, printers, and screen readers.

One problem with HTML that you may have noticed is that various Web browsers developed their own unique flavors of HTML to provide customers with new and useful features not available with other browsers. For example, the Netscape browser saw a need for frames, so it introduced a version of HTML that included the frameset and frame elements, both of which were not part of standard HTML at that time. Likewise, Microsoft saw a need for internal frames and introduced the iframe element into Internet Explorer— another innovation that represented a departure from standard HTML. Although these extensions were later adopted into the official HTML specifications by the World Wide Web Consortium (W3C), many other extensions were not adopted—for example, Internet Explorer's marquee element used to create blocks of scrolling text. The result can some- times be a confusing mixture of competing HTML standards—one kind of HTML for each browser and, even worse, for each browser version. Although the innovations offered by Netscape, Microsoft, and others certainly increased the scope and power of HTML, they did so at the expense of clarity. Web designers could no longer create Web sites without taking a lot of time and effort to ensure their sites worked across various browsers and browser versions.

A second problem with HTML is that it can be applied inconsistently. For example, the following code does not follow HTML specifications because the h1 element has not been closed with an ending </h1> tag:

```
<body>
   <h1>Web Page Title
</body>
```

Although this code does not follow the correct syntax, most browsers render it correctly. Likewise, the following code would likely be interpreted correctly even though the col- span attribute value is not enclosed in quotation marks:

```
<td colspan=2>Heading</td>
```

Although a browser that is very forgiving of mistakes in syntax might seem beneficial to the Web page designer, it also can cause confusion as different Web pages employ HTML code in markedly different ways. This behavior also affects the browser design. By mak- ing allowances for inconsistently applied HTML code, the source code for the browser must be larger and more complex to deal with all contingencies. This can become an issue for browsers that run on handheld devices, which are more limited in the space they allot for software. So it is actually better for everyone if Web page code adheres to certain standards for content and structure. The path to a cleaner version of HTML involved rewriting HTML in terms of XML.

XML and XHTML

Extensible Markup Language or **XML** can be thought of as "SGML light"—a language like SGML used to create markup languages but without SGML's complexity and size. XML has been used to create several markup languages, including MathML for mathematical content, CML for documenting chemical structures, and MusicML for describing musical scores. Individual users can also create their own markup languages tailored for specific needs. For example, a business might design an XML document that contains elements for recording inventory and pricing data. This code

```
<work>
    <work-number>K. 331</work-number>
    <work-title>Piano Sonata in A Major</work-title>
</work>
<identification>
    <creator type="composer">Wolfgang Amadeus Mozart</creator>
    <rights>Copyright 2003 Recordare LLC</rights>
</identification>
```

is an excerpt from a MusicML document describing Mozart's *Piano Sonata in A Major*. Aside from the different tag names, the appearance of this code is very similar to what you've seen with HTML, which is to be expected because both are markup languages. This leads to **XHTML**, which is a reformulation of HTML written in XML. As with HTML and XML, the W3C maintains the specifications and standards for XHTML. The W3C has released or is in the process of developing different versions of XHTML. Figure 9-2 summarizes these versions.

| Figure 9-2 | Versions of XHTML |

Version	Date Released	Description
XHTML 1.0	2001	This version is a reformulation of HTML 4.01 in XML and combines the strength of HTML 4.0 with the power of XML. XHTML brings the rigor of XML to Web pages and provides standards for more robust Web content on a wide range of browser platforms.
XHTML 1.1	2002	A minor update to XHTML 1.0 that allows for modularity and simplifies writing extensions to the language.
XHTML 2.0	not yet released	The latest version, designed to remove most of the presentational features left in HTML. XHTML 2.0 is not backward-compatible with XHTML 1.1.
XHTML 5.0	not yet released	A version of HTML 5.0 written under the specifications of XML; unlike XHTML 2.0, XHTML 5.0 will be backward-compatible with XHTML 1.1.

The most widely supported version of XHTML is XHTML 1.0, with the specifications most closely matching the specifications for HTML 4.0 (the latest W3C version of HTML at the time of this writing). XHTML 1.1 is a restructuring of XHTML 1.0 in which different elements are placed within modules. This allows browsers to support only the portions of the XHTML language that are relevant to their needs. Figure 9-3 describes some of the different modules in XHTML 1.1.

XHTML 1.1 modules | Figure 9-3

Module	Use	Supported Elements and Attributes
Structure	Used to define the basic structure of the document	body, head, html, title
Metainformation	Used to add meta-information to the document	meta
Text	Used for text content	abbr, acronym, address, blockquote, br, cite, code, dfn, div, em, h1, h2, h3, h4, h5, h6, kbd, p, pre, q, samp, span, strong, var
Presentation	Used for presentational elements	b, big, hr, i, small, sub, sup, tt
List	Used for list content	dl, dt, dd, ol, ul, li
Object	Used for embedded objects	object, param
Image	Used for inline images	img
Client-side Image Map	Used for client-side image maps	area, map
Hypertext	Used for links	a
Frames	Used for frames	frameset, frame, noframes
Iframe	Used for inline frames	iframe
Forms	Used for Web forms	button, fieldset, form, input, label, legend, select, optgroup, option, textarea
Table	Used for Web tables	caption, col, colgroup, table, tbody, td, tfoot, th, thead, tr
Scripting	Used for adding scripts to the document	noscript, script
Style Sheet	Used for accessing style sheets	style
Style Attribute	Used for adding the style attribute to individual elements	attribute: style attribute (deprecated)
Legacy	Used for deprecated elements and attributes	basefont, center, dir, font, isindex, menu, s, strike, uattributes: align, alink, background, bgcolor, color, face, link, size, text, type, vlink

For example, an aural browser that works only with text might support only modules that deal with text content, and not modules that deal with images or embedded objects. This enables browser developers to reduce the sizes of their applications to fit the requirements of specific devices. Browser developers can also use XHTML Basic, a version of XHTML 1.1 that limits the modules to those useful with handheld devices.

XHTML 2.0 is still in draft form and so it is not supported in the Web community. When completed, this version is expected to represent a great departure from previous versions of XHTML and HTML. In fact, documents written in XHTML 2.0 will not be backward-compatible with earlier XHTML versions—a point that concerns many developers. The development of XHTML 2.0 will likely require the development of new XHTML modules or revisions to existing XHTML modules. For this reason, a great deal of development effort is also going into HTML 5.0 (and its XML version, XHTML 5.0), which will provide more support for multimedia elements as well as features for entering and retrieving data.

In the end, any future version of XHTML must have wide-ranging browser support before it can be easily adopted for general use. Browser support does not occur automatically, nor is acceptance of any revisions to XHTML uniform across all browsers. So even after the specifications for new versions of XHTML are finalized, it will be many years before XHTML 1.0 can be entirely replaced.

Creating an XHTML Document

Because XHTML documents are also considered XML documents, the first line of an XHTML file contains a prolog indicating that the document adheres to the syntax rules of XML. The form of the XML prolog is

```
<?xml version="value" encoding="type" ?>
```

where the version attribute indicates the XML version of the document and the encoding attribute specifies character encoding. XHTML documents are written in XML 1.0. The encoding depends on the character set being used; but unless you are including special international characters, you can set the encoding value to UTF-8 (for a discussion of encoding and character sets, see Tutorial 2). So for most XHTML documents, you can include the following prolog:

```
<?xml version="1.0" encoding="UTF-8" ?>
```

Reference Window | **Adding an XML Prolog**

- To declare that a document is written in XML, enter
  ```
  <?xml version="value" encoding="type" ?>
  ```
  as the first line of the file, where the version attribute indicates the XML version of the document and the encoding attribute specifies the character encoding.
- For XHTML documents, use the prolog
  ```
  <?xml version="1.0" encoding="UTF-8" ?>
  ```
  where *row1*, *row2*, *row3*, etc. are the heights of the rows in pixels or percentages.

Tip

You can also indicate the encoding used in your XHTML file by adding a meta element to the head section with the content attribute set to the MIME type and character set employed in the document.

The first thing you need to do for Tom's Wizard Works file is to add an XML prolog.

To insert an XML prolog:

1. Return to the **works.htm** file in your text editor.

2. At the top of the file, insert the following XML prolog, as shown in Figure 9-4:

   <?xml version="1.0" encoding="UTF-8" ?>

Figure 9-4 | **Inserting the XML prolog**

```
<?xml version="1.0" encoding="UTF-8" ?>
<html>
<head>
```

3. Save your changes to the file.

Note that the prolog is not strictly required for XHTML documents and can be omitted. You should also be aware that older browsers might not be able to interpret XHTML documents that start with a prolog, though this has become less of a problem in recent years.

Creating Well-Formed Documents

To make XML documents follow specific rules for content and structure, they are evaluated with an XML parser. An **XML parser** is a program that checks the document for errors in syntax and content, and reports any errors it finds. An XML document that employs the correct syntax is known as a **well-formed** document, as shown in Figure 9-5.

Testing for well-formedness | Figure 9-5

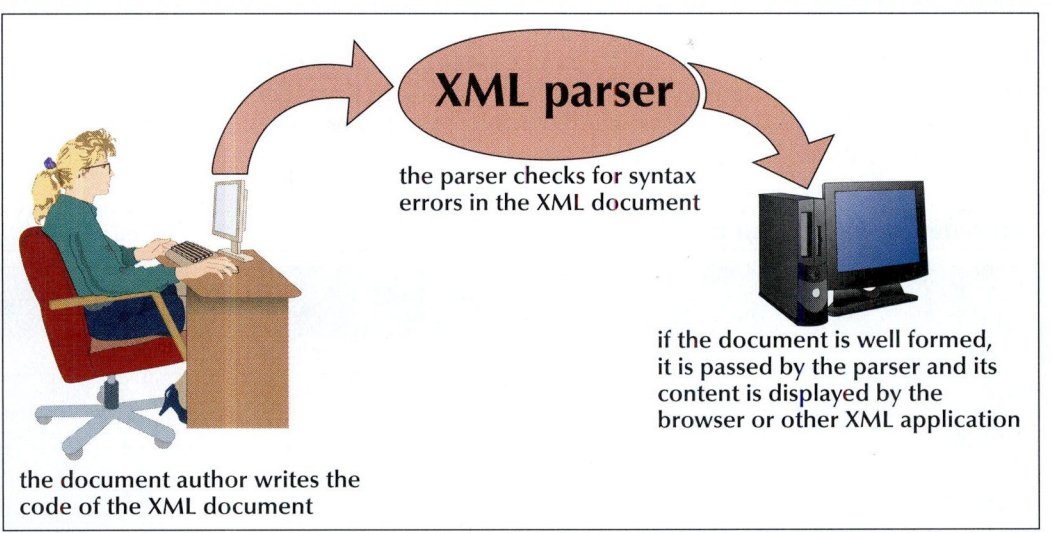

XML parser

the parser checks for syntax errors in the XML document

if the document is well formed, it is passed by the parser and its content is displayed by the browser or other XML application

the document author writes the code of the XML document

With HTML, browsers usually accept documents that violate HTML syntax as long as the violation is not too severe. However, an XML parser will reject any XML document that is not well formed. For example, the sample code described earlier

```
<body>
    <h1>Web Page Title
</body>
```

is not an example of well-formed code because it violates the basic rule that every two-sided tag must have both an opening and closing tag. When you write XHTML code, it's important to be familiar with all of the rules of proper syntax. Figure 9-6 lists seven syntax requirements that all XML documents (and therefore all XHTML documents) must follow.

Rules for well-formed XML | Figure 9-6

Rule	Incorrect	Correct
Element names must be lowercase	`<P>This is a paragraph.</P>`	`<p>This is a paragraph.</p>`
Elements must be properly nested	`<p>This text is <b>bold. </p></b>`	`<p>This text is <b>bold. </b></p>`
All elements must be closed	`<p>This is the first paragraph.` `<p>This is the second paragraph.`	`<p>This is the first paragraph.</p>` `<p>This is the second paragraph.</p>`
Empty elements must be terminated	`This is a line break `	`This is a line break `
Attribute names must be lowercase	`<td ALIGN="right">`	`<td align="right">`
Attribute values must be quoted	`<table width=620>`	`<table width="620">`
Attributes must have values	`<option selected>`	`<option selected="selected">`

In addition to the rules specified in Figure 9-6, all XML documents must also include a single root element that contains all other elements. For XHTML, that root element is the html element. You should already be familiar with most of these rules because you've been working with well-formed HTML from the first tutorial. However, if you examine older Web pages you may find document code that violates that basic syntax, but which most browsers nonetheless support.

In some older HTML documents, you might find cases of **attribute minimization**, a situation in which some attributes lack attribute values. XHTML does not allow attribute minimization. Figure 9-7 lists the minimized attributes that are in some HTML documents, along with their XHTML-compliant versions.

Figure 9-7 **Attribute minimization in HTML and XHTML**

HTML	XHTML
compact	compact="compact"
checked	checked="checked"
declare	declare="declare"
readonly	readonly="readonly"
disabled	disabled="disabled"
selected	selected="selected"
defer	defer="defer"
ismap	ismap="ismap"
nohref	nohref="nohref"
noshade	noshade="noshade"
nowrap	nowrap="nowrap"
multiple	multiple="multiple"
noresize	noresize="noresize"

For example, in earlier versions of HTML, the following code was used to indicate that a radio button should be selected by default:

```
<input type="radio" checked>
```

In XHTML, this code would be rewritten as

```
<input type="radio" checked="checked" />
```

Failure to make this change would cause the XHTML document to be rejected as not well formed.

Tip

A minimized attribute can be updated to XHTML by using the name of the attribute as the attribute's value.

Creating Valid XHTML Documents

In addition to being well formed, XML documents can also be checked to see if they are valid. A **valid** document is a well-formed document that also contains only approved elements, attributes, and other features of the language. If the code

```
<body>
   <mainhead>Web Page Title</mainhead>
</body>
```

were entered into an XHTML file, the code would be considered well formed because it complies with the syntax rules of XML—but it would not constitute valid XHTML code because XHTML does not support the <mainhead> tag. To specify what the correct content and structure is for a document, the developers of an XML-based language can create a collection of rules called the **document type definition** or **DTD**. As shown in Figure 9-8, an XML parser tests the content of the document against the rules in the DTD. If it does not conform to those rules, the parser will reject the document as not valid.

Testing for validity   Figure 9-8

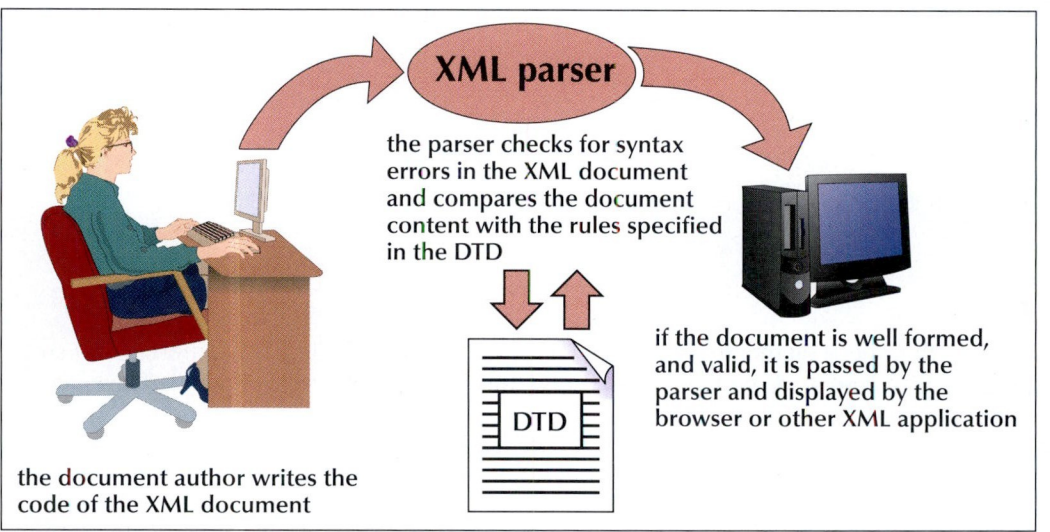

the document author writes the code of the XML document

the parser checks for syntax errors in the XML document and compares the document content with the rules specified in the DTD

if the document is well formed, and valid, it is passed by the parser and displayed by the browser or other XML application

For example, an XML document for a business might contain elements that store the name of each product in inventory. The DTD for that document could require that each product name element be accompanied by an id attribute value, and that no products share the same name or id. An XML parser would reject any XML document for that business that didn't satisfy those rules, even if the document was well formed. In this way, XML differs from HTML which does not include a mechanism to force Web page authors to adhere to rules for syntax and content.

Transitional, Frameset, and Strict DTDs

There are several different DTDs associated with HTML and XHTML documents. Some of the DTDs represent older versions of HTML. For example, if you want to create a document that is validated only against the standards of HTML 2.0, there is a DTD available for that. However, for most purposes you'll focus on the three DTDs used with XHTML 1.0:

- **transitional:** The transitional DTD supports many of the presentational features of HTML, including the deprecated elements and attributes. It is best used for older documents that contain deprecated features.
- **frameset:** The frameset DTD is used for documents containing frames and also supports deprecated elements and attributes.
- **strict:** The strict DTD does not allow any presentational features or deprecated HTML elements and attributes, and does not support frames or inline frames. It is best used for documents that must strictly conform to the latest standards.

If you need to support older browsers, you should use the transitional DTD, which recognizes deprecated elements and attributes such as the font element and the bgcolor attribute. If you need to support older browsers in a framed Web site, you should use the frameset DTD. If you only need to support more current browsers and want to weed out any use of deprecated features, and you have no need to support frames, then you should use the strict DTD.

In addition to browser-specific elements (such as Internet Explorer's marquee element), the following elements are not allowed under the strict DTD:

- applet
- basefont
- center
- dir
- font
- frame
- frameset
- iframe
- isindex
- menu
- noframes
- s
- strike
- u

Note that these elements are allowed in the transitional DTD. The frameset DTD supports these elements as well as the frame, frameset, and noframes elements. Therefore, the code

```
<font color="red">Wizard Works</font>
```

which uses the deprecated font element to format text, would be considered valid code under the transitional and frameset DTDs but not under the strict DTD.

In addition to prohibiting the use of certain elements, the strict DTD also enforces a particular structure on the document. For example, you cannot place a block-level element within an inline element. Figure 9-9 lists the prohibited child elements under the strict DTD.

Figure 9-9   **Child elements prohibited under the strict DTD**

Element	Prohibited Children
inline element	block-level elements
body	a, abbr, acronym, b, bdo, big, br, button, cite, code, dfn, em, i, img, input, kbd, label, map, object, q, samp, select, small, span, strong, sub, sup, textarea, tt, var
button	button, form, fieldset, iframe, input, isindex, label, select, textarea
blockquote	a, abbr, acronym, b, bdo, big, br, button, cite, code, dfn, em, i, img, input, kbd, label, map, object, q, samp, select, small, span, strong, sub, sup, textarea, tt, var
form	a, abbr, acronym, b, bdo, big, br, cite, code, dfn, em, form, i, img, kbd, map, object, q, samp, small, span, strong, sub, sup, tt, var
label	label
pre	big, img, object, small, sub, sup
all other page elements	big, small

For example, the following code would be disallowed under the strict DTD because it places an inline image as a child of the body element:

```
<body>
   <img src="logo.jpg" alt="Wizard Works" />
</body>
```

However, you could make this code compliant with the strict DTD by placing the inline image within a paragraph:

```
<body>
   <p><img src="logo.jpg" alt="Wizard Works" /></p>
</body>
```

The goal of this rule is to enforce the inline nature of the img element. Because an inline image is displayed inline within a block element such as a paragraph, it should not be found outside of that context. For the same reason, form elements like the input or select elements should be found only within a form, not outside of one.

Finally, all three DTDs require that the following elements be present in every valid XHTML document:

- html
- head
- title
- body

Although the html, head, and body elements are generally expected under HTML, XHTML requires that every valid document include the title element as well. Any XHTML document that omits the title element is rejected.

The Valid Use of Attributes

DTDs also include different rules for attributes and their use. Under the strict DTD, deprecated attributes are not allowed. A list of these prohibited attributes with their corresponding elements is displayed in Figure 9-10.

Figure 9-10 ▶ **Prohibited attributes under the strict DTD**

Element	Prohibited Attributes
a	target
area	target
base	target
body	alink, bgcolor, link, text, vlink,
br	clear
caption	align
div	align
dl	compact
form	name, target
h*n*	align
hr	align, noshade, size, width
img	align, border, hspace, name, vspace
input	align
li	type, value
link	target
map	name
object	align, border, hspace, vspace
ol	compact, start
p	align
pre	width
script	language
table	align, bgcolor
td	bgcolor, height, nowrap, width
th	bgcolor, height, nowrap, width
tr	bgcolor
ul	type, compact

Many of the attributes listed in Figure 9-10 are so-called presentational attributes because they define how the browser should render the associated element on the Web page. All of the attributes listed in Figure 9-10 are supported in the transitional and frameset DTDs. Therefore, the code

```
<img src="logo.jpg" alt="Wizard Works" align="left" />
```

which uses the align attribute to float an inline image on the left margin of the page, would not be valid under the strict DTD because the align attribute is prohibited; however, it would be allowed under the frameset and transitional DTDs. To make this code valid under all three DTDs, you could replace the align attribute with an inline style that employs the float style:

```
<img src="logo.jpg" alt="Wizard Works" style="float: left" />
```

You may also find that you must make changes to older HTML code in the use of the name attribute. The strict DTD requires the use of the id attribute in place of the name attribute, so the tags

```
<a name="top">
<form name="order">
```

```
<img name="logo" />
<map name="parkmap">
```

would be written in strict XHTML as

```
<a id="top">
<form id="order">
<img id="logo" />
<map id="parkmap">
```

Finally, unlike the transitional and frameset DTDs, the strict DTD does not support the target attribute. This means that you cannot open links in secondary browser windows if you want your code to be strictly compliant with XHTML. This decision was not greeted with enthusiasm by many developers, so the target attribute was reintroduced in XHTML 1.1 as part of the Target module. If your users' browsers support XHTML 1.1 and the Target module, you can use the target attribute in all of your links.

Whereas some attributes are prohibited, others are required. A list of the required attributes and the elements they're associated with is shown in Figure 9-11.

Tip

The transitional and frameset DTDs also require the use of the id attribute, but do not reject documents that contain both the name and id attributes. For those DTDs, it's best to include both attributes if you want to make your code backward-compatible.

Required XHTML attributes ◁ **Figure 9-11**

Element	Required Attributes
applet	height, width
area	alt
base	href
basefont	size
bdo	dir
form	action
img	alt, src
map	id
meta	content
optgroup	label
param	name
script	type
style	type
textarea	cols, rows

For example, an inline image is valid only if it contains both the src and alt attributes, and a form element is valid only if it contains an action attribute.

Although the list of rules for well-formed and valid documents may seem long and onerous, they simply reflect good coding practice. You would not, for example, want to create a Web page without a page title, or an inline image without alternate text. In addition to being required for valid well-formed code, there are many advantages to using DTDs. Perhaps their most significant advantage is the help they provide in troubleshooting documents. If you create or edit your XHTML code by hand, you can easily make mistakes in syntax, content, or structure. Using a DTD enables you to test your document and correct any mistakes.

Inserting the DOCTYPE Declaration

To specify which DTD is used by the XHTML document, you add a DOCTYPE declaration directly after the XML prolog. The syntax of the DOCTYPE declaration for a general XML document is

```
<!DOCTYPE root type "id" "url">
```

where *root* is the name of the root element of the document, *type* identifies the type of DTD (either PUBLIC or SYSTEM), *id* is an id associated with the DTD, and *url* is the location of an external file containing the DTD rules. For XHTML documents, you set the value *root* to html and the *type* value to PUBLIC. Web browsers do not need to store the location of the external file containing the rules of any of the three DTDs. Therefore, the DOCTYPE declaration for XHTML documents has the simpler form

```
<!DOCTYPE html PUBLIC "id">
```

where *id* is the id for the DTD. Figure 9-12 lists the complete DOCTYPE declarations for different versions of HTML and XHTML. Note that you can validate a document not only against different versions of XHTML 1.0, but even down to the W3C's specifications for HTML 2.0, which can be beneficial if you need to develop code for older browser versions. You can access the most recent versions of these DTDs on the W3C Web site.

Figure 9-12 ▷ **DOCTYPE declarations for different versions of HTML and XHTML**

DTD	DOCTYPE
HTML 2.0	`<!DOCTYPE html PUBLIC "-//IETF//DTD HTML 2.0//EN">`
HTML 3.2	`<!DOCTYPE html PUBLIC "-//W3C//DTD HTML 3.2 Final//EN">`
HTML 4.01 strict	`<!DOCTYPE html PUBLIC "-//W3C//DTD HTML 4.01//EN"` `"http://www.w3.org/TR/html4/strict.dtd">`
HTML 4.01 transitional	`<!DOCTYPE html PUBLIC "-//W3C//DTD HTML 4.01 Transitional//EN"` `"http://www.w3.org/TR/html4/loose.dtd">`
HTML 4.01 frameset	`<!DOCTYPE html PUBLIC "-//W3C//DTD HTML 4.01 Frameset//EN"` `"http://www.w3.org/TR/html4/frameset.dtd">`
XHTML 1.0 strict	`<!DOCTYPE html PUBLIC "-//W3C//DTD XHTML 1.0 Strict//EN"` `"http://www.w3.org/TR/xhtml1/DTD/xhtml1-strict.dtd">`
XHTML 1.0 transitional	`<!DOCTYPE html PUBLIC "-//W3C//DTD XHTML 1.0 Transitional//EN"` `"http://www.w3.org/TR/xhtml1/DTD/xhtml1-transitional.dtd">`
XHTML 1.0 frameset	`<!DOCTYPE html PUBLIC "-//W3C//DTD XHTML 1.0 Frameset//EN"` `"http://www.w3.org/TR/xhtml1/DTD/xhtml1-frameset.dtd">`
XHTML 1.1	`<!DOCTYPE html PUBLIC "-//W3C//DTD XHTML 1.1//EN"` `"http://www.w3.org/TR/xhtml11/DTD/xhtml11.dtd">`

Setting the Document DTD

- To apply the XHTML 1.0 strict DTD, add the following line after the XML declaration:
  ```
  <!DOCTYPE html PUBLIC "-//W3C//DTD XHTML 1.0 Strict//EN"
   "http://www.w3.org/TR/xhtml1/DTD/xhtml1-strict.dtd">
  ```
- To apply the XHTML 1.0 transitional DTD, use the following:
  ```
  <!DOCTYPE html PUBLIC "-//W3C//DTD XHTML 1.0 Transitional//EN"
   "http://www.w3.org/TR/xhtml1/DTD/xhtml1-transitional.dtd">
  ```
- To apply the XHTML 1.0 frameset DTD, use the following:
  ```
  <!DOCTYPE html PUBLIC "-//W3C//DTD XHTML 1.0 Frameset//EN"
   "http://www.w3.org/TR/xhtml1/DTD/xhtml1-frameset.dtd">
  ```

Tom suggests that you associate the Wizard Works Web site with the transitional DTD for XHTML 1.0. To do that, you'll add the DOCTYPE declaration for XHTML 1.0 transitional. Because the code for the DOCTYPE declaration can be long and complicated, a text file with the declarations from Figure 9-12 has been created for you to copy from.

To insert a DOCTYPE declaration:

▶ 1. In your text editor, open the **dtd_list.txt** file from the tutorial.09\tutorial folder included with your Data Files.

▶ 2. Copy the DOCTYPE declaration for the XHTML 1.0 transitional DTD—the third DTD from the bottom of the file.

▶ 3. Close the file and return to the **works.htm** file in your text editor.

▶ 4. Directly after the XML prolog, paste the copied DOCTYPE declaration. Figure 9-13 highlights the revised code in the file.

Inserting the DOCTYPE declaration ◀ **Figure 9-13**

```
<?xml version="1.0" encoding="UTF-8" ?>

<!DOCTYPE html PUBLIC "-//W3C//DTD XHTML 1.0 Transitional//EN"
   "http://www.w3.org/TR/xhtml1/DTD/xhtml1-transitional.dtd">

<html>
<head>
```

▶ 5. Save your changes to the file.

Setting the XHTML Namespace

Another modification you can make to the works.htm file is to add a namespace declaration to the html element. Understanding the concept of a namespace requires looking more into how XML operates. As was noted earlier, XHTML is only one of hundreds of languages built on the foundation of XML. For example, another XML-based language, MathML, is used for documents containing mathematical content, symbols, equations, and operations. For a math professor interested in creating a Web site, MathML provides many elements and attributes not available with HTML or XHTML. It would be useful for the professor to have a document language that combined features from both XHTML and MathML.

Recall from the history of HTML that browser developers dealt with the issue of needing new features in their documents by adding extensions to the HTML language. XML (and through it, XHTML) deals with this problem by allowing elements and attributes from several different XML-based languages to be combined within a single document. Ideally, therefore, our math professor could combine elements of XHTML and MathML in his document without having to invent a new language or modify the specifications of an old one.

The problem is that you need a way of identifying which element goes with which language. This is done by using namespaces. A **namespace** is a unique identifier for the elements and attributes originating from one particular language, such as XHTML or MathML. There are two types of namespaces: default and local. For now you'll only focus on the default namespace. A **default namespace** is the namespace that is assumed to be applied to the root element and any element within it—which includes, by default, any element within the document. To declare a default namespace, you add the xmlns (XML namespace) attribute

```
<root xmlns="namespace">
```

to the markup tag for the document's root element, where *root* is the name of the root element and *namespace* is the namespace id. Every XML-based language has a namespace id. For example, if you wish to declare that the elements in your document belong to the XHTML namespace by default, you would add the following attribute to the opening <html> tag:

```
<html xmlns="http://www.w3.org/1999/xhtml">
```

The namespace id for XHTML looks like a url, but it's not treated as one by the XML parser. The id can actually be any string of characters as long as it uniquely identifies the document namespace. For XHTML, it was decided to use http://www.w3.org/1999/xhtml as the unique identifier.

Reference Window | **Setting the XHTML Namespace**

- To set XHTML as the default namespace for a document, add the xmlns attribute to the html element with the following value:
  ```
  <html xmlns="http://www.w3.org/1999/xhtml">
  ```

If you don't intend to combine different XML-based languages within the same document, it's still a good idea to add a namespace to an XHTML file. In practical terms, an XHTML document is still interpretable by most browsers without a namespace. However, the W3C requires that the XHTML namespace be added to the html element to avoid any possible confusion in the future when mixed documents become more prevalent. Tom would like you to add the default namespace to his works.htm file.

To add the XHTML namespace:

▶ **1.** Locate the opening <html> tag in the **works.htm** file.

▶ **2.** Within the tag, insert the following attribute, as shown in Figure 9-14:
```
xmlns="http://www.w3.org/1999/xhtml"
```

```
<?xml version="1.0" encoding="UTF-8" ?>

<!DOCTYPE html PUBLIC "-//W3C//DTD XHTML 1.0 Transitional//EN"
  "http://www.w3.org/TR/xhtml1/DTD/xhtml1-transitional.dtd">

<html xmlns="http://www.w3.org/1999/xhtml">
<head>
```

▶ **3.** Close the file, saving your changes.

▶ **4.** If you want to take a break before starting the next session, you can close any open files or programs now.

Namespaces in Compound Documents | InSight

One of the features of XML is the ability to combine several languages into a single document. For the elements of the different languages to coexist, you assign one language as the default namespace for the document so that all elements are assumed to belong to that language. Elements that do not belong to the default namespace belong instead to a **local namespace**. The existence of a local namespace is indicated by adding a prefix to the markup tag as follows

```
<prefix:element> ...</prefix:element>
```

where *prefix* is the prefix for the local namespace and *element* is the name of element within that local namespace. For example, the following code contains elements from both XHTML and MathML (the markup language for mathematical documents):

```
<p>
   <ml:mi>x</ml:mi>
   <ml:mo>+</ml:mo>
   <ml:mn>1</ml:mn>
</p>
```

The namespace prefix for MathML is ml, and the MathML element names are mi, mo, and mn. To create a local namespace, you add the attribute

```
xmlns:prefix="namespace"
```

to the html root element, where *prefix* is the prefix you'll use to mark elements in this local namespace and *namespace* is the namespace id. Every XML-based language has a unique namespace id. For example, to declare a local namespace for MathML, you would add the following code to the html element:

```
<html xmlns:ml="http://www.w3.org/1998/math/MathML">
```

Most browsers do not include built-in support to render elements from non-XHTML languages, but you can often add support for different XML-based languages by installing browser add-ins. You can also create style sheets to display non-XHTML elements on your Web page. See your browser's documentation for more information.

With the addition of the XHTML namespace, you have converted the Tom's HTML document into XHTML format. In the next session, you'll test this document to determine whether it passes the W3C tests for well-formedness and validity.

1. What is a well-formed document? What is a valid document?
2. Why is the following code not well formed?:

   ```
   <img src="logo.jpg" alt="Wizard Works">
   ```

   How would you correct it?

3. Why is the following code not well formed?:

   ```
   <input type="radio" disabled />
   ```

   How would you correct it?

4. Why is the following code not valid under strict XHTML?:

   ```
   <blockquote>
       For more information go to the <a href="faq.htm"FAQ page</a>
   </blockquote>
   ```

   Suggest a correction for the problem.

5. Why is the following code not valid under strict XHTML?:

   ```
   <img src="logo.jpg" alt="Wizard Works" align="right" />
   ```

   How would you fix it?

6. Why is the following code not valid under transitional XHTML?:

   ```
   <map name="parkmap"> ... </map>
   ```

   Suggest a change to the code that would correct the problem and make the code backward-compatible with older browsers.

7. What declaration would you add to an XHTML document to associate it with the XHTML strict DTD?
8. What line do you add to the start of your file to declare it as an XML document?

Session 9.2

Testing under XHTML Transitional

In the last session you converted Tom's Web page document from HTML format into XHTML format. By adding the DOCTYPE declaration and XML namespace, you can test the document for well-formedness and validity. To test the document, you must submit the file to an XML parser. There are several parsers available on the Web. You'll use the one hosted on the W3C Web site.

To access the W3C validator page:

▶ 1. Use your browser to open the Web page at **http://validator.w3.org**.

▶ 2. Click the **Validate by File Upload** tab on the Web page.

   Trouble? Depending on the current format of the validator page, it might not exactly match the figures and screen shots in this session. Use whatever buttons or forms exist on the Web page.

▶ **3.** Click the **Browse** button and locate the **works.htm** file from the tutorial.09\tutorial folder included with your Data Files.

▶ **4.** Select the file and click the **Open** button. The filename and path will be displayed in the File input box, as shown in Figure 9-15.

Selecting a file for validation ◀ **Figure 9-15**

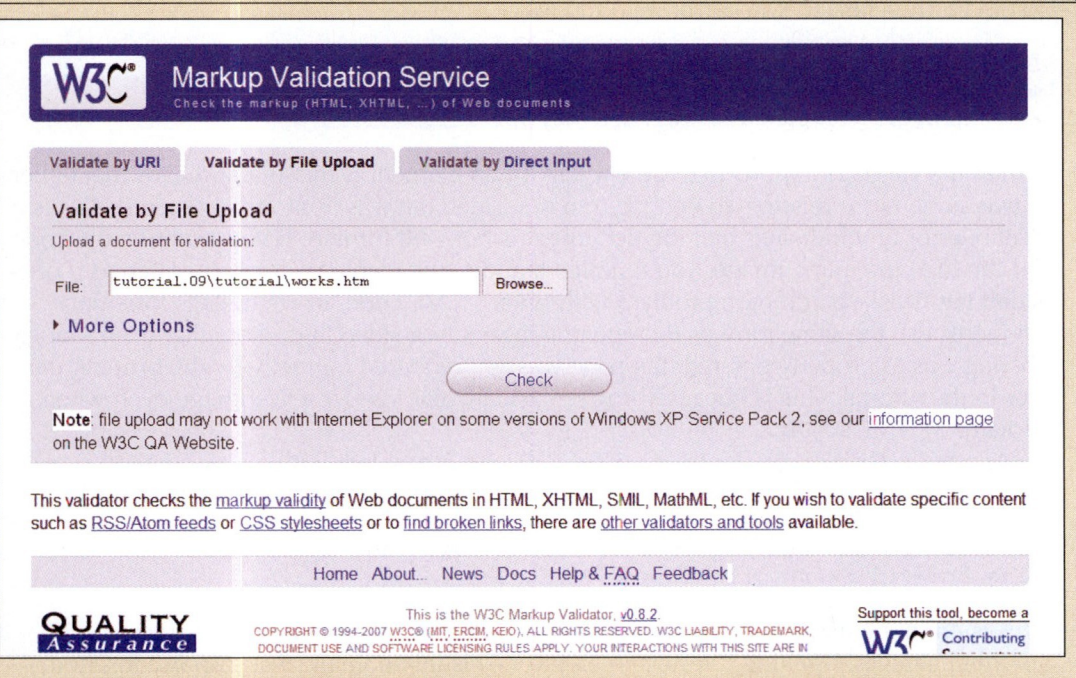

▶ **5.** Click the **Check** button. The validator reports several errors in the file, as shown in Figure 9-16.

Results of the first validation test ◀ **Figure 9-16**

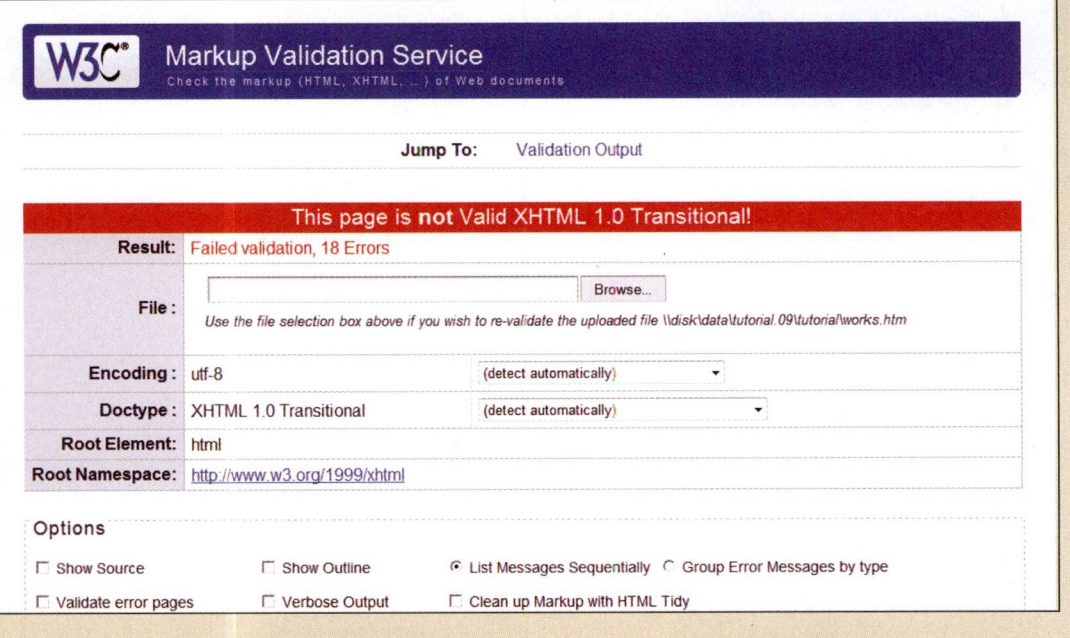

> **Tip**
>
> You can test a different DTD on the validator page without editing the file by selecting the DTD from the Doctype list box.

▶ **6.** Scroll down the Web page to read the validator's summary of the errors.

A total of 18 errors were reported by the validator. This doesn't mean that there are 18 separate mistakes in the file. In some cases, the same mistake results in several errors being noted in the report, and fixing one mistake can result in several of the errors reported by the validator being resolved. In a large error list, it's unlikely that you can fix everything at once. It's best to fix the most obvious mistakes first to reduce the size of the list, leaving the more subtle errors to be fixed last. Tom wants you to examine the error list in more detail. The first error reported was:

Line 28, column 55: **end tag for "img" omitted, but OMITTAG NO was specified**
`<img src="logo.jpg" alt="Wizard Works" align="left">`

When the validator reports that the end tag for an element is missing, it means that either a two-sided tag is missing an end tag or a one-sided tag was improperly entered. This is a syntax error and indicates that the document is not well formed. If you examine the code for the logo.jpg inline image, you'll notice that the img element was not written as a one-sided tag. This is a common problem with older HTML code, in which tags for empty elements use the same form as the opening tags of two-sided tags. Note that even though the tag was improperly entered, the page was still rendered correctly by the browser earlier in the tutorial. This is because browsers usually can render a Web page even when it violates XHTML syntax.

Another error reported by the browser indicates a problem with the document's validity:

Line 52, column 40: **required attribute "alt" not specified**
`<img src="firework.gif" align="right">`

This is an inline image without the alt attribute. Because the alt attribute is required for all inline images, omitting it results in an error. This inline image was also not inserted using a one-sided tag, resulting in a syntax error as well. You'll fix these errors and resubmit the file for testing.

To fix and resubmit the file:

► 1. Return to the **works.htm** file in your text editor.

► 2. Locate the img element for the logo.jpg file and change it to a one-sided tag using the proper syntax.

► 3. Locate the img element for the firework.gif image, add the attribute

   `alt=""`

   and change the tag to a one-sided tag. Figure 9-17 shows the revised code in the file.

Modifying the img elements in the document ◀ **Figure 9-17**

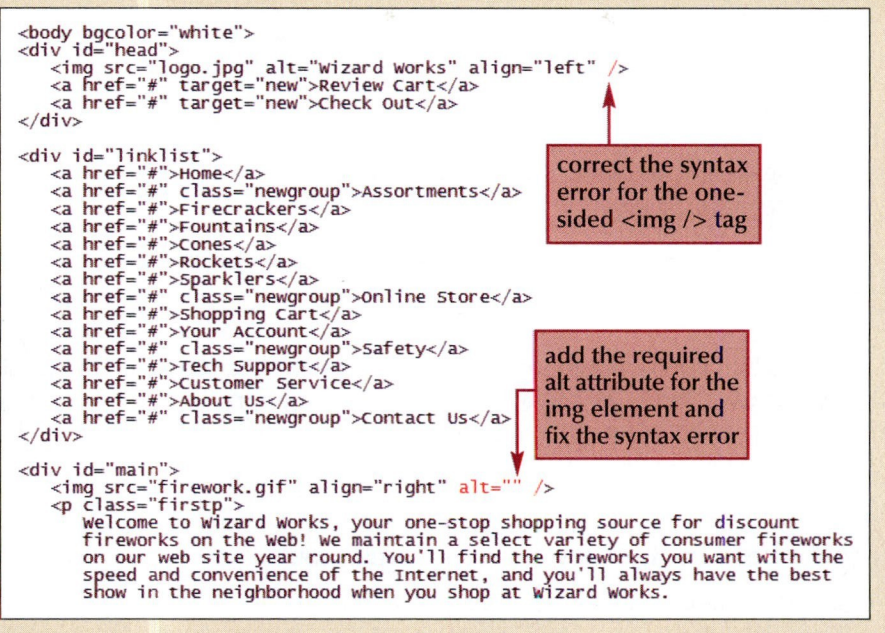

```
<body bgcolor="white">
<div id="head">
    <img src="logo.jpg" alt="wizard Works" align="left" />
    <a href="#" target="new">Review Cart</a>
    <a href="#" target="new">Check Out</a>
</div>

<div id="linklist">
    <a href="#">Home</a>
    <a href="#" class="newgroup">Assortments</a>
    <a href="#">Firecrackers</a>
    <a href="#">Fountains</a>
    <a href="#">Cones</a>
    <a href="#">Rockets</a>
    <a href="#">Sparklers</a>
    <a href="#" class="newgroup">Online Store</a>
    <a href="#">Shopping Cart</a>
    <a href="#">Your Account</a>
    <a href="#" class="newgroup">Safety</a>
    <a href="#">Tech Support</a>
    <a href="#">Customer Service</a>
    <a href="#">About Us</a>
    <a href="#" class="newgroup">Contact Us</a>
</div>

<div id="main">
    <img src="firework.gif" align="right" alt="" />
    <p class="firstp">
    welcome to wizard Works, your one-stop shopping source for discount
    fireworks on the web! we maintain a select variety of consumer fireworks
    on our web site year round. You'll find the fireworks you want with the
    speed and convenience of the Internet, and you'll always have the best
    show in the neighborhood when you shop at wizard works.
</div>
```

> correct the syntax error for the one-sided <img /> tag

> add the required alt attribute for the img element and fix the syntax error

▶ **4.** Save your changes to the file.

▶ **5.** Return to your Web browser and refresh or reload the Web page to resubmit the validation check on the **works.htm** file. You might be queried as to whether or not you wish to resend the previous information. If so, click the **Retry** or **OK** button.

Trouble? If clicking the Refresh or Reload button does not resubmit the page for testing, you can click the Browse button on the form to reselect the works.htm file from the tutorial.09\tutorial folder, and then click the Revalidate button.

Figure 9-18 shows the new validation report.

Tip

To test the code from international documents, select a different encoding value from the Encoding list box on the validator page.

Results of the second validation test ◀ **Figure 9-18**

W3C Markup Validation Service
Check the markup (HTML, XHTML, ...) of Web documents

Jump To: Validation Output

This page is **not** Valid XHTML 1.0 Transitional!

Result:	Failed validation, 12 Errors
File :	[ ] Browse... *Use the file selection box above if you wish to re-validate the uploadeded file \\disk\data\tutorial.09\tutorial\works.htm \tutorial\works.htm*
Encoding :	utf-8 — (detect automatically)
Doctype :	XHTML 1.0 Transitional — (detect automatically)
Root Element:	html
Root Namespace:	http://www.w3.org/1999/xhtml

Options

☐ Show Source   ☐ Show Outline   ⦿ List Messages Sequentially   ○ Group Error Messages by type

☐ Validate error pages   ☐ Verbose Output   ☐ Clean up Markup with HTML Tidy

By fixing these errors, you reduced the size of the error list from 18 to 12. You can trim that down even more. The first error in the latest list states

Line 59, column 5: **document type does not allow element "p" here; missing one of "object", "applet", "map", "iframe", "button", "ins", "del" start-tag**
`<p>`

which can indicate that an element has been improperly nested within the p element—but read on. Another error states

Line 78, column 5: **tag for "p" omitted, but OMITTAG NO was specified**
`</div>`

which indicates that the paragraph element was not properly closed with the closing `</p>` tag. In this case, the same mistake has caused both errors. By not closing the paragraph element, it appears that other elements have been improperly placed inside of it. By adding the closing tag, both errors should be corrected.

To fix the errors in the Web page paragraphs:

▶ 1. Return to the **works.htm** file in your text editor.

▶ 2. Locate the three paragraph elements in the main section and add closing `</p>` tags to each paragraph, as shown in Figure 9-19.

Figure 9-19 ▶ **Closing the paragraph elements**

```
<div id="main">
    <img src="firework.gif" align="right" alt="" />
    <p class="firstp">
        Welcome to Wizard Works, your one-stop shopping source for discount
        fireworks on the Web! We maintain a select variety of consumer fireworks
        on our web site year round. You'll find the fireworks you want with the
        speed and convenience of the Internet, and you'll always have the best
        show in the neighborhood when you shop at Wizard Works.</p>
    <p>
        We supply quality fireworks to buy online at wholesale prices. Our
        professional fireworks display team is available to design and organize
        your display; or if you want to organize your own fireworks party, our
        experienced fireworks designers have selected the best fireworks for the
        occasion. We've made it easy for you to buy on-line for delivery direct
        to your home.</p>
    <p>
        We also create customized fireworks and displays for special needs. Please
        contact one of our design engineers to see if we can create a display for
        your special event. Be sure to order special event fireworks early to ensure
        on-time delivery.</p>
```

▶ 3. Save your changes and return to the W3C validator page. Click the **Refresh** or **Reload** button in your browser to redo the validation check. As shown in Figure 9-20, the page should now pass the validation check under the XHTML 1.0 transitional DTD.

Successful validation under XHTML transitional ◀ **Figure 9-20**

W3C Markup Validation Service
Check the markup (HTML, XHTML, ...) of Web documents

Jump To: Congratulations · Icons

This Page Is Valid XHTML 1.0 Transitional!

Result: Passed validation

File: [_____] Browse...
Use the file selection box above if you wish to re-validate the uploaded file \\disk\data\tutorial.09\tutorial\works.htm \tutorial\works.htm

Encoding: utf-8   (detect automatically) ▼

Doctype: XHTML 1.0 Transitional   (detect automatically) ▼

Root Element: html

Root Namespace: http://www.w3.org/1999/xhtml

Options

☐ Show Source   ☐ Show Outline   ⦿ List Messages Sequentially   ○ Group Error Messages by type

☐ Validate error pages   ☐ Verbose Output   ☐ Clean up Markup with HTML Tidy

Testing under XHTML Strict

Now that the Web page has passed the validation check for XHTML 1.0 transitional, Tom wants the page tested under XHTML 1.0 strict. To perform this test, you first must change the DOCTYPE declaration to use the strict XHTML 1.0 DTD.

To change the DOCTYPE declaration:

▶ **1.** Reopen the **dtd_list.txt** file from the tutorial.09\tutorial folder in your text editor. Copy the DOCTYPE declaration for XHTML 1.0 strict and then close the file.

▶ **2.** Return to the **works.htm** file in your text editor.

▶ **3.** Paste the copied DOCTYPE declaration into the file, replacing the previous declaration for XHTML 1.0 transitional. Figure 9-21 highlights the revised code in the file.

Pasting the XHTML 1.0 strict DOCTYPE declaration ◀ **Figure 9-21**

```
<?xml version="1.0" encoding="UTF-8" ?>

<!DOCTYPE html PUBLIC "-//W3C//DTD XHTML 1.0 Strict//EN"
    "http://www.w3.org/TR/xhtml1/DTD/xhtml1-strict.dtd">

<html xmlns="http://www.w3.org/1999/xhtml">
<head>
```

With the new DOCTYPE declaration pasted into the works.htm file, you can retest the document using the same validator page on the W3C Web site.

To test the file under the strict DTD:

▶ **1.** Save your changes to the **works.htm** file.

> **2.** Return to the W3C validator page. Click the **Refresh** or **Reload** button in your browser to redo the validation check. As shown in Figure 9-22, the page fails the test under XHTML 1.0 strict.

| Figure 9-22 | Results of the XHTML strict validation test |

Tip

You can view extended comments on your page errors by checking the Verbose Output check box on the validator page.

Five errors are reported by the W3C validator page. The first two are:

```
Line 26, column 14: there is no attribute "bgcolor"
<body bgcolor="white">
Line 28, column 48: there is no attribute "align"
<img src="logo.jpg" alt="Wizard Works" align="left" />
```

Both errors reference presentational attributes that are not supported under the XHTML 1.0 strict DTD. The first attribute, bgcolor, is used to set the background color of the Web page. The align attribute referenced in the second error message is used to float the inline image on the left page margin. You can fix both errors by removing the attributes and replacing them with the background-color and float styles added to the ww.css style sheet.

To replace the attributes with styles:

> **1.** Return to the **works.htm** file in your Web browser.

> **2.** Delete the attribute

```
bgcolor="white"
```

from the opening <body> tag.

> **3.** Go down two lines in the file and delete the attribute

```
align="left"
```

from the <img /> tag for the logo.jpg file.

> **4.** Scroll down the file and delete the attribute

```
align="right"
```

from the <img /> tag for the firework.gif graphic.

5. Save your changes to the file and then open the **ww.css** file in your text editor.

6. Add the style

   ```
   background-color: white
   ```

   to the list of style properties for the body element.

7. Directly below the styles for the #head a:hover selector, insert the following style declaration for images nested within the #head selector:

   ```
   #head img {float: left}
   ```

8. Directly below the styles for the #main selector, insert the following style declaration:

   ```
   #main img {float: right}
   ```

   Figure 9-23 highlights the revised code in the style sheet file.

Modifying the ww.css style sheet ◁ **Figure 9-23**

```
body              {background-image: url(back.jpg); background-repeat: repeat-y;
                   font-size: 16px; margin-right: 20px; background-color: white}
#head             {position: absolute; top: 0px; left: 0px; width: 100%; font-size: 16px;
                   font-family: sans-serif; background-color: white; text-align: right;
                   border-bottom: 2px solid black; padding-top: 5px}
#head a           {color: white; background-color: blue; font-size: 10px; font-weight: bold;
                   text-decoration: none; text-align: center; border: 5px outset white;
                   width: 100px; padding: 2px; margin-left: 20px}
#head a:hover     {color: black; background-color: yellow; border: 5px inset white}
#head img         {float: left}
#linklist         {position: absolute; top: 125px; left: 0px; font-size: 14px;
                   font-weight: bold; font-family: sans-serif; width: 140px; padding: 10px}
#linklist a       {color: rgb(247,233,64); text-decoration: none; display: block}
#linklist a:hover {color: white; text-decoration: underline}
#linklist .newgroup {margin-top: 10px}
#main             {position: absolute; top: 125px; left: 160px}
#main img         {float: right}
.firstp:first-letter {font-size: 300%; line-height: 0.8; float: left}
address           {border-top: 2px solid black; font-style: normal; font-size: 10px;
                   font-family: sans-serif; text-align: center; margin-top: 15px}
```

9. Save your changes to the file, and then return to the **W3C validator page** in your Web browser. Refresh or reload the **works.htm** page and verify that the number of errors in the page has dropped to three.

The next error reported by the validator is:

```
Line 29, column 22: there is no attribute "target"
<a href="#" target="_new">Review Cart</a>
```

The target attribute is not supported in XHTML strict, so it will have to be removed from the Web page. This means that if Tom wants to work with XHTML strict, he will not be able to direct his hypertext links to new browser windows or tabs.

To remove the target attribute:

1. Return to the **works.htm** file in your Web browser.

2. Delete the attribute

   ```
   target="_new"
   ```

   from the hypertext links for the Review Cart and Check Out links located at the top of the Web page body.

▶ **3.** Save your changes to the file and then reload or refresh the **W3C validator page** in your Web browser. The number of errors in the Web page has dropped to two.

| InSight | **The target Attribute and Strict XHTML** |

The decision not to support the target attribute under strict XHTML was a controversial one. Many Web page designers prefer to have some links open in new browser windows or tabs, rather than in the window or tab that displays their site, to allow users to stay at their site while also browsing on other sites.

One problem is that the ability to open a new window or tab is strictly browser-dependent. For example, cell phones and PDAs don't support opening new windows, and those devices are becoming increasingly important tools for viewing the Web. Another argument is that the action of opening a link in a new window should be left to the user's preference; it should not be forced on users by the Web site designer. Most browsers provide users the ability to choose where to open links, and that is where the decision should reside. Finally, there is the opinion that opening new browser windows for the user is actually confusing to new users who can get lost as the number of open windows increases with each site they visit.

However, despite these reasons, many Web designers still want to direct links to new browser windows. One way to allow a link to be opened in a new window but still retain valid code under XHTML strict is to use JavaScript to open the link. The following code shows a JavaScript command that can be added to any hypertext link to force the link to open in a new window:

```
<a href="url" onclick="window.open(this.href); return false;"
            onkeypress="window.open(this.href); return false;">
   linked text
</a>
```

Note that for this approach to work, the user's browser must have JavaScript enabled. This is the default state for most browsers. However, if JavaScript is not enabled, the JavaScript code will be ignored and the link will open in the current browser window or tab.

The last two errors in the works.htm file involve using the <font> tag and the color attribute. The reported errors are as follows:

Line 73, column 18: **there is no attribute "color"**

```
<font color="blue">Wizard Works</font> &#183;
```

Line 73, column 24: **element "font" undefined**

```
<font color="blue">Wizard Works</font> &#183;
```

To fix this problem, you'll remove the unsupported font element and color attribute, replacing them with the following supported code:

```
<span style="color: blue">Wizard Works</span> &#183;
```

Make this change to the works.htm file.

To replace the font and color attributes:

▶ **1.** Return to the **works.htm** file in your text editor.

▶ **2.** Scroll to the bottom of the file and replace

```
<font color="blue">Wizard Works</font>
```

with the following, as shown in Figure 9-24:

```
<span style="color: blue">Wizard Works</span>
```

Replacing the font element and color attribute Figure 9-24

```
<address>
    <span style="color: blue">Wizard Works</span> &#183;
    4311 Tower Street &#183;
    Ashland, KY  41105 &#183;
    (606) 555-3188
</address>
</div>
```

3. Save your changes to the file and then reload or refresh the **W3C validator page** in your Web browser. As shown in Figure 9-25, the validator should now report that the code for the works.htm file passes validation under XHTML strict.

Successful validation under XHTML strict Figure 9-25

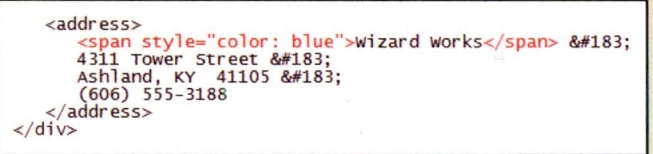

Jump To:	Congratulations · Icons

This Page Is Valid XHTML 1.0 Strict!

Result:	Passed validation
File :	[_____] Browse... *Use the file selection box above if you wish to re-validate the upload file \\disk\data\tutorial.09\tutorial\works.htm* \tutorial\works.htm
Encoding :	utf-8 (detect automatically) ▾
Doctype :	XHTML 1.0 Strict (detect automatically) ▾
Root Element:	html
Root Namespace:	http://www.w3.org/1999/xhtml

Options

☐ Show Source   ☐ Show Outline   ⦿ List Messages Sequentially ○ Group Error Messages by type

☐ Validate error pages   ☐ Verbose Output   ☐ Clean up Markup with HTML Tidy

Once you have a document that passes the validation test, you might want to make a note of this on your Web page. The W3C provides code that you can paste into your document to advertise this fact. Tom suggests that you add this code to the Wizard Works Web page.

To insert the W3C validation notice:

1. Scroll to the bottom of the **W3C validator page** and select the code sample directly to the right of the second validation icon image (the blue image).

2. Click **Edit** from your browser menu and then click **Copy**.

3. Return to the **works.htm** file in your text editor and paste the following code directly below the closing </address> tag, as shown in Figure 9-26:

```
<p>
    <a href="http://validator.w3.org/check?uri=referer">
        <img src="http://www.w3.org/Icons/valid-xhtml10-blue"
             alt="Valid XHTML 1.0 Strict" height="31" width="88" />
    </a>
</p>
```

You can indent the code to make it easier to read.

Figure 9-26

Inserting the code for the W3C validation icon

```
<address>
    <span style="color: blue">Wizard Works</span> &#183;
    4311 Tower Street &#183;
    Ashland, KY  41105 &#183;
    (606) 555-3188
</address>

<p>
    <a href="http://validator.w3.org/check?uri=referer">
        <img src="http://www.w3.org/Icons/valid-xhtml10-blue"
            alt="Valid XHTML 1.0 Strict" height="31" width="88" />
    </a>
</p>

</div>
```

▶ **4.** Save your changes to the **works.htm** file and then close it.

▶ **5.** Reopen **works.htm** in your Web browser. As shown in Figure 9-27, the validation icon appears in the bottom-right corner of the page.

Figure 9-27

Final Wizard Works page

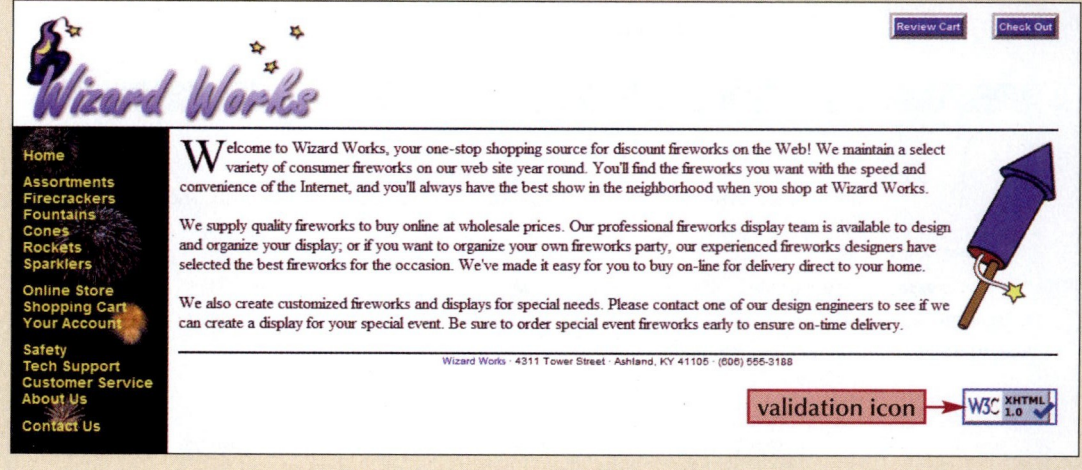

You show the completed Web page to Tom. He's pleased with your work in updating the file to meet the specifications for XHTML. He is sure that these changes will help the Web site in the future as the company tries to stay current with the latest developments in XHTML.

Using Style Sheets and XHTML

Although XHTML and HTML files are simple text documents, not all text is the same. Browsers and parsers distinguish between two types of text: parsed character data and unparsed character data. **Parsed character data** or **PCDATA** is text that is processed (parsed) by a browser or parser. The following code is an example of PCDATA:

```
<title>Wizard Works</title>
```

When a browser encounters this string of characters, it processes it and uses that information to change the text of the browser's title bar. In PCDATA, you cannot enter character symbols such as <, >, and & directly into a document as text because they are used to process information. The < and > symbols are used to mark the beginning and end of element tags.

The & symbol is used to indicate a special character. If you want to display a < symbol in your document, for example, you must use the special character symbol <.

Unparsed character data or **CDATA** is text that is not processed by the browser or parser. In CDATA, you can use any character you like without worrying about it being misinterpreted—browsers and parsers essentially ignore it. The DTDs for XML and XHTML specify whether an element contains CDATA or PCDATA. Most elements contain PCDATA. This prevents document authors from putting symbols such as < into the element content.

However, this also has an impact on embedded style sheets. The content of an embedded style sheet is treated as PCDATA, meaning that a parser attempts to process the information contained in the style sheet's characters. This can cause problems if the style sheet contains a character that could be processed by the parser. For example, the following embedded style sheet contains the > character, which a parser would interpret as the end of an element tag:

```
<style type="text/css">
    p > img {float: left}
</style>
```

A parser encountering this code would probably invalidate the document (assuming that the code didn't crash the page entirely). This problem also occurs with JavaScript (a topic you'll cover in the next tutorial), in which the <, >, and & symbols are frequently used.

One way of dealing with this problem is to use a special construct called a **CDATA section**, which marks a block of text as CDATA so that parsers ignore any text within it. The syntax of the CDATA section is

```
<![CDATA[
    text
]]>
```

where *text* is the content that you want treated as CDATA. To apply this to your style sheet, you could place the CDATA section within the style element as follows:

```
<style type="text/css">
<![CDATA[
    p > img {float: left}
]]>
</style>
```

The problem with this solution is that many browsers do not understand or recognize CDATA sections, and this can cause problems in displaying your page. In the end, the best solution is often to replace all embedded style sheets in XHTML documents with external style sheets. This has the added advantage of completely removing style from content because all the styles are placed in separate files. Note that this is not an issue if the embedded style sheet doesn't contain any characters that can't be processed by the XML parser.

Review | **Session 9.2 Quick Check**

1. An XHTML transitional validation test reports the following error:

   ```
   Line 51, column 3:
     tag for "br" omitted, but OMITTAG NO was specified
   <br>
   ```

   Suggest a possible cause of the error and how you would correct it.

2. A validation test under XHTML 1.0 strict reports the following error:

   ```
   Line 59, column 12: there is no attribute "align"
   <p align="left">
   ```

   Suggest a possible cause of the error and how you would correct it.

3. A validation test under XHTML 1.0 strict reports the following error:

   ```
   Line 22, column 14: there is no attribute "name"
   <form name="orders">
   ```

   Suggest a possible cause of the error and how you would correct it.

4. Suggest how to write code for a hypertext link to open in a new browser window and still be valid under the XHTML strict DTD.
5. What is the difference between PCDATA and CDATA?
6. Why would you want to place an embedded style sheet within a CDATA section?

Review | **Tutorial Summary**

In this tutorial, you learned how to create and work with XHTML documents. The first session reviewed the history of XHTML and its development from XML. You learned about well-formed and valid documents as well as the different DTDs associated with XHTML. The session then discussed how certain coding practices in HTML documents would lead to syntax errors in XHTML. The session examined the XML prolog and DOCTYPE declarations, as well as issues around specifying the XHTML namespace. The session concluding by discussing how XHTML can be used with other XML languages to create combined documents. In the second session you learned how to use an online validator to test a document for well-formedness and validity. The tutorial concluded with a discussion of the syntax issues surrounding embedded styles sheets.

Key Terms

attribute minimization	frameset DTD	UCS
CDATA	local namespace	Unicode
CDATA section	namespace	Universal Character Set
character encoding	parsed character data	unparsed character data
character set	parser	valid
default namespace	PCDATA	well formed
document type definition	strict DTD	XML parser
DTD	transitional DTD	

Practice | **Review Assignments**

Practice the skills you learned in the tutorial using the same case scenario.

Data Files needed for the Review Assignments: back.jpg, dtd_list.txt, founttxt.htm, and logo.jpg

Tom has another file that he wants you to update to XHTML. This page contains an order form for some of the fountains sold by Wizard Works. The file has some older HTML elements and syntax in it, so he wants you to confirm that the file is well formed and valid after you've updated it for XHTML. Figure 9-28 shows a preview of the completed Web page.

Figure 9-28

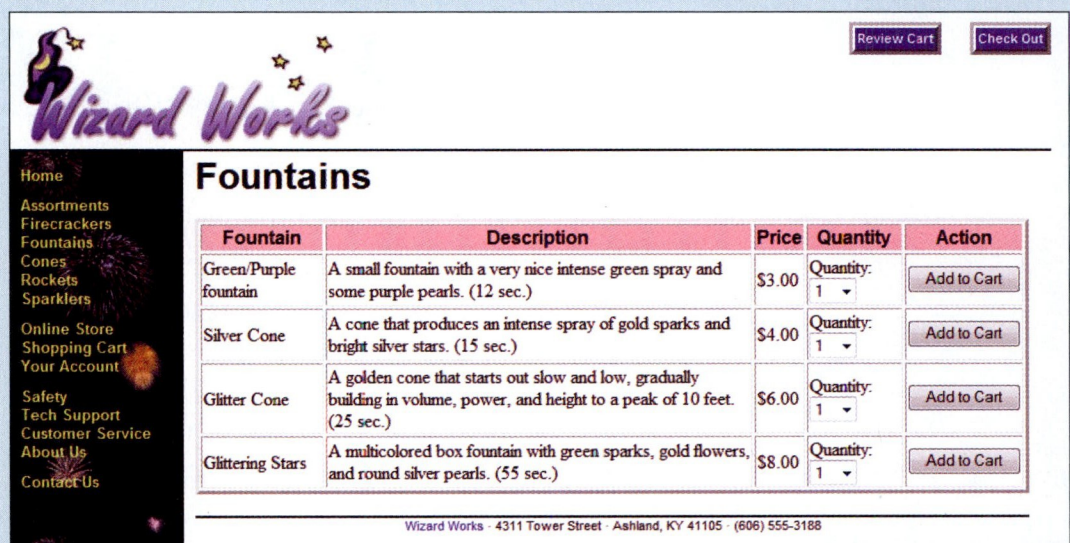

Complete the following:

1. Use your text editor to open **founttxt.htm** from the tutorial.09\review folder included with your Data Files. Enter *your name* and *the date* in the comment section of the file and save the file as **fountain.htm** in the same folder.
2. Insert an XML prolog at the top of the file, setting the version number to 1.0 and the character encoding to UTF-8.
3. Below the XML prolog, insert a DOCTYPE declaration indicating that this document conforms to the XHTML 1.0 strict DTD (you can copy the code for this declaration from the **dtd_list.txt** file in the tutorial.09\review folder).
4. Set the default namespace for the document to the XHTML namespace.
5. Use a validator to test whether the document is well formed and valid under the XHTML 1.0 strict DTD. If any deprecated presentational attributes are found, replace them with the equivalent inline style. Note that when this form is run, its action should use the CGI script at *http://wizardworksstore.com/cgi/cart*.
6. After the document passes XHTML 1.0 strict, save your changes and view the page in your Web browser to ensure that it still looks like Figure 9-28.
7. Submit your completed files to your instructor.

| Apply | | Case Problem 1 |

Use the skills you learned in this tutorial to convert an online menu to XHTML format.

Data Files needed for this Case Problem: breakfst.jpg, breaktxt.htm, dinner.jpg, dinnrtxt.htm, dtd_list.txt, lunch.jpg, lunchtxt.htm, and tan.jpg

Kelsey's Diner   You've been asked to update the Web pages for Kelsey's Diner, a popular restaurant in Worcester, Massachusetts. Cindy Towser, the manager of the diner, would like the pages that display her breakfast, lunch, and dinner menus updated so that they comply with XHTML standards. A preview of one of the menu pages is shown in Figure 9-29.

Figure 9-29

Complete the following:

1. Use your text editor to open **breaktxt.htm**, **lunchtxt.htm**, and **dinnrtxt.htm** from the tutorial.09\case1 folder included with your Data Files. Enter *your name* and *the date* in the comment section of each file and save the files as **breakfst.htm**, **lunch.htm**, and **dinner.htm**, respectively, in the same folder.

2. Go to the **breakfst.htm** file in your text editor and insert an XML prolog at the top of the file. Use the default values for the version and encoding attributes.

3. After the XML prolog, insert a DOCTYPE declaration for the XHTML 1.0 strict DTD (you may copy the entry from the **dtd_list.txt** file in the tutorial.09\case1 folder for the code of this declaration).

4. Set the default namespace of the document to the XHTML namespace.

5. Test the file on the validator and make a note of the errors reported. Here are some possible ways to fix the errors:

   - Convert any deprecated presentational attributes to an embedded style.
   - Correct syntax errors for one-sided tags.
   - Replace any prohibited attributes (such as the name attribute) with an equivalent valid attribute.
   - Replace the formatting done with the b and font elements with a span element and an embedded style.

6. Save your changes to **breakfst.htm** and continue to test the file until it passes the XHTML 1.0 strict validation test.

7. Repeat Steps 2 through 6 for the **lunch.htm** and **dinner.htm** files.

8. Test the completed Web site on your browser and verify that you can move among the pages by clicking the image map links in the logo at the top of the page.

9. Submit your completed files to your instructor.

| Apply | **\| Case Problem 2** |

Use the skills you've learned in this tutorial to update an old product page.

Data Files needed for this Case Problem: cassini.jpg, dtd_list.txt, gargtxt.htm, gbar.jpg, glogo.jpg, maa.jpg, and oneil.jpg

Middle Age Arts   Nicole Swanson is the head of the Web site team at Middle Age Arts, a company that creates and sells replicas of historical European works of art for home and garden use. She has recently started a project to update the old HTML code in the site's many pages. She's asked you to update the page describing the company's collection of decorative gargoyles. She wants the page to comply with XHTML 1.0 strict standards. Figure 9-30 shows a preview of the completed Web page.

Figure 9-30

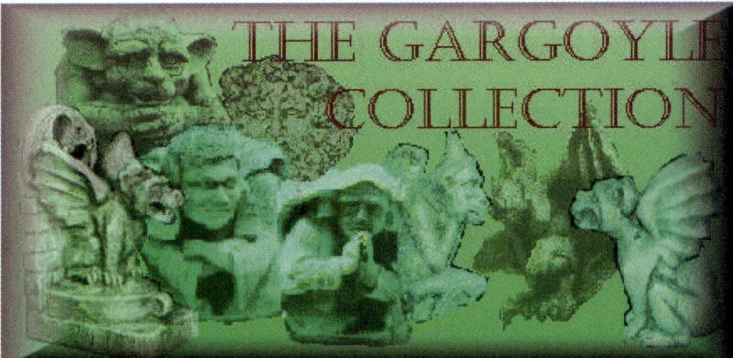

Middle Age Arts

Home Page
View the catalog
Place an order

About Gargoyles

Gargoyle Products

Other Collections

The Vatican Collection
The Rodin Collection
Renaissance Masters

From the President

This month Middle Age Arts introduces the Gargoyle Collection. I'm really excited about this new set of classical figures.

The collection contains faithful reproductions of gargoyles from some of the famous cathedrals of Europe, including Notre Dame, Rheims, and Warwick Castle. All reproductions are done to exacting and loving detail.

The collection also contains original works by noted artists such as Susan Bedford and Antonio Salvari. Our expert artisans have produced some wonderful and whimsical works, perfectly suited for home or garden use.

Don't delay, order your gargoyle today.

Irene O'Neil
President

What can you do with a gargoyle?

Don't think you need a gargoyle? Think again. Gargoyles are useful as:

- Bird baths
- Bookends
- Paperweights
- Pen holders
- Wind chimes

Go to our catalog for more ideas!

Profile of the Artist

This month's artist is Michael Cassini. Michael has been a professional sculptor for ten years. He  has won numerous awards, including the prestigious *Reichsman Cup* and an Award of Merit at the 2007 Tuscany Arts Competition.

Michael specializes in recreations of gargoyles from European cathedrals. You'll usually find Michael staring intently at the church walls in northern France. His work is represented by the *Turin Gargoyle*, a great addition to our Gargoyle Collection.

Complete the following:

1. Use your text editor to open **gargtxt.htm** from the tutorial.09\case2 folder included with your Data Files. Enter *your name* and *the date* in the comment section and save the file as **gargoyle.htm** in the same file.
2. Insert an XML prolog at the top of the file. Use the standard attribute defaults for an XHTML file.

3. After the XML prolog, insert a DOCTYPE declaration for the XHTML 1.0 strict DTD.

4. Set the default namespace of the document to the XHTML namespace.

5. Test the file on the validator. Fix the errors as follows:

   • Convert the attributes for the body element into styles in an embedded style sheet. (*Hint*: The link, alink, and vlink attributes are used to set the colors of hyperlinks, active links, and visited links in the Web page.)

   • Use proper syntax for any empty elements.

   • Set the color and text alignment of an h4 element using an inline style.

   • Ensure that all two-sided tags are properly closed.

   • Use the float style to align all inline images.

   • Use an inline style to set a table cell's width and background color.

   • Remove all deprecated elements and attributes.

6. Save your final version of the file once it passes the validation test for XHTML 1.0 strict, and then test it in your browser to ensure that it looks like Figure 9-30.

7. Submit your completed files to your instructor.

Challenge	**Case Problem 3**

Explore how to create a valid XHTML document using the frameset DTD.

Data Files needed for this Case Problem: cast.htm, castles.jpg, casttxt.htm, dtd_list.txt, hebd.htm, hebdtxt.htm, hebrides.jpg, high.htm, highland.jpg, hightxt.htm, lake.htm, lake.jpg, laketxt.htm, scottxt.htm, tourlist.gif, and tslogo.gif

Travel Scotland! Travel Scotland! is an online Web site that books tours of Scotland and the British Isles. You've recently been hired by Travel Scotland! to update the company's Web site. Fiona Findlay, the head of advertising for the company, has given you a set of pages in a framed Web site that describe four of the company's tours. She would like you to update the code so that it complies with XHTML standards for the transitional and frameset DTDs. A preview of the completed Web site is shown in Figure 9-31.

Figure 9-31

Complete the following:

1. Use your text editor to open the files **casttxt.htm**, **hebdtxt.htm**, **hightxt.htm**, **laketxt. htm**, and **scottxt.htm** from the tutorial.09\case3 folder included with your Data Files. Enter *your name* and *the date* in the comment section of each file and then save the files as **casttour.htm**, **hebdtour.htm**, **hightour.htm**, **laketour.htm**, and **scotland.htm,** respectively, in the same folder.

2. Go to the **scotland.htm** file in your text editor and insert an XML prolog at the top of the file.

3. Below the XML prolog, insert a DOCTYPE declaration that indicates that this file conforms to the standards for XHTML 1.0 transitional.

4. Set the default namespace to the XHTML namespace.

⊕ **EXPLORE**   5. Enclose the styles from the embedded style sheet within a CDATA section.

6. Save your changes and submit the page for validation. Correct any errors reported by the validator. (*Hint*: If alternate text is required for the image map hot spots, use the text displayed in the **tourlist.gif** graphic.)

7. Go to the **casttour.htm** file in your text editor and insert an XML prolog at the top of the file.

⊕ **EXPLORE**   8. Specify that the document uses the XHTML 1.0 frameset DTD and the XHTML namespace.

⊕ **EXPLORE**   9. Save your changes and submit the page for validation. Correct any errors in syntax or validity under the frameset DTD.

⊕ **EXPLORE**   10. Repeat Steps 7 through 9 for the **hebdtour.htm**, **hightour.htm**, and **laketour.htm** files.

11. Test the Web site in your browser to verify that the inline frames and the framed pages work correctly.

12. Submit your completed files to your instructor.

| Create | **Case Problem 4** |

Test your knowledge of XHTML by creating a well-formed valid document for an educational site.

Data Files needed for this Case Problem: address.txt, astro.txt, chem.txt, dtd_list.txt, elect.txt, eng.txt, mwslogo.gif, and physics.txt

Maxwell Scientific   Maxwell Scientific is an online Web site that sells science kits and educational products. Chris Todd, the head of the Web site development team, is leading an effort to update the company's Web site. He has given you some text files and graphic images. You may supplement this material with any additional files and resources at your disposal. Your job will be to develop this material into a Web site that is compliant with XHTML 1.0 strict standards. To ensure that the completed Web page is both well formed and valid, he wants you to test it on a validator before submitting it to him.

Complete the following:

1. Use your text editor to create the following HTML files in the tutorial.09\case4 folder: **astro.htm**, **chem.htm**, **elect.htm**, **eng.htm**, and **physics.htm**. Include *your name* and *the date* in a comment section for each file, along with a description of the purpose of the page.

2. Use the content from the **address.txt**, **astro.txt**, **chem.txt**, **elect.txt**, **eng.txt**, and **physics.txt** to create the content of each Web page. The design of the Web site and each individual page is up to you. Store any styles you create in an external style sheet named **mw.css** in the tutorial.09\case4 folder.

3. Each page should be designed as an XHTML 1.0 strict document. Include all necessary declarations and namespaces.
4. Test all of your pages against a validator to ensure that each page fulfills the requirements of the XHTML 1.0 strict DTD.
5. Submit your completed files to your instructor.

| Review | **Quick Check Answers** |

Session 9.1

1. An XML document that employs the correct syntax is known as well formed. A well-formed XML document that also contains the correct content is known as a valid document.

2. It employs the wrong syntax for the img element, it should be:

   ```
   <img src="logo.jpg" alt="Wizard Works" />
   ```

3. The disabled attribute has no value. The correct form is:

   ```
   <input type="radio" disabled="disabled" />
   ```

4. The blockquote element cannot contain the a element as a child element. You can correct this problem by nesting the <a> within a paragraph or other block-level element.

5. The align attribute is not a support attribute in the strict DTD. You can correct this as follows:

   ```
   <img src="logo.jpg" alt="Wizard Works" style="float: right" />
   ```

6. The map element requires the id attribute to be valid. The following is a valid form:

   ```
   <map name="parkmap" id="parkmap">
   ```

7. `<!DOCTYPE html PUBLIC "-//W3C//DTD XHTML 1.0 Strict//EN" "http://www.w3.org/TR/xhtml1/DTD/xhtml1-strict.dtd">`

8. `<?xml version="1.0" encoding="UTF-8" standalone="no" ?>`

Session 9.2

1. The br element should be created with an empty tag as

   ```
   <br />
   ```

2. The align attribute is not supported under XHTML 1.0 strict because it is a presentational attribute used to align text or page content. You can achieve the same result by applying the style text-align: left to the paragraph element.

3. The error occurs because under the strict DTD there is no support for the name attribute within the <form> tag. Replace the name attribute with the id attribute as follows:

   ```
   <form id="orders">
   ```

4. Use the following JavaScript commands within the <a> tag for the hypertext link:

   ```
   onclick="window.open(this.href); return false;"onkeypress="window.
   open(this.href); return false;">
   ```

5. CDATA or character data is text that is not processed by the browser or XML parser. PCDATA or parsed character data is processed by the browser or the XML parser and so will be interpreted in terms of the rules of syntax for XML.

6. To force the browser or XML parser to treat the style sheet commands as character data and not as text to be processed, thereby avoiding the situation where style sheet code will be interpreted as XHTML code.

Ending Data Files

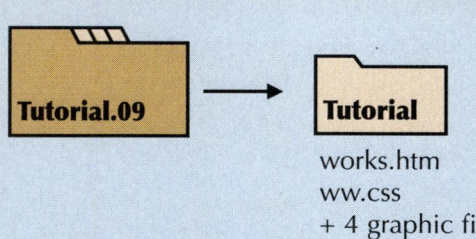

Tutorial.09 →

Tutorial

works.htm
ww.css
+ 4 graphic files

Review

fountain.htm
+ 2 graphic files

Case1

breakfst.htm
dinner.htm
lunch.htm
+ 4 graphic files

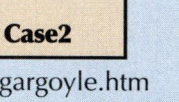

Case2

gargoyle.htm
+ 5 graphic files

Case3

casttour.htm
hebdtour.htm
hightour.htm
laketour.htm
scotland.htm
+ 4 HTML files
+ 6 graphic files

Case4

astro.htm
chem.htm
elect.htm
eng.htm
mw.css
physics.htm
+ 1 graphic file

Programming with JavaScript

Hiding E-Mail Addresses on a Library Web Site

Case | Monroe Public Library

Kate Howard is the head of technical services at Monroe Public Library in Monroe, Ohio. One of her jobs is to maintain the library's Web site. In previous years, the library has made its staff directory, including e-mail links to library employees, available online. Kate thinks that this is an important part of making the library more accessible to everyone. However, Kate has become concerned about the security issues involved with making the staff's e-mail addresses so accessible. Kate is aware that e-mail addresses can be scanned from an HTML file and used to send junk mail to the recipients.

She would like to have some way of scrambling the e-mail addresses within the HTML code while still making them viewable when the page is rendered by a Web browser. Kate has approached you for help in writing a program to accomplish this.

Starting Data Files

Tutorial.10 →

Tutorial
mpl.jpg
mplstyles.css
mpltxt.htm
spam.js

Review
mpl2txt.htm
mplstyles.css
random.js
+ 11 graphic files

Case1
datetime.js
skymaptxt.htm
skyweb.css
+ 26 graphic files

Case2
ads.js
fronttxt.htm
random.js
styles.css
+ 7 graphic files

Case3
back.jpg
functions.js
sunday.htm - saturday.htm
todaytxt.htm
+ 2 style sheets

Case4
functions.js
logo.jpg

Session 10.1

Introducing JavaScript

You meet with Kate to discuss her goals regarding the e-mail addresses on the library's staff directory page. She shows you the content and page layout she has created.

To open the staff directory page:

▶ 1. Use your text editor to open **mpltxt.htm** from the tutorial.10\tutorial folder included with your Data Files. Enter **your name** and **the date** in the comment section at the top of the file and save the file as **mpl.htm** in the same folder.

▶ 2. Take some time to scroll through the document to become familiar with its contents and structure.

▶ 3. Open **mpl.htm** in your Web browser. Figure 10-1 shows the initial appearance of the Web page.

Note that the staff directory table contains a column in which Kate wants to insert links to each employee's e-mail address; right now the column is empty.

Figure 10-1 | **Monroe Public Library Staff page**

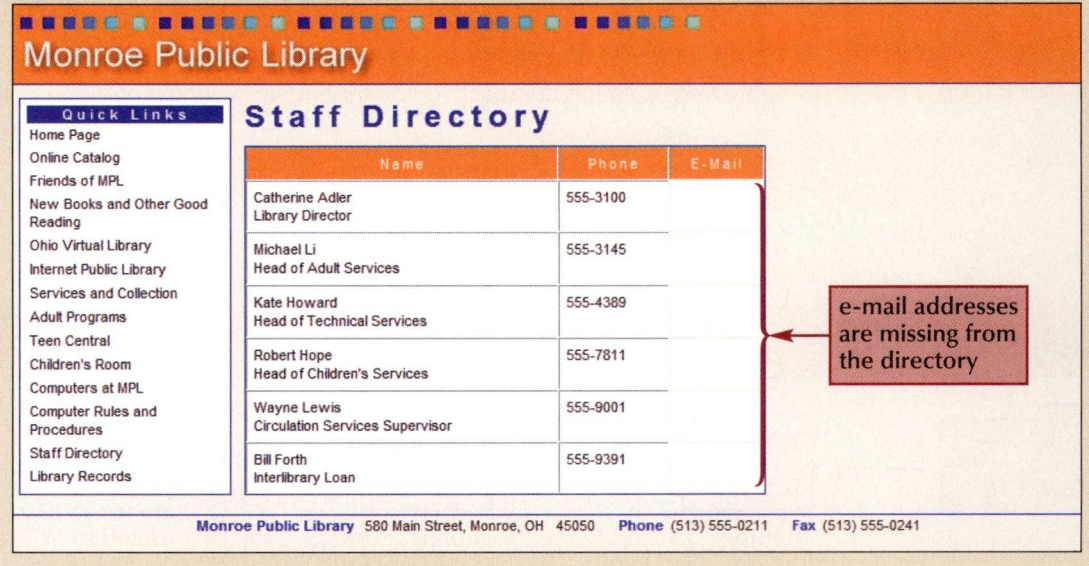

Although the staff directory page has proven invaluable in making library employees more responsive to the needs of the public, Kate is concerned about the security risks of putting e-mail addresses in that directory. Kate is most concerned about spam. **Spam** is essentially junk e-mail—messages that advertise products and services not requested by the recipient. A **spammer** is a person who sends these unsolicited e-mails, sometimes in bulk e-mailings involving tens of thousands of recipients. Aside from the annoyance of receiving unsolicited e-mail, spam costs companies thousands—and sometimes millions—of dollars each year by consuming valuable resources on mail servers and other devices forced to process the messages. Spam also reduces productivity by forcing employees to wade through numerous spam messages every day to find messages that are truly relevant.

One way that spammers collect e-mail addresses is through the use of e-mail harvesters. An **e-mail harvester** is a program that scans documents, usually Web pages, looking for e-mail addresses. Any e-mail address the harvester finds within the document code is added to a database, which can then be used for sending spam. So by putting the staff's e-mail addresses in the HTML code for the staff directory, Kate is also making them available to e-mail harvesters. See Figure 10-2.

Harvesting e-mail addresses | Figure 10-2

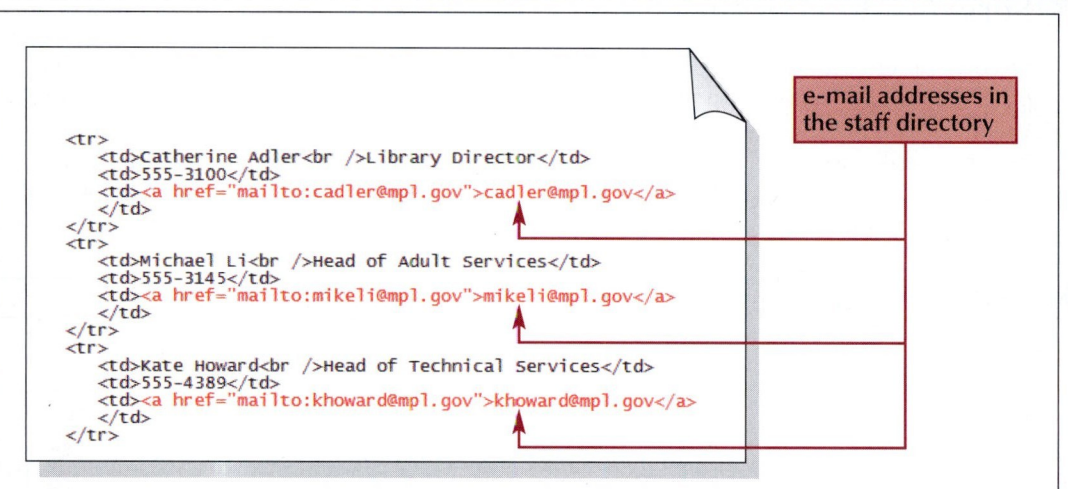

Kate would like you to scramble the e-mail addresses so that they don't appear within the Web page code; but when a browser loads and renders the page for a user, the e-mail addresses are unscrambled. See Figure 10-3. This mechanism will thwart most e-mail harvesters examining the document's HTML code while making the addresses available to users viewing the page on the Web. Note that some e-mail harvesters can still view both the underlying code and the page as they are rendered by a browser, so the proposed scrambling method is not 100% effective. However, because this technique will thwart many e-mail harvesters, Kate accepts it as a compromise solution.

Scrambling e-mail addresses | Figure 10-3

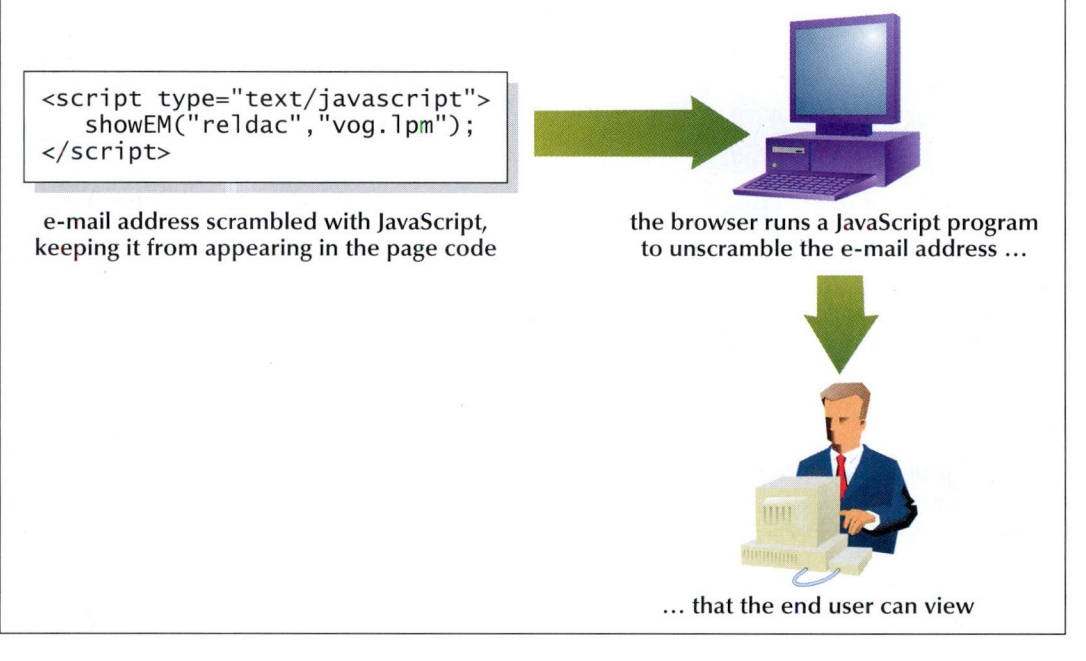

Neither HTML nor XHTML has features that allow you to scramble and unscramble the e-mail addresses from Kate's staff directory. This is not a standard function of Web browsers either. Therefore, you'll have to write a program to do this. Kate doesn't want library patrons to have to download any special applications; she wants the scrambling and unscrambling to appear behind the scenes of the library Web page. After some discussion, you decide that JavaScript is well suited to this task. You'll start on this project by first finding out just what JavaScript is and how to use it.

Server-Side and Client-Side Programming

Programming on the Web comes in two types: server-side programming and client-side programming. In **server-side programming**, a program is placed on the server that hosts a Web site. The program is then used to modify the contents and structure of Web pages. In some cases, users can interact with the program, requesting that specific information be displayed on a page, but the interaction is done remotely from the user to the server. See Figure 10-4.

Figure 10-4	Server-side programming

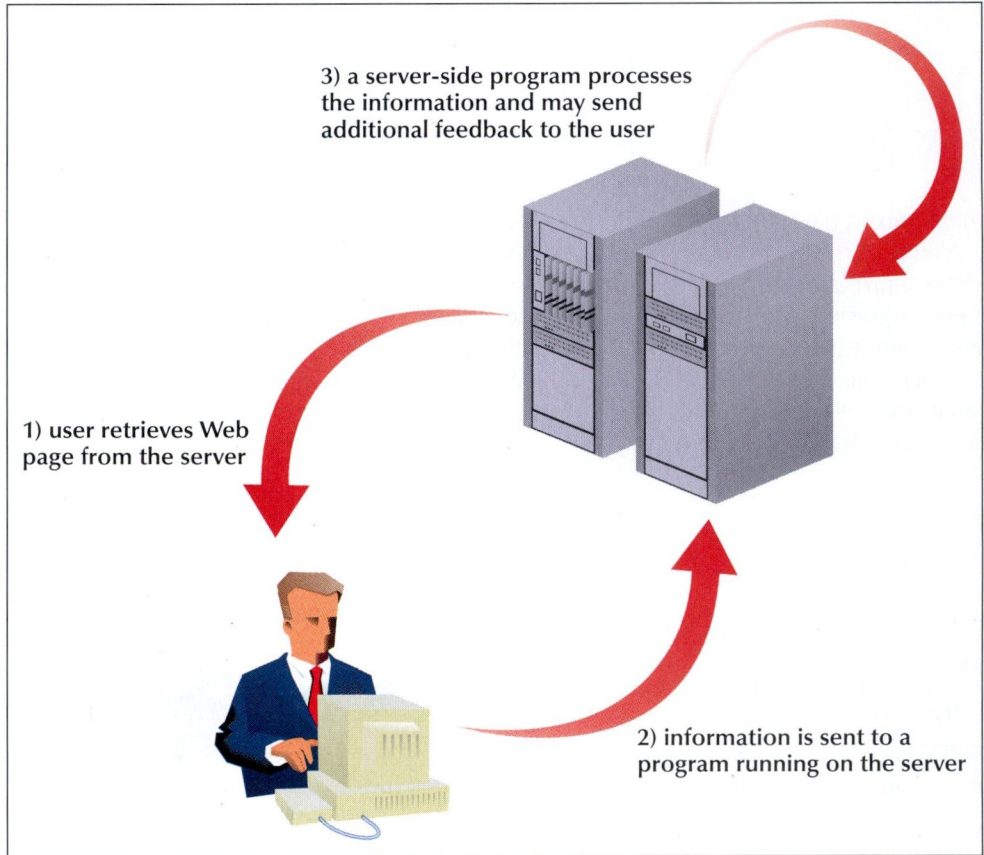

3) a server-side program processes the information and may send additional feedback to the user

1) user retrieves Web page from the server

2) information is sent to a program running on the server

There are advantages and disadvantages to this approach. A program running on a server can be connected to a database containing information not usually accessible to end users, enabling them to perform tasks not available on the client side. This enables Web pages to support such features as online banking, credit card transactions, and discussion groups. However, server-side programs use Web server resources, and in some cases a server's system administrator might place limitations on access to server-side programs to prevent users from continually accessing the server and potentially overloading the system. If the system is overloaded, an end user might have to sit through long delays as the server-side program handles multiple requests for information and action.

Client-side programming solves many of these problems by running programs on each user's computer rather than remotely off the server. See Figure 10-5.

Client-side programming ◀ Figure 10-5

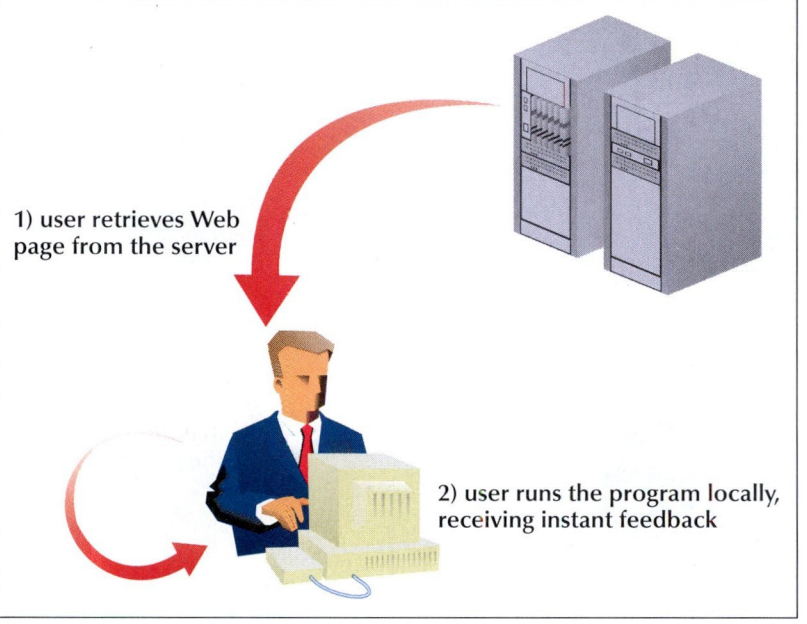

1) user retrieves Web page from the server

2) user runs the program locally, receiving instant feedback

Computing is thereby distributed so that the server is not overloaded with program-related requests. Client-side programs also tend to be more responsive because users do not have to wait for data to be sent over the Internet to a Web server. However, client-side programs can never completely replace server-side programming. For example, jobs such as running a search or processing a purchase order must be run from a central server because only the server contains the database needed to complete these types of operations.

In many cases, a combination of server-side and client-side programming is used. For example, Web forms typically use client-side programs to validate a user's entries (such as ensuring that all address information has been completely entered) and use server-side programs to submit the validated form for further processing (such as sending a purchase order to a central database). See Figure 10-6.

Figure 10-6   Combining client-side and server-side programming

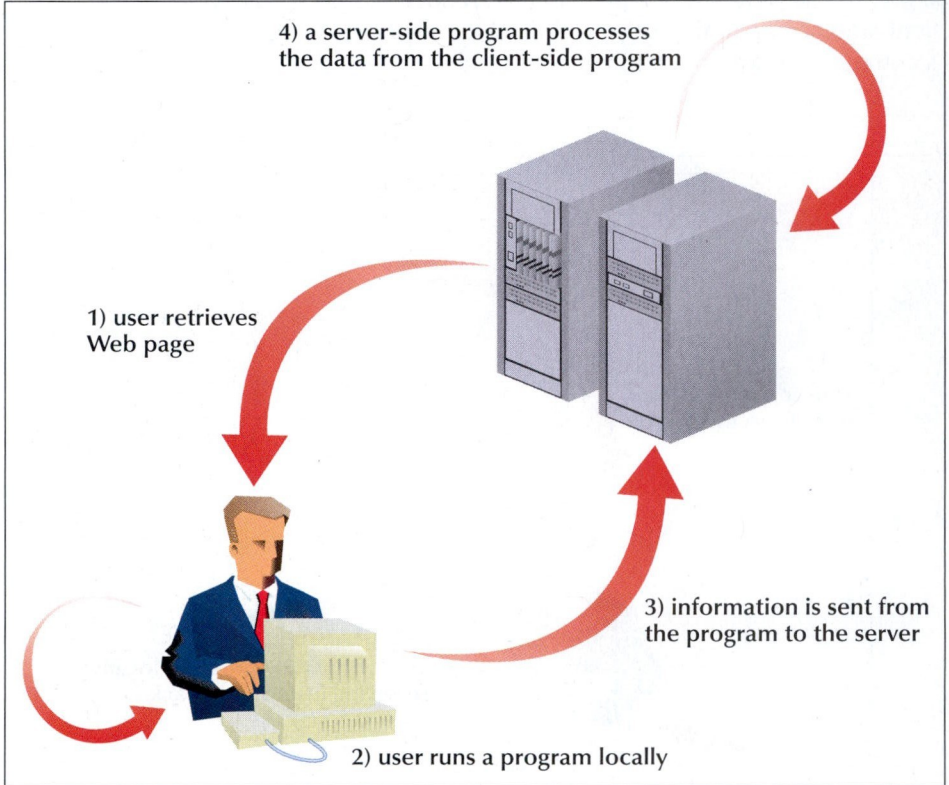

4) a server-side program processes the data from the client-side program

1) user retrieves Web page

3) information is sent from the program to the server

2) user runs a program locally

In this tutorial you'll work only with client-side programming. However, it's important to be aware that in many cases, a complete Web program includes both client-side and server-side elements.

The Development of JavaScript

Several programming languages can be run on the client side. One client-side programming language that you worked with in Tutorial 7 is Java. When Java was introduced, its advantages were quickly apparent and it was soon in wide use in many different browsers. However, creating a Java applet required access to the Java Development Kit (JDK), so nonprogrammers found it difficult to write their own Java applets.

To simplify this process, a team of developers from Netscape and Sun Microsystems created a subset of Java called **JavaScript**, which was different from Java in several important ways. Java is a **compiled language**, meaning that the program code must be submitted to a compiler that manipulates it, translating the code into a more basic language that machines can understand. For Java, this compiled code is the Java applet. Therefore, to create and run a program written in a compiled language, you need both the compiler and an application or operating system that can run the compiled code.

On the other hand, JavaScript is an **interpreted language**, meaning that the program code is executed directly without compiling. You need only two things to use JavaScript: 1) a text editor to write the JavaScript commands, and 2) a Web browser to run the commands and display the results. This means that JavaScript code can be inserted directly into an HTML or XHTML file, or placed in a separate text file that is linked to the Web page. JavaScript is not as powerful a computing language as Java, but it is simpler to use and meets the needs of most users who want to create programmable Web pages. Figure 10-7 highlights some of the key differences between Java and JavaScript.

Comparing Java and JavaScript ◄ Figure 10-7

Java	JavaScript
A compiled language	An interpreted language
Requires the JDK (Java Development Kit) to create the applet	Requires a text editor
Requires a Java virtual machine or interpreter to run the applet	Requires a browser that can interpret JavaScript code
Applet files are distinct from the HTML and XHTML code	JavaScript programs are integrated with HTML and XHTML code
Source code is hidden from the user	Source code is accessible to the user
Powerful, requiring programming knowledge and experience	Simpler, requiring less programming knowledge and experience
Secure; programs cannot write content to the hard disk	Secure; programs cannot write content to the hard disk; however, there are more security holes than in Java
Programs run on the client side	Programs run on the client side

Through the years, JavaScript has undergone several revisions. Internet Explorer actually supports a slightly different version of JavaScript called **JScript**. Although JScript is almost identical to JavaScript, some JavaScript commands are not supported in JScript, and vice versa. In addition, although it is tempting to use commands available in the latest JavaScript or JScript versions, these commands might prevent your programs from running on older browsers. For these reasons, you should always test your JavaScript programs on a variety of Web browsers.

Because of the proliferation of competing versions and revisions of scripting languages, the responsibility for developing a scripting standard has been transferred to an international body called the **European Computer Manufacturers Association** (**ECMA**). The standard developed by the ECMA is called **ECMAScript**—though browsers still refer to it as JavaScript. Other client-side programming languages are also available to Web page designers, such as the Internet Explorer scripting language **VBScript**. However, because of the nearly universal support for JavaScript, you'll use this language for your work on the library Web site.

Working with the Script Element

JavaScript programs can be placed directly in an HTML file or they can be saved in an external text file. Placing JavaScript code in a Web page file means that users only need to retrieve one file from the server. In addition, because the code and the page it affects are both within the same file, it can be easier to locate and fix programming errors. However, if you place the code in a separate file, the programs you write can be shared by the different pages on your Web site. In this tutorial, you'll work with JavaScript code entered into an HTML file as well as code stored in an external file. You'll first examine how to insert JavaScript code directly into an HTML file.

Creating a Script Element

Scripts are entered into an HTML or XHTML file using the script element. The syntax of the script element is

```
<script type="mime-type">
   script commands
</script>
```

where *mime-type* defines the language in which the script is written and *script commands* are commands written in the scripting language. The type attribute is required for XHTML documents and should be used for HTML documents as well. The MIME type for JavaScript programs is text/javascript; meaning that for JavaScript programs, you would use the following form:

```
<script type="text/javascript">
   JavaScript commands
</script>
```

You might see other ways of entering script elements into Web page code. In earlier versions of HTML, the language attribute was used in place of the type attribute to indicate the script language. For older browsers, you indicate that the scripting language is JavaScript using the following form:

```
<script language="JavaScript">
   JavaScript commands
</script>
```

The language attribute has been deprecated and is not supported by strict applications of XHTML, so you should use the type attribute in its place if you want to conform with current standards.

Note that the script element can be used with programming languages other than JavaScript. Other client-side scripting languages are identified by using a different value for the type attribute. For example, if you use VBScript from Microsoft, the MIME type is text/vbscript. You won't use VBScript in this tutorial.

Reference Window | **Creating a Script Element**

- To place a JavaScript script element into the Web page, insert the two-sided tag
  ```
  <script type="mime-type">
     script commands
    </script>
  ```
  where *mime-type* defines the language in which the script is written and *script commands* are commands written in the scripting language.
- For JavaScript programs, set the *mime-type* to text/javascript.

Placing the Script Element

When a browser encounters a script element within a file, it treats any lines within the element as commands to be run. Script elements are processed in the order in which they appear within an HTML file; there is no limit to the number of script elements that you can use within a Web page. Scripts can be placed in either the head section or the body section of a document. When placed in the body section, a browser interprets and runs them as it loads the different elements of the Web page. Although a single page can contain many script elements, the browser still can work with them as a single unit. So JavaScript commands that are created in one script element can be referenced by commands in other script elements.

Writing a JavaScript Statement

Now that you've reviewed some of the basics involved in entering JavaScript into your HTML files, you'll examine how to enter JavaScript code. Every JavaScript program consists of a series of statements. Each **statement**—also known as a **command**—is a single line that indicates an action for the browser to take. A statement should end in a semicolon, employing the syntax

```
JavaScript statement;
```

where *JavaScript statement* is the code that the browser runs. The semicolon is the official way of notifying the browser that it has reached the end of the statement. Most browsers are very forgiving and still interpret most statements correctly even if you neglect to include the ending semicolon. However, it is good programming practice to include the semicolons and some browsers require them.

JavaScript and XML Parsers | InSight

Using JavaScript code within an XHTML file can lead to problems because XHTML parsers attempt to process the symbols in JavaScript code. Because character symbols such as angle brackets (<>) and the ampersand (&) are often used in JavaScript programs, this can lead to a page being rejected by an XHTML parser. To avoid this problem, you can place your JavaScript code within a CDATA section as follows:

```
<script type="text/javascript">
<![CDATA[
   JavaScript code
]]>
</script>
```

where *JavaScript code* is the code contained in the JavaScript program. The CDATA section marks the text of the JavaScript code as data that should not be processed by XHTML parsers. Unfortunately, the CDATA section is not well supported by current browsers.

A third alternative is not to embed your scripts within XHTML files at all, but instead to place them in external files. This practice has the added advantage of separating program code from page content. If you need to create valid XHTML documents, this is probably the best solution.

Writing Output to a Web Document

The first JavaScript program you add to Kate's document is a program that writes the text of an e-mail address into the Web page. Although you could enter the e-mail address directly, you use this opportunity to experiment with JavaScript. You also build on this simple statement as you progress through the rest of the tutorial. You insert the e-mail address for Catherine Adler as the first entry in the staff directory. Her e-mail address is cadler@mpl.gov. To write this text to the Web document, you insert the following statement:

```
<script type="text/javascript">
   document.write("cadler@mpl.gov");
</script>
```

This document.write() statement tells the browser to send the text string cadler@mpl.gov to the Web page document. To see how your browser applies this command, enter the script element and command into Kate's mpl.htm file.

To write text to the Web page using JavaScript:

▶ 1. Return to the **mpl.htm** in your text editor.

▶ 2. Locate the table cell after the entry for Catherine Adler and insert the following code, as shown in Figure 10-8:

```
<script type="text/javascript">
   document.write("cadler@mpl.gov");
</script>
```

Figure 10-8	Inserting a script element

```
<tr>
    <td>Catherine Adler<br />Library Director</td>
    <td>555-3100</td>
    <td>
        <script type="text/javascript">
            document.write("cadler@mpl.gov");
        </script>
    </td>
</tr>
```

script to write content to the Web document

▶ 3. Save your changes to the file and then reload **mpl.htm** in your Web browser. As shown in Figure 10-9, the text of Catherine's e-mail address should appear in the staff directory.

Figure 10-9	Text generated by JavaScript

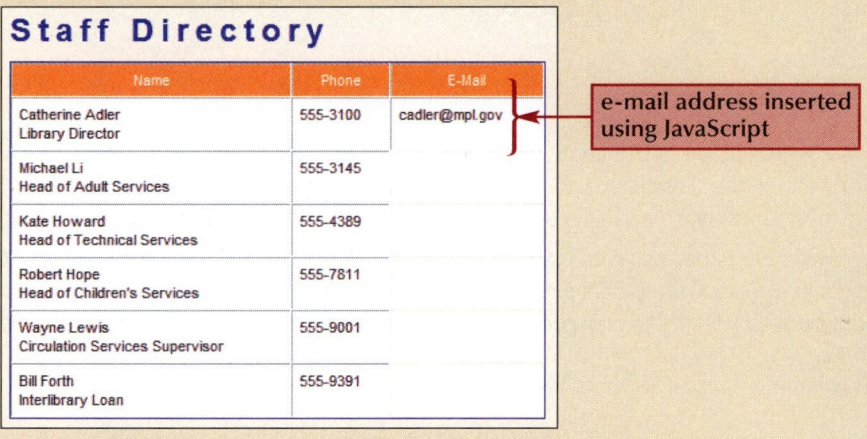

Staff Directory

Name	Phone	E-Mail
Catherine Adler Library Director	555-3100	cadler@mpl.gov
Michael Li Head of Adult Services	555-3145	
Kate Howard Head of Technical Services	555-4389	
Robert Hope Head of Children's Services	555-7811	
Wayne Lewis Circulation Services Supervisor	555-9001	
Bill Forth Interlibrary Loan	555-9391	

e-mail address inserted using JavaScript

Trouble? Internet Explorer might display a yellow alert bar at the top of the browser window with a warning that it has restricted access to active content for security reasons. This is done to enable users to prevent their browsers from running unwanted scripts. To run the script, click the information bar and choose Allow Blocked Content from the pop-up menu, and then click Yes in the dialog box that follows.

Note that the placement of the script element tells the browser where to place the new text. Because the script element is placed between the opening and closing <td> tags, the text generated by the script is placed there as well. In more advanced JavaScript programs, you can direct your output to specific locations in the Web page document—but that's beyond the scope of this tutorial.

The document.write() Method

The document.write() method, which you just used to display the e-mail text, is one of the basic ways in JavaScript to send output to the Web document. Why is it called a method? In JavaScript, many commands involve working with objects in the Web page and browser. An **object** is any item—from the browser window itself to a document displayed in the browser to an element displayed within the document. Even the mouse pointer, the window scrollbars, or the browser application itself can be treated as an object. A **method** is a process by which JavaScript manipulates or acts upon the properties of an object. In this case, you've used the write() method to write new text into the document object. The document.write() method has the general syntax

```
document.write("text");
```

where *text* is a string of characters that you want written to the Web document. The text string can also include HTML tags. For example, the following statement writes the text Monroe Public Library marked as an h1 heading into a document:

```
document.write("<h1>Monroe Public Library</h1>");
```

When a browser encounters this statement, it places the text and the markup tags into the document and renders that text as if it had been entered directly into the HTML file.

Kate wants the e-mail addresses in the staff directory to appear as hypertext links. This requires placing the e-mail addresses within <a> tags and adding the href attribute value indicating the destination of each link. For example, the code to create a link for Catherine Adler's e-mail address is:

```
<a href="mailto:cadler@mpl.gov">cadler@mpl.gov</a>
```

Writing this text string requires you to include quotation marks around the href attribute value. Because text strings created with the document.write() method must be enclosed in quotes as well, you have to place one set of quotes within another. This is done by using both single and double quotation marks. If you want to write a double quotation mark as part of the code sent to the document, you enclose the quotation marks within single quotation marks. To write single quotation marks, you enclose them within a set of double quotation marks. The type of quotation mark must always be different. If you try to enclose double quotes within another set of double quotes, the browser won't know when the quoted text string begins and ends. The following JavaScript code encloses the href attribute value in single quotes and uses double quotes to mark the entire text to be written to the Web page document:

```
document.write("<a href='mailto:cadler@mpl.gov'>");
document.write("cadler@mpl.gov");
document.write("</a>");
```

Note that this example places the entire code into three separate document.write() commands. Although you could use one long text string, it might be more difficult to read and to type without making a mistake. A browser treats these consecutive commands as one long string of text to be written into the document.

Tip

Another method to write text to the Web page is the document.writeln() method, which is identical to the document.write() method except that it adds a line break to the end of the text.

Writing to the Web Page

- To write text to the Web page with JavaScript, use the method
  ```
  document.write("text")
  ```
  where *text* is the HTML code to be written to the Web page.

You're ready to add the code for the link to Catherine Adler's e-mail address.

To write the e-mail link for Catherine Adler:

1. Return to the **mpl.htm** file in your text editor.

2. Directly after the opening <script> element, insert the following command:
   ```
   document.write("<a href='mailto:cadler@mpl.gov'>");
   ```

3. Directly before the closing </script> tag, insert the following command:
   ```
   document.write("</a>");
   ```
   Figure 10-10 shows the revised code in the file.

Figure 10-10 Inserting several document.write() commands

```
<tr>
    <td>Catherine Adler<br />Library Director</td>
    <td>555-3100</td>
    <td>
        <script type="text/javascript">
            document.write("<a href='mailto:cadler@mpl.gov'>");
            document.write("cadler@mpl.gov");
            document.write("</a>");
        </script>
    </td>
</tr>
```

4. Save your changes and then reopen **mpl.htm** in your Web browser.

5. Hover your mouse pointer over the e-mail address to verify that it is a link. As shown in Figure 10-11, the link to the e-mail address should appear in the browser's status bar.

Viewing an e-mail link ◀ Figure 10-11

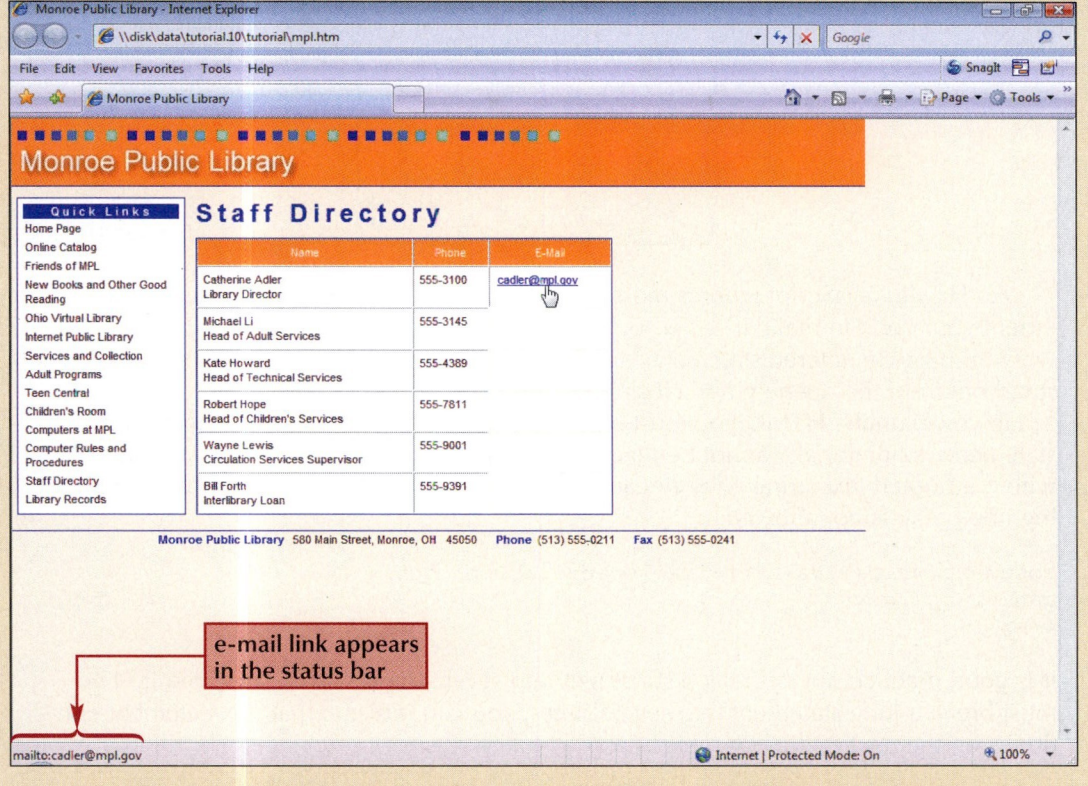

Trouble? If the link does not appear, verify that you included the opening and closing quotation marks in the JavaScript commands you just entered.

6. If you want to take a break before starting the next session, you can close any open files or programs now.

Understanding JavaScript Syntax

Besides the use of semicolons, there are some other syntax rules you should keep in mind when writing JavaScript statements. JavaScript is case sensitive so you must pay attention to whether or not letters are capitalized. For example, the following statements are not equivalent as far as JavaScript is concerned:

```
document.write("</a>");
Document.write("</a>");
```

The first command writes the HTML tag </a> to a Web page document. The second command is not recognized by a browser as a legitimate command and results in an error message. Figure 10-12 shows the error message generated by the Internet Explorer browser. The browser does not recognize the word Document (as opposed to document) and so cannot process the command. You'll examine how to handle this type of error later in this tutorial.

Figure 10-12 ▶ **An Internet Explorer error message resulting from improper case**

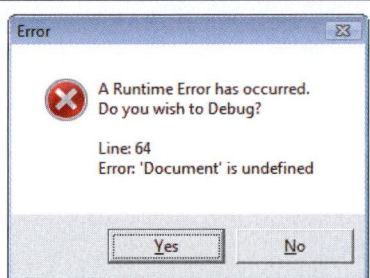

Like HTML, JavaScript ignores most occurrences of extra white space so you can indent your code to make it easier to read. You can see examples of this in Figure 10-10, where the newly entered statements are indented several spaces to make the commands stand out from the opening and closing <script> tags.

However, unlike HTML, you must be careful about line breaks occurring within a statement. A line break cannot be placed within the name of a JavaScript command or within a quoted text string without causing an error in the code. For example, the following line break is not allowed:

```
document.write("<a href='mailto:cadler@mpl.gov'>
cadler@mpl.gov
</a>");
```

It is good practice not to break a statement into several lines if you can avoid it. If you must break a long statement into several lines, you can indicate that the statement continues on the next line using a backslash, as follows:

```
document.write("<a href='mailto:cadler@mpl.gov'> \
cadler@mpl.gov \
</a>");
```

If the line break occurs within a quoted text string, you can also break the string into several distinct text strings placed over several lines by adding a plus symbol (+) at the end of each line, as follows:

```
document.write("<a href='mailto:cadler@mpl.gov'>" +
"cadler@mpl.gov" +
"</a>");
```

The + symbol used in this command combines several text strings into a single text string. However, breaking a single statement into several lines is usually not recommended because of the possibility of introducing errors into the code. It should be done only with very long and complicated statements.

Supporting Non-JavaScript Browsers | InSight

For browsers that don't support scripts or that have their support for client-side scripts disabled, you can specify alternative content using the noscript element. The syntax of the noscript element is

```
<noscript>
   alternative content
</noscript>
```

where *alternative content* is the content a browser should display in place of accessing and running the script. For example, the following code displays a text message indicating that the page requires the use of JavaScript:

```
<script type="text/javascript">
   JavaScript statements
</script>
<noscript>
      <p>This page requires JavaScript. Please turn on JavaScript
         if your browser supports it and reload the page.</p>
</noscript>
```

Browsers that support client-side scripts and have that support enabled ignore the content of the noscript element.

You've completed the first phase of creating a script to scramble e-mail addresses in Kate's staff directory. At this point you've worked on learning how to create and run JavaScript code to write text to a Web document. In the next session you'll add the ability to create and work with variables and functions.

Session 10.1 Quick Check | Review

1. What is a client-side program? What is a server-side program?
2. What tag do you enter in your HTML code to create a script element for the JavaScript programming language?
3. What JavaScript command writes the text Public Library as an h2 heading to a Web document?
4. What JavaScript command would you enter to write the following tag to a Web document?

   `<h2 id="sub">Public Library</h2>`

5. How do you enter a single JavaScript statement on two lines?
6. Why would the following command produce an error message?

   `document.Write("Monroe Public Library");`

7. What code should you enter in an HTML file to display the following paragraph for browsers that don't support JavaScript?

   `<p><i>JavaScript required</i></p>`

Session 10.2

Working with Variables

In the previous session you learned how to write page content to a Web page using the document.write() method. Because you used this method to specify a text string explicitly, the code did little more than what you could have accomplished by entering the e-mail link directly into an HTML tag. However, the document.write() method is much more powerful and versatile when used in conjunction with variables. A **variable** is a named item in a program that stores information. Most JavaScript programs use variables to represent values and text strings. Variables are useful because they can store information created in one part of a program and use that information elsewhere. Variable values can also change as the program runs, enabling the program to display different values under varying conditions.

Declaring a Variable

It's common practice to introduce variables in your code by declaring them. **Declaring** a variable tells the JavaScript interpreter to reserve memory space for the variable. The statement to declare a variable is

```
var variable;
```

where *variable* is the name assigned to the variable. For example, the following statement creates a variable named emLink:

```
var emLink;
```

You can declare multiple variables by entering the variable names in a comma-separated list. The following statement declares three variables named emLink, userName, and emServer:

```
var emLink, userName, emServer;
```

JavaScript imposes some limits on variable names:

- The first character must be either a letter or an underscore character (_).
- The remaining characters can be letters, numbers, or underscore characters.
- Variable names cannot contain spaces.
- You cannot use words that JavaScript has reserved for other purposes. For example, you cannot name a variable document.write.

Like other aspects of the JavaScript language, variable names are case sensitive. The variable names emLink and emlink represent two different variables. One common programming mistake is to forget this important fact and to use uppercase and lowercase letters interchangeably in variable names.

Assigning a Value to a Variable

Once a variable has been created or declared, you can assign it a value. The statement to assign a value to a variable is

```
variable = value;
```

where *variable* is the variable name and *value* is the value assigned to the variable. For example, the following statement stores the text string cadler in a variable named userName:

```
userName = "cadler";
```

You can combine the variable declaration and the assignment of a value in a single statement. The following statements declare the userName and emServer variables, and set their initial values:

```
var userName = "cadler", emServer = "mpl.gov";
```

Note that declaring a variable with the var keyword is not required in JavaScript. The first time you use a variable, JavaScript creates the variable in computer memory. The following statement both creates the director variable (if it has not already been declared in a previous statement) and assigns it an initial value:

```
director = "Catherine Adler";
```

Although it's not required, it's considered good programming style to include the var command whenever you create a variable. Doing so helps you keep track of the variables a program uses and also makes it easier for others to read and interpret your code.

Tip

To make your code easier to interpret, place all of your variable declarations at the beginning of your program, along with comments describing the purpose of each variable.

Declaring a JavaScript Variable | Reference Window

- To declare a JavaScript variable, run the statement
     ```
     var variable
     ```
  where *variable* is the name assigned to the variable.
- To declare a JavaScript variable and set its initial value, use
     ```
     var variable = value;
     ```
  where *value* is the initial value of the variable.

Using what you've learned about variables, you're ready to add two variables to the script element you created in the last session. The first variable, userName, will store the text string cadler, which is Catherine Adler's username on the library's mail server. The second variable, emServer, will store the text string mpl.gov, which is the domain name of the mail server. Later you'll revise this code to place different values in these variables, but you start with these two fixed values. By breaking up Catherine Adler's e-mail address into two parts, you'll make it easier to hide the e-mail address from e-mail harvesters.

To create two JavaScript variables:

1. Return to the **mpl.htm** file in your text editor.

2. Locate the script element you created in the last session. Directly below the opening <script> tag, insert the following code, as shown in Figure 10-13:

```
var userName = "cadler";
var emServer = "mpl.gov";
```

Figure 10-13 | **Declaring JavaScript variables**

```
<tr>
    <td>Catherine Adler<br />Library Director</td>
    <td>555-3100</td>
    <td>
        <script type="text/javascript">
            var userName = "cadler";
            var emServer = "mpl.gov";

            document.write("<a href='mailto:cadler@mpl.gov'>");
            document.write("cadler@mpl.gov");
            document.write("</a>");
        </script>
    </td>
</tr>
```

3. Save your changes to the file.

Working with Data Types

So far, the examples you've explored have used variables that store text strings. However, JavaScript variables can store different types of information. The type of information stored in a variable is referred to as its **data type**. JavaScript supports the following data types:

- numeric value
- text string
- Boolean value
- null value

A **numeric value** is any number, such as 13, 22.5, or -3.14159. Numbers can also be expressed in scientific notation, such as 5.1E2 for the value 5.1×10^2 (or 510). Numeric values are specified without any quotation marks. So if you wished to store the value 2007 in the year variable, you would use the statement

```
year = 2007;
```

rather than

```
year = "2007";
```

A **text string** is any group of characters, such as "Hello" or "Happy Holidays!" or "421 Sunrise Lane." Text strings must be enclosed within either double or single quotation marks, but not both. The string value 'Hello' is acceptable, but the string value "Hello' is not.

A **Boolean value** indicates the truth or falsity of a statement. There are only two Boolean values: true and false. For example, the following statement sets the value of the useSafari variable to true and the value of the useIE variable to false:

```
useSafari = true;
useIE = false;
```

Tip

If a Boolean variable's value is left undefined, it is interpreted by JavaScript as having a value of false.

Boolean values are most often used in programs that must act differently based on different conditions. The useSafari variable cited above might be used in a program that tests whether a user is running the Safari browser. If the value is set to true, the program might be written to run differently for the user than if the value were set to false.

Finally, a **null value** indicates that no value has yet been assigned to the variable. This can also be done explicitly using the keyword null in assigning a value to the variable, as in the statement

```
emLink = null;
```

or implicitly by simply declaring the variable without assigning it a value, as follows:

```
var emLink;
```

In either case, the emLink variable will have a null value until it is assigned a value using one of the other data types.

In JavaScript, a variable's data type is always determined by the context in which it is used. This means that a variable can switch from one data type to another within a single program. In the following two statements, the variable Month starts out as a numeric variable with an initial value of 5, but then becomes a text string variable containing the text March:

```
Month = 5;
Month = "March";
```

When variables are not strictly tied to specific data types like this, programmers refer to the language as a **weakly typed language**; JavaScript is one such language. Other programming languages are **strongly typed languages**, forcing the programming to explicitly identify a variable's data type. In those languages, the above code would result in an error because a given variable cannot store more than one type of data.

A weakly typed language such as JavaScript relieves the programmer from the task of assigning a data type to a variable. However, this can lead to unpredictable results if you aren't careful. For example, in JavaScript the + symbol can be used with either numeric values or text strings. When used with numeric values, it returns the sum of the values—so that the code

```
var total = 5 + 4;
```

stores the value 9 in the total variable. When used with text strings, the + symbol combines the text strings—so that the code

```
var emLink = "cadler" + "@" + "mpl.gov";
```

stores the text string cadler@mpl.gov in the emLink variable. However, when used with both text strings and numeric values, the + symbol treats the numeric value as a text string so that the code

```
x = 5;
y = "4";
z = x+y;
```

stores the text string 54 in the z variable because the y variable stores "4" as a text string, not a number. This result is not readily apparent from the code without a prior understanding of how JavaScript handles text and numeric values. This is one of the limitations of a weakly typed language in which data types are inferred by the rules of the language and not by the programmer.

To see how the + symbol works with text string variables, you'll add a third variable to your script. The emLink variable will be used to store the complete e-mail address for Catherine Adler by combining the userName variable with the emServer variable.

To create the emLink variable:

1. Return to the **mpl.htm** file in your text editor.

2. Directly below the command to create the emServer variable, insert the following command, as shown in Figure 10-14:

```
var emLink = userName + "@" + emServer;
```

Figure 10-14 | **Creating the emLink variable**

```
<script type="text/javascript">
    var userName = "cadler";
    var emServer = "mpl.gov";
    var emLink = userName + "@" + emServer;

    document.write("<a href='mailto:cadler@mpl.gov'>");
    document.write("cadler@mpl.gov");
    document.write("</a>");
</script>
```

> the value stored in the emLink variable is cadler@mpl.gov

▶ **3.** Save your changes to the file.

After you've created a variable, you can use it in JavaScript statements in place of the value it contains. The following code writes the text string Monroe Public Library to a Web page:

```
var libName = "Monroe Public Library";
document.write(libName);
```

You can also use the + symbol to combine a variable with a text string and then write the combined text string to the document. The following statements send the text string

```
<p>Welcome to the Monroe Library</p>
```

to the Web document:

```
var libName = "Monroe Library";
document.write("<p>Welcome to the "+libName+"</p>");
```

You can use the document.write() command with the variables you've already created to write the hypertext link for Catherine Adler's e-mail address. The code is as follows:

```
document.write("<a href='mailto:" + emLink + "'>");
document.write(emLink);
document.write("</a>");
```

If the text string cadler@mpl.gov is stored in the emLink variable, these commands will write the following code to the Web page:

```
<a href='mailto:cadler@mpl.gov'>
caldler@mpl.gov
</a>
```

Notice that the document.write() command nests single quotes within double quotes so that the HTML code written to the Web page includes the value of the href attribute within a set of single quotation marks. You'll add this JavaScript code to the Web page, replacing the previous document.write() commands.

To replace the document.write() commands in the script:

▶ **1.** Return to the **mpl.htm** file in your text editor.

▶ **2.** Replace the three document.write() commands in the script with the following code, as shown in Figure 10-15:

```
document.write("<a href='mailto:" + emLink + "'>");
document.write(emLink);
document.write("</a>");
```

Writing the value of the emLink variable to the Web page | **Figure 10-15**

```
<script type="text/javascript">
    var userName = "cadler";
    var emServer = "mpl.gov";
    var emLink = userName + "@" + emServer;

    document.write("<a href='mailto:" + emLink + "'>");
    document.write(emLink);
    document.write("</a>");
</script>
```

3. Save your changes to the file and then reload **mpl.htm** in your Web browser. The hypertext link for Catherine Adler's e-mail address should remain unchanged from what was shown earlier in Figure 10-11.

Creating a JavaScript Function

So far, in writing code for the staff directory page, you've focused on the e-mail address of only one person. However, five other individuals are listed in the staff directory. If you wanted to use JavaScript to write the e-mail links for the rest of the directory, you could repeat the code you used for Catherine Adler's entry five more times. However, JavaScript provides a simpler way of doing this.

When you want to reuse the same JavaScript commands throughout your Web page, you store the commands in a function. A **function** is a collection of commands that performs an action or returns a value. Every function includes a **function name**, which identifies it, and a set of commands that are run when the function is called. Some functions also require **parameters**, which are variables associated with the function. The general syntax of a JavaScript function is

```
function function_name(parameters){
    JavaScript commands
}
```

where *function_name* is the name of the function, *parameters* is a comma-separated list of variables used in the function, and *JavaScript commands* are the statements run by the function. Function names, like variable names, are case sensitive. For example, weekDay and WEEKDAY are treated as different function names. A function name must begin with a letter or underscore (_) and cannot contain any spaces. The following is an example of a function named showMsg() that writes a paragraph to a Web document:

```
function showMsg() {
    document.write("<p>Welcome to the Monroe Library</p>");
}
```

There are no parameters to this function. If you had stored the name of the library in a function parameter named libName, the showMsg() function would look as follows:

```
function showMsg(libName) {
    document.write("<p>Welcome to the" + libName +"</p>");
}
```

If the libName parameter had the value Monroe Public Library, then the HTML code

```
<p>Welcome to the Monroe Public Library</p>
```

would be sent to the Web document.

Rather than rewrite the code for generating the e-mail link for each person in the staff directory, you'll put the commands in a function named showEM(). The code for the showEM() function is as follows:

```
function showEM(userName,emServer) {
    var emLink = userName+"@" + emServer;
    document.write("<a href='mailto:" + emLink + "'>");
    document.write(emLink);
    document.write("</a>");
}
```

Compare the code for this function to the script you created in Figure 10-15. Note that userName and emServer variables from that earlier code are used here as parameters of the showEM() function.

Add the showEM() function to the document head of the mpl.htm file.

To insert the showEM() function:

▶ **1.** Return to the **mpl.htm** file in your text editor.

▶ **2.** Directly above the closing </head> tag, insert the following script element and function, as shown in Figure 10-16:

```
<script type="text/javascript">
    function showEM(userName,emServer) {
        var emLink = userName + "@"+emServer;
        document.write("<a href='mailto:" + emLink + "'>");
        document.write(emLink);
        document.write("</a>");
    }
</script>
```

Figure 10-16 ▶ **Inserting the showEM() function**

```
<title>Monroe Public Library</title>
<link href="mplstyles.css" rel="stylesheet" type="text/css" />

<script type="text/javascript">
    function showEM(userName, emServer) {
        var emLink = userName + "@" + emServer;
        document.write("<a href='mailto:" + emLink + "'>");
        document.write(emLink);
        document.write("</a>");
    }
</script>
</head>
```

Calling a Function

When a browser encounters a function, it bypasses it without executing any of the code it contains. The function is executed only when called by another JavaScript command. If the function has any parameters, the initial values of the parameters are set when the function is called. The expression to call a function and run the commands it contains has the following form:

function_name(parameter values)

where *function_name* is the name of the function and *parameter values* is a comma-separated list of values that match the parameters of the function. For example, to call the showMsg() function described earlier using the text string Monroe Public Library as the value of the libName parameter, you would run the command

```
showMsg("Monroe Public Library");
```

The HTML code

```
<p>Welcome to the Monroe Public Library</p>
```

would be written to the document.

Parameter values can also themselves be variables. The following commands store the library name in a text string variable named libText and call the showMsg() function using that variable as the parameter value:

```
var libText="Cutler Public Library";
```

```
showMsg(libText);
```

The result is that the following HTML code is written to the Web document:

```
<p>Welcome to the Cutler Public Library</p>
```

Functions can be called repeatedly with different parameter values to achieve different results. For example, the following code calls the showMsg() function twice with different parameter values to display two welcome paragraphs for the Monroe and Cutler Public Libraries:

```
var libText = "Monroe Public Library";
showMsg(libText);
var libText2 = "Cutler Public Library";
showMsg(libText2);
```

You can use a function call to run the showEM() function you just entered. To write a hypertext link for Catherine Adler's e-mail address, the function call is as follows:

```
showEM("cadler","mpl.gov");
```

As a result, the userName parameter has an initial value of cadler and the emServer parameter has the initial value of mpl.gov. You're ready to replace the commands you entered earlier to write the hypertext link for Catherine Adler's e-mail address with this function call.

To call the showEM() function:

▶ 1. Return to the **mpl.htm** file in your text editor, and scroll down the file to the script element containing the JavaScript code for Catherine Adler's e-mail address.

▶ 2. Replace all of the commands within the script element with the following command, as shown in Figure 10-17:

```
showEM("cadler","mpl.gov");
```

Figure 10-17 | Calling the showEM() function

```
<tr>
    <td>Catherine Adler<br />Library Director</td>
    <td>555-3100</td>
    <td>

        <script type="text/javascript">
            showEM("cadler","mpl.gov");
        </script>

    </td>
</tr>
```

▶ **3.** Save your changes to the file and then reload **mpl.htm** in your Web browser. The link to Catherine Adler's e-mail address should once again appear in the staff table, unchanged from Figure 10-11.

Using the function call gives the same result as the code you used earlier. However, the great advantage is that you can reuse the showEM() function for other e-mail addresses in the staff directory by simply changing the parameter values. You don't have to reenter all four of the program lines. For longer programs this is a substantial improvement.

Reference Window | **Creating and Calling a JavaScript Function**

- To create a JavaScript function that performs an action, insert the structure
  ```
  function function_name(parameters){
      JavaScript commands
  }
  ```
  where *function_name* is the name of the function, *parameters* is a comma-separated list of variable names used in the function, and *JavaScript commands* are the statements run by the function.
- To create a JavaScript function that returns a value, use
  ```
  function function_name(parameters){
      JavaScript commands
      return value;
  }
  ```
  where *value* is the value returned by the function.
- To call a JavaScript function, run the command
  ```
  function_name(values)
  ```
  where *function_name* is the name of the JavaScript function and *values* is a comma-separated list of values for each of the parameters of the function.

Kate asks you to call the showEM() function for the other e-mail addresses in the staff table.

To add the remaining e-mail addresses:

▶ **1.** Return to the **mpl.htm** file in your text editor.

▶ **2.** Locate the entry for Michael Li. His e-mail address is mikeli@mpl.gov. Add the following script element to the empty table cell that directly follows the Michael Li entry:

```
<script type="text/javascript">
    showEM("mikeli","mpl.gov");
</script>
```

3. Kate Howard's e-mail address is khoward@mpl.gov. Insert the following script element in the empty table cell for her entry in the staff directory:

```
<script type="text/javascript">
   showEM("khoward","mpl.gov");
</script>
```

Trouble? You can use the copy and paste feature of your text editor because the additions you'll make to the file in these steps are so similar. If you're not sure where to place these script elements, refer to Figure 10-18.

4. Robert Hope's e-mail address is rhope@mpl.gov. Enter the following script element for his entry:

```
<script type="text/javascript">
   showEM("rhope","mpl.gov");
</script>
```

5. Wayne Lewis's e-mail address is wlewis@mpl.gov. Enter the following script element in the empty table cell for his entry:

```
<script type="text/javascript">
   showEM("wlewis","mpl.gov");
</script>
```

6. Bill Forth's e-mail address is bforth@mpl.gov. Enter the following code in the empty table cell for his entry:

```
<script type="text/javascript">
   showEM("bforth","mpl.gov");
</script>
```

Figure 10-18 shows the revised code in the mpl.htm file.

Inserting the remaining e-mail addresses **Figure 10-18**

```
<tr>
   <td>Michael Li<br />Head of Adult Services</td>
   <td>555-3145</td>
   <td>
      <script type="text/javascript">
         showEM("mikeli","mpl.gov");
      </script>
   </td>
</tr>
<tr>
   <td>Kate Howard<br />Head of Technical Services</td>
   <td>555-4389</td>
   <td>
      <script type="text/javascript">
         showEM("khoward","mpl.gov");
      </script>
   </td>
</tr>
<tr>
   <td>Robert Hope<br />Head of Children's Services</td>
   <td>555-7811</td>
   <td>
      <script type="text/javascript">
         showEM("rhope","mpl.gov");
      </script>
   </td>
</tr>
<tr>
   <td>Wayne Lewis<br />Circulation Services Supervisor</td>
   <td>555-9001</td>
   <td>
      <script type="text/javascript">
         showEM("wlewis","mpl.gov");
      </script>
   </td>
</tr>
<tr>
   <td>Bill Forth<br />Interlibrary Loan</td>
   <td>555-9391</td>
   <td>
      <script type="text/javascript">
         showEM("bforth","mpl.gov");
      </script>
   </td>
</tr>
```

> **7.** Save your changes to the file and reload **mpl.htm** in your Web browser. Figure 10-19 shows the complete list of e-mail addresses in the staff directory. Verify that each e-mail address is a hypertext link by hovering your mouse pointer over the address text and observe the destination of the link in the browser's status bar.

Figure 10-19 ▶ **The complete list of e-mail address links in the staff directory**

Name	Phone	E-Mail
Catherine Adler Library Director	555-3100	cadler@mpl.gov
Michael Li Head of Adult Services	555-3145	mikeli@mpl.gov
Kate Howard Head of Technical Services	555-4389	khoward@mpl.gov
Robert Hope Head of Children's Services	555-7811	rhope@mpl.gov
Wayne Lewis Circulation Services Supervisor	555-9001	wlewis@mpl.gov
Bill Forth Interlibrary Loan	555-9391	bforth@mpl.gov

> **8.** If you want to take a break before starting the next session, you can close any open files and programs now.

Creating a Function to Return a Value

You created the showEM() function to perform the action of writing a text string to your Web document. The other use of functions is to return a calculated value. For a function to return a value, it must include a return statement. The syntax of a function that returns a value is

```
function function_name(parameters){
   JavaScript commands
   return value;
}
```

where *value* is the calculated value that is returned by the function. For example, the following CalcArea() function calculates the area of a rectangular region by multiplying the region's length and width:

```
function CalcArea(length, width) {
   var area = length*width;
   return area;
}
```

In this function, the value of the area variable is returned by the function. You can then call the function to retrieve this value. The following code uses the function to calculate the area of a rectangle whose dimensions are 8 × 6 units:

```
var x = 8;
var y = 6;
var z = CalcArea(x,y);
```

The first two commands assign the values 8 and 6 to the x and y variables, respectively. The values of both of these variables are then sent to the CalcArea() function as the values of the length and width parameters. The CalcArea() function uses these values to calculate the area, which it then returns, assigning that value to the z variable. As a result of these commands, a value of 48 is assigned to the z variable.

Functions that return a value can be placed within larger expressions. For example, the following code calls the CalcArea() function within an expression that multiplies the area value by 2:

```
var z = CalcArea(x,y)*2;
```

When this command is run, the value of the CalcArea() function is returned, multiplied by 2, and then stored in the z variable. Using the above parameter values, the value of the z variable is 96.

Functions and Variable Scope | InSight

As you've seen, the commands within a function are run only when called. This has an impact on how variables within the function are treated. Every variable you create has a property known as **scope**, which indicates where you can reference a variable within the Web page. A variable's scope can be either local or global. A variable created within a JavaScript function has **local scope** and can be referenced only within that function. Variables with local scope are sometimes referred to as **local variables**. In the function you created in this session, the emLink variable has local scope and can be referenced only within the showEM() function. Parameters such as the userName and emServer parameters from the showEM() function also have local scope and are not recognized outside of the function in which they're used. When the showEM() function stops running, those variables and their values are not held in the computer memory and their values can no longer be accessed.

Variables not declared within functions have **global scope** and can be referenced from within all script elements on the Web page. Variables with global scope are often referred to as **global variables**.

You've successfully added the showEM() function to the staff directory page. In the next session you'll continue to add features to that function, including the ability to scramble and unscramble e-mail addresses to further hide them from e-mail harvesters.

Session 10.2 Quick Check | Review

1. Specify the JavaScript command to declare a variable named weekday with an initial value of Friday.
2. Describe two uses of the + symbol.
3. What are the four data types supported by JavaScript?
4. Specify the JavaScript command to write the code

   ```
   <img src='file' alt='' />
   ```

   to the Web page, where *file* is the value stored in the fileName variable.

5. What are the two purposes of a JavaScript function?
6. Write a JavaScript function named CalcVol() to calculate the volume of a rectangular solid. The function should have three parameters named x, y, and z, and return the value of a variable named Vol that is equal to x*y*z.
7. Write the JavaScript statement to call the CalcVol() function with values of x = 3, y = 10, and z = 4, storing the result of the function in a variable named TotalVol.
8. What is variable scope?

Session 10.3

Accessing an External JavaScript File

You show your work on the staff directory to Kate. She's happy that you were able to use JavaScript to generate the e-mail addresses, but she's still concerned that the text of each employee's username and mail server are present in the document as parameter values of the showEM() function. She would like to have those values hidden from any e-mail harvesters that might be scanning the document code. You discuss the issue with a programmer friend who sends you a file containing the following function:

```
function stringReverse(textString) {
   if (!textString) return '';
   var revString='';
   for (i = textString.length-1; i>=0; i--)
      revString+=textString.charAt(i);
   return revString;
}
```

Interpreting the code contained within this function is beyond the scope of this tutorial, but for now it is sufficient to know in general what the function does. The function has a single parameter named textString, which stores a string of characters. The function then creates a variable name revString that stores the characters from textString in reverse order, and that reversed text string is returned by the function. For example, if you called the function in the statements

```
userName = stringReverse("reldac");
emServer = stringReverse("vog.lpm");
```

the userName variable would have the value cadler, and the emServer variable would have the value mpl.gov (the text strings reldac and vog.lpm in reverse order). You show this function to Kate and she agrees that this will be sufficient to hide the actual username and server name from most e-mail address harvesters.

The stringReverse() function has already been entered for you and stored in a file named spam.js. To access JavaScript code and functions placed in external files, you employ the same script element you've been using to insert JavaScript commands directly into the staff directory document. The code to access an external script file is

```
<script src="url" type="mime-type"></script>
```

where *url* is the URL of the external document and *mime-type* is the language of the code in the external script file. For example, to access the code in the spam.js file, you would add the following script element to your Web document:

```
<script type="text/javascript" src="spam.js"></script>
```

Tip

Place all script elements that reference external files in the document head so that those programs are immediately loaded by the Web browser and can be referenced by any code within the Web page.

It's a common practice for JavaScript programmers to create libraries of functions located in external files that are easily accessible to pages on the entire Web site. Any new functions added to the external file are then instantly accessible to each Web page without having to edit the contents of those pages. External files containing JavaScript commands and functions always have the file extension .js to distinguish them from files containing script commands from other languages.

When a browser encounters a script element that points to an external file, it loads the contents of the external file into the Web document just as if the programmer had entered the code from the external file directly into the Web file. See Figure 10-20.

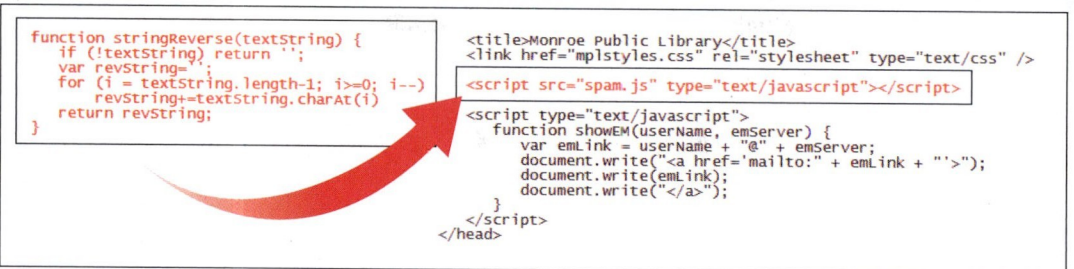

Accessing an External JavaScript File

| Reference Window

- To access the code stored in an external file, add the script element
  ```
  <script src="url" type="mime-type"></script>
  ```
  to the Web page, where *url* is the URL of the external document and *mime-type* is the language of the code in the external script file.
- For JavaScript files, set the *mime-type* to text/javascript.
- JavaScript files usually have the file extension .js.

You insert a script element into the staff directory page to access the code from the spam.js file.

To access the code in the spam.js file:

1. Return to the **mpl.htm** file in your text editor.

2. Directly above the opening <script> tag in the head section of the file, insert the following script element, as shown in Figure 10-21:

```
<script src="spam.js" type="text/javascript"></script>
```

Inserting a link to an external script file ◀ Figure 10-21

```
<title>Monroe Public Library</title>
<link href="mplstyles.css" rel="stylesheet" type="text/css" />

<script src="spam.js" type="text/javascript"></script>

<script type="text/javascript">
    function showEM(userName, emServer) {
        var emLink = userName + "@" + emServer;
        document.write("<a href='mailto:" + emLink + "'>");
        document.write(emLink);
        document.write("</a>");
    }
</script>
</head>
```

Next you'll want to confirm that the stringReverse() function from the spam.js file is working correctly. To test the function, call it to reverse the text string values of the user-Name and emServer parameters in the showEM() function.

To test the stringReverse() function:

1. Scroll down to the showEM() function.

2. Insert the following two lines of code at the top of the function, as shown in Figure 10-22:

```
userName = stringReverse(userName);
emServer = stringReverse(emServer);
```

Figure 10-22	Calling the stringReverse() function

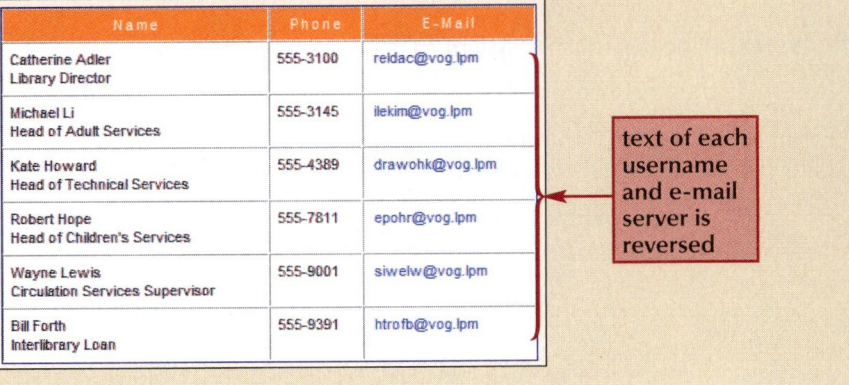

```
<script type="text/javascript">
    function showEM(userName, emServer) {

        userName = stringReverse(userName);
        emServer = stringReverse(emServer);

        var emLink = userName + "@" + emServer;
        document.write("<a href='mailto:" + emLink + "'>");
        document.write(emLink);
        document.write("</a>");
    }
</script>
```

reverse the order of the characters in the userName and emServer parameters

3. Save your changes to the file, and then reload **mpl.htm** in your Web browser. As shown in Figure 10-23, the text of the username and mail server portions of each employee's e-mail address appears reversed on the Web page.

Figure 10-23	Staff directory with e-mail addresses reversed

Name	Phone	E-Mail
Catherine Adler Library Director	555-3100	reldac@vog.lpm
Michael Li Head of Adult Services	555-3145	ilekim@vog.lpm
Kate Howard Head of Technical Services	555-4389	drawohk@vog.lpm
Robert Hope Head of Children's Services	555-7811	epohr@vog.lpm
Wayne Lewis Circulation Services Supervisor	555-9001	siwelw@vog.lpm
Bill Forth Interlibrary Loan	555-9391	htrofb@vog.lpm

text of each username and e-mail server is reversed

The stringReverse() function appears to be working correctly. Of course, you don't want the e-mail addresses to be reversed in the rendered document; you want those addresses to appear correctly. Instead, you want the code within the document reversed to thwart e-mail harvesters. This means that you need to enter the username and e-mail server names in reverse order.

To change the userName and emServer parameter values:

1. Return to the **mpl.htm** file in your text editor.

2. Scroll down the file to the script element for Catherine Adler's e-mail address and change the value of the userName parameter from cadler to **reldac**. Change the value of the emServer parameter from mpl.gov to **vog.lpm**.

3. Change the parameter values for Michael Li's e-mail address to **ilekim** and **vog.lpm**.

4. Change the parameter values for Katherine Howard's e-mail address to **drawohk** and **vog.lpm**.

▶ **5.** Change the parameter values for Robert Hope's e-mail address to **epohr** and **vog.lpm**.

▶ **6.** Change the parameter values for Wayne Lewis's e-mail address to **siwelw** and **vog.lpm**.

▶ **7.** Finally, change the parameter values for Bill Forth's e-mail address to **htrofb** and **vog.lpm**. Figure 10-24 highlights the revised code in the file.

Entering the reversed userName and emServer parameter values ◀ Figure 10-24

```html
<tr>
    <td>Catherine Adler<br />Library Director</td>
    <td>555-3100</td>
    <td>
        <script type="text/javascript">
            showEM("reldac","vog.lpm");
        </script>
    </td>
</tr>

<tr>
    <td>Michael Li<br />Head of Adult Services</td>
    <td>555-3145</td>
    <td>
        <script type="text/javascript">
            showEM("ilekim","vog.lpm");
        </script>
    </td>
</tr>
<tr>
    <td>Kate Howard<br />Head of Technical Services</td>
    <td>555-4389</td>
    <td>
        <script type="text/javascript">
            showEM("drawohk","vog.lpm");
        </script>
    </td>
</tr>
<tr>
    <td>Robert Hope<br />Head of Children's Services</td>
    <td>555-7811</td>
    <td>
        <script type="text/javascript">
            showEM("epohr","vog.lpm");
        </script>
    </td>
</tr>
<tr>
    <td>Wayne Lewis<br />Circulation Services Supervisor</td>
    <td>555-9001</td>
    <td>
        <script type="text/javascript">
            showEM("siwelw","vog.lpm");
        </script>
    </td>
</tr>
<tr>
    <td>Bill Forth<br />Interlibrary Loan</td>
    <td>555-9391</td>
    <td>
        <script type="text/javascript">
            showEM("htrofb","vog.lpm");
        </script>
    </td>
</tr>
```

▶ **8.** Save your changes to the file and reload **mpl.htm** in your Web browser. As shown in Figure 10-25, the text characters of the e-mail addresses for staff members now appear in the correct order.

Figure 10-25 ▶ **Final staff directory page**

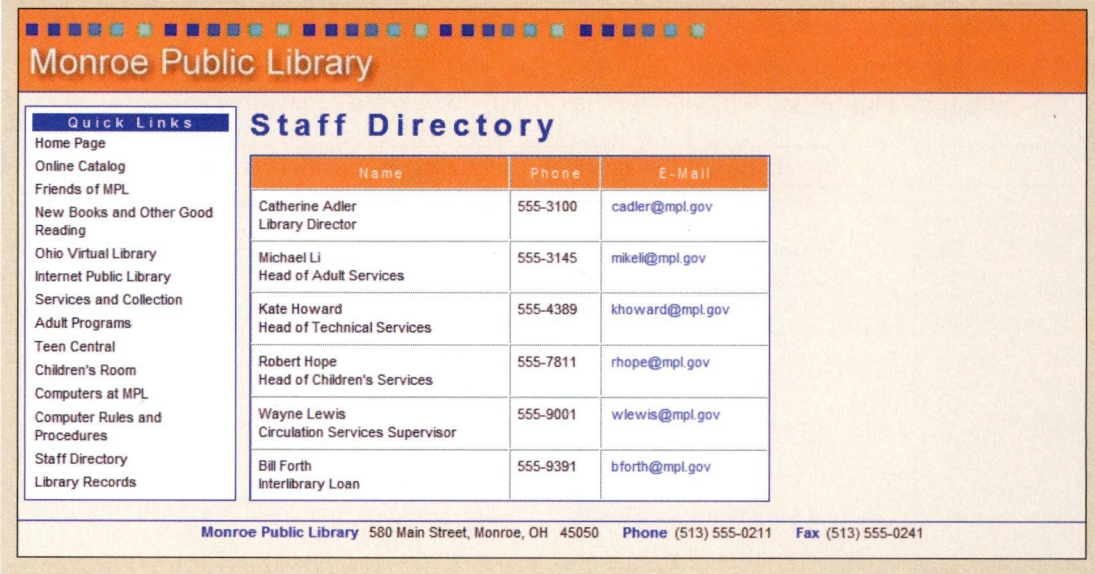

You review your progress with Kate. As she scans through the code in the HTML file, she's pleased to note that none of the e-mail addresses for the six staff members appears in any readable form. By breaking the e-mail addresses into two parts (the userName and the emServer parts) and entering the text in reverse order, you have effectively hidden the actual addresses from harvesting programs.

Commenting JavaScript Code

Kate is pleased to see how JavaScript can unscramble the e-mail addresses and present them to users in a readable form. However, she is concerned that in the future, she might forget how this program is designed to work. She would like you to add some comments to the code you created.

Inserting Single-Line and Multiline Comments

Commenting your code is an important programming practice. It helps other people who examine your code to understand what your programs are designed to do and how they work. It can even help you in the future when you return to edit the programs you've written and need to recall the programming choices you made. In JavaScript, comments can be added to script elements on either single or multiple lines. The syntax of a single-line comment is

```
// comment text
```

where *comment text* is the JavaScript comment. Single-line comments can be placed within the same line as a JavaScript command, making it easier to interpret each command in your code. The following is an example of a JavaScript statement that includes a single-line comment:

```
document.write(emLink); // write e-mail address to the Web page
```

For more extended comments, you place the comment text on several lines using the following structure:

```
/*
   comment text spanning
   several lines
*/
```

The following is an example of a multiline comment applied to a JavaScript program:

```
/*
   The showEM() function displays a link to the user's e-mail address.
   The text of the user and e-mail server names are entered in
   reverse order to thwart e-mail harvesters.
*/
```

Inserting JavaScript Comments | Reference Window

- To insert a single-line comment into a JavaScript program, use
  ```
  // comment text
  ```
  where *comment text* is the JavaScript comment. Single-line comments can be placed on the same line as a JavaScript command.
- To insert several lines of comments, use the following:
  ```
  /*
     comment text spanning
     several lines
  */
  ```

Kate would like you to add comments to the showEM() function you created.

To add comments to your JavaScript code:

1. Return to the **mpl.htm** file in your text editor.

2. Add the following multiline comment directly below the opening function statement for the showEM() function:

   ```
   /*
      The showEM() function displays a link to the user's
      e-mail address.
      The text of the user and e-mail server names are entered in
      reverse order to thwart e-mail harvesters.
   */
   ```

3. Add the following single-line comment to the end of the line that reverses the value of the userName parameter:

   ```
   // reverse the text of the userName parameter
   ```

4. Add the following comment to the end of the line that reverses the value of the emServer parameter:

   ```
   // reverse the text of the emServer parameter
   ```

5. Finally, add the following comment to the end of the line creating the emLink variable:

   ```
   // combine the text of userName and emServer
   ```

   Figure 10-26 displays these comments in the mpl.htm file.

Figure 10-26   **Adding comments to the showEM() function**

```
<script type="text/javascript">
    function showEM(userName, emServer) {
        /*
           The showEM() function displays a link to the user's e-mail address.
           The text of the user and e-mail server names are entered in
           reverse order to thwart e-mail harvesters.
        */

        userName = stringReverse(userName); // reverse the text of the userName parameter
        emServer = stringReverse(emServer); // reverse the text of the emServer parameter

        var emLink = userName + "@" + emServer; // combine the text of userName and emServer
        document.write("<a href='mailto:" + emLink + "'>");
        document.write(emLink);
        document.write("</a>");
    }
</script>
```

▶ **6.** Close the **mpl.htm** file, saving your changes.

▶ **7.** Reopen **mpl.htm** in your Web browser and verify that you have not introduced any errors by adding comments to the showEM() function.

▶ **8.** You can close any open files or programs now.

You show the commented version of the showEM() function to Kate. She agrees that it will help her better remember the purpose of the function and how the function works.

Using Comments to Hide JavaScript Code

Comments have another purpose besides documenting the code used in a JavaScript application. Older browsers that do not support JavaScript can present a problem for Web designers. If such browsers encounter JavaScript commands, they might display the program code as part of the Web page body. To avoid this problem, you can hide a script from these browsers using both HTML and JavaScript comment lines. The following is the syntax for doing this:

```
<script type="text/javascript">
   <!--Hide from nonJavaScript browsers
        JavaScript commands
   // Stop hiding from older browsers -->
</script>
```

When a Web browser that doesn't support scripts encounters this code, it ignores the <script> tag, as it does any tag it doesn't recognize. The next line it sees is the start of the HTML comment tag, which doesn't close until the arrow symbol (-->) in the second-to-last line. This means that the browser ignores the entire JavaScript program. It similarly ignores the final </script> tag.

On the other hand, a browser that does support JavaScript recognizes the <script> tag and ignores any HTML tags found between the <script> and </script> tags. Therefore, in this example, it bypasses the comment tag in the second line and processes the JavaScript program as written. The JavaScript comment, which starts with the double slash symbol (//) in the second-to-last line, is included to help other users understand and interpret your code.

Hiding JavaScript code from older browsers is not as important as it once was, so you will not add this feature to the JavaScript code for the staff directory page.

Debugging Your JavaScript Programs

As you work with JavaScript, you will inevitably encounter scripts that fail to work because of an error in the code. To fix a problem with a program, you need to debug it. **Debugging** is the process of searching code to locate a source of trouble. To debug a program, you must first determine the type of error present in your code.

There are three types of errors: load-time errors, run-time errors, and logical errors. A **load-time error** occurs when a script is first loaded by the browser. As the page loads, the browser reads through the code looking for mistakes in syntax. For example, suppose you had neglected to include the closing parenthesis, as in the following command from the showEM() function:

```
document.write("</a>";
```

In this case, you would be making a mistake in the syntax of the document.write() method. When a load-time error is uncovered, the JavaScript interpreter halts loading the script. Depending on the browser, an error message might also appear. Figure 10-27 shows the message generated by the above error in Internet Explorer. An error message can include the line number and character number of the error. This does not mean that the error occurred at this location in the document—the source of the trouble could be much earlier in the script. The message simply indicates the location at which the JavaScript interpreter was forced to cancel loading the script.

Reporting a load-time error Figure 10-27

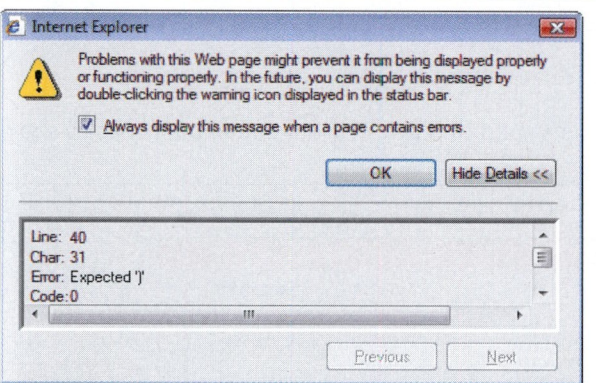

A **run-time error** occurs after a script has been successfully loaded and is being executed. In a run-time error, the mistake occurs when the browser cannot complete a line of code. One common source of a run-time error is mislabeling a variable name. For example, the line of code

```
document.write(emlink);
```

in the showEM() function would result in the run-time error shown in Figure 10-28.

| Figure 10-28 | ▶ | **Reporting a run-time error** |

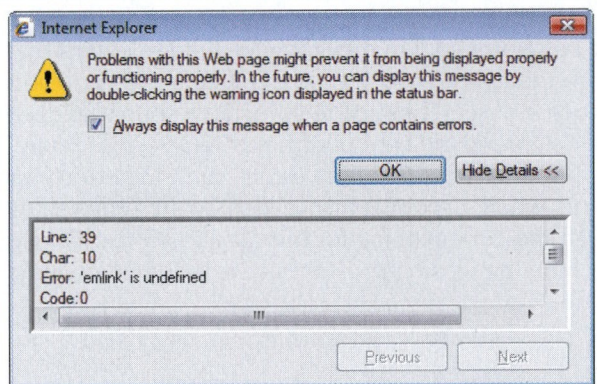

The mistake in this line of code is that there is no variable named emlink in the showEM() function—the variable name should be emLink (recall that variable names are case sensitive). When a browser attempts to write the contents of the emlink variable to the Web document, it discovers that no such variable exists and reports the run-time error. When a JavaScript interpreter catches a run-time error, it halts execution of the script and displays an error message indicating the location where it was forced to quit.

Logical errors are free from syntax and structural mistakes, but result in incorrect results. A logical error is often the hardest to fix and sometimes requires you to meticulously trace every step of your code to detect the mistake. Suppose you had incorrectly entered the line of code to create the emLink variable, placing the server name before the username, as follows:

```
var emLink = emServer + "@" + userName;
```

In this case, a browser would display the list of e-mail addresses as shown in Figure 10-29.

| Figure 10-29 | ▶ | **Displaying a logical error** |

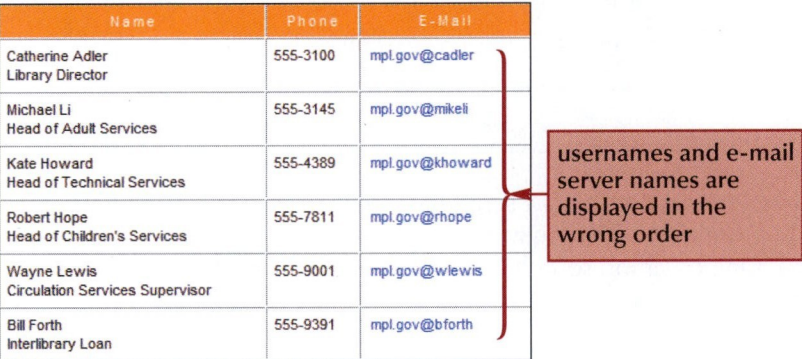

Although the browser did not report any mistakes, this is obviously not the way Kate wants e-mail addresses displayed!

Common Mistakes in JavaScript Programs | InSight

When you begin writing JavaScript programs, you will invariably encounter mistakes in your code. Some common sources of programming error include:

- Misspelling a variable name: For example, if you named a variable ListPrice, then misspellings or incorrect capitalization—such as listprice, ListPrices, or list_price—will result in the program failing to run correctly.
- Mismatched parentheses or braces: The following code results in an error because the function lacks the closing brace:

  ```
  function Area(width, height) {
     var size = width*height;
  ```

- Mismatched quotes: If you neglect the closing quotes around a text string, JavaScript treats the text string as an object or variable, resulting in an error. The following code results in an error because the closing double quote is missing from the firstName variable:

  ```
  var firstName = "Sean';
  var lastName = "Lee";
  document.write(firstName+" " + lastName);
  ```

- Missing quotes: When you combine several text strings using the + symbol, you might neglect to quote all text strings. For example, the following code generates an error because of the missing quotes around the <br /> tag:

  ```
  document.write("MidWest Student Union" + <br />);
  ```

As you become more experienced in writing JavaScript code, you'll be able to quickly spot these types of errors, making it easier for you to debug your programs.

Debugging Tools and Techniques

There are several techniques you can employ to avoid making programming mistakes and to quickly locate the mistakes you do make. One is to write **modular code**, which is code that entails breaking up a program's different tasks into smaller, more manageable chunks. A common strategy when creating modular code is to use functions that perform a few simple tasks. The different functions can then be combined and used in a variety of ways.

If you do encounter a logical error in which the incorrect results are displayed by the browser, you can monitor the changing values of your variables using an alert dialog box. An **alert dialog box** is a dialog box generated by JavaScript that displays a text message with an OK button. Clicking the OK button closes the dialog box, allowing the browser to resume running the JavaScript code. The command to create an alert dialog box is

```
alert(text);
```

where *text* is the text string that you want displayed in the dialog box. You can also use a variable name in place of a text string. For example, the command

```
alert(emLink);
```

displays the current value of the emLink variable. Figure 10-30 shows the appearance of this dialog box for the first entry in the library staff directory. Alert dialog boxes are useful in determining what is happening to your variable values while a program is running.

Figure 10-30 ▶ **Displaying a variable value in an alert dialog box**

Browsers also offer various tools for debugging JavaScript programs. Microsoft offers the **Microsoft Script Debugger**, a debugger available for use with its Internet Explorer browser running under Windows XP. The Microsoft Script Debugger is available for free from the Microsoft Web site and is also included with the Microsoft Office XP suite. When the Microsoft Script Debugger is installed on your system, it displays a prompt when it encounters a load-time or run-time error in one of your scripts. See Figure 10-31.

Figure 10-31 ▶ **Runtime Error dialog box**

Tip

To enable script debugging on Internet Explorer, you might have to turn on script debugging from the Advanced tab on the Internet Explorer Options dialog box.

Clicking the Yes button opens the Microsoft Script Debugger window, highlighting the source of the error. As shown in Figure 10-32, the source of this particular error is that the showEM() function was referenced as showem(). Because function names are case sensitive, the browser was unable to locate the function and reported an error. You can learn more about the script debugger using the online help provided with the Microsoft Script Debugger or at the Microsoft Web site.

Microsoft Script Debugger window ◀ Figure 10-32

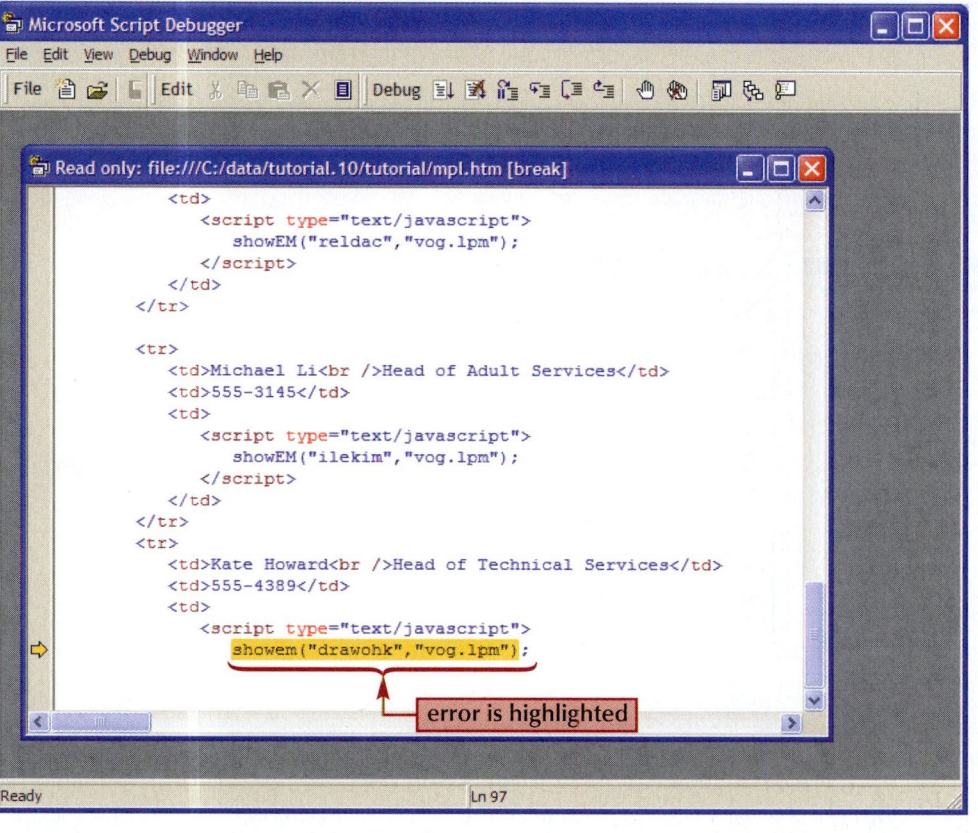

Firefox also provides the **Firefox Error Console** that displays all of the errors generated within the current document. To view the list of errors, type javascript: in the address bar as shown in Figure 10-33.

Figure 10-33 ▶ **Accessing the Firefox Error Console**

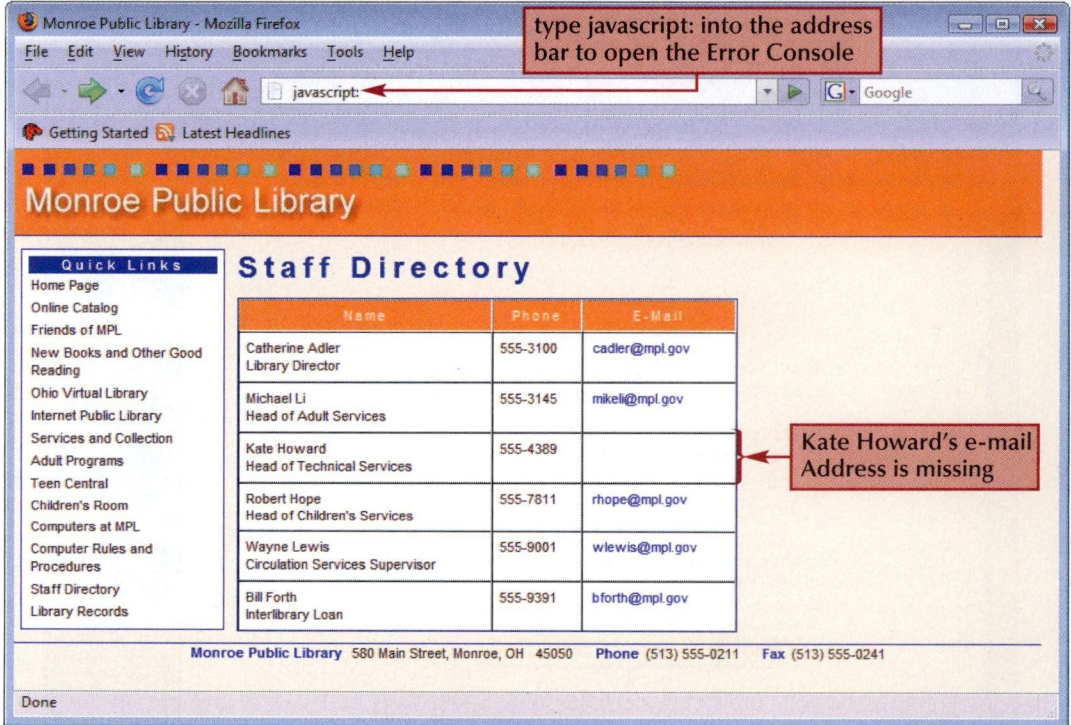

The Error Console appears as another Firefox browser window, as shown in Figure 10-34. Within the Error Console is an Evaluate box in which you can insert JavaScript commands to evaluate your code and variable values at the point at which the error occurred.

Figure 10-34 ▶ **The Firefox Error Console**

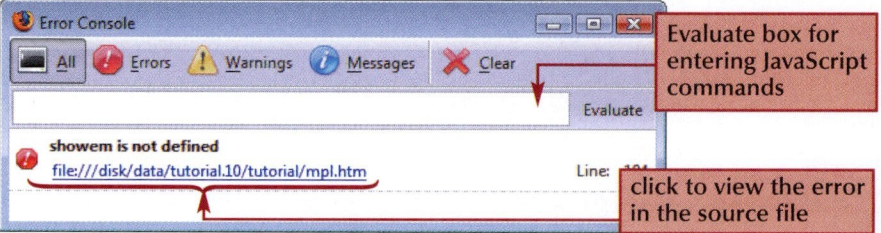

The Error Console also includes a hypertext link to another Firefox window that displays the code for the source file. The point at which the error was first detected (not necessarily the source of the error) is highlighted in this window, as shown in Figure 10-35.

Highlighting the source of the error ◄ **Figure 10-35**

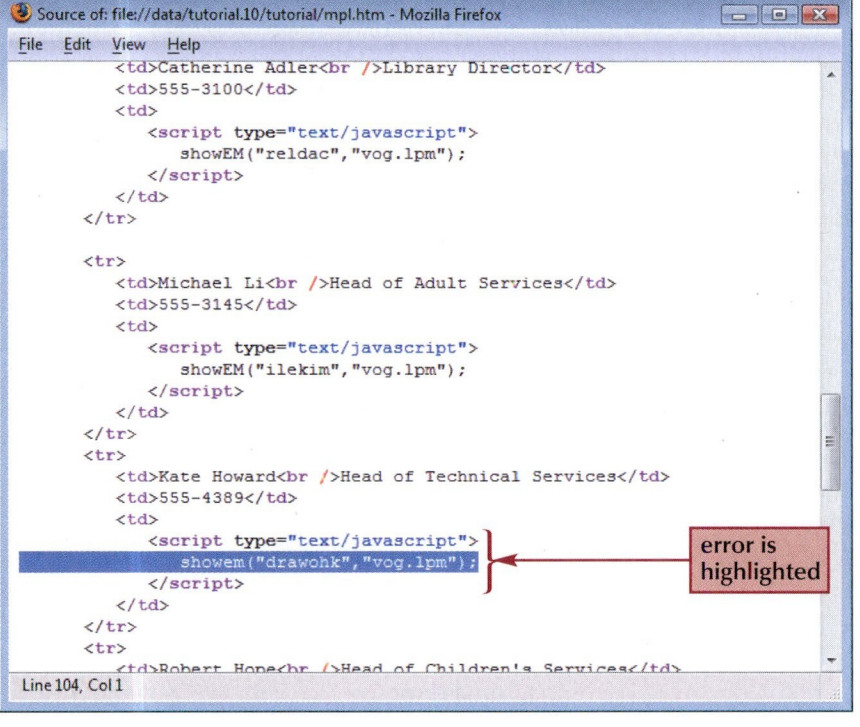

You can learn more about Firefox's Error Console by using the online help in the console window. Because errors inevitably creep into any programming task you undertake, it's important to be familiar with the various debugging tools available to you.

You've completed your work on the staff directory for the Monroe Public Library. Kate will call you again as other issues with the library's Web site arise.

Session 10.3 Quick Check | Review

1. Specify the code to access the JavaScript file library.js.
2. Specify the code to enter the single-line JavaScript comment Library of JavaScript functions.
3. Specify the code to enter following multiline JavaScript comment:
   ```
   The library.js file contains a collection of
   JavaScript functions for use with the file index.htm
   ```
4. What is debugging?
5. What code would you enter to display the value of the userName variable in an alert dialog box?
6. What are the three types of errors generated by mistakes in a JavaScript program?
7. Your code has a misspelled variable name. What type of error will result from the mistake?

In this tutorial you learned how to create and run Web page programs written in the JavaScript language. In the first session, you learned about the history of JavaScript and how it compares to Java. You then studied how to create a script element and how to use JavaScript to write text to a Web document. In the second session, you learned how to create and use variables as well as how to write and call a JavaScript function. The third session examined how to access code in external JavaScript files. The session then demonstrated how to document your code with comments. The tutorial concluded with a discussion of common scripting errors and an overview of some tools and techniques you can use to ensure that your code is error free.

Key Terms

alert dialog box	function	null value
Boolean value	function name	numeric value
client-side programming	global scope	object
command	global variable	parameter
compiled language	human input validation	run-time error
data type	interpreted language	scope
debugging	JavaScript	server-side programming
declaring	JScript	spam
ECMA	load-time error	spammer
ECMAScript	local scope	statement
e-mail harvester	local variable	strongly typed language
European Computer	logical error	text string
Manufacturers	method	variable
Association	Microsoft Script Debugger	VBScript
Firefox Error Console	modular code	weakly typed language

| Practice | **Review Assignments** |

Practice the skills you learned in the tutorial using the same case scenario.

Data Files needed for the Review Assignments: 0.jpg through 9.jpg, mpl2txt.htm, mpl.jpg, mplstyles.css, and random.js

Kate has a new assignment for you. One of the pages on the Monroe Public Library Web site is the library records page, which contains sensitive information about library patrons and the books they have checked out. Kate has created a Web form in which a staff member enters a username and password before getting access to the library records. However, Kate has heard that some hackers create programs that search for Web forms that open confidential pages. One technique of these hackers is to have automated programs that submit thousands of username/password combinations, hoping to break into the system. Kate knows that some sites use human input validation to thwart these programs.

Human input validation is a technique that requires the entry of some piece of information that humans can easily enter, but automated programs cannot. One approach is to display a series of images containing numbers or letters and request that the user enter the numbers or letters being displayed. Because most automated programs can't "see" images, they cannot answer this question; most humans, on the other hand, can enter the requested information without trouble. Kate suggests you write a program that shows five images, each displaying a random number between 0 and 9. In addition to entering a username and password, users will be required to enter the numbers they see on the screen. Figure 10-36 shows a preview of the completed Web page.

| Figure 10-36 |

Your job is to write a script to display the random images. The images have been stored in files named 0.jpg through 9.jpg. To help you, Kate has located a file that contains a JavaScript function to return a random integer from 0 to *size*, where *size* is the largest integer to be returned. The name of the function is randomInteger, so to call the function, you use the command

```
randomInteger(size)
```

For example, to return a random integer from 0 to 5, you would run the command

```
randomInteger(5)
```

The randomInteger() function has been saved for you in the random.js file.

Complete the following:

1. Use your text editor to open **mpl2txt.htm** from the tutorial.10\review folder included with your Data Files. Enter *your name* and *the date* in the comment section of the file and save the file as **mpl2.htm** in the same folder.

2. In the head section, just above the closing </head> tag, insert a script element that accesses the code in the random.js file.

3. Add a second script element for the code that you'll add to the mpl2.htm file.

4. Within the second script element, create a function named showImg(). The purpose of this function is to write an inline image tag into the current document. The function has no parameters. Add the following statements to the function:

   a. Add the following multiline comment to the start of the function, just below the opening showImg() function statement:

   ```
   The showImg() function displays a random image from the
   0.jpg through 9.jpg files.
    The random image is designed to thwart hackers attempting to enter
   the library records database by requiring visual confirmation.
   ```

   b. Declare a variable named imgNumber equal to the value returned by the randomInteger() function. Use 9 as the value of the size parameter in the randomInteger() function.

   c. Append the statement that creates the imgNumber variable with the following single-line comment:

   ```
   Return a random number from 0 to 9.
   ```

   d. Insert a command that writes the text

   ```
   <img src='imgNumber.jpg' alt='' />
   ```

   to the document, where *imgNumber* is the value of the imgNumber variable.

5. Scroll down to the bottom of the file and locate the last table cell in the document. Within this empty table cell, insert a script element.

6. Within the script element, call the showImg() function five times. You do not need to specify a parameter value.

7. Save your changes to the file.

8. Open **mpl2.htm** in your Web browser. Verify that each time you refresh the Web page, a different sequence of five image numbers appears at the bottom of the Web form. Debug your code as necessary using any of the tools or techniques described in this tutorial.

9. Submit your completed files to your instructor.

Apply | Case Problem 1

Use the skills you learned in this tutorial to create an online star map.

Data Files needed for this Case Problem: datetime.js, mask.gif, sky0.jpg through sky23.jpg, skymaptxt.htm, skyweb.css, and skyweb.jpg

SkyWeb Astronomy　　Dr. Andrew Weiss of Central Ohio University maintains an astronomy page called SkyWeb for his students. On his Web site he discusses many aspects of astronomy and stargazing. One of the tools of the amateur stargazer is a planisphere, which is a handheld device composed of two flat disks: one disk shows a map of the constellations, and the other disk contains a window corresponding to the part of the sky that is visible at a given time and date. When a user rotates the second disk to the current date and time, the constellations that appear in the window correspond to the constellations currently visible in the nighttime sky.

Dr. Weiss has asked for your help in constructing an online planisphere for his Web site. He has created 24 different sky charts, named sky0.jpg through sky23.jpg, that represent 24 different rotations of the nighttime sky. He has also created an image containing a transparent window through which a user can view a selected sky chart. A preview of the completed Web page is shown in Figure 10-37.

Figure　10-37

The Planisphere figure showing the SkyWeb online planisphere with sky chart for March 9, 2011, 11:22 pm.

| Home Page | The Night Sky | The Moon | The Planets | The Messier Objects | Stars |

Dr. Weiss has designed the page layout. He needs your help in creating JavaScript code to display the current date and time, and to display the correct sky chart for that date and time. To do this, you've been provided with two functions:

- The showDateTime() function, which returns the current date and time in the text string

      Month Day, Year, hour:time am/pm

where *Month* is the name of the current month, *Day* is the current day, *Year* is the current year, *hour* is the current hour, *minute* is the current minute, and am/pm changes based on the current time.

- The getMap() function, which returns a number from 0 to 23. The number matches the number of the sky map image to show based on the current date and time.

Both functions have been placed in an external JavaScript file named datetime.js.

Complete the following:

1. Use your text editor to open the **skymaptxt.htm** file from the tutorial.10\case1 folder included with your Data Files. Enter *your name* and *the date* in the comment section of the file. Save the file as **skymap.htm** in the same folder.
2. Directly below the link element in the head section, insert a script element accessing the datetime.js file.
3. Below the script element, insert another script element that contains the following statements:
   a. Insert a multiline comment containing the following text:
      **timeStr is a text string containing the current date and time
      mapNum is the number of the map to display in the planisphere**
   b. Declare a variable named timeStr equal to the value returned from the showDateTime() function.
   c. Declare a variable named mapNum equal to the value returned from the getMap() function.
4. Scroll down the file to the div element with id value maps and replace the line
   ```
   <img id="sky" src="sky0.jpg" alt="" />
   ```
   with a script element that writes the following HTML code:
   `<img id='sky' src='mapNum.jpg' alt='' />`
   where *mapNum* is the value of the mapNum variable.
5. Scroll down a few lines and replace the date/time value January 1, 2011, 12:00 a.m. with a script element that writes the value of the timeStr variable to the Web page.
6. Save your changes to the file and then open **skymap.htm** in your Web browser. Verify that the planisphere displays the current date and time.

⊕ EXPLORE
7. If you're able to modify the date/time settings on your computer, change the date and time and then reload or refresh the page to verify that the date/time value changes and that the map also changes. Debug your code as necessary.
8. Submit your completed files to your instructor.

Apply | **Case Problem 2**

Use JavaScript to display random banner ads.

Data Files needed for this Case Problem: ad1.jpg through ad5.jpg, ads.js, fp.jpg, fronttxt.htm, logo.jpg, random.js, and styles.css

Ridgewood Herald Tribune Maria Ramirez manages advertising accounts for the *Ridgewood Herald Tribune* in Ridgewood, New Jersey. Recently, the paper has put more of its content online. To offset the cost of the Web site, Maria is selling ad space on the company's home page. She is looking at creating banner ads to be displayed on the paper's masthead, with each ad linked to the advertiser's Web site. Because ad space on the paper's home page is the most valuable, Maria has decided to sell space to five companies, with the selection of the banner ad determined randomly each time a user opens the page.

Maria has asked for your help in writing the JavaScript code to display banner ads randomly. She has provided a collection of functions that will be useful to you:

- The randInt() function, which returns random integers from 1 to *n*. To call the randInt() function, use the following expression:

  `randInt(n)`

- The adDescription() function, which returns the description of the *n*th ad from a list of ad descriptions. To call the function, use the following expression:

  `adDescription(n)`

- The adLink() function, which returns the URL of the *n*th ad of the collection. To call the function, use the following expression:

  `adLink(n)`

The random.js file contains the randInt() function. The ads.js file contains the adDescription() and adLink() functions. Figure 10-38 shows a preview of the completed Web page with one of the random banner ads displayed at the top of the page.

Figure 10-38

Complete the following:

1. Use your text editor to open the **fronttxt.htm** file from the tutorial.10\case2 folder included with your Data Files. Enter *your name* and *the date* in the comment section of the file. Save the file as **front.htm** in the same folder.

2. After the link element in the head section, insert a script element accessing the functions in the random.js file.

3. Insert another script element accessing the functions in the ads.js file.

4. Scroll down the file to the div element with the id ads. Replace the content of the div element with a script element containing the following statements:

    a. Declare a variable named rNumber equal to the value returned from the randInt() function using 5 as the parameter value. Append the following comment to the statement:

        ```
        generate a random integer from 1 to 5
        ```

    b. Declare a variable named rAd equal to the text string returned from the adDescription() function using rNumber as the parameter value. Append the following comment to the statement:

        ```
        description of the random ad
        ```

    c. Declare a variable named rLink equal to the URL returned from the adLink() function using rNumber as the parameter value. Append the following comment:

        ```
        URL of the random ad
        ```

    d. Insert a command to write the text

        ```
        <a href="url">
            <img src="adn.jpg" alt="description"/>
        </a>
        ```

        to the Web document, where *url* is the value of the rLink variable, *n* is the value of the rNumber variable, and *description* is the value of the rAd variable.

5. Save your changes to the file.

6. Open **front.htm** in your Web browser. Refresh the Web page multiple times, verifying that different banner ads appear each time the page is refreshed. Debug your code as necessary.

7. Submit your completed files to your instructor.

| Challenge | **Case Problem 3** |

Explore how to write a script to display the daily calendar of events at a student union.

Data Files needed for this Case Problem: back.jpg, friday.htm, functions.js, monday. htm, mw.css, saturday.htm, schedule.css, sunday.htm, thursday.htm, todaytxt.htm, tuesday.htm, and wednesday.htm

Midwest Student Union   Sean Lee manages the Web site for the student union at MidWest University in Salina, Kansas. The student union provides daily activities for the students on campus. As Web site manager, part of Sean's job is to keep the Web site up to date on the latest activities sponsored by the union. At the beginning of each week, she revises a set of seven Web pages detailing the events for each day in the upcoming week.

Sean would like the Web site to display the current day's schedule in an inline frame within the Web page named Today at the Union. To do this, her Web page must be able to determine the day of the week and then load the appropriate file into the frame. She would also like the Today at the Union page to display the current day and date. Figure 10-39 shows a preview of the page she wants you to create.

Figure 10-39

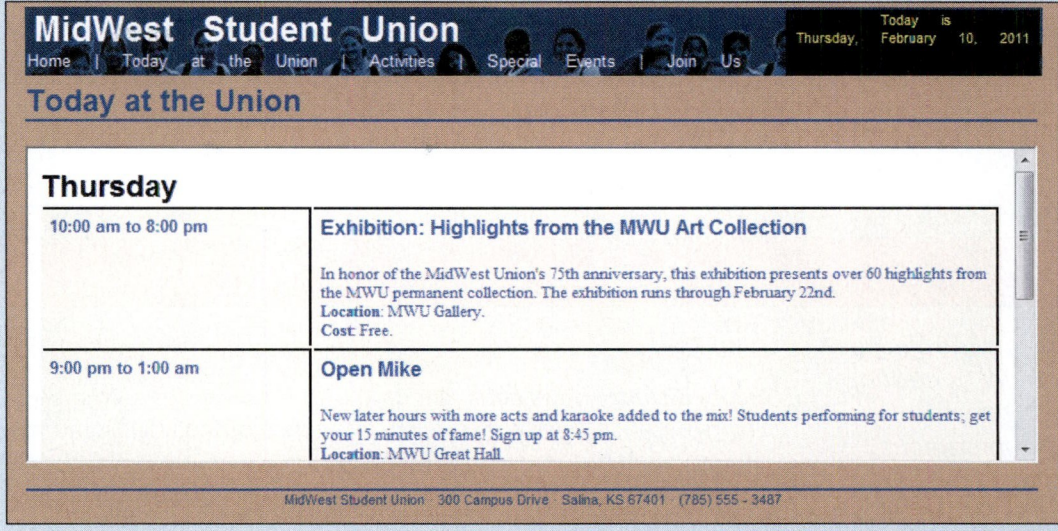

Sean has created the layout of the page, and she needs you to write the scripts to insert the current date and the calendar of events for the current day. To assist you, she has located two functions:

- The showDate() function, which returns a text string containing the current date in the format *Weekday, Month Day, Year*. The function has no parameter values.
- The weekDay() function, which returns a text string containing the name of the current weekday, from Sunday through Saturday. This function also has no parameter values.

The two functions are stored in an external JavaScript file named functions.js. The daily schedules have been stored in files named sunday.htm through saturday.htm.

Complete the following:

1. Use your text editor to open the **todaytxt.htm** file from the tutorial.10\case3 folder included with your Data Files. Enter *your name* and *the date* in the comment section of the file and save it as **today.htm**.

2. In the head section just above the closing </head> tag, insert a script element accessing the functions.js file.

3. Scroll down the file and locate the div element with the id dateBox. Within this element insert a script element. The script should run the following two commands:
   a. Write the following HTML code to the Web page:
      ```
      Today is <br />
      ```

EXPLORE

   b. Write the text string returned by the showDate() function to the Web document.

4. Scroll down the file and locate the h2 heading Today at the Union. Within the empty paragraph that follows this heading, insert another script element. Within the script element, do the following:
   a. Insert the following multiline comment:
      ```
      Display the daily schedule in an inline frame.
      Daily schedules are stored in the files
      sunday.htm through saturday.htm.
      ```

EXPLORE

   b. Insert a command to write the HTML code
      ```
      <iframe src='weekday.htm'></iframe>
      ```
   to the Web page, where *weekday* is the text string returned by the weekDay() function.

5. Save your changes to the document.

6. Open **today.htm** in your Web browser. Verify that it shows the current date and that the daily schedule matches the current weekday.

 EXPLORE

7. If you have the ability to change your computer's date and time, change the date to different days of the week and refresh the Web page. Verify that the date and the daily schedule change to match the new date you selected. Debug your code as necessary.

8. Submit your completed files to your instructor.

Create | **Case Problem 4**

Test your knowledge of JavaScript by creating a splash screen displaying famous birthdays.

Data Files needed for this Case Problem: functions.js and logo.jpg

HappyBirthdayNews.com   Linda Chi is the owner of a Web site called HappyBirthdayNews.com that specializes in birthday gifts and memorabilia. To make her site more interesting for users, Linda wants to create a splash screen that displays the current date and a famous birthday occurring on that date. She has asked for your help in writing the JavaScript code to generate the welcome message. She has designed the page's style and content, and has also located the following JavaScript functions:

- The showDate() function, which returns the current date in the text string *Weekday, Month Day, Year*, where *Weekday* is the day of the week, *Month* is the name of the month, *Day* is the day of the month, and *Year* is the four-digit year value. The showDate() function has no parameters.

- The dayNumber() function, which returns the day number of the current date, ranging from 1 (the first day of the year) to 366 (the last day of the year). The dayNumber() function has no parameters.

- The showBirthDay() function, which returns a text string describing a famous birthday on the given date. The function has a single parameter—*day*—which is equal to the day number of the famous birthday you want to view.

The three functions have already been saved for you in a file named functions.js. Figure 10-40 shows one possible solution to this problem.

Figure 10-40

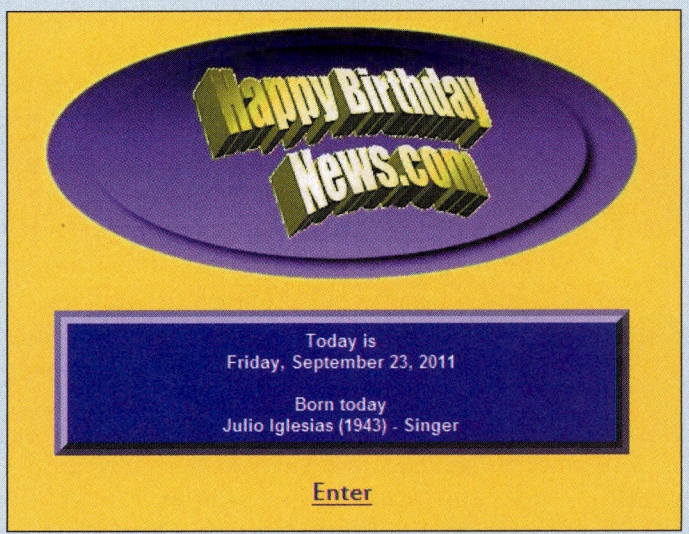

Complete the following:

1. Use your text editor to create the file **birthday.htm** and save it in the tutorial.10\case4 folder included with your Data Files. Create a comment section containing *your name* and *the date* as well as a brief description of the Web page.

2. Create a splash screen introducing the HappyBirthday.com Web site. The content and design of the site are up to you. You can use the **logo.jpg** graphic file as the logo for the Web site and supplement it with any other content or graphics you find.

3. Use your knowledge of JavaScript to add the following features to the Web page:
   - A page element that displays the current date
   - A page element that displays the name of a famous person born on that date
   - Any comments that document each of the variables you use in writing your JavaScript code and any functions you create

4. Save your changes to the file and then open it in your Web browser. Verify that the page displays the current date and a famous person's birthday for that date.

⊕ EXPLORE

5. If you're able to change the date on your computer's clock, change the date and refresh the Web page. Verify that the page displays the new date and a new famous birthday. Debug your code as necessary.

6. Submit your completed files to your instructor.

Review | **Quick Check Answers**

Session 10.1

1. A client-side program is a program that is run on a user's computer, usually with a Web browser. A server-side program runs off of a Web server.

2. `<script type="text/javascript"> ... </script>`

3. `document.write("<h2>Public Library</h2>");`

4. `document.write('<h2 id="sub">Public Library</h2>');`

5. Place the backslash (\) symbol at the end of the line to indicate that the statement continues on the next line.

6. JavaScript is case sensitive, so this statement should read:

   `document.write("Monroe Public Library");`

7. `<noscript>`

      `<p><i>JavaScript required</i></p>`

   `</noscript>`

Session 10.2

1. `var weekday = "Friday";`

2. To calculate the sum of numeric values or to combine text strings into a single text string

3. numeric, text, Boolean, and null

4. `document.write("<img src='" + fileName + "' alt='' />");`

5. To perform an action or to return a value

6. `function CalcVol(x, y, z) {`

      `Vol = x*y*z;`

      `return Vol;`

   `}`

7. `TotalVol = CalcVol(3, 10, 4);`
8. Scope indicates where you can reference a variable within the Web page.

Session 10.3

1. `<script src="library.js" type="text/javascript"></script>`
2. `// Library of JavaScript functions.`
3. ```
   /*
       The library.js file contains a collection of
       JavaScript functions for use with the file index.htm
   */
   ```
4. Debugging is the process of searching code to locate a source of trouble.
5. `alert(userName);`
6. load-time error, run-time error, and logical error
7. a run-time error

Ending Data Files

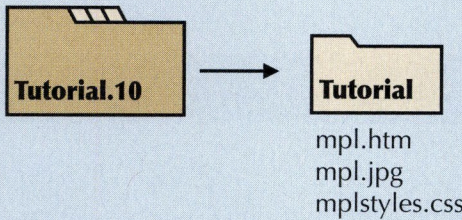

Tutorial.10 → **Tutorial**

mpl.htm
mpl.jpg
mplstyles.css
spam.js

Review

mpl2.htm
mplstyles.css
random.js
+ 11 graphic files

Case1

datetime.js
skymap.htm
skyweb.css
+ 26 graphic files

Case2

ads.js
front.htm
random.js
style.css
+ 7 graphic files

Case3

back.jpg
functions.js
sunday.htm - saturday.htm
today.htm
+ 2 style sheets

Case4

birthday.htm
functions.js
logo.jpg
styles.css
   ```

Reality Check

The Web is constantly changing, offering users new and innovative ways of presenting information and exchanging data. Some of the greatest innovations do not always come from large and well-financed companies, but from entrepreneurs who see ways of bringing something new to the Internet community. In this exercise you will explore the dynamic world of the Web.

Please be sure *not* to include any personal information of a sensitive nature in the files you create to be submitted to your instructor for this exercise. Later on, you can update the files with such information for your personal use.

1. Research the history and development of some of the most important sites on the Web and prepare a report exploring what new features those sites brought to the Web. For example, how did sites such as Google, MySpace, and YouTube change our perception of the Internet? What features did these sites offer that had not previously been part of the Web?

2. Explore the impact that new technology has had on Web page development and the development of XHTML. Focus on the impact of MP3 players, cell phones, and high-speed wireless connections.

3. The most dominant browser on the market is Internet Explorer, but it does not always follow the specifications set forth by the World Wide Web Consortium (W3C). One of the challenges for a Web site designer is the different standards used by Internet Explorer compared to Web browsers that do follow the W3C recommendations. Investigate many of the key differences between Internet Explorer and the W3C specifications for CSS and HTML. Also examine how Web designers resolve these differences.

4. When a Web site changes its content, it's useful to be able to notify users of that fact. One way of informing users of new and interesting material is by creating a feed of the site using RSS. Explore the concepts behind RSS, including the use of RSS in creating audio and video feeds for podcasts.

5. All information on the Web is stored on Web servers. Users interact with the Web using Web browsers run on their PCs and Macintoshes. One approach to make communication between the server and the browser more seamless is called AJAX. Do a Web search on AJAX technology and examine how AJAX has affected the way users interact with Web servers.

6. How is the Web changing? Examine some of the latest trends in the development of the Web. Research the goals of the languages currently in development by the W3C. How will these new languages change the way people design Web sites in the future?

7. Assume that you're a designer who wishes to create a Web site that reports on issues involved with Web page design and changes to the Web. Create a Web site that summarizes what you've learned about the changing nature of the Web. The design and content of the Web site is up to you, but the site should include the following features:

   - At least three pages, one each describing a different aspect of the changing nature of the Web
   - A convenient list of links to enable users to quickly access topics of interest on your Web site
   - Links to all external sites containing the information you've gathered

- At least one external style sheet used by all of the pages on your Web site
- At least one Web table listing some of the information you've gathered for your report
- A Web form in which users can sign up for a newsletter about the changing nature of the Web and HTML
- At least one example of an inline frame that displays the contents of an external Web site
- An audio or video clip introducing your site's contents to the viewer (if you have the ability to create or locate a clip)

8. All of your code should be compliant with the XHTML 1.0 strict DTD. Test your code to ensure its validity.
9. Submit your completed files to your instructor.

Objectives

- Create an image with irregular line wrap
- Insert and format a Web table
- Insert and format an inline frame
- Embed an MP3 sound clip
- Insert and format a Web form

Creating a Music School Web Site

Case | Young Notes

Brenda is the owner of Young Notes, a private music school that has recently opened in Brownwood, Texas. She has asked for your help in setting up the school's Web site. Eventually the Web site will be extensive, covering all of the services offered by the school, but for now Brenda wants you to create a site with five Web pages. The first page will contain the site's home page, describing the Young Notes school. The second page will contain a description of the lessons offered by the school and will include a Web table with a fee schedule. The third page will contain a list of a few members of the Young Notes staff. Brenda wants the staff biographies to appear within an inline frame on the Web page. The fourth page will contain a list of upcoming Young Notes concerts and recitals. Brenda wants you to include a sound clip from last year's Honors Award Concert. The last page will display a Web form that students and their parents can submit to get more information about Young Notes.

Brenda has created much of the site's content and many of the site's styles. She needs you to add a graphic image of a Young Notes student, a table with information on lessons, an inline frame for the staff biographies, a sound clip from last year's concert, and a form for prospective families to fill out to get more information about the school. She also needs you to insert styles into her style sheets for these new elements and to link the Web pages together. Once you're finished, she will use your work as a starting point for planning the final version of the site.

Starting Data Files

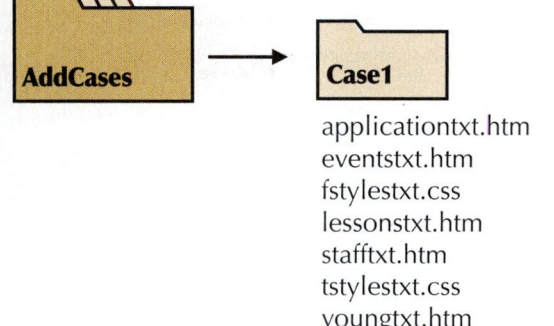

AddCases → Case1

applicationtxt.htm
eventstxt.htm
fstylestxt.css
lessonstxt.htm
stafftxt.htm
tstylestxt.css
youngtxt.htm
ystylestxt.css
+ 4 HTML files
+ 1 style sheet
+ 11 graphic files
+ 1 MP3 file

Complete the following:

1. Use your text editor to open the **applicationtxt.htm**, **eventstxt.htm**, **fstylestxt.css**, **lessonstxt.htm**, **stafftxt.htm**, **tstylestxt.css**, **youngtxt.htm**, and **ystylestxt.css** files from the addcases/case1 folder included with your Data Files. Enter *your name* and *the date* in the comment section of each file. Save the files as **application.htm**, **events.htm**, **fstyles.css**, **lessons.htm**, **staff.htm**, **tstyles.css**, **young.htm**, and **ystyles.css**, respectively, in the same folder.

2. Go to the **young.htm** file in your text editor. This file contains the Young Notes home page. Brenda wants you to add a graphic of a student to the page with an irregular line wrap around the image. Figure AC1-1 shows a preview of the completed page.

Figure AC1-1

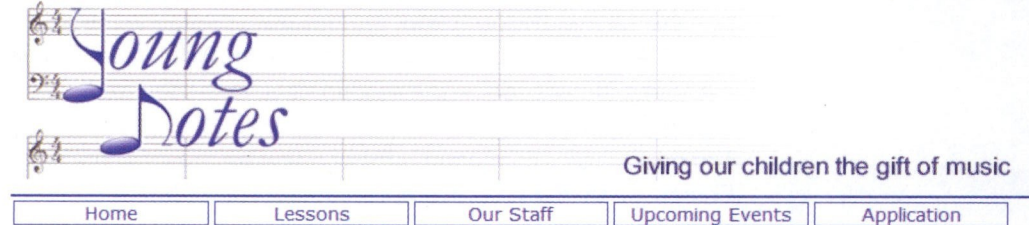

The Young Notes Mission Statement

Young Notes is dedicated to the idea that everyone has the ability to perform and appreciate music and that a life begun with the gift of music will grow in joy.

Our Philosophy

There are few things as rewarding as being able to play a role in the growth of a student's musical talent. New doors open when a student discovers a composer, attends a concert, learns a new piece, or performs for an appreciative audience. We want our students to have a positive experience, establish good practice habits, and have fun. We accept the responsibility of providing the finest instruction for each of our students, of continuing to study and practice our musical art, and of being active members of the community, fully engaged in bringing music to our neighbors.

Why Choose Young Notes?

The Young Notes music program is so much more than music lessons. We strive to give our students the best music education possible. Here are a few things that set us apart:

○ Family Friendly We have programs for everyone in your family! With instruction for just about every instrument, we can arrange lessons for the whole family at one convenient time.

○ Highly Qualified Instructors Young Notes has some of the area's best teachers. Take a look at our instructor bios.

○ Orientation Interviews Finding a good student/teacher match is essential to a student's success. We offer "get to know you" complementary lessons to match each student to the right teacher.

○ Performance With an ongoing schedule of recitals, music festivals, and contests (competitive and non-competitive), students have a chance to hone their performance skills in a friendly, supportive environment.

○ Open Rooms During specified hours you can come in and practice! Call our office to schedule a time.

We look forward to seeing you soon at Young Notes!

Young Notes · 175 South Avenue · Brownwood, TX 76801 · (325) 555 - 0155 · info@youngnotesschool.com

3. To insert the graphic, add five inline image elements at the top of the first paragraph after the initial h2 heading. Set the source of the inline images to **student1.jpg** through **student5.jpg**. Specify an empty text string for the alt attribute.

4. Link the **young.htm** file to the **ystyles.css** style sheet and then close the file, saving your changes.

5. Go to the **ystyles.css** style sheet in your text editor. At the bottom of the file, insert a style to float all img elements nested with the #main selector on the right margin, but only when the right margin is clear of other floating elements. Set the margin around the image elements to 0 pixels, except for the left margin, which should be set to 10 pixels.

6. Save the **ystyles.css** file, and then open the **young.htm** file in your Web browser. Verify that the page resembles that shown in Figure AC1-1 and that the text of the home page wraps around the graphic files that comprise the student image.

7. Go to the **lessons.htm** file in your text editor. This file contains a short summary of the music lessons offered by Young Notes. Figure AC1-2 shows a preview of the completed Web page.

Figure AC1-2

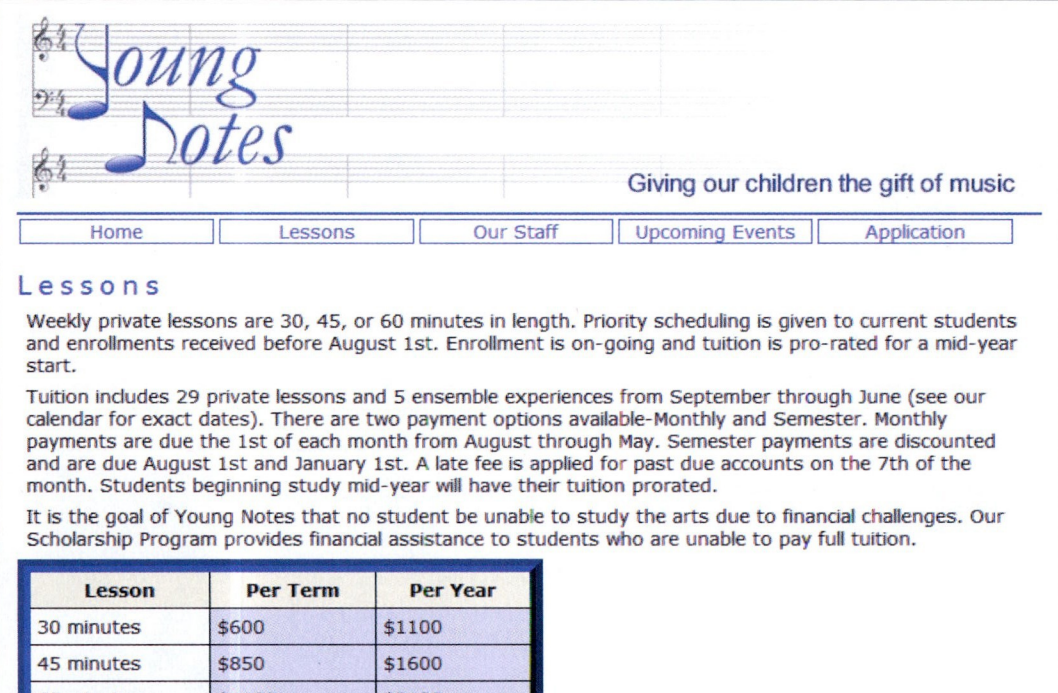

8. At the bottom of the file directly above the last paragraph, insert a Web table containing the following elements.
   a. A table heading row group consisting of one row with three heading cells containing the text Lesson, Per Term, and Per Year.
   b. A table body row group containing three rows of table data cells with the values shown in Figure AC1-2.
   c. A column group containing one column element belonging to the firstCol class and another column element belonging to the feeColumns class. The feeColumns element should span two columns in the Web table.

9. Link the **lessons.htm** file to the **tstyles.css** style sheet and then close the file, saving your changes.

10. Go to the **tstyles.css** file in your text editor. Add the following styles to the style sheet.

    a. Set the font size of the table element to 14 pixels. Add a 10-pixel offset border with the color value (68, 76, 169) around the table. Set the table borders to collapse in case of conflicts with other borders. Set the width of the table to 400 pixels.

    b. Set the background color of the table heading row group to ivory.

    c. Vertically align the text of all table header and table data cells with the top of the cell. Add 5 pixels of padding to those cells. Surround those cells with a 1-pixel-wide solid black border.

    d. Change the background color of table columns belonging to the feeColumns class to the value (232, 232, 255).

11. Close the file, saving your changes, and then in your browser, view the Lessons page. Verify that the layout and format of the Web table resemble that shown in figure AC1-2.

12. Go to the **staff.htm** file in your text editor. This file contains the code for the Young Notes staff page. The biographies of four staff members will appear within an inline frame. The code for the four bio pages has already been done for you. Figure AC1-3 shows a preview of the completed staff page.

Figure AC1-3

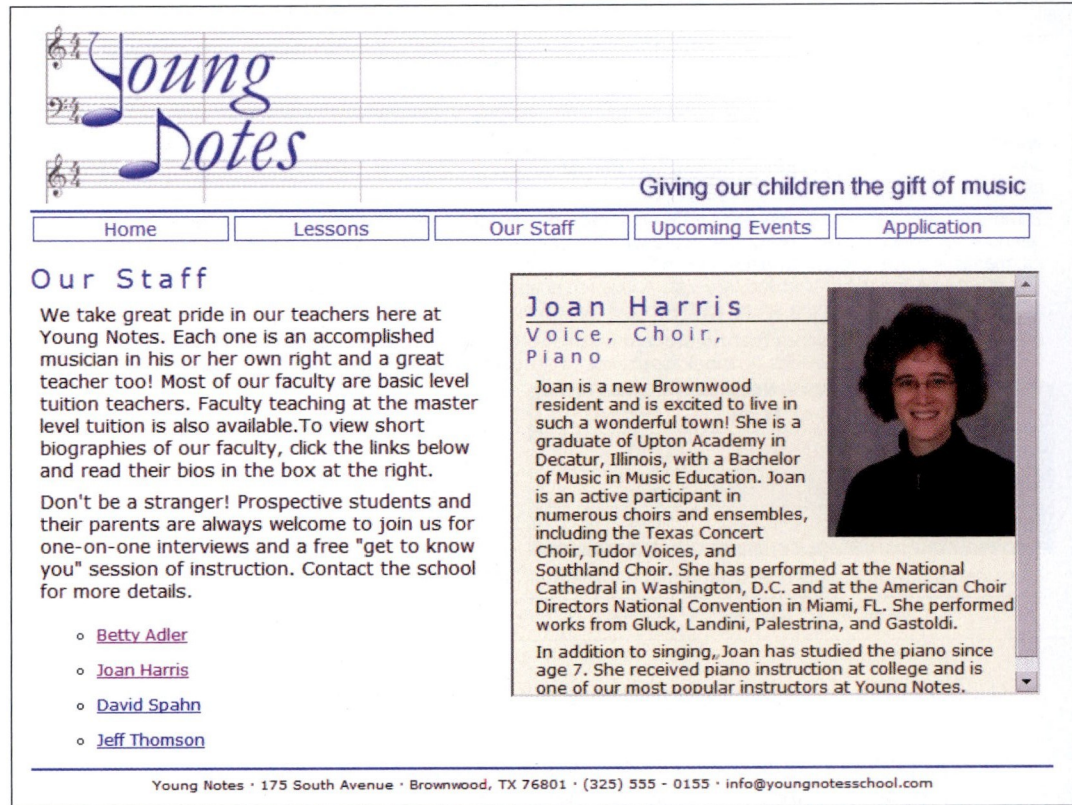

13. Directly above the Our Staff h2 heading, insert an inline frame. Add the following attributes to the frame:

    a. Set the source of the frame to the **badler.htm** file.

    b. Give the frame the name and id bio.

    c. Set the width and height of the frame to 400 pixels by 320 pixels.

    d. Set the margin height and width to 10 pixels.

14. Scroll down to the unordered list of hypertext links for the four staff members listed in this page. Set the target of the four links to open in the bio inline frame you created.

15. Close the **staff.htm** file, saving your changes, and then return to the **ystyles.css** file in your text editor.

16. Add a style to float inline images within the #main selector on the right margin. Set the margin around the inline frame to 10 pixels.

17. Close the **ystyles.css** file, saving your changes. Go to the Our Staff page in your Web browser and verify that each of the four staff bios appears within the inline frame you created.

18. Go to the **events.htm** file in your text editor. This file lists the upcoming events sponsored by Young Notes. Brenda wants you to add an embedded sound clip from a concert performed last year. Figure AC1-4 shows a preview of the page with the embedded sound clip.

Figure AC1-4

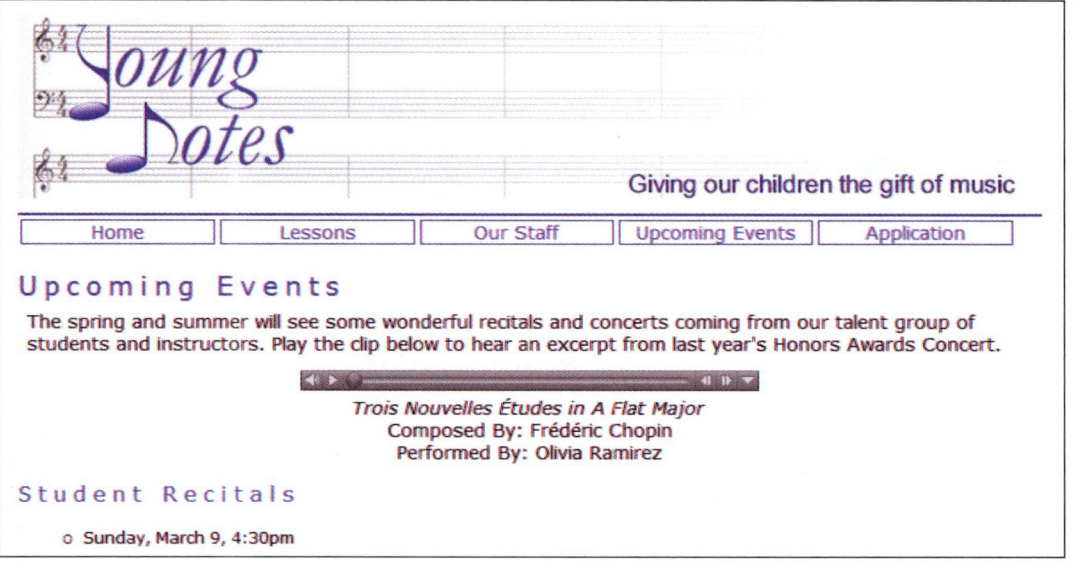

19. In the empty second paragraph directly above the <br /> tag, insert the embedded sound clip using the QuickTime player. Embed the clip as follows:

   a. Use the IE conditional comments to create different HTML code for IE and non-IE browsers.

   b. Embed the chopin.mp3 file with dimensions of the clip being 350 pixels wide by 26 pixels high.

   c. Set the mime-type of the audio file to audio/mpeg.

   d. For IE browsers, embed the clip as an ActiveX object. Include the appropriate class id and codebase values.

   e. Display the QuickTime controls for the player, and do not have the clip start automatically.

   f. For older browsers that do not support the <object> tag, display the clip using the <embed> tag. Set the attribute values of the <embed> tag to match what you set with the <object> tag.

   g. If the browser does not support embedded sound clips, display a hypertext link to the chopin.mp3 file.

20. Close the **events.htm** file, saving your changes. Go to the Upcoming Events page in your Web browser and verify that the embedded sound clip appears under the paragraph text.

21. If you can turn off support for embedded sound clips within your browser, turn off the support and verify that the page displays a link to the chopin.mp3 file.

22. Go to the **application.htm** file in your text editor. In this file you'll insert a Web form that students and adults can fill out and submit to find out more information about Young Notes. Figure AC1-5 shows a preview of the Web page you'll create.

Figure AC1-5

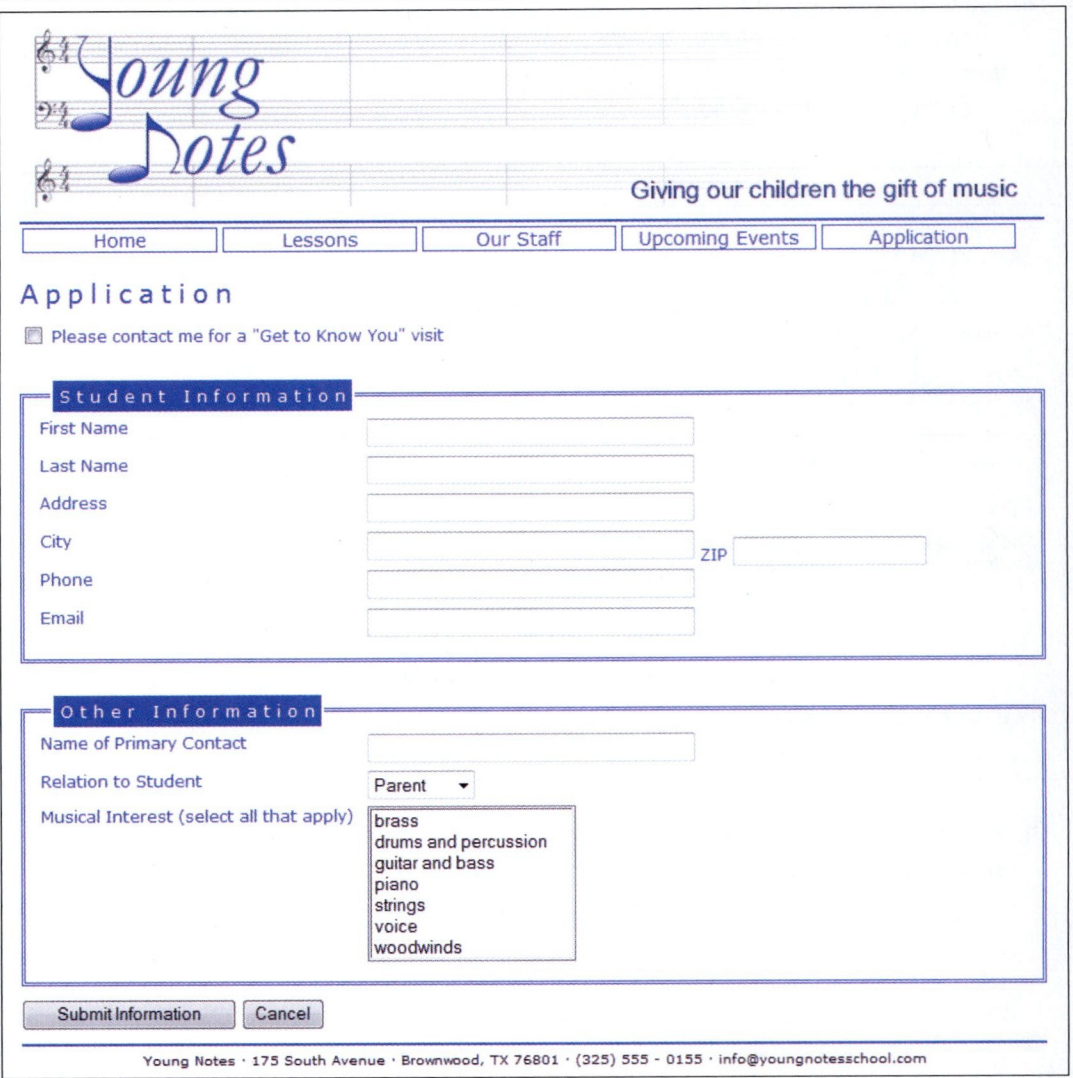

23. Directly below the Application h2 heading, insert a form element. Set the name and id the form to interestForm. Have the form access the CGI script located at *www.youngnotesschool.orgcgi-bin/interest* using the post method.

24. Within the form insert a hidden field named email. Set the value of the hidden field to the e-mail address, info@youngnotesschool.org.

25. Insert a check box field named call. Next to the check box insert a label containing the text, Please contact me for a "Get to Know You" visit.

26. Create a fieldset with the id contactFields and the legend Student Information. Within the fieldset insert the following:
    a. An input box for the fName field. Directly before the input box insert a label for the fName field containing the text, First Name.
    b. Insert a label with the text Last Name, associated with the lName field. Add an input box for the lName field directly after the label.
    c. Insert a label with the text Address, associated with the address field. Add an input box for the text field directly after the label.
    d. Insert a label with the text City, associated with the city field. Add an input box for the city field directly after the label.
    e. Insert a label for the text ZIP, associated with the zip field. Add an input box for the zip field directly after the label.
    f. Insert a label for the phone field containing the text Phone, associated with the phone field. Add an input box for the phone field directly after the label.
    g. Insert a label for the email field containing the text Email, associated with the email field. Add an input box for the email field directly after the label.
    h. Place all of the labels and input box within the contactFields fieldset, within the blockEntry class, except the label and input box for the zip field.
    i. Insert line breaks by placing the <br /> tag after the input boxes for the fName, lName, zip, and phone fields.
27. Below the contactFields field set, insert another field set with the id otherFields. Add the legend containing the text Other Information.
28. Add the following elements to the otherFields field set:
    a. Insert a label containing the text Name of Primary Contact, and associated with the pcontact field. After the label insert an input box for the pcontact field.
    b. Insert a label for the ctype field containing the text Relation to Student. After the label insert a selection list for the ctype field and containing the options Parent and Guardian. The values of the two options are also Parent and Guardian.
    c. Insert a label for the interest field containing the text Musical Interest (select all that apply). After the label insert a selection list containing the text shown in Figure AC1-5. The option values associated with text are: brass, drums, guitar, piano, strings, voice, and woodwinds. Set the size of the selection list to seven entries and allow users to select multiple options from the list.
    d. Place all of the labels, input boxes, and selection lists from the fieldset in the blockEntry class.
    e. Insert line breaks after the pcontact input box and the ctype selection list using the <br /> element.
29. After the otherFields field set, insert a submit button and a cancel button containing the text Submit Information, and Cancel, respectively.
30. Link the **application.htm** file to the **fstyles.css** style sheet. Close the **application.htm** file, saving your changes.
31. Go to the **fstyles.css** file in your text editor. Add the following styles to the style sheet:
    a. Set the font size of the form element to 12 pixels and the font color to the value (68, 76, 169). Set the top and bottom margins of the form to 10 pixels.
    b. Add a 3-pixel double border in the color value (68, 76, 169) to all field sets in the form. Set the top and bottom margin of field sets to 10 pixels. Set the left and right margins of the field sets to 0 pixels. Set the padding of the field sets to 5 pixels.
    c. Display field set legends in a white font on a background color value of (68, 76, 169). Set the letter spacing, padding, and margin of the field set legends to 5 pixels.

    d. Place all labels belonging to the blockEntry class in the form using absolute positioning. Set the value of the large style property to 30 pixels.

    e. Set the width of all input boxes belonging to the blockEntry class to 250 pixels. Set the left margin of those input boxes to 250 pixels as well. Set the bottom margin to 5 pixels.

    f. Set the left margin of all selection lists in the blockEntry class to 250 pixels. Set the bottom margin of those selection lists to 5 pixels.

32. Save your changes to the file, and then go to the Application page in the Young Notes Web site. Verify that the layout and content of the application form resemble that shown in Figure AC1-5.

33. Submit your completed files to your instructor.

Ending Data Files

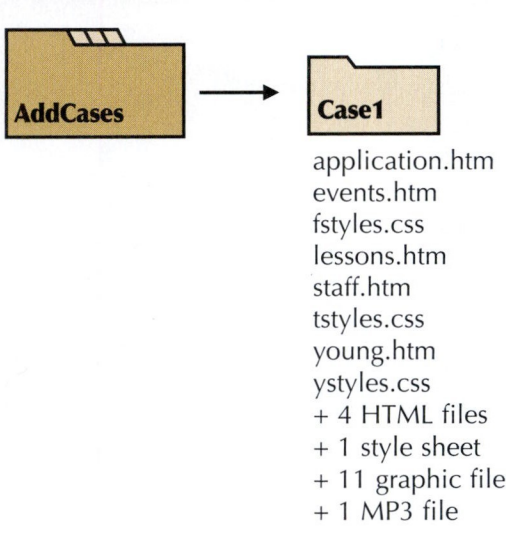

AddCases → Case1

application.htm
events.htm
fstyles.css
lessons.htm
staff.htm
tstyles.css
young.htm
ystyles.css
+ 4 HTML files
+ 1 style sheet
+ 11 graphic files
+ 1 MP3 file

Objectives

- Convert an HTML document to XHTML
- Add rounded corners to a box
- Create a drop-cap
- Generate content with JavaScript
- Create a style sheet for printed output
- Generate content with CSS

Creating a Culinary Web Site

Case | Cornucopia Online

Gary Kendrick is the owner and manager of a shop selling gourmet products. Gary's company began under the name *Cornucopia* and is based in his hometown of Bristol, Connecticut. The store originally was a small shop in which Gary raised and sold turkeys—still a main feature of the company. As the company grew in popularity, Gary branched out into other fields and products, eventually moving its operations to the Web under the name *Cornucopia Online*.

The company has been in operation for several years and Gary is looking at revising the Web site's design and layout. He has hired you as part of his Web site development team. Some of the work on the new design has already been completed; he would like you to complete the design of the site's home page and work on the Recipe of the Week page.

Because of the store's origins in selling turkeys and other poultry, Gary is aware that Thanksgiving and the holidays are a busy time for Cornucopia Online. So, besides the HTML code you'll write, Gary also wants you to add a JavaScript program to the site's home page that will display a countdown message informing customers of the number of days remaining until Thanksgiving.

Starting Data Files

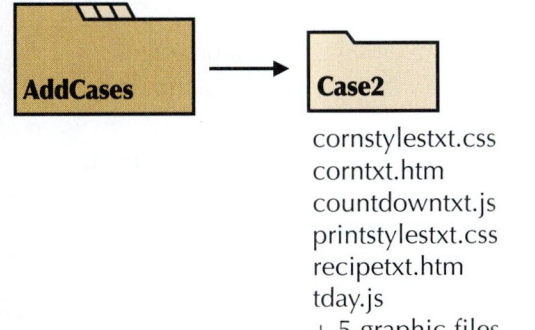

AddCases → Case2

cornstylestxt.css
corntxt.htm
countdowntxt.js
printstylestxt.css
recipetxt.htm
tday.js
+ 5 graphic files

Complete the following:

1. Use your text editor to open the **cornstylestxt.css**, **corntxt.htm**, **countdowntxt.js**, **printstylestxt.css** and **recipetxt.htm** files from the addcases/case2 folder included with your Data Files. Enter *your name* and *the date* in the comment section of each file. Save the files as **cornstyles.css**, **corn.htm**, **countdown.js**, **printstyles.css**, and **recipe.htm**, respectively, in the same folder.

2. Go to the **corn.htm** file in your text editor. This file will be used for the Cornucopia Online home page. A preview of the final version of the page is shown in Figure AC2-1.

Figure AC2-1

3. Link the page to the **cornstyles.css** style sheet.

4. Change the file from an HTML file into an XHTML file by adding an xml prolog, a DOCTYPE declaration for the XHTML strict DTD, and an xml namespace attribute to the opening <html> tag.

5. Gary wants to have a decorative border around the contents of the main div element. To create this decorative border, enclose the contents of the main div element (but not the main div element itself) within a set of four container div elements with id names, bottom, left, corner, and boxContent.

6. Gary also wants to create a drop-cap effect for the first paragraph of text on the home page. Locate the article div element and set the id of the first paragraph within that container to the value firstPara.

7. Save your changes, and then open the **cornstyles.css** file in your text editor.

8. At the bottom of the file, insert a style declaration for the first line of the firstPara div element to display the text of the first line in small capital letters.

9. Insert a style declaration that applies the following styles to the first letter of the firstPara div element:
   a. Float the text on the left margin.
   b. Set the font size to 350% of the normal font size.
   c. Set the line height to 0.8 and the margin to 5 pixels to the right and below the letter, but 0 pixels to the left and above.
   d. Display the first letter in a serif font with the text color value (173, 89, 28).

10. For the #corner selector, display the **corner.jpg** graphic image in the bottom left corner of the element, without repeating. Display the **bottom.jpg** image at the bottom of the div element with the id bottom. Repeat the image only horizontally. Display the **left.jpg** image on the left edge of the div element with the id left. Tile the image only vertically.

11. Set the width of the element with the id boxContent to 740 pixels. Set the padding size to 40 pixels at the bottom and left edge of the element and 0 pixels at the top and right edges.

12. Save your changes, and then open **corn.htm** in your Web browser. Verify that the drop-cap, first line, and decorative borders match Figure AC2-1.

13. Gary has located some JavaScript programs to display the current date and to calculate the number of days until Thanksgiving from the current date. The program to display the current date is named showDate(). The program to calculate the days until Thanksgiving is called daysToThanksgiving(). He's stored both of these programs in the **tday.js** file. Return to the **corn.htm** file in your text editor and insert an external script element pointing to the **tday.js** external JavaScript file.

14. Gary wants you to store the code that writes the days until Thanksgiving in another external script file. Open the **countdown.js** file in your text editor and insert a function named countdown(). The function has no parameters, but should include commands to write the following HTML code to the Web document:
```
Today is: <br />
date
<br /><br /> There are:
days
days until Thanksgiving
```
where *date* is the text returned by the showDate() function and *days* is the text returned by the daysToThanksgiving() function. Neither function requires a parameter value.

15. Close **countdown.js**, saving your changes, and then return to the **corn.htm** file in your text editor. Insert an external script element pointing to the **countdown.js** file.

16. Scroll down to the div element with the id head. Within this div container, insert another div element with the id countdown. Within that div element, insert a script element that calls the countdown() function.

17. Close the **corn.htm** file, saving your changes, and then return to the **cornstyles.css** file in your text editor. At the bottom of the file, insert a style declaration that applies the following format to the countdown div element:
   a. Set the width of the element to 150 pixels and the top/bottom margins to 10 pixels. Set the left/right margins to 0 pixels.

   b. Set the padding to 5 pixels.
   c. Set the font size to 10 pixels.
   d. Float the div element on the right margin.
   e. Add a 2-pixel solid border with the color value (173, 89, 28).

18. Close **cornstyles.css**, saving your changes, and then reload **corn.htm** in your Web browser. Verify that in the upper-right corner there is a box with a message as in Figure AC2-1, indicating the date and the number of days until Thanksgiving.

19. Open **recipe.htm** in your text editor. The page displays the Recipe of the Week, shown in Figure AC2-2.

Figure AC2-2

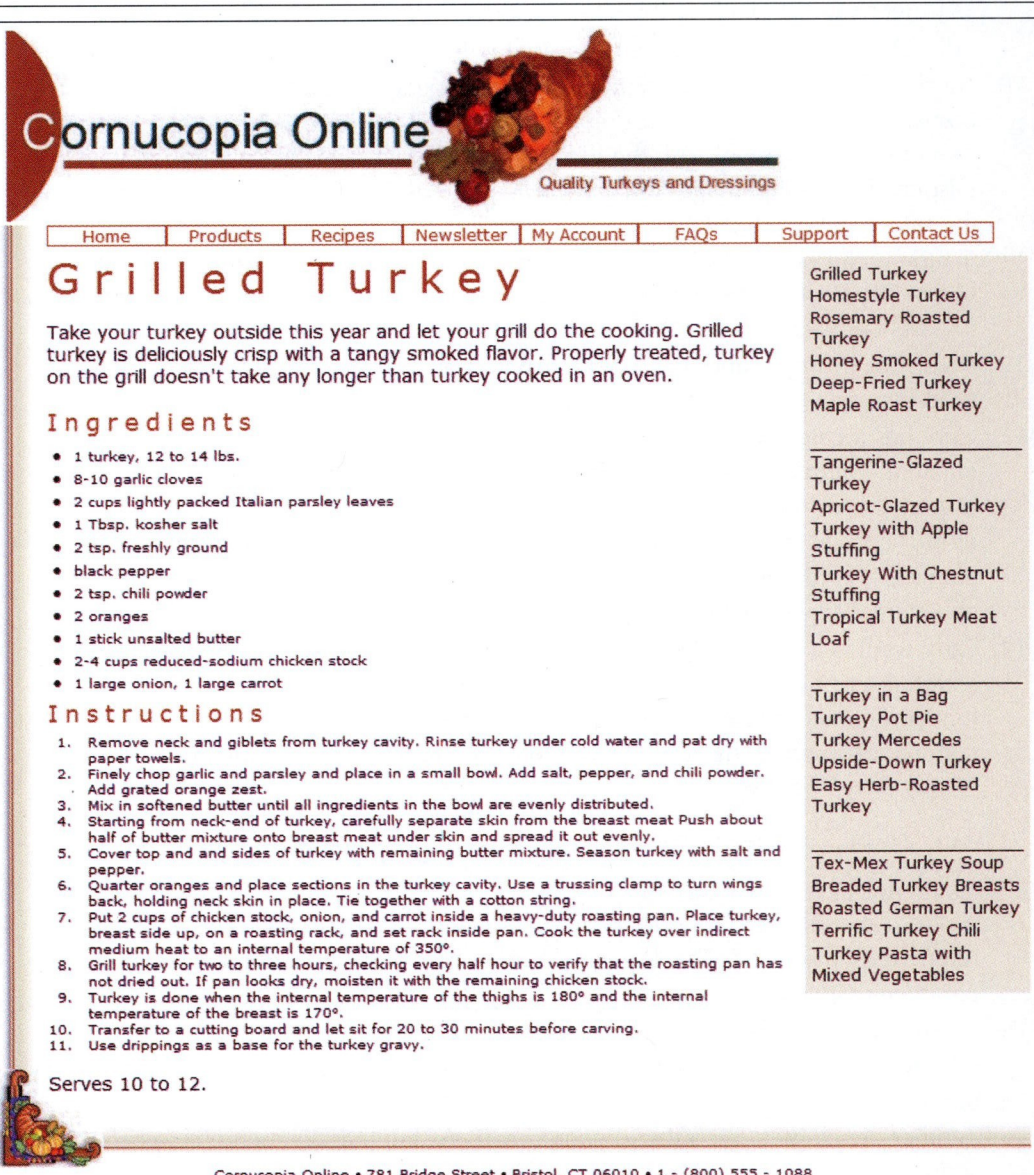

20. Change the format of the file from HTML to XHTML using the XHTML script DTD.

21. Insert a link to the **cornstyles.css** style sheet.

22. As you did for the **corn.htm** file, enclose the contents of the main div element with four container div elements with ids, bottom, left, corner, and boxContent.
23. Save your changes to the file, and then open **recipe.htm** in your Web browser. Verify that the layout and design resemble that shown in Figure AC2-2.
24. Gary wants the printed version of this page to display just the recipe for grilled turkey. Figure AC2-3 shows a preview of the printed output. To create a style sheet for printed output, go to the **printstyles.css** file in your text editor.

Figure AC2-3

Cornucopia Online Recipe Page

Recipe of the Week: Grilled Turkey

Take your turkey outside this year and let your grill do the cooking. Grilled turkey is deliciously crisp with a tangy smoked flavor. Properly treated, turkey on the grill doesn't take any longer than turkey cooked in an oven.

Ingredients

- 1 turkey, 12 to 14 lbs.
- 8-10 garlic cloves
- 2 cups lightly packed Italian parsley leaves
- 1 Tbsp. kosher salt
- 2 tsp. freshly ground
- black pepper
- 2 tsp. chili powder
- 2 oranges
- 1 stick unsalted butter
- 2-4 cups reduced-sodium chicken stock
- 1 large onion, 1 large carrot

Instructions

1. Remove neck and giblets from turkey cavity. Rinse turkey under cold water and pat dry with paper towels.
2. Finely chop garlic and parsley and place in a small bowl. Add salt, pepper, and chili powder. Add grated orange zest.
3. Mix in softened butter until all ingredients in the bowl are evenly distributed.
4. Starting from neck-end of turkey, carefully separate skin from the breast meat Push about half of butter mixture onto breast meat under skin and spread it out evenly.
5. Cover top and and sides of turkey with remaining butter mixture. Season turkey with salt and pepper.
6. Quarter oranges and place sections in the turkey cavity. Use a trussing clamp to turn wings back, holding neck skin in place. Tie together with a cotton string.
7. Put 2 cups of chicken stock, onion, and carrot inside a heavy-duty roasting pan. Place turkey, breast side up, on a roasting rack, and set rack inside pan. Cook the turkey over indirect medium heat to an internal temperature of 350°.
8. Grill turkey for two to three hours, checking every half hour to verify that the roasting pan has not dried out. If pan looks dry, moisten it with the remaining chicken stock.
9. Turkey is done when the internal temperature of the thighs is 180° and the internal temperature of the breast is 170°.
10. Transfer to a cutting board and let sit for 20 to 30 minutes before carving.
11. Use drippings as a base for the turkey gravy.

Serves 10 to 12.

25. Insert an @page rule that defines the size of the printed output as an 8½ × 11″ sheet of paper, with ½″ margins, in portrait orientation.

26. Add a style to prevent the display of the elements with the head, links, and links2 ids. Also hide the address element.

27. Add a style to display h1 and h2 headings in a sans-serif font.

28. For h1 headings, insert a style that automatically inserts the text Recipe of the Week: directly before the h1 heading text.

29. Close the **printstyles.css** file, saving your changes.

30. Return to the **recipe.htm** file in your text editor. Insert a link to the **printstyles.css** file, indicating that this style sheet should only be used for print media.

31. Indicate that the **cornstyles.css** style sheet should be used only for screen media.

32. Close the **recipe.htm** file, saving your changes. Reload the file in your Web browser and either print the page or use the print preview feature of your Web browser to confirm that the print layout resembles that shown in Figure AC2-3. (Note: Internet Explorer does not support the CSS style to insert content, so the printed heading under IE will read just Grilled Turkey.)

33. Using an XHTML validator, test whether the **corn.htm** and **recipe.htm** files pass validation under the strict XHTML DTD. Correct errors until the files pass validation.

34. Submit your completed files to your instructor.

Ending Data Files

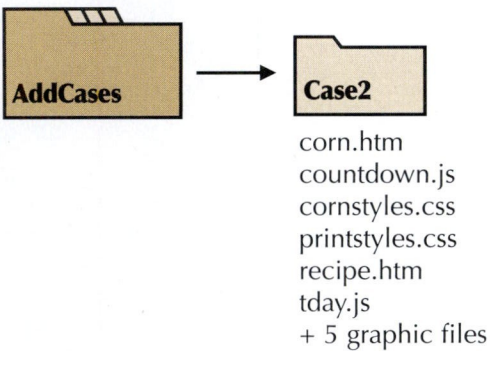

corn.htm
countdown.js
cornstyles.css
printstyles.css
recipe.htm
tday.js
+ 5 graphic files

Objectives

- Design a complete Web site from scratch
- Create an online survey form
- Generate content using a JavaScript function
- Create a style sheet for a complete Web site
- Test a Web site against the XHTML strict DTD

Creating an Online Newsletter

Case | Twin Life Magazine

Twin Life is a magazine created for parents of twins, triplets, and other multiple-birth children. Recently the company has decided to go online and publish parts of its monthly magazine on the World Wide Web. Elise Howard, the magazine's editor, has asked you to create a Web site for the contents of *Twin Life*.

Elise envisions a total of five Web pages for the site: a front page, a news page, a monthly features page, a page of special articles, and a customer survey page. She gave you a disk containing text files of the articles and image files she wants you to include. You are free to supplement these files with any other appropriate material.

Starting Data Files

AddCases → **Case3**

calendar.txt   recipe.txt
chicago.txt   roles.txt
CreditRoll.class   staff.txt
dates.js   survey.txt
deliver.txt   talk.txt
editor.txt   twintips.txt
mbirths.txt   + 8 graphic files
rates.txt

Complete the following:

1. Use your text editor to create the following html files: **articles.htm**, **feature.htm**, **news.htm**, **survey.htm**, **twinlife.htm**, and **twinstyles.css** in the addcases/case3 folder included with your Data Files. Enter *your name, the date,* and *a description* in the comment section of each file.

2. The **twinlife.htm** file should contain the home page for the newsletter. The **articles.htm** should contain a page of articles about twins and child care. The **feature.htm** should contain an advice column and a recipe of the month. The **news.htm** file should contain a page of news stories. Finally, the **survey.htm** should contain a Web form requesting information from newsletter subscribers. Use the text files for the content of these pages, though you are free to supplement these pages with additional material.

3. The design of the Web site is up to you, but it should incorporate the following:
   - Each page should be written to the standards of the XHTML strict DTD.
   - The page should have at least one Web form, a Web table, and an inline frame.
   - All formatting should be done in the **twinstyles.css** style sheet.
   - Each page should contain links to all of the other pages in the Web site so that users can easily navigate from one page to another.

4. The list of upcoming events (found in the **calendar.txt** file) should be displayed in a scrolling window, using the CreditRoll.class Java applet. You need to determine the values of each parameter in the applet, aside from the TEXTx parameters.

5. The home page should display the current date. Use the showDate() function from the dates.js JavaScript file to generate the text of the current date.

6. The magazine's logo (**twinlogo.gif**) should include an image map linking to the five Web pages in the Web site. You will have to determine the coordinates for each hotspot using either your image editing software or an image map editor.

7. A Submit button and a Reset button should be included with the online survey form. The form should be submitted to a CGI script at: *http://www.twinlifemag.com/cgi/survey*.

8. Test all of the files in your Web site against a validator to verify that they pass validation under the XHTML strict DTD.

9. Submit the completed files to your instructor.

Ending Data Files

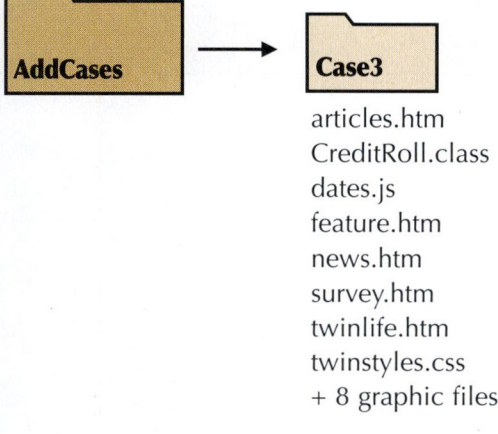

AddCases → **Case3**

articles.htm
CreditRoll.class
dates.js
feature.htm
news.htm
survey.htm
twinlife.htm
twinstyles.css
+ 8 graphic files

Creating an XML Document

Developing a Document for a Cooking Web Site

Case | thehelpfulcook.com

Tara Anderson runs a Web site called thehelpfulcook.com, where people who share her love for cooking can post their favorite recipes. The Web site has been a big success and Tara is looking into changing how she stores her recipe data.

Recently, Tara investigated XML as a potential means of organizing information about cooking and ingredients. She's learned that XML has some advantages in presenting structured content like recipes. Data stored in an XML document can be integrated with the company's Web site and, through the use of style sheets, Tara can present XML data to her site's users.

Tara believes that her Web site eventually will move to a model that relies on a combination of HTML, XML, and style sheets to record and share cooking recipes. To move in that direction, she wants to start investigating how to display a simple recipe using XML. She has asked for your help in creating a small demonstration document for this purpose.

Starting Data Files

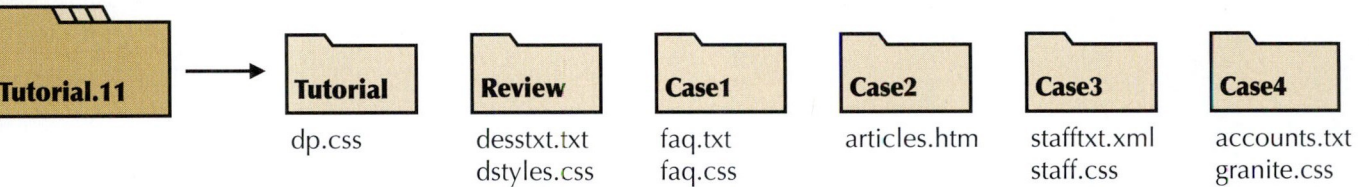

Tutorial.11 → Tutorial — dp.css

Review — desstxt.txt / dstyles.css

Case1 — faq.txt / faq.css

Case2 — articles.htm

Case3 — stafftxt.xml / staff.css

Case4 — accounts.txt / granite.css

Session 11.1

Introducing XML

XML stands for **Extensible Markup Language**. A **markup language** is a language that describes the structure and contents of documents, specifically documents that contain data. The term **extensible** means capable of being extended and modified. Thus, XML is a markup language that can be extended and modified to match the needs of the document author and the data being recorded. The following short history lesson may help you better understand how XML fits in with HTML, another markup language.

The Roots of XML

XML has its roots in the **Standard Generalized Markup Language (SGML)**, a language introduced in 1980 that describes the structure and contents of any machine-readable information. SGML is **device-independent** and **system-independent**, meaning that documents written in SGML can be used, in theory, on almost any type of device under almost any type of operating system. An SGML programmer concentrates on the data stored in an SGML document, not how that document will be rendered. SGML has been the chosen vehicle for creating structured documents in businesses and government organizations of all sizes. For example, think of the daunting task of documenting all of the parts used in a jet airplane, while simultaneously creating a structure that engineers, mechanics, and developers can use to quickly retrieve and edit that information. SGML provides tools to manage documentation projects of this magnitude.

However, because of its power, scope, and flexibility, SGML is a difficult language to learn and apply. The official specification for SGML is more than 150 pages long and covers some scenarios and cases that are rarely encountered by even the most experienced programmer. As a result, the use of SGML is often limited to those organizations that can afford the cost and overhead of maintaining complex SGML environments. For example, SGML would not be suited for the World Wide Web, where Web page authors need a language that is easy to use.

One purpose of SGML is to create **SGML applications**, which are markup languages based on the SGML architecture that can be applied to specific, not general, types of information. One such SGML application is Hypertext Markup Language (HTML). As an SGML application, HTML shares several of the SGML properties, such as device-independence. However, because HTML is an SGML application written for a specific purpose, it does not have SGML's expensive overhead.

The Limits of HTML

Despite its popularity, HTML has some limitations and flaws that frustrate Web developers. One major problem occurred when the Web became a source of information storage and retrieval, a task for which HTML was not designed. For example, Tara might create the following Web document to describe a shopping list of produce items for her Web site:

```
<h2>Shopping List</h2>
<h3>Ingredients</h3>
<ol>
    <li>Apples ($2.99/bag)</li>
    <li>Grapes ($2.49/bag)</li>
    <li>Onions ($2.99/bag)</li>
    <li>Red Leaf Lettuce ($1.50/bunch)</li>
    <li>Mushrooms ($1.79/carton)</li>
</ol>
```

This document has two headings: an h2 heading for the "Shopping List" title and an h3 heading for the "Ingredients" title. In addition, the document contains an ordered list describing each food item in the shopping list with the price of each item in parentheses. Although the h2 heading, h3 heading, and other elements in this document provide information to the browser about how the document is structured, they don't tell anything about the information the page contains. After all, this same document structure could be used in the following online music store page:

```
<h2>Kind of Blue</h2>
<h3>Miles Davis</h3>
<ol>
   <li>So What (9:22)</li>
   <li>Freddie Freeloader (9:46)</li>
   <li>Blue in Green (5:37)</li>
   <li>All Blues (11:33)</li>
   <li>Flamenco Sketches (9:26)</li>
</ol>
```

As long as your only concern is placing text on a Web page, it makes no difference whether the page is about mushrooms or music. However, if you want a search engine to quickly scan this document and extract information about the artist or music tracks, it would help if the document structure told the search engine something about the document contents. Without being able to determine whether a particular tag refers to the title, music track, price, or artist, it's difficult to locate that precise piece of information.

A second limitation of HTML for data storage is that it is limited to a set of predefined elements, and cannot be expanded to accommodate different types of information. In some cases, browser manufacturers have expanded the versions of HTML they support to offer new features, as Netscape did by introducing frames and as Internet Explorer did by offering inline frames. However, nothing in the language enables an individual Web author to expand the scope of HTML to meet the needs of a particular Web document.

One result of these browser modifications to HTML was a confusing mix of competing HTML standards—often one for each browser and, indeed, each browser version. Although the innovations offered by Netscape, Internet Explorer, and others did much to increase the scope, power, and popularity of HTML, they did so at the expense of clarity. Web authors could not easily create Web sites without taking into account all of the browser differences.

A final limitation of HTML is that it can be inconsistently applied. For example, the syntax of HTML instructs the Web page author to enclose all attribute values in single or double quotation marks and to match all opening tags with ending tags. However, to make HTML easier for nonprogrammers, most browsers will accept violations of these basic syntax rules. Indeed, many early HTML editors also routinely violated these types of syntax rules. Even though this lack of enforced standards made it easier to write HTML code, it also meant that browser code had to be more cumbersome than necessary to accommodate all of the various lapses in HTML syntax perpetrated by some Web authors and editing programs.

As a result, there were several reasons to look for a new language standard that would more easily extend to new information types, be customizable, require stricter adherence to the syntax of the language, and provide meaning and structure to the information contained within each document. This language was to be XML.

Exploring the Concepts Behind XML

XML can be thought of as "SGML light." Like SGML, XML is a language used to create vocabularies for other markup languages, but it does not have SGML's complexity and expansiveness. The standards for XML are developed and maintained by the World Wide Web Consortium (W3C).

XML Design Goals

When the W3C started planning the language, it established design goals for XML that included the following:

1. XML must be easily usable over the Internet. Because the Web is a major source of information sharing, XML had to be compatible with the major Web protocols such as HTTP and MIME.

2. XML must support a wide variety of applications. XML should not be limited to the Web; it must also be effective for other applications, such as databases, word processing, spreadsheets, financial transactions, and voice mail.

3. XML must be compatible with SGML. Because XML is a subset of SGML, many software tools developed for SGML should be adaptable for XML.

4. It must be easy to write programs that process XML documents. One of HTML's greatest strengths is its simplicity. XML should emulate this characteristic by making it easy for even nonprogrammers to write XML code.

5. XML documents should be clear and easily understandable by nonprogrammers. Like HTML, XML documents should be text files. The contents of an XML document should follow a logical, tree-like structure. Element names should be intuitively clear to anyone reading the XML code.

6. The design of XML must be exact and concise. The specifications for XML should not be as all-encompassing and sprawling as SGML.

7. XML documents must be easy to create. For XML to be practical, XML documents need to be as easy to create as HTML documents.

8. Terseness in XML markup is of minimal importance. As improvements in bandwidth have speeded up data exchange over the Internet, terseness (keeping document size small) was not as important as making document code understandable and easy to use.

Creating an XML Vocabulary

Like SGML, XML can be used to create **XML applications** or **XML vocabularies**, which are markup languages tailored to contain specific pieces of information. If Tara wanted to create a vocabulary for the recipes stored on thehelpfulcook.com, she might enter the following markup tags in her document:

```
<title>Asian Dipping Sauce</title>
<author>Barbara Ferris</author>
<ingredients>
   <ingredient amt="1/2 cup">soy sauce</ingredient>
   <ingredient amt="1/2 cup">plum sauce</ingredient>
   <ingredient amt="1/2 cup">pineapple juice</ingredient>
   <ingredient amt="1/2 cup">ketchup</ingredient>
   <ingredient amt="1/4 cup">scallions, finely sliced</ingredient>
   <ingredient amt="3 tbsps">cilantro, chopped</ingredient>
   <ingredient amt="2 tbsps">fresh ginger, minced</ingredient>
   <ingredient amt="2 tbsps">fresh garlic, minced</ingredient>
</ingredients>
```

You'll explore the structure and syntax of this document further in the next session. But even without knowing much about XML, you can already infer a lot about the type of information this document contains. You can quickly see that this document contains information on a recipe titled "Asian Dipping Sauce" that was submitted to thehelpfulcook.com by Barbara Ferris. The sauce is made up of soy sauce, plum sauce, pineapple juice, ketchup, scallions, cilantro, ginger, and garlic. The amount of each ingredient is specified in the amt attribute. For example, the recipe calls for 3 tablespoons of chopped cilantro.

The title, author, ingredients, and ingredient elements in this example do not come from any particular XML specification. Rather, they are custom elements that Tara might create specifically for use on her Web site. Tara could create additional elements describing things such as the steps in preparing the sauce, the category of food that this sauce belongs to, and a classification that indicates whether this is a simple, medium, or difficult recipe to produce. In this way, Tara can create her own XML vocabulary that deals specifically with the type of data she records for thehelpfulcook.com.

Standard XML Vocabularies

If Tara wanted to share the vocabulary that she uses for thehelpfulcook.com with other recipe sites and cooking applications, she would use a standard vocabulary that is accepted throughout the industry. As XML grew in popularity, standard vocabularies were developed across a wide range of disciplines. For example, chemists need to describe chemical structures containing hundreds of atoms bonded to other atoms and molecules. To meet this need, an XML vocabulary called the **Chemical Markup Language (CML)** was developed, which codes molecular information. Figure 11-1 shows an example of a CML document used to store information on the ammonia molecule.

Ammonia molecule described using CML ◄ Figure 11-1

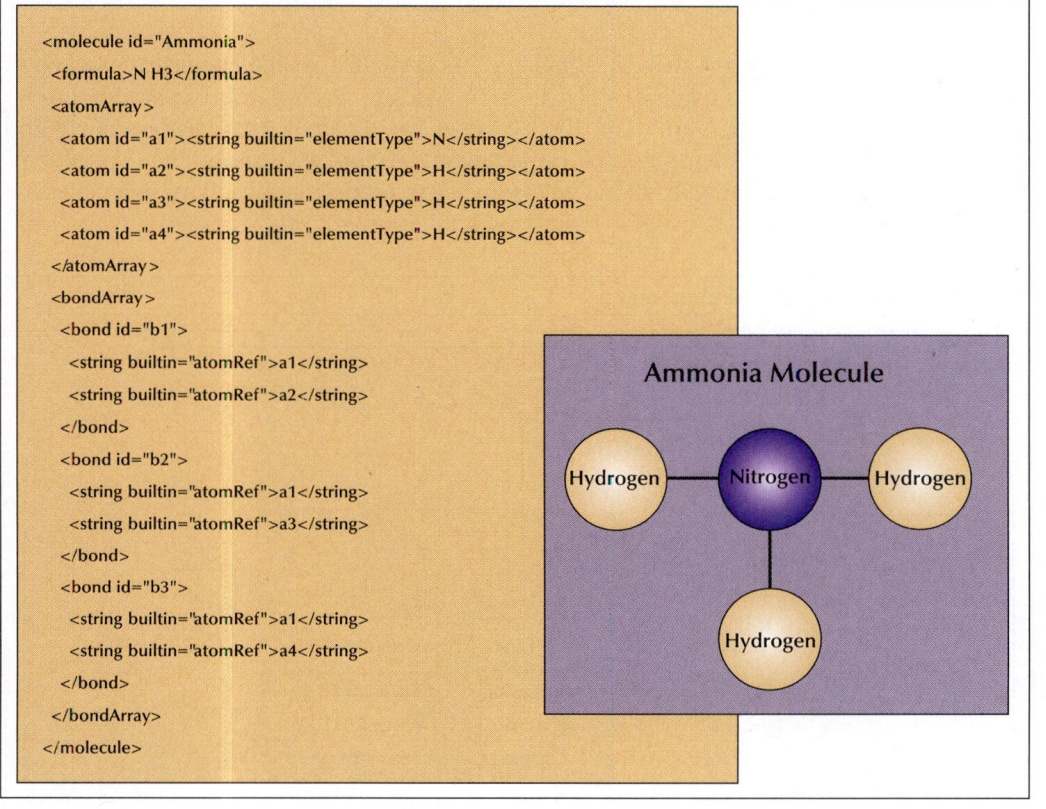

```
<molecule id="Ammonia">
 <formula>N H3</formula>
 <atomArray>
  <atom id="a1"><string builtin="elementType">N</string></atom>
  <atom id="a2"><string builtin="elementType">H</string></atom>
  <atom id="a3"><string builtin="elementType">H</string></atom>
  <atom id="a4"><string builtin="elementType">H</string></atom>
 </atomArray>
 <bondArray>
  <bond id="b1">
   <string builtin="atomRef">a1</string>
   <string builtin="atomRef">a2</string>
  </bond>
  <bond id="b2">
   <string builtin="atomRef">a1</string>
   <string builtin="atomRef">a3</string>
  </bond>
  <bond id="b3">
   <string builtin="atomRef">a1</string>
   <string builtin="atomRef">a4</string>
  </bond>
 </bondArray>
</molecule>
```

Another XML application, **MathML**, is used to store and evaluate mathematical operations, constants, and equations. XML vocabularies have even been developed that describe music notation and lyrics. Figure 11-2 lists a few of the many vocabularies that have been developed under XML.

Figure 11-2 ▶ **XML vocabularies**

XML Vocabulary	Description
Channel Definition Format (CDF)	Automatic delivery of information from Web publishers to PCs, PDAs, cell phones, and other information devices
Chemical Markup Language (CML)	Coding of molecular and chemical information
Extensible Hypertext Markup Language (XHTML)	HTML written as an XML application
Mathematical Markup Language (MathML)	Presentation and evaluation of mathematical equations and operations
Music Markup Language (MML)	Display and organization of music notation and lyrics
Open Financial Exchange (OFX)	Exchange of financial data between financial institutions, businesses, and consumers via the Internet
Really Simple Syndication (RSS)	Distribution of news headlines and syndicated columns
Synchronized Multimedia Integration Language (SMIL)	Editing of interactive audiovisual presentations involving streaming audio, video, text, and any other media type
Voice Extensible Markup Language (VoiceXML)	Creating audio dialogues that feature synthesized speech, digitized audio, and speech recognition

Tip

You can learn more about several standard XML vocabularies at the W3C site, *www.w3.org*.

One of the more important XML vocabularies is **XHTML (Extensible Hypertext Markup Language)**, which is a reformulation of HTML as an XML application. You'll examine some properties of XHTML as you learn more about XML in the upcoming tutorials. You might find all of these acronyms and languages a bit overwhelming. Figure 11-3 shows the relationship between SGML, HTML, and XML, along with some of the various applications associated with SGML and XML.

Figure 11-3 ▶ **Markup languages and vocabularies**

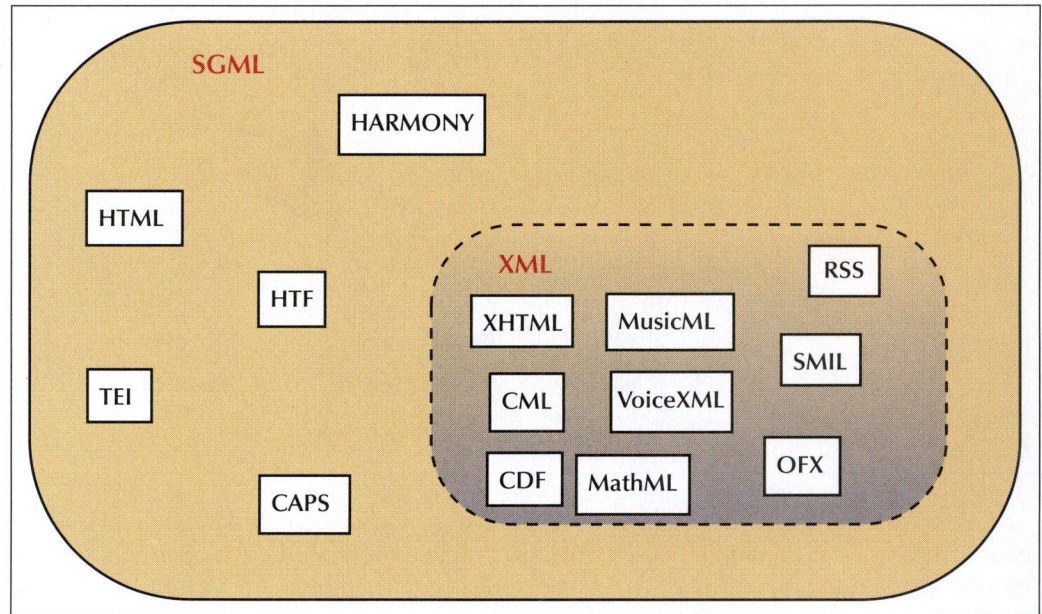

DTDs and Schemas

For different users to effectively share a vocabulary, rules have to be developed that specifically control what code and content a document from that vocabulary might have. This is done by attaching either a **document type definition (DTD)** or a **schema** to the XML document containing the data. Both DTDs and schemas contain rules for how data in a document vocabulary should be structured. For example, Tara can create a DTD or schema to require each recipe document to contain the recipe title, the person who submitted it, a list of ingredients, and a list of the steps to prepare the dish. DTDs and schemas are not required, but they can help to ensure that an XML document follows a specific vocabulary. All the standard vocabularies listed in Figure 11-2 have DTDs to ensure that people in a given industry or area work from the same guidelines.

To create a DTD or a schema, you only need access to a text editor. Both DTDs and schemas can be accessed as external text files. DTDs can also be included within XML documents.

Well-Formed and Valid XML Documents

To ensure a document's compliance with XML rules, it can be tested against two standards: Is it well-formed? Is it valid? A **well-formed** document contains no syntax errors and satisfies the general specifications for XML code as laid out by the W3C. At a minimum, an XML document must be well-formed or it will not be readable by programs that process XML code.

If an XML document is part of a vocabulary with a defined DTD or schema, it also needs to be tested to ensure that it satisfies the rules of that vocabulary. An XML document that satisfies the rules of a DTD or schema (in addition to being well-formed) is said to be a **valid document**. In this tutorial, you'll look only at the basic syntax rules of XML to create well-formed documents. You'll learn how to test documents for validity in later tutorials.

Creating an XML Document

You are ready to create your first XML document. Like HTML documents, XML documents can be created with a basic text editor such as Notepad or TextEdit. More sophisticated XML editors are available that can make it easier to design documents, but they are not required for the thehelpfulcook.com project.

The Structure of an XML Document

An XML document consists of three parts: the prolog, the document body, and the epilog. The **prolog** includes the following parts:

- An XML declaration indicating that the document is written in the language of XML
- Comment lines used to provide additional information about the document contents (optional)
- Processing instructions for a program reading the XML document (optional)
- A document type declaration to provide information about the rules used in the document's vocabulary (optional)

The prolog is followed by the **document body**, which contains the document's contents in a hierarchical tree structure. An optional **epilog** appears after the document body and contains any final comments or processing instructions.

The XML Declaration

The first part of the prolog (the first line in any XML document) is the **XML declaration**, which signals to the program reading the file that the document is written in XML and provides information about how that code is to be interpreted by the program. The syntax of the XML declaration is

```
<?xml version="version" encoding="encoding" standalone="yes|no" ?>
```

where *version* is the version of the XML specification being used in the document and *encoding* identifies the character set used in the document. The default version value is 1.0. You can also specify a version value of 1.1. However, not much difference exists between the 1.0 and 1.1 specifications.

Because different languages use different character sets, the encoding declaration allows XML to be used across a range of written languages. The default encoding scheme is UTF-8, which matches most English language characters as well as characters from other languages such as Japanese and Korean. However, if the XML document contains special characters such as ö or _, you might need to use an extended character set. For example, setting the encoding value to ISO-8859-1 tells a program reading the document that characters from the ISO-8859-1 (Latin-1) character set are being used in the document. This character set includes many characters from non-English Western European languages.

Finally, the standalone attribute indicates whether the document contains any references to external files. If so, such references usually point to DTDs contained in external files. A standalone value of yes indicates that the document is self-contained, and a value of no indicates that the document requires additional information from external documents. The default value is no.

The sample XML declaration

```
<?xml version="1.0" encoding="UTF-8" standalone="yes" ?>
```

indicates that the XML version is 1.0, the UTF-8 (English language) encoding scheme is being used, and the document is self-contained. If you instead entered the XML declaration

```
<?xml version="1.0" ?>
```

a processor would apply the UTF-8 encoding scheme and assume that the document has a standalone value of no by default. Remember, XML is case sensitive. You cannot change the XML declaration to uppercase letters. A prolog opening with

```
<?XML VERSION="1.0" ENCODING="UTF-8" STANDALONE="YES" ?>
```

would result in an error because the code is entered in uppercase. In addition, quotation marks must surround the values in a declaration. An XML declaration of

```
<?xml version=1.0 encoding=UTF-8 standalone=no ?>
```

would also result in an error because the quotation marks are missing around the attribute values.

Creating an XML Declaration | Reference Window

- To create an XML declaration, enter the code

  ```
  <?xml version="version" encoding="encoding" standalone="yes|no" ?>
  ```

  in the first line of an XML document, where *version* is the version of the XML specification being used in the document, *encoding* identifies the character codes used in the document, and the standalone attribute indicates whether the XML processor needs access to external documents when parsing the document.

You'll start creating the first XML document by writing the declaration for an XML recipe document to be used by thehelpfulcook.com.

To create the XML declaration for a recipe document:

▶ 1. Use your text editor to open a blank document.

   Trouble? Your instructor may direct you to use an XML document editor. If you don't know how to use the text editor or the XML editor, ask your instructor or technical resource person for help.

▶ 2. Type the following line as the first line in your document:

   ```
   <?xml version="1.0" encoding="UTF-8" standalone="yes" ?>
   ```

▶ 3. Save your document as **recipes.xml** in the tutorial.11/tutorial folder included with your Data Files.

   Trouble? Some text editors will automatically assign the .txt extension to the text file. If that is the case, you need to specify the .xml extension. Type recipes.xml in the File name box, click All Files from the Save as Type list box, and then click the Save button.

   Trouble? If you use a word processor such as Microsoft Word, you must save the document as a text file (with the .xml extension) and not in the word processor's native format.

Inserting Comments

Tara wants you to include information in the document about its purpose, contents, and author. One way of doing this is with commented text. Although comments may appear anywhere within an XML document, it's a good idea to include comments in the prolog to help users viewing the XML code to understand the document and its contents. XML comments follow the same syntax as HTML comments:

```
<!-- comment text -->
```

where *comment text* is the text of the XML comment. You will use this form to add comments to the recipes.xml file describing its contents and purpose.

Tip

Comments cannot contain double hyphens or be nested within other comments.

To insert an XML comment:

▶ 1. In your text editor, add the following comment lines to the recipes.xml file directly below the XML declaration, replacing *your name* and *the date* with your name and the current date, as shown in Figure 11-4:

```
<!--
    Recipes from thehelpfulcook.com

    Filename: recipes.xml
    Author:    your name
    Date:      the date

-->
```

Figure 11-4 ▶ **XML comment**

```
<?xml version="1.0" encoding="UTF-8" standalone="yes" ?>
<!--
    Recipes from thehelpfulcook.com

    Filename: recipes.xml
    Author:    Tara Anderson
    Date:      3/1/2012

-->
```

▶ 2. Save the recipes.xml file, and then close it.

XML and RSS | InSight

One of the more important XML vocabularies on the Internet is **Really Simple Syndication (RSS)**, which is the language used for distributing news articles or any content that changes on a regular basis to a group of subscribers. Subscribers to an RSS site can receive periodic updates using a software program called a **feed reader** or an **aggregator**. These feed readers can be built into commonly used software. One example of a feed reader is the Apple program iTunes, which allows users to automatically retrieve audio and video feeds in the form of **podcasts** that can be played on the user's portable MP3 player or iPod. Although the content delivered by the podcast is audio or video, the language that organizes and describes that content is RSS. Most current browsers contain some type of built-in feed reader to allow users to retrieve and view feeds from within their browser window. RSS frees the user from having to manually retrieve information from the Internet. After a site's contents have been made available through RSS, the user can have that information automatically retrieved by his or her feed reader.

Because an RSS file is written in XML, the RSS code follows the conventions of all XML documents. For example, the following are the first lines of an RSS file from the Podcast Alley Web site (*www.podcastalley.com*) used to distribute audio content to interested subscribers:

```
<?xml version="1.0" encoding="UTF-8"?>
<!-- generator="PodcastAlley 1.0" -->
<rss version="2.0">
   <channel>
   <title>Podcast Alley Podcaster Interviews</title>
   <description>Podcast Interviews on Podcast Alley.</description>
   <link>http://www.podcastalley.com</link>
...
   </channel>
</rss>
```

After the initial prolog, the rest of the document is used to indicate what kind of information is available to the user, when it was made available, the format of the information, and where to retrieve it. The channel, title, description, and link elements are all part of the RSS vocabulary.

Another language used for Web feeds is **Atom**. Atom was developed in response to the confusion that resulted from competing versions of RSS that made it difficult for developers to move forward with the creation of news feed sites. Like RSS, Atom is an XML vocabulary, so Atom documents must follow the same basic rules of any well-formed XML document.

At this point, you've finished the XML document's prolog. In the next session, you'll add content to Tara's document, providing information on a recipe for Asian grilled steaks.

Session 11.1 Quick Check | Review

1. Define the term "extensible." How does the concept of extensibility relate to XML?
2. What is SGML and why was SGML not used for authoring pages on the Web?
3. What is an SGML application? Provide one example of an SGML application.
4. Name three limitations of HTML that led to the development of XML.
5. What is an XML vocabulary? Provide an example of an XML vocabulary.
6. What are the three parts of an XML document?
7. What XML declaration specifies that an XML document supports version 1.0, uses the ISO-8859-1 encoding scheme, and does not require information from other documents?

8. In an XML document, what XML code creates the comment text, "Entry extracted from the thehelpfulcook.com database"?
9. How is podcasting related to XML?

Session 11.2

Working with Elements

To complete Tara's XML recipe document, you'll add elements describing a steak recipe. **Elements** are the basic building blocks of XML files that contain data to be stored in the document. The content is stored between an **opening tag** and a **closing tag**. The syntax of an XML element is

```
<element>content</element>
```

where *element* is the name given to the element, *content* represents the content of the element, *<element>* is the opening tag, and *</element>* is the closing tag. Element names are usually selected by XML authors to be descriptive of element contents. Tara can store the name of the person who submitted the recipe by using the following line of code:

```
<author>Tanya Evans</author>
```

The following are a few important points to remember about XML elements:

- Element names are case sensitive. For example, the element name "recipe" is considered different from "RECIPE."
- Element names must begin with a letter or the underscore character (_) and cannot contain blank spaces. For example, "First Name" is not a valid element name, but "First_Name" is a valid name.
- Element names cannot begin with the letters "xml" because those characters are reserved for special XML commands.
- The name in an element's closing tag must match the name in the opening tag.

For example, the following element text would result in an error because the opening tag is capitalized and the closing tag is not, meaning that they are not recognized as the opening and closing tags for the same element:

```
<AUTHOR>Tanya Evans</author>
```

Reference Window | **Marking XML Elements**

- To mark an XML element, enter
  ```
  <element>content</element>
  ```
  where *element* is the name given to the element, *content* represents the content of the element, *<element>* is the element's opening tag, and *</element>* is the closing tag.
- To mark an empty element, use the following tag:
  ```
  <element />
  ```

Empty Elements

Not all elements contain content. An **open element** or **empty element** is an element that contains no content. Empty element tags are entered using a one-sided tag obeying the syntax

```
<element />
```

where *element* is the name of the empty element. Note that an empty element consists of a single tag—it has no opening and closing tags.

Empty XML elements are similar to HTML's collection of empty elements, such as the <hr /> tag for horizontal lines or the <img /> tag for inline graphics. If empty elements contain no content, why use them in an XML document? One reason is to mark certain sections of the document for programs reading it. For example, Tara might use an empty element to distinguish one group of recipes from another. As you'll see, empty elements can also contain attributes that can be used to store information. Finally, empty elements can be used to reference external documents containing nontextual data such as the <img /> tag used to reference graphic image files.

> **Tip**
>
> You can enter empty elements as two-sided tags with no content: *<element></element>*. Most programmers prefer the one-sided tag syntax to avoid confusion with two-sided tags, which normally contain content.

Nesting Elements

In addition to text content, elements can also contain other elements. An element contained within another element is said to be a **nested element**. In the following example, multiple ingredient elements are nested within the ingredients element:

```
<ingredients>
    <ingredient>1/2 cup soy sauce</ingredient>
    <ingredient>1/2 cup plum sauce</ingredient>
    <ingredient>1/2 cup pineapple juice</ingredient>
</ingredients>
```

XML uses familial names to refer to the hierarchical relationships between elements. A nested element is a **child element** of its **parent element**. Elements that are side-by-side in a document's hierarchy are **sibling elements**. In the above code, each ingredient element is a sibling of the other ingredient elements, and each is a child of the ingredients element.

One common syntactical error in creating an XML document is to improperly nest one element within another. XML does not allow the opening and closing tags of parent and child elements to overlap. The XML code

```
<recipe>Grilled Steak <author>Tanya Evans</recipe></author>
```

is not well-formed because the recipe element does not completely enclose the author element. The closing </recipe> tag should be moved outside of the </author> tag to prevent any overlap of the element tags, as follows:

```
<recipe>Grilled Steak <author>Tanya Evans</author></recipe>
```

> **Tip**
>
> Make your code easier to read by indenting child elements.

The Element Hierarchy

The familial relationship of parent, child, and sibling extends throughout the entire document body. All the elements in the body are children of a single element called the **root element** or **document element**. Figure 11-5 shows a sample XML document with its hierarchy represented in a tree diagram. The root element in this document is the recipes element. The XML declaration and comments are not included in the tree structure of the document body.

Figure 11-5   **XML document and corresponding tree structure**

```
<?xml version="1.0" ?>
<!- Recipes from thehelpfulcook.com -->
<recipes>
   <recipe>
      <title>Grilled Steak Sauce</title>
      <author>Tanya Evans</author>
      <ingredients>
         <ingredient>1/2 cup soy sauce</ingredient>
         <ingredient>1/2 cup plum sauce</ingredient>
         <ingredient>1/2 cup pineapple juice</ingredient>
      </ingredients>
   </recipe>
</recipes>
```

An XML document must include a root element to be considered well-formed. The following document code is not well-formed because it lacks a single root element containing all other elements in the document body:

```
<?xml version="1.0" ?>
<!-- Recipes from thehelpfulcook.com -->

<title>Grilled Flank Steak with Asian Sauce</title>
<author>Tanya Evans</author>
<ingredients>
   <ingredient>1/2 cup soy sauce</ingredient>
   <ingredient>1/2 cup plum sauce</ingredient>
   <ingredient>1/2 cup pineapple juice</ingredient>
</ingredients>
```

Charting the Element Hierarchy

A quick way to view the overall structure of a document body is to chart the elements in a tree structure like the one shown in Figure 11-5. This can become confusing, however, when a single element has several children of the same type. For example, the ingredients element in Figure 11-5 contains three ingredient elements. Other recipes will have differing numbers of ingredients. It would be useful to have a general tree diagram that indicates whether a particular child element can occur zero times, once, or several times within a parent. Figure 11-6 displays the shorthand code you will see in the tree diagrams in this and subsequent tutorials to indicate the general structure of the document body.

Symbol to indicate the number of child elements   **Figure 11-6**

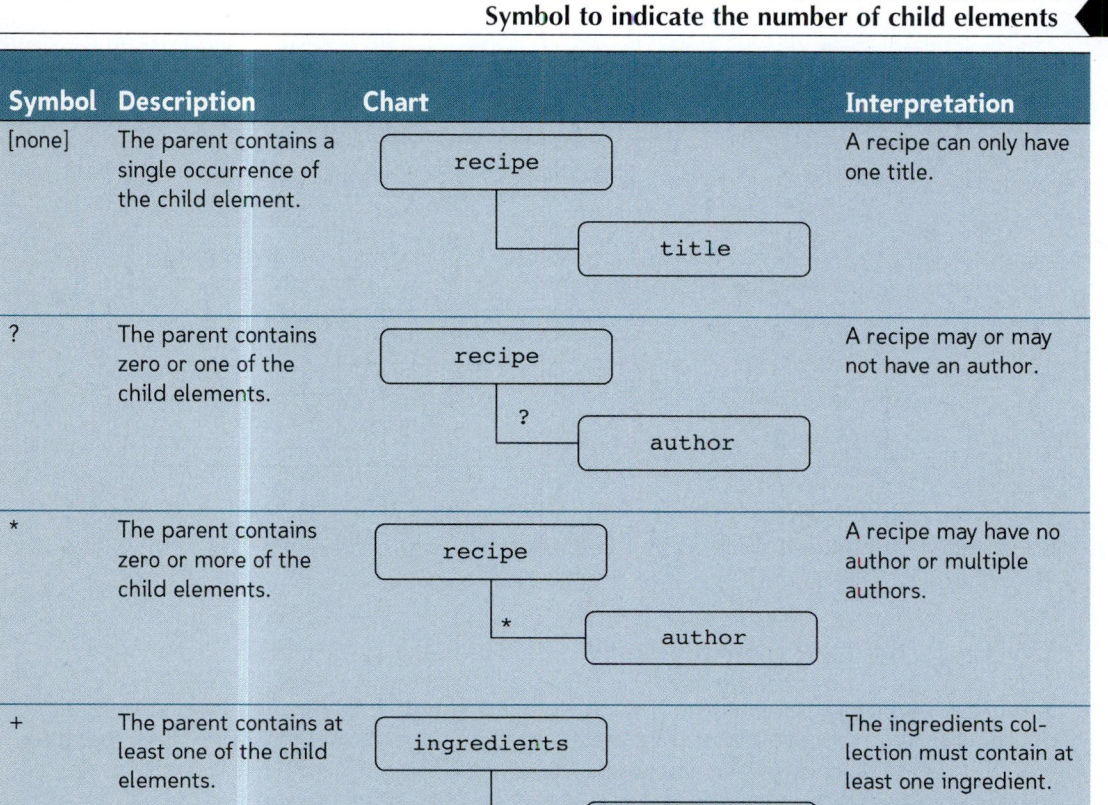

Symbol	Description	Chart	Interpretation
[none]	The parent contains a single occurrence of the child element.	recipe → title	A recipe can only have one title.
?	The parent contains zero or one of the child elements.	recipe → ? author	A recipe may or may not have an author.
*	The parent contains zero or more of the child elements.	recipe → * author	A recipe may have no author or multiple authors.
+	The parent contains at least one of the child elements.	ingredients → + ingredient	The ingredients collection must contain at least one ingredient.

Figure 11-7 shows how to apply these symbols to the XML document you'll create for Tara. According to this chart, the recipe document can contain any number of recipes, but each recipe must have one title, zero or one servings element, zero or multiple authors, one ingredients collection, and one collection of cooking directions. Within the ingredients and directions collections, the document must contain at least one ingredient and one step, respectively.

Figure 11-7 ▷ **Tree structure of the recipes.xml document**

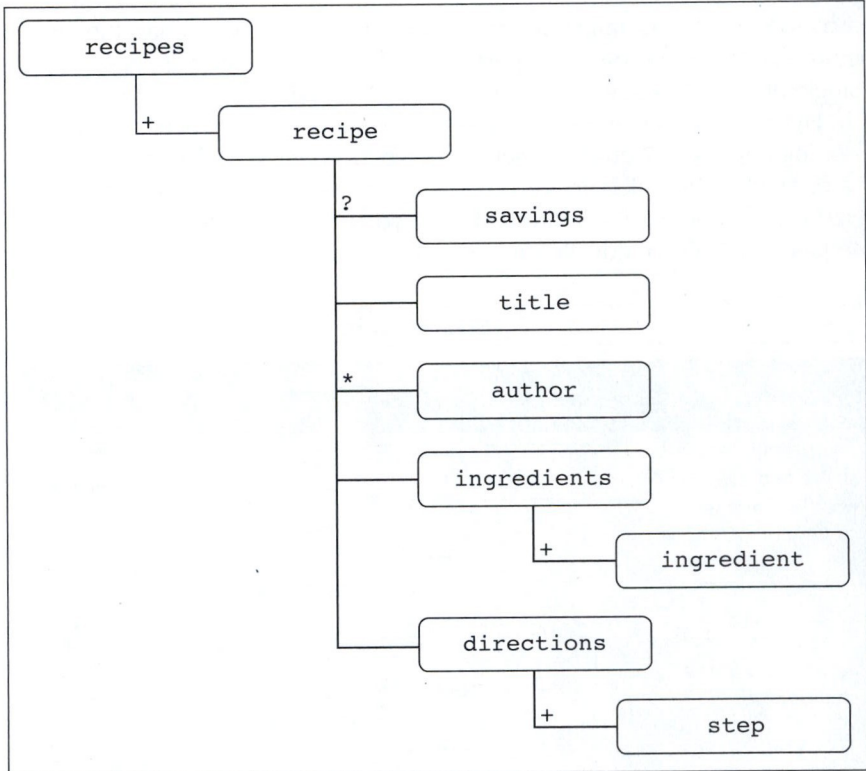

The symbols ?, *, and + are part of the code used in creating DTDs to validate XML documents. Using these symbols in a tree diagram will prepare you to learn more about DTDs later on.

Writing the Document Body

You are ready to use the features of XML elements you reviewed in Tara's recipes document. Tara wants you to add the details of the recipe shown in Figure 11-8. Because you will create your own XML vocabulary for this document, you'll use descriptive element names for all the element items.

Recipe for the thehelpfulcook.com Web site   Figure 11-8

Grilled Flank Steak with Asian Sauce
by: Tanya Evans
Servings: 6

Ingredients
- 1/2 cup soy sauce
- 1/2 cup plum sauce
- 1/2 cup pineapple juice
- 1/2 cup ketchup
- 1/4 cup scallions, finely sliced
- 3 tbsps cilantro, chopped
- 2 tbsps fresh ginger, minced
- 2 tbsps fresh garlic, minced
- 2 flank steaks, about 1-1/4 lbs each

Directions
1. Combine the marinade ingredients in a medium bowl.
2. Trim the flank steaks of surface fat.
3. Place the steaks and marinade in a sealed plastic bag and refrigerate for 3 to 6 hours.
4. Remove the steaks from the bag and boil the marinade in a small saucepan for 1 full minute.
5. Let steaks stand at room temperature for 20 to 30 minutes.
6. Grill steaks over direct high heat (500°) for 8 to 10 minutes, turning once halfway through.
7. Remove steaks from the grill and let rest for 3 to 5 minutes.
8. Cut steaks across the grain into thin strips and serve with the marinade sauce.

You'll add this information to the recipes.xml document using recipes as the root element of the document and placing the recipe, title, author, servings, ingredients, and directions as descendant elements of the root. To make the code more readable, you'll indent each child element a few spaces to the right of its parent. This common practice makes XML code more readable and has no impact on how the code is interpreted by a program that opens it.

To insert XML elements in the recipes.xml document:

1. Return to the **recipes.xml** file in your text editor.

2. At the bottom of the file, insert the following elements and content, as shown in Figure 11-9:

```
<recipes>
   <recipe>
      <title>Grilled Flank Steak with Asian Sauce</title>
      <author>Tanya Evans</author>
      <servings>6</servings>
   </recipe>
</recipes>
```

Figure 11-9 **XML elements and content**

```
<?xml version="1.0" encoding="UTF-8" standalone="yes" ?>
<!--
    Recipes from thehelpfulcook.com

    Filename: recipes.xml
    Author:   Tara Anderson
    Date:     3/1/2012


-->

<recipes>
    <recipe>
        <title>Grilled Flank Steak with Asian Sauce</title>
        <author>Tanya Evans</author>
        <servings>6</servings>
    </recipe>
</recipes>
```

Next, you'll add the elements for both the recipe ingredients and the recipe directions.

To add the remaining XML elements to the recipes.xml document:

▶ **1.** Directly below the servings element, insert the following ingredients:

```
<ingredients>
    <ingredient>1/2 cup soy sauce</ingredient>
    <ingredient>1/2 cup plum sauce</ingredient>
    <ingredient>1/2 cup pineapple juice</ingredient>
    <ingredient>1/2 cup ketchup</ingredient>
    <ingredient>1/4 cup scallions, finely sliced</ingredient>
    <ingredient>3 tbsps cilantro, chopped</ingredient>
    <ingredient>2 tbsps fresh ginger, minced</ingredient>
    <ingredient>2 tbsps fresh garlic, minced</ingredient>
    <ingredient>2 flank steaks, about 1-1/4 lbs each</ingredient>
</ingredients>
```

▶ **2.** Below the list of ingredients, insert the following cooking directions:

```
<directions>
    <step>Combine the marinade ingredients in a medium bowl.</step>
    <step>Trim the flank steaks of surface fat.</step>
    <step>Place the steaks and marinade in a sealed plastic bag and
refrigerate for 3 to 6 hours.</step>
    <step>Remove the steaks from the bag and boil the marinade in a
small saucepan for 1 full minute.</step>
    <step>Let steaks stand at room temperature for 20 to 30 minutes.
</step>
    <step>Grill steaks over direct high heat (500 degrees) for 8 to 10
minutes, turning once halfway through.</step>
    <step>Remove steaks from the grill and let rest for 3 to 5
minutes.</step>
    <step>Cut steaks across the grain into thin strips and serve with
the marinade sauce.</step>
</directions>
```

Figure 11-10 highlights the added elements.

The ingredients and directions elements | Figure 11-10

```
<recipes>
    <recipe>
        <title>Grilled Flank Steak with Asian Sauce</title>
        <author>Tanya Evans</author>
        <servings>6</servings>

        <ingredients>
            <ingredient>1/2 cup soy sauce</ingredient>
            <ingredient>1/2 cup plum sauce</ingredient>
            <ingredient>1/2 cup pineapple juice</ingredient>
            <ingredient>1/2 cup ketchup</ingredient>
            <ingredient>1/4 cup scallions, finely sliced</ingredient>
            <ingredient>3 tbsps cilantro, chopped</ingredient>
            <ingredient>2 tbsps fresh ginger, minced</ingredient>
            <ingredient>2 tbsps fresh garlic, minced</ingredient>
            <ingredient>2 flank steaks, about 1-1/4 lbs each</ingredient>
        </ingredients>

        <directions>
            <step>Combine the marinade ingredients in a medium bowl.</step>
            <step>Trim the flank steaks of surface fat.</step>
            <step>Place the steaks and marinade in a sealed plastic bag and
                refrigerate for 3 to 6 hours.</step>
            <step>Remove the steaks from the bag and boil the marinade in
                a small saucepan for 1 full minute.</step>
            <step>Let steaks stand at room temperature for 20 to
                30 minutes.</step>
            <step>Grill steaks over direct high heat (500 degrees) for 8 to
                10 minutes, turning once halfway through.</step>
            <step>Remove steaks from the grill and let rest for 3 to 5
                minutes.</step>
            <step>Cut steaks across the grain into thin strips and serve with
                the marinade sauce.</step>
        </directions>

    </recipe>
</recipes>
```

▶ **3.** Save your changes to the file.

Working with Attributes

Every element in an XML document can contain one or more attributes. An **attribute** describes a feature or characteristic of an element. The syntax for adding an attribute to an element is

```
<element attribute="value"> ... </element>
```

or in the case of an empty element

```
<element attribute="value" />
```

Here, *attribute* is the attribute's name and *value* is the attribute's value. Attribute values are text strings and must always be enclosed within either single or double quotation marks. For example, if Tara wants to include the amount of each ingredient as an attribute of the ingredient element, she could enter the following code:

```
<ingredient amount="1/2 cup">soy sauce</ingredient>
```

Because attribute values are considered text strings, they can contain spaces and almost any character other than angle brackets (< >). You can choose any name for an attribute, subject to the following constraints:

- Attribute names are case sensitive. For example, an attribute named "Amount" is different from an attribute named "amount".
- Attribute names must begin with a letter or an underscore (_) and cannot contain blank spaces.
- Attribute names cannot begin with the text string "xml".
- An attribute name can appear only once within an element.

Adding an Attribute to an Element

- To add an attribute to an element, use

  ```
  <element attribute="value"> ... </element>
  ```
  or
  ```
  <element attribute="value" />
  ```
  where *attribute* is the attribute's name and *value* is the attribute's value.

Tara wants you to add attributes to the recipe element specifying the group that the recipe belongs to and the nationality of the dish.

To insert an attribute in the recipe element:

▶ **1.** Go to the opening <recipe> tag within the recipes.xml file.

▶ **2.** Within the opening tag, insert the following attributes, as shown in Figure 11-11:

   ```
   group="beef" nationality="asian"
   ```

Figure 11-11 ▷ **Attributes added to the recipes element**

```
<recipes>
   <recipe group="beef" nationality="asian">
      <title>Grilled Flank Steak with Asian Sauce</title>
      <author>Tanya Evans</author>
      <servings>6</servings>
```

▶ **3.** Save your changes to the file.

InSight | **When to Use Attributes**

It's not always clear when to use attribute values rather than inserting a new element. For example, you could have placed the group and nationality attributes for the recipe element as child elements in the following form:

```
<recipe>
   <group>beef</group>
   <nationality>asian</nationality>
...
</recipe>
```

Some XML developers argue that attributes should never be used because they add to the document's complexity, and information placed within an element is more easily accessible by programs reading the document. Others argue that attributes should be used for any data read by an application processing the document, but not of interest to the general reader. For example, Tara might want to mark her recipes with an ID number. But because the ID number itself is not important to people viewing her Web site, it should be placed as an attribute value.

One rule of thumb is that if a value is something you want displayed, place it in an element; otherwise, place it in an attribute. Another rule of thumb is to place content within elements, but to place information describing or identifying that content within an attribute. This can be a difficult distinction to make in most cases.

Using Character and Entity References

Tara wants to change the word "degree" used in the document to the ° symbol. To place symbols in an XML document, you insert **character references**, which identify symbols based on the character's code number from the ISO/IEC international character set. The **ISO/IEC character set** is an international numbering system for referencing characters from virtually any language. For example, the degree symbol ° has the code number 176. To insert a symbol based on its character code, you use the character reference

```
&#nnn;
```

where *nnn* is the character code number. In this case, you would enter the following code into the XML document to insert a reference to the ° symbol:

```
&#176;
```

XML also supports **entity references**, which are named references to special symbols or extra content found in external files or extended text strings. The syntax of an entity reference is

```
&entity;
```

where *entity* is the name assigned to the entity. XML supports five entity references, used for the symbols >, <, &, ', and ". Individual browsers might support additional entity references, but they are not part of the XML standards. Figure 11-12 lists these five entity references as well as character code references used for other symbols.

Tip

Make sure to end every entity reference with a semicolon. Failure to include the semicolon results in a document that is not well-formed.

Character references ◀ **Figure 11-12**

Symbol	Character Code	Entity Name	Description
>	>	>	Greater than
<	<	<	Less than
'	&#27;	'	Apostrophe (single quote)
"	&#22;	"	Double quote
&	&	&	Ampersand
©	©		Copyright
®	®		Registered trademark
™	™		Trademark
°	°		Degree
½	½		One-half
¼	¼		One-fourth
£	£		Pound sign
€	€		Euro sign
¥	¥		Yen sign

A common mistake in XML documents is to forget that the XML processor interprets every ampersand (&) as a character reference and not as a character. For example, the code

```
<author>Tanya Evans & Dale Stevens</author>
```

results in an error message because the & symbol is not followed by a recognized character reference number or entity name. To avoid this problem, you need to use the & or & character reference in place of the ampersand symbol, as follows:

```
<author>Tanya Evans &amp; Dale Stevens</author>
```

When the document is processed, the XML parser will display the following text:

```
Tanya Evans & Dale Stevens
```

Character references are sometimes used to store the text of HTML code within an XML element. For example, to store the HTML tag

```
<img src="logo.gif" />
```

in an element named htmlcode, you need to use character references to reference the ", <, and > symbols contained in the HTML tag, as shown in the following code:

```
<htmlcode>&#60;img src=&#22;logo.gif&#22; /&#62;</htmlcode>
```

The code

```
<htmlcode><img src="logo.gif" /></htmlcode>
```

would not give the same result because an XML processor would attempt to interpret

```
<img src="logo.gif" />
```

as an empty element and not as a text string within the htmlcode element.

You will modify the recipes.xml document, replacing the word "degrees" with a character reference for the ° symbol. In addition, you'll replace the 1/2 and 1/4 ingredient measurements with the $\frac{1}{2}$ and $\frac{1}{4}$ symbols.

To insert character references for nonalphanumeric symbols:

1. Within the recipes.xml file, scroll to the first four ingredient elements, and then replace the 1/2 cup measurements with the **½** character reference. The fraction will appear as the $\frac{1}{2}$ symbol.

2. In the fifth ingredient element, replace the 1/4 cup measurement with the **¼** character reference. The fraction will appear as the $\frac{1}{4}$ symbol.

3. In the last ingredient element, replace the 1-1/4 weight measure with the **1¼** character reference. The measurement will appear as 1 $\frac{1}{4}$.

4. Scroll down to the sixth step element, and then replace the word "degrees" with the **°** character reference. The ° symbol will appear instead of the word "degrees."

   Figure 11-13 highlights the changed text in the file.

Character references added to the recipes.xml file ◀ Figure 11-13

```
<ingredients>
    <ingredient>&#189; cup soy sauce</ingredient>
    <ingredient>&#189; cup plum sauce</ingredient>
    <ingredient>&#189; cup pineapple juice</ingredient>
    <ingredient>&#189; cup ketchup</ingredient>
    <ingredient>&#188; cup scallions, finely sliced</ingredient>
    <ingredient>3 tbsps cilantro, chopped</ingredient>
    <ingredient>2 tbsps fresh ginger, minced</ingredient>
    <ingredient>2 tbsps fresh garlic, minced</ingredient>
    <ingredient>2 flank steaks, about 1&#188; lbs each</ingredient>
</ingredients>

<directions>
    <step>Combine the marinade ingredients in a medium bowl.</step>
    <step>Trim the flank steaks of surface fat.</step>
    <step>Place the steaks and marinade in a sealed plastic bag and
        refrigerate for 3 to 6 hours.</step>
    <step>Remove the steaks from the bag and boil the marinade in
        a small saucepan for 1 full minute.</step>
    <step>Let steaks stand at room temperature for 20 to
        30 minutes.</step>
    <step>Grill steaks over direct high heat (500&#176;) for 8 to
        10 minutes, turning once halfway through.</step>
    <step>Remove steaks from the grill and let rest for 3 to 5
        minutes.</step>
    <step>Cut steaks across the grain into thin strips and serve with
        the marinade sauce.</step>
</directions>
```

▶ **5.** Save your changes to the file.

Understanding Text Characters and Whitespace

As you've seen from working on the recipes.xml file, XML documents consist only of text characters. However, text characters fall into three categories: parsed character data, character data, and whitespace. To appreciate how different programs interpret the contents and code of XML documents, it's important to understand the distinctions between these categories.

Parsed Character Data

Parsed character data (pcdata), consists of all the characters that XML treats as part of a document's XML code. This includes characters found in:

- the XML declaration
- the opening and closing tags of an element
- empty element tags
- character or entity references
- comments
- processing instructions

Parsed character data is also found in other XML features, which you'll learn about in later tutorials, such as processing instructions and document type declarations. The presence of pcdata can cause unexpected errors to occur within a document. Because an element may contain nested child elements, XML treats any element content as potential pcdata. This means that symbols such as &, <, or >, which are all used in creating markup tags or entity references, are parsed by programs reading the document. As a result, the line

```
<temperature> >100 degrees </temperature>
```

would result in an error because the > symbol in the temperature value is viewed as the end of a markup tag and, without any accompanying markup tag characters, the document is rejected as being not well-formed. To avoid this problem, you would have to replace the > symbol with either the character reference > or the entity reference >. The content of the temperature element should therefore be entered as:

```
<temperature> &gt;100 degrees </temperature>
```

Character Data

After you account for parsed character data, the remaining symbols constitute a document's actual contents, known as **character data**. Character data is not processed, but instead is treated as pure data content. One purpose of character and entity references is to convert pcdata into character data. When the program reading an XML document encounters an entity reference such as >, it converts the entity reference into the corresponding character data symbol—in this case, >.

Whitespace

The third type of character that an XML document can contain is whitespace. **Whitespace** refers to nonprintable characters such as spaces (created by pressing the Spacebar), new line characters (created by pressing the Enter key), or tab characters (created by pressing the Tab key). Processers reading an XML document must determine whether whitespace represents actual content or is used to make the code more readable. For example, the code shown earlier in Figure 11-9 is indented to make it more readable to the user. However, this does not have any impact on how the XML document's contents or structure is interpreted.

HTML applies **whitespace stripping**, in which consecutive occurrences of whitespace are treated as a single space. Whitespace stripping allows HTML authors to format a document to be readable without affecting its appearance in browsers. Because of this, the HTML code

```
<p>This is a
   paragraph</p>
```

is treated the same as

```
<p>This is a paragraph</p>
```

Whitespace is treated slightly differently in XML. No whitespace stripping occurs for element content, which means that the content of the XML element

```
<paragraph>This is    a
      paragraph</paragraph>
```

is interpreted as

```
This is    a
      paragraph
```

preserving both the new line character and all the blank spaces. Be aware, however, that not all applications that read XML documents apply this interpretation. For example, the Internet Explorer browser applies whitespace stripping to the element content in XML code in the same way it applies it to HTML code.

When whitespace appears in places other than element content, XML treats it in the following manner:

- Whitespace is ignored when it is the only character data between element tags. This allows XML authors to format a document to be readable without affecting its contents or structure.
- Whitespace is ignored within a document's prolog and epilog, and within any element tags.
- Whitespace within an attribute value is not ignored and is treated as part of the attribute value.

The effect of these rules is that whitespace is ignored in XML documents unless it is part of the document's data content. Note that this is not the case with Internet Explorer, which ignores whitespace wherever it appears in the document.

Creating a CDATA Section

Sometimes an XML document needs to store large blocks of text containing the < and > symbols. For example, consider placing a tutorial about HTML in an XML document. In such cases, it would be cumbersome to replace all of the < and > symbols with the < and > character references, and the code itself would be difficult to read.

As an alternative to using character references, you can place large blocks of text in a CDATA section. A **CDATA section** is a block of text that is designated as character data that any program reading the XML document will not attempt to parse. The syntax for creating a CDATA section is

```
<![CDATA[
    character data
]]>
```

where *character data* is text contained within the section. A CDATA section can contain most markup characters, such as <, >, and &, and these characters are interpreted as text rather than markup commands. In addition, a CDATA section:

- can be placed anywhere within a document
- cannot be nested within other CDATA sections
- cannot be empty

The only sequence of symbols that may not occur within a CDATA section is]]> because this marker is used to end the CDATA section.

The following example shows an element named htmlcode that contains a CDATA section, which is used to store several HTML tags for the thehelpfulcook.com Web site:

```
<htmlcode>
<![CDATA[
    <h1>thehelpfulcook.com</h1>
    <h2>An online source of recipes and cooking tips</h2>
]]>
</htmlcode>
```

In this example, XML treats the text as character data, not pcdata; a processor would not read the <h1> and <h2> characters as element tags. You can place any large block of text within a CDATA section to avoid inadvertently inserting a character that would be misinterpreted by an XML processor (such as the ampersand symbol).

You will insert a description element into the recipes.xml file that describes each recipe. To ensure that the description is treated as character data, you will place it within a CDATA section.

Tip

Whitespace used within a CDATA section is preserved when viewed in Internet Explorer, but ignored when viewed in other browsers.

To create a CDATA section:

▶ 1. Directly below the title element in the recipes.xml file, insert the following CDATA section, as shown in Figure 11-14:

```
<description>
  <![CDATA[
  A flavorful marinade adds a touch of zest to this classic
  steak recipe. The dish is best served with green beans
  & rice. We recommend complementing the marinade spices with
  a pale ale or a Pinot Noir.
  ]]>
</description>
```

| Figure 11-14 | CDATA section |

```
<recipes>
  <recipe group="beef" nationality="asian">
    <title>Grilled Flank Steak with Asian Sauce</title>
    <description>
      <![CDATA[
      A flavorful marinade adds a touch of zest to this classic
      steak recipe. The dish is best served with green beans
      & rice. We recommend complementing the marinade spices with
      a pale ale or a Pinot Noir.
      ]]>
    </description>
    <author>Tanya Evans</author>
    <servings>6</servings>
```

▶ 2. Save your changes to the file.

In this session, you added the last element to the recipes.xml file. In the next session, you will format the document's appearance for display in a Web browser.

| Review | **Session 11.2 Quick Check** |

1. Why is the following code in error?

   `<Title>Grilled Steak</title>`

2. What is the root element?
3. What is an empty element?
4. What are sibling elements?
5. What is the difference between character data and parsed character data?
6. Name three ways to insert the ampersand (&) symbol into the contents of an XML document without it being treated as parsed character data.
7. What is a CDATA section?
8. Describe how whitespace is handled within an XML document.

Session 11.3

Processing an XML Document

Now that you have created the content for Tara's recipe document, you can work with that content. A program that reads and interprets an XML document is called an **XML processor** or **XML parser**. A parser has several functions. First, a parser interprets a document's code and verifies that it satisfies all the XML specifications for document structure and syntax.

XML parsers are strict. If even one tag is omitted or one lowercase character should be uppercase, the parser reports an error and rejects the document. This may seem excessive, but that rigidity was built into XML to eliminate the ability of viewers to interpret how the code is displayed—much like HTML gives Web browsers wide discretion in interpreting markup code. The end result is that XML code accepted by one parser should be accepted by others. A second function of an XML parser is to interpret pcdata in a document and resolve any character or entity references found within the document. Finally, an XML document may contain processing instructions that tell the parser exactly how the document should be read and interpreted. The job of the parser is to interpret these instructions and carry them out. Figure 11-15 outlines the complete process from document creation to final presentation.

XML document being parsed | Figure 11-15

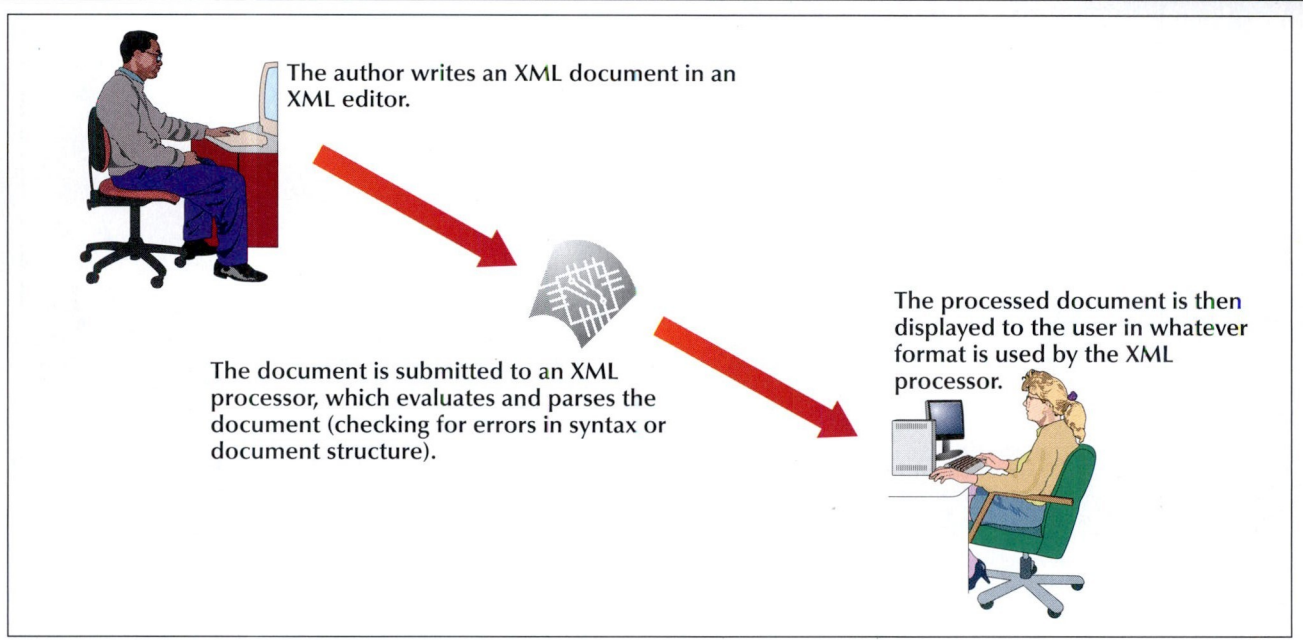

The author writes an XML document in an XML editor.

The document is submitted to an XML processor, which evaluates and parses the document (checking for errors in syntax or document structure).

The processed document is then displayed to the user in whatever format is used by the XML processor.

Most current Web browsers include an XML parser of some type. Microsoft developed an XML parser called **MSXML** for its Internet Explorer browser. MSXML was introduced as an add-on for Internet Explorer version 4.0, and was built directly into the Web browser for Internet Explorer versions 5.0 and above. There are several versions of MSXML. At the time of this writing, the most current version is MSXML 6.0, which ships with installations of Windows Vista and is downloadable from the Microsoft Web site for Windows XP and Windows 2003. The most commonly used version is MSXML 3.0, which is supported by Windows 2000 and above. The current version of Microsoft Office includes MSXML 4.0 along with built-in tools to support XML within Microsoft Office applications. New versions of MSXML are backward-compatible with earlier versions; and unless you are programming your own XML tools, you do not need to worry about which version of MSXML is installed on your system.

Starting with version 6.0, the Netscape browser included a built-in XML parser. Opera versions 8.0 and above include an XML parser, as do all versions of Mozilla Firefox and Apple Safari.

When an XML document is submitted to a browser, the XML parser built into the browser first checks for syntax errors. If it finds none, the browser displays the contents of the document. Older browsers might display only the data content; newer browsers display both the data and the document's tree structure. Current browsers usually display XML documents in an expandable/collapsible outline format that allows users to hide nested elements. The various parts of the document may be color coded, making it easier to read and interpret.

You'll open Tara's recipes.xml file in your Web browser to see how the document is displayed by the XML parser built into your browser.

To view the recipes.xml file in your browser:

▶ 1. Start your Web browser, and open the **recipes.xml** file from the tutorial.11\tutorial folder. Figure 11-16 shows the contents of the file as it appears within the Internet Explorer browser window. Note that the character references you inserted in the previous session—¼ and ½ and °—appear as ¼, ½, and °, respectively, in the rendered document.

Figure 11-16 ▶ **XML document viewed in a browser**

```
<?xml version="1.0" encoding="UTF-8" standalone="yes" ?>
<!--
    Recipes from thehelpfulcook.com

    Filename: recipes.xml
    Author:   Tara Anderson
    Date:     3/1/2012

-->
<recipes>
  <recipe group="beef" nationality="asian">
    <title>Grilled Flank Steak with Asian Sauce</title>
    <description>
      <![CDATA[
        A flavorful marinade adds a touch of zest to this classic
        steak recipe. The dish is best served with green beans
        & rice. We recommend complementing the marinade spices with
        a pale ale or a Pinot Noir.

      ]]>
    </description>
    <author>Tanya Evans</author>
    <servings>6</servings>
    <ingredients>
      <ingredient>½ cup soy sauce</ingredient>
      <ingredient>½ cup plum sauce</ingredient>
      <ingredient>½ cup pineapple juice</ingredient>
      <ingredient>½ cup ketchup</ingredient>
      <ingredient>¼ cup scallions, finely sliced</ingredient>
      <ingredient>3 tbsps cilantro, chopped</ingredient>
      <ingredient>2 tbsps fresh ginger, minced</ingredient>
      <ingredient>2 tbsps fresh garlic, minced</ingredient>
      <ingredient>2 flank steaks, about 1¼ lbs each</ingredient>
    </ingredients>
    <directions>
      <step>Combine the marinade ingredients in a medium bowl.</step>
      <step>Trim the flank steaks of surface fat.</step>
      <step>Place the steaks and marinade in a sealed plastic bag and refrigerate for 3 to 6 hours.</step>
      <step>Remove the steaks from the bag and boil the marinade in a small saucepan for 1 full minute.</step>
      <step>Let steaks stand at room temperature for 20 to 30 minutes.</step>
      <step>Grill steaks over direct high heat (500°) for 8 to 10 minutes, turning once halfway through.</step>
      <step>Remove steaks from the grill and let rest for 3 to 5 minutes.</step>
      <step>Cut steaks across the grain into thin strips and serve with the marinade sauce.</step>
    </directions>
  </recipe>
</recipes>
```

the CDATA displayed as it is entered into the XML file

the ½ character reference appears as ½

the ¼ character reference appears as ¼

the ° character reference appears as °

Trouble? If the recipes.xml file looks different from that shown in Figure 11-16, you are probably using a different browser and/or browser version than was used in this figure. Continue with Step 2.

Trouble? If you are running Internet Explorer for Windows and the recipes.xml file opened in another application, XML documents are probably associated with Notepad or another application besides the Internet Explorer browser. To open an XML document in Internet Explorer, locate the file in Windows Explorer, right-click the file icon, point to Open With, and then click Internet Explorer from the list of available programs.

2. If you are running a browser that displays the contents of the document in outline form, click the **minus (–)** symbols in front of the <ingredients> and <directions> tags. The browser collapses the elements nested within those two tags, as shown in Figure 11-17.

Document tree collapsed **Figure 11-17**

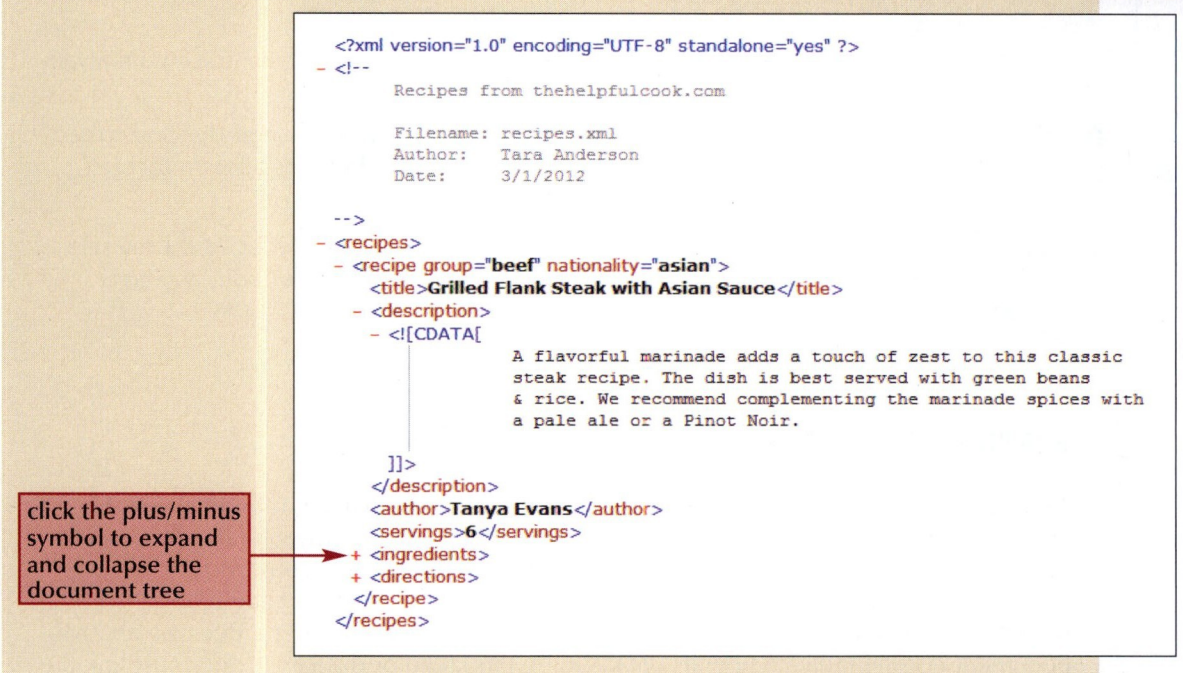

click the plus/minus symbol to expand and collapse the document tree

Because the XML file is well-formed, the browser has no trouble rendering the document's content. Tara now wants to see how browsers respond to an XML document that is not well-formed. She asks you to intentionally introduce an error into the recipes.xml file to verify that the error is flagged by the browser.

To introduce an error into the recipes.xml file:

1. Return to the **recipes.xml** file in your text editor.

2. Scroll to the bottom of the file, and then change the closing tag from </recipes> to **</RECIPES>**. This change will result in an error because the closing tag no longer exactly matches the text of the opening tag.

3. Save your changes to the file, and then reload **recipes.xml** in your Web browser. An error message similar to the one shown in Figure 11-18 appears.

Figure 11-18 ▸ **Error message produced by a document that is not well-formed**

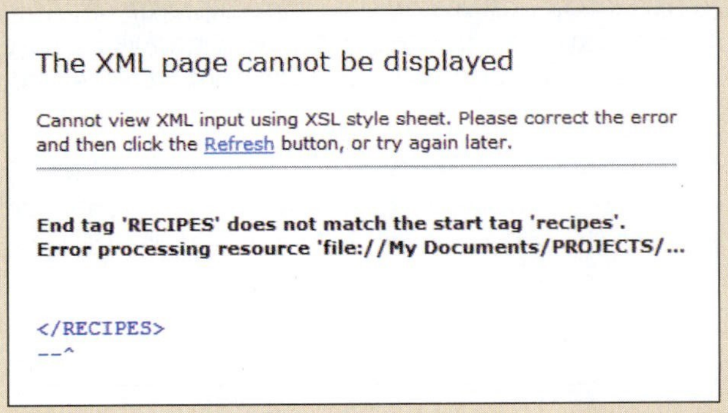

The XML page cannot be displayed

Cannot view XML input using XSL style sheet. Please correct the error and then click the Refresh button, or try again later.

End tag 'RECIPES' does not match the start tag 'recipes'.
Error processing resource 'file://My Documents/PROJECTS/...

```
</RECIPES>
--^
```

Trouble? If you do not see an error message, your browser does not contain a validating XML parser. Continue with Step 4.

▸ **4.** Return to the **recipes.xml** file in your text editor, and then change the closing tag </RECIPES> back to **</recipes>**. The opening and closing tags again match exactly.

▸ **5.** Save your changes to the file, and then reload **recipes.xml** in your Web browser, verifying that the browser once again displays the document without any error messages.

Formatting XML Data with CSS

Tara wants to share this XML document with other users by placing it on the Web. However, she wants the data to be formatted in a visually attractive way. She does not want to display the contents in the default hierarchical format shown in Figure 11-16.

XML documents do not include any information about how they should be rendered. Rendering is determined solely by the parser processing the document. Because an XML document doesn't indicate how its data is to be formatted or displayed, you must link the document to an external style sheet to specify its appearance. The XML document and the style sheet are then combined by an XML parser to render a single formatted document, as shown in Figure 11-19.

Combining an XML document and a style sheet ◄ **Figure 11-19**

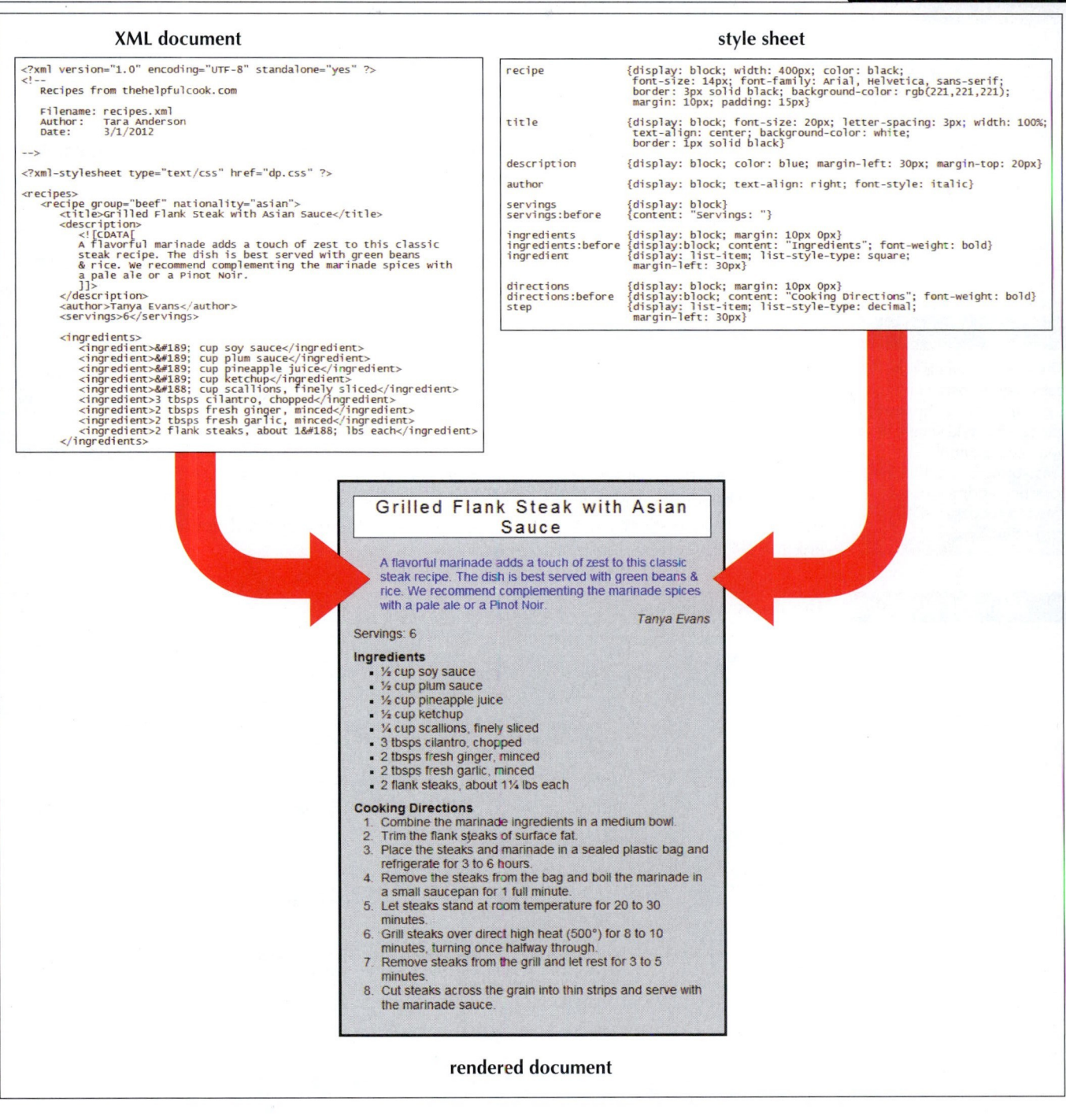

rendered document

Cascading Style Sheets (CSS), the standard developed for use with HTML on the Web, can also be used with the elements in any XML document. If you are already familiar with HTML and CSS, you are well on your way to formatting XML data. You will apply a style sheet to Tara's document. CSS styles are applied to an XML element using the style declaration

```
selector {attribute1:value1; attribute2:value2; ...}
```

where *selector* identifies an element (or a set of elements with each element separated by a comma) from the XML document; *attribute1*, *attribute2*, and so on are CSS style attributes; and *value1*, *value2*, and so forth are values of the CSS styles. For example, the following style declaration displays the text of the author element in a red boldface type:

```
author {color:red; font-weight: bold;}
```

You can use CSS to add extra text to the display of XML documents with the content style. To insert extra text before an element, use the style

```
selector:before {content: "text";}
```

where *text* is the text you wanted displayed before the element or elements identified by *selector*. To insert extra text after an element, use the style declaration

```
selector:after {content: "text";}
```

where *text* is the text you wanted displayed after the element or elements identified by *selector*. Note that adding text using the content style does not modify the contents of the XML document, only how that document is displayed by the browser.

Tara already created styles for the elements of the recipes.xml file, which she stored in an external style sheet named dp.css. The content of the dp.css file is shown in Figure 11-20. The style sheet contains styles for each of the elements in Tara's document. To see how the styles in this style sheet will affect the appearance of the recipes.xml document, you must link the XML document to the style sheet.

Tip

The content style is not currently supported by the Internet Explorer browser, so use XSL style sheets if you need a completely cross-browser solution for inserting additional text into the rendered XML document.

Figure 11-20 ▶ **The dp.css style sheet**

```
recipe            {display: block; width: 400px; color: black;
                   font-size: 14px; font-family: Arial, Helvetica, sans-serif;
                   border: 3px solid black; background-color: rgb(221,221,221);
                   margin: 10px; padding: 15px}

title             {display: block; font-size: 20px; letter-spacing: 3px; width: 100%;
                   text-align: center; background-color: white;
                   border: 1px solid black}

description       {display: block; color: blue; margin-left: 30px; margin-top: 20px}

author            {display: block; text-align: right; font-style: italic}

servings          {display: block}
servings:before   {content: "Servings: "}

ingredients       {display: block; margin: 10px 0px}
ingredients:before {display:block; content: "Ingredients"; font-weight: bold}
ingredient        {display: list-item; list-style-type: square;
                   margin-left: 30px}

directions        {display: block; margin: 10px 0px}
directions:before {display:block; content: "Cooking Directions"; font-weight: bold}
step              {display: list-item; list-style-type: decimal;
                   margin-left: 30px}
```

Inserting a Processing Instruction

You create a link from the XML document to the style sheet through the use of a processing instruction. A **processing instruction** is a command that tells the XML parser how to process the document. Processing instructions have the general form

```
<?target instruction ?>
```

where *target* identifies the program (or object) to which the processing instruction is directed and *instruction* is information that the document passes on to the parser for processing. Usually the instruction takes the form of attributes and attribute values. For example, the processing instruction to access and link the contents of an XML document to a style sheet is

```
<?xml-stylesheet type="style" href="url" ?>
```

where *style* is the type of style sheet the XML processor will be accessing, and *url* is the name and location of the style sheet. In this example, xml-stylesheet is the processing instruction's target, and the other items within the tag are processing instructions that identify the type and location of the style sheet. For a cascading style sheet, the style should be text/css.

Attaching a Style Sheet to an XML Document | Reference Window

- To attach a CSS style sheet to an XML document, insert the command
  ```
  <?xml-stylesheet type="text/css" href="url" ?>
  ```
  within the XML document's prolog, where *url* is the name and location of the CSS file.

You'll add a processing instruction to the recipes.xml file to access the styles in the dp.css file.

To link the recipes.xml file to the dp.css style sheet:

1. Return to the **recipes.xml** file in your text editor.

2. Directly above the opening <recipes> tag, insert the following processing instruction, as shown in Figure 11-21:

   ```
   <?xml-stylesheet type="text/css" href="dp.css" ?>
   ```

Processing instruction ◄ **Figure 11-21**

```
<?xml-stylesheet type="text/css" href="dp.css" ?>

<recipes>
    <recipe group="beef" nationality="asian">
        <title>Grilled Flank Steak with Asian Sauce</title>
        <description>
            <![CDATA[
            A flavorful marinade adds a touch of zest to this classic
            steak recipe. The dish is best served with green beans
            & rice. We recommend complementing the marinade spices with
            a pale ale or a Pinot Noir.
            ]]>
        </description>
        <author>Tanya Evans</author>
        <servings>6</servings>
```

3. Save your changes to the file, and then close it.

4. Reopen or refresh **recipes.xml** in your Web browser. Figure 11-22 shows the contents of the recipes.xml file with the dp.css style sheet applied to the file's contents. The browser uses the specified style sheet in place of its default styles.

Figure 11-22 The recipes document formatted with the dp.css style sheet

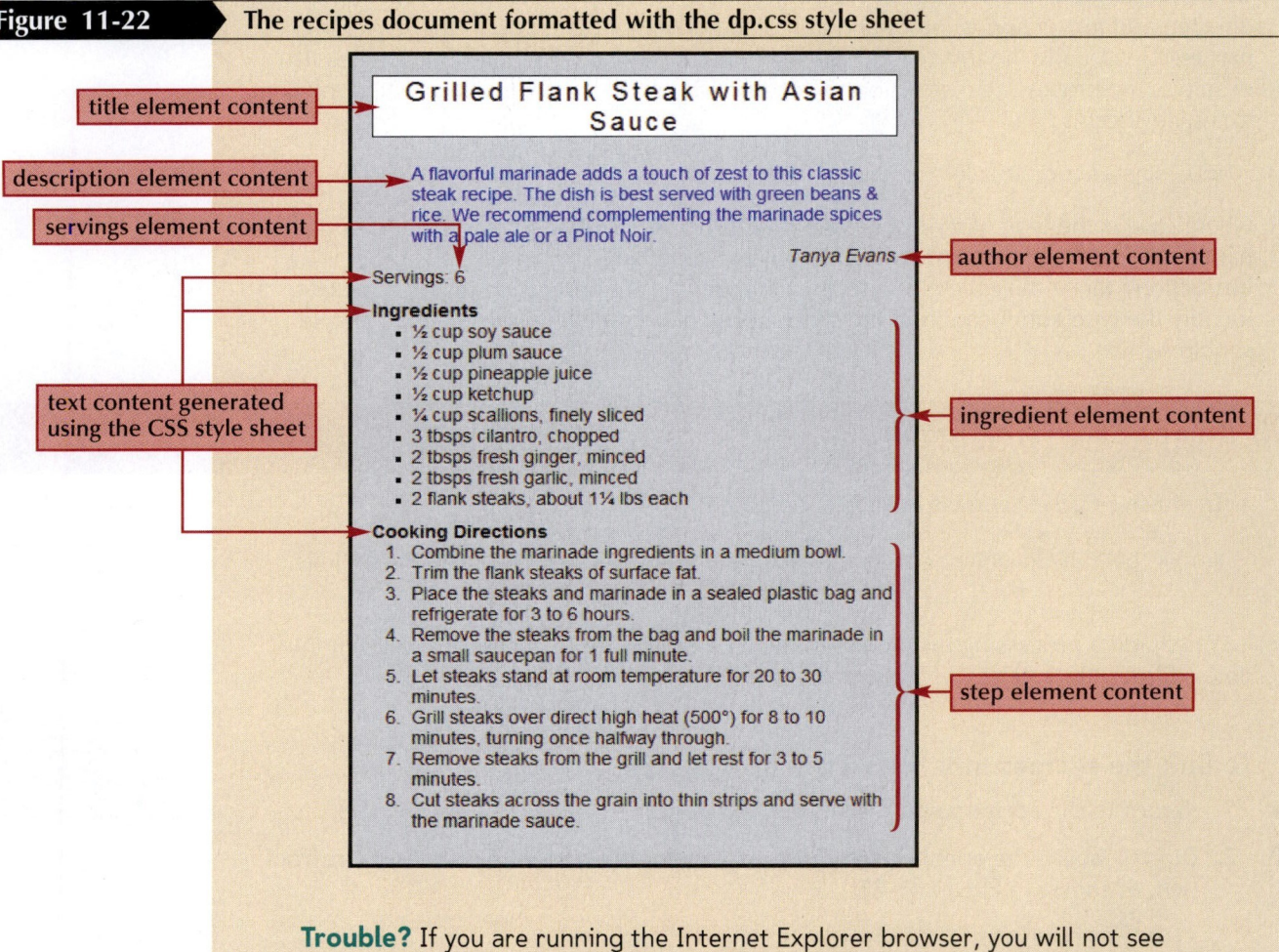

Trouble? If you are running the Internet Explorer browser, you will not see Servings: before the number 6 nor will you see the Ingredients and Cooking Directions headings. If you are running the Firefox browser, the numbered list of cooking direction steps will all be numbered with a zero. The Web page shown in Figure 11-22 was generated by the Opera Web browser.

Creating Style Sheets for XML with XSL | InSight

CSS is only one way of applying a style to the contents of an XML document. Another way is with the Extensible Stylesheet Language. **Extensible Stylesheet Language (XSL)** is a style sheet language developed specifically for XML. XSL is actually an XML vocabulary, so any XSL style sheet must follow the rules of well-formed XML. XSL works by transforming the contents of an XML document into another document format. For example, an XSL style sheet can be used to take the contents of an XML document and create an HTML file that can be displayed in any Web browser. The HTML code generated by the XSL style sheet can itself be linked to a CSS file.

XSL is not limited to generating HTML code. With XSL, the contents of an XML document can be transformed into code used by word processors such as Microsoft Word. Another possibility is that one XML document can be transformed into another. Web browsers often use internal XSL style sheets to display XML document. The outline form of Tara's document that was shown in Figure 11-16 is actually the XML document as transformed by an XSL style sheet built into the browser's XML parser. This style sheet is used by the browser until a different style sheet is specified by a processing instruction in the XML document.

Tara is pleased with the formatted document you created. Tara and the members of her Web team will get back to you as they continue to work on adding XML content to the thehelpfulcook.com Web site. Eventually, they will move the entire library of recipes into a collection of XML documents based on the vocabulary that Tara will develop with your assistance.

Session 11.3 Quick Check | Review

1. What is an XML parser?
2. What happens if you attempt to open an XML document that contains syntax errors in an XML parser?
3. What do you need to format the contents of an XML document?
4. What CSS style declaration displays the TITLE element in a bold font?
5. What is a processing instruction?
6. What code links an XML document to a style sheet file named standard.css?

Tutorial Summary | Review

This tutorial introduced the XML markup language. In the first session, you studied the background and theory behind XML. You learned how XML relates to SGML and HTML. You also saw how XML can be used to create vocabularies for specialized pieces of information. In the second session, you created an XML document and worked with elements and attributes as well as with character data, parsed character data, and whitespace in XML documents. You also used entities to insert characters not found on the keyboard. In the third session, you learned about the use of XML parsers and Web browsers to display the contents of an XML document. The tutorial concluded with a look at the use of style sheets with XML.

Key Terms

aggregator
Atom
attribute
CDATA section
character data
character reference
Chemical Markup
   Language (CML)
child element
closing tag
device-independent
document body
document element
document type
   definition (DTD)
element
empty element
entity reference
epilog
extensible

Extensible Hypertext Markup
   Language (XHTML)
Extensible Markup
   Language (XML)
Extensible Stylesheet
   Language (XSL)
feed reader
ISO/IEC character set
markup language
MathML
MSXML
nested element
open element
opening tag
parent element
parsed character
   data (pcdata)
podcast
processing instruction
prolog

Really Simple
   Syndication (RSS)
root element
schema
SGML application
sibling element
Standard Generalized
   Markup Language (SGML)
system-independent
valid document
well-formed
whitespace
whitespace stripping
XHTML
XML
XML application
XML declaration
XML parser
XML processor
XML vocabulary
XSL

| Review Assignments

Data Files needed for the Review Assignments: desstxt.txt, dstyles.css

Tara has another document that she wants you to create for the thehelpfulcook.com Web site. She wants to start including dessert recipes in the XML documents she has been creating. Tara saved a sample dessert recipe in a text file and wants you to use the contents of that file in an XML document. Figure 11-23 shows the structure of the document that she wants you to create.

Figure 11-23

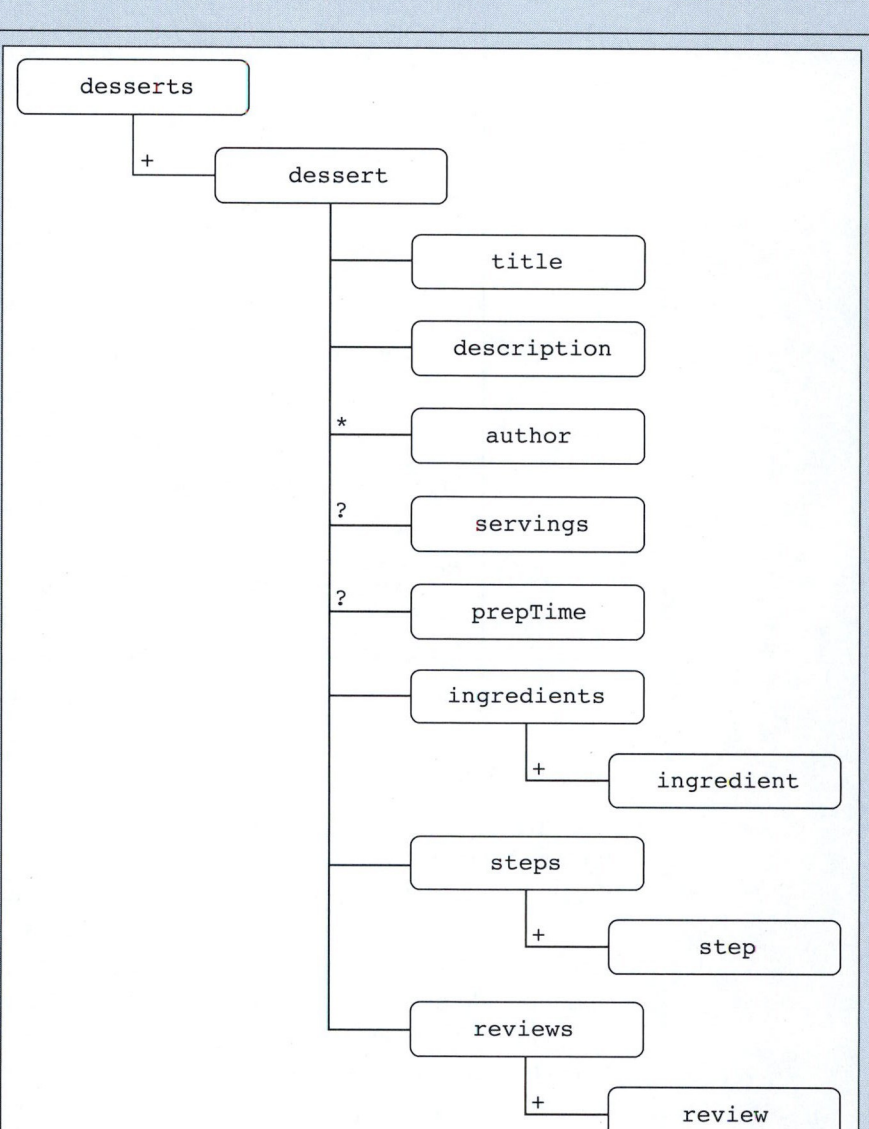

Tara provided a CSS style sheet for the dessert recipes. Figure 11-24 shows a preview of her sample XML document formatted with her CSS style sheet.

Figure 11-24

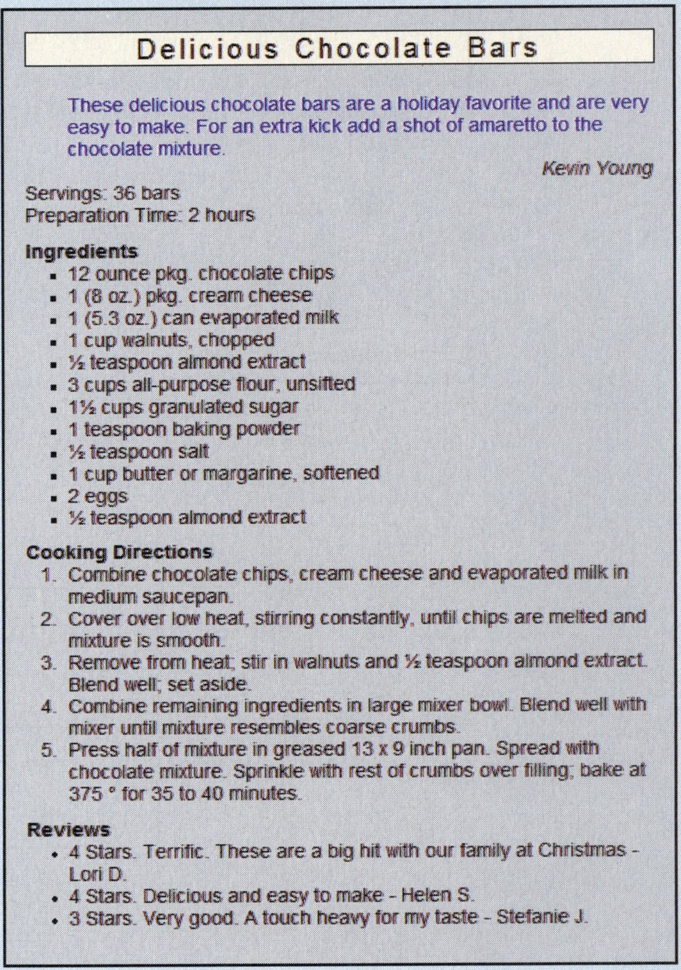

Delicious Chocolate Bars

These delicious chocolate bars are a holiday favorite and are very easy to make. For an extra kick add a shot of amaretto to the chocolate mixture.

Kevin Young

Servings: 36 bars
Preparation Time: 2 hours

Ingredients
- 12 ounce pkg. chocolate chips
- 1 (8 oz.) pkg. cream cheese
- 1 (5.3 oz.) can evaporated milk
- 1 cup walnuts, chopped
- ½ teaspoon almond extract
- 3 cups all-purpose flour, unsifted
- 1½ cups granulated sugar
- 1 teaspoon baking powder
- ½ teaspoon salt
- 1 cup butter or margarine, softened
- 2 eggs
- ½ teaspoon almond extract

Cooking Directions
1. Combine chocolate chips, cream cheese and evaporated milk in medium saucepan.
2. Cover over low heat, stirring constantly, until chips are melted and mixture is smooth.
3. Remove from heat; stir in walnuts and ½ teaspoon almond extract. Blend well; set aside.
4. Combine remaining ingredients in large mixer bowl. Blend well with mixer until mixture resembles coarse crumbs.
5. Press half of mixture in greased 13 x 9 inch pan. Spread with chocolate mixture. Sprinkle with rest of crumbs over filling; bake at 375 ° for 35 to 40 minutes.

Reviews
- 4 Stars. Terrific. These are a big hit with our family at Christmas - Lori D.
- 4 Stars. Delicious and easy to make - Helen S.
- 3 Stars. Very good. A touch heavy for my taste - Stefanie J.

Complete the following:

1. Use your text editor to create a file named **desserts.xml**, saving the file in the tutorial.11/review folder.
2. Create a prolog at the top of the document, indicating that this is an XML document using the UTF-8 encoding scheme and that it is a standalone document.
3. Below the XML declaration, insert the comment **Desserts from thehelpfulcook.com** and then add three additional comment lines containing the filename, *your name* as the page's author, and the *current date*.
4. Place the content from the **desstxt.txt** file in the tutorial.11/review folder into the XML document, using the structure indicated in Figure 11-23.
5. Indent the element tags to make the code easier to read and understand.
6. Enclose the contents of the description element in a CDATA section.
7. Replace all occurrences of 1/2 with a character reference to the ¹/₂ symbol. Replace the word "degrees" in the fifth step of the recipe with a character reference to the ° symbol.
8. Add a processing instruction to the document, linking it to the **dstyles.css** style sheet.

9. Save your changes to the file, open **desserts.xml** in your Web browser, and then verify that the completed document contains no errors and that its format resembles that shown in Figure 11-24. (*Hint*: Under the Internet Explorer browser, the Servings, Ingredients, Cooking Directions, and Reviews headings will not appear. Under the Firefox browser, the steps will not be numbered sequentially.)

10. Submit the completed files to your instructor.

| Apply | | **Case Problem 1** |

Use the skills you learned in this tutorial to create an FAQ document for a computer manufacturer.

Data Files needed for this Case Problem: faq.css, faq.txt

Jackson Electronics   Located in Santa Fe, New Mexico, Jackson Electronics is a privately held manufacturer of consumer digital products such as scanners, printers, and digital cameras. Originally founded by Pete Jackson in 1948 as an office supply store, Jackson Electronics has thrived over the years with innovative thinking and effective use of cutting-edge technology. Alison Greely is one of the Webmasters for the Jackson Electronics Web site. Her primary responsibility is to maintain information on the frequently asked questions (FAQs) section of the site. Alison wants to convert her documents into XML format. She has given you a text file containing FAQs for two of Jackson Electronics' products: the ScanMaster scanner and the DigiCam digital camera. Figure 11-25 shows the structure she wants to apply to the document.

Figure 11-25

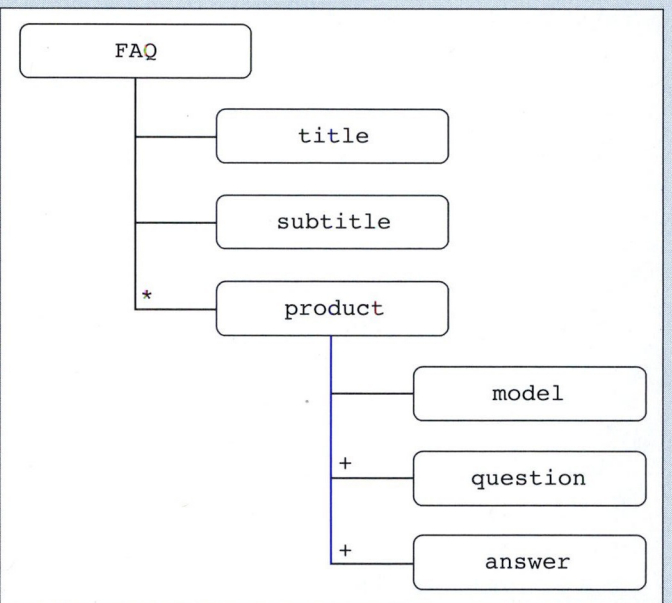

You will convert this text file to an XML document and then link it to the CSS style sheet that Alison has provided. Figure 11-26 shows a preview of the document rendered in a Web browser.

Figure 11-26

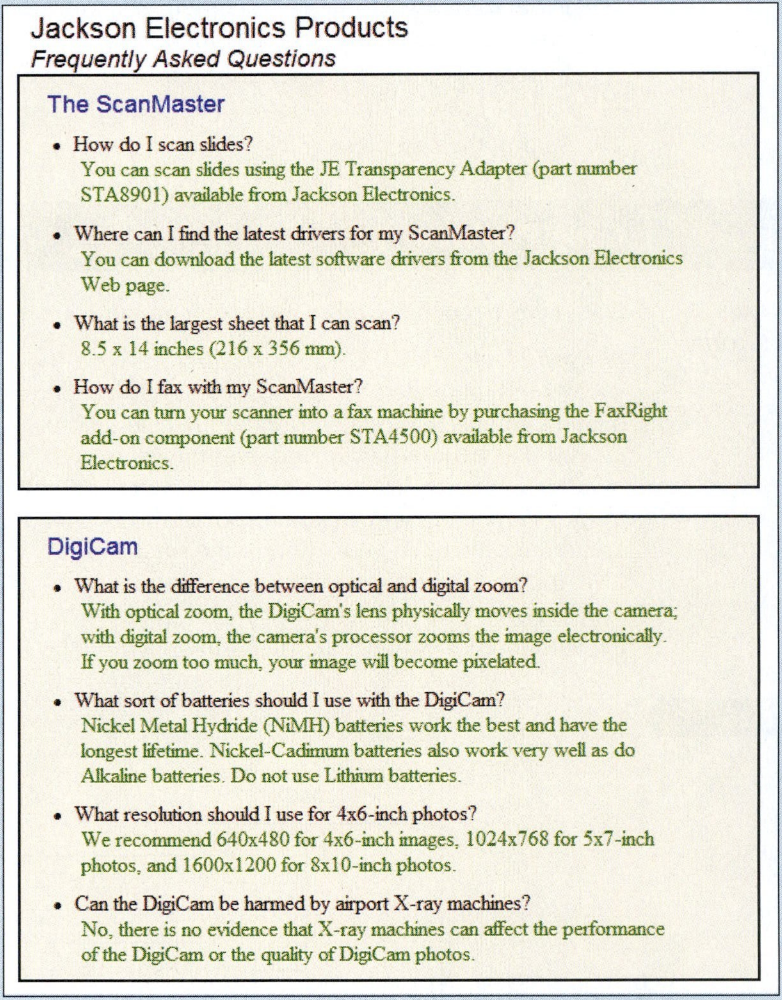

Jackson Electronics Products
Frequently Asked Questions

The ScanMaster

- How do I scan slides?
  You can scan slides using the JE Transparency Adapter (part number STA8901) available from Jackson Electronics.

- Where can I find the latest drivers for my ScanMaster?
  You can download the latest software drivers from the Jackson Electronics Web page.

- What is the largest sheet that I can scan?
  8.5 x 14 inches (216 x 356 mm).

- How do I fax with my ScanMaster?
  You can turn your scanner into a fax machine by purchasing the FaxRight add-on component (part number STA4500) available from Jackson Electronics.

DigiCam

- What is the difference between optical and digital zoom?
  With optical zoom, the DigiCam's lens physically moves inside the camera; with digital zoom, the camera's processor zooms the image electronically. If you zoom too much, your image will become pixelated.

- What sort of batteries should I use with the DigiCam?
  Nickel Metal Hydride (NiMH) batteries work the best and have the longest lifetime. Nickel-Cadimum batteries also work very well as do Alkaline batteries. Do not use Lithium batteries.

- What resolution should I use for 4x6-inch photos?
  We recommend 640x480 for 4x6-inch images, 1024x768 for 5x7-inch photos, and 1600x1200 for 8x10-inch photos.

- Can the DigiCam be harmed by airport X-ray machines?
  No, there is no evidence that X-ray machines can affect the performance of the DigiCam or the quality of DigiCam photos.

Complete the following:

1. Using your text editor, open **faq.txt** from the tutorial.11/case1 folder, and then save the document as **faq.xml**.
2. Create a prolog at the top of the document, indicating that this is an XML document using version 1.0 of XML. You do not need to include any other information in the XML declaration.
3. After the XML declaration, insert the comment **ScanMaster and DigiCam FAQ** and then add additional comments that contain *your name* and the *current date*.
4. Create a root element named **FAQ**.
5. Enclose the text "Jackson Electronics Products" in a **title** element, and set the text "Frequently Asked Questions" in an element named **subtitle**.
6. Create two **product** elements. Within each product element, insert a **model** element containing the name of the product.
7. Within both product elements, enclose each question in the text file within a **question** element.
8. Within both product elements, enclose each answer in the document within an **answer** element, and place the text of those answers within a CDATA section.

9. Add a processing instruction to the prolog to apply the **faq.css** style sheet to this document.

10. Save your changes to the file, open **faq.xml** in your Web browser, and then verify that the appearance and layout of the document resemble that shown in Figure 11-26 and that the browser reports no errors.

11. Submit your completed files to your instructor.

| Challenge | | Case Problem 2 |

Learn basic features of RSS as you create an RSS news feed containing articles for a surfing Web site.

Data File needed for this Case Problem: articles.htm

ripwave.com   Kei-lani Malia of Kailua, Hawaii, works for the surfing Web site ripwave.com. The site caters to surfing enthusiasts who are interested in following the results from amateur and professional competitions around the world. Kei-lani wants to create a news feed containing articles that can be automatically downloaded to ripwave. com subscribers. News feeds are typically written in the RSS markup language, an XML vocabulary. You will help Kei-lani develop this news feed, learning some basic features of RSS in the process.

RSS contains several elements and attributes designed for describing and distributing articles on the Internet. A slimmed-down version of a typical document tree for an RSS document is shown in Figure 11-27.

Figure 11-27

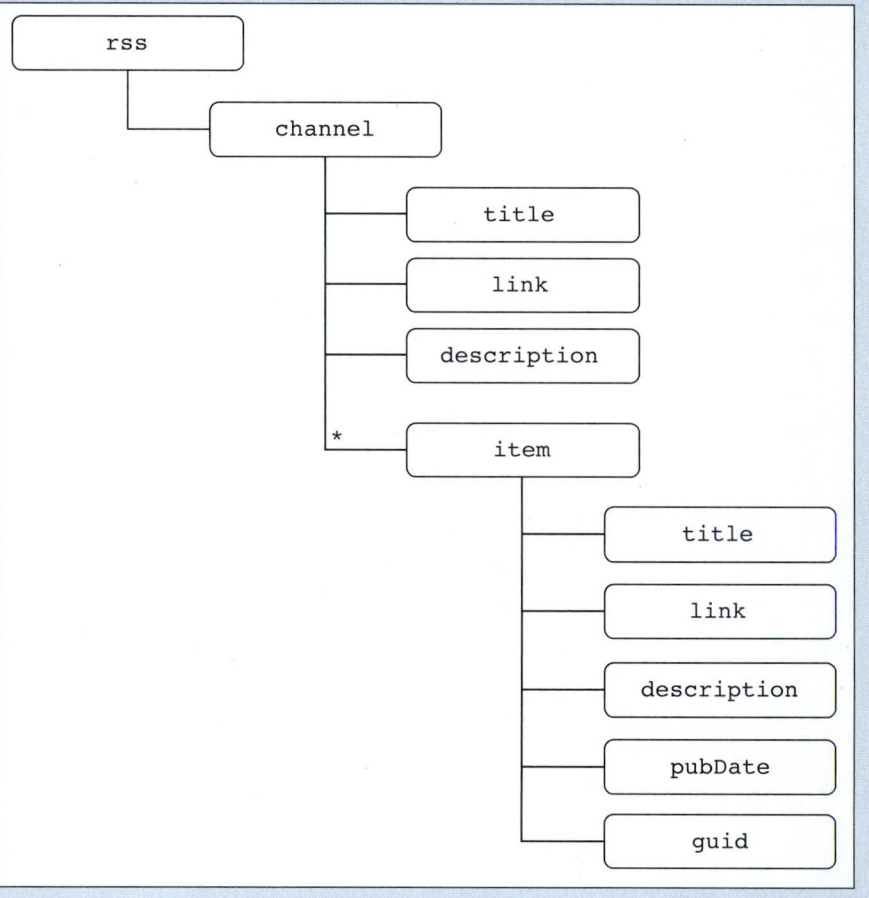

You will create an RSS document from the raw text that Kei-lani prepared. Using your work as a starting point, Kei-lani hopes to create a customized news feed service for all ripwave.com subscribers.

Complete the following:

1. Use your text editor to create a file named **ripwave.xml** in the tutorial.11/case2 folder.

2. Create a prolog at the top of the document, indicating that this is an XML document using version 1.0 of XML and that the characters are encoded under UTF-8.

3. After the XML declaration, add the comment **This is a news feed from ripwave.com linking to the latest news reports on international surfing competitions.** followed by the filename, *your name*, and the **current date**.

4. Insert the root element **rss** into the document. The rss element indicates that this file is written in the RSS language. Add a version attribute to the rss element, setting its value to **2.0**.

5. Within the rss element, insert the **channel** element.

6. Within the channel element, insert one title element containing the text **ripwave.com News Feed**. Add a link element pointing to the URL **http://www.ripwave.com/Site/asp**. Add the description element containing the text **Keep up with the news from the world of competitive surfing with the latest results and articles about your favorite surfers.**

7. Add three **item** elements to the document. RSS documents can contain multiple item elements, with each item element describing a different news feed item.

8. Each item element contains several child elements. Make the following additions to the first item element in the document:
   a. Insert a **title** element that provides a title for the first news item. Set the title of the first item to **Kai Harris wins the San Diego ASP World Junior Championship**.
   b. Insert a **link** element. The purpose of the link element is to provide a hypertext link to the source of the news item. The link to the first news item is **http://www. ripwave.com/articles/art8711asp**.
   c. Insert a **description** element that contains the text of the news item. For the first item, take the text from the **articles.htm** file in the tutorial.11/case2 folder, using the paragraph text (not the heading) of the first article in the document. Include the HTML markup tags found in the article.
   d. Enclose the article text you inserted into the description element in the last step within a CDATA section.
   e. Add a **pubDate** element. The purpose of the pubDate element is to indicate the publication date of the news item. Enter a value of **Tue, 10 Apr 2012 13:59:56 EST** for this first news item.
   f. Enter a **guid** element. The purpose of the guid element is to provide a unique identifier for the news item. Enter an identifier of **http://www.ripwave.com/ articles8711**.
   g. The guid element has an attribute named **isPermaLink**. The purpose of the isPermaLink attribute is to indicate whether the guid element points to a permanent link to the file. Set the value of this attribute to **true**.

9. Enter content for the next item element in your RSS document. Add the following child elements:
   a. Set the **title** content to **Koke Triumphs at Pro Am Malaysia**.
   b. Set the **link** content to **http://www.ripwave.com/articles/art8704.asp**.

   c. Insert the HTML markup for the paragraphs (not the heading) of the second news article from the articles.htm file into the **description** element. As before, enclose the HTML markup tags within a CDATA section.

   d. Set the **pubDate** content to **Tue, 10 Apr 2012 06:42:13 EST**.

   e. Set the **guid** element to the value **http://www.ripwave.com/articles8704** with an **isPermaLink** attribute value of **true**.

10. Enter content for the last of the three news item elements in your RSS document. Add the following child elements:

   a. Set the **title** content to **Pauline Li drives Kata Surf Club to victory in Crown Club Series**.

   b. Set the **link** content to **http://www.ripwave.com/articles/art8693.asp**.

   c. Set the **description** content to the HTML markup for the third article in the articles.htm file; again only using the paragraphs from the news article (not the heading) and enclosing the markup tags within a CDATA section.

   d. Set the **pubDate** to **Mon, 9 Apr 2012 10:25:45 EST**.

   e. Set the **guid** element to the value **http://www.ripwave.com/articles8693** with a value for the **isPermaLink** attribute of **true**.

11. Save your changes to the file, and then close it.

12. Open **ripwave.xml** in your Web browser. Verify that there are no errors in the document.

13. Submit the completed files to your instructor.

Challenge	**Case Problem 3**

Explore how to create a well-formed XML document.

Data Files needed for this Case Problem: staff.css, stafftxt.xml

Biotech, Inc.   Located in Dallas, Texas, Biotech, Inc. (BI) was created in April 2002 as a result of the merger of four smaller biotechnology research concerns. Linda Abrahams is a human resource representative for BI. Most recently, she has been entering employee data into an XML document and is running into a few problems. When she opened the document in her Web browser, the browser reported several syntax errors. Linda doesn't know how to solve the problem. You will help her by cleaning up the code.

Complete the following:

1. Start your text editor, open the **stafftxt.xml** file from the tutorial.11/case3 folder, enter *your name* and the *current date* in the comment section, and then save the file as **staff.xml**.

2. Open **staff.xml** in your Web browser.

⊕ EXPLORE

3. Using the information about the document's syntax errors reported by your Web browser, locate and fix the errors. (*Hint*: The browser will report only one error at a time. After you fix one error and reload the file, the browser displays the next error in the file, if one exists.)

4. After you have fixed all the syntax errors, link the **staff.xml** document to the **staff.css** style sheet.

5. Add a **gender** attribute to each Employee element in the document. Set the value of the gender attribute to **male** for male employees and **female** for female employees.

6. Display **staff.xml** in your Web browser.

⊕ EXPLORE

7. Draw the tree structure for the contents of the staff.xml file.

8. Submit your completed files to your instructor.

Create	**Case Problem 4**

Test your knowledge of XML by creating an XML document for a life insurance company.

Data Files needed for this Case Problem: accounts.txt, granite.css

Granite Mutual Life   Brian Carlson is an accounts manager for Granite Mutual Life in Eagan, Minnesota. He has created a text document containing personal information for all the accounts in his portfolio. However, the financial applications used by Granite Mutual Life need that data in an XML document using a specific XML vocabulary. You will convert Brian's text file to an XML document and then display that information in a Web page.

Complete the following:

1. Using the contents of the **accounts.txt** file in the tutorial.11\case4 folder, create an XML document named **accounts.xml** saved in the same folder.

2. The accounts.xml file should contain the following items:
   - The root element of the document should be named **Accounts**. The Accounts element should contain multiple occurrences of a child element named **Client**.
   - The Client element should have five child elements: **Name**, **Address**, **Phone**, **E-mail**, and **Account_Total**.
   - The Client element should have a single attribute named **ID** containing the customer ID number of each person (customer ID numbers begin with the letters "CS" followed by four digits).
   - The Name element should contain two child elements named **First** and **Last**, storing the first and last names of each person in Brian's accounts list.
   - The Address element should contain the following child elements: **Street**, **City**, **State**, and **Zip**, which contain the individual parts of the client's address.
   - The Phone element should contain the client's phone number.
   - The E-mail element should contain the client's e-mail address.
   - The Account_Total element should contain the current amount of money each client has invested with Granite Mutual Life.

3. Within the document's prolog, insert a comment describing the purpose of the document. Include the filename, ***your name***, and the ***current date*** in the comment text.

4. Attach the **accounts.xml** file to a CSS style sheet named **granite.css**.

5. Open **accounts.xml** in your Web browser and verify that there are no errors reported by the XML parser within the browser.

6. Submit your completed files to your instructor.

Review	**Quick Check Answers**

Session 11.1

1. Extensible means capable of being extended and modified. XML can be expanded by creating new elements and attributes for different pieces of information, and by allowing authors to create vocabularies tailored to specific information sources.

2. SGML stands for Standard Generalized Markup Language, which describes the structure and contents of any machine-readable information and is device-independent and system-independent. Although SGML was used to develop HTML, SGML is complicated and requires a complex environment; whereas Web page authors need a language that is easy to learn, manage, and implement.

3. a markup language created using SGML, such as HTML

4. HTML is not designed to describe information. HTML is not easily extended to different types of information. HTML does not impose rigid standards for syntax and therefore can be inconsistently applied.

5. a markup language created with XML and tailored to contain specific types of information, such as MathML, ChemML, XHTML, and RSS

6. prolog, document body, and epilog

7. `<?xml version="1.0" encoding="ISO-8859-1" standalone="yes" ?>`

8. `<!-- Entry extracted from the thehelpfulcook.com database -->`

9. The contents of a podcast are organized in an RSS document that feed readers can retrieve and read. RSS is an XML vocabulary, so RSS documents must satisfy the syntax requirements of XML.

Session 11.2

1. The case of the opening and closing tags does not match.

2. the element at the top of the document hierarchy; all other elements in the document are children of the root element

3. an element that contains no content, although it might contain one or more attributes whose values might be used by XML parsers

4. elements that share a common parent element

5. Parsed character data, or pcdata, consists of all those characters that XML treats as parts of markup tags. After you remove parsed character data, the symbols remaining constitute a document's actual content, known as character data, which is not parsed by the XML processor or assumed to contain XML commands.

6. use a CDATA section or the `&#38;` or `&amp;` character references

7. a section marked off as containing character data and not parsed character data

8. Whitespace is ignored in XML documents unless it is part of the document's data content.

Session 11.3

1. a program that reads an XML document and can test whether the document is well-formed and, in some cases, valid

2. The parser reports an error and rejects the document.

3. a style sheet (usually a CSS or XSL style sheet)

4. `TITLE {font-weight: bold;}`

5. a command that provides instructions to be run by XML parsers

6. `<?xml-stylesheet type="text/css" href="standard.css" ?>`

Ending Data Files

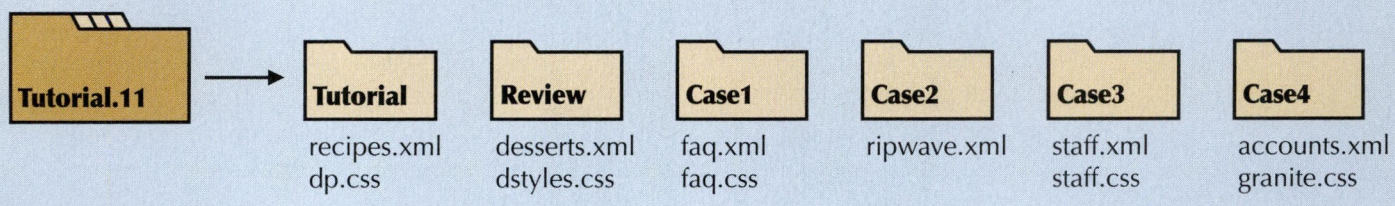

Tutorial.11 →

Tutorial
recipes.xml
dp.css

Review
desserts.xml
dstyles.css

Case1
faq.xml
faq.css

Case2
ripwave.xml

Case3
staff.xml
staff.css

Case4
accounts.xml
granite.css

Objectives

Session 12.1
- Understand compound documents and the problem of name collision
- Declare a namespace for an XML vocabulary
- Apply a namespace to an element
- Create a default namespace
- Apply a namespace to an attribute

Session 12.2
- Declare a namespace within a CSS style sheet
- Apply a namespace to a style selector
- Use the escape character to apply a namespace to a selector
- Create a compound document containing XML and XHTML elements and attributes

Working with Namespaces

Combining XML Vocabularies in a Compound Document

Case | Jackson Electronics

Gail Oglund is an information technician at one of the assembly plants for Jackson Electronics, a manufacturer of computers and peripherals. Part of Gail's job is to design and create reports for manufacturing orders. Gail needs to compare the orders for printers, computers, and other products against the parts on hand needed to assemble them.

Recently, the company has been considering storing manufacturing information in XML documents. Several XML vocabularies have been developed for this task. One vocabulary is used to track the quantity of each part currently available at the assembly plant. Another vocabulary is used to record the assembled models that the plant must produce during the current week.

Gail wants to produce a single document that combines information from both vocabularies. She also wants to display the document as a Web page on the plant's intranet, so the finished document needs to include elements from the XHTML vocabulary as well. You will produce a sample document that Gail can use as a model for future projects.

Note: Support for the integration of different XML vocabularies within a single document varies from browser to browser. Some of the examples in this tutorial will not work under specific browsers. When that is the case, the text indicates which browser is unable to completely render the document.

Starting Data Files

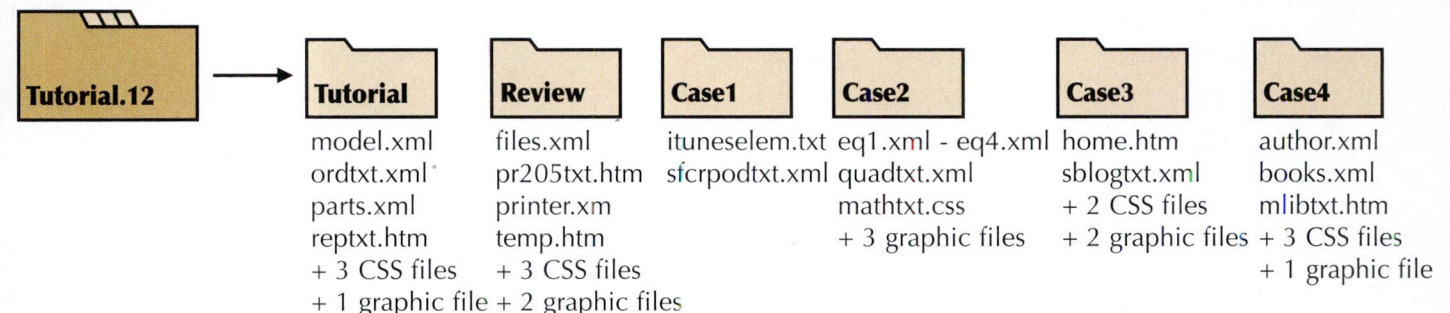

Tutorial	Review	Case1	Case2	Case3	Case4
model.xml	files.xml	ituneselem.txt	eq1.xml - eq4.xml	home.htm	author.xml
ordtxt.xml	pr205txt.htm	sfcrpodtxt.xml	quadtxt.xml	sblogtxt.xml	books.xml
parts.xml	printer.xm		mathtxt.css	+ 2 CSS files	mlibtxt.htm
reptxt.htm	temp.htm		+ 3 graphic files	+ 2 graphic files	+ 3 CSS files
+ 3 CSS files	+ 3 CSS files				+ 1 graphic file
+ 1 graphic file	+ 2 graphic files				

Session 12.1

Combining XML Vocabularies

At the Jackson Electronics assembly plant where Gail works, XML vocabularies have been developed for several tasks. One vocabulary was created to track the number of parts currently available at the plant, and another was created to store the orders that need to be assembled.

The tree structure of the vocabulary for tracking available parts is shown in Figure 12-1. The elements in this vocabulary include the title of each part, the part description, and the number of each part currently in stock. Gail stored data on the parts required to assemble Jackson Electronics' Laser4C color printer in the parts.xml file.

Figure 12-1   **Tree structure of the parts vocabulary**

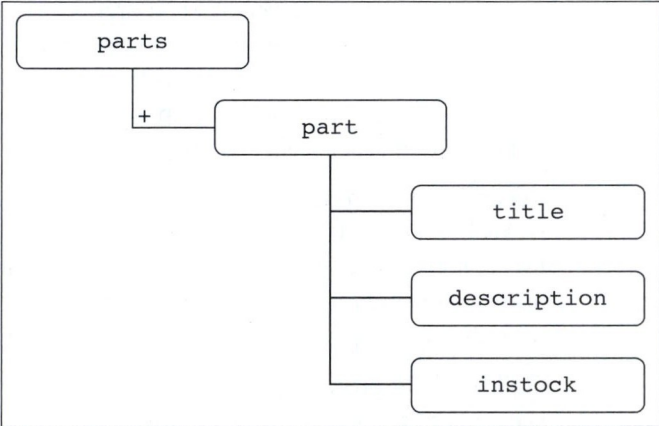

Gail created an accompanying external CSS style sheet for this document in the parts.css file. Figure 12-2 shows the Web page that is generated when the style sheet is applied to the contents of the parts.xml file.

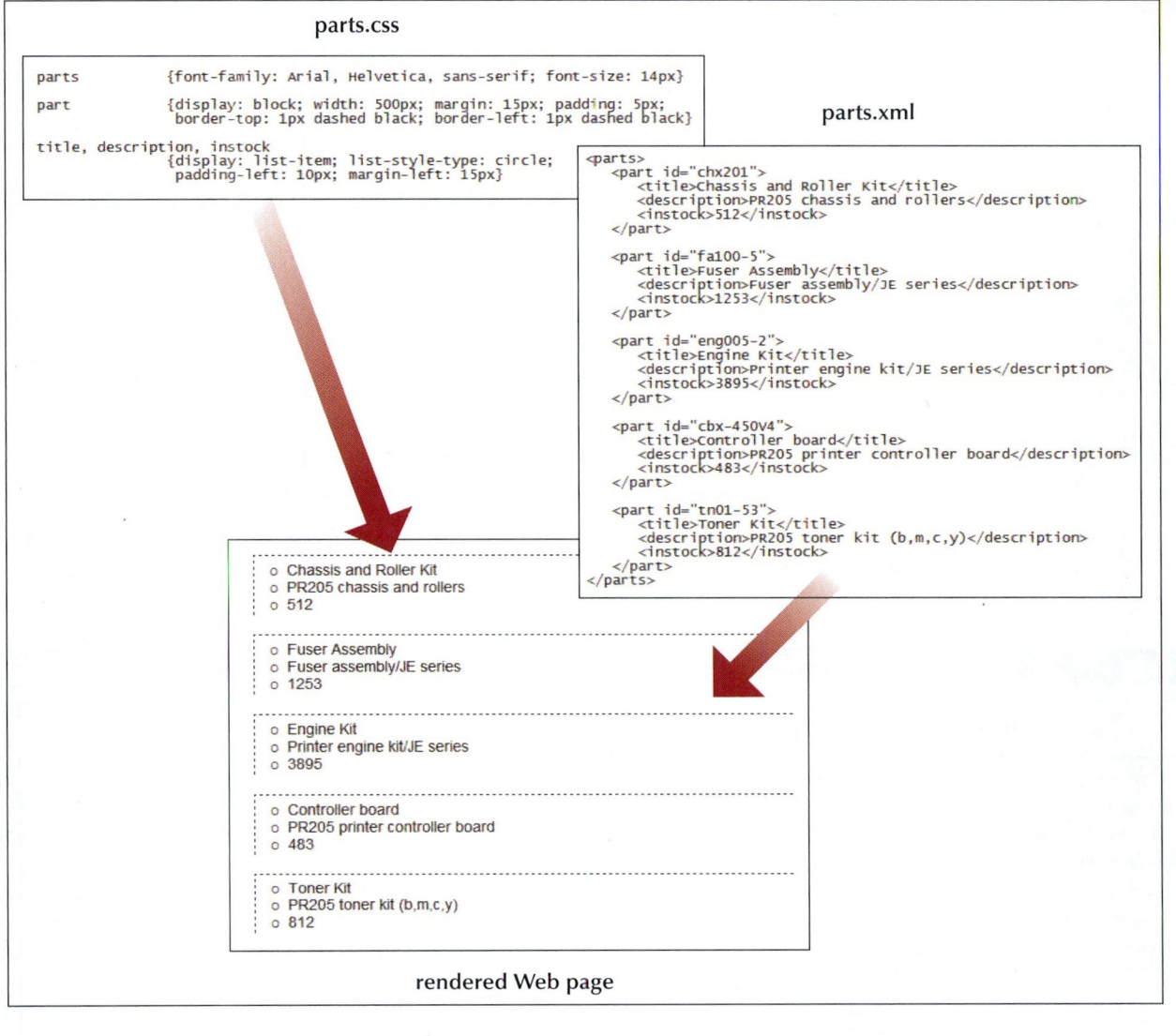

parts.css

```
parts              {font-family: Arial, Helvetica, sans-serif; font-size: 14px}

part               {display: block; width: 500px; margin: 15px; padding: 5px;
                    border-top: 1px dashed black; border-left: 1px dashed black}

title, description, instock
                   {display: list-item; list-style-type: circle;
                    padding-left: 10px; margin-left: 15px}
```

parts.xml

```
<parts>
    <part id="chx201">
        <title>Chassis and Roller Kit</title>
        <description>PR205 chassis and rollers</description>
        <instock>512</instock>
    </part>

    <part id="fa100-5">
        <title>Fuser Assembly</title>
        <description>Fuser assembly/JE series</description>
        <instock>1253</instock>
    </part>

    <part id="eng005-2">
        <title>Engine Kit</title>
        <description>Printer engine kit/JE series</description>
        <instock>3895</instock>
    </part>

    <part id="cbx-450v4">
        <title>Controller board</title>
        <description>PR205 printer controller board</description>
        <instock>483</instock>
    </part>

    <part id="tn01-53">
        <title>Toner Kit</title>
        <description>PR205 toner kit (b,m,c,y)</description>
        <instock>812</instock>
    </part>
</parts>
```

```
    o Chassis and Roller Kit
    o PR205 chassis and rollers
    o 512

    o Fuser Assembly
    o Fuser assembly/JE series
    o 1253

    o Engine Kit
    o Printer engine kit/JE series
    o 3895

    o Controller board
    o PR205 printer controller board
    o 483

    o Toner Kit
    o PR205 toner kit (b,m,c,y)
    o 812
```

rendered Web page

The tree structure for the vocabulary describing printer models built by Jackson Electronics is shown in Figure 12-3. The vocabulary contains elements for a model's title, description, and type; the number of models that need to be assembled; and the parts required for the assembly. Gail used this vocabulary to create a document showing the order information for the Laser4C printer. She stored this information in the model.xml file.

Figure 12-3 ▶ **Tree structure of the models vocabulary**

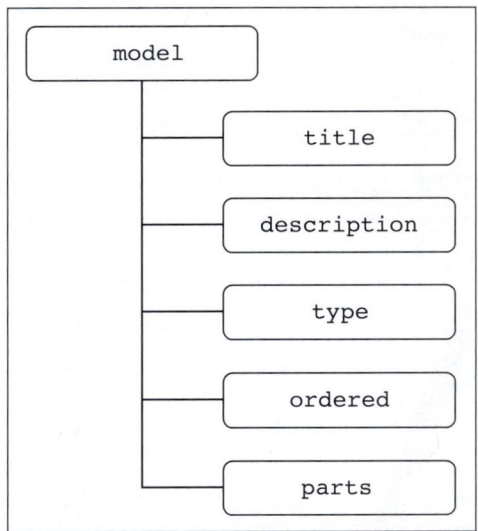

Gail created a CSS style sheet for this document as well, in the model.css file. Figure 12-4 shows the Web page that is generated when the style sheet is applied to the contents of the model.xml file.

Figure 12-4 ▶ **Style sheet and contents of the model.xml file**

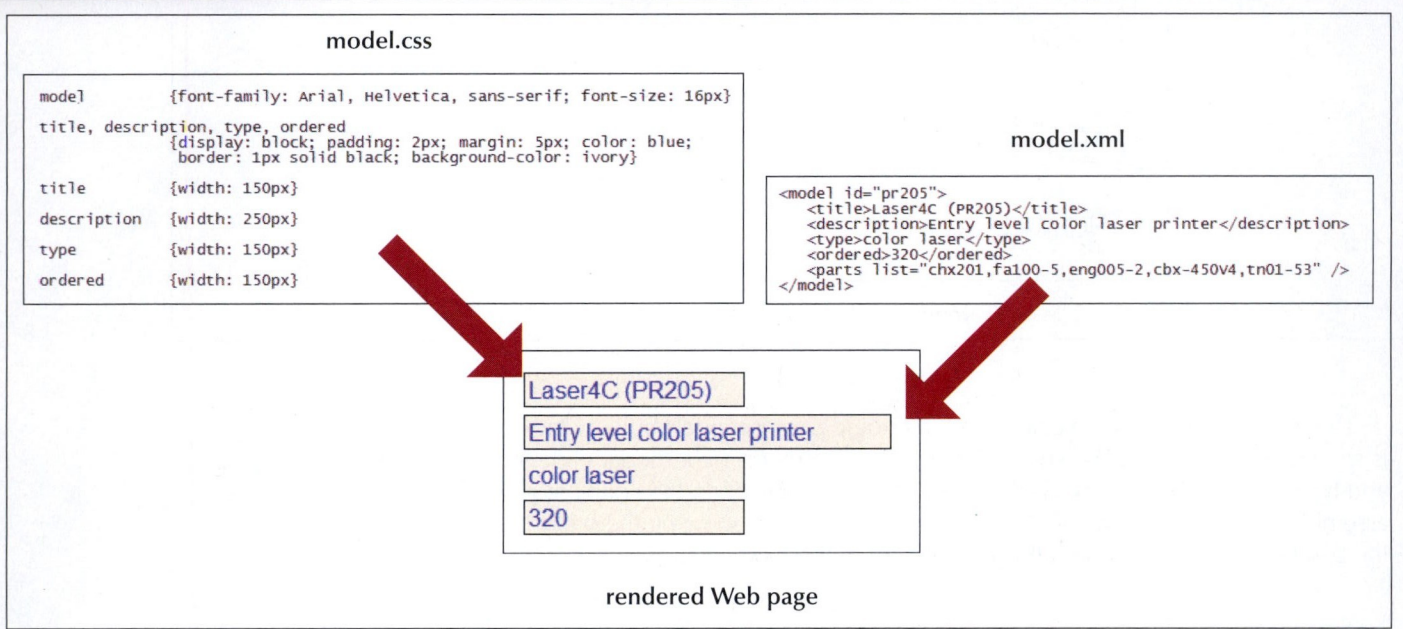

Gail wants to combine the two XML documents in a single report so she can see at a glance how many models of the Laser4C printer are on order and how many of the necessary parts are available to meet those orders. She also wants the report to include the usual features found in Web pages, such as headings, tables, inline images, and descriptive text. Figure 12-5 shows a preview of how she wants the page to appear.

Proposed report page combining multiple vocabularies ◀ Figure 12-5

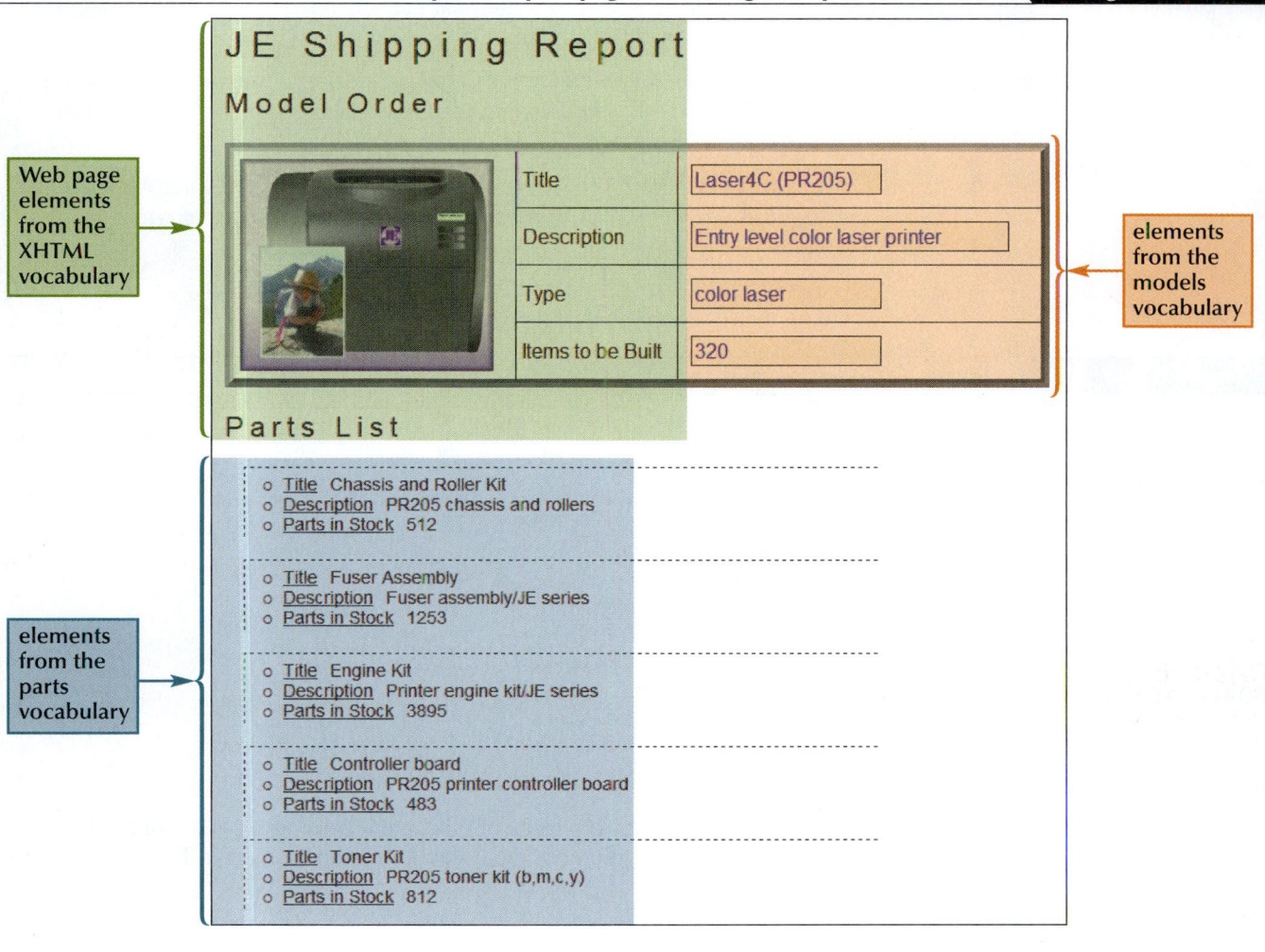

The final document that Gail wants to produce must include elements from three XML vocabularies: the parts vocabulary, the models vocabulary, and the XHTML vocabulary. A document that combines several vocabularies is known as a **compound document**. Gail wants you to work with her XML files to create a sample compound document that she can use as a model for future projects.

Creating a Compound Document

You'll start by combining the elements from the parts and models vocabularies, storing the result in a new file named order.xml. To display the contents of this compound document, you will use the style sheet rules defined in the parts.css and model.css style sheets. You'll create these three files now.

To create the parts.css, model.css, and order.xml files:

▶ 1. Use your text editor to open **partstxt.css** from the tutorial.12/tutorial folder included with your Data Files, enter **your name** and **the date** in the comment section, save the file as **parts.css** in the same folder, and then close the file.

> **2.** Use your text editor to open **modtxt.css** from the tutorial.12/tutorial folder, enter *your name* and *the date* in the comment section, save the file as **model.css** in the same folder, and then close the file.

> **3.** Use your text editor to open **ordtxt.xml** from the tutorial.12/tutorial folder, enter *your name* and *the date* in the comment section at the top of the file, and then save the file as **order.xml**.

> **4.** At the bottom of the order.xml file, insert the following two processing instructions to link the order.xml document to the parts.css and model.css style sheets, as shown in Figure 12-6:

```
<?xml-stylesheet type="text/css" href="parts.css" ?>
<?xml-stylesheet type="text/css" href="model.css" ?>
```

Figure 12-6 ▶ **Links to the parts.css and model.css style sheets**

```
<?xml version="1.0" encoding="UTF-8" standalone="yes" ?>
<!--
    New Perspectives on XHTML and XML
    Tutorial 12
    Tutorial Case

    Jackson Electronics Order Report
    Author: Gail Oglund
    Date:   3/1/2012

    Filename:          order.xml
    Supporting Files: model.css, parts.css
-->

<?xml-stylesheet type="text/css" href="parts.css" ?>
<?xml-stylesheet type="text/css" href="model.css" ?>
```

> **5.** Save your changes to the file.

Next, you'll copy and paste the elements from the model.xml and parts.xml file into the order.xml file. The structure of the document you'll create is shown in Figure 12-7.

Structure of the order.xml document ◀ Figure 12-7

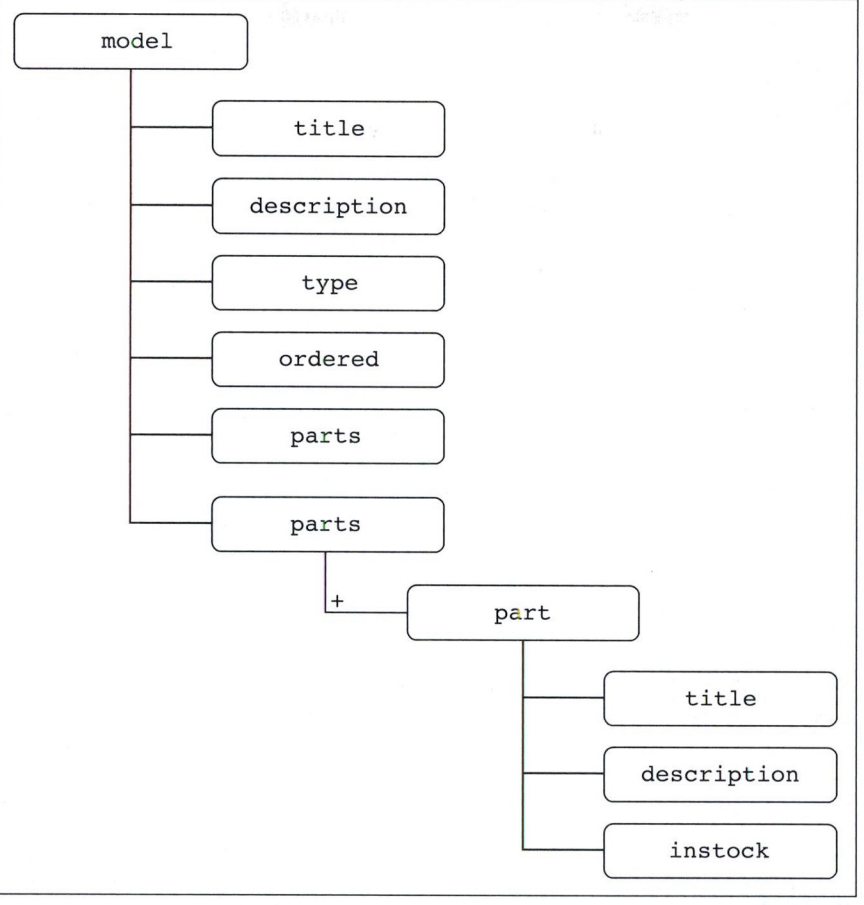

To copy and paste from the model.xml and order.xml files:

▶ **1.** Use your text editor to open the **model.xml** file from the tutorial.12/tutorial folder.

▶ **2.** Copy the contents of the document from the opening `<model>` tag through the closing `</model>` tag, and then close the model.xml file without saving any changes you may have inadvertently made.

▶ **3.** Return to the **order.xml** file in your text editor, and then paste the model.xml elements at the bottom of the file.

▶ **4.** Use your text editor to open **parts.xml** from the tutorial.12/tutorial folder, copy the contents of the file from the opening `<parts>` tag through the closing `</parts>` tag, and then close the parts.xml file without saving any changes you may have inadvertently made.

▶ **5.** Return to the **order.xml** file, and then paste the parts elements directly before the closing `</model>` tag. Figure 12-8 highlights the revised contents of the order.xml file.

Figure 12-8 **Compound document with content from the models and parts vocabularies**

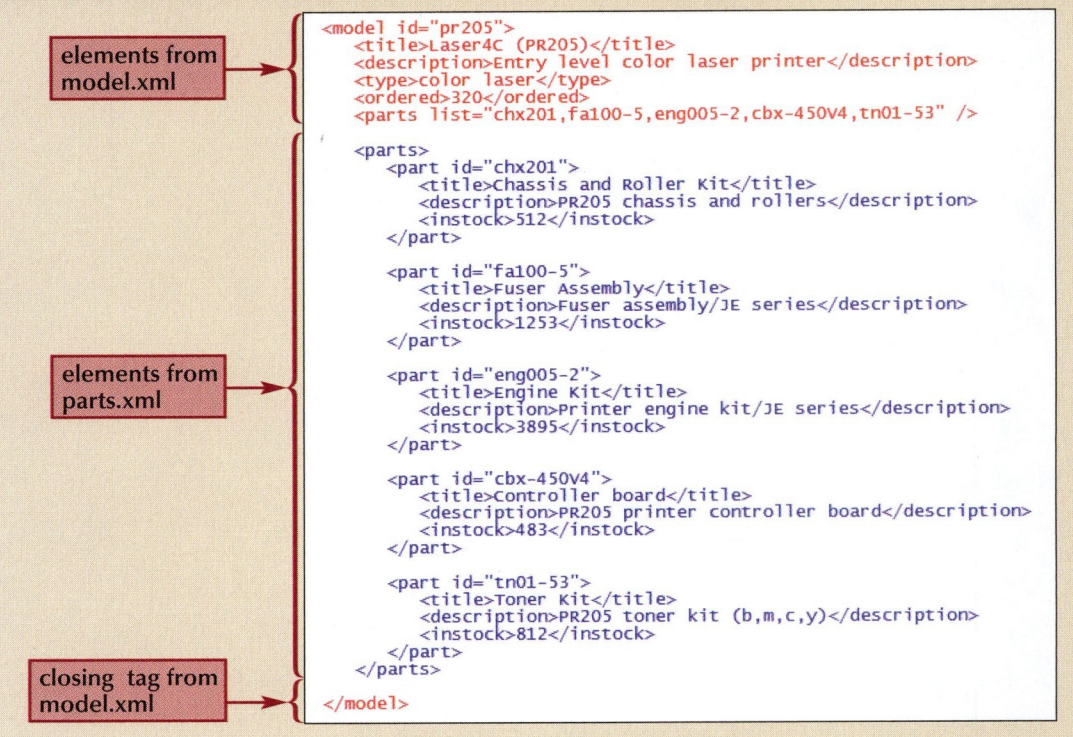

elements from model.xml

elements from parts.xml

closing tag from model.xml

```
<model id="pr205">
    <title>Laser4C (PR205)</title>
    <description>Entry level color laser printer</description>
    <type>color laser</type>
    <ordered>320</ordered>
    <parts list="chx201,fa100-5,eng005-2,cbx-450V4,tn01-53" />

    <parts>
        <part id="chx201">
            <title>Chassis and Roller Kit</title>
            <description>PR205 chassis and rollers</description>
            <instock>512</instock>
        </part>

        <part id="fa100-5">
            <title>Fuser Assembly</title>
            <description>Fuser assembly/JE series</description>
            <instock>1253</instock>
        </part>

        <part id="eng005-2">
            <title>Engine Kit</title>
            <description>Printer engine kit/JE series</description>
            <instock>3895</instock>
        </part>

        <part id="cbx-450V4">
            <title>Controller board</title>
            <description>PR205 printer controller board</description>
            <instock>483</instock>
        </part>

        <part id="tn01-53">
            <title>Toner Kit</title>
            <description>PR205 toner kit (b,m,c,y)</description>
            <instock>812</instock>
        </part>
    </parts>

</model>
```

You'll open this compound document in your Web browser to see how it looks.

To view the compound document in a Web browser:

1. Save your changes to the order.xml file.

2. Open **order.xml** in your Web browser. See Figure 12-9.

Laser4C (PR205)

Entry level color laser printer

color laser

320

style of the model content

○ Chassis and Roller Kit
○ PR205 chassis and rollers
○ 512

○ Fuser Assembly
○ Fuser assembly/JE series
○ 1253

○ Engine Kit
○ Printer engine kit/JE series
○ 3895

○ Controller board
○ PR205 printer controller board
○ 483

○ Toner Kit
○ PR205 toner kit (b,m,c,y)
○ 812

style of the parts content

Laser4C (PR205)

Entry level color laser printer

color laser

320

Chassis and Roller Kit

PR205 chassis and rollers

○ 512

Fuser Assembly

Fuser assembly/JE series

○ 1253

Engine Kit

Printer engine kit/JE series

○ 3895

Controller board

PR205 printer controller board

○ 483

Toner Kit

PR205 toner kit (b,m,c,y)

○ 812

**style of the combined document
mixes up the styles from the two
source documents**

Trouble? If your browser displays the contents of the XML document in outline format rather than the rendered Web page, there may be an error in the <?xml-stylesheet ...> processing instructions. Check your code against the code shown in Figure 12-6.

The styles applied to the compound document are quite different from the styles applied to the two individual documents shown in Figures 12-2 and 12-4. Specifically, the styles used for each part's title and description have changed. What went wrong? The problem comes from combining elements with the same name from two different XML vocabularies.

Understanding Name Collision

When you create a compound document, the same element name may be used in more than one of the vocabularies. In the order compound document, several names are repeated in the structures of the parts and models vocabularies. For instance, both vocabularies use the title and description names. In the parts vocabulary, these elements describe a particular part; in the models vocabulary, these same element names describe a fully assembled model. The parts element is also used in both vocabularies. In the parts vocabulary, the parts element contains a collection of part elements. In the models vocabulary, the parts element is an empty element that contains an attribute listing the part element ids. The duplication of these element names is an example of **name collision**, which occurs when the same element name from different XML vocabularies is used within a compound document.

Figure 12-10 identifies the duplicated element names from the models and parts vocabularies that appear in the order.xml compound document. When you combined the contents of the model.xml and parts.xml documents, the styles associated with the element names from the different vocabularies got mixed up. As a result, the format of the combined Web page looks nothing like the rendered pages of the two source documents.

Figure 12-10 **Name collision in the order.xml file**

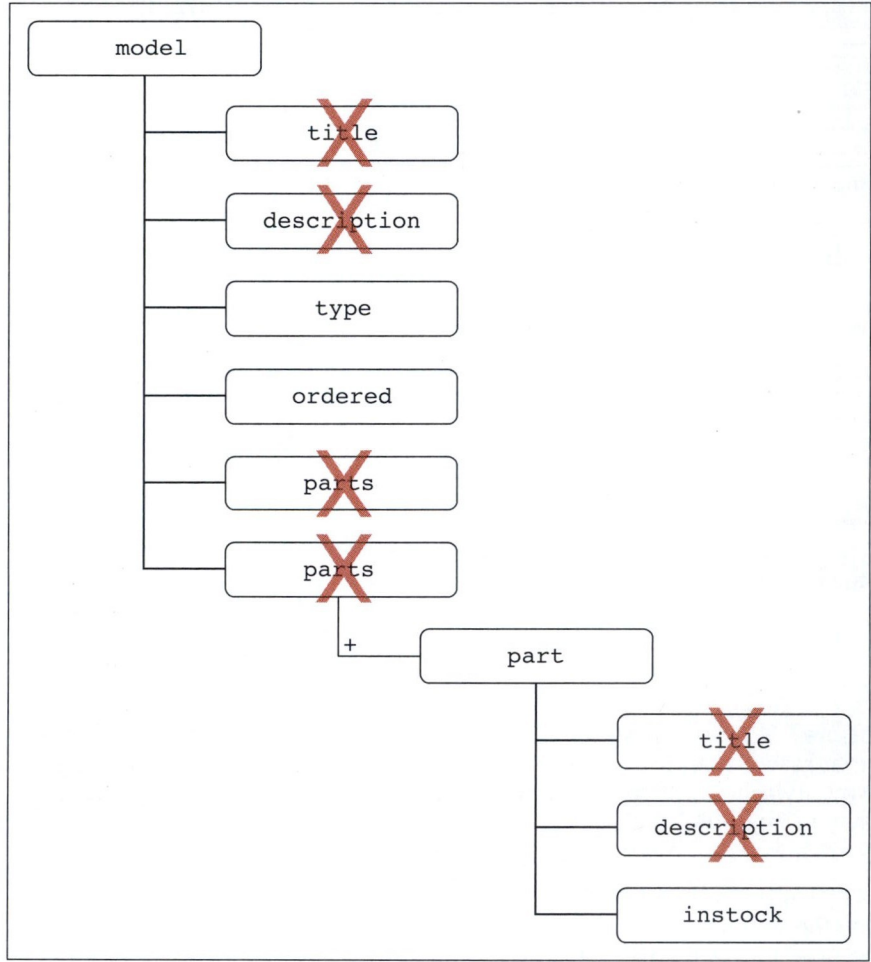

Jackson Electronics could have been more careful in choosing element names to prevent name collisions among different vocabularies. However, name collisions are often unavoidable. After all, one benefit of XML vocabularies is the ability to use simple element names to describe data. Creating complex element names to avoid name collision eliminates this benefit. Moreover, there are other XML vocabularies such as XHTML over which Gail has no control. XHTML element names such as title and address are certain to be found in thousands of XML vocabularies.

Gail could avoid combining elements from different vocabularies in the same document to prevent name collisions; however, this would make XML a poor information tool. Instead, Gail needs a mechanism that distinguishes elements in one vocabulary from elements in another vocabulary. XML provides such a mechanism with namespaces.

Working with Namespaces

A **namespace** is a defined collection of element and attribute names. For example, the collection of element and attribute names from Gail's models vocabulary could define a single namespace. Likewise, the element and attribute names from the parts vocabulary could constitute a different namespace. Applying a namespace to an XML document involves two steps:

1. Declare the namespace.
2. Identify the elements and attributes within the document that belong to that namespace.

You'll start by looking at how to declare a namespace.

Declaring a Namespace

To declare a namespace, you add the attribute

```
<element xmlns:prefix="uri"> ... </element>
```

to an element within an XML document, where *element* is the element in which the namespace is declared, *prefix* is a string of characters that you'll add to element and attribute names to associate them with the declared namespace, and *uri* is a **Uniform Resource Identifier (URI)**—a text string that uniquely identifies a resource. In this case, the URI is the declared namespace. For example, the following code declares a namespace with the URI *http://jacksonelx.com/models*, associating that URI with the prefix mod within the model element:

```
<model xmlns:mod="http://jacksonelx.com/models"> ... </model>
```

The number of namespace attributes that can be declared within an element is unlimited. A namespace that has been declared within an element can be applied to any descendant of the element. Some XML authors add all namespace declarations to the document's root element so that the namespace is available to all elements within the document.

Understanding URIs | InSight

The URI used in namespaces looks like a Web address used to create a link to a Web site; however, that is not its purpose. The purpose of a URI is simply to provide a unique string of characters that identify a resource.

One version of a URI is the Uniform Resource Locator (URL), which is used to identify the location of a resource (such as a Web page) on the Web. There is a good reason to also use URLs as a basis for identifying namespaces. If an XML vocabulary is made widely available, the namespace associated with that vocabulary needs to be unique. URLs serve as a built-in mechanism on the Web for generating unique addresses. For example, the home page of Gail's company, Jackson Electronics, has the Web address

```
http://jacksonelx.com
```

which provides customers with a unique location to access all of Jackson Electronics' online services and products. To ensure the uniqueness of any namespaces associated with the vocabularies developed for Jackson Electronics documents, it makes sense to use the Jackson Electronics Web address as a foundation. Note that although the URI doesn't actually need to point to a real site on the Web, it is often helpful to place documentation at the site identified by the URI so that users can go there to learn more about the XML vocabulary being referenced.

Using URLs is widely accepted in declaring namespaces, but you can use almost any unique string identifier, such as JacksonElectronicsModelNS or PR205X299x. The main requirement is that a URI is unique so that it is not confused with the URIs of other namespaces.

Gail wants you to create namespaces for the parts and models vocabularies. You will declare both namespaces in the root element of the order.xml file, assigning mod as the prefix for the models namespace and pa as the prefix for elements of the parts namespace. The URIs for the two namespaces will be *http://jacksonelx.com/models* and *http://jacksonelx.com/parts*. These URIs do not point to actual sites on the Web, but they do provide unique URIs for the two namespaces.

To declare the model and parts namespaces:

▶ **1.** Return to the **order.xml** file in your text editor.

▶ **2.** Within the opening `<model>` tag, insert the following namespace declarations, as shown in Figure 12-11:

```
xmlns:mod="http://jacksonelx.com/models"
xmlns:pa="http://jacksonelx.com/parts"
```

Figure 12-11 ▶ **Namespace declarations for models and parts**

```
<model id="pr205" xmlns:mod="http://jacksonelx.com/models"
                   xmlns:pa="http://jacksonelx.com/parts">

<title>Laser4C (PR205)</title>
<description>Entry level color laser printer</description>
<type>color laser</type>
<ordered>320</ordered>
<parts list="chx201,fa100-5,eng005-2,cbx-450v4,tn01-53" />
```

Reference Window | **Declaring a Namespace**

- To declare a namespace, add the attribute
    `<element xmlns:prefix="uri"> ... </element>`
  to an element in the document, where *element* is the element in which the namespace is declared, *prefix* is the namespace prefix, and *uri* is the URI of the namespace.
- To declare a default namespace, add the xmlns attribute without specifying a prefix as follows:
    `<element xmlns="uri"> ...`

Applying a Namespace to an Element

After you declare a namespace, you have to indicate which elements in the document belong to that namespace. To apply an XML namespace to an element, you qualify the element's name. A **qualified name (qname)** is an element name consisting of two parts: the **namespace prefix** that identifies the namespace, and the **local part** or **local name** that identifies the element or attribute within that namespace. The general form for applying a qualified name to a two-sided tag is

`<prefix:element> ... </prefix:element>`

where *prefix* is the namespace prefix and *element* is the local part. An element name without such a prefix is referred to as an **unqualified name**. Until now, you've worked only with unqualified names. To change the element names in the model.xml document from unqualified to qualified names, you could declare and apply the following namespace prefixes:

```
<mod:model xmlns:mod="http://jacksonelx.com/models">
   <mod:title>Laser4C (PR205)</mod:title>
   <mod:description>Entry level color laser printer</mod:description>
   <mod:type>color laser</mod:type>
   <mod:ordered>320</mod:ordered>
   <mod:parts list="chx201,fa100-5,eng005-2,cbx-450V4,tn01-53" />
</mod:model>
```

The opening <model> tag includes both the namespace prefix and the xmlns attribute to declare the namespace. This indicates that the model element itself is part of the namespace that it declares.

In the order.xml document, the mod prefix is used for elements from the models namespace and the pa prefix is used for elements from the parts namespace. You will apply these namespaces to the elements in the document that belong to one or the other namespace.

To apply the models and parts namespaces:

▶ 1. Add the **mod:** prefix to the opening and closing tags of each element in the models namespace, as shown in Figure 12-12.

Models namespace prefix — Figure 12-12

```
<mod:model id="pr205" xmlns:mod="http://jacksonelx.com/models"
                       xmlns:pa="http://jacksonelx.com/parts">

   <mod:title>Laser4C (PR205)</mod:title>
   <mod:description>Entry level color laser printer</mod:description>
   <mod:type>color laser</mod:type>
   <mod:ordered>320</mod:ordered>
   <mod:parts list="chx201,fa100-5,eng005-2,cbx-450V4,tn01-53" />

   <parts>
      <part id="chx201">
         <title>Chassis and Roller Kit</title>
         <description>PR205 chassis and rollers</description>
         <instock>512</instock>
      </part>

      <part id="fa100-5">
         <title>Fuser Assembly</title>
         <description>Fuser assembly/JE series</description>
         <instock>1253</instock>
      </part>

      <part id="eng005-2">
         <title>Engine Kit</title>
         <description>Printer engine kit/JE series</description>
         <instock>3895</instock>
      </part>

      <part id="cbx-450V4">
         <title>Controller board</title>
         <description>PR205 printer controller board</description>
         <instock>483</instock>
      </part>

      <part id="tn01-53">
         <title>Toner Kit</title>
         <description>PR205 toner kit (b,m,c,y)</description>
         <instock>812</instock>
      </part>
   </parts>
</mod:model>
```

mod namespace prefix identifies elements from the models vocabulary

Tip

You can quickly replace all instances of the prefix using the search and replace feature in your text editor.

▶ 2. Add the **pa:** prefix to the opening and closing tags of each element in the parts namespace, as shown in Figure 12-13.

Figure 12-13 ▶ Parts namespace prefix

```
<mod:model id="pr205" xmlns:mod="http://jacksonelx.com/models"
                      xmlns:pa="http://jacksonelx.com/parts">

    <mod:title>Laser4C (PR205)</mod:title>
    <mod:description>Entry level color laser printer</mod:description>
    <mod:type>color laser</mod:type>
    <mod:ordered>320</mod:ordered>
    <mod:parts list="chx201,fa100-5,eng005-2,cbx-450V4,tn01-53" />

    <pa:parts>
        <pa:part id="chx201">
            <pa:title>Chassis and Roller Kit</pa:title>
            <pa:description>PR205 chassis and rollers</pa:description>
            <pa:instock>512</pa:instock>
        </pa:part>

        <pa:part id="fa100-5">
            <pa:title>Fuser Assembly</pa:title>
            <pa:description>Fuser assembly/JE series</pa:description>
            <pa:instock>1253</pa:instock>
        </pa:part>

        <pa:part id="eng005-2">
            <pa:title>Engine Kit</pa:title>
            <pa:description>Printer engine kit/JE series</pa:description>
            <pa:instock>3895</pa:instock>
        </pa:part>

        <pa:part id="cbx-450V4">
            <pa:title>Controller board</pa:title>
            <pa:description>PR205 printer controller board</pa:description>
            <pa:instock>483</pa:instock>
        </pa:part>

        <pa:part id="tn01-53">
            <pa:title>Toner Kit</pa:title>
            <pa:description>PR205 toner kit (b,m,c,y)</pa:description>
            <pa:instock>812</pa:instock>
        </pa:part>
    </pa:parts>

</mod:model>
```

pa namespace prefix identifies elements from the parts vocabulary

▶ **3.** Save your changes to the order.xml file.

Because you added several namespace prefixes to the various elements in the order.xml document, it's a good idea to verify that no syntax errors appear in the file. You can do this by reloading the file in your Web browser.

To check for syntax errors in the order.xml file:

▶ **1.** Reload or refresh **order.xml** in your Web browser. If you are using Firefox, Opera, or Safari, the Web page should look unchanged from the page shown in Figure 12-9. If you are using Internet Explorer, you should see the data content of the order.xml file without any formatting, as shown in Figure 12-14.

Figure 12-14 ▶ The order.xml file as it appears in Internet Explorer

Laser4C (PR205) Entry level color laser printer color laser 320 Chassis and Roller Kit PR205 chassis and rollers 512 Fuser Assembly Fuser assembly/JE series 1253 Engine Kit Printer engine kit/JE series 3895 Controller board PR205 printer controller board 483 Toner Kit PR205 toner kit (b,m,c,y) 812

Trouble? If your browser reports a syntax error, you may have neglected to include all the namespace prefixes shown in Figures 12-12 and 12-13. Return to the order.xml file in your text editor and verify that you have included all of the prefixes, including the prefixes in the closing tags, and then repeat Step 1.

Applying a Default Namespace

Although you used namespace prefixes for all the elements in the order.xml document, this is not always required. You can declare a **default namespace** by omitting the prefix in the namespace declaration. Any descendant element or attribute is then considered part of this namespace unless a different namespace is declared within one of the child elements. The syntax to create a default namespace is:

```
<element xmlns="uri"> ... </element>
```

To define the models namespace as the default namespace for model elements, for example, you could enter the following code:

```
<model xmlns="http://jacksonelx.com/models">
    <title>Laser4C (PR205)</title>
    <description>Entry level color laser printer</description>
    <type>color laser</type>
    <ordered>320</ordered>
    <parts list="chx201,fa100-5,eng005-2,cbx-450V4,tn01-53" />
</model>
```

In this case, all the elements, including the model element, are considered part of the models namespace. The advantage of default namespaces is that they make the code easier to read and write because you do not have to add the namespace prefix to each element. The disadvantage, however, is that an element's namespace is not readily apparent from the code. Still, many compound documents use a default namespace that covers most of the elements in the document, and assign namespace prefixes to elements from other XML vocabularies.

Working with Attributes

Like an element name, an attribute can be qualified by adding a namespace prefix. The syntax to qualify an attribute is

```
<element prefix:attribute="value"> ... </element>
```

where *prefix* is the namespace prefix and *attribute* is the attribute name. For example, the following code assigns both the model element and the id attribute to the same models namespace:

```
<mod:model xmlns:mod="http://jacksonelx.com/models"
           mod:id="pr205">
...
</mod:model>
```

Unlike element names, there is no default namespace for attribute names. Default namespaces apply to elements, but not to attributes. An attribute name without a prefix is assumed to belong to the same namespace as the element that contains it. Thus, the id attribute in the following code is automatically assumed to belong to the models namespace, even though it lacks the mod prefix:

```
<mod:model xmlns:mod="http://jacksonelx.com/models"
           id="pr205">
...
</mod:model>
```

Because an attribute is automatically associated with the namespace of its element, you rarely need to qualify an attribute name. The only exception occurs when an attribute from one namespace needs to be used in an element from another namespace. For example, XHTML uses the class attribute to associate elements belonging to a common group or class. You could attach the class attribute from the XHTML namespace to elements from other namespaces. Because the class attribute is often used in CSS to apply common formats to groups of elements, using the class attribute in other XML elements would apply this feature of CSS to those elements as well.

For Gail's document, there is no need to assign attributes to namespaces, so you will not add this feature to the order.xml file.

Reference Window | **Applying a Namespace**

- To apply a namespace to an element, add the namespace prefix
  ```
  <prefix:element> ... </prefix:element>
  ```
  to the element's opening and closing tags, where *prefix* is the namespace prefix and *element* is the local part of the qualified element name. If no prefix is specified, the element is assumed to be part of the default namespace.
- To apply a namespace to an attribute, add the namespace prefix
  ```
  <element prefix:attribute="value"> ... </element>
  ```
  to the attribute name, where *attribute* is the attribute name. An attribute is by default part of the namespace of its containing element.

InSight | **Uniform Resource Names**

Another type of URI is a **Uniform Resource Name (URN)**. A URN provides a persistent name for a resource, independent of that resource's location. URNs take the form

```
urn:NID:NSS
```

where *NID* is the namespace identifier and *NSS* is a text string specific to that namespace. The *NID* indicates how to interpret the text string in the *NSS*. For example, the following URN uniquely identifies a book by its ISBN (a common numbering system for books and other library materials):

```
urn:isbn:0-619-01969-7
```

If a URL can be thought of as a unique address of a specific location, a URN can be thought of as a unique name that is associated with a specific item. URNs are rarely used in place of URLs, but this may change in the future.

Gail is pleased with the work that you've done applying namespaces to her document, but she wonders why it has not had an effect on the appearance of the Web page in some of her browsers, and why it has entirely removed the formatting in Internet Explorer. In the next session, you'll address this problem by applying namespaces to the styles in CSS style sheets.

Review | **Session 12.1 Quick Check**

1. What is a name collision?
2. What is a namespace? How do namespaces prevent the problem of name collisions?
3. Explain why namespace URIs do not necessarily point to sites on the Web.
4. What attribute would you add to a document's root element to declare a namespace with the URI *http://ns.doc.book* and the prefix book?

5. How would you modify the code `<author>David Stevens</author>` to indicate that the element belongs to the book namespace declared in the previous question?

6. What attribute would you add to the root element in Question 4 to make the book namespace the default namespace for all elements in the document?

7. How would you change the code `<book isbn="0-1969-7">Blue Moon</book>` to explicitly indicate that the isbn attribute belongs to the book namespace?

8. If any attribute name is unqualified, what namespace is it presumed to belong to?

Session 12.2

Adding a Namespace to a Style Sheet

In the previous session, you added namespaces to Gail's document. Your next task is to add namespace support to the style sheets she designed. Recall from the previous tutorial that to apply a CSS style to an XML element, you use the style declaration

```
selector {attribute1:value1; attribute2:value2; ...}
```

where *selector* references an element or elements in the XML document. So, to set the width of the title element, you could enter the following style declaration:

```
title {width: 150px}
```

If an element has a qualified name such as mod:title, do not include the prefix in the selector name, as follows:

```
mod:title {width: 150px}
```

This doesn't work with style sheets because CSS reserves the colon character for pseudo-elements and pseudoclasses. Instead, you have to declare a namespace in the style sheet and then reference that namespace in the selector.

Declaring a Namespace

To declare a namespace in a style sheet, you add the rule

```
@namespace prefix "uri";
```

to the CSS style sheet, where *prefix* is the namespace prefix and *uri* is the URI of the namespace. Both the prefix and the URI must match the prefix and URI used in the XML document. So, to declare the models namespace in Gail's style sheet, you would add the following rule:

```
@namespace mod "http://jacksonelx.com/models";
```

Note that the prefix (mod) and the URI (*http://jacksonelx.com/models*) match the prefix and URI you entered in the previous session.

As with XML documents, the namespace prefix is optional. If the namespace prefix is omitted, the URI in the @namespace rule is considered to be the default namespace for the selectors in the style sheet. Any @namespace rules in the style sheet must come after all @import and @charset rules, and before any style declarations.

Tip

If a namespace prefix is declared more than once, only the last instance is used in the style sheet.

Applying a Namespace to a Selector

After you have declared a namespace in a style sheet, you can associate selectors with that namespace by adding the namespace prefix to each selector name separated with the | symbol, as follows:

```
prefix|selector {attribute1:value1; attribute2:value2; ...}
```

For example, the style declaration

```
mod|title {width: 150px}
```

applies the width style to all title elements that belong to the models namespace. You can also use the wildcard symbol (*) to apply a style to any element within a namespace or to elements across different namespaces. For example, the style declaration

```
mod|* {font-size: 12pt}
```

applies the font-size style to any element within the models namespace. Similarly, the declaration

```
*|title {width: 150px}
```

sets a width of 150 pixels to any element named title from any namespace. If you omit the namespace prefix from a selector, its style is also applied to all namespaces. For example, the declaration

```
title {width: 150px}
```

applies to all elements named title in any namespace. This is the reason that the styles from the style sheets got mixed up in the order.xml Web page. Because of the name collisions, the browser applied the style from one namespace to elements in another namespace. Now that you know how to distinguish namespaces, this will not be a problem.

You will add @namespace rules to the style sheets in the model.css and parts.css files.

To declare namespaces in the model.css and parts.css style sheets:

1. Open the **model.css** style sheet in your text editor.

2. Directly after the opening comment tags, insert the following namespace declaration:

   ```
   @namespace mod "http://jacksonelx.com/models";
   ```

3. Add the namespace prefix **mod|** to each selector in the style sheet, as shown in Figure 12-15.

Figure 12-15   **The models namespace applied to the model.css style sheet**

```
@namespace mod "http://jacksonelx.com/models";
mod|model        {font-family: Arial, Helvetica, sans-serif; font-size: 16px}
mod|title, mod|description, mod|type, mod|ordered
                 {display: block; padding: 2px; margin: 5px; color: blue;
                  border: 1px solid black; background-color: ivory}
mod|title        {width: 150px}
mod|description  {width: 250px}
mod|type         {width: 150px}
mod|ordered      {width: 150px}
```

4. Save your changes to the file.

5. Open the **parts.css** style sheet in your text editor, and then, directly above the first style declaration, insert the following namespace declaration:

   `@namespace pa "http://jacksonelx.com/parts";`

6. Add the namespace prefix **pal** to each selector in the style sheet, as shown in Figure 12-16.

The parts namespace applied to the parts.css style sheet   Figure 12-16

```
@namespace pa "http://jacksonelx.com/parts";

pa|parts            {font-family: Arial, Helvetica, sans-serif; font-size: 14px}

pa|part             {display: block; width: 500px; margin: 15px; padding: 5px;
                    border-top: 1px dashed black; border-left: 1px dashed black}

pa|title, pa|description, pa|instock
                    {display: list-item; list-style-type: circle;
                    padding-left: 10px; margin-left: 15px}
```

7. Save your changes to the style sheet.

Defining Namespaces with the Escape Character

Not all browsers support the use of the @namespace rule. When the specifications for XML 1.0 were first posted, no support existed for namespaces. Several competing proposals were circulated for adding namespace support to XML and CSS. One proposal, which was not adopted but was implemented in the Internet Explorer browser, was to insert the backslash escape character (\) before the colon character in the namespace prefix. So, for Internet Explorer to apply a style to an element from a particular namespace, you use the declaration

```
prefix\:selector {attribute1:value1; attribute2:value2; ...}
```

where *prefix* is the namespace prefix used in the XML document. For example, the declaration for the title element in the models namespace is:

```
mod\:title {width: 150px}
```

You can apply the same style to several elements in the namespace by using the * symbol. For example, the following declaration sets the width of all elements in the models namespace to 150 pixels:

```
mod\:* {width: 150px}
```

Other browsers such as Firefox, Opera, and Safari do not support this method with XML documents. If you want to support the widest range of browsers, you must duplicate the styles in the style sheet using both methods.

Gail wants the style sheets to work across a wide range of browsers, so you will add style declarations using the escape character format.

To apply the escape character format to the model.css and parts.css style sheets:

1. Return to the **model.css** style sheet in your text editor.

2. Copy the six style declarations in the document, and then paste the declarations below the comment, "Insert CSS namespace escape styles here."

> **3.** Change the format of the namespace prefixes from **|** to **\:** in each of the pasted style declarations, as shown in Figure 12-17.

Figure 12-17 | **Escape character in the model.css style sheet**

```
@namespace mod "http://jacksonelx.com/models";

mod|model            {font-family: Arial, Helvetica, sans-serif; font-size: 16px}

mod|title, mod|description, mod|type, mod|ordered
                     {display: block; padding: 2px; margin: 5px; color: blue;
                      border: 1px solid black; background-color: ivory}

mod|title            {width: 150px}

mod|description      {width: 250px}

mod|type             {width: 150px}

mod|ordered          {width: 150px}


/* Insert CSS namespace escape styles here */

mod\:model           {font-family: Arial, Helvetica, sans-serif; font-size: 16px}

mod\:title, mod\:description, mod\:type, mod\:ordered
                     {display: block; padding: 2px; margin: 5px; color: blue;
                      border: 1px solid black; background-color: ivory}

mod\:title           {width: 150px}

mod\:description     {width: 250px}

mod\:type            {width: 150px}

mod\:ordered         {width: 150px}
```

namespace format supported by Internet Explorer

> **4.** Save your changes to the model.css file, and then close the file.

> **5.** Return to the **parts.css** style sheet in your text editor. You will add similar escape characters to the style declarations in this style sheet.

> **6.** Copy the three style declarations, and then paste the copied text at the bottom of the file.

> **7.** Change the format of the pasted declarations from **|** to **\:** as shown in Figure 12-18.

Figure 12-18 | **Escape character in the parts.css style sheet**

```
@namespace pa "http://jacksonelx.com/parts";

pa|parts             {font-family: Arial, Helvetica, sans-serif; font-size: 14px}

pa|part              {display: block; width: 500px; margin: 15px; padding: 5px;
                      border-top: 1px dashed black; border-left: 1px dashed black}

pa|title, pa|description, pa|instock
                     {display: list-item; list-style-type: circle;
                      padding-left: 10px; margin-left: 15px}

/* Insert CSS namespace escape styles here */

pa\:parts            {font-family: Arial, Helvetica, sans-serif; font-size: 14px}

pa\:part             {display: block; width: 500px; margin: 15px; padding: 5px;
                      border-top: 1px dashed black; border-left: 1px dashed black}

pa\:title, pa\:description, pa\:instock
                     {display: list-item; list-style-type: circle;
                      padding-left: 10px; margin-left: 15px}
```

namespace format supported by Internet Explorer

> **8.** Save your changes to the parts.css file, and then close the file.

Now that you've added namespace support (using both methods) to the model.css and parts.css style sheets, you will test that your Web browser displays the appropriate styles for repeated elements in the order document.

To view the styles applied to elements from both the models and parts namespaces:

▶ **1.** Use your browser to open the **order.xml** file. As shown in Figure 12-19, styles for the elements in the models and parts namespaces are correctly applied. Compare this page with the one shown in Figure 12-9, in which the styles were mixed up between the two namespaces.

Web page combining styles from both namespaces ◀ Figure 12-19

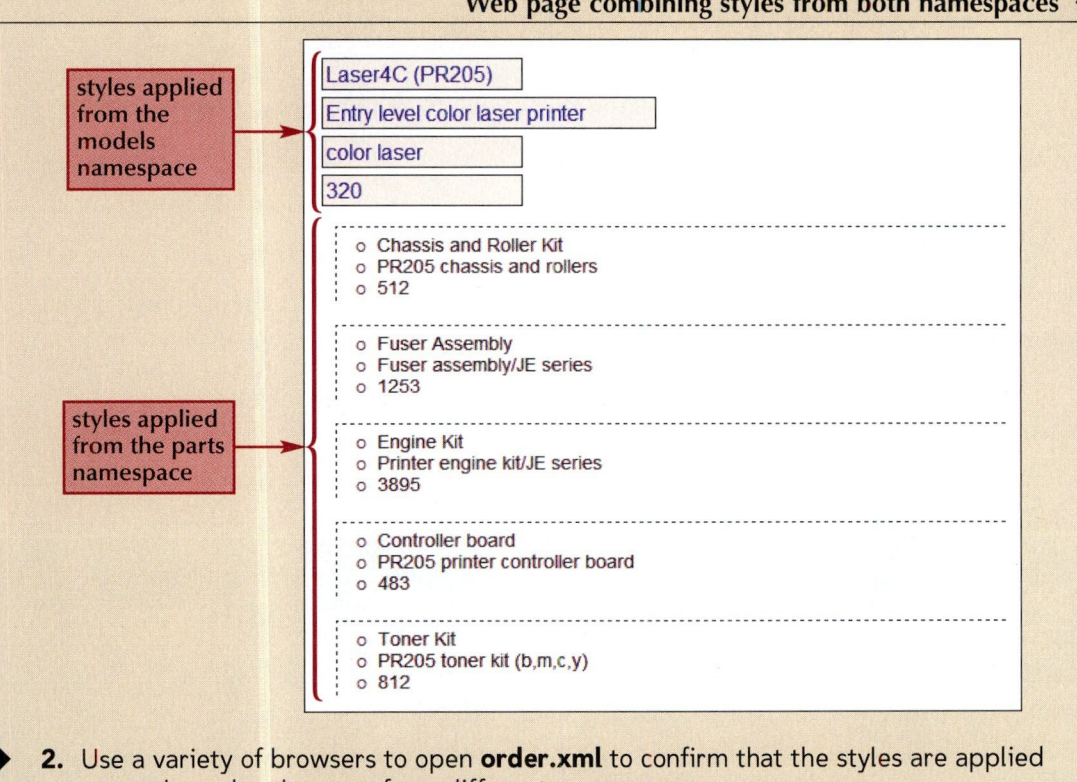

▶ **2.** Use a variety of browsers to open **order.xml** to confirm that the styles are applied correctly to the elements from different namespaces.

Gail is pleased that you were able to work out the problems with the style sheets and the namespaces. The Web page contains all the data that Gail wants. However, it does not contain any descriptive text. Gail wants you to add a third XML vocabulary to the document—one that includes page elements that describe the purpose and content of the report. To do this, you'll add elements from XHTML.

Reference Window | **Declaring and Applying a Namespace in a CSS Style**

- To declare a namespace in a CSS style sheet, add the rule
    `@namespace prefix "uri";`
  before any style declarations, where *prefix* is the namespace prefix and *uri* is the namespace URI. If no prefix is specified, the namespace URI is the default namespace for selectors in the style sheet.
- To apply a namespace to a selector, use the form
    `prefix|selector {attribute1:value1; attribute2:value2; ...}`
  where *prefix* is the namespace prefix and *selector* is a selector for an element or group of elements in the document.
  For Internet Explorer browsers, use the following form to apply a namespace to a selector:
    `prefix\:selector {attribute1:value1; attribute2:value2; ...}`

Combining Standard Vocabularies

So far you've worked only with the custom XML vocabularies that Gail has created for the Jackson Electronics assembly plant. The standard vocabularies that are shared throughout the world such as XHTML, RSS, and MathML can also be combined within single documents. Many of these standard vocabularies have unique URIs, some of which are listed in Figure 12-20.

Figure 12-20 | Namespace URIs for standard vocabularies

Vocabulary	Namespace URI
CDF	http://www.microsoft.com/standards/channels.dtd
CML	http://www.xml-cml.org/dtd/cml1_0_1.dtd
MathML	http://www.w3.org/1998/Math/MathML
iTunes Podcast	http://www.itunes.com/dtds/podcast-1.0.dtd
RSS 1.0	http://purl.org/rss/1.0/
SMIL	http://www.w3.org/2001/SMIL20/Language
SVG	http://www.w3.org/2000/svg
VoiceXML	http://www.w3.org/2001/vxml
XForms	http://www.w3.org/2002/xforms
XHTML	http://www.w3.org/1999/xhtml
XML Schema	http://www.w3.org/2001/XMLSchema
XSLT	http://www.w3.org/1999/XSL/Transform

As XML continued to develop as the standard language for sharing markup data, Web browsers extended and improved their ability to support documents that combine multiple vocabularies. At the time of this writing, both Firefox and Opera supported documents that combine both the XHTML and MathML languages. Internet Explorer will support MathML only if an add-in is installed with the application. Currently, Safari does not support MathML at all.

To show how these different vocabularies can work together, Figure 12-21 demonstrates an XML document that uses XHTML to mark an h1 heading and a paragraph, but uses elements from MathML to mark elements of a mathematical equation. The Firefox browser, using a built-in style sheet that can cope with elements from both languages, displays the entire document.

A compound XHTML and MathML document | Figure 12-21

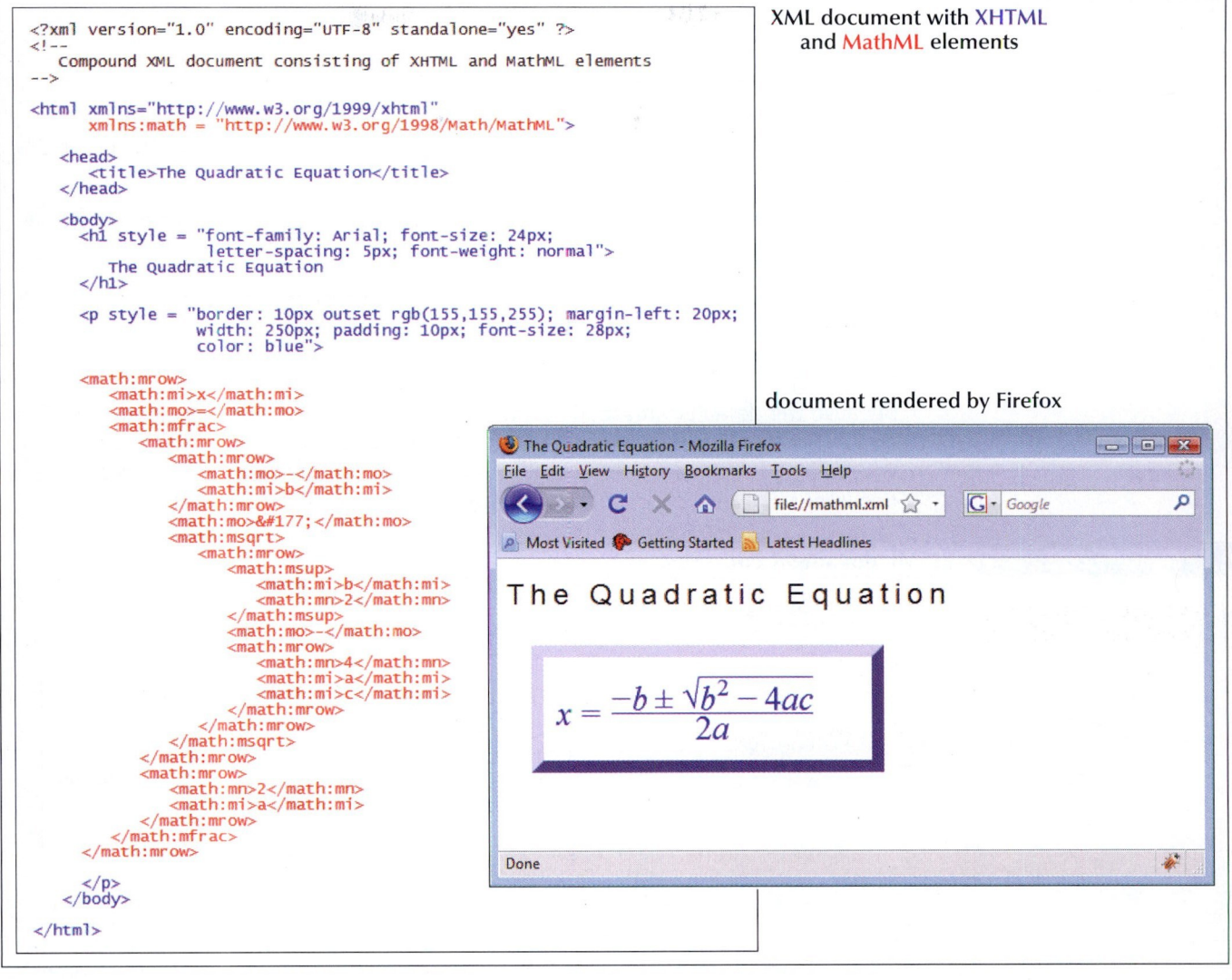

XML document with XHTML and MathML elements

```
<?xml version="1.0" encoding="UTF-8" standalone="yes" ?>
<!--
    Compound XML document consisting of XHTML and MathML elements
-->
<html xmlns="http://www.w3.org/1999/xhtml"
      xmlns:math = "http://www.w3.org/1998/Math/MathML">

   <head>
      <title>The Quadratic Equation</title>
   </head>

   <body>
      <h1 style = "font-family: Arial; font-size: 24px;
                  letter-spacing: 5px; font-weight: normal">
         The Quadratic Equation
      </h1>

      <p style = "border: 10px outset rgb(155,155,255); margin-left: 20px;
                 width: 250px; padding: 10px; font-size: 28px;
                 color: blue">

      <math:mrow>
         <math:mi>x</math:mi>
         <math:mo>=</math:mo>
         <math:mfrac>
            <math:mrow>
               <math:mrow>
                  <math:mo>-</math:mo>
                  <math:mi>b</math:mi>
               </math:mrow>
               <math:mo>&#177;</math:mo>
               <math:msqrt>
                  <math:mrow>
                     <math:msup>
                        <math:mi>b</math:mi>
                        <math:mn>2</math:mn>
                     </math:msup>
                     <math:mo>-</math:mo>
                     <math:mrow>
                        <math:mn>4</math:mn>
                        <math:mi>a</math:mi>
                        <math:mi>c</math:mi>
                     </math:mrow>
                  </math:mrow>
               </math:msqrt>
            </math:mrow>
            <math:mrow>
               <math:mn>2</math:mn>
               <math:mi>a</math:mi>
            </math:mrow>
         </math:mfrac>
      </math:mrow>

      </p>
   </body>

</html>
```

document rendered by Firefox

There are also specialized browsers that can display compound documents combining two or more specific vocabularies. Jumbo, for example, can display compound documents that employ XHTML and CML (Chemical Markup Language). These browsers include built-in support and style sheets for the elements of those vocabularies. As you've seen, though, the elements of almost any XML document can be displayed in a Web browser if the style sheets are designed to work with the elements of the XML vocabulary.

Adding XML to an HTML Document

You can also use namespaces to add XML elements to an HTML file. In this situation, you would leave the HTML elements in the default namespace, but provide namespace prefixes for all the non-HTML elements.

Gail already entered the HTML code for the manufacturing report. She needs you to combine this document with the XML elements from the parts and models namespaces. Before you can create a compound document combining three different markup languages, you need to convert Gail's HTML file into an XHTML file. This can be done by adding an xml declaration at the top of the file and by setting the default namespace of the document to the XHTML vocabulary. As listed in Figure 12-20, the URI of the XHTML namespace is *http://www.w3.org/1999/xhtml.*

To convert the HTML file to an XHTML file:

1. Use your text editor to open the **reptxt.htm** file from the tutorial.12/tutorial folder, enter ***your name*** and ***the date*** in the comment section, and then save the file as **report.htm** in the same folder.
2. Insert the following xml declaration as the very first line in the file (above the comment section):

```
<?xml version="1.0" encoding="UTF-8" standalone="yes" ?>
```

3. Add the following attribute to the opening <html> tag:

```
xmlns="http://www.w3.org/1999/xhtml"
```

Because the default namespace points to the URI for XHTML, every element in the document that lacks a namespace prefix is considered part of the XHTML vocabulary. This means you do not have to modify any of the element tags in Gail's document. Figure 12-22 shows the revised report.htm file.

Figure 12-22 HTML document converted to XHTML

xml prolog

xhtml namespace

```
<?xml version="1.0" encoding="UTF-8" standalone="yes" ?>
<!--
   New Perspectives on XHTML and XML
   Tutorial 12
   Tutorial Case

   Jackson Electronics Shipping Report
   Author: Gail Oglund
   Date:    3/1/2012

   Filename:         report.xml
   Supporting Files: model.css, parts.css, pr205.jpg, report.css
-->

<html xmlns="http://www.w3.org/1999/xhtml">
<head>
   <title>Jackson Electronics Shipping Order</title>
   <link rel="stylesheet" href="report.css" type="text/css" />
</head>
```

Next, you'll add the parts element to the report.htm file. Because this element comes from another namespace, you'll also add the namespace declaration to the <html> tag and insert a link element to link Gail's report to the parts.css style sheet.

To add the elements of the parts vocabulary:

1. Return to the **order.xml** file in your text editor.
2. Copy the contents of the document from the opening `<pa:parts>` tag through the closing `</pa:parts>` tag.
3. Return to the **report.htm** file in your text editor, and then paste the copied elements directly below the h2 heading, Parts List, near the bottom of the file. See Figure 12-23.

The parts elements inserted from the parts vocabulary ◄ Figure 12-23

```
<h2>Parts List</h2>
<pa:parts>
    <pa:part id="chx201">
        <pa:title>Chassis and Roller Kit</pa:title>
        <pa:description>PR205 chassis and rollers</pa:description>
        <pa:instock>512</pa:instock>
    </pa:part>

    <pa:part id="fa100-5">
        <pa:title>Fuser Assembly</pa:title>
        <pa:description>Fuser assembly/JE series</pa:description>
        <pa:instock>1253</pa:instock>
    </pa:part>

    <pa:part id="eng005-2">
        <pa:title>Engine Kit</pa:title>
        <pa:description>Printer engine kit/JE series</pa:description>
        <pa:instock>3895</pa:instock>
    </pa:part>

    <pa:part id="cbx-450V4">
        <pa:title>Controller board</pa:title>
        <pa:description>PR205 printer controller board</pa:description>
        <pa:instock>483</pa:instock>
    </pa:part>

    <pa:part id="tn01-53">
        <pa:title>Toner Kit</pa:title>
        <pa:description>PR205 toner kit (b,m,c,y)</pa:description>
        <pa:instock>812</pa:instock>
    </pa:part>
</pa:parts>
</body>
```

▶ **4.** Add the following attribute to the opening <html> tag:

```
xmlns:pa="http://jacksonelx.com/parts"
```

▶ **5.** Below the link element that links the report.htm file to the report.css style sheet, insert the following link element to link the parts.css style sheet to the document:

```
<link rel="stylesheet" href="parts.css" type="text/css" />
```

Figure 12-24 shows the revised contents of the report.htm file.

Parts namespace added to the XHTML document ◄ Figure 12-24

```
<html xmlns="http://www.w3.org/1999/xhtml"
      xmlns:pa="http://jacksonelx.com/parts">
<head>
    <title>Jackson Electronics Shipping Order</title>
    <link rel="stylesheet" href="report.css" type="text/css" />
    <link rel="stylesheet" href="parts.css" type="text/css" />
</head>
```

parts namespace →

linking to the parts.css style sheet →

▶ **6.** Save your changes to the file, and then open **report.htm** in your Web browser. As shown in Figure 12-25, the Web page shows a combination of XHTML elements and elements from the parts vocabulary.

Figure 12-25 **Elements from the parts namespace displayed in the report page**

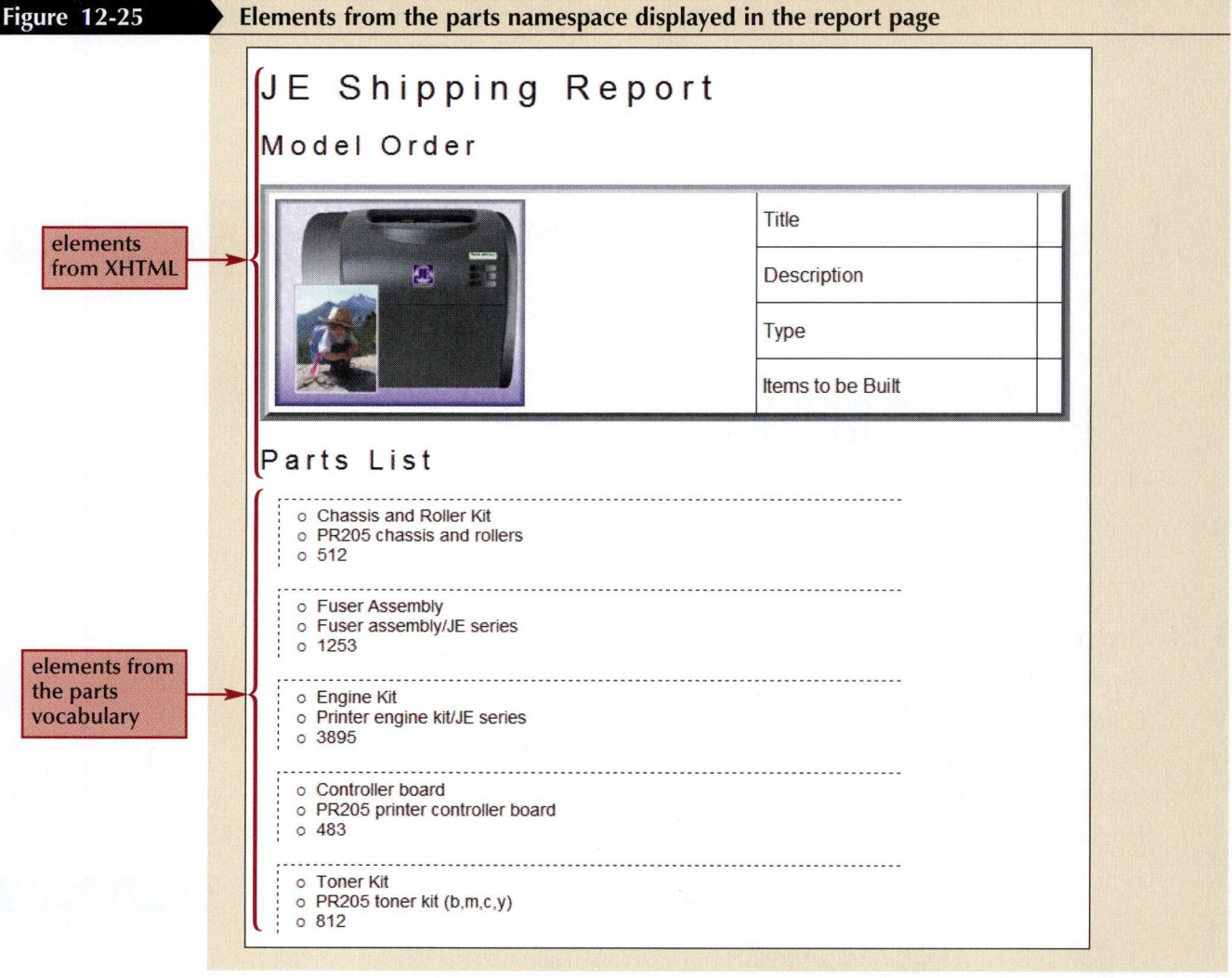

Gail wants descriptive text added to each of the bulleted items in the parts list. She's already created a style for descriptive text enclosed within a span element. She wants you to add the appropriate span elements to each item in the parts list.

To describe the items in the parts list:

▶ **1.** Return to the **report.htm** file in your text editor.

▶ **2.** Scroll down to the first title element in the parts namespace, and then, directly after the opening `<pa:title>` tag, insert the following text:

   `<span>Title</span>`

▶ **3.** In the next line, directly after the opening `<pa:description>` tag, insert the following text:

   `<span>Description</span>`

▶ **4.** In the next line, directly after the opening `<pa:instock>` tag, insert the following text:

   `<span>Parts in Stock</span>`

5. Repeat Steps 2 through 4 for the four remaining parts in the list. Figure 12-26 shows the newly inserted text.

Descriptive XHTML elements ◄ Figure 12-26

```
<h2>Parts List</h2>
<pa:parts>
   <pa:part id="chx201">
      <pa:title><span>Title</span>Chassis and Roller Kit</pa:title>
      <pa:description><span>Description</span>PR205 chassis and rollers</pa:description>
      <pa:instock><span>Parts in Stock</span>512</pa:instock>
   </pa:part>

   <pa:part id="fa100-5">
      <pa:title><span>Title</span>Fuser Assembly</pa:title>
      <pa:description><span>Description</span>Fuser assembly/JE series</pa:description>
      <pa:instock><span>Parts in Stock</span>1253</pa:instock>
   </pa:part>

   <pa:part id="eng005-2">
      <pa:title><span>Title</span>Engine Kit</pa:title>
      <pa:description><span>Description</span>Printer engine kit/JE series</pa:description>
      <pa:instock><span>Parts in Stock</span>3895</pa:instock>
   </pa:part>

   <pa:part id="cbx-450v4">
      <pa:title><span>Title</span>Controller board</pa:title>
      <pa:description><span>Description</span>PR205 printer controller board</pa:description>
      <pa:instock><span>Parts in Stock</span>483</pa:instock>
   </pa:part>

   <pa:part id="tn01-53">
      <pa:title><span>Title</span>Toner Kit</pa:title>
      <pa:description><span>Description</span>PR205 toner kit (b,m,c,y)</pa:description>
      <pa:instock><span>Parts in Stock</span>812</pa:instock>
   </pa:part>
</pa:parts>
</body>
```

6. Save your changes to the file, and then reload **report.htm** in your Web browser. As shown in Figure 12-27, descriptive text appears next to each item in the parts list.

Descriptive XHTML titles in the parts list ◄ Figure 12-27

Parts List

```
o  Title  Chassis and Roller Kit
o  Description  PR205 chassis and rollers
o  Parts in Stock  512
----------------------------------------
o  Title  Fuser Assembly
o  Description  Fuser assembly/JE series
o  Parts in Stock  1253
----------------------------------------
o  Title  Engine Kit
o  Description  Printer engine kit/JE series
o  Parts in Stock  3895
----------------------------------------
o  Title  Controller board
o  Description  PR205 printer controller board
o  Parts in Stock  483
----------------------------------------
o  Title  Toner Kit
o  Description  PR205 toner kit (b,m,c,y)
o  Parts in Stock  812
```

Finally, you'll add information from the model elements to Gail's report. Once again, you'll have to insert a namespace declaration for these elements and add a link to the model.css style sheet.

To add elements from the models vocabulary:

▶ **1.** Return to the **report.htm** file in your text editor, and then add the following namespace declaration to the opening `<html>` tag:

```
xmlns:mod="http://jacksonelx.com/models"
```

▶ **2.** Add the following link to the document's head:

```
<link rel="stylesheet" href="model.css" type="text/css" />
```

▶ **3.** In the table cell directly after the Title table heading, insert the following element:

```
<mod:title>Laser4C (PR205)</mod:title>
```

▶ **4.** In the table cell directly after the Description table heading, insert the following element:

```
<mod:description>Entry level color laser
printer</mod:description>
```

▶ **5.** In the table cell directly after the Type table heading, insert the following element:

```
<mod:type>color laser</mod:type>
```

▶ **6.** In the table cell directly after the Items to be Built table heading, insert the following element:

```
<mod:ordered>320</mod:ordered>
```

▶ **7.** Add the following tag directly after the opening `<body>` tag to include the root element of the models vocabulary:

```
<mod:model id="pr205">
```

▶ **8.** Directly before the closing `</body>` tag, insert the following closing tag for the root model element:

```
</mod:model>
```

Figure 12-28 shows the newly added elements in the report.htm file.

Elements added from the models vocabulary   Figure 12-28

```html
<html xmlns="http://www.w3.org/1999/xhtml"
      xmlns:pa="http://jacksonelx.com/parts"
      xmlns:mod="http://jacksonelx.com/models">
<head>
   <title>Jackson Electronics Shipping Order</title>
   <link rel="stylesheet" href="report.css" type="text/css" />
   <link rel="stylesheet" href="parts.css" type="text/css" />
   <link rel="stylesheet" href="model.css" type="text/css" />
</head>

<body>
   <mod:model id="pr205">
   <h1>JE Shipping Report</h1>
   <h2>Model Order</h2>

   <table>
   <tr>
      <td rowspan="4"><img src="pr205.jpg" alt="" /></td>
      <th>Title</th>
      <td><mod:title>Laser4C (PR205)</mod:title></td>
   </tr>
   <tr>
      <th>Description</th>
      <td><mod:description>Entry level color laser printer</mod:description></td>
   </tr>
   <tr>
      <th>Type</th>
      <td><mod:type>color laser</mod:type></td>
   </tr>
   <tr>
      <th>Items to be Built</th>
      <td><mod:ordered>320</mod:ordered></td>
   </tr>
   </table>
```

```html
      <pa:part id="tn01-53">
         <pa:title><span>Title</span>Toner Kit</pa:title>
         <pa:description><span>Description</span>PR205 toner kit (b,m,c,y)</pa:description>
         <pa:instock><span>Parts in Stock</span>812</pa:instock>
      </pa:part>
   </pa:parts>
   </mod:model>

</body>

</html>
```

▶ **9.** Save your changes to the file, and then close the file.

▶ **10.** Reopen **report.htm** in your Web browser. Figure 12-29 shows the format of the completed compound document.

Figure 12-29 | **Completed compound report page**

JE Shipping Report
Model Order

Title	Laser4C (PR205)
Description	Entry level color laser printer
Type	color laser
Items to be Built	320

elements from the models vocabulary

Parts List

- Title Chassis and Roller Kit
- Description PR205 chassis and rollers
- Parts in Stock 512

- Title Fuser Assembly
- Description Fuser assembly/JE series
- Parts in Stock 1253

- Title Engine Kit
- Description Printer engine kit/JE series
- Parts in Stock 3895

- Title Controller board
- Description PR205 printer controller board
- Parts in Stock 483

- Title Toner Kit
- Description PR205 toner kit (b,m,c,y)
- Parts in Stock 812

Gail is pleased with the final Web page. She'll bring the completed documents to the programming staff so that they can work on automating the process. In the future, she hopes to have software in place that will automatically pull model and parts data from their source files and combine those elements with elements of the XHTML language.

Compound Documents and Podcasting | InSight

One area where compound documents appear is podcasting. Information about the location and content of podcasts is written in the XML vocabulary language RSS. As you learned in the previous tutorial, RSS is used for syndicating text, video, or audio content. However, if you want to list your podcast on Apple's iTunes Music Store to make it more accessible to the general population, you have to add elements that are not part of RSS, but specific to the needs of iTunes. Therefore, the final podcast document has elements from both RSS and the iTunes vocabulary.

To declare the iTunes namespace, you add the following attribute to the root rss element of the podcast document:

```
<rss version="2.0"
     xmlns:itunes="http://www.itunes.com/dtds/podcast-1.0.dtd">
```

After you have declared the iTunes namespace, you can populate the rest of the document with iTunes-specific elements. The following text shows a portion of a compound document describing a podcast channel using elements from both RSS and iTunes:

```
<channel>
    <title>Jazz Pod Sessions</title>
    <link>http://jazzsessionpod.com</link>
    <description>Enjoy jazz music from JPS</description>
    <itunes:author>David Hmong</itunes:author>
    <itunes:category text="Music">
        <itunes:category text="Jazz" />
    </itunes:category>
...
</channel>
```

The iTunes-specific elements listed here—author and category—will be displayed in Apple's iTunes Music Store, providing additional information to potential subscribers of the feed. To augment the descriptions of individual episodes, you add iTunes-specific elements to each <item> tag in the RSS document. The following shows part of the code for one episode of the Jazz Pod Sessions podcast:

```
<item>
    <title>Jazz at Carnegie Hall</title>
    <itunes:subtitle>Famous Concerts</itunes:subtitle>
    <itunes:summary>Jazz from Carnegie Hall</itunes:summary>
    <itunes:author>Various</itunes:author>
    <itunes:duration>59:23</itunes:duration>
...
</item>
```

This particular episode highlights famous jazz concerts at Carnegie Hall. The code uses iTunes-specific elements to provide a subtitle for the show, a summary, the show's author, and the duration of the show in minutes and seconds.

The iTunes elements listed here represent only a fraction of the elements you can add to podcast code. You can learn more about podcasting and how to write compound documents involving both RSS and iTunes by visiting Apple's Web site.

1. What rule do you add to a CSS style sheet to declare a namespace with the URI *http://ns.doc.book* and the namespace prefix book?
2. What rule do you add to a CSS style sheet to make the namespace in Question 1 the default namespace for all selectors in the style sheet?
3. Using the namespace rule in Question 1, how would you modify the selector for the author element to indicate that it belongs to the book namespace?
4. How would you modify the selector in Question 3 to work with the Internet Explorer browser?
5. A document written in the SVG vocabulary has a root element named svg. How would you modify this element to indicate that the default namespace for the document is the SVG namespace?
6. You want to include elements from MathML and SVG in an XHTML document. How would you modify the root element html to indicate the presence of these three XML vocabularies? Assume that the default namespace is XHTML, and that elements from the MathML namespace have the prefix MM and elements from the SVG namespace have the prefix SVG.
7. An RSS document has the following content:

   ```
   <?xml version="1.0"?>
   <rss version="2.0">
      <channel>
         <title>Econ Report</title>
         <link>http://www.dol.gov/</link>
         <description>Weekly Economic Reports</description>
         <language>en-us</language>
         <pubDate>Feb 3, 2012 04:00:00 GMT</pubDate>
      </channel>
   </rss>
   ```

   How would you modify this code to create a compound document that contains the following img element:

   ```
   <img src="stock.jpg" alt="Stock Chart" />
   ```

   Insert the img element directly below the pubDate element and indicate that the element belongs to the XHTML namespace by using xhtml as the namespace prefix. Be sure to add the XHTML namespace declaration to the root element of this document.

8. How would you modify the root element of an RSS document to include support for the iTunes namespace?

Tutorial Summary | Review

In this tutorial, you learned how to create compound documents that combine elements and attributes from several XML vocabularies. In the first session, you learned how combining vocabularies in a single document can result in name collision. To solve the problem of name collision, you saw how to declare and apply namespaces to elements and attributes within a document. You also learned how namespaces can be associated with URIs to provide a unique identification for each vocabulary in a document. In the second session, you learned how to modify CSS style sheets for the major browsers to accommodate namespaces. The tutorial ended by examining how to create an XHTML document that combines features from XHTML and other XML vocabularies.

Key Terms

compound document	namespace	Uniform Resource
default namespace	namespace prefix	Name (URN)
local name	qualified name (qname)	unqualified name
local part	Uniform Resource	
name collision	Identifier (URI)	

Practice		Review Assignments

Practice the skills you learned in the tutorial using the same case scenario.

Data Files needed for the Review Assignments: files.xml, filestxt.css, je.css, logo.jpg, pr205.jpg, pr205txt.htm, printer.xml, printtxt.css, temp.htm

Gail talked to Jeff Drake about your work in creating compound documents involving several XML vocabularies. Jeff has a problem similar to Gail's with his work on the Jackson Electronics Web site. The company has created several XML vocabularies for the Web site. One vocabulary contains descriptive information about the company's products. Another contains a list of downloadable files for updating drivers, software, and product firmware. Jeff wants to combine information from the two vocabularies into a single Web page along with elements from XHTML. Figure 12-30 shows a preview of the completed Web page.

Figure 12-30

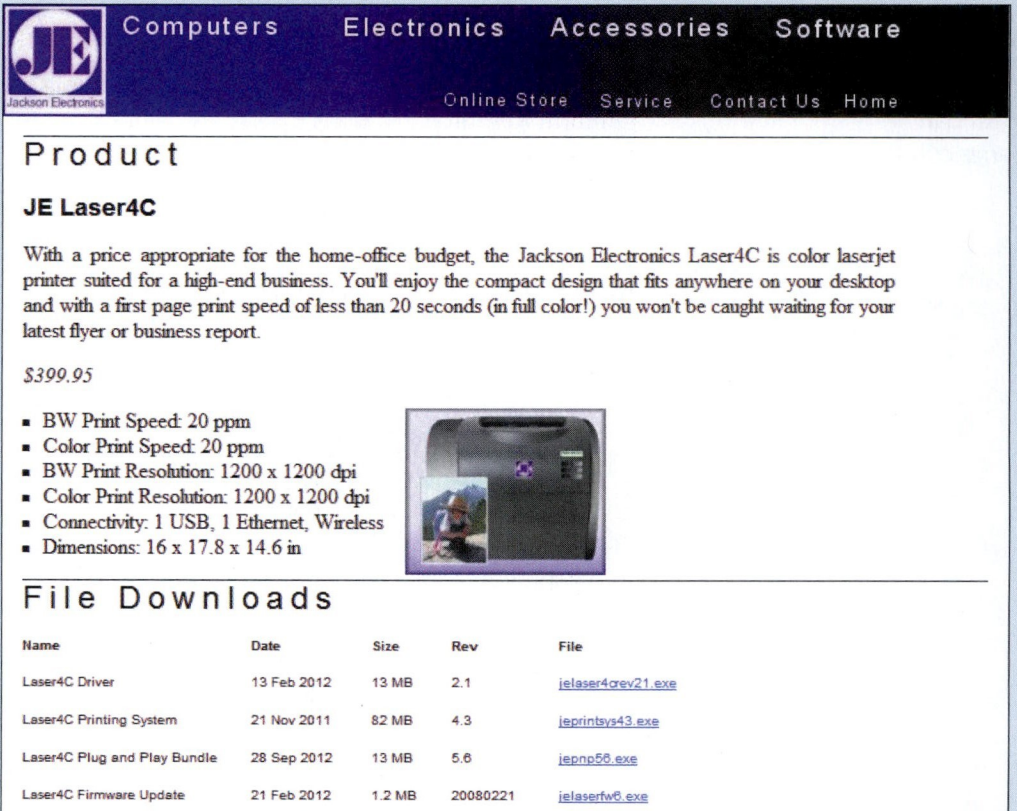

Jeff has already created much of the Web page as well as the style sheets for the different elements in the three vocabularies. He needs you to edit the style sheets so that they support namespaces, and then combine the elements in a single compound document.

Complete the following:

1. In your text editor, open the **printtxt.css** style sheet located in the tutorial.12/review folder, enter *your name* and *the date* in the comment section, and then save the file as **printer.css** in the same folder.

2. Below the initial comment section, insert a rule creating the printer namespace with the prefix **prnt** and the URI *http://jacksonelx.com/printers*. Edit all the selectors in the style sheet so they belong to this namespace. Copy the style declarations and paste them at the bottom of the file. Change the selector names to use the escape code syntax employed by Internet Explorer. Save your changes to the file, and then close it.

3. In your text editor, open the **filestxt.css** style sheet from the tutorial.12/review folder, enter *your name* and *the date* in the comment section, and then save the file as **files.css** in the same folder. Insert a rule declaring the download namespace. The prefix of the namespace should be **dwnld** and the URI should be *http://jacksonelx.com/files*. Make all the selectors in the style sheet belong to this namespace using both the namespace style and escape codes. Save your changes to the file, and then close it.

4. In your text editor, open the **pr205txt.htm** file from the tutorial.12/review folder, enter *your name* and *the date* in the comment section, and then save the file as **pr205.htm** in the same folder.

5. Change the document into an XHTML file by inserting an xml declaration at the top of the file.

6. Add attributes to the root element html, making the XHTML namespace the default namespace for elements in the document. Add namespaces for the printer, and then download namespaces using the same prefixes and URIs you used in the printer.css and files.css style sheets.

7. Below the `<h1>` Product heading tag, copy and paste the name, description, and price elements from the printer.xml document. Place those three elements in the printer namespace.

8. Directly above the h1 File Downloads heading, copy and paste the specs and item elements from the printer.xml file. Place those elements in the printer namespace.

9. Directly above the closing `</body>` tag, copy and paste the elements from the files.xml document. Place those elements in the download namespace.

10. Enclose the contents of each item element from the download namespace within an `<a>` tag, with the href attribute set to the file temp.htm.

11. Add link elements to the head section of the file with links to the printer.css and files.css style sheets.

12. Save your changes to the file, and then close it.

13. Open **pr205.htm** in your Web browser. Verify that the layout of the page resembles that shown in Figure 12-30, and that the links in the File Downloads section are pointed at the temp.htm file. Check your results in Internet Explorer and other major browsers to ensure that the resulting page is cross-browser compatible.

14. Submit the completed assignment to your instructor.

Apply | **Case Problem 1**

Use the skills you learned in this tutorial to create a compound document containing elements from the RSS and iTunes namespaces.

Data Files needed for this Case Problem: sfcrpodtxt.xml, ituneselem.txt

The SF Control Room   You work as an assistant to Kevin Vinter, a noted science writer and science fiction author. Kevin recently started a Web site called the SF Control Room, where he'll post articles and stories about science and science fiction as well as host discussion forums for his fans and colleagues. He's also interested in starting a podcast in which he'll provide readings from his stories and essays. Kevin asked you to set up the podcast. Because podcasts are created from XML documents written in the language of RSS, you will create a sample RSS document linking to two episodes of the SF Control Room podcast. You also want to promote the podcast on the iTunes Music Store, so you'll augment the RSS file with elements from the iTunes vocabulary. Figure 12-31 shows a tree diagram highlighting some of the elements from both vocabularies that you'll place in the document.

Figure 12-31

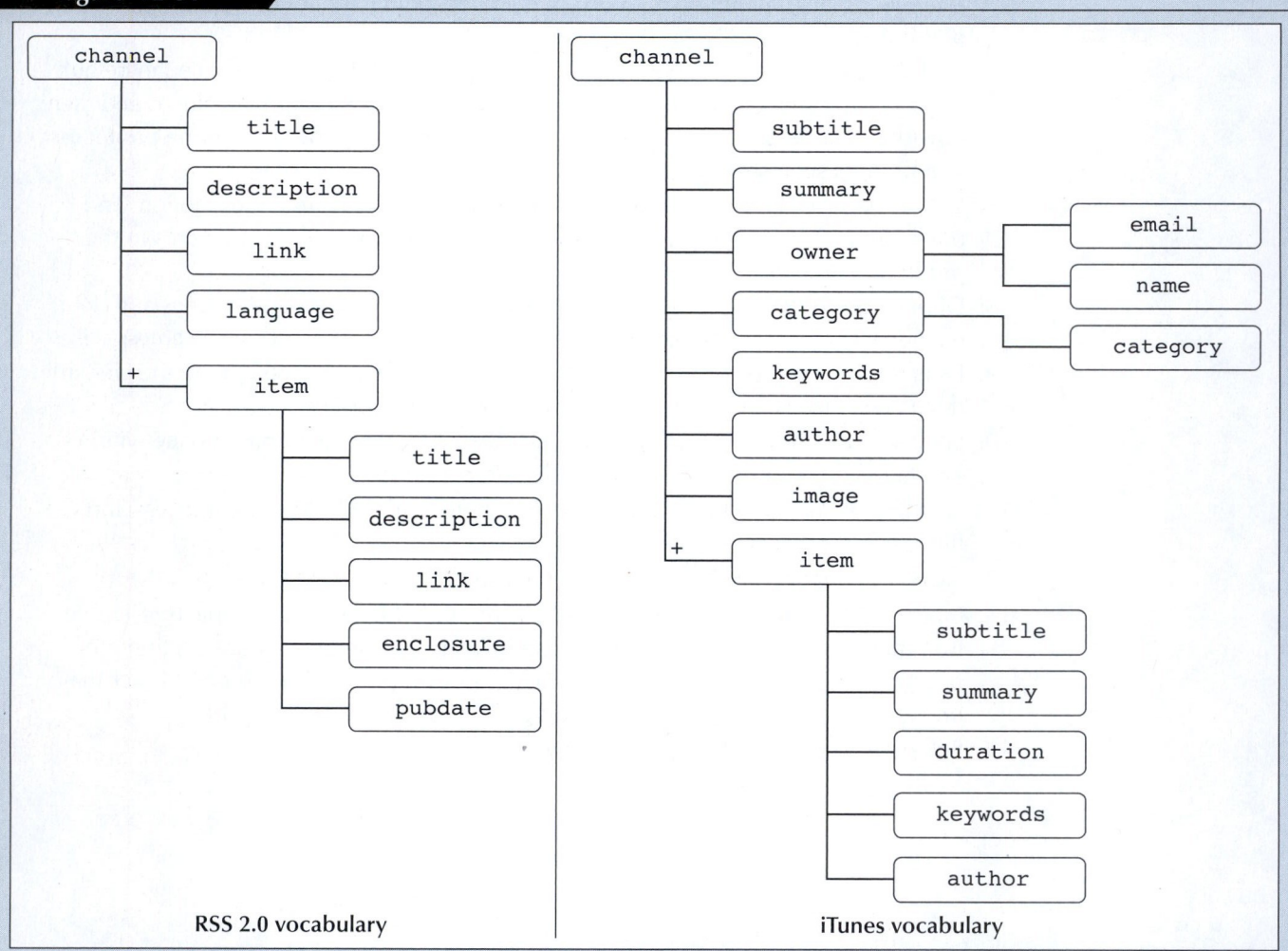

RSS 2.0 vocabulary

iTunes vocabulary

You've already received an RSS file containing the RSS elements and a text file containing iTunes-related information on the podcast and podcast episodes. Your job will be to create a compound element combining the features of the two vocabularies.

Note: Safari for the Macintosh has specific tools for handling RSS documents that cause the compound document created in this case to not be rendered. Test your answers to this case problem using another major browser such as Firefox, Internet Explorer, or Opera.

Complete the following:

1. In your text editor, open the **sfcrpodtxt.xml** file from the tutorial.12/case1 folder, enter *your name* and *the date* in the comment section, and then save the file as **sfcrpod.xml** in the same folder.

2. Add a namespace declaration to the root rss element, declaring the iTunes namespace. Use **itunes** as the namespace prefix.

3. In your text editor, open the **ituneselem.txt** file from the tutorial.12/case1 folder. This file contains the content for the different iTunes elements. Using this file as a reference, complete the rest of the content in the RSS document.

4. Return to the **sfcrpod.xml** file in your text editor. Add the subtitle and summary iTunes elements as child elements of the channel element. Place both elements in the iTunes namespace and use the text indicated in the ituneselem.txt file as the content of the two elements.

5. Below the summary element, insert the iTunes owner element. The owner element indicates the owner of the podcast for the iTunes Music Store. Within the owner element, insert two elements named **email** and **name** containing Kevin Vinter's e-mail address and name, respectively. Make sure these elements belong to the iTunes namespace.

6. Specify the category of the podcast using the iTunes category element. The name of the category is contained in an attribute of the category element named text. Insert two category elements, one nested inside the other. The outer category element should have a text attribute value of **Arts**, and the inner category element should have a text attribute value of **Literature**.

7. Complete the iTunes channel by adding iTunes elements for the podcast's keywords, author, and image.

8. Add iTunes elements that describe each podcast episode. Podcast episodes are marked with the item element. Kevin's document has two episodes. Add the subtitle, summary, duration, keywords, and author elements for each of the two episodes.

9. Save your changes to the file, and then load **sfcrpod.xml** in your Web browser. Verify that there are no errors reported in the document.

10. Submit the completed compound document to your instructor.

Challenge	**Case Problem 2**

Explore how to create a compound document containing elements from XHTML and MathML vocabularies.

Data Files needed for this Case Problem: back.jpg, eq1.xml, eq2.xml, eq3.xml, eq4.xml, logo.jpg, mathtxt.css, quadtxt.xml, side.jpg

MathWeb   Professor Laureen Cole of Coastal University is creating a Web site called MathWeb to use for online tutorials on mathematical topics. Laureen has been reading about the XML vocabulary MathML and how it can be used to display mathematical equations and information. She's asked you to create a compound XML document containing elements from XHTML and MathML. Figure 12-32 shows a preview of the page that you will create.

Figure 12-32

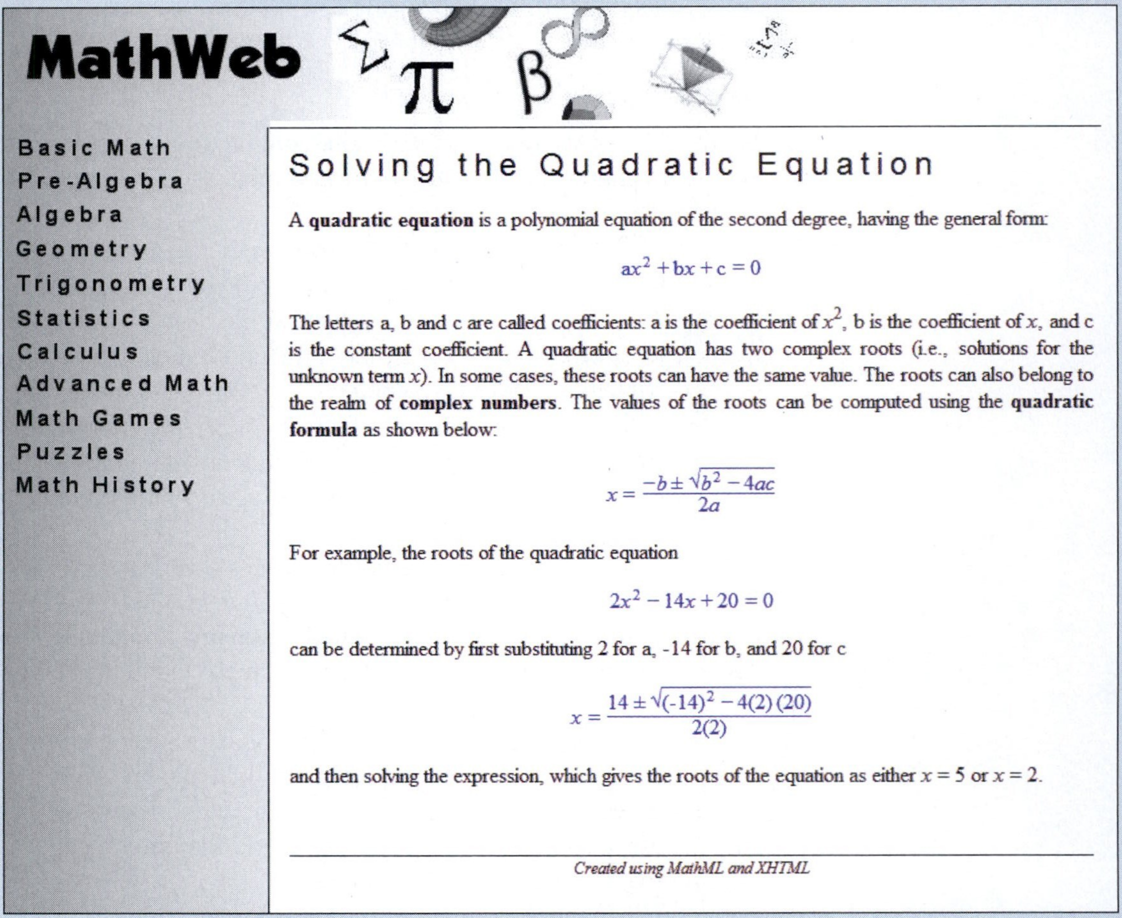

MathWeb

Basic Math
Pre-Algebra
Algebra
Geometry
Trigonometry
Statistics
Calculus
Advanced Math
Math Games
Puzzles
Math History

Solving the Quadratic Equation

A **quadratic equation** is a polynomial equation of the second degree, having the general form:

$$ax^2 + bx + c = 0$$

The letters a, b and c are called coefficients: a is the coefficient of x^2, b is the coefficient of x, and c is the constant coefficient. A quadratic equation has two complex roots (i.e., solutions for the unknown term x). In some cases, these roots can have the same value. The roots can also belong to the realm of **complex numbers**. The values of the roots can be computed using the **quadratic formula** as shown below:

$$x = \frac{-b \pm \sqrt{b^2 - 4ac}}{2a}$$

For example, the roots of the quadratic equation

$$2x^2 - 14x + 20 = 0$$

can be determined by first substituting 2 for a, -14 for b, and 20 for c

$$x = \frac{14 \pm \sqrt{(-14)^2 - 4(2)(20)}}{2(2)}$$

and then solving the expression, which gives the roots of the equation as either $x = 5$ or $x = 2$.

Created using MathML and XHTML

Laureen already created the content for the mathematical equations that she wants on her Web site. She wants you to complete the Web page.

Note: *Safari for the Macintosh has specific tools for handling RSS documents that cause the compound document created in this case to not be rendered. Test your answers to this case problem using another major browser such as Firefox, Internet Explorer, or Opera.*

Complete the following:

1. In your text editor, open **quadtxt.xml** from the tutorial.12/case2 folder, enter *your name* and *the date* in the comment section, and then save the document as **quad.xml** in the same folder.
2. Directly below the comment section, insert a processing instruction that links this document to the math.css style sheet.

⊕ EXPLORE

3. Within the root element html, insert two namespace declarations for the XHTML and MathML namespaces. Make XHTML the default namespace of the document. Use the prefix **m** for all elements belonging to the MathML namespace.
4. Scroll down to the paragraph element with the id eq1. Within this paragraph, paste the MathML elements from the **eq1.xml** file located in the tutorial.12/case2 folder. Apply the MathML namespace to these pasted elements.

5. Repeat Step 4 for the paragraphs with the ids eq2 through eq4, pasting the elements from the **eq2.xml** through **eq4.xml** files. In each case, apply the MathML namespace to the pasted elements.

6. Save your changes to the file, and then close it.

7. In your text editor, open the **mathtxt.css** file from the tutorial.12/case2 folder, enter *your name* and *the date* in the comment section, and then save the file as **math.css** in the same folder.

8. Directly below the comment section, insert a rule declaring the MathML namespace using the same prefix and URI you used in the quad.xml file.

9. At the bottom of the style sheet, insert style declarations to display any element named mrow from the MathML namespace in blue. Use both syntax methods to apply this style.

10. Save your changes to the style sheet, and then close it.

⊕ EXPLORE
11. Open the **quad.xml** file in either the Firefox or the Opera browser. Verify that the MathML equations appear as shown in Figure 12-32. If you are using a browser that does not support MathML, verify that the XML document opens without a syntax error being reported.

12. Submit the completed project to your instructor.

Challenge	**Case Problem 3**

Explore how to create a compound document combining XHTML and RSS.

Data Files needed for this Case Problem: home.htm, hometxt.css, links.jpg, newstxt.css, sblogger.jpg, sblogtxt.xml

Sblogger Steve Lavent runs a sports blog called Sblogger with links to sports sites, online chats, and Steve's unique commentary on the daily events in the world of sports. Steve wants to display the current headlines on his home page as an RSS feed with any HTML elements added to the RSS document as a wrapper around the news headlines. Eventually he'll automate this process using scripts on his Web server. For now, he wants you to design a sample XML document that combines XHTML and RSS elements. A preview of the Sblogger home page is shown in Figure 12-33.

Figure 12-33

SBLOGGER
Sports Blogging with a Difference

News Sites

ESPN
Sportsline
Sports Illustrated
CNN
MSNBC
Fox Sports

Columnists

Thomas Bacon
Steve Carls
Debbie Eggert
Frank Franks
Bob Mitchell
Sean Smith
Tom Upham
Mary Yancy

Blogs

Captain X
Die Yankees
Die BoSoxers
Packer Heaven
FBall Blog
Couch Potato
Sports Roundup
Fat, Drunk, and ...

Archives

January
February
March
April
May
June
July

Check that Pen!

ESPN is reporting that Houston running back JT Olson has come to terms with the team, signing a three-year deal for $12 million. "I'm really happy with the contract," claims JT, "and I'm looking forward to holding out next year for a new contract after winning the rushing title." Yo Texas, check JT's pen to make sure it wasn't filled with disappearing ink!

A Cheesy Monument

Green Bay native Jeff Miller loves Packers QB Todd Rodgers. And he loves the Packers. And he loves cheese. So what could be more natural than carving a life-size statue of his beloved player in a huge block of gouda? Speaking of natural, Jeff's wife is starting to complain about the natural odor of the monument. "I suppose I'll have to give it up," sighs Jeff. For his next creation, Jeff can do the entire porous GB defense ... in swiss cheese; or he can simply do a statue of beleagured GB defense back Chris Conners in toast.

Jenkins on Ice

Retired b-baller Dennis Jenkins announced today that he has signed a contract with "Long Sleep" to have his body frozen before death, to be revived only when medical science has discovered a cure to the aging process. "Lots of guys get frozen for cancer and stuff, " explains the always-entertaining Jenkins, "I just want to return once they can give me back my eternal youth.[sic]" Perhaps Jenkins is also hoping medical science can cure his free-throw shooting - 47% and falling during his last year in the league.

A reader tells us that Jenkins may not be aware that part of the process of "Long Sleep" is to remove the head, keeping only the brain to be revived. This would be a problem for Jenkins since he would be left with his least-valuable asset.

Posted: 8/10/2012 @11:39 am Comments (39) Trackback (1)

Current Headlines

Carson leads PGA
Brett Carson took a three stroke lead into the final round of the PGA Championship at Whistling Straits with a birdie on the final hole.

Groveny Signs Deal
New York signed leading defenseman Steve Groveny to a 2-year contract on Thursday.

Olson Out for Two Weeks
Kansas City QB Drew Olson will miss two weeks of practice due to a sprained knee, team officials announced this morning.

Soccer Season Delayed
The start of Spain's soccer season will be delayed for two weeks because of financial problems and fallout from a league-wide drug scandal.

Gregg Called Up
Steve Gregg was recalled to the majors after allowing two hits in six innings in his third start for Triple-A Akron.

Steve already created the style sheets, RSS code, and HTML elements for the Web page. He needs you to combine all these elements in a single XML file.

Complete the following:

1. In your text editor, open **sblogtxt.xml** from the tutorial.12/case3 folder, enter *your name* and *the date* in the comment section, and then save the file as **sblogger.xml** in the same folder.

2. Directly below the comment section, insert two processing instructions to link the file to the home.css and news.css style sheets.

3. Within the root element rss, declare the XHTML namespace using **html** as the namespace prefix.

4. Below the opening `<rss>` tag, insert the opening `<html>` tag. Place this element in the XHTML namespace.

5. In your text editor, open the **home.htm** file from the tutorial.12/case3 folder, copy the elements from the file starting with the opening `<head>` tag through the opening `<div>` tag for the news feed section, and then paste these elements into the sblogger.xml document directly above the opening `<channel>` tag.

 EXPLORE

6. Apply the XHTML namespace to all of the pasted HTML elements.

7. Directly below the closing `</channel>` tag, insert the closing `</div>`, `</body>`, and `</html>` tags. Place these three elements in the XHTML namespace.

8. Save your changes to the file, and then close it.

9. In your text editor, open the **hometxt.css** style sheet from the tutorial.12/case3 folder, enter *your name* and *the date* in the comment section, and then save the file as **home.css** in the same folder.

10. Directly below the comment section, insert a rule declaring the XHTML namespace using the same namespace prefix you used in the sblogger.xml file.

11. Place all of the selectors in the style sheet in the XHTML namespace using both forms.

12. Save your changes to the file, and then close it.

13. In your text editor, open the **newstxt.css** style sheet from the tutorial.12/case3 folder, enter *your name* and *the date* in the comment section, and then save the file as **news.css** in the same folder.

⊕ EXPLORE 14. Directly below the comment section, declare all four of the RSS namespaces declared in the sblogger.xml document, using the same namespace prefixes.

⊕ EXPLORE 15. Add style declarations in both formats to hide all of the elements from the sy and dc namespaces. (*Hint*: Use the display: none style.)

16. Save your changes to the file, and then close it.

17. Open **sblogger.xml** in your Web browser. Verify that the XHTML elements are properly formatted and that the headings from the RSS news feed appear in a box on the right margin of the page, as shown in Figure 12-33. If you open the Web page in the Apple Safari browser, you may not see the document as shown in Figure 12-33.

18. Submit your completed project to your instructor.

Create	**Case Problem 4**

Test your knowledge of compound documents by combining several vocabularies in a single XHTML file.

Data Files needed for this Case Problem: authortxt.css, bookstxt.css, mlibtxt.htm, books.xml, author.xml, library.css, bml.jpg

Bozeman Public Library   Brett Vironque works on the Web development team for the Bozeman Public Library in Bozeman, Montana. The team is considering updating its system to incorporate XML documents. He wants you to create a sample Web page in which information on an author and a list of books by that author are displayed on the page. He's provided you with two XML documents: one describing the author and the other describing the books. There is a great deal of overlap in the element names from the two vocabularies, so you'll have to use namespaces to distinguish the elements from the two vocabularies.

Complete the following:

1. In your text editor, open the **authortxt.css**, **bookstxt.css**, and **mlibtxt.htm** files from the tutorial.12/case4 folder, enter *your name* and *the date* in the comment section of each file, and then save the files as **author.css**, **books.css**, and **mlib.htm**, respectively, in the same folder.

2. Convert the mlib.htm file to an XHTML file by adding an XML declaration and adding **XHTML** as the default namespace to the root html element.

3. Add the author and books namespace declarations to the root element. Use the prefix **bk** for the books namespace and the URI *http://bmlib.com/books*. Use the prefix **au** for the author namespace and the URI *http://bmlib.com/author*.

4. Add link elements to the document head, linking the mlib.htm file to the author.css and books.css style sheet files.

5. Scroll down to the div element with the id maincontent. Within this div element, insert the contents of the **books.xml** file located in the tutorial.12/case4 folder. Place all the pasted elements in the books namespace.

6. Go to the div element with the id mainsidebar. Within this element, insert the contents of the **author.xml** file. Place all the pasted elements in the author namespace.

7. Save your changes to the mlib.htm file, and then close it.

8. In your text editor, go to the **author.css** file, and then place the style declarations for each element in the author namespace. Ensure that your code works under all browsers. Save your changes to the file, and then close it.

9. In your text editor, go to the **books.css** file, and then place the style declarations for each element in the books namespace. Ensure that your code works under all browsers. Save your changes to the file, and then close it.

10. Open **mlib.htm** in your Web browser, verifying that the styles for the XHTML, author, and books vocabularies have been properly applied.

11. Submit the completed project to your instructor.

Review | **Quick Check Answers**

Session 12.1

1. A name collision occurs when two elements from different XML vocabularies share the same name in a compound document.

2. A namespace is a defined collection of element and attribute names. By placing XML vocabularies in different namespaces, elements from the different vocabularies can share the same name without confusion.

3. A URI is a unique text string that identifies the namespace, and many namespaces use URLs because they point to unique locations on the Internet. However, it is not required that the URI point to an actual site.

4. `xmlns:book="http://ns.doc.book"`

5. `<book:author>David Stevens</book:author>`

6. `xmlns="http://ns.doc.book"`

7. `<book book:isbn="0-1969-7">Blue Moon</book>`

8. the element containing it

Session 12.2

1. `@namespace book "http://ns.doc.book";`

2. `@namespace "http://ns.doc.book";`

3. `book|author`

4. `book\:author`

5. `<svg xmlns="http://www.w3.org/2000/svg">`

6. ```
<html xmlns="http://www.w3.org/1999/xhtml"
      xmlns:MM="http://www.w3.org/1998/Math/MathML"
      xmlns:SVG="http://www.w3.org/2000/svg">
```

7. ```
<?xml version="1.0"?>
<rss version="2.0">
   <channel>
      <title>Econ Report</title>
      <link>http://www.dol.gov/</link>
      <description>Weekly Economic Reports</description>
```

```
      <language>en-us</language>
      <pubDate>Feb 3, 2012 04:00:00 GMT</pubDate>
      <xhtml:img src="stock.jpg" alt="Stock Chart" />
   </channel>
 </rss>
```
8. `<rss version="2.0"`
```
      xmlns:itunes="http://www.itunes.com/dtds/podcast-1.0.dtd">
 ...
 </rss>
```

Ending Data Files

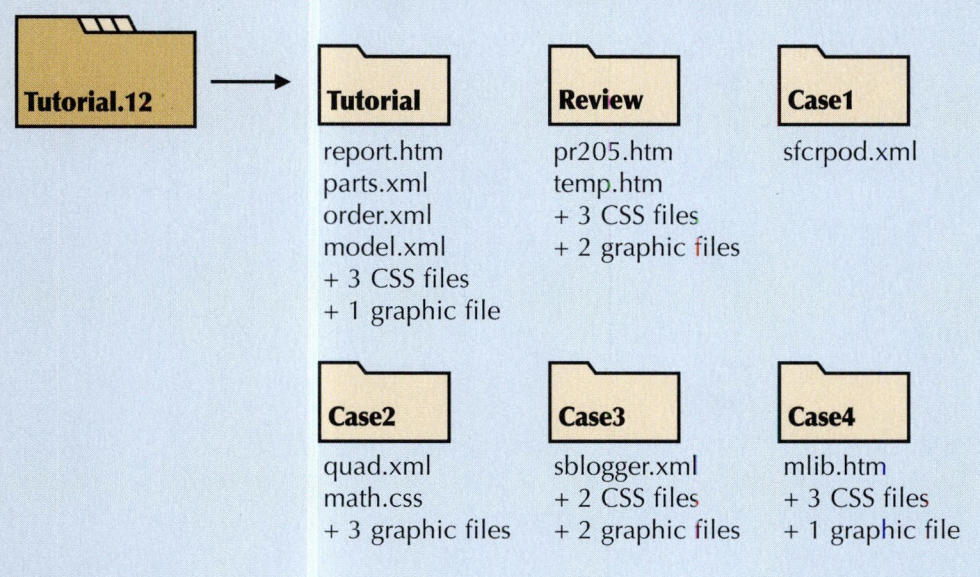

Tutorial.12 →

Tutorial
report.htm
parts.xml
order.xml
model.xml
+ 3 CSS files
+ 1 graphic file

Review
pr205.htm
temp.htm
+ 3 CSS files
+ 2 graphic files

Case1
sfcrpod.xml

Case2
quad.xml
math.css
+ 3 graphic files

Case3
sblogger.xml
+ 2 CSS files
+ 2 graphic files

Case4
mlib.htm
+ 3 CSS files
+ 1 graphic file

Objectives

Session 13.1
- Review the principles of data validation
- Create a DOCTYPE
- Specify the content of an XML element
- Define the structure of child elements

Session 13.2
- Set rules for attribute content
- Set attribute values
- Define optional and required attributes
- Accommodate namespaces in a DTD

Session 13.3
- Place internal and external content in an entity
- Create entity references
- Store code in parameter entities
- Create comments and conditional sections
- Create entities for non-character data

Validating Documents with DTDs

Working with Document Type Definitions

Case | Butterfly Garden

Samantha Shen works at Butterfly Garden, an online store that sells butterfly and moth larvae to hobbyists and collectors. The order of Lepidoptera (the insect order comprising moths and butterflies) includes more than 180,000 species. Although Butterfly Garden has nowhere near that many samples in its catalog, the shop does have an extensive holding and its customer base is expanding as more people take up the butterfly hobby. Part of Samantha's job at Butterfly Garden is to record information about the store's customers, including the individual orders they place.

Samantha is starting to use XML to record this information, and has created a sample XML document containing information on customers and their orders. Samantha knows that her document needs to be well formed, following the XML syntax rules exactly, but she also wants the document to follow certain rules regarding content. For example, data on each customer must include the customer's name, phone number, and address. Each customer order must contain a complete list of the items purchased, including the date the order was placed. You will create an XML document for Samantha that adheres to both the rules of XML and the rules Samantha set up for the document's content and structure.

Note: *To complete this tutorial, you will need to have access to Internet Explorer for Windows or an XML parser capable of validating an XML document based on a DTD.*

Starting Data Files

Tutorial.13 →

Tutorial
orderstxt.xml
codestxt.dtd

Review
gardtxt.xml
kitstxt.xml
samptxt.xml
kitstxt.dtd
samptxt.dtd

Case1
edltxt.xml
teamstxt.dtd

Case2
clockstxt.xml
clockstxt.dtd

Case3
modelstxt.xml
partstxt.xml
pixaltxt.xml
modelstxt.dtd
partstxt.dtd

Case4
listtxt.xml
lhousetxt.dtd
members.txt

Demo
validate_dtd.htm
+ 3 graphic files

Session 13.1

Creating a Valid Document

Samantha has collected information about Butterfly Garden's customers. To keep the information to a manageable size, Samantha created a sample document for you to work on, limiting it to three customers and their orders. Figure 13-1 shows a table of the information she entered for those customers.

Figure 13-1 | **Customer orders table**

Customer		Orders		Item	Qty.	Price
Name:	Mr. David Lynn	orderID:	or1031	BF100P	1	299.95
custID:	cust201	Date:	8/1/2012	BFGK10	1	49.95
Type:	home	orderID:	or1142	MWT15	2	52.23
Address:	211 Fox Street	Date:	9/14/2012	MBL25	3	124.44
	Greenville, NH 03048					
Phone:	(603) 555-1812					
E-mail:	dlynn@nhx.net					
Name:	Mrs. Jean Kaufmann	orderID:	or1089	HME100	1	39.95
custID:	cust202	Date:	8/11/2012	MP12	2	89.95
Type:						
Address:	411 East Oak Avenue 54656					
	Sparta, WI					
Phone:	(608) 555-4033					
E-mail:	jk@truedreams.com					
Name:	Riverfront High School	orderID:	or1120	PLBK70	2	79.95
custID:	cust203	Date:	9/15/2012			
Type:	school					
Address:	55 Washburn Lane					
	Monroe, MI 48161					
Phone:	(811) 555-2987					

For each customer, Samantha recorded the customer's name, ID, type (home, school, or business), address, phone number, and e-mail address. Each customer has placed one or more separate orders. For convenience, Samantha has grouped each customer order within an orders element. For each order, Samantha recorded the order's ID number and date. Finally, within each order, she entered the items purchased and the quantity and price of each item. Samantha placed this information in an XML document, which you will open now.

To open the orders document:

▶ 1. Use your text editor to open **orderstxt.xml** from the tutorial.13/tutorial folder, enter **your name** and **the date** in the comment section of the file, and then save the file as **orders.xml**. Figure 13-2 shows the contents of the orders.xml document for the first customer.

First customer in the orders.xml document ◀ Figure 13-2

```
<customers>
    <customer custID="cust201" custType="home">
        <name title="Mr.">David Lynn</name>
        <address>
            <![CDATA[
            211 Fox Street
            Greenville, NH 03048
            ]]>
        </address>
        <phone>(603) 555-1812</phone>
        <email>dlynn@nhx.net</email>
        <orders>
            <order orderID="or1031" orderBy="cust201">
                <orderDate>8/1/2012</orderDate>
                <items>
                    <item itemPrice="299.95">BF100P</item>
                    <item itemPrice="49.95">BFGK10</item>
                </items>
            </order>
            <order orderID="or1142" orderBy="cust201">
                <orderDate>9/14/2012</orderDate>
                <items>
                    <item itemPrice="52.23" itemQty="2">MWT15</item>
                    <item itemPrice="124.44" itemQty="3">MBL25</item>
                </items>
            </order>
        </orders>
    </customer>
</customers>
```

▶ **2.** Examine the contents of the orders.xml document. In particular, compare the elements entered in the document with the table shown in Figure 13-1.

Some elements in Samantha's document, such as the name and phone elements, should appear only once for each customer, whereas other elements such as the order and item elements can appear multiple times. The email element is optional: Two customers have an e-mail address and one does not. Some of the attributes are also optional: The title attribute is not needed when the customer is a company and the itemQty attribute is used only when the number of items ordered is greater than 1.

Samantha created the diagram shown in Figure 13-3 to better illustrate the structure of the elements and attributes in her document. Recall that the + symbol in front of an element indicates that at least one child element must be present in the document, and the ? symbol indicates the presence of zero children or one child. Samantha's diagram shows that the customers, orders, and items elements must have at least one customer, order, or item child, respectively, and that the email element is optional. Samantha also indicated the presence of element attributes below each element name. Optional attributes are surrounded by square brackets. The document has three optional attributes: the custType attribute associated with the customer element, the title attribute associated with the name element, and the itemQty attribute associated with the item element.

Figure 13-3 **Structure of the orders.xml document**

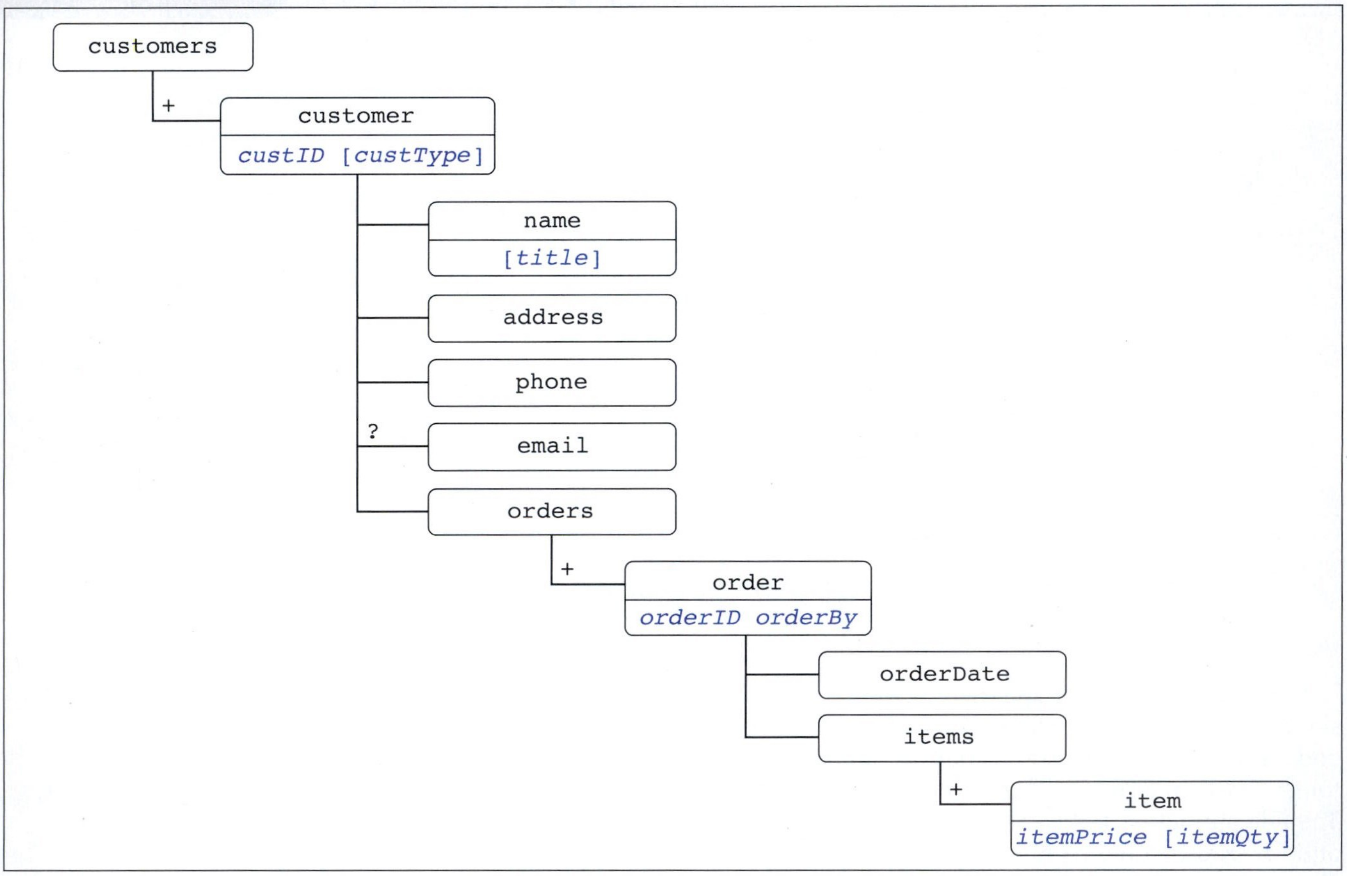

To keep accurate and manageable records, Samantha must maintain this structure in her document. She wants to ensure that the customer information includes the address and phone number for each customer, the items the customer ordered, and the date the order was placed. In XML terms, this means that the document must be well formed and valid.

Declaring a DTD

One way to create a valid document is to design a DTD for the document. Recall that a DTD is a collection of rules that define the content and structure of an XML document. Used in conjunction with an XML parser that supports data validation, a DTD can:

- Ensure that all required elements are present in the document
- Prevent undefined elements from being used in the document
- Enforce a specific data structure on document contents
- Specify the use of element attributes and define their permissible values
- Define default values for attributes
- Describe how parsers should access non-XML or nontextual content

A DTD is attached to a document in a statement called a **document type declaration**, which is more simply referred to as a **DOCTYPE**. The DOCTYPE must be added to the document prolog after the XML declaration and before the document's root element. The purpose of the DOCTYPE is to either specify the rules of the DTD or provide information to the parser about where those rules can be located. Each XML document can have only one DOCTYPE.

Because DTDs can be placed either within an XML document or in an external file, you can divide a DOCTYPE into two parts: an internal subset and an external subset. The **internal subset** contains rules and declarations from the DTD, which are placed directly into the document, and has the form

```
<!DOCTYPE root
[
    statements
]>
```

where *root* is the name of the document's root element and *statements* are declarations and rules from the DTD.

For example, the root element of the orders.xml document is customers, so any DOCTYPE in the orders.xml document has to specify customers as the value for the *root* parameter, as follows

```
<!DOCTYPE customers
[
    statements
]>
```

where again *statements* are declarations and rules from the DTD.

When the DTD is located in an external file, the DOCTYPE includes an **external subset** that indicates the location of this file. Locations can be defined using either a system identifier or a public identifier. With a **system identifier**, you specify the location of the DTD file. The DOCTYPE has the form

```
<!DOCTYPE root SYSTEM "uri">
```

where *root* is again the document's root element and *uri* is the URI of the external file. For example, if Samantha places the DTD for the orders.xml document in an external file named rules.dtd, she can add the following system identifier to the DOCTYPE:

```
<!DOCTYPE customers SYSTEM "rules.dtd">
```

When an XML vocabulary becomes widely used, developers seek to make the DTD easily accessible. This is done by creating a name for the DTD, which is called a **public identifier** or a **formal public identifier**. The public identifier provides the XML parser with information about the DTD, including the owner or author of the DTD, and the language in which the DTD is written. The syntax of a DOCTYPE involving a public identifier is

```
<!DOCTYPE root PUBLIC "id" "uri">
```

where *root* is the document's root element, *id* is the public identifier, and *uri* is the system location of the DTD (included in case the XML parser cannot process the document solely based on the information provided by the public identifier). In one sense, the public identifier acts like the namespace URI because it doesn't specify a physical location for the DTD, but instead provides the DTD with a unique name that can be recognized by an XML parser. For example, XHTML documents that conform strictly to standards employ the following DOCTYPE:

```
<!DOCTYPE html PUBLIC "-//W3C//DTD XHTML 1.0 Strict//EN"
"http://www.w3.org/TR/xhtml1/DTD/xhtml1-strict.dtd">
```

Tip

The *root* value in the DOCTYPE must match the name of the XML document's root element or else the document will be rejected as invalid.

The public identifier is "-//W3C//DTD XHTML 1.0 Strict//EN", a string of characters that XML parsers recognize as the identifier for the XHTML strict DTD. An XML parser that recognizes this public identifier can use it to try to retrieve the DTD associated with the XML vocabulary used in the document. If the parser cannot retrieve the DTD based on the public identifier, it can access it from the system location provided by *http://www.w3.org/TR/xhtml1/DTD/xhtml1-strict.dtd*. As you can see, the system identifier acts as a backup to the public identifier. Most standard XML vocabularies such as XHTML and RSS have public identifiers. However, a customized XML vocabulary such as the one Samantha created for Butterfly Garden may not have a public identifier.

InSight | Interpreting the Public Identifiers

The public identifier is simply a public name given to a DTD that the XML parser can use to process and validate the document. The parser can use the public identifier to find the latest version of the DTD on the Internet. Each public identifier name has the structure

```
standard//owner//description//language
```

where *standard* indicates whether the DTD is a recognized standard, *owner* is the owner or developer of the DTD, *description* is a description of the XML vocabulary for which the DTD is developed, and *language* is a two-letter abbreviation of the language employed by the DTD. For example, the identifier for the XHTML vocabulary

```
-//W3C//DTD XHTML 1.0 Strict//EN
```

can be interpreted in the following manner: The initial - character tells the parser that the DTD is not a recognized standard. DTDs that meet approved ISO (Internal Organization for Standardization) standards begin with the symbols ISO, whereas DTDs that meet an approved non-ISO standard begin with the + symbol. The next part of the id, W3C, indicates that this DTD is owned and developed by the W3C (World Wide Web Consortium) and that it is used for the XHTML 1.0 Strict vocabulary. Finally, the closing EN characters indicate that the DTD is written in English.

If the XML parser has an internal catalog for working with public identifiers, it can use the information contained in the public identifier to work with the DTD. However, public identifiers are not a requirement, so you should always include a system location for your public DTDs to support parsers that do not work with public identifiers.

In writing code, you might create DOCTYPEs with both internal and external subsets. A DTD that is shared among many different XML documents would be placed within an external file, whereas rules or declarations specific to an individual XML document would be placed within the internal subset. A DOCTYPE that combines both internal and external subsets has the following form:

```
<!DOCTYPE root SYSTEM "URI"
[
    declarations
]>
```

If the DTD has a public identifier, the DOCTYPE has the following form:

```
<!DOCTYPE root PUBLIC  "id" "URI"
[
    declarations
]>
```

When a DOCTYPE contains both an internal and an external subset, the internal subset takes precedence over the external subset when conflict arises between the two. This is useful when an external subset is shared among several documents. The external subset would define some basic rules for all of the documents and the internal subset would define rules that are specific to each document, as illustrated in Figure 13-4. In this way, internal and external DTDs work in the same manner as embedded and external style sheets. An XML environment composed of several documents and vocabularies might use both internal and external DTDs.

Internal and external DTDs ◄ **Figure 13-4**

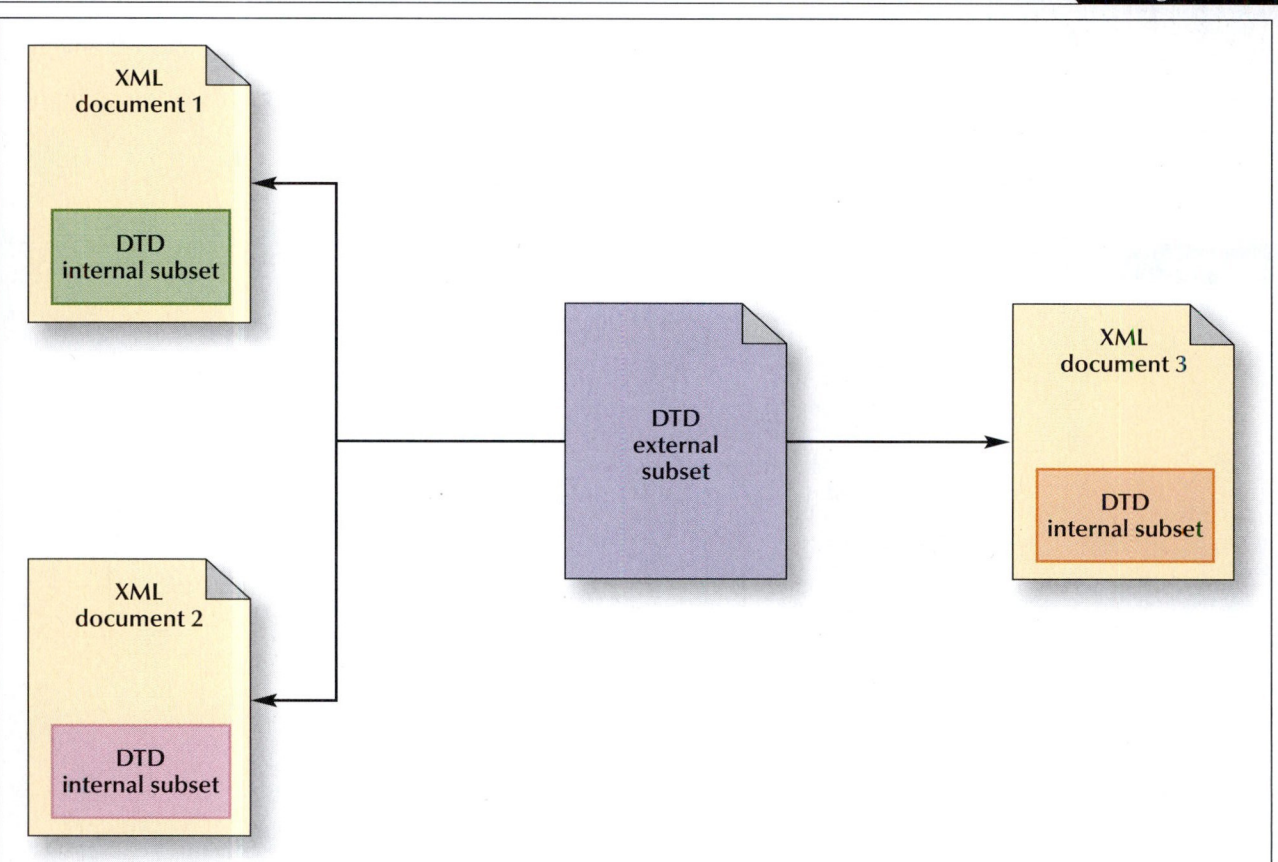

Declaring a DTD | Reference Window

- To declare an internal DTD subset, use the DOCTYPE

  ```
  <!DOCTYPE root
  [
      declarations
  ]>
  ```

  where *root* is the name of the document's root element, and *declarations* are the statements that constitute the DTD.
- To declare an external DTD subset with a system location, use the DOCTYPE

  ```
  <!DOCTYPE root SYSTEM "uri">
  ```

  where *uri* is the URI of the external DTD file.
- To declare an external DTD subset with a public location, use the DOCTYPE

  ```
  <!DOCTYPE root PUBLIC "id" "uri">
  ```

  where *id* is the public identifier of the DTD.

Writing the Document Type Declaration

Samantha wants you to place the DTD directly in her XML document so she can easily compare the DTD to the document content. You will insert a DOCTYPE into the orders. xml file, leaving its contents blank for the moment.

To insert a DOCTYPE into the orders.xml document:

▶ **1.** Directly above the opening <customers> tag, insert the following DOCTYPE, as shown in Figure 13-5:

```
<!DOCTYPE customers
[

]>
```

| Figure 13-5 | **Inserted DOCTYPE** |

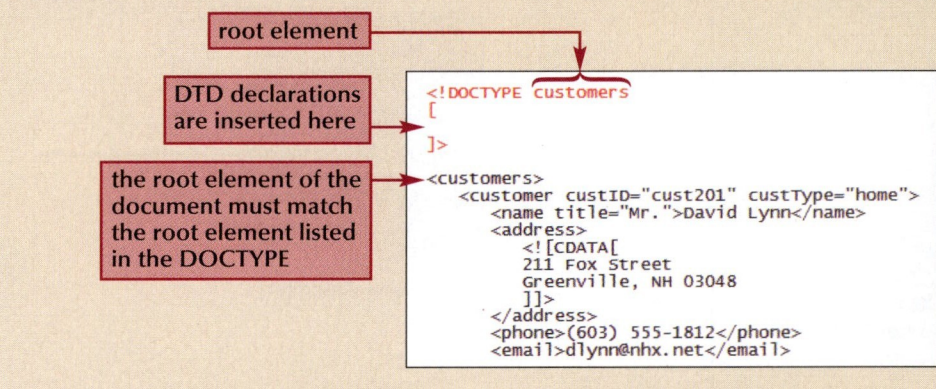

▶ **2.** Save your changes to the file.

Now that you have added a DOCTYPE to Samantha's document, you can begin adding statements to the DTD to define the structure and content of her XML vocabulary.

Declaring Document Elements

In a valid document, every element must be declared in the DTD. An **element type declaration** (also called an **element declaration**), specifies an element's name and indicates what kind of content the element can contain. It can even specify the order in which elements appear in the document. The syntax of an element declaration is

```
<!ELEMENT element content-model>
```

where *element* is the name of the element and *content-model* specifies what type of content the element contains. The element name is case sensitive. So, if the element name is PRODUCTS, it must be entered as PRODUCTS (not Products or products) in the element declaration. Remember that element names cannot contain any spaces or reserved symbols such as < or >. The *content-model* will specify one of the five following possibilities for the element content:

- The element can contain only parsed character data.
- The element can contain only child elements.
- The element cannot store any content.

- The element can store any type of content or no content at all.
- The element stores both parsed character data and child elements.

Generally, elements contain parsed character data or child elements. For example, in Samantha's document, the phone element contains a text string that stores the customer's phone number. On the other hand, the customer element contains five elements (name, address, phone, email, and orders). The next sections explore each type in more detail.

Elements Containing Any Type of Content

The most general type of content model is ANY, which allows an element to store any type of content. The syntax to allow any element content is:

```
<!ELEMENT element ANY>
```

For example, the declaration

```
<!ELEMENT product ANY>
```

in the DTD would allow the product element to contain any type of content (or none at all). Any of the following content in the XML document would satisfy this element declaration:

```
<product>PLBK70 Painted Lady Breeding Kit</product>
```

or

```
<product />
```

or

```
<product>
   <name>PLBK70</name>
   <type> Painted Lady Breeding Kit</type>
</product>
```

Allowing an element to contain any type of content has little value in document validation. After all, the idea behind validation is to enforce a particular set of rules on elements and their content; allowing any content defeats the purpose of a rule.

Empty Elements

The EMPTY content model is reserved for elements that store no content. The syntax for an empty element declaration is:

```
<!ELEMENT element EMPTY>
```

The element declaration

```
<!ELEMENT img EMPTY>
```

would require the img element to be entered as an empty element:

```
<img />
```

Attempting to add content to an empty element would result in XML parsers rejecting the document as invalid.

Elements Containing Parsed Character Data

The #PCDATA content model is reserved for elements that can store parsed character data and is declared as follows:

```
<!ELEMENT element (#PCDATA)>
```

For example, the declaration

```
<!ELEMENT name (#PCDATA)>
```

permits the following element in an XML document:

```
<name>Lea Ziegler</name>
```

An element declaration employing the #PCDATA content model does not allow for child elements. As a result, a name element containing the child elements

```
<name>
   <first>Lea</first>
   <last>Ziegler</last>
</name>
```

is not considered valid because child elements are not considered parsed character data.

The name, address, phone, email, orderDate, and item elements in the orders.xml document contain only parsed character data. Samantha wants you to add declarations for these elements to the DTD.

To declare elements containing parsed character data in the orders.xml document:

▶ 1. Within the DOCTYPE declaration, insert the following element declarations, as shown in Figure 13-6:

```
<!ELEMENT name (#PCDATA)>
<!ELEMENT address (#PCDATA)>
<!ELEMENT phone (#PCDATA)>
<!ELEMENT email (#PCDATA)>
<!ELEMENT orderDate (#PCDATA)>
<!ELEMENT item (#PCDATA)>
```

Figure 13-6 ▸ **Element declarations**

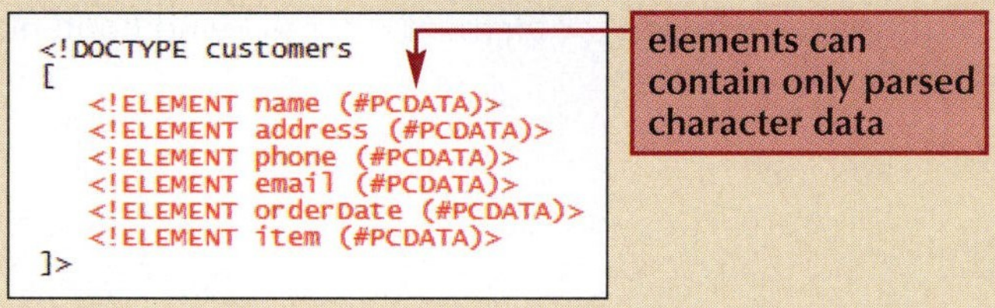

```
<!DOCTYPE customers
[
   <!ELEMENT name (#PCDATA)>
   <!ELEMENT address (#PCDATA)>
   <!ELEMENT phone (#PCDATA)>
   <!ELEMENT email (#PCDATA)>
   <!ELEMENT orderDate (#PCDATA)>
   <!ELEMENT item (#PCDATA)>
]>
```

elements can contain only parsed character data

▶ 2. Save your changes to the file.

Specifying Element Content

- To declare that an element may contain any type of content, insert the declaration
  ```
  <!ELEMENT element ANY>
  ```
  where *element* is the element name.
- To declare an empty element containing no content whatsoever, use the following declaration:
  ```
  <!ELEMENT element EMPTY>
  ```
- To declare that an element may contain only parsed character data, use the following declaration:
  ```
  <!ELEMENT element (#PCDATA)>
  ```

Working with Child Elements

Next, you will consider how to declare an element that contains only child elements. The syntax for such a declaration is

```
<!ELEMENT element (children)>
```

where *element* is the parent element and *children* is a listing of its child elements. The simplest form for the listing consists of a single child element associated with a parent. For example, the declaration

```
<!ELEMENT customer (phone)>
```

indicates that the customer element can contain only a single child element named phone. The following document would be invalid under this element declaration because the customer element is shown with two child elements: name and phone:

```
<customer>
    <name>Lea Ziegler</name>
    <phone>555-2819</phone>
</customer>
```

For content that involves multiple child elements, you can specify the elements in a sequence or you can specify a choice of elements.

Specifying an Element Sequence

A **sequence** is a list of elements that follow a defined order. The syntax to specify child elements in a sequence is

```
<!ELEMENT element (child1, child2, ...)>
```

where *child1*, *child2*, etc., represents the sequence of child elements within the parent. The order of the child elements in an XML document must match the order defined in the element declaration. For example, the following element declaration defines a sequence of three child elements for each customer:

```
<!ELEMENT customer (name, phone, email)>
```

Under this declaration, the following document is valid:

```
<customer>
    <name>Lea Ziegler</name>
    <phone>(813) 555-8931</phone>
    <email>LZiegler@tempmail.net</email>
</customer>
```

However, even though the elements and their contents are identical in the following document, the document is not valid because the sequence doesn't match the defined order:

```
<customer>
   <name>Lea Ziegler</name>
   <email>LZiegler@tempmail.net</email>
   <phone>(813) 555-8931</phone>
</customer>
```

Specifying an Element Choice

Rather than defining a sequence of child elements, the element declaration can define a **choice** of possible elements. The syntax used to specify an element choice is

```
<!ELEMENT element (child1 | child2 | ...)>
```

where *child1*, *child2*, etc., are the possible child elements of the parent. For example, the following declaration allows the customer element to contain either the name or the company element:

```
<!ELEMENT customer (name | company)>
```

With this declaration, either of the following documents is valid:

```
<customer>
   <name>Lea Ziegler</name>
</customer>
```

or

```
<customer>
   <company>VTech Productions</company>
</customer>
```

However, under this declaration, a document cannot include both the name and company elements because the choice model allows only one of the child elements listed.

An element declaration can combine both a sequence and a choice of child elements. For example, the following declaration limits the customer element to three child elements, the first of which is either the name or the company element, followed by the phone, and then the email element:

```
<!ELEMENT customer ((name | company), phone, email)>
```

Under this declaration, either of the following sample documents is valid:

```
<customer>
   <name>Lea Ziegler</name>
   <phone>(813) 555-8931</phone>
   <email>LZiegler@tempmail.net</email>
</customer>
```

or

```
<customer>
   <company>VTech Productions</company>
   <phone>(813) 555-8931</phone>
   <email>LZiegler@tempmail.net</email>
</customer>
```

However, a customer element that does not start with either a name element or a company element followed by the phone and email elements would be invalid.

Specifying Child Elements

- To declare the order of child elements, use the declaration
    ```
    <!ELEMENT element (child1, child2, ...)>
    ```
  where *child1*, *child2*, ... is the order in which the child elements must appear within the parent element.
- To allow for a choice of child elements, use the declaration
    ```
    <!ELEMENT element (child1 | child2 | ...)>
    ```
  where *child1*, *child2*, ... are the possible children of the parent element.

Modifying Symbols

So far, all the content models you have seen assume that each child element occurs once within its parent. If you need to specify duplicates of the same element, you could repeat the element name in the list. For example, the following element declaration indicates that the customer element must contain two phone elements:

```
<!ELEMENT customer (phone, phone)>
```

However, rarely will you specify the exact number of duplicate elements. Instead, DTDs use more general numbering with a **modifying symbol** that specifies the number of occurrences of each element. The three modifying symbols are the question mark (?), the plus sign (+), and the asterisk (*). These are the same modifying symbols you saw when creating a tree diagram for an XML document. As before, the ? symbol indicates that an element occurs zero times or one time, the + symbol indicates that an element occurs at least once, and the * symbol indicates that an element occurs zero times or more. There are no other modifying symbols. If you want to specify an exact number of child elements, such as the two phone elements discussed above, you must repeat the element names that number of times.

In the orders.xml document, the customers element must contain at least one element named customer. The element declaration for this is:

```
<!ELEMENT customers (customer+)>
```

A modifying symbol is placed directly after the element it modifies. You can also include modifying symbols in element sequences. For example, in Samantha's document, each customer element contains the name, address, phone, and email elements, but the email element is optional, occurring either zero times or one time. The element declaration for this is:

```
<!ELEMENT customer (name, address, phone, email?)>
```

The three modifying symbols can also modify entire element sequences or choices. You do this by placing the character immediately following the closing parenthesis of the sequence or choice. When applied to a sequence, the modifying symbol is used to repeat the sequence. For example, the declaration

```
<!ELEMENT order (orderDate, items)+>
```

indicates that the child element sequence (orderDate, items) can be repeated one or more times within each order element. Of course, each time the sequence is repeated, the orderDate element must appear first, followed by the items element.

When applied to a choice model, the modifying symbols allow for multiple combinations of each child element. The declaration

```
<!ELEMENT customer (name | company)+>
```

allows any of the following lists of child elements:

```
name
company
name, company
name, name, company
name, company, company, name
```

The only requirement is that the combined total of name and company elements be greater than zero.

Applying Modifying Symbols

- To specify that an element can appear zero times or one time, use
  ```
  item?
  ```
  in the element declaration in the DTD where *item* is an element name, or the list or sequence of elements.
- To specify one or more occurrences of an item, use:
  ```
  item+
  ```
- To specify zero or more occurrences of an item, use:
  ```
  item*
  ```

Now that you have seen how to specify the occurrences of child elements, you can add these declarations to the DTD for Samantha's document. The declarations can be entered in any order, but it's useful to insert the declarations in the order in which the elements appear in the document. You can also insert blank lines between groups of declarations to make the code easier to read.

Tip

DTDs make no provision to specify the exact number of child elements. To specify that an element contains exactly three child elements, enter the sequence *child, child, child* into the declaration.

To declare the child elements:

1. At the top of the list of declarations in the DTD of the orders.xml file, insert the following element declaration to specify that the root customers element must contain at least one customer element:

   ```
   <!ELEMENT customers (customer+)>
   ```

2. Below the customers declaration, insert a blank line and the following declaration to specify that the customer element must contain the name, address, phone, an optional email address, and an orders element:

   ```
   <!ELEMENT customer (name, address, phone, email?, orders)>
   ```

3. Below the declaration for the email element, insert the following declaration to specify that the orders element must contain at least one order:

   ```
   <!ELEMENT orders (order+)>
   ```

4. Below the orders declaration, insert a blank line and the following declaration to specify that each order contains the orderDate element and a list of items that were ordered:

   ```
   <!ELEMENT order (orderDate, items)>
   ```

5. Below the orderDate declaration, insert the following declaration to specify that each items element must contain at least one item, and then insert another blank line:

   ```
   <!ELEMENT items (item+)>
   ```

   Figure 13-7 shows the complete element declaration in the DTD.

Declarations for the child elements ◀ Figure 13-7

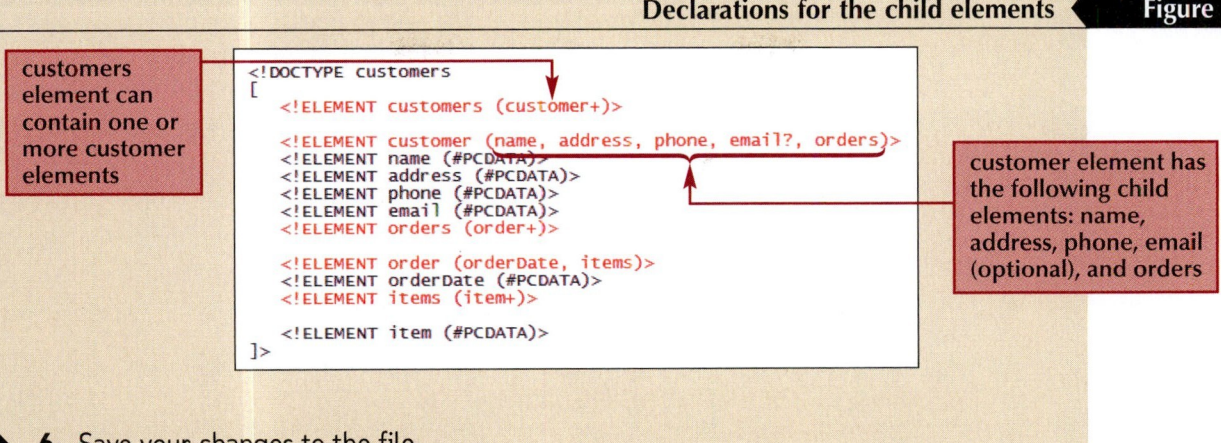

customers element can contain one or more customer elements

```
<!DOCTYPE customers
[
    <!ELEMENT customers (customer+)>

    <!ELEMENT customer (name, address, phone, email?, orders)>
    <!ELEMENT name (#PCDATA)>
    <!ELEMENT address (#PCDATA)>
    <!ELEMENT phone (#PCDATA)>
    <!ELEMENT email (#PCDATA)>
    <!ELEMENT orders (order+)>

    <!ELEMENT order (orderDate, items)>
    <!ELEMENT orderDate (#PCDATA)>
    <!ELEMENT items (item+)>

    <!ELEMENT item (#PCDATA)>
]>
```

customer element has the following child elements: name, address, phone, email (optional), and orders

▶ **6.** Save your changes to the file.

To see how these element declarations represent the structure of the document, compare Figure 13-7 with the tree diagram shown earlier in Figure 13-3.

DTDs and Mixed Content | InSight

An XML element is not constrained to have either parsed character data or child elements; it might have both in what is known as **mixed content**. For example, the title element in the following code contains both the text of the title and a collection of subtitle elements:

```
<title>The Importance of Being Earnest
    <subtitle>A Trivial Comedy for Serious People</subtitle>
    <subtitle>by Oscar Wilde</subtitle>
</title>
```

To declare mixed content in a DTD, you use the following declaration:

```
<!ELEMENT element (#PCDATA | child1 | child2 | ...)*>
```

This declaration applies the * modifying symbol to a choice of parsed character data or child elements. Because the * symbol is used with a choice list, the element can contain any number of occurrences of child elements or text strings of parsed character data, or it can contain no content at all. For example, the declaration

```
<!ELEMENT title (#PCDATA | subtitle)*>
<!ELEMENT subtitle (#PCDATA)>
```

allows the title element to contain any number of text strings of parsed character data interspersed by subtitle elements. The subtitle elements themselves contain only parsed character data.

Although very flexible, elements with mixed content do not add much defined structure to a document. You can specify only the names of the child elements, and you cannot constrain the order in which those child elements appear or control the number of occurrences for each element. An element might contain only text or it might contain any number of child elements in any order. For this reason, it is best not to work with mixed content if you want a tightly structured document (which, after all, is one reason for creating a DTD).

At this point you have defined a structure for the elements in the orders.xml file, but you haven't defined the attributes associated with those elements. You will add attribute declarations in the next session.

1. What code would you enter to connect your document to a DTD stored in the file books.dtd (assume that the name of the root element is Inventory)?
2. What declaration would you enter to allow the book element to contain any content?
3. What declaration would you enter to specify that the video element is empty?
4. What declaration would you enter to indicate that the book element can contain only parsed character data?
5. What declaration would you enter to indicate that the book element contains only a single child element named author?
6. What declaration would you enter to indicate that the book element can contain one or more child elements named author?
7. What declaration would you enter to allow the book element to contain a choice of mixed content, including parsed character data or child elements named author or title?

Session 13.2

Declaring Attributes

In the previous session, you defined the structure of Samantha's document by declaring all the elements in the orders.xml document and indicating what type of content each element could contain. However, for the document to be valid, you must also declare all the attributes associated with those elements. You must indicate whether the attribute is required or optional, and you must indicate what kinds of values are allowed in the attribute. Finally, you can indicate whether the attribute has a default value associated with it. Figure 13-8 describes all the attributes that Samantha intends to use in the orders.xml document along with the properties of each element.

Figure 13-8 | Attributes used in orders.xml

Element	Attributes	Description	Required?	Default Value(s)
customer	custID	Customer ID number	Yes	none
	custType	Customer type	No	"home", "school", or "business"
name	title	Title associated with the customer's name	No	"Mr.", "Mrs.", or "Ms."
Order	orderID	Order ID number	Yes	none
	orderBy	ID of the customer placing the order	Yes	none
item	itemPrice	Item price	Yes	none
	itemQty	Quantity of the item ordered	No	"1"

For example, every customer element must have a custID attribute to record the customer ID value, but it is optional to have a custType attribute to indicate the type of customer placing the order. If the custType attribute is included, it must have a value of "home" or "school" or "business". If a custID attribute is omitted from the customer element or if the value of the custType is not "home" or "school" or "business", the document will be declared invalid.

To enforce these attribution properties, you must add an **attribute-list declaration** to the document's DTD. The attribute-list declaration:

- Lists the names of all the attributes associated with a specific element
- Specifies the data type of each attribute
- Indicates whether each attribute is required or optional
- Provides a default value for each attribute, if necessary

The syntax for declaring a list of attributes is

```
<!ATTLIST element attribute1 type1 default1
                  attribute2 type2 default2
                  attribute3 type3 default3 ... >
```

where *element* is the name of the element associated with the attributes, *attribute* is the name of an attribute, *type* is the attribute's data type, and *default* indicates whether the attribute is required and whether it has a default value. In practice, declarations for elements with multiple attributes are often easier to interpret if the attributes are declared separately rather than in one long declaration. The following is an equivalent form in the DTD:

```
<!ATTLIST element attribute1 type1 default1>
<!ATTLIST element attribute2 type2 default2>
<!ATTLIST element attribute3 type3 default3>
...
```

XML parsers combine the different statements into a single attribute declaration. If a processor encounters more than one declaration for the same attribute, it ignores the second statement. Attribute-list declarations can be located anywhere within the document type declaration, although it is often easiest to work with attribute declarations that are located adjacent to the declaration for the element with which they are associated.

Declaring Attributes in a DTD | Reference Window

- To declare a list of attributes associated with an element, enter the declaration

```
<!ATTLIST element attribute1 type1 default1
                  attribute2 type2 default2
                  attribute3 type3 default3 ...>
```

  or

```
<!ATTLIST element attribute1 type1 default1 >
<!ATTLIST element attribute2 type2 default2 >
<!ATTLIST element attribute3 type3 default3 >
...
```

  where *element* is the element associated with the attributes, *attribute* is the name of an attribute, *type* is the attribute's data type, and *default* indicates whether the attribute is required and whether it has a default value.

As a first step in adding attributes to the DTD for the orders.xml document, you will declare the names of the attributes and the elements they are associated with in the document. (Because you are not yet going to include the data type and default values for the attributes, these attribute declarations are incomplete and would be rejected by any XML parser.)

To declare the attributes in the orders.xml document:

▶ 1. If you took a break after the previous session, make sure the orders.xml file is open in your text editor.

▶ 2. Below the customer declaration, insert the following two declarations to indicate that the customer element contains two attributes named custID and custType:

```
<!ATTLIST customer custID>
<!ATTLIST customer custType>
```

▶ 3. Below the declaration for the name element, insert the following declaration to indicate that the name element contains a title attribute:

```
<!ATTLIST name title>
```

▶ 4. Below the declaration for the order element, insert the following two declarations to indicate that the order element contains two attributes named orderID and orderBy:

```
<!ATTLIST order orderID>
<!ATTLIST order orderBy>
```

Tip

To make your code easier to read, place your attribute lists next to the element declaration in the DTD.

▶ 5. Below the declaration for the item element, insert the following attribute declarations to indicate that the item element contains attributes named itemPrice and itemQty:

```
<!ATTLIST item itemPrice>
<!ATTLIST item itemQty>
```

Figure 13-9 shows the newly inserted text with the list of attributes associated with each element.

Figure 13-9   **Declarations for the attribute names**

```
<!DOCTYPE customers
[
    <!ELEMENT customers (customer+)>

    <!ELEMENT customer (name, address, phone, email?, orders)>
    <!ATTLIST customer custID>
    <!ATTLIST customer custType>

    <!ELEMENT name (#PCDATA)>
    <!ATTLIST name title>

    <!ELEMENT address (#PCDATA)>
    <!ELEMENT phone (#PCDATA)>
    <!ELEMENT email (#PCDATA)>
    <!ELEMENT orders (order+)>

    <!ELEMENT order (orderDate, items)>
    <!ATTLIST order orderID>
    <!ATTLIST order orderBy>

    <!ELEMENT orderDate (#PCDATA)>
    <!ELEMENT items (item+)>

    <!ELEMENT item (#PCDATA)>
    <!ATTLIST item itemPrice>
    <!ATTLIST item itemQty>
]>
```

Working with Attribute Types

The next step in defining these attributes is to specify the type of data each attribute can contain. Attribute values can consist only of character data, but you can control the format of those characters. Figure 13-10 lists the different data types that DTDs support for attribute values. Each data type gives you a varying degree of control over the attribute's content. You will investigate each of these types in greater detail, starting with character data.

Attribute types | Figure 13-10

Attribute Value	Description
CDATA	Character data
enumerated list	A list of possible attribute values
ID	A unique text string
IDREF	A reference to an ID value
IDREFS	A list of ID values separated by white space
ENTITY	A reference to an external unparsed entity
ENTITIES	A list of entities separated by whitespace
NMTOKEN	An accepted XML name
NMTOKENS	A list of XML names separated by whitespace
NOTATION	A name of a notation defined in the DTD

Character Data

Attribute values specified as character data (CDATA) can contain almost any data except those characters reserved by XML for other purposes (such as the <, >, and & characters). To declare an attribute value as character data, you add the CDATA data type to the attribute declaration with the following syntax:

```
<!ATTLIST element attribute CDATA default>
```

For example, the price of each item in Samantha's document is expressed in character data. To indicate this in the DTD, you would add the following CDATA attribute type to the declaration for the itemPrice attribute:

```
<!ATTLIST item itemPrice CDATA default>
```

Any of the following attribute values are allowed under this declaration even though the meaning of the itemPrice value differs from one item to another:

```
<item itemPrice="29.95"> ... </item>
<item itemPrice="$29.95"> ... </item>
<item itemPrice="£29.95"> ... </item>
```

Note that the £ symbol in this example is treated as character data.

In Samantha's document, two attributes contain character data: itemPrice and itemQty. You will add this information to their attribute declarations.

To specify that an attribute contains character data:

▶ **1.** Within the attribute declarations for itemPrice and itemQty in the orders.xml file, insert the type **CDATA** as shown in Figure 13-11.

Character data type added to the attribute declarations | Figure 13-11

```
<!ELEMENT item (#PCDATA)>
<!ATTLIST item itemPrice CDATA>
<!ATTLIST item itemQty CDATA>
]>
```

attribute values are composed of character data

▶ **2.** Save your changes to the file.

Although it might seem strange that values of the itemQty attribute are expressed in character data rather than integers or numbers, this is because no such attribute type exists for DTDs. To indicate that an attribute value must be an integer or a number, you use schemas—a topic you will study in the next tutorial.

Enumerated Types

The CDATA data type allows for almost any string of characters, but in some cases you will want to restrict the attribute to a set of possible values. For example, Samantha uses the custType attribute to indicate whether a customer is making purchases for a school, a business, or home use. She needs to restrict the custType attribute to values of "school", "home", or "business". Attributes that are limited to a set of possible values are known as **enumerated types**. The general form of an attribute declaration that uses an enumerated type is

```
<!ATTLIST element attribute (value1 | value2 | value3 | ...) default >
```

where *value1*, *value2*, etc., are allowed values for the specified attribute. To limit the value of the custType attribute to "school" or "home" or "business", Samantha can include the following enumerated type in the declaration:

```
<!ATTLIST customer custType (school | home | business) default>
```

Under this declaration, any custType attribute whose value is not "school", "home", or "business" causes parsers to reject the document as invalid. Samantha wants you to add this enumerated type to the DTD as well as an enumerated type to specify the enumerated values for the title attribute of the name element.

To declare an enumerated data type:

1. Within the custType attribute declaration, insert the data type **(school | home | business)** to specify the enumerated values for the custType attribute.

2. Within the title attribute declaration for the name element, insert the data type **(Mr. | Mrs. | Ms.)** to specify the enumerated values for the title attribute. Figure 13-12 shows the revised DTD.

Figure 13-12 ▶ **Enumerated attribute values**

```
<!DOCTYPE customers
[
    <!ELEMENT customers (customer+)>

    <!ELEMENT customer (name, address, phone, email?, orders)>
    <!ATTLIST customer custID>
    <!ATTLIST customer custType (school | home | business)>

    <!ELEMENT name (#PCDATA)>
    <!ATTLIST name title (Mr. | Mrs. | Ms.)>
```

values of the title attribute are limited to "Mr.", "Mrs.", or "Ms."

Another type of enumerated attribute is a notation. A **notation** associates the value of an attribute with a <!NOTATION> declaration that is inserted elsewhere in the DTD. Notations are used when an attribute value refers to a file containing nontextual data, such as a graphic image or a video clip. You will learn more about notations and how to work with nontextual data in the next session.

Tokenized Types

Tokenized types are character strings that follow certain specified rules (known as **tokens**) for format and content. DTDs support four kinds of tokens: IDs, ID references, name tokens, and entities.

An **ID token** is used when an attribute value must be unique within the document. In Samantha's document, the customer element contains the custID attribute, storing a unique ID for each customer. To prevent users from entering the same custID value for different customers, Samantha can define the attribute type for the custID attribute as follows:

```
<!ATTLIST customer custID ID default>
```

Under this declaration, the following elements are valid:

```
<customer custID="Cust021"> ... </customer>
<customer custID="Cust022"> ... </customer>
```

However, the following elements would not be valid because the same custID value is used more than once:

```
<customer custID="Cust021"> ... </customer>
<customer custID="Cust021"> ... </customer>
```

After an ID value has been declared in a document, other attribute values can reference it using the IDREF token. An attribute declared as an **IDREF token** must have a value equal to the value of an ID attribute located somewhere in the same document. This enables an XML document to contain cross-references between one element and another. The attribute declaration for an ID reference is:

```
<!ATTLIST element attribute IDREF default>
```

For example, the order element in Samantha's document has an attribute named orderBy, which contains the ID of the customer who placed the order. Because this is an ID reference, Samantha can ensure that the orderBy value refers to an actual customer using the following declaration:

```
<!ATTLIST order orderBy IDREF default>
```

When an XML parser encounters this attribute, it searches the XML document for an ID value that matches the value of the orderBy attribute. If it doesn't find one, the parser rejects the document as invalid. You cannot specify that an XML parser limit its search to only particular elements or attributes. Any attribute that has been declared by the data type ID is a candidate for an ID reference.

Attributes can contain multiple IDs and ID references that are placed in lists, with each entry separated by whitespace. For example, Samantha might list all the orders made by a certain customer as an attribute of the customer element as in the following sample code:

```
<customer orders="OR3413 OR3910 OR5310">

...
   <order orderID="OR3413"> ... </order>
   <order orderID="OR3910"> ... </order>
   <order orderID="OR5310"> ... </order>
...
</customer>
```

Each ID listed in the orders attribute must match an ID value located elsewhere in the document. If it does not, Samantha would want the document to be declared invalid.

To declare that an attribute contains a list of IDs, you apply the following IDS attribute to the attribute declaration:

```
<!ATTLIST element attribute IDS default>
```

To declare that an attribute contains a list of ID references, you use the following IDREFS attribute type:

```
<!ATTLIST element attribute IDREFS default>
```

For the code sample above, to indicate that the orders attribute contains a list of ID references and to indicate the orderID attribute is considered to contain IDs, you would enter the following attribute declarations in the DTD:

```
<!ATTLIST customer orders IDREFS default>
<!ATTLIST order orderID ID default>
```

As with the IDREF token, all of the IDs listed in an IDREFS token must be found in an ID located somewhere in the file, or parsers will reject the document as invalid. However, nothing in the attribute declaration defines in which attributes the referenced ID will be located. So, although the orders attribute defined above must reference an ID value, it is not forced to find that ID value only in the order attribute.

In Samantha's document, the custID and orderID attributes contain ID values, while the orderBy attribute contains a reference to the customer ID. Samantha wants you to declare the custID and orderID attributes as ID data types and the orderBy attribute as belonging to the IDREF data type.

To declare attributes as IDs and ID references:

1. Within the custID and orderID attribute declarations, insert the data type **ID** to ensure that each custID value in the document is unique.

2. Within the orderBy attribute declaration, insert the data type **IDREF** to ensure that each orderBy value references an ID value somewhere in the document. See Figure 13-13.

Figure 13-13 ▶ Attribute IDs and IDREFs

```
<!DOCTYPE customers
[
    <!ELEMENT customers (customer+)>

    <!ELEMENT customer (name, address, phone, email?, orders)>
    <!ATTLIST customer custID ID>                              ◄── each custID value
    <!ATTLIST customer custType (school | home | business)>        must be unique in
                                                                   the document
    <!ELEMENT name (#PCDATA)>
    <!ATTLIST name title (Mr. | Mrs. | Ms.)>

    <!ELEMENT address (#PCDATA)>
    <!ELEMENT phone (#PCDATA)>
    <!ELEMENT email (#PCDATA)>
    <!ELEMENT orders (order+)>

    <!ELEMENT order (orderDate, items)>
    <!ATTLIST order orderID ID>                                    each orderBy
    <!ATTLIST order orderBy IDREF>  ◄──                            value must
                                                                   reference an ID
    <!ELEMENT orderDate (#PCDATA)>                                 value somewhere
    <!ELEMENT items (item+)>                                       in the document

    <!ELEMENT item (#PCDATA)>
    <!ATTLIST item itemPrice CDATA>
    <!ATTLIST item itemQty CDATA>
]>
```

The **NMTOKEN (name token)** data type is used with character data whose values must be valid XML names. This means that NMTOKEN data types can contain letters, numbers, and the symbols underscore (_), hyphen (-), period (.), and colon (:), but not whitespace characters such as blank spaces or line returns. This constraint makes name tokens less flexible than character data, which can contain whitespace characters. If Samantha wants to make sure that an attribute value is always a valid XML name, she can use the NMTOKEN type instead of the CDATA type. When an attribute contains more than one name token, you define the attribute using the **NMTOKENS** data type and separate each name token in the list with a blank space.

Declaring Attribute Types | Reference Window

- To indicate that an attribute contains character data, use
  ```
  attribute CDATA
  ```
  where *attribute* is the name of the attribute.
- To constrain an attribute value to a list of possible values, use
  ```
  attribute (value1 | value2 | value3 | ...)
  ```
  where *value1*, *value2*, etc., are allowed values for the attribute.
- To indicate that an attribute contains ID values, use the following declaration:
  ```
  attribute ID
  ```
- To indicate that an attribute contains a whitespace-separated list of ID values, use the following declaration:
  ```
  attribute IDS
  ```
- To indicate that an attribute contains a reference to an ID value, use the following declaration:
  ```
  attribute IDREF
  ```
- To indicate that an attribute contains a whitespace-separated list of references to ID values, use the following declaration:
  ```
  attribute IDREFS
  ```
- To constrain an attribute to an XML name containing only letters, numbers, and the punctuation symbols underscore (_), hyphen (-), period (.), and colon (:), but no whitespace, use the following declaration:
  ```
  attribute NMTOKEN
  ```
- To constrain an attribute to a whitespace-separated list of XML names, use the following declaration:
  ```
  attribute NMTOKENS
  ```

Working with Attribute Defaults

The final part of an attribute declaration is the attribute default, which defines whether an attribute value is required, optional, assigned a default value, or fixed to a specified value. Figure 13-14 shows the entry in the attribute declaration for each of these four possibilities.

Figure 13-14 ▶ Attribute defaults

Attribute Default	Description
#REQUIRED	The attribute must appear with every occurrence of the element.
#IMPLIED	The attribute is optional.
"default"	The attribute is optional. If an attribute value is not specified, a validating XML parser will supply the default value.
#FIXED "default"	The attribute is optional. If an attribute value is specified, it must match the default value.

Figure 13-8 showed how Samantha outlined the properties for the attributes in the orders.xml document. Based on this outline, a customer ID value is required for every customer. To indicate this in the DTD, you add the #REQUIRED value to the attribute declaration, as follows:

```
<!ATTLIST customer custID ID #REQUIRED>
```

On the other hand, Samantha does not always record whether a customer represents a school, home, or business, so you add the #IMPLIED value to the custType attribute to indicate that this attribute is optional. The following shows the complete attribute declaration for the custType attribute:

```
<!ATTLIST customer custType (school | home | business) #IMPLIED>
```

If an XML parser encounters a customer element without a custType attribute, it doesn't invalidate the document, but instead assumes a blank value for the attribute.

Another attribute from Samantha's document is the itemQty attribute, which indicates the quantity of each item on the order. The itemQty attribute is optional; but unlike the custType attribute, which gets a blank value if omitted, Samantha wants XML parsers to assume a value of "1" if no value has been specified for the itemQty value. The complete attribute declaration for the itemQty attribute is:

```
<!ATTLIST item itemQty CDATA "1">
```

The last type of attribute default is #FIXED default, which fixes the attribute to a specified default value. If you omit the attribute from the element, an XML parser supplies the default value. If you include the attribute, the attribute value must be equal to default or the document is invalid.

Now that you've seen how to work with attribute defaults, you can complete the attribute declarations by adding the default specifications.

To specify attribute defaults in the orders.xml document:

1. Add **#REQUIRED** to the custID, orderID, orderBy, and itemPrice attribute declarations to indicate that these are required attributes.

2. Add **#IMPLIED** to the custType and title attributes to indicate that these are optional attributes.

3. Add **"1"** to the itemQty attribute to indicate that this is the default value of the attribute if no attribute value is entered in the document. Figure 13-15 shows the final form of all of the attribute declarations in the DTD.

```
<!DOCTYPE customers
[
   <!ELEMENT customers (customer+)>

   <!ELEMENT customer (name, address, phone, email?, orders)>
   <!ATTLIST customer custID ID #REQUIRED>
   <!ATTLIST customer custType (school | home | business) #IMPLIED>

   <!ELEMENT name (#PCDATA)>
   <!ATTLIST name title (Mr. | Mrs. | Ms.) #IMPLIED>

   <!ELEMENT address (#PCDATA)>
   <!ELEMENT phone (#PCDATA)>
   <!ELEMENT email (#PCDATA)>
   <!ELEMENT orders (order+)>

   <!ELEMENT order (orderDate, items)>
   <!ATTLIST order orderID ID #REQUIRED>
   <!ATTLIST order orderBy IDREF #REQUIRED>

   <!ELEMENT orderDate (#PCDATA)>
   <!ELEMENT items (item+)>

   <!ELEMENT item (#PCDATA)>
   <!ATTLIST item itemPrice CDATA #REQUIRED>
   <!ATTLIST item itemQty CDATA "1">
]>
```

#IMPLIED indicates that the attribute is optional and may be omitted from the element

#REQUIRED indicates that the attribute must always be included with the element

▶ **4.** Save your changes to the file.

Specifying the Attribute Default | Reference Window

- Within an attribute declaration, insert one of the following attribute defaults:

  `#REQUIRED`

  for an attribute that must appear with every occurrence of the element;

  `#IMPLIED`

  for an optional attribute;

  `"default"`

  for an optional attribute that has a *default* value when omitted; or

  `#FIXED "default"`

  for an optional attribute that must be fixed to the *default* value.

Validating an XML Document

You are ready to test whether the orders.xml document is valid under the rules Samantha has specified. To test for validity, an XML parser must be able to compare the XML document with the rules established in the DTD. The Web has many excellent sources for validating parsers, including Web sites in which you can upload an XML document for free to have it validated against an internal or external DTD.

The Internet Explorer browser version 6.0 and above has its own built-in XML parser, MSXML. However, the validation commands of the MSXML parser are only accessible to the programmer, not to the general user of the browser. This tutorial provides a Web page that was created for you to validate XML documents using the MSXML parser. You will use this Web page to validate Samantha's orders.xml document.

To validate the orders.xml file:

▶ 1. Use your Internet Explorer for Windows browser to open the **validate_dtd.htm** file from the tutorial.13/demo folder included with your Data Files.

Trouble? If you don't have access to the Internet Explorer for Windows browser, talk to your instructor or technical resource person about getting access to a different XML parser to validate your documents, or search the Web for online or free XML parsers and validators.

Trouble? If Internet Explorer displays a yellow bar blocking the operation of validator, click the yellow bar to activate it.

▶ 2. On the Web page, click the **Browse** button. The Choose File dialog box opens.

▶ 3. Navigate to the **tutorial.13/tutorial** folder, click the **orders.xml** file, and then click the **Open** button. The reference to the selected file appears in the Web page.

▶ 4. On the Web page, click the **Validate** button. As shown in Figure 13-16, the Web page reports that the orders.xml file has no validation errors, followed by a file listing of the orders.xml contents.

| Figure 13-16 | ▶ Internet Explorer validation Web page |

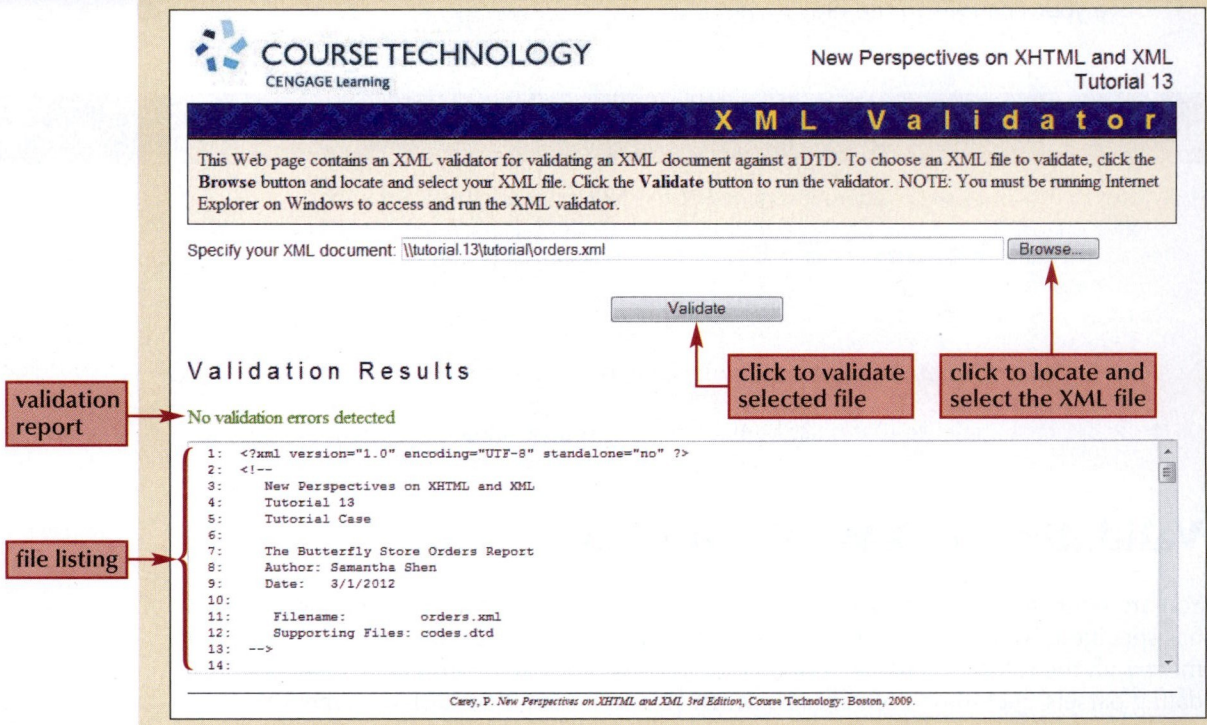

Trouble? If Internet Explorer warns you of a potential security risk, click the Yes button to continue.

Trouble? If a validation error is reported by the Web page, there is an error in the DTD code. Return to the orders.xml file in your text editor and check your DTD code against the code shown in Figure 13-15. Your code should match exactly, including the use of uppercase and lowercase letters. Fix any discrepancies, and then repeat this set of steps to re-validate the document.

Although the file is valid, it is a good learning experience to place a few intentional errors into your XML code to see how validation errors are discovered and reported. You will add the following errors to your document:

- The inclusion of an element not listed in the DTD
- The inclusion of an attribute not listed in the DTD
- An attribute declared as an ID reference that does not reference any ID value in the document

Each of these errors should cause the document to be rejected by the XML parser as invalid.

To add intentional errors to the orders.xml file:

1. Return to the **orders.xml** file in your text editor.

2. Scroll down to the first customer, David Lynn, and then, directly below the phone element, add the following new fax element, which the XML parser will flag as an error because the element has not been declared in the DTD:

   ```
   <fax>(603) 555-1814</fax>
   ```

3. Scroll down to the first order element with the orderID or1031, and then add the following new attribute, which the XML parser will flag as an error because the attribute has not been declared in the DTD:

   ```
   recvdBy="Dawn Young"
   ```

4. Change the value of the orderBy attribute for this order from cust201 to **cust210**. Because no ID attribute entered into this document has the value cust210, the XML parser will flag this as an error. Figure 13-17 highlights the new and revised code in the document.

Intentional errors added to the orders.xml file | **Figure 13-17**

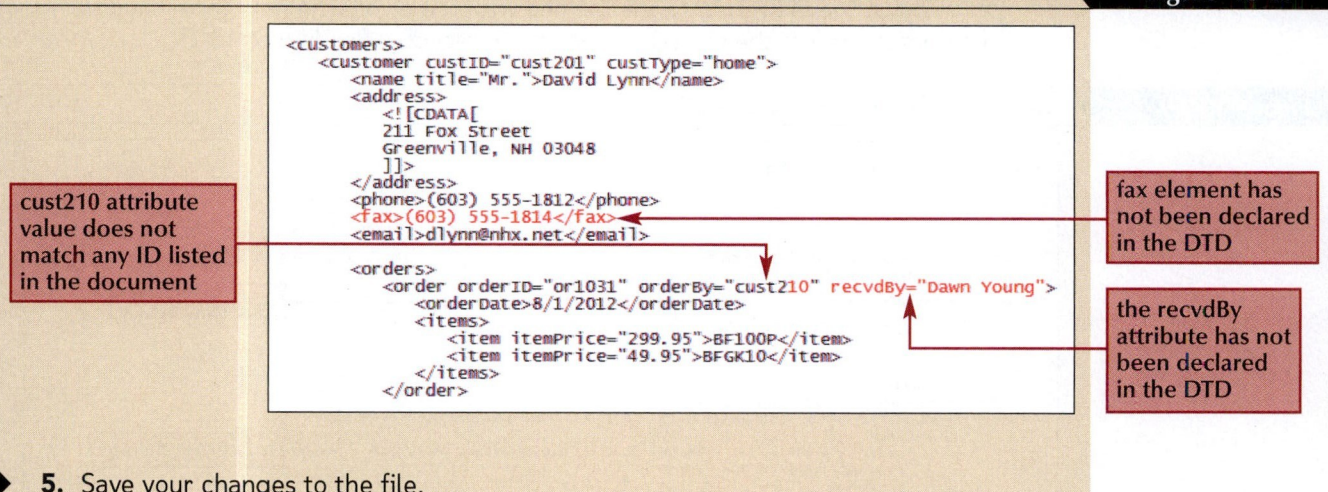

cust210 attribute value does not match any ID listed in the document

fax element has not been declared in the DTD

the recvdBy attribute has not been declared in the DTD

5. Save your changes to the file.

You will again validate the orders.xml file to test whether these three errors are caught and reported by the XML parser. Because of how the MSXML parser built into the IE browser operates, only the first error the parser catches is listed. After the parser finds an error, it stops loading the XML document, preventing it from finding subsequent errors.

To validate the revised orders.xml file:

▶ 1. Return to the **validate_dtd.htm** file in your Internet Explorer browser.

▶ 2. On the Web page, click the **Validate** button. The parser reports an error with the fax element. The parser is expecting a child element named email or orders. Because fax was not listed as a child element in the DTD, the orders.xml file is rejected.

▶ 3. Scroll down the file listing to see the line with the error highlighted in the listing of the orders.xml contents. See Figure 13-18.

Figure 13-18	Validation error due to an invalid element

Validation Results

Validation Failed

Validation error reported at: Line 53 at Character 12
    <fax>(603) 555-1814</fax>
Reason: Element content is invalid according to the DTD/Schema.   ◄── reason for error
Expecting: email, orders.

```
47:           <![CDATA[
48:           211 Fox Street
49:           Greenville, NH 03048
50:           ]]>
51:        </address>
52:        <phone>(603) 555-1812</phone>
**53**     <fax>(603) 555-1814</fax>    ◄── location of error
54:        <email>dlynn@nhx.net</email>
55:
56:        <orders>
57:           <order orderID="or1031" orderBy="cust210" recvdBy="Dawn Young">
58:              <orderDate>8/1/2012</orderDate>
59:              <items>
60:                 <item itemPrice="299.95">BF100P</item>
```

▶ 4. Return to the **orders.xml** file in your text editor, remove the fax element that you entered in the previous set of steps, and then save your changes to the file.

▶ 5. Return to the **validate_dtd.htm** Web page, click the **Validate** button, and then scroll down the file listing to see the line with the error. The next error caught by the parser involves the undeclared attribute recvdBy. See Figure 13-19.

Figure 13-19	Validation error due to an invalid attribute

Validation Results

Validation Failed

Validation error reported at: Line 55 at Character 73
    <order orderID="or1031" orderBy="cust210" recvdBy="Dawn Young">
Reason: The attribute 'recvdBy' on this element is not defined in the DTD/Schema.   ◄── reason for error

```
48:           211 Fox Street
49:           Greenville, NH 03048
50:           ]]>
51:        </address>
52:        <phone>(603) 555-1812</phone>
53:        <email>dlynn@nhx.net</email>
54:        <orders>
**55**        <order orderID="or1031" orderBy="cust210" recvdBy="Dawn Young">    ◄── location of error
56:              <orderDate>8/1/2012</orderDate>
57:              <items>
58:                 <item itemPrice="299.95">BF100P</item>
59:                 <item itemPrice="49.95">BFGK10</item>
60:              </items>
61:           </order>
```

▶ 6. Return to the **orders.xml** file in your text editor, remove the recvdBy attribute and its attribute value from the first order element, and then save your changes to the file.

▶ **7.** Return to the **validate_dtd.htm** Web page, click the **Validate** button, and then scroll down the file listing to see the line with the error. The parser finds the last error in the document, the one in which the cust210 value does not reference any ID value found in the document. See Figure 13-20.

Validation error due to a missing ID value   **Figure 13-20**

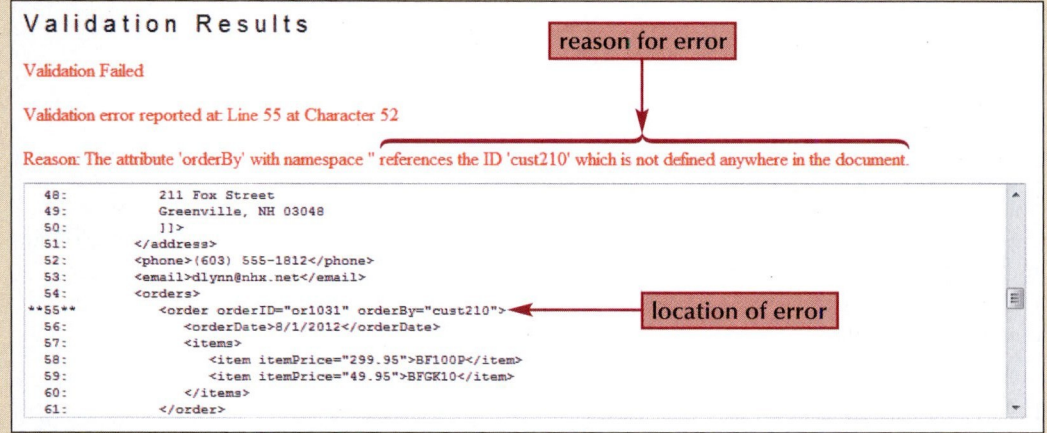

```
Validation Results

Validation Failed

Validation error reported at: Line 55 at Character 52

Reason: The attribute 'orderBy' with namespace '' references the ID 'cust210' which is not defined anywhere in the document.

48:          211 Fox Street
49:          Greenville, NH 03048
50:        ]]>
51:      </address>
52:      <phone>(603) 555-1812</phone>
53:      <email>dlynn@nhx.net</email>
54:      <orders>
**55**        <order orderID="or1031" orderBy="cust210">
56:            <orderDate>8/1/2012</orderDate>
57:            <items>
58:               <item itemPrice="299.95">BF100P</item>
59:                <item itemPrice="49.95">BFGK10</item>
60:            </items>
61:        </order>
```

reason for error

location of error

▶ **8.** Return to the **orders.xml** file in your text editor, change the orderBy attribute value for the first order element from cust210 back to **cust201**, and then save your changes to the file.

▶ **9.** Return to the **validate_dtd.htm** Web page, click the **Validate** button, and then verify that the parser reports no errors in the orders.xml file.

InSight	**Reconciling DTDs and Namespaces**

One drawback with DTDs is that they are not namespace-aware, so you cannot create a set of validation rules for elements and attributes belonging to a particular namespace. To get around this limitation, you can work with namespace prefixes, applying a validation rule to the element's qualified name. For example, if the phone element is placed in the customers namespace using the cu namespace prefix

```
<cu:phone>(315) 555-1812</cu:phone>
```

then the element declaration in the DTD would need to include the same element name qualification:

```
<!ELEMENT cu:phone (#PCDATA)>
```

In essence, the DTD treats a qualified name as the complete element name including the namespace prefix, colon, and local name. It doesn't recognize the namespace prefix as significant. Any namespace declarations in a document must also be included in the DTD for the document to be valid. This is usually done using a fixed datatype for the namespace's URI. For example, if the root element in a document declares the customers namespace using the attribute value

```
<cu:customers xmlns:cu="http://www.butterfly.com/customers">
```

then the DTD should include the following attribute declaration:

```
<!ATTLIST cu:customers xmlns:cu CDATA #FIXED
"http://www.butterfly.com/customers">
```

The drawback to mixing namespaces and DTDs is that you must know the namespace prefix used in an XML document, and the DTD must be written to conform to that namespace. This makes it difficult to perform validation on a wide variety of documents that might employ any number of possible namespace prefixes. In addition, there is no way of knowing what namespace a prefix in the DTD points to because DTDs do not include a mechanism for matching a prefix to a namespace URI. It is also difficult to validate a compound document using standard vocabularies such as XHTML because you cannot easily modify the standard DTDs to accommodate the namespaces in your document.

If you need to validate compound documents that employ several namespaces, a better solution is to use schemas, which is a validation tool that does support namespaces.

In this session, you defined the content and structure of Samantha's document in a DTD. In the next session, you will work with entities and nontextual content in the DTD and learn about the DTDs associated with some of the standard XML vocabularies.

Review	**Session 13.2 Quick Check**

1. What attribute declaration creates an optional text string for the title attribute within the book element?
2. A play element has a required attribute named type, which can have one of four possible values: Romance, Tragedy, History, and Comedy. Enter the appropriate attribute declaration in the play element.
3. What is the main difference between an attribute with the CDATA type and one with the NMTOKEN type?
4. A book element has a required ID attribute named ISBN. Enter the appropriate attribute declaration in the book element.
5. An author element has an optional attribute named booksBy, which contains a whitespace-separated list of ISBNs for the books the author has written. If ISBN is an ID attribute for another element in the document, what declaration would you use for the booksBy attribute?

6. A book element has an optional attribute named inStock that can have the value yes or no. The default value is yes. What is the declaration for the inStock attribute?

Session 13.3

Introducing Entities

In the orders.xml document, Samantha inserted product codes for the different items ordered by customers. For example, the first customer in the file, Mr. David Lynn, ordered four items with the product codes BF100P, BFGK10, MWT15, and MBL25. Each of these product codes is associated with a longer text description of the product. Figure 13-21 shows the product codes and descriptions for all of the items in the orders.xml file.

Tip

For a long text string that will be repeated throughout an XML document, avoid data entry errors by placing the text string in its own entity.

Product codes and descriptions — **Figure 13-21**

Product Code	Description
BF100P	Butterfly farm pop-up self-erecting portable greenhouse
BFGK10	Field of Dreams backyard butterfly garden kit
HME100	Hummingbird Hawkmoth (Manduca Sexta), 100 eggs
MBL25	Monarch Butterfly, 6-12 larvae
MP12	Monarch Pupae (Danaus Plexippus), 12 pupae
MWT15	Giant Milkweed Tree (Calotropis Ssp.), 1 crown flower
PLBK70	Painted Lady classroom breeding kit, 70 larvae

Samantha wants some way to reference the longer text descriptions of these items without having to enter the descriptions into each order in her document. You can do this with entities. You have already worked with entities to insert special character strings into an XML document. XML supports the following five built-in entities:

- **&** for the & character
- **<** for the < character
- **>** for the > character
- **'** for the ' character
- **"** for the " character

When an XML parser encounters these entities, it can display the corresponding character symbol. With a DTD, you can create a customized set of entities corresponding to text strings such as Samantha's product descriptions, files, or nontextual content that you want referenced by the XML document. When the XML parser encounters one of your customized entities, it will also be able to display the corresponding character text.

Working with General Entities

To create a customized entity, you add an entity to the document's DTD. Entities are classified based on where the entity will be applied, where the entity's content is located, and finally what type of content is referenced by the entity. Entities that are used within the XML document are known as **general entities**. Another type of entity, a parameter entity, is used within a DTD. You will learn about parameter entities later in this session.

Entities can reference content found either within an external file or within the DTD itself. An entity that references content found in an external file is called an **external entity**, whereas an entity whose content is found within the DTD is known as an **internal entity**.

Finally, the content referenced by the entity can be either parsed or unparsed. A **parsed entity** references text that can be readily interpreted or parsed by an application reading the XML document. Parsed entities can reference characters, words, phrases, paragraphs, or entire documents. The only requirement is that the text be well formed. An entity that references content that either is nontextual or cannot be interpreted by the XML parser is an **unparsed entity**. One example of an unparsed entity is an entity that references a graphic image file.

Each class of entity is declared slightly differently in the DTD. You'll start by creating a parsed entity for character data located in the XML document.

Creating Parsed Entities

To create an internal parsed entity, you add the entity declaration

```
<!ENTITY entity "value">
```

to the DTD, where *entity* is the name you assigned to the entity and *value* is the text string associated with the entity. The entity name follows the same rules that apply to all XML names: The name can have no blank spaces and must begin with either a letter or an underscore. The entity value itself must be well-formed XML text. This can be a simple text string or it can be well-formed XML code. For example, to store the product description for the product with the item code MBL25, you would add the following entity to the document's DTD:

```
<!ENTITY MBL25 "Monarch Butterfly, 6-12 larvae">
```

You can add markup tags to any entity declaration by including them in the entity value, as follows:

```
<!ENTITY MBL25 "<desc>Monarch Butterfly, 6-12 larvae</desc>">
```

Any text is allowed for an entity's value, as long as it corresponds to well-formed XML. The entity declaration

```
<!ENTITY MBL25 "<desc>Monarch Butterfly, 6-12 larvae">
```

would result in an invalid document when the entity is processed by the XML parser because it lacks the closing </desc> tag in the entity's value. Entity values must be well formed within themselves without reference to other entities or document content. You couldn't, for example, place the closing </desc> tag in another entity declaration or within the XML document itself.

For longer text strings that would not easily fit within the value of an entity declaration, you can place the content in an external file. To create a parsed entity that references content from an external file, you use the declaration

```
<!ENTITY entity SYSTEM "uri">
```

where *entity* is again the entity's name and *uri* is the URI of the external file containing the entity's content. The following entity declaration references the content of the description.xml file:

```
<!ENTITY MBL25 SYSTEM "description.xml">
```

The description.xml file must contain well-formed XML content. However, it should not contain an xml declaration. Because XML documents can contain only one xml declaration, placing a second one in a document via an external entity results in an error.

An external entity can also reference a public location using the declaration

```
<!ENTITY entity PUBLIC "id" "uri">
```

where *id* is the public identifier and *uri* is the system location of the external file (included in case the XML parser doesn't recognize the public identifier). A public location for an external entity might look like the following:

```
<!ENTITY MBL25 PUBLIC "-//BFS//MBL25 INFO" "description.xml">
```

In this case, the public identifier "-//BFS//MBL25 INFO" is used by an XML parser to load the external content corresponding to the MBL25 entity. If that ID is not recognized, the parser falls back to the system location of the description.xml file. In this way, external entities behave like DOCTYPEs that reference external DTDs from either public or system locations.

Declaring General Parsed Entities | Reference Window

- To declare a parsed internal entity, use the declaration
  ```
  <!ENTITY entity "value">
  ```
  where *entity* is the entity's name and *value* is the entity's value.
- To declare a parsed external entity from a system location, use the declaration
  ```
  <!ENTITY entity SYSTEM "uri">
  ```
  where *uri* is the URI of the external file containing the entity value.
- To declare a parsed external entity from a public location, use the declaration
  ```
  <!ENTITY entity PUBLIC "id" "uri">
  ```
  where *id* is the public identifier for the external file.

Referencing a General Entity

After a general entity has been declared in a DTD, it can be referenced anywhere within the body of the XML document. The syntax for referencing a general entity is the same as referencing one of the five built-in XML entities, namely

```
&entity;
```

where *entity* is the entity's name as declared in the DTD. For example, if the MBL25 entity is declared in the DTD as

```
<!ENTITY MBL25 "Monarch Butterfly, 6-12 larvae">
```

you can reference the entity's value in the XML document with

```
<item>&MBL25;</item>
```

and any XML parser encountering this entity reference will be able to expand the entity into its referenced value, namely:

```
<item>Monarch Butterfly, 6-12 larvae</item>
```

The fact that the entity's value is expanded into the code of the XML document is one reason why entity values must correspond to well-formed XML code. Because of the way entities are parsed, you cannot include the & symbol as part of an entity's value. XML parsers interpret the & symbol as a reference to another entity and attempt to resolve the reference. If you need to include the & symbol, you should use the built-in entity reference &. You also cannot use the % symbol in an entity's value because, as you'll learn later in this session, this is the symbol used for inserting parameter entities.

Reference Window | **Referencing a General Entity**

- To reference a general entity within an XML document, enter
  `&entity;`
  where *entity* is the entity name declared in the DTD associated with the XML document.

Samantha wants you to declare parsed entities for all the product codes in the orders.xml document. Because these product codes could also be used in the other XML documents she's working on, you will place the declarations in an external DTD file named codes.dtd. This way, Samantha can reuse the entity names without having to reenter the DTD code.

To create the entity declarations in an external DTD file:

1. If you took a break after the previous session, make sure the orders.xml file is open in your text editor.

2. Use your text editor to open the **codestxt.dtd** file from the tutorial.13/tutorial folder, enter **your name** and **the date** in the comment section, and then save the file as **codes.dtd** in the same folder.

3. Add the following entity declarations below the comment section, as shown in Figure 13-22:

   ```
   <!ENTITY BF100P "Butterfly farm pop-up self-erecting portable
   greenhouse">
   <!ENTITY BFGK10 "Field of Dreams backyard butterfly garden kit">
   <!ENTITY HME100 "Hummingbird Hawkmoth (Manduca Sexta), 100 eggs">
   <!ENTITY MBL25 "Monarch Butterfly, 6-12 larvae">
   <!ENTITY MP12 "Monarch Pupae (Danaus Plexippus), 12 pupae">
   <!ENTITY MWT15 "Giant Milkweed Tree (Calotropis Ssp.),
   1 crown flower">
   <!ENTITY PLBK70 "Painted Lady classroom breeding kit, 70 larvae">
   ```

Figure 13-22 | **Creating general entities**

```
<!ENTITY BF100P "Butterfly farm pop-up self-erecting portable greenhouse">
<!ENTITY BFGK10 "Field of Dreams backyard butterfly garden kit">
<!ENTITY HME100 "Hummingbird Hawkmoth (Manduca Sexta), 100 eggs">
<!ENTITY MBL25 "Monarch Butterfly, 6-12 larvae">
<!ENTITY MP12 "Monarch Pupae (Danaus Plexippus), 12 pupae">
<!ENTITY MWT15 "Giant Milkweed Tree (Calotropis Ssp.), 1 crown flower">
<!ENTITY PLBK70 "Painted Lady classroom breeding kit, 70 larvae">
```

4. Save your changes to the file.

Because you placed these entity declarations in an external DTD file, you need some way of linking the orders.xml document to that DTD. One way would be to revise the DOCTYPE to include the codes.dtd file along with the internal declarations you already have created; another option is to use a parameter entity.

Working with Parameter Entities

Just as you use general entities when you want to insert content into an XML document, you use a **parameter entity** when you want to insert content into the DTD itself. With parameter entities, a DTD can be broken into smaller chunks, or **modules**, placed in different files. Imagine a team of programmers working on a DTD for a large XML vocabulary such as XHTML, containing hundreds of elements and attributes. Rather than placing all the declarations within a single file, individual programmers could work on sections suited to their expertise. Parameter entities also enable XML programmers to reuse large blocks of DTD code without retyping the same code multiple times. The declaration to create a parameter entity is similar to the declaration for a general entity, with the syntax

```
<!ENTITY % entity "value">
```

where *entity* is the name of the parameter entity and *value* is the text referenced by the parameter entity. Like general entities, parameter entities can also reference external content in either system or public locations. The declarations for external parameter entities are

```
<!ENTITY % entity SYSTEM "uri">
```

or

```
<!ENTITY % entity PUBLIC "id" "uri">
```

where *uri* is the location of the external file containing DTD content and *id* is a public identifier for the parameter entity. For example, the following code shows an internal parameter entity for a collection of elements and attributes:

```
<!ENTITY % books
    "<!ELEMENT Book (Title, Author)>
     <!ATTLIST Book Pages CDATA #REQUIRED>
     <!ELEMENT Title (#PCDATA)>
     <!ELEMENT Author (#PCDATA)>"
>
```

If you place these elements and attributes in an external DTD file named books.dtd, you could declare the following external parameter entity to access the content of that document:

```
<!ENTITY % books SYSTEM "books.dtd">
```

After a parameter has been declared, you can reference it within the DTD using the statement

```
%entity;
```

where *entity* is the name assigned to the parameter entity. Parameter entity references can be placed only where a declaration would regularly occur, such as within an internal or external DTD. You *cannot* insert a parameter entity reference within the element content of an XML document. For example, to reference the books parameter entity described above, you would enter the following line into the DTD:

```
%books;
```

Figure 13-23 shows how parameter entities can be used to combine DTDs from multiple files into a single (virtual) DTD.

Figure 13-23 ▷ **DTDs combined with parameter entities**

books.dtd

```
<!ELEMENT Book (Title, Author)>
<!ATTLIST Book Pages CDATA #REQUIRED>
<!ELEMENT Title (#PCDATA)>
<!ELEMENT Author (#PCDATA)>
```

magazines.dtd

```
<!ELEMENT Magazine (Name)>
<!ATTLIST Magazine Publisher CDATA #REQUIRED>
<!ELEMENT Name (#PCDATA)>
```

```
<!ENTITY % books SYSTEM "books.dtd">
<!ENTITY % mags SYSTEM "magazines.dtd">

%books;
%mags;
```

```
<!ENTITY % books SYSTEM "books.dtd">
<!ENTITY % mags SYSTEM "magazines.dtd">

<!ELEMENT Book (Title, Author)>
<!ATTLIST Book Pages CDATA #REQUIRED>
<!ELEMENT Title (#PCDATA)>
<!ELEMENT Author (#PCDATA)>
<!ELEMENT Magazine (Name)>
<!ATTLIST Magazine Publisher CDATA #REQUIRED>
<!ELEMENT Name (#PCDATA)>
```

XML parser expands the parameter entity references into the DTD

Reference Window | **Declaring and Referencing a Parameter Entity**

- To declare an internal parameter entity, add the line
    ```
    <!ENTITY % entity "value">
    ```
    to the DTD, where *entity* is the entity's name and *value* is the entity value.
- To declare an external parameter entity for a system location, use
    ```
    <!ENTITY % entity SYSTEM "uri">
    ```
    where *uri* is the URI of the system file.
- To declare an external parameter entity for a public location, use
    ```
    <!ENTITY % entity PUBLIC "id" "uri">
    ```
    where *id* is the public identifier.
- To reference a parameter entity, add the statement
    ```
    %entity;
    ```
    to the DTD, where *entity* is the name of the parameter entity.

Samantha wants you to add a parameter entity to the DTD within the orders.xml file to load the contents of the codes.dtd file you just created. You will name the parameter entity itemCodes.

To insert the itemCodes parameter entity:

▶ 1. Return to the **orders.xml** file in your text editor.

▶ 2. Add the following entity declaration at the bottom of the internal DTD:

```
<!ENTITY % itemCodes SYSTEM "codes.dtd">
```

3. Insert the following reference directly below the parameter entity for the codes.dtd file to add a reference to the parameter entity:

```
%itemCodes;
```

Figure 13-24 shows the completed DTD.

Reference to the codes.dtd file   **Figure 13-24**

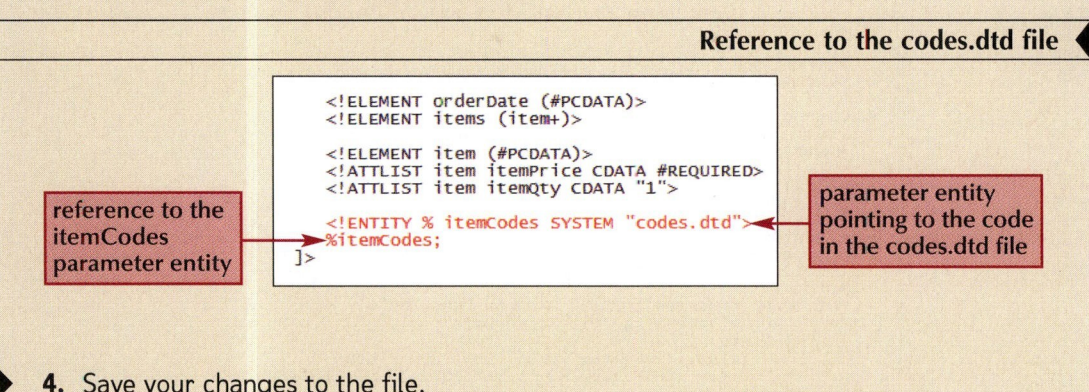

reference to the itemCodes parameter entity

parameter entity pointing to the code in the codes.dtd file

```
<!ELEMENT orderDate (#PCDATA)>
<!ELEMENT items (item+)>

<!ELEMENT item (#PCDATA)>
<!ATTLIST item itemPrice CDATA #REQUIRED>
<!ATTLIST item itemQty CDATA "1">

<!ENTITY % itemCodes SYSTEM "codes.dtd">
%itemCodes;
]>
```

4. Save your changes to the file.

With the parameter entity added to the DTD to access the contents of the codes.dtd file, you can insert entity references in the body of the XML document, replacing Samantha's product codes.

To add entity references:

1. Return to the **orders.xml** file in your text editor.

2. Locate the first product code for the first customer item, and then change BF100P to **&BF100P;** to replace the product code with an entity reference.

3. Locate the second product code and change BFGK10 to **&BFGK10;** to replace the product code with an entity reference. See Figure 13-25.

General entities   **Figure 13-25**

```
<customers>
    <customer custID="cust201" custType="home">
        <name title="Mr.">David Lynn</name>
        <address>
            <![CDATA[
            211 Fox Street
            Greenville, NH 03048
            ]]>
        </address>
        <phone>(603) 555-1812</phone>
        <email>dlynn@nhx.net</email>
        <orders>
            <order orderID="or1031" orderBy="cust201">
                <orderDate>8/1/2012</orderDate>
                <items>
                    <item itemPrice="299.95">&BF100P;</item>
                    <item itemPrice="49.95">&BFGK10;</item>
                </items>
            </order>
```

reference to the BFGK10 general entity

4. Change the five remaining product codes in the document to entity references by inserting an ampersand (&) before the product code and a semicolon (;) after the product code. Figure 13-26 shows the rest of the revised orders.xml file with the modified item values highlighted in red.

Figure 13-26 The orders.xml file with all general entities

```
          <order orderID="or1142" orderBy="cust201">
              <orderDate>9/14/2012</orderDate>
              <items>
                  <item itemPrice="52.23" itemQty="2">&MWT15;</item>
                  <item itemPrice="124.44" itemQty="3">&MBL25;</item>
              </items>
          </order>
      </orders>
  </customer>

  <customer custID="cust202">
      <name title="Mrs.">Jean Kaufmann</name>
      <address>
          <![CDATA[
          411 East Oak Avenue
          Sparta, WI   54656
          ]]>
      </address>
      <phone>(608) 555-4033</phone>
      <email>jk@truedreams.com</email>
      <orders>
          <order orderID="or1089" orderBy="cust202">
              <orderDate>8/11/2012</orderDate>
              <items>
                  <item itemPrice="39.95">&HME100;</item>
                  <item itemPrice="89.95" itemQty="2">&MP12;</item>
              </items>
          </order>
      </orders>
  </customer>

  <customer custID="cust203" custType="school">
      <name>Riverfront High School</name>
      <address>
          <![CDATA[
          55 Washburn Lane
          Monroe, MI   48161
          ]]>
      </address>
      <phone>(811) 555-2987</phone>
      <orders>
          <order orderID="or1120" orderBy="cust203">
              <orderDate>9/15/2012</orderDate>
              <items>
                  <item itemPrice="79.95" itemQty="2">&PLBK70;</item>
              </items>
```

With the entity references added to Samantha's document, you can check whether their values are resolved in your Web browser. At the time of this writing, only Internet Explorer can resolve content placed in external entities and DTDs. The built-in XML parsers in browsers such as Safari and Firefox do not allow for this.

To view the entity values with the Internet Explorer browser:

1. Save your changes to the orders.xml file.

2. Open **orders.xml** in Internet Explorer. As shown in Figure 13-27, when viewed in Internet Explorer's outline format, the values of all seven product codes are displayed.

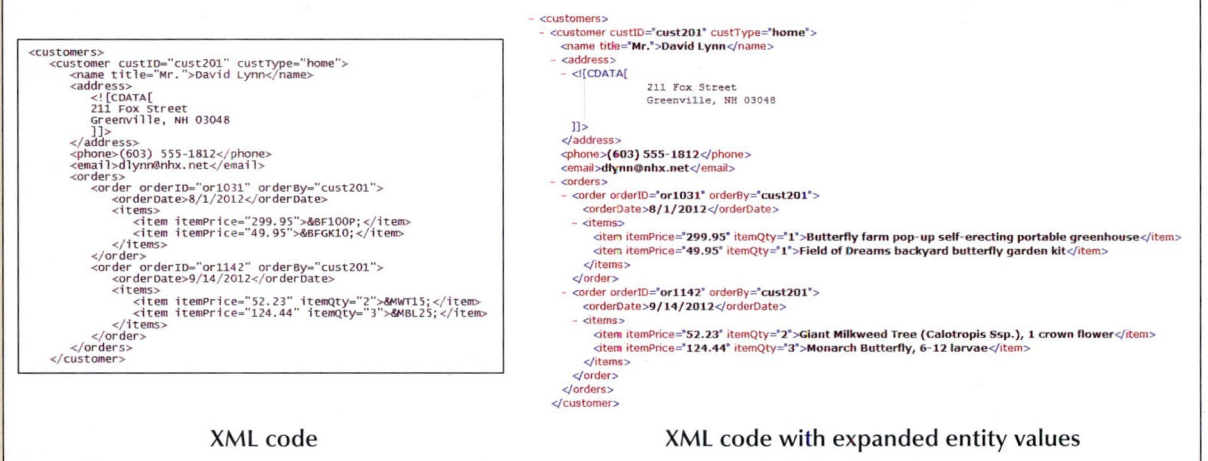

XML code   XML code with expanded entity values

Trouble? If you opened the file with a browser other than Internet Explorer, you may not see the entity values resolved in the rendered page. Firefox and Safari report a parsing error due to an undefined entity. You will fix this problem shortly.

Of the major browsers at the time of this writing, only Internet Explorer for Windows supports the use of external entities in combination with DTDs. In particular, Firefox and other Mozilla browsers use a built-in XML parser called Expat, which does not support resolution of external entities. The reason is that if an entity declaration is placed in a file on a remote Web server, the XML parser has to establish a TCP/IP connection with the remote file, which might not always be possible. Thus, to ensure that an XML document can be properly read and rendered, Expat requires entities to be part of the internal DTD. This situation might be resolved in future releases of these browsers, so Samantha does not want you to completely remove the code you entered. However, to remove the error message within these browsers, you can copy the entity declarations from the codes.dtd file and paste them into the internal DTD.

To copy and paste the general entities:

▶ 1. Return to the **codes.dtd** file in your text editor and copy the seven entity declarations.

▶ 2. Return to the **orders.xml** file in your text editor and paste the entity declarations at the top of the DTD. See Figure 13-28.

Figure 13-28	Entities pasted in the internal DTD

```
<!DOCTYPE customers
[
   <!ENTITY BF100P "Butterfly farm pop-up self-erecting portable greenhouse">
   <!ENTITY BFGK10 "Field of Dreams backyard butterfly garden kit">
   <!ENTITY HME100 "Hummingbird Hawkmoth (Manduca Sexta), 100 eggs">
   <!ENTITY MBL25 "Monarch Butterfly, 6-12 larvae">
   <!ENTITY MP12 "Monarch Pupae (Danaus Plexippus), 12 pupae">
   <!ENTITY MWT15 "Giant Milkweed Tree (Calotropis Ssp.), 1 crown flower">
   <!ENTITY PLBK70 "Painted Lady classroom breeding kit, 70 larvae">

   <!ELEMENT customers (customer+)>

   <!ELEMENT customer (name, address, phone, email?, orders)>
   <!ATTLIST customer custID ID #REQUIRED>
   <!ATTLIST customer custType (school | home | business) #IMPLIED>

   <!ELEMENT name (#PCDATA)>
   <!ATTLIST name title (Mr. | Mrs. | Ms.) #IMPLIED>

   <!ELEMENT address (#PCDATA)>
   <!ELEMENT phone (#PCDATA)>
   <!ELEMENT email (#PCDATA)>
   <!ELEMENT orders (order+)>

   <!ELEMENT order (orderDate, items)>
   <!ATTLIST order orderID ID #REQUIRED>
   <!ATTLIST order orderBy IDREF #REQUIRED>

   <!ELEMENT orderDate (#PCDATA)>
   <!ELEMENT items (item+)>

   <!ELEMENT item (#PCDATA)>
   <!ATTLIST item itemPrice CDATA #REQUIRED>
   <!ATTLIST item itemQty CDATA "1">

   <!ENTITY % itemCodes SYSTEM "codes.dtd">
   %itemCodes;
]>
```

3. Save the orders.xml file, and then open **orders.xml** in the Firefox browser and verify that the browser displays the extended descriptions associated with each product code.

   Trouble? If you are running Safari or Opera as your Web browser, remove the last two lines of the DTD that create and reference the external parameter entities. At the time of this writing, neither of these browsers can resolve such external entities within the DTD.

Inserting Comments into a DTD

Samantha is pleased with your work on creating the DTD for the sample XML document. However, she is concerned that the code in the DTD might be confusing to other programmers. She suggests that you add a few lines of comments. Comments in a DTD follow the same syntax as comments in XML. The specific form of a DTD comment is

```
<!--comment-->
```

where *comment* is the text of the DTD comment. Whitespace is ignored within a comment, so you can spread comment text over several lines without affecting DTD code.

To add comments to the DTD:

1. Return to the **orders.xml** file in your text editor.

2. Above the first general entity (for the BF100P product code), insert the following comment line:

   ```
   <!-- Product code descriptions inserted as general entities -->
   ```

> **3.** Above the first parameter entity linking the DTD to the codes.dtd file, insert the following comment line:
>
> ```
> <!-- codes.dtd contains a list of product codes (IE browser only) -->
> ```
>
> Figure 13-29 shows the final form of the DTD for the orders.xml file.

DTD comments   Figure 13-29

```
<!DOCTYPE customers
[
<!-- Product code descriptions inserted as general entities -->
    <!ENTITY BF100P "Butterfly farm pop-up self-erecting portable greenhouse">
    <!ENTITY BFGK10 "Field of Dreams backyard butterfly garden kit">
    <!ENTITY HME100 "Hummingbird Hawkmoth (Manduca Sexta), 100 eggs">
    <!ENTITY MBL25 "Monarch Butterfly, 6-12 larvae">
    <!ENTITY MP12 "Monarch Pupae (Danaus Plexippus), 12 pupae">
    <!ENTITY MWT15 "Giant Milkweed Tree (Calotropis Ssp.), 1 crown flower">
    <!ENTITY PLBK70 "Painted Lady classroom breeding kit, 70 larvae">

    <!ELEMENT customers (customer+)>

    <!ELEMENT customer (name, address, phone, email?, orders)>
    <!ATTLIST customer custID ID #REQUIRED>
    <!ATTLIST customer custType (school | home | business) #IMPLIED>

    <!ELEMENT name (#PCDATA)>
    <!ATTLIST name title (Mr. | Mrs. | Ms.) #IMPLIED>

    <!ELEMENT address (#PCDATA)>
    <!ELEMENT phone (#PCDATA)>
    <!ELEMENT email (#PCDATA)>
    <!ELEMENT orders (order+)>

    <!ELEMENT order (orderDate, items)>
    <!ATTLIST order orderID ID #REQUIRED>
    <!ATTLIST order orderBy IDREF #REQUIRED>

    <!ELEMENT orderDate (#PCDATA)>
    <!ELEMENT items (item+)>

    <!ELEMENT item (#PCDATA)>
    <!ATTLIST item itemPrice CDATA #REQUIRED>
    <!ATTLIST item itemQty CDATA "1">
<!-- codes.dtd contains a list of product codes (IE browser only) -->
    <!ENTITY % itemCodes SYSTEM "codes.dtd">
    %itemCodes;
]>
```

> **4.** Save your changes to the **orders.xml** file, and then close the file.

Creating Conditional Sections

When you're creating a new DTD, it is useful to try out different combinations of declarations. You can do this by using a **conditional section**, which is a section of the DTD that is processed only in certain situations. The syntax for creating a conditional section is

```
<![keyword[
   declarations
]]>
```

where *keyword* is either INCLUDE (for a section of declarations that you want parsers to interpret) or IGNORE (for the declarations that you want parsers to pass over). For example, the following code creates two sections of declarations—one for Magazine elements and another for Book elements:

```
<![IGNORE[
   <!ELEMENT Magazine (Name)>
   <!ATTLIST Magazine Publisher CDATA #REQUIRED>
   <!ELEMENT Name (#PCDATA)>
]]>
```

```
<![INCLUDE[
  <!ELEMENT Book (Title, Author)>
  <!ATTLIST Book Pages CDATA #REQUIRED>
  <!ELEMENT Title (#PCDATA)>
  <!ELEMENT Author (#PCDATA)>
]]>
```

An XML parser processing this DTD will run the declarations involving the Book element, but will ignore the declarations involving the Magazine element. As you experiment with the DTD's structure, you can enable a section by changing its keyword from IGNORE to INCLUDE.

One effective way of creating IGNORE sections is to create a parameter entity that defines whether those sections should be included, and to use the value of the entity as the keyword for the conditional section. For example, the following UseFullDTD entity has a value of IGNORE, which causes the conditional section that follows it to be ignored by the XML parser:

```
<!ENTITY % UseFullDTD "IGNORE">

<![ %UseFullDTD; [
  <!ELEMENT Magazine (Name)>
  <!ATTLIST Magazine Publisher CDATA #REQUIRED>
  <!ELEMENT Name (#PCDATA)>
]]>
```

By changing the value of UseFullDTD from IGNORE to INCLUDE, you can add any conditional section that uses this entity reference to the document's DTD. This enables you to switch multiple sections in the DTD off and on by editing a single line in the file, which is most useful when several conditional sections are scattered throughout a long DTD. Rather than locating and changing each conditional section, you can switch the sections on and off by changing the parameter entity's value.

Conditional sections can be applied only to external DTDs. Although they may be useful in other contexts, you cannot apply them to the DTD in Samantha's document because it uses only an internal DTD.

Working with Unparsed Data

In this session, you worked with creating entities for character data. For a DTD to validate either binary data, such as images or video clips, or character data that is not well formed, you also need to work with unparsed entities. Because an XML parser cannot work with this type of data directly, a DTD needs to include instructions for how to treat the unparsed entity.

The first step is to declare a notation, which identifies the data type of the unparsed data. A notation must supply a name for the data type and provide clues about how applications should handle the data. Notations must reference external content (because that content must contain nontextual data) and you must specify an external location. One option is to use a system location, which you specify with the code

```
<!NOTATION notation SYSTEM "uri">
```

where *notation* is the notation's name and *uri* is a system location that gives the XML parser clues about how the data should be handled. The other option is to specify a public location, using the declaration

```
<!NOTATION notation PUBLIC "id" "uri">
```

where *id* is a public identifier recognized by XML parsers. The URI for the resource can be either a program that can work with the unparsed data or the actual data type. For example, if Samantha wanted to include references in the orders.xml document to graphic image files stored in the JPEG format, she could enter the following notation in the document's DTD:

```
<!NOTATION jpeg SYSTEM "paint.exe">
```

Because an XML parser doesn't know how to handle graphic data, this notation associates the paint.exe program with the jpeg data type. If you don't want to specify a particular program, you could instead indicate the data type by using the mime-type value with the following notation:

```
<!NOTATION jpeg SYSTEM "image/jpeg">
```

In this case, an XML parser associates the jpeg notation with the image/jpeg data type as long as the operating system already knows how to handle JPEG files. After a notation is declared, you can create an unparsed entity that references specific items that use that notation. The syntax to declare an unparsed entity is

```
<!ENTITY entity SYSTEM "uri" NDATA notation>
```

where *entity* is the name of the entity referencing the notation, *uri* is the URI of the unparsed data, and *notation* is the name of the notation that defines the data type for the XML parser. Again, you can also provide a public location for the unparsed data if an XML parser supports it, using the following form:

```
<!ENTITY entity PUBLIC "id" "uri" NDATA notation>
```

For example, the following declaration creates an unparsed entity named BF100PIMG that references the graphic image file bf100p.jpg:

```
<!ENTITY BF100PIMG SYSTEM "bf100p.jpg" NDATA jpeg>
```

After you create an entity to reference unparsed data, that entity can be associated with attribute values by using the ENTITY data type in the attribute declaration. If Samantha wanted to add an image attribute to every item element in the orders.xml document, she could insert the following attribute declaration in the DTD:

```
<!ATTLIST item image ENTITY #REQUIRED>
```

With this declaration added, Samantha could then add the image attribute to the XML document, using the BF100PIMG entity as the attribute's value, as follows:

```
<item image="BF100PIMG">
```

It's important to understand precisely what this code does and does not accomplish: It tells XML parsers what kind of data is represented by the BF100PIMG entity and it provides clues on how to interpret the data stored in the bf100p.jpg file, but it does not tell parsers anything else. Whether an application reading the XML document opens a device to display the image file depends solely on the program itself. Remember that the purpose of XML is to create structured documents, but not necessarily to tell programs how to render the data in a document. If a validating XML parser reads the <item> tag described above, it probably wouldn't try to read the graphic image file, but it might check to see whether the file is there. By doing so, the parser would confirm that the document is complete in its content and in all its references to unparsed data.

Current Web browsers do not support mechanisms for validating and rendering unparsed data declared in the DTDs of XML documents, so you will not add this feature to the orders.xml file.

> **Tip**
>
> As an alternative to notations, you can place the URL listing the resource for nontextual content in an element or attribute and then allow your application to work with that element or attribute value directly.

Validating Standard Vocabularies

All of your work in this tutorial involved the custom XML vocabulary developed by Samantha for orders submitted to Butterfly Garden. Most of the standard XML vocabularies in popular use have existing DTDs associated with them. To validate a document used with a standard vocabulary, you usually have to access an external DTD located on a Web server or rely upon a DTD built into your XML parser. Figure 13-30 lists the DOCTYPE declarations for some popular XML vocabularies.

Figure 13-30 ▶ DOCTYPE declarations for standard vocabularies

Vocabulary	DOCTYPE
XHTML 1.0 strict	`<!DOCTYPE html PUBLIC "//W3C//DTD XHTML 1.0 Strict//EN" "http://www.w3.org/TR/xhtml1/DTD/xhtml1-strict.dtd">`
XHTML 1.0 transitional	`<!DOCTYPE html PUBLIC "-//W3C//DTD XHTML 1.0 Transitional//EN" "http://www.w3.org/TR/xhtml1/DTD/xhtml1-transitional.dtd">`
XHTML 1.0 frameset	`<!DOCTYPE html PUBLIC "-//W3C//DTD XHTML 1.0 Frameset//EN" "http://www.w3.org/TR/xhtml1/DTD/xhtml1-frameset.dtd">`
XHTML 1.1	`<!DOCTYPE html PUBLIC "-//W3C//DTD XHTML 1.1//EN" "http://www.w3.org/TR/xhtml11/DTD/xhtml11.dtd">`
MathML 1.01	`<!DOCTYPE math SYSTEM "http://www.w3.org/Math/DTD/mathml1/mathml.dtd">`
MathML 2.0	`<!DOCTYPE math PUBLIC "-//W3C//DTD MathML 2.0//EN" "http://www.w3.org/TR/MathML2/dtd/mathml2.dtd">`
SVG 1.1 basic	`<!DOCTYPE svg PUBLIC "-//W3C//DTD SVG 1.1 Basic//EN" "http://www.w3.org/Graphics/SVG/1.1/DTD/svg11-basic.dtd">`
SVG 1.1 full	`<!DOCTYPE svg PUBLIC "-//W3C//DTD SVG 1.1//EN" "http://www.w3.org/Graphics/SVG/1.1/DTD/svg11.dtd">`
SMIL 1.0	`<!DOCTYPE smil PUBLIC "-//W3C//DTD SMIL 1.0//EN" "http://www.w3.org/TR/REC-smil/SMIL10.dtd">`
SMIL 2.0	`<!DOCTYPE SMIL PUBLIC "-//W3C//DTD SMIL 2.0//EN" "http://www.w3.org/TR/REC-smil/2000/SMIL20.dtd">`
VoiceXML 2.1	`<!DOCTYPE vxml PUBLIC "-//W3C//DTD VOICEXML 2.1//EN" "http://www.w3.org/TR/voicexml21/vxml.dtd">`

For example, to validate an XHTML document against the XHTML 1.0 strict standard, you would add the following code to the document header:

```
<?xml version="1.0" encoding="UTF-8" standalone="no" ?>
<!DOCTYPE html PUBLIC "-//W3C//DTD XHTML 1.0 Strict//EN"
   "http://www.w3.org/TR/xhtml1/DTD/xhtml1-strict.dtd">

<html>

</html>
```

The W3C provides an online validator at *http://validator.w3.org* that you can use to validate HTML, XHTML, MathML, and SVG. The validator works with files placed on the Web or uploaded via a Web form.

Most standard vocabularies make their DTDs available online for inspection. Studying the DTDs of other XML vocabularies is a great way to learn how to design your own. Figure 13-31 shows the part of the DTD for XHTML 1.0 that sets the syntax rules for the br (line break) element. The DTD includes substantial use of parameter entities to allow the same set of attributes to be shared among the many elements of XHTML. For example, the coreattrs parameter entity contains a list of core attributes used by most XHTML elements. The StyleSheet and Text parameter entities contain code that sets the data type for style sheets and title attributes. From the DTD, you can quickly see that the four core attributes of XHTML are the id, class, style, and title attributes; and although they are available to almost all elements in the XHTML language, they are not required attributes. The specifications for the br element are fairly simple. Other elements of the XHTML language have more complicated rules, but all are based on the principles discussed in this tutorial.

XHTML 1.0 strict DTD for the br element ◄ Figure 13-31

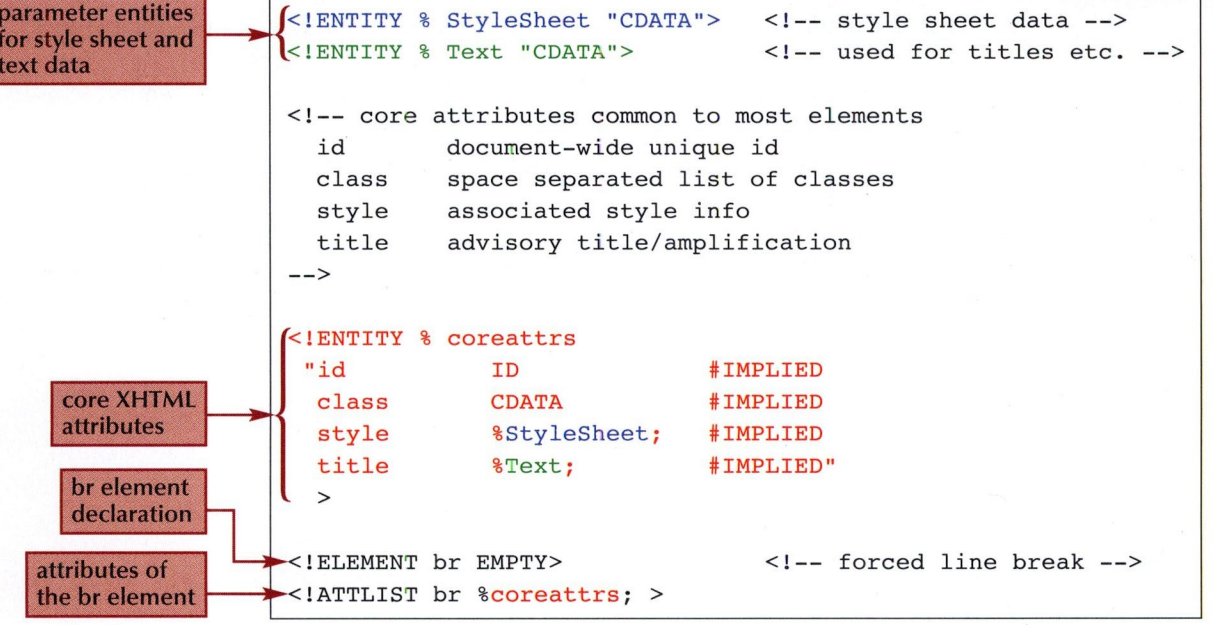

parameter entities for style sheet and text data

core XHTML attributes

br element declaration

attributes of the br element

```
<!ENTITY % StyleSheet "CDATA">    <!-- style sheet data -->
<!ENTITY % Text "CDATA">          <!-- used for titles etc. -->

<!-- core attributes common to most elements
   id          document-wide unique id
   class       space separated list of classes
   style       associated style info
   title       advisory title/amplification
-->

<!ENTITY % coreattrs
  "id          ID              #IMPLIED
   class       CDATA           #IMPLIED
   style       %StyleSheet;    #IMPLIED
   title       %Text;          #IMPLIED"
  >

<!ELEMENT br EMPTY>               <!-- forced line break -->
<!ATTLIST br %coreattrs; >
```

InSight | **Advantages and Disadvantages of DTDs**

DTDs are the common standard for validating XML documents, but they do have some serious limitations. Because a DTD is not written in the XML language, XML parsers must support the syntax and language requirements needed to interpret DTD code. DTDs are also limited in the data types they support. For example, you cannot specify that an element or attribute's value be limited to only integers or text strings entered in a specific format. Nor can you exactly specify the structure of a document other than a general description of the number or choice of child elements. Finally, DTDs do not support namespaces and thus are of limited value in compound documents.

However, DTDs are a recognized and long-supported standard. Therefore, you should have little problem finding parsers and applications to validate your XML documents based on a DTD. DTDs also support entities, providing a mechanism for referencing nontextual content from your XML file.

If the limitations of DTDs are a severe hindrance to validating your XML documents, another standard—schemas—provides support for an extended list of data types and can be easily adapted to compound documents involving several namespaces.

You have completed your work on Samantha's document. She will use the DTD you developed to ensure that any new data added to the orders.xml document conforms to the standards you established.

Review | **Session 13.3 Quick Check**

1. What is the difference between a general entity and a parameter entity?
2. What is the difference between a parsed entity and an unparsed entity?
3. What declaration stores the text string "<Title>Hamlet</Title>" as a general entity named Play? What command references this entity in a document?
4. What declaration stores the contents of the plays.xml file as a general entity named Plays?
5. What code stores the contents of the plays.dtd file as a parameter entity named Works?
6. What is a notation?
7. How do you reference the image file shakespeare.gif in an unparsed entity named Portrait? Assume that this entity is using a notation named GIF.

Tutorial Summary | Review

In this tutorial, you learned how to create well-formed and valid documents using DTDs. The first session reviewed the basic principles of document validation, showing how to declare a document type definition. The session examined two types of DTDs, internal and external, and explained the benefits of each. The rest of the session showed how to set syntax rules for elements, specifying the element content and the structure of any child elements. The second session focused on working with attributes. It covered the various attribute types and the DTD declarations for setting rules for attribute values. The session then explored how to validate an XML document. It concluded with a look at the challenges that namespaces provide for data validation. The third session focused on entities. It looked at the different types of entities and explored how to insert entity references into an XML document. The session also examined how to use parameter entities to combine different DTDs into a single file and how to create references to noncharacter data. The tutorial concluded with a brief look at how DTDs are used with standard XML vocabularies such as XHTML.

Key Terms

attribute-list declaration	general entity	NMTOKENS
choice	ID token	notation
conditional section	IDREF token	parameter entity
DOCTYPE	internal entity	parsed entity
document type declaration	internal subset	public identifier
element declaration	mixed content	sequence
element type declaration	modifying symbol	system identifier
enumerated types	module	tokenized types
external entity	name token	tokens
external subset	NMTOKEN	unparsed entity
formal public identifier		

Note: In the problems that follow, each of the XML documents to be validated include intentional errors. Part of your job is to find and correct those errors using the validation report from the DTDs you create.

Practice	**Review Assignments**

Practice the skills you learned in the tutorial using the same case scenario.

Data Files needed for the Review Assignments: gardtxt.xml, kitstxt.dtd, kitstxt.xml, samptxt.dtd, samptxt.xml

Samantha needs your help with two documents. One document lists some of Butterfly Garden's egg, larvae, and pupae samples. The other document provides information on Butterfly Garden's butterfly kits and equipment. Figure 13-32 shows the tree structures of the two XML vocabularies.

Figure 13-32

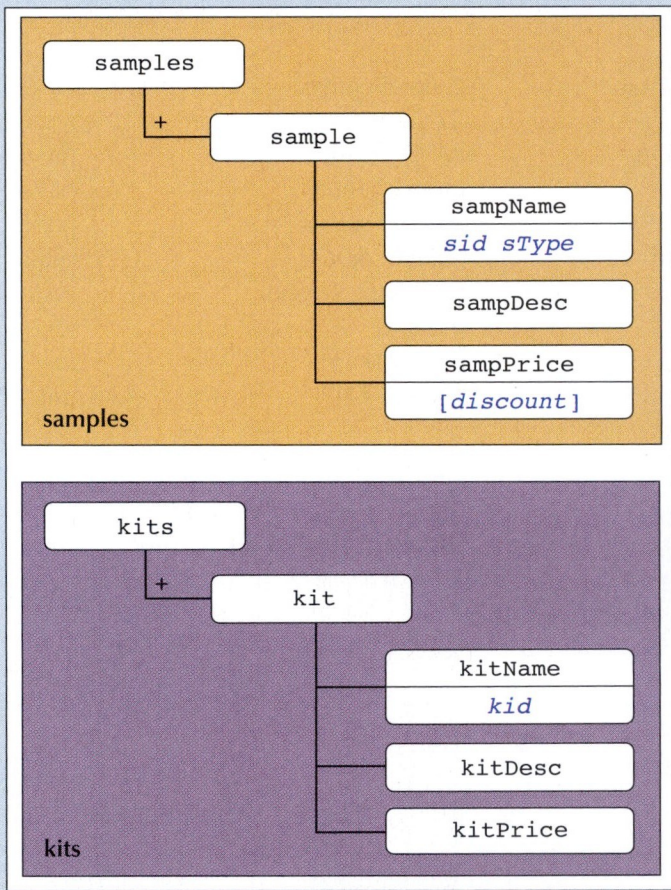

The samples vocabulary contains a root element named samples with one or more occurrences of the sample element containing information on butterfly and moth samples. The sample element contains three child elements: sampName, sampDesc, and sampPrice. The sampName element stores the name of the product sample and supports two attributes: sid, an ID number of the sample, and sType, the type of sample (eggs, larvae, or pupae). The sampDesc and sampPrice elements store a description of the product sample and its price. The sampPrice element also supports an optional discount attribute that indicates whether a student discount is available for the moth or butterfly sample.

The kits vocabulary contains the root element kits with one or more kit elements. Each kit element has three child elements named kitName, kitDesc, and kitPrice, providing the name, description, and sales price, respectively, of the kit or equipment sold by Butterfly Garden. The kitName element contains an attribute named kid, which contains an ID number of the kit.

From these two documents, Samantha wants to create a master document containing a list of both sample and kit offerings. As you did with Samantha's orders document, it is important to enforce a document structure to ensure that information recorded in these documents is valid. Therefore, part of your task will be to combine the DTDs from the samples and kits vocabularies into a single DTD for the compound document. None of the element names overlap, so you do not need to use namespaces in this document.

Complete the following:

1. Using your text editor, open the **kitstxt.dtd**, **kitstxt.xml**, **samptxt.dtd**, **samptxt.xml**, and **gardtxt.xml** files from the tutorial.13/review folder, enter *your name* and *the date* in the comment section of each file, and then save the files as **kits.dtd, kits.xml**, **samples.dtd**, **samples.xml**, and **garden.xml**, respectively.

2. Review the contents of the samples.xml file, which contains the list of butterfly and moth samples, and then, within the **samples.dtd** file, declare the following elements:

    a. The **samples** element, containing at least one occurrence of the child element sample

    b. The **sample** element, containing three child elements in the sequence sampName, sampDesc, sampPrice

    c. The **sampName**, **sampDesc**, and **sampPrice** elements, each containing parsed character data

3. Add the following attribute declarations to the samples.dtd file:

    a. The sampName element, containing a required **sid** attribute as an ID

    b. The sampName element, containing a required **sType** attribute equal to eggs, larvae, or pupae

    c. The sampPrice element, containing an optional **discount** attribute equal to either yes or no

4. Save your changes to the samples.dtd file, and then close it.

5. Review the contents of the kits.xml file and then declare the following elements in the **kits.dtd** file:

    a. The **kits** element, containing at least one occurrence of the child element kit

    b. The **kit** element, containing three child elements in the sequence kitName, kitDesc, and kitPrice

    c. The **kitName**, **kitDesc**, and **kitPrice** elements, each containing parsed character data

6. Specify that the kitName element contains a required ID attribute named **kid**.

7. Save the kits.dtd file, and then close it.

8. In the **garden.xml** file, insert an internal DTD for the root element **productList** directly after the comment section and before the opening <productList> tag.

9. Within the internal DTD, declare the following items:
   a. The **productList** element, containing the child element sequence kits, samples
   b. An external general entity named **kitsList**, referencing the kits.xml file
   c. An external general entity named **samplesList**, referencing the samples.xml file
   d. An external parameter entity named **kitsDTD**, referencing the kits.dtd file
   e. An external parameter entity named **samplesDTD**, referencing the samples.dtd file

10. Below the entity declarations within the DTD, insert references to the kitsDTD and samplesDTD parameters. Add the DTD comments **kits list DTD** and **samples list DTD** to the corresponding lines of code.

11. Within the productList element, insert references for the kitsList and samplesList entities.

12. Save your changes to the garden.xml file.

13. Use Internet Explorer with the **validate_dtd.htm** file in the tutorial.13\demo folder or another program to validate the garden.xml file. There are three validation errors from the kits.xml file and one from the samples.xml file. Fix the errors until the garden.xml file passes the validation test.

14. Open the **garden.xml** file in the Internet Explorer browser and verify that the contents of the kits.xml and samples.xml files appear in the document.

15. Submit the completed and validated project to your instructor.

Apply		**Case Problem 1**

Use the skills you learned in this tutorial to validate a document of sports data.

Data Files needed for this Case Problem: edltxt.xml, teamstxt.dtd

Professional Basketball Association Kurt Vaughn works for the Professional Basketball Association (PBA) and is responsible for coordinating information and statistics for the PBA's many developmental leagues. Part of Kurt's job is to maintain a document that lists the starting lineup for each team and provides statistics on individual players. Kurt asked for your help in creating XML documents that maintain a consistent document structure. He has created a sample document describing six teams from the Eastern Developmental League (EDL). The document lists the five starting players on each team, including the following statistics about each player: PPG (points per game), RPG (rebounds per game), and Assists (assists per game). Figure 13-33 shows a tree diagram of the vocabulary. Note that the PPG, RPG, and Assists attributes are all optional.

Figure 13-33

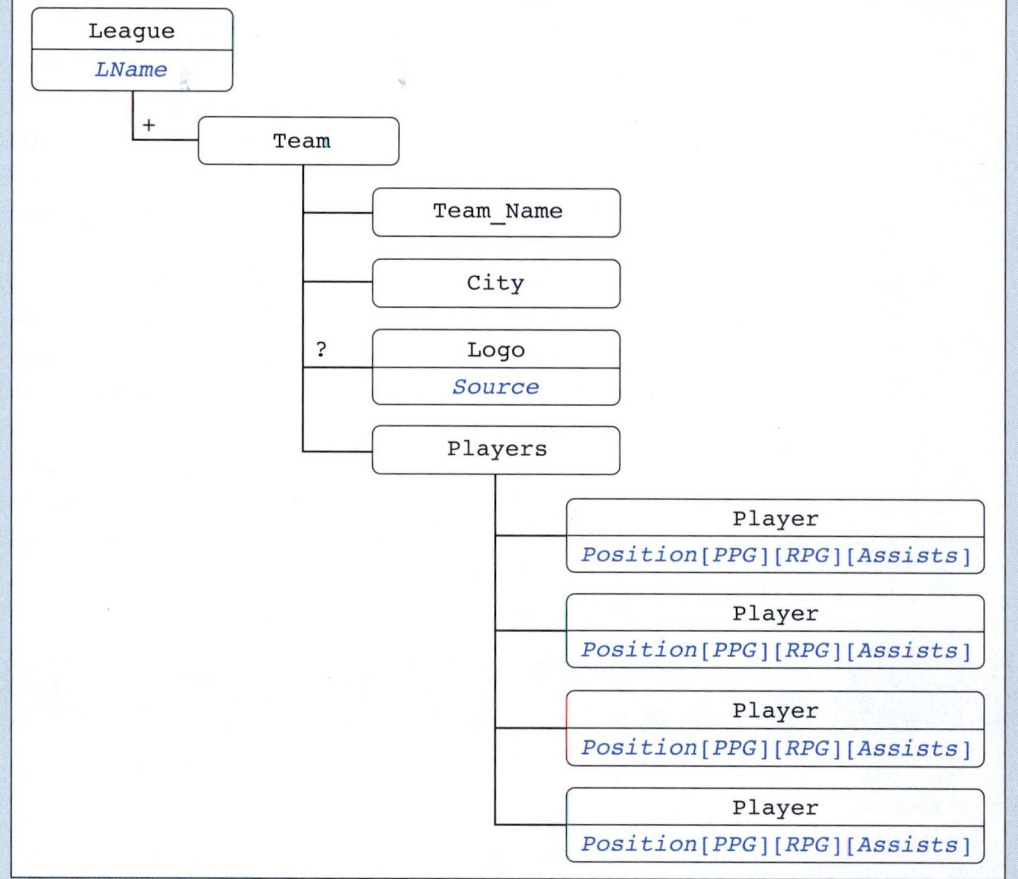

The document also contains an element that stores information about graphic files of team logos. The logo element is optional. Any DTD you create for this document also must work with the unparsed data contained in these graphic files.

Complete the following:

1. Using your text editor, open **edltxt.xml** and **teamstxt.dtd** from the tutorial.13/case1 folder, enter *your name* and *the date* in the comment section of each file, and then save the files as **edl.xml** and **teams.dtd**, respectively.

2. Review the contents of the edl.xml file and then, within the **teams.dtd** file, declare the following elements:

   a. The **League** element, containing at least one occurrence of the child element Team

   b. The **Team** element, containing child elements in the sequence Team_Name, City, Logo (optional), and Players

   c. The **Team_Name** and **City** elements, containing parsed character data

   d. The **Logo** element as an empty element

   e. The **Players** element, containing five child elements, each named Player

   f. The **Player** element, containing parsed character data

3. Declare the following required attributes in the DTD:

   a. The League element should contain a single attribute named **LName** containing character data.

b. The Logo element should contain an entity attribute named **Source**.

c. The Player element should contain an attribute named **Position** with values limited to Center, Forward, or Guard.

d. The Player element should also contain three optional attributes named **PPG**, **RPG**, and **Assists**, all containing character data.

⊕ EXPLORE

4. Declare a notation named BMP with a system location equal to "image/bmp".

5. Save the teams.dtd file, and then close it.

6. In the **edl.xml** file, directly after the comment section, insert a DOCTYPE that references the system location teams.dtd.

⊕ EXPLORE

7. Add an internal subset to the DTD and, within the subset, create three unparsed entities. Each entity should reference the BMP notation. The first entity should be named **Tigers** and reference the Tigers.bmp file. The second entity should be named **Raiders** and reference the Raiders.bmp file. Finally, the third entity should be named **Storm** and reference the Storm.bmp file.

8. Save your changes to the edl.xml file.

9. Test the **edl.xml** file in Internet Explorer using the **validate_dtd.htm** Web page from the tutorial.13\demo folder or another validating parser available to you. Correct any reported errors to make the document valid.

10. Submit the completed and validated project to your instructor.

Apply | Case Problem 2

Use the skills you learned in this tutorial to validate a museum collection document.

Data Files needed for this Case Problem: clockstxt.dtd, clockstxt.xml

The Heritage Museum   Irena Gorski is an archivist at the Heritage Museum in State College, Pennsylvania. The museum is exploring how to transfer its listings to XML format, and Irena has begun by creating a sample document of the museum's extensive collection of clocks. A schematic of the vocabulary she's developing is shown in Figure 13-34.

Figure 13-34

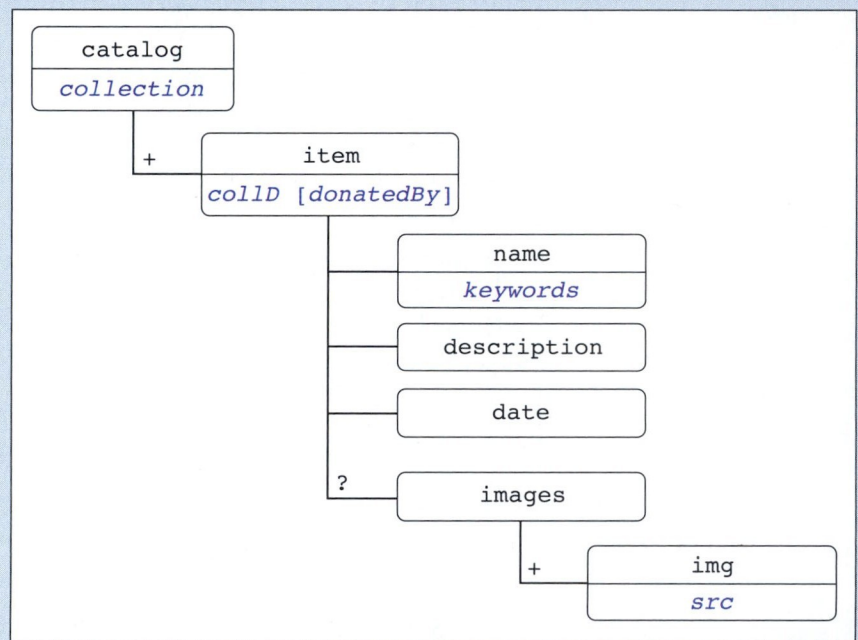

The vocabulary Irena designed has a root element named catalog with one or more item elements. Each item element contains the name of the item, a description, the estimated date of the item, and, in some cases, a list of image files containing pictures of the item. Irena also added attributes to indicate the type of collection the items come from, the collection ID for each item, who donated the item, a list of keywords associated with the item, and the source of any image file. You will assist Irena by creating a DTD based on her XML vocabulary and then use it to validate her sample document.

Complete the following:

1. Using your text editor, open **clockstxt.dtd** and **clockstxt.xml** from the tutorial.13/case2 folder, enter *your name* and *the date* in the comment section of each file, and then save the files as **clocks.dtd** and **clocks.xml**, respectively.

2. In the **clocks.dtd** file, declare the following elements:
   a. The **catalog** element, containing one or more item elements
   b. The **item** element, containing the following sequence of child elements: name, description, date, and (optionally) images
   c. The **name**, **description**, and **date** elements, containing only parsed character data
   d. The **images** element, containing one or more img elements
   e. The **img** element, containing empty content

3. Declare the following attributes in the DTD:
   a. The **collection** attribute, a required attribute of the catalog element, containing a valid XML name
   b. The **collID** attribute, a required ID attribute of the item element
   c. The **donatedBy** attribute, an optional attribute of the item element, containing character data
   d. The **keywords** attribute, a required attribute of the name element, containing a list of valid XML names
   e. The **src** attribute, a required attribute of the img element, containing character data

4. Save your changes to the clocks.dtd file.

5. In the **clocks.xml** file, directly after the comment section, insert a DOCTYPE that references the system location clocks.dtd.

6. Save your changes to the clocks.xml file.

7. Validate the **clocks.xml** file in Internet Explorer using the **validate_dtd.htm** file from the tutorial.13\demo folder or another validating parser. Correct any reported errors to make the file valid.

8. Submit the completed and validated project to your instructor.

| Challenge | **Case Problem 3** |

Explore how to use both DTDs and namespaces in a compound document.

Data Files needed for this Case Problem: modelstxt.dtd, modelstxt.xml, partstxt.dtd, partstxt.xml, pixaltxt.xml

Pixal Products Kristin Laughlin processes orders for an assembly plant for Pixal Products. As part of her job, she has created several XML vocabularies dealing with model orders and the parts available to assemble them. She wants to create a compound document combining information from the models and parts vocabularies. She also wants to validate any data entered into her documents, and asks you to develop DTDs. Because she is creating compound documents that combine elements from the models and parts namespaces, she needs the DTDs to work with namespaces. Figure 13-35 shows the tree structure of the compound document.

Figure 13-35

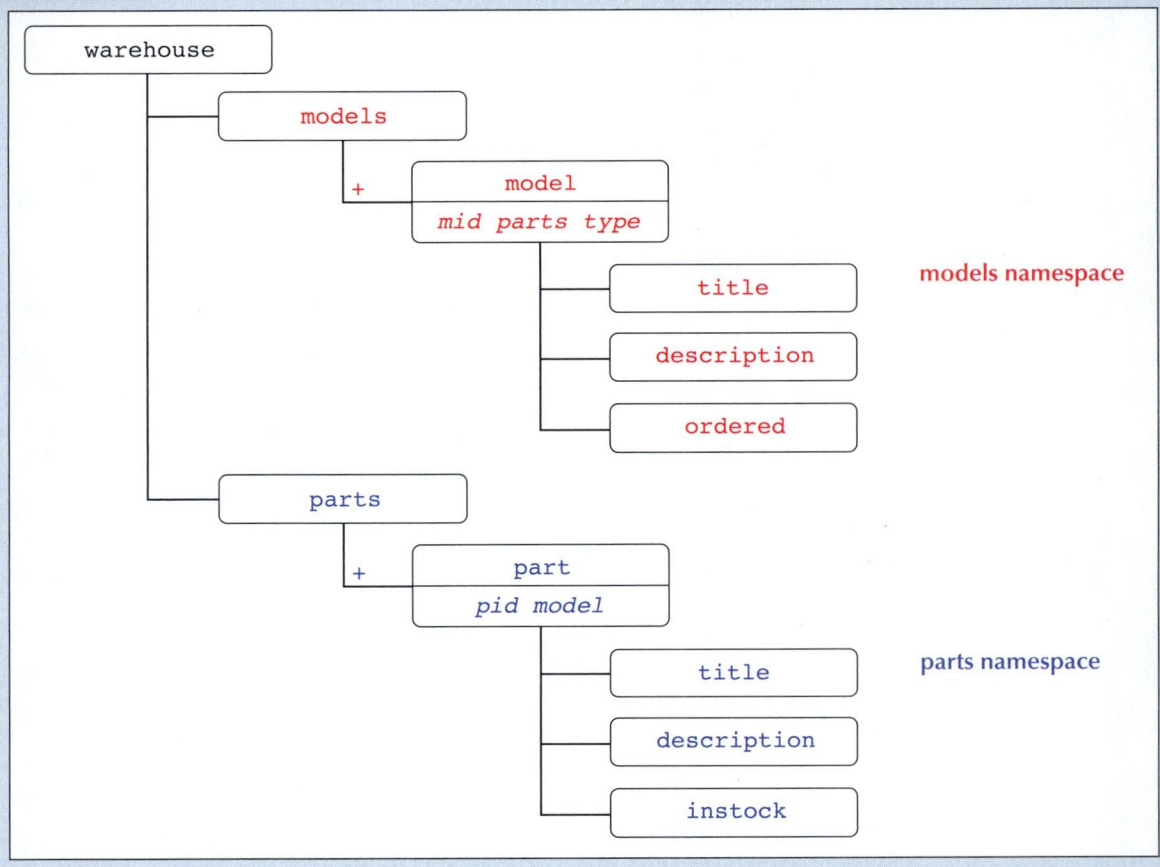

Kristin wants you to create separate DTDs for the models and parts namespaces, and then use entities to read the information from different XML documents into a master compound document. Figure 13-36 shows a schematic of the file relationships in Kristin's proposed project.

Figure 13-36

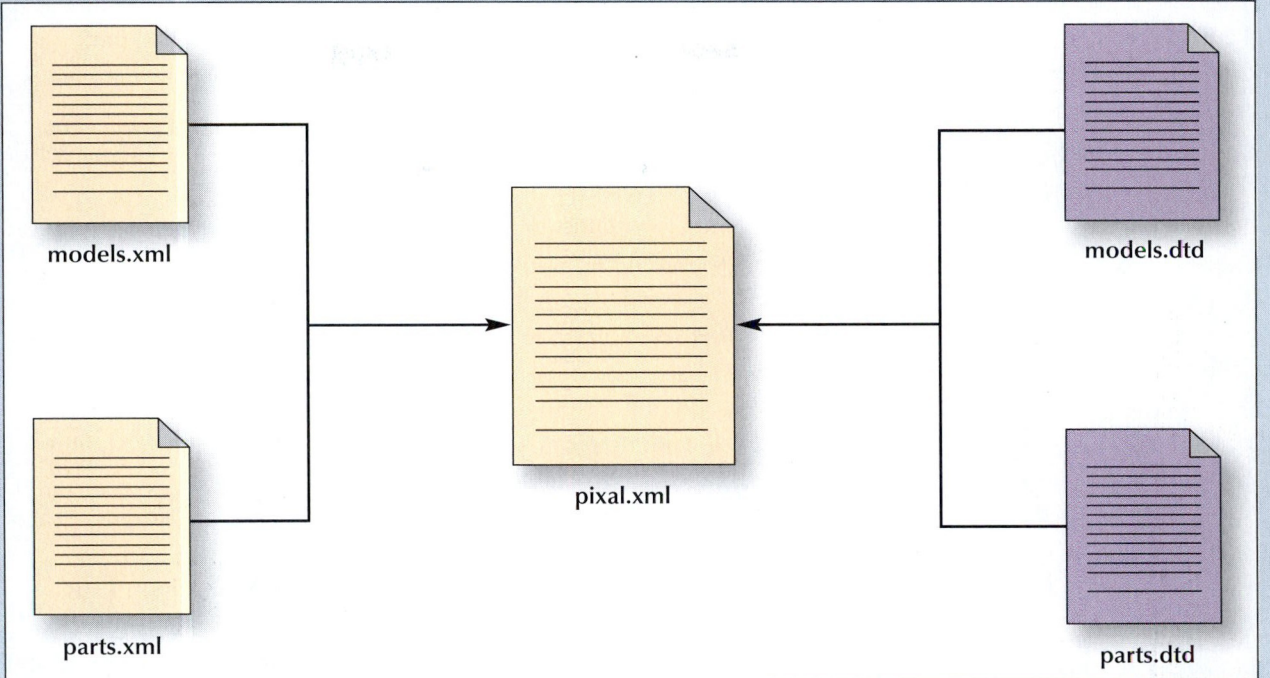

models.xml

parts.xml

pixal.xml

models.dtd

parts.dtd

Complete the following:

1. Using your text editor, open the **modelstxt.dtd**, **modelstxt.xml**, **partstxt.dtd**, **partstxt.xml**, and **pixaltxt.xml** files from the tutorial.13/case3 folder, enter *your name* and *the date* in the comment section of each file, and then save the files as **models.dtd**, **models.xml**, **parts.dtd**, **parts.xml**, and **pixal.xml**, respectively.

2. In the **models.xml** file, place all the elements in the namespace *http://pixalproducts.com/models* with the namespace prefix **m**. Save your changes to the file.

3. In the **parts.xml** file, place all the elements in the namespace *http://pixalproducts.com/parts* with the namespace prefix **p**. Save your changes to the file.

4. In the **models.dtd** file, add the following element declarations (being sure to include the namespace prefix m with all of the element names):

   a. The **models** element, containing at least one child element named model

   b. The **model** element, containing the following sequence of child elements: title, description, and ordered

   c. The **title**, **description**, and **ordered** elements, containing parsed character data

✦EXPLORE 5. Add an attribute declaration to the models element to declare the *http://pixalproducts.com/models* namespace as a fixed value.

6. Add the following attribute declarations to the model element:

   a. An ID attribute named **mid**

   b. An attribute named **parts**, containing a list of ID references

   c. An attribute named **type**, whose value is limited to scanner, color_laser, bw_laser, inkjet, and camera

7. Save your changes to the models.dtd file.

8. In the **parts.dtd** file, add the following element declarations (being sure all element references in the document include the p namespace prefix):
   a. The **parts** element, containing at least one child element named part
   b. The **part** element, containing the following sequence of child elements: title, description, and instock
   c. The **title**, **description**, and **instock** elements, containing parsed character data
9. Add the following attribute declarations:
   a. The parts element contains an attribute declaring the *http://pixalproducts.com/parts* namespace as a fixed value.
   b. The part element contains an ID attribute named **pid**.
   c. The part element should also include a **model** attribute containing a list of ID references.
10. Save your changes to the parts.dtd file.
11. In the **pixal.xml** file, add the root element warehouse to the document belonging to the default namespace *http://pixalproducts.com*.

⊕ **EXPLORE** 12. Between the comment section and the opening <warehouse> tag, insert an internal DTD subset with the following declarations:
   a. The **warehouse** element, containing the two child elements: m:models and p:parts
   b. A fixed attribute of the warehouse element declaring the *http://pixalproducts.com* namespace
   c. A parameter entity named **modelsDTD** pointing to the models.dtd file
   d. A parameter entity named **partsDTD** pointing to the parts.dtd file
   e. An external entity named **modelsList** pointing to the models.xml file
   f. An external entity named **partsList** pointing to the parts.xml file
13. At the end of the internal DTD subset, insert references to the modelsDTD and partsDTD parameters.
14. Within the warehouse element, insert references to the modelsList and partsList entities.
15. Save your changes to the pixal.xml file, and then close it.

⊕ **EXPLORE** 16. Validate the **pixal.xml** file in Internet Explorer using the **validate_dtd.htm** file from the tutorial.13\demo folder or another validating parser. Correct any reported errors to make the file valid. The parts.xml and models.xml files each contain a couple of errors. (*Hint*: All the ID references must point to actual IDs in the compound document and use the same capitalization.)
17. Submit the completed and validated project to your instructor.

| Create | **Case Problem 4** |

Test your knowledge of DTDs by creating a DTD for a contribution list.

Data Files needed for this Case Problem: lhousetxt.dtd, listtxt.xml, members.txt

The Lighthouse Charitable Trust   Sela Voight is the Membership Coordinator for The Lighthouse, a charitable organization located in central Kentucky. One of her responsibilities is to maintain a membership list of people in the community who have contributed to The Lighthouse. Members can belong to one of three categories: Platinum, Gold, and Premium. The categories assist Sela in defining her fundraising goals and strategies to reach those goals.

Currently, most of the data that Sela has compiled resides in text files. To be a more effective fundraiser, she wants to convert this data into an XML document and ensure that the resulting document follows some specific guidelines. You will create the XML document for her.

Complete the following:

1. Using your text editor, open the **lhousetxt.dtd** and **listtxt.xml** files from the tutorial.13/case4 folder, insert *your name* and *the date* in the comment section, and then save the files as **lhouse.dtd** and **list.xml**, respectively.

2. Using the data stored in the **members.txt** file in the tutorial.13\case4 folder for the document content, create a document structure in the **list.xml** file. The appearance of the document is up to you, but it should include the following features:

    a. A root element named **list** should contain several member elements.

    b. Each member element should contain the following child elements, which should appear no more than once within the member element: **name**, **address**, **phone**, **email** (optional), **contribution**, **contact**, and **notes** (optional).

    c. The **member** element contains an attribute named level that identifies the donor level: Platinum, Gold, or Premium. This is a required attribute for each member.

3. In the **lhouse.dtd** file, use the structure you created in the list.xml file as a model for this external DTD subset. Save and close the file.

4. Apply your DTD to the contents of the list.xml file. Save your changes to the list.xml file, and then close it.

5. Test the **list.xml** file to verify its validity. Correct any reported errors.

6. Submit the completed and validated project to your instructor.

Review	**| Quick Check Answers**

Session 13.1

1. `<!DOCTYPE Inventory SYSTEM "books.dtd">`
2. `<!ELEMENT book ANY>`
3. `<!ELEMENT video EMPTY>`
4. `<!ELEMENT book (#PCDATA)>`
5. `<!ELEMENT book (author)>`
6. `<!ELEMENT book (author+)>`
7. `<!ELEMENT book (#PCDATA | author | title)*>`

Session 13.2

1. `<!ATTLIST book title CDATA #IMPLIED>`
2. `<!ATTLIST play type (Romance | Tragedy | History | Comedy) #REQUIRED>`
3. NMTOKEN types cannot contain blank spaces.
4. `<!ATTLIST book ISBN ID #REQUIRED>`
5. `<!ATTLIST author booksBy IDREFS #IMPLIED>`
6. `<!ATTLIST book inStock (yes | no) "yes">`

Session 13.3

1. General entities are used only with the contents of an XML document. Parameter entities are used only with the contents of a DTD.
2. Parsed entities consist entirely of well-formed XML content. Unparsed entities are constructed from non-XML data, including nontextual data.

3. `<!ENTITY Play "<Title>Hamlet</Title>">`
   `&Play;`
4. `<!ENTITY Plays SYSTEM "plays.xml">`
5. `<!ENTITY % Works SYSTEM "plays.dtd">`
6. A notation is a resource that an XML parser uses to handle or identify unparsed data.
7. `<!ENTITY Portrait SYSTEM "shakespeare.gif" NDATA GIF>`

Ending Data Files

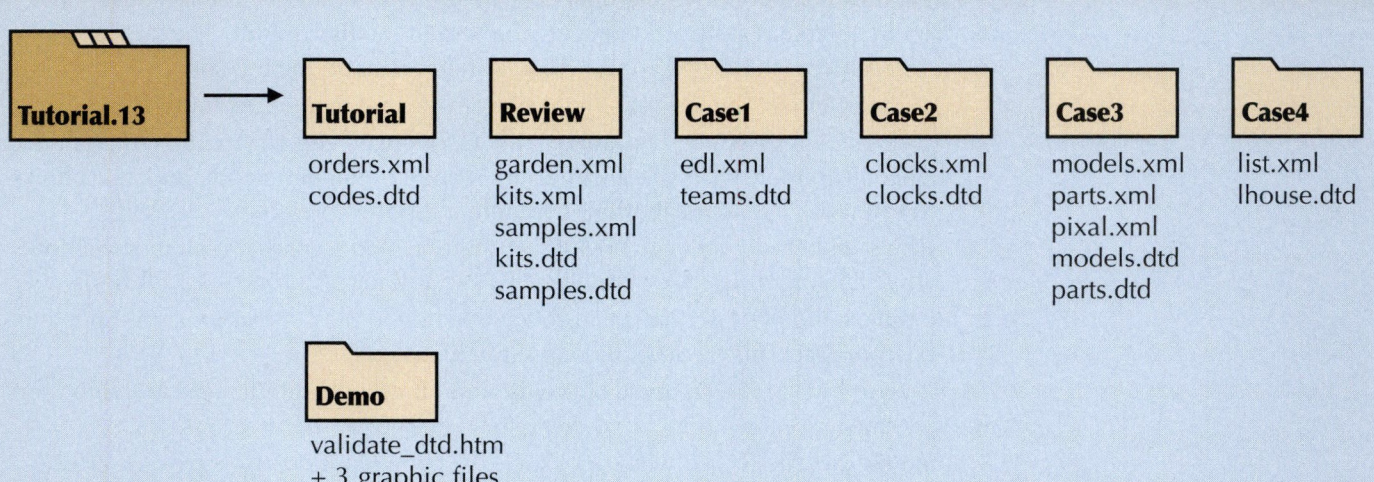

Tutorial.13 →

Tutorial
orders.xml
codes.dtd

Review
garden.xml
kits.xml
samples.xml
kits.dtd
samples.dtd

Case1
edl.xml
teams.dtd

Case2
clocks.xml
clocks.dtd

Case3
models.xml
parts.xml
pixal.xml
models.dtd
parts.dtd

Case4
list.xml
lhouse.dtd

Demo
validate_dtd.htm
+ 3 graphic files

Objectives

Validating Documents with Schemas

Exploring the XML Schema Vocabulary

Case | University Hospital

Allison Grant is a project coordinator at the Clinical Cancer Center (CCC) of University Hospital, where she manages the center's various ongoing research projects. Allison wants to use XML to create structured documents containing information on the different studies and the patients enrolled in those studies. Eventually, the XML documents can be used as a data resource for the center's intranet, enabling investigators to view project and patient data online.

Accuracy is important to the CCC. Allison needs to know that the data she enters is error free. Some studies are limited to patients of a certain age, medical condition, or gender, and Allison must be able to confirm that the patient data in her XML documents matches the criteria for the studies. Allison also needs to create compound documents from the various XML vocabularies she's created. For example, she may need to create a document that combines patient information with information on the study itself.

DTDs cannot fulfill Allison's needs. DTDs have a limited range of data types and provide no way to deal with numeric data. Also, DTDs and namespaces do not mix well. However, schemas can work with a wide range of data types and do a better job than DTDs in supporting namespaces and compound documents. Allison asks you to develop schemas for the XML documents that she's already created.

Starting Data Files

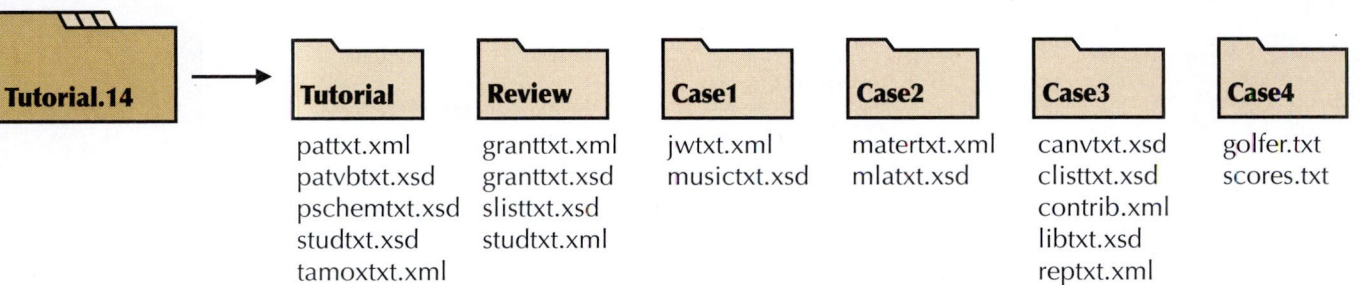

Tutorial.14 →

Tutorial
pattxt.xml
patvbtxt.xsd
pschemtxt.xsd
studtxt.xsd
tamoxtxt.xml

Review
granttxt.xml
granttxt.xsd
slisttxt.xsd
studtxt.xml

Case1
jwtxt.xml
musictxt.xsd

Case2
matertxt.xml
mlatxt.xsd

Case3
canvtxt.xsd
clisttxt.xsd
contrib.xml
libtxt.xsd
reptxt.xml

Case4
golfer.txt
scores.txt

Demo
validate_schema.htm
+ 3 graphic files

Session 14.1

Introducing XML Schema

You and Allison meet at the hospital to discuss her work for the Clinical Cancer Center. She has brought along a file named patients.xml, which contains a list of patients participating in a study examining the effects of the drug Tamoxifen on breast cancer. You'll open this file now.

To open the patients document:

▶ **1.** Use your text editor to open **pattxt.xml** from the tutorial.14\tutorial folder, enter **your name** and **the date** in the comment section, and then save the file as **patients.xml**. See Figure 14-1.

Figure 14-1 ▶ **Contents of the patients.xml document**

```
<patients>
   <patient patID="MR890-041-02" onStudy="TBC-080-5">
      <lastName>Dibbs</lastName>
      <firstName>Cynthia</firstName>
      <dateOfBirth>1949-05-22</dateOfBirth>
      <age>62</age>
      <stage>II</stage>
      <performance scale="Karnofsky">0.81</performance>
   </patient>

   <patient patID="MR771-121-10" onStudy="TBC-080-5">
      <lastName>Wilkes</lastName>
      <firstName>Karen</firstName>
      <dateOfBirth>1963-02-24</dateOfBirth>
      <age>48</age>
      <stage>II</stage>
      <comment>Dropped out of study.</comment>
      <performance scale="Karnofsky">0.84</performance>
   </patient>

   <patient patID="MR701-891-05" onStudy="TBC-080-5">
      <lastName>Sanchez</lastName>
      <firstName>Olivia</firstName>
      <dateOfBirth>1962-08-14</dateOfBirth>
      <age>49 years old</age>
      <stage>II</stage>
      <comment>Possibly stage I/II</comment>
      <comment>Karnofsky performance rating unavailable.</comment>
      <performance scale="Bell">0.89</performance>
   </patient>

   <patient patID="MR805-891-08" onStudy="TBC-080-5">
      <lastName>Russell</lastName>
      <firstName>Alice</firstName>
      <dateOfBirth>1956-9-14</dateOfBirth>
      <age>55</age>
      <stage>II</stage>
      <performance scale="Karnofsky">1.76</performance>
   </patient>

   <patient patID="mr815-741-03" onStudy="tbc-080-5">
      <lastName>Browne</lastName>
      <firstName>Brenda</firstName>
      <dateOfBirth>1968-04-25</dateOfBirth>
      <age>39</age>
      <stage>I</stage>
      <performance scale="Karnosfky">0.88</performance>
   </patient>

</patients>
```

> ▶ **2.** Examine the contents of the document, paying close attention to the order of the elements and the values of the elements and attributes.

Figure 14-2 shows the tree structure of the XML vocabulary used in the document. For each patient element in the document, Allison inserted two attributes: patID and onStudy. The first contains the patient's medical record number and the second contains the ID of the study in which the patient is enrolled. She's collected each patient's first and last name, date of birth, age, breast cancer stage, and health performance score. Each patient element can contain multiple comment elements for any additional information that a study's investigator wants to add.

Structure of the patients vocabulary ◀ **Figure 14-2**

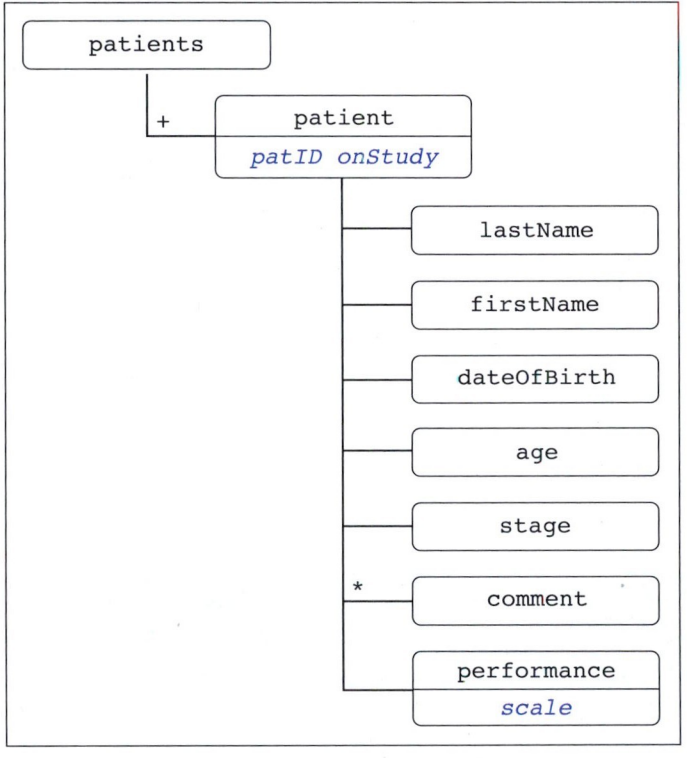

The patients.xml file contains the initial patients entered into the Tamoxifen study, but eventually it will contain more entries. As more patients are added, Allison wants to ensure that the new data obeys the study's eligibility guidelines. For example, patients must be at least 21 years of age to give informed consent. Every patient must have a valid medical record number. For the Tamoxifen study, patients must be diagnosed with either Stage I or Stage II cancer. You and Allison discuss whether a DTD can validate a document with this type of data.

The Limits of DTDs

DTDs are commonly used for validation largely because of XML's origins as an offshoot of SGML. SGML originally was designed for text-based documents, such as reports and technical manuals. As long as data content is limited to simple text, DTDs work well for validation. However, as XML began being used for a wider range of document content, developers searched for an alternative to the DTDs.

One complaint about DTDs is their lack of data types. For example, Allison can declare an age element in the DTD, but she cannot specify that the age element may contain only numbers or that those numbers fall within a specified range of values. She can declare a dateOfBirth element, but a DTD doesn't have the ability to force that element to contain only dates. DTDs simply do not provide the control over data that Allison requires. DTDs also do not recognize namespaces, so they are not well suited to compound documents in which content from several vocabularies needs to be validated. This is a concern for Allison because her job at the CCC will involve developing several XML vocabularies that will often be combined into single documents.

Finally, DTDs employ a syntax called **Extended Backus Naur Form (EBNF)**, which is different from the syntax used for XML. This means that the document's author must be able to work not only with the syntax of XML, but with EBNF as well. For developers who want to work with only one language, this could be a concern.

Because XML stands for *Extensible* Markup Language, you can use XML to document the structure and content of other XML documents. This is the idea behind schemas.

Schemas and DTDs

A schema is an XML document that contains validation rules for an XML vocabulary. When applied to a specific XML file, the document to be validated is called the **instance document** because it represents a specific instance of the rules defined in the schema. Schemas have several advantages over DTDs. XML parsers need to understand only XML, so all the tools used to create an instance document can also be applied to designing the schema. Schemas also support more data types, including data types for numbers and dates as well as custom data types for special needs. Additionally, schemas are more flexible than DTDs in dealing with mixed content, and they provide support for namespaces, making it easier to validate compound documents. Figure 14-3 summarizes some of the more important differences between schemas and DTDs.

Figure 14-3   **Comparison of schemas and DTDs**

Feature	Schemas	DTDs
Document language	XML	Extended Backus Naur Form (EBNF)
Standards	multiple standards	one standard
Supported data types	44	10
Customized data types	yes	no
Mixed content	easy to develop	difficult to develop
Namespaces	completely supported	only namespace prefixes are supported
Entities	no	yes

Tip

You should validate your document using either a DTD or a schema but not both because some XML parsers validate the document under one and ignore the other, causing the document to be rejected.

If schemas are so useful, why do you need DTDs? First, DTDs represent an older standard for XML documents and are more widely supported. DTDs are simpler to create and maintain than schemas because the language itself is easier to work with. This is partly due to the fact that DTDs are more limited than schemas. Thus, DTDs are easier to set up for basic documents that don't require much validation.

Schema Vocabularies

Unlike DTDs, a single standard doesn't exist for schemas. Instead, developers created several schema vocabularies to serve different needs of the XML developer. Figure 14-4 describes some of these schema vocabularies.

Schema	Description
XML Schema	The most widely used schema standard, XML Schema is developed and maintained by the W3C and is designed to handle a broad range of document structures. It is also referred to as XSD.
Document Definition Markup Language (DDML)	One of the original schema languages, DDML (originally known as XSchema) was created to replicate all DTD functionality in a schema. DDML does not support any data types beyond what could be found in DTDs.
XML Data	One of the original schema languages, XML Data was developed by Microsoft to replace DTDs.
XML Data Reduced (XDR)	XDR is a subset of the XML Data schema, primarily used prior to the release of XML Schema.
Regular Language for XML (RELAX)	A simple alternative to the W3C's XML schema standard, RELAX provides much of the same functionality as DTDs, with additional support for namespaces and data types. RELAX does not support entities or notations.
Tree Regular Expressions (TREX)	A TREX schema specifies a pattern for an XML document's structure and content, and thus identifies a class of XML documents that match the pattern. TREX has been merged with RELAX into RELAX NG.
RELAX NG (Regular Language for XML Next Generation)	RELAX NG is the current version of RELAX, combining the features of RELAX and TREX.
Schematron	The Schematron schema represents documents using a tree pattern, allowing support for document structures that might be difficult to represent in traditional schema languages.

Support for a particular schema depends solely on the XML parser being used for validation. Before applying any of the schemas listed in Figure 14-4, you must verify the level of support offered by your application for that particular schema. XML Schema, developed by the W3C in March 2001, is the most widely adopted schema standard. This tutorial focuses primarily on XML Schema, although many of the concepts involved with XML Schema can be applied to the other schema vocabularies.

> **Tip**
>
> You can convert a DTD to XML Schema format using the dtd2xs converter, available at *www.w3.org/XML/Schema*.

Starting a Schema File

As you saw in the previous tutorial, DTDs can be placed within the instance document or within an external file. Schemas, however, are always placed in an external file. XML Schema files also end with the .xsd file extension. Allison already created a blank XML Schema file for you to work on. You will open this file.

To start work on the XML Schema file:

▶ 1. Use your text editor to open **pschemtxt.xsd** from the tutorial.14\tutorial folder, and then enter *your name* and *the date* in the comment section.

▶ 2. Save the file as **pschema.xsd**.

The root element in any XML Schema document is the schema element. For a parser to recognize that the document is written in the XML Schema vocabulary, the schema element must include a declaration for the XML Schema namespace using the URI *http://www.w3.org/2001/XMLSchema*. The general structure of an XML Schema file is

```
<?xml version="1.0" ?>
<schema xmlns="http://www.w3.org/2001/XMLSchema">
    content
</schema>
```

where *content* is the list of elements and attributes that define the rules of the instance document. By convention, the namespace prefix xsd or xs is assigned to the XML Schema namespace to identify elements and attributes that belong to the XML Schema vocabulary. Keeping well-defined namespaces in an XML Schema document becomes very important when you start creating schemas for compound documents involving several namespaces. The usual form of an XML Schema document is therefore:

```
<?xml version="1.0" ?>
<xs:schema xmlns:xs="http://www.w3.org/2001/XMLSchema">
    content
</xs:schema>
```

This tutorial assumes a namespace prefix of xs in discussing the elements and attributes of the XML Schema language. However, you can choose to use a different prefix in your own XML Schema documents. You can also set XML Schema as the document's default namespace and not need any prefix. The only requirement is that you be consistent in the use of a namespace prefix.

You will add the root schema element to the pschema.xsd file, placing it in the XML Schema namespace with the xs namespace prefix.

To insert the schema element in the pschema.xsd file:

▶ **1.** Directly below the comment section, insert the following code, as shown in Figure 14-5:

```
<xs:schema xmlns:xs="http://www.w3.org/2001/XMLSchema">
</xs:schema>
```

Figure 14-5 | **XML Schema root element**

```
<?xml version="1.0" encoding="UTF-8" ?>
<!--
    New Perspectives on XHTML and XML
    Tutorial 14
    Tutorial Case

    Patient list schema
    Author: Allison Grant
    Date:   3/1/2012

    Filename:        pschema.xsd
    Supporting Files:
-->

<xs:schema xmlns:xs="http://www.w3.org/2001/XMLSchema">
</xs:schema>
```

XML Schema namespace URI

▶ **2.** Save your changes to the file.

- To create an XML Schema document, insert the structure
  ```
  <schema xmlns="http://www.w3.org/2001/XMLSchema">
     content
  </schema>
  ```
  in the file, where *content* consists of the elements and attributes of XML Schema used in defining the rules of the instance document.
- To apply a namespace prefix (customarily xs or xsd) to the elements and attributes of the XML Schema vocabulary, use the following structure:
  ```
  <xs:schema xmlns:xs="http://www.w3.org/2001/XMLSchema">
     content
  </xs:schema>
  ```

Understanding Simple and Complex Types

XML Schema supports two types of content: simple and complex. A **simple type** contains a single value, such as the value of an attribute or the textual content of an element. A **complex type** contains two or more values or elements placed within a defined structure. Examples of complex types include elements that contain attributes in addition to a text value or an element that contains child elements. Figure 14-6 lists examples of both simple and complex types.

Simple and complex types of content   **Figure 14-6**

Simple Types	Complex Types
An element containing only text	**An empty element containing attributes**
`<subject>Cynthia Dibbs</subject>`	`<subject name="Cynthia Dibbs" age="62" />`
An attribute	**An element containing text and an attribute**
`age="62"`	`<subject age="62">Cynthia Dibbs</subject>`
	An element containing child elements

	`<subject>`
	   `<name>Cynthia Dibbs</name>`
	   `<age>62</age>`
	`</subject>`

	An element containing child elements and an attribute

	`<subject age="62">`
	   `<name>Cynthia Dibbs</name>`
	`</subject>`

The patients.xml file contains several examples of simple and complex types. These are listed in Figure 14-7. Note that all attributes in the document are, by default, simple types. The patients, patient, and performance elements are complex types because they contain either nested child elements or attributes. The lastName, firstName, dateOfBirth, age, stage, and comment elements are all simple types because they contain only element text.

Figure 14-7 | **Simple and complex types in the patients.xml document**

Item	Contains	Content Type
patients	nested child elements	complex
patient	nested child elements	complex
patID	an attribute value	simple
onStudy	an attribute value	simple
lastName	element text	simple
firstName	element text	simple
dateOfBirth	element text	simple
age	element text	simple
stage	element text	simple
comment	element text	simple
performance	an attribute	complex
scale	an attribute value	simple

The distinction between simple and complex types is important in XML Schema because the code to define a simple type differs greatly from the code to define a complex type. You will start writing the schema for Allison's document by defining all of the simple types found in the patients.xml file.

Defining a Simple Type Element

An element in the instance document containing only text and no attributes or child elements is defined in XML Schema using the <xs:element> tag

```
<xs:element name="name" type="type" />
```

where *name* is the name of the element in the instance document and *type* is the type of data stored in the element. The data type can be one of XML Schema's built-in data types, or it can be a data type defined by the schema author. If you use a built-in data type, you must indicate that it belongs to the XML Schema namespace because it is a feature of the XML Schema language. The code to use a built-in data type is therefore

```
<xs:element name="name" type="xs:type" />
```

where *type* is a data type supported by XML Schema. Note that if you use a different namespace prefix or declare XML Schema as the default namespace for the document, the prefix will be different.

Perhaps the most commonly used data type in XML Schema is string, which allows an element to contain any text string. For example, in the patients.xml file, the lastName element contains the text of the patient's last name. To indicate that this element contains string data, you would add the following element to the XML Schema file:

```
<xs:element name="lastName" type="xs:string" />
```

For now, you will define the data type of each simple type element as a simple text string. You'll revise these declarations in the next session, when you examine the wide variety of data types supported by XML Schema as well as learn how to define your own data types.

To declare the simple type elements in the patients.xml file:

▶ **1.** Within the schema root element, insert the following simple type elements, as shown in Figure 14-8, being sure to match the case:

```
<xs:element name="lastName" type="xs:string" />
<xs:element name="firstName" type="xs:string" />
<xs:element name="dateOfBirth" type="xs:string" />
<xs:element name="age" type="xs:string" />
<xs:element name="stage" type="xs:string" />
<xs:element name="comment" type="xs:string" />
```

Elements defined as simple types ◀ **Figure 14-8**

```
<xs:schema xmlns:xs="http://www.w3.org/2001/XMLSchema">

    <xs:element name="lastName" type="xs:string" />
    <xs:element name="firstName" type="xs:string" />
    <xs:element name="dateOfBirth" type="xs:string" />
    <xs:element name="age" type="xs:string" />
    <xs:element name="stage" type="xs:string" />
    <xs:element name="comment" type="xs:string" />

</xs:schema>
```

simple type elements

element contains only a simple text string

▶ **2.** Save your changes to the file.

Defining a Simple Type Element | Reference Window

- To define a simple type element, enter
    ```
    <xs:element name="name" type="type" />
    ```
    where *name* is the element name in the instance document and *type* is the data type.
- To use a data type built into the XML Schema language, place *type* in the XML Schema namespace as follows:
    ```
    <xs:element name="name" type="xs:type" />
    ```

Defining an Attribute

The other simple type content found in Allison's document is the attribute value. To define an attribute in XML Schema, use the <xs:attribute> tag

```
<xs:attribute name="name" type="type" default="default"
fixed="fixed"/>
```

where *name* is the name of the attribute, *type* is the data type, *default* is the attribute's default value, and *fixed* is a fixed value for the attribute. The default and fixed attributes are optional. You use them to specify a default attribute value (applied when no attribute value is entered in the instance document) or to fix an attribute to a specific value.

Attributes use the same collection of data types that simple type elements do. For example, the following code defines the Gender attribute, indicating that it contains a text string with a default value of female:

```
<xs:attribute name="Gender" type="xs:string" default="female" />
```

The patients.xml file has three attributes: patID, onStudy, and scale. None of these attributes has a default or fixed value. You will add the attribute declarations to the schema file below the element declarations you just created.

To define the attributes used in the patients.xml file:

▶ **1.** Add the following attribute definitions to the schema, as shown in Figure 14-9:

```
<xs:attribute name="patID" type="xs:string" />
<xs:attribute name="onStudy" type="xs:string" />
<xs:attribute name="scale" type="xs:string" />
```

Figure 14-9 ▶ **Attributes defined as simple types**

```
<xs:schema xmlns:xs="http://www.w3.org/2001/XMLSchema">

    <xs:element name="lastName" type="xs:string" />
    <xs:element name="firstName" type="xs:string" />
    <xs:element name="dateOfBirth" type="xs:string" />
    <xs:element name="age" type="xs:string" />
    <xs:element name="stage" type="xs:string" />
    <xs:element name="comment" type="xs:string" />

    <xs:attribute name="patID" type="xs:string" />
    <xs:attribute name="onStudy" type="xs:string" />
    <xs:attribute name="scale" type="xs:string" />

</xs:schema>
```

attribute definitions

attribute contains only a simple text string

▶ **2.** Save your changes to the file.

- To declare an attribute, use the syntax
  ```
  <xs:attribute name="name" type="type" default="default"
  fixed="fixed" />
  ```
  where *name* is the element name in the instance document and *type* is the data type of the element. The default and fixed values are optional.
- For data types that are part of the XML Schema vocabulary, place *type* in the XML Schema namespace, as follows:
  ```
  <xs:attribute name="name" type="xs:type" default="default"
  fixed="fixed" />
  ```

Defining a Complex Type Element

The three attributes you defined are not yet associated with any elements in Allison's document. To do that, you must first define the elements containing each of these attributes. Because those elements contain attributes, they are considered complex elements. The basic structure for defining a complex type element with XML Schema is

```
<xs:element name="name">
   <xs:complexType>
      declarations
   </xs:complexType>
</xs:element>
```

where *name* is the name of the element and *declarations* are declarations that declare the type of content contained within the element. This content could include nested child elements, basic text, attributes, or any combination of the three. As shown in Figure 14-6, the following four complex type elements usually appear in an instance document:

- An empty element containing only attributes
- An element containing text content and attributes but no child elements
- An element containing child elements but no attributes
- An element containing both child elements and attributes

XML Schema applies a different code structure to each of these four possibilities. You will start by looking at the definition for an empty element that contains one or more attributes.

Defining an Element Containing Only Attributes

The code to define the attributes of an empty element is

```
<xs:element name="name">
    <xs:complexType>
        attributes
    </xs:complexType>
</xs:element>
```

where *name* is the name of the element in the instance document and *attributes* is the set of simple type elements that define the attributes associated with the element. For example, the empty element

```
<subject name="Cynthia Dibbs" age="62" />
```

has two attributes: name and age. The code for this complex type element has the following structure:

```
<xs:element name="subject">
    <xs:complexType>
        <xs:attribute name="name" type="xs:string" />
        <xs:attribute name="age" type="xs:string" />
    </xs:complexType>
</xs:element>
```

The order of the attribute declarations is unimportant. XML Schema allows attributes to be entered in any order within a complex type element.

Defining an Element Containing Attributes and Basic Text

If an element in the instance document contains attributes and text content but no child elements, the structure that declares the elements and attributes takes a different form. In these cases, the definition needs to indicate that the element contains simple content and a collection of one or more attributes. The structure of the element definition is

```
<xs:element name="name">
    <xs:complexType>
        <xs:simpleContent>
            <xs:extension base="type">
                attributes
            </xs:extension>
        </xs:simpleContent>
    </xs:complexType>
</xs:element>
```

where *type* is the data type of the element's content (or xs:*type* if the data type is part of the XML Schema vocabulary) and *attributes* is a list of the attributes associated with the element. The purpose of the simpleContent element in this code is to indicate that the element contains only text and no nested child elements. The <xs:extension> tag is used to extend this definition to include the list of attributes. The simpleContent and extension elements are important tools used by XML Schema to derive new data types and to define complex content. In this case, you are using them to define a complex element that contains a text value and is associated with one or more attributes.

One such element in the patients.xml file is the performance element. The following is a sample of the type of content stored in this element:

```
<performance scale="Karnofsky">0.81</performance>
```

The following code defines this element and associates it with the scale attribute:

```
<xs:element name="performance">
   <xs:complexType>
      <xs:simpleContent>
         <xs:extension base="xs:string">
            <xs:attribute name="scale" type="xs:string" />
         </xs:extension>
      </xs:simpleContent>
   </xs:complexType>
</xs:element>
```

In this code, the base attribute in the <xs:extension> element sets the data type for the performance element. At this point, you are assuming that the performance element contains a text string. You also set the data type of the scale attribute to xs:string, indicating that it contains a text string.

Referencing an Element or Attribute Definition

You have already defined the scale attribute in the pschema.xsd file. You could revise the code to nest that attribute definition within the definition of the performance element. However, XML Schema allows for a great deal of flexibility in writing complex types. Rather than repeating that earlier attribute declaration within the performance element, you can create a reference to it. The code to create a reference to an element or attribute definition is

```
<xs:element ref="elemName" />
<xs:attribute ref="attName" />
```

Tip

To repeat an attribute or element definition, simplify the schema by defining the attribute or element once and then reference that definition wherever it is used.

where *elemName* is the name used in an element definition and *attName* is the name used in an attribute definition. The following code references the scale attribute from within the performance element:

```
<xs:attribute name="scale" type="xs:string" />

<xs:element name="performance">
   <xs:complexType>
      <xs:simpleContent>
         <xs:extension base="xs:string">
            <xs:attribute ref="scale" />
         </xs:extension>
      </xs:simpleContent>
   </xs:complexType>
</xs:element>
```

You will add the definition of the performance element to the pschema.xsd file.

To define the performance element:

▶ 1. Below the declaration for the scale attribute in the pschema.xsd file, add the following complex type declaration, as shown in Figure 14-10:

```
<xs:element name="performance">
   <xs:complexType>
      <xs:simpleContent>
         <xs:extension base="xs:string">
```

```
            <xs:attribute ref="scale" />
        </xs:extension>
      </xs:simpleContent>
    </xs:complexType>
  </xs:element>
```

Complex type element containing text and an attribute ◄ **Figure 14-10**

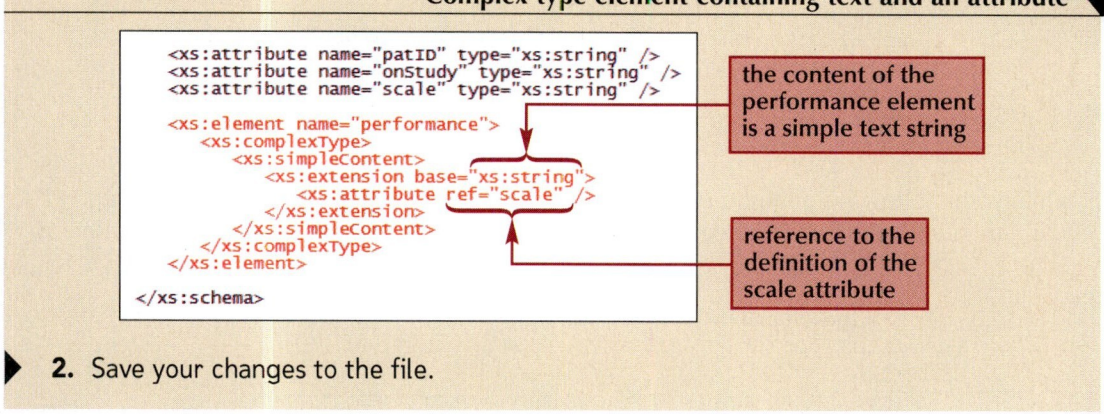

the content of the performance element is a simple text string

reference to the definition of the scale attribute

▶ **2.** Save your changes to the file.

Defining an Element with Nested Children

Next, you will examine complex elements that contain nested child elements but no attributes or text. To define this type of complex element, use the structure

```
<xs:element name="name">
    <xs:complexType>
        <xs:compositor>
            elements
        </xs:compositor>
    </xs:complexType>
</xs:element>
```

where *name* is the name of the element, *compositor* defines how the child elements are organized, and *elements* is a list of the nested child elements. You can choose any of the following compositors to define the organization of the child elements:

• **sequence**—requires the child elements to appear in the order listed in the schema
• **choice**—allows any *one* of the child elements listed to appear in the instance document
• **all**—allows any of the child elements to appear in any order in the instance document; however, they must appear either only once or not at all

For example, the following code assigns four child elements—street, city, state, and country—to the address element. Because the definition uses the sequence compositor, the document is invalid if the address element doesn't contain all these child elements in the specified order.

```
<element name="address">
    <xs:complexType>
        <xs:sequence>
            <xs:element name="street" type="xs:string" />
            <xs:element name="city" type="xs:string" />
            <xs:element name="state" type="xs:string" />
            <xs:element name="country" type="xs:string" />
        </xs:sequence>
    </xs:complexType>
</xs:element>
```

The following definition allows the sponsor element to have an element named parent or guardian. Because the definition uses the choice compositor, the sponsor element can contain either element, but not both.

```
<xs:element name="sponsor">
   <xs:complexType>
      <xs:choice>
         <xs:element name="parent" type="xs:string" />
         <xs:element name="guardian" type="xs:string" />
      </xs:choice>
   </xs:complexType>
</xs:element>
```

Finally, the following definition uses the all compositor to allow the Family element to contain elements named Father or Mother. The Family element can also contain neither a Father nor a Mother element.

```
<xs:element name="Family">
   <xs:complexType>
      <xs:all>
         <xs:element name="Father" type="xs:string" />
         <xs:element name="Mother" type="xs:string" />
      </xs:all>
   </xs:complexType>
</xs:element>
```

Tip

A complex element can contain only one all compositor. You cannot combine the all compositor with the choice or sequence compositor.

The choice and sequence compositors can be nested and combined. The following definition uses two choice compositors nested within a sequence compositor to allow the Account element to contain either the Person or Company element followed by either the Cash or Credit element:

```
<xs:element name="Account">
   <xs:complexType>
      <xs:sequence>
         <xs:choice>
            <xs:element name="Person" type="xs:string" />
            <xs:element name="Company" type="xs:string" />
         </xs:choice>
         <xs:choice>
            <xs:element name="Cash" type="xs:string" />
            <xs:element name="Credit" type="xs:string" />
         </xs:choice>
      </xs:sequence>
   </xs:complexType>
</xs:element>
```

Defining an Element Containing Nested Elements and Attributes

The next complex element you will consider is an element containing both child elements and attributes. To define an element with this kind of content, use the structure

```
<xs:element name="name">
   <xs:complexType>
      <xs:compositor>
         elements
      </xs:compositor>
      attributes
   </xs:complexType>
</xs:element>
```

where *name* is the name of the element; *compositor* is either sequence, choice, or all; *elements* is a list of child elements nested within the element; and *attributes* is a list of attribute definitions associated with the element. This is the same structure used for elements containing nested children except that a list of attributes is included. For example, the patient element from Allison's patients.xml file contains two attributes (patID and onStudy) and seven child elements (lastName, firstName, dateOfBirth, age, stage, comment, and performance). You already defined the content for the two attributes and seven child elements, so you can insert references to those earlier definitions in the code, as follows:

```
<xs:element name="patient">
    <xs:complexType>
        <xs:sequence>
            <xs:element ref="lastName" />
            <xs:element ref="firstName" />
            <xs:element ref="dateOfBirth" />
            <xs:element ref="age" />
            <xs:element ref="stage" />
            <xs:element ref="comment" />
            <xs:element ref="performance" />
        </xs:sequence>

        <xs:attribute ref="patID" />
        <xs:attribute ref="onStudy" />
    </xs:complexType>
</xs:element>
```

You will add this definition of the patient element to the pschema.xsd file.

To define the patient element in the pschema.xsd file:

▶ **1.** Below the definition of the performance element, insert the following code, as shown in Figure 14-11:

```
<xs:element name="patient">
    <xs:complexType>
        <xs:sequence>
            <xs:element ref="lastName" />
            <xs:element ref="firstName" />
            <xs:element ref="dateOfBirth" />
            <xs:element ref="age" />
            <xs:element ref="stage" />
            <xs:element ref="comment" />
            <xs:element ref="performance" />
        </xs:sequence>

        <xs:attribute ref="patID" />
        <xs:attribute ref="onStudy" />
    </xs:complexType>
</xs:element>
```

Figure 14-11   **Element containing both child elements and attributes**

```
<xs:element name="performance">
   <xs:complexType>
      <xs:simpleContent>
         <xs:extension base="xs:string">
            <xs:attribute ref="scale" />
         </xs:extension>
      </xs:simpleContent>
   </xs:complexType>
</xs:element>

<xs:element name="patient">
   <xs:complexType>
      <xs:sequence>
         <xs:element ref="lastName" />
         <xs:element ref="firstName" />
         <xs:element ref="dateOfBirth" />
         <xs:element ref="age" />
         <xs:element ref="stage" />
         <xs:element ref="comment" />
         <xs:element ref="performance" />
      </xs:sequence>

      <xs:attribute ref="patID" />
      <xs:attribute ref="onStudy" />
   </xs:complexType>
</xs:element>

</xs:schema>
```

child elements of the patient element (elements must be entered in the specified order)

attributes of the patient element

2. Save your changes to the file.

The only element from the patients.xml file you haven't yet declared is the root patients element. This element has no attributes but does contain the patient element as a child. The definition of this element

```
<xs:element name="patients">
   <xs:complexType>
      <xs:sequence>
         <xs:element ref="patient" />
      </xs:sequence>
   </xs:complexType>
</xs:element>
```

references the definition of the patient element that you created earlier. You will add this definition to the file.

To define the patients element in the pschema.xsd file:

1. Below the definition of the patient element, insert the following code, as shown in Figure 14-12:

```
<xs:element name="patients">
   <xs:complexType>
      <xs:sequence>
         <xs:element ref="patient" />
      </xs:sequence>
   </xs:complexType>
</xs:element>
```

Element containing only child elements ◀ Figure 14-12

```
<xs:element name="patient">
    <xs:complexType>
        <xs:sequence>
            <xs:element ref="lastName" />
            <xs:element ref="firstName" />
            <xs:element ref="dateOfBirth" />
            <xs:element ref="age" />
            <xs:element ref="stage" />
            <xs:element ref="comment" />
            <xs:element ref="performance" />
        </xs:sequence>

        <xs:attribute ref="patID" />
        <xs:attribute ref="onStudy" />
    </xs:complexType>
</xs:element>

<xs:element name="patients">
    <xs:complexType>
        <xs:sequence>
            <xs:element ref="patient" />
        </xs:sequence>
    </xs:complexType>
</xs:element>

</xs:schema>
```

the patients element contains the patient element as a child and no other content

2. Save your changes to the file.

Specifying Mixed Content | InSight

One limitation of using DTDs is their inability to define mixed content, which is an element that contains both a text string and child elements. You can specify the child elements with a DTD, but you cannot constrain their order or number. XML Schema gives you more control over mixed content. To specify that an element contains both text and child elements, add the mixed attribute to the <complexType> tag. When the mixed attribute is set to the value true, XML Schema assumes that the element contains both text and child elements. The structure of the child elements can then be defined with the conventional method. For example, the XML content

```
<Summary>
    Patient <Name>Cynthia Davis</Name> was enrolled in
    the <Study>Tamoxifen Study</Study> on 8/15/2003.
</Summary>
```

can be declared in the schema file using the following complex type:

```
<element name="Summary">
    <complexType mixed="true">
        <sequence>
            <element name="Name" type="string"/>
            <element name="Study" type="string"/>
        </sequence>
    </complexType>
</element>
```

XML Schema allows text content to appear before, between, and after any child element.

Reference Window | **Defining Complex Type Elements**

- To define an empty element containing one or more attributes, use

```
<xs:element name="name">
   <xs:complexType>
      attributes
   </xs:complexType>
</xs:element>
```

where *name* is the element name and *attributes* is a list of attributes associated with the element.

- To define an element containing text content and one or more attributes, use

```
<xs:element name="name">
   <xs:complexType>
      <xs:simpleContent>
         <xs:extension base="type">
            attributes
         </xs:extension>
      </xs:simpleContent>
   </xs:complexType>
</xs:element>
```

where *type* is the data type of the text content of the element.

- To define an element containing only nested child elements, use

```
<xs:element name="name">
   <xs:complexType>
      <xs:compositor>
         elements
      </xs:compositor>
   </xs:complexType>
</xs:element>
```

where *elements* is a list of the child elements, and *compositor* is sequence, choice, or all.

- To define an element containing both attributes and nested child elements, use the following:

```
<xs:element name="name">
   <xs:complexType>
      <xs:compositor>
         elements
      </xs:compositor>
   </xs:complexType>
   attributes
</xs:element>
```

At this point, you have defined all of the simple and complex types in Allison's document. Next you will refine your schema by adding code that defines exactly how these simple and complex types are used and what kind of data they can contain.

Indicating Required Attributes

An attribute may or may not be required with a particular element. To indicate whether an attribute is required, the use attribute can be added to a statement that assigns the attribute to an element. The general syntax of the use attribute is

```
<xs:element name="name">
   <xs:complexType>
      element content
      <xs:attribute properties use="use" />
   </xs:complexType>
</xs:element>
```

where *name* is the name of the element containing the attribute, *element content* is XML Schema code that defines the content and structure of the element, *properties* is XML Schema code that defines the data type and properties of the attribute, and *use* has one of the following three values:

- **required**—The attribute must always appear with the element.
- **optional**—The use of the attribute is optional with the element.
- **prohibited**—The attribute cannot be used with the element.

For example, in Allison's document, the scale attribute is required with every performance element. To force the instance document to follow this rule, you add the use attribute to the definition of the scale attribute:

```
<xs:attribute name="scale" type="xs:string" use="required" />
```

If you neglect to add the use attribute to an element declaration, the XML parser assumes that the attribute is optional. The use attribute is only applied when assigning an attribute to a specific element from the instance document. After all, an attribute might be required for one element and optional for another.

The three attributes in Allison's document—patID, onStudy, and scale—are all required for the document to be valid. You will indicate this in the schema by specifying the use of each attribute.

Tip

If you apply the use property to an attribute without reference to the element containing the attribute, the XML Schema code will be rejected as invalid.

To indicate a required attribute in the pschema.xsd file:

1. Go to the code defining the performance element, and then, within the line that references the scale attribute, add `use="required"` to indicate that this attribute is required when used with the performance element.

2. Within the code that defines the patient element, add `use="required"` to the references to the patID and onStudy attributes to indicate that these are also required attributes when used with the patient element. Figure 14-13 highlights the revised code in the schema.

Required attributes ◀ **Figure 14-13**

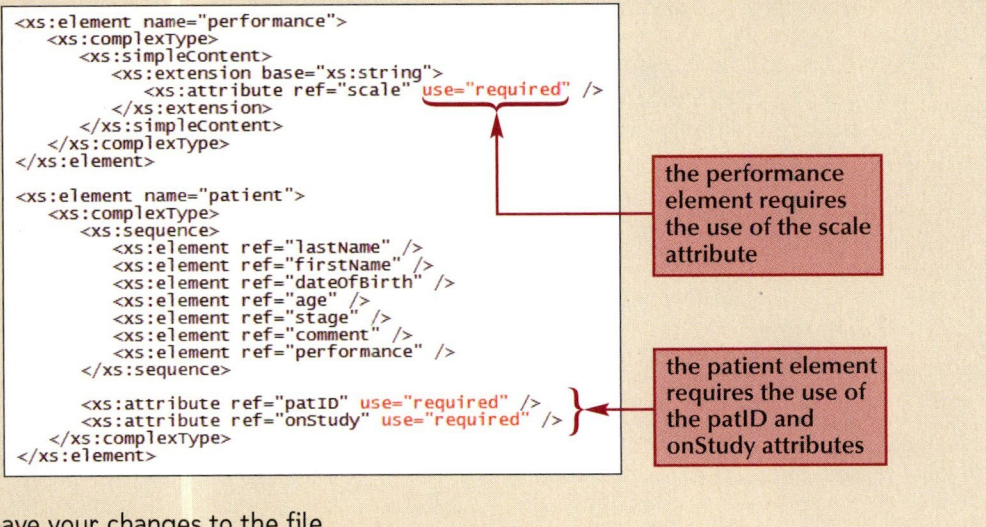

```
<xs:element name="performance">
    <xs:complexType>
        <xs:simpleContent>
            <xs:extension base="xs:string">
                <xs:attribute ref="scale" use="required" />
            </xs:extension>
        </xs:simpleContent>
    </xs:complexType>
</xs:element>

<xs:element name="patient">
    <xs:complexType>
        <xs:sequence>
            <xs:element ref="lastName" />
            <xs:element ref="firstName" />
            <xs:element ref="dateOfBirth" />
            <xs:element ref="age" />
            <xs:element ref="stage" />
            <xs:element ref="comment" />
            <xs:element ref="performance" />
        </xs:sequence>

        <xs:attribute ref="patID" use="required" />
        <xs:attribute ref="onStudy" use="required" />
    </xs:complexType>
</xs:element>
```

the performance element requires the use of the scale attribute

the patient element requires the use of the patID and onStudy attributes

3. Save your changes to the file.

Specifying the Number of Child Elements

The previous code samples assumed that each element in the list appeared once and only once. This is not always the case. For example, Allison's document contains information on one or more patients, so you need to allow for one or more patient elements. To specify the number of times an element appears in the instance document, you can apply the minOccurs and maxOccurs attributes

```
<xs:element name="name" type="type" minOccurs="value" maxOccurs="value"
/>
```

to the element definition, where the minOccurs *value* defines the minimum times the element can occur and the maxOccurs *value* defines the maximum number of times the element can occur. For example, the following element declaration specifies that the patient element must appear one to three times in the instance document:

```
<xs:element name="patient" type="xs:string" minOccurs="1" maxOccurs="3"
/>
```

Tip

A minOccurs value of 0 and a maxOccurs value of unbounded are equivalent to the * character in a DTD. Likewise, values of 1 and unbounded are equivalent to the + character, and values of 0 and 1 are equivalent to the ? character.

Any time the minOccurs attribute is set to 0, the element is optional. The maxOccurs attribute can be any positive value, or it can have a value of unbounded for unlimited occurrences of the element. If a value is specified for the minOccurs attribute but the maxOccurs attribute is missing, the value of the maxOccurs attribute is assumed to be equal to the value of the minOccurs attribute. Finally, if both attributes are missing, the element is assumed to occur only once.

The patient element occurs one or more times in Allison's document, and the comment element occurs zero or more times. All the other elements occur only once. You will add the appropriate minOccurs and maxOccurs values to the schema for the patient and comment elements.

To set the occurrences of the patient and comment elements in the pschema.xsd file:

▶ 1. Go to the code that references the comment element in the pschema.xsd file and add the properties `minOccurs="0" maxOccurs="unbounded"` to allow for zero or more occurrences of the comment element.

▶ 2. Go to the code that references the patient element and add the properties `minOccurs="1" maxOccurs="unbounded"` to allow for one or more occurrences of the patient element. Figure 14-14 highlights the new code in the schema.

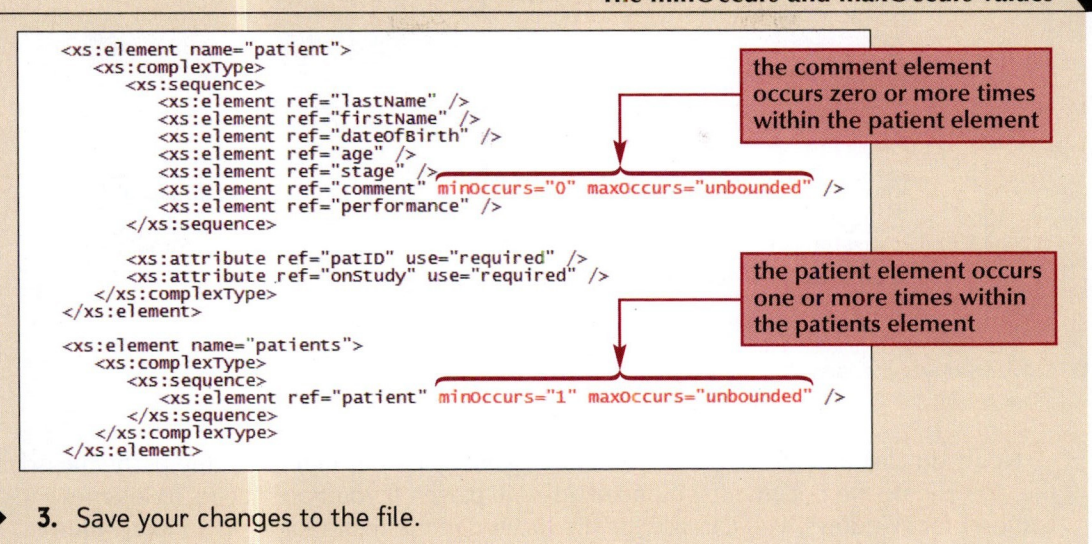

The minOccurs and maxOccurs values   Figure 14-14

```
<xs:element name="patient">
    <xs:complexType>
        <xs:sequence>
            <xs:element ref="lastName" />
            <xs:element ref="firstName" />
            <xs:element ref="dateOfBirth" />
            <xs:element ref="age" />
            <xs:element ref="stage" />
            <xs:element ref="comment" minOccurs="0" maxOccurs="unbounded" />
            <xs:element ref="performance" />
        </xs:sequence>

        <xs:attribute ref="patID" use="required" />
        <xs:attribute ref="onStudy" use="required" />
    </xs:complexType>
</xs:element>

<xs:element name="patients">
    <xs:complexType>
        <xs:sequence>
            <xs:element ref="patient" minOccurs="1" maxOccurs="unbounded" />
        </xs:sequence>
    </xs:complexType>
</xs:element>
```

the comment element occurs zero or more times within the patient element

the patient element occurs one or more times within the patients element

3. Save your changes to the file.

Applying a Schema to an Instance Document

Now that you have created the schema for the patients.xml document, you are ready to validate it. To attach a schema to the document, you must first declare the XML Schema Instance namespace in the document and then specify the location of the schema file. To declare the XML Schema Instance namespace, you add the following element to the root element of the instance document:

```
xmlns:xsi="http://www.w3.org/2001/XMLSchema-instance"
```

The prefix xsi is commonly used for the XML Schema Instance namespace, although you can specify a different prefix in your documents.

The attribute you use to specify the location of the schema file depends on whether the instance document is associated with a namespace. If there is no namespace, add the attribute

```
xsi:noNamespaceSchemaLocation="schema"
```

to the root element, where *schema* is the location and name of the schema file. Note that the attribute requires the xsi namespace prefix because it is an attribute from the XML Schema Instance namespace.

Allison has not yet placed the contents of her patients document in a namespace, so you will add the following attribute to the root patients element:

```
xsi:noNamespaceSchemaLocation="pschema.xsd"
```

You'll explore how to apply schemas to documents that belong to a namespace in the third session of this tutorial.

To apply a schema to the patients document:

1. Return to the **patients.xml** file in your text editor.

2. Within the patients element, add the following attributes, as shown in Figure 14-15:

```
xmlns:xsi="http://www.w3.org/2001/XMLSchema-instance"
xsi:noNamespaceSchemaLocation="pschema.xsd"
```

| Figure 14-15 | Schema applied to a document without a namespace |

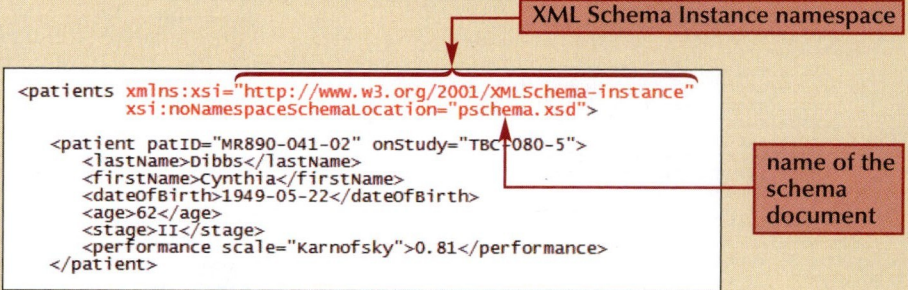

3. Save your changes to the file.

Now you can validate Allison's document against the rules defined in the pschema.xsd file. To validate the document, you need an XML parser. If you have access to Internet Explorer for Windows, you can use the file located in the demo folder to validate your documents against their schemas. If not, you can use one of the free or commercial XML validating parsers available on the Web.

To validate the patients document:

1. Use Internet Explorer to open the **validate_schema.htm** file from the tutorial.14\demo folder.

2. Click the **Browse** button, locate and select the **patients.xml** file from the tutorial.14\tutorial folder, and then click the **Open** button in the Choose File dialog box. The reference to the file appears on the validation page.

3. Click the **Validate** button. The Web page reports that the patients.xml file has no validation error. See Figure 14-16.

| Figure 14-16 | Validation results for the patients.xml file |

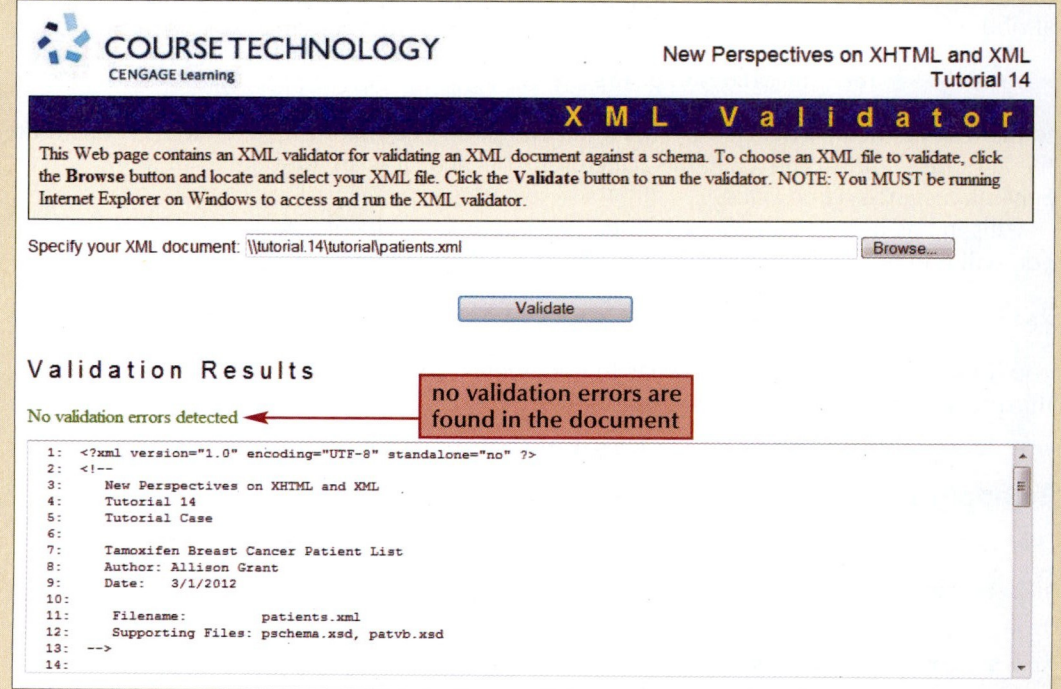

Tip

Your instance document could also fail validation due to errors in the schema file. You can test your schema file for errors by submitting the schema code to the W3C online validator at *www.w3.org/ 2001/03/webdata/xsv*.

Trouble? If you receive an error message, the code of the patients.xml and pschema.xsd files in your text editor may have an error. Compare your schema code to that shown in Figure 14-14. Common mistakes include forgetting to insert the namespace prefix before XML Schema attribute and element names, mismatching the upper- and lowercase letters, and forgetting to add closing tags to the two-sided elements.

Allison suggests that you add an intentional error to the patients.xml file to confirm that the document is rejected as invalid. You will add a second stage element to the first patient's data. Because the schema you wrote assumes only one stage element per patient, this should result in an invalid document.

To add an error to the patients.xml file:

1. Return to the **patients.xml** file in your text editor and add the following line to the information on the first patient in the document, as shown in Figure 14-17:

   `<stage>III</stage>`

Second stage element added to the patients.xml file   **Figure 14-17**

```
<patients xmlns:xsi="http://www.w3.org/2001/XMLSchema-instance"
          xsi:noNamespaceSchemaLocation="pschema.xsd">

    <patient patID="MR890-041-02" onStudy="TBC-080-5">
        <lastName>Dibbs</lastName>
        <firstName>Cynthia</firstName>
        <dateOfBirth>1949-05-22</dateOfBirth>
        <age>62</age>
        <stage>II</stage>
        <stage>III</stage>
        <performance scale="Karnofsky">0.81</performance>
    </patient>
```

a second stage element is not valid according to the schema

2. Save your changes to the file, and then return to the **validate_schema.htm** file in the Internet Explorer browser.

3. Click the **Validate** button. The document is rejected as invalid due to the unexpected extra stage element. See Figure 14-18.

Validation error   **Figure 14-18**

Validation Results

Validation Failed

Validation error reported at: Line 24 at Character 14
  `<stage>III</stage>`
Reason: Element content is invalid according to the DTD/Schema.
Expecting: comment, performance.

description of the error

```
17:
18:         <patient patID="MR890-041-02" onStudy="TBC-080-5">
19:             <lastName>Dibbs</lastName>
20:             <firstName>Cynthia</firstName>
21:             <dateOfBirth>1949-05-22</dateOfBirth>
22:             <age>62</age>
23:             <stage>II</stage>
**24**        <stage>III</stage>
25:             <performance scale="Karnofsky">0.81</performance>
26:         </patient>
27:
28:         <patient patID="MR771-121-10" onStudy="TBC-080-5">
29:             <lastName>Wilkes</lastName>
30:             <firstName>Karen</firstName>
```

location of the validation error

> ► **4.** Return to the **patients.xml** file in your text editor, delete the extra stage element you entered in Step 1, and then save your changes to the file.
>
> ► **5.** Revalidate the document and confirm that it passes the validation test.

Allison is pleased with the initial work you've done in designing a schema for the patients document. However, you have not implemented all the rules that Allison wanted. You'll do that in the next session as you learn about data types and how to apply them.

Review | **Session 14.1 Quick Check**

1. What is a schema? What is an instance document?
2. How do schemas differ from DTDs?
3. What is a simple type? What is a complex type?
4. How do you declare a simple type element named Weight containing string data?
5. How do you declare a complex type element named Contact containing the child elements Mail and/or Phone? (Assume that the Mail and Phone elements are simple type elements containing text strings.)
6. The Book element contains simple text and a Title attribute. What code would you enter into the schema file to define this complex type element?
7. What code would you enter into a schema to create a reference to an attribute named patientID?
8. What attribute would you add to the root element of an instance document to attach it to a schema file named Schema1.xsd? Assume that no namespace has been assigned to the schema file and that you are using the XML Schema vocabulary.

Session 14.2

Validating with Built-In Data Types

The schema you designed for the patients document uses the string data type for all element and attribute content, which allows users to enter any text string into those items. Allison wants to ensure that dates are entered in the proper form, that only positive integers are entered for the patient ages, and that the patient and study IDs follow a prescribed pattern. You can do all of these using data types supported by XML Schema.

XML Schema supports two general categories of data types: built-in and user-derived. A **built-in data type** is part of the XML Schema language. A **user-derived data type** is a data type defined by the schema's author. You'll first work with the built-in data types before creating your own.

XML Schema divides its built-in data types into two classes: primitive and derived. A **primitive data type**, also called a **base type**, is one of 19 fundamental data types that are not defined in terms of other types. A **derived data type** is a data type that is developed from one of the base types. Figure 14-19 provides a schematic diagram of all 44 built-in data types.

XML Schema built-in data types   **Figure 14-19**

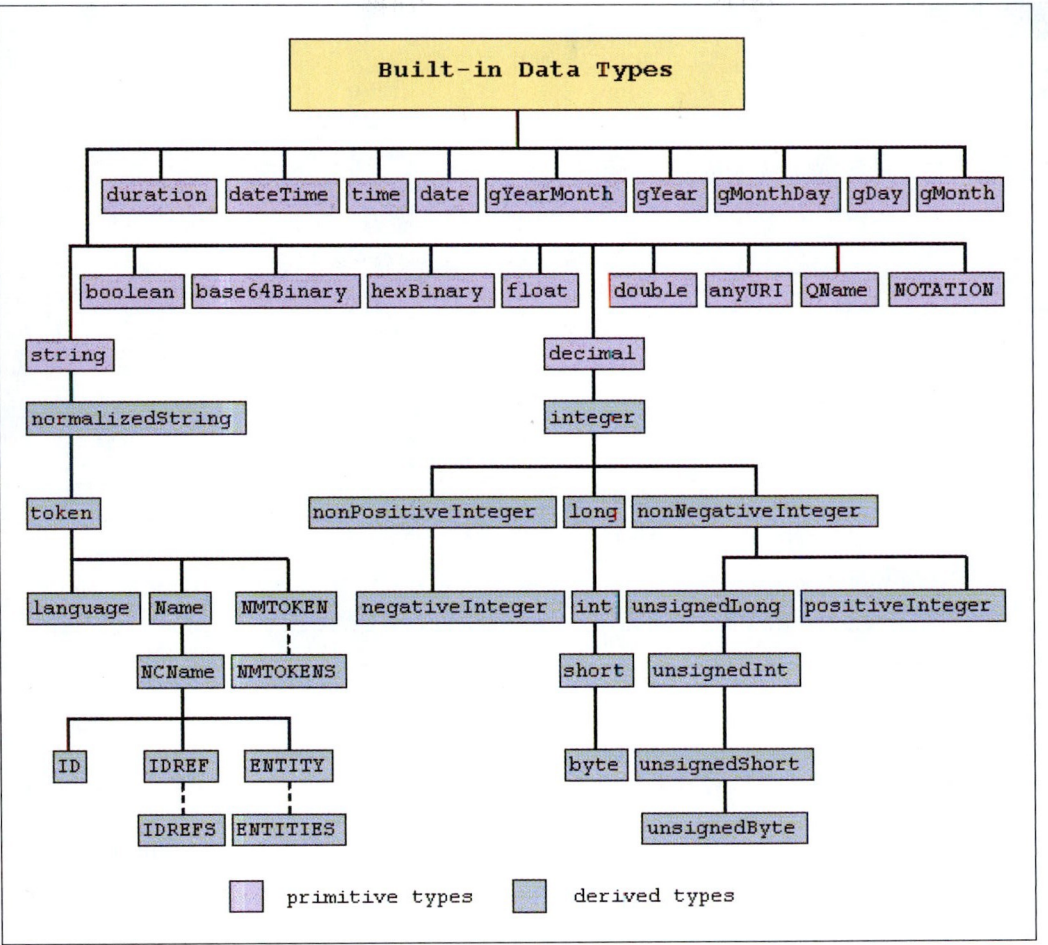

Tip

All built-in data types are part of the XML Schema vocabulary and must be placed in the XML Schema namespace.

Derived data types share many of the same characteristics as the primitive data types they are derived from, but with one or two additional restrictions or modifications. To see how this is done, you'll examine the string data types.

String Data Types

In the previous session, you used only the primitive string type, allowing almost any text string in the elements and attributes of Allison's document. The string data type is the most general of XML Schema's built-in data types. For that reason, it is not very useful if you need to exert more control over element and attribute values in an instance document. XML Schema provides several derived data types that enable you to restrict text strings. Figure 14-20 describes some of these types.

Figure 14-20 ▶ **String data types**

Data Type	Description
xs:string	A text string containing all legal characters from the ISO/IEC character set, including all whitespace characters
xs:normalizedString	A text string in which all whitespace characters are replaced with blank spaces
xs:token	A text string in which blank spaces are replaced with a single blank space; opening and closing spaces are removed
xs:NMTOKEN	A text string containing valid XML names with no whitespace
xs:NMTOKENS	A list of NMTOKEN data values separated by whitespace
xs:Name	A text string similar to the NMTOKEN data type except that names must begin with a letter or the character : or -
xs:NCName	A "noncolonized name," derived from the Name data type but restricting the use of colons anywhere in the name
xs:ID	A unique ID name found nowhere else in the instance document
xs:IDREF	A reference to an ID value found in the instance document
xs:IDREFS	A list of ID references separated by whitespace
xs:ENTITY	A value matching an unparsed entity defined in a DTD
xs:ENTITIES	A list of entity values matching an unparsed entity defined in a DTD

Some of the other data types in the list should be familiar from the previous tutorial. For example, the ID type allows text strings containing unique ID values, and the IDREF and IDREFS data types allow only text strings that contain references to ID values located in the instance document.

Each patient in Allison's document has a patID attribute that uniquely identifies the patient. You will apply the ID data type to this attribute.

To apply the ID data type:

1. If you took a break after the previous session, make sure the patients.xml and pschema.xsd files are open in your text editor and the validate_schema.htm file is open in Internet Explorer.

2. Return to the **pschema.xsd** file in your text editor.

3. Scroll down the document and locate the definition for the patID attribute.

4. Change the type value from xs:string to **xs:ID** as shown in Figure 14-21. Because the ID data type is built into XML Schema, all elements and attributes from the XML Schema vocabulary must be identified using the xs namespace prefix.

Figure 14-21 ▶ **ID data type**

patID values must be unique IDs

```
<xs:attribute name="patID" type="xs:ID" />
<xs:attribute name="onStudy" type="xs:string" />
<xs:attribute name="scale" type="xs:string" />
```

Numeric Data Types

Unlike DTDs, XML Schema supports numeric data types. Most numeric types are derived from four primitive data types: decimal, double, float, and boolean. Figure 14-22 lists some of the XML Schema numeric data types.

Numeric data types ◄ **Figure 14-22**

Data Type	Description
xs:decimal	A decimal number in which the decimal separator is always a dot (.) with a leading + or - character allowed; no nonnumeric characters are allowed, nor is exponential notation.
xs:integer	An integer
xs:nonPositiveInteger	An integer less than or equal to zero
xs:negativeInteger	An integer less than zero
xs:nonNegativeInteger	An integer greater than or equal to zero
xs:positiveInteger	An integer greater than zero
xs:float	A floating point number allowing decimal values and values in scientific notation; infinite values can be represented by -INF and INF; nonnumeric values can be represented by NaN.
xs:double	A double precision floating point number
xs:boolean	A Boolean value that has the value true, false, 0, or 1

Allison entered the ages of all the patients in the Tamoxifen study, and she wants you to validate that the values of the age element have been entered as positive integers. She also recorded a numeric score for each patient's performance on a medical evaluation test. The score values range from 0 to 1. She wants the data type for the performance element to be decimal.

To apply the positiveInteger and decimal data types:

▶ **1.** Change the data type for the age element from xs:string to **xs:positiveInteger**.

▶ **2.** Change the base value of the performance element from xs:string to **xs:decimal**. Because performance is a complex type element containing text and attributes, you add the data type to the base attribute in the simpleContent element. Figure 14-23 shows the revised code.

Numeric data types ◄ **Figure 14-23**

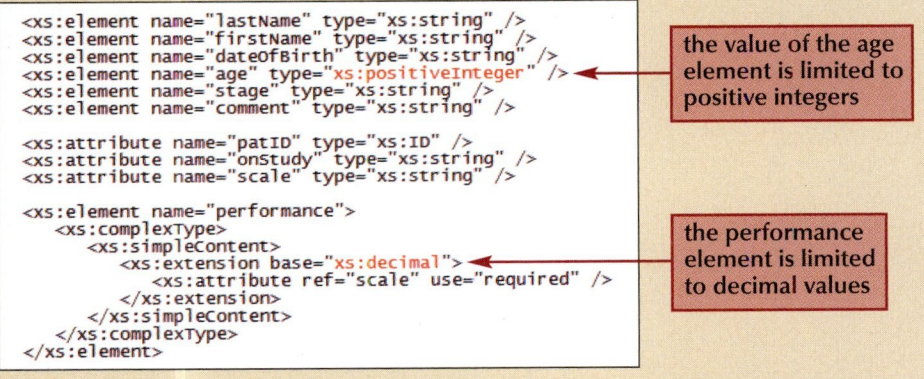

```
<xs:element name="lastName" type="xs:string" />
<xs:element name="firstName" type="xs:string" />
<xs:element name="dateOfBirth" type="xs:string" />
<xs:element name="age" type="xs:positiveInteger" />
<xs:element name="stage" type="xs:string" />
<xs:element name="comment" type="xs:string" />

<xs:attribute name="patID" type="xs:ID" />
<xs:attribute name="onStudy" type="xs:string" />
<xs:attribute name="scale" type="xs:string" />

<xs:element name="performance">
    <xs:complexType>
        <xs:simpleContent>
            <xs:extension base="xs:decimal">
                <xs:attribute ref="scale" use="required" />
            </xs:extension>
        </xs:simpleContent>
    </xs:complexType>
</xs:element>
```

the value of the age element is limited to positive integers

the performance element is limited to decimal values

Trouble? If your code differs from the code in Figure 14-23, you did not enter the data types exactly as specified. A misspelling or change of case will cause the XML parser to reject the entire schema file and report the instance document as invalid. Correct any inconsistencies in the code.

Dates and Times

XML Schema provides several data types for dates, times, and durations. However, XML Schema does not allow for any flexibility in the date and time format. Date values must be entered in the format

yyyy-mm-dd

where *yyyy* is the four-digit year value, *mm* is the two-digit month value, and *dd* is the two-digit day value. Month values range from 01 to 12, and day values range from 01 to 31 (depending on the month). The date value

`2012-01-08`

would be valid under XML Schema, but the date

`2012-1-8`

would not because its month and day values are not two-digit integers.

Times in XML Schema must be entered using 24-hour (or military) time. The format is

`hh:mm:ss`

where *hh* is the hour value ranging from 00 to 23, and *mm* and *ss* are the minutes and seconds values ranging from 00 to 59. No data type exists for expressing time in the 12-hour AM/PM format, but you can create a custom data type for that time pattern. In the time format, each time value (hours, minutes, and seconds) must be specified. Thus, the time value

`15:45`

would be invalid because it does not specify a value for seconds. Figure 14-24 summarizes the different date and time formats supported by XML Schema.

Tip

To support date strings such as 1/8/2012 or Jan. 8, 2012, you must create your own date type or use one of the data type libraries created by other XML developers.

Date and time data types   Figure 14-24

Data Type	Description
xs:datetime	A date and time entered in the format *yyyy-mm-ddThh:mm:ss* where *yyyy* is the four-digit year, *mm* is the two-digit month, *dd* is the two-digit day, *T* is the time zone, *hh* is the two-digit hour, *mm* is the two-digit minute, and *ss* is the two-digit second
xs:date	A date entered in the format *yyyy-mm-dd*
xs:time	A time entered in the format *hh:mm:ss*
xs:gYearMonthDay	A date based on the Gregorian calendar entered in the format *yyyy-mm-dd* (equivalent to xs:date)
xs:gYearMonth	A date entered in the format *yyyy-mm* (no day is specified)
xs:gYear	A year entered in the format *yyyy*
xs:gMonthDay	A month and day entered in the format *--mm-dd*
xs:gMonth	A month entered in the format *--mm*
xs:gDay	A day entered in the format *---dd*
xs:duration	A time duration entered in the format *PyYmMdDhHmMsS* where *y, m, d, h, m,* and *s* are the duration values in years, months, days, hours, minutes, and seconds respectively; an optional negative sign is also permitted to indicate a negative time duration

Allison recorded each patient's date of birth in her XML document and entered the value into the dateOfBirth element. You will apply the date data type to values of this element to confirm that she entered all the date values correctly.

To apply the date data type:

▶ 1. Locate the declaration for the dateOfBirth element and change the data type to **xs:date**, as shown in Figure 14-25.

Date data type   Figure 14-25

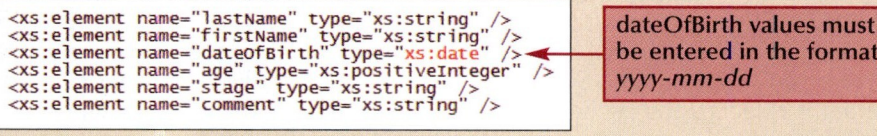

```
<xs:element name="lastName" type="xs:string" />
<xs:element name="firstName" type="xs:string" />
<xs:element name="dateOfBirth" type="xs:date" />
<xs:element name="age" type="xs:positiveInteger" />
<xs:element name="stage" type="xs:string" />
<xs:element name="comment" type="xs:string" />
```

dateOfBirth values must be entered in the format *yyyy-mm-dd*

▶ 2. Save your changes to the pschema.xsd file.

Applying Built-In XML Schema Data Types | Reference Window

- For any string content, use the data type xs:string.
- For an ID value, use xs:ID.
- For a reference to an ID value, use xs:IDREF.
- For a decimal value, use xs:decimal.
- For an integer value, use xs:integer.
- For a positive integer, use xs:positiveInteger.
- For a date in the format *yyyy-mm-dd*, use xs:date.
- For time in the format *hh:mm:ss*, use xs:time.

With the data types you added to the pschema.xsd file, you will validate the contents of the patients.xml file to verify that Allison's data matches the rules of the schema.

To validate the patients.xml file:

▶ 1. Return to the **validate_schema.htm** file in Internet Explorer or access another XML parser.

▶ 2. If necessary, click the **Browse** button to locate and select the **patients.xml** file from the tutorial.14\tutorial folder.

▶ 3. Click the **Validate** button. As shown in Figure 14-26, the validator reports an error in the patients.xml file. The age for one of the patients has been entered as "49 years old" rather than the integer value 49. You will fix this problem and revalidate the file.

| Figure 14-26 | Invalid age reported |

Validation Results

Validation Failed

Validation error reported at: Line 41 at Character 26
    <age>49 years old</age>
Reason: Error parsing '49 years old' as integer datatype.
The element: 'age' has an invalid value according to its data type.

```
34:        <performance scale="Karnofsky">0.84</performance>
35:      </patient>
36:
37:      <patient patID="MR701-891-05" onStudy="TBC-080-5">
38:        <lastName>Sanchez</lastName>
39:        <firstName>Olivia</firstName>
40:        <dateOfBirth>1962-08-14</dateOfBirth>
**41**    <age>49 years old</age>
42:        <stage>II</stage>
43:        <comment>Possibly stage I/II</comment>
44:        <comment>Karnofsky performance rating unavailable.</comment>
45:        <performance scale="Bell">0.89</performance>
46:      </patient>
47:
```

Trouble? If the validator reports the error "Validation error reported at Line 16 at Character 55. xsi:noNamespaceSchemaLocation="pschema.xsd">. Reason: The element 'patients' is used but not declared in the DTD/Schema," you have made an error in entering the XML Schema code, such as mistyping a data type name. The validator rejected the pschema.xsd file and cannot validate the document, starting with the root element patients. Return to the pschema.xsd file, check your code against that shown in the figures, and then repeat this set of steps.

▶ 4. Return to the **patients.xml** file in your text editor, change the age value for the patient from 49 years old to **49**, and then save your changes to the file.

▶ 5. Return to the **validate_schema.htm** Web page, and then click the **Validate** button. The next validation error appears, as shown in Figure 14-27. In this error, the date of birth has been entered in the improper format of 1956-9-14 rather than 1956-09-14.

Validation Results

Validation Failed

Validation error reported at: Line 51 at Character 31
    <dateOfBirth>1956-9-14</dateOfBirth>
Reason: Error parsing '1956-9-14' as date datatype.
The element: 'dateOfBirth' has an invalid value according to its data type.

```
47:
48:        <patient patID="MR805-891-08" onStudy="TBC-080-5">
49:            <lastName>Russell</lastName>
50:            <firstName>Alice</firstName>
**51**         <dateOfBirth>1956-9-14</dateOfBirth>
52:            <age>55</age>
53:            <stage>II</stage>
54:            <performance scale="Karnofsky">1.76</performance>
55:        </patient>
56:
57:        <patient patID="mr815-741-03" onStudy="tbc-080-5">
58:            <lastName>Browne</lastName>
59:            <firstName>Brenda</firstName>
60:            <dateOfBirth>1968-04-25</dateOfBirth>
```

▶ **6.** Return to the **patients.xml** file in your text editor, change the date of birth from 1956-9-14 to `1956-09-14`, and then save your changes to the file.

▶ **7.** Return to the **validate_schema.htm** Web page, and then click the **Validate** button to confirm that the patients.xml file is now valid based on the schema you created.

Deriving Customized Data Types

In addition to the built-in data types, you also need to create some new data types to fully validate Allison's document. Allison has laid out the following rules for the elements and attributes in her document:

• Patients must be at least 21 years of age.
• The stage of the breast cancer must be I or II.
• The performance score must fall between 0 and 1.
• The value of the performance scale attribute must be either Bell or Karnofsky.

XML Schema has no built-in data types for these rules, but you can use XML Schema to derive your own data types. The code to derive a new data type is

```
<xs:simpleType name="name">
    rules
</xs:simpleType>
```

where *name* is the name of the user-defined data type and *rules* is the list of statements that define the properties of that data type. This structure is also known as a **named simple type** because it defines simple type content under a name provided by the schema author. A simple type without a name is known as an **anonymous simple type**. One advantage of creating a named simple type is that you reference that simple type elsewhere in your schema using the simple type name.

Each new data type must be derived from a preexisting data type found in either XML Schema or a user-defined vocabulary. The three components involved in deriving a new data type are the:

- **value space**—The set of values that correspond to the data type; for example, a positiveInteger data type consists of the numbers 1, 2, 3, etc., but does not contain 0, negative integers, fractions, or text strings.
- **lexical space**—The set of textual representations of the value space; for example, the floating data type supports the value 42, which can be represented in several ways (such as 42, 42.0, or 4.2E01).
- **facets**—The properties that distinguish one data type from another; facets can include such properties as text string length or a range of allowable values; for example; a facet that distinguishes the integer data type from the positiveInteger data type is the fact that positive integers are constrained to the realm of positive numbers.

New data types are created by manipulating the properties of these three components. You can do this by:

1. Creating a list based on preexisting data types
2. Creating a union of one or more of the preexisting data types
3. Restricting the values of a preexisting data type

You'll start by examining how to create a list of data types.

Deriving a List Data Type

A **list data type** is a list of values separated by whitespace, in which each item in the list is derived from an established data type. You already have seen a couple of examples of list data types found in XML Schema, including the xs:ENTITIES and xs:IDREFS lists. In these cases, the list data types are derived from XML Schema's xs:ENTITY and xs:IDREF data types. The syntax for deriving a customized list data type is

```
<xs:simpleType name="name">
   <xs:list itemType="type" />
</xs:simpleType>
```

where *name* is the name assigned to the list data type and *type* is the data type from which each item in the list is derived. For example, clinical studies at the University Hospital often involve recording patients' weekly white blood cell counts, where each blood cell count is entered as a decimal value. An element containing this information might appear as follows:

```
<wbc>15.1 15.8 12.0 9.3 7.1 5.2 4.3 3.4</wbc>
```

To create a data type for this information, you could define the following named simple type:

```
<xs:simpleType name="wbcList">
   <xs:list itemType="xs:decimal" />
</xs:simpleType>
```

In this case, you have a data type named wbcList that contains a list of decimal values. To apply this new data type to the wbc element, you reference the data type in the definition as follows:

```
<xs:element name="wbc" type="wbcList" />
```

Notice that the type value does not have the xs namespace prefix because wbcList is not part of the XML Schema vocabulary; it is a named simple type created by the schema author.

Tip

A list data type must always use whitespace as the delimiter. You cannot use commas or other non-whitespace characters.

Deriving a Union Data Type

A **union data type** is based on the value and/or lexical spaces from two or more preexisting data types. Each base data type is known as a **member data type**. The syntax for deriving a union data type is

```
<xs:simpleType name="name">
    <xs:union memberTypes="type1 type2 type3 ..." />
</xs:simpleType>
```

where *type1*, *type2*, *type3*, etc. are the member types that constitute the union. XML Schema also allows unions to be created from nested simple types. The syntax is

```
<xs:simpleType name="name">
    <xs:union>
        <xs:simpleType>
            rules1
        </xs:simpleType>
        <xs:simpleType>
            rules2
        </xs:simpleType>
    </xs:union>
...
</xs:simpleType>
```

where *rules1*, *rules2*, etc. are the rules for creating different user-derived data types. For example, when collecting data on white blood cell counts, Allison might have precise counts as well as more narrative levels—such as high, normal, or low—to record in her research. As a result of this variety, the wbc element might look as follows:

```
<wbc>15.9 high 14.2 9.8 normal low 5.3</wbc>
```

To validate this element containing a mixture of numeric and descriptive measures, she could create the derived data type

```
<xs:simpleType name="wbcType">
    <xs:union memberTypes="xs:decimal xs:Name"/>
</xs:simpleType>
```

so that the parser will accept any value as long as it is either a decimal value or a text string of the Name type. Next, she would use this data type to derive a list type based on the union data type

```
<xs:simpleType name="wbcList">
    <xs:list itemType="wbcType"/>
</xs:simpleType>
```

allowing the wbc element to contain a list consisting of either decimal values or XML names.

Deriving a Restricted Data Type

The final kind of derived data type is a **restricted data type**, in which a restriction is placed on the facets of a preexisting data type, such as an integer data type that is constrained to fall within a range of values. XML Schema provides 12 constraining facets that can be used to derive new data types, which are described in Figure 14-28.

Figure 14-28 ▸ **Constraining facets**

Facet	Description
enumeration	Constrains the data to a specified list of values
length	Specifies the length of the data in characters (for text strings) or items (for lists)
maxLength	Specifies the maximum length of the data in characters (for text strings) or items (for lists)
minLength	Specifies the minimum length of the data in characters (for text strings) or items (for lists)
pattern	Constrains the lexical space of the data to follow a specific character pattern
whiteSpace	Controls the use of blanks in the lexical space of the data; the whiteSpace facet has three values: preserve (preserve all whitespace) replace (replace all tabs, carriage returns, and line feed characters with blank spaces) collapse (collapse all consecutive occurrences of whitespace to a single blank space, remove any leading or trailing whitespace)
maxExclusive	Constrains the data to be less than a maximum value
maxInclusive	Constrains the data to be less than or equal to a maximum value
minExclusive	Constrains the data to be greater than a minimum value
minInclusive	Constrains the data to be greater than or equal to a minimum value
fractionDigits	Specifies the maximum number of decimal places to the right of the decimal point in the data value
totalDigits	Specifies the maximum number of decimals in the data value

Constraining facets are applied to a base type using the structure

```
<xs:simpleType name="name">
   <xs:restriction base="type">
      <xs:facet1 value="value1" />
      <xs:facet2 value="value2" />
   </xs:restriction>
</xs:simpleType>
```

where *type* is the data type on which the restricted data type is based; *facet1*, *facet2*, etc., are constraining facets; and *value1*, *value2*, etc., are values for each constraining facet. In Allison's document, the age of each patient must be at least 21. The restricted data type would use the minInclusive facet to restrict the age value to at least 21. The code for the ageType data type therefore would be

```
<xs:simpleType name="ageType">
   <xs:restriction base="xs:integer">
      <xs:minInclusive value="21" />
   </xs:restriction>
</xs:simpleType>
```

forcing the age values to be integers with a minimum value of 21. You will add this data type to the schema and apply it to the age element.

To create the ageType data type:

▶ 1. Return to the **pschema.xsd** file in your text editor.

▶ 2. Below the declaration for the performance element, insert the following code to constrain the age element to at least 21:

```
<xs:simpleType name="ageType">
   <xs:restriction base="xs:integer">
      <xs:minInclusive value="21" />
   </xs:restriction>
</xs:simpleType>
```

▶ 3. Change the data type for the age element from xs:positiveInteger to `ageType`. Figure 14-29 shows the revised code in the schema. You do *not* include the xs namespace prefix when referencing the data type because ageType is not part of the XML Schema vocabulary.

The ageType data type | Figure 14-29

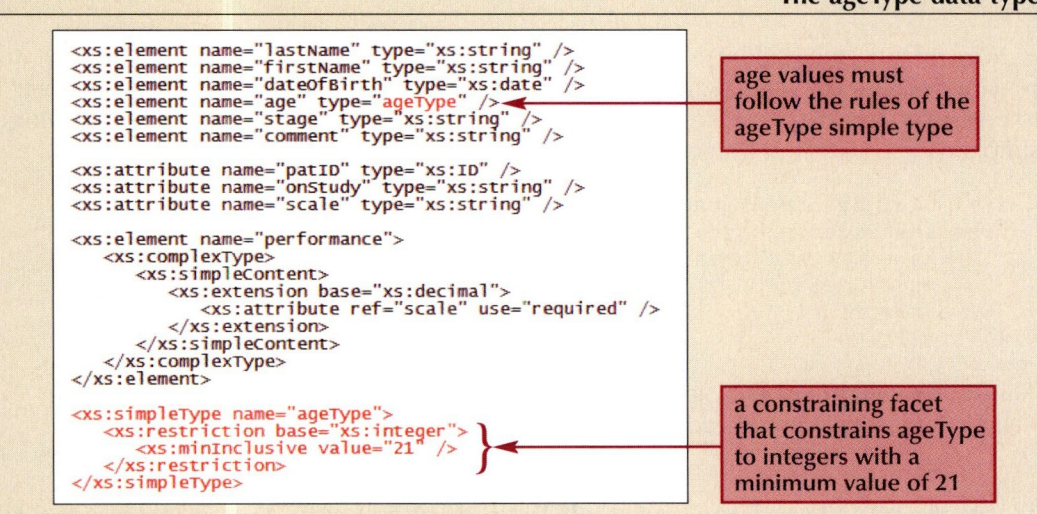

```
<xs:element name="lastName" type="xs:string" />
<xs:element name="firstName" type="xs:string" />
<xs:element name="dateOfBirth" type="xs:date" />
<xs:element name="age" type="ageType" />
<xs:element name="stage" type="xs:string" />
<xs:element name="comment" type="xs:string" />

<xs:attribute name="patID" type="xs:ID" />
<xs:attribute name="onStudy" type="xs:string" />
<xs:attribute name="scale" type="xs:string" />

<xs:element name="performance">
   <xs:complexType>
      <xs:simpleContent>
         <xs:extension base="xs:decimal">
            <xs:attribute ref="scale" use="required" />
         </xs:extension>
      </xs:simpleContent>
   </xs:complexType>
</xs:element>

<xs:simpleType name="ageType">
   <xs:restriction base="xs:integer">
      <xs:minInclusive value="21" />
   </xs:restriction>
</xs:simpleType>
```

age values must follow the rules of the ageType simple type

a constraining facet that constrains ageType to integers with a minimum value of 21

Facets can also be used to define a lower and upper range for data. In Allison's data, performance scores range from 0 to 1, with 0 and 1 excluded as possible values. To create a data type for this interval, you use the minExclusive and maxExclusive facets, setting the value of the minExclusive facet to 0 and the value of the maxExclusive facet to 1. You will use these two facets to create a data type named perfType for the performance element.

To derive the perfType data type in the pschema.xsd file:

▶ 1. Below the ageType simple type, insert the following code to constrain the performance element to decimal values between 0 and 1:

```
<xs:simpleType name="perfType">
   <xs:restriction base="xs:decimal">
      <xs:minExclusive value="0" />
      <xs:maxExclusive value="1" />
   </xs:restriction>
</xs:simpleType>
```

▶ 2. Change the data type in the performance element from xs:decimal to `perfType`. See Figure 14-30.

Figure 14-30 | **The perfType data type**

```
<xs:element name="performance">
   <xs:complexType>
      <xs:simpleContent>
         <xs:extension base="perfType">
            <xs:attribute ref="scale" use="required" />
         </xs:extension>
      </xs:simpleContent>
   </xs:complexType>
</xs:element>

<xs:simpleType name="ageType">
   <xs:restriction base="xs:integer">
      <xs:minInclusive value="21" />
   </xs:restriction>
</xs:simpleType>

<xs:simpleType name="perfType">
   <xs:restriction base="xs:decimal">
      <xs:minExclusive value="0" />
      <xs:maxExclusive value="1" />
   </xs:restriction>
</xs:simpleType>
```

performance must follow the rules of the perfType simple type

a constraining facet that constrains perfType values to decimals greater than 0 and less than 1

When data values belong to a set of values rather than a range, you can create a list of possible values using the enumeration element. Allison wants values of the stage element to be limited to either I for Stage I cancer patients or II for Stage II patients. The following simple type restricts the element to only these two possible values:

```
<xs:simpleType name="stageType">
   <xs:restriction base="xs:string">
      <xs:enumeration value="I" />
      <xs:enumeration value="II" />
   </xs:restriction>
</xs:simpleType>
```

Allison also needs a similar structure to restrict the value of the scale attribute to either Bell or Karnofsky. You will add both of these enumerated types to the schema.

To create the stageType and scaleType data types in the pschema.xsd file:

1. Below the ageType simple type, insert the following code to restrict the stage to I or II:

```
<xs:simpleType name="stageType">
   <xs:restriction base="xs:string">
      <xs:enumeration value="I" />
      <xs:enumeration value="II" />
   </xs:restriction>
</xs:simpleType>
```

2. Insert the following code to restrict the scale to Bell or Karnofsky:

```
<xs:simpleType name="scaleType">
   <xs:restriction base="xs:string">
      <xs:enumeration value="Bell" />
      <xs:enumeration value="Karnofsky" />
   </xs:restriction>
</xs:simpleType>
```

3. Change the data type of the stage element from xs:string to `stageType`.

4. Change the data type of the scale attribute from xs:string to `scaleType`. Figure 14-31 highlights the revised code.

The stageType and scaleType data types | Figure 14-31

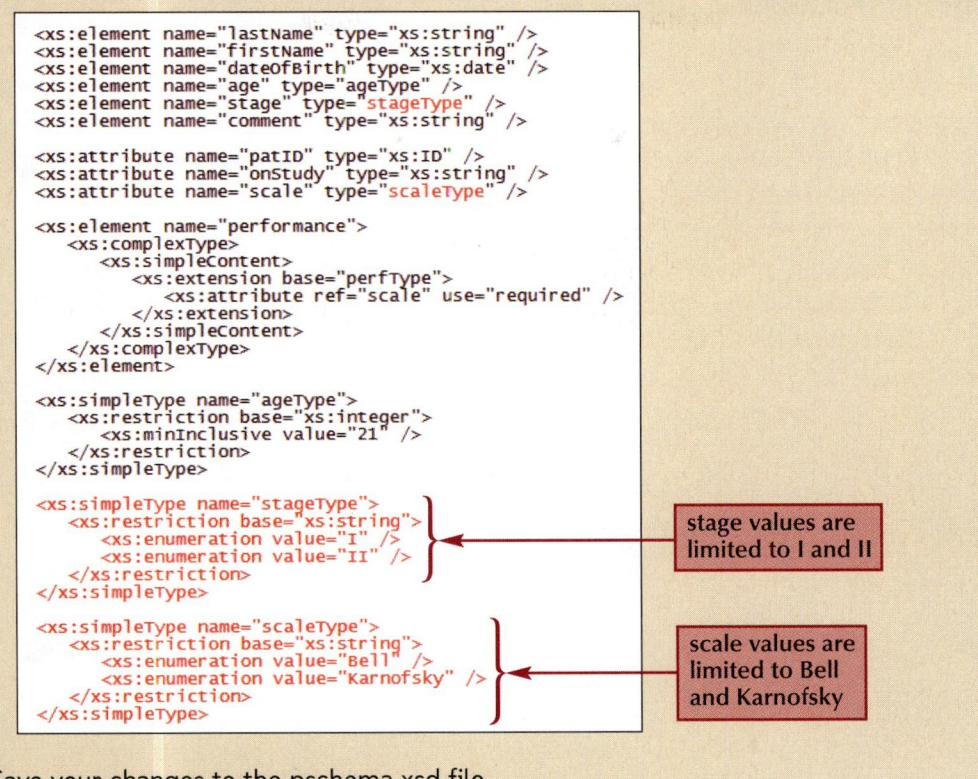

```
<xs:element name="lastName" type="xs:string" />
<xs:element name="firstName" type="xs:string" />
<xs:element name="dateOfBirth" type="xs:date" />
<xs:element name="age" type="ageType" />
<xs:element name="stage" type="stageType" />
<xs:element name="comment" type="xs:string" />

<xs:attribute name="patID" type="xs:ID" />
<xs:attribute name="onStudy" type="xs:string" />
<xs:attribute name="scale" type="scaleType" />

<xs:element name="performance">
    <xs:complexType>
        <xs:simpleContent>
            <xs:extension base="perfType">
                <xs:attribute ref="scale" use="required" />
            </xs:extension>
        </xs:simpleContent>
    </xs:complexType>
</xs:element>

<xs:simpleType name="ageType">
    <xs:restriction base="xs:integer">
        <xs:minInclusive value="21" />
    </xs:restriction>
</xs:simpleType>

<xs:simpleType name="stageType">
    <xs:restriction base="xs:string">
        <xs:enumeration value="I" />
        <xs:enumeration value="II" />
    </xs:restriction>
</xs:simpleType>

<xs:simpleType name="scaleType">
    <xs:restriction base="xs:string">
        <xs:enumeration value="Bell" />
        <xs:enumeration value="Karnofsky" />
    </xs:restriction>
</xs:simpleType>
```

stage values are limited to I and II

scale values are limited to Bell and Karnofsky

5. Save your changes to the pschema.xsd file.

Reference Window | **Deriving Custom Data Types**

- To derive a list of preexisting data types, use
  ```
  <xs:simpleType name="name">
    <xs:list itemType="type"/>
  </xs:simpleType>
  ```
  where *name* is the name of the custom data type and *type* is the data type on which it is based.

- To derive a union of two or more preexisting data types, use
  ```
  <xs:simpleType name="name">
    <xs:union memberTypes="type1 type2 type3 ..."/>
  </xs:simpleType>
  ```
  where *type1*, *type2*, *type3*, etc., are the member types that constitute the union and upon which the custom data type is based. Alternatively, use the nested form
  ```
  <xs:simpleType name="name">
    <xs:union>
        <xs:simpleType>
            rules1
        </xs:simpleType>
        <xs:simpleType>
            rules2
        </xs:simpleType>
  ...
      </xs:union>
    </xs:simpleType>
  ```
  where *rules1*, *rules2*, etc., are the rules that define the different data types in the union.

- To derive a data type by restricting the values of a preexisting data type, use
  ```
  <xs:simpleType name="name">
    <xs:restriction base="type">
        <xs:facet1 value="value1" />
        <xs:facet2 value="value2" />
    </xs:restriction>
  </xs:simpleType>
  ```
  where *facet1*, *facet2*, etc., are constraining facets, and *value1*, *value2*, etc., are values for the constraining facets.

Before editing this schema further, you will test the revised schema against the current contents of the patients.xml file.

To validate the custom data types in the patients.xml file:

▶ **1.** Return to the **validate_schema.htm** file in your Internet Explorer browser and with the **patients.xml** file still selected, click the **Validate** button. As shown in Figure 14-32, the validator encounters an error because a performance score greater than 1 has been entered for a patient. The correct value is 0.76, not 1.76.

Invalid performance score value | Figure 14-32

Validation Results

Validation Failed

Validation error reported at: Line 54 at Character 44
   <performance scale="Karnofsky">1.76</performance>
Reason: maxExclusive constraint failed.
The element: 'performance' has an invalid value according to its data type.

```
47:
48:        <patient patID="MR805-891-08" onStudy="TBC-080-5">
49:            <lastName>Russell</lastName>
50:            <firstName>Alice</firstName>
51:            <dateOfBirth>1956-09-14</dateOfBirth>
52:            <age>55</age>
53:            <stage>II</stage>
**54**         <performance scale="Karnofsky">1.76</performance>
55:        </patient>
56:
57:        <patient patID="mr815-741-03" onStudy="tbc-080-5">
58:            <lastName>Browne</lastName>
59:            <firstName>Brenda</firstName>
60:            <dateOfBirth>1968-04-25</dateOfBirth>
```

Trouble? If you receive a different error message, you probably have an error in your schema code. Check your code against that shown in Figures 14-29 through 14-31 and make the necessary corrections. You can also validate your schema code using the schema validator at *www.w3.org/2001/03/webdata/xsv*.

2. Go to the **patients.xml** file in your text editor, change the value from 1.76 to `0.76`, and then save your changes to the file.

3. Return to the **validate_schema.htm** file in your Internet Explorer browser, and then click the **Validate** button. Figure 14-33 shows a second validation error in which the value of the scale attribute was entered as Karnosfky rather than Karnofsky. You will correct this typographical error.

Invalid performance scale | Figure 14-33

Validation Results

Validation Failed

Validation error reported at: Line 63 at Character 38
   <performance scale="Karnosfky">0.88</performance>
Reason: enumeration constraint failed.
The attribute: 'scale' has an invalid value according to its data type.

```
55:        </patient>
56:
57:        <patient patID="mr815-741-03" onStudy="tbc-080-5">
58:            <lastName>Browne</lastName>
59:            <firstName>Brenda</firstName>
60:            <dateOfBirth>1968-04-25</dateOfBirth>
61:            <age>39</age>
62:            <stage>I</stage>
**63**         <performance scale="Karnosfky">0.88</performance>
64:        </patient>
65:
66:   </patients>
67:
```

4. Go to the **patients.xml** file in your text editor, change Karnosfky to `Karnofsky`, and then save your changes to the file.

▶ **5.** Return to the **validate_schema.htm** file in your Internet Explorer browser, and then click the **Validate** button to revalidate the file. The file passes the validation test.

Deriving Data Types Using Regular Expressions

Allison has two final restrictions to place on data values stored in her patient records:

- Each patient's medical record number must be entered in the form MR###-###-## where # is a digit from 0 to 9.
- The study name must follow the form *AAA-###-#* where *A* is a capital letter from A through Z and # is a digit from 0 to 9.

These rules involve the representation of the values, so you need to create a restriction based on the lexical space. One way of doing this is through a regular expression.

Introducing Regular Expressions

A **regular expression** is a text string that defines a character pattern. Regular expressions can be created to define patterns for phone numbers, postal address codes, e-mail addresses, and in the case of Allison's document, personal IDs. To apply a regular expression in a data type, you create the simple type

```
<xs:simpleType name="name">
   <xs:restriction base="type">
      <xs:pattern value="regex" />
   </xs:restriction>
</xs:simpleType>
```

where *regex* is a regular expression pattern. The most basic pattern specifies the characters that must appear in valid data. The following regular expression forces the value of the data type to be the text string ABC:

```
<xs:pattern value="ABC" />
```

Any other combination of letters, including the use of lowercase letters, would be invalid.

Instead of a pattern involving specific characters, you usually want a more general pattern involving **character types** that represent different kinds of characters. The general form of a character type is

```
\char
```

where *char* represents a specific character type. Character types can include digits, word characters (any uppercase or lowercase letter, digit, or underscore character [_]), boundaries around words (any text string containing only word characters), and whitespace characters. Figure 14-34 describes the code for representing each of these character types.

Character Type	Description
\d	A digit from 0 to 9
\D	A non-digit character
\w	A word character (an upper- or lowercase letter, a digit, or an underscore (_)
\W	A non-word character
\b	A boundary around a word (a text string of word characters)
\B	The absence of a boundary around a word
\s	A whitespace character (a blank space, tab, new line, carriage return, or form feed)
\S	A non-whitespace character
.	Any character

Regular expression character types — Figure 14-34

For example, the character type for a single digit is \d. To create a regular expression representing three digits, you would apply the following pattern:

```
<xs:pattern value="\d\d\d" />
```

Any text string that contains three digits would match this pattern. Thus, the text strings 012 or 921 would match this pattern, but 1,020 or 54 would not.

For more general patterns, characters can also be grouped into lists called **character sets** that specify exactly what characters or ranges of characters are allowed in the pattern. The syntax of a character set is

```
[chars]
```

where *chars* is the set of characters in the character set. For example, the pattern

```
<xs:pattern value="[dog]" />
```

matches any of the characters "d", "o", or "g". Because characters can be sorted alphabetically or numerically, character sets can also be created for a range of characters using the general syntax

```
[char1 - charN]
```

where *char1* is the first character in the range and *charN* is the last letter in the range. To create a range of lowercase letters, you would use the following pattern:

```
<xs:pattern value="[a-z]" />
```

Any lowercase letter would be matched by this pattern. You can also match numeric values. The following matches any digit from 1 to 5:

```
<xs:pattern value="[1-5]" />
```

Figure 14-35 lists many of the common character sets used in regular expressions.

Tip

In a regular expression, the opposite of a character type is indicated by a capital letter. So \d represents a single digit, and \D represents any character that is *not* a digit.

Figure 14-35 ▶ Regular expression character lists

Character Set	Description
[chars]	Match any character in the chars list
[^chars]	Do not match any character in chars
[char1-charN]	Match any character in the range char1 through charN
[^char1-charN]	Do not match any character in the range char1 through charN
[a-z]	Match any lowercase letter
[A-Z]	Match any uppercase letter
[a-zA-Z]	Match any letter
[0-9]	Match any digit from 0 to 9
[0-9a-zA-Z]	Match any digit or letter

The regular expressions you've looked at so far have involved individual characters. To specify the number of occurrences for a particular character or group of characters, a **quantifier** can be appended to a character type or set. Figure 14-36 lists the different quantifiers used in regular expressions. Some of these quantifiers should be familiar from your work with DTDs.

Figure 14-36 ▶ Regular expression quantifiers

Quantifier	Description
*	Repeat 0 or more times
?	Repeat 0 or 1 time
+	Repeat 1 or more times
{n}	Repeat exactly n times
{n,}	Repeat at least n times
{n,m}	Repeat at least n times but no more than m times

As you saw earlier, to specify a pattern of three consecutive digits, you can use the following regular expression:

```
\d\d\d
```

Tip

On the Web, you can find libraries of predefined regular expression patterns that can be applied to text strings such as phone numbers, postal codes, credit card numbers, and Social Security numbers.

Alternatively, you can employ the quantifier {3} using the pattern

```
<xs:pattern value="\d{3}" />
```

which also defines a pattern of three digits. To validate a string of uppercase characters of any length, you use the * quantifier, as follows:

```
<xs:pattern value="[A-Z]*" />
```

The following pattern allows for a text string of uppercase letters from zero to ten characters long:

```
<xs:pattern value="[A-Z]{0,10}" />
```

- To derive a data type based on a regular expression pattern, use

```
<xs:simpleType name="name">
  <xs:restriction base="type">
    <xs:pattern value="regex" />
  </xs:restriction>
</xs:simpleType>
```

where *name* is the name of the derived data type, *type* is a preexisting data type on which the derived type is based, and *regex* is a regular expression defining the pattern of characters in the data.

Applying a Regular Expression

You have only scratched the surface of what regular expressions can do. The topic of regular expressions could fill an entire tutorial by itself. However, you have covered enough to be able to comply with Allison's request that all ID strings be in the format MR###-###-##, where # is a digit from 0 to 9. The pattern for this expression is

```
<xs:pattern value="MR\d{3}-\d{3}-\d{2}" />
```

where the character type \d represents a single digit and the quantifiers {3} and {2} indicate that the digits must be repeated three and two times, respectively. Study IDs must follow the *AAA-###-#* pattern, where *A* is any uppercase letter and # is a digit. The regular expression for this pattern is:

```
<xs:pattern value="[A-Z]{3}-\d{3}-\d" />
```

This pattern uses the character set and quantifier [A-Z]{3} to represent any string of three uppercase letters. You will create data types named mrType and studyType based on these patterns.

To derive a data type based on a regular expression:

1. Return to the **pschema.xsd** file in your text editor and insert the following code directly below the declaration for the scale attribute to set the pattern for the medical record values:

```
<xs:simpleType name="mrType">
  <xs:restriction base="xs:ID">
    <xs:pattern value="MR\d{3}-\d{3}-\d{2}" />
  </xs:restriction>
</xs:simpleType>
```

The base type is xs:ID, indicating that this custom data type will be derived from unique ID values in the document.

2. Add the following code to derive the studyType data type to specify the pattern for the study IDs:

```
<xs:simpleType name="studyType">
  <xs:restriction base="xs:string">
    <xs:pattern value="[A-Z]{3}-\d{3}-\d" />
  </xs:restriction>
</xs:simpleType>
```

3. Change the data type of the patID attribute from xs:ID to **mrType**.

> **4.** Change the data type of the onStudy attribute from xs:string to `studyType`. Figure 14-37 shows the revised code of the schema file.

| Figure 14-37 | The mrType and studyType data types |

```
<xs:attribute name="patID" type="mrType" />
<xs:attribute name="onStudy" type="studyType" />
<xs:attribute name="scale" type="scaleType" />

<xs:simpleType name="mrType">
    <xs:restriction base="xs:ID">
        <xs:pattern value="MR\d{3}-\d{3}-\d{2}" />
    </xs:restriction>
</xs:simpleType>

<xs:simpleType name="studyType">
    <xs:restriction base="xs:string">
        <xs:pattern value="[A-Z]{3}-\d{3}-\d" />
    </xs:restriction>
</xs:simpleType>
```

> values must be unique IDs of the form MR###-###-##, where # is a digit

> values must be text strings of the form AAA###-###-#, where A is an uppercase letter and # is a digit

> **5.** Save your changes to the pschema.xsd file.

Next, you will validate Allison's document to ensure that all the medical record numbers and study IDs match the patterns you defined.

To validate the medical record numbers and the study IDs:

> **1.** Return to the **validate_schema.htm** file in your Internet Explorer browser, and then, if necessary, locate and select the **patients.xml** file from the tutorial.14\ tutorial folder.

> **2.** Click **Validate** button to validate the document. The validator encounters an error because the medical record number for the last patient is mr815-741-03 rather than MR815-741-03. See Figure 14-38.

| Figure 14-38 | Invalid patID value |

Validation Results

Validation Failed

Validation error reported at: Line 57 at Character 54
  <patient patID="mr815-741-03" onStudy="tbc-080-5">
Reason: pattern constraint failed.
The attribute: 'patID' has an invalid value according to its data type.

> mr815-741-03 should be MR815-741-03

```
  54:         <performance scale="Karnofsky">0.76</performance>
  55:     </patient>
  56:
**57**     <patient patID="mr815-741-03" onStudy="tbc-080-5">
  58:         <lastName>Browne</lastName>
  59:         <firstName>Brenda</firstName>
  60:         <dateOfBirth>1968-04-25</dateOfBirth>
  61:         <age>39</age>
  62:         <stage>I</stage>
  63:         <performance scale="Karnofsky">0.88</performance>
  64:     </patient>
  65:
  66: </patients>
```

Trouble? If you receive a different error message, you probably have an error in your code. Check your schema for errors in the code, making corrections as needed, and then repeat Step 2.

3. Go to the **patients.xml** file in your text editor, change value of the patID attribute for the last patient from mr815-741-03 to `MR815-741-03`, and then save your changes to the file.

4. Return to the Internet Explorer browser, and then press the **Validate** button to revalidate the patients.xml file. Figure 14-39 shows a second validation error caused by entering the value of the onStudy attribute as tbc-080-5 rather than TBC-080-5. You will correct this problem.

Invalid onStudy number — **Figure 14-39**

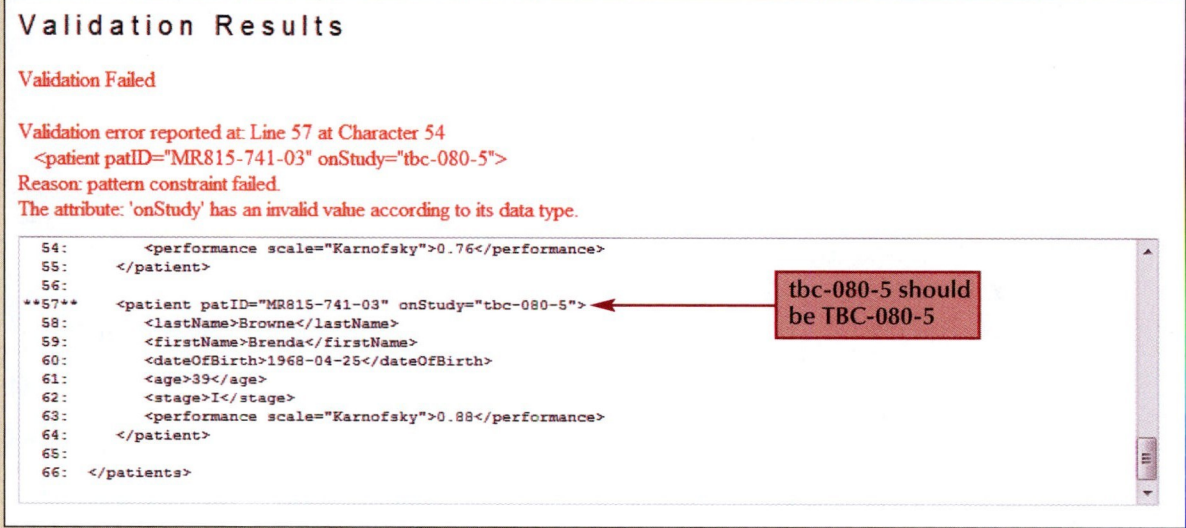

```
Validation Results

Validation Failed

Validation error reported at: Line 57 at Character 54
  <patient patID="MR815-741-03" onStudy="tbc-080-5">
Reason: pattern constraint failed.
The attribute: 'onStudy' has an invalid value according to its data type.

  54:          <performance scale="Karnofsky">0.76</performance>
  55:      </patient>
  56:
**57**     <patient patID="MR815-741-03" onStudy="tbc-080-5">        tbc-080-5 should
  58:          <lastName>Browne</lastName>                            be TBC-080-5
  59:          <firstName>Brenda</firstName>
  60:          <dateOfBirth>1968-04-25</dateOfBirth>
  61:          <age>39</age>
  62:          <stage>I</stage>
  63:          <performance scale="Karnofsky">0.88</performance>
  64:      </patient>
  65:
  66:  </patients>
```

5. Go to the **patients.xml** file in your text editor, change tbc-080-5 to `TBC-080-5`, and then save your changes.

6. Return to the Internet Explorer browser, and then click the **Validate** button to revalidate the patients.xml file. The file should be valid based on the rules in the schema.

InSight | **Deriving Data Types and Inheritance**

You can use XML Schema to create a library of new data types. You can use every new data type you create as a base for creating yet another type. For example, you can start with a data type for integer values, use that to define a new data type for positive integers, use that to define a type for positive integers between 1 and 100, and so forth. However, unless you are creating a list or a union, every new type represents a restriction of one or more facets in a preexisting type.

In some cases, you might want to fix a facet so that any new types based upon it cannot modify it. For example, if Allison had defined the age data type to have a minimum value of 18, she might want to prevent any future data types based on age from being able to change that minimum value. She can do so by applying the following fixed attribute to the minInclusive facet:

```
<xs:minInclusive value="18" fixed="true" />
```

From this point forward, any new data type based on the age type will have its minimum value set at 18. Fixing a facet makes the data type library less flexible and should be used only in situations where changing the facet value would dramatically alter the original meaning of the data type. For example, legal reasons might require the minimum age value to be set at 18, so that every study in Allison's cancer document must allow for patients of that age.

You can also use XML Schema to prevent any new data types from being created from an existing type. This is done using the final attribute

```
<xs:simpleType name="name" final="derivation">
   . . .
</xs:simpleType>
```

where *name* is the name of the new data type and *derivation* indicates which methods of creating new data types are prohibited (list, union, restriction, or all). For example, the following code defines the age data type and prohibits it from being used in deriving a new data type through a union or a list:

```
<xs:simpleType name="age" final="union list">
   . . .
</xs:simpleType>
```

When the final attribute is omitted or set to an empty text string, XML Schema will allow for any kinds of derivations of the original type.

You have completed work on creating custom data types using named simple types. In the next session, you will explore how to create custom complex types and how to structure your schema to work with compound documents involving several different XML vocabularies from different namespaces.

Review | **Session 14.2 Quick Check**

1. Enter a definition for a data type named Weight containing only decimal data.
2. Enter the attribute definition for the itemIDs attribute containing a list of ID references.
3. Define a data type named VisitDates containing a list of dates.
4. Define a data type named Status that contains either a decimal or a text string.
5. Define a data type named Party limited to one of the following: Democrat, Republican, or Independent.
6. Define a data type named Percentage limited to decimal values falling between 0 and 1 (inclusive).

7. Define a data type named SocSecurity containing a text string matching the pattern ###-##-####, where # is a digit from 0 to 9.

Session 14.3

Working with Named Types

In the previous session, you used named simple types to create your own library of customized data types for Allison's document. XML Schema also allows schema authors to create customized complex types. The advantage of creating a complex type is that a complex structure of elements and attributes can be stored as a single entity. For example, consider the following child element containing the complex content of two nested elements named firstName and lastName:

```
<xs:element name="client">
   <xs:complexType>
      <xs:sequence>
         <xs:element name="firstName" type="xs:string" />
         <xs:element name="lastName" type="xs:string" />
      </xs:sequence>
   </xs:complexType>
</xs:element>
```

The complex type applied to the client element is called an **anonymous complex type** because no name attribute is used in the opening <xs:complexType> tag. However, because such firstName/lastName child elements occur frequently in many kinds of XML documents, it would be helpful if you could store this structure rather than reentering it over and over again. You can do this by naming the structure and creating a **named complex type** that can be used elsewhere in the schema. For example, you could enter the following code to create a complex type named fullName that is unassigned to any particular element:

```
<xs:complexType name="fullName">
   <xs:sequence>
      <xs:element name="firstName" type="xs:string" />
      <xs:element name="lastName" type="xs:string" />
   </xs:sequence>
</xs:complexType>
```

This named complex type could then be applied to any complex type element using the type attribute (just as you used the type attribute to apply a customized simple type in the previous session). For example, to apply this same structure to complex type elements named client and salesperson, you could add the following code to the schema:

```
<xs:element name="client" type="fullName" />
<xs:element name="salesperson" type="fullName" />
```

Because they both use the complex type fullName, the client and the salesperson elements have the same complex structure: two child elements named firstName and lastName, both containing text strings.

Named Model Groups

Named complex types are not the only structures you can create to reuse in schemas. Another structure is a named model group. As the name suggests, a **named model group** is a collection, or group, of elements. Named model groups are created using the structure

```
<xs:group name="name">
   elements
</xs:group>
```

where *name* is the name of the model group, and *elements* is a collection of element declarations. The element declarations must be enclosed within a sequence, choice, or all compositor. The following code creates a model group named fullName that contains two elements:

```
<xs:group name="fullName">
   <xs:sequence>
      <xs:element name="firstName" type="xs:string" />
      <xs:element name="lastName" type="xs:string" />
   </xs:sequence>
</xs:group>
```

To apply a named model group to an element declaration, you use the ref attribute. For example, to reference the fullName model group from the client element, you use the following code:

```
<xs:element name="client">
   <xs:complexType>
      <xs:group ref="fullName"/>
   </xs:complexType>
</xs:element>
```

As with named complex types, model groups are useful when a document contains element declarations or code that you want to repeat throughout the schema.

Named Attribute Groups

Attributes can also be grouped into collections called **named attribute groups**. This is particularly useful for attributes that apply to several different elements in the instance document. The syntax for a named attribute group is

```
<xs:attributeGroup name="name">
   attributes
</xs:attributeGroup>
```

where *name* is the name of the attribute group and *attributes* is a collection of attributes assigned to the group. For example, one of Allison's documents might contain the following element to identify a physician:

```
<doctor docID="DR251" dept="Pediatrics">
   Curt Hurley
</doctor>
```

Both the docID and dept attributes may need to be used in other elements. To place both of these within an attribute group named docInfo, you could create the following named attribute group:

```
<xs:attributeGroup name="docInfo">
   <xs:attribute name="docID" type="xs:string" use="required" />
   <xs:attribute name="dept" type="xs:string" use="required" />
</xs:attributeGroup>
```

To use the docInfo attribute group with the doctor element, you would create a reference to the group as follows:

```
<xs:element name="doctor" type="deptData" />

<xs:complexType name="deptData">
   <xs:simpleContent>
      <xs:extension base="xs:string">
         <xs:attributeGroup ref="docInfo" />
      </xs:extension>
   </xs:simpleContent>
</xs:complexType>
```

This code not only references an attribute group, it also uses a named complex type to simplify the declaration of the doctor element.

Designing a Schema

There are many different ways to design a schema. As you have seen, you can create objects such as named complex types and then reuse them through the schema file, or you can nest one complex type inside of another. The way you design the layout of your schema file can impact how that schema is interpreted and applied to the instance document.

One important issue in schema design is determining the scope of the different objects declared within the schema. XML Schema recognizes two types of scope: global and local. Objects with **global scope** are direct children of the root schema element that can be referenced throughout the schema document. One advantage of creating objects with global scope is that you reuse code several times in the same schema file without having to rewrite it. Objects with **local scope** can only be referenced within the object in which they are defined. In a large and sprawling schema file, it can be an advantage to keep all definitions confined to a local scope rather than referenced throughout a long document. This distinction between global and local scope leads to three basic schema designs: flat catalog, Russian doll, and Venetian blind.

Flat Catalog Design

In a **flat catalog design**—sometimes referred to as a **salami slice design**—all element and attribute definitions have global scope. Figure 14-40 shows an example of a flat catalog design, highlighting the different elements and attributes. Every element and attribute definition is a direct child of the root schema element and thus has been defined globally.

| Figure 14-40 | Flat catalog design with all attributes and elements defined globally |

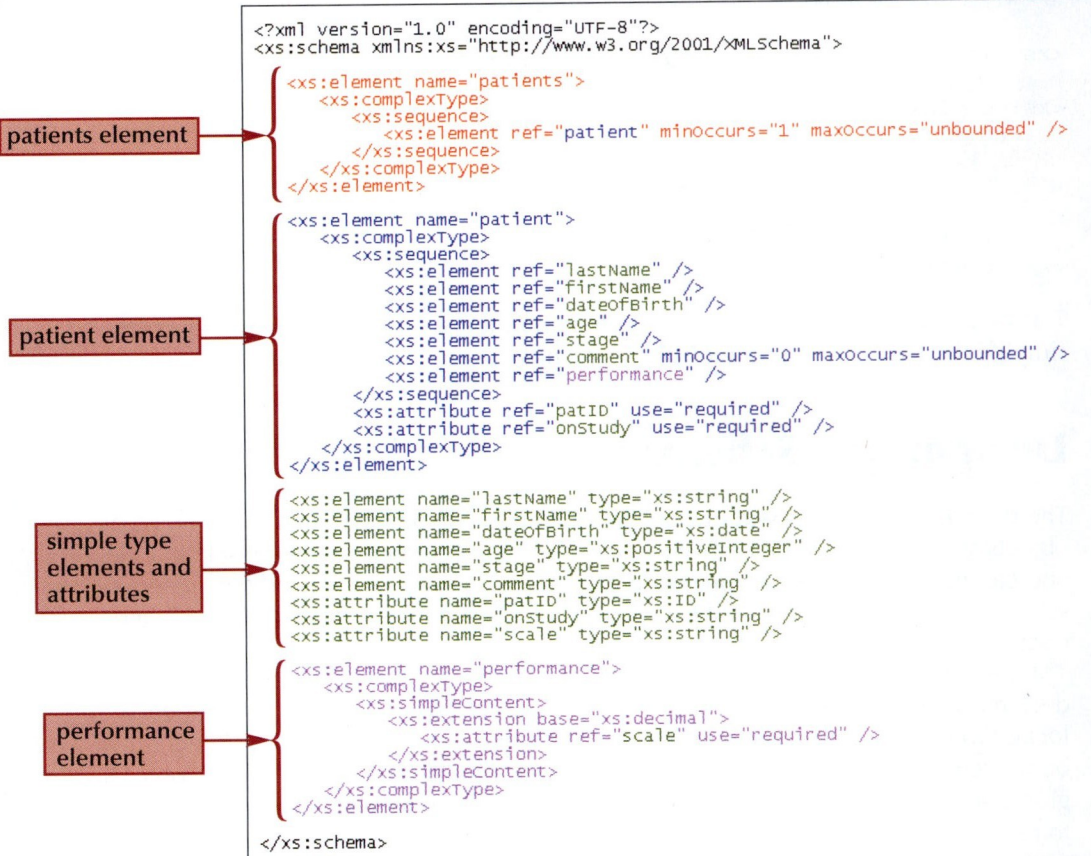

The pschema.xsd file you have been working on is written as a flat catalog structure with every element and attribute declared as a child of the root schema element.

Russian Doll Design

A **Russian doll design** has only one global element with everything else nested inside of it, much like Russian dolls nest one inside another. Figure 14-41 shows the schema from Figure 14-40 reorganized into a Russian doll design. The only declaration with global scope is for the patients element; all other declarations are made locally, nested inside of the patients element.

Russian doll design with a single global element definition   Figure 14-41

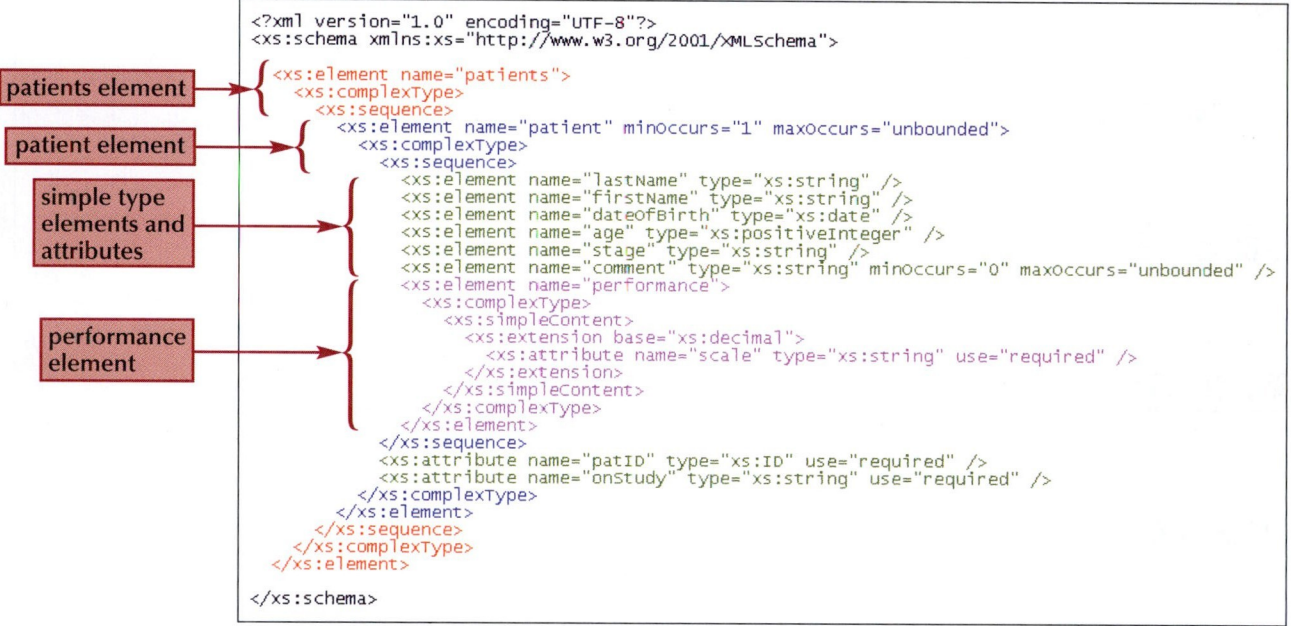

```
<?xml version="1.0" encoding="UTF-8"?>
<xs:schema xmlns:xs="http://www.w3.org/2001/XMLSchema">

  <xs:element name="patients">
    <xs:complexType>
      <xs:sequence>
        <xs:element name="patient" minOccurs="1" maxOccurs="unbounded">
          <xs:complexType>
            <xs:sequence>
              <xs:element name="lastName" type="xs:string" />
              <xs:element name="firstName" type="xs:string" />
              <xs:element name="dateOfBirth" type="xs:date" />
              <xs:element name="age" type="xs:positiveInteger" />
              <xs:element name="stage" type="xs:string" />
              <xs:element name="comment" type="xs:string" minOccurs="0" maxOccurs="unbounded" />
              <xs:element name="performance">
                <xs:complexType>
                  <xs:simpleContent>
                    <xs:extension base="xs:decimal">
                      <xs:attribute name="scale" type="xs:string" use="required" />
                    </xs:extension>
                  </xs:simpleContent>
                </xs:complexType>
              </xs:element>
            </xs:sequence>
            <xs:attribute name="patID" type="xs:ID" use="required" />
            <xs:attribute name="onStudy" type="xs:string" use="required" />
          </xs:complexType>
        </xs:element>
      </xs:sequence>
    </xs:complexType>
  </xs:element>

</xs:schema>
```

Labels (left side):
- patients element
- patient element
- simple type elements and attributes
- performance element

Russian doll designs mimic the nesting structure of the elements in the instance document. The root element of the instance document becomes the top element declaration in the schema. All child elements within the root element are similarly nested in the schema. A Russian doll design is much more compact than a flat catalog, but the multiple levels of nested elements can be confusing. Also, the element and attribute declarations cannot be reused elsewhere in the schema because they are made locally (other than the single root element).

Venetian Blind Design

A **Venetian blind design** is similar to a flat catalog, except that instead of declaring elements and attributes globally, it creates named types and references those types within a single global element. Figure 14-42 shows the schema file in a Venetian blind design. In this layout, the only globally declared element is the patients element. All other elements and attributes are placed within element or attribute groups or, in the case of the performance element, within a named complex type.

| Figure 14-42 | Venetian blind design with element and attribute groups and named complex types |

```
<?xml version="1.0" encoding="UTF-8"?>
<xs:schema xmlns:xs="http://www.w3.org/2001/XMLSchema">

    <xs:element name="patients">
        <xs:complexType>
            <xs:sequence>
                <xs:element name="patient" type="pType" minOccurs="1" maxOccurs="unbounded" />
            </xs:sequence>
        </xs:complexType>
    </xs:element>

    <xs:complexType name="pType">
        <xs:group ref="childElements" />
        <xs:attributeGroup ref="patientAtt" />
    </xs:complexType>

    <xs:group name="childElements">
        <xs:sequence>
            <xs:element name="lastName" type="xs:string" />
            <xs:element name="firstName" type="xs:string" />
            <xs:element name="dateOfBirth" type="xs:date" />
            <xs:element name="age" type="xs:positiveInteger" />
            <xs:element name="stage" type="xs:string" />
            <xs:element name="comment" type="xs:string" minOccurs="0" maxOccurs="unbounded" />
            <xs:element name="performance" type="perfType" />
        </xs:sequence>
    </xs:group>

    <xs:attributeGroup name="patientAtt">
        <xs:attribute name="patID" type="xs:ID" />
        <xs:attribute name="onStudy" type="xs:string" />
    </xs:attributeGroup>

    <xs:complexType name="perfType">
        <xs:simpleContent>
            <xs:extension base="xs:decimal">
                <xs:attribute name="scale" type="xs:string" use="required" />
            </xs:extension>
        </xs:simpleContent>
    </xs:complexType>

</xs:schema>
```

Labels pointing to sections of the code:
- **patients element** → `<xs:element name="patients">` block
- **pType complex type** → `<xs:complexType name="pType">` block
- **childElements group** → `<xs:group name="childElements">` block
- **patientAtt group** → `<xs:attributeGroup name="patientAtt">` block
- **perfType complex type** → `<xs:complexType name="perfType">` block

A Venetian blind design represents a compromise between flat catalogs and Russian dolls. Although the various element and attribute groups and named types are declared globally (and can be reused throughout the schema), the declarations for the elements and attributes for the instance document are local and nested within element and attribute groups. Only the root element from the instance document—in this case, the patients element—is defined globally.

Which schema layout you use depends on several factors. If the schema has several lines of code that need to be repeated, you probably want to use a flat catalog or Venetian blind design. If you are interested in a compact schema that mirrors the structure of the instance document, you should use a Russian doll design. Figure 14-43 summarizes some of the differences between the three layouts.

Comparison of schema designs   Figure 14-43

Feature	Flat Catalog (Salami Slice)	Russian Doll	Venetian Blind
Global and local declarations	All declarations are global.	The schema contains one single global element; all other declarations are local.	The schema contains one single global element; all other declarations are local.
Nesting of elements	Element declarations are not nested.	Element declarations are nested within a single global element.	Element declarations are nested within a single global element referencing named complex types, element groups, and attribute groups.
Reusability	Element declarations can be reused throughout the schema.	Element declarations can only be used once.	Named complex types, element groups, and attribute groups can be reused throughout the schema.
Interaction with namespaces	If a namespace is attached to the schema, all elements need to be qualified in the instance document.	If a namespace is attached to the schema, only the root element needs to be qualified in the instance document.	If a namespace is attached to the schema, only the root element needs to be qualified in the instance document.

Rather than continuing to work on the flat catalog design for the schema file, Allison wants you to switch to a Venetian blind design. She thinks that the Venetian blind layout maintains the flexibility of a flat catalog, while providing a structure similar to the contents of her instance document. Making the change will also make it easier to apply a namespace to the schema and instance document, as you'll see shortly. Allison already created a version of the schema file in a Venetian blind layout.

To open the Venetian blind version of the schema:

▶ 1. If you took a break after the previous session, make sure the patients.xml and pschema.xsd files are open in your text editor and the validate_schema.htm file is open in Internet Explorer.

▶ 2. Use your text editor to open the **patvbtxt.xsd** file from the tutorial.14\tutorial folder, enter **your name** and **the date** in the comment section, and then save the file as **patvb.xsd**.

▶ 3. Review the contents of the schema file, noting the use of named types, element groups, and attribute groups. Note that only the patients element is declared globally.

Associating a Schema with a Namespace

Allison has learned that several XML vocabularies have been developed for the different research projects at the hospital. To avoid confusion with other vocabularies, Allison reserved the URI *http://uhosp.edu/patients/ns* as the URI for the patients vocabulary. She needs you to place her patients document and the schema you developed for it in this namespace.

Targeting a Namespace

To associate the rules of a schema with a namespace, you declare the namespace of the instance document in the schema element and then make that namespace the target of the schema using the targetNamespace attribute. The code to set the schema namespace is

```
<xs:schema xmlns:xs="http://www.w3.org/2001/XMLSchema"
          xmlns="prefix:uri"
          targetNamespace="uri">

...
</xs:schema>
```

where *prefix* is the prefix of the namespace and *uri* is the URI of the namespace. The *prefix* is optional. You can omit it to make the namespace of the instance document the default namespace. For example, to associate Allison's schema file with the namespace of the patients vocabulary, you would modify the schema element as follows:

```
<xs:schema xmlns:xs="http://www.w3.org/2001/XMLSchema"
          xmlns="http://uhosp.edu/patients/ns"
          targetNamespace="http://uhosp.edu/patients/ns">

...
</xs:schema>
```

Any customized data types, named types, elements, element groups, or attributes created in the schema are considered part of the target namespace. This allows you to make validation rules part of an XML vocabulary. For example, the age element is part of the patients vocabulary, as is the rule that the age element must have a minimum value of 21.

If you use the vocabulary's namespace as the default namespace for the schema, you do not have to qualify any references to those customized objects. On the other hand, if you apply a prefix to the namespace, references to those objects must be qualified by that prefix. Figure 14-44 shows both possibilities: one in which references to objects from the XML Schema vocabulary are qualified, and the other in which XML Schema is the default namespace but references to customized objects are qualified.

Qualified names in a schema | Figure 14-44

```
<xs:schema xmlns:xs="http://www.w3.org/2001/XMLSchema"
           xmlns="http://uhosp.edu/patients/ns"
           targetNamespace="http://uhosp.edu/patients/ns">

   <xs:element name="patients">
      <xs:complexType>
         <xs:sequence>
            <xs:element name="patient" type="pType" minOccurs="1" maxOccurs="unbounded" />
         </xs:sequence>
      </xs:complexType>
   </xs:element>

   <xs:complexType name="pType">
      <xs:group ref="childElements" />
      <xs:attributeGroup ref="patientAtt" />
   </xs:complexType>

   <xs:group name="childElements">
      <xs:sequence>
         <xs:element name="lastName" type="xs:string" />
         <xs:element name="firstName" type="xs:string" />
         <xs:element name="dateOfBirth" type="xs:date" />
         <xs:element name="age" type="ageType" />
         <xs:element name="stage" type="stageType" />
         <xs:element name="comment" type="xs:string" minOccurs="0" maxOccurs="unbounded" />
         <xs:element name="performance" type="perfComplex" />
      </xs:sequence>
   </xs:group>
```

the XML Schema namespace is qualified

```
<schema xmlns="http://www.w3.org/2001/XMLSchema"
        xmlns:pat="http://uhosp.edu/patients/ns"
        targetNamespace="http://uhosp.edu/patients/ns">

   <element name="patients">
      <complexType>
         <sequence>
            <element name="patient" type="pat:pType" minOccurs="1" maxOccurs="unbounded" />
         </sequence>
      </complexType>
   </element>

   <complexType name="pType">
      <group ref="pat:childElements" />
      <attributeGroup ref="pat:patientAtt" />
   </complexType>

   <group name="childElements">
      <sequence>
         <element name="lastName" type="string" />
         <element name="firstName" type="string" />
         <element name="dateOfBirth" type="date" />
         <element name="age" type="pat:ageType" />
         <element name="stage" type="pat:stageType" />
         <element name="comment" type="string" minOccurs="0" maxOccurs="unbounded" />
         <element name="performance" type="pat:perfComplex" />
      </sequence>
   </group>
```

the patients namespace is qualified

You will modify Allison's schema file, using *http://uhosp.edu/patients/ns* as the default and target namespace of the schema.

To associate the schema with a namespace:

▶ 1. Add the following attributes to the root schema element from the **patvb.xsd** file, as shown in Figure 14-45:

```
xmlns="http://uhosp.edu/patients/ns"
targetNamespace="http://uhosp.edu/patients/ns"
```

Figure 14-45 ▶ **Namespace applied to a schema**

```
<xs:schema xmlns:xs="http://www.w3.org/2001/XMLSchema"
           xmlns="http://uhosp.edu/patients/ns"
           targetNamespace="http://uhosp.edu/patients/ns">

   <xs:element name="patients">
      <xs:complexType>
         <xs:sequence>
            <xs:element name="patient" type="pType" minOccurs="1" maxOccurs="unbounded" />
         </xs:sequence>
      </xs:complexType>
   </xs:element>
```

▶ **2.** Save your changes to the patvb.xsd file, and then close the file.

Reference Window | **Targeting a Namespace**

- To target a schema to a namespace, add the attributes
    prefix:xmlns="*uri*"
    targetNamespace="*uri*"
  to the schema element, where *prefix* is the optional prefix of the namespace and *uri* is the URI of the namespace.

Applying the Namespace to the Instance Document

In the first session, you validated the patients.xml document without a namespace by adding the attribute

```
xsi:noNamespaceSchemaLocation="schema"
```

to the root element, where *schema* is the location and name of the schema file. Because you now have a namespace associated with the document, you need to replace that attribute with

```
xsi:schemaLocation="uri schema"
```

where *uri* is the URI of the document's namespace and *schema* is again the location and name of a schema file that belongs to that namespace. A single document might be associated with several namespaces, each associated with its own schema. If so, the locations are entered in the following pairs:

```
xsi:schemaLocation="uri1 schema1 uri2 schema2 uri3 schema3 ..."
```

where *uri1*, *uri2*, etc., are the URIs of the different namespaces, and *schema1*, *schema2*, etc., are the schemas associated with each namespace. Because the content of the patients document is associated with only the *http://uhosp.edu/patients/ns* namespace from the patvb.xsd file, you will enter the following attribute to the root patient element:

```
xsi:schemaLocation="http://uhosp.edu/patients/ns patvb.xsd"
```

To apply the schema to the patients document:

▶ **1.** Return to the **patients.xml** file in your text editor, and then save the file as **patients_ns.xml** in the tutorial.14\tutorial folder.

2. Place the document in the patients namespace by adding the following declaration to the patients element:

```
xmlns="http://uhosp.edu/patients/ns"
```

3. Remove the xsi:noNamespaceSchemaLocation attribute, replacing it with the following:

```
xsi:schemaLocation="http://uhosp.edu/patients/ns patvb.xsd"
```

Figure 14-46 shows the revised code of the file.

Schema namespace attached to the patients_ns.xml file ◀ Figure 14-46

```
<patients xmlns:xsi="http://www.w3.org/2001/XMLSchema-instance"
          xmlns="http://uhosp.edu/patients/ns"
          xsi:schemaLocation="http://uhosp.edu/patients/ns patvb.xsd">

   <patient patID="MR890-041-02" onStudy="TBC-080-5">
      <lastName>Dibbs</lastName>
      <firstName>Cynthia</firstName>
      <dateOfBirth>1949-05-22</dateOfBirth>
      <age>62</age>
      <stage>II</stage>
      <performance scale="Karnofsky">0.81</performance>
   </patient>
```

4. Validate the **patients_ns.xml** document using the **validate_schema.htm** file in your Internet Explorer browser or another validating parser. Figure 14-47 shows the validation result.

Validation error in the patients_ns.xml file ◀ Figure 14-47

Validation Results

Validation Failed

Validation error reported at: Line 19 at Character 54
  <patient patID="MR890-041-02" onStudy="TBC-080-5">
Reason: Element content is invalid according to the DTD/Schema.
Expecting: patient.

```
 10:
 11:     Filename:        patients.xml
 12:     Supporting Files: pschema.xsd, patvb.xsd
 13:  -->
 14:
 15:  <patients xmlns:xsi="http://www.w3.org/2001/XMLSchema-instance"
 16:          xmlns="http://uhosp.edu/patients/ns"
 17:          xsi:schemaLocation="http://uhosp.edu/patients/ns patvb.xsd">
 18:
**19**    <patient patID="MR890-041-02" onStudy="TBC-080-5">
 20:        <lastName>Dibbs</lastName>
 21:        <firstName>Cynthia</firstName>
 22:        <dateOfBirth>1949-05-22</dateOfBirth>
 23:        <age>62</age>
```

The validator reports a rather cryptic error message: "Element content is invalid according to the DTD/Schema. Expecting: patient." The document has become invalid after adding support for namespaces.

Qualified and Unqualified Names

The validation error is due to the way scope affects how a schema is applied to the instance document. In XML Schema, any element or attribute with global scope must be entered as a qualified name (i.e., with a namespace prefix). The reason is that elements and attributes with global scope are attached to the schema's target namespace, while elements and attributes declared locally are not. In the instance document, this is reflected by qualifying those global elements or attributes.

This fact may impact your choice of schema designs. In a flat catalog, all elements and attributes are declared globally, so each element and attribute must be qualified in the instance document. Because Venetian blind and Russian doll designs have a single global element, only the root element must be qualified in the instance document. By switching from the flat catalog to the Venetian blind layout, you avoided having to change every element and attribute name in the instance document into a qualified name.

To create a valid instance document, you will return to the patients_ns.xml file and add a namespace prefix to the patients namespace.

To qualify the patients element:

▶ 1. Return to the **patients_ns.xml** file in your text editor.

▶ 2. Change the namespace declaration to:

```
xmlns:pat="http://uhosp.edu/patients/ns"
```

▶ 3. Add the **pat:** namespace prefix to both the opening and closing tags of the patients element. See Figure 14-48.

Figure 14-48	The patients element qualified

```
<pat:patients xmlns:xsi="http://www.w3.org/2001/XMLSchema-instance"
              xmlns:pat="http://uhosp.edu/patients/ns"
              xsi:schemaLocation="http://uhosp.edu/patients/ns patvb.xsd">

    <patient patID="MR890-041-02" onStudy="TBC-080-5">
        <lastName>Dibbs</lastName>
        <firstName>Cynthia</firstName>
        <dateOfBirth>1949-05-22</dateOfBirth>
        <age>62</age>
        <stage>II</stage>
        <performance scale="Karnofsky">0.81</performance>
    </patient>



    <patient patID="MR815-741-03" onStudy="TBC-080-5">
        <lastName>Browne</lastName>
        <firstName>Brenda</firstName>
        <dateOfBirth>1968-04-25</dateOfBirth>
        <age>39</age>
        <stage>I</stage>
        <performance scale="Karnofsky">0.88</performance>
    </patient>

</pat:patients>
```

You don't have to qualify the child elements and attributes of the patients element because none of them were declared globally in the patvb.xsd schema file. Only the patients element was defined globally, which is why it is the only element that requires a qualified name.

▶ 4. Save your changes to the **patients_ns.xml** file, and then revalidate the document using the Internet Explorer validator or another validator to verify that the document is now valid based on the rules of the schema.

Applying a Schema to an Instance Document | Reference Window

- To apply a schema to a document without a namespace, add the attributes
  ```
  xmlns:xsi="http://www.w3.org/2001/XMLSchema-instance"
  xsi:noNamespaceSchemaLocation="schema"
  ```
  to the instance document's root element, where *schema* is the schema file associated with the document.
- To apply a schema to a document with a namespace, add the attributes
  ```
  xmlns:xsi="http://www.w3.org/2001/XMLSchema-instance"
  xmlns:prefix="uri"
  xsi:schemaLocation="uri schema"
  ```
  to the instance document's root element, where *prefix* is the namespace prefix, *uri* is the URI of the namespace, and *schema* is the schema file. All global elements and attributes declared in the schema must be qualified in the instance document.

You can force all elements and attributes to be qualified, regardless of their scope, by adding the elementFormDefault and attributeFormDefault attributes

```
<xs:schema
    elementFormDefault="qualify"
    attributeFormDefault="qualify">

...
</xs:schema>
```

to the root schema element in the schema file, where *qualify* is either qualified or unqualified, specifying whether all the elements and attributes of the instance document must be qualified. The default value of both of these attributes is unqualified except for globally defined elements and attributes, which must always be qualified. To require all elements to be qualified but not all attributes (other than globally declared attributes), enter the following code into the schema element:

```
<xs:schema
    elementFormDefault="qualified"
    attributeFormDefault="unqualified">

...
</xs:schema>
```

This is a common setup in which you want to explicitly qualify each element name with a namespace prefix.

You can also set the qualification for individual elements or attributes by applying the form attribute

```
<xs:element name="name" form="qualify" />
<xs:attribute name="name" form="qualify" />
```

to the definitions in the schema, where *qualify* is again either qualified or unqualified. The element declaration

```
<xs:element name="patient" form="qualified" />
```

requires the patient element to be qualified in the instance document, whether it has been declared globally or locally in the schema.

Tip

Many XML developers consider the best practice is to qualify all elements in the instance document to avoid confusion about which elements belong to which namespaces.

Validating a Compound Document

Allison has been working on a second XML vocabulary, one that documents the features of the different clinical studies sponsored by the hospital. The structure of that vocabulary is shown in Figure 14-49.

Figure 14-49 | **Structure of the study vocabulary**

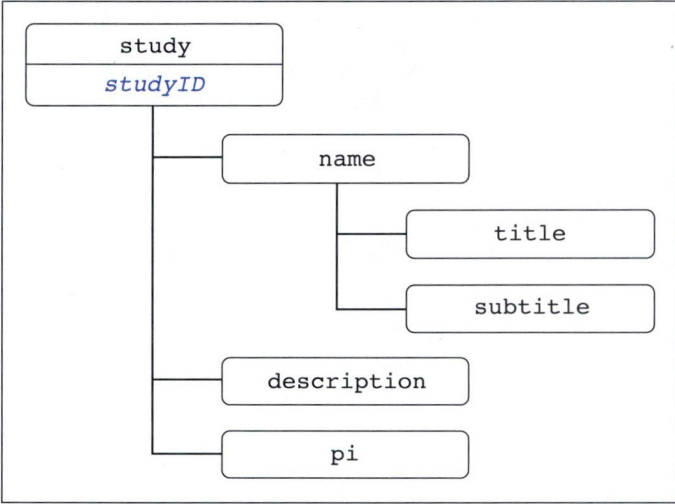

So far, the study vocabulary contains only basic information about the clinical studies: It records the title and subtitle of the study, a description of the study, and the name of the study's principal investigator (PI). As Allison continues to develop XML documents, she will add more elements and attributes to this vocabulary. Allison already has created a schema and instance document based on this vocabulary. You will open both of those files now.

To view the schema and instance files for the study vocabulary:

1. Use your text editor to open the **studtxt.xsd** file from the tutorial.14\tutorial folder, enter *your name* and *the date* in the comment section, and then save the file as **study.xsd**.

2. Review the contents and structure of the study schema shown in Figure 14-50. This schema uses a Russian doll design, with study being the only element declared globally in the file. Allison already entered the target namespace of this vocabulary using a URI of *http://uhosp/studies/ns*.

Schema for the study vocabulary — **Figure 14-50**

```
<xs:schema xmlns:xs="http://www.w3.org/2001/XMLSchema"
           xmlns="http://uhosp/studies/ns"
           targetNamespace="http://uhosp/studies/ns">

   <xs:element name="study">
      <xs:complexType>
         <xs:sequence>
            <xs:element name="name">
               <xs:complexType>
                  <xs:sequence>
                     <xs:element name="title" type="xs:string" />
                     <xs:element name="subtitle" type="xs:string" />
                  </xs:sequence>
               </xs:complexType>
            </xs:element>
            <xs:element name="description" type="xs:string" />
            <xs:element name="pi" type="xs:string" />
         </xs:sequence>
         <xs:attribute name="studyID" type="xs:ID" />
      </xs:complexType>
   </xs:element>

</xs:schema>
```

3. Use your text editor to open the **tamoxtxt.xml** file from the tutorial.14\tutorial folder, enter *your name* and *the date* in the comment section, and then save the file as **tamoxifen.xml**. The contents of the tamoxifen.xml file shown in Figure 14-51 contain basic information on a clinical cancer study that investigates the efficacy of the drug Tamoxifen on Stage I and Stage II cancer patients. Allison already placed this document in the URI *http://uhosp/studies/ns* and qualified the root element named study with a namespace prefix.

Contents of the tamoxifen.xml file — **Figure 14-51**

```
<std:study studyID="TBC-080-5"
           xmlns:xsi="http://www.w3.org/2001/XMLSchema-instance"
           xmlns:std="http://uhosp/studies/ns"
           xsi:schemaLocation="http://uhosp/studies/ns study.xsd">

   <name>
      <title>Tamoxifen Breast Cancer Study</title>
      <subtitle>Randomized Phase 3 Clinical Trial</subtitle>
   </name>
   <description>This is a phase 3 clinical cancer trial in which
               stage I and stage II breast cancer patients are
               randomly assigned to either Tamoxifen or a placebo.
               The endpoints of the study are long-term mortality
               and quality of life measures.
   </description>
   <pi>Dr. Diane West</pi>

</std:study>
```

4. Validate the **tamoxifen.xml** file using the **validate_schema.htm** file under Internet Explorer or another validating parser to confirm that the tamoxifen.xml file contains no validation errors.

Allison wants to combine the information about the Tamoxifen Breast Cancer Study and the list of patients enrolled in that study in a single compound document. Figure 14-52 shows a schematic diagram of the document involving elements and attributes from both vocabularies. You can create such a document by copying the elements and attributes from the patients_ns.xml file and pasting them into the tamoxifen.xml file.

Figure 14-52 Compound document combining the study and patients vocabularies

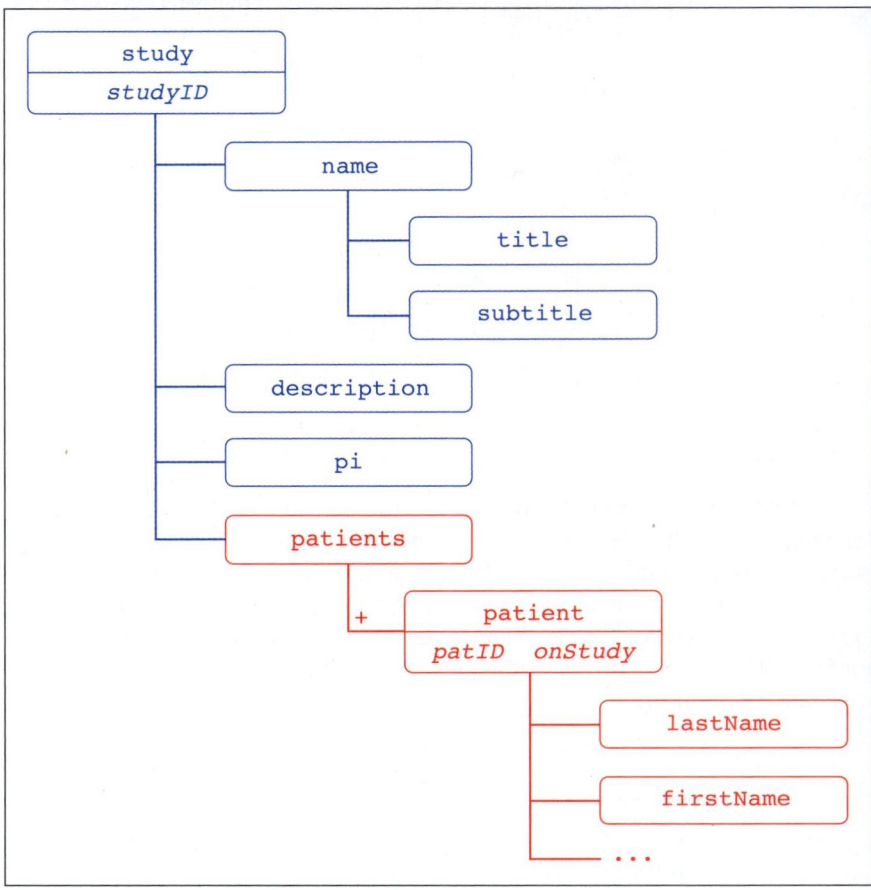

You will create the compound document.

To create the compound document:

▶ 1. Go to the **patients_ns.xml** file in your text editor, and then copy the contents of the document from the opening <pat:patients> tag through the closing </pat:patients> tag. Do not copy any of the document prolog.

▶ 2. Return to the **tamoxifen.xml** file in your text editor, and then paste the copied content into the file, directly between the pi element and the closing </std:study> tag.

▶ 3. Remove the XML Schema instance namespace attribute from the opening <pat:patients> tag in the patients element because it is already declared in the study element. Figure 14-53 shows the compound document containing elements from both the study and patients vocabularies.

```
<std:study studyID="TBC-080-5"
          xmlns:xsi="http://www.w3.org/2001/XMLSchema-instance"
          xmlns:std="http://uhosp/studies/ns"
          xsi:schemaLocation="http://uhosp/studies/ns study.xsd">

  <name>
      <title>Tamoxifen Breast Cancer Study</title>
      <subtitle>Randomized Phase 3 Clinical Trial</subtitle>
  </name>
  <description>This is a phase 3 clinical cancer trial in which
              stage I and stage II breast cancer patients are
              randomly assigned to either Tamoxifen or a placebo.
              The endpoints of the study are long-term mortality
              and quality of life measures.
  </description>
  <pi>Dr. Diane West</pi>

  <pat:patients xmlns:pat="http://uhosp.edu/patients/ns"
              xsi:schemaLocation="http://uhosp.edu/patients/ns patvb.xsd">

    <patient patID="MR890-041-02" onStudy="TBC-080-5">
        <lastName>Dibbs</lastName>
        <firstName>Cynthia</firstName>
        <dateOfBirth>1949-05-22</dateOfBirth>
        <age>62</age>
        <stage>II</stage>
        <performance scale="Karnofsky">0.81</performance>
    </patient>
```

```
    <patient patID="MR815-741-03" onStudy="TBC-080-5">
        <lastName>Browne</lastName>
        <firstName>Brenda</firstName>
        <dateOfBirth>1968-04-25</dateOfBirth>
        <age>39</age>
        <stage>I</stage>
        <performance scale="Karnofsky">0.88</performance>
    </patient>

  </pat:patients>

</std:study>
```

▶ **4.** Save your changes to the file, and then revalidate the **tamoxifen.xml** file. The validator should report an error indicating that the element content is invalid according to the schema.

Allison's document describing the Tamoxifen study and its patients is invalid because nothing in the study schema allows for a list of patients. For the document to be valid, you must add this information to the schema file. One advantage of schemas is that you can combine multiple schemas into a single document. XML Schema provides two ways of adding one schema file to another: inclusion and importing.

Including and Importing Schemas

You include a schema file when you want to combine schema files from the same namespace. This might be the case if one schema file contains a collection of customized data types that you want shared among many different files, and another schema file contains a collection of elements and attributes that define the structure of a particular document. To include a schema, you add the element

```
<xs:schema attributes>
   <xs:include schemaLocation="schema" />

...

</xs:schema>
```

as a child of the root schema element, where *attributes* are the attributes that describe the schema such as its namespace, and *schema* is the name of the schema file to be included. The effect is to combine the two schema files into a single schema that can then be applied to a specific instance document. In an environment in which large and complex XML vocabularies are developed, different teams might work on different parts of the schema, using the include element to combine the different parts into a finished product. Rather than one large and complex schema file, you can break the schema into smaller, more manageable files that can be shared and combined.

The other way to combine schemas is through importing, which is used when the schemas come from different namespaces. The syntax of the import element is

```
<xs:schema attributes>
   <xs:import namespace="uri" schemaLocation="schema" />

...
</xs:schema>
```

where *uri* is the URI of the namespace for the imported schema and *schema* is again the name of the schema file. For example, to import the contents of the patients schema into Allison's study schema, you would add the following import element to the study.xsd schema file:

```
<xs:import namespace="http://uhosp.edu/patients/ns"
      schemaLocation="patvb.xsd" />
```

A schema can contain any number of include and import elements. Each must be globally declared as a direct child of the root schema element. You will use the import element to import the patvb.xsd schema file into the study.xsd file.

To import the patvb.xsd schema file:

1. Return to the **study.xsd** file in your text editor.

2. Directly below the opening tag of the schema element, insert the following import element, as shown in Figure 14-54:

   ```
   <xs:import namespace="http://uhosp.edu/patients/ns"
         schemaLocation="patvb.xsd" />
   ```

Figure 14-54 | Imported schema

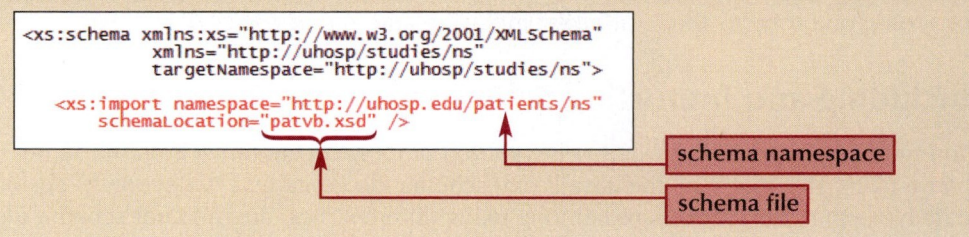

schema namespace

schema file

Referencing Objects from Other Schemas

After a schema is imported into another schema file, any objects it contains with global scope can be referenced in that file. To reference an object from an imported schema, you must declare the namespace of the imported schema in the schema element. You can then reference the object using the ref attribute or the type attribute for customized simple and complex types.

Allison wants the patients element to be placed directly after the pi element in this schema. You will add the reference to that element to the schema.

To reference the patients element in the study.xsd file:

1. Add the following namespace declaration to the root schema element:

   ```
   xmlns:pat="http://uhosp.edu/patients/ns"
   ```

2. Insert the following element reference directly below the pi element declaration:

   ```
   <xs:element ref="pat:patients" />
   ```

   The element reference is qualified with a namespace prefix to indicate to the validator that this reference points to a global object found in the patients namespace. Figure 14-55 shows the revised schema code.

The study and patients schemas combined in a single file | Figure 14-55

```
<xs:schema xmlns:xs="http://www.w3.org/2001/XMLSchema"
        xmlns="http://uhosp/studies/ns"
        targetNamespace="http://uhosp/studies/ns"
        xmlns:pat="http://uhosp.edu/patients/ns">        ◄── declaring the
                                                              patients namespace

    <xs:import namespace="http://uhosp.edu/patients/ns"
        schemaLocation="patvb.xsd" />

    <xs:element name="study">
        <xs:complexType>
            <xs:sequence>
                <xs:element name="name">
                    <xs:complexType>
                        <xs:sequence>
                            <xs:element name="title" type="xs:string" />
                            <xs:element name="subtitle" type="xs:string" />
                        </xs:sequence>
                    </xs:complexType>
                </xs:element>
                <xs:element name="description" type="xs:string" />
                <xs:element name="pi" type="xs:string" />
                <xs:element ref="pat:patients" />        ◄── referencing the patients
            </xs:sequence>                                   element declaration from
            <xs:attribute name="studyID" type="xs:ID" />    the patients namespace
        </xs:complexType>
    </xs:element>

</xs:schema>
```

3. Save your changes to the file.

> **4.** Use the **validate_schema.htm** Web page in your Internet Explorer browser or another validating parser to confirm that the tamoxifen.xml file passes validation as it draws its rules for content and structure from the two different schema files.
>
> **5.** Close any open files or applications.

This example provides a glimpse of the power and flexibility of schemas in working with multiple vocabularies and namespaces. In more advanced applications, large schema structures can be created to validate equally complex XML environments involving dozens of documents and vocabularies. The XML Schema language is also flexible enough to provide control over which elements and attributes are validated and how they are validated.

Allison is pleased with the work you have done in creating a schema for the compound document describing the features of the Tamoxifen Breast Cancer Study and the patients enrolled in it.

Review | Session 14.3 Quick Check

1. What is a named complex type? What is an anonymous complex type?
2. What code would you enter to create an element group named address containing elements named street, city, state, and zip? Assume that each of the elements is a string data type.
3. What is a flat catalog design and how does it differ from a Russian doll design?
4. What attributes would you add to a schema element to target the schema in the namespace *http://jazzwarehouse.com/sales*? Assume that the namespace is also the default namespace for the schema.
5. What attribute would you add to the top element in an instance document to attach it to a schema file named jazz.xsd with the namespace *http://jazzwarehouse.com/sales*?
6. If a schema is associated with a namespace, what must you do to every element and attribute in the instance document that has been declared with global scope in the schema file?
7. What attribute would you add to the root schema element to force every element to be qualified in the instance document?
8. How does importing a schema file differ from including a schema file, with respect to the namespace of the schema?

This tutorial covered how to perform validation using XML Schema. The first session introduced the topic of schemas, discussed different schema vocabularies, and compared them to DTDs. The session continued with the creation of a basic schema that declared simple type elements, attributes, and a variety of complex type elements. The session concluded with a validation of an XML document based on that schema.

The second session focused on the topic of data types. It began by exploring the wide variety of built-in XML Schema data types used for text strings, numeric values, and dates and times. The session then looked at how to create customized data types for lists and unions, and it examined restrictions on the value space, lexical space, and facets of a base data type. It provided a brief introduction to regular expressions and demonstrated how to create a regular expression for an ID value.

The third session looked at schema structures and compared three schema designs. It then demonstrated how to merge schemas with namespaces and how to validate a compound document based on several XML vocabularies and associated schemas.

Key Terms

anonymous complex type	global scope	regular expression
anonymous simple type	instance document	restricted data type
base type	lexical space	Russian doll design
built-in data type	list data type	salami slice design
character set	local scope	simple type
character type	member data type	union data type
complex type	named attribute group	user-derived data type
derived data type	named complex type	value space
Extended Backus Naur	named model group	Venetian blind design
Form (EBNF)	named simple type	
facet	primitive data type	
flat catalog design	quantifier	

Note: In the Case Problems, some XML documents include intentional errors. Part of your job is to find and correct those errors using validation reports from the schemas you create.

Practice	**Review Assignments**

Practice the skills you learned in the tutorial using the same case scenario.

Data Files needed for this Review Assignment: granttxt.xml, granttxt.xsd, slisttxt.xsd, studtxt.xml

Each study at the University Hospital's Clinical Cancer Center receives funding from a federal, state, local, or private agency grant. Allison has created an XML vocabulary containing information about the different grants that have been awarded to the center. She wants you to create a schema to validate grant information. Allison has also added more information to the studies XML vocabulary for information on individual research projects. Figure 14-56 shows the structures of the grant and studies vocabularies.

Figure 14-56

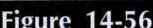

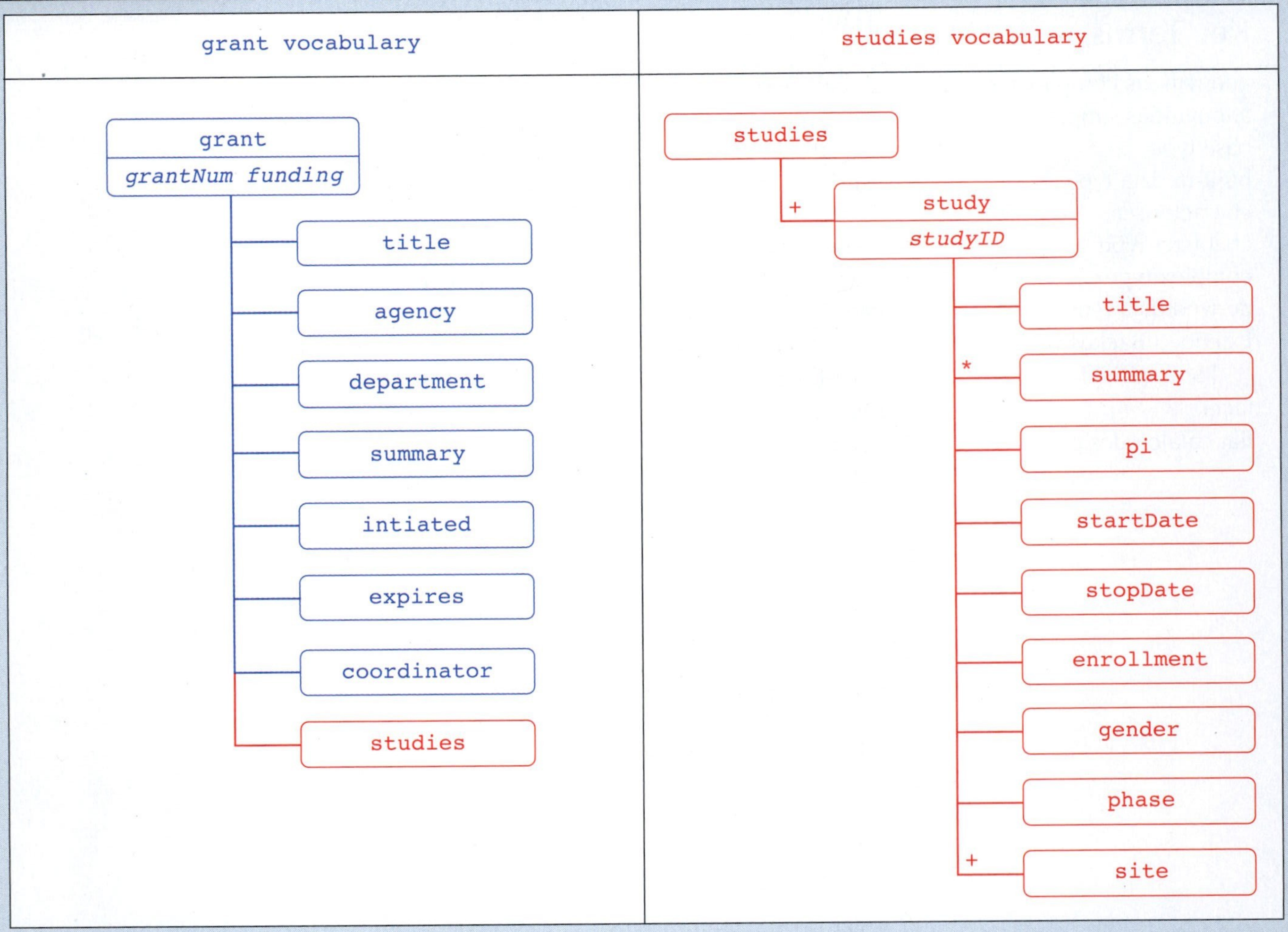

A description of the elements and attributes used in both vocabularies is shown in Figure 14-57.

Figure 14-57

Vocabulary	Element or Attribute	Description
grant	grant	The root element
	grantNum	ID number of the grant with the format *AAAAAA-####-##*, where *A* is an uppercase letter and # is a digit
	funding	Funding agency (federal, state, local, or private)
	title	Grant title
	agency	Granting agency
	department	Hospital department
	summary	Summary of grant
	initiated, expires	Date the grant starts and ends
	coordinator	Name of grant coordinator
studies	studies	The root element
	study	Element storing information on each study
	studyID	ID number of the study in the format CCC-###-##, where # is a digit
	title	Study title
	summary	An optional summary describing the study
	pi	The study's principal investigator
	startDate, stopDate	The date the study starts and ends
	enrollment	The number of patients enrolled in the study
	gender	The gender of patients in the study (female, male, or all)
	phase	The study phase (1, 2, or 3)
	site	The site where the study took place (multiple possible sites)

Allison already created a document containing information on one particular grant and another document containing a list of studies funded by that grant. She wants both documents validated based on schemas you create. Finally, she wants you to create and validate a compound document containing both grant and study information.

Complete the following:

1. Using your text editor, open the **granttxt.xml**, **granttxt.xsd**, **slisttxt.xsd**, **and studtxt.xml** files from the tutorial.14\review folder, enter *your name* and *the date* in the comment section of each file, and then save the files as **grant.xml**, **grant.xsd**, **slist.xsd** and **studies.xml**, respectively.

2. Go to the **grant.xsd** file in your text editor. Add the root schema element to the document and declare the XML Schema namespace using the xs prefix. Set the default namespace of the document to the URI *http://uhosp.edu/grant/ns* and also make this URI the target namespace of the schema.

3. Create the following named simple types:
   a. **grantType**, based on the ID data type and restricting the regular expression pattern `[A-Z]{6}-\d{4}-\d{2}`
   b. **fundingType**, based on the string data type and restricted to the following values: federal, state, local, and private

4. Using a Russian doll design, declare the **grant** element containing the following sequence of nested child elements: title, agency, department, summary, initiated, expires, and coordinator. Set the following properties for the nested elements:

   a. All of the child elements should contain string data except the initiated and expires elements, which contain dates.

   b. The grant element should also support two attributes: grantNum and funding. The **grantNum** attribute contains grantType data while the **funding** attribute contains fundingType data.

5. Save your changes to the grant.xsd file.

6. Go to the **grant.xml** file in your text editor. Within the root element, declare the XML Schema instance namespace using the **xsi** namespace prefix. Declare the grant namespace using the URI *http://uhosp.edu/grant/ns* and the namespace prefix **gr**. Apply the schema from the grant namespace *http://uhosp.edu/grant/ns*, referencing the schema file grant.xsd.

7. Change the name of the grant element to a qualified name by adding the **gr** prefix to the opening and closing tags.

8. Save your changes to the grant.xml file and then validate the document. Correct any validation errors you discover in the instance document. (*Hint*: You can also test your schema file for errors. You can use the online validator at *www.w3.org/2001/03/webdata/xsv*.)

9. Go to the **slist.xsd** file in your text editor. Insert the root schema element and declare the XML Schema namespace using the **xs** prefix. Set the default namespace and namespace target to the URI *http://uhosp.edu/studies/ns*.

10. Declare the following named simple types:

    a. **studyIDType**, based on the ID data type and restricted to the regular expression pattern
    `ccc-\d{3}-\d{2}`

    b. **genderType**, based on the string data type and limited to the values: female, male, and all

    c. **phaseType**, based on the positive integer data type and having a maximum value of 3 (inclusive)

11. Apply a Venetian blind layout to this schema by doing the following:

    a. Create an element group named **studyElements** containing the following sequence of elements: title, summary, pi, startDate, stopDate, enrollment, gender, phase, and site.

    b. The title, summary, pi, and site elements contain string data.

    c. The startDate and stopDate elements contain dates.

    d. The enrollment element contains a nonnegative integer.

    e. The gender and phase elements contain genderType and phaseType data, respectively.

    f. The summary element can occur 0 times. The site element must occur at least once, but its upper limit is unbounded. All other elements are assumed to occur only once.

12. Create a complex type named **studyType**. Within this complex type, do the following:

    a. Insert a reference to the studyElements element group.

    b. Insert the studyID attribute containing studyIDType data.

13. Create a complex type named **studies**. Within this element, insert an element sequence containing the study element. The study element contains studyType data and must occur at least once.

14. Save your changes to the slist.xsd file and then go to the **studies.xml** file in your text editor. Declare the XML Schema instance namespace in the root element using the **xsi** prefix. Declare the studies namespace using the URI *http://uhosp.edu/studies/ns* with the namespace prefix **std**. Set the location of the schema to the *http://uhosp.edu/studies/ns* namespace referencing the slist.xsd file.

15. Qualify the name of the studies root element by adding the **std** namespace prefix.

16. Save your changes to the studies.xml file and then validate the document. Correct any errors the validator discovers in the instance document.

17. With both the grant and studies documents validated, create a compound document combining elements from both vocabularies. Return to the **studies.xml** file in your text editor and copy the document body including the opening and closing tags of the studies element. Go to the **grant.xml** file in your text editor. Directly after the coordinator element, paste the copied contents of the studies.xml file. Remove the XML Schema instance namespace declaration from the studies element. Save your changes to the file.

18. Create a schema for the compound document by returning to the **grant.xsd** file in your text editor. Within the root element, declare the studies namespace using the *http://uhosp.edu/studies/ns* URI and the **std** namespace prefix.

19. Directly after the opening tag of the schema element, import the contents of the slist.xsd schema file specifying *http://uhosp.edu/studies/ns* as the namespace URI.

20. Directly after the declaration for the coordinator element, insert an element reference to the studies element located in the studies namespace. Save your changes to the grant.xsd file.

21. Validate the contents of the grant.xml file, which now contains elements from both the grant and studies namespaces.

22. Submit the completed and validated project to your instructor.

| Apply | **Case Problem 1** |

Use the skills you learned in this tutorial to validate a music catalog.

Data Files needed for this Case Problem: jwtxt.xml, musictxt.xsd

The Jazz Warehouse   Richard Brooks is working on an XML document to store the inventory of vintage albums sold by the Jazz Warehouse. Figure 14-58 shows the structure of the vocabulary employed in the document.

Figure 14-58

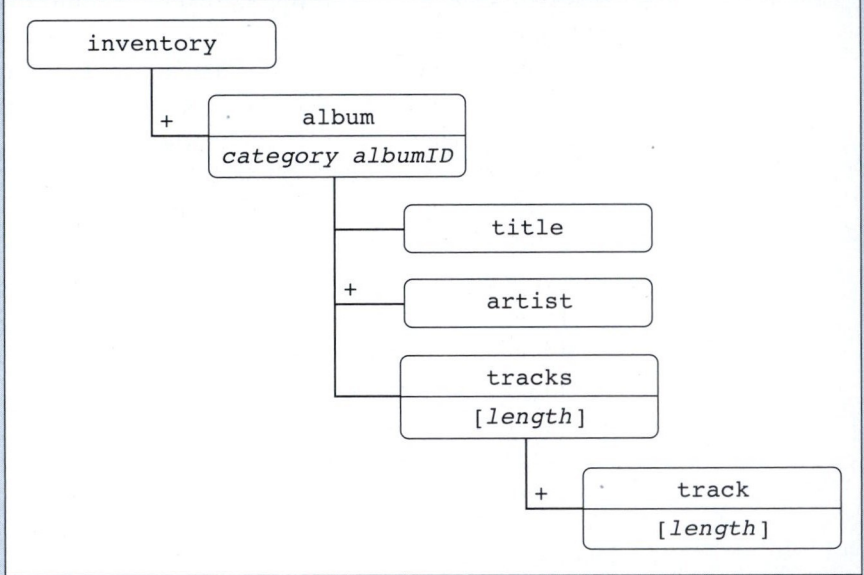

A description of the elements and attributes used in the music catalog is shown in Figure 14-59.

Figure 14-59

Element or Attribute	Description
inventory	The root element
album	Element storing information about each album
category	The album category (New Orleans, Swing, Bebop, Modern)
albumID	Album ID number in the form JW######, where # is a digit
title	The album title
artist	The album artist (there may be more than one)
tracks	Element storing information on the album tracks
length	An optional attribute storing the length (in *hours:minutes:seconds*) of an entire album or track
track	The name of an individual album track

Richard needs your help in creating a schema that will validate the data he has already entered and will enter in the future. To keep the code compact, you'll use a Russian doll design for the schema layout. Richard is not planning to use this schema with other XML documents, so you do not have to define a namespace for the vocabulary he created.

Complete the following:

1. Using your text editor, open the **jwtxt.xml** and **musictxt.xsd** files from the tutorial.14\case1 folder, enter *your name* and *the date* in the comment section of each file, and then save the files as **jw.xml** and **music.xsd**, respectively.

2. Go to the **music.xsd** file in your text editor and insert the root schema element. Declare the XML Schema namespace with **xsd** as the namespace prefix.

3. Define the following data types:

   a. **albumIDType**, based on the ID data type and restricted to the regular expression pattern
      `JW\d{6}`

   b. **jazzType**, based on the string data type and limited to enumerated values: New Orleans, Swing, Bebop, and Modern

4. Create a Russian doll layout by first declaring the inventory complex element type and then nesting the album element within it. The album must occur at least once, but its upper limit is unbounded.

5. Within the album declaration, insert the following:

   a. A sequence of the child elements: **title**, **artist**, and **tracks**. The title and artist elements contain the string data type. The artist element can occur one or more times.

   b. The tracks element is a complex type element and contains at least one track element. The tracks element also contains an optional length attribute containing time data.

   c. Declare two attributes named **category** and **albumID**. The category attribute is required and contains jazzType data. The albumID attribute is also required and contains albumIDType data.

6. Save your changes to the music.xsd file, and then close it.

7. Go to the **jw.xml** file in your text editor. Within the root inventory element, declare the XML Schema instance namespace. Use **xsi** as the namespace prefix. Attach the schema file music.xsd to this instance document, indicating that the schema and instance document do not belong to any namespace.

8. Save your changes to the jw.xml file, and then validate the file. Correct any data entry errors you find in the instance document until no validation errors are reported. (*Hint:* You can also test your schema file for errors using the online validator at *www.w3.org/2001/03/webdata/xsv*.)

9. Submit your complete and validated project to your instructor.

| Apply | | Case Problem 2 |

Use the skills you learned in this tutorial to validate a list of library materials.

Data Files needed for this Case Problem: matertxt.xml, mlatxt.xsd

Bozeman Public Library   Keisha Rodgers is part of the IT department for the Montana Library Association based in Bozeman, Montana. One of her responsibilities in the upcoming year is to convert the database of library holdings into XML format. As part of this process, she's asked for your help in developing the schema that will be used to validate the XML documents. She has created a sample document to work on. Eventually your work will be used in a much larger system. The structure of the sample document is shown in Figure 14-60.

Figure 14-60

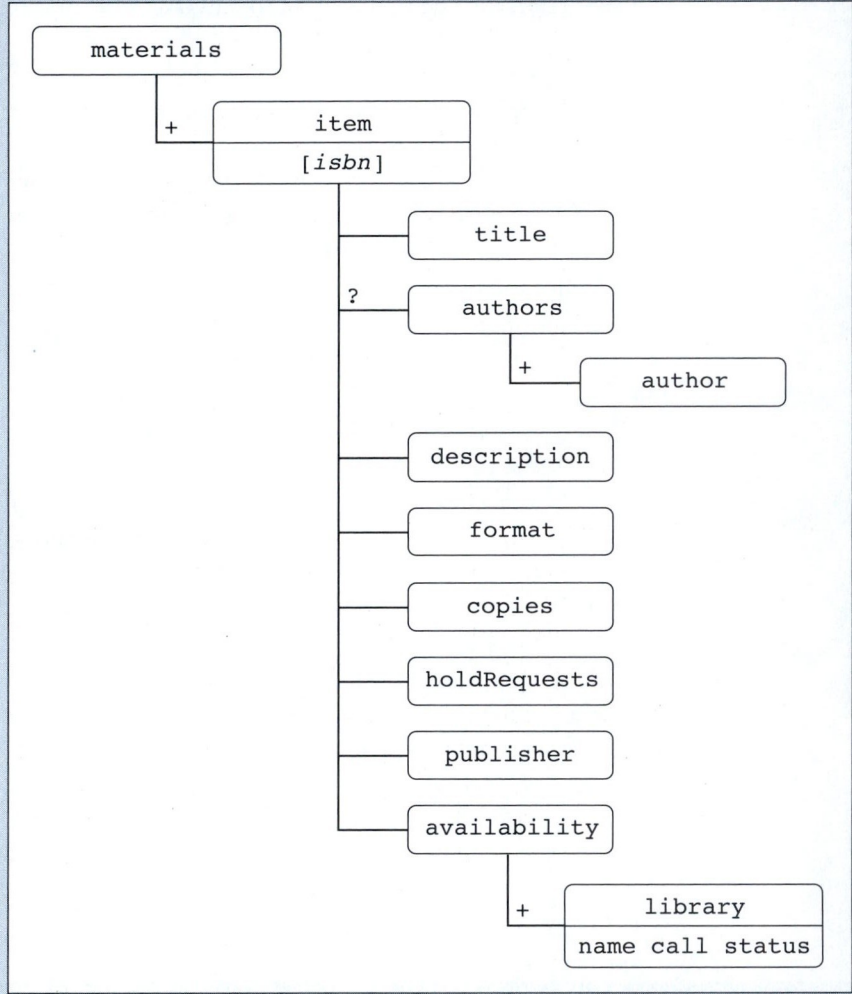

Figure 14-61 describes the elements and attributes in this sample document as well as the rules that govern the data that can be entered into a valid document.

Figure 14-61

Element or Attribute	Description
materials	The root element
item	Element containing information about each item in the library
isbn	An optional attribute in the form of 10 digits or 9 digits followed by the letter x
title	The title of the item
authors	An optional element containing a list of authors
author	The name of an author of the item
description	A description of the item
format	The item's format (book, cassette, cd, dvd, newspaper, periodical, or vhs)
copies	A positive integer indicating the number of copies of item in the library system
holdRequests	A non-negative integer indicating the number of hold requests library patrons have placed on the item
publisher	The name of the publisher of the item
availability	A list of the libraries stocking the item (Ashfield, Billings, Bozeman, Great Falls, or Helena)
library	An empty element containing information about the library stocking the item
name	The name of the library
call	The item's call number at the library
status	The current status of the item (In Library or Checked Out)

Your job will be to express this document structure and set of rules in terms of the XML Schema language, and then validate Keisha's document on the schema you created.

Complete the following:

1. Using your text editor, open the **matertext.xml** and **mlatxt.xsd** files from the tutorial.14\case2 folder, enter *your name* and *the date* in the comment section of each file, and then save the files as **materials.xml** and **mla.xsd**, respectively.

2. Go to the **mla.xsd** file in your text editor and insert the root schema element. Set the default namespace and the target of the schema to the URI *http://montanalib.org/holdings/ns*. Insert the namespace for the XML Schema vocabulary using the namespace prefix **xs**.

3. Define the simple data type **isbnType**, restricting its value to a text string corresponding to the regular expression

   \d{9}[\d|X]

4. Define the simple data type **materialType**, limiting its values to: book, cassette, cd, dvd, newspaper, periodical, or vhs.

5. Define the simple data type **libType**, limiting its values to: Ashfield, Billings, Bozeman, Great Falls, or Helena.

6. Define the simple data type **statusType**, limiting its values to: In Library or Checked Out.

7. Create a named complex type named **authorType**. The purpose of this complex type is to define the structure of the author element. Within this definition, insert a sequence containing the author element occurring at least once in the instance document. The author element contains a text string but no attributes or child elements.

8. Create a named complex type named **availabilityType**. The complex type contains a sequence of library elements that occurs at least once in the instance document. Each library element is an empty element but contains three attributes: name, call, and status. The name attribute contains libType data. The call attribute contains string data. The status attribute contains statusType data. Each attribute is required.

9. Create a named complex type named **itemType**. This type is used to define the elements nested within the item element. Add the following sequence of elements to the complex type:
   a. The **title** element, containing a text string
   b. The **authors** element, containing authorType data (set the minOccurs and maxOccurs values so that this element is optional, occurring at most once)
   c. The **description** element, containing a text string
   d. The **format** element, containing materialType data
   e. The **copies** element, containing a positive integer
   f. The **holdRequests** element, containing a non-negative integer
   g. The **publisher** element, containing a text string
   h. The **availability** element, containing availabilityType data

10. Declare as a global element the **materials** element. Define the element to have a sequence of elements of the item element occurring at least once. Set the data type of the item element to itemType.

11. Save your changes to the mla.xsd file.

12. Return to the **materials.xml** file in your text editor. Add the XML Schema Instance namespace to the root materials element using **xsi** as the namespace prefix. Add the materials namespace *http://montanalib.org/holdings/ns* to the root element using the namespace prefix **mla**. Attach the schema file mla.xsd to the document, specifying *http://montanalib.org/holdings/ns* as the namespace URI.

13. Save your changes to the file, and then validate the document. Correct any errors you find in the instance document. (*Hint:* You can also test your schema file for errors using the validator at *www.w3.org/2001/03/webdata/xsv*.)

14. Submit your completed and validated project to your instructor.

| Challenge | | **Case Problem 3** |

Explore how to create a library of custom simple and complex data types.

Data Files needed for this Case Problem: canvtxt.xsd, clisttxt.xsd, contrib.xml, libtxt.xsd, reptxt.xml

EPAC-MO EPAC-MO is an environmental political action committee operating in central Missouri. Sudha Bhatia manages fundraising reports for the committee and has been using XML to record information on contributors and canvassers who collect donations. She has developed a vocabulary for the canvassers to record each canvasser's name, address, and total amount collected. She has also developed a vocabulary for contributions, recording each contributor's name, address, and total amount donated. Sudha wants your help in developing a schema to validate the information she puts in her documents. Because Sudha will create a compound document displaying information on both canvassers and contributions, she needs the schema to combine information from several namespaces. Figure 14-62 shows the tree structure for the vocabulary of the compound document.

Figure 14-62

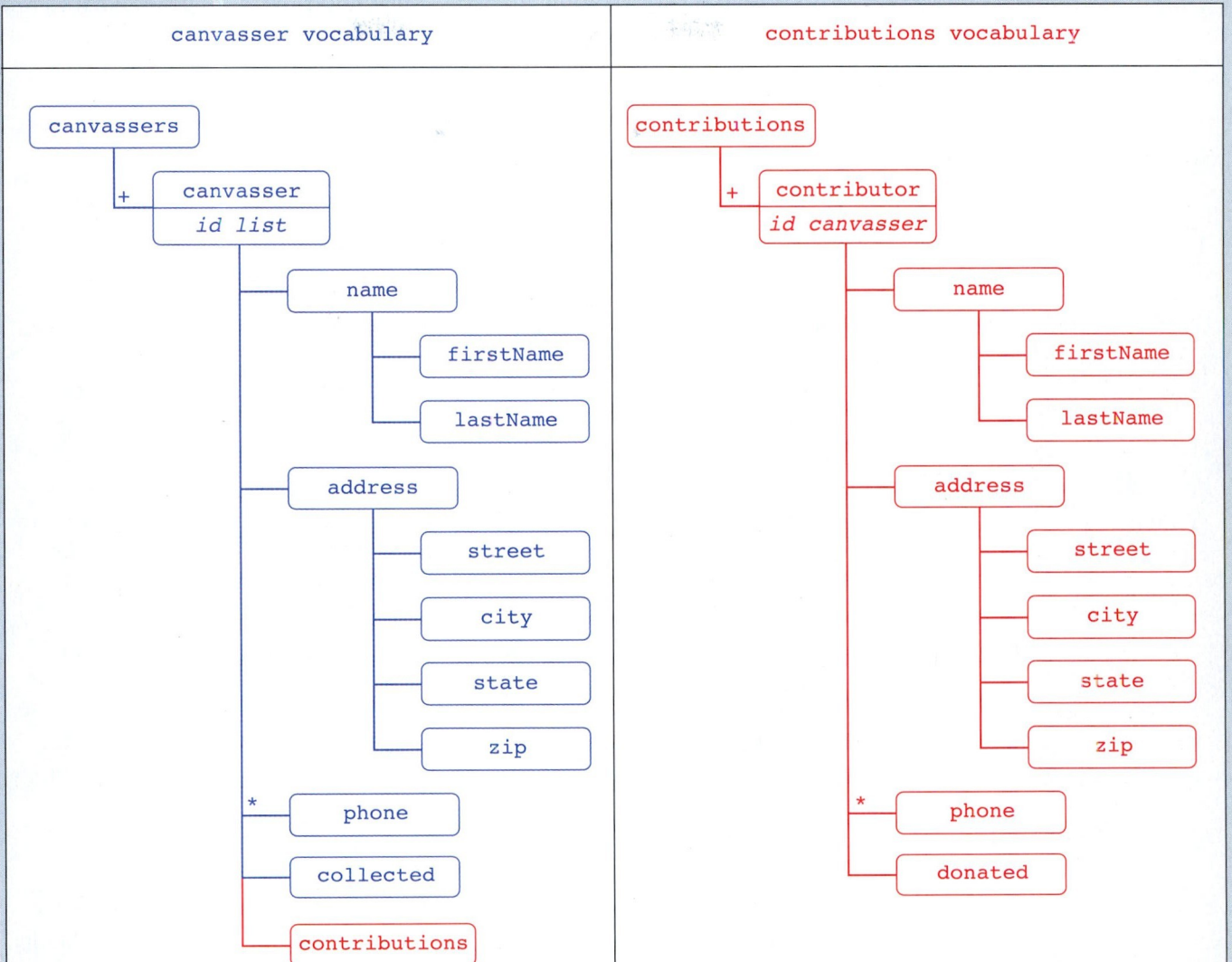

Several simple and complex types, such as the name and address elements, are repeated in both vocabularies. Rather than repeating the definitions in both schemas, you will place the definitions for these common elements in a third schema containing a library of common data types. You will import that schema into the schema files for both the canvasser and contributions vocabularies.

Complete the following:

1. Use your text editor to open the **canvtxt.xsd**, **clisttxt.xsd**, **libtxt.xsd**, and **reptxt.xml** files from the tutorial.14\case3 folder, enter *your name* and *the date* in the comment section of each file, and then save the files as **canvlist.xsd**, **clist.xsd**, **lib.xsd**, and **report.xml**, respectively.

2. Go to the **lib.xsd** file in your text editor. Within this schema, you'll create a library of data types. Add the root schema element and insert the declaration for the XML Schema namespace using the **xs** prefix. Set the default namespace and target of the schema to the URI *http://epacmo.org/library*.

EXPLORE

3. Create the following simple data types:
   a. **stateType**, based on the string data type and limited to two uppercase letters
   b. **zipType**, based on the integer data type consisting of five characters—the first of which is a digit from 1 to 9 and the remaining four are digits from 0 to 9
   c. **phoneType**, based on the string data type consisting of eight characters—the first character being a digit from 1 to 9, followed by two more digits from 0 to 9, followed by a hyphen and then four more digits from 0 to 9

4. Create a complex type named **nameType** containing the following sequence of elements: firstName and lastName. Both elements contain text strings and no attributes or child elements.

5. Create a complex type named **addressType** containing the following sequence of elements: **street**, **city**, **state**, and **zip**. The street and city elements contain string data. The state element contains stateType data. The zip element contains zipType data.

6. Save your changes to the lib.xsd file, close the file, and then go to the **clist.xsd** file in your text editor. You will create the schema for the contributions vocabulary in this file.

7. Insert the root schema element, declaring the XML Schema namespace with the **xs** prefix. Declare the library namespace using the URI *http://epacmo.org/library* and the namespace prefix **lib**. Set the default namespace and the schema target to the URI *http://epacmo.org/contributors*.

8. Import the lib.xsd schema file using the URI of the library namespace.

9. Using a Russian doll design, insert the declaration for the complex type element **contributions**. The element contains the child element contributor, which occurs at least once in the instance document.

10. The **contributor** element is also a complex type element containing the child elements name, address, phone, and donated, and the attributes id and canvasser. The phone element may occur any number of times.

EXPLORE

11. Set the data types of the elements and attributes of the contributor element as follows:
    a. The **name** element, containing nameType data (taken from the library namespace)
    b. The **address** element, containing addressType data (taken from the library namespace)
    c. The **phone** element, containing phoneType data (taken from the library namespace)
    d. The **donated** element, containing positive integer data
    e. The **id** attribute, containing ID data
    f. The **canvasser** attribute, containing an ID reference

12. Save your changes to the clist.xsd file, close the file, and then go to the **canvlist.xsd** file in your text editor. This file contains the schema for the canvasser vocabulary.

13. Insert the root schema element, declaring the XML Schema namespace with the **xs** prefix. Declare the library namespace using the **lib** prefix and the URI *http:// epacmo.org/library,* and the contributors namespace using the **clist** prefix and the URI *http://epacmo.org/contributors*. Set the default namespace and the schema target to the URI *http://epacmo.org/canvassers*.

14. Import the library and contributors schemas using the appropriate namespace URIs and schema locations.

15. Using a Russian doll design, declare the complex type element **canvassers**. The element has a single child element, canvasser, that occurs at least once. The canvasser element contains the following sequence of child elements: name, address, phone, collected, and an element that references the contributions element from the contributions namespace. The phone element can occur any number of times. The canvasser element also contains the id and list attributes.

16. As with the contributions schema, the name, address, and phone elements contain nameType, addressType, and phoneType data, respectively, taken from the lib vocabulary. The collected element contains positive integers. The id attribute contains ID data. The list attribute contains a list of ID references.

17. Save your changes to the file, close the file, and then go to the **report.xml** file in your text editor.

18. Within the root canvassers element, declare the XML Schema instance namespace using the prefix **xsi**. Declare the canvassers namespace using the prefix **canvlist**. Declare the contributions namespace using the prefix **contlist**. Attach schema from the canvlist.xsd file using the appropriate namespace.

19. Change the opening and closing tags of the canvassers element to a qualified name using the **canvlist** namespace prefix. Change the opening and closing tags of the two contributions elements to qualified names using the **contlist** namespace prefix. Save your changes.

20. Go to the **contrib.xml** file in your text editor. Copy and paste the contributor information for contributors c001, c002, and c004 within the first set of contributions tags in the report.xml file. Copy and paste the contributor information for contributors c003, c005, and c006 from the contrib.xml file within the second set of contributions tags in the report.xml file.

◆ EXPLORE

21. Save your changes to the report.xml file, and then validate the file. Correct any mistakes found in the document.

22. Submit the completed and validated project to your instructor.

Create | **Case Problem 4**

Test your knowledge of schemas by creating a schema.

Data Files needed for this Case Problem: golfer.txt, scores.txt

Fairway Views   David Hwu runs a sports information service for golfing enthusiasts called Fairway Views. He is interested in storing information about professional golfers and tournament scores in a collection of XML documents. You will help him develop some XML vocabularies and the schemas to validate his documents. One XML vocabulary will store information on individual golfers. Another vocabulary stores information on scoring results from major tournaments.

David has provided you with two text files of sample data. One text file contains information about the golfer Brett Bierson. The other text file contains Brett's scores from a recent tournament. David wants you to create a compound document combining information from both vocabularies and a pair of schemas to validate that sample file.

Complete the following:

1. Use your text editor to open the **golfer.txt** and **scores.txt** files from the tutorial.14\ case4 folder, and then study the contents of the files. Based on the contents of these two files, develop two XML vocabularies: one to describe the information from the golfer.txt file and the other to describe the information from the scores.txt file. The structure of the two vocabularies is up to you, but it should include examples of attributes and nested child elements.

2. Place the golfer vocabulary in the namespace *http://fairwayviews.com/golfers/ns* and the scores vocabulary in the namespace *http://fairwayviews.com/scores/ns*.

3. Create a compound document named **golfer.xml** that includes data from both the golfer and the scores vocabularies. Include a comment section in the file that describes the content and purpose of the document.

4. Create a schema file named **scores.xsd** that can be used to validate the content from the scores vocabulary. The layout and structure of the schema is up to you, but it should contain examples of the following:
   - A customized data type restricting the value of a built-in XML Schema data type
   - A named complex type that describes the structure of a complex element
   - An attribute that employs the IDREF data type

5. Create a schema file named **golfers.xsd** that can be used to validate the golfer vocabulary. The schema should demonstrate how to import the scores schema and include the following features:
   - Attributes with data values limited to nonnegative and positive integers
   - An attribute containing an ID value
   - An element containing a floating point value

6. Apply the two schemas you created to your compound document, **golfer.xml**. Validate the file to ensure that there are no errors. (*Hint:* You can also test your schema file for errors using the validator at *www.w3.org/2001/03/webdata/xsv.*)

7. Submit the completed and validated project to your instructor.

Review | **Quick Check Answers**

Session 14.1

1. A schema is an XML document that can validate the content and structure of other XML documents. An instance document is the XML document to be validated by a given schema.

2. Schemas support namespaces and work with combined documents better than DTDs. Schemas support more data types and enable the user to easily create customized data types.

3. A simple type element contains a single value, such as the value of an attribute or the textual content of an element. A complex type element contains structured content in the form of child elements and/or attributes.

4. `<xs:element name="Weight" type="xs:string" />`

```
5. <xs:element name="Contact">
      <xs:complexType>
         <xs:all>
            <xs:element name="Mail" type "xs:string" />
            <xs:element name="Phone" type "xs:string" />
         </xs:all>
      </xs:complexType>
   </xs:element>
6. <xs:element name="Book">
      <xs:complexType>
         <xs:simpleType>
            <xs:extension base="xs:string">
               <xs:attribute name="Title" type="xs:string" />
            </xs:extension>
         </xs:simpleType>
      </xs:complexType>
   </xs:element>
7. <xs:attribute ref="patientID" />
8. xmlns:xsi="http://www.w3.org/2001/XMLSchema-instance
   "xsi:noNamespaceSchemaLocation="Schema1.xsd"
```

Session 14.2

```
1. <xs:element name="Weight" type="xs:decimal" />
2. <xs:attribute name="itemIDs" type="xs:IDREFS" />
3. <xs:simpleType name="VisitDates">
      <xs:list itemType="xs:date" />
   </xs:simpleType>
4. <xs:simpleType name="Status">
      <xs:union memberTypes="xs:decimal xs:string" />
   </xs:simpleType>
5. <xs:simpleType name="Party">
      <xs:restriction base="xs:string">
         <xs:enumeration value="Democrat" />
         <xs:enumeration value="Republican" />
         <xs:enumeration value="Independent" />
      </xs:restriction>
   </xs:simpleType>
6. <xs:simpleType name="Percentage">
      <xs:restriction base="xs:decimal">
         <xs:minInclusive value="0" />
         <xs:maxInclusive value="1" />
      </xs:restriction>
   </xs:simpleType>
7. <xs:simpleType name="SocSecurity">
      <xs:restriction base="xs:string">
         <xs:pattern value="\d{3}-\d{2}-\d{4}" />
      </xs:restriction>
   </xs:simpleType>
```

Session 14.3

1. A named complex type is a complex type with a value assigned to the name attribute. An anonymous complex type has no name value.

2.
```
<xs:group name="address">
    <xs:sequence>
        <xs:element name="street" type="xs:string" />
        <xs:element name="city" type="xs:string" />
        <xs:element name="state" type="xs:string" />
        <xs:element name="zip" type="xs:string" />
    </xs:sequence>
</xs:group>
```

3. A flat catalog is a schema design in which all element and attribute declarations are global. In a Russian doll design, only one element is global and the rest of the elements and attributes are nested within that one global element.

4.
```
xmlns="http://jazzwarehouse.com/sales"
targetNamespace="http://jazzwarehouse.com/sales"
```

5. `xsi:schemaLocation="http://jazzwarehouse.com/sales jazz.xsd"`

6. You must qualify the global element and attributes with a namespace prefix.

7. `elementFormDefault="qualified"`

8. An included schema must belong to the same target namespace as the current schema. An imported schema belongs to a different namespace.

Ending Data Files

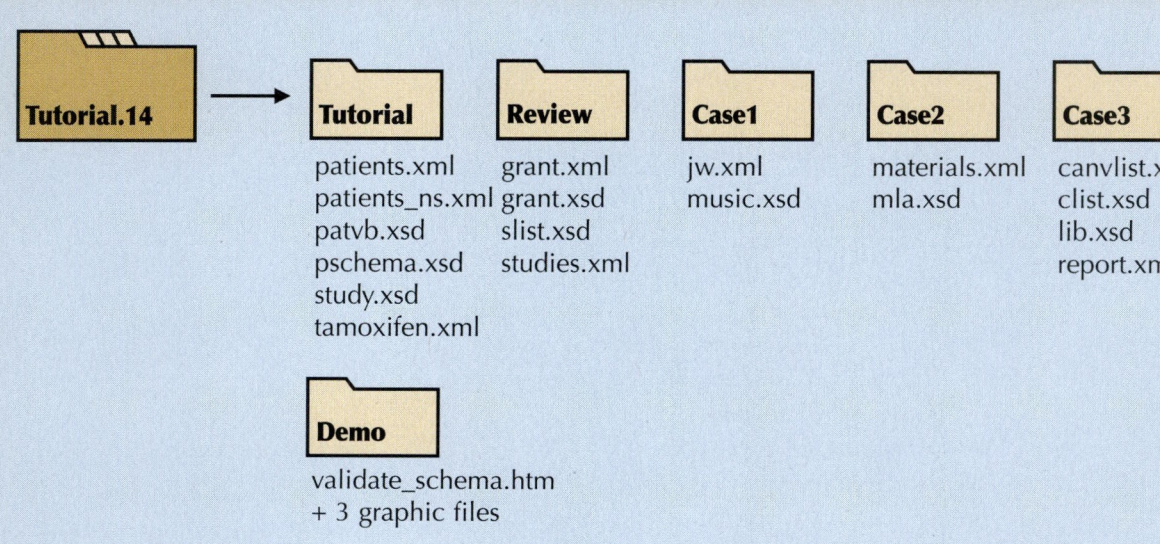

Tutorial.14 →

Tutorial
patients.xml
patients_ns.xml
patvb.xsd
pschema.xsd
study.xsd
tamoxifen.xml

Review
grant.xml
grant.xsd
slist.xsd
studies.xml

Case1
jw.xml
music.xsd

Case2
materials.xml
mla.xsd

Case3
canvlist.xsd
clist.xsd
lib.xsd
report.xml

Case4
golfer.xml
golfers.xsd
scores.xsd

Demo
validate_schema.htm
+ 3 graphic files

Reality Check

XML is a powerful tool for developed structured documents whose content can be tested against a collection of rules defined in a DTD or schema. Expand your knowledge of the uses of XML by doing the following:

1. Use the Web to search for a specific XML vocabulary written for an industry or area of study. Write a report summarizing the features and use of this vocabulary.
2. Design your own XML vocabulary for a field of study that interests you. Your vocabulary should include the following features:
   a. Elements containing textual content
   b. Elements containing child elements
   c. Attributes containing textual content
   d. XML-supported entities
3. Write a summary documenting your vocabulary for other users.
4. Create an instance document based on your XML vocabulary.
5. Write a DTD to validate your instance document based on your vocabulary. Confirm that your instance document passes validation.
6. Write a schema to validate your instance document. Your schema should include the following features:
   a. One or more custom data types
   b. A named complex type
   c. A named model group
   d. A named attribute group
   e. Schema contents laid out in a Venetian blind design
7. Apply your schema to your instance document and verify that your instance document passes validation.
8. Create a second XML vocabulary in the same field of study as your first. Document your vocabulary for other users.
9. Create a namespace for both of your vocabularies.
10. Create a compound document combining elements and attributes from both of your vocabularies.
11. Create a second schema file to validate the contents of your second XML vocabulary.
12. Apply your combined schemas to your compound document and confirm that the compound document passes validation.
13. Document your code and describe what you've learned from creating your own system of XML documents.
14. Submit the completed project to your instructor.

Color Names and Color Values

Appendix A

Both HTML and XHTML allow you to define colors using either color names or color values. HTML and XHTML support a list of 16 basic color names. Most browsers also support an extended list of color names, which are listed in the following table along with their RGB and hexadecimal values. The 16 color names supported by HTML and XHTML appear highlighted in the table. Web-safe colors appear in a bold font.

If you want to use only Web-safe colors, limit your RGB values to 0, 51, 153, 204, and 255 (or limit your hexadecimal values to 00, 33, 66, 99, CC, and FF). For example, an RGB color value of (255, 51, 204) would be Web safe, while an RGB color value of (255, 192, 128) would not.

Starting Data Files

There are no starting Data Files needed for this appendix.

Color Name	RGB Value	Hexadecimal Value
aliceblue	(240,248,255)	#F0F8FF
antiquewhite	(250,235,215)	#FAEBD7
aqua	**(0,255,255)**	**#00FFFF**
aquamarine	(127,255,212)	#7FFFD4
azure	(240,255,255)	#F0FFFF
beige	(245,245,220)	#F5F5DC
bisque	(255,228,196)	#FFE4C4
black	**(0,0,0)**	**#000000**
blanchedalmond	(255,235,205)	#FFEBCD
blue	**(0,0,255)**	**#0000FF**
blueviolet	(138,43,226)	#8A2BE2
brown	(165,42,42)	#A52A2A
burlywood	(222,184,135)	#DEB887
cadetblue	(95,158,160)	#5F9EA0
chartreuse	(127,255,0)	#7FFF00
chocolate	(210,105,30)	#D2691E
coral	(255,127,80)	#FF7F50
cornflowerblue	(100,149,237)	#6495ED
cornsilk	(255,248,220)	#FFF8DC
crimson	(220,20,54)	#DC1436
cyan	**(0,255,255)**	**#00FFFF**
darkblue	(0,0,139)	#00008B
darkcyan	(0,139,139)	#008B8B
darkgoldenrod	(184,134,11)	#B8860B
darkgray	(169,169,169)	#A9A9A9
darkgreen	(0,100,0)	#006400

Color Name	RGB Value	Hexadecimal Value
darkkhaki	(189,183,107)	#BDB76B
darkmagenta	(139,0,139)	#8B008B
darkolivegreen	(85,107,47)	#556B2F
darkorange	(255,140,0)	#FF8C00
darkorchid	(153,50,204)	#9932CC
darkred	(139,0,0)	#8B0000
darksalmon	(233,150,122)	#E9967A
darkseagreen	(143,188,143)	#8FBC8F
darkslateblue	(72,61,139)	#483D8B
darkslategray	(47,79,79)	#2F4F4F
darkturquoise	(0,206,209)	#00CED1
darkviolet	(148,0,211)	#9400D3
deeppink	(255,20,147)	#FF1493
deepskyblue	(0,191,255)	#00BFFF
dimgray	(105,105,105)	#696969
dodgerblue	(30,144,255)	#1E90FF
firebrick	(178,34,34)	#B22222
floralwhite	(255,250,240)	#FFFAF0
forestgreen	(34,139,34)	#228B22
fuchsia	**(255,0,255)**	**#FF00FF**
gainsboro	(220,220,220)	#DCDCDC
ghostwhite	(248,248,255)	#F8F8FF
gold	(255,215,0)	#FFD700
goldenrod	(218,165,32)	#DAA520
gray	(128,128,128)	#808080
green	(0,128,0)	#008000
greenyellow	(173,255,47)	#ADFF2F
honeydew	(240,255,240)	#F0FFF0
hotpink	(255,105,180)	#FF69B4

Color Name	RGB Value	Hexadecimal Value
indianred	(205,92,92)	#CD5C5C
indigo	(75,0,130)	#4B0082
ivory	(255,255,240)	#FFFFF0
khaki	(240,230,140)	#F0E68C
lavender	(230,230,250)	#E6E6FA
lavenderblush	(255,240,245)	#FFF0F5
lawngreen	(124,252,0)	#7CFC00
lemonchiffon	(255,250,205)	#FFFACD
lightblue	(173,216,230)	#ADD8E6
lightcoral	(240,128,128)	#F08080
lightcyan	(224,255,255)	#E0FFFF
lightgoldenrodyellow	(250,250,210)	#FAFAD2
lightgreen	(144,238,144)	#90EE90
lightgrey	(211,211,211)	#D3D3D3
lightpink	(255,182,193)	#FFB6C1
lightsalmon	(255,160,122)	#FFA07A
lightseagreen	(32,178,170)	#20B2AA
lightskyblue	(135,206,250)	#87CEFA
lightslategray	(119,136,153)	#778899
lightsteelblue	(176,196,222)	#B0C4DE
lightyellow	(255,255,224)	#FFFFE0
lime	**(0,255,0)**	**#00FF00**
limegreen	(50,205,50)	#32CD32
linen	(250,240,230)	#FAF0E6
magenta	**(255,0,255)**	**#FF00FF**
maroon	(128,0,0)	#800000
mediumaquamarine	(102,205,170)	#66CDAA
mediumblue	(0,0,205)	#0000CD
mediumorchid	(186,85,211)	#BA55D3

Color Name	RGB Value	Hexadecimal Value
mediumpurple	(147,112,219)	#9370DB
mediumseagreen	(60,179,113)	#3CB371
mediumslateblue	(123,104,238)	#7B68EE
mediumspringgreen	(0,250,154)	#00FA9A
mediumturquoise	(72,209,204)	#48D1CC
mediumvioletred	(199,21,133)	#C71585
midnightblue	(25,25,112)	#191970
mintcream	(245,255,250)	#F5FFFA
mistyrose	(255,228,225)	#FFE4E1
moccasin	(255,228,181)	#FFE4B5
navajowhite	(255,222,173)	#FFDEAD
navy	**(0,0,128)**	**#000080**
oldlace	(253,245,230)	#FDF5E6
olive	**(128,128,0)**	**#808000**
olivedrab	(107,142,35)	#6B8E23
orange	(255,165,0)	#FFA500
orangered	(255,69,0)	#FF4500
orchid	(218,112,214)	#DA70D6
palegoldenrod	(238,232,170)	#EEE8AA
palegreen	(152,251,152)	#98FB98
paleturquoise	(175,238,238)	#AFEEEE
palevioletred	(219,112,147)	#DB7093
papayawhip	(255,239,213)	#FFEFD5
peachpuff	(255,218,185)	#FFDAB9
peru	(205,133,63)	#CD853F
pink	(255,192,203)	#FFC0CB
plum	(221,160,221)	#DDA0DD
powderblue	(176,224,230)	#B0E0E6
purple	**(128,0,128)**	**#808080**

Color Name	RGB Value	Hexadecimal Value
red	**(255,0,0)**	**#FF0000**
rosybrown	(188,143,143)	#BC8F8F
royalblue	(65,105,0)	#4169E1
saddlebrown	(139,69,19)	#8B4513
salmon	(250,128,114)	#FA8072
sandybrown	(244,164,96)	#F4A460
seagreen	(46,139,87)	#2E8B57
seashell	(255,245,238)	#FFF5EE
sienna	(160,82,45)	#A0522D
silver	(192,192,192)	#C0C0C0
skyblue	(135,206,235)	#87CEEB
slateblue	(106,90,205)	#6A5ACD
slategray	(112,128,144)	#708090
snow	(255,250,250)	#FFFAFA
springgreen	(0,255,127)	#00FF7F
steelblue	(70,130,180)	#4682B4
tan	(210,180,140)	#D2B48C
teal	(0,128,128)	#008080
thistle	(216,191,216)	#D8BFD8
tomato	(255,99,71)	#FF6347
turquoise	(64,224,208)	#40E0D0
violet	(238,130,238)	#EE82EE
wheat	(245,222,179)	#F5DEB3
white	**(255,255,255)**	**#FFFFFF**
whitesmoke	(245,245,245)	#F5F5F5
yellow	**(255,255,0)**	**#FFFF00**
yellowgreen	(154,205,50)	#9ACD32

HTML Character Entities

Appendix B

The following table lists the extended character set for HTML, also known as the ISO Latin-1 Character Set. You can specify characters by name or by numeric value. For example, you can use either ® or ® to specify the registered trademark symbol, ®.

Not all browsers recognize all code names. Some older browsers that support only the HTML 2.0 standard do not recognize × as a code name, for instance. Code names that older browsers may not recognize are marked with an asterisk in the following table.

CHARACTER	CODE	CODE NAME	DESCRIPTION
	&#09;		Tab
	&#10;		Line feed
	&#32;		Space
!	&#33;		Exclamation mark
"	&#34;	&quot;	Double quotation mark
#	&#35;		Pound sign
$	&#36;		Dollar sign
%	&#37;		Percent sign
&	&#38;	&amp;	Ampersand
'	&#39;		Apostrophe
(	&#40;		Left parenthesis
)	&#41;		Right parenthesis
*	&#42;		Asterisk
+	&#43;		Plus sign
,	&#44;		Comma
-	&#45;		Hyphen
.	&#46;		Period
/	&#47;		Forward slash
0 - 9	0–9		Numbers 0–9
:	&#58;		Colon
;	&#59;		Semicolon
<	&#60;	&lt;	Less than sign

CHARACTER	CODE	CODE NAME	DESCRIPTION
=	=		Equal sign
>	>	>	Greater than sign
?	?		Question mark
@	@		Commercial at sign
A – Z	A–Z		Letters A–Z
[	[		Left square bracket
\	\		Back slash
]	]		Right square bracket
^	^		Caret
_	_		Horizontal bar (underscore)
`	`		Grave accent
a – z	a–z		Letters a–z
{	{		Left curly brace
|	|		Vertical bar
}	}		Right curly brace
~	~		Tilde
,	‚		Comma
ƒ	ƒ		Function sign (florin)
"	„		Double quotation mark
…	…		Ellipsis
†	†		Dagger
‡	‡		Double dagger
ˆ	ˆ		Circumflex

CHARACTER	CODE	CODE NAME	DESCRIPTION
‰	&#137;		Permil
Š	&#138;		Capital S with hacek
‹	&#139;		Left single angle
Œ	&#140;		Capital OE ligature
	–		Unused
'	&#145;		Single beginning quotation mark
'	&#146;		Single ending quotation mark
"	&#147;		Double beginning quotation mark
"	&#148;		Double ending quotation mark
•	&#149;		Bullet
–	&#150;		En dash
—	&#151;		Em dash
~	&#152;		Tilde
™	&#153;	™*	Trademark symbol
š	&#154;		Small s with hacek
›	&#155;		Right single angle
œ	&#156;		Lowercase oe ligature
Ÿ	&#159;		Capital Y with umlaut
		*	Non-breaking space
¡	&#161;	¡*	Inverted exclamation mark
¢	&#162;	¢*	Cent sign
£	&#163;	£*	Pound sterling
¤	&#164;	¤*	General currency symbol

CHARACTER	CODE	CODE NAME	DESCRIPTION
¥	&#165;	¥*	Yen sign
¦	&#166;	¦*	Broken vertical bar
§	&#167;	§*	Section sign
¨	&#168;	¨*	Umlaut
©	&#169;	©*	Copyright symbol
ª	&#170;	ª*	Feminine ordinal
«	&#171;	«*	Left angle quotation mark
¬	&#172;	¬*	Not sign
	&#173;	­*	Soft hyphen
®	&#174;	®*	Registered trademark
¯	&#175;	¯*	Macron
°	&#176;	°*	Degree sign
±	&#177;	±*	Plus/minus symbol
²	&#178;	²*	Superscript 2
³	&#179;	³*	Superscript 3
´	&#180;	´*	Acute accent
µ	&#181;	µ*	Micro sign
¶	&#182;	¶*	Paragraph sign
·	&#183;	·*	Middle dot
ç	&#184;	¸*	Cedilla
¹	&#185;	¹*	Superscript 1
º	&#186;	º*	Masculine ordinal
»	&#187;	»*	Right angle quotation mark

CHARACTER	CODE	CODE NAME	DESCRIPTION
¼	&#188;	¼*	Fraction one-quarter
½	&#189;	½*	Fraction one-half
¾	&#190;	¾*	Fraction three-quarters
¿	&#191;	¿*	Inverted question mark
À	&#192;	&Agrave;	Capital A, grave accent
Á	&#193;	&Aacute;	Capital A, acute accent
Â	&#194;	&Acirc;	Capital A, circumflex accent
Ã	&#195;	&Atilde;	Capital A, tilde
Ä	&#196;	&Auml;	Capital A, umlaut
Å	&#197;	&Aring;	Capital A, ring
Æ	&#198;	&Aelig;	Capital AE ligature
Ç	&#199;	&Ccedil;	Capital C, cedilla
È	&#200;	&Egrave;	Capital E, grave accent
É	&#201;	&Eacute;	Capital E, acute accent
Ê	&#202;	&Ecirc;	Capital E, circumflex accent
Ë	&#203;	&Euml;	Capital E, umlaut
Ì	&#204;	&Igrave;	Capital I, grave accent
Í	&#205;	&Iacute;	Capital I, acute accent
Î	&#206;	&Icirc;	Capital I, circumflex accent
Ï	&#207;	&Iuml;	Capital I, umlaut
Ð	&#208;	Ð*	Capital ETH, Icelandic
Ñ	&#209;	&Ntilde;	Capital N, tilde
Ò	&#210;	&Ograve;	Capital O, grave accent

CHARACTER	CODE	CODE NAME	DESCRIPTION
Ó	&#211;	&Oacute;	Capital O, acute accent
Ô	&#212;	&Ocirc;	Capital O, circumflex accent
Õ	&#213;	&Otilde;	Capital O, tilde
Ö	&#214;	&Ouml;	Capital O, umlaut
×	&#215;	×*	Multiplication sign
Ø	&#216;	&Oslash;	Capital O slash
Ù	&#217;	&Ugrave;	Capital U, grave accent
Ú	&#218;	&Uacute;	Capital U, acute accent
Û	&#219;	&Ucirc;	Capital U, circumflex accent
Ü	&#220;	&Uuml;	Capital U, umlaut
Ý	&#221;	&Yacute;	Capital Y, acute accent
Þ	&#222;	&THORN;	Capital THORN, Icelandic
ß	&#223;	&szlig;	Small sz ligature
à	&#224;	&agrave;	Small a, grave accent
á	&#225;	&aacute;	Small a, acute accent
â	&#226;	&acirc;	Small a, circumflex accent
ã	&#227;	&atilde;	Small a, tilde
ä	&#228;	&auml;	Small a, umlaut
å	&#229;	&aring;	Small a, ring
æ	&#230;	&aelig;	Small ae ligature
ç	&#231;	&ccedil;	Small c, cedilla
è	&#232;	&egrave;	Small e, grave accent
é	&#233;	&eacute;	Small e, acute accent

CHARACTER	CODE	CODE NAME	DESCRIPTION
ê	&#234;	&ecirc;	Small e, circumflex accent
ë	&#235;	&euml;	Small e, umlaut
ì	&#236;	&igrave;	Small i, grave accent
í	&#237;	&iacute;	Small i, acute accent
î	&#238;	&icirc;	Small i, circumflex accent
ï	&#239;	&iuml;	Small i, umlaut
ð	&#240;	&eth;	Small eth, Icelandic
ñ	&#241;	&ntilde;	Small n, tilde
ò	&#242;	&ograve;	Small o, grave accent
ó	&#243;	&oacute;	Small o, acute accent
ô	&#244;	&ocirc;	Small o, circumflex accent
õ	&#245;	&otilde;	Small o, tilde
ö	&#246;	&ouml;	Small o, umlaut
÷	&#247;	÷*	Division sign
ø	&#248;	&oslash;	Small o slash
ù	&#249;	&ugrave;	Small u, grave accent
ú	&#250;	&uacute;	Small u, acute accent
û	&#251;	&ucirc;	Small u, circumflex accent
ü	&#252;	&uuml;	Small u, umlaut
ý	&#253;	&yacute;	Small y, acute accent
þ	&#254;	&thorn;	Small thorn, Icelandic
ÿ	&#255;	&yuml;	Small y, umlaut

Placing a Document on the World Wide Web

Appendix C

Once you complete work on a Web page, you're probably ready to place it on the World Wide Web for others to see. To make a file available on the World Wide Web, it must be located on a computer connected to the Web called a **Web server**.

Your **Internet Service Provider (ISP)**—the company or institution through which you have Internet access—probably has a Web server available for your use. Because each Internet Service Provider has a different procedure for storing Web pages, you should contact your ISP to learn its policies and procedures. Generally you should be prepared to do the following:

- Extensively test your files with a variety of browsers and under different display conditions. Eliminate any errors and design problems before you place the page on the Web.
- Check the links and inline objects in each of your documents to verify that they point to the correct filenames. Verify your filename capitalization—some Web servers distinguish between a file named "Image.gif" and one named "image.gif." To be safe, use only lowercase letters in all your filenames.
- If your links use absolute pathnames, change them to relative pathnames.
- Find out from your ISP the name of the folder into which you'll be placing your HTML documents. You may also need a special user name and password to access this folder.
- Use FTP, an Internet protocol for transferring files, or e-mail to place your pages in the appropriate folder on your ISP's Web server. This capability is built in to some Web browsers, including Internet Explorer and Netscape, allowing you to easily transfer files to your Web server.
- Decide on a name for your Web site (such as "http://www.jackson_electronics.com"). Choose a name that will be easy for customers and interested parties to remember and return to.
- If you select a special name for your Web site, you may have to register it. Registration information can be found at http://www.internic.net. Your ISP may also provide this service for a fee. Registration is necessary to ensure that any name you give to your site is unique and not already in use. Usually you will have to pay a yearly fee to use a special name for your Web site.

Once you've completed these steps, your work will be available on the World Wide Web in a form that is easy for users to access.

Starting Data Files

There are no starting Data Files needed for this appendix.

Making the Web More Accessible

Appendix D

Studies indicate that about 20% of the population has some type of disability. Many of these disabilities do not affect an individual's ability to interact with the Web. However, other disabilities can severely affect an individual's ability to participate in the Web community. For example, on a news Web site, a blind user could not see the latest headlines. A deaf user would not be able to hear a news clip embedded in the site's main page. A user with motor disabilities might not be able to move a mouse pointer to activate important links featured on the site's home page.

Disabilities that inhibit an individual's ability to use the Web fall into four main categories:

- **Visual disability:** A visual disability can include complete blindness, color-blindness, or an untreatable visual impairment.
- **Hearing disability:** A hearing disability can include complete deafness or the inability to distinguish sounds of certain frequencies.
- **Motor disability:** A motor disability can include the inability to use a mouse, to exhibit fine motor control, or to respond in a timely manner to computer prompts and queries.
- **Cognitive disability:** A cognitive disability can include a learning disability, attention deficit disorder, or the inability to focus on large amounts of information.

While the Web includes some significant obstacles to full use by disabled people, it also offers the potential for contact with a great amount of information that is not otherwise cheaply or easily accessible. For example, before the Web, in order to read a newspaper, a blind person was constrained by the expense of Braille printouts and audio tapes, as well as the limited availability of sighted people willing to read the news out loud. As a result, blind people would often only be able to read newspapers after the news was no longer new. The Web, however, makes news available in an electronic format and in real-time. A blind user can use a browser that converts electronic text into speech, known as a **screen reader**, to read a newspaper Web site. Combined with the Web, screen readers provide access to a broader array of information than was possible through Braille publications alone.

> "The power of the Web is in its universality. Access by everyone regardless of disability is an essential aspect."
>
> — Tim Berners-Lee, W3C Director and inventor of the World Wide Web

Starting Data Files

There are no starting Data Files needed for this appendix.

In addition to screen readers, many other programs and devices—known collectively as assistive technology or adaptive technology—are available to enable people with different disabilities to use the Web. The challenge for the Web designer, then, is to create Web pages that are accessible to everyone, including (and perhaps especially) to people with disabilities. In addition to being a design challenge, for some designers, Web accessibility is the law.

Working with Section 508 Guidelines

In 1973, Congress passed the Rehabilitation Act, which aimed to foster economic independence for people with disabilities. Congress amended the act in 1998 to reflect the latest changes in information technology. Part of the amendment, **Section 508**, requires that any electronic information developed, procured, maintained, or used by the federal government be accessible to people with disabilities. Because the Web is one of the main sources of electronic information, Section 508 has had a profound impact on how Web pages are designed and how Web code is written. Note that the standards apply to federal Web sites, but not to private sector Web sites; however, if a site is provided under contract to a federal agency, the Web site or portion covered by the contract has to comply. Required or not, though, you should follow the Section 508 guidelines not only to make your Web site more accessible, but also to make your HTML code more consistent and reliable. The Section 508 guidelines are of interest not just to Web designers who work for the federal government, but to all Web designers.

The Section 508 guidelines encompass a wide range of topics, covering several types of disabilities. The part of Section 508 that impacts Web design is sub-section 1194.22, titled

§ 1194.22 Web-based intranet and internet information and applications.

Within this section are 15 paragraphs, numbered (a) through (p), which describe how each facet of a Web site should be designed so as to maximize accessibility. Let's examine each of these paragraphs in detail.

Graphics and Images

The first paragraph in sub-section 1194.22 deals with graphic images. The standard for the use of graphic images is that

§1194.22 (a) A text equivalent for every nontext element shall be provided (e.g., via "alt", "longdesc", or in element content).

In other words, any graphic image that contains page content needs to include a text alternative to make the page accessible to visually impaired people. One of the simplest ways to do this is to use the alt attribute with every inline image that displays page content. For example, in Figure D-1, the alt attribute provides the text of a graphical logo for users who can't see the graphic.

Figure D-1 **Using the alt attribute**

```
<img src="jkson.jpg" alt="Jackson Electronics" />
```

Not every graphic image requires a text alternative. For example, a decorative image such as a bullet does not need a text equivalent. In those cases, you should include the alt attribute, but set its value to an empty text string. You should never neglect to include the alt attribute. If you are writing XHTML-compliant code, the alt attribute is required. In other cases, screen readers and other nonvisual browsers will recite the filename of a graphic image file if no value is specified for the alt attribute. Since the filename is usually of no interest to the end-user, this results in needless irritation.

The alt attribute is best used for short descriptions that involve five words or less. It is less effective for images that require long descriptive text. You can instead link these images to a document containing a more detailed description. One way to do this is with the longdesc attribute, which uses the syntax

```
<img src="url" longdesc="url" />
```

where `url` for the longdesc attribute points to a document containing a detailed description of the image. Figure D-2 shows an example that uses the longdesc attribute to point to a Web page containing a detailed description of a sales chart.

Using the alt attribute **Figure D-2**

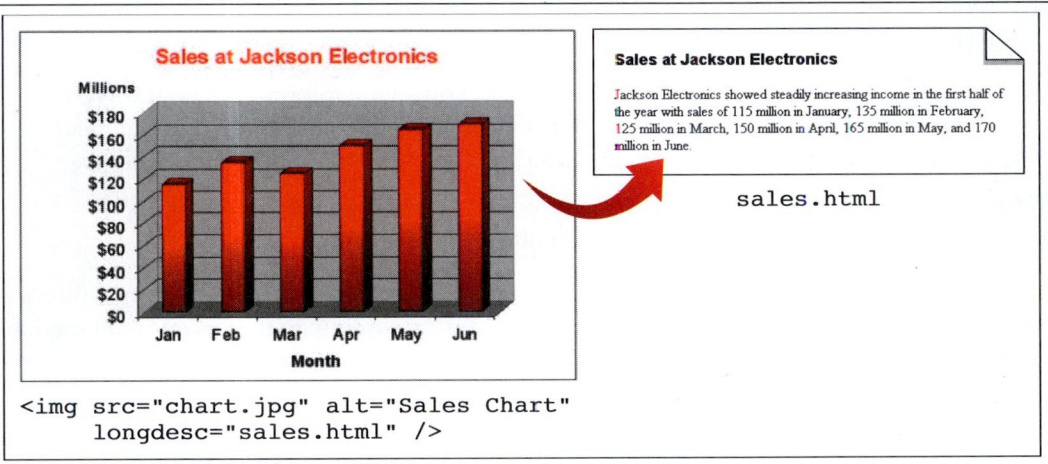

```
<img src="chart.jpg" alt="Sales Chart"
     longdesc="sales.html" />
```

In browsers that support the longdesc attribute, the attribute's value is presented as a link to the specified document. However, since many browsers do not yet support this attribute, many Web designers currently use a D-link. A **D-link** is an unobtrusive "D" placed next to the image on the page, which is linked to an external document containing a fuller description of the image. Figure D-3 shows how the sales chart data can be presented using a D-link.

Figure D-3 ▶ **Using a D-link**

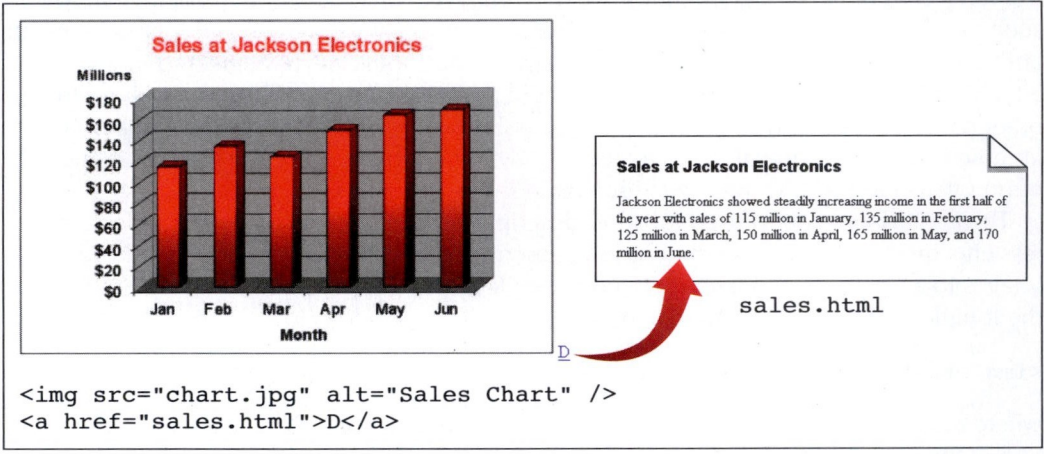

```
<img src="chart.jpg" alt="Sales Chart" />
<a href="sales.html">D</a>
```

To make your page accessible to visually-impaired users, you will probably use a combination of alternative text and linked documents.

Multimedia

Audio and video have become important ways of conveying information on the Web. However, creators of multimedia presentations should also consider the needs of deaf users and users who are hard of hearing. The standard for multimedia accessibility is

§1194.22 (b)   Equivalent alternatives for any multimedia presentation shall be synchronized with the presentation.

This means that any audio clip needs to be accompanied by a transcript of the audio's content, and any video clip needs to include closed captioning. Refer to your multimedia software's documentation on creating closed captioning and transcripts for your video and audio clips.

Color

Color is useful for emphasis and conveying information, but when color becomes an essential part of the site's content, you run the risk of shutting out people who are color blind. For this reason the third Section 508 standard states that

§1194.22 (c)   Web pages shall be designed so that all information conveyed with color is also available without color, for example from context or markup.

About 8% of men and 0.5% of women are afflicted with some type of color blindness. The most serious forms of color blindness are:

- **deuteranopia**: an absence of green sensitivity; deuteranopia is one example of red-green color blindness, in which the colors red and green cannot be easily distinguished.
- **protanopia**: an absence of red sensitivity; protanopia is another example of red-green color blindness.
- **tritanopia**: an absence of blue sensitivity. People with tritanopia have much less loss of color sensitivity than other types of color blindness.
- **achromatopsia**: absence of any color sensitivity.

The most common form of serious color blindness is red-green color blindness. Figure D-4 shows how each type of serious color blindness would affect a person's view of a basic color wheel.

Types of color blindness ◀ **Figure D-4**

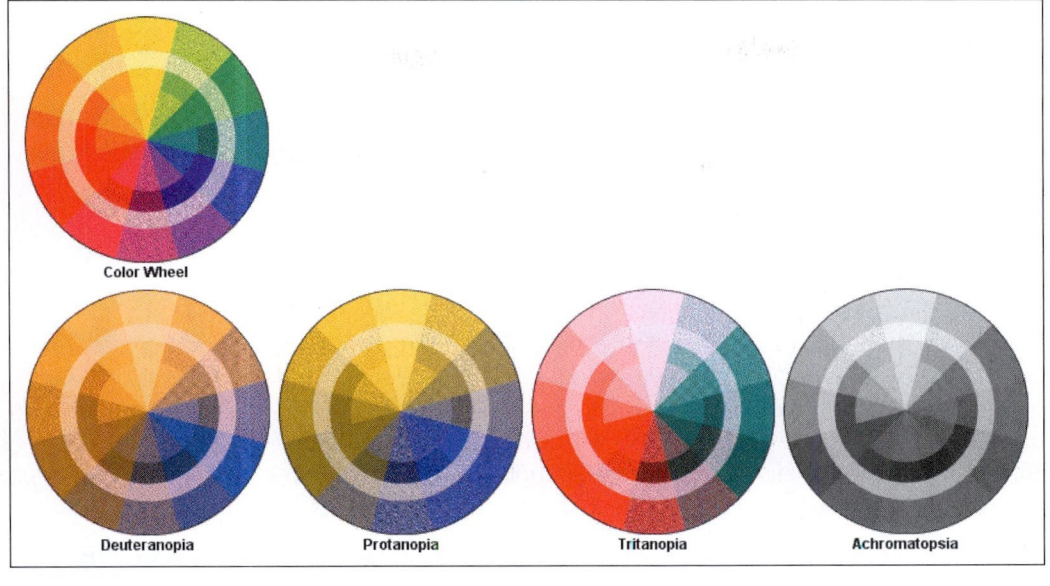

Color combinations that are easily readable for most people may be totally unreadable for users with certain types of color blindness. Figure D-5 demonstrates the accessibility problems that can occur with a graphical logo that contains green text on a red background. For people who have deuteranopia, protanopia, or achromatopsia, the logo is much more difficult to read.

The effect of color blindness on graphical content ◀ **Figure D-5**

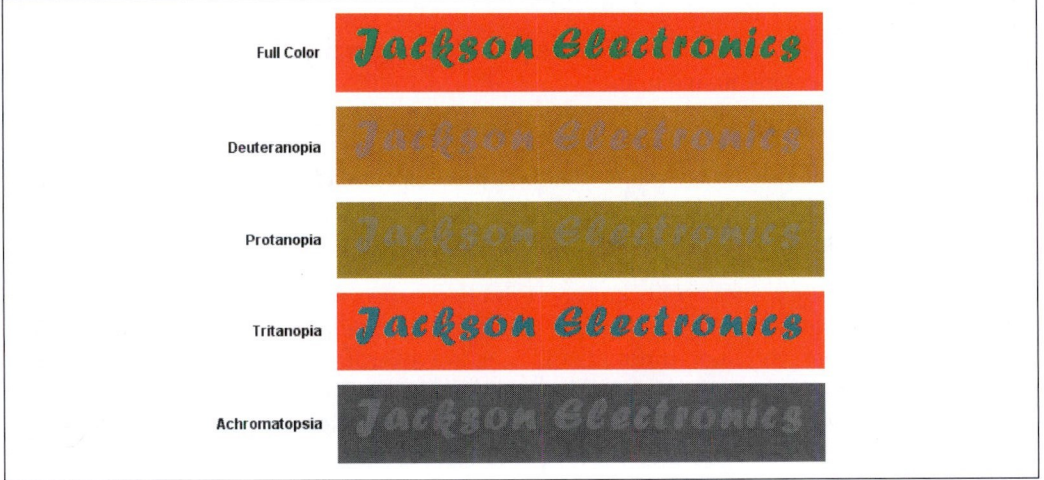

To make your page more accessible to people with color blindness, you can do the following:

• Provide noncolor clues to access your page's content. For example, some Web forms indicate required entry fields by displaying the field names in a red font. You can supplement this for color blind users by marking required fields with a red font *and* with an asterisk or other special symbol.
• Avoid explicit references to color. Don't instruct your users to click a red button in a Web form when some users are unable to distinguish red from other colors.
• Avoid known areas of color difficulty. Since most color blindness involves red-green color blindness, you should avoid red and green text combinations.

- Use bright colors, which are the easiest for color blind users to distinguish.
- Provide a grayscale or black and white alternative for your color blind users, and be sure that your link to that page is easily viewable.

Several sites on the Web include tools you can use to test your Web site for color blind accessibility. You can also load color palettes into your graphics software to see how your images will appear to users with different types of color blindness.

Style Sheets

By controlling how a page is rendered in a browser, style sheets play an important role in making the Web accessible to users with disabilities. Many browsers, such as Internet Explorer, allow a user to apply their own customized style sheet in place of the style sheet specified by a Web page's designer. This is particularly useful for visually impaired users who need to display text in extra large fonts with a high contrast between the text and the background color (yellow text on a black background is a common color scheme for such users). In order to make your pages accessible to those users, Section 508 guidelines state that

§1194.22 (d) **Documents shall be organized so they are readable without requiring an associated style sheet.**

To test whether your site fulfills this guideline, you should view the site without the style sheet. Some browsers allow you to turn off style sheets; alternately, you can redirect a page to an empty style sheet. You should modify any page that is unreadable without its style sheet to conform with this guideline.

Image Maps

Section 508 provides two standards that pertain to image maps:

§1194.22 (e) **Redundant text links shall be provided for each active region of a server-side image map.**

and

§1194.22 (f) **Client-side image maps shall be provided instead of server-side image maps except where the regions cannot be defined with an available geometric shape.**

In other words, the *preferred* image map is a client-side image map, unless the map uses a shape that cannot be defined on the client side. Since client-side image maps allow for polygonal shapes, this should not be an issue; however if you must use a server-side image map, you need to provide a text alternative for each of the map's links. Because server-side image maps provide only map coordinates to the server, this text is necessary in order to provide link information that is accessible to blind or visually impaired users. Figure D-6 shows a server-side image map that satisfies the Section 508 guidelines by repeating the graphical links in the image map with text links placed below the image.

Figure D-6 ▶ **Making a server-side image map accessible**

Client-side image maps do not have the same limitations as server-side maps because they allow you to specify alternate text for each hotspot within the map. For example, if the image map shown in Figure D-6 were a client-side map, you could make it accessible using the following HTML code:

```
<img src="servermap.jpg" alt="Jackson Electronics"
usemap="#links" />
<map name="links">
<area shape="rect" href="home.html" alt="home"
coords="21,69,123,117" />
<area shape="rect" href="products.html" alt="products"
coords="156,69,258,117" />
<area shape="rect" href="stores.html" alt="stores"
coords="302,69,404,117" />
<area shape="rect" href="support.html" alt="support"
coords="445,69,547,117" />
</map>
```

Screen readers or other nonvisual browsers use the value of the alt attribute within each <area /> tag to give users access to each area. However, because some older browsers cannot work with the alt attribute in this way, you should also include the text alternative used for server-side image maps.

Tables

Tables can present a challenge for disabled users, in particular those who employ screen readers or other nonvisual browsers. To render a Web page, these browsers employ a technique called **linearizing**, which processes Web page content using a few general rules:

1. Convert all images to their alternative text.
2. Present the contents of each table one cell at a time, working from left to right across each row before moving down to the next row.
3. If a cell contains a nested table, that table is linearized before proceeding to the next cell.

Figure D-7 shows how a nonvisual browser might linearize a sample table.

Figure D-7 ▶ **Linearizing a table**

	table							linearized content

	Model	Processor	Memory	DVD Burner	Modem	Network Adapter
Desktop PCs						
	Paragon 2.4	Intel 2.4GHz	256MB	No	Yes	No
	Paragon 3.7	Intel 3.7GHz	512MB	Yes	Yes	No
	Paragon 5.9	Intel 5.9GHz	1024MB	Yes	Yes	Yes

linearized content:

Desktop PCs
Model
Processor
Memory
DVD Burner
Modem
Network Adapter
Paragon 2.4
Intel 2.4 GHz
256MB
No
Yes
No
Paragon 3.7
Intel 3.7GHz
512MB
Yes
Yes
No
Paragon 5.9
Intel 5.9GHz
1024MB
Yes
Yes
Yes

One way of dealing with the challenge of linearizing is to structure your tables so that they are easily interpreted even when linearized. However, this is not always possible, especially for tables that have several rows and columns or may contain several levels of nested tables. The Section 508 guidelines for table creation state that

§1194.22 (g) Row and column headers shall be identified for data tables.

and

§1194.22 (h) Markup shall be used to associate data cells and header cells for data tables that have two or more logical levels of row or column headers.

To fulfill the 1194.22 (g) guideline, you should use the <th> tag for any table cell that contains a row or column header. By default, header text appears in a bold centered font; however, you can override this format using a style sheet. Many nonvisual browsers can search for header cells. Also, as a user moves from cell to cell in a table, these browsers can announce the row and column headers associated with each cell. So, using the <th> tag can significantly reduce some of the problems associated with linearizing.

You can also use the scope attribute to explicitly associate a header with a row, column, row group, or column group. The syntax of the scope attribute is

```
<th scope="type"> … </th>
```

where *type* is either row, column, rowgroup, or colgroup. Figure D-8 shows how to use the scope attribute to associate the headers with the rows and columns of a table.

Using the scope attribute ◀ **Figure D-8**

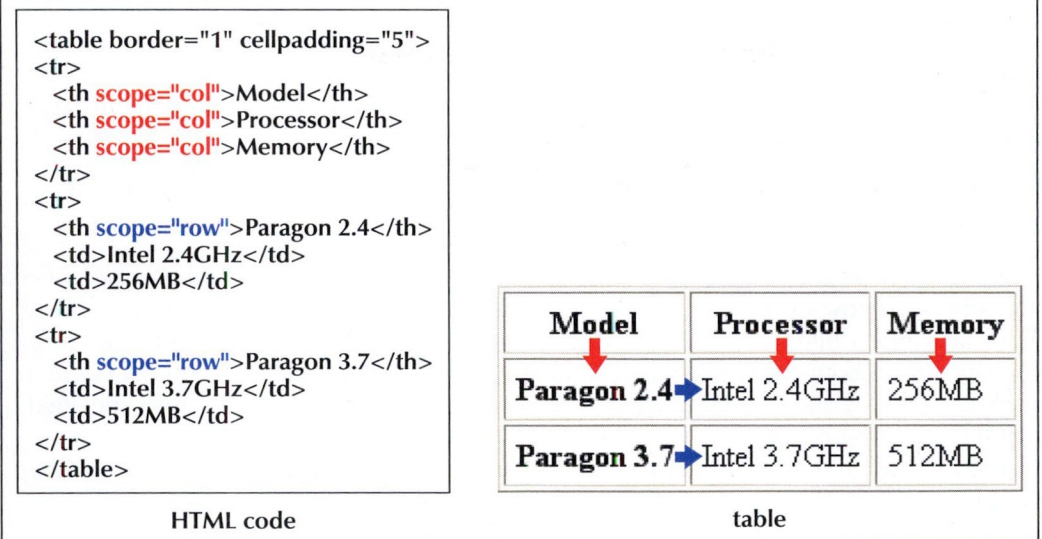

```
<table border="1" cellpadding="5">
<tr>
  <th scope="col">Model</th>
  <th scope="col">Processor</th>
  <th scope="col">Memory</th>
</tr>
<tr>
  <th scope="row">Paragon 2.4</th>
  <td>Intel 2.4GHz</td>
  <td>256MB</td>
</tr>
<tr>
  <th scope="row">Paragon 3.7</th>
  <td>Intel 3.7GHz</td>
  <td>512MB</td>
</tr>
</table>
```

HTML code   table

A nonvisual browser that encounters the table in Figure D-8 can indicate to users which rows and columns are associated with each data cell. For example, the browser could indicate that the cell value, "512MB" is associated with the Memory column and the Paragon 3.7 row.

For more explicit references, HTML also supports the headers attribute, which specifies the cell or cells that contain header information for a particular cell. The syntax of the headers attribute is

```
<td headers="ids"> … </td>
```

where *ids* is a list of id values associated with header cells in the table. Figure D-9 demonstrates how to use the headers attribute.

Using the headers attribute ◀ **Figure D-9**

```
<table>
<tr>
  <th id="c1">Model</th>
  <th id="c2">Processor</th>
  <th id="c3">Memory</th>
</tr>
<tr>
  <th id="r1" headers="c1">Paragon 2.4</th>
  <td headers="r1 c2">Intel 2.4GHz</td>
  <td headers="r1 c3">256MB</td>
</tr>
<tr>
  <th id="r2" headers="c1">Paragon 3.7</th>
  <td headers="r2 c2">Intel 3.7GHz</td>
  <td headers="r2 c3">512MB</td>
</tr>
</table>
```

Model	Processor	Memory
Paragon 2.4	Intel 2.4GHz	256MB
Paragon 3.7	Intel 3.7GHz	512MB

HTML code   table

Note that some older browsers do not support the scope and headers attributes. For this reason, it can be useful to supplement your tables with caption and summary attributes in order to provide even more information to blind and visually impaired users. See Tutorial 4 for a more detailed discussion of these elements and attributes.

Frame Sites

When a nonvisual browser opens a frame site, it can render the contents of only one frame at a time. Users are given a choice of which frame to open. So, it's important that the name given to a frame indicate the frame's content. For this reason, the Section 508 guideline for frames states that

§1194.22 (i) Frames shall be titled with text that facilitates frame identification and navigation.

Frames can be identified using either the title attribute or the name attribute, and different nonvisual browsers use different attributes. For example, the Lynx browser uses the name attribute, while the IBM Home Page Reader uses the title attribute. For this reason, you should use both attributes in your framed sites. If you don't include a title or name attribute in the frame element, some nonvisual browsers retrieve the document specified as the frame's source and then use that page's title as the name for the frame.

The following code demonstrates how to make a frame site accessible to users with disabilities.

```
<frameset cols="25%, *">
    <frame src="title.htm" title="banner" name="banner" />
    <frameset rows="100, *">
        <frame src="links.htm" title="links" name="links" />
        <frame src="home.htm" title="documents" name="documents" />
    </frameset>
</frameset>
```

Naturally, you should make sure that any document displayed in a frame follows the Section 508 guidelines.

Animation and Scrolling Text

Animated GIFs, scrolling marquees, and other special features can be a source of irritation for any Web user; however, they can cause serious problems for certain users. For example, people with photosensitive epilepsy can experience seizures when exposed to a screen or portion of a screen that flickers or flashes within the range of 2 to 55 flashes per second (2 to 55 Hertz). For this reason, the Section 508 guidelines state that

§1194.22 (j) Pages shall be designed to avoid causing the screen to flicker with a frequency greater than 2 Hz and lower than 55 Hz.

In addition to problems associated with photosensitive epilepsy, users with cognitive or visual disabilities may find it difficult to read moving text, and most screen readers are unable to read moving text. Therefore, if you decide to use animated elements, you must ensure that each element's flickering and flashing is outside of the prohibited range, and you should not place essential page content within these elements.

Scripts, Applets and Plug-ins

Scripts, applets, and plug-ins are widely used to make Web pages more dynamic and interesting. The Section 508 guidelines for scripts state that

§1194.22 (l) When pages utilize scripting languages to display content, or to create interface elements, the information provided by the script shall be identified with functional text that can be read by adaptive technology.

Scripts are used for a wide variety of purposes. The following list describes some of the more popular uses of scripts and how to modify them for accessibility:

- **Pull-down menus**: Many Web designers use scripts to save screen space by inserting pull-down menus containing links to other pages in the site. Pull-down menus are usually accessed with a mouse. To assist users who cannot manipulate a mouse, include keyboard shortcuts to all pull-down menus. In addition, the links in a pull-down menu should be repeated elsewhere on the page or on the site in a text format.
- **Image rollovers**: Image rollovers are used to highlight linked elements. However, since image rollovers rely on the ability to use a mouse, pages should be designed so that rollover effects are not essential for navigating a site or for understanding a page's content.
- **Dynamic content**: Scripts can be used to insert new text and page content. Because some browsers designed for users with disabilities have scripting turned off by default, you should either not include any crucial content in dynamic text, or you should provide an alternate method for users with disabilities to access that information.

Applets and plug-ins are programs external to a Web page or browser that add special features to a Web site. The Section 508 guideline for applets and plug-ins is

§1194.22 (m) When a Web page requires that an applet, plug-in or other application be present on the client system to interpret page content, the page must provide a link to a plug-in or applet that complies with §1994.21(a) through (i).

This guideline means that any applet or plug-in used with your Web site must be compliant with sections §1994.21(a) through (i) of the Section 508 accessibility law, which deal with accessibility issues for software applications and operating systems. If the default applet or plug-in does not comply with Section 508, you need to provide a link to a version of that applet or plug-in which does. For example, a Web page containing a Real Audio clip should have a link to a source for the necessary player. This places the responsibility on the Web page designer to know that a compliant application is available before requiring the clip to work with the page.

Web Forms

The Section 508 standard for Web page forms states that

§1194.22 (n) When electronic forms are designed to be completed on-line, the form shall allow people using assistive technology to access the information, field elements, and functionality required for completion and submission of the form, including all directions and cues.

This is a general statement that instructs designers to make forms accessible, but it doesn't supply any specific instructions. The following techniques can help you make Web forms that comply with Section 508:

- **Push buttons** should always include value attributes. The value attribute contains the text displayed on a button, and is rendered by different types of assistive technology.
- **Image buttons** should always include alternate text that can be rendered by nonvisual browsers.
- **Labels** should be associated with any input box, text area box, option button, checkbox, or selection list. The labels should be placed in close proximity to the input field and should be linked to the field using the label element.
- **Input boxes** and **text area boxes** should, when appropriate, include either default text or a prompt that indicates to the user what text to enter into the input box.
- **Interactive form elements** should be triggered by either the mouse or the keyboard.

The other parts of a Web form should comply with other Section 508 standards. For example, if you use a table to lay out the elements of a form, make sure that the form still makes sense when the table is linearized.

Links

It is common for Web designers to place links at the top, bottom, and sides of every page in their Web sites. This is generally a good idea, because those links enable users to move quickly and easily through a site. However, this technique can make it difficult to navigate a page using a screen reader, because screen readers move through a page from the top to bottom, reading each line of text. Users of screen readers may have to wait several minutes before they even get to the main body of a page, and the use of repetitive links forces such users to reread the same links on each page as they move through a site. To address this problem, the Section 508 guidelines state that

§1194.22 (o)   A method shall be provided that permits users to skip repetitive navigation links.

One way of complying with this rule is to place a link at the very top of each page that allows users to jump to the page's main content. In order to make the link unobtrusive, it can be attached to a transparent image that is one pixel wide by one pixel high. For example, the following code lets users of screen readers jump to the main content of the page without needing to go through the content navigation links on the page; however, the image itself is invisible to other users and so does not affect the page's layout or appearance.

```
<a href="#main">
   <img src="spacer.gif" height="1" width="1" alt="Skip to main
content" />
</a>


...


<a name="main"> </a>
page content goes here …
```

One advantage to this approach is that a template can be easily written to add this code to each page of the Web site.

Timed Responses

For security reasons, the login pages of some Web sites automatically log users out after a period of inactivity, or if users are unable to log in quickly. Because disabilities may prevent some users from being able to complete a login procedure within the prescribed time limit, the Section 508 guidelines state that

§1194.22 (p)   When a timed response is required, the user shall be alerted and given sufficient time to indicate that more time is required.

The guideline does not suggest a time interval. To satisfy Section 508, your page should notify users when a process is about to time out and prompt users whether additional time is needed before proceeding.

Providing a Text-Only Equivalent

If you cannot modify a page to match the previous accessibility guidelines, as a last resort you can create a text-only page:

§1194.22 (k) **A text-only page, with equivalent information or functionality, shall be provided to make a Web site comply with the provisions of this part, when compliance cannot be accomplished in any other way. The content of the text-only pages shall be updated whenever the primary page changes.**

To satisfy this requirement, you should:

- Provide an easily accessible link to the text-only page.
- Make sure that the text-only page satisfies the Section 508 guidelines.
- Duplicate the essential content of the original page.
- Update the alternate page when you update the original page.

By using the Section 508 guidelines, you can work towards making your Web site accessible to everyone, regardless of disabilities.

Understanding the Web Accessibility Initiative

In 1999, the World Wide Web Consortium (W3C) developed its own set of guidelines for Web accessibility called the **Web Accessibility Initiative (WAI)**. The WAI covers many of the same points as the Section 508 rules, and expands on them to cover basic Web site design issues. The overall goal of the WAI is to facilitate the creation of Web sites that are accessible to all, and to encourage designers to implement HTML in a consistent way.

The WAI sets forth 14 guidelines for Web designers. Within each guideline is a collection of checkpoints indicating how to apply the guideline to specific features of a Web site. Each checkpoint is also given a priority score that indicates how important the guideline is for proper Web design:

- **Priority 1:** A Web content developer **must** satisfy this checkpoint. Otherwise, one or more groups will find it impossible to access information in the document. Satisfying this checkpoint is a basic requirement for some groups to be able to use Web documents.
- **Priority 2:** A Web content developer **should** satisfy this checkpoint. Otherwise, one or more groups will find it difficult to access information in the document. Satisfying this checkpoint will remove significant barriers to accessing Web documents.
- **Priority 3:** A Web content developer **may** address this checkpoint. Otherwise, one or more groups will find it somewhat difficult to access information in the document. Satisfying this checkpoint will improve access to Web documents.

The following table lists WAI guidelines with each checkpoint and its corresponding priority value. You can learn more about the WAI guidelines and how to implement them by going to the World Wide Web Consortium Web site at *www.w3.org*.

WAI Guidelines	Priority
1. Provide equivalent alternatives to auditory and visual content	
1.1 Provide a text equivalent for every nontext element (e.g., via "alt", "longdesc", or in element content). *This includes:* images, graphical representations of text (including symbols), image map regions, animations (e.g., animated GIFs), applets and programmatic objects, ascii art, frames, scripts, images used as list bullets, spacers, graphical buttons, sounds (played with or without user interaction), stand-alone audio files, audio tracks of video, and video.	1
1.2 Provide redundant text links for each active region of a server-side image map.	1
1.3 Until user agents can automatically read aloud the text equivalent of a visual track, provide an auditory description of the important information of the visual track of a multimedia presentation.	1
1.4 For any time-based multimedia presentation (e.g., a movie or animation), synchronize equivalent alternatives (e.g., captions or auditory descriptions of the visual track) with the presentation.	1
1.5 Until user agents render text equivalents for client-side image map links, provide redundant text links for each active region of a client-side image map.	3
2. Don't rely on color alone	
2.1 Ensure that all information conveyed with color is also available without color, for example from context or markup.	1
2.2 Ensure that foreground and background color combinations provide sufficient contrast when viewed by someone having color deficits or when viewed on a black and white screen. [Priority 2 for images, Priority 3 for text].	2
3. Use markup and style sheets and do so properly	
3.1 When an appropriate markup language exists, use markup rather than images to convey information.	2
3.2 Create documents that validate to published formal grammars.	2
3.3 Use style sheets to control layout and presentation.	2
3.4 Use relative rather than absolute units in markup language attribute values and style sheet property values.	2
3.5 Use header elements to convey document structure and use them according to specification.	2
3.6 Mark up lists and list items properly.	2
3.7 Mark up quotations. Do not use quotation markup for formatting effects such as indentation.	2
4. Clarify natural language usage	
4.1 Clearly identify changes in the natural language of a document's text and any text equivalents (e.g., captions).	1
4.2 Specify the expansion of each abbreviation or acronym in a document where it first occurs.	3
4.3 Identify the primary natural language of a document.	3
5. Create tables that transform gracefully	
5.1 For data tables, identify row and column headers.	1
5.2 For data tables that have two or more logical levels of row or column headers, use markup to associate data cells and header cells.	1
5.3 Do not use a table for layout unless the table makes sense when linearized. If a table does not make sense, provide an alternative equivalent (which may be a linearized version).	2
5.4 If a table is used for layout, do not use any structural markup for the purpose of visual formatting.	2
5.5 Provide summaries for tables.	3
5.6 Provide abbreviations for header labels.	3

WAI Guidelines	Priority
6. Ensure that pages featuring new technologies transform gracefully	
6.1 Organize documents so they may be read without style sheets. For example, when an HTML document is rendered without associated style sheets, it must still be possible to read the document.	1
6.2 Ensure that equivalents for dynamic content are updated when the dynamic content changes.	1
6.3 Ensure that pages are usable when scripts, applets, or other programmatic objects are turned off or not supported. If this is not possible, then provide equivalent information on an alternative accessible page.	1
6.4 For scripts and applets, ensure that event handlers are input device-independent.	2
6.5 Ensure that dynamic content is accessible or provide an alternative presentation or page.	2
7. Ensure user control of time-sensitive content changes	
7.1 Until user agents allow users to control flickering, avoid causing the screen to flicker.	1
7.2 Until user agents allow users to control blinking, avoid causing content to blink (i.e., change presentation at a regular rate, such as turning on and off).	2
7.3 Until user agents allow users to freeze moving content, avoid movement in pages.	2
7.4 Until user agents provide the ability to stop the refresh, do not create periodically auto-refreshing pages.	2
7.5 Until user agents provide the ability to stop auto-redirect, do not use markup to redirect pages automatically. Instead, configure the server to perform redirects.	2
8. Ensure direct accessibility of embedded user interfaces	
8.1 Make programmatic elements such as scripts and applets directly accessible or compatible with assistive technologies [Priority 1 if functionality is important and not presented elsewhere, otherwise Priority 2.]	2
9. Design for device-independence	
9.1 Provide client-side image maps instead of server-side image maps except where the regions cannot be defined with an available geometric shape.	1
9.2 Ensure that any element with its own interface can be operated in a device-independent manner.	2
9.3 For scripts, specify logical event handlers rather than device-dependent event handlers.	2
9.4 Create a logical tab order through links, form controls, and objects.	3
9.5 Provide keyboard shortcuts to important links (including those in client-side image maps), form controls, and groups of form controls.	3
10. Use interim solutions	
10.1 Until user agents allow users to turn off spawned windows, do not cause pop-ups or other windows to appear and do not change the current window without informing the user.	2
10.2 Until user agents support explicit associations between labels and form controls, ensure that labels are properly positioned for all form controls with implicitly associated labels.	2
10.3 Until user agents (including assistive technologies) render side-by-side text correctly, provide a linear text alternative (on the current page or some other) for *all* tables that lay out text in parallel, word-wrapped columns.	3
10.4 Until user agents handle empty controls correctly, include default, place-holding characters in edit boxes and text areas.	3
10.5 Until user agents (including assistive technologies) render adjacent links distinctly, include nonlink, printable characters (surrounded by spaces) between adjacent links.	3
11. Use W3C technologies and guidelines	
11.1 Use W3C technologies when they are available and appropriate for a task and use the latest versions when supported.	2
11.2 Avoid deprecated features of W3C technologies.	2
11.3 Provide information so that users may receive documents according to their preferences (e.g., language, content type, etc.)	3
11.4 If, after best efforts, you cannot create an accessible page, provide a link to an alternative page that uses W3C technologies, is accessible, has equivalent information (or functionality), and is updated as often as the inaccessible (original) page.	1

WAI Guidelines	Priority
12. Provide context and orientation information	
12.1 Title each frame to facilitate frame identification and navigation.	1
12.2 Describe the purpose of frames and how frames relate to each other if this is not obvious from frame titles alone.	2
12.3 Divide large blocks of information into more manageable groups where natural and appropriate.	2
12.4 Associate labels explicitly with their controls.	2
13. Provide clear navigation mechanisms	
13.1 Clearly identify the target of each link.	2
13.2 Provide metadata to add semantic information to pages and sites.	2
13.3 Provide information about the general layout of a site (e.g., a site map or table of contents).	2
13.4 Use navigation mechanisms in a consistent manner.	2
13.5 Provide navigation bars to highlight and give access to the navigation mechanism.	3
13.6 Group related links, identify the group (for user agents), and, until user agents do so, provide a way to bypass the group.	3
13.7 If search functions are provided, enable different types of searches for different skill levels and preferences.	3
13.8 Place distinguishing information at the beginning of headings, paragraphs, lists, etc.	3
13.9 Provide information about document collections (i.e., documents comprising multiple pages).	3
13.10 Provide a means to skip over multiline ASCII art.	3
14. Ensure that documents are clear and simple	
14.1 Use the clearest and simplest language appropriate for a site's content.	1
14.2 Supplement text with graphic or auditory presentations where they will facilitate comprehension of the page.	3
14.3 Create a style of presentation that is consistent across pages.	3

Checking Your Web Site for Accessibility

As you develop your Web site, you should periodically check it for accessibility. In addition to reviewing the Section 508 and WAI guidelines, you can do several things to verify that your site is accessible to everyone:

- Set up your browser to suppress the display of images. Does each page still convey all of the necessary information?
- Set your browser to display pages in extra large fonts and with a different color scheme. Are your pages still readable under these conditions?
- Try to navigate your pages using only your keyboard. Can you access all of the links and form elements?
- View your page in a text-only browser. (You can use the Lynx browser for this task, located at *www.lynx.browser.org.*)
- Open your page in a screen reader or other nonvisual browser. (The W3C Web site contains links to several alternative browsers that you can download as freeware or on a short-term trial basis in order to evaluate your site.)
- Use tools that test your site for accessibility. (The WAI pages at the W3C Web site contains links to a wide variety of tools that report on how well your site complies with the WAI and Section 508 guidelines.)

Following the accessibility guidelines laid out by Section 508 and the WAI will result in a Web site that is not only more accessible to a wider audience, but whose design is also cleaner, easier to work with, and easier to maintain.

HTML and XHTML Elements and Attributes

Appendix E

This appendix provides descriptions of the major elements and attributes of HTML and XHTML. The elements and attributes represent the specifications of the W3C; therefore, they might not all be supported by the major browsers. Also, in some cases, an element or attribute is not part of the W3C specifications, but instead is an extension offered by a particular browser. Where this is the case, the element or attribute is listed with the supporting browser indicated in parentheses. Likewise, many elements and attributes have been deprecated by the W3C. Deprecated elements and attributes are supported by most browsers, but their use is discouraged.

Where appropriate, the appendix lists the version number in which each element and attribute was introduced. For example, an HTML version number of 2.0 for the <base /> tag means that it is supported by HTML 2.0 *and above*. Version numbers for XHTML refer to the support under the XHTML strict DTD. An asterisk next to the XHTML version number means that the element or attribute is supported under the XHTML transitional or frameset DTD, but not the strict DTD.

The following data types are used throughout this appendix:

- *char*   A single text character
- *char code*   A character encoding
- *color*   An HTML color name or hexadecimal color value
- *date*   A date and time in the format: *yyyy-mm-ddThh:mm:ssTIMEZONE*
- *integer*   An integer value
- *mime-type*   A MIME data type, such as "text/css", "audio/wav", or "video/x-msvideo"
- *mime-type list*   A comma-separated list of mime-types
- **option1**|*option2*| …   The value is limited to the specified list of *options*; a default value, if it exists, is displayed in **bold**
- *script*   A script or a reference to a script
- *styles*   A list of style declarations
- *text*   A text string
- *text list*   A comma-separated list of text strings
- *url*   The URL for a Web page or file
- *value*   A numeric value
- *value list*   A comma-separated list of numeric values

Starting Data Files

There are no starting Data Files needed for this appendix.

General Attributes

Several attributes are common to many page elements. Rather than repeating this information each time it occurs, the following tables summarize these attributes.

Core Attributes

The following four attributes, which are laid out in the specifications for HTML and XHTML, apply to all page elements and are supported by most browser versions.

Attribute	Description	HTML	XHTML
class="*text*"	Specifies the class or group to which an element belongs	4.0	1.0
id="*text*"	Specifies a unique identifier to be associated with the element	4.0	1.0
style="*styles*"	Defines an inline style for the element	4.0	1.0
title="*text*"	Provides an advisory title for the element	2.0	1.0

Language Attributes

The Web is designed to be universal and has to be adaptable to languages other than English. So, another set of attributes provides language support. This set of attributes is not as widely supported by browsers as the core attributes are. As with the core attributes, they can be applied to most page elements.

Attribute	Description	HTML	XHTML
dir="**ltr**|rtl"	Indicates the text direction as related to the lang attribute; a value of ltr displays text from left to right; a value of rtl displays text from right to left	4.0	1.0
lang="*text*"	Identifies the language used in the page content	4.0	1.0

Form Attributes

The following attributes can be applied to most form elements or to a Web form itself, but not to other page elements.

Attribute	Description	HTML	XHTML
accesskey="*char*"	Indicates the keyboard character that can be pressed along with the accelerator key to access a form element	4.0	1.0
disabled="disabled"	Disables a form field for input	4.0	1.0
tabindex="*integer*"	Specifies a form element's position in a document's tabbing order	4.0	1.0

Internet Explorer Attributes

Internet Explorer supports a collection of attributes that can be applied to almost all page elements. Other browsers do not support these attributes or support them only for a more limited collection of elements.

Attribute	Description
accesskey="*char*"	Indicates the keyboard character that can be pressed along with the accelerator key to access the page element
contenteditable="true|false|**inherit**"	Specifies whether the element's content can be modified online by the user
disabled="disabled"	Disables the page element for input
hidefocus="true|**false**"	Controls whether the element provides a visual indication of whether the element is in focus
tabindex="*integer*"	Specifies the position of the page element in the tabbing order of the document
unselectable="on|**off**"	Specifies whether the element can be selected by the user

Event Attributes

To make Web pages more dynamic, HTML and XHTML support event attributes that identify scripts to be run in response to an event occurring within an element. For example, clicking a main heading with a mouse can cause a browser to run a program that hides or expands a table of contents. Each event attribute has the form

event = "*script*"

where *event* is the name of the event attribute and *script* is the name of the script or command to be run by the browser in response to the occurrence of the event within the element.

Core Events

The general event attributes are part of the specifications for HTML and XHTML. They apply to almost all page elements.

Attribute	Description	HTML	XHTML
onclick	The mouse button is clicked.	4.0	1.0
ondblclick	The mouse button is double-clicked.	4.0	1.0
onkeydown	A key is pressed down.	4.0	1.0
onkeypress	A key is initially pressed.	4.0	1.0
onkeyup	A key is released.	4.0	1.0
onmousedown	The mouse button is pressed down.	4.0	1.0
onmousemove	The mouse pointer is moved within the element's boundaries.	4.0	1.0
onmouseout	The mouse pointer is moved out of the element's boundaries.	4.0	1.0
onmouseover	The mouse pointer hovers over the element.	4.0	1.0
onmouseup	The mouse button is released.	4.0	1.0

Document Events

The following list of event attributes applies not to individual elements within the page, but to the entire document as it is displayed within the browser window or frame.

Attribute	Description	HTML	XHTML
onafterprint	The document has finished printing (IE only).		
onbeforeprint	The document is about to be printed (IE only).		
onload	The page is finished being loaded.	4.0	1.0
onunload	The page is finished unloading.	4.0	1.0

Form Events

The following list of event attributes applies either to the entire Web form or fields within the form.

Attribute	Description	HTML	XHTML
onblur	The form field has lost the focus.	4.0	1.0
onchange	The value of the form field has been changed.	4.0	1.0
onfocus	The form field has received the focus.	4.0	1.0
onreset	The form has been reset.	4.0	1.0
onselect	Text content has been selected in the form field.	4.0	1.0
onsubmit	The form has been submitted for processing.	4.0	1.0

Internet Explorer Data Events

The following list of event attributes applies to elements within the Web page capable of data binding. Note that these events are supported only by the Internet Explorer browser.

Attribute	Description
oncellchange	Data has changed in the data source.
ondataavailable	Data has arrived from the data source.
ondatasetchange	The data in the data source has changed.
ondatasetcomplete	All data from the data source has been loaded.
onrowenter	The current row in the data source has changed.
onrowexit	The current row is about to be changed in the data source.
onrowsdelete	Rows have been deleted from the data source.
onrowsinserted	Rows have been inserted into the data source.

Internet Explorer Events

The Internet Explorer browser supports a wide collection of customized event attributes. Unless otherwise noted, these event attributes can be applied to any page element and are not supported by other browsers or included in the HTML or XHTML specifications.

Attribute	Description
onactive	The element is set to an active state.
onafterupdate	Data has been transferred from the element to a data source.
onbeforeactivate	The element is about to be set to an active state.
onbeforecopy	A selection from the element is about to be copied to the Clipboard.
onbeforecut	A selection from the element is about to be cut to the Clipboard.
onbeforedeactivate	The element is about to be deactivated.
onbeforeeditfocus	The element is about to become active.
onbeforepaste	Data from the Clipboard is about to be pasted into the element.
onbeforeunload	The page is about to be unloaded.
onbeforeupdate	The element's data is about to be updated.
onblur	The element has lost the focus.
oncontextmenu	The right mouse button is activated.
oncontrolselect	Selection using a modifier key (Ctrl for Windows, Command for Macintosh) has begun within the element.
oncopy	Data from the element has been copied to the Clipboard.
oncut	Data from the element has been cut to the Clipboard.
ondrag	The element is being dragged.
ondragdrop	The element has been dropped into the window or frame.
ondragend	The element is no longer being dragged.
ondragenter	The dragged element has entered a target area.
ondragleave	The dragged element has left a target area.
ondragover	The dragged element is over a target area.
ondragstart	The element has begun to be dragged.
ondrop	The dragged element has been dropped.
onerrorupdate	The data transfer to the element has been cancelled.
onfocus	The element has received the focus.
onfocusin	The element is about to receive the focus.
onfocusout	The form element has just lost the focus.
onhelp	The user has selected online help from the browser.
oninput	Text has just been entered into the form field.
onlosecapture	The element has been captured by the mouse selection.
onmouseenter	The mouse pointer enters the element's boundaries.
onmouseleave	The mouse pointer leaves the element's boundaries.
onmousewheel	The mouse wheel is moved.
onmove	The browser window or element has been moved by the user.
onmoveend	Movement of the element has ended.
onmovestart	The element has begun to move.
onpaste	Data has been pasted from the Clipboard into the element.

Attribute	Description
onpropertychange	One or more of the element's properties has changed.
onreadystatechange	The element has changed its ready state.
onresize	The browser window or element has been resized by the user.
onscroll	The scroll bar position within the element has been changed (also supported by other browsers).
onselectstart	Selection has begun within the element.
onstop	The page is finished loading.

HTML and XHTML Elements and Attributes

The following table contains an alphabetic listing of the elements and attributes supported by HTML, XHTML, and the major browsers. Some attributes are not listed in this table, but are described instead in the general attributes tables presented in the previous section of this appendix.

Element/Attribute	Description	HTML	XHTML
`<!-- text -->`	Inserts a comment into the document (comments are not displayed in therendered page)	2.0	1.0
`<!doctype>`	Specifies the Document Type Definition for a document	2.0	1.0
`<a> </a>`	Marks the beginning and end of a link	2.0	1.0
`accesskey="char"`	Indicates the keyboard character that can be pressed along with the accelerator key to activate the link	4.0	1.0
`charset="text"`	Specifies the character encoding of the linked document	4.0	1.0
`coords="value list"`	Specifies the coordinates of a hotspot in a client-side image map; the value list depends on the shape of the hotspot: shape="rect" "left, right, top, bottom"shape="circle" "x_center, y_center, radius"shape="poly" "x1, y1, x2, y2, x3, y3, ..."	4.0	1.0
`href="url"`	Specifies the URL of the link	3.2	1.0
`hreflang="text"`	Specifies the language of the linked document	4.0	1.0
`name="text"`	Specifies a name for the enclosed text, allowing it to be a link target	2.0	1.0
`rel="text"`	Specifies the relationship between the current page and the link specified by the href attribute	2.0	1.0
`rev="text"`	Specifies the reverse relationship between the current page and the linkspecified by the href attribute	2.0	1.0
`shape="rect|circle| polygon"`	Specifies the shape of the hotspot	4.0	1.0
`title="text"`	Specifies the pop-up text for the link	2.0	1.0
`target="text"`	Specifies the target window or frame for the link	4.0	1.0
`type="mime-type"`	Specifies the data type of the linked document	4.0	1.0
`<abbr> </abbr>`	Marks abbreviated text	4.0	1.0
`<acronym> </acronym>`	Marks acronym text	3.0	1.0
`<address> </address>`	Marks address text	2.0	1.0

Element/Attribute	Description	HTML	XHTML
`<applet> </applet>`	Embeds an applet into the browser (deprecated)	3.2	1.0*
`align="absmiddle|absbottom|baseline|bottom|center|left|middle|right|texttop|top"`	Specifies the alignment of the applet with the surrounding text	3.2	1.0*
`alt="text"`	Specifies alternate text for the applet (deprecated)	3.2	1.0*
`archive="url"`	Specifies the URL of an archive containing classes and other resources to be used with the applet (deprecated)	4.0	1.0*
`code="url"`	Specifies the URL of the applet's code/class (deprecated)	3.2	1.0*
`codebase="url"`	Specifies the URL of all class files for the applet (deprecated)	3.2	1.0*
`datafld="text"`	Specifies the data source that supplies bound data for use with the applet	4.0	
`datasrc="text"`	Specifies the ID or URL of the applet's data source	4.0	
`height="integer"`	Specifies the height of the applet in pixels	3.2	1.0*
`hspace="integer"`	Specifies the horizontal space around the applet in pixels (deprecated)	3.2	1.0*
`mayscript="mayscript"`	Permits access to the applet by programs embedded in the document		
`name="text"`	Specifies the name assigned to the applet (deprecated)	3.2	1.0*
`object="text"`	Specifies the name of the resource that contains a serialized representation of the applet (deprecated)	4.0	1.0*
`src="url"`	Specifies an external URL reference to the applet		
`vspace="integer"`	Specifies the vertical space around the applet in pixels (deprecated)	3.2	1.0*
`width="integer"`	Specifies the width of the applet in pixels (deprecated)	3.2	1.0*
`<area />`	Marks an image map hotspot	3.2	1.0
`alt="text"`	Specifies alternate text for the hotspot	3.2	1.0
`coords="value list"`	Specifies the coordinates of the hotspot; the value list depends on the shape of the hotspot: shape="rect" "left, right, top, bottom" shape="circle" "x_center, y_center, radius" shape="poly" "x1, y1, x2, y2, x3, y3, ..."	3.2	1.0
`href="url"`	Specifies the URL of the document to which the hotspot points	3.2	1.0
`nohref="nohref"`	Specifies that the hotspot does not point to a link	3.2	1.0
`shape="rect|circle|polygon"`	Specifies the shape of the hotspot	3.2	1.0
`target="text"`	Specifies the target window or frame for the link	3.2	1.0*
`<b> </b>`	Marks text as bold	2.0	1.0
`<base />`	Specifies global reference information for the document	2.0	1.0
`href="url"`	Specifies the URL from which all relative links in the document are based	2.0	1.0
`target="text"`	Specifies the target window or frame for links in the document	2.0	1.0*
`<basefont />`	Specifies the font setting for the document text (deprecated)	3.2	1.0*
`color="color"`	Specifies the text color (deprecated)	3.2	1.0*
`face="text list"`	Specifies a list of fonts to be applied to the text (deprecated)	3.2	1.0*
`size="integer"`	Specifies the size of the font range from 1 (smallest) to 7 (largest) (deprecated)	3.2	1.0*

Element/Attribute	Description	HTML	XHTML
`<bdo> </bdo>`	Indicates that the enclosed text should be rendered with the direction specified by the dir attribute	4.0	1.0
`<bgsound />`	Plays a background sound clip when the page is opened (IE and Opera only)		
`balance="integer"`	Specifies the balance of the volume between the left and right speakers where balance ranges from -10,000 to 10,000 (IE and Opera only)		
`loop="integer|` `infinite"`	Specifies the number of times the clip will be played (a positive integeror infinite) (IE and Opera only)		
`src="url"`	Specifies the URL of the sound clip file (IE and Opera only)		
`volume="integer"`	Specifies the volume of the sound clip, where the volume ranges from -10,000 to 0 (IE and Opera only)		
`<big> </big>`	Increases the size of the enclosed text relative to the default font size	3.0	1.0
`<blink> </blink>`	Blinks the enclosed text on and off		
`<blockquote>` `</blockquote>`	Marks content as quoted from another source	2.0	1.0
`align="left|` `center|right"`	Specifies the horizontal alignment of the content		
`cite="url"`	Provides the source URL of the quoted content	4.0	1.0
`clear="none|left|` `right|all"`	Prevents content from rendering until the specified margin is clear	3.0*	
`<body> </body>`	Marks the page content to be rendered by the browser	2.0	1.0
`alink="color"`	Specifies the color of activated links in the document (deprecated)	3.2	1.0*
`background="url"`	Specifies the background image file used for the page (deprecated)	3.0	1.0*
`bgcolor="color"`	Specifies the background color of the page (deprecated)	3.2	1.0*
`bgproperties="fixed"`	Fixes the background image in the browser window (IE only)		
`bottommargin="integer"`	Specifies the size of the bottom margin in pixels (IE only)		
`leftmargin="integer"`	Specifies the size of the left margin in pixels		
`link="color"`	Specifies the color of unvisited links (deprecated)	3.2	1.0*
`marginheight="integer"`	Specifies the size of the margin above and below the page (Netscape 4 only)		
`marginwidth="integer"`	Specifies the size of the margin to the left and right of the page (Netscape 4 only)		
`nowrap="false|true"`	Specifies whether the content wraps using normal HTML line-wrapping conventions (IE only)		
`rightmargin="integer"`	Specifies the size of the right margin in pixels (IE only)		
`scroll="yes|no"`	Specifies whether to display a scroll bar (IE only)		
`text="color"`	Specifies the color of page text (deprecated)	3.2	1.0*
`topmargin="integer"`	Specifies the size of the top page margin in pixels (IE only)		
`vlink="color"`	Specifies the color of previously visited links (deprecated)	3.2	1.0*
` `	Inserts a line break into the page	2.0	1.0
`clear="none|left|` `right|all"`	Displays the line break only when the specified margin is clear (deprecated)	3.2	1.0*
`<button> </button>`	Creates a form button	4.0	1.0
`datafld="text"`	Specifies the column from a data source that supplies bound data for the button (IE only)		
`dataformatas="html|` `plaintext|text"`	Specifies the format of the data in the data source bound with the button (IE only)		

Element/Attribute	Description	HTML	XHTML
`datasrc="url"`	Specifies the URL or ID of the data source bound with the button (IE only)		
`name="text"`	Provides the name assigned to the form button	4.0	1.0
`type="submit|reset|button"`	Specifies the type of form button	4.0	1.0
`value="text"`	Provides the value associated with the form button	4.0	1.0
`<caption> </caption>`	Creates a table caption	3.0	1.0
`align="bottom|center|left|right|top"`	Specifies the alignment of the caption (deprecated)	3.0	1.0*
`valign="top|bottom"`	Specifies the vertical alignment of the caption		
`<center> </center>`	Centers content horizontally on the page (deprecated)	3.2	1.0*
`<cite> </cite>`	Marks citation text	2.0	1.0
`<code> </code>`	Marks text used for code samples	2.0	1.0
`<col> </col>`	Defines the settings for a column or group of columns	4.0	1.0
`align="left|right|center"`	Specifies the alignment of the content of the column(s)	4.0	1.0
`bgcolor="color"`	Specifies the background color of the column(s)		
`char="char"`	Specifies a character in the column used to align column values	4.0	1.0
`charoff="integer"`	Specifies the offset in pixels from the alignment character specified in the char attribute	4.0	1.0
`span="integer"`	Specifies the number of columns in the group	4.0	1.0
`valign="top|middle|bottom|baseline"`	Specifies the vertical alignment of the content in the column(s)	4.0	1.0
`width="integer"`	Specifies the width of the column(s) in pixels	4.0	1.0
`<colgroup> </colgroup>`	Creates a container for a group of columns	4.0	1.0
`align="left|right center"`	Specifies the alignment of the content of the column group	4.0	1.0
`bgcolor="color"`	Specifies the background color of the column group		
`char="char"`	Specifies a character in the column used to align column group values	4.0	1.0
`charoff="integer"`	Specifies the offset in pixels from the alignment character specified in the char attribute	4.0	1.0
`span="integer"`	Specifies the number of columns in the group	4.0	1.0
`valign="top|middle|bottom|baseline"`	Specifies the vertical alignment of the content in the column group	4.0	1.0
`width="integer"`	Specifies the width of the columns in the group in pixels	4.0	1.0
`<dd> </dd>`	Marks text as a definition within a definition list	2.0	1.0
`<del> </del>`	Marks text as deleted from the document	3.0	1.0
`cite="url"`	Provides the URL for the document that has additional information about the deleted text	3.0	1.0
`datetime="date"`	Specifies the date and time of the text deletion	3.0	1.0
`<dfn> </dfn>`	Marks the defining instance of a term	3.0	1.0
`<dir> </dir>`	Contains a directory listing (deprecated)	2.0	1.0*
`compact="compact"`	Permits use of compact rendering, if available (deprecated)	2.0	1.0*

Element/Attribute	Description	HTML	XHTML
`<div> </div>`	Creates a generic block-level element	3.0	1.0
`align="left|center right|justify"`	Specifies the horizontal alignment of the content (deprecated)	3.0	1.0*
`datafld="text"`	Indicates the column from a data source that supplies bound data for the block (IE only)		
`dataformatas="html |plaintext|text"`	Specifies the format of the data in the data source bound with the block (IE only)		
`datasrc="url"`	Provides the URL or ID of the data source bound with the block (IE only)		
`nowrap="nowrap"`	Specifies whether the content wraps using normal HTML line-wrapping conventions	3.0*	
`<dl> </dl>`	Encloses a definition list using the dd and dt elements	2.0	1.0
`compact="compact"`	Permits use of compact rendering, if available (deprecated)	2.0	1.0*
`<dt> </dt>`	Marks a definition term in a definition list	2.0	1.0
`nowrap="nowrap"`	Specifies whether the content wraps using normal HTML line-wrapping conventions		
`<em> </em>`	Marks emphasized text	2.0	1.0
`<embed> </embed>`	Places an embedded object into the page (not part of the W3C specifications, but supported by most major browsers)		
`align="bottom|left |right|top"`	Specifies the alignment of the object with the surrounding content		
`autostart="true |false"`	Starts the embedded object automatically when the page is loaded		
`height="integer"`	Specifies the height of the object in pixels		
`hidden="true|false"`	Hides the object on the page		
`hspace="integer"`	Specifies the horizontal space around the object in pixels		
`name="text"`	Provides the name of the embedded object		
`pluginspage="url"`	Provides the URL of the page containing information on the object		
`pluginurl="url"`	Provides the URL of the page for directly installing the object		
`src="url"`	Provides the location of the file containing the object		
`type="mime-type"`	Specifies the mime-type of the embedded object		
`units="text"`	Specifies the measurement units of the object		
`vspace="integer"`	Specifies the vertical space around the object in pixels		
`width="integer"`	Specifies the width of the object in pixels		
`<fieldset> </fieldset>`	Places form fields in a common group	4.0	1.0
`align="left|center |right"`	Specifies the alignment of the contents of the field set (IE only)		
`datafld="text"`	Indicates the column from a data source that supplies bound data for the field set (IE only)		
`dataformatas="html| plaintext|text"`	Specifies the format of the data in the data source bound with the field set (IE only)		
`datasrc="url"`	Provides the URL or ID of the data source bound with the field set (IE only)		
`<font> </font>`	Formats the enclosed text (deprecated)	3.2	1.0*
`color="color"`	Specifies the color of the enclosed text (deprecated)	3.2	1.0*
`face="text list"`	Specifies the font face(s) of the enclosed text (deprecated)	3.2	1.0*
`size="integer"`	Specifies the size of the enclosed text, with values ranging from 1 (smallest) to 7 (largest); a value of +integer increases the font size relative to the font size specified in the basefont element (deprecated)	3.2	1.0*

Element/Attribute	Description	HTML	XHTML
\<form\> \</form\>	Encloses the contents of a Web form	2.0	1.0
accept="*mime-type list*"	Lists mime-types that the server processing the form will handle	4.0	1.0
accept-charset= "*char code*"	Specifies the character encoding that the server processing the form will handle	4.0	1.0
action="*url*"	Provides the URL to which the form values are to be sent	2.0	1.0
autocomplete="on|off"	Enables automatic insertion of information in fields in which the user has previously entered data (IE only)		
enctype="*mime-type*"	Specifies the mime-type of the data to be sent to the server for processing; the default is "application/x-www-form-urlencoded"	2.0	1.0
method="**get**|post"	Specifies the method of accessing the URL specified in the action attribute	2.0	1.0
name="*text*"	Specifies the name of the form	2.0	1.0
target="*text*"	Specifies the frame or window in which output from the form should appear	4.0	1.0
\<frame\> \</frame\>	Marks a single frame within a set of frames	4.0	1.0*
border="*integer*"	Specifies the thickness of the frame border in pixels (Netscape 4 only)		
bordercolor="*color*"	Specifies the color of the frame border		
frameborder="1|0"	Determines whether the frame border is visible (1) or invisible (0); Netscape also supports values of yes or no	4.0	1.0*
longdesc="*url*"	Provides the URL of a document containing a long description of the frame's contents	4.0	1.0*
marginheight= "*integer*"	Specifies the space above and below the frame object and the frame's borders, in pixels	4.0	1.0*
marginwidth="*integer*"	Specifies the space to the left and right of the frame object and the frame's borders, in pixels	4.0	1.0*
name="*text*"	Specifies the name of the frame	4.0	1.0*
noresize="noresize"	Prevents users from resizing the frame	4.0	1.0*
scrolling="**auto**| yes|no"	Specifies whether the browser will display a scroll bar with the frame	4.0	1.0*
src="*url*"	Provides the URL of the document to be displayed in the frame	4.0	1.0*
\<frameset\> \</frameset\>	Creates a collection of frames	4.0	1.0*
border="*integer*"	Specifies the thickness of the frame borders in the frameset in pixels (not part of the W3C specifications, but supported by most browsers)		
bordercolor="*color*"	Specifies the color of the frame borders		
cols="*value list*"	Arranges the frames in columns with the width of each column expressed either in pixels, as a percentage, or using an asterisk (to allow the browser to choose the width)	4.0	1.0*
frameborder="1|0"	Determines whether frame borders are visible (1) or invisible (0); (not part of the W3C specifications, but supported by most browsers; Netscape also supports values of yes or no)		
framespacing="*integer*"	Specifies the amount of space between frames in pixels (IE only)		
rows="*value list*"	Arranges the frames in rows with the height of each column expressed either in pixels, as a percentage, or using an asterisk (to allow the browser to choose the height)	4.0	1.0*

Element/Attribute	Description	HTML	XHTML
`<hi> </hi>`	Marks the enclosed text as a heading, where i is an integer from 1 (the largest heading) to 6 (the smallest heading)	2.0	1.0
`align="left|center|right|justify"`	Specifies the alignment of the heading text (deprecated)	3.0	1.0*
`<head> </head>`	Encloses the document head, containing information about the document	2.0	1.0
`profile="url"`	Provides the location of metadata about the document	4.0	1.0
`<hr />`	Draws a horizontal line (rule) in the rendered page	2.0	1.0
`align="left|center|right"`	Specifies the horizontal alignment of the line (deprecated)	3.2	1.0*
`color="color"`	Specifies the color of the line		
`noshade="noshade"`	Removes 3-D shading from the line (deprecated)	3.2	1.0*
`size="integer"`	Specifies the height of the line in pixels or as a percentage of the enclosing element's height (deprecated)	3.2	1.0*
`width="integer"`	Specifies the width of the line in pixels or as a percentage of the enclosing element's width (deprecated)	3.2	1.0*
`<html> </html>`	Encloses the entire content of the HTML document	2.0	1.0
`version="text"`	Specifies the version of HTML being used	2.0	1.1
`xmlns="text"`	Specifies the namespace prefix for the document		1.0
`<i> </i>`	Displays the enclosed text in italics	2.0	1.0
`<iframe> </iframe>`	Creates an inline frame in the document	4.0	1.0*
`align="bottom|left|middle|top|right"`	Specifies the horizontal alignment of the frame with the surrounding content (deprecated)	4.0	1.0*
`datafld="text"`	Indicates the column from a data source that supplies bound data for the inline frame (IE only)		4.0
`dataformatas="html|plaintext|text"`	Specifies the format of the data in the data source bound with the inline frame (IE only)		4.0
`datasrc="url"`	Provides the URL or ID of the data source bound with the inline frame (IE only)		4.0
`frameborder="1|0"`	Specifies whether to display a frame border (1) or not (0)	4.0	1.0*
`height="integer"`	Specifies the height of the frame in pixels	4.0	1.0*
`hspace="integer"`	Specifies the space to the left and right of the frame in pixels	4.0	1.0*
`longdesc="url"`	Indicates the document containing a long description of the frame's content	4.0	1.0*
`marginheight="integer"`	Specifies the space above and below the frame object and the frame's borders, in pixels	4.0	1.0*
`marginwidth="integer"`	Specifies the space to the left and right of the frame object and the frame's borders, in pixels	4.0	1.0*
`name="text"`	Specifies the name of the frame	4.0	1.0*
`scrolling="auto|yes|no"`	Determines whether the browser displays a scroll bar with the frame	4.0	1.0*
`src="url"`	Indicates the document displayed within the frame	4.0	1.0*
`vspace="integer"`	Specifies the space to the top and bottom of the frame in pixels	4.0	1.0*
`width="integer"`	Specifies the width of the frame in pixels	4.0	1.0*

Element/Attribute	Description	HTML	XHTML
`<ilayer> </ilayer>`	Creates an inline layer used to display the content of an external document (Netscape 4 only)		
`above="text"`	Specifies the name of the layer displayed above the current layer (IE only)		
`background="url"`	Provides the URL of the file containing the background image (IE only)		
`below="text"`	Specifies the name of the layer displayed below the current layer (IE only)		
`bgcolor="color"`	Specifies the layer's background color (IE only)		
`clip="top, left, bottom, right"`	Specifies the coordinates of the viewable region of the layer (IE only)		
`height="integer"`	Specifies the height of the layer in pixels (IE only)		
`left="integer"`	Specifies the horizontal offset of the layer in pixels (IE only)		
`pagex="integer"`	Specifies the horizontal position of the layer in pixels (IE only)		
`pagey="integer"`	Specifies the vertical position of the layer in pixels (IE only)		
`src="url"`	Provides the URL of the document displayed in the layer (IE only)		
`top="integer"`	Specifies the vertical offset of the layer in pixels (IE only)		
`visibility="hide|inherit|show"`	Specifies the visibility of the layer (IE only)		
`width="integer"`	Specifies the width of the layer in pixels (IE only)		
`z-index="integer"`	Specifies the stacking order of the layer (IE only)		
`<img> </img>`	Inserts an inline image into the document	2.0	1.0
`align="left|right| top|texttop| middle|absmiddle| baselines|bottom| absbottom"`	Specifies the alignment of the image with the surrounding content (deprecated)	2.0	1.0*
`alt="text"`	Specifies alternate text to be displayed in place of the image	2.0	1.0
`border="integer"`	Specifies the width of the image border (deprecated)	3.2	1.0*
`controls="control"`	For video images, displays a playback control below the image (IE only)		
`datafld="text"`	Names the column from a data source that supplies bound data for the image (IE only)		
`dataformatas="html| plaintext|text"`	Specifies the format of the data in the data source bound with the image (IE only)		
`datasrc="url"`	Provides the URL or ID of the data source bound with the image (IE only)		
`dynsrc="url"`	Provides the URL of a video or VRML file (IE and Opera only)		
`height="integer"`	Specifies the height of the image in pixels	3.0	1.0
`hspace="integer"`	Specifies the horizontal space around the image in pixels (deprecated)	3.0	1.0*
`ismap="ismap"`	Indicates that the image can be used as a server-side image map	2.0	1.0
`longdesc="url"`	Provides the URL of a document containing a long description of the image	4.0	1.0
`loop="integer"`	Specifies the number of times the video will play (IE and Opera only)		
`lowsrc="url"`	Provides the URL of the low-resolution version of the image (IE and Netscape only)		
`name="text"`	Specifies the image name	4.0	1.0*

Element/Attribute	Description	HTML	XHTML
src="*url*"	Specifies the image source file	2.0	1.0
start="fileopen|mouseover"	Indicates when to start the video clip (either when the file is opened or when the mouse hovers over the image) (IE and Opera only)		
suppress="true|false"	Suppresses the display of the alternate text and the placeholder icon until the image file is located (Netscape 4 only)		
usemap="*url*"	Provides the location of a client-side image associated with the image (not well-supported when the URL points to an external file)	3.2	1.0
vspace="*integer*"	Specifies the vertical space around the image in pixels (deprecated)	3.2	1.0*
width="*integer*"	Specifies the width of the image in pixels	3.0	1.0
<input> </input>	Marks an input field in a Web form	2.0	1.0
align="left|right|top|texttop|middle|absmiddle|baseline|bottom|absbottom"	Specifies the alignment of the input field with the surrounding content (deprecated)	2.0	1.0*
alt="*text*"	Specifies alternate text for image buttons and image input fields	4.0	1.0
checked="checked"	Specifies that the input check box or input radio button is selected	2.0	1.0
datafld="*text*"	Indicates the column from a data source that supplies bound data for the input field	4.0	
dataformatas="html|plaintext|text"	Specifies the format of the data in the data source bound with the input field	4.0	
datasrc="*url*"	Provides the URL or ID of the data source bound with the input field	4.0	
height="*integer*"	Specifies the height of the image input field in pixels (not part of the W3C specifications, but supported by many browsers)		
hspace="*integer*"	Specifies the horizontal space around the image input field in pixels (not part of the W3C specifications, but supported by many browsers)		
ismap="ismap"	Enables the image input field to be used as a server-side image map	4.0	1.1
maxlength="*integer*"	Specifies the maximum number of characters that can be inserted into a text input field	2.0	1.0
name="text"	Specifies the name of the input field	2.0	1.0
readonly="readonly"	Prevents the value of the input field from being modified	2.0	1.0
size="*integer*"	Specifies the number of characters that can be displayed at one time in an input text field	2.0	1.0
src="*url*"	Indicates the source file of an input image field	2.0	1.0
type="button|checkbox|file|hidden|image|password|radio|reset|submit|text"	Specifies the type of input field	2.0	1.0
usemap="url"	Provides the location of a client-side image associated with the image input field (not well-supported when the URL points to an external file)	4.0	1.0
value="*text*"	Specifies the default value of the input field	2.0	1.0
vspace="*integer*"	Specifies the vertical space around the image input field in pixels (not part of the W3C specifications, but supported by many browsers)		
width="*integer*"	Specifies the width of an image input field in pixels (not part of the W3C specifications, but supported by many browsers)		

Element/Attribute	Description	HTML	XHTML
`<ins> </ins>`	Marks inserted text	3.0	1.0
`cite="url"`	Provides the URL for the document that has additional information about the inserted text	3.0	1.0
`datetime="date"`	Specifies the date and time of the text insertion	3.0	1.0
`<isindex />`	Inserts an input field into the document for search queries (deprecated)	2.0	1.0*
`action="url"`	Provides the URL of the script used to process the sindex data		1.0
`prompt="text"`	Specifies the text to be used for the input prompt (deprecated)	3.0	1.0*
`<kbd> </kbd>`	Marks keyboard-style text	2.0	1.0
`<label> </label>`	Associates the enclosed content with a form field	4.0	1.0
`datafld="text"`	Indicates the column from a data source that supplies bound data for the label (IE only)		
`dataformatas="html|plaintext|text"`	Specifies the format of the data in the data source bound with the label (IE only)		
`datasrc="url"`	Provides the URL or ID of the data source bound with the label (IE only)		
`for="text"`	Provides the ID of the field associated with the label	4.0	1.0
`<layer> </layer>`	Creates a layer used to display the content of external documents; unlike the ilayer element, layer elements are absolutely positioned in the page (Netscape 4 only)		
`above="text"`	Specifies the name of the layer displayed above the current layer (Netscape 4 only)		
`background="url"`	Provides the URL of the file containing the background image (Netscape 4 only)		
`below="text"`	Specifies the name of the layer displayed below the current layer (Netscape 4 only)		
`bgcolor="color"`	Specifies the layer's background color (Netscape 4 only)		
`clip="top, left, bottom, right"`	Specifies the coordinates of the viewable region of the layer (Netscape 4 only)		
`height="integer"`	Specifies the height of the layer in pixels (Netscape 4 only)		
`left="integer"`	Specifies the horizontal offset of the layer in pixels (Netscape 4 only)		
`pagex="integer"`	Specifies the horizontal position of the layer in pixels (Netscape 4 only)		
`pagey="integer"`	Specifies the vertical position of the layer in pixels (Netscape 4 only)		
`src="url"`	Provides the URL of the document displayed in the layer (Netscape 4 only)		
`top="integer"`	Specifies the vertical offset of the layer in pixels (Netscape 4 only)		
`visibility="hide|inherit|show"`	Specifies the visibility of the layer (Netscape 4 only)		
`width="integer"`	Specifies the width of the layer in pixels (Netscape 4 only)		
`z-index="integer"`	Specifies the stacking order of the layer (Netscape 4 only)		
`<legend> </legend>`	Marks the enclosed text as a caption for a field set	4.0	1.0
`align="bottom|left|top|right"`	Specifies the alignment of the legend with the field set; Internet Explorer also supports the center option (deprecated)	4.0	1.0*

Element/Attribute	Description	HTML	XHTML
`<li> </li>`	Marks an item in an ordered (ol), unordered (ul), menu (menu), or directory (dir) list	2.0	1.0
`type="A|a|I|i` `|1|disc|square` `|circle"`	Specifies the bullet type associated with the list item: a value of "1" is the default for ordered list; a value of "disc" is the default for unordered list (deprecated)	3.2	1.0*
`value="integer"`	Sets the value for the current list item in an ordered list; subsequent list items are numbered from that value (deprecated)	3.2	1.0*
`<link />`	Creates an element in the document head that establishes the relationship between the current document and external documents or objects	2.0	1.0
`charset="char code"`	Specifies the character encoding of the external document	4.0	1.0
`href="url"`	Provides the URL of the external document	2.0	1.0
`hreflang="text"`	Indicates the language of the external document	4.0	1.0
`media="all|aural|` `braille|handheld|` `print|projection|` `screen|tty|tv"`	Indicates the media in which the external document is presented	4.0	1.0
`name="text"`	Specifies the name of the link		
`rel="text"`	Specifies the relationship between the current page and the link specified by the href attribute	2.0	
`rev="text"`	Specifies the reverse relationship between the current page and the link specified by the href attribute	2.0	1.0
`target="text"`	Specifies the target window or frame for the link	4.0	1.0*
`title="text"`	Specifies the title of the external document	2.0	1.0
`type="mime-type"`	Specifies the mime-type of the external document	4.0	1.0
`<map> </map>`	Creates an element that contains client-side image map hotspots	3.2	1.0
`name="text"`	Specifies the name of the image map	3.2	1.0*
`<marquee> </marquee>`	Displays the enclosed text as a scrolling marquee (not part of the W3C specifications, but supported by most browsers)		
`behavior="alternate` `|scroll|slide"`	Specifies how the marquee should move		
`bgcolor="color"`	Specifies the background color of the marquee		
`datafld="text"`	Indicates the column from a data source that supplies bound data for the marquee		
`dataformatas="html|` `plaintext|text"`	Indicates the format of the data in the data source bound with the marquee		
`datasrc="url"`	Provides the URL or ID of the data source bound with the marquee		
`direction="down|` `left|right|up"`	Specifies the direction of the marquee		
`height="integer"`	Specifies the height of the marquee in pixels		
`hspace="integer"`	Specifies the horizontal space around the marquee in pixels		
`loop="integer|` `infinite"`	Specifies the number of times the marquee motion is repeated		
`scrollamount=` `"integer"`	Specifies the amount of space, in pixels, between successive draws of the marquee text		
`scrolldelay="integer"`	Specifies the amount of time, in milliseconds, between marquee actions		
`truespeed="truespeed"`	Indicates whether the scrolldelay value should be set to its exact value; otherwise any value less than 60 milliseconds is rounded up		

Element/Attribute	Description	HTML	XHTML
vspace="integer"	Specifies the vertical space around the marquee in pixels		
width="integer"	Specifies the width of the marquee in pixels		
<menu> </menu>	Contains a menu list (deprecated)	2.0	1.0*
compact="compact"	Reduces the space between menu items (deprecated)	2.0	1.0*
start="integer"	Specifies the starting value of the items in the menu list		
type="A|a|I|i |1|disc|square| circle|none"	Specifies the bullet type associated with the list items	3.2	1.0*
<meta> </meta>	Creates an element in the document's head section that contains information and special instructions for processing the document	2.0	1.0
content="text"	Provides information associated with the name or http-equiv attributes	2.0	1.0
http-equiv="text"	Provides instructions to the browser to request the server to perform different http operations	2.0	1.0
name="text"	Specifies the type of information specified in the content attribute	2.0	1.0
scheme="text"	Supplies additional information about the scheme used to interpret the content attribute	4.0	1.0
<nobr> </nobr>	Disables line wrapping for the enclosed content (not part of the W3C specifications, but supported by most browsers)		
<noembed> </noembed>	Encloses alternate content for browsers that do not support the embed element (not part of the W3C specifications, but supported by most browsers)		
<noframe> </noframe>	Encloses alternate content for browsers that do not support frames	4.0	1.0*
<nolayer> </nolayer>	Encloses alternate content for browsers that do not support the layer or ilayer elements (Netscape 4 only)		
<noscript> </noscript>	Encloses alternate content for browsers that do not support client-side scripts	4.0	1.0
<object> </object>	Places an embedded object (image, applet, sound clip, video clip, etc.) into the page	4.0	1.0
archive="url"	Specifies the URL of an archive containing classes and other resources preloaded for use with the object	4.0	1.0
align="absbottom| absmiddle|baseline |bottom|left| middle|right| texttop|top"	Aligns the object with the surrounding content (deprecated)	4.0	1.0*
border="integer"	Specifies the width of the border around the object (deprecated)	4.0	1.0*
classid="url"	Provides the URL of the object	4.0	1.0
codebase="url"	Specifies the base path used to resolve relative references within the embedded object	4.0	1.0
codetype="mime-type"	Indicates the mime-type of the embedded object's code	4.0	1.0
data="url"	Provides the URL of the object's data file	4.0	1.0
datafld="text"	Identifies the column from a data source that supplies bound data for the embedded object	4.0	
dataformatas="html| plaintext|text"	Specifies the format of the data in the data source bound with the embedded object	4.0	
datasrc="url"	Provides the URL or ID of the data source bound with the embedded object	4.0	

Element/Attribute	Description	HTML	XHTML
declare="declare"	Declares the object without embedding it on the page	4.0	1.0
height="integer"	Specifies the height of the object in pixels	4.0	1.0
hspace="integer"	Specifies the horizontal space around the image in pixels	4.0	1.0
name="text"	Specifies the name of the embedded object	4.0	1.0
standby="text"	Specifies the message displayed by the browser while loading the embedded object	4.0	1.0
type="mime-type"	Indicates the mime-type of the embedded object	4.0	1.0
vspace="integer"	Specifies the vertical space around the embedded object	4.0	1.0
width="integer"	Specifies the width of the object in pixels	4.0	1.0
<ol> </ol>	Contains an ordered list of items	2.0	1.0
compact="compact"	Reduces the space between ordered list items (deprecated)	2.0	1.0*
start="integer"	Specifies the starting value in the list (deprecated)	3.2	1.0
type="A|a|I|i|1"	Specifies the bullet type associated with the list items (deprecated)	3.2	1.0*
<optgroup> </optgroup>	Contains a group of option elements in a selection field	4.0	1.0
label="text"	Specifies the label for the option group	4.0	1.0
<option> </option>	Formats an option within a selection field	2.0	1.0
label="text"	Supplies the text label associated with the option	4.0	1.0
selected="selected"	Selects the option by default	2.0	1.0
value="text"	Specifies the value associated with the option	2.0	1.0
<p> </p>	Marks the enclosed content as a paragraph	2.0	1.0
align="**left**|center |right|justify"	Horizontally aligns the contents of the paragraph (deprecated)	3.0	1.0*
<param> </param>	Marks parameter values sent to an object element or an applet element	3.2	1.0
name="text"	Specifies the parameter name	3.2	1.0
type="mime-type"	Specifies the mime-type of the resource indicated by the value attribute	4.0	1.0
value="text"	Specifies the parameter value	3.2	1.0
valuetype="**data**| ref|object"	Specifies the data type of the value attribute	4.0	1.0
<plaintext> </plaintext>	Marks the enclosed text as plain text (not part of the W3C specifications, but supported by most browsers)		
<pre> </pre>	Marks the enclosed text as preformatted text, retaining white space from the document	2.0	1.0
width="integer"	Specifies the width of preformatted text, in number of characters (deprecated)	2.0	1.0*
<q> </q>	Marks the enclosed text as a quotation	3.0	1.0
cite="url"	Provides the source URL of the quoted content	4.0	1.0
<s> </s>	Marks the enclosed text as strikethrough text (deprecated)	3.0	1.0*
<samp> </samp>	Marks the enclosed text as a sequence of literal characters	2.0	1.0
<script> </script>	Encloses client-side scripts within the document; this element can be placed within the head or the body element or it can refer to an external script file	3.2	1.0
charset="char code"	Specifies the character encoding of the script	4.0	1.0
defer="defer"	Defers execution of the script	4.0	1.0
event="text"	Specifies the event that the script should be run in response to	4.0	

Element/Attribute	Description	HTML	XHTML
for="*text*"	Indicates the name or ID of the element to which the event attribute refers to	4.0	
language="*text*"	Specifies the language of the script (deprecated)	4.0	1.0*
src="*url*"	Provides the URL of an external script file	4.0	1.0
type="*mime-type*"	Specifies the mime-type of the script	4.0	1.0
<select> </select>	Creates a selection field (drop-down list box) in a Web form	2.0	1.0
align="left|right| top|texttop| middle|absmiddle| baseline|bottom| absbottom"	Specifies the alignment of the selection field with the surrounding content (deprecated)	3.0*	
datafld="*text*"	Identifies the column from a data source that supplies bound data for the selection field	4.0	
dataformatas="html| plaintext|text"	Specifies the format of the data in the data source bound with the selection field	4.0	
datasrc="*url*"	Provides the URL or ID of the data source bound with the selection field	4.0	
multiple="multiple"	Allows multiple sections from the field	2.0	1.0
name="*text*"	Specifies the selection field name	2.0	1.0
size="*integer*"	Specifies the number of visible items in the selection list	2.0	1.0
<small> </small>	Decreases the size of the enclosed text relative to the default font size	3.0	1.0
<span> </span>	Creates a generic inline element	3.0	1.0
datafld="*text*"	Identifies the column from a data source that supplies bound data for the inline element (IE only)		
dataformatas="html| plaintext|text"	Specifies the format of the data in the data source bound with the inline element (IE only)		
datasrc="*url*"	Provides the URL or ID of the data source bound with the inline element (IE only)		
<strike> </strike>	Marks the enclosed text as strikethrough text (deprecated)	3.0	1.0*
<strong> </strong>	Marks the enclosed text as strongly emphasized text	2.0	1.0
<style> </style>	Encloses global style declarations for the document	3.0	1.0
media="all|aural| braille|handheld| print|projection| screen|tty|tv|"	Indicates the media of the enclosed style definitions	4.0	1.0
title="*text*"	Specifies the style of the style definitions	4.0	1.0
type="*mime-type*"	Specifies the mime-type of the style definitions	4.0	1.0
****	Marks the enclosed text as subscript text	3.0	1.0
****	Marks the enclosed text as superscript text	3.0	1.0
<table> </table>	Encloses the contents of a Web table	3.0	1.0
align="left|center |right"	Aligns the table with the surrounding content (deprecated)	3.0	1.0*
background="*url*"	Provides the URL of the table's background image (not part of the W3C specifications, but supported by most browsers)		
bgcolor="*color*"	Specifies the background color of the table (deprecated)	4.0	1.0*
border="*integer*"	Specifies the width of the table border in pixels	3.0	1.0
bordercolor="*color*"	Specifies the table border color (IE and Netscape 4 only)		

Element/Attribute	Description	HTML	XHTML
`bordercolordark="color"`	Specifies the color of the table border's shaded edge (IE only)		
`bordercolorlight="color"`	Specifies the color of the table border's unshaded edge (IE only)		
`cellpadding="integer"`	Specifies the space between the table data and the cell borders in pixels	3.2	1.0
`cellspacing="integer"`	Specifies the space between table cells in pixels	3.2	1.0
`cols="integer"`	Specifies the number of columns in the table		
`datafld="text"`	Indicates the column from a data source that supplies bound data for the table	4.0	
`dataformatas="html| plaintext|text"`	Specifies the format of the data in the data source bound with the table	4.0	
`datapagesize="integer"`	Sets the number of records displayed within the table	4.0	1.1
`datasrc="url"`	Provides the URL or ID of the data source bound with the table	4.0	
`frame="above|below |border|box| hsides|lhs|rhs| void|vside"`	Specifies the format of the borders around the table	4.0	1.0
`height="integer"`	Specifies the height of the table in pixels (not part of the W3C specifications, but supported by most browsers)		
`hspace="integer"`	Specifies the horizontal space around the table in pixels (not part of the W3C specifications, but supported by most browsers)		
`rules="all|cols| groups|none|rows"`	Specifies the format of the table's internal borders or gridlines	4.0	1.0
`summary="text"`	Supplies a text summary of the table's content	4.0	1.0
`vspace="integer"`	Specifies the vertical space around the table in pixels		
`width="integer"`	Specifies the width of the table in pixels	3.0	1.0
`<tbody> </tbody>`	Encloses the content of the Web table body	4.0	1.0
`align="left|center |right|justify|char"`	Specifies the alignment of the contents in the cells of the table body	4.0	1.0
`bgcolor="color"`	Specifies the background color of the table body		
`char="char"`	Specifies the character used for aligning the table body contents when the align attribute is set to "char"	4.0	1.0
`charoff="integer"`	Specifies the offset in pixels from the alignment character specified in the char attribute	4.0	1.0
`valign="baseline| bottom|middle|top"`	Specifies the vertical alignment of the contents in the cells of the table body	4.0	1.0
`<td> </td>`	Encloses the data of a table cell	3.0	1.0
`abbr="text"`	Supplies an abbreviated version of the contents of the table cell	4.0	1.0
`align="left|center |right"`	Specifies the horizontal alignment of the table cell data	3.0	1.0
`background="url"`	Provides the URL of the background image file		
`bgcolor="color"`	Specifies the background color of the table cell (deprecated)	4.0	1.0*
`bordercolor="color"`	Specifies the color of the table cell border (IE only)		
`bordercolordark="color"`	Specifies the color of the table cell border's shaded edge (IE only)		

Element/Attribute	Description	HTML	XHTML
bordercolorlight= "*color*"	Specifies the color of the table cell border's unshaded edge (IE only)		
char="*char*"	Specifies the character used for aligning the table cell contents when the align attribute is set to "char"	4.0	1.0
charoff="*integer*"	Specifies the offset in pixels from the alignment character specified in the char attribute	4.0	1.0
colspan="*integer*"	Specifies the number of columns the table cell spans	3.0	1.0
headers="*text*"	Supplies a space-separated list of table headers associated with the table cell	4.0	1.0
height="*integer*"	Specifies the height of the table cell in pixels (deprecated)	3.2	1.0*
nowrap="nowrap"	Disables line-wrapping within the table cell (deprecated)	3.0	1.0*
rowspan="*integer*"	Specifies the number of rows the table cell spans	3.0	1.0
scope="col|colgroup |row|rowgroup"	Specifies the scope of the table for which the cell provides data	4.0	1.0
valign="top|**middle** |bottom"	Specifies the vertical alignment of the contents of the table cell	3.0	1.0
width="*integer*"	Specifies the width of the cell in pixels (deprecated)	3.2	1.0*
<textarea> </textarea>	Marks the enclosed text as a text area input box in a Web form	2.0	1.0
datafld="*text*"	Specifies the column from a data source that supplies bound data for the text area box	4.0	
dataformatas="html| plaintext|text"	Specifies the format of the data in the data source bound with the text area box	4.0	
datasrc="*url*"	Provides the URL or ID of the data source bound with the text area box	4.0	
cols="*integer*"	Specifies the width of the text area box in characters	2.0	1.0
name="*text*"	Specifies the name of the text area box	2.0	1.0
readonly="readonly"	Specifies the value of the text area box, cannot be modified	4.0	1.0
rows="*integer*"	Specifies the number of visible rows in the text area box	2.0	1.0
wrap="off|**soft**|hard"	Specifies how text is wrapped within the text area box and how that text-wrapping information is sent to the server-side program; in earlier versions of Netscape Navigator, the default value is "off" (Netscape accepts the values "off," "virtual," and "physical.")		
<tfoot> </tfoot>	Encloses the content of the Web table footer	4.0	1.0
align="left|center |right|justify|char"	Specifies the alignment of the contents in the cells of the table footer	4.0	1.0
bgcolor="*color*"	Specifies the background color of the table body (not part of the W3C specifications, but supported by many browsers)		
char="*char*"	Specifies the character used for aligning the table footer contents when the align attribute is set to "char"	4.0	1.0
charoff="*integer*"	Specifies the offset in pixels from the alignment character specified in the char attribute	4.0	1.0
valign="baseline| bottom|middle|top"	Specifies the vertical alignment of the contents in the cells of the table footer	4.0	1.0
<th> </th>	Encloses the data of a table header cell	3.0	1.0
abbr="*text*"	Supplies an abbreviated version of the contents of the table cell	4.0	1.0
align="**left**|center |right"	Specifies the horizontal alignment of the table cell data	3.0	1.0
axis="*text list*"	Provides a list of table categories that can be mapped to a table hierarchy	3.0	1.0

Element/Attribute	Description	HTML	XHTML
background="*url*"	Provides the URL of the background image file (not part of the W3C specifications, but supported by many browsers)		
bgcolor="*color*"	Specifies the background color of the table cell (deprecated)	4.0	1.0*
bordercolor="*color*"	Specifies the color of the table cell border (IE only)		
bordercolordark="*color*"	Specifies the color of the table cell border's shaded edge (IE only)		
bordercolorlight= "*color*"	Specifies the color of the table cell border's unshaded edge (IE only)		
char="*char*"	Specifies the character used for aligning the table cell contents when the align attribute is set to "char"	4.0	1.0
charoff="*integer*"	Specifies the offset in pixels from the alignment character specified in the char attribute	4.0	1.0
colspan="*integer*"	Specifies the number of columns the table cell spans	3.0	1.0
headers="*text*"	A space-separated list of table headers associated with the table cell	4.0	1.0
height="*integer*"	Specifies the height of the table cell in pixels (deprecated)	3.2	1.0*
nowrap="nowrap"	Disables line-wrapping within the table cell (deprecated)	3.0	1.0*
rowspan="*integer*"	Specifies the number of rows the table cell spans	3.0	1.0
scope="col| colgroup|row|rowgroup"	Specifies the scope of the table for which the cell provides data	4.0	1.0
valign="top|**middle** |bottom"	Specifies the vertical alignment of the contents of the table cell	3.0	1.0
width="*integer*"	Specifies the width of the cell in pixels (deprecated)	3.2	1.0*
<thead> </thead>	Encloses the content of the Web table header	4.0	1.0
align="left|center |right|justify|char"	Specifies the alignment of the contents in the cells of the table header	4.0	1.0
bgcolor="*color*"	Specifies the background color of the table body		
char="*char*"	Specifies the character used for aligning the table header contents when the align attribute is set to "char"	4.0	1.0
charoff="*integer*"	Specifies the offset in pixels from the alignment character specified in the char attribute	4.0	1.0
valign="baseline| bottom|middle|top"	Specifies the vertical alignment of the contents in the cells of the table header	4.0	1.0
<title> </title>	Specifies the title of the document, placed in the head section of the document	2.0	1.0
<tr> </tr>	Encloses the content of a row within a Web table	3.0	1.0
align="left|center |right"	Specifies the horizontal alignment of the data in the row's cells	3.0	1.0
background="*url*"	Provides the URL of the background image file for the row		
bgcolor="*color*"	Specifies the background color of the row (deprecated)	4.0	1.0*
bordercolor="*color*"	Specifies the color of the table row border (IE only)		
bordercolordark="*color*"	Specifies the color of the table row border's shaded edge (IE only)		
bordercolorlight= "*color*"	Specifies the color of the table row border's unshaded edge (IE only)		
char="*char*"	Specifies the character used for aligning the table row contents when the align attribute is set to "char"	4.0	1.0
charoff="*integer*"	Specifies the offset in pixels from the alignment character specified in the char attribute	4.0	1.0

Element/Attribute	Description	HTML	XHTML
height="*integer*"	Specifies the height of the table row in pixels		
valign="baseline|bottom|*middle*|top"	Specifies the vertical alignment of the contents of the table row	3.0	1.0
<tt> </tt>	Marks the enclosed text as teletype or monospaced text	2.0	1.0
<u> </u>	Marks the enclosed text as underlined text (deprecated)	3.0	1.0*
<ul> </ul>	Contains an unordered list of items	2.0	1.0
compact="compact"	Reduces the space between unordered list items (deprecated)	2.0	1.0*
type="disc|square|circle"	Specifies the bullet type associated with the list items (deprecated)	3.2	1.0*
<var> </var>	Marks the enclosed text as containing a variable name	2.0	1.0
<wbr />	Forces a line-break in the rendered page (not part of the W3C specifications, but supported by many browsers)		
<xml> </xml>	Encloses XML content (also referred to as a "data island") or references an external XML document (IE only)		
ns="*url*"	Provides the URL of the XML data island (IE only)		
prefix="*text*"	Specifies the namespace prefix of the XML content (IE only)		
src="*url*"	Provides the URL of an external XML document (IE only)		
<xmp> </xmp>	Marks the enclosed text as preformatted text, preserving the white space of the source document; replaced by the pre element (deprecated)	2.0	

Cascading Style Sheets

Appendix F

This appendix describes the selectors, units, and attributes supported by Cascading Style Sheets (CSS). Version numbers indicate the lowest version that supports the given selector, unit, or attribute. This appendix focuses on CSS1 and CSS2 styles. It does not include all of the CSS3 styles due to the state of CSS3's development and current level of browser support for CSS3. You should always check your code against different browsers and browser versions to ensure that your page is being rendered correctly. Additional information about CSS can be found at the World Wide Web Consortium Web site at *www.w3.org*.

Starting Data Files

There are no starting Data Files needed for this appendix.

Selectors

The general form of a style declaration is:

selector {attribute1:value1; attribute2:value2; ...}

where *selector* is the selection of elements within the document to which the style will be applied; *attribute1, attribute2*, etc. are the different style attributes; and *value1, value2*, etc. are values associated with those styles. The following table shows some of the different forms that a selector can take.

Selector	Matches	CSS
*	All elements in the document	2.0
e	An element, *e*, in the document	1.0
e1, e2, e3, …	A group of elements, *e1, e2, e3*, in the document	1.0
e1 e2	An element *e2* nested within the parent element, *e1*	1.0
e1 > e2	An element *e2* that is a child of the parent element, *e1*	2.0
e1+e2	An element, *e2*, that is adjacent to element *e1*	2.0
e1.class	An element, *e1*, belonging to the *class* class	1.0
.class	Any element belonging to the *class* class	1.0
#id	An element with the id value *id*	1.0
[att]	The element contains the *att* attribute	2.0
[att="val"]	The element's *att* attribute equals "*val*"	2.0
[att~="val"]	The element's *att* attribute value is a space-separated list of "words," one of which is exactly "*val*"	2.0
[att|="val"]	The element's *att* attribute value is a hyphen-separated list of "words" beginning with "val"	3.0
[att^="val"]	The element's *att* attribute begins with "*val*"	3.0
[att$="val"]	The element's *att* attribute ends with "*val*"	3.0
[att*="val"]	The element's *att* attribute contains the value "*val*"	3.0
[ns|att]	References all *att* attributes in the *ns* namespace	3.0

Pseudo-Elements and Pseudo-Classes

Pseudo-elements are elements that do not exist in HTML code but whose attributes can be set with CSS. Many pseudo-elements were introduced in CSS2.

Pseudo-Element	Matches	CSS
e:after {content: "text"}	Text content, *text*, that is inserted at the end of an element, *e*	2.0
e:before {content: "text"}	Text content, *text*, that is inserted at the beginning of an element, *e*	2.0
e:first-letter	The first letter in the element, *e*	1.0
e:first-line	The first line in the element, *e*	1.0

Pseudo-classes are classes of HTML elements that define the condition or state of the element in the Web page. Many pseudo-classes were introduced in CSS2.

Pseudo-Class	Matches	CSS
:canvas	The rendering canvas of the document	
:first	The first printed page of the document (used only with print styles created with the @print rule)	2.0
:last	The last printed page of the document (used only with print styles created with the @print rule)	2.0
:left	The left side of a two-sided printout (used only with print styles created with the @print rule)	2.0
:right	The right side of a two-sided printout (used only with print styles created with the @print rule)	2.0
:root	The root element of the document (the html element in HTML and XHTML documents)	
:scrolled-content	The content that is scrolled in the rendering viewport (Netscape only)	
:viewport	The rendering viewport of the document (Netscape only)	
:viewport-scroll	The rendering viewport of the document plus the scroll bar region (Netscape only)	
e:active	The element, e, is being activated by the user (usually applies only to hyperlinks)	1.0
e:empty	The element, e, has no content (Netscape only)	
e:first-child	The element, e, which is the first child of its parent element	2.0
e:first-node	The first occurrence of the element, e, in the document tree	
e:focus	The element, e, has received the focus of the cursor (usually applies only to Web form elements)	2.0
e:hover	The mouse pointer is hovering over the element, e (usually applies only to hyperlinks)	2.0
e:lang(text)	Sets the language, text, associated with the element, e	2.0
e:last-child	The element, e, that is the last child of its parent element	2.0
e:last-node	The last occurrence of the element, e, in the document tree (Netscape only)	
e:link	The element, e, has not been visited yet by the user (applies only to hyperlinks)	1.0
e:not	Negate the selector rule for the element, e, applying the style to all e elements that do not match the selector rules (Netscape only)	
e:visited	The element, e, has been already visited by the user (to only the hyperlinks)	1.0

@ Rules

CSS supports different "@ rules" designed to run commands within a style sheet. These commands can be used to import other styles, download font definitions, or define the format of printed output.

@ Rule	Description	CSS
@charset "*encoding*"	Defines the character set encoding used in the style sheet (this must be the very first line in the style sheet document)	2.0
@import url(*url*) *media*	Imports an external style sheet document into the current style sheet, where *url* is the location of the external style sheet and *media* is a comma-separated list of media types (optional)	1.0
@media *media* {*style declaration*}	Defines the media for the styles in the *style declaration* block, where *media* is a comma-separated list of media types	2.0
@namespace *prefix* url(*url*)	Defines the namespace used by selectors in the style sheet, where *prefix* is the local namespace prefix (optional) and *url* is the unique namespace identifier; the @namespace rule must come before all CSS selectors (Netscape only)	
@page *label pseudo-class* {*styles*}	Defines the properties of a printed page, where *label* is a label given to the page (optional), *pseudo-class* is one of the CSS pseudo-classes designed for printed pages, and *styles* are the styles associated with the page	2.0

Miscellaneous Syntax

The following syntax elements do not fit into the previous categories but are useful in constructing CSS style sheets.

Item	Description	CSS
style !important	Places high importance on the preceding *style*, overriding the usual rules for inheritance and cascading	1.0
/* *comment* */	Attaches a *comment* to the style sheet	1.0

Units

Many style attribute values use units of measurement to indicate color, length, angles, time, and frequencies. The following table describes the measuring units used in CSS.

Units	Description	CSS
Color	**Units of color**	
name	A color name; all browsers recognize 16 base color names: aqua, black, blue, fuchsia, gray, green, lime, maroon, navy, olive, purple, red, silver, teal, white, and yellow	1.0
#rrggbb	The hexadecimal color value, where rr is the red value, gg is the green value, and bb is the blue value	1.0
#rgb	A compressed hexadecimal value, where the r, g, and b values are doubled so that, for example, #A2F = #AA22FF	1.0
rgb(red, green, blue)	The decimal color value, where red is the red value, green is the green value, and blue is the blue value	1.0
rgb(red%, green%, blue%)	The color value percentage, where red% is the percent of maximum red, green% is the percent of maximum green, and blue% is the percent of maximum blue	1.0
Length	**Units of length**	
auto	Keyword which allows the browser to automatically determine the size of the length	1.0
em	A relative unit indicating the width and the height of the capital "M" character for the browser's default font	1.0
ex	A relative unit indicating the height of the small "x" character for the browser's default font	1.0
px	A pixel, representing the smallest unit of length on the output device	1.0
in	An inch	1.0
cm	A centimeter	1.0
mm	A millimeter	1.0
pt	A point, approximately 1/72 inch	1.0
pc	A pica, approximately 1/12 inch	1.0
%	A percent of the width or height of the parent element	1.0
xx-small	Keyword representing an extremely small font size	1.0
x-small	Keyword representing a very small font size	1.0
small	Keyword representing a small font size	1.0
medium	Keyword representing a medium-sized font	1.0
large	Keyword representing a large font	1.0
x-large	Keyword representing a very large font	1.0
xx-large	Keyword representing an extremely large font	1.0
Angle	**Units of angles**	
deg	The angle in degrees	2.0
grad	The angle in gradients	2.0
rad	The angle in radians	2.0

Units	Description	CSS
Time	**Units of time**	
ms	Time in milliseconds	2.0
s	Time in seconds	2.0
Frequency	**Units of frequency**	
hz	The frequency in hertz	2.0
khz	The frequency in kilohertz	2.0

Attributes and Values

The following table describes the attributes and values for different types of elements. The attributes are grouped into categories to help you locate the features relevant to your particular design task.

Attribute	Description	CSS
Aural	**Styles for Aural Browsers**	
azimuth: *location*	Defines the location of the sound, where *location* is left-side, far-left, left, center-left, center, center-right, right, far-right, right-side, leftward, rightward, or an angle value	2.0
cue: url(*url1*) url(*url2*)	Adds a sound to an element: if a single value is present, the sound is played before and after the element; if two values are present, the first is played before and the second is played after	2.0
cue-after: url(*url*)	Specifies a sound to be played immediately after an element	2.0
cue-before: url(*url*)	Specifies a sound to be played immediately before an element	2.0
elevation: *location*	Defines the vertical location of the sound, where *location* is below, level, above, lower, higher, or an angle value	2.0
pause: *time1 time2*	Adds a pause to an element: if a single value is present, the pause occurs before and after the element; if two values are present, the first pause occurs before and the second occurs after	2.0
pause-after: *time*	Adds a pause after an element	2.0
pause-before: *time*	Adds a pause before an element	2.0
pitch: *value*	Defines the pitch of a speaking voice, where *value* is x-low, low, medium, high, x-high, or a frequency value	2.0
pitch-range: *value*	Defines the pitch range for a speaking voice, where *value* ranges from 0 to 100; a low pitch range results in a monotone voice, whereas a high pitch range sounds very animated	2.0
play-during: url(*url*) mix repeat *type*	Defines a sound to be played behind an element, where *url* is the URL of the sound file; mix overlays the sound file with the sound of the parent element; repeat causes the sound to be repeated, filling up the available time; and *type* is auto to play the sound only once, none to play nothing but the sound file, or inherit	2.0
richness: *value*	Specifies the richness of the speaking voice, where *value* ranges from 0 to 100; a low value indicates a softer voice, whereas a high value indicates a brighter voice	2.0
speak: *type*	Defines how element content is to be spoken, where *type* is normal (for normal punctuation rules), spell-out (to pronounce one character at a time), none (to suppress the aural rendering), or inherit	2.0

Attribute	Description	CSS
speak-numeral: *type*	Defines how numeric content should be spoken, where *type* is digits (to pronounce one digit at a time), continuous (to pronounce the full number), or inherit	2.0
speak-punctuation: *type*	Defines how punctuation characters are spoken, where *type* is code (to speak the punctuation literally), none (to not speak the punctuation), or inherit	2.0
speech-rate: *value*	Defines the rate of speech, where *value* is x-slow, slow, medium, fast, x-fast, slower, faster, or a value in words per minute	2.0
stress: *value*	Defines the maximum pitch, where *value* ranges from 0 to 100; a value of 50 is normal stress for a speaking voice	2.0
voice-family: *text*	Defines the name of the speaking voice, where *text* is male, female, child, or a text string indicating a specific speaking voice	2.0
volume: *value*	Defines the volume of a voice, where *value* is silent, x-soft, soft, medium, loud, x-loud, or a number from 0 (lowest) to 100 (highest)	2.0
Backgrounds	**Styles applied to an element's background**	
background: *color* url(*url*) *repeat attachment position*	Defines the background of the element, where *color* is a CSS color name or value, *url* is the location of an image file, *repeat* defines how the background image should be repeated, *attachment* defines how the background image should be attached, and *position* defines the position of the background image	1.0
background-attachment: *type*	Specifies how the background image is attached, where *type* is inherit, scroll (move the image with the page content), or fixed (fix the image and not scroll)	1.0
background-color: *color*	Defines the color of the background, where *color* is a CSS color name or value; the keyword "inherit" can be used to inherit the background color of the parent element, or "transparent" can be used to allow the parent element background image to show through	1.0
background-image: url(*url*)	Specifies the image file used for the element's background, where *url* is the URL of the image file	1.0
background-position: *x y*	Sets the position of a background image, where *x* is the horizontal location in pixels, as a percentage of the width of the parent element, or the keyword "left", "center", or "right", *y* is the vertical location in pixels, as a percentage of the height and of the parent element, or the keyword, "top", "center", or "bottom"	1.0
background-repeat: *type*	Defines the method for repeating the background image, where *type* is no-repeat, repeat (to tile the image in both directions), repeat-x (to tile the image in the horizontal direction only), or repeat-y (to tile the image in the vertical direction only)	1.0
Block-Level Styles	**Styles applied to block-level elements**	
border: *length style color*	Defines the border style of the element, where *length* is the border width, *style* is the border design, and *color* is the border color	1.0
border-bottom: *length style color*	Defines the border style of the bottom edge of the element	1.0
border-left: *length style color*	Defines the border style of the left edge of the element	1.0
border-right: *length style color*	Defines the border style of the right edge of the element	1.0
border-top: *length style color*	Defines the border style of the top edge of the element	1.0

Attribute	Description	CSS
border-color: *color*	Defines the color applied to the element's border using a CSS color unit	1.0
border-bottom-color: *color*	Defines the color applied to the bottom edge of the element	1.0
border-left-color: *color*	Defines the color applied to the left edge of the element	1.0
border-right-color: *color*	Defines the color applied to the right edge of the element	1.0
border-top-color: *color*	Defines the color applied to the top edge of the element	1.0
border-style: *style*	Specifies the design of the element's border (dashed, dotted, double, groove, inset, none, outset, ridge, or solid)	1.0
border-style-bottom: *style*	Specifies the design of the element's bottom edge	1.0
border-style-left: *style*	Specifies the design of the element's left edge	1.0
border-style-right: *style*	Specifies the design of the element's right edge	1.0
border-style-top: *style*	Specifies the design of the element's top edge	1.0
border-width: *length*	Defines the width of the element's border, in a unit of measure or using the keyword "thick", "medium", or "thin"	1.0
border-width-bottom: *length*	Defines the width of the element's bottom edge	1.0
border-width-left: *length*	Defines the width of the element's left edge	1.0
border-width-right: *length*	Defines the width of the element's right edge	1.0
border-width-top: *length*	Defines the width of the element's top edge	1.0
margin: *top right bottom left*	Defines the size of the margins around the top, right, bottom, and left edges of the element, in one of the CSS units of length	1.0
margin-bottom: *length*	Defines the size of the element's bottom margin	1.0
margin-left: *length*	Defines the size of the element's left margin	1.0
margin-right: *length*	Defines the size of the element's right margin	1.0
margin-top: *length*	Defines the size of the element's top margin	1.0
padding: *top right bottom left*	Defines the size of the padding space within the top, right, bottom, and left edges of the element, in one of the CSS units of length	1.0
padding-bottom: *length*	Defines the size of the element's bottom padding	1.0
padding-left: *length*	Defines the size of the element's left padding	1.0
padding-right: *length*	Defines the size of the element's right padding	1.0
padding-top: *length*	Defines the size of the element's top padding	1.0

Attribute	Description	CSS
Content	**Styles to attach additional content to elements**	
content: *text*	Generates a text string to attach to the content of the element	2.0
content: attr(*attr*)	Returns the value of the *attr* attribute from the element	2.0
content: close-quote	Attaches a close quote using the characters specified in the quotes style	2.0
content: counter(*text*)	Generates a counter using the text string *text* attached to the content (most often used with list items)	2.0
content: counters(*text*)	Generates a string of counters using the comma-separated text string *text* attached to the content (most often used with list items)	2.0
content: no-close-quote	Prevents the attachment of a close quote to an element	2.0
content: no-open-quote	Prevents the attachment of an open quote to an element	2.0
content: open-quote	Attaches an open quote using the characters specified in the quotes style	2.0
content: url(*url*)	Attaches the content of an external file indicated in the *url* to the element	2.0
counter-increment: *id integer*	Defines the element to be automatically incremented and the amount by which it is to be incremented, where *id* is an identifier of the element and *integer* defines by how much	2.0
counter-reset: *id integer*	Defines the element whose counter is to be reset and the amount by which it is to be reset, where *id* is an identifier of the element and *integer* defines by how much	2.0
quotes: *text1 text2*	Defines the text strings for the open quotes (*text1*) and the close quotes (*text2*)	2.0
Display Styles	**Styles that control the display of the element's content**	
clip: rect(*top, right, bottom, left*)	Defines what portion of the content is displayed, where *top, right, bottom*, and *left* are distances of the top, right, bottom, and left edges from the element's top-left corner; use a value of auto to allow the browser to determine the clipping region	2.0
display: *type*	Specifies the display type of the element, where *type* is one of the following: block, inline, inline-block, inherit, list-item, none, run-in, table, inline-table, table-caption, table-column, table-cell, table-column-group, table-header-group, table-footer-group, table-row, or table-row-group	1.0

Attribute	Description	CSS
height: *length*	Specifies the height of the element in one of the CSS units of length	1.0
min-height: *length*	Specifies the minimum height of the element	2.0
min-width: *length*	Specifies the minimum width of the element	2.0
max-height: *length*	Specifies the maximum height of the element	2.0
max-width: *length*	Specifies the maximum width of the element	2.0
overflow: *type*	Instructs the browser how to handle content that overflows the dimensions of the element, where *type* is auto, inherit, visible, hidden, or scroll	2.0
overflow-x: *type*	Instructs the browser how to handle content that overflows the element's width, where *type* is auto, inherit, visible, hidden, or scroll (IE only)	
overflow-y: *type*	Instructs the browser on how to handle content that overflows the element's height, where *type* is auto, inherit, visible, hidden, or scroll (IE only)	
text-overflow: *type*	Instructs the browser on how to handle text overflow, where *type* is clip (to hide the overflow text) or ellipsis (to display the … text string) (IE only)	
visibility: *type*	Defines the element's visibility, where *type* is hidden, visible, or inherit	2.0
width: *length*	Specifies the width of the element in one of the CSS units of length	1.0
Fonts and Text	**Styles that format the appearance of fonts and text**	
color: *color*	Specifies the color of the element's foreground (usually the font color)	1.0
font: *style variant weight size/line-height family*	Defines the appearance of the font, where *style* is the font's style, *variant* is the font variant, *weight* is the weight of the font, *size* is the size of the font, *line-height* is the height of the lines, and *family* is the font face; the only required attributes are *size* and *family*	1.0
font-family: *family*	Specifies the font face used to display text, where *family* is sans-serif, serif, fantasy, monospace, cursive, or the name of an installed font	1.0
font-size: *value*	Specifies the size of the font in one of the CSS units of length	1.0
font-size-adjust: *value*	Specifies the aspect *value* (which is the ratio of the font size to the font's ex unit height)	2.0
font-stretch: *type*	Expands or contracts the font, where *type* is narrower, wider, ultra-condensed, extra-condensed, condensed, semi-condensed, normal, semi-expanded, extra-expanded, or ultra-expanded	2.0
font-style: *type*	Specifies a style applied to the font, where *type* is normal, italic, or oblique	1.0
font-variant: *type*	Specifies a variant of the font, where *type* is inherit, normal, or small-caps	1.0
font-weight: *value*	Defines the weight of the font, where *value* is 100, 200, 300, 400, 500, 600, 700, 800, 900, normal, lighter, bolder, or bold	1.0
letter-spacing: *value*	Specifies the space between letters, where *value* is a unit of length or the keyword "normal"	1.0
line-height: *value*	Specifies the height of the lines, where *value* is a unit of length or the keyword, "normal"	1.0

Attribute	Description	CSS
text-align: *type*	Specifies the horizontal alignment of text within the element, where *type* is inherit, left, right, center, or justify	1.0
text-decoration: *type*	Specifies the decoration applied to the text, where *type* is blink, line-through, none, overline, or underline	1.0
text-indent: *length*	Specifies the amount of indentation in the first line of the text, where *length* is a CSS unit of length	1.0
text-shadow: *color* *x y blur*	Applies a shadow effect to the text, where *color* is the color of the shadow, *x* is the horizontal offset in pixels, *y* is the vertical offset in pixels, and *blur* is the size of the blur radius (optional); multiple shadows can be added with shadow effects separated by commas	2.0
text-transform: *type*	Defines a transformation applied to the text, where *type* is capitalize, lowercase, none, or uppercase	1.0
vertical-align: *type*	Specifies how to vertically align the text with the surrounding content, where *type* is baseline, middle, top, bottom, text-top, text-bottom, super, sub, or one of the CSS units of length	1.0
white-space: *type*	Specifies the handling of white space (blank spaces, tabs, and new lines), where *type* is inherit, normal, pre (to treat the text as preformatted text), or nowrap (to prevent line-wrapping)	1.0
word-spacing: *length*	Specifies the amount of space between words in the text, where *length* is either a CSS unit of length or the keyword "normal" to use normal word spacing	1.0
Layout	**Styles that define the layout of elements**	
bottom: *y*	Defines the vertical offset of the element's bottom edge, where *y* is either a CSS unit of length or the keyword "auto" or "inherit"	2.0
clear: *type*	Places the element only after the specified margin is clear of floating elements, where *type* is inherit, none, left, right, or both	1.0
float: *type*	Floats the element on the specified margin with subsequent content wrapping around the element, where *type* is inherit, none, left, right, or both	1.0
left: *x*	Defines the horizontal offset of the element's left edge, where *x* is either a CSS unit of length or the keyword "auto" or "inherit"	2.0
position: *type*	Defines how the element is positioned on the page, where *type* is absolute, relative, fixed, static, and inherit	1.0
right: *x*	Defines the horizontal offset of the element's right edge, where *x* is either a CSS unit of length or the keyword "auto" or "inherit"	2.0
top: *y*	Defines the vertical offset of the element's top edge, where *y* is a CSS unit of length or the keyword "auto" or "inherit"	2.0
z-index: *value*	Defines how overlapping elements are stacked, where *value* is either the stacking number (elements with higher stacking numbers are placed on top) or the keyword "auto" to allow the browser to determine the stacking order	2.0
Lists	**Styles that format lists**	
list-style: *type image position*	Defines the appearance of a list item, where *type* is the marker type, *image* is the URL of the location of an image file used for the marker, and *position* is the position of the marker	1.0
list-style-image: url(*url*)	Defines image used for the list marker, where *url* is the location of the image file	1.0

Attribute	Description	CSS
list-style-type: *type*	Defines the marker type used in the list, where *type* is disc, circle, square, decimal, decimal-leading-zero, lower-roman, upper-roman, lower-alpha, upper-alpha, or none	1.0
list-style-position: *type*	Defines the location of the list marker, where *type* is inside or outside	1.0
marker-offset: *length*	Defines the distance between the marker and the enclosing list box, where *length* is either a CSS unit of length or the keyword "auto" or "inherit"	2.0
Outlines	**Styles to create and format outlines**	
outline: *color style width*	Creates an outline around the element content, where *color* is the color of the outline, *style* is the outline style, and *width* is the width of the outline	2.0
outline-color: *color*	Defines the color of the outline	2.0
outline-style: *type*	Defines the style of the outline, where *type* is dashed, dotted, double, groove, inset, none, outset, ridge, solid, or inherit	2.0
outline-width: *length*	Defines the width of the outline, where *length* is expressed in a CSS unit of length	2.0
Printing	**Styles for printed output**	
page: *label*	Specifies the page design to apply, where *label* is a page design created with the @page rule	2.0
page-break-after: *type*	Defines how to control page breaks after the element, where *type* is avoid (to avoid page breaks), left (to insert a page break until a left page is displayed), right (to insert a page break until a right page is displayed), always (to always insert a page break), auto, or inherit	2.0
page-break-before: *type*	Defines how to control page breaks before the element, where *type* is avoid left, always, auto, or inherit	2.0
page-break-inside: *type*	Defines how to control page breaks within the element, where *type* is avoid, auto, or inherit	2.0
marks: *type*	Defines how to display crop marks, where *type* is crop, cross, none, or inherit	2.0
size: *width height orientation*	Defines the size of the page, where *width* and *height* are the width and the height of the page and *orientation* is the orientation of the page (portrait or landscape)	2.0
orphans: *value*	Defines how to handle orphaned text, where *value* is the number of lines that must appear within the element before a page break is inserted	2.0
widows: *value*	Defines how to handle widowed text, where *value* is the number of lines that must appear within the element after a page break is inserted	2.0
Scrollbars and Cursors	**Styles to format the appearance of scrollbars and cursors**	
cursor: *type*	Defines the cursor image used, where *type* is n-resize, ne-resize, e-resize, se-resize, s-resize, sw-resize, w-resize, nw-resize, crosshair, pointer, move, text, wait, help, auto, default, inherit, or a URL pointing to an image file; individual browsers also support dozens of other cursor types	2.0
scrollbar-3dlight-color: *color*	Defines the *color* of the outer top and left edge of the slider (IE only)	
scrollbar-arrow-color: *color*	Defines the *color* of the scroll bar directional arrows (IE only)	

Attribute	Description	CSS
scrollbar-base-color: *color*	Defines the *color* of the scroll bar button face, arrow, slider, and slider tray (IE only)	
scrollbar-darkshadow-color: *color*	Defines the *color* of the outer bottom and right edges of the slider (IE only)	
scrollbar-face-color: *color*	Defines the *color* of the button face of the scroll bar arrow and slider (IE only)	
scrollbar-highlight-color: *color*	Defines the *color* of the inner top and left edges of the slider (IE only)	
scrollbar-shadow-color: *color*	Defines the *color* of the inner bottom and right edges of the slider (IE only)	
Special Effects	**Styles to create special visual effects**	
filter: *type parameters*	Applies transition and filter effects to elements, where *type* is the type of filter and *parameters* are parameter values specific to the filter (IE only)	
Tables	**Styles to format the appearance of tables**	
border-collapse: *type*	Determines whether table cell borders are separate or collapsed into a single border, where *type* is separate, collapse, or inherit	2.0
border-spacing: *length*	If separate borders are used for table cells, defines the distance between borders, where *length* is a CSS unit of length or inherit	2.0
caption-side: *type*	Defines the position of the caption element, where *type* is bottom, left, right, top, or inherit	2.0
empty-cells: *type*	If separate borders are used for table cells, defines whether to display borders for empty cells, where *type* is hide, show, or inherit	2.0
speak-header: *type*	Defines how table headers are spoken in relation to the data cells, where *type* is always, once, or inherit	2.0
table-layout: *type*	Defines the algorithm used for the table layout, where *type* is auto (to define the layout once all table cells have been read), fixed (to define the layout after the first table row has been read), or inherit	2.0

JavaScript Objects, Properties, Methods, and Event Handlers

Appendix G

This appendix defines some of the important JavaScript objects, properties, methods, and event handlers. The JavaScript object is listed first, followed by any properties, methods, and event handlers associated with it.

Where a particular object, property, method, or event handler is supported only in a specific browser, this fact is noted in the table.

As always, you should test your code against a variety of browsers to ensure support.

JavaScript Elements	Description
Anchor	An anchor in the document (use the anchor name)
Properties	
accessKey	The hotkey that gives the element focus
charset	The character set of the linked document
coords	The coordinates of the object, used with the shape attribute
hreflang	The language code of the linked resource
name	The name of the anchor
nameProp	The string holding the filename portion of the URL in the href
shape	The string defining the shape of the object
tabIndex	The numeric value that indicates the tab order for the object
text	The anchor text
type	Specifies the media type in the form of a MIME type for the link target
Methods	
blur( )	Removes focus from the element
handleEvent (*event*)	Causes the Event instance *event* to be processed
focus( )	Gives the element focus
Applet	A Java applet in the document
Properties	
align	Specifies alignment, for example, "left
alt	Specifies alternative text for the applet
altHTML	Specifies alternative text for the applet
archive	A list of URLs
code	The URL for the applet class file
codeBase	The base URL for the applet
height	The height of the object in pixels
hspace	The horizontal margin to the left and the right of the applet
name	The name of the applet
object	The name of the resource that contains a serialized representation of the applet
vspace	The vertical margin above and below the applet
width	The width of the object in pixels
Area	An area defined in an image map
Properties	
accessKey	The hotkey that gives the element focus
alt	Alternative text to the graphic
cords	Defines the coordinates of the object
hash	The anchor name from the URL
host	The host and domain names from the URL
hostname	The hostname from the URL
href	The entire URL
pathname	The pathname from the URL

JavaScript Elements	Description
port	The port number from the URL
protocol	The protocol from the URL
search	The query portion from the URL
shape	The shape of the object, for example, "default", "rect", "circle", or "poly"
tabIndex	Numeric value that indicates the tab order for the object
target	The target attribute of the <area> tag
Methods	
getSelection()	Returns the value of the current selection3.0
Event Handlers	
onDblClick()	Runs when the area is double-clicked
onMouseOut()	Runs when the mouse leaves the area
onMouseOver()	Runs when the mouse enters the area
Array	An array object
Properties	
index	For an array created by a regular expression match, the zero-based index of the match in the string
input	Reflects the original string against which the regular expression was matched
length	The next empty index at the end of the array
prototype	A mechanism to add properties to an array object
Methods	
concat(*array*)	Combines two arrays and stores the result in a third array named *array*
join(*string*)	Stores each element in a text string named *string*
pop( )	"Pops" the last element of the array and reduces the length of the array by 1
push(*arg1, arg2, ...*)	"Pushes" the elements in the list to the end of the array and returns the new length
reverse( )	Reverses the order of the elements in the array
shift( )	Removes the first element from an array, returns that element, and shifts all other elements down one index
slice(*array, begin,end*)	Extracts a portion of the array, starting at the index number *begin* and ending at the index number *end*; the elements are then stored in *array*
sort(*function*)	Sorts the array based on the function named *function*; if *function* is omitted, the sort applies dictionary order to the array
splice(*start,howMany,* [,*item1*[,*item2* [,…]]])	Removes *howMany* elements from the array, beginning at index *start* and replaces the removed elements with the *itemN* arguments (if passed); returns an array of the deleted elements
toString( )	Returns a string of the comma-separated values of the array
unshift([Item1 [,item2[,…]]])	Inserts the items to the front of an array and returns the new length of the array
Button	A push button in an HTML form (use the button's name)
Properties	
accessKey	Indicates the hotkey that gives the element focus
align	Specifies the alignment of the element, for example, "right"
disabled	A Boolean indicating whether the element is disabled

JavaScript Elements	Description
enabled	Indicates whether the button has been enabled
form	The name of the form containing the button
name	The name of the button element
size	Indicates the width of the button in pixels
tabIndex	Indicates the tab order for the object
type	The value of the type attribute for the <button> tag
value	The value of the button element
Methods	
blur()	Removes focus from the button
click()	Emulates the action of clicking the button
focus()	Gives focus to the button
Event Handlers	
onBlur	Runs when the button loses the focus
onClick	Runs when the button is clicked
onFocus	Runs when the button receives the focus
onMouseDown	Runs when the mouse button is pressed
onMouseUp	Runs when the mouse button is released
Checkbox	A check box in an HTML form
Properties	
accessKey	Indicates the hotkey that gives the element focus
align	Specifies the alignment of the element, for example, "right"
checked	Indicates whether the check box is checked
defaultChecked	Indicates whether the check box is checked by default
disabled	Boolean indicating whether the element is disabled
enabled	Indicates whether the check box is enabled
form	The name of the form containing the check box
name	The name of the check box element
size	Indicates the width of the check box in pixels0
status	Boolean indicating whether the check box is currently selected
tabIndex	Indicates the tab order for the object
type	The value of the type attribute for the <input> tag
value	The value of the check box element
Methods	
blur()	Removes the focus from the check box
click()	Emulates the action of clicking on the check box
focus()	Gives focus to the check box
Event Handlers	
onBlur	Runs when the check box loses the focus
onClick	Runs when the check box is clicked
onFocus	Runs when the check box receives the focus

JavaScript Elements	Description
Date	An object containing information about a specific date or the current date; dates are expressed either in local time or in UTC (Universal Time Coordinates), otherwise known as Greenwich Mean Time
Methods	
getDate()	Returns the day of the month, from 1 to 31
getDay()	Returns the day of the week, from 0 to 6 (Sunday = 0, Monday = 1, etc.)
getFullYear()	Returns the year portion of the date in four-digit format
getHours()	Returns the hour in military time, from 0 to 23
getMilliseconds()	Returns the number of milliseconds
getMinutes()	Returns the minute, from 0 to 59
getMonth()	Returns the value of the month, from 0 to 11 (January = 0, February = 1, etc.)
getSeconds()	Returns the seconds
getTime()	Returns the date as an integer representing the number of milliseconds since December 31, 1969, at 18:00:00
getTimezoneOffset()	Returns the difference between the local time and Greenwich Mean Time in minutes
getYear()	Deprecated. Returns the number of years since 1900; for example, 1996 is represented by '96'—this value method is inconsistently applied after the year 1999
getUTCDate()	Returns the UTC getDate() value
getUTCDay()	Returns the UTC getDay() value
getUTCFullYear()	Returns the UTC getFullYear() value
getUTCHours()	Returns the UTC getHours() value
getUTCMilliseconds()	Returns the UTC getMilliseconds() value
getUTCMinutes()	Returns the UTC getMinutes() value
getUTCMonth()	Returns the UTC getMonth() value
getUTCSeconds()	Returns the UTC getSeconds() value
getUTCTime()	Returns the UTC getTime() value
getUTCYear()	Returns the UTC getYear() value
setDate(*date*)	Sets the day of the month to the value specified in *date*
setFullYear(*year*)	Sets the year to the four-digit value specified in *year*
setHours(*hour*)	Sets the hour to the value specified in *hour*
setMilliseconds(*milliseconds*)	Sets the millisecond value to *milliseconds*
setMinutes(*minutes*)	Sets the minute to the value specified in *minutes*
setMonth(*month*)	Sets the month to the value specified in *month*
setSeconds(*seconds*)	Sets the second to the value specified in *seconds*
setTime(*time*)	Sets the time using the value specified in *time*, where *time* is a variable containing the number of milliseconds since December 31, 1969, at 18:00:00
setYear(*year*)	Sets the year to the value specified in *year*
toDateString()	Returns a date as a string value
toLocaleDateString()	Returns a date as a string value
toTimeString()	Returns a time as a string value

JavaScript Elements	Description
toGMTString()	Converts the current date to a text string in Greenwich Mean Time
toLocaleString()	Converts a date object's date to a text string, using the date format the Web browser is set up to use
toSource	String representing the source code of the object
toString()	String representation of a Date object
toUTCString()	Date converted to string using UTC
UTC()	Milliseconds since December 31, 18:00:00, using UTC
UTC(*date*)	Returns *date* in the form of the number of milliseconds since December 31, 1969, at 18:00:00 for Universal Coordinated Time
setUTCDate(*date*)	Applies the setDate() method in UTC time
setUTCFullYear(*year*)	Applies the setFullYear() method in UTC time
setUTCHours(*hour*)	Applies the setHours() method in UTC time
setUTCMilliseconds (*milliseconds*)	Applies the setMilliseconds() method in UTC time
setUTCMinutes(*minutes*)	Applies the setMinutes() method in UTC time
setUTCMonth(*month*)	Applies the setMonth() method in UTC time
setUTCSeconds(*seconds*)	Applies the setSeconds() method in UTC time
setUTCTime(*time*)	Applies the setTime() method in UTC time
setUTCYear(*year*)	Applies the setYear() method in UTC time
dir	A directory listing element in the document
Properties	
compact	A Boolean indicating whether the listing should be compacted
div	A <div> (block container) element in the document
Properties	
align	Alignment of the element
document	An HTML document (child of Window)
Properties	
alinkColor	The color of active hypertext links in the document
all[ ]	An array of each of the HTML tags in the document
anchors[ ]	An array of the anchors in the document
applets[ ]	An array of the applets in the document
attributes[ ]	A collection of attributes for the element
bgColor	The background color of the document
body	Reference to the <body> element object of the document
charset	A string containing the character set of the document
characterSet	A string containing the character set of the document
childNodes[ ]	A collection of child nodes of the object
classes.*class.tag.style*	Deprecated; the *style* associated with the element in the document with the class name *class* and the tag name *tag*
cookie	A text string containing the document's cookie values

JavaScript Elements	Description
designMode	Specifies whether design mode is on or off
dir	A string holding the text direction of text enclosed in the document
doctype	Reference to the DocumentType object for the document
documentElement	Reference to the root node of the document object hierarchy
domain	The domain of the document
embeds	An array of the embedded objects in the document
expando	A Boolean dictating whether instance properties can be added to the object (*IE only*)
fgColor	The text color used in the document
firstChild	Reference to the first child node of the element, if one exists
form	A form within the document (the form itself is also an object)
forms	An array of the forms in the document
implementation	An object with method *hasFeature(feature, level)* that returns a Boolean indicating if the browser supports the feature given in the string *feature* at the DOM level passed in the string *level*
lastChild	Reference to the last child node of the element, if one exists
lastModified	The date the document was last modified
layers	An array of layer objects
linkColor	The color of hypertext links in the document
links	An array of the links within the document
localName	A string indicating the "local" XML name for the object
location	The URL of the document
media	The media for which the document is intended
nextSibling	Reference to next sibling of the node
nodeName	A string containing the name of the node, the name of the tag to which the object corresponds
nodeValue	A string containing value within the node
ownerDocument	Reference to the document in which the element is contained
parentNode	Reference to the parent of the object
parentWindow	Reference to the window that contains the document
previousSibling	Reference to the previous sibling of the node
protocol	A string containing the protocol used to retrieve the document—its full name
referrer	The URL of the document containing the link that the user accessed to get to the current document
security	A string that contains information about the document's certificate
styleSheets[ ]	Collection of style sheets in the document
title	The title of the document
URL	The URL of the document
vlinkColor	The color of followed hypertext links
XMLDocument	Reference to the top-level node of the XML DOM exposed by the document
XSLDocument	Reference to the top-level node of the XSL DOM exposed by the document

JavaScript Elements	Description
Methods	
addEventListener (whichEvent, handler, direction)	Instructs the object to execute the function *handler* whenever an event of the type stated in *whichEvent* occurs; *direction* is a Boolean telling which phase to fire; use true for capture and false for bubbling
appendChild(newChild)	Appends *newChild* to the end of the node's childNodes[ ] list
attachEvent(whichHandler, theFunction)	Attaches the function *theFunction* as a handler specified by the string *whichHandler*
clear()	Clears the contents of the document window
cloneNode(cloneChildren)	Clones the node and returns the new clone
close()	Closes the document stream
createAttribute(name)	Returns a new attribute node of a name given by string *name*
createComment(data)	Returns a new comment node with the text given by *data*
createElement(tagName)	Returns a new element object that corresponds to *tagName*
createEventObject ([eventObj])	Creates and returns a new Event instance to pass to *fireEvent()*
createStyleSheet ([url [,index]])	Creates a new styleSheet object from the Stylesheet at the URL in the string *url* and inserts it into the document at index *index*
createTextNode(data)	Returns a new text node with value given by *data*
detachEvent(whichHandler, theFunction)	Instructs the object to stop executing *theFunction* as a handler given the string *whichHandler*
dispatchEvent(event)	Causes *event* to be processed by the appropriate handler; is used to redirect events
fireEvent(handler [, event])	Fires the event handler given by *handler*
focus()	Gives focus to the document and fires *onfocus* handler
getElementById(id)	Returns the element with *id* (or *name*) that is equal to *id*
getElementByName(name)	Gets a collection of elements with *id* (or *name*) that is equal to *name*
getElementByTagName (tagname)	Gets a collection of elements corresponding to *tagname*
getSelection()	Returns the selected text from the document
hasAttributes()	Returns a Boolean showing if any attributes are defined for the node
hasChildNodes()	Returns a Boolean showing if the node has children
insertBefore(newChild, refChild)	Inserts the node *newChild* in front of *refChild* in the *childNodes*[ ] list of *refChild*'s parent node
isSupported(feature [, version])	Returns a Boolean showing which feature and version identified in the arguments is supported
normalize()	Merges adjacent text nodes in the subtree rooted at this element
open()	Opens the document stream
recalc([forceAll])	If *forceAll* is *true*, all dynamic properties are reevaluated
removeChild(oldChild)	Removes *oldChild* from the node's children and returns a reference to the removed node
removeEventListener (whichEvent, handler, direction)	Removes the function *handler* for the event declared in *whichEvent* for the phase stated in the Boolean *direction*

JavaScript Elements	Description
replaceChild(newChild, oldChild)	Replaces the node's child node *oldChild* with the node *newChild*
setActive()	Sets the document as the current element but does not give it focus
write()	Writes to the document window
writeln()	Writes to the document window on a single line (used only with preformatted text)
Event Handlers	
onClick	Runs when the document is clicked
onDblClick	Runs when the document is double-clicked
onKeyDown	Runs when a key is pressed down
onKeyPress	Runs when a key is initially pressed
onKeyUp	Runs when a key is released
onLoad	Runs when the document is initially loaded
onMouseDown	Runs when the mouse button is pressed down
onMouseUp	Runs when the mouse button is released
onUnLoad	Runs when the document is unloaded
Error	This object gives information about the error that occurred during runtime
Properties	
description	Describes the nature of the error
lineNumber	The line number that generated the error
number	The numeric value of the Microsoft-specific error number
File, FileUpload	A file upload element in an HTML form (use the FileUpload box's name)
Properties	
accessKey	Indicates the hotkey that gives the element focus
disabled	A Boolean signifying if the element is disabled
form	The form object containing the FileUpload box
name	The name of the FileUpload box
size	The width in pixels
tabIndex	A numeric value of the width in pixels
type	The type attribute of the FileUpload box
value	The pathname of the selected file in the FileUpload box
Methods	
blur()	Removes the focus from the FileUpload box
focus()	Gives the focus to the FileUpload box
handleEvent(*event*)	Invokes the event handler for the specified *event*
select()	Selects the input area of the FileUpload box
Event Handlers	
onBlur	Runs when the focus leaves the FileUpload box
onChange	Runs when the value in the FileUpload box is changed
onFocus	Runs when the focus is given to the FileUpload box

JavaScript Elements	Description
`Form`	`An HTML form (use the form's name)`
Properties	
acceptCharset	Specifies a list of character encodings for input data to be accepted by the server processing the form
action	The location of the CGI script that receives the form values
autocomplete	Specifies whether form autocompletion is on or off
elements[ ]	An array of elements within the form
encoding	The type of encoding used in the form
enctype	Specifies the MIME type of submitted data
length	The number of elements in the form
method	The type of method used when submitting the form
name	The name of the form
target	The name of the window into which CGI output should be directed
Methods	
handleEvent(*event*)	Invokes the event handler for the specified *event*
reset()	Resets the form
submit()	Submits the form to the CGI script
urns(*urn*)	Retrieves a collection of all elements to which the behavior of string *urn* is attached
Event Handlers	
onReset	Runs when the form is reset
onSubmit	Runs when the form is submitted
`Frame`	`A frame window (use the frame's name)`
Properties	
document	The current document in the frame window
frames	An array of frames within the frame window
length	The length of the frames array
name	The name of the frame
parent	The name of the window that contains the frame
self	The name of the current frame window
top	The name of the topmost window in the hierarchy of frame windows
window	The name of the current frame window
Methods	
alert(*message*)	Displays an Alert box with the text string *message*
blur()	Removes the focus from the frame
clearInterval(*ID*)	Cancels the repeated execution
clearTimeout(*ID*)	Cancels the delayed execution *ID*
confirm(*message*)	Displays a Confirm box with the text string *message*
open(*URL, name, features*)	Opens a URL in the frame with the name *name* and a feature list indicated by *features*
print()	Displays the Print dialog box

JavaScript Elements	Description
prompt(*message, response*)	Displays a Prompt dialog box with the text string *message* and the default value *response*
setInterval(*expression, time*)	Runs an *expression* after *time* milliseconds
setTimeout(*expression, time*)	Runs an *expression* every *time* milliseconds
Event Handlers	
onBlur	Runs when the focus is removed from the frame
onFocus	Runs when the frame receives the focus
onMove	Runs when the frame is moved
onResize	Runs when the frame is resized
h1...h6	Heading level element in the document
Properties	
align	The alignment of the element, for example, "right"
head	Corresponds to the <head> element in the document
Properties	
profile	A list of the URLs for data properties and legal values
hidden	A hidden field on an HTML form (use the name of the hidden field)
Properties	
form	The name of the form containing the hidden field
name	The name of the hidden field
type	The type of the hidden field
value	The value of the hidden field
history	An object containing information about the Web browser's history list
Properties	
current	The current URL in the history list
length	The number of items in the history list
next	The next item in the history list
previous	The previous item in the history list
Methods	
back()	Navigates back to the previous item in the history list
forward()	Navigates forward to the next item in the history list
go(*location*)	Navigates to the item in the history list specified by the value of *location*; the *location* variable can be either an integer or the name of the Web page
hr	A horizontal rule element in the document
Properties	
align	Alignment of the object, for example, "right"
color	The color of the rule
noShade	A Boolean indicating that the rule is not to be shaded
size	The size (height) of the rule in pixels
width	The width of the rule in pixels

JavaScript Elements	Description
`html`	Corresponds to the `<html>` element in the document
Properties	
version	The DTD version for the document
`iframe`	An inline frame element in the document
Properties	
align	The alignment of the object, for example, "right"
allowTransparency	A Boolean specifying whether the background of the frame can be transparent
border	The width of the border around the frame
contentDocument	The document that corresponds to the content of this frame
contentWindow	The window that corresponds to this frame
frameBorder	String of "0" (no border) or "1" (show border)
height	The height of the frame in pixels
longdesc	The URL of a long description for the frame
marginHeight	Vertical margins in pixels
marginWidth	Horizontal margins in pixels
name	The name of the frame
width	The width of the frame in pixels
`image`	An inline image (use the name assigned to the image)
Properties	
align	Specifies the alignment of the object, for example, "left", "right", or "center"
alt	A string containing alternative text for the image
border	The width of the image border in pixels
complete	A Boolean value indicating whether the image has been completely loaded by the browser
height	The height of the image in pixels
hspace	The horizontal space around the image in pixels
isMap	A Boolean indicating whether the image is a server-sid image map
longDesc	The URL for a more detailed description of the image
loop	An integer indicating how many times the image is to loop when activated
lowSrc	Specifies a URL for a lower-resolution image to display
lowsrc	The value of the lowsrc property of the `<img>` tag
name	The name of the image
nameProp	Indicates the name of the file given in the *src* attribute of the `<img>` tag
src	The URL of the image
style	Reference to the inline *Style* object for the element
useMap	Contains a URL to use as a client-side image map
vspace	The vertical space around the image in pixels
width	The width of the image in pixels
Methods	
handleEvent(*event*)	Invokes the event handler for the specified *event*

JavaScript Elements	Description
Event Handlers	
onAbort	Runs when the image load is aborted
onError	Runs when an error occurs while loading the image
onKeyDown	Runs when a key is pressed down
onKeyPress	Runs when a key is pressed
onKeyUp	Runs when a key is released
onLoad	Runs when the image is loaded
implementation	Information about the DOM technologies the browser supports (child of Document)
Methods	
hasFeature(feature [, version])	A Boolean indicating if the browser supports the feature at the DOM level given in version
label	A form field label in the document
Properties	
accessKey	Indicates the hotkey that gives the element focus
form	The form that encloses the label
layer	A document layer (use the name of the layer); deprecated in favor of the standard <div> element (NS 4.0 only)
Properties	
above	The layer above the current layer (NS 4.0 only)
background	The background image of the layer (NS 4.0 only)
below	The layer below the current layer (NS 4.0 only)
bgColor	The background color of the layer (NS 4.0 only)
clip.bottom, clip.height, clip.left, clip.right, clip.top, clip.width	The size and position of the layer's clipping area (NS 4.0 only)
document	The document containing the layer (NS 4.0 only)
name	The value of the *name* or *id* attribute for the layer (NS 4.0 only)
left	The x-coordinate of the layer (NS 4.0 only)
pageX	The x-coordinate relative to the document (NS 4.0 only)
pageY	The y-coordinate relative to the document (NS 4.0 only)
parentLayer	The containing layer (NS 4.0 only)
siblingAbove	The layer above in the zIndex (NS 4.0 only)
siblingBelow	The layer below in the zIndex (NS 4.0 only)
src	The URL of the layer document (NS 4.0 only)
top	The y-coordinate of the layer (NS 4.0 only)
visibility	The state of the layer's visibility (NS 4.0 only)
zIndex	The zIndex value of the layer (NS 4.0 only)
Methods	
handleEvent(event)	Invokes the event handler for the specified *event* (NS 4.0 only)
load(source, width)	Loads a new URL into the layer from *source* with the specified *width* (NS 4.0 only)

JavaScript Elements	Description
moveAbove(*layer*)	Moves the layer above *layer (NS 4.0 only)*
moveBelow(*layer*)	Moves the layer below *layer (NS 4.0 only)*
moveBy(*x, y*)	Moves the *x* pixels in the *x*-direction, and the *y* pixels in the *y*-direction *(NS 4.0 only)*
moveTo(*x, y*)	Moves the upper-left corner of the layer to the specified0 (*x, y*) coordinate *(NS 4.0 only)*
moveToAbsolute(*x, y*)	Moves the layer to the specified coordinate (*x, y*) within the page *(NS 4.0 only)*
resizeBy(*width, height*)	Resizes the layer by the specified *width* and *height (NS 4.0 only)*
resizeTo(*width, height*)	Resizes the layer to the specified *height* and *width (NS 4.0 only)*
Event Handlers	
onBlur	Runs when the focus leaves the layer *(NS 4.0 only)*
onFocus	Runs when the layer receives the focus *(NS 4.0 only)*
onLoad	Runs when the layer is loaded *(NS 4.0 only)*
onMouseOut	Runs when the mouse leaves the layer *(NS 4.0 only)*
onMouseOver	Runs when the mouse hovers over the layer *(NS 4.0 only)*
legend	A `<legend>` (fieldset caption) element in the document
Properties	
accessKey	Indicates the hotkey
align	Specifies the alignment of the element, for example, "right"
form	The form in which the element is enclosed
link	A link within an HTML document (use the name of the link)
Properties	
accessKey	Indicates the hotkey that gives the element focus
charset	The character set of the linked document
coords	Defines the coordinates of the object
disabled	A Boolean indicating whether the element is disabled
hash	The anchor name from the link's URL
host	The host from the link's URL
hostname	The hostname from the link's URL
href	The link's URL
hreflang	Indicates the language code of the linked resource
media	The media the linked document is intended for
nameProp	Holds the filename portion of the URL in the *href*
pathname	The path portion of the link's URL
port	The port number of the link's URL
protocol	The protocol used with the link's URL
search	The search portion of the link's URL
target	The target window of the hyperlinks
text	The text used to create the link
type	Specifies the media type in the form of a MIME type for the ink target
Methods	
handleEvent(*event*)	Invokes the event handler for the specified *event*

JavaScript Elements	Description
Event Handlers	
onClick	Runs when the link is clicked
onDblClick	Runs when the link is double-clicked
onKeyDown	Runs when a key is pressed down
onKeyPress	Runs when a key is initially pressed
onKeyUp	Runs when a key is released
onMouseDown	Runs when the mouse button is pressed down on the link
onMouseOut	Runs when mouse moves away from the link
onMouseOver	Runs when the mouse hovers over the link
onMouseUp	Runs when the mouse button is released
location	The location of the document
Properties	
hash	The location's anchor name
host	The location's hostname and port number
href	The location's URL
pathname	The path portion of the location's URL
port	The port number of the location's URL
protocol	The protocol used with the location's URL
Methods	
Assign(*url*)	Assigns the URL in the string *url* to the object
reload()	Reloads the location
replace(*url*)	Loads a new location with the address *url*
map	Corresponds to a <map> (client-side image map)element in the document
Properties	
Areas[ ]	A collection of *areas* enclosed by the object
Name	String holding the name of the image map
Math	An object used for advanced mathematical calculations
Properties	
E	The value of the base of natural logarithms (2.7182...)
LN10	The value of the natural logarithm of 10
LN2	The value of the natural logarithm of 2
LOG10E	The base 10 logarithm of E
LOG2E	The base 2 logarithm of E
PI	The value of pi (3.1416...)
SQRT1_2	The square root of $\frac{1}{2}$
SQRT2	The square root of 2
Methods	
abs(*number*)	Returns the absolute value of *number*
acos(*number*)	Returns the arc cosine of *number* in radians
asin(*number*)	Returns the arc sine of *number* in radians

JavaScript Elements	Description
atan(*number*)	Returns the arc tangent of *number* in radians
atan2()	Returns the arc tangent of the quotient of its arguments
ceil(*number*)	Rounds *number* up to the next-highest integer
cos(*number*)	Returns the cosine of *number*, where *number* is an angle expressed in radians
exp(*number*)	Raises the value of E (2.7182...) to the value of *number*
floor(*number*)	Rounds *number* down to the next-lowest integer
log(*number*)	Returns the natural logarithm of *number*
max(*number1, number2*)	Returns the greater of *number1* and *number2*
min(*number1, number2*)	Returns the lesser of *number1* and *number2*
pow(*number1, number2*)	Returns the value of *number1* raised to the power of *number2*
random()	Returns a random number between 0 and 1
round(*number*)	Rounds *number* to the closest integer
sin(*number*)	Returns the sine of *number*, where *number* is an angle expressed in radians
sqrt(*number*)	Returns the square root of *number*
tan(*number*)	Returns the tangent of *number*, where *number* is an angle expressed in radians
toString(*number*)	Converts *number* to a text string

menu	A <menu> (menu list) element in the document
Properties	
compact	A Boolean signifying whether the list should be compacted

navigator	An object representing the browser currently in use
Properties	
appCodeName	The code name of the browser
appName	The name of the browser
appVersion	The version of the browser
cookieEnabled	A Boolean signifying whether persistent cookies are enabled
language	The language of the browser
mimeTypes	An array of the MIME types supported by the browser
oscpu	A string containing the operating system
platform	The platform on which the browser is running
plugins	An array of the plug-ins installed on the browser
preference	Allows a signed script to get and set certain Navigator preferences (*NS 4.0 only*)
userAgent	The user-agent text string sent from the client to the Web serve
Methods	
javaEnabled()	Indicates whether the browser supports Java
plugins.refresh()	Checks for newly installed plug-ins
taintEnabled()	Specifies whether data tainting is enabled

Option	An option from a selection list (use the name of the option or the index value from the options array)
Properties	
defaultSelected	A Boolean indicating whether the option is selected by default
disabled	A Boolean indicating whether the element is disabled
index	The index value of the option
label	Alternate text for the option as specified in the *label* attribute

JavaScript Elements	Description
selected	A Boolean indicating whether the option is currently selected
text	The text of the option as it appears on the Web page
value	The value of the option
param	Corresponds to an occurrence of a `<param>` element in the document
Properties	
name	The name of the parameter
type	The type of the value when *valueType* is "ref"
value	The value of the parameter
valueType	Provides more information about how to interpret value; usually "data", "ref", or "object"
Password	A password field in an HTML form (use the name of the password field)
Properties	
defaultValue	The default password
name	The name of the password field
type	The type value of the password field
value	The value of the password field
Methods	
focus()	Gives the password field the focus
blur()	Leaves the password field
select()	Selects the password field
Event Handlers	
onBlur	Runs when the focus leaves the password field
onFocus	Runs when the password field receives the focus
plugin	A plug-in object in the Web page
Properties	
description	The description of the plug-in
filename	The plug-in filename
length	The number of MIME types supported by the plug-in
name	The name of the plug-in
popup	A popup window object created by using the createPopup() method in IE (*IE only*)
Properties	
document	Reference to the window's document (*IE only*)
isOpen	A Boolean indicating if the window is open (*IE only*)
Radio	A radio button in an HTML form (use the radio button's name)
PropertiesZ	
accessKey	Indicates the hotkey that gives the element focus
align	A string specifying the alignment of the element, for example, "right"
alt	Alternative text for the button

JavaScript Elements	Description
checked	A Boolean indicating whether a specific radio button has been checked
defaultChecked	A Boolean indicating whether a specific radio button is checked by default
defaultValue	The initial value of the button's *value* attribute
disabled	A Boolean indicating whether the element is disabled
form	The name of the form containing the radio button
name	The name of the radio button
type	The type value of the radio button
value	The value of the radio button
Methods	
blur()	Removes the focus from the radio button
click()	Clicks the radio button
focus()	Gives focus to the radio button
handleEvent(*event*)	Invokes the event handler for the specified *event*
Event Handlers	
onBlur	Runs when the focus leaves the radio button
onClick	Runs when the radio button is clicked
onFocus	Runs when the radio button receives the focus
RegExp	An object used for searching regular expressions
Properties	
global	Specifies whether to use a global pattern match
ignoreCase	Specifies whether to ignore case in the search string
input	The search string
lastIndex	Specifies the index at which to start matching the next string
lastMatch	The last matched characters
lastParen	The last parenthesized substring match
leftContext	The substring preceding the most recent match
multiline	Specifies whether to search on multiple lines
rightContext	The substring following the most recent match
source	The string pattern
Methods	
compile()	Compiles a regular search expression
exec(*string*)	Executes the search for a match to *string*
test(*string*)	Tests for a match to *string*
Reset	A reset button in an HTML form (use the name of the reset button)
Properties	
accessKey	Indicates the hotkey that gives the element focus
align	Specifies the alignment of the element, for example, "right"
alt	Alternative text for the button

JavaScript Elements	Description
defaultValue	Contains the initial value of the button
disabled	A Boolean indicating whether the element is disabled
form	The name of the form containing the reset button
name	The name of the reset button
type	The type value of the reset button
value	The value of the reset button
Methods	
blur()	Removes the focus from the reset button
click()	Clicks the reset button
focus()	Gives the focus to the reset button
handleEvent(*event*)	Invokes the event handler for the specified *event*
Event Handlers	
onBlur	Runs when the focus leaves the reset button
onClick	Runs when the reset button is clicked
onFocus	Runs when the reset button receives the focus
screen	An object representing the user's screen
Properties	
availHeight	The height of the screen, minus toolbars or any other permanent objects
availWidth	The width of the screen, minus toolbars or any other permanent objects
colorDepth	The number of possible colors in the screen
height	The height of the screen
pixelDepth	The number of bits per pixel in the screen
width	The width of the screen
Script	Corresponds to a <script> element in the document
Properties	
charset	The character set used to encode the script
defer	A Boolean indicating whether script execution may be deferred
src	The URL of the external script
text	The contents of the script
type	The value of the type attribute
Select	A selection list in an HTML form (use the name of the selection list)
Properties	
disabled	A Boolean indicating whether the element is disabled
form	The name of the form containing the selection list
length	The number of *options* in the selection list
multiple	A Boolean indicating whether multiple *options* may be selected
name	The name of the selection list
options[ ]	An array of options within the selection list; see the options object for more information on working with individual selection list options
selectedIndex	The index value of the selected option from the selection list

JavaScript Elements	Description
size	The number of options that are visible at one time
tabIndex	Numeric value that indicates the tab order for the object
type	The type value of the selection list
value	The *value* of the currently selected option
Methods	
add(element, before)	Adds the *option* referenced by the *element* to the list of options before the *option* referenced by *before*; if *before* is null, it is added at the end
blur()	Removes the focus from the selection list
focus()	Gives the focus to the selection list
handleEvent(*event*)	Invokes the event handler for the specified *event*
remove(index)	Removes the option at index *index* from the list of *options*
Event Handlers	
onBlur	Runs when the focus leaves the selection list
onChange	Runs when the focus leaves the selection list and the value of the selection list is changed
onFocus	Runs when the selection list receives the focus
String	An object representing a text string
Properties	
length	The number of characters in the string
Methods	
anchor(*name*)	Converts the string into a hypertext link anchor with the name *name*
big()	Displays the string using the <big> tag
blink()	Displays the string using the <blink> tag
bold()	Displays the string using the <b> tag
charAt(*index*)	Returns the character in the string at the location specified by *index*
charCodeAt(position)	Returns an unsigned integer of the Unicode value of the haracter at index *position*
concat(*string2*)	Concatenates the string with the second text string *string2*
fixed()	Displays the string using the <tt> tag
fontColor(*color*)	Sets the color attribute of the string
fontSize(*value*)	Sets the size attribute of the string
indexOf(*string, start*)	Searches the string, beginning at the *start* character, and returns the index value of the first occurrence of the string *string*
italics()	Displays the string using the <i> tag
lastIndexOf(*string, start*)	Searches the string, beginning at the *start* character, and locates the index value of the last occurrence of the string *string*
link(*href*)	Converts the string into a hypertext link pointing to the URL *href*
match(*expression*)	Returns an array containing the matches based on the regular expression *expression*
replace(*expression, new*)	Performs a search based on the regular expression *expression* and replaces the text with *new*
search(*expression*)	Performs a search based on the regular expression *expression* and returns the index number

JavaScript Elements	Description
slice(*begin*, *end*)	Returns a substring between the *begin* and the *end* index values; the *end* index value is optional
small()	Displays the string using the <small> tag
split(*separator*)	Splits the string into an array of strings at every occurrence of the *separator* character
strike()	Displays the string using the <strike> tag
sub()	Displays the string using the <sub> tag
substr(*begin*, *length*)	Returns a substring starting at the *begin* index value and continuing for *length* characters; the *length* parameter is optional
substring(*begin*, *end*)	Returns a substring between the *begin* and the *end* index values; the *end* index value is optional
sup()	Displays the string using the <sup> tag
toLowerCase()	Converts the string to lowercase
toUpperCase()	Converts the string to uppercase
style	This corresponds to an instance of a <style> element in the page
Properties	
disabled	A Boolean indicating whether the element is disabled
sheet	The styleSheet object corresponding to the element
styleSheet	The styleSheet object corresponding to the element
type	The value of the *type* attribute for the style sheet
Submit	A submit button in an HTML form (use the name of the submit button)
Properties	
accessKey	String indicating the hotkey that gives the element focus
alt	Alternative text for the button
defaultValue	The initial value of the button's *value* attribute
disabled	A Boolean indicating whether the element is disabled
form	The name of the form containing the submit button
name	The name of the submit button
tabIndex	Numeric value that indicates the tab order for the object
type	The type value of the submit button
value	The value of the submit button
Methods	
blur()	Removes the focus from the submit button
click()	Clicks the submit button
focus()	Gives the focus to the submit button
handleEvent(*event*)	Invokes the event handler for the specified *event*
Event Handlers	
onBlur	Runs when the focus leaves the submit button
onClick	Runs when the submit button is clicked
onFocus	Runs when the submit button receives the focus

JavaScript Elements	Description
Text	An input box from an HTML form (use the name of the input box)
Properties	
accessKey	A string indicating the hotkey that gives the element focus
defaultValue	The default value of the input box
disabled	A Boolean indicating whether the element is disabled
form	The form containing the input box
maxLength	The maximum number of characters the field can contain
name	The name of the input box
size	The width of the field in characters
tabIndex	The numeric value that indicates t1he tab order for the object
type	The type value of the input box
value	The value of the input bo
Methods	
blur()	Removes the focus from the input box
focus()	Gives the focus to the input box
handleEvent(*event*)	Invokes the event handler for the specified *event*
select()	Selects the input box
Event Handlers	
onBlur	Runs when the focus leaves the input box
onChange	Runs when the focus leaves the input box and the input box value changes
onFocus	Runs when the input box receives the focus
onSelect	Runs when some of the text in the input box is selected
Textarea	A text area box in an HTML form (use the name of the text area box)
Properties	
accessKey	Indicates the hotkey that gives the element focus
cols	The number of columns of the input area
defaultValue	The default value of the text area box
enabled	Indicates whether a text area field is enabled using a Boolean
form	The form containing the text area box
name	The name of the text area box
rows	The number of rows of the input area
tabIndex	Numeric value that indicates the tab order for the object
type	The type value of the text area box
value	The value of the text area box
Methods	
blur()	Removes the focus from the text area box
focus()	Gives the focus to the text area box
handleEvent(*event*)	Invokes the event handler for the specified *event*
select()	Selects the text area box
Event Handlers	
onBlur	Runs when the focus leaves the text area box
onChange	Runs when the focus leaves the text area box and the text area box value changes
onFocus	Runs when the text area box receives the focus
onKeyDown	Runs when a user presses a key
onKeyPress	Runs when a user presses or holds down a key
onKeyUp	Runs when a user releases a key
onSelect	Runs when some of the text in the text area box is selected

JavaScript Elements	Description
`window`	The document window

Properties

clipboardData	Provides access to the OS's clipboard
defaultStatus	The default message shown in the window's status bar
directories	A Boolean specifying whether the Netscape 6 "directories" button is visible.
document	The document displayed in the window
frameElement	The *Frame* in which the window is enclosed
frames	An array of frames within the window (see the frames object for properties and methods applied to individual frames)
history	A list of visited URLs
innerHeight	The height of the window's display area
innerWidth	The width of the widow's display area
length	The number of frames in the window
location	The URL loaded into the window
locationbar.visible	A Boolean indicating the visibility of the window's location bar
menubar.visible	A Boolean indicating the visibility of the window's menu bar
name	The name of the window
opener	The name of the window that opened the current window
outerHeight	The height of the outer area of the window
outerWidth	The width of the outer area of the window
pageXOffset	The *x*-coordinate of the window
pageYOffset	The *y*-coordinate of the window
parent	The name of the window containing this particular window
personalbar.visible	A Boolean indicating the visibility of the window's personal bar
screen	The browser's *screen* object
screenLeft	The *x*-coordinate in pixels of the left edge of the client area of the browser window
screenTop	The *y*-coordinate in pixels of the top edge of the client area of the browser window
scrollbars.visible	A Boolean indicating the visibility of the window's scroll bars
scrollX	How far the window is scrolled to the right
scrollY	How far the window is scrolled down
self	The current window
status	The message shown in the window's status bar
statusbar.visible	A Boolean indicating the visibility of the window's status bar
toolbar.visible	A Boolean indicating the visibility of the window's toolbar
top	The name of the topmost window in a hierarchy of windows
window	The current window

Methods

alert(*message*)	Displays the text contained in *message* in a dialog box
back()	Loads the previous page in the window
blur()	Removes the focus from the window
captureEvents()	Sets the window to capture all events of a specified type
clearInterval(*ID*)	Clears the interval for *ID*, set with the SetInterval method
clearTimeout()	Clears the timeout, set with the setTimeout method
close()	Closes the window
confirm(*message*)	Displays a confirmation dialog box with the text *message*
createPopup(*arg*)	Creates a popup window and returns a reference to the new popup object
disableExternalCapture	Disables external event capturing
enableExternalCapture	Enables external event capturing

JavaScript Elements	Description
find(*string, case, direction*)	Displays a Find dialog box, where *string* is the text to find in the window, *case* is a Boolean indicating whether the find is case-sensitive, and *direction* is a Boolean indicating whether the find goes in the backward direction (all of the parameters are optional)
focus()	Gives focus to the window
forward()	Loads the next page in the window
handleEvent(*event*)	Invokes the event handler for the specified *event*
moveBy(*horizontal, vertical*)	Moves the window by the specified amount in the *horizontal* and *vertical* directions
moveTo(*x, y*)	Moves the window to the *x*- and *y*-coordinates
open()	Opens the window
print()	Displays the Print dialog box
prompt(*message, default_text*)	Displays a Prompt dialog box with the text *message* (the default message is *default_text*)
releaseEvents(*event*)	Releases the captured events of a specified *event*
resizeBy(*horizontal, vertical*)	Resizes the window by the amount in the *horizontal* and *vertical* directions
resizeTo(*width, height*)	Resizes the window to the specified *width* and *height*
routeEvent(*event*)	Passes the *event* to be handled natively
scroll(*x, y*)	Scrolls the window to the *x, y* coordinate
scrollBy(*x, y*)	Scrolls the window by *x* pixels in the *x*-direction and *y* pixels in the *y*-direction
scrollTo(*x, y*)	Scrolls the window to the *x, y* coordinate
setActive( )	Sets the window to be active but does not give it the focus
setCursor(*type*)	Changes the cursor to *type*
setInterval(*expression, time*)	Evaluates the *expression* every *time* milliseconds have passed
setTimeout(*expression, time*)	Evaluates the *expression* after *time* milliseconds have passed
sizeToContent( )	Resizes the window so all contents are visible
stop()	Stops the window from loading
Event Handlers	
onBlur	Runs when the window loses the focus
onDragDrop	Runs when the user drops an object on or within the window
onError	Runs when an error occurs while loading the page
onFocus	Runs when the window receives the focus
onLoad	Runs when the window finishes loading
onMove	Runs when the window is moved
onResize	Runs when the window is resized
onUnload	Runs when the window is unloaded

JavaScript Operators, Keywords, and Syntactical Elements

Appendix H

The following table lists some of the important JavaScript operators, keywords, and syntactical elements. The first operators listed in the table are the assignment operators, used to assign values to variables and to document objects. The next operators are the arithmetic operators, used for performing arithmetic calculations on variables (addition, subtraction, multiplication, and division). The comparison operators are next and are used primarily in conditional expressions and in program loops. The JavaScript keywords listed in the table are special names reserved by JavaScript. The logical operators are used for evaluating whether an expression is true or false, and are primarily used in conditional expressions and in program loops. The last part of the table contains special syntax elements for marking the end of a program or for inserting a JavaScript comment.

Operators	Description
Assignment	**Operators used to assign values to variables**
=	Assigns the value of the variable on the right to the variable on the left ($x = y$)
+=	Adds the two variables and assigns the result to the variable on the left ($x += y$ is equivalent to $x = x + y$)
-=	Subtracts the variable on the right from the variable on the left and assigns the result to the variable on the left ($x- = y$ is equivalent to $x = x - y$)
*=	Multiplies the two variables together and assigns the result to the variable on the left ($x *= y$ is equivalent to $x = x * y$)
/=	Divides the variable on the left by the variable on the right and assigns the result to the variable on the left ($x /= y$ is equivalent to $x = x / y$)
&=	Combines two expressions into a single expression (x &= y is equivalent to $x = x \& y$)
%=	Divides the variable on the left by the variable on the right and assigns the remainder to the variable on the left ($x \%= y$ is equivalent to $x = x \% y$)
Arithmetic	**Operators used for arithmetic functions**
+	Adds two variables together ($x + y$)
-	Subtracts the variable on the right from the variable on the left ($x - y$)
*	Multiplies two variables together ($x * y$)
/	Divides the variable the left by the variable on the right (x / y)
%	Calculates the remainder after dividing the variable on the left by the variable on the right ($x \% y$)
++	Increases the value of a variable by 1 ($x ++$ is equivalent to $x = x + 1$)
&	Combines two expressions ($x \& y$) Decreases the value of variable by 1 ($x --$ is equivalent to $x = x - 1$)
-	Changes the sign of a variable ($- x$)
Comparison	**Operators used for comparing expressions**
==	Returns true when the two expressions are equal ($x == y$)
!=	Returns true when the two expressions are not equal ($x != y$)
!==	Returns true when the values of the two expressions are equal ($x !== y$)
>	Returns true when the expression on the left is greater than the expression on the right ($x > y$)
<	Returns true when the expression on the left is less than the expression on the right ($x < y$)
>=	Returns true when the expression on the left is greater than or equal to the expression on the right ($x >= y$)
<=	Returns true when the expression on the left is less than or equal to the expression on the right ($x <= y$)

Operators	Description
Conditional	**Operators used to determine values based on conditions that are either true or false**
(condition) ? *value1 : value2*	If *condition* is true, then this expression equals *value1*; otherwise it equals *value2*
Keywords	**JavaScript keywords are reserved by JavaScript**
infinity	Represents positive infinity (often used with comparison operators)
this	Refers to the current object
var	Declares a variable
with	Allows the declaration of all the properties for an object without directly referencing the object each time
Logical	**Operators used for evaluating true and false expressions**
^	The XOR (exclusive OR) operator
!	Reverses the Boolean value of the expression
&&	Returns true only if both expressions are true (also known as an AND operator)
||	Returns true when either expression is true (also known as an OR operator)
		Returns true if the expression is false and false if the expression is true (also known as a NEGATION operator)
Syntax	**Syntactical elements**
;	Indicates the end of a command line
/ comments *\/*	Used for inserting *comments* within a JavaScript command line
// comments	Used to create a line of *comments*

Working with Cookies

Appendix I

Introducing Cookies

A **cookie** is a piece of information stored in a text file that a Web browser places on a user's computer. Typically, cookies contain data to be accessed the next time a user visits a particular Web site. For example, many online stores use cookies to store users' addresses and credit card information. This enables a store to access previously entered information from a cookie the next time a repeat user makes a purchase, freeing the user from reentering this material.

Where a browser places a cookie file depends on the browser. Netscape stores cookies in a single text file named cookie.txt. Internet Explorer stores cookies in a separate text file, typically in the Windows/Cookies folder. Browsers limit each cookie to 4 kilobytes in size, and a computer can generally not store more than 300 cookies at one time. If a browser tries to store more than 300 cookies, the oldest cookies are deleted to make room.

Cookies, the Web Server, and CGI Scripts

The first implementation of cookies was with a CGI script running on a Web server. A CGI script can retrieve the cookie information and perform some action based on the information in the file. The process works as follows:

1. A user accesses the Web site and sends a request to the CGI script on the Web server, either by filling out an order form or by some other process that calls the CGI script.
2. The CGI script determines whether a cookie for the user exists.
3. If no cookie is detected, the Web server sends a form, or page, for a user to enter the information needed by the cookie. This information is then sent to the CGI script for processing.
4. If a cookie is found, the CGI script retrieves that information and creates a new page, or modifies the current page, based on the information contained in the cookie.

Information is exchanged using the same Hypertext Transfer Protocol (HTTP) used for retrieving the contents of the Web page. This is because each transfer includes a header section that contains information about the document (such as its MIME data type) and allows for general information in the form:

```
field-name: field-value
```

These field-name/field-value pairs contain information that can be stored in a user's cookie.

To store this information on a Web server, a Web programmer must add the Set-Cookie statement to the header section of the CGI script. The Set-Cookie statement is used the first time the user accesses the Web page. Four parameters are often set with cookies: name, expires, path, and domain. The syntax is:

```
Set-Cookie: name=text; expires=date; path=text; domain=text; secure
```

The name parameter defines the name of the cookie, and its value cannot contain spaces, commas, or semicolons. The expire parameter indicates the date the information expires; if no expire parameter is included, the cookie expires when the user's browsing session ends. The path parameter indicates the URL path portion to which that cookie applies; setting this value to "/" allows the cookie to be accessed from any folder within the Web site. The domain parameter specifies the URL domain portion to which the cookie applies (usually the domain name of the current document). Finally, the secure parameter indicates that the data should be transferred over a secure link—one that uses file encryption.

Once the initial cookie is created, the browser sends the Cookie statement in the header section of the transfer the next time the user accesses the Web page. The syntax of this statement is

```
Cookie: name1:value1; name2:value2; ...
```

where *name1* is the first field name (whatever that might be) and *value1* is the value of the first field. The statement can contain as many field/value pairs as needed by the Web page so long as the total size of the cookie doesn't exceed 4 kilobytes.

Once the Web server retrieves the cookie field names and values, the CGI script processes them. Because CGI programming is beyond the scope of this book, you will focus on working with cookies on the client side with JavaScript.

Working with the Cookie Property

JavaScript uses the cookie property of the document object to retrieve and update cookie information. The cookie property is simply a text string containing all of the field/value pairs used by the cookie, with each pair separated by a semicolon. To set a value for a cookie, you would use the document.cookie property with the form

```
document.cookie='cookie1=OrderForm; expires=Mon, 08-Apr-
2006 12:00:00 GMT; path="/"; secure';
```

where the cookie contains the cookie1 field with the value OrderForm. This particular cookie expires at noon on Monday, April 8, 2006. Because the path value equals "/", this cookie is accessible from any folder within the Web site. The secure property has been set, so any transfer of information involving this cookie must use file encryption. Note that this is a long text string, with the string value enclosed in single quotation marks.

If your Web page had an online form named "Orders", you could create additional field/value pairs using the form names and values as follows:

```
document.cookie='cookie1=OrderForm; name='+document.Orders.Name.
value+'; custid=+'document.Orders.CustId.value;
```

Here, two additional fields have been added to the cookie: name and custid. The values for these fields are taken respectively from the Name field and the CustId field in the Orders form.

Reading a Cookie

One of the challenges of working with cookies in JavaScript is reading the cookie information. To do this you need to extract the appropriate information from the cookie's text string and place that information in the appropriate JavaScript variables. You can use several of JavaScript's string functions to help with this task. To start, create a function named "readCookie(fname)", where "fname" is the name of the field whose value you want to retrieve. The initial code looks like

```
function readCookie(fname) {
    var cookies=document.cookie;
}
```

where the text string of the cookie is stored in the cookies variable. In the text string, each field name is followed by an equal sign, so you can use the indexOf( ) method (see Appendix G) to locate the occurrence of the text string "fname=", where *fname* is the field name you want to retrieve. You'll store this location in a variable named startname. The command is:

```
startname=cookies.indexOf(fname+"=");
```

For example, if fname="custid" in the text string below, startname would have a value of 33, because custid starts with the thirty-third character in the text string.

```
cookie1=OrderForm; name=Brooks; custid=20010; type=clothes
```

What if the field name is not found in the cookie? In this case, startname has a value of -1, and you can create an If...Else conditional statement to handle this contingency. To simplify things for this example, you'll assume that this is not a concern, and continue.

Next you need to locate the field's value. This value is placed after the equal sign and continues until you reach a semicolon indicating the end of the field's value, or until you reach the end of the text string. The field's value then starts one space after the first equal sign after the field's name. You'll locate the beginning of the field value, using the same indexOf( ) method, and store that location in the startvalue variable. The command is:

```
startvalue=cookies.indexOf("=", startname)+1;
```

Here, you locate the text string "=", starting at the point startname in the cookies text string. You add one to whatever value is returned by the indexOf() method. In the text string

```
cookie1=OrderForm; name=Brooks; custid=20010; type=clothes
```

the value of the startvalue variable is 40, because the "2" in "20010" is the fortieth character in the string.

Next you locate the end of the field's value, which is the first semicolon after the startvalue character. If the field is the last value in the text string, there is no semicolon at the end, so the indexOf( ) method returns a value of -1. If that occurs, you'll use the length of the text string to locate the value's end. Once again, using the indexOf( ) method, you'll store this value in the endvalue variable. The JavaScript command is:

```
endvalue=cookies.indexOf(";",startvalue);
if(endvalue==-1) {
    endvalue=cookies.length;
}
```

In the text string below, the value of the endvalue variable for the custid field is 45.

```
cookie1=OrderForm; name=Brooks; custid=20010; type=clothes
```

To extract the field's value and store it in a variable named fvalue, use the substring( ) method

```
fvalue=cookies.substring(startvalue, endvalue);
```

where the startvalue indicates the start of the substring and the endvalue marks the substring's end. The complete readCookie(fname) function looks as follows:

```
function readCookie(fname) {
   var cookies=document.cookie;
   var startname=cookies.indexOf(fname+"=");
   var startvalue=cookies.indexOf("=", startname)+1;
   var endvalue=cookies.indexOf(";",startvalue);
   if(endvalue==-1) {
     endvalue=cookies.length;
   }
   var fvalue=cookies.substring(startvalue, endvalue);
return fvalue;
}
```

In a JavaScript program, calling the function

```
readCookie("custid");
```

would return a value of 20010, which is the customer id value stored in the cookie file. You should review this example carefully, paying close attention to the use of the indexOf( ) method and the substring( ) method.

Encoding Cookies

Values in the cookie text string cannot contain spaces, semicolons, or commas. This can be a problem if you are trying to store phrases or sentences. The solution to this problem is to encode the value, using the same type of encoding scheme that is used in URLs (which also cannot contain spaces, commas, and semicolons) or in the mailto action. JavaScript includes the escape( ) method for encoding your text strings. Encoding replaces blank spaces, semicolons, and commas with special characters. For example, if you want to insert an Address field in your cookie that contains a street number and an address, you could use the following JavaScript command:

```
document.cookie='Address='+escape(document.Orders.Address.value);
```

To read a text string that has been encoded, you use JavaScript's unescape( ) method. For example, you could replace the command that stores the field value in the fvalue variable in the readCookie( ) function with the following command:

```
var fvalue=unescape(cookies.substring(startvalue, endvalue));
```

This command removes any encoding characters and replaces them with the appropriate spaces, semicolons, commas, and so forth.

Glossary/Index

Note: Boldface entries include definitions.

Special Characters

* (asterisk), HTML 719

+ (plus sign), HTML 719

? (question mark), HTML 719

A

absolute path A path that specifies a file's precise location within a computer's folder structure. HTML 71

absolute positioning A style that enables you to place an element at specific coordinates either on a page or within a containing element. HTML 227–230

absolute unit A unit that is fixed in size regardless of the device rendering the Web page, specified in one of five standard units of measurement: mm (millimeters), cm (centimeters), in (inches), pt (points), and pc (picas). HTML 143–144

access key A single key on the keyboard that you type in conjunction with the Alt key for Windows users, or the Control key for Macintosh users, to jump to one of the control elements in a form. HTML 365

ActiveX A technology developed by Microsoft involving reusable software components that can be run from within a variety of Windows programs. HTML 424–429

classid attribute, HTML 425, HTML 426–427

codebase attribute, HTML 425–427

inserting ActiveX controls, HTML 426

Internet Explorer conditional comments, HTML 427–429

add-on An extra component added to a program (such as a Web browser) to provide a feature or capability not included in the program. HTML 413

aggregator A software program that provides periodic updates to subscribers of an RSS site; also called a feed reader. HTML 627

AIFF/AIFC file format, HTML 416

alert dialog box A dialog box generated by JavaScript that displays a text message with an OK button. HTML 599–600

alignment

aligning cell contents with HTML, HTML 297–298

aligning text vertically, HTML 152

characters, HTML 298

vertical, in HTML, HTML 298–299

American Standard Code for Information Interchange. *See* ASCII (American Standard Code for Information Interchange)

amplitude The height of a sound wave, relating to the sound's volume-the higher the amplitude, the louder the sound. HTML 413

anchor, HTML 78

animated GIF An image composed of several images that are displayed one after the other, creating the illusion of motion. HTML 154

anonymous complex type A complex type in XML Schema that is defined without a name. HTML 822

anonymous simple type A simple type in XML Schema that is defined without a name. HTML 795

applet A mini application, not a stand-alone application, running in conjunction with a hosting program such as a Web browser, such as a Java program. HTML 454–463

applet element, HTML 463–464

embedding, HTML 456–457

inserting parameters, HTML 457–463

applet element, HTML 463–464

applet window A window in which an applet runs; the window can be resized and positioned anywhere within a Web page. HTML 455

ARPANET The precursor to the Internet-a wide area network which started with two network nodes located at UCLA and Stanford connected by a single phone line. HTML 2

ASCII (American Standard Code for Information Interchange) The character set representing the alphabet of English characters/, HTML 43

aspect ratio The ratio of a frame, usually 4:3. HTML 431

asterisk (*), modifying symbol, HTML 719

Atom An XML vocabulary used for Web feeds that was developed in response to the confusion that resulted from competing versions of RSS. HTML 627

attribute A markup tag that controls the use, behavior, and in some cases the appearance of an element in an HTML document; a description of a feature or characteristic of an element. HTML 34–37, HTML 635–636, HTML 677–678, HTML 722–731

character data, HTML 725–726

declaring, HTML 722–724

defaults, HTML 729–731

defining, HTML 773–774

defining elements containing attributes and basic text, HTML 775–776

defining elements containing nested elements and attributes, HTML 778–781

defining elements containing only attributes, HTML 775

enumerated types, HTML 726

fields in forms, HTML 364

forms, HTML 391–392

hypertext, HTML 98–102

id attribute, HTML 74–77

presentational, HTML 37

referencing attribute definitions, HTML 776–777

required, indicating, HTML 782–783

style, HTML 34–36

tokenized types, HTML 727–729

types, HTML 724–729

XHTML, HTML 535–537, HTML 548–550

attribute minimization In some older HTML documents, a situation in which some attributes lack attribute values; XHTML does not allow attribute minimization. HTML 532

attribute selector A declaration used to select an element based on the element's attributes. HTML 203–205

attribute-list declaration A declaration in the document's DTD that lists the names of all the attributes associated with a specific element, specifies the data type of each attribute, indicates whether each attribute is required or optional, and provides a default value for each attribute, if necessary. HTML 723

AU file format, HTML 416

audio, digital, HTML 413–417

augmented linear structure A structure for a Web page that is similar to a linear structure, but which contains links in addition to those that move only forward and backward. HTML 63

B

background

formatting, HTML 157–159

images, HTML 159–161

style, HTML 161

background sound, HTML 429

bandwidth A measure of the amount of data that can be sent through a communication pipeline each second. HTML 411–412